Discovering PSYCHOLOGY

Wolf's Clothing, #2 (collage, 36" × 24", 1990)

The stunning artwork that appears on the cover and chapter-opening pages of *Psychology* was created by Phoebe Beasley, an award-winning artist and lithographer. Ms. Beasley's luminous oil paint and tissue paper collages capture the unique, yet universal, life experiences of all kinds of people. Similarly, psychologists study a wide range of human experiences—creativity, love, memory, dreaming, sexuality, growing up and growing old—looking for the general patterns underlying the expression of human individuality. The personal narratives portrayed in Beasley's work, like those in Don and Sandy Hockenbury's chapter Prologues, help us understand and appreciate human behavior.

Discovering PSYCHOLOGY

FOURTH EDITION

Don H. Hockenbury
Tulsa Community College

Sandra E. Hockenbury

Worth Publishers

Publisher: Catherine Woods
Acquisitions Editor: Charles Linsmeier
Executive Development Editor: Sharon Balbos
Marketing Manager: Kate Nurre
Associate Managing Editor: Tracey Kuehn
Project Editor: Anthony Calcara
Media & Supplements Editor: Andrea Musick
Production Manager: Barbara Seixas
Art Director/Cover Designer: Barbara Reingold
Text Designer: Lissi Sigillo
Layout Designers: Lee Ann Mahler and Lyndall Culbertson
Photo Editors: Cecilia Varas and Donna Ranieri
Illustration Coordinator: Bill Page
Line Art: Dragonfly Media Group, Chris Notarile, and J/B Woolsey Associates
Cover Art: Phoebe Beasley
Composition: Compset, Inc., and TSI Graphics
Printing and Binding: RR Donnelley

Library of Congress Control Number: 2006901717

ISBN-13: 978-0-7167-7654-3
ISBN-10: 0-7167-7654-5

Fifth printing

Illustration credits and permissions start on page IC-1 and constitute an extension of the copyright
page.

Worth Publishers
41 Madison Avenue
New York, New York 10010
212-576-9400
www.worthpublishers.com

Faculty Services: 800-446-8923
Technical Support: 800-936-6899

To the loving memory of our fathers,

Ken and Erv

About the Authors

Don and Sandy Hockenbury are the authors of *Psychology* and *Discovering Psychology*. As an author team, they bring their unique talents and abilities to the teaching of introductory psychology.

Don H. Hockenbury is an Assistant Professor of Psychology at Tulsa Community College. Don received his B.S. in psychology and his M.A. in clinical psychology from the University of Tulsa. Before he began his teaching career, Don worked in psychiatric facilities and in private practice. With over 20 years of experience in teaching introductory psychology, Don appreciates the challenges of engaging the diverse students of today's college classrooms and of showing them the scientific nature and the personal relevance of psychology. Before co-authoring *Psychology* and *Discovering Psychology*, Don served as a reviewer and supplements author for several psychology textbooks. Don is an associate member of the American Psychological Association and a member of the American Psychological Society and the American Association for the Advancement of Science. Don was recently honored with the Tulsa Community College Award for Teaching Excellence.

Sandra E. Hockenbury is a science writer who specializes in psychology. Sandy received her B.A. from Shimer College and her M.A. from the University of Chicago, where she was also a Research Associate at the Institute of Social and Behavioral Pathology. Prior to co-authoring *Psychology* and *Discovering Psychology*, Sandy worked for several years as a psychology editor in both academic and college textbook publishing. Sandy's particular areas of interest are cross-cultural psychology, comparative cognition, and nonconscious processes. Sandy has also taught as an adjunct faculty member at Tulsa Community College. She is a member of the American Psychological Society and the American Association for the Advancement of Science.

Don and Sandy's 16-year-old daughter, Laura, enjoys science, rock-climbing, playing piano, improvisational comedy, and clowning. Laura is a member of Tender Loving Clowns, a volunteer group, and as her alter ego "Dandy," performs for children and adults at nonprofit events. Laura has also become quite versatile in assisting with house repairs. In a lapse of judgment, the Hockenburys recently moved to a bigger but creaky old house in a historic section of Tulsa. Also actively participating in house repairs are brothers Tom Cat and Bob Cat (a.k.a. "The Boys"). Despite being co-authors of numerous publications who try to write in a mechanically challenged house with a teenage daughter and two rambunctious cats, the Hockenburys are still happily married. On most days.

brief contents

contents

chapter 1
Introduction and Research Methods

chapter 2
Neuroscience and Behavior

chapter 3
Sensation and Perception

chapter 4
Consciousness and Its Variations

chapter 5
Learning

chapter 6
Memory

chapter 7
Thinking, Language, and Intelligence

chapter 8
Motivation and Emotion

chapter 9
Lifespan Development

chapter 10
Personality

chapter 11
Social Psychology

chapter 12
Stress, Health, and Coping

chapter 13
Psychological Disorders

chapter 14
Therapies

appendix A
Statistics: Understanding Data

Marie D. Thomas   California State University, San Marcos

appendix B
Industrial/Organizational Psychology

Marie Waung   University of Michigan, Dearborn

to the instructor

Welcome to the fourth edition of Hockenbury & Hockenbury *Discovering Psychology*!

For those of you who are using Hockenbury & Hockenbury *Discovering Psychology* for the first time, this faculty preface will help orient you to the many features of our text, its supplements, and its media package. If you want to get the most out of our book and teaching package, reading this preface will be well worth your time.

To those of you who used a previous edition of Hockenbury & Hockenbury *Discovering Psychology*, thank you for helping make our text a success! Rest assured that, once again, we have taken several steps to help make your transition to the new edition as smooth and easy as possible. As we've done previously, we have assembled a complete, detailed, and page-referenced list of changes in the new edition. You can find that list and other helpful materials in the Instructor's Section of the *Discovering Psychology,* Fourth Edition, companion Web site.

We've been gratified by the enthusiastic response to the three previous editions of *Discovering Psychology*. We've especially enjoyed the many e-mails we've received from students who felt that the book was speaking directly to them. Students and faculty alike told us how much they appreciated *Discovering Psychology*'s distinctive voice, its inviting learning environment, the engaging writing style, and the clarity of explanations on every page—qualities we've maintained in the fourth edition.

Like the three previous editions, the fourth edition reflects our heartfelt belief that psychology is the most exciting science that exists. More so than any other science, psychology speaks to students' lives. Psychology provides a wealth of meaningful and practical insights about behavior and mental processes. Our desire to communicate the excitement and relevance of our scientific discipline to students is one of the main reasons we've spent the last 17 years of our lives researching and writing the first four editions of *Discovering Psychology*.

The fourth edition of *Discovering Psychology* continues to reflect our commitment to the goals that have guided us as teachers and authors. Once again, we invite you to explore every page of the new edition of *Discovering Psychology* so that you can see firsthand how we:

- Communicate both the scientific rigor and personal relevance of psychology
- Clearly explain psychological concepts and how they are linked
- Present controversial topics in an impartial and even-handed fashion
- Show how classic psychological studies help set the stage for today's research
- Personalize historical figures in psychology with interesting details about their lives
- Encourage and model critical and scientific thinking
- Expand student awareness of cultural and gender influences

- Create a student-friendly, personal learning environment
- Actively engage diverse students, including adult learners
- Provide an effective pedagogical system that helps students develop more effective learning strategies and test for retention

What's New in the Fourth Edition

We began the revision process with the thoughtful recommendations and feedback we received from our reviewers and colleagues. We also had face-to-face dialogues with approximately 200 students at three different colleges. Another 600 students gave us feedback through our Web site and classroom surveys.

We are very proud of the fact that student feedback continues to play an important role in shaping our text. Students not only provide constructive—and sometimes creative—suggestions concerning our text and learning aids, but many also read and give us feedback about new and revised text sections. We continue to be impressed by how conscientiously most students approach the task of improving *Discovering Psychology* for future students.

In this edition, we also benefited from the research assistance of 14 psychology graduate students at Rutgers University. The graduate students helped us by surveying the research literature in their different areas of psychology specialization. Their efforts were greatly appreciated!

After carefully evaluating the feedback from faculty and students, we arrived at several goals for the fourth edition of *Discovering Psychology,* including the following:

Streamline discussions and add new information without adding to the overall length of *Discovering Psychology*

We began the revision process with a commitment to make space for new discussions and information by revising and streamlining current content. Without sacrificing coverage of classic research, theories, or key concepts that provide the foundations of psychological knowledge, we added a wealth of new topics and coverage. We're pleased to report that we met our goal: we added just ten pages in overall length to the fourth edition of *Discovering Psychology.*

Update, update, update with more than 700 new research citations, more than half published in 2004, 2005, and 2006

Faculty have told us how much they appreciate our efforts to present interesting and current psychology research to students. Keeping up with our incredibly diverse and productive discipline is an ongoing process. Just so you know, we personally subscribe to 29 print and 4 electronic journals, and we regularly monitor numerous psychology, neuroscience, and life science Web sites. The result of all these research efforts? There are over 700 new references in the fourth edition of *Discovering Psychology,* more than half of which are from 2004, 2005, or 2006. Interested faculty are welcome to download a complete list of the new references in *Discovering Psychology,* which can be found in the Instructor's Section of our companion Web site.

The 700+ new citations reflect the many new and updated topics and discussions in the fourth edition of *Discovering Psychology*. What follows is just a sample of some of the new and updated topics:

- A new Critical Thinking Box, "Abuse at Abu Ghraib: Why Do Ordinary People Commit Evil Acts?" Incorporating Milgram's classic research on obedience and Zimbardo's Stanford Prison Experiment, the box provides an even-handed discussion of the situational factors that contributed to the mistreatment of Iraqi detainees by American military personnel (pp. 462–463)

- Added coverage of people who resist obeying illegal or immoral orders, and suggestions for resisting authority under such conditions (p. 464)

- How observational learning principles have been applied in entertainment–education programs to promote social changes and healthy behaviors in Mexico, Africa, and Asia (pp. 209–212)

- New research on neurogenesis and the role of neural stem cells in brain development (pp. 59, 62–63)

- New prologue story about the sensory and perceptual changes experienced by Mike May, a man who regained low-level eyesight after more than 40 years of being completely blind (pp. 83–84)

- New section on brain plasticity, including how learning the new skill of juggling produced distinct changes in brain structure (pp. 75–77)

- New discussion and illustration of the sensory processing of fast and slow pain signals (pp. 102–104)

- New discussion of the principles of genetics, featuring the contemporary interactionist perspective on genes and environment, and the surprising conclusions of the International Human Genome Sequencing Consortium (pp. 352–355)

- A new Science Versus Pseudoscience Box, "Brain Myths" (p. 70)

- The growing evidence for the effectiveness of virtual reality therapy in the treatment of phobias and posttraumatic stress disorder (p. 559)

- How the reward system of the brain is "hijacked" by drugs, leading to addiction, craving, and relapse (p. 158)

- Updated research on the viral infection theory of schizophrenia (p. 538–539)

- Updated and expanded discussion of Renée Baillargeon's research on infant cognitive development (pp. 372–373)

- How brain-imaging is transforming our views of the adolescent brain (p. 377)

- The progressive destruction of brain tissue in Alzheimer's disease as revealed by brain imaging (p. 252)

- Latest findings on the role of the newly discovered hormone, ghrelin, in hunger, along with a new illustration depicting the association of neurochemical messengers and hunger signals (pp. 304–306)

- Expanded treatment of Vygotsky's theory of cognitive development (p. 373)

Expanded Focus on Neuroscience Feature

The Focus on Neuroscience feature, implemented in the last edition of *Discovering Psychology*, proved to be very popular with both instructors and students. As you'll see, we've added several new Focus on Neuroscience boxes and updated or replaced many that were in the third edition. As brain-imaging technology has moved into the mainstream of psychology research, it has yielded fascinating insights into the relationship among the brain, behavior, and mental processes. Modern neuroscience techniques have also shed light on some of the classic problems and controversies in psychology. Here are a few of the questions addressed by the Focus on Neuroscience features:

- Why do addictive drugs produce such irresistible cravings?
- How does the brain change and develop during adolescence?
- How does Alzheimer's disease affect the brain?
- How does the brain change in response to learning a new motor skill?
- Why do we enjoy looking at attractive people?
- Why is falling in love such an intoxicating experience?
- Does psychotherapy affect the brain?

Although we've increased our neuroscience coverage, we've stayed keenly attuned to the goal of presenting these findings in language that is accessible to students. We also felt that it was very important to present neuroscience findings in the context of established psychological knowledge about a particular behavior. Thus, you'll find the new Focus on Neuroscience features positioned close to the broader psychological discussion of a particular topic. A complete listing of the Focus on Neuroscience features appears later in this preface.

Major Chapter Revisions

As you page through our new edition, you will encounter new examples, boxes, photos, and illustrations in every chapter. There are numerous new topics and discussions. Although every chapter has been updated, you'll find major changes with significant new material in three particular chapters: Chapter 3, Sensation and Perception; Chapter 6, Memory; and Chapter 9, Lifespan Development. We'd like to draw your attention to some of those significant changes.

Chapter 3, Sensation and Perception

Chapter 3 opens with a new Prologue, "Learning to See." The Prologue tells the remarkable story of Mike May, a businessman, inventor, and world traveler who just happens to have been blind since a freak accident at the age of 3. Forty years later, he regained sight in one eye. We weave Mike's story throughout the chapter as we describe his rediscovery of the visual world. Fascinating in its own right, Mike's experience is also the perfect vehicle for students to understand the role the brain plays in perception. Mike's story helps illustrate many key ideas in this chapter, including:

- the difference between sensation and perception;
- the effects of experience on the development of visual pathways in the brain;
- how perceptual abilities, including depth perception and motion perception, are influenced by experience with the sensory world; and
- how susceptibility to even the most compelling visual illusions is related to visual experience.

You will encounter other changes in Chapter 3 as well. There is an entirely new discussion of pain that includes a new graphic illustrating fast and slow pain pathways, a discussion of pain sensitization and phantom limb pain, and gender differences in pain. Rounding out our enhanced coverage of pain is an expanded Application, "Strategies to Control Pain." The application now includes a discussion of complementary and alternative medicine, and a critical review of magnet therapy. Finally, we've added some fascinating new research on the quest to discover human pheromones.

Chapter 6, Memory

In response to the explosion of research in this area of psychology, this chapter has been reorganized and updated to present a contemporary understanding of memory. As we added new material, however, we were careful to retain our coverage of classic studies and maintain our student-friendly approach with many examples and applications to everyday life. Among the additions and changes:

- coverage of the role of interference in short-term memory;
- new discussion of Baddeley's working memory model;
- new section on absent-mindedness and prospective memory failures;
- new table of suggestions for avoiding prospective memory failures;
- new research on encoding failure;
- the effects of schemas and scripts on memory distortions;
- section on forgetting now precedes material on imperfect and false memories;
- new section describing recent studies on the development of faulty and false memories;
- new real-world examples of the misinformation effect and eyewitness misidentification
- new box summarizing research findings on déjà vu;
- new box discussing 2004 research on H.M.'s surprising knowledge about people who became famous after his surgery;
- new Focus on Neuroscience feature detailing brain tissue loss in Alzheimer's disease;
- expanded Application, "Superpower Your Memory in Just Minutes Per Day!"

Chapter 9, Lifespan Development

A new Prologue introduces the chapter themes. The section on genetics has been completely rewritten, providing a clear explanation of the contemporary understanding of the role of genes in development. Gone is the "genotype-as-blueprint" analogy that was once widely accepted, replaced by the new understanding of the flexibility of gene expression and the importance of the gene–environment interaction. Also covered are some of the latest findings by the International Genome Sequencing Consortium.

Other major changes include a new treatment of adolescent physical development and puberty. The discussion of adolescence has been expanded to include new research on factors that influence the timing of puberty, the effects of early and late maturation, and the importance of romantic and sexual relationships in adolescence. A new Focus on Neuroscience feature details the recent findings on brain development throughout the adolescent and early adulthood years. The section on cognitive development has been updated and expanded, and now includes more substantial coverage of Lev Vygotsky's influential theory.

NEW Test Bank with Question Graphics Feature

Those of you who have used previous editions of our text know that we are also the authors of the Test Bank, a distinction that is unique among all the other introductory psychology textbooks published. And, in fact, we use our own Test Bank each and every semester in teaching multiple sections of introductory psychology. From firsthand experience, we appreciate how important it is for you to have a wide selection of high-quality multiple-choice, true–false, and short-answer essay test questions. In this edition we have added or replaced over 500 new test items. The full Test Bank now contains over 6,000 questions. And, for the first time, we have added graphics to the Test Bank so that you can include line art when generating and printing your tests. You can read more about this feature in the preface to the Test Bank.

Enhanced Web Companion Site

In response to student feedback, we have expanded the review activities that are available on the Web companion site that accompanies the fourth edition of *Discovering Psychology*. Many of you already know that we are actively involved in providing materials for the Web site for both students and faculty. For example, we write the self-scoring practice quizzes and the crossword puzzles for each chapter. Among the enhancements for the fourth edition: each chapter has two self-scoring practice quizzes; the new crossword puzzles have an online "hint" feature; students will be able to save crosswords and return to them later. Other media enhancements are discussed later in this preface.

Expanded Resources for Instructors

With the invaluable assistance of Skip Pollock, Mesa Community College; Claudia Cochran, El Paso Community College; and Beth Finders, St. Charles Community College, the Instructor's Resources now include a cleaner, more intuitive organization, advice on teaching the nontraditional student, new popular video suggestions, and revised "Psychology in the News" topics. Features that faculty have found useful in previous editions, such as the detailed chapter outlines, continue to be part of the Instructor's Resources. As we'll describe in "The Supplements" section, we have some significant new additions to our video and CD resources for the fourth edition, most importantly Worth Publishers' newest video series *Moving Images: Exploring Discovering Psychology Through Film,* the Instructor's Resource CD-ROM, and the Instructor's Resource eLibrary.

Features of *Discovering Psychology*

For all that is new in the fourth edition, we were careful to maintain the unique elements that have been so well received in the previous editions. Every feature and element in our text was carefully developed and serves a specific purpose. From comprehensive surveys, reviewers, and our many discussions with faculty and students, we learned what elements people wanted in a text and why they thought those features were important tools that enhanced the learning process. We also surveyed the research literature on text comprehension, student learning, and memory. In the process, we acquired many valuable insights from the work of cognitive and educational psychologists. Described below are the main features of *Discovering Psychology* and how these features enhance the learning process.

The Narrative Approach

As you'll quickly discover, our book has a very distinctive voice. From the very first page of this text, the reader comes to know us as people and teachers through carefully selected stories and anecdotes. Some of our friends and relatives also graciously allowed us to share stories about their lives. The stories are quite varied—some are funny, others are dramatic, and some are deeply personal. All of them are true.

Associate the new with the old in some natural and telling way, so that the interest, being shed along from point to point, finally suffuses the entire system of objects. . . . Anecdotes and reminiscences [should] abound in [your] talk; and the shuttle of interest will shoot backward and forward, weaving the new and the old together in a lively and entertaining way.

William James, *Talks to Teachers* (1899)

The stories we tell reflect one of the most effective teaching methods—the *narrative approach.* In addition to engaging the reader, each story serves as a pedagogical springboard to illustrate important concepts and ideas. Every story is used to connect new ideas, terms, and ways of looking at behavior to information with which the student is already familiar.

Prologues

As part of the narrative approach, every chapter begins with a **Prologue,** a true story about ordinary people with whom most students can readily identify. Each Prologue effectively introduces the chapter's themes and lays the groundwork for explaining why the topics treated by the chapter are important. The Prologue establishes a link between familiar experiences and new information—a key ingredient in facilitating learning. Later in the chapter, we return to the people and stories introduced in the Prologue, further reinforcing the link between familiar experiences and new ways of conceptualizing them.

Logical Organization, Continuity, and Clarity

As you read the chapters in *Discovering Psychology,* you'll see that each chapter tells the story of a major topic in psychology in a logical way that flows continuously from beginning to end. Themes are clearly established in the first pages of the chapter. Throughout the chapter, we come back to those themes as we present subtopics and specific research studies. Chapters are very thoughtfully organized so that students can easily see how ideas are connected. The writing is carefully paced to maximize student interest and comprehension. Rather than simply mentioning terms and findings, we explain concepts clearly. And we use concrete analogies and everyday examples, rather than vague or flowery metaphors, to help students grasp abstract concepts and ideas.

Paradoxically, one of the ways that we maintain narrative continuity throughout each chapter is through the use of in-text boxes. The boxes provide an opportunity to explore a particular topic in depth without losing the narrative thread of the chapter.

The **In Focus boxes** do just that—they focus on interesting topics in more depth than the chapter's organization would allow. These boxes highlight interesting research, answer questions that students commonly ask, or show students how psychological research can be applied in their own lives. The fourth edition of *Discovering Psychology* includes the following In Focus boxes:

- Questions About the Use of Animals in Psychological Research (p. 32)
- The Puzzle of the Left-Hander (p. 72)
- Do Pheromones Influence Human Behavior? (p. 100)
- What You Really Want to Know About Sleep (p. 136)
- What You Really Want to Know About Dreams (p. 146)
- Watson, Classical Conditioning, and Advertising (p. 182)
- Biological Preparedness and Conditioned Fears: What Gives You the Creeps? (p. 188)
- Changing the Behavior of Others: Alternatives to Punishment (p. 195)
- Déjà Vu: An Illusion of Memory (p. 236)
- H.M. and Famous People (p. 251)
- Does a High IQ Score Predict Success in Life? (p. 278)
- Explaining Those Amazing Identical-Twin Similarities (p. 424)
- Gender Differences in Responding to Stress: "Tend-and-Befriend" or "Fight-or-Flight?" (p. 498)

Scientific Emphasis

Many first-time psychology students walk into the classroom operating on the assumption that psychology is nothing more than common sense or a collection of personal opinions. Clearly, students need to come away from an introductory psychology course with a solid understanding of the scientific nature of the discipline. To help you achieve that goal, in every chapter we show students how the scientific method has been applied to help answer different kinds of questions about behavior and mental processes.

Because we carefully guide students through the details of specific experiments and studies, students develop a solid understanding of how scientific evidence is gathered and the interplay between theory and research. And because we rely on original rather than secondary sources, students get an accurate presentation of both classic and contemporary psychological studies.

One unique way that we highlight the scientific method in *Discovering Psychology* is with our trademark **Science Versus Pseudoscience** boxes. In these boxes, students see the importance of subjecting various claims to the standards of scientific evidence. These boxes promote and encourage scientific thinking by focusing on topics that students frequently ask about in class. The fourth edition of *Discovering Psychology* includes the following Science Versus Pseudoscience boxes:

- What Is a Pseudoscience? (p. 20)
- Phrenology: The Bumpy Road to Scientific Progress (p. 58)
- Brain Myths (p. 70)
- Subliminal Perception (p. 87)
- Graphology: The "Write" Way to Assess Personality? (p. 427)
- EMDR: Can You Wave Your Fears Away? (pp. 572–573)

Critical Thinking Emphasis

Another important goal of *Discovering Psychology* is to encourage the development of critical thinking skills. To that end, we do not present psychology as a series of terms, definitions, and facts to be skimmed and memorized. Rather, we try to give students an understanding of how particular topics evolved. In doing so, we also demonstrate the process of challenging preconceptions, evaluating evidence, and revising theories based on new evidence. In short, every chapter shows the process of psychological research—and the important role played by critical thinking in that enterprise.

Because we do not shrink from discussing the implications of psychological findings, students come to understand that many important issues in contemporary psychology are far from being settled. Even when research results are consistent, how to interpret those results can sometimes be the subject of considerable debate. As the authors of the text, we very deliberately try to be evenhanded and fair in presenting both sides of controversial issues. In encouraging students to join these debates, we often challenge them to be aware of how their own preconceptions and opinions can shape their evaluation of the evidence.

Beyond discussions in the text proper, every chapter includes one or more **Critical Thinking** boxes. These boxes are carefully designed to encourage students to think about the broader implications of psychological research—to strengthen and refine their critical thinking skills by developing their own position on questions and issues that don't always have simple answers. Each Critical Thinking box ends with two or three questions that you can use as a written assignment or for classroom discussions. The fourth edition of *Discovering Psychology* includes the following Critical Thinking boxes:

- What Is Critical Thinking? (p. 16)
- Assessing the Violent Video Game Study (p. 30)
- ESP: Can Perception Occur Without Sensation? (pp. 108–109)
- Is Hypnosis a Special State of Consciousness? (pp. 152–153)
- Is Human Freedom Just an Illusion? (pp. 196–197)
- Does "Reel" Violence Cause Real Aggressive Behavior? (pp. 210–211)
- The Memory Wars: Recovered or False Memories? (pp. 244–245)
- The Persistence of Unwarranted Beliefs (p. 270)
- Has Evolution Programmed Us to Overeat? (p. 309)
- Emotion in Nonhuman Animals: Laughing Rats, Silly Elephants, and Smiling Dolphins? (pp. 336–337)
- The Effects of Child Care on Attachment and Development (pp. 362–363)
- Are Women Really More Emotional Than Men? (p. 329)
- Freud Versus Rogers on Human Nature (p. 413)
- Abuse at Abu Ghraib: Why Do Ordinary People Commit Evil Acts? (p. 462)
- Do Personality Factors Cause Disease? (p. 492)
- Are People with a Mental Illness as Violent as the Media Portray Them? (p. 508)
- Does Smoking Cause Depression and Other Psychological Disorders? (pp. 524–525)

Cultural Coverage

As you can see in Table 1 on page xxiv, we weave cultural coverage throughout many discussions in the text. But because students are usually unfamiliar with cross-cultural psychology, we also highlight specific topics in **Culture and Human Behavior** boxes. These boxes increase student awareness of the importance of culture in many areas of human experience. They are unique in that they go beyond simply describing cultural differences in behavior. They show students how cultural influences shape behavior and attitudes, including the student's own behavior and attitudes. The fourth edition of *Discovering Psychology* includes the following Culture and Human Behavior boxes:

- What Is Cross-Cultural Psychology? (pp. 12)
- Culture and the Müller-Lyer Illusion: The Carpentered-World Hypothesis (p. 120)
- Cultural Differences in Early Memories (p. 227)
- The Effect of Language on Perception (pp. 272–273)
- Stereotype Threat: Performing When There's a "Threat in the Air" (p. 290)
- Evolution and Mate Preferences (p. 314)
- Where Does the Baby Sleep? (p. 361)
- Conflict Between Adolescents and Their Parents (p. 379)
- Explaining Failure and Murder: Culture and Attributional Biases (p. 445)
- The Stress of Adapting to a New Culture (p. 481)
- Travel Advisory: The Jerusalem Syndrome (p. 535)
- Cultural Values and Psychotherapy (p. 574)

Table 1 Integrated Cultural Coverage

Page(s)	Topic	Page(s)	Topic
In addition to the topics covered in the Culture and Human Behavior boxes, cultural influences are addressed in the following discussions:		311	Cultural attitudes associated with the prevalence of eating disorders
10–12	Cross-cultural perspective in contemporary psychology	326	Culture and achievement motivation
21	Cross-cultural study of "pace of life" as example of naturalistic observation	328	Culturally universal emotions
49	Effect of traditional Chinese acupuncture on endorphins	329	Cross-cultural research on gender and emotional expressiveness
103–104	Pain experience affected by cultural learning experiences	330	Culture and emotional experience
122	Use of acupuncture in traditional Chinese medicine for pain relief	331	Cross-cultural studies of psychological arousal associated with emotions
145	Dream themes in different cultures	334	Universal facial expressions
154–155	Meditation in different cultures	335–337	Culture, cultural display rules, and emotional expression
155–156	Research collaboration between Tibetan Buddhist monks and western neuroscientists	359	Cultural influences on temperament
156–157	Use of psychoactive drugs in different cultures	360	Cross-cultural studies of attachment
157	Racial and ethnic differences in drug metabolism rate	362–363	Native language and infant language development
157	Cultural norms and patterns of drug use	363–364	Cross-cultural research on infant-directed speech
157	Differences in alcohol use by U.S. ethnic groups	364	Culture and patterns of language development
161–162	Tobacco and caffeine use in different cultures	365	Culture's influence on gender and gender roles
164	Peyote use in religious ceremonies in other cultures	373	Influence of culture on cognitive development
196–197	Clash of B. F. Skinner's philosophy with American cultural ideals and individualistic orientation	378–379	Cultural influences on timing of adolescent romantic relationships
209–212	Cross-cultural application of observational learning principles in entertainment-education programming in Mexico, Latin America, Asia, and Africa	385	Culture and images of aging
		398–399	Cultural influences on Freud's psychoanalytic theory
230	Cross-cultural research on tip-of-the-tongue phenomenon	406–407	Cultural influences on Jung's personality theory
271–273	Properties of language that are common to all cultures	408	Jung on archetypal images, including mandalas, in different cultures
274	Development of Nicaraguan Sign Language as cross-cultural evidence of innate human predisposition to develop language	408–409	Cultural influences on the development of Horney's personality theory
		409–410	Freud's impact on Western culture
277	Historical misuse of IQ tests to evaluate immigrants	413	Rogers on cultural factors in the development of antisocial behavior
277–279	Potential effect of culture on intelligence test performance	421–422	Cross-cultural research on the universality of the five-factor model of personality
279	Wechsler's recognition of the importance of culture and ethnicity in developing the WAIS intelligence test	440–442	Cultural conditioning and the "what is beautiful is good" myth
282–283	Role of culture in Gardner's definition and theory of intelligence	443–446	Attributional biases in individualistic versus collectivistic cultures
283–284	Role of culture in Sternberg's definition and theory of intelligence	450–454	Stereotypes, prejudice, and group identity
286	IQ and cross-cultural comparison of educational differences	452	Ethnocentrism
287–288	Effect of culture on IQ score comparisons	456	Influence of cultural norms on conformity
287–288	Rapid gains in IQ scores in different nations	464–465	Cross-cultural comparisons of destructive social influence
288–289	Cross-cultural studies of group discrimination and IQ	478	Cross-cultural research on life events and stress
289–291	Role of culture in tests and test-taking behavior	480	Cultural differences as source of stress
302–303	Culture's effects on food preferences and eating behavior	489	Cross-cultural research on the benefits of perceived control
307	Cross-cultural data on percentage of population who are overweight	499–500	Effect of culture on coping strategies

Table continues

Table 1 Integrated Cultural Coverage *continued*

Page(s)	Topic	Page(s)	Topic
507	Role of culture in distinguishing between normal and abnormal behavior	530	Role of culture in dissociative experiences
		536–537	Prevalence of schizophrenia in different cultures
509	Use of DSM categories to compile cross-cultural data on prevalence of psychological disorders	541	Findings from the Finnish Adoptive Family Study of Schizophrenia
514	Cultural variants of panic disorder and panic attacks	552	Use of interpersonal therapy to treat depression in Uganda
515	Taijin kyofusho, a culture-specific disorder related to social phobia	571	Impact of cultural differences on effectiveness of psychotherapy
519	Cultural influences in obsessions and compulsions	576	Efficacy of traditional herbal treatment for psychotic symptoms in India
526	Cultural expectations and diagnosis of personality disorders		

Gender Coverage

Gender influences and gender differences are described in many chapters. Table 2 shows the integrated coverage of gender-related issues and topics in *Discovering Psychology*. To help identify the contributions made by female researchers, the full names of researchers are provided in the References section at the end of the text. When researchers are identified using initials instead of first names (as APA style recommends), many students automatically assume that the researchers are male.

Table 2 Integrated Gender Coverage

Page(s)	Topic	Page(s)	Topic
4	Titchener's inclusion of female graduate students in his psychology program in the late 1800s	159	Gender and rate of metabolism of alcohol
		159	Gender and binge drinking among college students
6	Contributions of Mary Whiton Calkins to psychology	166–167	Gender differences in effects of MDMA (ecstasy) on the brain
6	Contributions of Margaret Floy Washburn to psychology		
23	Gender and video game playing among college students	176	Women as research assistants in Pavlov's laboratories
54–56	Endocrine system and effects of sex hormones	210–211	Gender and the long-term effects of viewing media violence
95	Gender differences in incidence of color blindness	272–273	Language, gender stereotypes, and gender bias
100	Gender differences in responses to human chemosignals (pheromones)	290	Test performance and the influence of gender stereotypes
		307	Gender and dieting behavior
101	Gender differences in olfactory function across cultures	308	Gender differences in rates of overweight and obesity
104	Gender differences in the perception of pain	309–310	Gender differences in activity level and metabolism
139	Gender differences in driving while sleepy and traffic accidents related to sleepiness	311	Gender differences in the prevalence of eating disorders
		314	Gender differences in mate preferences
140	Gender differences in stress-related insomnia following terrorist attacks	315–316	Sex differences in the pattern of human sexual response
140	Gender differences in incidence of some sleep disorders	316–317	Sexual motivation and sexual behavior
145	Gender differences in dream content	316–319	Sexual orientation

Table continues

Table 2 Integrated Gender Coverage *continued*

Page(s)	Topic	Page(s)	Topic
319–322	Sexual attitudes and behavior	494–495	Gender differences in providing social support and effects of social support
322	Sex differences in prevalence of sexual problems and dysfunctions	494–495	Gender differences in susceptibility to the stress contagion effect
328	Gender similarities and differences in experience and expression of emotion	494–495	Gender and social networks
329	Gender differences in emotional expression	498	Gender differences in responding to stress— the "tend-and-befriend" response
355	Sex differences in genetic transmission of recessive characteristics	510	Gender differences in the prevalence of psychological disorders
365	Definitions of gender, gender role, and gender identity	514	Gender differences in prevalence of phobias
365–366	Development of gender identity and gender roles	515	Gender differences in prevalence of social phobia and taijin kyofusho
365–366	Sex differences in early childhood behavior	517	Gender differences in prevalence of posttraumatic stress disorder
366–367	Theories of gender-role development		
366–367	Gender stereotypes and gender roles	522	Gender differences in prevalence of major depression and seasonal affective disorder
374–375	Gender differences in timing of the development of primary and secondary sex characteristics	523	Lack of gender differences in prevalence of bipolar disorder
375–376	Gender and accelerated puberty in father-absent homes	527–528	Gender differences in incidence of paranoid personality disorder
376	Gender differences in effects of early and late maturation	528	Gender differences in incidence of antisocial personality disorder
382	Gender differences in friendship patterns and age of first marriage	529	Gender differences in incidence of borderline personality disorder
384	Gender differences in single parent, head-of-household status	537–538	Paternal age and incidence of schizophrenia
385	Gender and patterns of career development and parenting responsibilities	542–543	Gender differences in number of suicide attempts and in numbers of suicide deaths
405–406	Gender identity development in Freud's psychoanalytic theory	556–557	Contributions of Mary Cover Jones to behavioral therapy
408	Sexual archetypes (anima, animus) in Jung's personality theory	584	Gender differences in sexual contact between therapists and clients
408–409	Horney's critique of Freud's view of female psychosexual development	B-10	Gender differences in management style
410–411	Critique of sexism in Freud's theory	B-12	Gender differences in reasons for wanting to telecommute
459	Gender similarities in results of Milgram's obedience studies		
479	Gender differences in frequency and source of daily hassles		

Neuroscience Coverage

Psychology and neuroscience have become intricately intertwined. Especially in the last decade, the scientific understanding of the brain and its relation to human behavior has grown dramatically. The imaging techniques of brain science—PET scans, MRIs, and functional MRIs—have become familiar terminology to many students, even if they don't completely understand the differences between them. To reflect that growing trend, we have increased our neuroscience coverage to show students how understanding the brain can help explain the complete range of human behavior, from the ordinary to the severely disturbed. Starting with Chapter 2, each chapter contains one or more **Focus on Neuroscience** discussions that are designed to complement the broader chapter discussion. Here is a complete list of the Focus on Neuroscience features in *Discovering Psychology*:

- Dissecting Einstein's Brain: Clues to a Genius? (p. 57)
- Understanding Brain-Imaging Techniques (pp. 60–61)
- Juggling and Brain Plasticity (p. 75)
- Vision, Experience, and the Brain (p. 93)
- Brain Changes During REM Sleep (p. 145)
- The Addicted Brain: Diminishing Rewards (p. 158)
- How Methamphetamines Erode the Brain (p. 163)
- Virtual Operant Conditioning: Remote-Controlled "Ratbots" (p. 202)
- Assembling Memories: Echoes and Reflections of Perception (p. 246)
- Mapping Brain Changes in Alzheimer's Disease (p. 252)
- Seeing Faces and Places in the Mind's Eye (p. 262)
- Dopamine Receptors and Obesity (p. 310)
- Emotions and the Brain (p. 333)
- The Adolescent Brain: A Work in Progress (p. 377)
- Romantic Love and the Brain (p. 320)
- Personality Traits and Patterns of Brain Activity (p. 421)
- Brain Reward When Making Eye Contact with Attractive People (p. 442)
- The Mysterious Placebo Effect (p. 485)
- The Hallucinating Brain (p. 534)
- Schizophrenia: A Wildfire in the Brain (p. 540)
- Comparing Psychotherapy and Antidepressant Medication (p. 581)

Chapter Applications

Among all the sciences, psychology is unique in the degree to which it speaks to our daily lives and applies to everyday problems and concerns. The **Application** at the end of each chapter provides an opportunity to present the findings from psychological research that address a wide variety of problems and concerns. In every Application, we present research-based information in a form that students can use to enhance everyday functioning. As you can see in the following list, topics range from improving self-control to overcoming gender differences in handling interpersonal conflict:

- Evaluating Media Reports About Psychology (pp. 34–35)
- Pumping Neurons: Maximizing Your Brain's Potential (pp. 77–78)
- Strategies to Control Pain (pp. 121–122)
- Improving Sleep and Mental Alertness (p. 168)
- Using Learning Principles to Improve Self-Control (p. 213)
- Superpower Memory in Minutes per Day! (p. 253–254)
- A Workshop on Creativity (pp. 292–293)
- Turning Your Goals into Reality (pp. 343–344)
- Raising Psychologically Healthy Children (pp. 389–390)
- Possible Selves: Imagine the Possibilities (pp. 431–432)
- The Persuasion Game (pp. 469–470)
- Minimizing the Effects of Stress (pp. 500–501)
- Understanding and Helping to Prevent Suicide (pp. 542–543)
- What to Expect in Psychotherapy (pp. 583–584)

The Pedagogical System

The pedagogical system in *Discovering Psychology* was carefully designed to help students identify important information, test for retention, and learn how to learn. It is easily adaptable to an SQ3R approach, for those instructors who have had success with that technique.

As described below, the different elements of this text form a pedagogical system that is very student-friendly, straightforward, and effective. We've found that it appeals to diverse students with varying academic and study skills, enhancing the learning process without being gimmicky or condescending. A special student preface titled **To the Student** on pages xli to xliv immediately before Chapter 1 describes the complete pedagogical system and how students can make the most of it.

The pedagogical system has four main components: (1) Advance Organizers, (2) Chapter Review, (3) the Student Study Guide, and (4) the *Discovering Psychology* fourth edition Web companion site. Major sections are introduced by an **Advance Organizer** that identifies the section's *Key Theme* followed by a bulleted list of *Key Questions*. Each Advance Organizer mentally primes the student for the important information that is to follow and does so in a way that encourages active learning. Students often struggle with trying to determine what's important to learn in a particular section or chapter. As a pedagogical technique, the Advance Organizer provides a guide that directs the student toward the most important ideas, concepts, and information in the section. It helps students identify main ideas and distinguish them from supporting evidence and examples.

There are several other in-chapter pedagogical aids. A clearly identified **Chapter Outline** provides an overview of topics and organization. Within the chapter, **Key Terms** are set in boldface type and defined in the margin. *Pronunciation guides* are included for difficult or unfamiliar words. Because students often have trouble identifying the most important theorists and researchers, names of **Key People** are set in boldface type within the chapter.

The **Chapter Review** at the end of each chapter contains several elements to help students review for exams. The chapter's **Key Points** are summarized and bulleted under each major section heading. This feature is followed by a page-referenced list of **Key Terms.** We also provide a page-referenced brief biography of **Key People** at the end of each chapter, mentioning again why each person is important.

Beyond the learning aids in the text, every new copy of *Discovering Psychology* comes with a free copy of the excellent **Study Guide** written by Cornelius Rea, Douglas College. Supplementing the study guide is the **Discovering Psychology Companion Web Site.** At the companion site, each chapter has *two 15-question self-scoring practice quizzes, flashcards for rehearsing key terms,* and *two interactive crossword puzzles.* The *Discovering Psychology* companion site also contains several other great features, including the Worth **Online Study Center,** which is designed to help students personally identify challenging concepts in order to master them (described on page xxxiii), Thomas Ludwig's award-winning **PsychSim 5** computer simulations, and **PsychQuest** interactive experiments and simulations. The companion Web site can be accessed at **www.DiscoveringPsychology.com**

The *Discovering Psychology* Teaching Package: Print Supplements

The comprehensive teaching package that accompanies *Discovering Psychology* is designed to help you save time and teach more effectively. Many elements of the supplements package will be particularly helpful to the adjunct or part-time instructor. This superb teaching package, expanded in the fourth edition, includes the following elements:

- **Instructor's Resources and Binder,** prepared by Skip Pollock, Mesa Community College; Claudia Cochran, El Paso Community College; Beth Finders, St. Charles Community College; Beverly Drinnin, Des Moines Area Community College; Wayne Hall, San Jacinto College-Central Campus; and Nancy Melucci, Los Angeles Community College District. The Instructor's Resources include an abundance of materials to aid instructors in planning their courses, including chapter learning objectives, detailed chapter outlines, lecture guides, classroom demonstrations and activities, student exercises, advice on teaching the nontraditional student, popular video suggestions, and "Psychology in the News" topics. Also included are two **Video Guides,** both written by Don and Sandy Hockenbury. These video guides tie the *Scientific American Teaching Modules* and *The Brain Teaching Modules* directly to the text. New to this edition, three **Faculty Guides** tie topics in the text to *Psychology: The Human Experience, The Worth Digital Media Archive,* and *The Mind Teaching Modules,* which provide the instructor with a rich array of opportunities to teach with media. Last but not least, the Instructor's Resources include **Crossword Puzzles,** also prepared by Don and Sandy Hockenbury. There are two crossword puzzles for each text chapter and one puzzle for each Appendix. The crossword puzzles are also available as interactive puzzles on the student section of the companion Web site.

- **Test Bank, written by Don and Sandra Hockenbury** This revised and enhanced printed Test Bank includes over 6,000 multiple-choice, true–false, and short-answer essay questions, plus Learning Objectives for each chapter that correspond to those in the Instructor's Resources. We have also added graphics to the Test Bank, so that you can include line art when generating and printing your tests. Each question is page-referenced to the textbook, identified as a factual/definitional or conceptual/analytical question, and keyed to the learning objective. The revision also includes more than 500 new questions.

- **Brownstone's *Diploma* Computerized Test Bank, Online Testing, and Gradebook** This versatile test-generating software allows instructors to edit, add, or scramble questions from the *Discovering Psychology* Fourth Edition Test Bank; format tests; and administer exams over a local area network or online. The Gradebook software allows you to track student progress and generate grade reports.

- **Full-color transparencies** with more than 200 images, charts, and photos from the text, including archival photographs of famous psychologists.

- **FREE! Study Guide for *Discovering Psychology,*** written by Cornelius Rea, Douglas College, New Westminster, British Columbia, Canada. The Study Guide is carefully designed to help students understand text information and prepare for exams. For every chapter, the Study Guide includes a Preview and an "At a Glance" section (both provide an overview of and objectives for the chapter). Each major topic includes a progress test, comprising multiple-choice, matching, and/or true–false questions. The Guide also contains "Graphic Organizers," which encourage students to complete graphs, charts, and flow diagrams that ultimately provide a visual synopsis of text material. End-of-chapter material includes "Something to Think About" sections, which contain thought-provoking questions designed to encourage critical thinking and application of the material.

■ **NEW!** *Pursuing Human Strengths: A Positive Psychology Guide* by Martin Bolt, Calvin College. Martin Bolt's new workbook aims to help students build up their psychological strengths. Closely following the research, this book provides a brief overview of 9 positive traits, such as hope, self-respect, commitment, and joy. It also offers self-assessment activities that help students gauge how much of the trait they have developed, and research-based suggestions for how they might work further toward fostering these traits.

■ *Psychology: The Human Experience* **Telecourse Student Guide,** written by Ken Hutchins, Orange Coast College. The Emmy-award–winning Coast Learning Systems telecourse titled *Psychology: The Human Experience* is based on Hockenbury & Hockenbury *Psychology,* the designated text to accompany the telecourse. Ken Hutchins, Don Hockenbury, and Sandra Hockenbury were members of the Faculty Advisory Committee and were closely involved in the development of the telecourse. The Telecourse Study Guide by Ken Hutchins draws clear connections between the text and the telecourse, helping students to get the most out of the learning experience.

■ **NEW! The** *Scientific American* **Psychology Reader, Second Edition,** is a collection of nine articles selected by Don and Sandra Hockenbury from recent issues of *Scientific American* magazine. The Hockenburys have written an introduction and preview of each article, as well as a series of thoughtful discussion questions to encourage classroom discussions.

■ *Improving the Mind and the Brain:* **A Scientific American Special Issue** This single-topic issue from *Scientific American* magazine features the latest findings from the most distinguished researchers in the field, including Fred Gage, Marguerite Holloway, Robert Sapolsky, and Steven E. Hyman.

■ *Scientific American Explores The Hidden Mind* In this special edition of *Scientific American* magazine, *The Hidden Mind* updates reports from some of the most notable neuroscientists studying the human brain, including Michael Gazzaniga, Antonio Damasio, Joseph LeDoux, Ursula Bellugi, and Doreen Kimura.

■ *Making Sense of Psychology on the Web* **with CD-ROM** by Connie K. Varnhagen, University of Alberta, is a brief booklet that helps students become discriminating Web users, locate reliable information, evaluate sites, and organize research. The guide includes a CD-ROM containing the award-winning Research Assistant HyperFolio, intuitive software that enables students to clip bits and pieces of Web sites and other electronic resources (snippets of text, illustrations, video clips, audio clips, and more) and compile them into worksheets and an easily accessible electronic filing cabinet.

■ *The Critical Thinking Companion,* **Second Edition,** by Jane Halonen, James Madison University, and Cynthia Gray, Alverno College. Tied to the main topics in introductory psychology, this engaging handbook includes six categories of critical thinking exercises: pattern recognition, practical problem solving, creative problem solving, scientific critical thinking, psychological reasoning, and perspective taking. The second edition has been updated to include six activities per chapter.

The *Discovering Psychology* Teaching Package: Media Supplements

- **NEW!** *eLibrary* **to accompany** *Discovering Psychology,* **Fourth Edition** www.worthpublishers.com/irel. The Hockenbury print and media supplements are regularly celebrated for their quality, abundance, and accuracy. However, the multiplicity of resources accompanying the text (combined with limited time) can be daunting. The eLibrary brings together the text and supplementary resources in a single, easy-to-use Web site, and includes a straightforward search engine (similar to Google) that allows you to quickly search for resources related to specific topics. You can quickly access content from the text and ancillary package and either download it or create a Web page to share with students.

- **NEW! Instructor's Resource CD-ROM to accompany** *Discovering Psychology,* **Fourth Edition** This newly customized presentation CD-ROM contains all text art and illustrations, as well as Outline, Illustration, and Enhanced Lecture PowerPoint slides. This new CD-ROM also includes an electronic version of the *Instructor's Resources.*

- **NEW!** *Moving Images: Exploring Psychology Through Film* **(available on DVD or VHS)** This new Worth Video Series includes short 3- to 10-minute video clips that span the introductory course and offer recent footage from a variety of academically sound sources, including Films for the Humanities and Sciences.

- **Worth Digital Media Archive CD-ROM (available on DVD or VHS)** This dual-platform Instructor's Presentation CD-ROM contains a rich collection of 42 digitized video clips of classic experiments and research. Footage includes Albert Bandura's Bobo doll experiment, Harold Takooshian's bystander studies, Piaget's conservation experiment, electrical brain stimulation, Harry Harlow's monkey experiments, Stanley Milgram's obedience study, and Ulric Neisser's selective attention studies. The *Digital Media Archive* clips on the CD are compressed in MPEG format and are compatible with Microsoft PowerPoint software. A **Faculty Guide** is available.

- *Psychology: The Human Experience* **Teaching Modules. (available on DVD or VHS)** This Emmy-award–winning series includes more than three hours of footage from the Introductory Psychology telecourse, *Psychology: The Human Experience*, produced by Coast Learning Systems in collaboration with Worth Publishers. Tied specifically to the Hockenbury text, these brief clips are ideal for lecture. Footage contains noted scholars, the latest research, and beautiful animations. A **Faculty Guide** is available.

- *Scientific American Frontiers* **Teaching Modules, Second Edition (available on DVD or VHS)** This collection of more than 30 video segments is adapted from the award-winning television series *Scientific American Frontiers*. Hosted by Alan Alda, these 8- to 12-minute teaching modules take your students behind the scenes to see how psychology research is actually conducted. The series features the work of such notable researchers as Daniel Schacter, Michael Gazzaniga, Steven Pinker, Benjamin Beck, Steve Sumi, Renée Baillargeon, Barry Beyerstein, Ray Hyman, Carl Rosengren, Laura Pettito, Barbara

Rothbaum, Robert Stickgold, and Irene Pepperberg. The **Faculty Guide** written by Don and Sandra Hockenbury links the modules to specific topics in *Discovering Psychology*. These video modules are an excellent resource to stimulate class discussion and interest on a variety of topics.

■ *The Brain* **Teaching Modules, Second Edition (available on DVD or VHS)** Along with new modules from the acclaimed PBS series, the second edition of *The Brain* Teaching Modules includes a **Faculty Guide** written by Don and Sandra Hockenbury that links the modules to specific topics in the fourth edition of *Discovering Psychology*. The second edition contains 10 new and 13 revised modules using added material, new audio, and new graphics. Individual segments range from 4 to 12 minutes in length, providing flexibility in highlighting specific topics.

■ *The Mind* **Teaching Modules, Second Edition. (available on DVD or VHS)** This revised and rich collection of 35 short clips dramatically enhances and illustrates key topics in the lectures and the text. The second edition contains updated segments on language processing, infant cognitive development, genetic factors in alcoholism, and living without memory (featuring a new interview with Clive Wearing). A **Faculty Guide** is available.

■ **Worth Image and Lecture Gallery at www.worthpublishers.com/ILG** Using the Image and Lecture Gallery, you can browse, search, and download all chapter art, illustrations, and prebuilt PowerPoint presentation files for all Worth titles. Users can also create personal folders for easy organization of materials.

■ **PowerPoint Slides** are available in three different formats and can be customized to fit your needs. Chapter art and text outlines make up two presentation formats. The third set, developed by longtime Hockenbury adopter Marian Gibney, Phoenix College, with contributions from Michelle Drapkin, Rutgers University, focuses on key terms and themes from the text and features tables, graphs, and figures from the text.

■ *PsychOnline* **(Course Management Version) by Thomas Ludwig, Hope College www.worthpublishers.com/psychonline** Housed in both WebCT and Blackboard, *PsychOnline* is a comprehensive instructor and student online solution for introductory psychology. Designed for use as a supplement for either Web-enhanced lecture courses or complete online courses, *PsychOnline* offers a rich, Web-based collection of interactive tutorials and activities for introductory psychology.

■ *PsychOnline 2.0* **by Thomas Ludwig, Hope College www.worthpublishers.com/psychonline2004** *PsychOnline 2.0* is a comprehensive online resource for introductory psychology. It includes more than 100 interactive tutorials and over 250 activities, plus the following new features: a Web-based interface that is easy to use and incorporate within your course; a self-guided study plan that includes a multiple-choice Diagnostic Test for each topic; and 20 modules from Thomas Ludwig's *PsychSim 5.0*.

■ **Online Course Materials** As a service for adopters using WebCT or Blackboard course management systems, Worth Publishers will provide the electronic instructor and student resources for this text in the appropriate format for their system. The files will be organized and prebuilt to match the specific software and can be easily downloaded (via the WebCT or Blackboard content showcases) directly onto the department server; they can be used to create entire online courses, to provide supplemental materials for existing courses, or for distance learning purposes. Course outlines, prebuilt quizzes, links, activities, and a whole array of materials are included, eliminating hours of work for instructors. Worth also supports the systems Angel and Desire2learn. For more information please visit www.bfwpub.com/lms.

■ **Personal Response System, offered by Worth Publishers, in partnership with EduCue.** The Personal Response System is the user-friendly way to make your class time more efficient, more interactive, and more effective. This wireless, remote system (about the size of a television remote control) lets you pause to ask questions and instantly record responses, as well as take attendance, direct students through lectures, gauge your students' understanding of the material, and much more. For each chapter, there are 8 to 10 questions (available in both Word and PowerPoint) that can be used in your PRS lecture. For more information, contact Worth Publishers at PRS@bfwpub.com.

■ **Hockenbury *Discovering Psychology* Companion Web Site at www.DiscoveringPsychology.com** provides students with a free online study guide, 24 hours a day, 7 days a week, with no access codes. Features include Learning Objectives, interactive Crossword Puzzles, Thinking Critically Web activities, annotated Web Links, Online Quizzes, and online versions of *PsychSim* and *PsychQuest* by Thomas Ludwig, Hope College. Instructors can download PowerPoint slides and access the Worth Image and Lecture Gallery.

■ **NEW! The Worth *Online Study Center 2.0* for *Discovering Psychology*, Fourth Edition** This new premium Web site helps students identify areas of potential weakness by combining a unique self-assessment tool with an intuitive search engine. Students can take a chapter-specific Self-Test and view a Study Plan generated directly from their results. After reviewing the various interactive resources and tutorials within the Study Plan, students can then take up to two more self-tests to see how they've improved their understanding of a certain topic. The *Online Study Center* also contains an online version of the *Discovering Psychology* textbook.

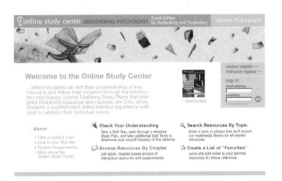

■ **REVISED! *PsychSim 5.0* by Thomas Ludwig, Hope College** Developed by leading multimedia author Thomas Ludwig, *PsychSim* is an award-winning program that offers a unique way for students to better understand the major concepts of general psychology. Version 5.0 contains new modules that place the student in the role of experimenter or subject in simulated research, or provide dynamic demonstrations illustrating fundamental psychology principles. Through *PsychSim,* students have a much deeper understanding of core psychological concepts by engaging in the discipline's classic experiments. Expanded to 42 modules, the new *PsychSim 5.0* is available to students on CD-ROM with an accompanying booklet.

■ ***PsychInquiry* for *Discovering Psychology*, Fourth Edition** Developed by leading multimedia author Thomas Ludwig (author of *PsychOnline, PsychSim,* and *PsychQuest*), this new CD-ROM contains dozens of highly interactive activities designed to help students learn about psychological research and improve their critical thinking. These activities enable students to work hands-on with descriptive, correlational, and experimental research (using observation, surveys, case studies, and experiments) to help them hone the critical thinking mindset required for psychological research. *PsychInquiry* activities are complete with animations, video, fresh illustrations, and self-assessment instruments that draw students into the discipline and introductory course. In addition to the coverage of core research concepts, *PsychInquiry* also offers a handful of more extensive research activities for use as classroom projects or lab assignments. Tied specifically to *Discovering Psychology,* Fourth Edition, the CD-ROM includes text-specific chapter quizzes, crossword puzzles, and flashcards (also available on the companion Web site).

- **Glosario/Glossary,** an online English–Spanish glossary, is tied to each of the textbook chapters. The Glosario/Glossary will help students whose native language is Spanish read and understand the text contents. Each glossary entry includes the English term and the Spanish term followed by the definition in Spanish plus text page references. Terms and definitions from the glossary are also available in flashcard format so students can quiz themselves on key terminology in their native language.

These print and media supplements are available to all qualified adopters of Hockenbury & Hockenbury *Discovering Psychology*. For more information about these supplements, contact your regional Worth/Freeman sales representative or call Faculty Services at 1-800-446-8923.

Acknowledgments

Many talented people contributed to this project. First, we would like to acknowledge the efforts of our supplements team that created materials specifically devoted to our book. Our thanks to:

- **Cornelius Rea** at Douglas College in British Columbia, Canada, for once again writing a very effective Student Study Guide.

- **Ken Hutchins** at Orange Coast College, Costa Mesa, California, for writing a thorough telecourse study guide that helps students get the most out of the new Coast Learning Systems Telecourse *Psychology: The Human Experience* and Hockenbury & Hockenbury *Psychology,* the text on which the telecourse is based.

- **Skip Pollock,** Mesa Community College; **Claudia Cochran,** El Paso Community College; **Beth Finders,** St. Charles Community College; **Nancy Melucci,** Los Angeles Community College District; **Bev Drinnin,** Des Moines Area Community College; and **Wayne Hall** of San Jacinto College for preparing comprehensive and substantially revised Instructor's Resources.

- **Marie Waung** at the University of Michigan at Dearborn for her exceptional appendix on industrial/organizational psychology.

- **Marie D. Thomas** at California State University, San Marcos, for providing a student-friendly statistics appendix.

- **Angela Ruiz Daudet,** translator of the English/Spanish Glosario/Glossary supplement to this text.

As colleagues who care as much as we do about teaching, they have our gratitude for their hard work and commitment to excellence.

We are indebted to our colleagues who acted as reviewers throughout the development of the fourth editions of *Psychology* and *Discovering Psychology*. Their thoughtful suggestions and advice helped us refine and strengthen the fourth edition. To each and every reviewer, thank you for generously sharing your time and candid thoughts with us:

Lise Abrams, University of Florida
Dave Alfano, Community College of Rhode Island
Mara Aruguete, Lincoln University

Harriet Bachner, Northeastern State University
Jacquelyn Beech, American River College
Jen Bizon, Texas A & M

Ann Brandt-Williams, Glendale Community College

Tom Carskadon, Mesa State

Beth Finders, St. Charles Community College

Mark Garrison, Kentucky State University

David Gersh, Houston Community College, Central

Karen Glendenning, Florida State University

Donald R. Green, Houston Community College, Southwest

Rodney Grisham, Indian River Community College

Judith Harackiewicz, University of Wisconsin

Terri L. Heck, Macomb Community College

Aeron Hicks, Fort Scott Community College

Sean Hill, Lewis & Clark Community College

Tasha Howe, Humbolt State University

Dave Kurz, Del Mar College

Kim MacLin, University of Northern Iowa

T. Darin Matthews, The Citadel

Maureen McCall, University of Louisville

Anne McCrea, Sinclair Community College

Julie Ann McIntyre, Russell Sage College

J. Mark McKellop, Juniata College

Penny S. McNatt, University of North Florida

Wendy L. Mills, San Jacinto College, North

Todd D. Nelson, California State University, Stanislaus

Ginger Osbourne, Santa Ana College

Skip Pollock, Mesa Community College

Jack Powell, Univeristy of Hartford

Russell Revlin, University of California, Santa Barbara

Edna Ross, University of Louisville

Heidi Smith, United States Air Force Academy

Keith Williams, Grand Valley State University

Kevin M.P. Woller, Rogers State University

We are especially delighted to acknowledge the valuable assistance of the following graduate students, all advanced psychology students at Rutgers University, for their many contributions to several chapters. We greatly appreciate your help in making the fourth edition of *Discovering Psychology* up to date. Good luck in your psychology careers!

Erica Briscoe

Thomas Cain

Florette Cohen

Jarret Crawford

Michelle Drapkin

Kim Fairchild

Robin Freyberg

Linda Kranitz

Amanda Moreno

Tami Musumeci

Christie Veitch

As we started to formulate our goals for the fourth edition of *Discovering Psychology*, we began by reviewing the comments, suggestions, and ideas from the reviewers who helped shape the earlier editions of our text. We would like to thank the following reviewers for their lasting contributions:

Harry Avis, Sierra College

Tricia Alexander, Long Beach City College

J. Michael Bailey, Northwestern University

Marie Banich, University of Illinois

Roy F. Baumeister, Case Western Reserve University

Tamara M. Beauboeuf, University of Houston–Downtown

Rebecca S. Bigler, University of Wisconsin

Connie Bosworth, El Paso Community College

Robert T. Brown, University of North Carolina/Wilmington

Mike Chase, Quincy University

Ann N. Dapice, Rogers University

B. David Das, Elgin Community College

Edward L. Deci, University of Rochester

Robin DesJardin, John Tyler Community College

Ernest Dzendolet, University of Massachusetts

David Eckerman, University of North Carolina

Robert Fisher, University of Texas

Peter Flynn, Northern Essex Community College

Elizabeth L. Glisky, University of Arizona

Kendra Gilds, Lane Community College

Harvey Ginsburg, Southwest Texas State University

Frank Hager, Allegany College

Diane F. Halpern, California State University

Richard Harland, West Texas A&M University

Jean Hill, New Mexico Highlands University

Sally Hill, Bakersfield College

Dean Hinshaw, Shasta College

Bryan Hoyt, Fort Hays State University

Edassery V. James, Purdue University–Calumet

Jon H. Kaas, Vanderbilt University

Louise Katz, Columbia State Community College

Mark Kelland, Lansing Community College

Beverly R. King, South Dakota State University

James E. King, University of Arizona

Alfred D. Kornfeld, Eastern Connecticut State University

Ilona Kovacs, Rutgers University

Linda Lawrence, University of New Mexico/Valencia

Laura Madson, New Mexico State University

Kam Majer, Glendale Community College

Brent Mallinckrodt, University of Missouri

Richard L. Mascolo, El Camino College

Nancy J. Melucci, El Camino College

Akira Miyake, University of Colorado at Boulder

Doug Mook, University of Virginia

Carolyn L. Morgan, University of Wisconsin/Whitewater

Joel Morgovsky, Brookdale Community College

Hajime Otani, Central Michigan University

W. Gerrod Parrott, Georgetown University

Joan Piroch, Coastal Carolina University

Kathleen Pope, Dixie College

Jack Powell, University of Hartford

James S. Previte, Victor Valley College

Debra Rowe, Oakland Community College

Harvey R. Schiffman, Rutgers University

N. Clayton Silver, University of Nevada, Las Vegas

Brett Silverstein, City College of New York

Nancy Simpson, Trident Technical College

Denise M. Sloan, Temple University

Gregory Snodgrass, Southwest Texas State University

Patricia Stephenson, Miami–Dade Community College

Mark Stewart, American River College

Ivonne Tjoe Fat, Rochester Community College

Richard W. Townsend, Miami–Dade Community College

Peter Urcuioli, Purdue University

Marie Waung, University of Michigan at Dearborn

David G. Webster, Georgia Southern University

Marcia Wehr, Santa Fe Community College

Eugene Winograd, Emory University

Brian W. Young, University of Nevada, Las Vegas

Cecelia K. Yoder, Oklahoma City Community College

Michael J. Zeller, Mankato State University

Worth Publishers

The remarkable people who make up Worth Publishers have a reputation for producing college textbooks of the highest quality. From the earliest stages of the editorial process to the last stages of production, their attention to every detail of this project never wavered. Each one of them played a critical role in helping us produce the best book possible.

Publisher Catherine Woods is always a reliable source of insight, encouragement, and advice. Catherine is truly a remarkable person, both professionally and personally. It is a privilege to call her our friend.

Acquisitions editor Charles Linsmeier made several contributions to our project. His conscientious attention to details and scheduling was especially helpful in making sure that the electronic and web-based supplements met the needs of faculty and students. In this edition, we also benefited from the helpful suggestions and organizational skills of freelance development editor Joan Brown.

The design of the fourth edition owes much of its effectiveness to the creative talents of art director Barbara Reingold, who patiently reworked numerous design elements until they were just right. We enjoyed the opportunity to work closely with designer Lee Ann Mahler, who achieved the seamless interaction of text, graphics, boxes, and features that you see on the pages of *Discovering Psychology*.

Many of the new photographs throughout this edition of *Discovering Psychology* appear due to the hard work of photo researchers Cecilia Varas and Donna Ranieri. The new and revised illustrations in the fourth edition represent the work of the artists at Dragonfly Media Group and Chris Notarile. And, we thank award-winning artist Phoebe Beasley for embracing the goals of our book and, once again, graciously allowing us to use her stunning collages for our cover and chapter opening images.

One of the great pleasures of the production process is working with associate managing editor Tracey Kuehn. Working diligently behind the scenes, Tracey never loses her cool (or anything else) throughout the sometimes nerve-racking production schedule. Tracey's expertise, creativity, and delightful sense of humor are invaluable as she tackles and resolves the inevitable problems that accompany a project of this complexity. Every step of the way, Tracey goes the extra mile to make sure the final product is as close to perfect as we can make it.

Project editor Anthony Calcara kept the seemingly unending stream of photos, figures, manuscript, and page proof flowing smoothly, coordinating a myriad of details with calm assurance. Copyeditor Karen Osborne, proofreader Lisa Kinne, and bibliographer Beverly Wehrli chased down the gremlins that seem to haunt publishing companies at night and managed to catch just about every one of them.

Up until the very last minute, production manager Barbara Seixas performed one miracle after another to bring the book to press on schedule. Barbara coordinated a bewildering array of technical details to deliver a beautifully produced book.

Supplements editors Andrea Musick, Eve Conte, Stacey Alexander, and Betty Probert brought a new level of expertise, reliability, and dedication to the development and production of a complex supplements package. They are awesome! With conscientious attention to a multitude of details, they expertly coordinated an integrated program of print, video, computer, and Internet supplements.

The dedication and enthusiasm of marketing manager Kate Nurre, who expertly coordinated advertising, marketing, and sales support efforts, helped launch the fourth edition with a bang. We also appreciate the support and leadership of Tom Scotty, national sales manager. Special thanks to our longtime friend and adopted family member, Steve Patrick, southwest regional manager.

Our Family and Friends

Finally, a few personal acknowledgments are in order. Several friends and family members kindly allowed us to share their stories with you. Sandy's mother, Fern, deserves particular thanks and recognition for her constant support and never-ending supply of funny stories. Sadly, we lost Erv since the publication of the last edition, but we know that he lives on in the stories we tell here as well as in our personal memories. We hope that our respect, love, and appreciation comes through in every story we tell! We also thank Janeen and Marty, Terry and Jean, Judy, and all the other members of our extended family for their support and encouragement. We are grateful to our niece Katie and to our good friends Asha and Paul, Marcia, and Nina and Mike for allowing us to tell their stories in our book. Had Richard lived to see *Discovering Psychology*, we know he would have been proud to be part of its pages. Special thanks also to our good friend Tom Gay, who challenged us to write this book 17 years ago and then guided us along the way. We continue to value Tom's wisdom, advice, and wonderful sense of humor.

Our daughter Laura has lived with this project since its inception and her own conception, as the two events very nearly coincided. Over the years, Laura became accustomed to postponing many simple pleasures of childhood "until the chapter was done." Now 16 years old, Laura is an independent-minded high school junior, aspiring biomechanical engineer, a dedicated pianist, and volunteer professional clown. She loves learning, reading, music, photography, clowning, sports, and above all, her two cats, Bob Cat and Tom Cat. And, making her parents laugh, of course. We are blessed to have a daughter who has been a constant source of joy and happiness, laughter and love throughout the writing process.

An Invitation

We hope that you will let us know how you and your students like the fourth edition of *Discovering Psychology*. And, as always, we welcome your thoughts, comments, and suggestions! You can write to us in care of Worth

Publishers, 41 Madison Avenue, 35th Floor, New York, NY 10010, or contact us via e-mail at:

DiscoveringPsychology@cox.net

Above all, we hope that your semester is an enjoyable and successful one as you introduce your students to the most fascinating and personally relevant science that exists.

With best wishes,

Learning from *Discovering Psychology*

Welcome to psychology! Our names are Don and Sandy Hockenbury, and we're the authors of your textbook. Every semester we teach several sections of introductory psychology. We wrote this text to help you succeed in the class you are taking. Every aspect of this book has been carefully designed to help you get the most out of your introductory psychology course. Before you begin reading, you will find it well worth your time to take a few minutes to familiarize yourself with the special features and learning aids in this book.

Learning Aids in the Text

Key Theme
- You can enhance your chances for success in psychology by using the learning aids that have been built into this textbook.

Key Questions
- What are the functions of the Prologue, Advance Organizers, Key Terms, and Key People?
- What are the functions of the different types of boxes in this text, and why should you read them?
- Where can you go to access a virtual study guide at any time of the day or night, and what study aids are provided?

First, take a look at the **Chapter Outline** at the beginning of each chapter. The Chapter Outline provides an overview of the main topics that will be covered in the chapter. You might also want to flip through the chapter and browse a bit so you have an idea of what's to come.

Next, read the chapter **Prologue**. The Prologue is a true story about real people. Some of the stories are humorous, some dramatic. We think you will enjoy this special feature, but it will also help you to understand the material in the chapter and why the topics are important. The Prologue will help you relate the new information in this book to experiences that are already familiar to you. In each chapter, we return to the people and stories introduced in the Prologue to illustrate important themes and concepts.

As you begin reading the chapter, you will notice several special elements. **Major Sections** are easy to identify because the heading is in red type. The beginning of each major section also includes an **Advance Organizer**—a short section preview that looks like the one above.

The **Key Theme** provides you with a preview of the material in the section to come. The **Key Questions** will help you focus on some of the most important material in the section. Keep the questions in mind as you read the section. They will help you identify the most important points in the chapter.

After you finish reading each section, look again at the Advance Organizer. Make sure that you can comfortably answer each question before you go on to the next section. If you want to maximize your understanding of the material, write out the answer to each question. You can also use the questions in the Advance Organizer to aid you in taking notes or outlining chapter sections.

Notice that some terms in the chapter are printed in **boldface,** or darker, type. Some of these **Key Terms** may already be familiar to you, but most will be new. The dark type signals that the term has a specialized meaning in psychology. Each Key Term is formally defined within a sentence or two of being introduced. The Key Terms are also defined in the margins, usually on the page on which they appear in text. Some Key Terms include a **pronunciation guide** to help you say the word correctly. Occasionally, we print words in *italic type* to signal either that they are boldfaced terms in another chapter or that they are specialized terms in psychology.

Certain names also appear in boldface type. These are the **Key People**—the researchers or theorists who are especially important within a given area of psychological study. Typically, Key People are the psychologists or other researchers whose names your instructor will expect you to know.

Reviewing for Examinations

The **Chapter Review** at the end of each chapter includes several elements to help you review what you have learned. The **Key Points** section provides a concise summary of the main ideas of the chapter. Because the Key Terms are boldfaced within the summary, you can see them again in the context in which they were introduced and used. All the chapter's **Key Terms** are listed, along with the pages on which they appear and are defined. You can check your knowledge of the Key Terms by defining each term in your own words, then comparing your definition to information on the page where it is discussed. Brief biographical sketches of the chapter's **Key People** appear at the end of each chapter, along with the numbers of the pages on which each person is discussed. These brief biographical sketches will help you remember why each scientist is important.

Special Features in the Text

Each chapter in *Discovering Psychology* has several boxes that focus on different kinds of topics. Take the time to read the boxes because they are an integral part of each chapter. They also present important information that you may be expected to know for class discussion or tests. There are four types of boxes:

- **Critical Thinking boxes** ask you to stretch your mind a bit, by presenting issues that are provocative or controversial. They will help you actively question the implications of the material that you are learning.

- **Science Versus Pseudoscience boxes** examine the evidence for various popular pseudosciences—from subliminal persuasion to graphology. These discussions will help teach you how to think scientifically and critically evaluate claims.

- **Culture and Human Behavior boxes** are another special feature of this text. Many students are unaware of the importance of cross-cultural research in contemporary psychology. These boxes highlight cultural differences in thinking and behavior. They will also sensitize you to the ways in which people's behavior, including your own, has been influenced by cultural factors.

- **In Focus boxes** present interesting information or research. Think of them as sidebar discussions. They deal with topics as diverse as déjà vu, human pheromones, whether animals dream, and why snakes give so many people the creeps.

There is also a special feature called **Focus on Neuroscience.** The Focus on Neuroscience sections provide clear explanations of intriguing studies that use brain-imaging techniques to study psychological processes. Among the topics that are highlighted: brain development during adolescence, schizophrenic hallucinations, mental images, drug addiction, and romantic love and the brain.

We think you'll find the **Application** section at the end of each chapter particularly helpful. Each Application provides concrete suggestions to help you deal with real-life concerns. These suggestions are based on psychological research, rather than opinions, anecdotes, or self-help philosophies. The Applications show you how psychology can be applied to a wide variety of everyday concerns. We hope that the Applications make a difference in your life. Because the Applications for Chapters 5, 6, and 8 deal with setting and achieving goals and enhancing motivation and memory, you may want to skip ahead and read them right after you finish this student preface.

There are two special appendices at the back of the text. The **Statistics: Understanding Data** appendix discusses how psychologists use statistics to summarize and draw conclusions from the data they have gathered. The **Industrial/Organizational Psychology** appendix describes the branch of psychology that studies human behavior in the workplace. Your instructor may assign one or both of these appendices, or you may want to read them on your own.

Also at the back of this text is a **Glossary** containing the definitions for all Key Terms in the book and the pages on which they are discussed in more detail. You can use the **Subject Index** to locate discussions of particular topics and the **Name Index** to locate particular researchers.

The *Discovering Psychology* Companion Web Site

The *Discovering Psychology* companion Web site provides you with a free virtual study guide, available 24 hours a day, 7 days a week. The companion Web site has a wealth of helpful study aids for each chapter in this book.

- You can print the **Learning Objectives** to provide a detailed list of the information that you should master for each chapter.

- You can take **Self-Scoring Quizzes** or use the **Flashcards** feature to test yourself on the Key Terms and Key People. The Web site also offers a Spanish-language version of the Flashcards.

- The **Interactive Crossword Puzzles** are a fun way to test your knowledge of Key Terms and ideas. There are two puzzles for each chapter and one for each appendix. There is also a "hint" feature if you get stuck on one of the crossword items.

- **Drag and Drop Figures** give you an opportunity to match Key Terms to the appropriate parts of a diagram or other graphic.

- **Interactive computer simulations**, **demonstrations**, and other **activities** are provided to help you apply and reinforce your understanding of important chapter concepts.

- **Critical Thinking Exercises** are linked to more than 100 other Web sites, and additional **Annotated Web Links** will allow you to explore psychology on the Internet.

You can access the Hockenbury companion Web site at the following Internet address:

www.DiscoveringPsychology.com

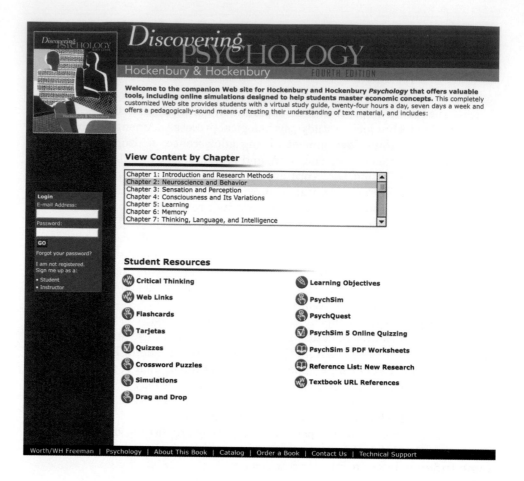

The Study Guide

Beyond the learning aids contained in each chapter and on the *Discovering Psychology* home page, we also highly recommend the excellent **Study Guide** that accompanies this text. The Study Guide was written by our colleague Cornelius Rea at Douglas College in New Westminster, British Columbia, Canada. Your bookstore should have copies available or will be happy to order it. If you did not receive a Study Guide when you purchased this text, you can order one through your college bookstore or through one of the online booksellers, such as Amazon.com or BarnesandNoble.com. The ISBN for the Study Guide is 0-7167-7655-3.

That's it! We hope you enjoy reading and learning from the fourth edition of *Discovering Psychology*. We welcome your thoughts or suggestions for the fifth edition of this book. You can write to us at the following address:

Don and Sandy Hockenbury
c/o Worth Publishers
41 Madison Avenue, 35th Floor
New York, NY 10010

Or you can contact us at our e-mail address:

DiscoveringPsychology@cox.net

Have a great semester!

Discovering PSYCHOLOGY

Second Circle Dance

Introduction and Research Methods

Prologue

Just a Game?

Walking into our 9:30 class on the Monday after Thanksgiving break, we could hear our students already engaged in a lively debate. Stacking our notebooks on the table at the front of the class, we started setting up the overhead projector. We were half-listening to the students talking and arguing when several words seemed to suddenly punctuate the air: *Columbine. Massacre. Plot. Guns. Jocks and preppies. Outcasts.*

We glanced at each other. *Another Columbine?*

"I remember how I felt in high school," Tanisha was saying. "It seemed like every other day was just another chance to get picked on. But I can't imagine wanting to kill everybody at school."

"Jared, what are you guys talking about?" Don asked as he fiddled with the focus on the overhead projector.

"There was this thing on the news this morning about the police arresting five high school students in Massachusetts who were supposedly planning a massacre like the one at Columbine," Jared explained.

"Did anyone get hurt?" Sandy asked.

"Nobody got hurt," Nicole answered. "This one girl warned her favorite teacher not to go to the high school because these other students were planning the attack."

"I was telling them that I heard this military psychologist talk at Holland Hall," Carla added. "He claimed that playing violent video games was involved in the school shootings at Columbine, Jonesboro, and that place in Kentucky."

"Was that the presentation by Dave Grossman?" Sandy asked.

"That was him!" Carla responded. "He had all these graphs showing how violent video games teach kids how to kill and make them think that shooting people is cool."

"I went to his talk," Don said. "Grossman made some interesting points."

"Man, that is so *not* true!" Kyle interjected. "I play *Quake III* and *Doom* all the time. They're fun! They're just shoot-'em-up video games!"

Kyle was one of those students who had stood out in class from the first day. Eighteen years old, six-foot-four, almost always wearing a red OU baseball cap and a "Students for Christ" T-shirt or sweatshirt, a professed Scooby-Doo addict, *and* the top-scoring student in all of his classes. Not the kind of young man that you'd expect to be spending his free time racking up kills on a video game.

"It may not affect you, Kyle, but I won't let either of my boys play those kinds of games," Kim said. "I think those boys at Columbine were addicted to those violent video games."

What Do Psychologists Study? Friendship and flirting, cooperation and confrontation. Public behavior, private thoughts. Happiness and hope, stress and pessimism. These are just a few of the wide range of topics studied in *psychology,* the science of behavior and mental processes. But whether psychologists study the behavior of a single brain cell or the behavior of a crowd on a college campus, they rely on the scientific method to guide their investigations.

"I don't think the video games had anything to do with it," Kyle insisted. "Those kids had other problems, serious psychological problems."

"Maybe so," Sandy said. "Still, it's an interesting question. I think there's quite a bit of research on that topic."

"Let's talk about this," Don said. "How could you test the claim that violent video games make people more aggressive?" As the discussion continued, we volunteered to look up some of the original research studies on the effects of video games and bring them to the next class. Later in the chapter, you'll see what we uncovered.

As this spontaneous class discussion demonstrated, psychology is a science that speaks to our lives in very real and meaningful ways. Indeed, many of the topics we cover strike a responsive chord in our students. As teachers, we've found that building on the many links between psychological knowledge and our students' personal experiences is a very effective way to learn about psychology.

Throughout this text, you'll see that we frequently relate new information to familiar experiences or use personal examples to illustrate abstract concepts. In linking familiar information to new information, our goal is to build a conceptual bridge between your existing knowledge and the new material that you need to learn. A key component of this approach is the Prologue that opens every chapter. Each Prologue is a true story about real people and events. The Prologue lays the groundwork for the chapter by introducing some of its major themes, and it shows you how those themes are linked to everyday life and familiar situations.

In this introductory chapter, we'll establish the foundation for the rest of the text. We'll build a bridge to the past as you learn about some of the key players who helped establish psychology as a science. One was the famous American psychologist William James. James was a master teacher who understood that information that is personally meaningful is better comprehended and remembered. We'll also establish a bridge to the present as we look at how psychologists investigate questions about behavior and mental processes—including whether playing violent video games can make people more aggressive. We hope that you, like our students, will see how psychological findings can make a difference in your own life.

Welcome to psychology!

Introduction

The Origins of Psychology

Key Theme
■ Today, psychology is defined as the science of behavior and mental processes, a definition that reflects psychology's origins and history.

Key Questions
■ How did philosophy and physiology affect the emergence of psychology as a science?
■ What roles did Wundt and James play in establishing psychology?
■ What were the early schools and approaches in psychology, and how did their views differ?

We begin this introductory chapter by stepping backward in time to answer several important questions: How did psychology begin? When did psychology begin? Who founded psychology as a science?

It's important to consider these historical issues for several reasons. First, students are often surprised at the wide range of topics studied by contemporary psychologists. Those topics can range from the behavior of a single brain cell to the behavior of people in groups, from prenatal development to old age, and from normal behavior and mental processes to severely maladaptive behavior and mental processes. As you become familiar with how psychology began and developed, you'll have a better appreciation for how it has come to encompass such diverse subjects.

Second, you need to understand how the definition of **psychology** has evolved over the past century to what it is today—*the science of behavior and mental processes.* Indeed, the history of psychology is the history of a field struggling to define itself as a separate and unique scientific discipline. The early psychologists struggled with such fundamental issues as:

- How should psychology be defined?
- What is the proper subject matter of psychology?
- Which areas of human experience should be studied?
- What methods should be used to investigate psychological issues?
- Should psychology include the study of nonhuman animal behavior?
- Should psychological findings be used to change or enhance human behavior?

These debates helped set the tone of the new science, define its scope, and set its limits. Over the past century, the shifting focus of these debates has influenced the topics studied, the emphasis given to particular areas, and the research methods used.

The Influence of Philosophy and Physiology

The earliest origins of psychology can be traced back several centuries to the writings of the great philosophers. More than 2,000 years ago, the Greek philosopher Aristotle wrote extensively about topics like sleep, dreams, the senses, and memory. He also described the traits and dispositions of different animals (Robinson, 1997). Many of Aristotle's ideas remained influential until the beginnings of modern science in the seventeenth century.

At that time, the French philosopher René Descartes (1596–1650) proposed a doctrine called *interactive dualism*—the idea that mind and body were separate entities that interact to produce sensations, emotions, and other conscious experiences. Today, psychologists continue to debate the relationship between mental activity and the brain.

Philosophers also laid the groundwork for another issue that would become central to psychology—the *nature–nurture issue.* For centuries, philosophers debated which was more important: the inborn *nature* of the individual or the environmental influences that *nurture* the individual. Psychologists continue to focus on this question, which today is usually framed in terms of *heredity versus environment.*

Such philosophical discussions influenced the topics that would be considered in psychology. But the early philosophers could advance the understanding of human behavior only to a certain point. Their methods were limited to intuition, observation, and logic.

The eventual emergence of psychology as a science hinged on advances in other sciences, particularly physiology. *Physiology* is a branch of biology that studies the functions and parts of living organisms, including humans. In the 1600s, physiologists were becoming interested in the human brain and its relation to behavior. By the early 1700s, it was discovered that damage to one side of the brain produced a loss of function in the opposite side of the body. By the early 1800s, the idea that different brain areas were related to different behavioral functions was being vigorously debated. Collectively, the early scientific discoveries made by physiologists were establishing the foundation for an idea that was to prove critical to the emergence of psychology—namely, that scientific methods could be applied to issues of human behavior and thinking.

psychology
The scientific study of behavior and mental processes.

Nature or Nurture? Both mother and son are clearly enjoying the experience of drawing together. Is the child's interest in art an expression of his natural tendencies, or is it the result of his mother's encouragement and teaching? Are such environmental factors more important than the child's inborn abilities? Originally posed by philosophers hundreds of years ago, such questions continue to interest psychologists today.

Wilhelm Wundt (1832–1920)
German physiologist Wilhelm Wundt is generally credited as being the founder of psychology as an experimental science. In 1879, he established the first psychology research laboratory in Leipzig, Germany. By the early 1900s, many American students had come to study at Wundt's facilities, which now occupied several floors at the university. By that time, Wundt's research had expanded to include such topics as cultural psychology and developmental psychology.

Wilhelm Wundt
The Founder of Psychology

By the second half of the 1800s, the stage had been set for the emergence of psychology as a distinct scientific discipline. The leading proponent of this idea was a German physiologist named **Wilhelm Wundt.** Wundt used scientific methods to study fundamental psychological processes, such as mental reaction times in response to visual or auditory stimuli. For example, Wundt tried to measure precisely how long it took a person to consciously detect the sight and sound of a bell being struck.

A major turning point in psychology occurred in 1874, when Wundt published his landmark text, *Principles of Physiological Psychology.* In this book, Wundt outlined the connections between physiology and psychology. He also promoted his belief that psychology should be established as a separate scientific discipline that would use experimental methods to study mental processes (Fancher, 1996). A few years later, in 1879, Wundt realized that goal when he opened the first psychology research laboratory at the University of Leipzig. Many regard this event as marking the formal beginning of psychology as an experimental science (Bringmann & others, 1997).

Wundt defined psychology as the study of consciousness and emphasized the use of experimental methods to study and measure consciousness. Until he died in 1920, Wundt exerted a strong influence on the development of psychology as a science. Two hundred students from around the world, including many from the United States, traveled to Leipzig to earn doctorates in experimental psychology under Wundt's direction (Benjamin, 1997). Over the years, some 17,000 students attended Wundt's afternoon lectures on general psychology, which often included demonstrations of devices he had developed to measure mental processes (Blumenthal, 1998).

Edward B. Titchener
Structuralism

One of Wundt's most devoted students was a young Englishman named **Edward B. Titchener.** After earning his psychology doctorate in Wundt's laboratory in 1892, Titchener accepted a position at Cornell University in Ithaca, New York. There he established a psychology laboratory that ultimately spanned 26 rooms.

Titchener eventually departed from Wundt's position and developed his own ideas on the nature of psychology. Titchener's approach, called *structuralism,* became the first major school of thought in psychology. **Structuralism** held that even our most complex conscious experiences could be broken down into elemental *structures,* or component parts, of sensations and feelings. To identify these structures of conscious thought, Titchener trained subjects in a procedure called *introspection.* The subjects would view a simple stimulus, such as a book, and then try to reconstruct their sensations and feelings immediately after viewing it. (In psychology, a *stimulus* is anything perceptible to the senses, such as a sight, sound, smell, touch or taste.) They might first report on the colors they saw, then the smells, and so on, in the attempt to create a total description of their conscious experience (Tweney, 1997).

In addition to being distinguished as the first school of thought in early psychology, Titchener's structuralism holds the dubious distinction of being the first school to disappear. With Titchener's death in 1927, structuralism as an influential school of thought in psychology essentially ended. But even before Titchener's death, structuralism was often criticized for relying too heavily on the method of introspection.

As noted by Wundt and other scientists, introspection had significant limitations (Blumenthal, 1998). First, introspection was an unreliable method of investigation. Different subjects often provided very different introspective reports about the same stimulus. Even subjects well trained in introspection varied in their responses to the same stimulus from trial to trial.

Edward B. Titchener (1867–1927)
Born in England, Titchener studied with Wundt in Germany and then became a psychology professor at Cornell University in 1892. In contrast to the psychology programs at both Harvard and Columbia Universities at the time, Titchener welcomed women into his graduate program at Cornell. In fact, more women completed their psychology doctorates under Titchener's direction than with any other male psychologist of his generation (Evans, 1991).

Second, introspection could not be used to study children or animals. Third, complex topics, such as learning, development, mental disorders, and personality, could not be investigated using introspection. In the end, the methods and goals of structuralism were simply too limited to accommodate the rapidly expanding interests of the field of psychology.

William James
Functionalism

By the time Titchener arrived at Cornell University, psychology was already well established in the United States. The main proponent of American psychology was one of Harvard's most outstanding teachers—**William James.** James had first become intrigued by the emerging science of psychology after reading one of Wundt's articles, entitled "Recent Advances in the Field of Physiological Psychology," in the late 1860s.

In the early 1870s, James began teaching a physiology and anatomy class at Harvard University. An intense, enthusiastic teacher, James was prone to changing the subject matter of his classes as his own interests changed (B. Ross, 1991). Gradually, his lectures came to focus more on psychology than on physiology. By the late 1870s, James was teaching classes devoted exclusively to the topic of psychology.

At about the same time, James began writing a comprehensive textbook of psychology, a task that would take him more than a decade. James's *Principles of Psychology* was finally published in two volumes in 1890. Despite its length of more than 1,400 pages, *Principles of Psychology* quickly became the leading psychology textbook. In it, James discussed such diverse topics as brain function, habit, memory, sensation, perception, and emotion. James's views had an enormous impact on the development of psychology in the United States (Bjork, 1997b).

James's ideas became the basis for a new school of psychology, called functionalism. **Functionalism** stressed the importance of how behavior *functions* to allow people and animals to adapt to their environments. Unlike structuralists, functionalists did not limit their methods to introspection. They expanded the scope of psychology research to include direct observation of living creatures in natural settings. They also examined how psychology could be applied to areas such as education, child rearing, and the work environment.

Both the structuralists and the functionalists thought that psychology should focus on the study of conscious experiences. But the functionalists had very different ideas about the nature of consciousness and how it should be studied. Rather than trying to identify the essential structures of consciousness at a given moment, James saw consciousness as an ongoing stream of mental activity that shifts and changes. As James wrote in *Talks to Teachers* (1899):

> Now the *immediate* fact which psychology, the science of mind, has to study is also the most general fact. It is the fact that in each of us, when awake (and often when asleep), *some kind of consciousness is always going on.* There is a stream, a succession of states, or waves, or fields (or whatever you please to call them), of knowledge, of feeling, of desire, of deliberation, etc., that constantly pass and repass, and that constitute our inner life. The existence of this is the primal fact, [and] the nature and origin of it form the essential problem, of our science.

Like structuralism, functionalism no longer exists as a distinct school of thought in contemporary psychology. Nevertheless, functionalism's twin themes of the importance of the adaptive role of behavior and the application of psychology to enhance human behavior continue to be evident in modern psychology (D. N. Robinson, 1993).

William James (1842–1910)
Harvard professor William James was instrumental in establishing psychology in the United States. In 1890, James published a highly influential text, *Principles of Psychology.* James's ideas became the basis of another early school of psychology, called *functionalism,* which stressed studying the adaptive and practical functions of human behavior.

structuralism
Early school of psychology that emphasized studying the most basic components, or structures, of conscious experiences.

functionalism
Early school of psychology that emphasized studying the purpose, or function, of behavior and mental experiences.

William James and His Students

Like Wundt, James profoundly influenced psychology through his students, many of whom became prominent American psychologists. Two of James's most notable students were G. Stanley Hall and Mary Whiton Calkins.

In 1878, **G. Stanley Hall** received the first PhD in psychology awarded in the United States. Hall founded the first psychology research laboratory in the United States at Johns Hopkins University in 1883. He also began publishing the *American Journal of Psychology,* the first U.S. journal devoted to psychology. Most important, in 1892, Hall founded the American Psychological Association and was elected its first president (Dewsbury, 2000). Today, the American Psychological Association (APA) is the world's largest professional organization of psychologists, with more than 150,000 members.

In 1890, **Mary Whiton Calkins** was assigned the task of teaching experimental psychology at a new women's college—Wellesley College. Calkins studied with James at nearby Harvard University. She completed all the requirements for a PhD in psychology. However, Harvard refused to grant her the PhD degree because she was a woman and at the time Harvard was not a coeducational institution.

Although never awarded the degree she had earned, Calkins made several notable contributions to psychology (Stevens & Gardner, 1982). She conducted research in many areas, including dreams, memory, and personality. In 1891, she established a psychological laboratory at Wellesley College. At the turn of the twentieth century, she wrote a well-received textbook, titled *Introduction to Psychology.* In 1905, Calkins was elected president of the American Psychological Association—the first woman, but not the last, to hold that position.

Just for the record, the first American woman to earn an official PhD in psychology was **Margaret Floy Washburn.** Washburn was Edward Titchener's first doctoral student at Cornell University. She strongly advocated the scientific study of the mental processes of different animal species. In 1908, she published an influential text, titled *The Animal Mind.* Her book summarized research on sensation, perception, learning, and other "inner experiences" of different animal species. In 1921, Washburn became the second woman elected president of the American Psychological Association (Carpenter, 1997).

G. Stanley Hall (1844–1924)
G. Stanley Hall helped organize psychology in the United States. Among his many achievements, Hall established the first psychology research laboratory in the United States and founded the American Psychological Association. In 1888, Hall became the first president of Clark University in Worcester, Massachusetts.

Mary Whiton Calkins (1863–1930)
Under the direction of William James, Mary Whiton Calkins completed all the requirements for a PhD in psychology. Calkins had a distinguished professional career, establishing a psychology laboratory at Wellesley College and becoming the first woman president of the American Psychological Association.

Margaret Floy Washburn (1871–1939)
After becoming the first American woman to earn an official PhD in psychology, Washburn went on to a distinguished career. Despite the discrimination against women that was widespread in higher education during the early twentieth century, Washburn made many contributions to psychology. She was the second woman to be elected president of the American Psychological Association.

Sigmund Freud

Psychoanalysis

Wundt, James, and other early psychologists emphasized the study of conscious experiences. But at the turn of the twentieth century, new approaches challenged the principles of both structuralism and functionalism.

In Vienna, Austria, a physician named **Sigmund Freud** was developing an intriguing theory of personality based on uncovering causes of behavior that were *unconscious,* or hidden from the person's conscious awareness. Freud's school of psychological thought, called **psychoanalysis,** emphasized the role of unconscious conflicts in determining behavior and personality.

Freud's psychoanalytic theory of personality and behavior was based largely on his work with his patients and on insights derived from self-analysis. Freud believed that human behavior was motivated by unconscious conflicts that were almost always sexual or aggressive in nature. Past experiences, especially childhood experiences, were thought to be critical in the formation of adult personality and behavior. According to Freud (1904), glimpses of these unconscious impulses are revealed in everyday life in dreams, memory blocks, slips of the tongue, and spontaneous humor. Freud believed that when unconscious conflicts became extreme, psychological disorders could result.

Freud's psychoanalytic theory of personality also provided the basis for a distinct form of psychotherapy. Many of the fundamental ideas of psychoanalysis continue to influence psychologists and other professionals in the mental health field. In Chapter 10, on personality, and Chapter 14, on psychotherapy, we'll explore Freud's views on personality in more detail.

Sigmund Freud (1856–1939)
In 1909, Freud (*front left*) and several other psychoanalysts were invited by G. Stanley Hall (*front center*) to participate in Clark University's 20th anniversary celebration in Worcester, Massachusetts. Freud delivered five lectures on psychoanalysis. Listening in the audience was William James, who later wrote to a friend that Freud struck him as "a man obsessed with fixed ideas" (Rosenzweig, 1997). Carl Jung (*front right*), who later developed his own theory of personality, also attended this historic conference. Ernest Jones, Freud's biographer and translator, is standing behind Hall.

John B. Watson

Behaviorism

The course of psychology changed dramatically in the early 1900s when another approach, called **behaviorism,** emerged as a dominating force. Behaviorism rejected the emphasis on consciousness promoted by structuralism and functionalism. It also flatly rejected Freudian notions about unconscious influences. Instead, behaviorism contended that psychology should focus its scientific investigations strictly on *overt behavior*—observable behaviors that could be objectively measured and verified.

Behaviorism is yet another example of the influence of physiology on psychology. Behaviorism grew out of the pioneering work of a Russian physiologist named **Ivan Pavlov.** Pavlov demonstrated that dogs could learn to associate a neutral stimulus, such as the sound of a bell, with an automatic behavior, such as reflexively salivating to food. Once an association between the sound of the bell and the food was formed, the sound of the bell alone would trigger the salivation reflex in the dog. Pavlov enthusiastically believed he had discovered the mechanism by which all behaviors were learned.

In the United States, a young, dynamic psychologist named **John B. Watson** shared Pavlov's enthusiasm. Watson (1913) championed behaviorism as a new school of psychology. Structuralism was still an influential perspective, but Watson strongly objected to both its method of introspection and its focus on conscious mental processes. As Watson (1924) wrote in his classic book, *Behaviorism:*

> Behaviorism, on the contrary, holds that the subject matter of human psychology *is the behavior of the human being.* Behaviorism claims that consciousness is neither a definite nor a usable concept. The behaviorist, who has been trained always as an experimentalist, holds, further, that belief in the existence of consciousness goes back to the ancient days of superstition and magic.

psychoanalysis
Personality theory and form of psychotherapy that emphasize the role of unconscious factors in personality and behavior.

behaviorism
School of psychology and theoretical viewpoint that emphasize the study of observable behaviors, especially as they pertain to the process of learning.

Three Key Scientists in the Development of Behaviorism Building on the pioneering research of Russian physiologist Ivan Pavlov, American psychologist John B. Watson founded the school of behaviorism. Behaviorism advocated that psychology should study observable behaviors, not mental processes. Following Watson, B. F. Skinner continued to champion the ideas of behaviorism. Skinner became one of the most influential psychologists of the twentieth century. Like Watson, he strongly advocated the study of observable behaviors rather than mental processes.

Ivan Pavlov (1849–1936)   John B. Watson (1878–1958)   B. F. Skinner (1904–1990)

The influence of behaviorism on American psychology was enormous. The goal of the behaviorists was to discover the fundamental principles of *learning*—how behavior is acquired and modified in response to environmental influences. For the most part, the behaviorists studied animal behavior under carefully controlled laboratory conditions.

Although Watson left academic psychology in the early 1920s, behaviorism was later championed by an equally forceful proponent—the famous American psychologist **B. F. Skinner.** Like Watson, Skinner believed that psychology should restrict itself to studying outwardly observable behaviors that could be measured and verified. In compelling experimental demonstrations, Skinner systematically used reinforcement or punishment to shape the behavior of rats and pigeons (Bjork, 1997a).

Between Watson and Skinner, behaviorism dominated American psychology for almost half a century (R. Evans, 1999a). During that time, the study of conscious experiences was largely ignored as a topic in psychology (Hilgard, 1992). In Chapter 5, on learning, we'll look at the lives and contributions of Pavlov, Watson, and Skinner in greater detail.

Carl Rogers
Humanistic Psychology

For several decades, behaviorism and psychoanalysis were the perspectives that most influenced the thinking of American psychologists. In the 1950s, a new school of thought emerged, called **humanistic psychology.** Because humanistic psychology was distinctly different from both psychoanalysis and behaviorism, it was sometimes referred to as the "third force" in American psychology (Cain, 2002).

Two Leaders in the Development of Humanistic Psychology Carl Rogers and Abraham Maslow were key figures in establishing humanistic psychology. Humanistic psychology emphasized the importance of self-determination, free will, and human potential. The ideas of Carl Rogers have been particularly influential in modern psychotherapy. Abraham Maslow's theory of motivation emphasized the importance of psychological growth.

Humanistic psychology was largely founded by American psychologist **Carl Rogers.** Like Freud, Rogers was influenced by his experiences with his psychotherapy clients. However, rather than emphasizing unconscious conflicts, Rogers emphasized the *conscious* experiences of his patients, including each person's unique potential for psychological growth and self-direction. In contrast to the behaviorists, who saw human behavior as being shaped and maintained by external causes, Rogers emphasized self-determination, free will, and the importance of choice in human behavior (Bozarth & others, 2002).

Abraham Maslow was another advocate of humanistic psychology. Maslow developed a theory of motivation that emphasized psychological growth, which we'll discuss in Chapter 8. Like psychoanalysis, humanistic psychology included not only influential theories of personality but also a form of psychotherapy, which we'll discuss in later chapters.

Carl Rogers (1902–1987)   Abraham Maslow (1908–1970)

By briefly stepping backward in time, you've seen how the debates among the key thinkers in psychology's history shaped the development of psychology as a whole. Each of the schools that we've described had an impact on the topics and methods of psychological research. As you'll see throughout this textbook, that impact has been a lasting one.

From the founding of Wundt's laboratory in 1879, psychology has evolved to its current status as a dynamic and multidimensional science. In the next section, we'll touch on some of the more recent developments in psychology's evolution. We'll also explore the diversity that characterizes contemporary psychology.

humanistic psychology
School of psychology and theoretical viewpoint that emphasize each person's unique potential for psychological growth and self-direction.

Contemporary Psychology

Key Theme
- As psychology has developed as a discipline, the topics it investigates have become progressively more diverse.

Key Questions
- How do the seven perspectives in psychology differ in emphasis and approach?
- What are psychology's major specialty areas?

Since the 1960s, the range of topics in psychology has become progressively more diverse. And, as psychology's knowledge base has increased, psychology itself has become more specialized (Bower, 1993). Rather than being dominated by a particular approach or school of thought, today's psychologists tend to identify themselves according to (1) the *perspective* they emphasize in investigating psychological topics and (2) the *specialty area* in which they have been trained and practice.

Major Perspectives in Psychology

Any given topic in contemporary psychology can be approached from a variety of perspectives. Each perspective discussed here represents a different emphasis or point of view that can be taken in studying a particular behavior, topic, or issue. As you'll see in this section, the influence of the early schools of psychology is apparent in the first four perspectives that characterize contemporary psychology.

The Biological Perspective

As we've already noted, physiology has played an important role in psychology since it was founded. Today, that influence continues, as is shown by the many psychologists who take the biological perspective. The *biological perspective* emphasizes studying the physical bases of human and animal behavior, including the nervous system, endocrine system, immune system, and genetics.

Interest in the biological perspective has grown in the last few decades, partly because of advances in technology and medicine. For example, in the late 1950s and early 1960s, medications were developed that helped control the symptoms of serious psychological disorders, such as schizophrenia and depression. The relative success of these new drugs sparked new questions about the interaction among biological factors and human behavior, emotions, and thought processes.

Equally important were technological advances that have allowed psychologists and other researchers to explore the human brain as never before. The development of the PET scan, MRI scan,

Psychology is the one discipline that uniquely encompasses the complex interplay between intrapersonal, biological, interpersonal, and socio-structural determinants of human functioning.

Albert Bandura (2001)

The Biological Perspective The physical aspects of behavior and mental processes are studied by biological psychologists. Psychologists and other scientists who specialize in the study of the brain and the rest of the nervous system are often called *neuroscientists.* Shown here is psychologist Suzanne Corkin, who heads up the Behavioral Neuroscience Laboratory at MIT (Massachusetts Institute of Technology). Corkin's research focuses on the brain mechanisms that underlie perception, memory, and thinking and other mental processes. She is also well known for her studies of the effects of brain injury on human memory. You'll read about Corkin's research in Chapter 6, on memory.

Studying Behavior from Different Psychological Perspectives Psychologists can study a particular behavior, topic, or issue from different perspectives. Consider the heroic efforts of the U.S. Coast Guard helicopter rescue teams in the first chaotic days after Hurricane Katrina devastated much of New Orleans. Trained to rescue people in life-or-death situations in turbulent open seas, the helicopter pilots and crew members criss-crossed the New Orleans skies, hour after hour, day after day, saving the lives of hundreds of people stranded by the flood waters.

Taking the *biological perspective*, a psychologist might study whether there are biological differences between the U.S. Coast Guard rescue workers and other people, such as the ability to stay calm and focused in the face of dangerous situations. A psychologist taking the *behavioral perspective* might look at how helping behaviors are learned and reinforced. Taking the *cognitive perspective*, another psychologist might investigate the kinds of mental processes that are involved in planning and carrying out the successful evacuation of thousands of desperate people from the rooftops of their submerged homes.

and functional MRI (fMRI) scan has allowed scientists to study the structure and activity of the intact brain. These and other advances have produced new insights into the biological bases of memory, learning, mental disorders, and other behaviors. In Chapter 2, we'll explore the biological foundations of behavior in detail.

The Psychodynamic Perspective

The key ideas and themes of Freud's landmark theory of psychoanalysis continue to be important among many psychologists, especially those working in the mental health field. As you'll see in Chapter 10, on personality, and Chapter 14, on therapies, many of Freud's ideas have been expanded or modified by his followers. Today, psychologists who take the *psychodynamic perspective* emphasize the importance of unconscious influences, early life experiences, and interpersonal relationships in explaining the underlying dynamics of behavior or in treating people with psychological problems.

The Behavioral Perspective

Watson and Skinner's contention that psychology should focus on observable behaviors and the fundamental laws of learning is evident today in the *behavioral perspective*. Contemporary psychologists who take the behavioral perspective continue to study how behavior is acquired or modified by environmental causes. Many psychologists who work in the area of mental health also emphasize the behavioral perspective in explaining and treating psychological disorders. In Chapter 5, on learning, and Chapter 14, on therapies, we'll discuss different applications of the behavioral perspective.

The Humanistic Perspective

The influence of the work of Carl Rogers and Abraham Maslow continues to be seen among contemporary psychologists who take the humanistic perspective. The *humanistic perspective* focuses on the motivation of people to grow psychologically, the influence of interpersonal relationships on a person's self-concept, and the importance of choice and self-direction in striving to reach one's potential. Like the psychodynamic perspective, the humanistic perspective is often emphasized among psychologists working in the mental health field. You'll encounter the humanistic perspective in the chapters on motivation (8), personality (10), and therapies (14).

The Cognitive Perspective

During the 1960s, psychology experienced a return to the study of how mental processes influence behavior (Evans, 1999b). This movement was called "the cognitive revolution" because it represented a break from traditional behaviorism. Cognitive psychology focused once again on the important role of mental processes in how people process and remember information, develop language, solve problems, and think.

The development of the first computers in the 1950s contributed to the cognitive revolution. Computers gave psychologists a new model for conceptualizing human mental processes—human thinking, memory, and perception could be understood in terms of an information-processing model. We'll consider the cognitive perspective in several chapters, including Chapter 7, on thinking, language, and intelligence.

The Cross-Cultural Perspective

More recently, psychologists have taken a closer look at how cultural factors influence patterns of behavior—the essence of the *cross-cultural perspective*. By the late 1980s, *cross-cultural psychology* had emerged in full force as large numbers of psychologists began studying the diversity of human behavior in different cultural settings and countries (Segall & others, 1998; Triandis, 1996). In the process, psychologists discovered that some well-established psychological findings were not as universal as they had thought.

For example, one well-established psychological finding was that people exert more effort on a task when working alone than when working as part of a group, a phenomenon called *social loafing*. First demonstrated in the 1970s, social loafing has been a common finding in many psychological studies conducted with American and European subjects. But when similar studies were conducted with Chinese participants during the 1980s, the opposite was found to be true (see Moghaddam & others, 1993). Chinese participants worked harder on a task when they were part of a group than when they were working alone.

These findings were just the tip of the iceberg. Today, psychologists are keenly attuned to the influence of cultural and ethnic factors on behavior. We have included Culture and Human Behavior boxes throughout this textbook to help sensitize you to the influence of culture on behavior—including your own. We describe cross-cultural psychology in more detail in Culture and Human Behavior Box 1.1 on page 12.

The Evolutionary Perspective

The newest psychological perspective to gain prominence is that of evolutionary psychology. **Evolutionary psychology** refers to the application of the principles of evolution to explain psychological processes and phenomena (Buss, 1999). The evolutionary perspective has grown out of a renewed interest in the work of English naturalist **Charles Darwin.** Darwin's first book on evolution, *On the Origin of Species by Means of Natural Selection,* was published in 1859.

The theory of evolution proposes that the individual members of a species compete for survival. Because of inherited differences, some members of a species are better adapted to their environment than are others. Organisms that inherit characteristics that increase their chances of survival in their particular habitat are more likely to survive, reproduce, and pass on their characteristics to their offspring. Conversely, individuals that inherit less-useful characteristics are less likely to survive, reproduce, and pass on their characteristics. This process reflects the principle of *natural selection:* The most adaptive characteristics are "selected" and perpetuated to the next generation.

How is evolutionary theory applied to psychology? Basically, psychologists who take the evolutionary perspective assume that psychological processes are also subject to the principle of natural selection. As David Buss (1995a) writes, a given psychological process exists in the form it does because it "solved a specific problem of individual survival or reproduction recurring over human evolutionary history." That is, those psychological processes that helped individuals adapt to their environments also helped them survive, reproduce, and pass those abilities on to their offspring.

As you consider the role of evolution in shaping modern psychological processes, keep a couple of things in mind. We tend to take the trappings of civilization—governments, transportation systems, factories and manufacturing, education, and organized medicine—for granted. But these aspects of everyday life developed only recently in the evolutionary history of *Homo sapiens.* What we think of as human history has existed for less than 10,000 years, since the earliest appearance of agriculture.

In contrast, our evolutionary ancestors spent more than *2 million years* as primitive hunter-gatherers. Our lives as humans living in agricultural, industrial, and postindustrial societies make up less than 1 percent of the time that humans spent as hunter-gatherers. The important point here is that a few thousand years are not long enough for sweeping evolutionary changes to take place. Psychological processes that were adaptations to a prehistoric way of life may continue to exist in the behavioral repertoire of people today. However, some of those processes may not necessarily be adaptive in our modern world (Cosmides & others, 1992).

evolutionary psychology
The application of principles of evolution, including natural selection, to explain psychological processes and phenomena.

The Evolutionary Perspective The evolutionary perspective analyzes behavior in terms of how it increases a species' chances to survive and reproduce. Comparing behaviors across species can often lead to new insights about the adaptive function of a particular behavior. For example, humans, monkeys, and apes are all members of the primate family. Close bonds with caregivers are essential to the primate infant's survival—whether that infant is a golden monkey at a wildlife preserve in northern China or a human infant at a family picnic in Norway. As you'll see in later chapters, the evolutionary perspective has been applied to many different areas of psychology, including human relationships, mate selection, eating behavior, and emotional responses (Caporael, 2001).

CULTURE AND HUMAN BEHAVIOR 1.1

What Is Cross-Cultural Psychology?

All cultures are simultaneously very similar and very different.

Harry Triandis (1994)

Culture is a broad term that refers to the attitudes, values, beliefs, and behaviors shared by a group of people and communicated from one generation to another (Matsumoto, 2000). A person's sense of cultural identity is influenced by such factors as ethnic background, nationality, race, religion, and language. When this broad definition is applied to people throughout the world, about 4,000 different cultures can be said to exist. Studying the differences among those cultures and examining the influences of culture on behavior are the fundamental goals of **cross-cultural psychology** (Betancourt & López, 1993; Segall & others, 1998).

People around the globe share many attributes: We all eat, sleep, form families, seek happiness, and mourn losses. Yet the way in which we express our human qualities can vary considerably among cultures. *What* we eat, *where* we sleep, and *how* we form families, define happiness, and express sadness can take very different forms in different cultures.

As we grow up within a given culture, we learn our culture's *norms,* or unwritten rules of behavior. Once those cultural norms are understood and internalized, we tend to act in accordance with them without too much thought. For example, according to the dominant cultural norms in the United States, infants and toddlers are not supposed to routinely sleep in the same bed as their parents. In many other cultures around the world, however, it's taken for granted that babies *will* sleep in the same bed as their parents or other adult relatives (Morelli & others, 1992). Members of these other cultures are often surprised and even shocked at the U.S. practice of separating infants and toddlers from their parents at night. (In Culture and Human Behavior Box 9.1 on page 361, we discuss this topic at greater length.)

Whether considering sleeping habits or hairstyles, most people share a natural tendency to accept their own cultural rules as defining what's "normal." This tendency to use your own culture as the standard for judging other cultures is called **ethnocentrism.** Although it may be a natural tendency, ethnocentrism can lead to the inability to separate ourselves from our own cultural backgrounds and biases so that we can understand the behaviors of others (Matsumoto, 2000). Ethnocentrism may also prevent us from being aware of how our behavior has been shaped by our own culture.

Some degree of ethnocentrism is probably inevitable, but extreme ethnocentrism can lead to intolerance for other cultures. If we believe that our way of seeing things or behaving is the only proper one, other ways of behaving and thinking may seem not only foreign, but ridiculous, inferior, wrong, or immoral.

In addition to influencing how we behave, culture affects how we define our sense of self (Kitayama & others, 1997; Markus & Kitayama, 1991, 1998). For the most part, the dominant cultures of the United States, Canada, Australia, New Zealand, and Europe can be described as individualistic cultures. **Individualistic cultures** emphasize the needs and goals of the individual over the needs and goals of the group (Triandis, 1996). In individualistic societies, social behavior is more strongly influenced by individual preferences and attitudes than by cultural norms and values. In such cultures, the self is seen as *independent,* autonomous, and distinctive. Personal identity is defined by individual achievements, abilities, and accomplishments.

In contrast, **collectivistic cultures** emphasize the needs and goals of the group over the needs and goals of the individual. Social behavior is more heavily influenced by cultural norms than by individual preferences and attitudes. In a collectivistic culture, the self is seen as being much more *interdependent* with others (Simon & others, 1995). Relationships with others and identification with a larger group, such as the family or tribe, are key components of personal identity. The cultures of Asia, Africa, and Central and South America tend to be collectivistic. According to Triandis (1995), about two-thirds of the world's population live in collectivistic cultures.

The distinction between individualistic and collectivistic societies is useful in cross-cultural psychology. Nevertheless, psychologists are careful not to assume that these generalizations are true of *every* member or *every* aspect of a given culture. Many cultures are neither completely individualistic nor completely collectivistic, but fall somewhere between the two extremes (Kagitçibasi, 1997). Equally important, psychologists recognize that there is a great deal of individual variation among the members of every culture (Gudykunst & Bond, 1997). It's important to keep that qualification in mind when cross-cultural findings are discussed, as they will be throughout this book.

The Culture and Human Behavior boxes that we have included in this book will help you learn about human behavior in other cultures. They will also help you understand how culture affects *your* behavior, beliefs, attitudes, and values as well. We hope you will find this feature both interesting and enlightening!

Cultural Differences in Subway Norms Like thousands of commuters in the United States, many commuters in Tokyo take the subway to work each day. In Japan, however, commuters line up politely behind white lines on the subway platform and patiently wait their turn to board the train. White-gloved conductors obligingly "assist" passengers in boarding by shoving them in from behind, cramming as many people into the subway car as possible. Clearly, the norms that govern subway-riding behavior are very different in American and Japanese cultures.

Specialty Areas in Psychology

The following list describes some of the important specialty areas in contemporary psychology, reflecting the enormous diversity of psychology today. Figure 1.1 shows the approximate percentage of American psychologists working in different specialty areas and employment settings.

Biological psychology focuses on the relationship between behavior and the body's physical systems, including the brain and the rest of the nervous system, the endocrine system, the immune system, and genetics.

Cognitive psychology investigates mental processes, including reasoning and thinking, problem solving, memory, perception, mental imagery, and language.

Experimental psychology is the term traditionally used to describe research focused on such basic topics as sensory processes, principles of learning, emotion, and motivation. However, note that experiments can be conducted by psychologists in every area of psychology.

Developmental psychology studies the physical, social, and psychological changes that occur at different ages and stages of the lifespan, from conception to old age.

Social psychology explores how people are affected by their social environments, including how people think about and influence others. Topics as varied as conformity, obedience, persuasion, interpersonal attraction, helping behavior, prejudice, aggression, and social beliefs are studied by social psychologists.

Personality psychology examines individual differences and the characteristics that make each person unique, including how those characteristics originated and developed.

Health psychology focuses on the role of psychological factors in the development, prevention, and treatment of illness. Health psychology includes such areas as stress and coping, the relationship between psychological factors and physical health, patient–doctor relationships, and ways of promoting health-enhancing behaviors.

Educational psychology studies how people of all ages learn. Educational psychologists help develop the instructional methods and materials used to train people in both educational and work settings. A related field, *school psychology,* focuses on designing programs that promote the intellectual, social, and emotional development of children, including children with special needs.

culture
The attitudes, values, beliefs, and behaviors shared by a group of people and communicated from one generation to another.

cross-cultural psychology
Branch of psychology that studies the effects of culture on behavior and mental processes.

ethnocentrism
The belief that one's own culture or ethnic group is superior to all others, and the related tendency to use one's own culture as a standard by which to judge other cultures.

individualistic cultures
Cultures that emphasize the needs and goals of the individual over the needs and goals of the group.

collectivistic cultures
Cultures that emphasize the needs and goals of the group over the needs and goals of the individual.

FIGURE 1.1 Specialty Areas and Employment Settings The pie chart on the left shows the specialty areas of psychologists who recently received their doctorates. The category "Other areas" includes such specialty areas as health psychology, forensic psychology, and sports psychology. The pie chart on the right shows psychologists' primary place of employment.

SOURCE: Frincke & Pate (2004).

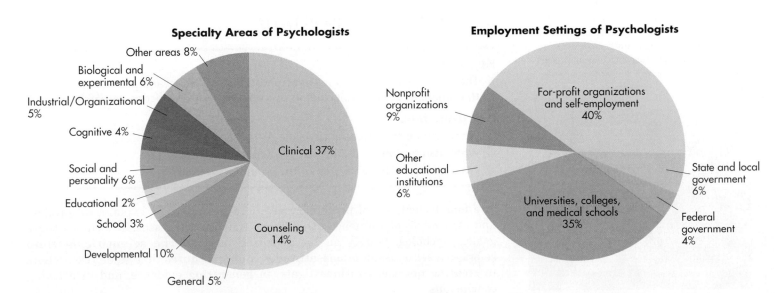

Specialty Areas of Psychologists

Other areas 8%
Biological and experimental 6%
Industrial/Organizational 5%
Cognitive 4%
Social and personality 6%
Educational 2%
School 3%
Developmental 10%
General 5%
Counseling 14%
Clinical 37%

Employment Settings of Psychologists

Nonprofit organizations 9%
Other educational institutions 6%
For-profit organizations and self-employment 40%
State and local government 6%
Federal government 4%
Universities, colleges, and medical schools 35%

School Psychology There are about 25,000 school psychologists in the United States who provide a variety of psychological services to children, adolescents, and families in public and private schools. School psychologists help teachers, school administrators, and parents understand how children learn and develop. Some of the activities that school psychologists perform include counseling and assessing students, consulting with parents and school staff, and working with outside agencies to promote learning and development.

Rx Privileges for Psychologists In 2004, Louisiana became the second state to grant prescription-writing privileges to properly trained psychologists, joining New Mexico, which enacted similar legislation in 2002 (Holloway, 2004a). After completing additional coursework and supervised clinical training, psychologists in these states are allowed to prescribe medications, like the antidepressant medications shown here, for symptoms of psychological disorders. Especially in rural areas underserved by mental health professionals, allowing trained psychologists to prescribe medications may help many people who have been unable to gain access to mental health care (Holloway, 2004b). Similar legislation is now pending in 18 other states.

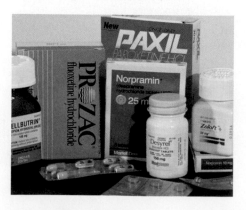

Industrial/organizational psychology is concerned with the relationship between people and work. This specialty includes such topics as worker productivity and job satisfaction, personnel selection and training, consumer reactions to a company's products or services, and the interaction between people and equipment.

Clinical psychology studies the causes, treatment, and prevention of different types of psychological disorders, such as anxiety or depression, eating disorders, and chronic substance abuse. Working in private practice, hospitals, or community mental health centers, clinical psychologists have extensive training in psychological disorders, psychotherapy techniques, and psychological testing. Along with conducting psychotherapy with individuals, clinical psychologists also work with married couples, families, and groups of unrelated people. A related specialty area is *counseling psychology,* which aims to improve everyday functioning by helping people cope more effectively with challenging situations and solve problems in daily living.

Like clinical psychologists, psychiatrists also study the causes, treatment, and prevention of psychological disorders. How are clinical psychologists and psychiatrists different? A *clinical psychologist* typically has a doctorate in psychology, which includes intensive training in treating people with psychological disorders. In contrast, a *psychiatrist* has a medical degree plus years of specialized training in the treatment of psychological disorders. Both clinical psychologists and psychiatrists can treat patients with psychological disorders. However, only psychiatrists can order medical procedures, like electroshock treatments, which are discussed in Chapter 14 on therapies. In most of the United States, psychiatrists and some other medical professionals, but not psychologists, can prescribe medications, but that is starting to change, as we discuss in the margin. Finally, a *psychoanalyst* is a clinical psychologist, psychiatrist, or other mental health professional with extensive training in Freud's psychoanalytic method of psychotherapy. In Chapter 14, we'll describe other workers in the mental health field, such as clinical social workers, licensed professional counselors, and marriage and family therapists.

Despite the diversity of their work settings and interests, psychologists share common methods of investigating facets of human behavior and mental processes. In the next section, we'll look at how psychologists are guided by the scientific method in their efforts to understand behavior and mental processes.

The Scientific Method

Key Theme
■ The scientific method is a set of assumptions, attitudes, and procedures that guide all scientists, including psychologists, in conducting research.

Key Questions
■ What are the four goals of psychology?
■ What assumptions and attitudes are held by psychologists?
■ What characterizes each step of the scientific method?

The four basic goals of psychology are to (1) describe, (2) explain, (3) predict, and (4) control or influence behavior and mental processes. To achieve these goals, psychologists rely on the scientific method. The **scientific method** refers to a set of assumptions, attitudes, and procedures that guide researchers in creating questions to investigate, in generating evidence, and in drawing conclusions.

Like all scientists, psychologists are guided by the basic scientific assumption that *events are lawful* (Rutherford & Ahlgren, 1991). When this scientific assumption is applied to psychology, it means that psychologists assume that behavior and mental processes follow consistent patterns. Psychologists are also guided by the assumption that *events are explainable*. Thus, psychologists assume that behavior and mental processes have a cause or causes that can be understood through careful, systematic study.

In striving to discover and understand consistent patterns of behavior, psychologists are *open-minded*. They are willing to consider new or alternative explanations of behavior and mental processes. However, their open-minded attitude is tempered by a healthy sense of *scientific skepticism*. That is, psychologists critically evaluate the evidence for new findings, especially those that seem contrary to established knowledge. And, in promoting new ideas and findings, psychologists are *cautious* in the claims they make.

Collectively, the assumptions and attitudes that psychologists assume reflect critical thinking. Ideally, you should assume the same set of attitudes as you approach the study of psychology. To learn how to be a better critical thinker, see Critical Thinking Box 1.2 on page 16.

The Steps in the Scientific Method
Seeking Answers

Like any science, psychology is based on **empirical evidence**—evidence that is the result of objective observation, measurement, and experimentation. As part of the overall process of producing empirical evidence, psychologists follow the four basic steps of the scientific method. In a nutshell, these steps are:

- Formulate a specific question that can be tested
- Design a study to collect relevant data
- Analyze the data to arrive at conclusions
- Report the results

Following the basic guidelines of the scientific method does not guarantee that valid conclusions will be reached. However, these steps do help guard against bias and minimize the chance for error and faulty conclusions. Let's look at some of the key concepts associated with each step of the scientific method.

Step 1. Formulate a Hypothesis That Can Be Tested Empirically

Once a researcher has identified a question or an issue to investigate, he or she must formulate a hypothesis that can be tested empirically. Formally, a **hypothesis** is a tentative statement that describes the relationship between two or more variables. A hypothesis is often stated as a specific prediction that can be empirically tested, such as "psychological stress increases the likelihood of physical illness."

The **variables** contained in any given hypothesis are simply the factors that can vary, or change. These changes must be capable of being observed, measured, and verified. The psychologist must provide an operational definition of each variable to be investigated. An **operational definition** defines the variable in terms of how it is to be measured, manipulated, or changed.

Operational definitions are important because many of the concepts that psychologists investigate—such as memory, happiness, or stress—can be measured in more than one way. In providing operational definitions of the variables in the study, the researcher spells out in very concrete and precise terms how the variables will be manipulated or measured. In this way, other researchers can understand exactly how the variables were measured or manipulated in a particular study.

scientific method
A set of assumptions, attitudes, and procedures that guide researchers in creating questions to investigate, in generating evidence, and in drawing conclusions.

empirical evidence
Evidence that is based upon objective observation, measurement, and/or experimentation.

hypothesis
(high-POTH-eh-sis) A tentative statement about the relationship between two or more variables.

variable
A factor that can vary, or change, in ways that can be observed, measured, and verified.

operational definition
A precise description of how the variables in a study will be manipulated or measured.

Formulating a Hypothesis: Do Dogs Look Like Their Owners? Hypotheses are often generated from everyday observations. For example, many people believe that pets resemble their owners. How could this hypothesis be scientifically tested? University of California–San Diego psychologists Michael Roy and Nicholas Christenfeld (2004, 2005) set out to test this hypothesis. They found that study participants were able to accurately match photos of dogs with photos of their owners—but only if the dogs were purebred. Other research has come to the same conclusion (Payne & Jaffe, 2005). The explanation? People tend to choose dogs that resemble themselves.

CRITICAL THINKING 1.2

What Is Critical Thinking?

As you'll see throughout this text, many issues in contemporary psychology are far from being settled. And although research findings may have been arrived at in a very objective manner, the *interpretation* of what findings mean and how they should be applied can be a matter of considerable debate. In short, there is a subjective side to *any* science. But this is especially important in psychology, because psychological research often involves topics and issues that apply directly to people's everyday concerns and behavior.

As you look at the evidence that psychology has to offer on many topics, we want to encourage you to engage in critical thinking. In general, critical thinking refers to *actively questioning* statements rather than blindly accepting them. More precisely, we define **critical thinking** as the active process of:

■ Trying to minimize the influence of preconceptions and biases while rationally evaluating evidence.

■ Determining the conclusions that can be drawn from the evidence.

■ Considering alternative explanations.

What are the key attitudes and mental skills that characterize critical thinking?

1. The critical thinker can assume other perspectives.

Critical thinkers are not imprisoned by their own points of view. Nor are they limited in their capacity to imagine life experiences and perspectives that are fundamentally different from their own. Rather, the critical thinker strives to understand and evaluate issues from many different angles.

BIZARRO   BY DAN PIRARO

CAPRICORN: TODAY IS A GOOD DAY TO MAKE IMPORTANT DECISIONS ABOUT YOUR LIFE BASED ON ARBITRARY NONSENSE WRITTEN BY AN ANONYMOUS STRANGER IN A NEWSPAPER.

2. The critical thinker is aware of biases and assumptions.

In evaluating evidence and ideas, critical thinkers strive to identify the biases and assumptions that are inherent in any argument. Critical thinkers also try to identify and minimize the influence of their *own* biases.

3. The critical thinker is flexible yet maintains an attitude of healthy skepticism.

Critical thinkers are open to new information, ideas, and claims. They genuinely consider alternative explanations and possibilities. However, this open-mindedness is tempered by a healthy sense of skepticism. The critical thinker consistently asks, "What evidence supports this claim?"

4. The critical thinker engages in reflective thinking.

Critical thinkers avoid knee-jerk responses. Instead, critical thinkers are *reflective*. Most

complex issues are unlikely to have a simple resolution. Therefore, critical thinkers resist the temptation to sidestep complexity by boiling an issue down to an either/or, yes/no kind of proposition. Instead, the critical thinker *expects* and *accepts* complexity (Halpern, 1998).

5. The critical thinker scrutinizes the evidence before drawing conclusions.

Critical thinkers strive to weigh all the available evidence *before* arriving at conclusions. And, in evaluating evidence, critical thinkers distinguish between *empirical evidence* and *opinions* based on feelings or personal experience.

As you can see, critical thinking is not a single skill, but rather a *set* of attitudes and thinking skills. As is true with any set of skills, you can get better at these skills with practice. That's one reason we've included Critical Thinking boxes in many chapters of this text.

You'll discover that these Critical Thinking boxes do not follow a rigid formula but are very diverse. Some will challenge your preconceptions about certain topics. Others will invite you to take sides in the debates of some of the most important contributors to modern psychology.

We hope you enjoy this feature!

Critical Thinking Questions

■ Why might other people want to discourage you from thinking critically?

■ In what situations is it probably most important for you to exercise critical thinking skills?

---

critical thinking
The active process of trying to minimize the influence of preconceptions and biases while rationally evaluating evidence, determining the conclusions that can be drawn from evidence, and considering alternative explanations.

For example, consider the hypothesis that negativity reduces marital stability (see Karney & Bradbury, 1995). To test this hypothesis, you would need to formulate an operational definition of each variable. How could you operationally define "negativity" and "marital stability"? What could you measure?

You could operationally define negativity in many different ways. For example, you might operationally define negativity as the number of arguments the couple has per month or as the number of critical comments each partner made about the other in a one-hour interview. In a similar way, you would have to devise an operational definition for marital stability, such as the number of times the couple has separated.

Step 2. Design the Study and Collect the Data

This step involves deciding which research method to use for collecting data. There are two basic categories of research methods—*descriptive* and *experimental*. Each research method answers different kinds of questions and provides different kinds of evidence.

Descriptive methods are research strategies for *observing* and *describing* behavior, including identifying the factors that seem to be associated with a particular phenomenon. Descriptive methods answer the who, what, where, and when kinds of questions about behavior. Who engages in a particular behavior? What factors or events seem to be associated with the behavior? Where does the behavior occur? When does the behavior occur? How often? In the next section, we'll discuss commonly used descriptive methods, including *naturalistic observation, surveys, case studies,* and *correlational studies.*

In contrast, the *experimental method* is used to show that one variable causes change in a second variable. In an experiment, the researcher deliberately varies one factor, then measures the changes produced in a second factor. Ideally, all experimental conditions are kept as constant as possible except for the factor that the researcher systematically varies. Then, if changes occur in the second factor, those changes can be attributed to the variations in the first factor.

Step 3. Analyze the Data and Draw Conclusions

Once observations have been made and measurements have been collected, the raw data need to be summarized and analyzed. Researchers use the methods of a branch of mathematics known as **statistics** to summarize, analyze, and draw conclusions about the data they have collected.

Researchers rely on statistics to determine whether their results support their hypotheses. They also use statistics to determine whether their findings are statistically significant. If a finding is **statistically significant,** it means that the results are not very likely to have occurred by chance. As a rule, statistically significant results confirm the hypothesis. Appendix A provides a more detailed discussion of the use of statistics in psychology research.

Keep in mind that statistical significance and practical significance are not necessarily the same thing. If a study involves a large number of participants, even small differences among groups of subjects may result in a statistically significant finding. But the actual average differences may be so small as to have little practical significance or importance. For example, a recent study tried to identify risk factors for people who attempt suicide (Mann & others, 1999). One statistically significant finding was that suicide attempters had fewer years of education (12.7 years) as compared to nonattempters (14 years). In practical terms, however, the difference was not substantial enough to be clinically meaningful in trying to help identify people who pose a suicide risk. So remember that a statistically significant result is simply one that is not very likely to have occurred by chance. Whether the finding is significant in the everyday sense of being important is another matter altogether.

A statistical technique called **meta-analysis** is increasingly being used in psychology to analyze the results of many research studies on a specific topic. Basically, meta-analysis involves pooling the results of several studies into a single analysis. By creating one large pool of data to be analyzed, meta-analysis can sometimes reveal overall trends that may not be evident in individual studies. Meta-analysis is especially useful when a particular issue has generated a large number of studies, some of which have produced weak or contradic-

---

statistics
A branch of mathematics used by researchers to organize, summarize, and interpret data.

statistically significant
A mathematical indication that research results are not very likely to have occurred by chance.

meta-analysis
A statistical technique that involves combining and analyzing the results of many research studies on a specific topic in order to identify overall trends.

Using Statistics to Predict College Success
How do you draw conclusions when there are many studies investigating the same basic question? Psychologist Steven Robbins and his colleagues (2004) used a statistical technique called *meta-analysis* to pool the results of more than 100 published studies investigating the psychological, social, and study skills most strongly associated with success in college. The researchers operationally defined "success in college" as cumulative grade point average (GPA). Beyond high school GPA and standardized test scores, the meta-analysis revealed that the strongest predictors of successful performance in college were two psychological factors related to motivation: *academic self-efficacy* and *achievement motivation*. As you'll read in Chapter 8, *self-efficacy* refers to the degree to which you are convinced of your ability to effectively meet the demands of a particular situation. *Achievement motivation* refers to your drive to excel, succeed, or outperform others on a particular task. Both of these motivational factors were more important in predicting college success than socioeconomic status, academic skills, or level of social or financial support.

tory results. When a large number of different factors have been implicated in a particular phenomenon, meta-analysis can help identify the most important factors.

Step 4. Report the Findings

For advances to be made in any scientific discipline, researchers must publish or share their findings with other scientists. In addition to reporting their results, psychologists provide a detailed description of the study itself, including the following:

- Who participated in the study
- How participants were selected
- How variables were operationally defined
- What procedures or methods were used
- How the data were analyzed
- What the results seem to suggest

Describing the precise details of the study makes it possible for other investigators to **replicate,** or repeat, the study. Replication is an important part of the scientific process. When a study is replicated and the same basic results are obtained again, scientific *confidence* that the results are accurate is increased. Conversely, if the replication of a study fails to produce the same basic findings, confidence in the original findings is reduced.

One way in which psychologists report their findings is by formally presenting their research at a professional conference. A researcher can also write a paper summarizing the study and submit it to one of the many psychology journals for publication. Before accepting papers for publication, most psychology journals send them to other psychologists to review. The reviewers critically evaluate different aspects of a study, including how the results were analyzed. If the study conforms to the principles of sound scientific research and contributes to the existing knowledge base, the paper is accepted for publication.

Throughout this text, you'll see citations that look like the following: (Anderson & Dill, 2000). These citations identify the sources of the research and ideas that are being discussed. The citation tells you the author or authors (Anderson & Dill) of the published study and the year (2000) in which the study was published. Using this information, you can find the complete reference in the alphabetized References section at the back of this text. The complete reference lists the authors' full names, the article title, and the journal or book in which the article was published. Figure 1.2 shows you how to interpret the different parts of a typical journal reference.

Claude Steele Presenting His Research Along with writing up their research in papers submitted for publication in peer-reviewed journals, psychologists also often discuss their research at national and regional psychology conferences. Here, Stanford University Professor Claude Steele discusses his research at the annual meeting of the American Psychological Society. Steele's research centers on *stereotype threat*, which refers to the ways that negative stereotypes can affect the performance of people who belong to stigmatized groups. We discuss Steele's influential research in chapter 7 (see Culture and Human Behavior Box 7.4 on page 290).

FIGURE 1.2 How to Read a Journal Reference Using the References section at the back of this text, you can find the complete source for each citation that appears in a chapter. This figure shows the different components of a typical journal reference. In the chapter itself, the citation for this particular reference would read "(Anderson & Dill, 2000)."

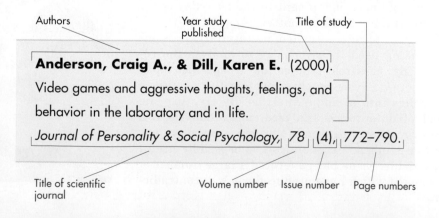

Authors — **Anderson, Craig A., & Dill, Karen E.** Year study published — (2000). Title of study — Video games and aggressive thoughts, feelings, and behavior in the laboratory and in life. *Journal of Personality & Social Psychology,* 78 (4), 772–790. Title of scientific journal — Volume number — Issue number — Page numbers

Building Theories
Integrating the Findings

As research findings accumulate from individual studies, eventually theories develop. A **theory,** or *model,* is a tentative explanation that tries to account for diverse findings on the same topic. Note that theories are *not* the same as hypotheses. A hypothesis is a specific question or prediction to be tested. In contrast, a theory integrates and summarizes a large number of findings and observations. Along with explaining existing results, a good theory often generates predictions and new hypotheses that can be tested by further research.

As you encounter different theories, try to remember that theories are *tools* for explaining behavior and mental processes, not statements of absolute fact. Like any tool, the value of a theory is determined by its usefulness. A useful theory is one that furthers the understanding of behavior, allows testable predictions to be made, and stimulates new research. Often, more than one theory proves to be useful in explaining a particular area of behavior or mental processes, such as the development of personality or the experience of emotion.

It's also important to remember that theories often reflect the *self-correcting nature of the scientific enterprise.* In other words, when new research findings challenge established ways of thinking about a phenomenon, theories are expanded, modified, and even replaced. Thus, as the knowledge base of psychology evolves and changes, theories evolve and change to produce more accurate and useful explanations of behavior and mental processes.

While the conclusions of psychology rest on empirical evidence gathered using the scientific method, the same is not true of *pseudoscientific* claims. As you'll read in Science Versus Pseudoscience Box 1.3 on page 20, pseudosciences often violate the basic rules of science.

replicate
To repeat or duplicate a scientific study in order to increase confidence in the validity of the original findings.

theory
A tentative explanation that tries to integrate and account for the relationship of various findings and observations.

descriptive research methods
Scientific procedures that involve systematically observing behavior in order to describe the relationship among behaviors and events.

naturalistic observation
The systematic observation and recording of behaviors as they occur in their natural setting.

Descriptive Research Methods

Key Theme
- ■ Descriptive research methods are used to systematically observe and describe behavior.

Key Questions
- ■ What are naturalistic observation and case study research, and why and how are they conducted?
- ■ What is a survey, and why is random selection important in survey research?
- ■ What are the advantages and disadvantages of each descriptive method?

Descriptive research methods are strategies for observing and describing behavior. Using descriptive methods, researchers can answer important questions, such as when certain behaviors take place, how often they occur, and whether they are related to other factors, such as a person's age, ethnic group, or educational level. As you'll see in this section, descriptive methods can provide a wealth of information about behavior, especially behaviors that would be difficult or impossible to study experimentally.

Naturalistic Observation
The Science of People- and Animal-Watching

When psychologists systematically observe and record behaviors as they occur in their natural settings, they are using the descriptive method called **naturalistic observation.** Usually, researchers engaged in naturalistic observation try to

SCIENCE VERSUS PSEUDOSCIENCE 1.3

What Is a Pseudoscience?

What do astrology, numerology, graphology, palmistry, aura reading, and crystal therapy have in common? All of these are examples of *pseudosciences.* The word *pseudo* means "fake" or "phony," so a pseudoscience is a *fake science.* More specifically, a **pseudoscience** is a theory, method, or practice that promotes claims in a way that appears to be scientific and plausible even though supporting empirical evidence is lacking or nonexistent (Lilienfeld & others, 2001; Shermer, 1997).

Some claims of paranormal phenomena also fall into the category of pseudoscience. **Paranormal phenomena** are alleged abilities or events that fall outside the range of normal experience and established scientific explanations. Examples of paranormal phenomena include *extrasensory perception* (ESP), such as mental telepathy, psychic predictions, and channeling (in which a spirit entity supposedly speaks through a human medium).

Many pseudoscientific claims violate a basic rule of science, called the **rule of falsifiability:** In order for a claim to be proved true, you must be able to identify some type of evidence that would refute the claim or prove that it is *false.* If there is no conceivable evidence that could disprove a claim, the claim is irrefutable—and examining evidence is pointless. *Irrefutable claims* often take the form of broad or vague statements that are essentially meaningless.

For instance, take the claim that "Wearing a quartz crystal will align your aura and balance your spiritual energy." How could such a statement be tested? Is there any kind of evidence that would *disprove* such a claim?

Pseudosciences often use anecdotes or *testimonials* as evidence to support their claims (Hines, 2003). For example, "My sister wore a quartz crystal for a year and she didn't catch a single cold!" Although such testimonials may sound convincing, they are *not* acceptable scientific evidence because they lack the basic controls used in experimental research. Many different factors could account for the

apparent success of the claim, some of which we'll describe in future chapters. These include simple coincidence, expectancy or placebo effects, misremembering, and illusory correlation. An **illusory correlation** is the mistaken belief that two factors or events are related when they are not—like the person's sister wearing a crystal and staying healthy.

Mixing established scientific facts with unfounded claims is another common pseudoscience strategy. For example, astrology claims that the gravitational forces of distant planets influence human personality and behavior on earth (Dean & others, 1996). But pseudosciences typically apply scientific principles in ways that are *not* substantiated by empirical evidence and are actually *contradicted* by scientific explanations. In the case of astrology, the gravitational effects of even the closest planets are far too weak to have any impact on earth-bound humans (Hines, 2003).

Many pseudosciences claim to enhance human behavior or abilities. To bolster the credibility of their claims, pseudosciences typically use lots of scientific jargon. Vague references to "leading researchers," "controlled psychological studies," "technological breakthroughs," and so forth may be cited without any documentation or specific sources.

One of our goals as the authors of your text is to help you develop the ability to think scientifically. This includes using scientific

thinking to evaluate claims about behavior or mental processes that seem farfetched. To help you understand how the scientific method could be used to test any claim, we created the **Is It TRUE?** model (Hockenbury & Hockenbury, 1999). Each letter of the word *TRUE* refers to a different step in the evaluation process, as follows:

T = Is It Testable? Can the claim be stated as a testable hypothesis? If the procedure to test the claim is an experiment, what are the independent and dependent variables? What are the operational definitions of the variables? What controls are needed for the test? If the claim is not testable, is there physical evidence to support the claim?

R = Is It Reliable? How many times was the claim tested? Has evidence for the claim been replicated? If the test was repeated by others, were the same results obtained?

U = Is It Unusual? Are the results significantly different from what you would expect if nothing more than chance or guessing were operating during the test?

E = Is It Explainable? How would a reasonable person explain the outcome? Are there other possible explanations for the outcome? If the results fail to provide support, how do proponents of the claim account for the results? Why might people be motivated to believe in the claim despite a lack of evidence supporting it?

Using the "Is It TRUE?" model can help you evaluate the evidence for or against pseudoscientific and paranormal claims. In the next few sections, we'll look at some of the strategies that psychologists and other scientists use to empirically test hypotheses and claims. And, in later chapters, you'll see how a variety of pseudoscience claims have stood up to scientific testing. We hope you enjoy the Science Versus Pseudoscience feature boxes throughout this text!

© 1999 by Sidney Harris

avoid being detected by their subjects, whether people or nonhuman animals. The basic goal of naturalistic observation is to detect the behavior patterns that exist naturally—patterns that might not be apparent in a laboratory or if the subjects knew they were being watched.

As you might expect, psychologists very carefully define the behaviors that they will observe and measure before they begin their research. Often, to increase the accuracy of the observations, two or more observers are used. In some studies, observations are videotaped or audiotaped so that the researchers can carefully analyze the details of the behaviors being studied.

One advantage of naturalistic observation is that it allows researchers to study human behaviors that cannot ethically be manipulated in an experiment. For example, suppose that a psychologist wants to study bullying behavior in children. It would not be ethical to deliberately create a situation in which one child is aggressively bullied by another child. However, it *would* be ethical to study bullying by observing aggressive behavior in children on a crowded school playground (Pepler & Craig, 1995).

As a research tool, naturalistic observation can be used wherever patterns of behavior can be openly observed—from the rain forests of the Amazon to fast-food restaurants, shopping malls, and singles' bars. Because the observations occur in the natural setting, the results of naturalistic observation studies can often be generalized more confidently to real-life situations than can the results of studies using artificially manipulated or staged situations (see Pepler & Craig, 1995).

Naturalistic Observation: Studying the "Pace of Life" Naturalistic observation can be used to study many different types of behavior. For example, social psychologist Robert Levine (1997) set out to compare the "pace of life" in 31 different countries. How could you operationally define the "pace of life"? One measure that Levine adopted was "the amount of time it took a pedestrian to walk a distance of 60 feet on a downtown city street." To collect the data, observers unobtrusively timed at least 35 male and 35 female pedestrians in each country (Levine & Norenzayan, 1999). The results? The fastest walkers were clocked in Ireland and the slowest in Brazil. Of the 31 countries, walkers in the United States were ranked as the 6th fastest, and Canadian walkers came in at 11th.

Case Studies
Details, Details, Details

A **case study** is an intensive, in-depth investigation of an individual or a small group of individuals. Case studies involve compiling a great deal of information, often from a variety of different sources, to construct a detailed picture of the person. The subject may be intensively interviewed, and his or her friends, family, and co-workers may be interviewed as well. Psychological records, medical records, and even school records may be examined. Other sources of information can include extensive psychological testing and observations of the person's behavior. Clinical psychologists and other mental health specialists routinely use case studies to develop a complete profile of a psychotherapy client.

Case studies are also used to investigate rare, unusual, or extreme conditions. Yet case studies often provide psychologists with information that can be used to help understand normal behavior. In Chapters 2 and 6, you'll see how case studies of people with brain damage have contributed to our understanding of such psychological functions as language and memory.

Surveys
(A) Always (B) Sometimes (C) You've Got to Be Kidding!

A direct way to find out about the behavior, attitudes, and opinions of people is simply to ask them. In a **survey,** people respond to a structured set of questions about their experiences, beliefs, behaviors, or attitudes. One key advantage offered by survey research is that information can be gathered from a much larger group of people than is possible with other research methods.

Typically, surveys involve a carefully designed questionnaire in a paper-and-pencil format that is distributed to a select group of people. Computer-based or Internet-based surveys have become increasingly more common. And, surveys

pseudoscience
A fake or false science that makes claims based on little or no scientific evidence.

paranormal phenomena
Alleged abilities or events that fall outside the range of normal experience and established scientific explanations.

rule of falsifiability
In order for a claim to be scientifically tested and proved true, there must be identifiable evidence that could prove the claim false.

illusory correlation
The mistaken belief that two factors or events are related when they are not.

case study
An intensive study of a single individual or small group of individuals.

survey
A questionnaire or interview designed to investigate the opinions, behaviors, or characteristics of a particular group.

are still often conducted over the telephone or in person, with the interviewer recording the person's responses. As with paper-and-pencil surveys, the interviewer usually asks a structured set of questions in a predetermined order. Such interview-based surveys are typically more expensive and time consuming than questionnaire-based surveys.

Surveys are seldom administered to everyone within the particular group or population under investigation. Instead, researchers usually select a **sample**—a segment of the larger group or population. Selecting a sample that is representative of the larger group is the key to getting accurate survey results. A **representative sample** very closely parallels, or matches, the larger group on relevant characteristics, such as age, sex, race, marital status, and educational level.

How do researchers select the participants so that they end up with a sample that is representative of the larger group? The most common strategy is to randomly select the sample participants. **Random selection** means that every member of the larger group has an equal chance of being selected for inclusion in the sample.

To illustrate how random selection works, let's look at how the sample was created for the *National Health and Social Life Survey* (abbreviated *NHSLS*). Conducted by researcher Robert T. Michael and his colleagues (1994) at the University of Chicago, the NHSLS focused on the sexual practices of American adults between the ages of 18 and 59. Here is Michael's description of how his team used random selection to choose the survey participants:

> Essentially, we chose at random geographic areas of the country, using the statistical equivalent of a coin toss to select them. Within these geographic regions, we randomly selected cities, towns, and rural areas. Within those cities and towns we randomly selected neighborhoods. Within those neighborhoods, we randomly selected households. . . . If there were two people living in a household who were in our age range, we flipped a coin to select which one to interview. If there were three people in the household, we did the equivalent of flipping a three-sided coin to select one of them to interview.

Notice that the participants who were interviewed in the NHSLS did *not* volunteer to participate in the survey. A specific individual was randomly selected through the process described. If that person refused to participate, someone else in the household could *not* substitute for that person. Using this random selection process, more than 3,000 people were interviewed for the National Health and Social Life Survey.

How closely did the NHSLS sample match important characteristics of the U.S. population? You can see for yourself by comparing the two columns in Table 1.1. Clearly, the random selection process used in the NHSLS resulted in a sample that very closely approximated the characteristics of the U.S. population as a whole.

In constructing the random sample for the National Health and Social Life Survey, the goal was to reflect the entire U.S. adult population. However, some surveys are designed to sample the experiences, behaviors, or opinions of a specific group of people. For example, researchers Craig Anderson and Karen Dill (2000) were interested in how much time young people spend playing video games, especially violent video games. They surveyed 227 college students taking introductory psychology classes at a large midwestern university. The students also completed some personality tests and a questionnaire on past delinquent behaviors.

Figure 1.3 shows some of the survey results. In general, the amount of time spent playing video games decreased as the participants advanced in their level of education. But even at the college level, 88 percent of the female students and 97 percent of the male students reported being regular video game players. *Super Mario Brothers, Tetris,* and *Mortal Kombat* were the most popular games.

Although Anderson and Dill's data are interesting, it's important to stress that their survey was not based on a random sample of U.S. youth. Consequently, all you can really conclude from this survey is what it indicated about the characteristics of the college students who participated. To make broader

Table 1.1

Comparing the NHSLS Sample and the U.S. Population

	NHSLS Sample	U.S. Population
Gender		
Men	44.6%	49.7%
Women	55.4	50.3
	100 %	100 %
Age		
18–24	15.9%	18.2%
25–29	14.5	14.3
30–39	31.3	29.5
40–49	22.9	22.7
50–59	15.3	15.3
	100 %	100 %
Education		
Less than high school	13.9%	15.8%
High school or equivalent	62.2	64.0
Any college	16.6	13.9
Advanced	7.3	6.3
	100 %	100 %
Marital Status		
Never married	28.2%	27.7%
Currently married	53.3	58.3
Divorced, separated	16.2	12.4
Widowed	2.3	1.6
	100 %	100 %
Race/Ethnicity		
White	76.5%	75.9%
Black	12.7	11.7
Hispanic	7.5	9.0
Other	3.3	3.3
	100 %	100 %

SOURCE: Michael & others (1994).

Using random selection, approximately 3,000 people were chosen for the sample used in the National Health and Social Life Survey (NHSLS). In this table, you can see that the overall characteristics of those in the NHSLS sample were very representative of the U.S. population as a whole.

generalizations about the video game habits and preferences of American youth, a survey based on a true random sample would be needed.

One potential problem with surveys and questionnaires is that people do not always answer honestly. Participants may misrepresent their personal characteristics or lie in their responses. These problems can be addressed in a well-designed survey. One strategy is to rephrase and ask the same basic question at different points in the survey or during the interview. The researchers can then compare the responses to make sure that the participant is responding honestly and consistently.

Correlational Studies
Looking at Relationships and Making Predictions

Key Theme

■ Correlational studies show how strongly two factors are related.

Key Questions

■ What is a correlation coefficient?

■ What is the difference between a positive correlation and a negative correlation?

■ Why can't correlational studies be used to demonstrate cause-and-effect relationships?

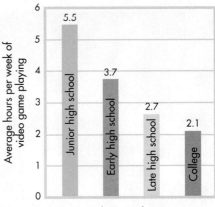

FIGURE 1.3 Time Spent Playing Video Games Anderson and Dill's (2000) survey of 227 college students revealed that the amount of time participants spent playing video games decreased as they attained higher levels of education. Notice that even at the college level, students reported playing video games for more than two hours per week on the average.

SOURCE: Adapted from data reported in Anderson & Dill (2000).

Along with answering the *who, what, where,* and *when* questions, the data gathered by descriptive research techniques can be analyzed to show how various factors are related. A **correlational study** examines how strongly two variables are related to, or associated with, each other. Correlations can be used to analyze the data gathered by any type of descriptive method.

To illustrate how correlational analysis can reveal links between different variables, let's return to the survey that Craig Anderson and Karen Dill (2000) conducted on video game playing by college students. Recall that Anderson and Dill collected data on the amount of time the participants spent playing different kinds of video games. The participants also filled out a questionnaire on past delinquent behavior and completed tests designed to measure different personality characteristics. Finally, Anderson and Dill compiled each student's cumulative grade point average.

Anderson and Dill wanted to know if there was any relationship between time spent playing video games and other factors, including personality attributes, delinquent behavior, or academic achievement. Once the data were collected from their survey participants, Anderson and Dill used statistical procedures to calculate a figure called a *correlation coefficient*.

A **correlation coefficient** is a numerical indicator of the strength of the relationship between two factors. A correlation coefficient always falls in the range from −1.00 to +1.00. The correlation coefficient has two parts—the number and the sign. The number indicates the *strength* of the relationship, and the sign indicates the *direction* of the relationship between the two variables.

More specifically, the closer a correlation coefficient is to 1.00, whether it is positive or negative, the stronger the correlation or association is between the two factors. Hence, a correlation coefficient of +.90 or −.90 represents a very strong association, meaning that the two factors almost always occur together. A correlation coefficient of +.10 or −.10 represents a very weak correlation, meaning that the two factors seldom occur together. (Correlation coefficients are discussed in greater detail in the Appendix on Statistics at the back of this book.)

Notice that correlation coefficients do not function like the algebraic number line. A correlation of −.80 represents a stronger relationship than does a correlation of +.10. The plus or minus sign in a correlation coefficient simply tells you the direction of the relationship between the two variables.

sample
A selected segment of the population used to represent the group that is being studied.

representative sample
A selected segment that very closely parallels the larger population being studied on relevant characteristics.

random selection
Process in which subjects are selected randomly from a larger group such that every group member has an equal chance of being included in the study.

correlational study
A research strategy that allows the precise calculation of how strongly related two factors are to each other.

correlation coefficient
A numerical indication of the magnitude and direction of the relationship (the *correlation*) between two variables.

Jazzing Up Your Love Life with Correlation Coefficients Using data from the University of Chicago's ongoing General Social Survey, researchers John Robinson and Geoffrey Godbey (1998) discovered that adult sexual behavior was positively correlated with certain musical preferences. After controlling for age and race, the researchers found that people who have a strong preference for jazz are 30 percent more sexually active than the average American. Liking other types of music, such as rock or rap, was unrelated to sexual activity. Does this mean that listening to jazz *causes* an increase in sexual activity? Not necessarily. Remember, a correlation between two factors does not necessarily indicate causality—only that the two factors co-vary in a systematic way.

A Perfect Positive Correlation: The Clock and the Bell Tower If a +1.00 correlation occurred between two variables, it would be termed a *perfect positive correlation*. This means that every time Factor A occurred, Factor B would also occur. This might seem to suggest that Factor A is causing Factor B to occur, but that's not necessarily the case. For example, every time the big hand on the clock tower gets to 12, two miles away the bell starts ringing. The two events are perfectly correlated yet, in this case, one does not cause the other.

A **positive correlation** is one in which the two factors vary in the *same* direction. That is, the two factors increase or decrease together. For example, Anderson and Dill found that there was a positive correlation of +.22 between the amount of time spent playing violent video games and aggressive personality characteristics. That is, as the amount of time spent playing violent video games *increased*, aggression scores on personality tests *increased*.

In contrast, a **negative correlation** is one in which the two variables move in opposite directions: As one factor decreases, the other increases. For example, Anderson and Dill found that there was a *negative* correlation of −.20 between the amount of time spent playing video games and academic achievement, as measured by cumulative college grade point average. As the amount of time spent playing video games *increased*, college grade point average *decreased*.

Given this basic information about correlation coefficients, what can we conclude about the relationship between the time spent playing video games and academic achievement? Or about exposure to violent video games and aggressive personality characteristics? Does the evidence allow us to conclude that playing video games *causes* a decrease in grade point average? Or that playing violent video games *causes* people to develop more aggressive personalities?

Not necessarily. For example, even if playing video games and getting poor grades were very strongly correlated, it's completely possible that some other factor is involved. For example, it could be that students who lack academic motivation tend to spend their free time playing video games rather than studying. Thus, it might be that a lack of academic motivation, rather than video games, is responsible for lower grades.

Similarly, consider the positive correlation between aggressive personality and amount of time spent playing violent video games. We cannot conclude that playing violent video games *causes* an increase in aggression. It's entirely possible that people who are more aggressive are attracted to violent video games or enjoy playing them. Thus, it could be that people with aggressive personalities are more likely to spend more time playing violent video games than people who are less aggressive.

Here is the critical point: Even if two factors are very strongly correlated, *correlation does not necessarily indicate causality*. A correlation tells you only that two factors seem to be related or that they co-vary in a systematic way. Although two factors may be very strongly correlated, correlational studies cannot be used to demonstrate a true cause-and-effect relationship. As you'll see in the next section, the experimental method is the only scientific strategy that can provide compelling evidence of a cause-and-effect relationship between two variables.

Even though you can't draw conclusions about causality from it, correlational research can be very valuable. First, correlational research can be used to rule out some factors and identify others that merit more intensive study. Second, the results of correlational research can sometimes allow you to make meaningful predictions. For example, when Anderson and Dill (2000) analyzed data from their survey, they discovered that there was a moderately strong correlation of +.46 between the amount of time spent playing violent video games and aggressive delinquent behavior, such as damaging public or private property. That is, the more time that was spent playing violent video games, the higher was the incidence of aggressive delinquent behavior. Looking at the overall results of their survey, Anderson and Dill concluded that there *were* legitimate reasons to be concerned about the potential negative consequences of long-term or excessive exposure to video games, especially violent video games. And, their findings led them to design an experiment to study the association between playing violent video games and actual aggressive behavior.

Each of the descriptive research methods we've looked at in this section can provide information about when behavior happens, how often it happens, and whether other factors or events are related to the behavior being studied. Next, we'll take an in-depth look at how Anderson and Dill used the experimental method to study the relationship between playing violent video games and aggressive behavior.

The Experimental Method

Key Theme
■ The experimental method is used to demonstrate a cause-and-effect relationship between two variables.

Key Questions
■ What were the hypothesis, independent variable, and dependent variable in the Anderson and Dill video game experiment?
■ What are the roles of random assignment, the experimental group, and the control group?
■ What are some important variations in experimental design, and what are the limitations of experiments?

The **experimental method** is a research method used to demonstrate a cause-and-effect relationship between changes in one variable and the effect that is produced on another variable. Conducting an experiment involves deliberately varying one factor, which is called the **independent variable.** The researcher then measures the changes, if any, that are produced in a second factor, called the **dependent variable.** The dependent variable is so named because changes in it *depend* on variations in the independent variable.

To the greatest degree possible, all other conditions in the experiment are held constant. Thus, when the data are analyzed, any changes that occur in the dependent variable can be attributed to the deliberate manipulation of the independent variable. In this way, an experiment can demonstrate a cause-and-effect relationship between the independent and dependent variables.

Do Violent Video Games Increase Aggressive Behavior?

Remember the chapter Prologue and our students' questions about the influence of video games on aggressive behavior? To help you understand the experimental method, let's look at part of an experiment conducted by psychologists Craig Anderson and Karen Dill.

Anderson and Dill (2000) wanted to study the effects of playing violent video games on behavior, especially aggressive behavior. In the previous section, we noted that Anderson and Dill conducted a correlational study based on questionnaires and personality measures that were administered to a large number of college students. Analysis of the data indicated that playing violent video games was strongly and positively correlated with two factors: aggressive delinquent behavior in real life and, to a lesser degree, aggressive personality characteristics. However, as Anderson and Dill noted, such correlational evidence *cannot* be used to draw conclusions about cause-and-effect relationships. Experimental evidence is needed to show that a causal relationship exists between two variables—in this case, between playing violent video games and exhibiting real-life aggression.

positive correlation
A finding that two factors vary systematically in the same direction, increasing or decreasing together.

negative correlation
A finding that two factors vary systematically in opposite directions, one increasing as the other decreases.

experimental method
A method of investigation used to demonstrate cause-and-effect relationships by purposely manipulating one factor thought to produce change in another factor.

independent variable
The purposely manipulated factor thought to produce change in an experiment; also called the *treatment of interest.*

dependent variable
The factor that is observed and measured for change in an experiment; thought to be influenced by the independent variable.

71%	Percentage of teenage boys who have played *Grand Theft Auto* video games
62%	Percentage of teenagers who play video games at least one hour per week

Source: (Crabtree, 2003)

The Hypothesis, Participants, and Random Assignment

Anderson and Dill set out to experimentally test the hypothesis that playing violent video games would increase aggressive behavior. The participants in their study were 210 undergraduate students—104 females and 106 males—taking an introductory psychology class. All students received partial credit in the class for voluntarily participating in the experiment. An alternate activity was available for class credit for students who did not want to participate in the study.

The researchers used a process called *random assignment* to assign participants to the different experimental groups. **Random assignment** means that all participants in the study have an equal chance of being assigned to any of the groups in the experiment. Random assignment is an important element of good experimental design, because it helps ensure that potential differences among the participants are spread out across all experimental conditions. And, because the same criteria are used to assign all participants to the different groups in the experiment, random assignment helps make sure that the assignment of participants is not biased in any way.

Violent Video Games and Aggressive Behavior As you can see in this screen shot from a best-selling video game, *Grand Theft Auto 3,* graphic violence is a core theme of many popular computer games. These games use realistic sounds and sophisticated 3-D visual effects. The player typically assumes the role of the main character, firing a variety of weapons and racking up points for killing and mutilating opponents or even innocent bystanders. Are such games harmless entertainment? Or do they encourage real-life aggressive behavior?

The Experimental and Control Groups

In this experiment, the *independent variable,* which is also sometimes referred to as the *treatment of interest,* was playing a violent video game. Those participants who were randomly assigned to play the violent video game constituted the **experimental group,** or the **experimental condition.** Participants in the experimental group go through all the different phases of the experiment and are exposed to the independent variable, or treatment of interest.

In any well-designed experiment, there is at least one **control group,** or **control condition.** In Anderson and Dill's experiment, the control group consisted of the participants who were assigned to play a *nonviolent* video game. In a typical experiment, the participants assigned to the control group go through all the experimental phases but are *not* exposed to the independent variable. Thus, the control group serves as a baseline against which changes in the experimental group can be compared.

How were the violent and nonviolent video games chosen? Anderson and Dill selected them on the basis of a previous study they had done in which participants rated several video games. That study had indicated that two video games were essentially the same in terms of difficulty, enjoyment, and frustration, but differed in the amount of violence. Those two video games were *Wolfenstein 3D* and *Myst.*

Here's the basic storyline of *Wolfenstein 3D:* It's World War II. You, the hero, have been imprisoned by the Nazis in the dungeon of Castle Wolfenstein. You escape (of course) and gain access to an arsenal of weapons, including a machine gun, a revolver, a knife, and a flame thrower. Your goal? Kill the Nazi guards as you make your way through the maze of tunnels and halls that wind through Castle Wolfenstein, progressively advancing in game levels so that you can kill the most nefarious Nazi of all—Adolf Hitler.

In contrast, *Myst* is an engaging, interactive game set on a mysterious island. Lush scenery, background music, and three-dimensional effects enhance the game, which was deliberately designed to be nonviolent. To play the game, you explore the island, uncover secrets, collect clues, and solve a variety of puzzles with logic and the information you've gathered.

The Dependent Variable: Aggressive Behavior

The hypothesis predicted that playing violent video games (the independent variable) would increase aggressive behavior (the dependent variable). How did Anderson and Dill operationally define "aggressive behavior"? Ethically, of course, the researchers could not create an experimental situation in which participants could actually attack or harm one another, either physically or otherwise. Instead, they used a standard measure of aggressive behavior called the *Competitive Reaction Time Task*.

Here's how the Competitive Reaction Time Task works. Two research participants are situated in different rooms, each wearing headphones and sitting in front of a computer screen. As soon as the participants hear a signal tone, each tries to push the mouse button faster than the opponent in the other room. Whichever participant loses the race gets blasted with noise through the headphones. There are a total of 25 reaction time races.

How does the Competitive Reaction Time Task provide a measure of aggressive behavior? Before each race, each participant sets the noise level and duration that will be delivered to his or her opponent if the opponent loses. Participants can choose a sound blast level that ranges from Level 1, which corresponds to 50 decibels, to a high of Level 10, which corresponds to a very loud 100 decibels. On their computer screens, the participants can see the penalty for losing that has been set by their opponents.

Because the players determine the penalty that will be delivered to the loser of the game, the Competitive Reaction Time Task allows researchers to precisely measure the level of aggression that a research participant is willing to mete out to another participant. In this experiment, then, Anderson and Dill operationally defined aggressive behavior as "the intensity and duration of noise blasts the participant chooses to deliver to the opponent."

Although the Competitive Reaction Time Task appears convincing, the game is actually rigged. The research participant is not really competing against another person in a different room. Instead, the computer is programmed so that each research participant experiences the exact same outcome—13 wins and 12 losses. The intensity and duration of the noise blasts that they receive when they lose are also predetermined, and they are the same for all participants.

The Experimental Procedure

To give participants ample playing experience with the assigned video game, the researchers had them come to the laboratory for two separate sessions approximately one week apart. When participants first arrived at the laboratory, they were told they were taking part in a study to investigate how people learn and develop skills at motor tasks such as those involved in playing video games and how these skills affect other mental and motor tasks. They were also told that they would be recorded in order to carefully analyze their motor skill development. To help make this believable, a VCR was set up and running near their computer, complete with bogus wires connecting the VCR and the computer.

During the first laboratory session, each participant was instructed on how to play the assigned video game. Then they played either *Wolfenstein 3D* or *Myst* for 30 minutes, depending on whether they were part of the experimental or control group. At the second laboratory session a week later, participants played their assigned video game for another 15-minute period. This was followed by the Competitive Reaction Time Task, in which they had multiple opportunities to

SIPRESS

"'GameBoy: A Memoir of Addiction,'
by Ronald Markowitz."

random assignment
The process of assigning participants to experimental conditions so that all participants have an equal chance of being assigned to any of the conditions or groups in the study.

experimental group or **experimental condition**
In an experiment, the group of participants who are exposed to all experimental conditions, including the independent variable or treatment of interest.

control group or **control condition**
In an experiment, the group of participants who are exposed to all experimental conditions, except the independent variable or treatment of interest; the group against which changes in the experimental group are compared.

FIGURE 1.4 The Experimental Design of Anderson and Dill's Violent Video Game Study

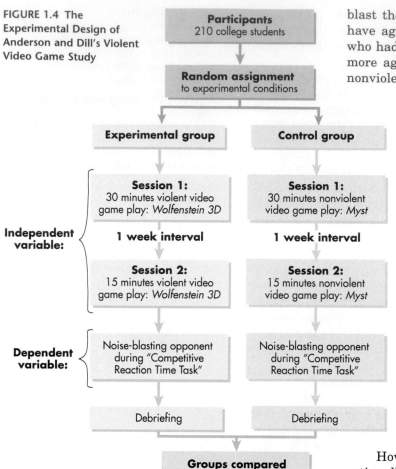

blast their opponent with noise. Given the opportunity to behave aggressively against an invisible opponent, would those who had just played *Wolfenstein 3D* (the violent game) behave more aggressively than those who had just played *Myst* (the nonviolent game)?

At the conclusion of the second experimental session, each participant received a debriefing statement that explained the study's actual hypotheses and procedures and debunked the cover story. The research assistant also answered any questions about the experiment. Figure 1.4 outlines the basic steps in this study.

The Results and Discussion

What did Anderson and Dill find? Let's look at the experimental results. As Figure 1.5 shows, there was a statistically significant difference between the experimental and control conditions. Students who had played *Wolfenstein 3D,* the violent game, scored higher on one measure of aggressive behavior than students who had played *Myst,* the nonviolent video game. On average, they delivered longer blasts of noise to their opponents. This result confirmed that participants who had played a violent video game behaved more aggressively than participants who had played a nonviolent video game.

However, remember that Anderson and Dill (2000) operationally defined aggressive behavior as "the intensity and duration of noise blasts the participant chooses to deliver to the opponent." Although there were statistically significant differences between the two groups on the *duration* of the noise blasts, the two groups did not differ significantly on *intensity* of the sound setting. In other words, playing the violent versus the nonviolent video game had no effect on how loudly the research participants blasted their opponents. The researchers were surprised by the lack of significant group differences on intensity of the noise blasts.

Nonetheless, combining these experimental results with Anderson and Dill's correlational study that we described earlier provides converging lines of real-world and laboratory evidence. As Anderson and Dill (2000) explain:

> In the laboratory, college students who played a violent video game behaved more aggressively toward an opponent than did students who had played a nonviolent video game. Outside the laboratory, students who reported playing more violent video games over a period of years also engaged in more aggressive behavior in their own lives. This convergence of findings across such disparate methods lends considerable strength to the main hypothesis that exposure to violent video games can increase aggressive behavior.

FIGURE 1.5 **Results of the Violent Video Game Experiment** In the graph you can see that briefly playing a violent video game increased aggressive behavior. As compared to those who played a nonviolent video game, the participants who played the violent video game blasted their opponents with longer noise bursts in the Competitive Reaction Time Task. The difference between the two groups was statistically significant.

SOURCE: Data adapted from Anderson & Dill (2000).

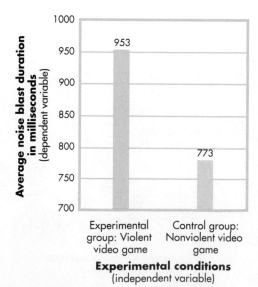

Reporting the Findings

Anderson and Dill's study was published in the *Journal of Personality and Social Psychology*, one of psychology's premier scientific journals. Needless to say, the study also attracted considerable media attention—and provoked considerable debate. Shortly before the study was published, Anderson testified before the U.S. Senate in a public hearing on "The Impact of Interactive Violence on Children."

Anderson argued that playing violent video games may be more harmful than watching violent television and movies (Anderson & others, 2003). Why? One reason is that the player takes on the role and identifies with the aggressor, especially in first-person shooter games like "Doom" or "Grand Theft Auto." Also, because the games are interactive, the player must actively choose to behave aggressively—or lose (Anderson & others, 2003).

Since the publication of Anderson and Dill's experiment, many more research studies have found links between violent video game play and aggression (see Anderson & others, 2004; APA, 2005). Analyzing numerous studies, the American Psychological Association came to this conclusion: Exposure to interactive, violent video games increases aggressive behavior, thoughts, and angry feelings, and decreases helpful behavior. Consequently, in August 2005, the APA passed a resolution calling for the reduction of violent content in interactive games that are marketed to children and adolescents. You can read the text of the APA resolution at: http://www.apa.org/releases/resolutiononvideoviolence.pdf

And how did our students in the 9:30 class react to the Anderson and Dill study? Kim was even more determined to keep her boys away from violent computer games. Kyle, however, remained unconvinced. "Maybe some people get more aggressive when they play those kinds of games," he argued. "But still, there's a big difference between playing some make-believe video game and killing real people." Tanisha had another idea: "Not everyone is as self-disciplined as you, Kyle. Maybe the effects aren't the same for everybody. Maybe some kids are very easily influenced by playing violent video games and we need to identify those kids."

"A new hypothesis!" Sandy exclaimed.

How did you respond to the results of this influential study? We asked the students in several of our classes to critically evaluate the Anderson and Dill video game study. We discuss some of their observations in Critical Thinking Box 1.4 on page 30.

Variations in Experimental Design

The design of any particular experiment depends on the issues being investigated. In this section, we'll look at a specific variation in experimental designs— the use of a placebo control group.

Placebo Control Group

Some experiments are designed to assess the effectiveness of a therapeutic treatment, such as a particular medication or a type of psychotherapy. In this kind of experiment, participants in the experimental group receive the independent variable, or treatment of interest—the actual drug or therapy. Other participants are assigned to a **placebo control group** and receive a placebo. A *placebo* is an inert substance or a treatment that has no known effects (Straus & von Ammon Cavanaugh, 1996). In a typical therapeutic effectiveness study, participants are told the purpose of the study and that they have a 50–50 chance of receiving the actual versus the placebo treatment.

For example, psychologist Paul Solomon and his colleagues (2002) used a placebo control group to test claims that an herb called *ginkgo biloba* improves memory, concentration, and mental focus in older adults. Participants were randomly assigned to two groups. One group took the manufacturer's recommended dosage of ginkgo biloba daily for six weeks, while the control group took

Psychologist Craig Anderson Testifying before the U.S. Senate Commerce Committee, Anderson said, "Of course, most people who consume high levels of violent media, adults or youth, do not end up in prison for violent crimes. The more relevant question is whether many (or most) people become more angry, aggressive, and violent as a result of being exposed to high levels of media violence. Are they more likely to slap a child or spouse when provoked? Are they more likely to drive aggressively and display 'road rage'? Are they more likely to assault co-workers? The answer is a clear 'yes.'"

Can Ginkgo Biloba Enhance Your Mental Abilities? Sales of the herbal supplement ginkgo biloba are booming: More than $300 million is spent on the dietary supplement every year in the United States alone. Manufacturers market the herb as a "cognitive enhancer," claiming that it improves memory, alertness, mental focus, and concentration, especially in older adults. Studies of ginkgo biloba's effectiveness have produced inconsistent results (see Gold & others, 2002). The use of a placebo control group in a recent study by Paul Solomon and his colleagues (2002) provided clear evidence, however, that ginkgo biloba was no more effective than a placebo in improving memory, mental alertness, or concentration.

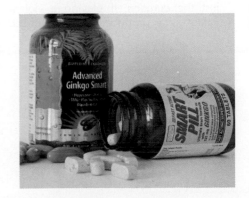

Assessing the Violent Video Game Study

Throughout this text, we will encourage you to develop a healthy sense of *scientific skepticism* and hone your *critical thinking skills* (see page 16). To get some practice exercising those skills, reread the discussion of the Anderson and Dill experiment. Do you see any weaknesses or problems with the study?

When we asked our students to critically evaluate the Anderson and Dill experiment, here are some of the issues that they identified:

DOONESBURY

- **The study lacked a no-treatment control group.** One of the most common criticisms our students voiced was that they wondered how people who *hadn't* played *any* video games would perform on the Competitive Reaction Time Task.

- **There was no baseline measurement.** Several astute students wondered why there wasn't a baseline session on the Competitive Reaction Time Task *before* the video games were introduced. A baseline would allow the researchers to directly compare aggressive behavior before and after playing violent or nonviolent video games.

- ***Myst* and *Wolfenstein 3D* are *too* different.** Many of our students were not convinced that most college students would rate *Wolfenstein 3D* and *Myst* as being equally "difficult, enjoyable, frustrating, and fast in action." Why not have the participants engage in a fast-action, nonviolent video game, such as *Tetris, DX-Ball 2,* or *WinBrickOut?*

- **There was no difference in one measure of aggression.** Many students noticed that there was no difference in the *intensity* of the noise blast delivered in the Competitive Reaction Time Task, just the *duration*. If playing a violent video game produced a strong effect, wouldn't you think that it would also have increased the *intensity* of the noise blast?

- **The laboratory tasks were artificial.** Several students thought that the experimental setup was unrealistic. For example, students who were habitual video game players commented that they rarely played a video game for just 15 or 30 minutes, especially an exciting one. Similarly, some students thought that blasting an unseen opponent with noise from a computer terminal was a far cry from aggressive behavior intended to hurt another person.

- **Does statistical significance automatically mean practical significance?** Look again at Figure 1.5. The average difference between the experimental and control group was 180 milliseconds. A *millisecond* is 1/1000th of a second. Thus, the blast duration difference, while statistically significant, was only about 1/6th of a second. In general, our students thought the difference was too small to have any kind of practical significance.

Critically evaluating evidence is an important part of the scientific process. To be fair, it's important that we point out that research on the effects of video games is still at a very early stage—and we have presented just *one* study here. Some of the issues identified by our students have been addressed in more recent research (see Anderson, 2004; Anderson & others, 2003). In fact, later studies have found stronger effects of violent video games on aggression (see Anderson & others, 2004). Finally, consider the *ethical* problems faced by psychologists in the area of human aggression. How do you design an experiment that realistically reflects aggressive behavior without harming your participants?

Critical Thinking Questions

- How compelling do you find the relationship between violent video games and aggression?

- How would you design a study to test the relationship between violent video games and aggression?

- Does the artificial nature of laboratory research make it less valid? Why or why not?

an identical dosage of capsules containing a placebo. At the beginning and end of the six-week study, all participants took a battery of cognitive tests.

The results? At the end of the six-week study, the test scores of *both* groups rose. However, there were no significant differences between the improvement in the placebo group and the improvement in the ginkgo biloba group. Because a placebo control group was used, the researchers were able to conclude that the participants' experience with the tests—simply taking the same tests twice—was probably the reason for the general improvement in test scores. This phenomenon is called a **practice effect.**

A placebo control group can also help researchers check for **expectancy effects,** which are changes that may occur simply because subjects expect change to occur. Expectancy effects are also sometimes referred to as *placebo effects.* Using this method, researchers can compare the effects of the actual treatment versus the expectancy effects, if any, that are demonstrated by the placebo control group.

In therapeutic effectiveness studies, researchers often use a double-blind technique. A **double-blind study** is one in which neither the participants nor the researcher who interacts with them is aware of the treatment or condition to which the participants have been assigned. For example, in the ginkgo biloba study, the researchers who interacted with the participants did not know which were receiving the placebo and which the actual treatment. The researchers who *did* know which participants had been assigned to each group did not interact with or evaluate the participants. In contrast, a *single-blind study* is one in which the researchers, but not the subjects, are aware of critical information.

The purpose of the double-blind technique is to guard against the possibility that the researcher will inadvertently display **demand characteristics,** which are subtle cues or signals that communicate what is expected of certain subjects (Kihlstrom, 1995, 2002). A behavior as subtle as smiling when dealing with some participants but not others could bias the outcome of a study.

Limitations of Experiments

The strength of a well-designed experiment is that it can provide convincing evidence of a cause-and-effect relationship between the independent and dependent variables. Experiments do have limitations, however. Because experiments are often conducted in highly controlled laboratory situations, they are frequently criticized for having little to do with actual behavior. That is, the artificial conditions of some experiments may produce results that do not *generalize* well, meaning that the results cannot be applied to real situations or to a more general population beyond the participants in the study. In order to make experimental conditions less artificial, experiments are sometimes conducted in a natural setting rather than in a laboratory.

Another limitation of the experimental method is that even when it is possible to create the conditions that the researchers want to study, it may be unethical to do so. In the final section of this chapter, we'll look at the kinds of ethical considerations that psychologists must take into account in conducting any kind of research.

Ethics in Psychological Research

Key Theme
- Psychological research conducted in the United States is subject to ethical guidelines developed by the American Psychological Association.

Key Questions
- What are five key provisions of the APA ethics code for research involving humans?
- Why do psychologists sometimes conduct research with nonhuman animals?

What might happen if you were to volunteer to participate in a psychology experiment or study? Are psychologists allowed to manipulate or control you without your knowledge or consent? Could a psychologist force you to reveal your innermost secrets? Could he or she administer electric shocks?

placebo control group
(pluh-SEE-bo) In an experiment, a control group in which the participants are exposed to a fake independent variable, or placebo. The effects of the placebo are compared to the effects of the actual independent variable, or treatment of interest, on the experimental group.

practice effect
Any change in performance that results from mere repetition of a task.

expectancy effects
Changes in a subject's behavior produced by the subject's belief that change should happen; also called *placebo effects.*

double-blind study
Experimental technique in which neither the participants nor the researcher interacting with the participants is aware of the group or condition to which the participants have been assigned.

demand characteristics
In a research study, subtle cues or signals expressed by the researcher that communicate the kind of response or behavior that is expected from the participant.

IN FOCUS 1.5

Questions About the Use of Animals in Psychological Research

The use of nonhuman animal subjects in psychological and other research is based on the premise that human life is intrinsically more valuable than animal life. Not everyone agrees with this position (see Herzog, 2005).

The American Psychological Association (1992) condones the use of animals in psychological research, but only under certain conditions. First, research using animal subjects must have an *acceptable scientific purpose.* Second, there must be a reasonable expectation that the research will (a) increase knowledge about behavior, (b) increase understanding of the species under study, or (c) produce results that benefit the health or welfare of humans or other animals.

What standards must psychologists meet in using animal subjects?

The American Psychological Association (1992) publishes the *Guidelines for Ethical Conduct in the Care and Use of Animals,* which you can read at: www.apa.org/science/animal2.html The APA Guidelines for animal care have been praised as being the most comprehensive set of guidelines of their kind. In addition, federal and state laws govern the care and use of research animals (Overmier & Carroll, 2001).

How common is the use of animal subjects in psychology research?

The majority of psychology research involves human subjects, not animals. Nonhuman animals are used in only about 7 to 8 percent of psychological studies conducted in a given year. About 90 percent of the animals used in psychological research are rodents and birds, primarily rats, mice, and pigeons. Only about 5 percent of the animals are monkeys and other primates. Use of dogs or cats is rare in psychological studies. The rest of the total includes a wide variety of creatures, from bats to sea snails (APA Committee on Animal Research and Ethics, 2004).

Why are animals used in psychological research?

Here are a few of the key reasons that psychologists might use animal subjects rather than human subjects in research:

1. Many psychologists are interested in the study of animal behavior for its own sake.

The branch of psychology that focuses on the study of the behavior of nonhuman animals is called **comparative psychology.** Some psychologists also do research in the area called *animal cognition,* which is the study of animal learning, memory, thinking, and language (Boysen & Hines, 1999).

Animal research is also pursued for its potential benefit to animals themselves. For example, psychological research on animal behavior has been used to improve the quality of life of animals in zoos and to increase the likelihood of survival of endangered species in the wild.

2. Animal subjects are sometimes used for research that could not feasibly be conducted on human subjects.

There are many similarities between human and animal behavior, but animal behavior tends to be less complex. Thus, it is sometimes easier to identify basic principles of behavior by studying animals. Psychologists can also observe some animals throughout their

entire lifespan, from the prenatal stage to old age. To track such changes in humans would take many decades of research. Finally, psychologists can exercise much greater control over animal subjects than over human subjects. If necessary, researchers can control every aspect of the animals' environment and even their genetic background.

In what areas of psychology has research using animals produced valuable information?

Psychological research with animal subjects has made essential contributions to virtually every area of psychology. Along with contributing to knowledge of the workings of the human brain, animal research has contributed to psychological knowledge in the areas of learning, memory, cognition, psychological disorders, therapies, and stress. Research with animals has produced significant gains in the treatment of many conditions, including substance abuse, spinal cord injury, hypertension, and sleep disorders (see Carroll & Overmier, 2001). Significant gains have also been made in helping animals, including the successful breeding and preservation of endangered species, improvements in the care of zoo animals, and the prevention of animal diseases (APA Committee on Animal Research and Ethics, 2004).

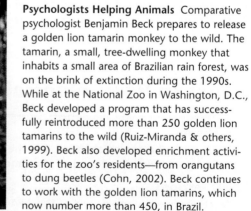

Psychologists Helping Animals Comparative psychologist Benjamin Beck prepares to release a golden lion tamarin monkey to the wild. The tamarin, a small, tree-dwelling monkey that inhabits a small area of Brazilian rain forest, was on the brink of extinction during the 1990s. While at the National Zoo in Washington, D.C., Beck developed a program that has successfully reintroduced more than 250 golden lion tamarins to the wild (Ruiz-Miranda & others, 1999). Beck also developed enrichment activities for the zoo's residents—from orangutans to dung beetles (Cohn, 2002). Beck continues to work with the golden lion tamarins, which now number more than 450, in Brazil.

The answer to all these questions is "no." The American Psychological Association (APA) has developed a strict code of ethics for conducting research with both human and animal subjects. This code is contained in a document called *Ethical Principles of Psychologists and Code of Conduct* (APA, 2002). You can access the complete guidelines at http://www.apa.org/ethics/.

comparative psychology
Branch of psychology that studies the behavior of different animal species.

In general, psychologists must respect the dignity and welfare of participants. Psychologists cannot deceptively expose research participants to dangerous or harmful conditions that might cause either physical or emotional harm. At most institutions, any psychological research using human or animal subjects must be approved by an ethics panel.

Not surprisingly, the ethical guidelines for research with human and animal subjects are somewhat different. However, the use of animals in psychological research is also governed by specific ethical guidelines (APA, 1992). These guidelines, as well as other issues, are discussed in In Focus Box 1.5.

Here are highlights of five key provisions in the 2002 APA ethical principles regulating research with human participants:

- **Informed consent and voluntary participation.** In reasonably understandable language, the psychologist must inform the participants of the purpose of the research, including significant factors that might influence a person's willingness to participate in the study, such as potential risks, discomfort, or unpleasant emotional experiences. The psychologist must also explain to the participants that they are free to decline to participate or to withdraw from the research at any time.

- **Students as research participants.** When research participation is a course requirement or an opportunity for extra credit, the student must be given the choice of an alternative activity to fulfill the course requirement or earn extra credit.

- **The use of deception.** Psychologists can use deceptive techniques as part of the study only when two conditions have been met: (1) It is not feasible to use alternatives that do not involve deception, and (2) the potential findings justify the use of deception because of their scientific, educational, or applied value.

- **Confidentiality of information.** In their writing, lectures, or other public forums, psychologists may not disclose personally identifiable information about research participants.

- **Information about the study and debriefing.** All participants must be provided with the opportunity to obtain information about the nature, results, and conclusions of the research. Psychologists are also obligated to *debrief* the participants and to correct any misconceptions that participants may have had about the research.

Who makes sure that these ethical guidelines are followed? First, all institutions where psychological research is conducted have ethics committees that must review and approve all research proposals. Second, the APA has established the Committee on Scientific and Professional Ethics, which investigates all complaints it receives. Any psychologist who is found to be in violation of the ethics code may be suspended or expelled from the APA.

> *Psychologists are committed to increasing scientific and professional knowledge of behavior and people's understanding of themselves and others and to the use of such knowledge to improve the condition of individuals, organizations, and society. Psychologists respect the dignity and worth of all people, and the rights of individuals to privacy, confidentiality, and self-determination.*
>
> American Psychological Association (2002)

Closing Thoughts

In this chapter, we've laid the foundation for exploring a wide range of topics in psychology. Like the students in our 9:30 class, you've probably found yourself questioning why people sometimes act the way they do. "Why would someone do such a thing?" is a common question in our psychology classes. Psychologists have applied the tools of science, sometimes very ingeniously, to understand why we humans do what we do. As you'll discover, whether it is dealing with the common experiences of everyday life or with more extreme events, psychology can provide many insights into human behavior and mental processes. As we share those insights with you, you'll learn not only about other people but about yourself as well. It's a fascinating journey and one that we look forward to sharing with you.

Psychologists and psychological findings are often featured in the media. Sometimes it's a researcher, such as Craig Anderson, who is being interviewed about the published results of a study that has caught the interest of the popular press. Or it may be a psychologist who is appearing on a television or radio talk show to discuss a particular topic, such as the degree to which parents influence a child's personality (Gardner & Herbert, 2002).

How can you evaluate the information about psychology and psychological topics reported in the mass media? The following guidelines will help you critically evaluate what you see and hear in the news.

1. Be especially skeptical of sensationalistic claims or findings.

News headlines proclaiming "discoveries" or "breakthroughs" in psychological research are designed to grab your attention. Almost always, if you listen or read further, you'll encounter a much more cautious tone in the statements of the psychologists themselves. As scientists, psychologists tend to be conservative in stating their research results so as not to mislead the public. Reporters, however, are sometimes more interested in attracting readers or viewers than in accurately portraying scientific results (Connor-Greene, 1993). As media psychologist Rhea Farberman (1999) explains:

> What the researcher sees in his or her research results—one piece of the overall research puzzle that can be applied within the limits of this particular study—is different from what the reporter wants to find in a research study—the all-encompassing headline. The challenge for the psychologist is how to translate the research into a meaningful sound bite.

Given the difficulty of compressing complicated information into a brief 10-second sound bite, it's common for researchers to be quoted out of context or for important qualifying statements to be left out by a reporter or producer (Farberman, 2003). A 60-minute interview may be edited down to just 30 seconds of air time.

2. Anecdotes are the essence of talk shows, not scientific evidence.

Psychology-related topics are standard fare on news and talk shows and even the so-called reality TV shows (Gardner & Herbert, 2002). Although such programs often feature psychologists with research experience and expertise in a particular area, the shows tend to quickly abandon discussions of scientific evidence in favor of anecdotal evidence.

Anecdotal evidence consists of personal stories told to confirm or support a particular claim. The personal stories are often dramatic, funny, or heartrending, making them subjectively very compelling. However, an anecdote by definition is one person's experience. There's no way to know if the person's experience is representative of other people's—or if it is exceptional or unusual. In contrast, descriptive and experimental research typically involves large groups of carefully selected subjects. When the number of participants in a study is small, researchers usually take that limitation into account when they draw conclusions from their findings.

3. Remember that the goal of "shock" radio and television is ratings.

Let's face it. The media are not educational institutions. They are a profit-driven industry, and the size of the audience is crucial to realizing those profits. So what draws viewers and listeners? Shock value is a big draw. As media psychologist Michael Broder (1999) explains, "It's not how nice, professional, smart, loyal, helpful, or thorough you are, but how well you attract numbers of people."

4. Look for the original source of professional publication.

When the media report on a study that has been conducted by a reputable researcher, the original source of professional publication is almost always noted in the news report. Usually, psychological research is published in a professional psychology journal before it is shared with the general public. For example, it was only *after* Craig Anderson and Karen Dill (2000) published their findings about playing violent video games in the *Journal of Personality and Social Psychology* that they discussed their findings with reporters. Even so, reporters don't always read the research report or understand the research issues under discussion. And they may add their own in-

terpretations to those of the researchers, thereby distorting or misrepresenting the actual findings (Farberman, 1999).

There's another reason why it's important to look for the original source of professional publication. The research published in most of the professional psychology journals is reviewed by peers. Before the research is accepted for publication, psychologists with expert knowledge in research methods and statistics review the study. In doing so, they verify that all aspects of the study were carefully designed to guard against erroneous conclusions. Thus, peer review helps ensure that psychological research adheres to the rigorous standards of scientific evidence.

5. Consider how the research was funded.

It costs money to conduct research. Research published in professional journals usually notes the funding sources in a footnote or endnote. Given that, would you be wary of research that was funded by a company or agency whose motive is to convince you to buy some product or service? Such situations do not necessarily invalidate the research, but they do raise concerns about conflicts of interest.

6. Consider the methods and operational definitions used.

At this point, you should understand the importance of such elements as control groups in experiments, operational definitions of variables, the use of multiple observers in descriptive research, random assignment of subjects to experimental conditions, and the use of a sample that is representative of the population being studied. Look for these elements in the description of the study to increase your confidence in the research findings.

7. Remember the distinction between correlation and causality.

Remember the correlation we mentioned between higher levels of sexual activity and a preference for jazz? Many research results reported in the mass media are correlational studies, yet the news reports imply that a cause-and-effect relationship has been discovered. From our earlier discussion, you now understand that two factors may be correlated, but one does not necessarily cause the other. It is entirely possible that a third factor is responsible for the behavior in question. As a general rule, whenever the words *link, tie, connection, association,* or *relationship* are used in headlines describing psychological findings, the research being described is correlational.

8. Skepticism is the rule, not the exception, in science.

It seems as if it is basic to human nature to look for easy answers to life's dilemmas—whether that involves increasing your motivation and self-discipline, improving your memory, combating stress, or enhancing relationships. As you'll see in the Applica-

tion sections at the end of each chapter, psychological research has much to say about these and other practical topics. But achieving these goals is rarely as easy as the popular press portrays it. Therefore, remember one final axiom in evaluating research claims reported in the media: If it sounds too good to be true, it probably is!

Chapter Review
Introduction and Research Methods

Key Points

Introduction: The Origins of Psychology

- **Psychology** is now defined as the scientific study of behavior and mental processes. However, the definition of psychology has evolved over time.

- Early philosophers, such as Aristotle and Descartes, used logic and intuition to understand psychological topics. Later, the discoveries of physiologists demonstrated that scientific methods could be applied to psychological topics.

- Wilhelm Wundt, a German physiologist, is credited with founding psychology as an experimental science. Wundt's student Edward B. Titchener established **structuralism,** the first school of psychology. The structuralists used introspection to try to identify the structures of conscious experiences.

- William James founded and promoted psychology in the United States. James established **functionalism,** a school of psychology that emphasized the adaptive role of behavior. James's students G. Stanley Hall and Mary Whiton Calkins were two important figures in early American psychology.

- Sigmund Freud established **psychoanalysis** as a theory of personality and form of psychotherapy. Psychoanalysis emphasized the role of unconscious conflicts in determining behavior and personality.

- **Behaviorism** was based on Ivan Pavlov's research and emerged in the early 1900s. Behaviorism was first championed by John Watson and further developed by B. F. Skinner. Behaviorism rejected the study of mental processes and emphasized the study of observable behavior, especially the principles of learning.

- Carl Rogers and Abraham Maslow promoted **humanistic psychology,** which emphasized psychological growth and the importance of choice in human behavior.

Contemporary Psychology

- Psychology has become progressively more diverse as a science. Topics can be approached from several different perspectives, which include the biological, psychodynamic, behavioral, humanistic, cognitive, cross-cultural, and **evolutionary psychology** perspectives.

- Important specialty areas of psychology include biological psychology, cognitive psychology, experimental psychology, developmental psychology, social psychology, personality psychology, health psychology, educational psychology, industrial/organizational psychology, and clinical psychology.

The Scientific Method

- The four goals of psychology are to describe, explain, predict, and influence human behavior and mental processes. Psychology is based on **empirical evidence.**

- Psychologists are trained in the **scientific method,** which has four steps: (1) generate a **hypothesis** that can be tested empirically, (2) design the study and collect the data, (3) analyze the data and draw conclusions, and (4) report the findings. **Variables** must be **operationally defined.**

- Research methods include descriptive methods and the experimental method. **Statistics** are used to analyze the data and to determine whether findings are **statistically significant. Meta-analysis** can be used to combine and analyze multiple studies on a single topic. Reporting the results of a study allows other researchers to **replicate** the study.

- As research findings accumulate from individual studies, **theories** or models develop to explain the different findings on a related topic. Theories are tools for understanding and explaining behavior and mental processes. Theories evolve and change as new evidence emerges.

Descriptive Research Methods

- **Descriptive research methods** are research strategies used to observe and describe behavior. The goal of **naturalistic observation** is to detect behavior patterns as they exist in their natural settings. The **case study** method involves intensive study of a single subject or a small group of subjects.

- **Surveys,** questionnaires, and interviews are administered to a **sample** of the larger group to be investigated. For results to be generalizable to the larger population, the sample must be a **representative sample.** Participants are usually chosen through **random selection.**

- **Correlational studies** investigate how strongly two factors are related to each other. The relationship is expressed in terms of a **correlation coefficient.** A **positive correlation** indicates that two factors vary in the same direction, whereas a **negative correlation** indicates that two factors vary in opposite directions.

- Even when two factors are strongly related, conclusions cannot be drawn about causality because a third factor may actually be responsible for the association. However, correlational evidence can be used to identify important relationships and to make meaningful predictions.

The Experimental Method

- The **experimental method** can demonstrate a cause-and-effect relationship between one variable and another. Experiments involve manipulating the **independent variable** and measuring the effects of the manipulation on the **dependent variable.**

- An experiment testing the effects of playing violent video games on aggressive behavior was used to help illustrate **random assignment** of subjects to experimental conditions, **experimental groups** compared to a **control group,** systematic manipulation of the independent variable, and objective measurement of the dependent variable.

- There are many variations in experimental design. A **placebo control group** can be used to check for **practice effects** and **expectancy effects.** The use of a **double-blind study** helps guard against **demand characteristics.** Although experiments can provide evidence of causality, they are sometimes criticized for creating artificial conditions. Not all questions can be studied experimentally.

Ethics in Psychological Research

- All psychological research is subject to regulations contained in an ethical code developed by the American Psychological Association. For research with human subjects, the ethical code requires that informed consent and voluntary participation must be ensured, student subjects must be given alternatives to participating in research, deceptive techniques can be used only under specific conditions, records are kept confidential, and participants are to be debriefed and allowed to learn more about the study.

- Research with animal subjects is also governed by an ethical code developed by the American Psychological Association.

Key Terms

psychology, p. 3

structuralism, p. 4

functionalism, p. 5

psychoanalysis, p. 7

behaviorism, p. 7

humanistic psychology, p. 8

evolutionary psychology, p. 11

culture, p. 13

cross-cultural psychology, p. 12

ethnocentrism, p. 12

individualistic cultures, p. 12

collectivistic cultures, p. 12

scientific method, p. 14

empirical evidence, p. 15

hypothesis, p. 15

variable, p. 15

operational definition, p. 15

critical thinking, p. 16

statistics, p. 17

statistically significant, p. 17

meta-analysis, p. 17

replicate, p. 18

theory, p. 19

descriptive research methods, p. 19

naturalistic observation, p. 19

pseudoscience, p. 20

paranormal phenomena, p. 20

rule of falsifiability, p. 20

illusory correlation, p. 20

case study, p. 21

survey, p. 21

sample, p. 22

representative sample, p. 22

random selection, p. 22

correlational study, p. 23

correlation coefficient, p. 23

positive correlation, p. 24

negative correlation, p. 24

experimental method, p. 25

independent variable, p. 25

dependent variable, p. 25

random assignment, p. 26

experimental group (experimental condition), p. 26

control group (control condition), p. 26

placebo control group, p. 29

practice effect, p. 31

expectancy effects, p. 31

double-blind study, p. 31

demand characteristics, p. 31

comparative psychology, p. 32

Key People

Mary Whiton Calkins (1863–1930)   American psychologist who conducted research on memory, personality, and dreams; established one of the first U.S. psychology research laboratories; first woman president of the American Psychological Association. (p. 6)

Charles Darwin (1809–1882)   English naturalist and scientist whose theory of evolution through natural selection was first published in *On the Origin of Species* in 1859. (p. 11)

Sigmund Freud (1856–1939)   Austrian physician and founder of psychoanalysis. (p. 7)

G. Stanley Hall (1844–1924)   American psychologist who established the first psychology research laboratory in the United States; founded the American Psychological Association. (p. 6)

William James (1842–1910)   American philosopher and psychologist who founded psychology in the United States and established the psychological school called functionalism. (p. 5)

Abraham Maslow (1908–1970)   American humanistic psychologist who developed a theory of motivation. (p. 8)

Ivan Pavlov (1849–1936)   Russian physiologist whose pioneering research on learning contributed to the development of behaviorism; discovered the basic learning process that is now called classical conditioning. (p. 7)

Carl Rogers (1902–1987)   American psychologist who founded the school of humanistic psychology. (p. 8)

B. F. Skinner (1904–1990)   American psychologist and leading proponent of behaviorism; developed a model of learning called operant conditioning; emphasized studying the relationship between environmental factors and observable behavior. (p. 8)

Edward B. Titchener (1867–1927)   British-born American psychologist who founded structuralism, the first school of psychology. (p. 4)

Margaret Floy Washburn (1871–1939)   American psychologist who was the first woman to earn a doctorate in psychology in the United States; published research on mental processes in animals. (p. 6)

John B. Watson (1878–1958)   American psychologist who founded behaviorism, emphasizing the study of observable behavior and rejecting the study of mental processes. (p. 7)

Wilhelm Wundt (1832–1920)   German physiologist who founded psychology as a formal science; opened first psychology research laboratory in 1879. (p. 4)

Web Companion   Review Activities

You can find additional review activities by going to **www.DiscoveringPsychology.com** and clicking on the *Discovering Psychology* 4th Edition text cover. At the Discovering Psychology Web Companion you'll find the chapter learning objectives, flashcards for key terms and key people, interactive crossword puzzles, self-scoring practice quizzes, and other materials to help you master the information in this chapter.

Red Moon Rising

Neuroscience and Behavior

Prologue Asha's Story

The headaches began without warning. A pounding, intense pain just over Asha's left temple. Asha just couldn't seem to shake it—the pain was unrelenting. She was uncharacteristically tired, too.

But our friend Asha, a 32-year-old university professor, chalked up her constant headache and fatigue to stress and exhaustion. After all, the end of her demanding first semester of teaching and research was drawing near. Still, Asha had always been very healthy and usually tolerated stress well. She didn't drink or smoke. And no matter how late she stayed up working on her lectures and research proposals, she still got up at 5:30 every morning to work out at the university gym.

There were other, more subtle signs that something was wrong. Asha's husband Paul noticed that she had been behaving rather oddly in recent weeks. For example, at Thanksgiving dinner, Asha had picked up a knife by the wrong end and tried to cut her turkey with the handle instead of the blade. A few hours later, Asha had made the same mistake trying to use scissors: She held the blades and tried to cut with the handle.

Asha laughed these incidents off, and for that matter, so did Paul. They both thought she was simply under too much stress. And when Asha occasionally got her words mixed up, neither Paul nor anyone else was terribly surprised. Asha was born in India, and her first language was Tulu. Although Asha was extremely fluent in English, she often got English phrases slightly wrong—like the time she said that Paul was a "straight dart" instead of a "straight arrow." Or when she said that it was "storming cats and birds" instead of "raining cats and dogs."

There were other odd lapses in language. "I would say something thinking it was correct," Asha recalled, "and people would say to me, 'What are you saying?' I wouldn't realize I was saying something wrong. I would open my mouth and just nonsense would come out. But it made perfect sense to me. At other times, the word was on the tip of my tongue—I knew I knew the word, but I couldn't find it. I would fumble for the word, but it would come out wrong. Sometimes I would slur words, like I'd try to say 'Saturday,' only it would come out 'salad-day.'"

On Christmas morning, Paul and Asha were with Paul's family, opening presents. Asha walked over to Paul's father to look at the pool cue he had received as a gift. As she bent down, she fell forward onto her father-in-law. At first, everyone thought Asha was just joking around. But then she fell to the floor, her body stiff. Seconds later, it was apparent that Asha had lost consciousness and was having a seizure.

Asha remembers nothing of the seizure or of being taken by ambulance to the hospital intensive care unit. She floated in and out of consciousness for the first day and night. A CAT scan showed some sort of blockage in Asha's brain. An MRI scan revealed a large white spot on the left side of her brain. At only 32 years of age, Asha had suffered a stroke—brain damage caused by a disruption of the blood flow to the brain.

She remained in the hospital for 12 days. It was only after Asha was transferred out of intensive care that both she and Paul began to realize just how serious the repercussions of the stroke were. Asha couldn't read or write and had difficulty comprehending what was being said. Although she could speak, she couldn't name even simple objects, such as a tree, a clock, or her doctor's tie. In this chapter, you will discover why the damage to Asha's brain impaired her ability to perform simple behaviors, like naming common objects.

Introduction
Neuroscience and Behavior

As we discussed in Chapter 1, **biological psychology** is the scientific study of the biological bases of behavior and mental processes. This area of research is also called *biopsychology* or *psychobiology*. All three terms emphasize the idea of a biological approach to the study of psychological processes. Biological psychology is one of the scientific disciplines that make important contributions to **neuroscience**—the scientific study of the nervous system. As *neuroscientists*, biopsychologists bring their expertise in behavior and behavioral research to this scientific endeavor. Some of the other scientific disciplines that contribute to neuroscience include *physiology, pharmacology, biology,* and *neurology*.

Neuroscience and biological psychology are not limited to the study of the brain and the nervous system. Throughout this textbook, you'll encounter questions that have been studied by neuroscientists. Here are some examples:

- How do we tell the difference between red and blue, sweet and sour, loud and soft? (Chapter 3)
- What happens in the brain when we sleep, dream, or meditate? (Chapter 4)
- What exactly is a memory, and how are memories stored in the brain? (Chapter 6)
- Why do we get hungry? How do emotions occur? (Chapter 8)
- How do emotions and attitudes affect our vulnerability to infection and disease? (Chapter 12)
- How does heredity influence our development? What role does genetics play in personality traits? (Chapters 9, 10, and 13)
- What role does abnormal brain chemistry play in psychological disorders? How do medications alleviate the symptoms of serious psychological disorders? (Chapters 13 and 14)

This chapter will lay an important foundation for the rest of this book by helping you develop a broad appreciation of the *nervous system*—the body's primary communication network. We'll start by looking at *neurons,* the basic cells of the nervous system. We'll also consider the organization of the nervous system and a closely linked communication network, the *endocrine system*. We'll then move on to a guided tour of the brain. We'll look at how certain brain areas are specialized to handle different functions, such as language, vision, and touch. In the Application, we'll discuss how the brain responds to environmental stimulation by literally altering its structure. And at several points, we'll return to Asha's story and tell you how she fared after her stroke.

Neuroscience and Behavior Maintaining your balance on a bicycle, smiling, talking with a friend—all your behaviors involve the complex integration of many physical processes working in harmony. For that matter, so does your ability to perceive and recognize the image in this photograph. What kinds of questions might neuroscientists ask about the common behaviors shown here?

The Neuron
The Basic Unit of Communication

Key Theme

■ Information in the nervous system is transmitted by specialized cells, called neurons.

Key Questions

■ What are the basic components of the neuron, and what are their functions?

■ What are glial cells, and what is their role in the nervous system?

■ What is an action potential, and how is it produced?

Communication throughout the nervous system takes place via **neurons**—cells that are highly specialized to receive and transmit information from one part of the body to another. Most neurons, especially those in your brain, are extremely small. A bit of brain tissue no larger than a grain of rice contains about 10,000 neurons! Your entire brain contains an estimated 100 *billion* neurons. Special magnifying equipment, such as an electron microscope, is usually used to study neurons.

Fortunately for neuroscientists, there are often striking similarities between the workings of the human nervous system and those of the nervous systems of many other creatures in the animal kingdom. Very simple creatures, such as sea snails and squid, tend to have larger neurons and simpler nervous systems than do humans. Neuroscientists have been able to closely observe the actions and reactions of a single neuron by studying the nervous systems of such simple animals.

Along with neurons, the human nervous system is made up of other types of specialized cells, called **glial cells** (see Figure 2.1). Glial cells outnumber neurons by about 10 to 1, but are much smaller. *Glia* is Greek for "glue," and at one time it was believed that glial cells were the glue that held the neurons of the brain together. Although they don't actually glue neurons together, glial cells do provide structural support for neurons. Glial cells also provide nutrition for neurons and remove waste products, including dead or damaged neurons. Beyond their support functions, evidence is growing that glial cells also play an active role in the signaling and communication of information between neurons (Haydon, 2001).

Neurons vary greatly in size and shape, reflecting their specialized functions. There are three basic types of neurons, each communicating different kinds of information. **Sensory neurons** convey information about the environment, such as light or sound, from specialized receptor cells in the sense organs to the brain. Sensory neurons also carry information from the skin and internal organs to the brain. **Motor neurons** communicate information to the muscles and glands of the body. Simply blinking your eyes activates thousands of motor neurons. Finally, **interneurons** communicate information *between* neurons. By far, most of the neurons in the human nervous system are interneurons, and many interneurons connect to other interneurons.

biological psychology
Specialized branch of psychology that studies the relationship between behavior and bodily processes and systems; also called *biopsychology* or *psychobiology*.

neuroscience
The study of the nervous system, especially the brain.

neuron
Highly specialized cell that communicates information in electrical and chemical form; a nerve cell.

glial cells
(GLEE-ull) Support cells that assist neurons by providing structural support, nutrition, and removal of cell wastes; manufacture myelin.

sensory neuron
Type of neuron that conveys information to the brain from specialized receptor cells in sense organs and internal organs.

motor neuron
Type of neuron that signals muscles to relax or contract.

interneuron
Type of neuron that communicates information from one neuron to the next.

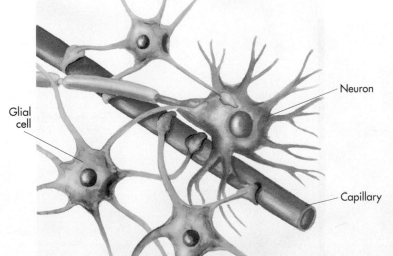

Glial cell

Neuron

Capillary

FIGURE 2.1 Glial Cells Glial cells greatly outnumber neurons in the brain. They provide support and nutrition for the neuron. One type of glial cell, shown here, provides a connection between neurons and blood vessels in the brain. Other types of glial cells form the myelin sheath, a fatty insulating substance wrapped around some neuron axons. Growing evidence suggests that glial cells are also involved in the signaling and communication of information between neurons (Haydon, 2001).

cell body
Processes nutrients and provides energy for the neuron to function; contains the cell's nucleus; also called the *soma*.

dendrites
Multiple short fibers that extend from the neuron's cell body and receive information from other neurons or from sensory receptor cells.

axon
The long, fluid-filled tube that carries a neuron's messages to other body areas.

Characteristics of the Neuron

Most neurons have three basic components: a *cell body, dendrites,* and an *axon* (see Figure 2.2). The **cell body,** also called the *soma,* contains structures that manufacture proteins and process nutrients, providing the energy the neuron needs to function. The cell body also contains the *nucleus,* which in turn contains the cell's genetic material—twisted strands of DNA called *chromosomes.*

Extending out from the cell body are many short, branching fibers, called **dendrites.** The term *dendrite* comes from a Greek word meaning "tree." If you have a good imagination, the intricate branching of the dendrites do often resemble the branches of a tree. Dendrites *receive* messages from other neurons or specialized cells. Dendrites with many branches have a greater surface area, which increases the amount of information the neuron can receive. Some neurons have thousands of dendrites.

The **axon** is a single, elongated tube that extends from the cell body in most, though not all, neurons. (Some neurons do not have axons.) Axons carry information *from* the neuron *to* other cells in the body, including other neurons, glands, and muscles. In contrast to the potentially large number of dendrites, a neuron has no more than one axon exiting from the cell body. However, many axons have branches near their tips that allow the neuron to communicate information to more than one target.

FIGURE 2.2 The Parts of a Typical Neuron
The drawing shows the location and function of key parts of a neuron. The photograph, made with the aid of an electron microscope, reveals actual cell bodies, dendrites, and axons in a cluster of neurons. The green coloring was added to provide contrast in the photograph to make the neurons more visible.

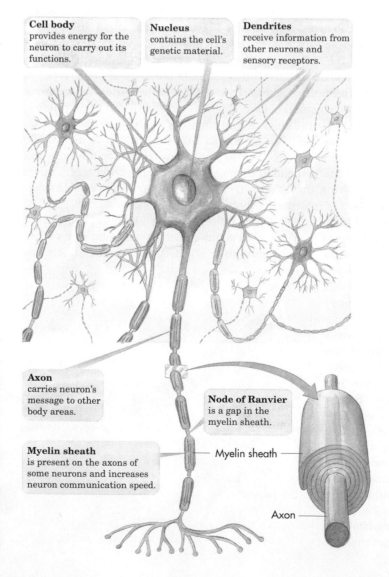

Cell body
provides energy for the neuron to carry out its functions.

Nucleus
contains the cell's genetic material.

Dendrites
receive information from other neurons and sensory receptors.

Axon
carries neuron's message to other body areas.

Node of Ranvier
is a gap in the myelin sheath.

Myelin sheath
is present on the axons of some neurons and increases neuron communication speed.

Myelin sheath

Axon

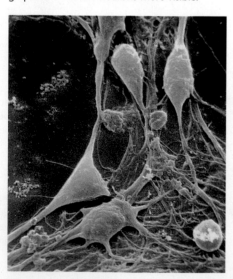

Axons can vary enormously in length. Most axons are very small; some are no more than a few thousandths of an inch long. Other axons are quite long. For example, the longest axon in your body is that of the motor neuron that controls your big toe. This neuron extends from the base of your spine into your foot. If you happen to be a seven-foot-tall basketball player, this axon could be four feet long! For most of us, of course, this axon is closer to three feet long.

The axons of many, though not all, neurons are surrounded by the **myelin sheath.** The myelin sheath is a white, fatty covering formed by special glial cells. In much the same way that you can bundle together electrical wires if they are insulated with plastic, myelin helps insulate one axon from the axons of other neurons. Rather than forming a continuous coating of the axon, the myelin sheath occurs in segments that are separated by small gaps where there is no myelin. The small gaps are called the *nodes of Ranvier,* or simply *nodes* (see Figure 2.2). Neurons wrapped in myelin communicate their messages up to 20 times faster than do unmyelinated neurons.

The importance of myelin becomes readily apparent when it is damaged. For example, *multiple sclerosis* is a disease that involves the degeneration of patches of the myelin sheath. This degeneration causes the transmission of neural messages to be slowed or interrupted, resulting in disturbances in sensation and movement. Muscular weakness, loss of coordination, and speech and visual disturbances are some of the symptoms that characterize multiple sclerosis.

Communication Within the Neuron
The All-or-None Action Potential

Essentially, the function of neurons is to transmit information throughout the nervous system. But exactly *how* do neurons transmit information? What form does this information take? In this section, we'll consider the nature of communication *within* a neuron, and in the following section we'll describe communication *between* neurons. As you'll see, communication in and between neurons is an electrochemical process.

In general, messages are gathered by the dendrites and cell body and then transmitted along the axon in the form of a brief electrical impulse called an **action potential.** The action potential is produced by the movement of electrically charged particles, called *ions,* across the membrane of the axon. Some ions are negatively charged, others positively charged.

Think of the axon membrane as a gatekeeper that carefully controls the balance of positive and negative ions on the interior and exterior of the axon. As the gatekeeper, the axon membrane opens and closes *ion channels* that allow ions to flow into and out of the axon.

Each neuron requires a minimum level of stimulation from other neurons or sensory receptors to activate it. This minimum level of stimulation is called the neuron's **stimulus threshold.** While waiting for sufficient stimulation to activate it, the neuron is said to be *polarized.* This means that there is a difference in the electrical charge between the inside and the outside of the axon.

More specifically, there is a greater concentration of negative proteins inside the neuron. Thus, the axon's interior is more negatively charged than is the exterior fluid surrounding the axon. The negative electrical charge is about −70 millivolts (thousandths of a volt) (see Figure 2.3). The −70 millivolts is referred to as the neuron's **resting potential.**

In this polarized, negative-inside/positive-outside condition, there are different concentrations of two particular ions: sodium and potassium. While the neuron is in resting potential, the fluid surrounding the axon contains a larger concentration of *sodium* ions than does the fluid within the axon. The fluid within the axon contains a larger concentration of *potassium* ions than is found in the fluid outside the axon.

myelin sheath
(MY-eh-lin) A white, fatty covering wrapped around the axons of some neurons that increases their communication speed.

action potential
A brief electrical impulse by which information is transmitted along the axon of a neuron.

stimulus threshold
The minimum level of stimulation required to activate a particular neuron.

resting potential
State in which a neuron is prepared to activate and communicate its message if it receives sufficient stimulation.

FIGURE 2.3 Electrical Changes During an Action Potential This graph shows the changing electrical charge of the neuron during an action potential. When the neuron depolarizes and ions cross the axon membrane, the result is a brief positive electrical impulse of +30 millivolts—the action potential. During the refractory period, the neuron reestablishes the resting potential negative charge of −70 millivolts and then is ready to activate again.

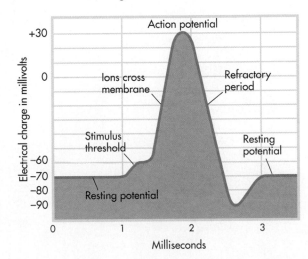

When sufficiently stimulated by other neurons or sensory receptors, the neuron *depolarizes*, beginning the action potential. At each successive axon segment, sodium ion channels open for a mere thousandth of a second. The sodium ions rush to the axon interior from the surrounding fluid, and then the sodium ion channels close. Less than a thousandth of a second later, the potassium ion channels open, allowing potassium to flow out of the axon and into the fluid surrounding it. Then the potassium ion channels close (see Figure 2.4). This sequence of depolarization and ion movement continues in a self-sustaining fashion down the entire length of the axon.

As this ion exchange occurs, the relative balance of positive and negative ions separated by the axon membrane changes. The electrical charge on the inside of the axon momentarily changes to a positive electrical charge of about +30 millivolts. The result is a brief positive electrical impulse that progressively occurs at each segment down the axon—the *action potential*.

Although it's tempting to think of the action potential as being conducted much as electricity is conducted through a wire, that's *not* what takes place in the neuron. The axon is actually a poor conductor of electricity. At each successive segment

FIGURE 2.4 Communication Within the Neuron: The Action Potential These drawings depict the ion channels in the membrane of a neuron's axon. When sufficiently stimulated, the neuron depolarizes and an action potential begins. At each progressive segment of the axon's membrane, sodium ion channels open and sodium ions rush into the interior of the axon. A split second later, the sodium ion channels close and potassium channels open, allowing potassium ions to flow out of the axon. As this sequence occurs, there is a change in the relative balance of positive and negative ions separated by the axon membrane. The electrical charge on the interior of the axon briefly changes from negative to positive. Once started, an action potential is self-sustaining and continues to the end of the axon. Following the action potential, the neuron repolarizes and reestablishes its negative electrical charge.

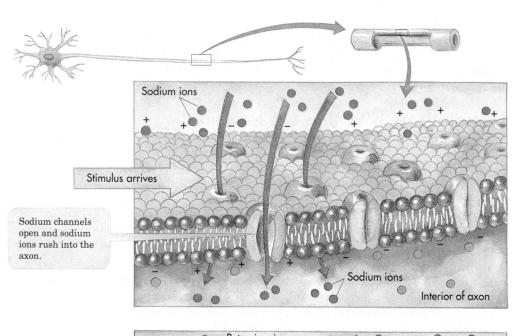

Sodium ions

Stimulus arrives

Sodium channels open and sodium ions rush into the axon.

Sodium ions

Interior of axon

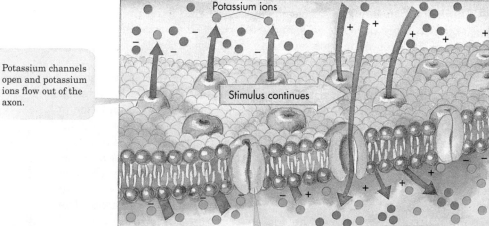

Potassium ions

Potassium channels open and potassium ions flow out of the axon.

Stimulus continues

The first sodium channels have closed, but those farther down the axon open, continuing the process of depolarization along the axon.

of the axon, the action potential is *regenerated* in the same way in which it was generated in the previous segment—by depolarization and the movement of ions.

Once the action potential is started, it is *self-sustaining* and continues to the end of the axon. In other words, there is no such thing as a partial action potential. Either the neuron is sufficiently stimulated and an action potential occurs, or the neuron is not sufficiently stimulated and an action potential does not occur. This principle is referred to as the **all-or-none law.**

Following the action potential, a *refractory period* occurs during which the neuron is unable to fire. This period lasts for about a thousandth of a second or less. During the refractory period, the neuron *repolarizes* and reestablishes the negative-inside/positive-outside condition. Like depolarization, repolarization occurs progressively at each segment down the axon. This process reestablishes the *resting potential* conditions so that the neuron is capable of firing again. The graph in Figure 2.3 on page 43 depicts the complete sequence from resting potential to action potential and back to resting potential.

For clarity, we've simplified some of the details involved in the action potential, but this is basically how information is communicated *within* the neuron. Remember, action potentials are generated in mere thousandths of a second. Thus, a single neuron can potentially generate hundreds of neural impulses per second. Given these minute increments of time, just how fast do neural impulses zip around the body?

The fastest neurons in your body communicate at speeds of up to 270 miles per hour. In the slowest neurons, messages creep along at about 2 miles per hour. This variation in communication speed is due to two factors: the axon diameter and the myelin sheath. The greater the axon's diameter, the faster the axon conducts action potentials. And, as we said earlier, myelinated neurons communicate faster than unmyelinated neurons. In myelinated neurons, the sodium ion channels are concentrated at each of the nodes of Ranvier where the myelin is missing. So, in myelinated neurons the action potential "jumps" from node to node rather than progressing down the entire length of the axon.

Communication Between Neurons
Bridging the Gap

Key Theme
- Communication between neurons takes place at the synapse, the junction between two adjoining neurons.

Key Questions
- How is information communicated at the synapse?
- What is a neurotransmitter, and what is its role in synaptic transmission?
- What are five important neurotransmitters, and how do psychoactive drugs affect synaptic transmission?

The primary function of a neuron is to communicate information to other cells, most notably other neurons. The point of communication between two neurons is called the **synapse.** At this communication junction, the message-*sending* neuron is referred to as the *presynaptic neuron*. The message-*receiving* neuron is called the *postsynaptic neuron*. For cells that are specialized to communicate information, neurons have a surprising characteristic: They don't touch each other. The presynaptic and postsynaptic neurons are separated by a tiny, fluid-filled space, called the **synaptic gap,** which is only about *five-millionths* of an inch wide.

The transmission of information between two neurons occurs in one of two ways: electrically or chemically. When communication is electrical, the synaptic gap is extremely narrow, and special ion channels serve as a bridge between the neurons. Electrical communication between the two neurons is virtually instantaneous.

all-or-none law
The principle that either a neuron is sufficiently stimulated and an action potential occurs or a neuron is not sufficiently stimulated and an action potential does not occur.

synapse
(SIN-aps) The point of communication between two neurons.

synaptic gap
(sin-AP-tick) The tiny space between the axon terminal of one neuron and the dendrite of an adjoining neuron.

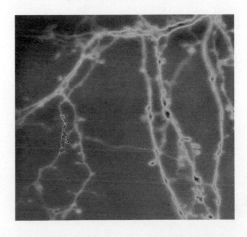

The Brain Capturing a Thought In the brain, as in the rest of the nervous system, information is transmitted by electrical impulses (red area) that speed from one neuron to the next.

axon terminals
Branches at the end of the axon that contain tiny pouches, or sacs, called synaptic vesicles.

synaptic vesicles
(sin-AP-tick VESS-ick-ulls) Tiny pouches or sacs in the axon terminals that contain chemicals called neurotransmitters.

neurotransmitters
Chemical messengers manufactured by a neuron.

synaptic transmission
(sin-AP-tick) The process through which neurotransmitters are released by one neuron, cross the synaptic gap, and affect adjoining neurons.

reuptake
The process by which neurotransmitter molecules detach from a postsynaptic neuron and are reabsorbed by a presynaptic neuron so they can be recycled and used again.

Although some neurons in the human nervous system communicate electrically, over 99 percent of the synapses in the brain use chemical transmission (Greengard, 2001). In general terms, chemical communication occurs when the presynaptic neuron creates a chemical substance that diffuses across the synaptic gap and is detected by the postsynaptic neuron. This one-way communication process between one neuron and another has many important implications for human behavior.

More specifically, here's how chemical communication takes place between neurons. As we've seen, when the presynaptic neuron is activated, it generates an action potential that travels to the end of the axon. At the end of the axon are several small branches called **axon terminals.** Floating in the interior fluid of the axon terminals are tiny sacs called **synaptic vesicles** (see Figure 2.5). The synaptic vesicles hold special chemical messengers manufactured by the neuron, called **neurotransmitters.**

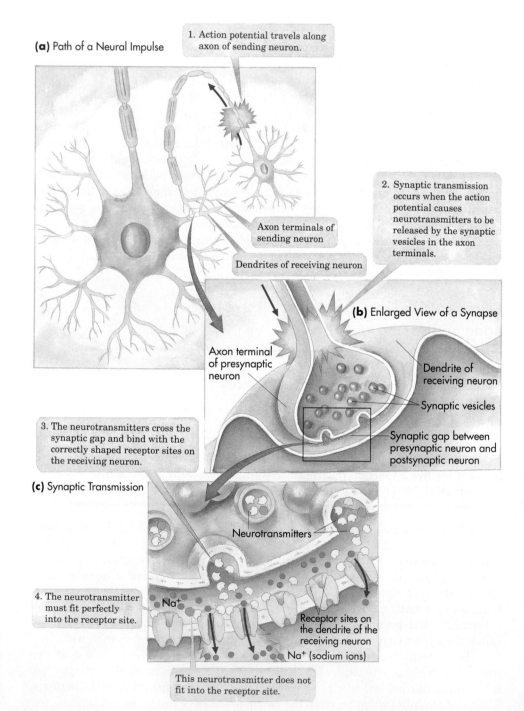

(a) Path of a Neural Impulse

1. Action potential travels along axon of sending neuron.

2. Synaptic transmission occurs when the action potential causes neurotransmitters to be released by the synaptic vesicles in the axon terminals.

Axon terminals of sending neuron

Dendrites of receiving neuron

(b) Enlarged View of a Synapse

Axon terminal of presynaptic neuron

Dendrite of receiving neuron

Synaptic vesicles

Synaptic gap between presynaptic neuron and postsynaptic neuron

3. The neurotransmitters cross the synaptic gap and bind with the correctly shaped receptor sites on the receiving neuron.

(c) Synaptic Transmission

Neurotransmitters

4. The neurotransmitter must fit perfectly into the receptor site.

Na⁺

Receptor sites on the dendrite of the receiving neuron

Na⁺ (sodium ions)

This neurotransmitter does not fit into the receptor site.

FIGURE 2.5 Communication Between Neurons: The Process of Synaptic Transmission
As you follow the steps in this progressive graphic, you can trace the sequence of synaptic transmission in which neurotransmitters are released by the sending, or presynaptic, neuron, cross the tiny fluid-filled space called the synaptic gap, and attach to receptor sites on the receiving, or postsynaptic, neuron.

When the action potential reaches the axon terminals, some of the synaptic vesicles "dock" on the axon terminal membrane, then release their neurotransmitters into the synaptic gap. These chemical messengers cross the synaptic gap and attach to *receptor sites* on the dendrites and other surfaces of the surrounding neurons. This journey across the synaptic gap is slower than electrical transmission but is still extremely rapid; it takes less than ten-millionths of a second. The entire process of transmitting information at the synapse is called **synaptic transmission.**

What happens to the neurotransmitter molecules after they've attached to the receptor sites of the postsynaptic neuron? Most often, they detach from the receptor and are reabsorbed by the presynaptic neuron so they can be recycled and used again. This process is called **reuptake.** Reuptake also occurs with many of the neurotransmitters that failed to attach to a receptor and are left floating in the synaptic gap. Neurotransmitter molecules that are not reabsorbed or that remain attached to the receptor site are broken down or destroyed by enzymes. As you'll see in the next section, certain drugs can interfere with both of these processes, prolonging the presence of the neurotransmitter in the synaptic gap.

The number of neurotransmitters that a neuron can manufacture varies. Some neurons produce only one type of neurotransmitter, whereas others manufacture three or more. Although estimates vary, scientists have thus far identified more than 100 different compounds that function as neurotransmitters in the brain (Greengard, 2001).

Each type of neurotransmitter has a chemically distinct, different shape. Like a key in a lock, a neurotransmitter's shape must precisely match that of a receptor site on the postsynaptic neuron for the neurotransmitter to affect that neuron. Keep in mind that the postsynaptic neuron can have many differently shaped receptor sites on its dendrites and other surfaces. Thus, it may accommodate several different neurotransmitters. The distinctive shapes of neurotransmitters and their receptor sites are shown schematically in Figure 2.6.

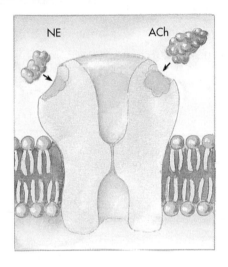

FIGURE 2.6 Neurotransmitter and Receptor Site Shapes Each neurotransmitter has a chemically distinct shape. Like a key in a lock, a neurotransmitter must perfectly fit the receptor site on the receiving neuron for its message to be communicated. In this figure, NE is the abbreviation for the neurotransmitter norepinephrine and ACh is the abbreviation for acetylcholine.

Excitatory and Inhibitory Messages

A neurotransmitter communicates either an excitatory or an inhibitory message to a postsynaptic neuron. An *excitatory message* increases the likelihood that the postsynaptic neuron will activate and generate an action potential. Conversely, an *inhibitory message* decreases the likelihood that the postsynaptic neuron will activate. If a postsynaptic neuron receives an excitatory and an inhibitory message simultaneously, the two messages cancel each other out.

It's important to note that the effect of any particular neurotransmitter depends on the particular *receptor* to which it binds. So, the same neurotransmitter can have an inhibitory effect on one neuron and an excitatory effect on another.

Depending on the number and kind of neurotransmitter chemicals that are bound to the receptor sites on the adjoining neurons, the postsynaptic neurons are more or less likely to activate. If the net result is a sufficient number of excitatory messages, the postsynaptic neuron depolarizes, generates an action potential, and releases its own neurotransmitters.

When released by a presynaptic neuron, neurotransmitter chemicals cross hundreds, even thousands, of synaptic gaps and affect the intertwined dendrites of adjacent neurons. Because the receiving neuron can have thousands of dendrites that intertwine with the axon terminals of many presynaptic neurons, the number of potential synaptic interconnections between neurons is mind-boggling. On the average, each neuron in the brain communicates directly with 1,000 other neurons (Greengard, 2001). Thus, in your brain alone, there are up to 100 *trillion* synaptic interconnections.

acetylcholine
(uh-*seet*-ull-KO-leen) Neurotransmitter that causes muscle contraction and is involved in memory function.

dopamine
(DOPE-uh-meen) Neurotransmitter involved in the regulation of bodily movement, thought processes, and rewarding sensations.

serotonin
(ser-ah-TONE-in) Neurotransmitter involved in sleep and emotions.

norepinephrine
(nor-ep-in-EF-rin) Neurotransmitter involved in learning and memory; also a hormone manufactured by adrenal glands.

GABA (gamma-aminobutyric acid)
Neurotransmitter that usually communicates an inhibitory message.

endorphins
(en-DORF-ins) Neurotransmitters that regulate pain perceptions.

Neurotransmitters and Their Effects

Your ability to perceive, feel, think, move, act, and react depends on the delicate balance of neurotransmitters in your nervous system. Too much or too little of a given neurotransmitter can have devastating effects. Yet neurotransmitters are present in only minuscule amounts in the human body. If you imagine trying to detect a pinch of salt dissolved in an Olympic-sized swimming pool, you will have some idea of the infinitesimal amounts of neurotransmitters present in brain tissue.

In this section, you'll see that researchers have linked abnormal levels of specific neurotransmitters to various physical and behavioral problems (see Table 2.1). Nevertheless, it's important to remember that any connection between a particular neurotransmitter and a particular effect is not a simple one-to-one relationship. Many behaviors are the result of the complex interaction of different neurotransmitters. Further, neurotransmitters sometimes have different effects in different areas of the brain.

Table 2.1

Summary of Important Neurotransmitters

Neurotransmitter	Primary Roles	Associated Disorders
Acetylcholine	Learning, memory	Alzheimer's disease
	Muscle contractions	
Dopamine	Movement	Parkinson's disease
	Thought processes	Schizophrenia
	Rewarding sensations	Drug addiction
Serotonin	Emotional states	Depression
	Sleep	
Norepinephrine	Physical arousal	Depression, stress
	Learning	
	Memory	
GABA	Inhibition of brain activity	Anxiety disorders
Endorphins	Pain perception	Opiate addiction
	Positive emotions	

Important Neurotransmitters

Acetylcholine, the first neurotransmitter discovered, is found in all motor neurons. It stimulates muscles to contract, including the heart and stomach muscles. Whether it is as simple as the flick of an eyelash or as complex as a back flip, all movement involves acetylcholine.

Acetylcholine is also found in many neurons in the brain, and it is important in memory, learning, and general intellectual functioning. People with *Alzheimer's disease,* which is characterized by progressive loss of memory and deterioration of intellectual functioning, have a severe depletion of several neurotransmitters in the brain, most notably acetylcholine.

The neurotransmitter **dopamine** is involved in movement, attention, learning, and pleasurable or rewarding sensations. Evidence suggests that the addictiveness of many drugs, including cocaine and nicotine, is related to their ability to increase dopamine activity in the brain (Nestler & Malenka, 2004; Self, 2005).

The degeneration of the neurons that produce dopamine in one brain area causes *Parkinson's disease,* which is characterized by rigidity, muscle tremors, poor balance, and difficulty in initiating movements. Symptoms can be alleviated by a drug called *L-dopa,* which converts to dopamine in the brain.

Nerve Gas and Acetylcholine By filtering the air, the gas mask protects this soldier against chemical weapons, like nerve gas. Nerve gas kills by causing acetylcholine to be continuously released by the motor neurons. Excessive acetylcholine builds up in the synaptic gap, causing muscle spasms that are so severe the victim is unable to breathe and quickly suffocates. Atropine is an effective antidote for nerve gas. When injected, atropine counteracts the effects of nerve gas by blocking acetylcholine receptor sites.

Excessive brain levels of dopamine are sometimes involved in the hallucinations and perceptual distortions that characterize the severe mental disorder called *schizophrenia*. Some antipsychotic drugs that relieve schizophrenic symptoms work by blocking dopamine receptors and reducing dopamine activity in the brain. Unfortunately, these antipsychotic drugs can also produce undesirable side effects. Because the drugs reduce dopamine in several different areas of the brain, long-term use sometimes produces symptoms that are very similar to those of Parkinson's disease. In the chapters on psychological disorders (Chapter 13) and therapies (Chapter 14), we'll discuss schizophrenia, dopamine, and antipsychotic drugs in more detail.

Michael J. Fox and Parkinson's Disease Actor Michael J. Fox was diagnosed with Parkinson's disease in 1990 at the age of 30. As the disease has progressed, Fox has experienced trembling, muscle stiffness, and difficulty initiating movements and speech. To help control the symptoms, he takes a medication containing L-dopa, which increases brain levels of the neurotransmitter dopamine. As Fox (1998) said in an interview, "The ugly truth is that I am flesh and blood and I am a bunch of neurotransmitters that may or may not work." Fox is keenly aware that the disease is progressive and, thus far, incurable. Fox left his hit TV series, *Spin City*, to devote himself to fundraising and increasing public awareness of Parkinson's disease. Among the estimated 1 million Americans who are afflicted with Parkinson's disease are former U.S. Attorney General Janet Reno and the Reverend Billy Graham.

The neurotransmitters **serotonin** and **norepinephrine** are found in many different brain areas. Serotonin is involved in sleep, moods, and emotional states, including depression. Antidepressant drugs such as *Prozac* increase the availability of serotonin in certain brain regions. Norepinephrine is implicated in the activation of neurons throughout the brain and helps the body gear up in the face of danger or threat. Norepinephrine also seems to be a key player in learning and memory retrieval. Like serotonin and dopamine, norepinephrine dysfunction is implicated in some mental disorders, especially depression (Holden, 2003).

GABA is the abbreviation for **gamma-aminobutyric acid,** a neurotransmitter found primarily in the brain. GABA usually communicates an inhibitory message to other neurons, helping to balance and offset excitatory messages. Alcohol makes people feel relaxed and less inhibited partly by increasing GABA activity, which reduces brain activity. Antianxiety medications, such as Valium and Xanax, also work by increasing GABA activity, which inhibits action potentials.

Endorphins: Regulating the Perception of Pain

In 1973, researchers Candace Pert and Solomon Snyder of Johns Hopkins University made the startling discovery that the brain contains receptor sites that are specific for the group of painkilling drugs called *opiates* (Pert & Snyder, 1973). Opiates include morphine, heroin, and codeine, all derived from the opium poppy. In addition to alleviating pain, opiates often produce a state of euphoria. Why would the brain have receptor sites for specific drugs like morphine? Pert, Snyder, and other researchers concluded that the brain must manufacture its own painkillers, morphinelike chemicals that act as neurotransmitters.

Within a few years, researchers identified a number of such chemicals manufactured by the brain (Snyder, 1984). Collectively, they are called **endorphins,** a term derived from the phrase *endogenous morphines*. (The word *endogenous* means "produced internally in the body.") Although chemically similar to morphine, endorphins are 100 times more potent. Today, it is known that endorphins are released in response to stress or trauma and that they reduce the perception of pain.

Researchers have found that endorphins are implicated in the pain-reducing effects of *acupuncture,* an ancient Chinese medical technique that involves inserting needles at various locations in the body (Ulett & Han, 2002). Endorphins are also associated with positive mood. For example, the "runner's high" associated with aerobic exercise has been attributed to endorphins. In marathon runners, endorphin levels have been found to increase up to four times over their normal levels (Mahler & others, 1989).

FIGURE 2.7 How Drugs Affect Synaptic Transmission Drugs affect brain activity by interfering with neurotransmitter functioning in the synapse. Drugs may also affect synaptic transmission by increasing or decreasing the amount of a particular neurotransmitter that is produced.

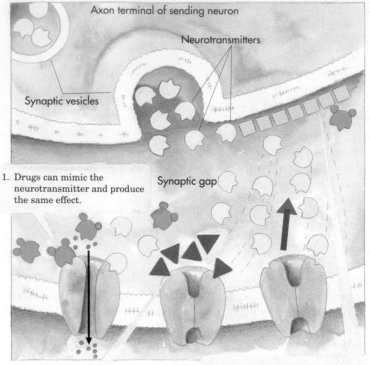

Axon terminal of sending neuron

Neurotransmitters

Synaptic vesicles

1. Drugs can mimic the neurotransmitter and produce the same effect.

Synaptic gap

2. Drugs can block the receptor site on the receiving neuron and prevent the effect of the neurotransmitter.

3. Drugs can block the reuptake of the neurotransmitter, increasing the effects of the neurotransmitter.

How Drugs Affect Synaptic Transmission

Much of what is known about different neurotransmitters has been learned from observing the effects of drugs and other substances. Many drugs, especially those that affect moods or behavior, work by interfering with the normal functioning of neurotransmitters in the synapse (Self, 2005).

As Figure 2.7 illustrates, some drugs increase or decrease the amount of neurotransmitter released by neurons. For example, the venom of a black widow spider bite causes acetylcholine to be released continuously by motor neurons, causing severe muscle spasms. Drugs may also affect the length of time the neurotransmitter remains in the synaptic gap, either increasing or decreasing the amount available to the postsynaptic receptor.

One way in which drugs can prolong the effects of the neurotransmitter is by blocking the reuptake of the neurotransmitter by the sending neuron. For example, Prozac inhibits the reuptake of serotonin, increasing the availability of serotonin in the brain. The illegal drug cocaine produces its exhilarating rush by interfering with the reuptake of dopamine (Volkow & others, 2003).

Drugs can also mimic specific neurotransmitters. When a drug is chemically similar to a specific neurotransmitter, it may produce the same effect as that neurotransmitter. It is partly through this mechanism that nicotine works as a stimulant. Nicotine is chemically similar to acetylcholine and can occupy acetylcholine receptor sites, stimulating skeletal muscles and causing the heart to beat more rapidly.

Alternatively, a drug can block the effect of a neurotransmitter by fitting into receptor sites and preventing the neurotransmitter from acting. For example, the drug *curare* blocks acetylcholine receptor sites, causing almost instantaneous paralysis. The brain sends signals to the motor neurons, but the muscles can't respond because the motor neuron receptor sites are blocked by the curare. Similarly, a drug called *naloxone* eliminates the effects of both endorphins and opiates by blocking opiate receptor sites.

The Nervous System and the Endocrine System
Communication Throughout the Body

Key Theme
■ Two major communication systems in the body are the nervous system and the endocrine system.

Key Questions
■ What are the divisions of the nervous system and their functions?
■ How is information transmitted in the endocrine system, and what are its major structures?
■ How do the nervous and endocrine systems interact to produce the fight-or-flight response?

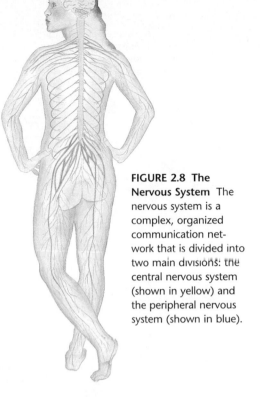

FIGURE 2.8 The Nervous System The nervous system is a complex, organized communication network that is divided into two main divisions: the central nervous system (shown in yellow) and the peripheral nervous system (shown in blue).

Specialized for communication, up to 1 *trillion* neurons are linked throughout your body in a complex, organized communication network called the **nervous system.** The human nervous system is divided into two main divisions: the *central nervous system* and the *peripheral nervous system* (see Figure 2.8). In order for even simple behaviors to occur, such as curling your toes or scratching your nose, these two divisions must function as a single, integrated unit. Yet each of these divisions is highly specialized and performs different tasks.

The neuron is the most important transmitter of messages in the central nervous system. In the peripheral nervous system, communication occurs along **nerves.** Nerves and neurons are not the same thing. Nerves are made up of large bundles of neuron axons. Unlike neurons, many nerves are large enough to be seen easily with the unaided eye.

The Central Nervous System

The **central nervous system (CNS)** includes the brain and the spinal cord. The central nervous system is so critical to your ability to function that it is entirely protected by bone—the brain by your skull and the spinal cord by your spinal column. Surrounding and protecting the brain and the spinal cord are three layers of membranous tissues, called the *meninges.* As an added measure of protection, the brain and spinal cord are suspended in *cerebrospinal fluid* to protect them from being jarred.

The central nervous system is aptly named. It is central to all your behaviors and mental processes. And it is the central processing center—every action, thought, feeling, and sensation you experience is processed through the central nervous system. The most important element of the central nervous system is, of course, the brain, which acts as the command center. We'll take a tour of the human brain in a later section.

Think of the spinal cord as an old-fashioned but very busy telephone switchboard, handling both incoming and outgoing messages. Sensory receptors send messages along sensory nerves to the spinal cord, then up to the brain. To activate muscles, the brain sends signals down the spinal cord, which are relayed out along motor nerves to the muscles.

Most behaviors are controlled by your brain. However, the spinal cord can produce **spinal reflexes**—simple, automatic behaviors that occur without any brain involvement. For example, the *withdrawal reflex* occurs when you touch a painful stimulus, such as something hot, electrified, or sharp. As you can see in Figure 2.9 on page 52, this simple reflex involves a loop of rapid communication among *sensory neurons,* which communicate sensation to the spinal cord; *interneurons,* which relay information within the spinal cord; and *motor neurons,* which signal the muscles to react.

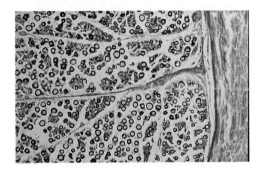

Nerves and Neurons Are Not the Same A cross section of a peripheral nerve is shown in this electron micrograph. Each black circle represents the end of one axon. As you can see, a nerve is actually composed of bundles of neuron axons.

nervous system
The primary internal communication network of the body; divided into the central nervous system and the peripheral nervous system.

nerves
Bundles of neuron axons that carry information in the peripheral nervous system.

central nervous system (CNS)
Division of the nervous system that consists of the brain and spinal cord.

spinal reflexes
Simple, automatic behaviors that are processed in the spinal cord.

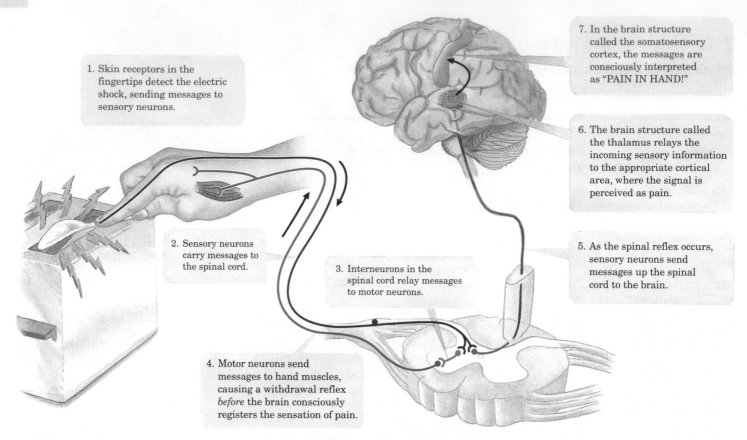

1. Skin receptors in the fingertips detect the electric shock, sending messages to sensory neurons.

2. Sensory neurons carry messages to the spinal cord.

3. Interneurons in the spinal cord relay messages to motor neurons.

4. Motor neurons send messages to hand muscles, causing a withdrawal reflex *before* the brain consciously registers the sensation of pain.

5. As the spinal reflex occurs, sensory neurons send messages up the spinal cord to the brain.

6. The brain structure called the thalamus relays the incoming sensory information to the appropriate cortical area, where the signal is perceived as pain.

7. In the brain structure called the somatosensory cortex, the messages are consciously interpreted as "PAIN IN HAND!"

FIGURE 2.9 A Spinal Reflex A spinal reflex is a simple, involuntary behavior that is processed in the spinal cord without brain involvement. If you shock yourself by using a wet spoon to pry a bagel out of a plugged-in toaster, you'll instantly pull your hand away from the painful stimulus—an example of the withdrawal reflex. The sequence shown above illustrates how the withdrawal reflex can occur before the brain processes the conscious perception of pain.

peripheral nervous system
(per-IF-er-ull) Division of the nervous system that includes all the nerves lying outside the central nervous system.

somatic nervous system
Subdivision of the peripheral nervous system that communicates sensory information to the central nervous system and carries motor messages from the central nervous system to the muscles.

autonomic nervous system
(aw-toe-NOM-ick) Subdivision of the peripheral nervous system that regulates involuntary functions.

Spinal reflexes are crucial to your survival. The additional few seconds that it would take you to consciously process sensations and decide how to react could result in serious injury. Spinal reflexes are also important as indicators that the neural pathways in your spinal cord are working correctly. That's why physicians test spinal reflexes during neurological examinations by tapping just below your kneecap for the knee-jerk spinal reflex or scratching the sole of your foot for the toe-curl spinal reflex.

The Peripheral Nervous System

The **peripheral nervous system** is the other major division of your nervous system. The word *peripheral* means "lying at the outer edges." Thus, the peripheral nervous system comprises all the nerves outside the central nervous system that extend to the outermost borders of your body, including your skin. The communication functions of the peripheral nervous system are handled by its two subdivisions: the *somatic nervous system* and the *autonomic nervous system*.

The **somatic nervous system** takes its name from the Greek word *soma*, which means "body." It plays a key role in communication throughout the entire body. First, the somatic nervous system communicates sensory information received by sensory receptors along sensory nerves *to* the central nervous system. Second, it carries messages *from* the central nervous system along motor nerves to perform voluntary muscle movements. All the different sensations that you're experiencing right now are being communicated by your somatic nervous system to your spinal cord and on to your brain. When you perform a voluntary action, such as turning a page of this book, messages from the brain are communicated down the spinal cord, then out to the muscles via the somatic nervous system.

The other subdivision of the peripheral nervous system is the **autonomic nervous system.** The word *autonomic* means "self-governing." Thus, the autonomic nervous system regulates *involuntary* functions, such as heartbeat, blood pressure, breathing, and digestion. These processes occur with little or no conscious involvement. This is fortunate, because if you had to mentally command your heart to beat or your stomach to digest the pizza you had for lunch, it would be difficult to focus your attention on anything else.

However, the autonomic nervous system is not completely self-regulating. By engaging in physical activity or purposely tensing or relaxing your muscles, you can increase or decrease autonomic activity. Emotions and mental imagery also influence your autonomic nervous system. Vividly imagining a situation that makes you feel angry, frightened, or even sexually aroused can dramatically increase your heart rate and blood pressure. A peaceful mental image can lower many autonomic functions.

The involuntary functions regulated by the autonomic nervous system are controlled by two different branches: the *sympathetic* and *parasympathetic nervous systems*. These two systems control many of the same organs in your body but cause them to respond in opposite ways (see Figure 2.10). In general, the sympathetic nervous system arouses the body to expend energy, and the parasympathetic nervous system helps the body conserve energy.

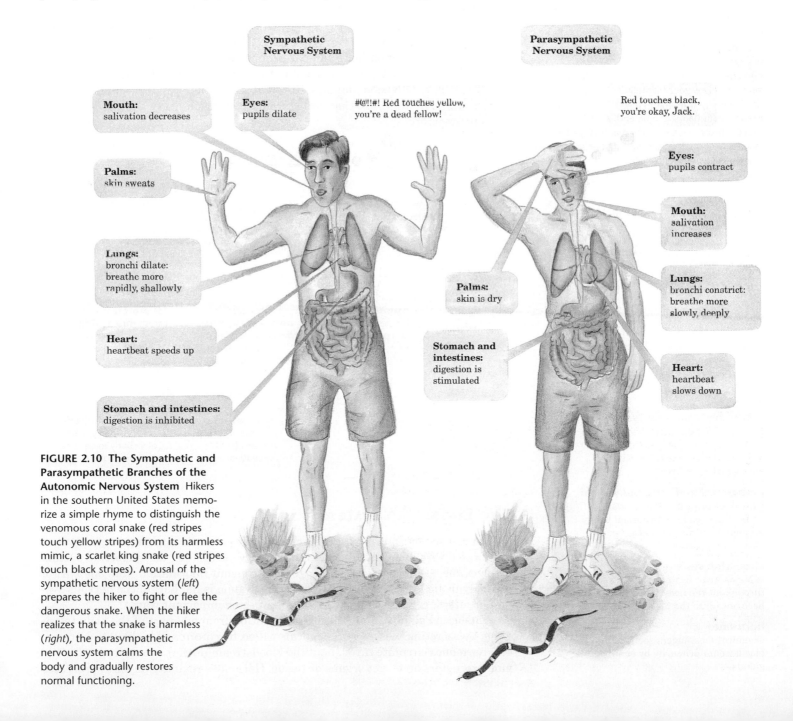

Sympathetic Nervous System

Parasympathetic Nervous System

Mouth: salivation decreases

Eyes: pupils dilate

#@!!#! Red touches yellow, you're a dead fellow!

Red touches black, you're okay, Jack.

Palms: skin sweats

Eyes: pupils contract

Mouth: salivation increases

Lungs: bronchi dilate: breathe more rapidly, shallowly

Palms: skin is dry

Lungs: bronchi constrict: breathe more slowly, deeply

Heart: heartbeat speeds up

Stomach and intestines: digestion is stimulated

Heart: heartbeat slows down

Stomach and intestines: digestion is inhibited

FIGURE 2.10 The Sympathetic and Parasympathetic Branches of the Autonomic Nervous System Hikers in the southern United States memorize a simple rhyme to distinguish the venomous coral snake (red stripes touch yellow stripes) from its harmless mimic, a scarlet king snake (red stripes touch black stripes). Arousal of the sympathetic nervous system (*left*) prepares the hiker to fight or flee the dangerous snake. When the hiker realizes that the snake is harmless (*right*), the parasympathetic nervous system calms the body and gradually restores normal functioning.

Activating the Sympathetic Nervous System The sympathetic branch of the autonomic nervous system gears the body up in response to perceived threats. This arousal of the body's systems prepares organisms to flee from danger or confront it head-on—the essence of the *fight-or-flight syndrome.* When the sympathetic nervous system activates in humans, tiny muscles in the skin contract, which elevates your hair follicles, producing the familiar sensation of "goose bumps" and making your hair stand on end. A similar process takes place in many mammals, making the fur or hair bristle, with rather spectacular results in this long-haired cat.

The **sympathetic nervous system** is the body's emergency system, rapidly activating bodily systems to meet threats or emergencies. When you are frightened, your breathing accelerates, your heart beats faster, digestion stops, and the bronchial tubes in your lungs expand. All these physiological responses increase the amount of oxygen available to your brain and muscles. Your pupils dilate to increase your field of vision, and your mouth becomes dry, because salivation stops. You begin to sweat in response to your body's expenditure of greater energy and heat. These bodily changes collectively represent the *fight-or-flight response*—they physically prepare you to fight or flee from a perceived danger. We'll discuss the fight-or-flight response in greater detail in Chapter 8, on emotion, and Chapter 12, on stress.

Whereas the sympathetic nervous system mobilizes your body's physical resources, the **parasympathetic nervous system** conserves and maintains your physical resources. It calms you down after an emergency. Acting much more slowly than the sympathetic nervous system, the parasympathetic nervous system gradually returns your body's systems to normal. Heart rate, breathing, and blood pressure level out. Pupils constrict back to their normal size. Saliva returns, and the digestive system begins operating again.

Although the sympathetic and parasympathetic nervous systems produce opposite effects, they act together, keeping the nervous system in balance (see Figure 2.11). Each division handles different functions, yet the whole nervous system works in unison so that both automatic and voluntary behaviors are carried out smoothly.

FIGURE 2.11 Organization of the Nervous System

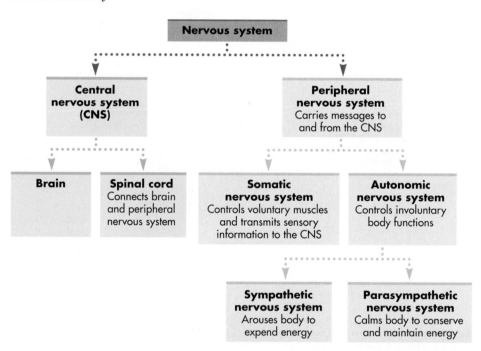

sympathetic nervous system
Branch of the autonomic nervous system that produces rapid physical arousal in response to perceived emergencies or threats.

parasympathetic nervous system
Branch of the autonomic nervous system that maintains normal bodily functions and conserves the body's physical resources.

endocrine system
(EN-doe-krin) System of glands located throughout the body that secrete hormones into the bloodstream.

hormones
Chemical messengers secreted into the bloodstream primarily by endocrine glands.

The Endocrine System

As you can see in Figure 2.12, the **endocrine system** is made up of glands that are located throughout the body. Like the nervous system, the endocrine system involves the use of chemical messengers to transmit information from one part of the body to another. Although the endocrine system is not part of the nervous system, it interacts with the nervous system in some important ways.

Endocrine glands communicate information from one part of the body to another by secreting messenger chemicals called **hormones** into the bloodstream. The hormones circulate throughout the bloodstream until they reach specific hormone receptors on target organs or tissue. Hormones regulate physical processes

Pineal gland
produces *melatonin*, which
helps regulate sleep–wake cycles

Hypothalamus
brain structure that controls the
pituitary gland; links nervous system
and endocrine system

Pituitary gland
regulates activities of several other
glands; produces *growth hormone*,
prolactin, and *oxytocin*

Thyroid gland
controls body metabolism rate

Adrenal glands
(adrenal cortex and adrenal medulla)
produce *epinephrine* (adrenaline) and
norepinephrine, which cause physical
arousal in response to danger, fear,
anger, stress, and other strong emotions

Pancreas
regulates blood sugar and insulin
levels; involved in hunger

Ovaries
secrete *estrogen* and *progesterone*, which
regulate female sexual development
and reproduction and influence sexual
behavior

Testes
secrete *testosterone*, which regulates
male sexual development and
reproduction and influences sexual
behavior

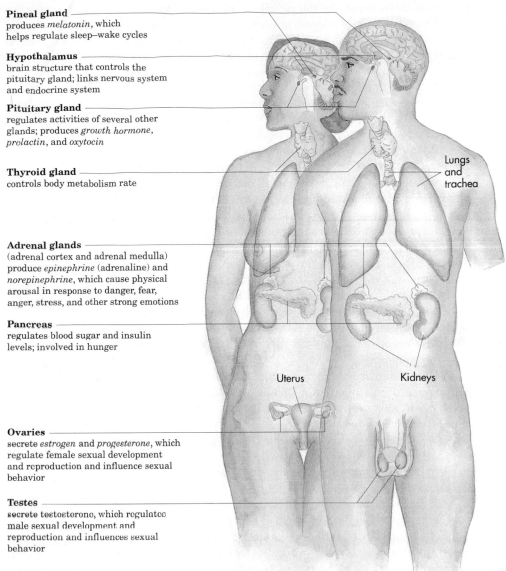

Lungs
and
trachea

Uterus

Kidneys

FIGURE 2.12 The Endocrine System The endocrine system and the nervous system are directly linked by the hypothalamus in the brain, which controls the pituitary gland. In turn, the pituitary releases hormones that affect the hormone production of several other endocrine glands. In the male and female figures shown here, you can see the location and main functions of several important endocrine glands.

and influence behavior in a variety of ways. Metabolism, growth rate, digestion, blood pressure, and sexual development and reproduction are just some of the processes that are regulated by the endocrine hormones. Hormones are also involved in emotional response and your response to stress.

Endocrine hormones are closely linked to the workings of the nervous system. For example, the release of hormones may be stimulated or inhibited by certain parts of the nervous system. In turn, hormones can promote or inhibit the generation of nerve impulses. Finally, some hormones and neurotransmitters are chemically identical. The same molecule can act as a hormone in the endocrine system and as a neurotransmitter in the nervous system.

In contrast to the rapid speed of information transmission in the nervous system, communication in the endocrine system takes place much more slowly. Hormones rely on the circulation of the blood to deliver their chemical messages to target organs, so it may take a few seconds or longer for the hormone to reach its target organ after it has been secreted by the originating gland.

The signals that trigger the secretion of hormones are regulated by the brain, primarily by a brain structure called the *hypothalamus*. (You'll learn more about the hypothalamus later in the chapter.) The hypothalamus serves as the main link between the endocrine system and the nervous system. The hypothalamus directly regulates

pituitary gland
(pih-TOO-ih-tare-ee) Endocrine gland attached to the base of the brain that secretes hormones that affect the function of other glands as well as hormones that act directly on physical processes.

adrenal glands
Pair of endocrine glands that are involved in the human stress response.

adrenal cortex
The outer portion of the adrenal glands.

adrenal medulla
The inner portion of the adrenal glands; secretes epinephrine and norepinephrine.

gonads
The endocrine glands that secrete hormones that regulate sexual characteristics and reproductive processes; *ovaries* in females and *testes* in males.

the release of hormones by the **pituitary gland,** a pea-sized gland just under the brain. The pituitary's hormones, in turn, regulate the production of other hormones by many of the glands in the endocrine system. This is why the pituitary gland is often referred to as the body's master gland. Under the direction of the hypothalamus, the pituitary gland controls hormone production in other endocrine glands.

The pituitary gland also produces some hormones that act directly. For example, the pituitary produces *growth hormone,* which stimulates normal skeletal growth during childhood. The pituitary gland can also secrete endorphins to reduce the perception of pain. In nursing mothers, the pituitary produces both *prolactin,* the hormone that stimulates milk production, and *oxytocin,* the hormone that produces the let-down reflex, in which stored milk is "let down" into the nipple.

Another set of glands, called the **adrenal glands,** is of particular interest to psychologists. The adrenal glands consist of the **adrenal cortex,** which is the outer gland, and the **adrenal medulla,** which is the inner gland. Both the adrenal cortex and the adrenal medulla produce hormones that are involved in the human stress response. As you'll see in Chapter 12, on stress, hormones secreted by the adrenal cortex also interact with the *immune system,* the body's defense against invading viruses or bacteria.

The adrenal medulla plays a key role in the fight-or-flight response, described earlier. When aroused, the sympathetic nervous system stimulates the adrenal medulla. In turn, the adrenal medulla produces *epinephrine* and *norepinephrine.* (You may be more familiar with the word *adrenaline,* which is another name for epinephrine.)

As they circulate through the bloodstream to the heart and other target organs, epinephrine and norepinephrine complement and enhance the effects of the sympathetic nervous system. These hormones also act as neurotransmitters, stimulating activity at the synapses in the sympathetic nervous system. The action of epinephrine and norepinephrine is a good illustration of the long-lasting effects of hormones. If you've noticed that it takes a while for you to calm down after a particularly upsetting or stressful experience, it's because of the lingering effects of epinephrine and norepinephrine in your body.

Also important are the **gonads,** or sex organs—the *ovaries* in women and the *testes* in men. In women, the ovaries secrete the hormones *estrogen* and *progesterone.* In men, the testes secrete male sex hormones called *androgens*, the most important of which is *testosterone*. Testosterone is also secreted by the adrenal glands in both males and females. In both males and females, the sex hormones influence sexual development, sexual behavior, and reproduction.

A Guided Tour of the Brain

Key Theme
- ■ The brain is a highly complex, integrated, and organized system of neurons.

Key Questions
- ■ What methods have been used to study the human brain, and how has each contributed to knowledge of the brain?
- ■ What are neural pathways?
- ■ How does the brain develop, and what is neurogenesis?

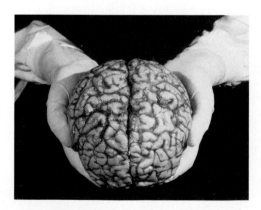

The Human Brain Weighing roughly three pounds, the human brain is about the size of a small cauliflower. Although your brain makes up only about 2 percent of your total body weight, it uses some 20 percent of the oxygen your body needs while at rest. The oxygen is used in breaking down glucose to supply the brain with energy.

Forget all the hype about the Internet. The *real* information superhighway is the human brain. In fact, the most complex mass of matter in the universe sits right between your two ears: your brain.

In this section we'll take you on a guided tour of the human brain. As your tour guides, our goal here is not to tell you everything that is known or suspected about

research involve systematically observing and recording the behavior of people whose brains have been damaged by illness or injury.

In a few instances, however, researchers have examined the brains of people with extraordinary talents, seeking neurological clues for their exceptional abilities (Burrell, 2005). We described one such attempt in the Focus on Neuroscience, on page 57.

Such case studies have provided valuable insights into behavior in such areas as memory, speech, emotion, movement, and personality. However, generalizing results from a case study must be done cautiously. Case studies usually focus on unusual situations or behaviors—in this case, brain disease or injury. Because these behaviors or situations are out of the ordinary, they may not reflect typical behavior.

Another potential limitation to information gleaned from studying the damaged brain is that brain injuries are rarely limited to specific, localized areas or contained within well-defined anatomical boundaries. It's often difficult to be sure exactly which brain area is responsible for specific behavioral problems. In addition, most behaviors involve the interaction of several different brain areas that are linked by networks of neuronal connections. Damage to one brain area may disrupt functioning in other areas that appear to be intact (Rorden & Karnath, 2004).

A related research method involves producing *lesions*—surgically altering, removing, or destroying specific portions of the brain—and observing subsequent behavior. In humans, lesions are sometimes produced for medical reasons, such as when part of the brain is surgically altered or removed to relieve uncontrollable seizures. Following such medical treatment, researchers can study the behavioral effects of the lesions. Lesions are sometimes produced in animals to systematically investigate the behavioral effects of damage in specific brain areas.

Researchers have also studied the behavioral effects of electrically stimulating specific brain areas. This procedure usually involves implanting tiny electrified disks or wires, called *bipolar electrodes*, into a specific brain area. Electrical stimulation causes activation of the neurons in the area around the tip of the electrode and usually produces the opposite behavioral effect of a lesion in the same brain area.

The invention of the **electroencephalograph** allowed scientists to record the brain's electrical activity through the use of large, disk-shaped electrodes placed harmlessly on a person's scalp. The graphic record of the brain's electrical activity that this instrument produces is called an *electroencephalogram,* abbreviated as *EEG*. Modern electroencephalographs provide sophisticated computerized analyses of the brain's electrical activity, recording the electrical activity of the brain from millisecond to millisecond.

As technology has become more advanced, so have the tools used to study the brain. In the Focus on Neuroscience on pages 60–61, we take a look at the new imaging techniques that allow neuroscientists to see the human brain at work.

The Developing Brain

Our guided tour will follow the same general sequence that the brain follows in its development before birth. By three weeks after conception, a sheet of primitive neural cells has formed. Just as you might roll a piece of paper to make a tube, this sheet curls to form the hollow *neural tube*. The neural tube is lined with *neural stem cells.* (Stem cells are cells that can divide indefinitely, renew themselves, and give rise to a variety of other types of cells.) The neural stem cells divide and multiply, producing other specialized cells that eventually give rise to neurons and glial cells.

Gradually, the top of the neural tube thickens into three bulges that will eventually form the three main regions of the brain: the *hindbrain, midbrain,* and *forebrain.* As the neural tube expands, it develops the cavities, called *ventricles,* that are found at the core of the fully developed brain. The ventricles are filled with cerebrospinal fluid, which cushions and provides nutrients for the brain and spinal cord. In the adult brain, the inner surface of the ventricles is lined with neural stem cells, forming what is called the *ventricular zone.*

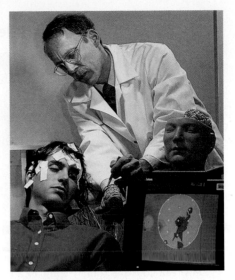

Monitoring Brain Activity The electroencephalograph measures the electrical activity of the brain using small electrodes that are harmlessly taped or pasted to a person's scalp. The rhythmical patterns of electrical activity are referred to as *brain waves.*

phrenology
(freh-NOL-uh-gee) A discredited pseudoscientific theory of the brain that claimed that personality characteristics, moral character, and intelligence could be determined by examining the bumps on a person's skull.

cortical localization
The notion that different functions are located or localized in different areas of the brain; also called *localization of function.*

electroencephalograph
An instrument that produces a graphic record of the brain's electrical activity by using electrodes placed on the scalp.

Human Embryo at Six Weeks Though the embryo is less than an inch long, the prominent structures of the hindbrain and the beginnings of the forebrain can clearly be seen at this early stage of prenatal development.

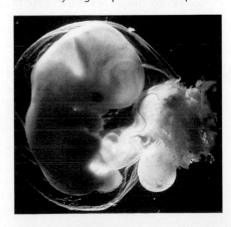

Neuroscience: Understanding Brain-Imaging Techniques

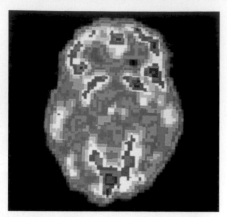 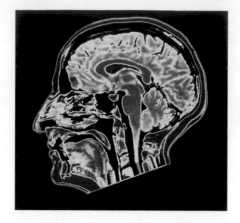 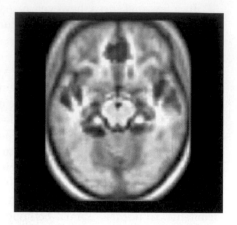

Positron emission tomography, or a PET scan, generates images of the brain's activity by tracking the brain's use of a radioactively tagged compound, such as glucose, oxygen, or a particular drug. An invasive procedure, PET involves injecting participants with a radioactive substance before the scan. The PET scan then measures the amount of the radioactively tagged substance used in thousands of brain areas while the person engages in some type of mental activity. Over the course of several minutes, the information is collected, analyzed, and averaged by computer. In the resulting color-coded images, the areas of greatest brain activity are indicated by red and yellow colors.

Magnetic resonance imaging, or MRI, is a noninvasive procedure that provides highly detailed images of the body's internal structures, including the brain. MRI is very versatile, producing thin "slice" images of body tissue from virtually any angle. As the person lies motionless in a long magnetic tube, powerful but harmless magnetic fields bombard the brain or other body area. In response to these magnetic fields, the molecules of the body generate electromagnetic signals, which are analyzed by computer to create the highly detailed images. Tissues with high concentrations of water, such as fat, appear lighter in color, while bone and other tissues with less water appear darker.

Functional magnetic resonance imaging, or fMRI, provides moment-by-moment images of the brain's changing activity. Using the same scanning hardware as an MRI, fMRI also tracks changes in the brain's blood flow and oxygen levels. Compared to PET scans, fMRI produces a much sharper picture and can detail much smaller brain structures. Another advantage of fMRI is that it provides a picture of brain activity averaged over seconds rather than the several minutes required by PET scans. Because fMRI is a noninvasive procedure, researchers can repeatedly scan a single subject. In an fMRI image, the areas of greatest brain activity are indicated by blue and yellow colors.

Commonly Used Brain-Imaging Techniques

Brain-scan images have become so commonplace in news articles and popular magazines that it's easy to forget just how revolutionary brain-imaging technology has been to the field of neuroscience (Posner & DiGirolamo, 2000). Shown above are the three types of brain-imaging techniques most commonly used in psychological research—**PET scans, MRI,** and **functional MRI,** which is abbreviated **fMRI**. The descriptions explain how each brain-imaging technique works and the kind of information it provides.

How Psychologists Use Brain-Imaging Technology

Like other scientific data-gathering methods described in Chapter 1, brain imaging is used for both descriptive and experimental research. A descriptive study utilizing brain scans might compare the brain structure or functioning of one carefully defined group of people with another. For example, MRI scans were used to compare London taxi drivers, who are required to have an encyclopedic knowledge of the city streets to pass their licensing exam, with matched participants who were not London taxi drivers (Maguire & others, 2000). The MRI scans showed that part of a brain structure involved in spatial memory, the *hippocampus,* was significantly larger in the experienced taxi drivers than in the control subjects. The size of the hippocampus was also positively correlated with the length of time the participants had been driving taxis in London. One implica-

tion of this study is that structures in the adult human brain can change in response to learning and environmental demands—an important topic that we'll explore later in the chapter.

Brain-imaging technology is also used in experimental research, especially in an important new field called cognitive neuroscience (Poldrack & Wagner, 2004). Integrating contributions from psychology, neuroscience, and computer science, **cognitive neuroscience** is the study of the neural basis of cognitive processes.

How is brain imaging used in cognitive neuroscience research? In a typical experiment, a brain scan is taken during a control task or condition, such as lying down with eyes closed. In the top row of PET scans in the image on the facing page, the control condition is shown in the middle PET scan. In that particular study, the control condition consisted of resting while staring at a fixed point.

The control scan is compared to brain scans taken while the participant is exposed to the experimental treatment or performing the experimental task. In the top row of PET scans, the first PET scan is the treatment task, which is labeled "Stimulation." More specifically, the treatment task in that study was looking at a flickering checkerboard pattern. The difference between the PET scans is calculated to determine the brain activity that can be attributed to the experimental condition (Gusnard & Raichle, 2001). In the chapters to come, you'll see several examples of experimental research that use brain-imaging techniques.

positron emission tomography (PET scan)
An invasive imaging technique that provides color-coded images of brain activity by tracking the brain's use of a radioactively tagged compound, such as glucose, oxygen, or a drug.

magnetic resonance imaging (MRI)
A noninvasive imaging technique that produces highly detailed images of the brain using electromagnetic signals generated by the brain in response to magnetic fields.

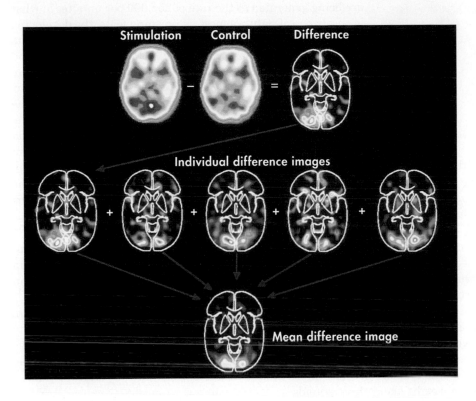

Stimulation   Control   Difference

Individual difference images

Mean difference image

Cognitive neuroscience research often follows the procedure shown on the left. In this particular study, the researchers used positron emission tomography to track changes in the participant's brain activity. In the *Control* condition, the participant's brain is scanned while looking at a fixed point on a blank screen. In the *Stimulation* (experimental) condition, the participant is scanned while engaged in the treatment task. In this study, the treatment task was looking at a flickering checkerboard pattern. After the control scan is "subtracted" from the experimental condition scan, the *Difference* image reveals the brain activity that is assumed to be uniquely attributable to the experimental task. In the next phase of the research (center row), difference images from the individual subjects are *combined and averaged*. This step helps minimize any idiosyncratic responses among the participants. It also provides a composite PET image identifying the brain regions selectively activated by the experimental task.

Potential Limitations of Brain-Imaging Studies

As technological advances occur, brain-imaging technology continues to improve, offering increasingly detailed pictures of the intact living brain. Nevertheless, brain-imaging research has some limitations (Racine & others, 2005). When you consider the results of brain-imaging studies, including those presented in this textbook, keep the following points in mind:

1. *Most brain-imaging studies involve small groups of subjects.* Because of the limited availability of sophisticated equipment and the high cost of brain-imaging technology, brain-scan research tends to involve small groups of subjects, often as few as a dozen or less. As is true with any research that involves a small number of participants, caution must be exercised in generalizing results to a wider population.

2. *Most brain-imaging studies involve simple aspects of behavior.* Human behavior is extraordinarily complex, and even seemingly simple tasks involve the smooth coordination of multiple brain regions (Rorden & Karnath, 2004). Reading this paragraph, for example, activates visual, language, memory, and auditory centers in your brain. As psychologist William Uttal (2001) observes, "The more complex the psychological process, the less likely it is that a narrowly circumscribed [brain] region uniquely associated with that process will be found."

3. *Knowing what brain area is involved may tell us little about the psychological process being investigated.* Knowing the brain location of a psychological process does not necessarily translate into an understanding of that process. For example, identifying a particular brain structure as being involved in fear does little to explain our psychological experience of fear (Miller & Keller, 2000). Snapshots of brain activity can only be interpreted within the context of psychological knowledge about the behavior being studied.

Looking at Brain-Scan Images

What should you notice when you look at a brain-scan image? First, read the text description carefully, so that you understand the task or condition that is being measured. Second, when a control-condition brain scan is shown, carefully compare the control scan with the treatment scan, noting how the two scans differ. Third, keep the limitations of brain-scan technology in mind, remembering that human experience is much too complex to be captured by a single snapshot of brain activity (Racine & others, 2005).

Although brain-imaging research has its limitations, the advent of sophisticated imaging technology has revolutionized our understanding of the human brain. But brain-imaging technology has also revealed just how much remains to be discovered about the most complex piece of matter known to exist in the universe—the human brain.

functional magnetic resonance imaging (fMRI)
A noninvasive imaging technique that uses magnetic fields to map brain activity by measuring changes in the brain's blood flow and oxygen levels.

cognitive neuroscience
The study of the neural basis of cognitive process that integrates contributions from psychology, neuroscience, and computer science.

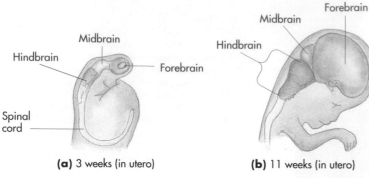

(a) 3 weeks (in utero)

(b) 11 weeks (in utero)

(c) At birth

FIGURE 2.13 The Sequence of Fetal Brain Development The human brain begins as a fluid-filled neural tube at about three weeks after conception. The hindbrain structures are the first to develop, followed by midbrain structures. The forebrain structures develop last, eventually coming to surround and envelop the hindbrain and midbrain structures.

neurogenesis
The development of new neurons.

During peak periods of brain development, new neurons are being generated at the rate of 250,000 per minute. In what is surely one of nature's most astonishing feats, the developing brain cells multiply, differentiate, and begin their migration to their final destination. Triggered by chemical signals and guided by the fibers of a special type of glial cells, the newly born neurons travel to specific locations (Nadarajah & Parnavelas, 2002). About halfway through the prenatal period, the production of new brain cells is virtually complete.

Eventually the new neurons reach their final destination and differentiate into specific types of neurons. They join with other developing neurons and begin forming the structures of the developing nervous system. But the process of neural development has only begun. The development of dendrites and synapses, as well as the extension of axons, begins before birth and continues throughout the lifespan (M.H. Johnson, 2001).

The fetal brain is constantly changing, forming as many as 2 million synaptic connections per second. Connections that are used are strengthened, while unused connections are pruned. By the end of fetal development, the forebrain structures eventually come to surround and envelop the hindbrain and midbrain structures (see Figure 2.13).

At birth, the infant's brain is only about one-fourth the size of an adult brain, weighing less than a pound. After birth, the neurons grow in size and continue to develop new dendrites. Myelin forms on axons in key areas of the brain, such as those involved in motor control. Axons also grow longer, and the branching at the ends of the axons becomes more dense. In adulthood, the fully mature human brain weighs about three pounds.

Neurogenesis

For many years, scientists believed that people and most animals did not experience **neurogenesis**—the development of new neurons—after birth. With the exception of birds, tree shrews, and some rodents, it was thought that the mature brain could lose neurons but could not grow new ones. But new studies offered compelling evidence that challenged that dogma (Gage, 2003; Gross, 2000).

First, research by psychologist Elizabeth Gould and her colleagues (1998) showed that adult marmoset monkeys were generating a significant number of new neurons every day in the *hippocampus,* a brain structure that plays a critical role in the ability to form new memories. Gould's groundbreaking research provided the first demonstration that new neurons could develop in an adult primate brain. Could it be that the human brain also has the capacity to generate new neurons in adulthood?

Researchers Peter Eriksson, Fred Gage, and their colleagues (1998) provided evidence that it does. The subjects were five adult cancer patients, whose ages ranged from the late fifties to the early seventies. These patients were all being given a drug used in cancer treatments to determine whether tumor cells are multiplying. The drug is incorporated into newly dividing cells and colors the cells. Using fluorescent lights, this chemical tracer can be detected in the newly created cells. The reasoning was that if new neurons were being generated, the drug would be present in their genetic material.

Within hours after each patient died, an autopsy was performed and the hippocampus was removed and examined. The results were unequivocal. In each patient, *hundreds* of new neurons had been generated since the drug had been administered, even though all the patients were over 50 years old (see accompanying photo). The conclusion? Contrary to the traditional scientific view, the hippocampus has the capacity to generate new neurons throughout the lifespan (Eriksson & others, 1998; Kempermann & Gage, 1999).

Neurogenesis in the Adult Human Brain Using laser microscopes to examine sections of the adult hippocampus, researchers Peter Eriksson and Fred Gage (1998) documented the presence of new neurons, shown in green, amid already established neurons, shown in red. In the area of the hippocampus studied, each cubic centimeter of brain tissue contained from 100 to 300 new neurons. New research on adult mice has shown that the newly generated neurons develop into fully functional neurons that form synaptic connections with existing cells in the hippocampus (van Praag & others, 2002).

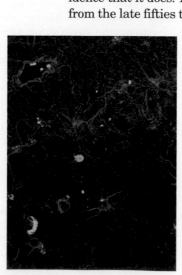

As new research on neurogenesis has exploded, new findings—and new questions—have arisen (Kempermann & others, 2004). For example, Gould and her colleagues (1999b, 2001) have found that new neurons develop and migrate to *multiple* brain regions in adult macaque monkeys. Stress, exercise, environmental complexity, and even social status have been shown to affect the rate of neurogenesis in rodents, birds, and monkeys (Gage, 2003; Kozorovitskiy & Gould, 2004; Mirescu & others, 2004). Whether these findings can be applied to the human brain remains unknown—and controversial (Rakic, 2002, 2004). Nevertheless, it is now generally accepted that neural stem cells in the human hippocampus develop into mature, functioning neurons (Gage, 2003). And, it appears that these new neurons are incorporated into the existing neural networks in the adult human brain.

In the next section, we'll continue our guided tour of the brain. Following the general sequence of the brain's development, we'll start with the structures at the base of the brain and work our way up to the higher brain regions, which are responsible for complex mental activity.

brainstem
A region of the brain made up of the hindbrain and the midbrain.

The Brainstem
Hindbrain and Midbrain Structures

Key Theme
- The brainstem includes the hindbrain and midbrain, located at the base of the brain.

Key Questions
- Why does damage to one side of the brain affect the opposite side of the body?
- What are the key structures of the hindbrain and midbrain, and what are their functions?

The major regions of the brain are illustrated in Figure 2.14, which can serve as a map to keep you oriented during our tour. At the base of the brain lie the hindbrain and, directly above it, the midbrain. Combined, the structures of the hindbrain and midbrain make up the brain region that is also called the **brainstem.**

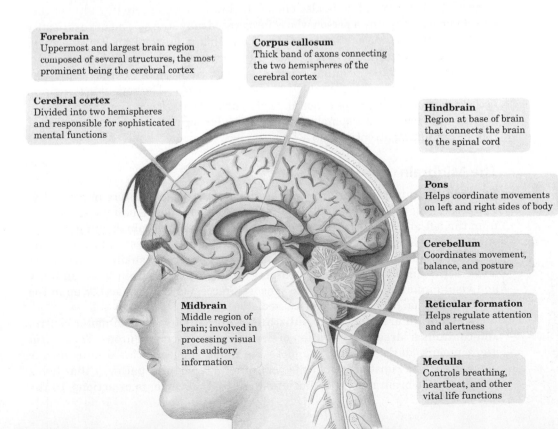

Forebrain
Uppermost and largest brain region composed of several structures, the most prominent being the cerebral cortex

Corpus callosum
Thick band of axons connecting the two hemispheres of the cerebral cortex

Cerebral cortex
Divided into two hemispheres and responsible for sophisticated mental functions

Hindbrain
Region at base of brain that connects the brain to the spinal cord

Pons
Helps coordinate movements on left and right sides of body

Cerebellum
Coordinates movement, balance, and posture

Reticular formation
Helps regulate attention and alertness

Midbrain
Middle region of brain; involved in processing visual and auditory information

Medulla
Controls breathing, heartbeat, and other vital life functions

FIGURE 2.14 Major Regions of the Brain This cross section of the human brain shows the primary structures that make up the hindbrain region (yellow labels), the midbrain region (blue label), and the forebrain region (pink labels). The hindbrain and midbrain regulate many of the most basic life functions, and the forebrain is involved in more sophisticated behaviors and higher mental processes.

hindbrain

A region at the base of the brain that contains several structures that regulate basic life functions.

medulla

(meh-DOOL-uh) A hindbrain structure that controls vital life functions such as breathing and circulation.

pons

A hindbrain structure that connects the medulla to the two sides of the cerebellum; helps coordinate and integrate movements on each side of the body.

cerebellum

(sare-uh-BELL-um) A large, two-sided hindbrain structure at the back of the brain; responsible for muscle coordination and maintaining posture and equilibrium.

reticular formation

(reh-TICK-you-ler) A network of nerve fibers located in the center of the medulla that helps regulate attention, arousal, and sleep; also called the *reticular activating system.*

midbrain

The middle and smallest brain region, involved in processing auditory and visual sensory information.

substantia nigra

(sub-STAN-she-uh NYE-gruh) An area of the midbrain that is involved in motor control and contains a large concentration of dopamine-producing neurons.

forebrain

The largest and most complex brain region, which contains centers for complex behaviors and mental processes; also called the *cerebrum.*

cerebral cortex

(suh-REE-brull or SARE-uh-brull) The wrinkled outer portion of the forebrain, which contains the most sophisticated brain centers.

cerebral hemispheres

The nearly symmetrical left and right halves of the cerebral cortex.

corpus callosum

A thick band of axons that connects the two cerebral hemispheres and acts as a communication link between them.

The Hindbrain

The **hindbrain** connects the spinal cord with the rest of the brain. Sensory and motor pathways pass through the hindbrain to and from regions that are situated higher up in the brain. Sensory information coming in from one side of the body crosses over at the hindbrain level, projecting to the opposite side of the brain. And outgoing motor messages from one side of the brain also cross over at the hindbrain level, controlling movement and other motor functions on the opposite side of the body. This is referred to as *contralateral organization.*

Contralateral organization accounts for why people who suffer strokes on one side of their brain experience muscle weakness or paralysis on the opposite side of their body. Our friend Asha, for example, suffered only minor damage to motor control areas in her brain. However, because the stroke occurred on the *left* side of her brain, what muscle weakness she did experience was localized on the *right* side of her body, primarily in her right hand.

Three structures make up the hindbrain—the medulla, the pons, and the cerebellum. The **medulla** lies directly above the spinal cord and contains centers active in the control of such vital autonomic functions as breathing, heart rate, and digestion. Because the medulla is involved in such critical life functions, damage to it can result in death. The medulla also controls a number of vital reflexes, such as swallowing, coughing, vomiting, and sneezing.

Above the medulla is a swelling of tissue called the **pons,** which represents the uppermost level of the hindbrain. Bulging out behind the pons is the large **cerebellum.** On each side of the pons, a large bundle of axons connects it to the cerebellum. The word *pons* means "bridge," and the pons is a bridge of sorts: Information from various other brain regions located higher up in the brain is relayed to the cerebellum via the pons.

The cerebellum functions in the control of balance, muscle tone, and coordinated muscle movements. It is also involved in the learning of habitual or automatic movements and motor skills, such as typing, writing, or gracefully backhanding a tennis ball.

Jerky, uncoordinated movements can result from damage to the cerebellum. Simple movements, such as walking or standing upright, may become difficult or impossible. The cerebellum is also one of the brain areas affected by alcohol consumption, which is why a person who is intoxicated may stagger and have difficulty walking a straight line or standing on one foot. (This is also why a police officer will ask a suspected drunk driver to execute these normally effortless movements.)

At the core of the medulla and the pons is a network of neurons called the **reticular formation,** or the *reticular activating system.* The reticular formation is composed of many groups of specialized neurons that project up to higher brain regions and down to the spinal cord. The reticular formation plays an important role in regulating attention and sleep.

The Midbrain

The **midbrain** is an important relay station that contains centers important to the processing of auditory and visual sensory information. Auditory sensations from the left and right ears are processed through the midbrain, helping you orient toward the direction of a sound. The midbrain is also involved in processing visual information, including eye movements, helping you visually locate objects and track their movements. After passing through the midbrain level, auditory and visual information is relayed to sensory processing centers farther up in the forebrain region, which will be discussed shortly.

A midbrain area called the **substantia nigra** is involved in motor control and contains a large concentration of dopamine-producing neurons. *Substantia nigra* means "dark substance," and as the name suggests, this area is darkly pigmented. The substantia nigra is part of a larger neural pathway that helps prepare other brain regions to initiate organized movements or actions. In the section on neurotransmitters, we noted that Parkinson's disease involves symptoms of abnormal movement, including difficulty initiating or starting a particular movement. Many of those movement-related symptoms are associated with the degeneration of dopamine-producing neurons in the substantia nigra.

The Forebrain

Key Theme
■ The forebrain includes the cerebral cortex and the limbic system structures.

Key Questions
■ What are the four lobes of the cerebral cortex and their functions?

■ What is the limbic system?

■ What functions are associated with the thalamus, hypothalamus, hippocampus, and amygdala?

Situated above the midbrain is the largest region of the brain: the **forebrain.** In humans, the forebrain, also called the *cerebrum*, represents about 90 percent of the brain. In Figure 2.15, you can see how the size of the forebrain has increased during evolution, although the general structure of the human brain is similar to that of other species (Clark & others, 2001). Many important structures are found in the forebrain region, but we'll begin by describing the most prominent—the cerebral cortex.

FIGURE 2.15 Evolution and the Cerebral Cortex The brains of these different animal species have many structures in common, including a cerebellum and cortex. However, the proportion devoted to the cortex is much higher in mammals than in species that evolved earlier, such as fish and amphibians. The relative size of the different structures reflects their functional importance (Kaas & Collins, 2001). The cross section of the human brain shows how the cerebral cortex has developed around and above more primitive brain structures.

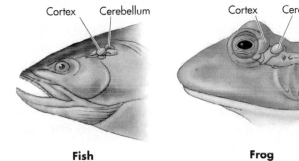

Fish

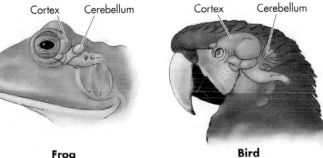

Frog

Bird

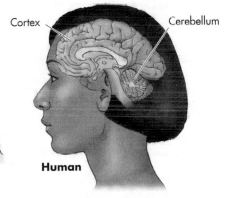

Human

The Cerebral Cortex

The outer portion of the forebrain, the **cerebral cortex,** is divided into two **cerebral hemispheres.** The word *cortex* means "bark," and much like the bark of a tree, the cerebral cortex is the outer covering of the forebrain. A thick bundle of axons, called the **corpus callosum,** connects the two cerebral hemispheres, as shown in Figure 2.16. The corpus callosum serves as the primary communication link between the left and right cerebral hemispheres.

The cerebral cortex is only about a quarter of an inch thick. It is mainly composed of glial cells and neuron cell bodies and axons, giving it a grayish appearance—which is why the cerebral cortex is sometimes described as being composed of *gray matter.* Extending inward from the cerebral cortex are white myelinated axons that are sometimes referred to as *white matter.* These myelinated axons connect the cerebral cortex to other brain regions.

Numerous folds, grooves, and bulges characterize the human cerebral cortex. The purpose of these ridges and valleys is easy to illustrate. Imagine a flat, three-foot by three-foot piece of paper. You can compact the surface area of this piece of paper by scrunching it up into a wad. In much the same way, the grooves and bulges of the cerebral cortex allow about three square feet of surface area to be packed into the small space of the human skull.

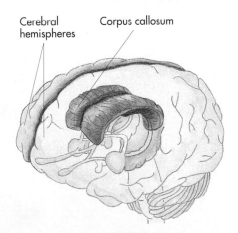

FIGURE 2.16 The Cerebral Hemispheres and the Corpus Callosum This transparent view of the brain shows the corpus callosum, the C-shaped bundle of axons that links the left and right hemispheres of the cerebral cortex.

temporal lobe
An area on each hemisphere of the cerebral cortex near the temples that is the primary receiving area for auditory information.

occipital lobe
(ock-SIP-it-ull) An area at the back of each cerebral hemisphere that is the primary receiving area for visual information.

parietal lobe
(puh-RYE-et-ull) An area on each hemisphere of the cerebral cortex located above the temporal lobe that processes somatic sensations.

frontal lobe
The largest lobe of each cerebral hemisphere; processes voluntary muscle movements and is involved in thinking, planning, and emotional control.

Look again at Figure 2.15 on page 65. The drawing of the human brain is cut through the center to show how the cerebral cortex has folded above and around the rest of the brain. In contrast to the numerous folds and wrinkles of the human cerebral cortex, notice the smooth appearance of the cortex in fish, amphibians, and birds. Mammals with large brains—such as cats, dogs, and nonhuman primates—also have wrinkles and folds in the cerebral cortex, but to a lesser extent than humans (Jarvis & others, 2005).

Each cerebral hemisphere can be roughly divided into four regions, or *lobes:* the *temporal, occipital, parietal,* and *frontal* lobes (see Figure 2.17). Each lobe is associated with distinct functions. Located near your temples, the **temporal lobe** contains the *primary auditory cortex,* which receives auditory information. At the very back of the brain is the **occipital lobe.** The occipital lobe includes the *primary visual cortex,* where visual information is received.

The **parietal lobe** is involved in processing bodily, or *somatosensory,* information, including touch, temperature, pressure, and information from receptors in the muscles and joints. A band of tissue on the parietal lobe, called the *somatosensory cortex,* receives information from touch receptors in different parts of the body.

Each part of the body is represented on the somatosensory cortex, but this representation is not equally distributed. Instead, body parts are represented in proportion to their sensitivity to somatic sensations. For example, your hands and face, which are very responsive to touch, have much greater representation on the somatosensory cortex than do the backs of your legs, which are far less sensitive to touch. If body areas were actually proportional to the amount of representation on the somatosensory cortex, humans would resemble the misshapen character on the right side of Figure 2.18.

The largest lobe of the cerebral cortex, the **frontal lobe,** is involved in planning, initiating, and executing voluntary movements. The movements of different body parts are represented in a band of tissue on the frontal lobe called the *primary motor cortex.* The degree of representation on the primary motor cortex for a particular body part reflects the diversity and precision of its potential movements, as shown on the left side of Figure 2.18. Thus, it's not surprising that almost one-third of the primary motor cortex is devoted to the hands and another third is devoted to facial muscles. The disproportionate representation of these two body areas on the primary motor cortex is reflected in the human capacity to produce an extremely wide range of hand movements and facial expressions.

FIGURE 2.17 Lobes of the Cerebral Cortex Each hemisphere of the cerebral cortex can be divided into four regions, or *lobes.* Each lobe is associated with distinct functions. The association areas, shaded in purple, make up most of the cerebral cortex.

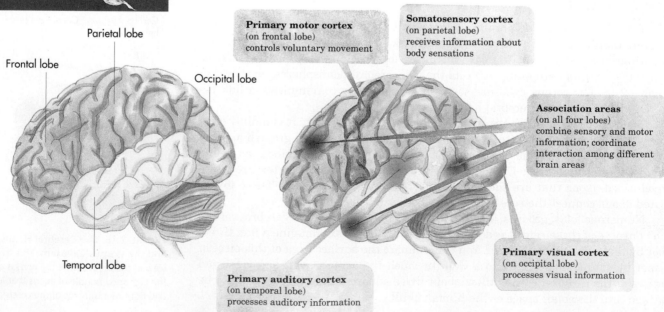

Frontal lobe

Parietal lobe

Occipital lobe

Temporal lobe

Primary motor cortex
(on frontal lobe)
controls voluntary movement

Somatosensory cortex
(on parietal lobe)
receives information about body sensations

Association areas
(on all four lobes)
combine sensory and motor information; coordinate interaction among different brain areas

Primary visual cortex
(on occipital lobe)
processes visual information

Primary auditory cortex
(on temporal lobe)
processes auditory information

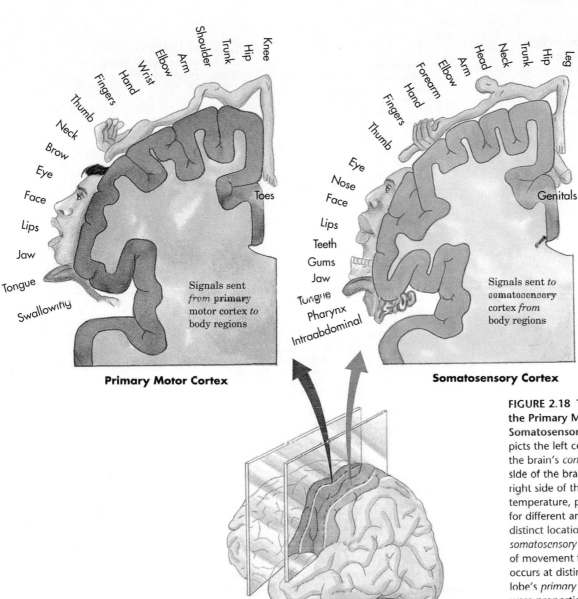

Primary Motor Cortex

Thumb
Fingers
Hand
Wrist
Elbow
Arm
Shoulder
Trunk
Hip
Knee
Neck
Brow
Eye
Face
Lips
Jaw
Tongue
Swallowing
Toes

Signals sent *from* primary motor cortex *to* body regions

Somatosensory Cortex

Fingers
Hand
Forearm
Elbow
Arm
Head
Neck
Trunk
Hip
Leg
Thumb
Eye
Nose
Face
Lips
Teeth
Gums
Jaw
Tongue
Pharynx
Intraabdominal
Genitals

Signals sent *to* somatosensory cortex *from* body regions

FIGURE 2.18 The Body's Representation on the Primary Motor Cortex and on the Somatosensory Cortex This illustration depicts the left cerebral hemisphere. Because of the brain's *contralateral organization,* the left side of the brain processes functions for the right side of the body, and vice versa. Touch, temperature, pressure, and pain sensations for different areas of the body occur at distinct locations on the parietal lobe's *somatosensory cortex.* Similarly, the initiation of movement for different parts of the body occurs at distinct locations on the frontal lobe's *primary motor cortex.* If body parts were proportional to their representation on the somatosensory cortex and primary motor cortex, they would look like the misshapen human figures on the outer edges of the drawings.

The primary sensory and motor areas found on the different lobes represent just a small portion of the cerebral cortex. The remaining bulk of the cerebral cortex consists mostly of three large *association areas.* These areas are generally thought to be involved in processing and integrating sensory and motor information. For example, the *prefrontal association cortex,* situated in front of the primary motor cortex, is involved in the planning of voluntary movements. Another association area includes parts of the temporal, parietal, and occipital lobes. This association area is involved in the formation of perceptions and in the integration of perceptions and memories.

The Limbic System

Beneath the cerebral cortex are several other important forebrain structures, which are components of the **limbic system.** The word *limbic* means "border," and as you can see in Figure 2.19 on page 68, the structures that make up the limbic system form a border of sorts around the brainstem. In various combinations, the limbic system structures form complex neural circuits that play critical roles in learning, memory, and emotional control (Squire & Knowlton, 1995).

limbic system
A group of forebrain structures that form a border around the brainstem and are involved in emotion, motivation, learning, and memory.

FIGURE 2.19 Key Structures of the Fore-brain and Limbic System In the cross-sectional view shown here, you can see the locations and functions of four important sub-cortical brain structures. In combination, these structures make up the *limbic system*, which regulates emotional control, learning, and memory.

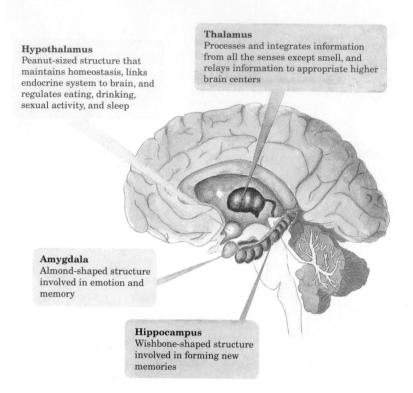

Hypothalamus
Peanut-sized structure that maintains homeostasis, links endocrine system to brain, and regulates eating, drinking, sexual activity, and sleep

Thalamus
Processes and integrates information from all the senses except smell, and relays information to appropriate higher brain centers

Amygdala
Almond-shaped structure involved in emotion and memory

Hippocampus
Wishbone-shaped structure involved in forming new memories

hippocampus
A curved forebrain structure that is part of the limbic system and is involved in learning and forming new memories.

thalamus
(THAL-uh-muss) A forebrain structure that processes sensory information for all senses, except smell, and relays it to the cerebral cortex.

hypothalamus
(hi-poe-THAL-uh-muss) A peanut-sized forebrain structure that is part of the limbic system and regulates behaviors related to survival, such as eating, drinking, and sexual activity.

Let's briefly consider some of the key limbic system structures and the roles they play in behavior.

The Hippocampus The **hippocampus** is a large structure embedded in the temporal lobe in each cerebral hemisphere (see Figure 2.19). The word *hippocampus* comes from a Latin word meaning "sea horse." If you have a vivid imagination, the hippocampus does look a bit like the curved tail of a sea horse. The hippocampus plays an important role in the ability to form new memories of events and information. As noted earlier, neurogenesis takes place in the adult hippocampus. The possible role of new neurons in memory formation is an active area of neuroscience research (Gross, 2000; Shors & others, 2001). In Chapter 6, we'll take a closer look at the role of the hippocampus and other brain structures in memory.

FIGURE 2.20 The Thalamus Almost all sensory and motor information going to and from the cerebral cortex is processed through the thalamus. This figure depicts some of the neural pathways from different regions of the thalamus to specific lobes of the cerebral cortex.

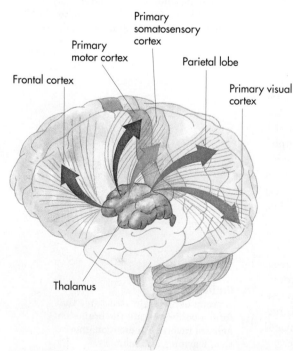

Primary somatosensory cortex

Primary motor cortex

Parietal lobe

Frontal cortex

Primary visual cortex

Thalamus

The Thalamus The word *thalamus* comes from a Greek word meaning "inner chamber." And indeed, the **thalamus** is a rounded mass of cell bodies located within each cerebral hemisphere. The thalamus processes and distributes motor information and sensory information (except for smell) going to and from the cerebral cortex. Figure 2.20 depicts some of the neural pathways going from the thalamus to the different lobes of the cerebral cortex. However, the thalamus is more than just a sensory relay station. The thalamus is also thought to be involved in regulating levels of awareness, attention, motivation, and emotional aspects of sensations.

The Hypothalamus *Hypo* means "beneath" or "below." As its name implies, the **hypothalamus** is located below the thalamus. Although it is only about the size of a peanut, the hypothalamus contains more than 40 neural pathways. These neural pathways ascend to other forebrain areas and descend to the midbrain, hindbrain, and spinal cord. The hypothalamus is involved in so many different functions, it is sometimes referred to as "the brain within the brain."

The hypothalamus regulates both divisions of the autonomic nervous system, increasing and decreasing such functions as heart rate and blood pressure. It also helps regulate a variety of behaviors related to survival, such as eating, drinking, frequency of sexual activity, fear, and aggression.

One area of the hypothalamus, called the *suprachiasmatic nucleus* (SCN), plays a key role in regulating daily sleep–wake cycles and other rhythms of the body. We'll take a closer look at the SCN in Chapter 4.

The hypothalamus exerts considerable control over the secretion of endocrine hormones by directly influencing the pituitary gland. The *pituitary gland* is situated just below the hypothalamus and is attached to it by a short stalk. The hypothalamus produces both neurotransmitters and hormones that directly affect the pituitary gland. As we noted in the section on the endocrine system, the pituitary gland releases hormones that influence the activity of other glands.

The Amygdala   The **amygdala** is an almond-shaped clump of neuron cell bodies at the base of the temporal lobe. The amygdala is involved in a variety of emotional response patterns, including fear, anger, and disgust. Studies with animals have shown that electrical stimulation of the amygdala can produce these emotions. In contrast, destruction of the amygdala reduces or disrupts behaviors that are linked to fear and rage. For example, when their amygdala is destroyed, monkeys lose their fear of natural predators, such as snakes. In humans, electrical stimulation of the amygdala produces feelings of fear and apprehension. The amygdala is also involved in learning and forming memories, especially those with a strong emotional component (LeDoux, 2000; McGaugh, 2004). In Chapter 8, we'll take a closer look at the amygdala's role in emotion.

amygdala
(uh-MIG-dull-uh) An almond-shaped forebrain structure that is part of the limbic system and is involved in emotion and memory.

Specialization in the Cerebral Hemispheres

Key Theme
- The two hemispheres of the cerebral cortex are specialized for different tasks, although they have many functions in common.

Key Questions
- How did Broca, Wernicke, and Sperry contribute to our knowledge of the brain?
- What is the corpus callosum, and what happens when it is cut?
- How do the functions of the right and left cerebral hemispheres differ?

If you were to hold a human brain in your hand, the two cerebral hemispheres would appear to be symmetrical. Although the left and right hemispheres are very similar in appearance, they are not identical. Anatomically, one hemisphere may be slightly larger than the other. There are also subtle differences in the sizes of particular structures, in the distribution of gray matter and white matter, and in the patterns of folds, bulges, and grooves that make up the surface of the cerebral cortex.

What about differences in the functions of the two hemispheres? In many cases, the functioning of the left and right hemispheres is symmetrical, meaning that the same functions are located in roughly the same places on each hemisphere. Examples of such functional symmetry include the primary motor cortex and the somatosensory cortex, which we discussed in the previous section. With regard to other important processes, however, the left and right cerebral hemispheres do differ—each cerebral hemisphere is specialized for particular abilities.

Here's a rough analogy. Imagine two computers that are linked through a network. One computer is optimized for handling word processing, the other for handling graphic design. Although specialized for different functions, the two computers actively share information and can communicate with each other across the network. In this analogy, the two computers correspond to the left and right cerebral hemispheres, and the network that links them is the corpus callosum.

The Corpus Callosum Brain tissue from the top of the brain has been cut away to expose the thick fibers of the corpus callosum, the structure that connects the left and right hemispheres of the brain. As you'll read in this section, cutting the corpus callosum eliminates the transfer of information between the two hemispheres, with some surprising consequences.

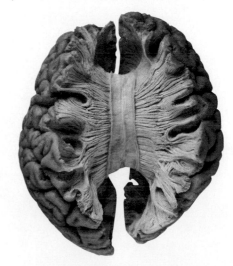

SCIENCE VERSUS PSEUDOSCIENCE 2.2

Brain Myths

Is it true that we only use 10 percent of our brain?

Think about the information presented in this chapter. Brain-imaging techniques clearly show, multiple brain areas are activated in response to even simple tasks, such as speaking or listening to music. Further, if we used only 10 percent of our brain, then people who have a stroke would probably not experience any obvious consequences. Of course, that's not what happens. There is *no* area of the brain that can be damaged without some kind of consequences. How well do you think you would function if a brain injury destroyed a "mere" 25 percent of your brain?

So where did the 10 percent myth come from?

The myth has been around since at least the early 1900s (Beyerstein, 1999). Some of those who perpetuate the 10 percent myth probably mean well, like teachers, coaches, and motivational speakers. Their basic message is that each of us should strive to reach our full potential. Others, however, are pseudoscientists or other charlatans hawking a product that they promise will enhance your creativity, psychic powers, intelligence, memory, or other hidden potential. But you will *never* hear a neuroscientist make the 10 percent claim.

Is the right brain responsible for creativity and intuition? Can you train your right brain?

There is no evidence that the right hemisphere is any more "intuitive" or "creative" than the left hemisphere (Corballis, 1999). Nor is there evidence that a teacher, however skilled, could somehow "educate" one side of your brain in isolation from the other. While it is true that each hemisphere is specialized for different abilities, you rely on the smooth, integrated functioning of *both* hemispheres to accomplish most tasks. This is especially true for such cognitively demanding tasks as artistic creativity, musical performance, or finding innovative solutions to complex problems.

As you'll see in this section, the first discoveries about the differing abilities of the two brain hemispheres were made more than a hundred years ago by two important pioneers in brain research, Pierre Broca and Karl Wernicke.

Language and the Left Hemisphere
The Early Work of Broca and Wernicke

FIGURE 2.21 Broca's and Wernicke's Areas of the Cerebral Cortex Broca's area, located in the lower frontal lobe, is involved in the production of speech. Wernicke's area, found in the temporal lobe, is important in the comprehension of written or spoken language. Damage to either of these areas will produce different types of speech disturbances, or aphasia. In most people, both areas are found on the left hemisphere.

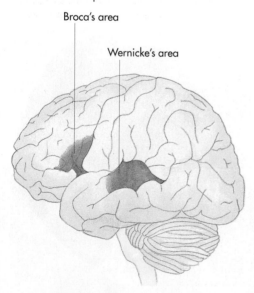

Broca's area

Wernicke's area

By the end of the 1700s it had already been well established that injury to one side of the brain could produce muscle paralysis or loss of sensation on the opposite side of the body. By the early 1800s, animal experiments had shown that specific functions would be lost if particular brain areas were destroyed. And, as discussed in Box 2.1 on phrenology (p. 58), scientists were beginning to debate the notion of **cortical localization,** or *localization of function*—the idea that particular areas of the human brain are associated with particular functions.

In the 1860s, more conclusive evidence for cortical localization was gathered by a French surgeon and neuroanatomist named **Pierre Paul Broca.** Broca treated a series of patients who had great difficulty speaking but could comprehend written or spoken language. Subsequent autopsies of these patients revealed a consistent finding—brain damage to an area on the *lower left frontal lobe.* Today, this area on the left hemisphere is referred to as *Broca's area,* and it is known to play a crucial role in speech production (see Figure 2.21).

About a decade after Broca's discovery, a young German neurologist named **Karl Wernicke** discovered another area in the left hemisphere that, when damaged, produced a different type of language disturbance. Unlike Broca's patients, Wernicke's patients had great difficulty understanding spoken or written communications. They could speak quickly and easily, but their speech sometimes made no sense. They sometimes used meaningless words or even nonsense syllables, though their sentences seemed to be grammatical. In response to the question "How are you feeling?" a patient might say something like, "Don't glow glover. Yes, uh, ummm, bick, bo chipickers the dallydoe mick more work mittle." Autopsies of these patients' brains revealed consistent damage to an area on the *left temporal lobe* that today is called *Wernicke's area* (see Figure 2.21).

The discoveries of Broca and Wernicke provided the first compelling clinical evidence that language and speech functions are performed primarily by the left cerebral hemisphere. If similar brain damage occurs in the exact same locations on the *right* hemisphere, these severe disruptions in language and speech are usually *not* seen.

The notion that one hemisphere exerts more control over or is more involved in the processing of a particular psychological function is termed **lateralization of function.** Speech and language functions are *lateralized* on the left hemisphere. Generally, the left hemisphere exerts greater control over speech and language abilities in virtually all right-handed and the majority of left-handed people. What about the left-handed people who don't fit this pattern? For more insights on hand preference and brain organization, see In Focus Box 2.3 on page 72.

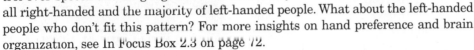

The language disruptions demonstrated by Broca's and Wernicke's patients represent different types of aphasia. **Aphasia** refers to the partial or complete inability to articulate ideas or understand spoken or written language because of brain injury or damage. There are many different types of aphasia.

People with *Broca's aphasia* find it difficult or impossible to produce speech, which is why it is often referred to as *expressive aphasia*. Despite their impairments in speaking, their comprehension of verbal or written words is relatively unaffected.

People with *Wernicke's aphasia* have great difficulty comprehending written or spoken communication, which is why it is often referred to as *receptive aphasia*. Although they can speak, they often have trouble finding the correct words.

At the beginning of this chapter, we described the symptoms experienced by our friend Asha in the weeks before and the months following her stroke. Asha, who is right-handed, experienced the stroke in her left hemisphere. About three days after her stroke, an MRI brain scan showed where the damage had occurred: the left temporal lobe.

Asha experienced many symptoms of Wernicke's aphasia. Talking was difficult, not because Asha couldn't speak, but because she had to stop frequently to search for the right words. Asha was unable to name even simple objects, like the cup on her hospital dinner tray or her doctor's necktie. She recognized the objects but was unable to say what they were. She had great difficulty following a normal conversation and understanding speech, both in English and in her native language, Tulu.

Asha also discovered that she had lost the ability to read. She could see the words on the page, but they seemed to have no meaning. Paul brought some of their Christmas cards to the hospital. Asha recalls, "When I realized I couldn't read the Christmas cards, I thought my life was over. I just lost it. I remember crying and telling the nurse, 'I have a doctorate and I can't read, write, or talk!'"

When we visited Asha in the hospital, we brought her a Christmas present: a portable cassette tape player with headphones and some tapes of relaxing instrumental music. Little did we realize how helpful the music would be for her. One tape was a recording of Native American flute music called *Sky of Dreams*. The music was beautiful and rather unusual, with intricate melodies and unexpected, complex harmonies. Although it was very difficult for Asha to follow normal speech, listening to *Sky of Dreams* was an entirely different experience. As Asha explained:

> I tried cranking up the music very high and it soothed me. I could sleep. At the time, the flute music seemed to be just perfectly timed with the way my brain was working. It was tuning out all the other noises so I could focus on just one thing and sleep. So I would play the music over and over again at a very high level. I did that for a long time because my mind was so active and jumbled that I couldn't think.

Paul Broca (1824–1880): Evidence for the Localization of Speech Paul Broca was already a famous scientist and surgeon when he announced in 1861 that he had discovered solid evidence for the localization of language functions in the human brain. His patient was an unpleasant middle-aged man universally known as Tan because that was the only word he could speak - aside from a single swear word when angered. Of normal intelligence, Tan could comprehend the speech of others but could not produce language himself. After Tan's death, an autopsy revealed a distinct lesion on the lower left frontal lobe. This area is still known as *Broca's area*.

Carl Wernicke (1040-1905): Evidence for the Localization of Language Comprehension Born in Poland but educated in Germany, psychiatrist and neurologist Carl Wernicke was only 26 when he published his findings on a type of aphasia that differed from that identified by Paul Broca. Wernicke's patients were unable to comprehend written or spoken language, although they could produce speech. Well-known for his research in clinical neurology, Wernicke published many articles and books, including a comprehensive textbook on psychiatry.

cortical localization
The notion that different functions are located or localized in different areas of the brain; also called *localization of function*.

lateralization of function
The notion that specific psychological or cognitive functions are processed primarily on one side of the brain.

aphasia
(uh-FAZE-yuh) The partial or complete inability to articulate ideas or understand spoken or written language because of brain injury or damage.

IN FOCUS 2.3

The Puzzle of the Left-Hander

Anatomically, our left and right hands are mirror images. Nevertheless, the vast majority of people use their right hand exclusively for tasks requiring dexterity. Only about 8 percent of the population are left-handed. Remarkably, this percentage has been consistent for more than 50 centuries. Even Stone Age cave drawings and tools indicate that our prehistoric ancestors were predominantly right-handed (Coren, 1992).

Almost all right-handed people display left-hemisphere dominance for speech and language functions (McManus, 2004). However, neurosurgeons have discovered a surprising pattern of differences in brain organization among left-handers.

Before brain surgery, each hemisphere can be separately anesthetized, allowing the hemisphere that controls speech functions to be identified. Using this technique, Theodore Rasmussen and Brenda Milner (1977) found that about 70 percent of left-handers show the same pattern as right-handers, with the left hemisphere dominant for language. About 15 percent of left-handed individuals show the opposite pattern, with language functions localized in the right hemisphere. The remaining 15 percent of left-handed individuals process language in both hemispheres. Other researchers, using fMRI, have found similar results (Knecht & others, 2000; Pujol & others, 1999).

The variability in brain organization among left-handed people may also account for the differences in degree of hand preference (Toga & Thompson, 2003). Right-handed people consistently perform virtually all tasks requiring dexterity with their right hands. But many left-handers show a pattern of mixed-handedness, preferring to use their right hand for some tasks. Your author Don, for example, writes

and holds a fork with his left hand. But he uses his right hand to swing a hammer, move the computer mouse, throw a ball, and play tennis.

Do the brains of right-handed and left-handed individuals differ in some fundamental way? Researchers have focused on differences in the size of the corpus callosum, the thick bundle of neuronal fibers connecting the two hemispheres. However, studies have been mixed. Some studies found that the corpus callosum is up to 11 percent larger in left-handed and ambidextrous individuals than in right-handed individuals (e.g., Habib & others, 1991; Moffat & others, 1998). Other studies find no differences in corpus callosum size based on handedness (e.g., Luders & others, 2003; Preuss & others, 2002).

What causes hand preference? Many theories have been proposed, but no one theory has succeeded in mustering unequivocal evidence. Some evidence suggests that genetics may be involved in determining handedness (Van Agtmael & others, 2001). If both parents are right-handed, the odds of their having a left-handed child are about 1 in 10. If one parent is left-handed and the other right-handed, the odds of their having a left-handed child are about 1 in 5. If both parents are left-handed, the odds of their having a left-handed child are approximately 1 in 4 (McManus & Bryden, 1992). And the incidence of left-handedness is higher among identical and fraternal twins than among singletons (Coren, 1994; Davis & Annett, 1994).

Adding some support to the idea of genetic determination, hand preference has been demonstrated before birth. Psychologist Peter G. Hepper and his colleagues (1990) used ultrasound to observe more than 200 developing fetuses. Approximately 95 percent preferred sucking

Left-Handed Orangutans Like humans, nonhuman primates show distinct hand preferences, but those preferences appear to vary by species, population, and task (Hopkins & Cantalupo, 2005). In one study, chimpanzees who were given a six-inch tube with peanut butter smeared in the middle used their *right* index finger to extract the peanut butter. Given the same task, gorillas were about equally right- and left-handed. But orangutans, like the one shown above, tend to be lefties, strongly favoring their left index finger (Hopkins & others, 2003, 2004). And, while studies have shown that captive chimpanzees tend to use their right hands to gesture and manipulate tools, wild chimpanzees are more likely to be left-handed (Hopkins & others, 2005; Lonsdorf & Hopkins, 2005).

their right thumb, and 5 percent preferred their left thumb. These figures correspond very closely to the number of left- and right-handed people in the population.

Despite considerable research, the bottom line is that psychologists still don't know what causes left-handedness. Nonetheless, these discoveries about the differences in handedness and cerebral organization underscore the human brain's tremendous flexibility and adaptability.

Asha's language functions were severely disrupted, yet she was able to listen to and appreciate instrumental music—even very complex music. Why? At the end of the next section, we'll offer a possible explanation for what seems to have been a disparity in Asha's cognitive abilities following her stroke.

Cutting the Corpus Callosum

The Split Brain

Since the discoveries by Broca and Wernicke, the most dramatic evidence illustrating the independent functions of the two cerebral hemispheres has come from a surgical procedure called the **split-brain operation.** This operation is used to stop or reduce recurring seizures in severe cases of epilepsy that can't be treated in any other fashion. The procedure involves surgically cutting the corpus callosum, the thick band of axons that connects the two hemispheres.

What was the logic behind cutting the corpus callosum? An epileptic seizure typically occurs when neurons begin firing in a disorganized fashion in one region of the brain. The disorganized neuronal firing quickly spreads from one hemisphere to the other via the corpus callosum. If the corpus callosum is cut, seizures should be contained in just one hemisphere, reducing their severity or eliminating them altogether. This is exactly what happened when the split-brain operation was first tried in this country in the 1940s (Springer & Deutsch, 1998).

Surprisingly, cutting the corpus callosum initially seemed to produce no noticeable effect on the patients, other than reducing their epileptic seizures. Their ability to engage in routine conversations and tasks seemed to be unaffected. On the basis of these early observations, some brain researchers speculated that the corpus callosum served no function whatsoever (see Gazzaniga, 1995). One famous psychologist, Karl Lashley, joked that its primary function seemed to be to keep the two hemispheres from sagging (Hoptman & Davidson, 1994).

In the 1960s, however, psychologist and neuroscientist **Roger Sperry** and his colleagues began unraveling the puzzle of the left and right hemispheres. Sperry and his colleagues used the apparatus shown in Figure 2.22 to test the abilities of split-brain patients. They would direct a split-brain subject to focus on a point in the middle of a screen, while briefly flashing a word or picture to the left or right of the midpoint.

Roger Sperry (1913–1994) For his pioneering research using split-brain patients to investigate the relationship between brain and behavior, Sperry received the 1981 Nobel Prize in Physiology or Medicine.

split-brain operation
A surgical procedure that involves cutting the corpus callosum.

FIGURE 2.22 The Experimental Setup in Split-Brain Research In a typical split-brain experiment, as shown here, the participant focuses his attention on the midpoint of the screen. Notice that he is unable to verbally identify the picture that is flashed to the nonverbal right hemisphere, but he is able to grasp the hammer with his left hand. In contrast, when the image of the apple is flashed to his verbal left hemisphere, he can easily name it.

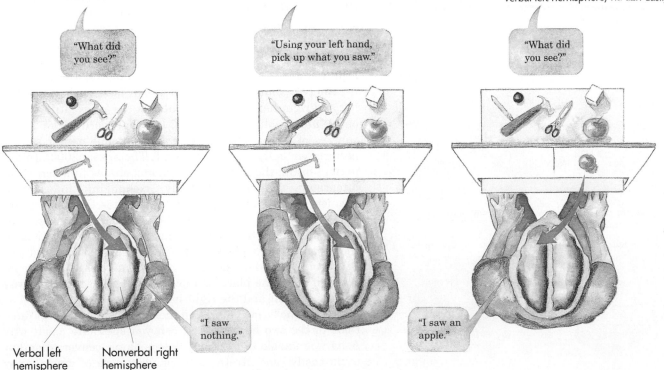

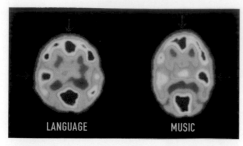

LANGUAGE   MUSIC

Specialization in the Left and Right Hemispheres The red arrow at the top of each PET scan points to the front of the brain. The red and yellow colors indicate the areas of greatest brain activity. Listening to speech involves a greater degree of activation of the language areas of the left hemisphere. Listening to music involves more activation in right-hemisphere areas. Notice, however, that there is some degree of activity in both hemispheres during these tasks.

FIGURE 2.23 Specialized Abilities of the Two Hemispheres Most people are left-hemisphere dominant for speech and language tasks, and right-hemisphere dominant for visual-spatial tasks. Although the hemispheres display some specialized abilities, many functions are symmetrical and performed the same way on both hemispheres.

Left-Hemisphere Dominance	GENERAL FUNCTION	Right-Hemisphere Dominance
Words Letters	VISION	Geometric patterns Faces Emotional expression
Language sounds	HEARING	Nonlanguage sounds Music
Verbal memory	MEMORY	Nonverbal memory
Speech Grammar rules Reading Writing Arithmetic	LANGUAGE	Emotional tone of speech
	SPATIAL ABILITY	Geometry Sense of direction Distance Mental rotation of shapes

In this procedure, visual information to the right of the midpoint is projected to the person's *left* hemisphere, and visual information to the left of the midpoint is projected to the *right* hemisphere. Behind the screen several objects were hidden from the split-brain subject. The subject could reach under a partition below the screen to pick up the concealed objects but could not see them (Sperry, 1982).

In a typical experiment, Sperry projected the image of an object concealed behind the screen, such as a hammer, to the left of the midpoint. Thus, the image of the hammer was sent to the right, nonverbal hemisphere. If a split-brain subject was asked to *verbally* identify the image flashed on the screen, he could not do so and often denied that anything had appeared on the screen. Why? Because his verbal left hemisphere had no way of knowing the information that had been sent to his right hemisphere. However, if a split-brain subject was asked to use his left hand to reach under the partition for the object that had been displayed, he would correctly pick up the hammer. This was because his left hand was controlled by the same right hemisphere that saw the image of the hammer.

Sperry's experiments reconfirmed the specialized language abilities of the left hemisphere that Broca and Wernicke had discovered more than a hundred years earlier. But notice, even though the split-brain subject's right hemisphere could not express itself verbally, it still processed information and expressed itself *nonverbally:* The subject was able to pick up the correct object.

Over the last four decades, researchers have gained numerous insights about the brain's lateralization of functions by studying split-brain patients, using brain-imaging techniques with normal subjects, and other techniques (Gazzaniga, 1998). On the basis of this evidence, researchers have concluded that—in most people—the left hemisphere is superior in language abilities, speech, reading, and writing.

In contrast, the right hemisphere is more involved in nonverbal emotional expression and visual-spatial tasks (Corballis & others, 2002). Deciphering complex visual cues, such as completing a puzzle or manipulating blocks to match a particular design, also relies on right-hemisphere processing (Gazzaniga, 1995). And the right hemisphere excels in recognizing faces and emotional facial cues, reading maps, copying designs, and drawing (Heller & others, 1998; Reuter-Lorenz & Miller, 1998). Finally, the right hemisphere shows a higher degree of specialization for musical appreciation or responsiveness—but not necessarily for musical ability, which involves the use of the left hemisphere as well (Springer & Deutsch, 1998).

Figure 2.23 summarizes the research findings for the different specialized abilities of the two hemispheres for right-handed people. As you look at the figure, it's important to keep two points in mind. First, the differences between the left and right hemispheres are almost always relative differences, *not* absolute differences. In other words, *both* hemispheres of your brain are activated to some extent as you perform virtually any task (Toga & Thompson, 2003). In the normal brain, the left and right hemispheres function in an integrated fashion, constantly exchanging information (Banich, 1998). Thus, Figure 2.23 indicates the hemisphere that typically displays greater activation or exerts greater control over a particular function. Second, many functions of the cerebral hemispheres, such as those involving the primary sensory and motor areas, *are* symmetrical. They are located in the same place and are performed in the same way on both the left and the right hemisphere.

Given the basic findings on the laterality of different functions in the two hemispheres, can you speculate about why Asha was unable to read or follow a simple conversation but could easily concentrate on a complex piece of music? Why were her language abilities so disrupted, while her ability to focus on and appreciate music remained intact after her stroke?

A plausible explanation has to do with the location of the stroke's damage on Asha's left temporal lobe. Because language functions are usually localized on the left hemisphere, the stroke produced serious disruptions in Asha's language abilities. However, her *right* cerebral hemisphere sustained no detectable damage. Because one of the right hemisphere's abilities is the appreciation of musical sounds, Asha retained the ability to concentrate on and appreciate music.

Plasticity
The Malleable Brain

Our tour of the human brain would not be complete without describing one last important characteristic of the brain: the brain's remarkable capacity to change in response to experience. Until the mid-1960s, neuroscientists believed—and taught—that by early adulthood the brain's physical structure

Neuroscience: Juggling and Brain Plasticity

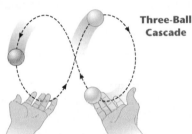

Three-Ball Cascade

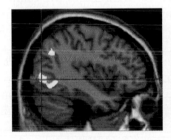 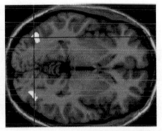

Learning a New Skill Makes Its Mark on the Brain The yellow in these MRIs shows the brain areas that temporarily increased by 3 to 4 percent in size in those participants who learned to juggle. These brain regions are involved in the ability to perceive, remember, and anticipate complex visual motions.

What happens to the brain when you learn a new, challenging skill? It is well known that learning affects the brain's functioning, but does it also affect the brain's physical structure?

Now German researcher Bogdan Draganski and his colleagues (2004) at the University of Regensburg have provided compelling experimental evidence that learning a new skill produces structural changes in the human brain. In their study, 24 young adults—21 women and 3 men— were assigned to either the "jugglers" or "nonjugglers" group. Members of both groups were given a baseline MRI scan. This baseline scan indicated that there were no significant regional brain differences between the two groups at the beginning of the study.

Then the participants in the juggler group had three months to practice and master a basic juggling routine—the classic three-ball cascade. If you've got three tennis balls handy, take a couple of minutes to try the three-ball cascade to get an idea of what the study participants had to master. When the particpants were able to show that they could juggle the three balls for at least 60 seconds, a second brain scan was performed. A second MRI brain scan was also carried out on the nonjugglers at the same point.

The researchers used a sophisticated whole-brain imaging technique to detect regional changes in gray and white matter. Compared to their baseline brain scans, the jugglers showed a 3 to 4 percent increase in the size of gray matter in two brain regions involved in perceiving, remembering, and anticipating complex visual motions. These

two regions are shown in yellow in the composite MRI scans shown above. In comparison, there were *no* brain changes in the scans of the nonjugglers over the same three-month period.

After the second brain scan, the participants in the juggling group were told to stop practicing their newly acquired skills. Three months later, the third and final round of brain scans were taken of both groups. Now, the same regions that had grown while the jugglers were practicing their skills every day had *decreased* in size. While still larger than before the participants had learned to juggle, the regions were 1 to 2 percent smaller than when the participants were juggling every day. In comparison, the same regions in the nonjuggling control group remained unchanged.

Because they couldn't take direct tissue samples of the affected brain areas, Draganski and his colleagues (2004) could not definitively identify the nature of the changes in the gray matter. However, it seems reasonable to suggest that the number and shape of neuronal dendrites and axon terminals probably increased, enhancing the communication ability of neurons (Grutzendler & others, 2002; Trachtenberg & others, 2002). It's also likely that the number of glial cells increased (Haydon, 2001).

As co-researcher Arne May (Draganski & others, 2004) noted, their results challenged prevailing views of the human central nervous system. "Human brains," he observed, "must be viewed as dynamic, changing with development and normal learning."

> *One of the great conceptual leaps of modern neuroscience has been the notion of neuroplasticity. . . . Scientists now know that even modest changes in the internal or external world can lead to structural changes in the brain.*
>
> Barry L. Jacobs (2004)

was *hard-wired* or fixed for life (Raisman, 2004). But today it's known that the brain's physical structure is literally sculpted by experience. The brain's ability to change function and structure is referred to as *brain plasticity,* or simply *plasticity.*

One form of plasticity is **functional plasticity,** which refers to the brain's ability to shift functions from damaged to undamaged brain areas. Depending on the location and degree of brain damage, stroke or accident victims often need to "relearn" once-routine tasks like speaking, walking, or reading. If the rehabilitation is successful, undamaged brain areas gradually assume the ability to process and execute the tasks (Celnik & Cohen, 2003; Mark & Taub, 2003).

But the brain can do more than just shift functions from one area to another. **Structural plasticity** refers to the brain's ability to physically change its structure in response to learning, active practice, or environmental stimulation. In the Focus on Neuroscience, "Juggling and Brain Plasticity," on page 75 we described an ingenious experiment that demonstrates structural plasticity in the human brain.

Closing Thoughts

In our exploration of neuroscience and behavior, we've traveled from the activities of individual neurons to the complex interaction of the billions of neurons that make up the human nervous system, most notably the brain. In the course of those travels, we presented four themes that are crucial to a scientific understanding of brain function: *localization, lateralization, integration,* and *plasticity.*

More than just a historical scientific oddity, phrenology's incorrect interpretation of bumps on the skull helped focus scientific debate on the notion of *localization*—the idea that different functions are localized in different brain areas. Although rejected in the early 1800s when Franz Gall was in his heyday, localization of brain functioning is well established today. The early clinical evidence provided by Broca and Wernicke, and the later split-brain evidence provided by Sperry and his colleagues, confirmed the idea of *lateralization*—that some functions are performed primarily by one cerebral hemisphere.

The ideas of localization and lateralization are complemented by another theme evident in this chapter—*integration.* Although the nervous system is highly specialized, even simple behaviors involve the highly integrated interaction of trillions of synapses. Your ability to process new information and experiences, your memories of previous experiences, your sense of who you are and what you know, your actions and reactions—all depend upon the harmony of the nervous system.

The story of Asha's stroke illustrated what can happen when that harmony is disrupted. Asha survived her stroke, but many people who suffer strokes do not. Of those who do survive a stroke, about one-third are left with severe impairments in their ability to function.

What happened to Asha? Fortunately, her story has a happy ending. Asha was luckier than many stroke victims—she was young, strong, and otherwise healthy. Asha's recovery was also aided by her high level of motivation, willingness to work hard, and sheer will to recover. After being discharged from the hospital, Asha began months of intensive speech therapy. Her speech therapist assigned a great deal of homework that consisted of repeatedly pairing pictures with words, objects with words, and words with objects.

Asha set a very high goal for herself: to return to teaching at the university the following fall semester. With the help of her husband, Paul, and her mother, Nalini, who traveled from India to help coach her back to full recovery, Asha made progressive and significant gains. With remarkable determination, Asha reached the goal she had set for herself. Eight months after her stroke, Asha returned to the classroom and her research lab.

Asha's Recovery After leaving the hospital, Asha began retraining her brain with speech therapy. Asha's husband Paul and her mother Nalini helped her with the speech drills. Day after day, Asha repeatedly paired words with objects or identified numbers, weekdays, or months. As Asha recalls, "My mom was a Montessori teacher for many years and she was incredibly patient with me, like she was with her own students and with us as children." As Asha gradually made progress, Nalini began taking her to stores. "She'd tell the clerk I was from India and that my English wasn't very good and ask them to please be patient with me. She basically forced me to talk to the sales clerks." Today, more than five years after the stroke, Asha has completely recovered and resumed teaching.

Today, more than five years after her stroke, the average person would never know that Asha had sustained significant brain damage. Other than an occasional tendency to "block" on familiar words—especially when she's very tired—Asha seems to have made a complete recovery.

Thus, Asha's story illustrates the final theme—the brain's remarkable *plasticity*. In the chapter Application, we take a closer look at how the brain responds to different types of environments. You will also learn how you can use the research to enhance your own dendritic potential!

functional plasticity
The brain's ability to shift functions from damaged to undamaged brain areas.

structural plasticity
The brain's ability to change its physical structure in response to learning, active practice, or environmental influences.

APPLICATION   Pumping Neurons: Maximizing Your Brain's Potential

It was 1962 when a group of neuroscientists led by psychologist Mark Rosenzweig published the unexpected finding that the brains of rats raised in *enriched environments* were significantly different from the brains of rats raised in *impoverished environments*.

The enriched environment is spacious, houses several rats, and has assorted wheels, ladders, tunnels, and objects to explore. The environment is also regularly changed for further variety. Some enriched environments have been designed to mimic an animal's natural environment (see Heyman, 2003). In the impoverished environment, a solitary rat lives in a small,

Rats in an Enriched Environment Compared with solitary rats raised in bare laboratory cages, rats raised in groups in an enriched environment, like the one shown here, show significant increases in brain growth and number of synaptic interconnections.

bare laboratory cage with only a water bottle and food tray to keep it company.

Consistently, researchers have found that enrichment increases the number and length of dendrites and dendritic branches, increases the number of glial cells, and enlarges the size of neurons (Cohen, 2003; Johnston & others, 1996). Recent studies have also shown that *neurogenesis* is enhanced in enriched environments, increasing the number or survival time of new neurons (Gould & Gross, 2002; van Praag & others, 2000). For example, moving adult rats into an enriched environment more than doubled the survival rate of new neurons in the hippocampus (Kempermann & Gage, 1999).

Enrichment produces more synaptic connections between brain neurons, while impoverishment decreases synaptic connections. With more synapses, the brain has a greater capacity to integrate and process

information and to do so more quickly. In young rats, enrichment increases the number of synapses in the cortex by as much as 20 percent (Kolb & Whishaw, 1998). Collectively, these changes result in increased processing and communication capacity in the brain. Behaviorally, enrichment has been shown to lead to enhanced performance on tasks designed to measure learning and memory, such as performance in different types of mazes (van Praag & others, 2000).

Even the aged brain can change in response to environmental stimulation. Researchers raised rats in impoverished environments until an age equivalent to that of 75 years in humans. (Ten days of rat life is roughly equivalent to one year of the human lifespan.) The rats were then placed in enriched environments until they reached the equivalent of 90 human years of age.

The senior-citizen rats showed significant increases in brain growth and synaptic interconnections (Diamond, 1988; Rosenzweig, 1996). In fact, no matter what the age of the rats studied, environmental enrichment or impoverishment had a significant impact on brain structure (Kempermann & others, 1998).

Who Moved My Exercise Wheel?

Neuroscientists have identified an additional factor that improves brain function, even in aging mammals: exercise. In one study, just a month of daily exercise helped reverse cognitive declines associated with aging in previously sedentary, elderly mice (van Praag & others, 2005). After having access to an exercise wheel for 30 days, mice who were the rodent equivalent of 70 years old learned to navigate a maze much faster than mice of the same age that did not exercise. They also had better memories of maze locations. Finally, the physically

Never Too Old to Learn
Virginia Hanley, 72, shows off the Web site that she created with other members of her computer club, the "Silver Stringers," who are all in their seventies and eighties. As the Silver Stringers demonstrate, a steep decline in intellectual and cognitive functioning is not an inevitable consequence of aging, especially if the environment is mentally stimulating (Kramer & Willis, 2002).

active elderly mice had a greatly increased rate of neurogenesis, and the new neurons functioned as well as new neurons generated in the brains of young mice. As study co-author Henriette van Praag (2005) points out, "Our findings show that it is never too late in life to start to exercise, and that doing so will likely delay the onset of aging-associated memory loss."

From Animal Studies to Humans

Enrichment studies have been carried out with many other species, including monkeys, cats, birds, honeybees, and even fruit flies (Kolb & Whishaw, 1998). In all cases, enriched environments are associated with striking changes in the brain, however primitive. As psychologists Bryan Kolb and Ian Whishaw (1998) observed, "Experience is a major force in shaping the nervous system of all animals."

Can the conclusions drawn from studies on rats, monkeys, and other animals be applied to human brains? Obviously, researchers cannot directly study the effects of enriched or impoverished environments on human brain tissue as they can with rats. However, psychologists and other researchers have amassed an impressive array of correlational evidence showing that the human brain also seems to benefit from enriched, stimulating environments (Rosenzweig, 1996).

For example, autopsy studies have compared the brains of university graduates with those of high school dropouts. The brains of university graduates had up to 40 percent more synaptic connections than those of high school dropouts (Jacobs & others, 1993).

Another line of evidence comes from several studies comparing symptoms of Alzheimer's disease in elderly individuals with different levels of education (Bennett & others, 2003; Stern & others, 1992, 1994). Autopsies showed that the more educated individuals had just as much damage to their brain cells as did the poorly educated individuals. However, because the better-educated people had more synaptic connections, their symptoms were much less severe than those experienced by the less educated people (see Melton, 2005).

Research has shown the importance of a stimulating lifestyle throughout the lifespan. For example, neurologist Robert Friedland and his colleagues (2001) discovered that people who had developed the symptoms of Alzheimer's disease by the age of 70 were much less active, both physically and intellectually, in early and middle adulthood—long before they developed symptoms of the disease—than healthy seniors who were free of Alzheimer's symptoms.

Analyzing the life histories of the Alzheimer's patients and the matched control group of healthy seniors, the researchers discovered that the healthy seniors had spent less time in passive pursuits than the Alzheimer's patients had. The healthy seniors had engaged in intellectually stimulating or creative hobbies, like reading, playing a musical instrument, woodworking, painting, or knitting. Solving puzzles and playing mind-challenging games like chess or board games were other intellectual activities that predicted a cognitively healthy old age. But there was *one* activity that the Alzheimer's patients had engaged in more than their healthy counterparts had: The Alzheimer's patients had spent a lot more time watching television.

The results of this study echo earlier research on intellectual enrichment: A mentally stimulating, intellectually challenging environment is associated with enhanced cognitive functioning. Just as physical activity strengthens the heart and muscles, mental activity strengthens the brain. Even in late adulthood, remaining mentally and physically active can help prevent or lessen mental decline (Colcombe & others, 2003; L. White & others, 1994).

More generally, the results of the enrichment research have fundamentally changed our understanding of the brain. As Kolb and Whishaw (1998) conclude, "Experience alters the synaptic organization of the brain in species as diverse as fruit flies and humans."

Pumping Neurons: Exercising Your Brain

So, here's the critical question: Are you a mental athlete—or a cerebral couch potato? Whatever your age, there seems to be a simple prescription for keeping your brain fit. According to neuroscientist Arnold Scheibel (1994), "Anything that's intellectually challenging can probably serve as a kind of stimulus for dendritic growth, which means it adds to the computational reserves in your brain." In short, you must actively exercise your brain cells. Try the new and unfamiliar. Here are just a few suggestions:

- If you are a "number" or "word" person, sign up for an art class.
- If you are a "math" or "spatial" person, start a personal journal or take a creative writing class.
- Unplug your television set for two weeks—or longer.
- Read, and read widely.
- Try all kinds of puzzles—word, visual, matching, and maze puzzles.
- Attend a play, an art exhibit, or a performance of classical or jazz music.
- Go to a museum.
- Read or reread a classic work of fiction or poetry.
- Pick a topic that interests you and research it on the Internet, following links to related Web sites.
- Sign up for a class on a subject outside your major.

Better yet, take a few minutes and generate your own list of mind-expanding opportunities!

Chapter Review
Neuroscience and Behavior

Key Points

Introduction: Neuroscience and Behavior

■ Psychological and biological processes are closely linked. **Biological psychologists** investigate the physical processes that underlie psychological experience and behavior. **Neuroscience** is the study of the nervous system, especially the brain.

The Neuron: The Basic Unit of Communication

■ Information in the nervous system is transmitted via cells specialized for communication, called **neurons. Glial cells** help neurons by providing nutrition, removing waste products, and producing the **myelin sheath.** There are three basic types of neurons: **sensory neurons, motor neurons,** and **interneurons.**

■ Most neurons have three basic components: a **cell body, dendrites,** and an **axon.** The axons of some neurons are wrapped in a myelin sheath, which speeds the rate at which neural messages are sent.

■ Within the neuron, information is communicated in the form of brief electrical messages called **action potentials.** The minimum level of stimulation required to activate a neuron is called the **stimulus threshold.** A neuron's **resting potential** is the state in which it is ready to activate and communicate its message if sufficiently stimulated. According to the **all-or-none law,** either a neuron is sufficiently stimulated and an action potential results, or it isn't sufficiently stimulated and an action potential doesn't occur.

■ The point of communication between two neurons is called the **synapse.** Neurons communicate information to other neurons either electrically or chemically. In chemical communication, **neurotransmitters** cross the **synaptic gap** and affect neighboring neurons. These neurotransmitters are held within **synaptic vesicles,** which float in **axon terminals.** The entire process of transmitting information at the synapse is called **synaptic transmission. Reuptake** is the process in which neurotransmitter molecules detach from the receptor and are reabsorbed and recycled. There are many different kinds of neurotransmitters, which send either excitatory or inhibitory messages to the receiving neuron. Some drugs influence behavior and mental processes by influencing neurotransmitter activity. Important neurotransmitters include **acetylcholine, dopamine, serotonin, norepinephrine, GABA,** and **endorphins.**

The Nervous System and the Endocrine System: Communication Throughout the Body

■ The **nervous system** is divided into two main divisions: the **central nervous system (CNS)** and the **peripheral nervous system.** The central nervous system is composed of the brain and the spinal cord. The spinal cord can produce **spinal reflexes.**

■ The peripheral nervous system consists of all the **nerves** outside the central nervous system. The two main subdivisions of the peripheral nervous system are the **somatic nervous system** and the **autonomic nervous system.** The autonomic nervous system is divided into the **sympathetic nervous system** and the **parasympathetic nervous system.**

■ The **endocrine system** is composed of glands that secrete **hormones** into the bloodstream, regulating many body functions, including physical growth, stress response, and sexual development. The endocrine system itself is regulated by the hypothalamus in the brain. Under the direction of the hypothalamus, the **pituitary gland** directly controls hormone production in other endocrine glands as well as hormones that act on physical processes. Another set of glands, called the **adrenal glands,** which include the **adrenal cortex** and the **adrenal medulla,** produce hormones that are involved in the human stress response. The **gonads** are endocrine glands that secrete hormones that regulate sexual characteristics and reproductive processes.

A Guided Tour of the Brain

■ Most psychological processes involve the integrated processing of information via neural pathways in multiple brain structures and regions.

■ Case studies of individuals with brain damage or injury have provided information about the brain's function. Researchers have also observed the behavioral effects of surgically altering or electrically stimulating a specific area of the brain. The **electroencephalograph** records the brain's electrical activity. Brain imaging is often used in **cognitive neuroscience** research. **MRI** scanners use magnetic signals to produce highly detailed images of the brain's structures. **PET** scans use radioactive substances to produce color-coded images of the brain's activity. **Functional MRI (fMRI)** scans track the brain's activity by measuring changes in blood flow in brain areas.

■ During prenatal development, the human brain begins as a fluid-filled neural tube, which ultimately forms the three key brain regions: the hindbrain, midbrain, and forebrain. Evidence now suggests that **neurogenesis,** the development of new neurons, can occur in the adult brain.

■ Combined, the hindbrain and midbrain structures constitute the **brainstem.** Sensory and motor pathways cross over in the **hindbrain.** The key structures of the hindbrain are the **medulla,** the **cerebellum,** and the **pons.** The **reticular formation** is located in the core of the medulla and the pons.

■ Auditory and visual information is integrated and coordinated in the **midbrain.** The **substantia nigra** is involved in motor control and contains a concentration of neurons that produce dopamine.

■ The outer portion of the **forebrain** is called the **cerebral cortex.** The cerebral cortex is divided into the left and right **cerebral hemispheres,** with the **corpus callosum** serving as the main communication link between them. Each hemisphere is divided into four lobes. The **temporal lobe** contains the primary auditory cortex. The **occipital lobe** contains the primary visual cortex. The **parietal lobe** contains the somatosensory cortex. The **frontal lobe** contains the primary motor cortex. The remainder of the cerebral cortex is composed of association areas.

■ The **limbic system** structures are found beneath the cerebral cortex and form neural circuits that play critical roles in learning, memory, and emotional control. The limbic system includes part of the frontal cortex and the **hippocampus, thalamus, hypothalamus,** and **amygdala.**

Specialization in the Cerebral Hemispheres

■ The notion that particular areas of the brain are associated with particular functions is called **cortical localization.**

In the mid-1800s, it was discovered that damage to the left hemisphere produced disruptions in speech and language called **aphasia.** Different forms of aphasia include Broca's aphasia and Wernicke's aphasia. Damage to the same areas of the right hemisphere did not produce aphasia. The notion that specific psychological or cognitive functions are processed primarily on one side of the brain is called **lateralization of function.**

■ More evidence for the specialized abilities of the two hemispheres has resulted from the **split-brain operation,** in which the corpus callosum connecting the two hemispheres is cut. Roger Sperry and his colleagues demonstrated the different strengths of each hemisphere in split-brain patients. The left hemisphere is specialized for language tasks, and the right hemisphere is specialized for visual-spatial tasks.

■ The human brain can change in response to environmental stimulation, training, or experience, displaying both **functional plasticity** and **structural plasticity.**

Key Terms

biological psychology, p. 40

neuroscience, p. 40

neuron, p. 41

glial cells, p. 41

sensory neuron, p. 41

motor neuron, p. 41

interneuron, p. 41

cell body, p. 42

dendrites, p. 42

axon, p. 42

myelin sheath, p. 43

action potential, p. 43

stimulus threshold, p. 43

resting potential, p. 43

all-or-none law, p. 45

synapse, p. 45

synaptic gap, p. 45

axon terminals, p. 46

synaptic vesicles, p. 46

neurotransmitters, p. 46

synaptic transmission, p. 46

reuptake, p. 46

acetylcholine, p. 48

dopamine, p. 48

serotonin, p. 48

norepinephrine, p. 48

GABA (gamma-aminobutyric acid), p. 48

endorphins, p. 48

nervous system, p. 51

nerves, p. 51

central nervous system (CNS), p. 51

spinal reflexes, p. 51

peripheral nervous system, p. 52

somatic nervous system, p. 52

autonomic nervous system, p. 52

sympathetic nervous system, p. 54

parasympathetic nervous system, p. 54

endocrine system, p. 54

hormones, p. 54

pituitary gland, p. 56

adrenal glands, p. 56

adrenal cortex, p. 56

adrenal medulla, p. 56

gonads, p. 56

phrenology, p. 59

cortical localization, p. 59

electroencephalograph, p. 59

positron emission tomography (PET scan), p. 60

magnetic resonance imaging (MRI), p. 60

functional magnetic resonance imaging (fMRI), p. 60

cognitive neuroscience, p. 60

neurogenesis, p. 62

brainstem, p. 63

hindbrain, p. 64

medulla, p. 64

pons, p. 64

cerebellum, p. 64

reticular formation, p. 64

midbrain, p. 64

substantia nigra, p. 64

forebrain, p. 65

cerebral cortex, p. 65

cerebral hemispheres, p. 65

corpus callosum, p. 65

temporal lobe, p. 66

occipital lobe, p. 66

parietal lobe, p. 66

frontal lobe, p. 66

limbic system, p. 67

hippocampus, p. 68

thalamus, p. 68

hypothalamus, p. 68

amygdala, p. 69

cortical localization, p. 70

lateralization of function, p. 71

aphasia, p. 71

split-brain operation, p. 73

functional plasticity, p. 76

structural plasticity, p. 76

Key People

Pierre Paul Broca (1824–1880)   French surgeon and neuroanatomist who in 1861 discovered an area on the lower left frontal lobe of the cerebral cortex that, when damaged, produces speech disturbances but no loss of comprehension. (p. 70)

Roger Sperry (1913–1994)   American psychologist who received the Nobel prize in 1981 for his pioneering research on brain specialization in split-brain patients. (p. 73)

Karl Wernicke (1848–1905)   German neurologist who in 1874 discovered an area on the left temporal lobe of the cerebral cortex that, when damaged, produces meaningless or nonsensical speech and difficulties in verbal or written comprehension. (p. 70)

Web Companion   Review Activities

You can find additional review activities by going to **www.DiscoveringPsychology.com** and clicking on the *Discovering Psychology* 4th Edition text cover. At the Discovering Psychology Web Companion you'll find the chapter learning objectives, flashcards for key terms and key people, interactive crossword puzzles, self-scoring practice quizzes, and other materials to help you master the information in this chapter.

Snow Mass Transit

Sensation and Perception

Prologue Learning to See

Mike was just 3 years old when a jar of fuel for a miner's lantern exploded in his face. The blast destroyed his left eye, and his right eye was severely damaged. For more than four decades, Mike May was completely blind.

But despite his blindness, Mike experienced—and accomplished—much more than most people ever dream of achieving. Always athletic, Mike played flag football in elementary school and wrestled and played soccer in high school and college. As an adult, he earned a master's degree in international affairs from Johns Hopkins University, went to work for the CIA, and then became a successful businessman.

He also learned to skydive, windsurf, water-ski, and snow-ski. How does a blind person ski down mountains? If you answered, "very carefully," you'd be wrong—at least in Mike's case. With a guide skiing in front of him shouting "left" or "right" to identify obstacles, Mike hurtled down the most difficult black diamond slopes at speeds up to 65 miles per hour. In fact, Mike has won several medals in national and international championships for blind downhill speed skiing.

It was through skiing that Mike met his wife, Jennifer. An accomplished skier herself, she volunteered to be his guide at a ski slope. Today, Mike and Jennifer and their two sons are all avid skiers (Abrams, 2002).

In the 1990s, Mike started a successful company that develops global positioning devices, along with other mobility devices, for the blind. The portable navigation system gives visually impaired people information about their location, landmarks, streets, and so forth wherever they travel. With his white cane and guide dog, Josh, Mike has traveled the world, both as a businessman and a tourist, ever optimistic and open to adventure. His personal motto: "There is always a way."

But in 1999, Mike's keen sensory world of touch, sounds, and aroma was on the verge of expanding. A new surgical technique became available that offered the chance that Mike's vision might be restored in his right eye. On March 7, 2000, Jennifer held her breath as the bandages were removed. "It was so unexpected—there was just a whoosh! of light blasting into my eye," Mike later recalled (May, 2002b). For the first time since he was 3 years old, Mike May could see.

And what was it like when Mike could see Jennifer for the first time? "It was incredible," he explained, "but the truth is, I knew exactly what she looked like, so it wasn't all that dramatic to see her. The same with my kids. Now, seeing other women or people that I can't touch, well, that's interesting because I couldn't see them before."

A Little Bit of Vision . . . Although Mike could "see" from the moment the bandages were removed from his eye *(left),* he still had trouble identifying objects, especially stationary ones. Mike tells this story of a walk down an unfamiliar street in Barcelona, Spain: "I picked my way through some street construction. I saw a fluorescent green object in my path and tapped it with my cane. It wasn't hard like a sign so I tapped it a bit harder as I still couldn't figure out visually what it was. I was startled as a burst of Spanish profanity came from the workman bent over digging out a hole in the sidewalk. He didn't take too kindly to me poking him in the behind with my cane. A little bit of vision can be dangerous sometimes" (May, 2004).

But what did Mike see? Anatomically, his right eye was now normal. But rather than being 20/20, his vision was closer to 20/1,000. What that means is his view of the world was very blurry. He could see colors, shapes, lines, shadows, light and dark patches. So why wasn't the world crystal clear?

Although the structures of his eye were working, his brain did not know how to interpret the signals it was receiving. As neuropsychologist Ione Fine (2002) explained, "Most people learn the language of vision between the age of birth and two years old. Mike has had to learn it as an adult." Indeed, there is much more to *seeing* than meets the eye.

Faces posed a particular challenge for Mike. During conversations, he found it very distracting to look at people's faces. As Mike wrote in his journal, "I can see their lips moving, eyelashes flickering, head nodding and hands gesturing. It was easiest to close my eyes or tune out the visual input. This was often necessary in order to pay attention to what they were saying" (May, 2004).

And what was it like the first time he went skiing, just weeks after his surgery? Mike was dazzled by the sight of the tall, dark green trees, the snow, and the distant peaks against the blue sky (May, 2004). But although you might think that vision, even blurry vision, would be a distinct advantage to an expert skier, this was not the case. Mike found it easier to ski with his eyes closed, with Jennifer skiing ahead and shouting out directions. With his eyes open, he was overwhelmed by all the visual stimuli and the frightening sense that objects were rushing toward him. "By the time I thought about and guessed at what the shadows on the snow meant, I would miss the turn or fall on my face. It was best to close my eyes," he explained.

Throughout this chapter, we will come back to Mike's story. We'll also tell you what neuropsychologists Ione Fine and Don MacLeod learned after conducting fMRI scans of Mike's brain. And, later in the chapter, we'll see how well you do at deciphering some visual illusions as compared to Mike.

Introduction

What Are Sensation and Perception?

Glance around you. Notice the incredible variety of colors, shades, shadows, and images. Listen carefully to the diversity of sounds, loud and soft, near and far. Focus on everything that's touching you—your clothes, your shoes, the chair you're sitting on. Now, inhale deeply through your nose and identify the aromas in the air.

With these simple observations you have exercised four of your senses: vision, hearing, touch, and smell. As we saw in Chapter 2, the primary function of the nervous system is communication—the transmission of information from one part of the body to the other. Where does that information come from? Put simply, your senses are the gateway through which your brain receives all its information about the environment. It's a process that is so natural and automatic that we typically take it for granted until it is disrupted by illness or injury. Nevertheless, as Mike's story demonstrates, people with one nonfunctional sense are amazingly adaptive. Often, they learn to compensate for the missing environmental information by relying on their other senses.

In this chapter, we will explore the overlapping processes of *sensation* and *perception*. **Sensation** refers to the detection and basic sensory experience of environmental stimuli, such as sounds, objects, and odors. **Perception** occurs when we integrate, organize, and interpret sensory information in a way that is meaningful. Here's a simple example to contrast the two terms. Your eyes' physical response to light, splotches of color, and lines reflects *sensation*. Integrating and organizing those sensations so that you interpret the light, splotches of color, and lines as a painting, a flag, or some other object reflects *perception*. Mike's visual world reflects this distinction. Although his eye was accurately transmitting visual information from his environment (*sensation*), his brain was unable to make sense out of the information (*perception*).

Where does the process of sensation leave off and the process of perception begin? There is no clear boundary line between the two processes as we actually experience them. In fact, many researchers in this area of psychology regard sensation and perception as a single process.

Although the two processes overlap, in this chapter we will present sensation and perception as separate discussions. In the first half of the chapter, we'll discuss the basics of *sensation*—how our sensory receptors respond to stimulation and transmit that information in usable form to the brain. In the second half of the chapter, we'll explore *perception*—how the brain actively organizes and interprets the signals sent from our *sensory receptors*.

Experiencing the World Through Our Senses Imagine biting into a crisp, red apple. All your senses are involved in your experience—vision, smell, taste, hearing, and touch. Although we're accustomed to thinking of our different senses as being quite distinct, all forms of sensation involve the stimulation of specialized cells called sensory receptors.

Basic Principles of Sensation

Key Theme
■ Sensation is the result of neural impulses transmitted to the brain from sensory receptors that have been stimulated by physical energy from the external environment.

Key Questions
■ What is the process of transduction?
■ What is a sensory threshold, and what are two main types of sensory thresholds?
■ How do sensory adaptation and Weber's law demonstrate that sensation is relative rather than absolute?

We're accustomed to thinking of the senses as being quite different from one another. However, all our senses involve some common processes. All sensation is a result of the stimulation of specialized cells, called **sensory receptors,** by some form of *energy*.

Imagine biting into a crisp, red apple. Your experience of hearing the apple crunch is a response to the physical energy of vibrations in the air, or *sound waves*. The sweet taste of the apple is a response to the physical energy of *dissolvable chemicals* in your mouth, just as the distinctive sharp aroma of the apple is a response to *airborne chemical molecules* that you inhale through your nose. The smooth feel of the apple's skin is a response to the *pressure* of the apple against your hand. And the mellow red color of the apple is a response to the physical energy of *light waves* reflecting from the irregularly shaped object into which you've just bitten.

Sensory receptors convert these different forms of physical energy into electrical impulses that are transmitted via neurons to the brain. The process by which a form of physical energy is converted into a coded neural signal that can be processed by the nervous system is called **transduction.** These neural signals are sent to the brain, where the perceptual processes of organizing and interpreting the coded messages occur. Figure 3.1 on page 86 illustrates the basic steps involved in sensation and perception.

sensation
The process of detecting a physical stimulus, such as light, sound, heat, or pressure.

perception
The process of integrating, organizing, and interpreting sensations.

sensory receptors
Specialized cells unique to each sense organ that respond to a particular form of sensory stimulation.

transduction
The process by which a form of physical energy is converted into a coded neural signal that can be processed by the nervous system.

FIGURE 3.1 The Basic Steps of Sensation and Perception

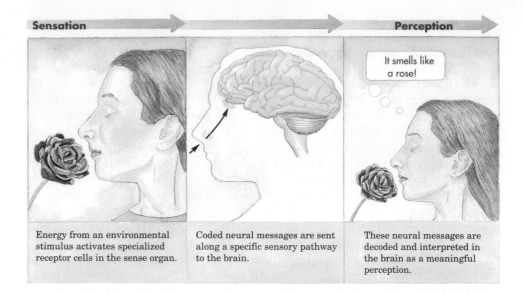

Sensation → **Perception**

Energy from an environmental stimulus activates specialized receptor cells in the sense organ.

Coded neural messages are sent along a specific sensory pathway to the brain.

These neural messages are decoded and interpreted in the brain as a meaningful perception.

It smells like a rose!

absolute threshold
The smallest possible strength of a stimulus that can be detected half the time.

difference threshold
The smallest possible difference between two stimuli that can be detected half the time; also called *just noticeable difference.*

Weber's law
(VAY-berz) A principle of sensation that holds that the size of the just noticeable difference will vary depending on its relation to the strength of the original stimulus.

Table 3.1

Absolute Thresholds

Sense	Absolute Threshold
Vision	A candle flame seen from 30 miles away on a clear, dark night
Hearing	The tick of a watch at 20 feet
Taste	One teaspoon of sugar in two gallons of water
Smell	One drop of perfume throughout a three-room apartment
Touch	A bee's wing falling on your cheek from a height of about half an inch

Psychologist Eugene Galanter (1962) provided these classic examples of the absolute thresholds for our senses. In each case, people are able to sense these faint stimuli at least half the time.

We are constantly being bombarded by many different forms of energy. For instance, at this very moment radio and television waves are bouncing around the atmosphere and passing through your body. However, sensory receptors are so highly specialized that they are sensitive only to very specific types of energy (which is lucky, or you might be seeing *I Love Lucy* reruns in your brain right now). So, for any type of stimulation to be sensed, the stimulus energy must first be in a form that can be detected by our sensory receptor cells. Otherwise, transduction cannot occur.

Sensory Thresholds

Along with being specialized as to the types of energy that can be detected, our senses are specialized in other ways as well. We do not have an infinite capacity to detect all levels of energy. To be sensed, a stimulus must first be strong enough to be detected—loud enough to be heard, concentrated enough to be smelled, bright enough to be seen. The point at which a stimulus is strong enough to be detected because it activates a sensory receptor cell is called a *threshold*. There are two general kinds of sensory thresholds for each sense—the absolute threshold and the difference threshold.

The **absolute threshold** refers to the smallest possible strength of a stimulus that can be detected half the time. Why just half the time? Because the minimum level of stimulation that can be detected varies from person to person and from trial to trial. Because of this human variability, researchers have arbitrarily set the limit as the minimum level of stimulation that can be detected half the time. Under ideal conditions (which rarely occur in normal daily life), our sensory abilities are far more sensitive than you might think (see Table 3.1). Can stimuli that are below the absolute threshold affect us? We discuss this question in Science versus Pseudoscience Box 3.1, "Subliminal Perception."

The other important threshold involves detecting the *difference* between two stimuli. The **difference threshold** is the smallest possible difference between two stimuli that can be detected half the time. Another term for the difference threshold is *just noticeable difference,* which is abbreviated *jnd.*

The just noticeable difference will *vary* depending on its relation to the original stimulus. This principle of sensation is called *Weber's law,* after the German physiologist Ernst Weber (1795–1878). **Weber's law** holds that for each sense, the size of a just noticeable difference is a constant proportion of the size of the initial stimulus. So, whether we can detect a change in the strength of a stimulus

SCIENCE VERSUS PSEUDOSCIENCE 3.1

Subliminal Perception

During the U.S. presidential election campaign of 2000, one political party (let's call them the "Democrats") accused the other political party (let's call them the "Republicans") of using subliminal techniques in a political ad. When the ad was played at slower-than-normal speed, the word "RATS" appeared in large white letters while the announcer criticized candidate Al Gore's prescription drug plan as one in which "bureaucrats decide." Democrats accused the Republicans of embedding a subliminal message in their ad, Republicans denied the accusation, and the firm that created the advertisement claimed that it was just a coincidence.

What are subliminal messages? Can they be used to persuade people to change their attitudes or buy products? **Subliminal perception** refers to the perception of stimuli that are below the threshold of conscious perception or awareness. (The word *limen* is Latin for "threshold.") Subliminal stimuli could be sounds presented too faintly for a person to consciously hear or visual images presented too rapidly for a person to consciously recognize.

Psychologists have studied subliminal perception for more than 60 years (e.g., Collier, 1940; A. C. Williams, 1938). But the idea that people's behavior could be manipulated by subliminal messages first attracted public attention in 1957. James Vicary, a marketing executive, claimed to have increased popcorn and Coca-Cola sales at a New Jersey movie theater by subliminally flashing the words "Eat popcorn" and "Drink Coke" during the movie.

Controlled tests, however, failed to replicate Vicary's claims (Bornstein, 1989). Vicary later admitted that his boast was a hoax to drum up customers for his failing marketing business (Pratkanis, 1992). Nevertheless, some people still believe that subliminal messages can exert a powerful and irresistible influence.

Subliminal Advertising in Politics In the original campaign ad, the words "RATS" appeared in large white letters, superimposed over the words "The Gore Prescription Plan." In a fraction of a second, "RATS" disappeared and the words "BUREAUCRATS DECIDE" appeared in smaller letters. If you were aware of the word's presence, you might have been able to spot it when the ad played at normal speed, but most viewers couldn't detect it.

Can your behavior be profoundly influenced by subliminal self-help tapes? By backward soundtracks on music albums? Or by vague sexual images or words embedded in advertisements? In a word, "no." Numerous studies have shown that subliminal self-help tapes do *not* produce the changes they claim to produce (e.g., Greenwald & others, 1991). Studies of backward soundtracks show that they have *no* effect (Begg & others, 1993; Swart & Morgan, 1992). And numerous studies on subliminal messages in advertising have shown that they do *not* influence consumer decisions (Trappey, 1996).

So, do subliminal stimuli have *any* effect? Surprisingly, the answer is a qualified "yes" (Bargh & Churchland, 1999; Epley & others, 1999). For example, in a 1959 study, Morris Eagle flashed subliminal images of a boy either angrily throwing a birthday cake or pleasantly presenting a birthday cake. When subjects were shown a picture of the same boy in a neutral posture, those who had been exposed to the angry image evaluated the boy's personality in much more negative terms than did those who had seen the pleasant image of the same boy. A more recent experiment showed that subliminally presenting subjects with a pleasant scene (cute kittens) or with an unpleasant scene (a skull) can influence how they judge a person shown in a neutral context (Krosnick & others, 1992).

Another area of research in subliminal perception involves a phenomenon called the mere exposure effect. The *mere exposure effect* refers to the fact that when people are repeatedly exposed to a novel stimulus, like a shape or a Chinese ideograph, their liking for that particular stimulus will increase (Zajonc, 2001). The mere exposure effect also holds true for subliminal exposure to stimuli (Bornstein, 1993; Murphy & others, 1995). For example, when people are exposed to a subliminal image of a geometric shape and later asked to pick the shape they prefer from a group of geometric shapes, they are more likely to choose the subliminally presented shape.

Today it is known that emotions, thoughts, and attitudes can be influenced by subliminal stimuli (Katkin & others, 2001; Merikle & Daneman, 1998). However, note that there is a difference between subliminal *perception* and subliminal *persuasion* (Epley & others, 1999). There is *no* evidence that subliminally presented stimuli can change behavior or personality in any long-lasting or significant way.

Rather, psychologists have found that the effects of subliminal stimuli tend to be weak and short-lived, usually lasting only seconds or minutes (Greenwald, 1992; Kihlstrom, 1993).

depends on the intensity of the *original* stimulus. For example, if you are holding a pebble (the original stimulus), you will notice an increase in weight if a second pebble is placed in your hand. But if you start off holding a very heavy rock (the original stimulus), you probably won't detect an increase in weight when the same pebble is balanced on it.

subliminal perception
The perception of stimuli that are below the threshold of conscious awareness.

What Weber's law underscores is that our psychological experience of sensation is *relative*. There is no simple, one-to-one correspondence between the objective characteristics of a physical stimulus, such as the weight of a pebble, and our psychological experience of it.

Sensory Adaptation

Suppose your best friend has invited you over for a spaghetti dinner. As you walk in the front door, you're almost overwhelmed by the odor of onions and garlic cooking on the stove. However, after just a few moments, you no longer notice the smell. Why? Because your sensory receptor cells become less responsive to a constant stimulus. This gradual decline in sensitivity to a constant stimulus is called **sensory adaptation.** Once again, we see that our experience of sensation is relative—in this case, relative to the *duration of exposure*.

Because of sensory adaptation, we become accustomed to constant stimuli, which allows us to quickly notice new or changing stimuli. This makes sense. If we were continually aware of all incoming stimuli, we'd be so overwhelmed with sensory information that we wouldn't be able to focus our attention. So, for example, once you manage to land your posterior on the sofa, you don't need to be constantly reminded that the sofa is beneath you.

Vision
From Light to Sight

Key Theme
- ■ The receptor cells for vision respond to the physical energy of light waves and are located in the retina of the eye.

Key Questions
- ■ What is the visible spectrum?
- ■ What are the key structures of the eye and their functions?
- ■ What are rods and cones, and how do their functions differ?

A lone caterpillar on the screen door, the pile of dirty laundry in the corner of the closet, a spectacular autumn sunset, the intricate play of color, light, and texture in a painting by Monet. The sense organ for vision is the eye, which contains receptor cells that are sensitive to the physical energy of *light*. Before we can talk about how the eye functions, we need to briefly discuss some characteristics of light as the visual stimulus.

What We See
The Nature of Light

Light is just one of many different kinds of electromagnetic energy that travel in the form of waves. Other forms of electromagnetic energy include X-rays, the microwaves you use to bake a potato, and the ultraviolet rays that give you a sunburn. The various types of electromagnetic energy differ in **wavelength,** which is the distance from one wave peak to another. Figure 3.2 shows the spectrum of different forms of electromagnetic energy.

Humans are capable of seeing only a minuscule portion of the electromagnetic energy range. In Figure 3.2, notice that the visible portion of the electromagnetic energy spectrum can be further divided into different wavelengths. As we'll discuss in more detail later, the different wavelengths of visible light correspond to our psychological perception of different colors.

---

sensory adaptation
The decline in sensitivity to a constant stimulus.

wavelength
The distance from one wave peak to another.

cornea
(CORE-nee-uh) A clear membrane covering the visible part of the eye that helps gather and direct incoming light.

pupil
The opening in the middle of the iris that changes size to let in different amounts of light.

iris
(EYE-riss) The colored part of the eye, which is the muscle that controls the size of the pupil.

lens
A transparent structure located behind the pupil that actively focuses, or bends, light as it enters the eye.

accommodation
The process by which the lens changes shape to focus incoming light so that it falls on the retina.

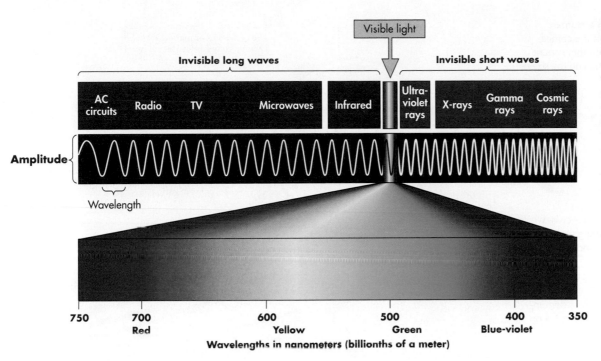

Visible light

Invisible long waves

Invisible short waves

| AC circuits | Radio | TV | Microwaves | Infrared | Ultra-violet rays | X-rays | Gamma rays | Cosmic rays |

Amplitude

Wavelength

750   700   600   500   400   350

Red   Yellow   Green   Blue-violet

Wavelengths in nanometers (billionths of a meter)

FIGURE 3.2 The Electromagnetic Spectrum We are surrounded by different kinds of electromagnetic energy waves, yet we are able to see only a tiny portion of the entire spectrum of electromagnetic energy. Some electronic instruments, like radio and television, are specialized receivers that detect a specific wavelength range. Similarly, the human eye is sensitive to a specific and very narrow range of wavelengths.

How We See
The Human Visual System

Suppose you're watching your neighbor's yellow and white tabby cat sunning himself on the front steps. How do you see the cat? Simply seeing a yellow tabby cat involves a complex chain of events. We'll describe the process of vision from the object to the brain. You can trace the path of light waves through the eye in Figure 3.3 on the next page.

How a Pit Viper Sees a Mouse at Night Does the world look different to other species? In many cases, yes. Each species has evolved a unique set of sensory capabilities. Pit vipers see infrared light, which we sense only as warmth. The mouse here has been photographed through an infrared viewer. The image shows how a pit viper uses its infrared "vision" to detect warm-blooded prey at night (Gould & Gould, 1994). Similarly, many insect and bird species can detect ultraviolet light, which is invisible to humans.

First, light waves reflected from the cat enter your eye, passing through the *cornea, pupil,* and *lens.* The **cornea,** a clear membrane that covers the front of the eye, helps gather and direct incoming light. The *sclera,* or white portion of the eye, is a tough, fibrous tissue that covers the eyeball except for the cornea. The **pupil** is the black opening in the eye's center. The pupil is surrounded by the **iris,** the colored structure that we refer to when we say that someone has brown eyes. The iris is actually a ring of muscular tissue that contracts or expands to precisely control the size of the pupil and thus the amount of light entering the eye. In dim light, the iris widens the pupil to let light in; in bright light, the iris narrows the pupil.

Behind the pupil is the **lens,** another transparent structure. In a process called **accommodation,** the lens thins or thickens to bend or focus the incoming light so that the light falls on the retina. If the eyeball is abnormally shaped, the lens may not properly focus the incoming light on the retina, resulting in a visual disorder. In nearsightedness, or *myopia,* distant objects appear blurry because the light reflected off the objects focuses in front of the retina. In farsightedness, or *hyperopia,* objects near the eyes appear blurry because light reflected off the objects is focused behind the retina. During middle age, another form of farsightedness often occurs, called *presbyopia.* Presbyopia is caused when the lens becomes brittle and inflexible. In *astigmatism,* an abnormally curved eyeball

FIGURE 3.3 Path of Light in a Human Eye Light waves pass through the cornea, pupil, and lens. The iris controls the amount of light entering the eye by controlling the size of the pupil. The lens changes shape to focus the incoming light onto the retina. As the light strikes the retina, the light energy activates the rods and cones. Signals from the rods and cones are collected by the bipolar cells, which transmit the information to the ganglion cells. The ganglion cell axons are bundled together to form the optic nerve, which transmits the information to the brain. The optic nerve leaves the eye at the optic disk, creating a blind spot in our visual field. (For a demonstration of the blind spot, see Figure 3.4 on the facing page.)

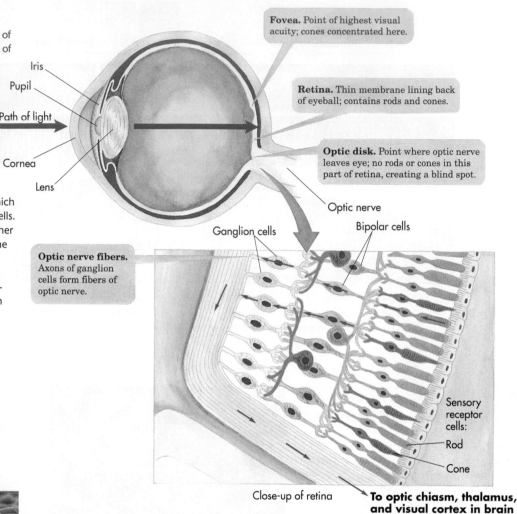

Fovea. Point of highest visual acuity; cones concentrated here.

Retina. Thin membrane lining back of eyeball; contains rods and cones.

Optic disk. Point where optic nerve leaves eye; no rods or cones in this part of retina, creating a blind spot.

Optic nerve

Ganglion cells   Bipolar cells

Optic nerve fibers. Axons of ganglion cells form fibers of optic nerve.

Sensory receptor cells:

Rod

Cone

Close-up of retina   **To optic chiasm, thalamus, and visual cortex in brain**

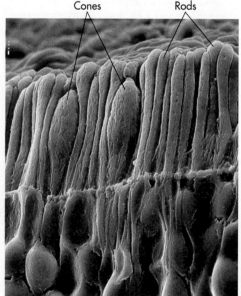

Cones   Rods

Slim Rods and Fat Cones The rods and cones in the retina are the sensory receptors for vision. They convert light into electrical impulses that are ultimately transmitted to the brain. This photograph shows the rods and cones magnified about 45,000 times. The rods are long and thin; the cones are shorter, fatter, and tapered at one end. As you can see, the rods and cones are densely packed in the retina, with many rods surrounding a single cone or pair of cones.

results in blurry vision for lines in a particular direction. Corrective glasses remedy these conditions by intercepting and bending the light so that the image falls properly on the retina. New surgical techniques, such as LASIK, correct visual disorders by reshaping the cornea so that light rays focus more directly on the retina.

The Retina
Rods and Cones

The **retina** is a thin, light-sensitive membrane that lies at the back of the eye, covering most of its inner surface (see Figure 3.3). Contained in the retina are the **rods** and **cones.** Because these sensory receptor cells respond to light, they are often called *photoreceptors*. When exposed to light, the rods and cones undergo a chemical reaction that results in a neural signal.

Rods and cones differ in many ways. First, as their names imply, rods and cones are shaped differently. Rods are long and thin, with blunt ends. Cones are shorter and fatter, with one end that tapers to a point. The eye contains far more rods than cones. It is estimated that each eye contains about 7 million cones and about 125 million rods!

Rods and cones are also specialized for different visual functions. Although both are light receptors, rods are much more sensitive to light than are cones. Once the rods are fully adapted to the dark, they are about a thousand times better than cones at detecting weak visual stimuli (Masland, 2001). We therefore rely primarily on rods for our vision in dim light and at night.

Rods and cones also react differently to *changes* in the amount of light. Rods adapt relatively slowly, reaching maximum sensitivity to light in about 30 minutes. In contrast, cones adapt quickly to bright light, reaching maximum sensitivity in about 5 minutes. That's why it takes several minutes for your eyes to adapt to the dim light of a darkened room but only a few moments to adapt to the brightness when you switch on the lights.

You may have noticed that it is difficult or impossible to distinguish colors in very dim light. This difficulty occurs because only the cones are sensitive to the different wavelengths that produce the sensation of color, and cones require much more light than rods do to function effectively. Cones are also specialized for seeing fine details and for vision in bright light.

Most of the cones are concentrated in the **fovea,** which is a region in the very center of the retina. Cones are scattered throughout the rest of the retina, but they become progressively less common toward the periphery of the retina. There are no rods in the fovea. Images that do not fall on the fovea tend to be perceived as blurry or indistinct. For example, focus your eyes on the word *For* at the beginning of this sentence. In contrast to the sharpness of the letters in *For,* the words to the left and right are somewhat blurry. The image of the outlying words is striking the peripheral areas of the retina, where rods are more prevalent and there are very few cones.

The Blind Spot

One part of the retina lacks rods and cones altogether. This area, called the **optic disk,** is the point at which the fibers that make up the optic nerve leave the back of the eye and project to the brain. Because there are no photoreceptors in the optic disk, we have a tiny hole, or **blind spot,** in our field of vision. To experience the blind spot, try the demonstration in Figure 3.4.

Why don't we notice this hole in our visual field? Some researchers have suggested that we simply don't notice that any information is missing because the blind spot is located in an area that has few receptors. Other researchers have suggested that the left eye compensates for the missing information in the right eye and vice versa. A more compelling explanation is that the brain actually fills in the missing background information (Ramachandran, 1992a, 1992b). In effect, the brain "paves over" the blind spot with the color and pattern of the surrounding visual information.

Processing Visual Information

Key Theme
- Signals from the rods and cones undergo preliminary processing in the retina before they are transmitted to the brain.

Key Questions
- What are the bipolar and ganglion cells, and how do their functions differ?
- How is visual information transmitted from the retina to the brain?
- What properties of light correspond to color perceptions, and how is color vision explained?

retina
(RET-in-uh) A thin, light-sensitive membrane located at the back of the eye that contains the sensory receptors for vision.

rods
The long, thin, blunt sensory receptors of the eye that are highly sensitive to light, but not to color, and that are primarily responsible for peripheral vision and night vision.

cones
The short, thick, pointed sensory receptors of the eye that detect color and are responsible for color vision and visual acuity.

fovea
(FO-vee-uh) A small area in the center of the retina, composed entirely of cones, where visual information is most sharply focused.

optic disk
Area of the retina without rods or cones, where the optic nerve exits the back of the eye.

blind spot
The point at which the optic nerve leaves the eye, producing a small gap in the field of vision.

ganglion cells
In the retina, the specialized neurons that connect to the bipolar cells; the bundled axons of the ganglion cells form the optic nerve.

FIGURE 3.4 Demonstration of the Blind Spot Hold the book a few feet in front of you. Close your right eye and stare at the insect spray can with your left eye. Slowly bring the book toward your face. At some point the spider will disappear because you have focused it onto the part of your retina where the blind spot is located. Notice, however, that you still perceive the spider web. That's because your brain has filled in information from the surrounding area.

Visual information is processed primarily in the brain. However, before visual information is sent to the brain, it undergoes some preliminary processing in the retina by specialized neurons called **ganglion cells.** This preliminary processing of visual data in the cells of the retina is possible because the retina develops from a bit of brain tissue that "migrates" to the eye during fetal development (see Hubel, 1995).

bipolar cells
In the retina, the specialized neurons that connect the rods and cones with the ganglion cells.

optic nerve
The thick nerve that exits from the back of the eye and carries visual information to the visual cortex in the brain.

optic chiasm
(KI-az-em) Point in the brain where the optic nerve fibers from each eye meet and partly cross over to the opposite side of the brain.

When the numbers of rods and cones are combined, there are over 130 million receptor cells in each retina. However, there are only about 1 million ganglion cells. How do just 1 million ganglion cells transmit messages from 130 million visual receptor cells?

Visual Processing in the Retina

Information from the sensory receptors, the rods and cones, is first collected by specialized neurons, called **bipolar cells** (see the lower part of Figure 3.3 on page 90). The bipolar cells then funnel the collection of raw data to the ganglion cells. Each ganglion cell receives information from the *photoreceptors* that are located in its *receptive field* in a particular area of the retina. In this early stage of visual processing, each ganglion cell combines, analyzes, and encodes the information from the photoreceptors in its receptive field before transmitting the information to the brain (Masland, 2001).

Signals from rods and signals from cones are processed differently in the ganglion cells. For the most part, a single ganglion cell receives information from only one or two cones but might well receive information from a hundred or more rods. The messages from these many different rods are combined in the retina before they are sent to the brain. Thus, the brain receives less specific visual information from the rods and messages of much greater visual detail from the cones.

As an analogy to how rod information is processed, imagine listening to a hundred people trying to talk at once over the same telephone line. You would hear the sound of many people talking, but individual voices would be blurred. Now imagine listening to the voice of a single individual being transmitted across the same telephone line. Every syllable and sound would be clear and distinct. In much the same way, cones use the ganglion cells to provide the brain with more specific visual information than is received from rods.

Because of this difference in how information is processed, cones are especially important in *visual acuity*—the ability to see fine details. Visual acuity is strongest when images are focused on the fovea because of the high concentration of cones there.

FIGURE 3.5 Neural Pathways from Eye to Brain The bundled axons of the ganglion cells form the optic nerve, which exits the retina at the optic disk. The optic nerves from the left and right eyes meet at the optic chiasm, then split apart. One set of nerve fibers crosses over and projects to the opposite side of the brain, and another set of nerve fibers continues along the same side of the brain. Most of the nerve fibers travel to the thalamus and then on to the visual cortex of the occipital lobe.

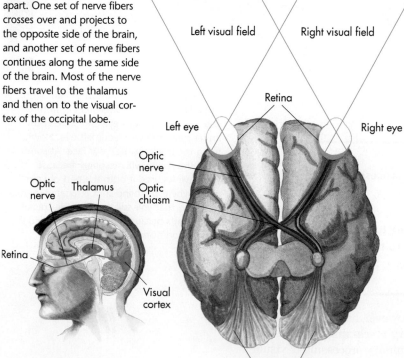

From Eye to Brain

How is information transmitted from the ganglion cells of the retina to the brain? The 1 million axons of the ganglion cells are bundled together to form the **optic nerve,** a thick nerve that exits from the back of the eye at the optic disk and extends to the brain (see Figure 3.5). The optic nerve has about the same diameter as a pencil. After exiting the eyes, the left and right optic nerves meet at the **optic chiasm.** Then the fibers of the left and right optic nerves split in two. One set of axons crosses over and projects to the opposite side of the brain. The other set of axons forms a pathway that continues along the same side of the brain (see Figure 3.5).

From the optic chiasm, most of the optic nerve axons project to the brain structure called the *thalamus.* This primary pathway seems to be responsible for processing information about form, color, brightness, and depth. A smaller number of axons follow a detour to areas in the *midbrain* before they make their way to the thalamus. This secondary pathway seems to be involved in processing information about the location of an object.

Neuroscience: Vision, Experience, and the Brain

(a)
Normal Control

(b)
Mike May

Scanning Mike's Brain The red, orange, and yellow colors In the left fMRI scan show the areas of the occipital lobe that are normally activated in response to faces. Blue and purple indicate the typical pattern of brain activity in response to objects. In contrast to a normal sighted individual, Mike's fMRI scan on the right shows only slight brain activation in response to objects and virtually no response to faces.

After Mike's surgery, his retina and optic nerve were completely normal. Formal testing showed that Mike had excellent color perception and that he could easily identify simple shapes and lines that were oriented in different directions. These abilities correspond to visual pathways that develop very early. Mike's motion perception was also very good. When thrown a ball, he could catch it more than 80 percent of the time.

Perceiving and identifying common objects, however, was difficult. Although Mike could "see" the object, he had to consciously use visual cues to work out its identity. For example, when shown the simple drawing above right, called a "Necker cube,"

Necker Cube Shown a stationary image of a Necker cube, Mike described it as "a square with lines." Only when the image began to rotate did Mike perceive it as a drawing of a cube.

Necker Cube

Mike described it as "a square with lines." But when shown the same image as a rotating image on a computer screen, Mike immediately identified it as a cube. Functional MRI scans showed that Mike's brain activity was nearly normal when shown a *moving* object.

What about more complex objects, like faces? Even three years after his surgery, Mike recognizes his wife and sons by their hair color, gait, and other clues, not by their faces. He can't tell whether a face is male or female, or whether its expression is happy or sad. Functional MRI scans revealed that when Mike is shown faces or objects, the part of the brain that is normally activated is silent (see brain scans).

For people with normal vision, recognizing complex three-dimensional objects—like tables, shoes, trees, or pencils—is automatic. But as Mike's story shows, these perceptual conclusions are actually based on experience and built up over time.

Neuroscientist Ione Fine and her colleagues (2003), who have studied Mike's visual abilities, believe that Mike's case indicates that some visual pathways develop earlier than others. Color and motion perception, they point out, develop early in infancy. But because people will continue to encounter new objects and faces throughout life, areas of the brain that are specialized to process faces and objects show plasticity. In Mike's case, these brain centers aren't developed.

Neuroscientists now know that there are several distinct neural pathways in the visual system, each responsible for handling a different aspect of vision (Zeki, 2001). Although specialized, the separate pathways are highly interconnected. From the thalamus, the signals are sent to the *visual cortex*, where they are decoded and interpreted.

Most of the receiving neurons in the visual cortex of the brain are highly specialized. Each responds to a particular type of visual stimulation, such as angles, edges, lines, and other forms, and even to the movement and distance of objects (Hubel, 1995; Livingstone & Hubel, 1988). These neurons are sometimes called *feature detectors* because they detect, or respond to, particular features or aspects of more complex visual stimuli. Reassembling the features into a recognizable image involves additional levels of processing in the visual cortex and other regions of the brain, including the *frontal lobes*.

Understanding exactly how neural responses of individual feature detection cells become integrated into the visual perceptions of faces and objects is a major goal in contemporary neuroscience (Palmeri & Gauthier, 2004; Cohen & Tong, 2001). As the Focus on Neuroscience illustrates, experience plays a key role in perception.

Color Vision

We see images of an apple, a banana, and an orange because these objects reflect light waves. But why do we perceive that the apple is red and the banana yellow? What makes an orange orange?

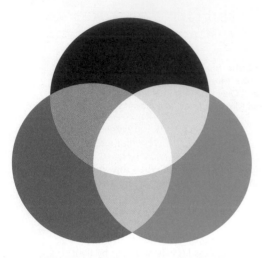

When Red + Blue + Green = White When light waves of different wavelengths are combined, the wavelengths are added together, producing the perception of a different color. Thus, when green light is combined with red light, yellow light is produced. When the wavelengths of red, green, and blue light are added together, we perceive the blended light as white.

color
The perceptual experience of different wavelengths of light, involving hue, saturation (purity), and brightness (intensity).

hue
The property of wavelengths of light known as color; different wavelengths correspond to our subjective experience of different colors.

saturation
The property of color that corresponds to the purity of the light wave.

brightness
The perceived intensity of a color, which corresponds to the amplitude of the light wave.

trichromatic theory of color vision
The theory that the sensation of color results because cones in the retina are especially sensitive to red light (long wavelengths), green light (medium wavelengths), or blue light (short wavelengths).

The Experience of Color
What Makes an Orange Orange?

To explain the nature of color, we must go back to the visual stimulus—light. Our experience of **color** involves three properties of the light wave. First, what we usually refer to as color is a property more accurately termed **hue.** Hue varies with the wavelength of light. Look again at Figure 3.2 on page 89. *Different wavelengths correspond to our subjective experience of different colors.* Wavelengths of about 400 nanometers are perceived as violet. Wavelengths of about 700 nanometers are perceived as red. In between are orange, yellow, green, blue, and indigo.

Second, the **saturation,** or *purity,* of the color corresponds to the purity of the light wave. Pure red, for example, produced by a single wavelength, is more *saturated* than pink, which is produced by a combination of wavelengths (red plus white light). In everyday language, saturation refers to the richness of a color. A highly saturated color is vivid and rich, whereas a less saturated color is faded and washed out.

The third property of color is **brightness,** or perceived intensity. Brightness corresponds to the amplitude of the light wave: the higher the amplitude, the greater the degree of brightness.

These three properties of color—hue, saturation, and brightness—are responsible for the amazing range of colors we experience. A person with normal color vision can discriminate from 120 to 150 color differences based on differences in hue, or wavelength, alone. When saturation and brightness are also factored in, we can potentially perceive millions of different colors (Bornstein & Marks, 1982).

Many people mistakenly believe that white light contains no color. White light actually contains all wavelengths, and thus all colors, of the visible part of the electromagnetic spectrum. A glass prism placed in sunlight creates a rainbow because it separates sunlight into all the colors of the visible light spectrum.

So we're back to the question: Why is an orange orange? Common sense tells us that the color of any object is an inseparable property of the object (unless we paint it, dye it, or spill spaghetti sauce on it). But, actually, *the color of an object is determined by the wavelength of light that the object reflects.* If your T-shirt is red, it's red because the cloth is *reflecting* only the wavelength of light that corresponds to the red portion of the spectrum. The T-shirt is *absorbing* the wavelengths that correspond to all other colors. An object appears white because it *reflects* all the wavelengths of visible light and absorbs none. An object appears black when it *absorbs* all the wavelengths of visible light and reflects none.

How We See Color

Color vision has interested scientists for hundreds of years. The first scientific theory of color vision, proposed by Hermann von Helmholtz (1821–1894) in the mid-1800s, was called the *trichromatic theory.* A rival theory, the *opponent-process theory,* was proposed in the late 1800s. Each theory was capable of explaining some aspects of color vision, but neither theory could explain all aspects of color vision. Technological advances in the last few decades have allowed researchers to gather direct physiological evidence to test both theories. The resulting evidence indicates that *both* theories of color vision are accurate. Each theory describes color vision at a different stage of visual processing (Hubel, 1995).

The Trichromatic Theory As you'll recall, only the cones are involved in color vision. According to the **trichromatic theory of color vision,** there are three varieties of cones. Each type of cone is especially sensitive to certain wavelengths— red light (long wavelengths), green light (medium wavelengths), and blue light (short wavelengths). For the sake of simplicity, we will refer to red-sensitive, green-sensitive, and blue-sensitive cones, but keep in mind that there is some

The Most Common Form of Color Blindness
To someone with red–green color blindness, these two photographs look almost exactly the same. People with this form of color blindness have normal blue-sensitive cones, but their other cones are sensitive to either red *or* green. Because of the way red–green color blindness is genetically transmitted, it is much more common in men than in women. People who are completely color blind and see the world only in shades of black, white, and gray are extremely rare—only one in a million people suffers from this disorder (Hurvich, 1981).

overlap in the wavelengths to which a cone is sensitive (Abramov & Gordon, 1994). A given cone will be *very* sensitive to one of the three colors and only slightly responsive to the other two.

When a color other than red, green, or blue strikes the retina, it stimulates a *combination* of cones. For example, if yellow light strikes the retina, both the red-sensitive and green-sensitive cones are stimulated; purple light evokes strong reactions from red-sensitive and blue-sensitive cones. The trichromatic theory of color vision received compelling research support in 1964, when George Wald showed that different cones were indeed activated by red, blue, and green light.

The trichromatic theory provides a good explanation for the most common form of **color blindness:** red–green color blindness. People with red–green color blindness cannot discriminate between red and green. That's because they have normal blue-sensitive cones, but their other cones are *either* red-sensitive or green-sensitive. Thus, red and green look the same to them. Because red–green color blindness is so common, stoplights are designed so that the location of the light as well as its color provides information to drivers. In vertical stoplights the red light is always on top, and in horizontal stoplights the red light is always on the far left.

The Opponent-Process Theory   The trichromatic theory cannot account for all aspects of color vision. One important phenomenon that the theory does not explain is the afterimage. An **afterimage** is a visual experience that occurs after the original source of stimulation is no longer present. To experience an afterimage firsthand, follow the instructions in Figure 3.6. What do you see?

Afterimages can be explained by the opponent-process theory of color vision, which proposes a different mechanism of color detection from the one set forth in the trichromatic theory. According to the **opponent-process theory of color vision,** there are four basic colors, which are divided into two pairs of color-sensitive neurons: red–green and blue–yellow. The members of each pair *oppose* each other. If red is stimulated, green is inhibited; if green is stimulated, red is inhibited. Green and red cannot both be stimulated simultaneously. The same is true for the blue–yellow pair. In addition, black and white act as an opposing pair. Color, then, is sensed and encoded in terms of its proportion of red OR green, and blue OR yellow.

For example, red light evokes a response of RED-YES–GREEN-NO in the red–green opponent pair. Yellow light evokes a response of BLUE-NO–YELLOW-YES. Colors other than red, green, blue, and yellow activate one member of each of these pairs to differing degrees. Purple stimulates the *red* of the red–green pair plus the *blue* of the blue–yellow pair. Orange activates *red* in the red–green pair and *yellow* in the blue–yellow pair.

Afterimages can be explained when the opponent-process theory is combined with the general principle of sensory

color blindness
One of several inherited forms of color deficiency or weakness in which an individual cannot distinguish between certain colors.

afterimage
A visual experience that occurs after the original source of stimulation is no longer present.

opponent-process theory of color vision
The theory that color vision is the product of opposing pairs of color receptors, red–green, blue–yellow, and black–white; when one member of a color pair is stimulated, the other member is inhibited.

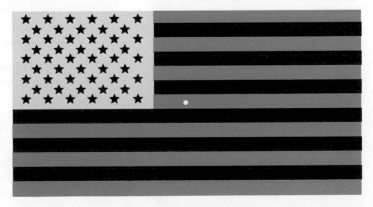

FIGURE 3.6 Demonstration of Afterimage
Stare at the white dot in the center of this oddly colored flag for about 30 seconds, and then look at a white wall or white sheet of paper. What do you see?

adaptation (Jameson & Hurvich, 1989). If you stare continuously at one color, sensory adaptation eventually occurs and your visual receptors become less sensitive to that color. What happens when you subsequently stare at a white surface?

If you remember that white light is made up of the wavelengths for *all* colors, you may be able to predict the result. The receptors for the original color have adapted to the constant stimulation and are temporarily "off duty." Thus they do not respond to that color. Instead, only the receptors for the opposing color will be activated, and you perceive the wavelength of only the *opposing* color. For example, if you stare at a patch of green, your green receptors eventually become "tired." The wavelengths for both green and red light are reflected by the white surface, but since the green receptors are "off," only the red receptors are activated. Staring at the green, black, and yellow flag in Figure 3.6 should have produced an afterimage of opposing colors: a red, white, and blue American flag.

An Integrated Explanation of Color Vision   At the beginning of this section we said that current research has shown that *both* the trichromatic theory and the opponent-process theory of color vision are accurate. How can both theories be right? It turns out that each theory correctly describes color vision at a *different level* of visual processing.

As described by the *trichromatic theory,* the cones of the retina do indeed respond to and encode color in terms of red, green, and blue. But recall that signals from the cones and rods are partially processed in the ganglion cells before being transmitted along the optic nerve to the brain. Researchers now believe that an additional level of color processing takes place in the ganglion cells.

As described by the *opponent-process theory,* the ganglion cells respond to and encode color in terms of opposing pairs (DeValois & DeValois, 1975). In the brain, the thalamus and visual cortex also encode color in terms of opponent pairs (Engel, 1999). Consequently, both theories contribute to our understanding of the process of color vision. Each theory simply describes color vision at a different stage of visual processing (Hubel, 1995).

Hearing
From Vibration to Sound

Key Theme
■ Auditory sensation, or hearing, results when sound waves are collected in the outer ear, amplified in the middle ear, and converted to neural messages in the inner ear.

Key Questions
■ How do sound waves produce different auditory sensations?
■ What are the key structures of the ear and their functions?
■ How do place theory and frequency theory explain pitch perception?

We have hiked in a desert area that was so quiet we could hear the whir of a single grasshopper's wings in the distance. And we have waited on a subway platform where the screech of metal wheels against metal rails forced us to cover our ears. The sense of hearing, or **audition,** is capable of responding to a wide range of sounds, from faint to blaring, simple to complex, harmonious to discordant. The ability to sense and perceive very subtle differences in sound is important to physical survival, social interactions, and language development. Most of the time, all of us are bathed in sound—so much so that moments of near-silence, like our experience in the desert, can seem almost eerie.

---

audition
The technical term for the sense of hearing.

loudness
The intensity (or amplitude) of a sound wave, measured in decibels.

amplitude
The intensity or amount of energy of a wave, reflected in the height of the wave; the amplitude of a sound wave determines a sound's loudness.

decibel
(DESS-uh-bell) The unit of measurement for loudness.

pitch
The relative highness or lowness of a sound, determined by the frequency of a sound wave.

frequency
The rate of vibration, or the number of sound waves per second.

timbre
(TAM-ber) The distinctive quality of a sound, determined by the complexity of the sound wave.

outer ear
The part of the ear that collects sound waves; consists of the pinna, the ear canal, and the eardrum.

eardrum
A tightly stretched membrane at the end of the ear canal that vibrates when hit by sound waves.

middle ear
The part of the ear that amplifies sound waves; consists of three small bones: the hammer, the anvil, and the stirrup.

inner ear
The part of the ear where sound is transduced into neural impulses; consists of the cochlea and semicircular canals.

cochlea
(COCK-lee-uh) The coiled, fluid-filled inner-ear structure that contains the basilar membrane and hair cells.

What We Hear

The Nature of Sound

Whether it's the ear-splitting screech of metal on metal or the subtle whir of a grasshopper's wings, *sound waves* are the physical stimuli that produce our sensory experience of sound. Usually, sound waves are produced by the rhythmic vibration of air molecules, but sound waves can be transmitted through other media, too, such as water. Our perception of sound is directly related to the physical properties of sound waves (see Figure 3.7).

One of the first things that we notice about a sound is how loud it is. **Loudness** is determined by the intensity, or **amplitude,** of a sound wave and is measured in units called **decibels.** Zero decibel represents the loudness of the softest sound that humans can hear, or the absolute threshold for hearing. As decibels increase, perceived loudness increases.

Pitch refers to the relative "highness" or "lowness" of a sound. Pitch is determined by the frequency of a sound wave. **Frequency** refers to the rate of vibration, or number of waves per second, and is measured in units called *hertz.* Hertz simply refers to the number of wave peaks per second. The faster the vibration, the higher the frequency, the closer together the waves are—and the higher the tone produced. If you pluck the high E and the low E strings on a guitar, you'll notice that the low E vibrates far fewer times per second than does the high E.

Most of the sounds we experience do not consist of a single frequency but are *complex,* consisting of several sound-wave frequencies. This combination of frequencies produces the distinctive quality, or **timbre,** of a sound, which enables us to distinguish easily between the same note played on a saxophone and on a piano. Every human voice has its own distinctive timbre, which is why you can immediately identify a friend's voice on the telephone from just a few words, even if you haven't talked to each other for years.

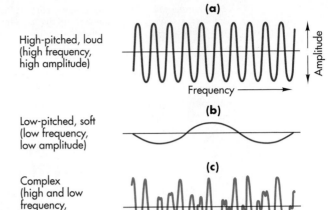

High-pitched, loud (high frequency, high amplitude)

Low-pitched, soft (low frequency, low amplitude)

Complex (high and low frequency, high and low amplitude)

FIGURE 3.7 Characteristics of Sound Waves The length of a wave, its height, and its complexity determine the loudness, pitch, and timbre that we hear. The sound produced by **(a)** would be high-pitched and loud. The sound produced by **(b)** would be soft and low. The sound in **(c)** is complex, like the sounds we usually experience in the natural world.

How We Hear

The Path of Sound

The ear is made up of the outer ear, the middle ear, and the inner ear. Sound waves are *collected* in the outer ear, *amplified* in the middle ear, and *transduced,* or *transformed into neural messages,* in the inner ear (see Figure 3.8 on page 98).

The **outer ear** includes the *pinna,* the *ear canal,* and the *eardrum.* The pinna is that oddly shaped flap of skin and cartilage that's attached to each side of your head. The pinna helps us pinpoint the location of a sound. But the pinna's primary role is to catch sound waves and funnel them into the ear canal. The sound wave travels down the ear canal, then bounces into the **eardrum,** a tightly stretched membrane. When the sound wave hits the eardrum, the eardrum vibrates, matching the vibrations of the sound wave in intensity and frequency.

The eardrum separates the outer ear from the **middle ear.** The eardrum's vibration is transferred to three tiny bones in the middle ear—the *hammer,* the *anvil,* and the *stirrup.* Each bone sets the next bone in motion. The joint action of these three bones almost doubles the amplification of the sound. The innermost bone, the stirrup, transmits the amplified vibration to the *oval window.* If the tiny bones of the middle ear are damaged or become brittle, as they sometimes do in old age, *conduction deafness* may result. Conduction deafness can be helped by a hearing aid, which amplifies sounds.

Like the eardrum, the oval window is a membrane, but it is many times smaller than the eardrum. The oval window separates the middle ear from the **inner ear.** As the oval window vibrates, the vibration is next relayed to an inner structure called the **cochlea,** a fluid-filled tube that's coiled in a spiral. The word *cochlea* comes from the Greek word for "snail," and the spiral shape of the cochlea does resemble a snail's shell. Although the cochlea is a very complex structure, it is quite tiny—no larger than a pea.

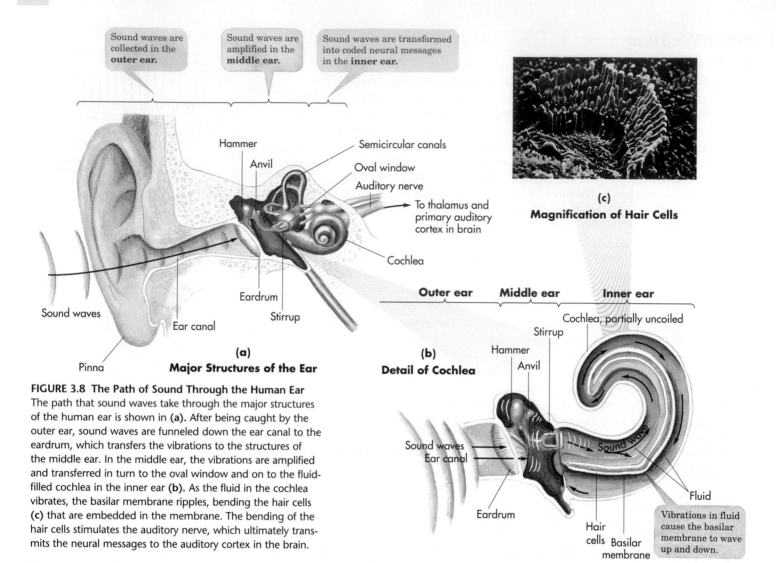

(c)
Magnification of Hair Cells

(a)
Major Structures of the Ear

(b)
Detail of Cochlea

FIGURE 3.8 The Path of Sound Through the Human Ear
The path that sound waves take through the major structures of the human ear is shown in **(a)**. After being caught by the outer ear, sound waves are funneled down the ear canal to the eardrum, which transfers the vibrations to the structures of the middle ear. In the middle ear, the vibrations are amplified and transferred in turn to the oval window and on to the fluid-filled cochlea in the inner ear **(b)**. As the fluid in the cochlea vibrates, the basilar membrane ripples, bending the hair cells **(c)** that are embedded in the membrane. The bending of the hair cells stimulates the auditory nerve, which ultimately transmits the neural messages to the auditory cortex in the brain.

Table 3.2

Decibel Level of Some Common Sounds

Decibels	Examples	Exposure Danger
180	Rocket launching pad	Hearing loss inevitable
140	Shotgun blast, jet plane	Any exposure is dangerous
120	Speakers at rock concert, sandblasting, thunderclap	Immediate danger
100	Chain saw, pneumatic drill	2 hours
90	Truck traffic, noisy home appliances, lawn mower	Less than 8 hours
80	Subway, heavy city traffic, alarm clock at 2 feet	More than 8 hours
70	Busy traffic, noisy restaurant	Critical level begins with constant exposure
60	Air conditioner at 20 feet, conversation, sewing machine	
50	Light traffic at a distance, refrigerator	
40	Quiet office, living room	
30	Quiet library, soft whisper	
0	Lowest sound audible to human ear	

As the fluid in the cochlea ripples, the vibration in turn is transmitted to the **basilar membrane,** which runs the length of the coiled cochlea. Embedded in the basilar membrane are the sensory receptors for sound, called **hair cells,** which have tiny, projecting fibers that look like hairs. Damage to the hair cells or auditory nerve can result in *nerve deafness,* which cannot be helped by a hearing aid. Exposure to loud noise can cause nerve deafness (see Table 3.2).

The hair cells bend as the basilar membrane ripples. It is here that transduction finally takes place: The physical vibration of the sound waves is converted into neural impulses. As the hair cells bend, they stimulate the cells of the auditory nerve, which carries the neural information to the thalamus and the auditory cortex in the brain.

The Chemical and Body Senses
Smell, Taste, Touch, and Position

Key Theme
■ Chemical stimuli produce the sensations of smell and taste, while pressure and other stimuli are involved in touch, pain, position, and balance sensations.

Key Questions
■ How do airborne molecules result in the sensation of an odor?
■ What are the primary tastes, and how does the sensation of taste arise?
■ How do fast and slow pain systems differ, and what is the gate-control theory of pain?
■ How are body sensations of movement, position, and balance produced?

The Chemical Senses: Smell and Taste Andrea Immer, the Dean of Wine Studies at the world-famous French Culinary Institute in New York City, is one of only ten women in the world to hold the title of Master Sommelier. Why does she sniff the wine before tasting it? Professional (and amateur) wine-tasters are keenly aware of the fact that the senses of smell and taste are closely intertwined. Specialized receptors in the nasal passages are able to detect the subtle aromas that differentiate among fine wines. A wine expert relies as much on her sense of smell as she does her sense of taste to evaluate the wine's overall quality (Simons & Noble, 2003).

The senses of smell and taste are closely linked. If you've ever temporarily lost your sense of smell because of a bad cold, you've probably noticed that your sense of taste was also disrupted. Even a hot fudge sundae tastes bland.

Smell and taste are linked in other ways, too. Unlike vision and hearing, which involve sensitivity to different forms of energy, the sensory receptors for taste and smell are specialized to respond to different types of *chemical* substances. That's why smell, or **olfaction,** and taste, or **gustation,** are sometimes called the "chemical senses" (Mombaerts, 2004).

People can get along quite well without a sense of smell. A surprisingly large number of people are unable to smell specific odors or lack a sense of smell completely, a condition called *anosmia.* Fortunately, humans gather most of their information about the world through vision and hearing. However, many animal species depend on chemical signals as their primary source of information.

Even for humans, smell and taste can provide important information about the environment. Tastes help us determine whether a particular substance is to be savored or spat out. Smells, such as the odor of a smoldering fire, leaking gas, or spoiled food, alert us to potential dangers.

How We Smell (Don't Answer That!)

The sensory stimuli that produce our sensation of an odor are *molecules in the air.* These airborne molecules are emitted by the substance we are smelling. We inhale them through the nose and through the opening in the palate at the back of the throat. In the nose, the molecules encounter millions of *olfactory receptor cells* located high in the nasal cavity.

Unlike the sensory receptors for hearing and vision, the olfactory receptors are constantly being replaced. Each cell lasts for only about 30 to 60 days. In 1991, neuroscientists Linda Buck and Richard Axel identified the odor receptors that are present on the hairlike fibers of the olfactory neurons. Like synaptic receptors, each odor receptor seems to be specialized to respond to molecules of a different chemical structure. When these olfactory receptor cells are stimulated by the airborne molecules, the stimulation is converted into neural messages that pass along their axons, bundles of which make up the *olfactory nerve.*

So far, hundreds of different odor receptors have been identified (Mombaerts, 2004). We don't have a separate receptor for each of the estimated 10,000 different odors that we can detect, however. Rather, each receptor is like a letter in an olfactory alphabet. Just as different combinations of letters in the alphabet are used to produce recognizable words, different combinations of olfactory receptors produce the sensation of distinct odors. Thus, the airborne molecules activate specific combinations of receptors. In turn, the brain identifies an odor by interpreting the *pattern* of olfactory receptors that are stimulated (Buck, 2000).

basilar membrane
(BAZ-uh-ler or BAZE-uh-ler) The membrane within the cochlea of the ear that contains the hair cells.

hair cells
The hairlike sensory receptors for sound, which are embedded in the basilar membrane of the cochlea.

olfaction
Technical name for the sense of smell.

gustation
Technical name for the sense of taste.

IN FOCUS 3.2

Do Pheromones Influence Human Behavior?

Many animals communicate by releasing **pheromones,** chemical signals that provide information about social and sexual status to other members of the same species (Dulac & Torello, 2003). Pheromones may mark territories and serve as warning signals to other members of the same species (Agosta, 1992). Ants use pheromones to mark trails for other ants, as do snakes and snails (Dusenberry, 1992). Pheromones are also extremely important in regulating sexual attraction, mating, and reproductive behavior in many animals (Dulac & Torello, 2003). A lusty male cabbage moth, for example, can detect pheromones released from a sexually receptive female cabbage moth that is several miles away.

Do humans produce pheromones as other animals do? The best evidence for the existence of human pheromones comes from studies of the female menstrual cycle by University of Chicago biopsychologist Martha McClintock (1992). While still a college student, McClintock (1971) set out to scientifically investigate the folk notion that women who live in the same dorm eventually develop synchronized menstrual periods. McClintock was able to show that the more time women spent together, the more likely their cycles were to be in sync.

Later research showed that smelling an unknown chemical substance in underarm sweat from female donors synchronized the recipients' menstrual cycles with

The Scent of Attraction Some perfume manufacturers claim that their products contain human pheromones that will make you "irresistible" to members of the opposite sex. But is there any evidence that pheromones affect human sexual attraction?

the donors' cycles (Preti & others, 1986; Stern & McClintock, 1998).

Since this finding, McClintock and her co-researchers have made a number of discoveries in their quest to identify human pheromones, which they prefer to call *human chemosignals.* Their search has narrowed to chemicals found in steroid compounds that are naturally produced by the human body and found in sweat, armpit hair, blood, and semen. In one study, Suma Jacob and McClintock (2000) found that exposure to the male or the female

steroid helped women maintain a positive mood after spending two hours filling out a tedious, frustrating questionnaire. Men's moods, however, tended to deteriorate after exposure to either steroid. PET scans of the women showed that exposure to the steroid increased activity in several key brain areas involved in emotion and attention, including the prefrontal cortex, amygdala, and cerebellum (Jacob & others, 2001).

No study as yet has shown that human chemosignals can function as an irresistible sexual signal (Benson, 2002). Rather than producing sexual attraction, McClintock (2001) believes, it's more likely that human chemosignals affect mood and emotional states.

Confirming this view, a new study by McClintock's lab showed that exposure to a chemical compound in the perspiration of breast-feeding mothers significantly increased sexual motivation in other, non-breast-feeding women (Spencer & others, 2004). The study's authors speculate that the presence of breast-feeding women acts as a social signal—an indicator that the social and physical environment is one in which pregnancy and breast-feeding will be supported.

Thus, rather than triggering specific behaviors, including sexual behavior, human chemosignals may be social signals, subliminally affecting social interactions and relationships in ways that we don't consciously recognize.

---

pheromones
Chemical signals released by an animal that communicate information and affect the behavior of other animals of the same species.

olfactory bulb
(ole-FACK-toe-ree) The enlarged ending of the olfactory cortex at the front of the brain where the sensation of smell is registered.

taste buds
The specialized sensory receptors for taste that are located on the tongue and inside the mouth and throat.

As shown in Figure 3.9, the olfactory nerves directly connect to the **olfactory bulb** in the brain, which is actually the enlarged ending of the *olfactory cortex* at the front of the brain. Axons from the olfactory bulb form the *olfactory tract.* These neural pathways project to different brain areas, including the temporal lobe and structures in the limbic system (Angier, 1995). The projections to the *temporal lobe* are thought to be part of the neural pathway involved in our conscious recognition of smells. The projections to the *limbic system* are thought to regulate our emotional response to odors.

The direct connection of olfactory receptor cells to areas of the cortex and limbic system is unique to our sense of smell. As discussed in Chapter 2, all other bodily sensations are first processed in the thalamus before being relayed to the higher brain centers in the cortex. Olfactory neurons are unique in another way, too. They are the only neurons that *directly* link the brain and the outside world (Axel, 1995). The axons of the sensory neurons that are located in your nose extend directly into your brain!

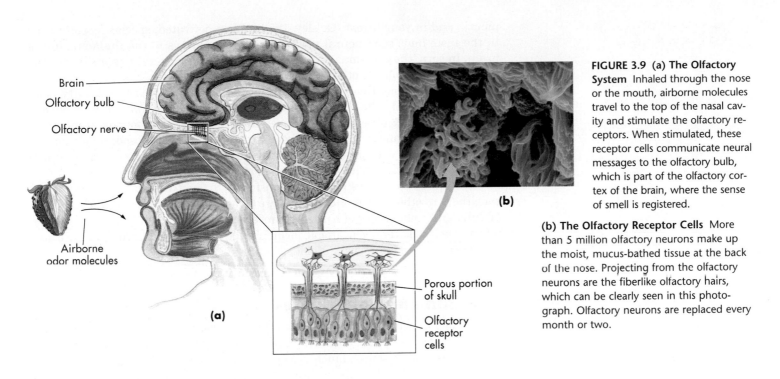

(a)

(b)

Brain
Olfactory bulb
Olfactory nerve

Airborne
odor molecules

Porous portion
of skull

Olfactory
receptor
cells

FIGURE 3.9 (a) The Olfactory System Inhaled through the nose or the mouth, airborne molecules travel to the top of the nasal cavity and stimulate the olfactory receptors. When stimulated, these receptor cells communicate neural messages to the olfactory bulb, which is part of the olfactory cortex of the brain, where the sense of smell is registered.

(b) The Olfactory Receptor Cells More than 5 million olfactory neurons make up the moist, mucus-bathed tissue at the back of the nose. Projecting from the olfactory neurons are the fiberlike olfactory hairs, which can be clearly seen in this photograph. Olfactory neurons are replaced every month or two.

As with the other senses, we experience sensory adaptation to odors when exposed to them for a period of time. In general, we reach maximum adaptation to an odor in less than a minute. We continue to smell the odor, but we have become about 70 percent less sensitive to it.

Taste
This Bud's for You!

Our sense of taste, or *gustation,* results from the stimulation of special receptors in the mouth. The stimuli that produce the sensation of taste are chemical substances in whatever you eat or drink. These substances are dissolved by saliva, allowing the chemicals to activate the **taste buds.** Each taste bud contains about 50 receptor cells that are specialized for taste.

The surface of the tongue is covered with thousands of little bumps with grooves in between (see Figure 3.10). These grooves are lined with the taste buds. Taste buds are also located on the insides of your cheeks, on the roof of your

FIGURE 3.10 Taste Buds (a) The photograph shows the surface of the tongue magnified hundreds of times. Taste buds are located in the grooves of the bumps on the surface of the tongue. **(b)** Embedded in the surface of the tongue are thousands of taste buds, the sensory receptor organs for taste. Each taste bud contains an average of 50 taste receptor cells. When activated, the taste receptor cells send messages to adjoining sensory neurons, which relay the information to the brain. Taste buds, like the olfactory neurons, are constantly being replaced. The life expectancy of a particular taste bud is only about 10 days.

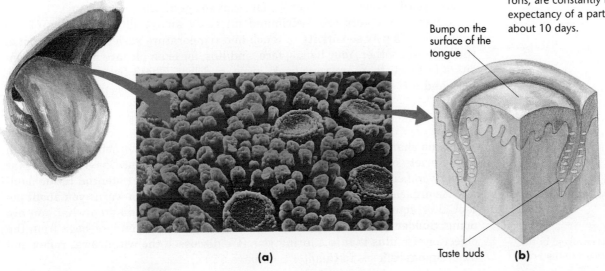

Bump on the
surface of the
tongue

Taste buds

(a)

(b)

mouth, and in your throat (Oakley, 1986). When activated, special receptor cells in the taste buds send neural messages along pathways to the thalamus in the brain. In turn, the thalamus directs the information to several regions in the cortex (O'Doherty, Rolls, & others, 2001b).

There were long thought to be four basic taste categories: sweet, salty, sour, and bitter. Recently, the receptor cells for a fifth basic taste, *umami,* were identified (Chaudhari & others, 2000). Loosely translated, *umami* means "yummy" or "delicious" in Japanese. *Umami* is the distinctive taste of monosodium glutamate and is associated with protein-rich foods and the savory flavor of Parmesan and other aged cheeses, mushrooms, seaweed, and meat.

Each taste bud shows maximum sensitivity to one particular taste and lesser sensitivity to other tastes. Most tastes are complex and result from the activation of different combinations of basic taste receptors. Taste is just one aspect of *flavor,* which involves several sensations, including the aroma, temperature, texture, and appearance of food (Simons & Noble, 2003).

The Skin and Body Senses

While vision, hearing, smell, and taste provide you with important information about your environment, another group of senses provides you with information that comes from a source much closer to home: your own body. In this section, we'll first consider the *skin senses,* which provide essential information about your physical status and your physical interaction with objects in your environment. We'll next consider the *body senses,* which keep you informed as to your position and orientation in space.

Touch

We usually don't think of our skin as a sense organ. But the skin is in fact the largest and heaviest sense organ. The skin of an average adult covers about 20 square feet of surface area and weighs about six pounds.

There are many different kinds of sensory receptors in the skin. Some of these sensory receptors are specialized to respond to just one kind of stimulus, such as pressure, warmth, or cold. Other skin receptors respond to more than one type of stimulus (Patapoutian & others, 2003).

One important receptor involved with the sense of touch, called the *Pacinian corpuscle,* is located beneath the skin. When stimulated by pressure, the Pacinian corpuscle converts the stimulation into a neural message that is relayed to the brain. If a pressure is constant, sensory adaptation takes place. The Pacinian corpuscle either reduces the number of signals sent or quits responding altogether (which is fortunate, or you'd be unable to forget the fact that you're wearing underwear).

Sensory receptors are distributed unevenly among different areas of the body, which is why sensitivity to touch and temperature varies from one area of the body to another. Your hands, face, and lips, for example, are much more sensitive to touch than are your back, arms, and legs. That's because your hands, face, and lips are much more densely packed with sensory receptors.

Pain

From the sharp sting of a paper cut to the dull ache of a throbbing headache, a wide variety of stimuli can trigger pain. **Pain** can be defined as an unpleasant sensory and emotional experience associated with actual or potential tissue damage. As unpleasant as it can be, pain helps you survive. Pain warns you about potential or actual injury, prompting you to pay attention and stop what you are doing. Sudden pain can trigger the withdrawal reflex as you jerk back from the object or stimulus that is injuring you. (We discussed the withdrawal reflex and other spinal reflexes in Chapter 2 on page 51.)

pain
The unpleasant sensation of physical discomfort or suffering that can occur in varying degrees of intensity.

nociceptors
Specialized sensory receptors for pain that are found in the skin, muscles, and internal organs.

substance P
A neurotransmitter that is involved in the transmission of pain messages to the brain.

Your body's pain receptors are called **nociceptors.** Nociceptors are actually small sensory fibers, called *free nerve endings,* in the skin, muscles, or internal organs. You have millions of nociceptors throughout your body, mostly in your skin (see Table 3.3). For example, your fingertips may have as many as 1,200 nociceptors per square inch. Your muscles and joints have fewer nociceptors. And, your internal organs have the smallest number of nociceptors.

Fast and Slow Pain Systems   To help illustrate pain pathways, imagine this scene: Don was trying to close a stuck window in our old house. As he wrapped his left hand on the top of the window and used his right hand to push down the lower edge, it suddenly came free and slammed shut, jamming his left fingertips between the upper and lower windows. As pain shot through him, he jerked the window back up to dislodge his mangled fingers, then headed to the kitchen for ice.

Don took little comfort in knowing that his injury had triggered two types of nociceptors: *A-delta fibers* and *C fibers*. The myelinated *A-delta fibers* represent the fast pain system. A-delta fibers transmit the sharp, intense, but short-lived pain of the immediate injury. The smaller, unmyelinated *C fibers* represent the slow pain system. As the sharp pain subsides, C fibers transmit the longer-lasting throbbing, burning pain of the injury (Hunt & Mantyh, 2001). The throbbing pain carried by the C fibers gradually diminishes as a wound heals over a period of days or weeks.

As shown in Figure 3.11, both the fast A-delta fibers and the slow C fibers transmit their messages to the spinal cord. Several neurotransmitters are involved in processing pain signals, but most C fibers produce a pain enhancer called substance P. **Substance P** stimulates free nerve endings at the site of the injury and also increases pain messages within the spinal cord (Budai, 2000).

Most of these messages from C fibers and A-delta fibers cross to the other side of the spinal cord, then to the brain. The fast pain messages travel to the thalamus, then to the somatosensory cortex, where the sensory aspects of the pain message is interpreted, such as the location and intensity of the pain. Interestingly, morphine and other opiates have virtually no effect on the fast pain system.

Table 3.3
Sensitivity of Different Body Areas to Pain

Most Sensitive	Least Sensitive
Back of the knee	Tip of the nose
Neck region	Sole of the foot
Bend of the elbow	Ball of the thumb

SOURCE: Geldard (1972)

FIGURE 3.11 Fast and Slow Pain Pathways
The fast pain pathway consists of myelinated A-delta fibers, shown in red, which project first to the thalamus and then on to the somatosensory cortex. Signals carried along this pathway produce the sensory aspects of pain—the sharp but short-lived pain of an immediate injury. In contrast, the slow pain pathway consists of unmyelinated C fibers, shown in blue. The slow pain pathway is much more involved with the emotional aspects of pain. The C fibers project to the thalamus and hypothalamus, then to limbic system structures, including the amygdala.

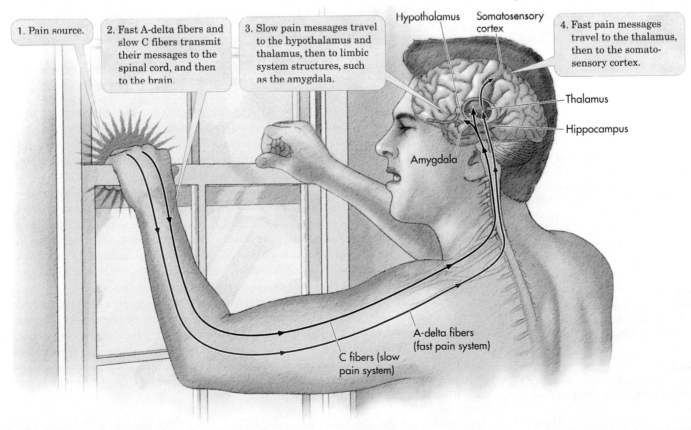

1. Pain source.

2. Fast A-delta fibers and slow C fibers transmit their messages to the spinal cord, and then to the brain.

3. Slow pain messages travel to the hypothalamus and thalamus, then to limbic system structures, such as the amygdala.

4. Fast pain messages travel to the thalamus, then to the somatosensory cortex.

Hypothalamus

Somatosensory cortex

Thalamus

Hippocampus

Amygdala

A-delta fibers (fast pain system)

C fibers (slow pain system)

Red-Headed Women and Pain Gender differences in pain have been extensively researched (see Fillingim, 2000). In general, women are more sensitive to pain than men. Studies also show that women respond better than men to some morphine-like pain medications called "kappa opioids" (Gear & others, 1996). Psychologist Jeffrey Mogil and his colleagues (2003) found that a gene associated with red hair and fair skin was implicated in the response to these pain medications. Women with two copies of this gene, like the three sisters above, experience much greater pain relief from kappa opioids than men or other women.

gate-control theory of pain
The theory that pain is a product of both physiological and psychological factors that cause spinal gates to open and relay patterns of intense stimulation to the brain, which perceives them as pain.

kinesthetic sense
(kin-ess-THET-ick) The technical name for the sense of location and position of body parts in relation to one another.

proprioceptors
(pro-pree-oh-SEP-ters) Sensory receptors, located in the muscles and joints, that provide information about body position and movement.

vestibular sense
(vess-TIB-you-ler) The technical name for the sense of balance, or equilibrium.

In contrast, slow pain messages follow a different route in the brain. From the spinal cord, the slow pain messages travel first to the hypothalamus and thalamus, and then to limbic system structures, such as the amygdala. Its connections to the limbic system suggest that the slow pain system is more involved in the emotional aspects of pain. Morphine and other opiates very effectively block painful sensations in the slow pain system (Lu & others, 2004).

Factors That Influence Pain "Gates" There is considerable individual variation in the experience of pain. When sensory pain signals reach the brain, the sensory information is integrated with psychological and situational information (Price, 1999). According to the **gate-control theory of pain,** depending on how the brain interprets the pain experience, it regulates pain by sending signals down the spinal cord that either open or close pain "gates," or pathways (Melzack & Wall, 1965, 1996). If, because of psychological, social, or situational factors, the brain signals the gates to open, pain is experienced or intensified. If for any of the same reasons the brain signals the gates to close, pain is reduced.

Anxiety, fear, and a sense of helplessness are just a few of the psychological factors that can intensify the experience of pain. Positive emotions, laughter, distraction, and a sense of control can reduce the perception of pain. As one example, consider the athlete who has conditioned himself or herself to minimize pain during competition. The experience of pain is also influenced by genetic factors, social and situational factors, and cultural learning experiences about the meaning of pain and how people should react to it (Mogil & others, 2003; Otis & others, 2004; Price, 2000). In the chapter Application on page 121, we discuss some helpful strategies that you can use to minimize pain.

Psychological factors also influence the release of *endorphins* and *enkephalins,* the body's natural painkillers (see Chapter 2). Endorphins and enkephalins are produced in the brain and spinal cord. They are released as part of the body's overall response to physical pain or stress. In the brain and spinal cord, endorphins and enkephalins inhibit the transmission of pain signals, including the release of substance P.

Sensitization: Unwarranted Pain One of the most frustrating aspects of pain management is that it can continue even after an injury has healed, such as after recovering from a spinal cord injury or severe burns. A striking example of this phenomenon is *phantom limb pain,* in which a person continues to experience intense painful sensations in a limb that has been amputated (Marx, 2004).

How can phantom limb pain be explained? Basically, the neurons involved in processing the pain signals undergo *sensitization.* Earlier in the chapter, we discussed *sensory adaptation,* in which sensory receptors become gradually less responsive to steady stimulation over time. Sensitization is the opposite of adaptation. In sensitization, pain pathways in the brain become increasingly *more* responsive over time (Woolf & Salter, 2000). It's like a broken volume control knob on your stereo that you can turn up, but not down or off.

As the pain circuits undergo sensitization, pain begins to occur in the absence of any sensory input. The result can be the development of persistent, *chronic pain* that continues after all indications are that the injury has healed (see Scholz & Woolf, 2002). In the case of phantom limb pain, sensitization has occurred in the pain transmission pathways from the site of the amputation. The sensitized pathways produce painful sensations that mentally feel as though they are coming from a limb that is no longer there.

Movement, Position, and Balance

The phone rings. Without looking up from your textbook, you reach for the receiver, pick it up, and guide it to the side of your head. You have just demonstrated your **kinesthetic sense**—the sense that involves the location and position of body parts in relation to one another. (The word *kinesthetics* literally means "feelings of motion.") The kinesthetic sense involves specialized sensory neurons, called **proprioceptors,** which are located in the muscles and joints. The proprioceptors constantly communicate information to the brain about changes in body position and muscle tension.

Closely related to the kinesthetic sense is the **vestibular sense,** which provides a sense of balance, or equilibrium, by responding to changes in gravity, motion, and body position. The two sources of vestibular sensory information, the *semicircular canals* and the *vestibular sacs,* are both located in the ear (see Figure 3.12). These structures are filled with fluid and lined with hairlike receptor cells that shift in response to motion, changes in body position, or changes in gravity.

When you experience environmental motion, like the rocking of a boat in choppy water, the fluids in the semicircular canals and the vestibular sacs are affected. Changes in your body's position, such as falling backward in a heroic attempt to return a volleyball serve, also affect the fluids. Your vestibular sense supplies the critical information that allows you to compensate for such changes and quickly reestablish your sense of balance.

Maintaining equilibrium also involves information from other senses, particularly vision. Under normal circumstances, this works to our advantage. However, when information from the eyes conflicts with information from the vestibular system, the result can be dizziness, disorientation, and nausea. These are the symptoms commonly experienced in motion sickness, the bane of many travelers in cars, on planes, on boats, and even in space. One strategy that can be used to combat motion sickness is to minimize sensory conflicts by focusing on a distant point or an object that is fixed, such as the horizon.

In the first part of this chapter, we've described how the body's senses respond to stimuli in the environment. Table 3.4 summarizes these different sensory systems. To make use of this raw sensory data, the brain must organize and interpret the data and relate them to existing knowledge. Next, we'll look at the process of perception—how we make sense out of the information that we receive from our environment.

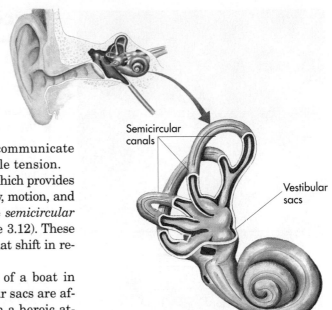

Semicircular canals

Vestibular sacs

FIGURE 3.12 The Vestibular Sense The vestibular sense provides our sense of balance, or equilibrium. Shown here are the two sources of vestibular sensory information, both located in the ear: the semicircular canals and the vestibular sacs. Both structures are filled with fluids that shift in response to changes in body position, gravity, or motion.

Table 3.4

Summary Table of the Senses

Sense	Stimulus	Sense Organ	Sensory Receptor Cells
Hearing (audition)	Sound waves	Ear	Hair cells in cochlea
Vision	Light waves	Eye	Rods and cones in retina
Color vision	Different wavelengths of light	Eye	Cones in retina
Smell (olfaction)	Airborne odor molecules	Nose	Hairlike receptor cells at top of nasal cavity
Taste (gustation)	Chemicals dissolved in saliva	Mouth	Taste buds
Touch	Pressure	Skin	Pacinian corpuscle
Pain	Tissue injury or damage; varied	Skin, muscles, and organs	Nociceptors
Movement (kinesthetic sense)	Movement of the body	None; muscle and joint tissue	Proprioceptors in muscle and joint tissue
Balance (vestibular sense)	Changes in position, gravity	Semicircular canals and vestibular sacs	Hairlike receptor cells in semicircular canals and vestibular sacs

Organizing Sensations into Meaningful Perceptions With virtually no conscious effort, the psychological process of perception allows you to integrate, organize, and interpret the lines, colors, and contours in this image as meaningful objects—a laughing child holding a panicky black cat in front of a Christmas tree. How did you reach those perceptual conclusions?

bottom-up processing
Information processing that emphasizes the importance of the sensory receptors in detecting the basic features of a stimulus in the process of recognizing a whole pattern; analysis that moves from the parts to the whole; also called *data-driven processing.*

top-down processing
Information processing that emphasizes the importance of the observer's knowledge, expectations, and other cognitive processes in arriving at meaningful perceptions; analysis that moves from the whole to the parts; also called *conceptually driven processing.*

Gestalt psychology
(geh-SHTALT) A school of psychology founded in Germany in the early 1900s that maintained that our sensations are actively processed according to consistent perceptual rules that result in meaningful whole perceptions, or *gestalts.*

figure–ground relationship
A Gestalt principle of perceptual organization that states that we automatically separate the elements of a perception into the feature that clearly stands out (the figure) and its less distinct background (the ground).

Perception

Key Theme
■ Perception refers to the process of integrating, organizing, and interpreting sensory information into meaningful representations.

Key Questions
■ What are bottom-up and top-down processing, and how do they differ?
■ What is Gestalt psychology?
■ What Gestalt principles determine our perceptions of objects and their relationship to their surroundings?

As we've seen, our senses are constantly registering a diverse range of stimuli from the environment and transmitting that information to the brain. But to make use of this raw sensory data, we must organize, interpret, and relate the data to existing knowledge.

Psychologists sometimes refer to this flow of sensory data from the sensory receptors to the brain as **bottom-up processing.** Also called *data-driven processing,* bottom-up processing is often at work when we're confronted with an ambiguous stimulus. For example, imagine trying to assemble a jigsaw puzzle one piece at a time, without knowing what the final picture will be. To accomplish this task, you would work with the individual puzzle pieces to build the image from the "bottom up," that is, from its constituent parts.

But as we interact with our environment, many of our perceptions are shaped by **top-down processing,** which is also referred to as *conceptually driven processing.* Top-down processing occurs when we draw on our knowledge, experiences, expectations, and other cognitive processes to arrive at meaningful perceptions, such as people or objects in a particular context.

Both top-down and bottom-up processing are involved in our everyday perceptions. As a simple illustration, look at the photograph above, which sits on Don's desk. Top-down processing was involved as you reached a number of perceptual conclusions about the image. You quickly perceived a little girl holding a black cat—our daughter Laura when she was three, holding her cat, Nubbin. You also perceived a child as a whole object even though the cat is actually blocking a good portion of the view of Laura.

But now look at the background in the photograph, which is more ambiguous. Deciphering these images involves both bottom-up and top-down processing. Bottom-up processes help you determine that behind the little girl looms a large, irregularly shaped, dark green object with brightly colored splotches on it. But what is it?

To identify the mysterious object, you must interpret the sensory data. Top-down processes help you identify the large green blotch as a Christmas tree—a conclusion that you probably would *not* reach if you had no familiarity with the way many Americans celebrate the Christmas holiday. The Christmas tree branches, ornaments, and lights are just fuzzy images, but other images work as clues—a happy child, a stuffed bear with a red-and-white stocking cap. Learning experiences create a conceptual knowledge base from which we can identify and interpret many objects, including kids, cats, and Christmas trees.

Clearly, bottom-up and top-down processing are both necessary to explain how we arrive at perceptual conclusions. But whether we are using bottom-up or top-down processing, a useful way to think about perception is to consider the basic perceptual questions we must answer in order to survive. We exist in an ever-changing environment that is filled with objects that may be standing still or moving, just like ourselves. Whether it's a bulldozer or a bowling ball, we need to be able to identify objects, locate objects in space, and, if they are moving, track their motion. Thus, our perceptual processes must help us organize our sensations to answer three basic, important questions: (1) What is it? (2) How far away is it? and (3) Where is it going?

In the next few sections, we will look at what psychologists have learned about the principles we use to answer these perceptual questions. Much of our discussion reflects the work of an early school of psychology called **Gestalt psychology,** which was founded by German psychologist **Max Wertheimer** in the early 1900s. The Gestalt psychologists emphasized that we perceive whole objects or figures *(gestalts)* rather than isolated bits and pieces of sensory information. Roughly translated, the German word *Gestalt* means a unified whole, form, or shape. Although the Gestalt school of psychology no longer formally exists, the pioneering work of the Gestalt psychologists established many basic perceptual principles (S. Palmer, 2002).

Max Wertheimer (1880–1943) Arguing that the whole is always greater than the sum of its parts, Wertheimer founded Gestalt psychology. Wertheimer and other Gestalt psychologists began by studying the principles of perception but later extended their approach to other areas of psychology.

The Perception of Shape
What Is It?

When you look around your world, you don't see random edges, curves, colors, or splotches of light and dark. Rather, you see countless distinct objects against a variety of backgrounds. Although to some degree we rely on size, color, and texture to determine what an object might be, we rely primarily on an object's *shape* to identify it.

Figure–Ground Relationship

How do we organize our perceptions so that we see an object as separate from other objects? The early Gestalt psychologists identified an important perceptual principle called the **figure–ground relationship,** which describes how this works. When we view a scene, we automatically separate the elements of that scene into the *figure,* which is the main element of the scene, and the *ground,* which is its background.

You can experience the figure–ground relationship by looking at a coffee cup on a table. The coffee cup is the figure, and the table is the ground. Notice that usually the figure has a definite shape, tends to stand out clearly, and is perceptually meaningful in some way. In contrast, the ground tends to be less clearly defined, even fuzzy, and usually appears to be behind and farther away than the figure.

The early Gestalt psychologists noted that figure and ground have vastly different perceptual qualities (N. Rubin, 2001). As Gestalt psychologist Edgar Rubin (1921) observed, "In a certain sense, the ground has no shape."

Survival and Figure–Ground Relationships
The natural camouflage that protects some animals, like this Brazilian moth, from predators illustrates the importance of figure–ground relationships in survival. When an animal's coloring and markings blend with its background, a predator cannot distinguish the animal (the *figure*) from its environment (the *ground*). In much the same way, military personnel and equipment are often concealed from enemy forces by clothing or tarps that are designed to blend in with the terrain, whether it be jungle, desert, forest, or snowy mountain range.

CRITICAL THINKING 3.3

ESP: Can Perception Occur Without Sensation?

Do you believe in ESP? If you do, you're not alone. A recent Gallup poll found that half of American adults believed in ESP (Newport & Stausberg, 2001). In fact, Americans spend over $600 million a year calling psychic hotlines (Nisbet, 1998).

ESP, or **extrasensory perception**, means the detection of information by some means other than through the normal processes of sensation. Forms of ESP include:

- *Telepathy*—direct communication between the minds of two individuals
- *Clairvoyance*—the perception of a remote object or event, such as sensing that a friend has been injured in a car accident
- *Psychokinesis*—the ability to influence a physical object, process, or event, such as bending a key or stopping a clock, without touching it
- *Precognition*—the ability to predict future events

The general term for such unusual abilities is *paranormal phenomena. Paranormal* means "outside the range of normal experience." Thus, these phenomena cannot be explained by known laws of science and nature. **Parapsychology** refers to the scientific investigation of claims of various paranormal phenomena. Contrary to what many people think, very few psychologists conduct any kind of parapsychological research.

Have you ever felt as if you had just experienced ESP? Consider the following two examples:

- Your sister was supposed to stop by around 7:00. It's now 7:15, and you "sense" that something has happened to her. Shortly after 8:00 she calls, informing you that she's been involved in a fender bender. Did you experience clairvoyance?
- Some years ago, Sandy had a vivid dream that our cat Nubbin got lost. The next morning, Nubbin sneaked out the back door, went for an unauthorized stroll in the woods, and was gone for three days. Did Sandy have a precognitive dream?

Such common experiences may be used to "prove" that ESP exists. However, two less extraordinary concepts can explain both occurrences: coincidence and the fallacy of positive instances.

Coincidence describes an event that occurs simply by chance. For example, you have over a thousand dreams per year, most of which are about familiar people and situations. By mere chance, *some* aspect of *some* dream will occasionally correspond with reality.

The *fallacy of positive instances* is the tendency to remember coincidental events that seem to confirm our belief about unusual phenomena and to forget all the instances that do not. For example, think of the number of times you've thought something happened to someone but nothing

did. Such situations are far more common than their opposites, but we quickly forget about the hunches that are not confirmed.

Why do people attribute chance events to ESP? Research has shown that believers in ESP are less likely to accurately estimate the probability of an event occurring by chance alone. Nonbelievers tend to be more realistic about the probability of events being the result of simple coincidence or chance (Blackmore, 1985).

Parapsychologists attempt to study ESP in the laboratory under controlled conditions. Many initially convincing demonstrations of ESP are later shown to be the result of research design problems or of the researcher's unintentional cuing of the subject. Occasionally, outright fraud is involved on the part of either the subject or experimenter (Randi, 1980, 1982).

Another problem involves *replication*. To be considered valid, experimental results must be able to be replicated, or repeated, by other scientists under identical laboratory conditions. To date, no parapsychology experiment claiming to show evidence of the existence of ESP has been successfully replicated (Hyman, 1994; Milton & Wiseman, 2001).

One active area of parapsychological research is the study of clairvoyance using an experimental procedure called the *ganzfeld procedure* (J. Palmer, 2003). (*Ganzfeld* is a German word that means "total field.") In a ganzfeld study, a "sender" in one room

ESP (extrasensory perception)
Perception of information by some means other than through the normal processes of sensation.

FIGURE 3.13 Figures Have Shape, but Ground Doesn't Which shape in **(b)** can also be found in **(a)**? The answer is that *both* shapes are in **(a)**. It's easy to spot the top shape because it corresponds to one of the shapes perceived as a *figure* in **(a)**. The bottom shape is harder to find because it is part of the *ground* or background of the total scene. Because we place more importance on figures, we're more likely to notice their shape while ignoring the shape of background regions.

SOURCE: Rubin (2001).

We notice the shape of the figure but *not* the shape of the background, even when that ground is used as a well-defined frame (see Figure 3.13). It turns out

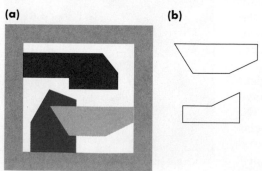

(a)　　　　　　　　**(b)**

that brain neurons *also* respond differently to a stimulus that is perceived as a figure versus a stimulus that is part of the ground (Baylis & Driver, 2001). Particular neurons in the cortex that responded to a specific shape when it was the shape of the figure did *not* respond when the same shape was presented as part of the background.

DILBERT   Scott Adams

attempts to communicate the content of pictures or short video clips to a receiver in a separate room. Isolated from all contact and wearing goggles and headphones to block external sensory stimuli, the "receiver" attempts to detect the image that is being sent.

One set of carefully controlled ganzfeld studies showed a "hit" rate that was well above chance, implying that some sort of transfer of information had taken place between sender and receiver (Bem & Honorton, 1994). These results, published in a well-respected psychology journal, *Psychological Bulletin,* led some psychologists to speculate that there might be something to extrasensory perception after all—and that the ganzfeld procedure might be the way to detect it. But other psychologists, like Ray Hyman (1994), argued that the study did *not* offer conclusive proof that ESP had been demonstrated.

In the past decade, many ganzfeld studies have been published, some showing positive results, some negative. Psychologists have used meta-analysis to try to determine whether the so-called ganzfeld effect has been successfully replicated. The verdict? British psychologists Julie Milton and Richard Wiseman (1999, 2001) concluded that the ganzfeld effect has *not* produced replicable evidence of an ESP effect in the laboratory. Other psychologists, however, dispute *that* conclusion with their own meta-analyses (Storm & Ertel, 2001). Most psychologists agree with Milton and Wiseman's (2001) bottom line: "The final verdict on [ESP] depends upon replication of an effect across experimenters under methodologically stringent conditions." To date, that bottom-line requirement has not been met.

Of course, the history of science is filled with examples of phenomena that were initially scoffed at and later found to be real. For example, the pain-relieving effects of acupuncture were initially dismissed by Western scientists as mere superstition or the power of suggestion.

However, controlled studies have shown that acupuncture does effectively relieve pain and may be helpful in treating other conditions (J. B. Murray, 1995; Ulett & others, 1998).

So keep an open mind about ESP, but also maintain a healthy sense of scientific skepticism. It is entirely possible that someday convincing experimental evidence will demonstrate the existence of ESP abilities (see Bem & Honorton, 1994; Milton & Wiseman, 2001; Storm & Ertel, 2001). In the final analysis, all psychologists, including those who accept the possibility of ESP, recognize the need for evidence that meets the requirements of the scientific method.

Critical Thinking Questions

- Why do you think that people who believe in ESP are less likely to attribute events to chance than people who don't think ESP is a real phenomenon?

- Can you think of any reasons why replication might be particularly elusive in research on extrasensory perception?

- Why is replication important in all psychological research, but particularly so in studies attempting to prove extraordinary claims, like the existence of ESP?

parapsychology
The scientific investigation of claims of paranormal phenomena and abilities.

The separation of a scene into figure and ground is not a property of the actual elements of the scene at which you're looking. Rather, your ability to separate a scene into figure and ground is a psychological accomplishment. To illustrate, look at the classic example shown in Figure 3.14. This perception of a single image in two different ways is called a *figure–ground reversal.*

Perceptual Grouping

Many of the forms we perceive are composed of a number of different elements that seem to go together (Prinzmetal, 1995). It would be

FIGURE 3.14 A Classic Example of Figure–Ground Reversal Figure–ground reversals illustrate the psychological nature of our ability to perceptually sort a scene into the main element and the background. If you perceive the white area as the figure and the dark area as the ground, you'll perceive a vase. If you perceive the dark area as the figure, you'll perceive two faces.

(a) The Law of Similarity

(b) The Law of Closure

(c) The Law of Good Continuation

(d) The Law of Proximity

FIGURE 3.15 The Gestalt Principles of Organization **(a)** The *law of similarity* is the tendency to perceive objects of a similar size, shape, or color as a unit or figure. Thus, you perceive four horizontal rows rather than six vertical columns of holiday cookies.

(b) The *law of closure* is the tendency to fill in the gaps in an incomplete image. Thus, you perceive the curved lines on the clock as smooth, continuous circles, even though they are interrupted by a person and the clock's hands.

(c) The *law of good continuation* is the tendency to group elements that appear to follow in the same direction as a single unit or figure. Thus, you tend to see the curved sections of the highways as continuous units.

(d) The *law of proximity* is the tendency to perceive objects that are close to one another as a single unit. Thus, you perceive these six people as two groups of three.

more accurate to say that we actively organize the elements to try to produce the stable perception of well-defined, whole objects. This is what perceptual psychologists refer to as "the urge to organize." What principles do we follow when we attempt to organize visual elements?

The Gestalt psychologists studied how the perception of visual elements becomes organized into patterns, shapes, and forms. They identified several laws, or principles, that we tend to follow in grouping elements together to arrive at the perception of forms, shapes, and figures. These principles include *similarity, closure, good continuation,* and *proximity.* Examples and descriptions of these perceptual laws are shown in Figure 3.15.

The Gestalt psychologists also formulated a general principle called the *law of Prägnanz,* or the *law of simplicity.* This law states that when several perceptual organizations of an assortment of visual elements are possible, the perceptual interpretation that occurs will be the one that produces the "best, simplest, and most stable shape" (Koffka, 1935). To illustrate, look at Figure 3.16. Do you perceive the image as two six-sided objects and one four-sided object? If you are following the law of Prägnanz, you don't. Instead, you perceptually organize the elements in the most cognitively efficient and simple way, perceiving them as three overlapping squares.

According to the Gestalt psychologists, the law of Prägnanz encompasses all the other Gestalt principles, including the figure–ground relationship. The implication of the law of Prägnanz is that our perceptual system works in an economical way to promote the interpretation of stable and consistent forms (van der Helm, 2000). The ability to efficiently organize elements into stable objects helps us perceive the world accurately. In effect, we actively and automatically construct a perception that reveals "the essence of something," which is roughly what the German word *Prägnanz* means.

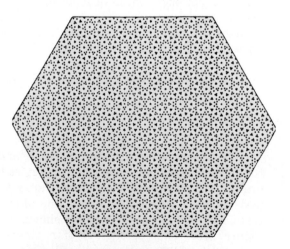

FIGURE 3.16 What Do You See? The law of simplicity refers to our tendency to efficiently organize the visual elements of a scene in a way that produces the simplest and most stable forms or objects. You probably perceived this image as that of three overlapping squares rather than as two six-sided objects and one four-sided object.

The Perceptual Urge to Organize As you scan this image, you'll experience firsthand the strong psychological tendency to organize visual elements to arrive at the perception of whole figures, forms, and shapes. Notice that as you shift your gaze across the pattern, you momentarily perceive circles, squares, and other geometric forms.

Depth Perception
How Far Away Is It?

Key Theme
■ Perception of distance and motion helps us gauge the position of stationary objects and predict the path of moving objects.

Key Questions
■ What are the monocular and binocular cues for distance or depth perception, and how does binocular disparity explain our ability to see three-dimensional forms in two-dimensional images?
■ What visual cues help us perceive distance and motion?
■ Why do we perceive the size and shape of objects as unchanging despite changes in sensory input?

BIZARRO   Dan Piraro

Being able to perceive the distance of an object has obvious survival value, especially regarding potential threats, such as snarling dogs or on-coming trains. But simply walking through your house or apartment also requires that you accurately judge the distance of furniture, walls, other people, and so forth. Otherwise, you'd be constantly bumping into doors, walls, and tables. The ability to perceive the distance of an object as well as the three-dimensional characteristics of an object is called **depth perception.**

Monocular Cues

We use a variety of cues to judge the distance of objects. The following cues require the use of only one eye. Hence, they are called **monocular cues** (*mono* means "one"). After familiarizing yourself with these cues, look at the photographs on the next page. Try to identify the monocular cues you used to determine the distance of the objects in each photograph.

1. *Relative size.* If two or more objects are assumed to be similar in size, the object that appears larger is perceived as being closer.

2. *Overlap.* When one object partially blocks or obscures the view of another object, the partially blocked object is perceived as being farther away. This cue is also called *interposition.*

3. *Aerial perspective.* Faraway objects often appear hazy or slightly blurred by the atmosphere.

4. *Texture gradient.* As a surface with a distinct texture extends into the distance, the details of the surface texture gradually become less clearly defined. The texture of the surface seems to undergo a gradient, or continuous pattern of change, from crisp and distinct when close to fuzzy and blended when farther away.

5. *Linear perspective.* Parallel lines seem to meet in the distance. For example, if you stand in the middle of a railroad track and look down the rails, you'll notice that the parallel rails seem to meet in the distance. The closer together the lines appear to be, the greater the perception of distance.

6. *Motion parallax.* When you are moving, you use the speed of passing objects to estimate the distance of the objects. Nearby objects seem to zip by faster than do distant objects. When you are riding on a commuter train, for example, houses and parked cars along the tracks seem to whiz by, while the distant downtown skyline seems to move very slowly.

depth perception
The use of visual cues to perceive the distance or three-dimensional characteristics of objects.

monocular cues
(moe-NOCK-you-ler) Distance or depth cues that can be processed by either eye alone.

Depth Perception In Action Several monocular cues combine to produce the illusion of depth in this photograph of the Ginza, a major shopping and entertainment district of Tokyo. See if you can identify examples of relative size, overlap, aerial perspective, texture gradient, and linear perspective.

Texture Gradient, Overlap, and Aerial Perspective Monocular cues are used to gauge distance of objects in a photograph. The tall grass appears crisp in the foreground and fuzzy in the background, an example of texture gradient. Similarly, haze blurs the foothills, creating the impression of even greater distance. The bushes are perceived as being closer than the house they overlap. Linear perspective is also evident in the parallel wheel tracks in the grass that seem to converge.

Relative Size, Linear Perspective, and Aerial Perspective Several monocular depth cues are operating in this photograph. Relative size is particularly influential: The very small image of the jogger and the decreasing size of the street lamps contribute to the perception of distance. Linear perspective is evident in the apparent convergence of the walkway railings. Aerial perspective contributes to the perception of depth from the hazy background.

Motion Parallax This photograph of waiters in India passing a tray from one train car to the next captures the visual flavor of motion parallax. Objects that whiz by faster are perceptually judged as being closer, as in the case here of the blurred ground and bushes. Objects that pass by more slowly are judged as being farther away, as conveyed by the clearer details of buildings and more distant objects.

When monocular cues are used by artists to create the perception of distance or depth in paintings, they are referred to as *pictorial cues*. If you look at the cover of this book, you can see how artist Phoebe Beasley used pictorial cues, including overlap and relative size, to create the perception of depth in her artwork.

Another monocular cue is *accommodation*. Unlike pictorial cues, accommodation utilizes information about changes in the shape of the lens of the eye to help us estimate distance. When you focus on a distant object, the lens is flat, but focusing on a nearby object causes the lens to thicken. Thus, to some degree, we use information provided by the muscles controlling the shape of the lens to judge depth. In general, however, we rely more on pictorial cues than on accommodation for depth perception.

Binocular Cues

Binocular cues for distance or depth perception require information from both eyes. One binocular cue is *convergence*—the degree to which muscles rotate your eyes to focus on an object. The more the eyes converge, or rotate inward, to focus on an object, the greater the strength of the muscle signals and the closer the object is perceived to be. For example, if you hold a dime about six inches in front of your nose, you'll notice the slight strain on your eye muscles as your eyes converge to focus on the coin. If you hold the dime at arm's length, less convergence is needed. Perceptually, the information provided by these signals from your eye muscles is used to judge the distance of an object.

binocular cues
(by-NOCK-you-ler) Distance or depth cues that require the use of both eyes.

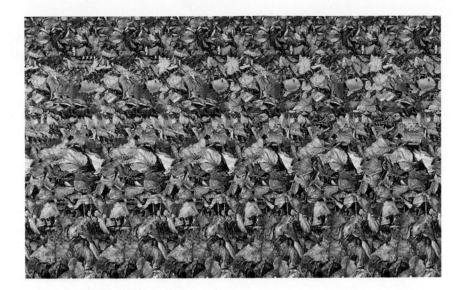

Binocular Disparity and the Perception of Depth in Stereograms This stereogram, *Rustling Hares,* was created by artist Hiroshi Kunoh (Kunoh & Takaoki, 1994). To see the three-dimensional images, first hold the picture close to your face. Focus your eyes as though you are looking at an object that is beyond the book and farther away. Without changing your focus, slowly extend your arms and move the picture away from you. The image of the leaves will initially be blurry, then details will come into focus and you should see three rabbits. The three-dimensional images that can be perceived in stereograms occur because of binocular disparity—each eye is presented with slightly different visual information.

Another binocular distance cue is *binocular disparity*. Because our eyes are set a couple of inches apart, a slightly different image of an object is cast on the retina of each eye. When the two retinal images are very different, we interpret the object as being close by. When the two retinal images are more nearly identical, the object is perceived as being farther away.

Here's a simple example that illustrates how you use binocular disparity to perceive distance. Hold a pencil just in front of your nose. Close your left eye, then your right. These images are quite different—that is, there is a great deal of binocular disparity between them. Thus you perceive the pencil as being very close. Now focus on another object across the room and look at it first with one eye closed, then the other. These images are much more similar. Because there is less binocular disparity between the two images, the object is perceived as being farther away. Finally, notice that with both eyes open, the two images are fused into one.

A *stereogram* is a picture that uses the principle of binocular disparity to create the perception of a three-dimensional image (Kunoh & Takaoki, 1994). Look at the stereogram shown above. When you first look at it, you perceive a two-dimensional picture of leaves. Although the pictorial cues of overlap and texture gradient provide some sense of depth to the image, the elements in the picture appear to be roughly the same distance from you.

However, a stereogram is actually composed of repeating columns of carefully arranged visual information. If you focus as if you are looking at some object that is farther away than the stereogram, the repeating columns of information will present a slightly different image to each eye. This disparate visual information then fuses into a single image, enabling you to perceive a three-dimensional image—three rabbits! To see the rabbits, follow the directions in the caption.

The Perception of Motion
Where Is It Going?

In addition to the ability to perceive the distance of stationary objects, we need the ability to gauge the path of moving objects, whether it's a baseball whizzing through the air, a falling tree branch, or an egg about to roll off the kitchen counter. How do we perceive movement?

As we follow a moving object with our gaze, the image of the object moves across the retina. Our eye muscles make microfine movements to keep the object in focus. We also compare the moving object to the background, which is usually stationary. When the retinal image of an object enlarges, we perceive the object

Mike and Motion Perception Catching a ball involves calculating an array of rapidly changing bits of visual information, including the ball's location, speed, and trajectory. Mike was especially appreciative of his newly regained motion perception. As Mike wrote in his journal, "Top on my list is being able to catch a ball in the air. This is pretty hard to do if you are totally blind, and now I can play ball with my boys and catch the ball 80 percent of the time it is thrown to me. I have spent half my life chasing a ball around in one way or another, so this is a big deal."

perceptual constancy
The tendency to perceive objects, especially familiar objects, as constant and unchanging despite changes in sensory input.

size constancy
The perception of an object as maintaining the same size despite changing images on the retina.

shape constancy
The perception of a familiar object as maintaining the same shape regardless of the image produced on the retina.

as moving toward us. Our perception of the speed of the object's approach is based on our estimate of the object's rate of enlargement (Schrater & others, 2001). Neural pathways in the brain combine information about eye-muscle activity, the changing retinal image, and the contrast of the moving object with its stationary background. The end result? We perceive the object as moving.

Neuroscientists do not completely understand how the brain's visual system processes movement. It's known that some neurons are highly specialized to detect motion in one direction but not in the opposite direction. Other neurons are specialized to detect motion at one particular speed. Research also shows that different neural pathways in the cerebral cortex process information about the depth of objects, movement, form, and color (Livingstone & Hubel, 1988; Zeki, 2001).

Psychologically, we tend to make certain assumptions when we perceive movement. For example, we typically assume that the *object,* or figure, moves while the background, or frame, remains stationary (Rock, 1995). Thus, as you visually follow a bowling ball down the alley, you perceive the bowling ball as moving and not the alley, which serves as the background.

Because we have a strong tendency to assume that the background is stationary, we sometimes experience an illusion of motion called *induced motion*. Induced motion was first studied by Gestalt psychologist **Karl Duncker** in the 1920s (King & others, 1998). Duncker (1929) had subjects sit in a darkened room and look at a luminous dot that was surrounded by a larger luminous rectangular frame. When the *frame* slowly moved to the right, the subjects perceived the *dot* as moving to the left.

Why did subjects perceive the dot as moving? Part of the explanation has to do with top-down processing. Perceptually, Duncker's subjects *expected* to see the smaller dot move within the larger rectangular frame, not the other way around. If you've ever looked up at a full moon on a windy night when the clouds were moving quickly across its face, you've probably experienced the induced motion effect. The combination of these environmental elements makes the moon appear to be racing across the sky.

Another illusion of apparent motion is called *stroboscopic motion*. First studied by Gestalt psychologist Max Wertheimer in the early 1900s, stroboscopic motion creates an illusion of movement with two carefully timed flashing lights (Wertheimer, 1912). A light briefly flashes at one location, followed about a tenth of a second later by another light briefly flashing at a second location. If the time interval and distance between the two flashing lights are just right, a very compelling illusion of movement is created.

Stroboscopic Motion and Movies The perception of smooth movements in a motion picture is due to stroboscopic motion. Much like this series of still photographs of a gymnast performing a back flip, a motion picture is actually a series of static photographs that are projected onto the screen at the rate of 24 frames per second, producing the illusion of smooth motion.

What causes the perception of stroboscopic motion? Although different theories have been proposed, researchers aren't completely sure. The perception of motion typically involves the movement of an image across the retina. However, during stroboscopic motion the image does *not* move across the surface of the retina. Rather, the two different flashing lights are detected at two different points on the surface of the retina. Somehow the brain's visual system combines this rapid sequence of visual information to arrive at the perceptual conclusion of motion, even though no movement has occurred. The perception of smooth motion in a movie is also due to stroboscopic motion.

Perceptual Constancies

Consider this scenario. As you're driving on a flat stretch of highway, a red SUV zips past you and speeds far ahead. As the distance between you and the SUV grows, its image becomes progressively smaller until it is no more than a dot on the horizon. Yet, even though the image of the SUV on your retinas has become progressively smaller, you don't perceive the vehicle as shrinking. Instead, you perceive its shape, size, and brightness as unchanged.

This tendency to perceive objects, especially familiar objects, as constant and unchanging despite changes in sensory input is called **perceptual constancy.** Without this perceptual ability, our perception of reality would be in a continual state of flux. If we simply responded to retinal images, our perceptions of objects would change as lighting, viewing angle, and distance from the object changed from one moment to the next. Instead, the various forms of perceptual constancy promote a stable view of the world.

Size and Shape Constancy

Size constancy is the perception that an object remains the same size despite its changing image on the retina. When our distance from an object changes, the image of the object that is cast on the retinas of our eyes also changes, yet we still perceive it to be the same size. The example of the red SUV illustrates the perception of size constancy. As the distance between you and the red SUV increased, you could eventually block out the retinal image of the vehicle with your hand, but you don't believe that your hand has suddenly become larger than the SUV. Instead, your brain automatically adjusts your perception of the vehicle's size by combining information about retinal image size and distance.

An important aspect of size constancy is that if the retinal image of an object does *not* change but the perception of its distance *increases,* the object is perceived as larger. To illustrate, try this: Stare at a 75-watt lightbulb for about 10 seconds. Then focus on a bright, distant wall. You should see an afterimage of the lightbulb on the wall that will look several times larger than the original lightbulb. Why? When you looked at the wall, the lingering afterimage of the lightbulb on your retina remained constant, but your perception of distance increased. When your brain combined and interpreted this information, your perception of the lightbulb's size increased. Remember this demonstration. We'll mention it again when we explain how some perceptual illusions occur.

Shape constancy is the tendency to perceive familiar objects as having a fixed shape regardless of the image they cast on our retinas. Try looking at a familiar object, such as a door, from different angles, as in the accompanying photograph. Your perception of the door's rectangular shape remains constant despite changes in its retinal image. Shape constancy has a greater influence on your perceptions than you probably realize (see Figure 3.17).

The Doors of Perception Each door in the photograph is positioned at a different angle and thus produces a differently shaped image on your retinas. Nevertheless, because of the perceptual principle of shape constancy, you easily identify all five shapes as rectangular doors.

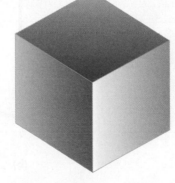

FIGURE 3.17 **How many right angles do you see?** Most people find 12 right angles in this drawing of a slightly tilted cube. But look again. There are *no* right angles in the drawing. Shape constancy leads you to perceive an image of a cube with right angles, despite the lack of sensory data to support that perception.

FIGURE 3.18 Illusory Contours The Gestalt principles of perceptual organization contribute to the illusion of triangular contours of this image. The second you look at this ambiguous image, you instantly reverse figure and ground so that the black circular regions become the ground, while the white region is visually favored as the figure. In organizing these visual fragments, which are lined up very precisely, the Gestalt principles of closure and good continuation contribute to the perceptual construction of a solid white triangle covering three black disks and an inverted triangle. The images produce a second intriguing illusion: The pure white illusory triangle seems brighter than the surrounding white paper.

Perceptual Illusions

Key Theme
■ Perceptual illusions underscore the idea that we actively construct our perceptual representations of the world according to psychological principles.

Key Questions
■ How can the Müller-Lyer and moon illusions be explained?
■ What do perceptual illusions reveal about perceptual processes?
■ What roles do perceptual sets, learning experiences, and culture play in perception?

Our perceptual processes are largely automatic and unconscious. On the one hand, this arrangement is mentally efficient. With a minimum of cognitive effort, we decipher our surroundings, answering important perceptual questions and making sense of the environment. On the other hand, because perceptual processing is largely automatic, we can inadvertently arrive at the wrong perceptual conclusion. When we misperceive the true characteristics of an object or an image, we experience a **perceptual illusion.**

During the past century, well over 200 perceptual illusions have been discovered. One famous perceptual illusion is shown in Figure 3.18. The perceptual contradictions of illusions are not only fascinating but can also shed light on how the normal processes of perception guide us to perceptual conclusions. Given the basics of perception that we've covered thus far, you're in a good position to understand how and why some famous illusions seem to occur.

The Müller-Lyer Illusion

FIGURE 3.19 The Müller-Lyer Illusion Compare the two photographs. Which *corner* line is longer? Now compare the two line drawings. Which center line is longer? In reality, the center lines in the photographs and the line drawings are all exactly the same length, which you can prove to yourself with a ruler.

Look at the center line made by the corners of the glass walls in photographs (a) and (c) in Figure 3.19. Which line is longer? If you said photograph (c), then you've just experienced the **Müller-Lyer illusion.** In fact, the two center lines are the same length, even though they *appear* to have different lengths. You can confirm that they are the same length by measuring them. The same illusion

(a)

(b)

(c)

(d)

occurs when you look at a simple line drawing of the Müller-Lyer illusion, shown in parts (b) and (d) of Figure 3.19.

The Müller-Lyer illusion is caused in part by visual depth cues that promote the perception that the center line in photograph (c) is *farther* from you (Gregory, 1968; Rock, 1995). When you look at photograph (c), the center line is that of a wall jutting away from you. When you look at drawing (d), the outward-pointing arrows create much the same visual effect—a corner jutting away from you. In Figure 3.19(a) and (b), visual depth cues promote the perception of *lesser* distance—a corner that is jutting toward you.

Size constancy also seems to play an important role in the Müller-Lyer illusion. Because they are the same length, the two center lines in the photographs and the line drawings produce retinal images that are the same size. However, as we noted in our earlier discussion of size constancy, if the retinal size of an object stays the same but the perception of its distance increases, we will perceive the object as being larger. Previously, we demonstrated this with the afterimage of a lightbulb that seemed much larger when viewed against a distant wall.

The same basic principle seems to apply to the Müller-Lyer illusion. Although all four center lines produce retinal images that are the same size, the center lines in images (c) and (d) are embedded in visual depth cues that make you perceive them as farther away. Hence, you perceive the center lines in these images as being longer, just as you perceived the afterimage of the lightbulb as being larger when viewed on a distant wall.

Keep in mind that the arrows pointing inward or outward are responsible for creating the illusion in the Müller-Lyer illusion. Take away those potent depth cues and the Müller-Lyer illusion evaporates. You perceive the two lines just as they are—the same length.

The Moon Illusion

Another famous illusion is one you've probably experienced firsthand—the **moon illusion,** shown in Figure 3.20. When a full moon is rising on a clear, dark night, it appears much larger when viewed on the horizon against buildings and trees than it does when viewed in the clear sky overhead. But the moon, of course, doesn't shrink as it rises. In fact, *the retinal size of the full moon is the same in all positions.* Still, if you've ever watched the moon rise from the horizon to the night sky, it does *appear* to shrink in size. What causes this illusion?

Part of the explanation has to do with our perception of the distance of objects at different locations in the sky (Kaufman & Kaufman, 2000; Rock, 1995). Researchers have found that people perceive objects on the horizon as farther away than objects that are directly overhead in the sky. The horizon contains many familiar distance cues, such as buildings, trees, and the smoothing of the texture of the landscape as it fades into the distance. The moon on the horizon is perceived as being *behind* these depth cues, so the depth perception cue of overlap adds to the perception that the moon on the horizon is farther away.

The moon illusion also involves the misapplication of the principle of size constancy. Like the afterimage of the glowing

FIGURE 3.20 The Moon Illusion Dispelled The *moon illusion* is subjectively very compelling. When viewed on the horizon, the moon appears to be much larger than when it is viewed higher in the sky. But as this time-lapse sequence of the moon rising over the Seattle skyline shows, the size of the moon remains the same as it ascends in the sky.

An Impossible Figure: Escher's *Waterfall* (1961) Impossible figures are visual riddles that capitalize on our urge to organize visual elements into a meaningful whole. Though not illusions in the true sense, these figures baffle our natural tendency to perceptually organize a scene. Dutch artist M. C. Escher (1898–1972) became famous for creating elaborate impossible figures, using perceptual principles to create complex visual puzzles. In most paintings, depth and distance cues are used to produce realistic scenes. But in Escher's work, the depth cues are often incompatible, producing a perceptual paradox. As you try to integrate the various perceptual cues in the drawing into a stable, integrated whole, you confront perceptual contradictions—such as the conclusion that water is running uphill. Escher was fascinated by the "psychological tension" created by such images (Schattschneider, 1990).

lightbulb, which looked larger on a distant wall, the moon looks larger when the perception of its distance increases. Remember, the retinal image of the moon is the *same* in all locations, as was the afterimage of the lightbulb. Thus, even though the retinal image of the moon remains constant, we perceive the moon as being larger because it seems farther away on the horizon (Kaufman & Kaufman, 2000).

If you look at a full moon on the horizon through a cardboard tube, you'll remove the distance cues provided by the horizon. The moon on the horizon shrinks immediately—and looks the same size as it does when directly overhead.

Mike and Perceptual Illusions

Perceptual illusions underscore the fact that what we see is *not* merely a simple reflection of the world, but our subjective perceptual interpretation of it. We've been developing and refining our perceptual interpretations from infancy onward. But what about Mike, who regained low vision after more than four decades of blindness?

Psychologist Ione Fine and her colleagues (2003) also assessed Mike's perceptual processing with a couple of perceptual illusions. For example, Mike was presented with an image containing illusory contours, shown at left. It's much like the more complex image we discussed in Figure 3.18 on page 116. When asked, "What is the 'hidden' shape outlined by the black apertures?" Mike had no response. However, when the form was outlined in red, Mike immediately perceived the red square.

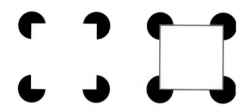

Now look at Figure 3.21 shown in the margin. Which tabletop is longer? If you used your keen perceptual skills and confidently said (a), you're wrong. If you responded as Mike did and said that the two tabletops are of identical size and shape, you'd be correct. You can use a ruler or tracing paper to verify this. This illusion is referred as the *Shepard Tables,* named after its creator, psychologist Roger Shepard (1990).

Why wasn't Mike susceptible to this compelling visual illusion? Partly, it's because he does not automatically use many of the depth perception cues we discussed earlier (Gregory, 2003). As psychologist Donald MacLeod explained, "Mike is impressively free from some illusions that beset normal vision, illusions that reflect the constructive processes involved in the perception of three-dimensional objects" (Abrams, 2002).

Although seeing is said to be believing, in the case of illusions, believing can lead to seeing something that isn't really there. As Mike gets more perceptual practice with the world, it will be interesting to see if he learns to fall for the same illusions that most of us do.

Like any psychological process, perception can be influenced by many factors, including our expectations. In the final section of this chapter, we'll consider how prior experiences and cultural factors can influence our perceptions of reality.

FIGURE 3.21 Which Tabletop Is Longer? The *Shepard Tables* illusion consists of two tables that are oriented in different directions. It capitalizes on our automatic use of depth perception cues to perceive what is really a two-dimensional drawing as three-dimensional objects. By relying on these well-learned depth perception cues, most people pick (a) as being the longer tabletop. In contrast, Mike May was oblivious to the perceptual illusion. He correctly responded that the two tabletops were the same size and shape (Fine & others, 2003). You can verify this with a ruler.

SOURCE: Illusion adapted from Shepard (1990).

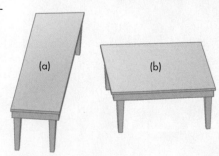

The Effects of Experience on Perceptual Interpretations

Our educational, cultural, and life experiences shape what we perceive. As a simple example, consider airplane cockpits. If your knowledge of the instruments contained in an airplane cockpit is limited, as is the case with your author Sandy, an airplane cockpit looks like a confusing, meaningless jumble of dials. But your author Don, who is a pilot, has a very different perception of an airplane cockpit. Rather than a blur of dials, he sees altimeters, VORs, airspeed and RPM indicators, and other instruments, each with a specific function. Our different perceptions of an airplane cockpit are shaped by our prior learning experiences.

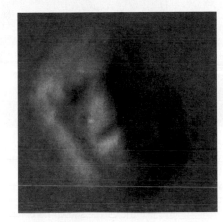

Learning experiences can vary not just from person to person but also from culture to culture. In Culture and Human Behavior Box 3.4 on the next page, we discuss the important role that experiences unique to a particular culture can play in the perception of illusions.

Past experience often predisposes us to perceive a situation in a particular way, even though other perceptions are possible. Consider this experience, which one of our students shared in class. As he was driving home late at night, he stopped at a convenience store to buy a pack of cigarettes. Standing at the counter and looking down as he rummaged through his wallet for some cash, he requested "a pack of Nows." When he looked up, the young female clerk had put a copy of *Penthouse* on the counter. Obviously, the clerk perceived what she had expected to hear.

This example illustrates the notion of **perceptual set**—the expectancies and predispositions that the observer brings to a perceptual situation. We're often mentally primed to interpret a particular perception in a particular way. Our perceptual sets are, of course, influenced by our prior learning experiences. One person's mystery dial is another person's altimeter.

Perceptual sets can exert a strong influence on the perceptual conclusions we reach. Perceptual sets usually lead us to reasonably accurate conclusions. If they didn't, we would develop new perceptual sets that were more accurate. But sometimes a perceptual set can lead us astray. For example, when the partially decomposed body of a large, hairy creature was discovered in upstate New York, it generated much excitement because the remains were perceived by several people as proof of the existence of "Bigfoot" (Hines, 2003). Scientists operating with a different perceptual set examined the dead creature and duly proclaimed it for what it was—the remains of a brown bear.

Similar examples of erroneous perceptual sets have occurred with supposed sightings of UFOs, the Loch Ness monster, mermaids, and ghosts. In each case, observers interpreted ambiguous stimuli in terms of the perceptual set they held in that situation and saw what their expectations led them to see.

The Face on Mars Was it built by ancient astronauts, or perhaps by the artisans of an ancient Martian civilization? Perceptual set led many people to see a "face" in this dimly lit rock formation on Mars photographed by NASA's *Viking 1* expedition. Higher-resolution photos taken at a later date revealed the mile-long "face" to be nothing more than one of many similar features sculpted into the planet's rocky surface by wind.

Visitors from Another Planet? Perceptual set may lead the avid believer in UFOs to see this photograph of unusual cloud formations as evidence for the existence of flying saucers.

perceptual set
The influence of prior assumptions and expectations on perceptual interpretations.

Culture and the Müller-Lyer Illusion: The Carpentered-World Hypothesis

The Gestalt psychologists believed that perceptual processes are inborn, a viewpoint called the *nativist position.* According to this position, people everywhere, whatever their background, see the world in the same way because they share the same perceptual rules. Other psychologists have advocated the *empiricist position,* believing that people actively construct their perceptions by drawing on their prior learning experiences, including cultural experiences.

The Müller-Lyer illusion has played a key role in the debate on this issue. Since the early 1900s, it has been known that people in industrialized societies are far more susceptible to the Müller-Lyer illusion than are people in some nonindustrialized societies (see Matsumoto, 2000). How can this difference be explained?

Cross-cultural psychologist Marshall Segall and his colleagues (1963, 1966) proposed the *carpentered-world hypothesis.* They suggested that people living in urban, industrialized environments have a great deal of perceptual experience in judging lines, corners, edges, and other rectangular, manufactured objects. Thus, people in carpentered cultures would be more susceptible to the Müller-Lyer illusion, which involves arrows mimicking a corner that is jutting toward or away from the perceiver.

In contrast, people who live in noncarpentered cultures more frequently encounter natural objects. In these cultures, perceptual experiences with straight lines and right angles are relatively rare. Segall predicted that people from these cultures would be less susceptible to the Müller-Lyer illusion.

A Noncarpentered Environment People who live in urban, industrialized environments have a great deal of perceptual experience with straight lines, edges, and right angles. In contrast, people who live in a noncarpentered environment, like the village shown here, have little experience with right angles and perfectly straight lines. Are people who grow up in a noncarpentered environment equally susceptible to the Müller-Lyer illusion?

To test this idea, Segall and his colleagues (1963, 1966) compared the responses of people living in carpentered societies, such as Evanston, Illinois, with those of people living in noncarpentered societies, such as remote areas of Africa. The results confirmed their hypothesis. The Müller-Lyer illusion was stronger for those living in carpentered societies. The findings provided strong support for the idea that culture could influence perception.

However, nativists were quick to suggest that Segall's results might be due to racial rather than cultural differences. After all, they pointed out, the non-Western subjects in

Segall's research were mostly Africans, and racial differences in eye pigmentation had been shown to affect the ability to visually detect contours (see Segall, 1994). Could the difference in illusion susceptibility be due to some sort of physiological difference rather than a cultural difference?

To address this issue, psychologist V. M. Stewart (1973) returned to Evanston and compared groups of white and African-American schoolchildren living there. Stewart found that the Evanston children, regardless of race, were equally susceptible to the Müller-Lyer illusion. She then compared groups of black African children in five different areas of Zambia—ranging from the very carpentered capital city of Lusaka to rural, noncarpentered areas of the country.

The results of this second comparison? The African children living in the carpentered society of Lusaka were just as susceptible to the illusion as were the white and African-American children living in Evanston. And the children living in the rural, noncarpentered countryside were far less susceptible. In other words, the children's race made no difference at all. What mattered was the children's experience, or lack of experience, with a carpentered environment.

Clearly, differences in susceptibility to the Müller-Lyer illusion underscore the important role that cultural experiences can play in shaping our perceptions. Segall (1994) summarized the empiricist view: "Every perception is the result of an interaction between a stimulus and a perceiver shaped by prior experience." Thus, people from very different cultural backgrounds might well perceive aspects of the world differently.

Closing Thoughts

From reflections of light waves to perceptual illusions, the world you perceive is the result of a complex interaction among distinctly dissimilar elements—environmental stimuli, sensory receptor cells, neural pathways, and brain mechanisms. Equally important are the psychological and cultural factors that help shape your perception of the world. As Mike's story illustrated, the world we experience relies not only on the functioning of our different sensory systems, but also on neural pathways sculpted by years of learning experiences from infancy onward.

Although he spent more than four decades totally blind, Mike never seemed to lack vision. With conviction, humor, and curiosity, he sought out a life of change and adventure. And he found it. Rather than expecting his surgery to fundamentally change his life, he simply welcomed the opportunity for new experiences. Throughout his life, Mike wrote, "I have sought change and thrive on it. I expected new and interesting experiences from getting vision as an adult but not that it would change my life" (May, 2004). As Mike points out, "My life was incredibly good before I had my operation. I've been very fortunate and had incredible opportunities, and so I can say that life was incredible. It was fantastic as a non-seeing person, and life is still amazing now that I have vision. That's been consistent between not seeing and seeing. Experiencing life to its fullest doesn't depend on having sight" (May, 2002b).

We hope that learning about Mike's experiences has provided you with some insights as to how your own life experiences have helped shape your perceptions of the world. In the Application, we'll provide you with some tips that we think you'll find useful in influencing your perceptions of painful stimuli.

"By getting some sight, I gained some new elements of my personality and lifestyle without rejecting the blindness. I am not a blind person or a sighted person. I am not even simply a visually impaired person. I am Mike May with his quirky sense of humor, graying hair, passion for life, and rather unusual combination of sensory skills."

APPLICATION Strategies to Control Pain

There are several strategies for controlling pain. Each of the following simple self-administered techniques can be useful for dealing with the everyday pain of a headache, an injury, or a trip to the dentist. Of course, the techniques described here are not a substitute for seeking appropriate medical attention, especially when pain is severe, recurring, or of unknown origin.

Self-Administered Strategies

1. Distraction

By actively focusing your attention on some nonpainful stimulus, you can often reduce pain (Cohen, 2002). For example, you can mentally count backward by sevens from 901, multiply pairs of two-digit numbers, draw different geometric figures in your mind, or count ceiling tiles. You can also focus on the details of a picture or other object.

Or, try our favorite strategy, which we'll dub the "iPod pain relief strategy." Intently listening to music, especially calming music, can reduce discomfort (Browning, 2001; Mitchell, 2002).

2. Imagery

Creating a vivid mental image can help control pain (T. Ball & others, 2003). Usually people create a pleasant and progressive scenario, such as walking along the beach or hiking in the mountains. Try to imagine all the different sensations involved, including the sights, sounds, aromas, touches, and tastes. The goal is to become so absorbed in your fantasy that you distract yourself from sensations of pain (Astin, 2004).

3. Relaxation

Deep relaxation can be a very effective strategy for deterring pain sensations (Benson, 1993; Turk & Nash, 1993). One simple relaxation strategy is deep breathing: Inhale deeply, then exhale very slowly and completely, releasing tension throughout your body. As you exhale, consciously note the feelings of relaxation and warmth you've produced in your body.

4. Counterirritation

The technique of counterirritation has been used for centuries. Counterirritation decreases pain by creating a strong, competing sensation that's mildly stimulating or irritating. People often do this naturally, as when they vigorously rub an injury or bite their lip during an injection.

How does rubbing the area where an injury has occurred reduce pain? The intense sensations of pain and the normal sensations of touch are processed through different nerve fibers going to the spinal cord. Increasing normal sensations of touch interferes with the transmission of high-intensity pain signals.

While undergoing a painful procedure, you can create and control a competing discomfort by pressing your thumbnail into your index finger. Focusing your attention on the competing discomfort may lessen your overall experience of pain.

5. Positive self-talk

This strategy involves making positive coping statements, either silently or out loud, during a painful episode or procedure (Cioffi & Holloway, 1993). Examples of positive self-talk include statements such as "It hurts, but I'm okay, I'm in control" and "I'm uncomfortable, but I can handle it."

Self-talk can also include redefining the pain. By using realistic and constructive thoughts about the pain experience in place of threatening or harmful thoughts, you can minimize pain. For example, an athlete in training might say, "The pain means my muscles are getting stronger." Or, consider the Marine Corps slogan: "Pain is weakness leaving the body."

Can Magnets Relieve Pain?

Our students frequently ask us about different *complementary and alternative medicines (CAM)*. Complementary and alternative medicines are a diverse group of health care systems, practices, or products that are *not* presently considered to be part of conventional medicine. Scientific evidence exists for some CAM therapies, such as the benefits of massage (Moyer & others, 2004). Therapies that are scientifically proven to be safe and effective usually become adopted by the mainstream health care system. However, the effectiveness and safety of many CAMs have not been proven by well-designed scientific studies.

Magnets are one popular CAM that has been used for many centuries to treat pain. In the United States, magnetic hairbrushes and insoles, magnetic salves, and clothes with magnets came into wide use after the Civil War, especially in some rural areas where few doctors were available. Healers claimed that magnetic fields existed in the blood, organs, or elsewhere in the body and that people became ill when their magnetic fields were depleted. Thus, healers marketed magnets as a means of "restoring" these magnetic fields (Basford, 2001; Ratterman & others, 2002).

Not much has changed in the last 150 years. Today, there are numerous magnetic products pitched to the public, especially over the Internet, to help control pain and promote healing. Manufacturers have put magnets in shoe insoles, mattress pads, belts, bracelets, and other jewelry. It is estimated that Americans spend about $500 million per year on magnets to treat pain. Worldwide, the estimate is $5 billion per year (Winemiller & others, 2003).

Do magnets relieve pain? To date, scientific research is inconclusive (Ratterman & others, 2002). The pain relief that some people experience could be due to a placebo effect and expectations that pain will decrease. Or, the relief could come from whatever holds the magnet in place, such as a warm bandage or the cushioned insole (Weintraub & others, 2003).

Strategies Pain Specialists Use

Beyond these self-administered strategies, pain specialists use a variety of techniques to control pain, including *hypnosis* and *painkilling drugs*. We'll discuss both of these topics in the next chapter. Two other pain-relieving strategies are *biofeedback* and *acupuncture*.

Biofeedback is a process of learning voluntary control over largely automatic body functions, such as heart rate, blood pressure, blood flow, and muscle tension. Using sensitive equipment that signals subtle changes in a specific bodily function, people can learn to become more keenly aware of their body's internal state. With the auditory or visual feedback provided by the biofeedback instrument, the person learns how to exercise conscious control over a particular bodily process.

For example, an individual who experiences chronic tension headaches might use biofeedback to learn to relax shoulder, neck, and facial muscles. In numerous studies, biofeedback has proven effective in helping many people who experience tension headaches, migraine headaches, jaw pain, and back pain (Astin, 2004; Scharff & others, 2002).

Pain Relief Through Acupuncture Acupuncture is one of the oldest, most commonly used medical procedures in the world. Acupuncture originated in China more than 2,500 years ago, but American acupuncture practices often incorporate medical traditions from Japan and Korea. It's estimated that over a million Americans receive acupuncture treatments each year. Does acupuncture work? In a recent large-scale study involving over 500 patients with arthritis of the knee, patients who received acupuncture experienced both greater pain relief and improved function than patients who received "sham" acupuncture (Berman & others, 2004).

Acupuncture is a pain-relieving technique that has been used in traditional Chinese medicine for thousands of years. Acupuncture involves inserting tiny needles at specific points in the body. The needles are then twirled, heated, or, as shown here, stimulated with a mild electrical current.

Research shows that acupuncture is beneficial in treating a variety of conditions involving pain. Although it is not yet understood exactly how acupuncture interrupts the transmission of pain signals, it is well-documented that acupuncture stimulates the release of endorphins (Ulett & Han, 2002). Acupuncture has been shown to be effective in postoperative surgical and dental pain, and it may be useful for such diverse conditions as headache, menstrual cramps, low back pain, and tennis elbow (National Center for Complementary and Alternative Medicine, 2002).

biofeedback
Technique that involves using auditory or visual feedback to learn to exert voluntary control over involuntary body functions, such as heart rate, blood pressure, blood flow, and muscle tension.

acupuncture
Ancient Chinese medical procedure involving the insertion and manipulation of fine needles into specific locations on the body to alleviate pain and treat illness; modern acupuncture may involve sending electrical current through the needles rather than manipulating them.

Chapter Review
Sensation and Perception

Introduction: What Are Sensation and Perception?

- **Sensation** refers to the response of sensory receptors in the sense organs to stimulation and the transmission of that information to the brain. **Perception** refers to the process through which the brain organizes and interprets sensory information.

- When **sensory receptors** are stimulated by an appropriate form of energy, **transduction** converts the energy into neural impulses, which are transmitted to the brain.

- Each sense is specialized in terms of the type and level of energy to which it will respond. Sensory thresholds include the **absolute threshold** and the **difference threshold**. **Weber's law** states that the just noticeable difference will vary depending on the strength of the original stimulus. **Sensory adaptation** takes place when the sensory receptor cells gradually decline in sensitivity to a constant stimulus.

Vision: From Light to Sight

- The sensory receptors for vision respond to light waves. The human eye is sensitive to a very narrow, specific range of **wavelengths** in the electromagnetic energy spectrum.

- Light waves enter the eye and pass through the **cornea** and the **pupil**. The **iris** controls how much light is allowed in. Behind the pupil is the **lens,** which focuses light on the **retina** through **accommodation**. The retina contains the sensory receptors for vision, the rods and cones.

- **Rods** are used for vision in dim light and for peripheral vision. **Cones** are used for color vision, for vision in bright light, and for seeing fine details. Cones are concentrated in the **fovea,** while rods are more prevalent in the periphery of the retina. There are no rods or cones in the **optic disk,** which creates a **blind spot** in the visual field.

- Rods and cones send information to the **bipolar** and **ganglion cells.** The ratio of cones to ganglion cells is much smaller than the ratio of rods to ganglion cells. The **optic nerve** fibers exit the back of each retina at the optic disk and meet at the **optic chiasm,** where some of the fibers cross over to the opposite side of the brain and then transmit information from the thalamus to the visual cortex. Feature detectors are highly specialized neurons in the visual cortex.

- **Color** is the psychological experience of different wavelengths of light and involves **hue, brightness,** and **saturation.** The color of an object is determined by the light wave it reflects. In combination, the **trichromatic theory** and the **opponent-process theory** explain color vision. The trichromatic theory explains red–green **color blindness** and color processing in the retina. The opponent-process theory explains **afterimages** and color processing in the ganglion cells and the brain.

Hearing: From Vibration to Sound

- The sense of hearing is called **audition.** The **loudness, pitch,** and **timbre** of a sound are determined by the **amplitude, frequency,** and complexity of a sound wave. Loudness is measured in **decibels.**

- Sound waves are collected in the **outer ear,** amplified by the **eardrum** in the **middle ear,** and transduced in the **inner ear.** The sensory receptors for hearing are the **hair cells,** which are located on the **basilar membrane** in the **cochlea.** The auditory nerve carries information to the thalamus and auditory cortex in the brain.

The Chemical and Body Senses: Smell, Taste, Touch, and Position

- The sensory receptors for smell (**olfaction**) and taste (**gustation**) are specialized to respond to chemical substances. The sensation of smell is caused by airborne molecules stimulating odor receptors on the olfactory receptor cells in the nasal lining. Olfactory information travels via the axons of the receptor cells to the **olfactory bulb** and is transmitted along the olfactory tract to different brain areas, including the temporal lobe and limbic system.

- Taste results from the stimulation of sensory receptors in the **taste buds,** which are located on the tongue and the inside of the mouth. When activated by chemical substances dissolved in saliva, the taste buds send neural messages to the thalamus in the brain. There are five primary tastes: sweet, salty, sour, bitter, and *umami.*

- The skin includes several kinds of sensory receptors, which are unevenly distributed among the parts of the body. The Pacinian corpuscle is the skin receptor that is sensitive to pressure.

- **Pain** occurs when **nociceptors** are stimulated. The fast pain system transmits signals that produce sensations of intense but short-lived pain, while the slow pain system transmits signals that produce sensations of dull, long-lasting pain. **Substance P** is a neurotransmitter that increases pain messages within the spinal cord. The **gate-control theory of pain** helps explain how psychological and other factors influence the subjective experience of pain.

- The **kinesthetic sense** involves the location and position of body parts in relation to one another, which is detected by specialized neurons called **proprioceptors.** The **vestibular sense** provides information about balance, equilibrium, and orientation.

Perception

- Both **bottom-up** and **top-down processing** are involved in everyday perception. The **Gestalt psychologists** emphasized the perception of *gestalts,* or whole forms.

- We rely primarily on shape to identify an object. **Figure–ground relationships** are important in distinguishing an object from its background. The Gestalt psychologists formulated several principles of perceptual organization, including the laws of proximity, similarity, closure, good continuation, and Prägnanz.

- **Depth perception** involves both monocular and binocular cues. **Monocular depth cues** include relative size, overlap, aerial perspective, texture gradient, linear perspective, motion parallax, and accommodation. **Binocular depth cues** include convergence and binocular disparity.

- The perception of movement involves integrating information from the eye muscles, the retina, and the environment. The illusion of induced motion is a result of our assumption that the background is stationary. The perception of strobo-scopic motion results from images being rapidly registered on the retina.

- Objects are perceived as stable despite changes in sensory input and retinal image, a concept called **perceptual constancy. Size constancy** and **shape constancy** are two important forms of perceptual constancy.

Perceptual Illusions

- **Perceptual illusions** are used to study perceptual principles. The **Müller-Lyer illusion** involves the principles of depth cues and size constancy. The **moon illusion** results from the principles of overlap and size constancy.

The Effects of Experience on Perceptual Interpretations

- Perceptual interpretations can be influenced by learning experiences, culture, and expectations. **Perceptual set** often determines the interpretation of an ambiguous stimulus.

Key Terms

sensation, p. 85

perception, p. 85

sensory receptors, p. 85

transduction, p. 85

absolute threshold, p. 86

difference threshold, p. 86

Weber's law, p. 86

subliminal perception, p. 87

sensory adaptation, p. 88

wavelength, p. 88

cornea, p. 89

pupil, p. 89

iris, p. 89

lens, p. 89

accommodation, p. 89

retina, p. 90

rods, p. 90

cones, p. 90

fovea, p. 91

optic disk, p. 91

blind spot, p. 91

ganglion cells, p. 91

bipolar cells, p. 92

optic nerve, p. 92

optic chiasm, p. 92

color, p. 94

hue, p. 94

saturation, p. 94

brightness, p. 94

trichromatic theory of color vision, pp. 94

color blindness, p. 95

afterimage, p. 95

opponent-process theory of color vision, p. 95

audition, p. 96

loudness, p. 97

amplitude, p. 97

decibel, p. 97

pitch, p. 97

frequency, p. 97

timbre, p. 97

outer ear, p. 97

eardrum, p. 97

middle ear, p. 97

inner ear, p. 97

cochlea, p. 97

basilar membrane, p. 98

hair cells, p. 98

olfaction, p. 99

gustation, p. 99

pheromones, p. 100

olfactory bulb, p. 100

taste buds, p. 101

pain, p. 102

nociceptors, p. 103

substance P, p. 103

gate-control theory of pain, p. 104

kinesthetic sense, p. 105

proprioceptors, p. 105

vestibular sense, p. 105

bottom-up processing, p. 106

top-down processing, p. 106

Gestalt psychology, p. 107

figure–ground relationship, p. 107

ESP (extrasensory perception), p. 108

parapsychology, p. 108

depth perception, p. 111

monocular cues, p. 111

binocular cues, p. 112

perceptual constancy, p. 115

size constancy, p. 115

shape constancy, p. 115

perceptual illusion, p. 116

Müller-Lyer illusion, p. 116

moon illusion, p. 117

perceptual set, p. 119

biofeedback, p. 122

acupuncture, p. 122

Key People

Karl Duncker (1903–1940) German Gestalt psychologist who is best known for his studies on the perception of motion; also studied the perception of pain and the effects of past experience on perception; immigrated to the United States in 1938. (p. 114)

Max Wertheimer (1880–1943) German psychologist who founded Gestalt psychology in the early 1900s, immigrated to the United States in 1933, studied the optical illusion of apparent movement, and described principles of perception. (p. 107)

Web Companion | Review Activities

You can find additional review activities by going to **www.DiscoveringPsychology.com** and clicking on the *Discovering Psychology* 4th Edition text cover. At the Discovering Psychology Web Companion you'll find the chapter learning objectives, flashcards for key terms and key people, interactive crossword puzzles, self-scoring practice quizzes, and other materials to help you master the information in this chapter.

Shaded Lives

Consciousness and Its Variations

Prologue

A Scream in the Night

Our friends Mike and Nina had been married for only four months, but they already had their nighttime routine down. Both of them needed to get up early in the morning—Nina worked the 7 A.M. to 3 P.M. shift as a neurology nurse, and Mike had to open the gift shop he managed at a large downtown hotel by 7:30 A.M. A confirmed night person, Nina had worked the 3-to-11 shift ever since she became a registered nurse. She had recently switched to the day shift so her schedule would mesh better with Mike's. But even after a couple of weeks, she was still having difficulty adjusting to the early-morning schedule. "My brain feels foggy until about noon," she complained to Mike.

One night, Nina and Mike crawled into bed, both exhausted. As they drifted off to sleep, Mike kept thinking about his job. His new boss had hinted that he really didn't like the way Mike was running the store. Mike closed his eyes and waited for his thoughts to slow down. As he relaxed, he thought about the shipment of greeting cards that was supposed to arrive early the next morning and imagined himself sorting through boxes at work. Just as he felt himself gently drifting off . . . "Ouch! Nina, stop kicking me!" he cried.

"I was sound asleep," Nina replied sleepily. "How could I have kicked you? You're imagining things, Michael. Just go to sleep."

Mike closed his eyes. A few moments later, he felt Nina's leg twitching and jerking against his, her breathing rhythmical as she snored lightly. He sighed and rolled over.

A few hours later, Mike was having a vivid dream about his new boss. His boss was standing at the top of a giant staircase, and Mike was at the bottom looking up. The dream scene switched quickly. Now Mike was at the top of a very tall escalator that wound around downward in a tight spiral in empty space, the escalator steps moving faster and faster. Terrified, he grabbed the edge of the escalator and held on, falling away, then struggling to swim back through midair. Suddenly, a blood-curdling scream cut through his dream.

Heart pounding, Mike jolted awake. *Am I dreaming?*

In the darkness, Nina screamed again.

Oh my God, there's someone in the apartment!

Mike leaped out of bed and fumbled for the baseball bat he kept underneath the bed. Shaking, he switched on the light. Nina was sitting up in bed, her eyes wide open, hands clasping her throat. Staring straight ahead, she screamed a third time, kicking at the blankets.

"Nina! What's wrong?!" Mike quickly scanned the bedroom. He ran out into the living room and turned on the lights. The front door was still securely locked and bolted from the inside. Baseball bat in hand, he ran into the kitchen. The back door was locked, the chain latch undisturbed. Completely baffled, he took a deep breath and walked back to the bedroom. "Nina, why did you scream?"

Nina didn't answer. She was slumped back down in bed, her eyes closed, sound asleep. She was the picture of blissful slumber. His heart still pounding, Mike stood in the doorway for another minute or so, watching Nina sleep. Nina sighed deeply and rolled over, snuggling toward Mike's side of the bed.

Finally, Mike shut off the lights and climbed into bed, his mind racing as he mentally replayed the incident. Now, every creak of the floor and rattle of the windows seemed to signal an intruder or some other danger. He glanced at the clock—12:47 A.M. Another 15 minutes passed before he got out of bed and padded into the kitchen. Reaching into the freezer for some ice cubes, he fixed himself a vodka and tonic. Toby, the cat, rounded the corner and joined him in the kitchen. As Toby rubbed up against his leg, Mike lit a cigarette and stared out the kitchen window into the darkness. *Why did Nina scream?*

In this chapter, we'll answer that question and tell you more about Nina's history of sleep disturbances. As you'll learn, this was not the first time—or the last—that Nina screamed in her sleep for no apparent reason.

Sleep and dreaming are among the topics that we'll cover in this chapter as we look at consciousness and how it changes over the course of each day. Psychologists have learned a great deal about the daily fluctuations of consciousness as well as about the different ways that alterations in consciousness can be induced, such as through the use of hypnosis, meditation, or psychoactive drugs.

Introduction

Consciousness

Experiencing the "Private I"

Key Theme

■ Consciousness refers to your immediate awareness of internal and external stimuli.

Key Questions

■ What did William James mean by the phrase *stream of consciousness*?
■ How has research on consciousness evolved over the past century?

Your immediate awareness of thoughts, sensations, memories, and the world around you represents the experience of **consciousness.** That the experience of consciousness can vary enormously from moment to moment is easy to illustrate. Imagine that we could videotape three one-minute segments of your conscious activities at different times while your psychology instructor lectures in class. What might those three one-minute segments of consciousness reveal? Here are just a few of the possibilities:

■ Focused concentration on your instructor's words and gestures

■ Drifting from one fleeting thought, memory, or image to another

consciousness
Personal awareness of mental activities, internal sensations, and the external environment.

- Awareness of physical sensations, such as the beginnings of a headache or the sharp sting of a paper cut
- Replaying an emotionally charged conversation and thinking about what you wish you had said
- Sexual fantasies
- Mentally rehearsing what you'll say and how you'll act when you meet a friend later in the day
- Wishful, grandiose daydreams about the future

Most likely, the three video clips would reveal very different scenes, dialogues, and content as your consciousness changed from one minute to the next. Yet even though your conscious experience is constantly changing, you don't experience your personal consciousness as disjointed. Rather, the subjective experience of consciousness has a sense of continuity. One stream of conscious mental activity seems to blend into another, effortlessly and seamlessly.

This characteristic of consciousness led the influential American psychologist **William James** (1892) to describe consciousness as a "stream" or "river." Although always changing, consciousness is perceived as unified and unbroken, much like a stream. Despite the changing focus of our awareness, our experience of consciousness as unbroken helps provide us with a sense of personal identity that has continuity from one day to the next.

The nature of human consciousness was one of the first topics to be tackled by the fledgling science of psychology in the late 1800s. In Chapter 1, we discussed how the first psychologists tried to determine the nature of the human mind through *introspection*—verbal self-reports that tried to capture the "structure" of conscious experiences. But because such self-reports were not objectively verifiable, many of the leading psychologists at the turn of the twentieth century rejected the study of consciousness. Instead, they emphasized the scientific study of *overt behavior*, which could be directly observed, measured, and verified.

> *Consciousness, then, does not appear to itself chopped up in bits. . . . It is nothing jointed; it flows. A "river" or a "stream" are the metaphors by which it is most naturally described. In talking of it hereafter, let us call it the stream of thought, or consciousness, of subjective life.*
>
> William James (1892)

Beginning in the late 1950s, many psychologists once again turned their attention to the study of consciousness. This shift occurred for two main reasons. First, it was becoming clear that a complete understanding of behavior would *not* be possible unless psychologists considered the role of conscious mental processes in behavior.

Second, although the experience of consciousness is personal and subjective, psychologists had devised more objective ways to study conscious experiences. For example, psychologists could often *infer* the conscious experience that seemed to be occurring by carefully observing behavior. Technological advances in studying brain activity were also producing intriguing correlations between brain activity and different states of consciousness.

Today, the scientific study of consciousness is incredibly diverse. Working from a variety of perspectives, psychologists and other neuroscientists are piecing together a picture of consciousness that takes into account the role of psychological, physiological, social, and cultural influences.

Mental Alertness, Circadian Cycles, and Traffic Accidents Most people experience a decrease in their level of mental alertness every afternoon around 3:00 PM. If you try to stay awake all night, you'll experience peak sleepiness at about 3:00 AM. One practical implication of this circadian fluctuation is that accidents are more likely when our mental alertness ebbs. In one study that analyzed more than 6,000 fatigue-related traffic accidents, the highest number of accidents occurred right around 3:00 AM. During the daytime, the rate of traffic accidents peaked during the mid-afternoon at about 3:00 PM. (Mitler, 1994; Stutts & others, 1999).

Biological and Environmental "Clocks" That Regulate Consciousness

Key Theme
■ Many body functions, including mental alertness, are regulated by circadian rhythms, which systematically vary over a 24-hour period.

Key Questions
■ How do sunlight, the suprachiasmatic nucleus, and melatonin regulate the sleep–wake cycle?
■ How do free-running conditions affect circadian rhythms?
■ What is jet lag, and how is it produced?

Throughout the course of the day, there is a natural ebb and flow to consciousness. The most obvious variation of consciousness that we experience is the daily sleep–wake cycle. But conscious states also change in more subtle ways.

For example, you've probably noticed that your mental alertness varies throughout the day in a relatively consistent way. Most people experience two distinct peaks of mental alertness: one in the morning, usually around 9:00 or 10:00 A.M., and one in the evening, around 8:00 or 9:00 P.M. In between these two peaks, you'll probably experience a slump in mental alertness at about 3:00 P.M. And, should you manage to stay awake, your mental alertness will probably reach its lowest point at about 3:00 A.M. One practical implication of this consistent daily pattern is the increase in the number of traffic accidents at the times when mental alertness is at its lowest points.

Mental alertness and the sleep–wake cycle are just two examples of the daily highs and lows you experience in a wide variety of bodily processes. These daily cycles are called **circadian rhythms.** The word *circadian* combines the Latin words for "about" and "day." So, the term *circadian rhythms* refers to biological processes that systematically vary over a period of about 24 hours.

You actually experience many different circadian rhythms that ebb and flow over the course of any given 24-hour period (see Table 4.1). Researchers have discovered over 100 bodily processes that rhythmically peak and dip each day, including blood pressure, the secretion of different hormones, and pain sensitivity.

Table 4.1

Examples of Human Circadian Rhythms

Function	Typical Circadian Rhythm
Peak mental alertness and memory functions	Two daily peaks: around 9:00 A.M. and 9:00 P.M.
Lowest body temperature	About 97°F around 4:00 A.M.
Highest body temperature	About 99°F around 4:00 P.M.
Peak physical strength	Two daily peaks: around 11:00 A.M. and 7:00 P.M.
Peak hearing, visual, taste, and smell sensitivity	Two daily peaks: around 3:00 A.M. and 6:00 P.M.
Lowest sensitivity to pain	Around 4:00 P.M.
Peak sensitivity to pain	Around 4:00 A.M.
Peak degree of sleepiness	Two daily peaks: around 3:00 A.M. and 3:00 P.M.
Peak melatonin hormone in blood	Between 1:00 A.M. and 3:00 A.M.
Peak allergic sensitivity to pollen and dust	Between 11:00 P.M. and 1:00 A.M.

SOURCES: Campbell (1997); Czeisler & Dijk (2001); Refinetti (2000); M. Young (2000).

circadian rhythm
(ser-KADE-ee-en) A cycle or rhythm that is roughly 24 hours long; the cyclical daily fluctuations in biological and psychological processes.

Normally, your circadian rhythms are closely synchronized with one another. For example, the circadian rhythm for the release of growth hormone is synchronized with the sleep–wake circadian rhythm so that growth hormone is released only during sleep.

The Suprachiasmatic Nucleus
The Body's Clock

Your many circadian rhythms are controlled by a master biological clock—a tiny cluster of neurons in the *hypothalamus* in the brain. As shown in Figure 4.1, this cluster of neurons is called the **suprachiasmatic nucleus,** abbreviated **SCN.** The SCN is the internal pacemaker that governs the timing of circadian rhythms, including the sleep–wake cycle (Saper & others, 2005).

Keeping the circadian rhythms synchronized with one another and on a 24-hour schedule also involves environmental time cues. The most important of these cues is bright light, especially sunlight. In people, light detected by special photoreceptors in the eye is communicated via the visual system to the SCN in the hypothalamus (Brainard & others, 2001a, 2001b).

How does sunlight help regulate the sleep–wake cycle and other circadian rhythms? As the sun sets each day, the decrease in available light is detected by the SCN through its connections with the visual system. In turn, the SCN triggers an increase in the production of a hormone called **melatonin.** Melatonin is manufactured by the *pineal gland,* an endocrine gland located in the brain.

Increased blood levels of melatonin make you sleepy and reduce activity levels. At night, blood levels of melatonin rise, peaking between 1:00 and 3:00 A.M. Shortly before sunrise, the pineal gland all but stops producing melatonin, and you soon wake up. As the sun rises, exposure to sunlight and other bright light suppresses melatonin levels, and they remain very low throughout the day. In this way, sunlight *entrains,* or sets, the SCN so that it keeps circadian cycles synchronized and operating on a 24-hour schedule.

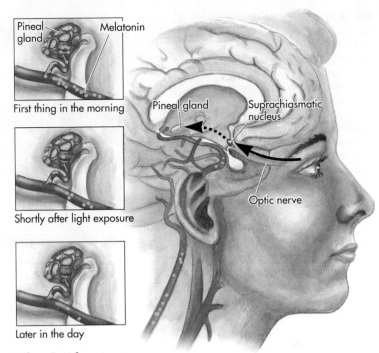

FIGURE 4.1 The Biological Clock Special photoreceptors in the retina regulate the effects of light on the body's circadian rhythms (Brainard & others, 2001a). In response to morning light, signals from these special photoreceptors are relayed via the optic nerve to the suprachiasmatic nucleus. In turn, the suprachiasmatic nucleus causes the pineal gland to reduce the production of melatonin, a hormone that causes sleepiness. As blood levels of melatonin decrease, mental alertness increases. Daily exposure to bright light, especially sunlight, helps keep the body's circadian rhythms synchronized and operating on a 24-hour schedule.

Life Without a Sundial
Free-Running Circadian Rhythms

Given that sunlight is responsible for setting your internal clock, what would happen to the timing of your circadian rhythms if they were allowed to "run free" in the absence of environmental time cues like sunlight and clocks? To create *free-running conditions,* researchers typically use underground isolation units. In some studies, they have even constructed rooms in caves. Volunteers live in these underground bunkers for weeks or months at a time, deprived of all environmental time cues.

Under free-running conditions, two distinct effects occur. First, in the absence of normal light, darkness, and other time cues, people tend to drift to the natural rhythm of the suprachiasmatic nucleus—roughly a 25-hour day, not a 24-hour day. Thus, people in a free-running condition go to sleep about an hour later each day. Exactly why the human sleep–wake cycle gravitates toward a 25-hour cycle—and under what conditions—is an issue that continues to be actively researched and debated (Roenneberg & others, 2003; Wright & others, 2001).

Second, under free-running conditions, circadian rhythms lose their normal synchronization with one another (Aschoff, 1993, 1994). All circadian rhythms become longer, but to different degrees. For example, normally the sleep–wake, body temperature, and melatonin cycles are closely coordinated. At about

suprachiasmatic nucleus (SCN)
(soup-rah-*kye*-az-MAT-ick) A cluster of neurons in the hypothalamus in the brain that governs the timing of circadian rhythms.

melatonin
(mel-ah-TONE-in) A hormone manufactured by the pineal gland that produces sleepiness.

Circadian Rhythms and the Blind Many blind people have free-running circadian cycles because they are unable to detect the light that normally sets the SCN. Like people deprived of environmental time cues, blind people can experience free-running melatonin, body temperature, and sleep–wake circadian cycles (Czeisler & others, 1995; Klerman & others, 1998). Consequently, many blind people suffer from recurring bouts of insomnia and other sleep problems.

3:00 A.M., your body temperature dips to its lowest point, just as melatonin is reaching its highest level and you are at your sleepiest. But in the absence of environmental cues, the sleep–wake, body temperature, and melatonin circadian rhythms become desynchronized, so that they are no longer properly coordinated with one another.

What happens when people leave the free-running condition and are once again exposed to normal daylight and darkness cues? Within days, sunlight resets the biological clock. Circadian rhythms become synchronized again and resume operating on a 24-hour rather than a 25-hour cycle (Lewy & Sack, 1987).

Circadian Rhythms and Sunlight
Some Practical Implications

The close tie between your internal biological clock and environmental time cues has some very important practical applications. For example, imagine that you leave Denver at 2:00 P.M. on a 10-hour flight to London. When you arrive in London, it's 7:00 A.M. and the sun is shining. However, your body is still on Denver time. As far as your internal biological clock is concerned, it's midnight.

The result? Your circadian rhythms are drastically out of synchronization with daylight and darkness cues. The psychological and physiological effects of this disruption in circadian rhythms can be severe. Thinking, concentration, and memory get fuzzy. You experience physical and mental fatigue, depression or irritability, and disrupted sleep. Collectively, these symptoms are called *jet lag*.

Although numerous physiological variables are involved in jet lag, the circadian cycle of the hormone melatonin plays a key role. When it's 10:00 A.M. in London, it's 3:00 A.M. in Denver. Since your body is still operating on Denver time, your melatonin production is peaking. Rather than feeling awake, you feel very sleepy, sluggish, and groggy. For many people, it can take a week or longer to adjust to such an extreme time change.

Jet Lag and the Direction of Travel Most people find it easier to adjust to the time changes when flying westward than eastward. Why? Flying westward adds hours to a traveler's day, which corresponds with the natural tendency of your internal body clock to drift toward longer days. As a general rule, it takes considerably longer to resynchronize your circadian rhythms to a new time zone when you fly eastward, which shortens your day.

You don't need to travel across multiple time zones to experience symptoms of jet lag. People who work night shifts or rotating shifts often suffer from jet lag symptoms because their circadian rhythms are out of sync with daylight and darkness time cues. Like Nina in the Prologue, nurses, doctors, and other medical personnel often have to work night shifts or rotating shifts. So do people working in law enforcement and the military, broadcasting and weather services, and other businesses that operate around the clock.

For night workers, the problem of being out of sync with the environmental clock is compounded every morning when they return home in the bright morning light. Exposure to bright morning light is a potent stimulus that can reset the body clock to a day schedule. Even traces of sunlight through curtains can prevent a person's body clock from staying in sync with the night work schedule. Because sunlight time cues exert such a powerful influence on circadian rhythms, many night-shift workers never fully adjust to a nighttime work schedule.

Sleep

Key Theme

■ Modern sleep research began with the invention of the EEG and the discovery that sleep is a state marked by distinct physiological processes and stages.

Key Questions

■ What are REM sleep and NREM sleep?

■ What characterizes sleep onset, each of the NREM sleep stages, and REM sleep?

■ What is the typical progression of sleep cycles, and how do sleep patterns change over the lifespan?

Birds do it. Giraffes do it. Cats do it a lot, mostly during the day. Dolphins do it, too, but only one brain hemisphere at a time. And, of course, you do it, and we do it, but not as much as we'd like to. Sleep, that is. In fact, if you live a long life, you'll spend approximately 22 years of your life sleeping.

From Aristotle to Shakespeare to Freud, history is filled with examples of scholars, writers, and scientists who have been fascinated by sleep and dreams. But prior to the twentieth century, there was no objective way to study the internal processes that might be occurring during sleep. Instead, sleep was largely viewed as a period of restful inactivity in which dreams sometimes occurred.

The Dawn of Modern Sleep Research

The invention of the **electroencephalograph** by German psychiatrist Hans Berger in the 1920s gave sleep researchers an important tool for measuring the rhythmic electrical activity of the brain (Stern, 2001). These rhythmical patterns of electrical activity are referred to as *brain waves*. The electroencephalograph produces a graphic record called an **EEG,** or **electroencephalogram.** By studying EEGs, sleep researchers have firmly established that brain-wave activity systematically changes throughout sleep.

Along with brain activity, today's sleep researchers monitor a variety of other physical functions during sleep. Eye movements, muscle movements, breathing rate, airflow, pulse, blood pressure, amount of exhaled carbon dioxide, body temperature, and breathing sounds are just some of the body's functions that are measured in contemporary sleep research (Ancoli-Israel, 1997; Cooper & Bradbury, 1994).

The next milestone in sleep research occurred in the early 1950s. Eugene Aserinsky, a graduate student at the University of Chicago, was working in the laboratory of renowned sleep researcher Nathaniel Kleitman. Using his 8-year-old son as a subject, Aserinsky discovered that particular EEG patterns during sleep were often associated with rapid movements of the sleeper's eyes (Morrison, 2003). Moreover, these periods of rapid eye movement were highly correlated with the subject's reports of dreaming. In 1953, Aserinsky and Kleitman published their findings, heralding the discovery of *rapid-eye-movement sleep,* usually abbreviated *REM sleep.*

Today, sleep researchers distinguish between two basic types of sleep. **REM sleep** is often called *active sleep* or *paradoxical sleep* because it is associated with heightened body and brain activity during which dreaming consistently occurs. **NREM sleep,** or *non-rapid-eye-movement sleep,* is often referred to as *quiet sleep* because the body's physiological functions and brain activity slow down during this period of slumber. NREM sleep is further divided into four stages, as we'll describe shortly.

electroencephalograph
(e-lec-tro-en-SEFF-uh-low-graph) An instrument that uses electrodes placed on the scalp to measure and record the brain's electrical activity.

EEG (electroencephalogram)
The graphic record of brain activity produced by an electroencephalograph.

REM sleep
Type of sleep during which rapid eye movements (REM) and dreaming usually occur and voluntary muscle activity is suppressed; also called *active sleep* or *paradoxical sleep.*

NREM sleep
Quiet, typically dreamless sleep in which rapid eye movements are absent; divided into four stages; also called *quiet sleep.*

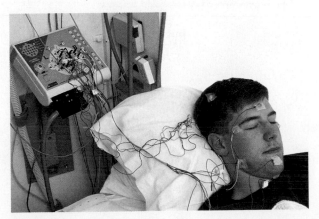

Monitoring Sleep Using electrodes that are attached harmlessly to the face and scalp, the electroencephalograph records the brain's electrical activity throughout the night. Although the equipment may look cumbersome and uncomfortable, people generally sleep just fine with all the wires attached.

The Onset of Sleep and Hypnagogic Hallucinations

Awake and reasonably alert as you prepare for bed, your brain generates small, fast brain waves, called **beta brain waves.** After your head hits the pillow and you close your eyes, your muscles relax. Your brain's electrical activity gradually gears down, generating slightly larger and slower **alpha brain waves.** As drowsiness sets in, your thoughts may wander and become less logical.

During this drowsy, presleep phase, you may experience odd but vividly realistic sensations. You may hear your name called or a loud crash, feel as if you're falling or floating, smell something burning, or see kaleidoscopic patterns or an unfolding landscape. These vivid sensory phenomena that occasionally occur during the transition from wakefulness to light sleep are called **hypnagogic hallucinations** (Mavromatis, 1987). Some hypnagogic hallucinations can be so vivid or startling that they cause a sudden awakening.

Probably the most common hypnagogic hallucination is the vivid sensation of falling. The sensation of falling is often accompanied by a *myoclonic jerk*—an involuntary muscle spasm of the whole body that jolts the person completely awake (Cooper, 1994). Also known as *sleep starts,* these experiences can seem really weird (or embarrassing) when they occur. But, you can rest assured, they are not abnormal. Almost all of our students have reported occasionally experiencing the hypnagogic hallucination of falling combined with a myoclonic jerk.

AH YES, THE OL' "SECONDS AWAY FROM BLISSFUL SLUMBER" BODY SPASM

FIGURE 4.2 The First 90 Minutes of Sleep
From wakefulness to the deepest sleep of stage 4 NREM, the brain's activity, measured by EEG recordings, progressively diminishes, as demonstrated by larger and slower brain waves. The four NREM stages occupy the first 50 to 70 minutes of sleep. Then, in a matter of minutes, the brain cycles back to smaller, faster brain waves, and the sleeper experiences the night's first episode of dreaming REM sleep, which lasts 5 to 15 minutes. During the rest of the night, the sleeper continues to experience 90-minute cycles of alternating NREM and REM sleep.

SOURCE: Based on Hobson (1995).

The First 90 Minutes of Sleep and Beyond

The course of a normal night's sleep follows a relatively consistent cyclical pattern. As you drift off to sleep, you enter NREM sleep and begin a progression through the four NREM sleep stages (see Figure 4.2). Each progressive NREM sleep stage is characterized by corresponding decreases in brain and body activity. On average, the progression through the first four stages of NREM sleep occupies the first 50 to 70 minutes of sleep.

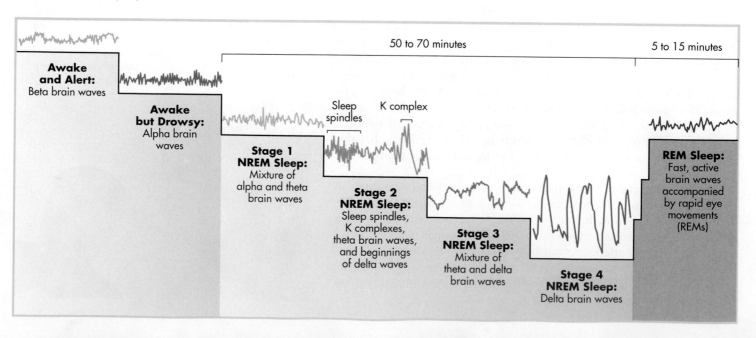

Awake and Alert: Beta brain waves

Awake but Drowsy: Alpha brain waves

Stage 1 NREM Sleep: Mixture of alpha and theta brain waves

Stage 2 NREM Sleep: Sleep spindles, K complexes, theta brain waves, and beginnings of delta waves

Stage 3 NREM Sleep: Mixture of theta and delta brain waves

Stage 4 NREM Sleep: Delta brain waves

REM Sleep: Fast, active brain waves accompanied by rapid eye movements (REMs)

50 to 70 minutes

5 to 15 minutes

Sleep spindles

K complex

Stage 1 NREM

As the alpha brain waves of drowsiness are replaced by even slower *theta brain waves,* you enter the first stage of sleep. Lasting only a few minutes, stage 1 is a transitional stage during which you gradually disengage from the sensations of the surrounding world. Familiar sounds, such as the hum of the refrigerator or the sound of traffic, gradually fade from conscious awareness. During stage 1 NREM, you can quickly regain conscious alertness if needed. Although hypnagogic experiences can occur in stage 1, less vivid mental imagery is common, such as imagining yourself engaged in some everyday activity, much as Mike imagined himself unpacking boxes at work. Although dreamlike, these images lack the unfolding, sometimes bizarre details of a true dream.

Stage 2 NREM

Stage 2 represents the onset of true sleep. Stage 2 sleep is defined by the appearance of **sleep spindles,** brief bursts of brain activity that last a second or two, and **K complexes,** single high-voltage spikes of brain activity (see Figure 4.2). Other than these occasional sleep spindles and K complexes, brain activity continues to slow down considerably. Breathing becomes rhythmical. Slight muscle twitches may occur. Theta waves are predominant in stage 2, but larger, slower brain waves, called *delta brain waves,* also begin to emerge. During the 15 to 20 minutes initially spent in stage 2, delta brain-wave activity gradually increases.

Stage 3 and Stage 4 NREM

Stages 3 and 4 of NREM are physiologically very similar. Both stages are defined by the amount of delta brain-wave activity. In combination, stages 3 and 4 are sometimes referred to as *slow-wave sleep.* When delta brain waves represent more than 20 percent of total brain activity, the sleeper is said to be in stage 3 NREM. When delta brain waves exceed 50 percent of total brain activity, the sleeper is said to be in stage 4 NREM.

During the 20 to 40 minutes spent in the night's first episode of stage 4 NREM, delta waves eventually come to represent 100 percent of brain activity. At that point, heart rate, blood pressure, and breathing rate drop to their lowest levels. Not surprisingly, the sleeper is almost completely oblivious to the world. Noises as loud as 90 decibels may fail to wake him. However, his muscles are still capable of movement. For example, if sleepwalking occurs, it typically happens during stage 4 NREM sleep (see In Focus Box 4.1 on page 136).

It can easily take 15 minutes or longer to regain full waking consciousness from stage 4. It's even possible to answer a ringing phone, carry on a conversation for several minutes, and hang up without ever leaving stage 4 sleep—and without remembering the conversation the next day. When people are briefly awakened by sleep researchers during stage 4 NREM and asked to perform some simple task, they often don't remember it the next morning.

beta brain waves
Brain-wave pattern associated with alert wakefulness.

alpha brain waves
Brain-wave pattern associated with relaxed wakefulness and drowsiness.

hypnagogic hallucinations
(hip-na-GAH-jick) Vivid sensory phenomena that occur during the onset of sleep.

sleep spindles
Short bursts of brain activity that characterize stage 2 NREM sleep.

K complex
Single but large high-voltage spike of brain activity that characterizes stage 2 NREM sleep.

Synchronized Sleepers As these time-lapse photographs show, couples who regularly sleep in the same bed tend to have synchronized sleep cycles. Since bed partners fall asleep at about the same time, they are likely to have similarly timed NREM–REM sleep cycles. The movements of this couple are also synchronized. Both sleepers shift position just before and after episodes of REM sleep.

IN FOCUS 4.1

What You Really Want to Know About Sleep

Why do I yawn? Is yawning contagious?

Research has contradicted the popular notion that too little oxygen or too much carbon dioxide causes yawning. Rather, yawning regulates and increases your level of arousal. Yawning is typically followed by an *increase* in activity level. Hence, you frequently yawn after waking up in the morning, while attempting to stay awake in the late evening, or when you're bored.

Reading about or even thinking about yawning can trigger the behavior. (Have you yawned yet?) Studies have shown that more than half of adults will yawn when they're shown videos of other people yawning. Although infants and children younger than age 5 don't display contagious yawning, it turns out that chimpanzees do. One explanation for contagious yawning is that it may have evolved as a social cue, helping groups to coordinate times of activity or rest.

Why do I get sleepy?

Research suggests that a naturally occurring compound in the body called *adenosine* may be the culprit. In studies with cats, prolonged wakefulness results in a sharp increase in adenosine levels, which reflect energy used for brain and body activity. As adenosine levels shoot up, so does the need for sleep. Slow-wave NREM sleep reduces adenosine levels. In humans, the common stimulant drug caffeine blocks adenosine receptors, promoting wakefulness.

Sometimes in the morning when I first wake up, I can't move. I'm literally paralyzed! Is this normal?

REM sleep is characterized by paralysis of the voluntary muscles, which keeps you from acting out your dreams. In a relatively common phenomenon called **sleep paralysis**, the paralysis of REM sleep carries over to the waking state for up to 10 minutes. If preceded by an unpleasant dream or hypnagogic experience, this sensation can be frightening. Sleep paralysis can also occur as you're falling asleep. In either case, the sleep paralysis lasts for only a few minutes. So, if this happens to you, relax—voluntary muscle control will soon return.

Do deaf people who use sign language sometimes "sleep sign" during sleep?

Yes.

Do the things people say when they talk in their sleep make any sense?

Sleeptalking typically occurs during NREM stages 3 and 4. There are many anecdotes of spouses who have supposedly engaged their sleeptalking mates in extended conversations, but sleep researchers have been unsuccessful in having extended dialogues with people who chronically talk in their sleep. As far as the truthfulness of the sleep-talker's utterances go, they're reasonably accurate insofar as they reflect whatever the person is responding to while asleep. By the way, not only do people talk in their sleep, but they can also sing in their sleep. In one case we know of, a little boy sleep-sang "Frosty the Snowman."

Is it dangerous to wake a sleepwalker?

It's not dangerous to wake a sleepwalker, it's just difficult, because sleepwalkers are in deep sleep. However, as sleepwalkers usually respond to verbal suggestions, it's relatively easy to guide them back to bed.

Sleepwalking may have a genetic component. Identical twins are much more likely to share this characteristic than are nontwin siblings. One college student confided to sleep researcher Jacob Empson (2002) that her whole family sleepwalked. She reported that one morning, her entire family woke up to find themselves seated around the kitchen table, where they had all gathered in their sleep!

SOURCES: J. R. Anderson & Meno (2003); J. R. Anderson & others (2004); Empson (2002); Ozbayrak & Berlin (1995); Platek & others (2003); Porkka-Heiskanen & others (1997); Provine (1989); Roenneberg & others, 2003; Saper & others, 2005; Spanos, McNulty, & others (1995a).

Thus far in our description, the sleeper is approximately 70 minutes into a typical night's sleep and immersed in deeply relaxed stage 4 NREM sleep. At this point, the sequence reverses. In a matter of minutes, the sleeper cycles back from stage 4 to stage 3 to stage 2 and enters a dramatic new phase: the night's first episode of REM sleep.

REM Sleep

During REM sleep, the brain becomes more active, generating smaller and faster brain waves (Hobson, 2005). Visual and motor neurons in the brain activate repeatedly, just as they do during wakefulness. Dreams usually occur during REM sleep. Although the brain is very active, voluntary muscle activity is suppressed, which prevents the dreaming sleeper from acting out those dreams.

REM sleep is accompanied by considerable physiological arousal. The sleeper's eyes dart back and forth behind closed eyelids—the rapid eye movements. Heart rate, blood pressure, and respirations can fluctuate up and down, sometimes extremely. Muscle twitches occur. In both sexes, sexual arousal may occur, which is not necessarily related to dream content.

sleep paralysis
A temporary condition in which a person is unable to move upon awakening in the morning or during the night.

This first REM episode tends to be brief, about 5 to 15 minutes. From the beginning of stage 1 NREM sleep through the completion of the first episode of REM sleep, about 90 minutes have elapsed.

Beyond the First 90 Minutes

Throughout the rest of the night, the sleeper cycles between NREM and REM sleep. Each cycle lasts about 90 minutes on average, but the duration of cycles may vary from 70 to 120 minutes. Usually, four more 90-minute cycles of NREM and REM sleep occur during the night. Just before and after REM periods, the sleeper typically shifts position.

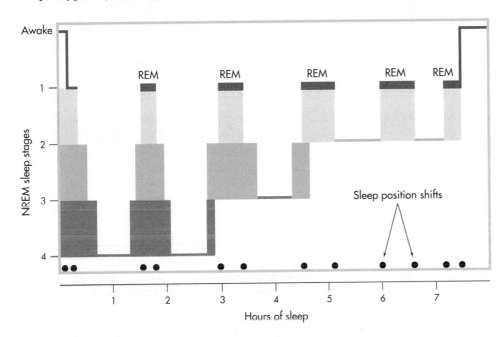

FIGURE 4.3 The 90-Minute Cycles of Sleep
During a typical night, you experience five 90-minute cycles of alternating NREM and REM sleep. The deepest stages of NREM sleep, stages 3 and 4, occur during the first two 90-minute cycles. Dreaming REM sleep episodes become progressively longer as the night goes on. Sleep position shifts, indicated by the dots, usually occur immediately before and after REM episodes.

SOURCE. Based on Hobson (1995).

The progression of a typical night's sleep cycles is depicted in Figure 4.3. Stages 3 and 4 NREM, slow-wave sleep usually occur only during the first two 90-minute cycles. As the night progresses, REM sleep episodes become increasingly longer and less time is spent in NREM. During the last two 90-minute sleep cycles before awakening, NREM sleep is composed primarily of stage 2 sleep and periods of REM sleep can last as long as 40 minutes. In a later section, we'll look at dreaming and REM sleep in more detail.

Changes in Sleep Patterns over the Lifespan

Over the course of our lives, the quantity and quality of our sleep change considerably (see Figure 4.4 on page 138). REM sleep begins long before birth, as scientists have discovered by using ultrasound to document fetal eye movements and by studying the sleep of premature infants. Four months before birth, REM sleep seems to constitute virtually all of fetal life. By one month before birth, the fetus demonstrates distinct sleep–wake cycles, spending around 12 hours each day in REM sleep (Mindell, 1997).

A newborn sleeps approximately 16 hours a day, about 50 percent of which is REM sleep. By the end of the first year of life, total sleep time drops to around 13 hours a day, about one-third of which is REM sleep.

In general, from birth onward, the average amount of time spent sleeping each day gradually decreases (see Figure 4.4). The amount of time devoted to REM sleep and slow-wave NREM sleep each night also gradually decreases over the lifespan (Bliwise, 1997). Young children can easily spend two hours or more each night in the deep sleep of stages 3 and 4 NREM. By early adulthood,

Sleep-Deprived Adolescents Teenagers require about 8.5 to 9 hours of sleep each night to be fully rested. However, only one out of seven U.S. teens actually gets that much sleep. Most adolescents report getting around 7 to 7.5 hours of sleep on school nights, which is probably why they sleep about 2 hours longer on weekends. Consequences of regular sleep loss include poor school performance, increased risk of accidents and injuries, and depressed mood (National Sleep Foundation, 2000).

FIGURE 4.4 Changes in REM and NREM Sleep Both the quality and quantity of sleep change over the lifespan. Even before birth, the cycles of REM and NREM sleep are evident. A newborn infant sleeps about 16 hours per day, with about 50 percent of sleep time devoted to REM. From birth onward, total sleep time, REM sleep, and NREM sleep slowly decrease. Time spent in stages 3 and 4, the deepest stages of NREM, also decreases over the lifespan.

SOURCE: Based on Hobson (1995).

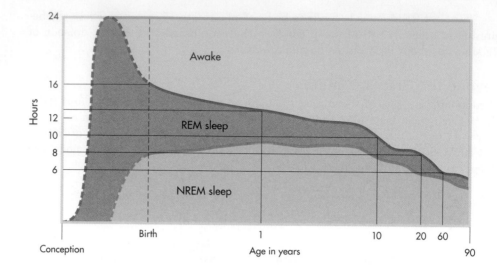

about an hour is spent in deep sleep each night. And by late adulthood, only about 20 minutes of a night's sleep is spent in stages 3 and 4 NREM sleep (Williams & others, 1994). By the time people reach their sixties, total sleep time averages about six hours per night and the quality of sleep is much more shallow.

Why Do We Sleep?

Key Theme

- Sleep deprivation studies demonstrate that we have a biological need for sleep, but the functions of sleep are not completely understood.

Key Questions

- What are REM and NREM rebound, and what insights do they provide into the function of sleep?
- How do the restorative and adaptive theories of sleep explain the function of sleep?

That we have a biological need for sleep is clearly demonstrated by *sleep deprivation studies* (see Siegel, 2005). After as little as one night's sleep deprivation, research subjects develop *microsleeps,* which are episodes of sleep lasting only a few seconds that occur during wakefulness. People who go without sleep for a day or more also experience disruptions in mood, mental abilities, reaction time, perceptual skills, and complex motor skills (Gökcebay & others, 1994).

Getting *less* sleep than you need (as many adults do) can also have negative effects. In one study, young men whose sleep was restricted to four hours a night for as few as six consecutive nights experienced harmful changes in metabolic and endocrine functioning (Spiegel & others, 1999). As sleep researcher Eve Van Cauter (1999) explained, "After only one week of sleep restriction, young, healthy males had glucose levels that were no longer normal. That's a rapid deterioration of the body's functions."

Sleep researchers have also selectively deprived people of different components of normal sleep. For example, to study the effects of *REM deprivation,* researchers wake sleepers whenever the monitoring instruments indicate that they are entering REM sleep. After several nights of being selectively deprived of REM sleep, the subjects are allowed to sleep uninterrupted. What happens? The first time subjects are allowed to sleep without interruption, they experience **REM rebound**—the amount of time spent in REM sleep increases by as much as 50 percent. Similarly, when people are selectively deprived of NREM stages 3 and 4, they experience *NREM rebound,* spending more time in NREM sleep.

REM rebound
A phenomenon in which a person who is deprived of REM sleep greatly increases the amount of time spent in REM sleep at the first opportunity to sleep uninterrupted.

restorative theory of sleep
The view that sleep and dreaming are essential to normal physical and mental functioning.

adaptive theory of sleep
The view that the unique sleep patterns of different animals evolved over time to help promote survival and environmental adaptation; also called the *evolutionary theory of sleep.*

sleep disorders
Serious disturbances in the normal sleep pattern that interfere with daytime functioning and cause subjective distress.

The phenomena of REM rebound and NREM rebound seem to indicate that the brain needs to make up for missing components of sleep. Clearly, we need both to sleep and to experience the full range of sleep stages. But what particular functions does sleep serve?

The **restorative theory of sleep** suggests that sleep promotes physiological processes that restore and rejuvenate the body and the mind (Gökcebay & others, 1994). According to this theory, NREM and REM sleep serve different purposes. NREM sleep is thought to be important for restoring the body, whereas REM sleep is thought to restore mental and brain functions (Maquet, 2001; Stickgold & others, 2001).

Evidence supporting the role of NREM sleep in restoring the body comes from studies that have demonstrated increased deep sleep following sleep deprivation, starvation, and strenuous athletic activity. In response to such stressors, the secretion of growth hormone, testosterone, prolactin, and other hormones increases during NREM sleep (Hirshkowitz & others, 1997).

The importance of REM sleep in mental and brain functions is suggested by the abundance of REM sleep in the developing fetus, in infants, and in young children and its subsequent decrease throughout adulthood (see Figure 4.4). Tentatively, this suggests that REM sleep plays some role in stimulating the high rate of brain development that occurs in the early stages of the lifespan.

In contrast to the restorative theory, the **adaptive theory of sleep** suggests that the sleep patterns exhibited by different animals, including humans, are the result of evolutionary adaptation (Webb, 1975). Also called the *evolutionary theory of sleep,* the basic idea is that different sleep patterns evolved as a way of preventing a particular species from interacting with the environment when doing so is most hazardous. Animals with few natural predators, such as gorillas and lions, sleep as much as 15 hours a day. In contrast, grazing animals, such as cattle and horses, tend to sleep in short bursts that total only about 4 hours per day (Siegel, 2005). Hibernation patterns of animals such as bears and gophers also coincide with periods during which environmental conditions pose the greatest threat to survival.

Although there is evidence to support both the restorative and the adaptive theories of sleep, many questions remain. The bottom line is that researchers still aren't sure exactly what physiological functions are served by sleep (Maquet, 2001; Morrison, 2003). Sleep may well fulfill multiple purposes.

Question: When Does an 800-Pound Predator Sleep? Answer: Any time it wants to! According to the adaptive theory of sleep, animals that have few predators, such as lions and polar bears, have the luxury of sleeping out in the open during daylight hours. Animals that are vulnerable to predators, such as giraffes and mice, sleep only fitfully or in well-protected nests (Siegel, 2005).

Sleep Disorders: Troubled Sleep

Key Theme
■ Sleep disorders take many different forms and are surprisingly common.

Key Questions
■ How is insomnia defined, and how common is it?
■ What are the most important parasomnias?
■ What is narcolepsy?

Sleep disorders are serious disturbances in the normal sleep pattern that interfere with daytime functioning and cause subjective distress (American Psychiatric Association, 2000a). Virtually everyone is seriously troubled by the quality or quantity of their sleep at some point. And, if you happen to be someone who regularly experiences sleep-related problems, you're not alone. According to a recent Sleep in America Poll, seven out of ten American adults report frequent sleep problems, including inadequate amounts of sleep. Other highlights from the National Sleep Foundation's annual surveys are presented in Table 4.2 on page 140.

The Perils of Driving While Drowsy According to studies reported by the National Highway Traffic Safety Administration (2003), drowsiness is blamed for at least 100,000 traffic accidents each year, causing more than 70,000 injuries—and 1,500 deaths. While many people in the United States get by with too little sleep, one group is especially prone to the effects of sleepiness behind the wheel—adult males age 25 or younger. Young male drivers have the highest number of traffic accidents that can be attributed to drowsiness (National Sleep Foundation, 2000).

insomnia
A condition in which a person regularly experiences an inability to fall asleep, to stay asleep, or to feel adequately rested by sleep.

restless legs syndrome (RLS)
A condition in which unpleasant sensations in the lower legs are accompanied by an irresistible urge to move the legs, temporarily relieving the unpleasant sensation but disrupting sleep.

Table 4.2

The National Sleep Foundation Survey: Asleep at the Wheel?

Key findings from the Sleep in America Poll, a national survey of randomly selected American adults:

- 37% reported being so sleepy during the day that it interfered with their daily activities.
- 40% compensated for sleep lost during the week by sleeping an extra hour or more on the weekends.
- 43% use caffeine to help them stay awake during the day.
- 51% have driven when drowsy during the past year.
- 17% have actually fallen asleep at the wheel in the past year.
- 1% have had a traffic accident due to being drowsy or falling asleep at the wheel.

SOURCE: National Sleep Foundation (2002, 2004).

Insomnia

By far the most common sleep complaint among adults is insomnia (Mahowald & Schenk, 2005). According to the 2002 National Sleep Foundation survey, 58 percent of adults are affected a few nights or more each week by at least one symptom of insomnia, such as waking up and being unable to go back to sleep.

Insomnia is not defined solely on the basis of the amount of time a person sleeps because people vary in how much sleep they need to feel refreshed. Rather, people are said to experience **insomnia** when they repeatedly complain about the quality or duration of their sleep, have difficulty going to sleep or staying asleep, or wake before it is time to get up.

For an estimated 12 million Americans, complaints of insomnia are related to a condition called **restless legs syndrome,** abbreviated **RLS.** People with RLS complain of unpleasant creeping, crawling, tingling, itching, or prickling sensations deep inside their lower legs accompanied by an irresistible urge to move (Mahowald & Schenk, 2005). These sensations are most prominent in the evening and at night, especially when the individual lies down or sits still for any length of time (Rothenberg, 1997). Moving the legs temporarily reduces the unpleasant sensations but also interferes with the person's ability to fall asleep or stay asleep.

More commonly, insomnia can often be traced to stressful life events, such as job or school difficulties, troubled relationships, the death of a loved one, or financial problems. Concerns about sleeping can add to whatever waking anxieties the person may already be experiencing. This can create a *vicious circle*—worrying about the inability to sleep makes troubled sleep even more likely, further intensifying anxiety.

Numerous studies have shown that behavior therapy and different medications are effective in the short-term treatment of insomnia (M. T. Smith & others, 2002). Behavioral techniques often help people develop better sleep habits. For example, a treatment called *stimulus control* conditions the person to associate the bed only with sleepiness and sleep, rather than with watching television, talking on the phone, or other nonsleep activities. Relaxation training and meditation, which we will discuss later in the chapter, are also commonly used to treat insomnia (Murtagh & Greenwood, 1995).

Educating people on sleep hygiene is often part of the successful treatment of insomnia. For example, many people troubled by the inability to sleep use alcohol or over-the-counter sleep medications to induce sleep. In the Prologue to this chapter, you saw how Mike resorted to a stiff drink to help him relax and go back to sleep. Although such remedies may temporarily help people fall asleep, both sleeping pills and alcohol disrupt normal sleep cycles, including REM sleep (Roehrs &

Insomnia Following the September 11th Attacks A surge in the number of Americans experiencing symptoms of insomnia occurred in the weeks and months following the terrorist attacks on the Pentagon and the World Trade Center on September 11, 2001. According to a survey conducted by the National Sleep Foundation (2002), seven out of ten Americans experienced one or more symptoms of insomnia, such as having trouble falling asleep at night or frequent awakenings during the night. The psychological toll of the attacks was more pronounced in women. Females were more likely than males (78 percent vs. 59 percent) to report that they had experienced symptoms of insomnia during the weeks immediately following the attacks.

Roth, 2001). Even the sleep-inducing medications sometimes prescribed by physicians to treat insomnia must be carefully managed to avoid drug dependence.

Sleep Apnea

The second most common sleep disorder, sleep apnea, affects some 20 million Americans (Carskadon & Taylor, 1997). In **sleep apnea,** the sleeper repeatedly stops breathing during the night. Carbon dioxide builds up in the blood, causing a momentary awakening, during which the sleeper snorts or gulps in air. Breathing may stop for as little as 10 seconds or for so long that the sleeper's skin turns blue before he or she wakes up. During a single night, more than 300 sleep apnea attacks can occur. Often the person has no recollection of the repeated awakenings but feels sleepy throughout the following day.

Sleep apnea is more common in men over the age of 50, especially those who are overweight, but also occurs in women and even children (Mahowald & Schenk, 2005). Special mouthpieces, weight loss, and surgical intervention have been effective in treating sleep apnea. For people who suffer from sleep apnea only when they sleep on their backs, treatment is sometimes as simple as sewing a tennis ball to the back of their pajama tops, which forces them to sleep on their sides (Saskin, 1997).

Sleepwalking and Night Terrors

Unlike insomnia, sleepwalking and night terrors are much more common in children than in adults. These sleep disturbances occur during the deepest stages of NREM sleep, stages 3 and 4. As noted previously, young children spend considerably more time each night in deep sleep than do adolescents or adults (Whyte & Schacter, 1995). Not surprisingly, most instances of bedwetting, or *nocturnal enuresis,* also tend to occur when the child is in deep sleep (Barclay & Houts, 1995a).

About 25 percent of all children experience at least one episode of **sleepwalking,** also known as *somnambulism.* Sleepwalking typically occurs during the first three hours after the child has gone to sleep. The child gets out of bed and moves about in a slow, poorly coordinated, automatic manner, usually with a blank, staring look on his face. Surprisingly, the sleepwalking child is usually able to navigate around objects without much difficulty. However, the child's general lack of awareness of his surroundings is evident. The sleepwalker may try to dress, eat, or go to the bathroom in the wrong location (Ozbayrak & Berlin, 1995).

Night terrors, or *sleep terrors,* also typically occur during stage 3 or 4 NREM sleep in the first few hours of sleep. Physiologically, a night terror is much more intense than a run-of-the-mill nightmare. The first sign of a night terror is sharply increased physiological arousal—restlessness, sweating, and a racing heart. Typically, the child experiencing night terrors abruptly sits up in bed and lets out a panic-stricken scream or cry for help as she thrashes about in bed or even sleepwalks. Terrified and disoriented, the child may struggle with a parent who tries to calm her down (Mahowald & Schenk, 2005).

Night terrors tend to be brief, usually lasting only a matter of seconds. Amazingly, the child almost immediately goes back to quiet sleep and wakes in the morning with no recollection of the incident. Unlike the unfolding dream story of a nightmare, night terrors are usually accompanied by a single but terrifying sensation, such as being crushed or falling. Often, the child imagines that she is choking or that a frightening figure is present, such as a threatening animal or monster (Kahn & others, 1991). Though dramatic, night terrors are not regarded as a true sleep disorder or psychological problem unless they occur frequently. For the vast majority of children who often experience night terrors, the problem usually resolves itself by early adolescence (Lask, 1995).

Our friend Nina, whom we described in the Prologue, is among the small percentage of people whose night terrors continue into adulthood. Just as when she

sleep apnea
(APP-nee-uh) A sleep disorder in which the person repeatedly stops breathing during sleep.

sleepwalking
A sleep disturbance characterized by an episode of walking or performing other actions during stage 3 or stage 4 NREM sleep; also called *somnambulism.*

night terrors
A sleep disturbance characterized by an episode of increased physiological arousal, intense fear and panic, frightening hallucinations, and no recall of the episode the next morning; typically occurs during stage 3 or stage 4 NREM sleep; also called *sleep terrors.*

Terror in the Night This print by French artist Jean Ignace Gérard is titled *The Nightmare.* However, the image of a monster lowering a weight on the sleeper's chest suggests instead the frightening experience of a night terror. Night terrors occur during NREM sleep and are almost always accompanied by a sensation of being crushed or smothered.

parasomnias

(pare-uh-SOM-nee-uz) A category of sleep disorders characterized by arousal or activation during sleep or sleep transitions; includes *sleepwalking, night terrors, sleep bruxism, sleep-related eating disorder,* and *REM sleep behavior disorder.*

REM sleep behavior disorder

A sleep disorder in which the sleeper acts out his or her dreams.

narcolepsy

(NAR-ko-lep-see) A sleep disorder characterized by excessive daytime sleepiness and brief lapses into sleep throughout the day.

cataplexy

A sudden loss of voluntary muscle strength and control that is usually triggered by an intense emotion.

An Episode of Cataplexy in Narcolepsy In this sequence of images, a man with narcolepsy experiences one of its most dramatic symptoms—cataplexy. Cataplexy involves the sudden and complete loss of muscle tone, and it is typically triggered by laughter, embarrassment, or some other type of emotional arousal. Although he is unable to move, the person remains conscious and aware of what is going on around him.

was a child, Nina doesn't remember her sleep terror episodes the next morning. However, her husband Mike has found that she seems most likely to experience a sleep terror episode when she is very tired or under stress.

Nina's parents told us that both Nina and her sister were sleepwalkers until their teenage years. As a child, Nina also experienced *sleep bruxism*—she would grind her teeth loudly in her sleep. Collectively, night terrors, sleepwalking, and sleep bruxism are referred to as **parasomnias,** a general category of sleep disorders that involve arousal or activation during sleep or sleep transitions (Mahowald & Schenk, 2005).

For example, consider the case of *sleep-related eating disorder,* which is most commonly diagnosed in women. People with this parasomnia will sleepwalk their way to the kitchen and compulsively eat, then awaken in the morning with no memory of the behavior. Although sweet-tasting foods like candy or cake are most commonly consumed, people will eat truly bizarre items, like raw bacon, cat food sandwiches, tubs of butter, slices of soap, or bouillon cube sandwiches (Schenk, 2003; Winkelman & others, 1999).

REM Sleep Behavior Disorder

Another, more serious parasomnia is **REM sleep behavior disorder** (Schenk & Mahowald, 2002). REM sleep behavior disorder typically affects men over the age of 50 and is characterized by the brain's failure to suppress voluntary muscle movements during REM sleep. Consequently, the dreamer acts out his dreams.

Interestingly, the dreams that are acted out in REM sleep behavior disorder are typically unusual for the dreamer. In one comprehensive review of REM sleep behavior disorder cases, 87 percent of the patients described feelings of fear and anger during dreams of being chased or attacked by unfamiliar people, animals, or insects (Schenk & Mahowald, 2002). Along with punching, kicking, yelling, and running, more complex behaviors have been reported, including attempting to leap through a window, setting fire to a bed, and firing an unloaded gun (Abad & Guilleminault, 2004). Tackling a chest of drawers or pummeling a bed partner are not uncommon. A key issue in REM sleep behavior disorder is protecting both the dreamer and his sleeping partner or housemates from such violent behavior.

REM sleep behavior disorder can occur as a side-effect of antidepressant or other medications. However, it is also associated with deterioration or damage in the brain regions that control arousal during sleep. In some cases, REM sleep behavior disorder is an early symptom of a neurological disorder, such as Parkinson's disease (Abad & Guilleminault, 2004; Mahowald & Schenck, 2005).

Narcolepsy

If you've ever tried to stay awake for 36 hours or longer, you know how incredibly sleepy you can get. That experience gives you an inkling of what life is like for people with narcolepsy. The most common, and most troubling, symptom of **narcolepsy** is excessive and recurring bouts of daytime sleepiness. People with narcolepsy experience an overwhelming sleepiness, lapsing into brief periods of sleep throughout the day that usually last an hour or less. These daytime sleep episodes occur regardless of how much nighttime sleep the person has had. They also often occur at inappropriate times, such as in the middle of a meeting.

The onset of these daytime sleep episodes is sometimes accompanied by frightening *hypnagogic hallucinations,* such as the house or building being on fire (see page 134). As the person awakens, he or she may briefly experience the sensation of being unable to move, which is termed *sleep paralysis* (see In Focus Box 4.1 on page 136). When these daytime sleep episodes occur suddenly, they are termed "sleep attacks."

Along with excessive daytime sleepiness, narcolepsy is often characterized by regular episodes of cataplexy. **Cataplexy** is the sudden loss of voluntary muscle strength and control, lasting from several seconds to several minutes. Cataplexy is usually triggered by a sudden, intense emotion, such as laughter, anger, or surprise. In mild episodes, the person's head may droop or facial muscles sag (Siegel, 2000). In more severe episodes, the person may completely lose muscle control. As shown in the accompanying series of photos, the person's knees buckle and he collapses on the floor.

The onset of narcolepsy typically occurs during adolescence, and it is considered a chronic, lifelong condition. Although estimates vary, approximately 250,000 Americans have narcolepsy, and it affects men and women equally (Zeman & others, 2004). Genetics seems to play an important role, as the disorder tends to run in families. Adding to the genetic evidence, scientists have identified the genes that produce narcoleptic symptoms in mice and dogs (Chemelli & others, 1999; Lin & others, 1999).

Although narcolepsy cannot be cured, a drug called *modafinil* (Provigil) reduces daytime sleepiness in people with narcolepsy (Baranski & others, 2004). Antidepressant medications can reduce episodes of cataplexy, hypnagogic hallucinations, and sleep paralysis. Stimulant drugs, such as Dexedrine and Ritalin, are also used to minimize narcoleptic symptoms.

Dreams and Mental Activity During Sleep

Key Theme
- A dream is an unfolding episode of vivid mental images that occurs during sleep.

Key Questions
- What patterns of brain activity are associated with dreaming sleep?
- How are dreams thought to aid memory consolidation?
- What do people dream about, and why don't we remember many of our dreams?

Dreams have fascinated people since the beginning of time. On average, about 25 percent of a night's sleep, or almost two hours every night, is spent dreaming. So, assuming you live to a ripe old age, you'll devote more than 50,000 hours, or about six years of your life, to dreaming.

Although dreams may be the most spectacular brain productions during sleep, they are *not* the most common. More prevalent is **sleep thinking,** which takes place during NREM sleep and consists of vague, uncreative, bland, and thoughtlike ruminations about real-life events (Hobson & Stickgold, 1995; Schatzman & Fenwick, 1994). For example, just before an important exam, students may review terms and concepts during NREM sleep.

In contrast to sleep thinking, a **dream** is an unfolding episode of mental images that is storylike, involving characters and events. According to sleep researcher J. Allan Hobson (1988), dreams have five basic characteristics:

- Emotions can be intense.
- Content and organization are usually illogical.
- Sensations are sometimes bizarre.
- Even bizarre details are uncritically accepted.
- Dream images are difficult to remember.

Many people believe that dreams occur only during REM sleep, but this is not the case. Dreams occur during both NREM and REM sleep (Rosenlicht & Feinberg, 1997). However, dreams during REM sleep are more frequent and of longer duration than are dreams during NREM sleep (Foulkes, 1997). When people are awakened during REM sleep, they will report a dream up to 90 percent of the time—even people who claim that they never dream.

sleep thinking
Repetitive, bland, and uncreative ruminations about real-life events during sleep.

dream
A storylike episode of unfolding mental imagery during sleep.

Dream Images Although people tend to emphasize visual imagery when they describe their dreams, sounds and physical sensations are also commonly present. Sensations of falling, flying, spinning, or trying to run may be experienced. We tend to dream of familiar people and places, but the juxtapositions of characters, objects, and events are typically illogical, even bizarre (Nielsen & Stenstrom, 2005). Nevertheless, the dreamer rarely questions a dream's details—until he or she wakes up!

People usually have four or five episodes of dreaming each night. Early-morning dreams, which can last as long as 40 minutes, are the dreams people are most likely to remember. Contrary to popular belief, dreams happen in real time, not in split seconds. In fact, dreamers tend to be quite accurate in estimating how long they've been dreaming (Empson, 2002).

The Brain During REM Sleep

What happens in the brain during REM sleep? Earlier in the chapter, we noted that EEG measurements show that the brain is highly active during REM sleep. In a series of PET scans of sleeping subjects, neuroscientist Allen Braun and his colleagues (1998) showed that the brain's activity during REM sleep is distinctly different from its activity during either wakefulness or slow-wave (NREM) sleep.

Braun found that both the primary visual cortex and the frontal lobes are essentially shut down during REM sleep. As we discussed in Chapter 2, the *primary visual cortex* is the area at the back of the brain that first registers visual information transmitted by the retinas of the eye. The *frontal lobes* are the brain areas responsible for higher-level cognitive processes, including reasoning, planning, and integrating perceptual information. Thus, during REM sleep, the sleeper is cut off from information about the external world *and* from the brain centers most involved in rational thought.

Other brain areas, however, are highly active during REM sleep. Activated areas include the *amygdala* and the *hippocampus,* structures of the limbic system that are involved in emotion, motivation, and memory (see Figure 2.20 on page 68). Also highly active are other parts of the brain's visual system that are involved in generating visual images (see Focus on Neuroscience on page 145).

These results suggest that the dreamer's uncritical acceptance of bizarre and chaotic dream images and narratives can be explained in terms of the inactivity of the frontal lobes—the very areas of the brain that are normally most active in analyzing and interpreting new information. In the absence of meaningful stimuli from the outside world, emotions and stored memories provide the raw data for the vivid visual images conjured up by the sleeping brain.

REM Sleep and Memory Consolidation

As you'll see in Chapter 6, *memory consolidation* refers to the gradual process of converting new memories into a long-term, relatively permanent form. Research suggests that sleep helps consolidate memories, especially *procedural memories* (Stickgold, 2005; Stickgold & others, 2001). Procedural memories are essentially memories for *how* to perform sequences of behaviors. For example, when you play the piano or a video game, you're drawing on your procedural memories.

Studies have shown that REM sleep increases after learning a novel task and that deprivation of REM sleep following training disrupts learning (Maquet, 2001). The importance of REM sleep was demonstrated in one study in which volunteers were trained on a simple but challenging perceptual task before going to sleep (Karni & others, 1994). Half the participants were repeatedly awakened during NREM sleep stages, while the other half were repeatedly awakened during REM sleep. The volunteers who enjoyed uninterrupted REM (dreaming) sleep improved their performance on the test the next day, but the participants whose REM sleep was disrupted did not.

While REM sleep appears to play an important role in memory consolidation, exactly how it does so is still unclear (Stickgold, 2005). Some studies have shown that brain areas activated during training on a particular task are actually *reactivated* during REM sleep (Louie & Wilson, 2001; Maquet & others, 2000). Thus, REM sleep seems to help stabilize the neural connections acquired through recent experience.

"Look, don't try to weasel out of this. It was my dream, but you had the affair in it."

Neuroscience: Brain Changes During REM Sleep

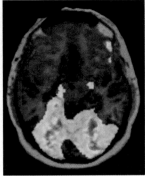
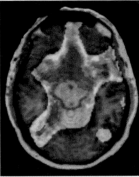

(a) REM sleep compared to wakefulness

(b) REM sleep compared to slow-wave sleep

These PET scans reveal how brain activity during REM sleep differs from wakefulness (scan *a*) and slow-wave sleep (scan *b*). The PET scans are color-coded: Yellow-red indicates areas of increased brain activity, and bluish-purple indicates areas of decreased brain activity.

Compared to wakefulness, scan (*a*) reveals that REM sleep involves decreased activity in the frontal lobes, which are involved in rational thinking, and the primary visual cortex, which processes external visual stimuli. The yellow-red areas indicate increased activity in visual areas associated with visual imagery—the images occurring in a dream.

Compared to slow-wave sleep, the yellow-red areas in scan (*b*) indicate that REM sleep is characterized by a sharp increase in areas of the limbic system that are associated with emotion, motivation, and memory. The activation of these brain areas reflects the intense emotions that often characterize dreams (Braun & others, 1998).

In combination, these two PET scans document the high degree of mental imagery and emotionality that takes place in the dreaming brain. But the brain changes that occur during REM sleep also show that the dreamer is cut off from the reality-testing functions of the frontal lobes—a fact that no doubt contributes to the sometimes bizarre nature of dreams.

What Do We Dream About?

Although nearly everyone can remember an unusually bizarre dream, most dreams are a reflection of everyday life, including people we know and familiar settings (Domhoff, 1999; Weinstein & others, 1991). Recall Mike's nightmare about his new boss, which was described in the Prologue. The giant staircase and spiral escalators were exaggerated versions of real architectural features of the atrium-style lobby of the hotel where he works.

Dream researcher Calvin Hall collected and analyzed over 10,000 dreams from hundreds of people. He found that a dream's themes often reflect the daily concerns of the dreamer (Hall & Van de Castle, 1966). Worries about exams, money, health, troubled relationships, or jobs are all likely to be reflected in our dreams—as was Mike's anxiety about his new boss.

Certain themes, such as falling, being chased, or being attacked, are surprisingly common across cultures. As you can see in Table 4.3, although thousands of miles apart and immersed in two very different cultures, American and Japanese college students share many dream themes. Surveys of dream content in many cultures have shown that dreamers around the world report more instances of negative events than of positive events (Domhoff, 1996). Instances of aggression are more common than are instances of friendliness, and dreamers are more likely to be victims of aggression than aggressors in their dreams. There is more aggression in men's dreams than in women's dreams, but women are more likely to dream that they are the victims of physical aggression.

Environmental cues *during* dreaming can also influence dream content. In sleep labs, researchers have played recordings of a rooster crowing, a bugle playing reveille, and a dog barking. Researchers have even sprayed water on sleeping subjects. Depending on the stimulus, up to half the dreamers incorporated the external stimulation into their dream content (Arkin & Antrobus, 1991).

Table 4.3

Common Dream Themes Across Cultures

	Percentage of Students Saying "Yes"	
	American	**Japanese**
Have you ever dreamed of . . . ?		
1. being attacked or pursued	77	91
2. falling	83	74
3. trying again and again to do something	71	87
4. school, teachers, studying	71	86
5. being frozen with fright	58	87
6. sexual experiences	66	68
7. arriving too late (e.g., missing train)	64	49
8. dead people as though alive	46	57
9. loved person being dead	57	42
10. being on the verge of falling	47	45
11. failing an examination	39	41
12. flying or soaring through air	34	46
13. being smothered, unable to breathe	44	33
14. seeing self as dead	33	35
15. being nude	43	17

SOURCE: Adapted from data reported in Empson (2002).

What You Really Want to Know About Dreams

If I fall off a cliff in my dreams and don't wake up before I hit the bottom, will I die?

The first obvious problem with this bit of folklore is that if you did die before you woke up, how would anyone know what you'd been dreaming about? Beyond this basic contradiction, studies have shown that about a third of dreamers can recall a dream in which they died or were killed. Dream sensations such as falling, soaring through the air, and being paralyzed seem to be universal.

Do animals dream?

Virtually all mammals experience sleep cycles in which REM sleep alternates with slow-wave NREM sleep. Animals clearly demonstrate perception and memory. They also communicate using vocalizations, facial expressions, posture, and gestures to show territoriality and sexual receptiveness. Thus, it's quite reasonable to conclude that the brain and other physiological changes that occur during animal REM sleep are coupled with mental images. One bit of anecdotal evidence supporting this idea involved a gorilla that had been taught sign language to communicate. The gorilla signed "sleep pictures," presumably referring to REM dream activity while it slept.

What do blind people "see" when they dream?

People who become totally blind before the age of 5 typically do not have visual dreams as adults. Even so, their dreams are just as complex and vivid as sighted people's dreams; they just involve other sensations—of sound, taste, smell, and touch.

Is it possible to control your dreams?

Yes, if you have lucid dreams. A *lucid dream* is one in which you become aware that you are dreaming while you are still asleep. About half of all people can recall at least one lucid dream, and some people frequently have lucid dreams. The dreamer can often consciously guide the course of a lucid dream, including backing it up and making it go in a different direction.

Can you predict the future with your dreams?

History is filled with stories of dream prophecies. Over the course of your life, you will have over 100,000 dreams. Simply by chance, it's not surprising that every now and then a dream contains elements that coincide with future events.

Are dreams in color or black and white?

Up to 80 percent of our dreams contain color. When dreamers are awakened and asked to match dream colors to standard color charts, soft pastel colors are frequently chosen.

SOURCES: Anch & others (1988); Blackmore (1998); Empson (2002); Halliday (1995); Hobson (2001); Hurovitz & others (1999); Schatzman & Fenwick (1994); Weinstein & others (1991).

Why Don't We Remember Our Dreams?

Even the best dream recallers forget the vast majority of their dreams—at least 95 percent, according to one estimate (Hobson, 1995). Why are dreams so much more difficult to remember than waking experiences? Several theories have been proposed, each with at least some evidence to support it.

As we'll discuss in more detail in Chapter 6, memory requires information to be processed and stored in such a way that it can be retrieved at a later time. One theory is that the fundamental changes in brain chemistry and functioning that occur during sleep fail to support such information processing and storage. For example, frontal lobe areas are involved in the formation of new memories. But as you read earlier, PET scans of sleeping volunteers have shown that the frontal lobes are inactive during REM sleep (Braun & others, 1998). Research has also shown that the neurotransmitters needed to acquire new memories—including serotonin, norepinephrine, and dopamine—are greatly reduced during REM sleep (Hobson, 2001; J. M. Siegel, 2001).

Some dreams are remembered, however, and several factors have been found to influence dream recall. First, you're much more likely to recall a dream if you wake up during it (Schredl & Montasser, 1997). When people are intentionally awakened during REM sleep, they usually recall the dream content. There are also individual differences in dream recall. Some people frequently remember their dreams in vivid detail. Other people hardly ever remember their dreams. Research has shown that people who are better at remembering visual details while awake are also better at recalling their dreams (Schredl & others, 1995).

Second, the more vivid, bizarre, or emotionally intense a dream is, the more likely it is to be recalled the following morning. Vivid dreams are also

"Off with his head! Off with his head!"

more likely to be remembered days or weeks after the dream has occurred (Hobson, 2001). In many respects, this is very similar to waking experiences. Whether you're awake or asleep, mundane and routine experiences are most likely to be forgotten.

Third, distractions on awakening interfere with our ability to recall dreams, as noted by psychologist Mary Calkins (1893) over a century ago:

> To recall a dream requires usually extreme and immediate attention to the content of the dream. Sometimes the slight movement of reaching for paper and pencil or of lighting one's candle seems to dissipate the dream-memory, and one is left with the tantalizing consciousness of having lived through an interesting dream-experience of which one has not the faintest memory.

Finally, it's difficult to remember *any* experience that occurs during sleep, not just dreams. Sleep researchers have found that people who are briefly awakened during the night to give reports or perform simple tasks frequently do not remember the incident the next morning. It seems clear, then, that the brain is largely programmed to forget not only the vast majority of dream experiences but also other experiences that happen during sleep.

Nightmares

An unpleasant anxiety dream that occurs during REM sleep is called a **nightmare.** Nightmares often produce spontaneous awakenings, during which the vivid and frightening dream content is immediately recalled. The general theme of nightmares is of being helpless or powerless in the face of great danger or destruction.

Nightmares are especially common in young children (Halliday, 1995). For example, when our daughter Laura was 4 years old, she told us about this vivid nightmare:

> There was a big monster chasing me and Nubbin the Cat! And we jumped on a golden horse but the monster kept chasing us! Then Nubbin jumped off and started to eat the monster. And then Mommy came and saved me! And then Daddy took a sword and killed the monster! And then me and Mommy and Nubbin rode the horse into the clouds.

Like Laura, young children often have nightmares in which they are attacked by an animal or monster. In dealing with a child who has experienced a nightmare, simple reassurance is a good first step, followed by an attempt to help the child understand the difference between an imaginary dream and a real waking experience. In adults, an occasional nightmare is a natural and relatively common experience (Wood & Bootzin, 1990). Nightmares are not considered indicative of a psychological or sleep disorder unless they frequently cause personal distress.

The Significance of Dreams

Key Theme
■ Theoretical approaches vary greatly in their explanations of the meaning of dreams.

Key Questions
■ How did Freud explain dreams?
■ How does the activation–synthesis model explain dreams?
■ What general conclusions can be drawn about the nature of dreams?

For thousands of years and throughout many cultures, dreams have been thought to contain highly significant, cryptic messages. Do dreams mean anything? Do they contain symbolic messages? In this final section on dreaming, we will look at two theories that try to account for the purpose of dreaming, starting with the most famous one.

nightmare
A frightening or unpleasant anxiety dream that occurs during REM sleep.

"Shouldn't Willis be in the bed and his imaginary monster under it?"

Freud on the Meaning of Dreams Dream intrepretation played an important role in Sigmund Freud's famous form of psychotherapy, called *psychoanalysis.* Freud believed that because psychological defenses are reduced during sleep, frustrated sexual and aggressive wishes are expressed symbolically in dreams. "In every dream an instinctual wish has to be represented as fulfilled," Freud (1933) wrote. According to Freud, we consciously remember the *manifest content,* or actual dream images. Hidden is what Freud called the *latent content*—the true, unconscious meaning of the dream which is disguised by the dream symbols.

Dream Researcher J. Allan Hobson Neuroscientist J. Allan Hobson developed the activation–synthesis model of dreaming with his colleague Robert McCarley. Although Hobson believes that dreams are the by-products of physiological processes in the brain, he does not believe that dreams are meaningless. Hobson (1999) observed, "Dreaming may be our most creative conscious state, one in which the chaotic, spontaneous recombination of cognitive elements produces novel configurations of information: new ideas. While many or even most of these ideas may be nonsensical, if even a few of its fanciful products are truly useful, our dream time will not have been wasted."

Sigmund Freud: Dreams as Fulfilled Wishes

In the chapters on personality and psychotherapy (Chapters 10 and 14), we'll look in detail at the ideas of **Sigmund Freud,** the founder of psychoanalysis. As we discussed in Chapter 1, Freud believed that sexual and aggressive instincts are the motivating forces that dictate human behavior. Because these instinctual urges are so consciously unacceptable, sexual and aggressive thoughts, feelings, and wishes are pushed into the unconscious, or *repressed.* However, Freud believed that these repressed urges and wishes could surface in dreams.

In his landmark work, *The Interpretation of Dreams* (1900), Freud wrote that dreams are the "disguised fulfillments of repressed wishes" and provide "the royal road to a knowledge of the unconscious mind." Freud believed that dreams function as a sort of psychological "safety valve" for the release of unconscious and unacceptable urges.

Freud (1904) believed that dreams have two components: the **manifest content,** or the dream images themselves, and the **latent content,** the disguised psychological meaning of the dream. For example, Freud (1911) believed that dream images of sticks, swords, and other elongated objects were phallic symbols, representing the penis. Dream images of cupboards, boxes, and ovens supposedly symbolized the vagina.

In many types of psychotherapy today, especially those that follow Freud's ideas, dreams are still seen as an important source of information about psychological conflicts. However, Freud's belief that dreams represent the fulfillment of repressed wishes has not been substantiated by psychological research (Fisher & Greenberg, 1996; Schatzman & Fenwick, 1994). Furthermore, research does not support Freud's belief that the dream images themselves—the manifest content of dreams—are symbols that disguise the dream's true psychological meaning (Domhoff, 1996).

The Activation–Synthesis Model of Dreaming

Armed with an array of evidence that dreaming involves the activation of different brain areas during REM sleep, researcher **J. Allan Hobson** and his colleague Robert McCarley first proposed a new model of dreaming in 1977. Called the **activation–synthesis model of dreaming,** this model maintains that dreaming is our subjective awareness of the brain's internally generated signals during sleep (Hobson, 1995; Hobson & Stickgold, 1995). Since it was first proposed, the model has evolved as new findings have been reported (Hobson & others, 1998; Stickgold & others, 2001).

Specifically, the activation–synthesis model maintains that the experience of dreaming sleep is due to the automatic activation of brainstem circuits at the base of the brain (see Figure 4.5). These circuits arouse more sophisticated brain areas, including visual and auditory pathways. As noted earlier, limbic system structures involved in emotion, such as the amygdala and hippocampus, are also activated during REM sleep. When we're awake, these pathways and brain structures are involved in registering stimuli from the external world. But rather than responding to stimulation from the external environment, the dreaming brain is responding to its own internally generated signals (Hobson, 2005).

In the absence of external sensory input, the activated brain combines, or synthesizes, these internally generated sensory signals and imposes meaning on them. The dream story itself is derived from a hodgepodge of memories, emotions, and sensations that are triggered by the brain's activation and chemical changes during sleep. According to this model, then, dreaming is essentially the brain synthesizing and integrating memory fragments, emotions, and sensations that are internally triggered (Hobson & others, 1998).

The activation–synthesis theory does *not* state that dreams are completely meaningless (Hobson & Stickgold, 1995). But if there is a meaning to dreams, that meaning lies in the deeply personal way in which the images are organized,

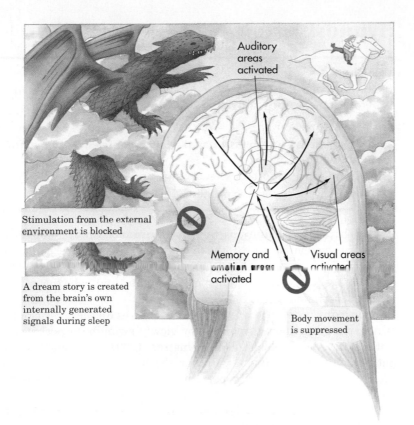

FIGURE 4.5 The Activation–Synthesis Model of Dreaming: Laura's Dream According to the activation–synthesis model, dreaming is caused by the activation of brainstem circuits that arouse other brain areas involved in sensations, emotions, and memories. The results of these internally generated signals are the dream images and sensations that the activated brain synthesizes, or combines. The dreaming person imposes a personal meaning on the dream story (Hobson & others, 1998).

Auditory areas activated

Stimulation from the external environment is blocked

A dream story is created from the brain's own internally generated signals during sleep

Memory and emotion areas activated

Visual areas activated

Body movement is suppressed

or synthesized. In other words, the meaning is to be found not by decoding the dream symbols, but by analyzing the way the dreamer makes sense of the progression of chaotic dream images.

Some Observations About the Meaning of Dreams

Subjectively, it seems obvious that at least some of our dreams mirror our real-life concerns, frustrations, anxieties, and desires. Less subjectively, this observation is consistent with sleep research on the content of dreams (Nielsen & Stenstrom, 2005; Weinstein & others, 1991). Large-scale analyses of dream reports demonstrate that dreams reflect the waking concerns and preoccupations of the dreamer (Domhoff, 1993, 1996). Thus, the topics you think about during the day are most likely to influence the topics you dream about at night (Nikles & others, 1998). Some dream researchers believe that most dreams, however chaotic or disorganized, are meaningfully related to the dreamers' current concerns, problems, and waking lives (Domhoff, 2003).

It may well be that the more bizarre aspects of dream sequences—the sudden scene changes, intense emotions, and vivid, unrealistic images—are due to physiological changes in the brain during REM and NREM sleep. Dream researcher David Foulkes (1993, 1997) argues that dreaming consciousness is no different from waking consciousness in its attempt to make sense of the information that is available to it. What differs is the *source* of the information. When we're awake, we monitor the external environment, making sense of the stimuli that impinge upon us from the environment as well as our own thoughts, feelings, and fantasies. During sleep, we try—as best we can—to make sense of the less orderly stimuli produced by the brain itself.

If nothing else, remember that the interpretation of dreams occurs when we're awake. It seems reasonable, then, to suggest that conscious speculations about the meaning of these elusive nightly productions might reveal more about the psychological characteristics of the interpreter than about the dream itself (Cartwright & Kas1991).

manifest content
In Freud's psychoanalytic theory, the elements of a dream that are consciously experienced and remembered by the dreamer.

latent content
In Freud's psychoanalytic theory, the unconscious wishes, thoughts, and urges that are concealed in the manifest content of a dream.

activation–synthesis model of dreaming
The theory that brain activity during sleep produces dream images (*activation*), which are combined by the brain into a dream story (*synthesis*).

hypnosis
(hip-NO-sis) A cooperative social inter-action in which the hypnotized person responds to the hypnotist's suggestions with changes in perception, memory, and behavior.

posthypnotic suggestion
A suggestion made during hypnosis that the person should carry out a specific instruction following the hypnotic session.

posthypnotic amnesia
The inability to recall specific informa-tion because of a hypnotic suggestion.

hypermnesia
(high-perm-NEE-zha) The supposed enhancement of a person's memory for past events through a hypnotic suggestion.

Hypnosis

Key Theme
- During hypnosis, people respond to suggestions with changes in perception, memory, and behavior.

Key Questions
- What characteristics are associated with responsiveness to hypnotic suggestions?
- What are some important effects of hypnosis?
- How has hypnosis been explained?

What is hypnosis? Definitions vary, but **hypnosis** can be defined as a cooperative social interaction in which the hypnotic participant responds to suggestions made by the hypnotist. These suggestions for imaginative experiences can produce changes in perception, memory, thoughts, and behavior (American Psychological Association, 2001).

For many people the word *hypnosis* conjures up the classic but sinister image of a hypnotist inducing hypnosis by slowly swinging a pocket watch back and forth. But, as psychologist John Kihlstrom (2001) explains, "The hypnotist does not hypnotize the individual. Rather, the hypnotist serves as a sort of coach or tutor whose job is to help the person become hypnotized." After experiencing hypnosis, some people are able to self-induce hypnosis.

The word *hypnosis* is derived from the Greek *hypnos,* meaning "sleep." The idea that the hypnotized person is in a sleeplike trance is still very popular among the general public. However, the phrase *hypnotic trance* is misleading and rarely used by researchers today (Wagstaff, 1999). When hypnotized, people do *not* lose control of their behavior. Instead, they typically remain aware of where they are, who they are, and what is transpiring.

Rather than being a sleeplike trance, hypnosis is characterized by highly focused attention, increased responsiveness to suggestions, vivid images and fantasies, and a willingness to accept distortions of logic or reality. During hypnosis, the person temporarily suspends her sense of initiative and voluntarily accepts and follows the hypnotist's instructions (Hilgard, 1986a).

Although most adults are moderately hypnotizable, people vary in their responsiveness to hypnotic suggestions. About 15 percent of adults are highly susceptible to hypnosis, and 10 percent are difficult or impossible to hypnotize (Hilgard, 1982; Register & Kihlstrom, 1986). Children tend to be more responsive to hypnosis than are adults, and children as young as 5 years old can be hypnotized (Kohen & Olness, 1993). Evidence suggests that the degree of susceptibility to hypnosis tends to run in families. For example, identical twins are more similar in their susceptibility to hypnosis than are fraternal twins (Nash, 2001).

The best candidates for hypnosis are individuals who approach the experience with positive, receptive attitudes. The expectation that you will be responsive to hypnosis also plays an important role (Kirsch & others, 1995; Spanos & others, 1993). People who are highly susceptible to hypnosis have the ability to become deeply absorbed in fantasy and imaginary experience. For instance, they easily become absorbed in reading fiction, watching movies, and listening to music (Barnier & McConkey, 1999; Kihlstrom, 2001).

Effects of Hypnosis

Deeply hypnotized subjects sometimes experience profound changes in their subjective experience of consciousness. They may report feelings of detachment from their bodies, profound relaxation, or sensations of timelessness. More commonly, hypnotized people converse normally and remain fully aware of their

How Is the Hypnotic State Produced? In a willing volunteer, hypnosis can be induced in a variety of ways, but swinging a pocket watch is usually not one of them. Instead, as psychologist Michael Nash demonstrates, hypnosis is more commonly induced by speaking in a calm, monotonous voice, suggesting that the person is becoming drowsy, sleepy, and progressively more relaxed. To help the volunteer focus her attention, the hypnotist may also ask her to concentrate on a simple visual stimulus, such as a spot on the wall.

surroundings. Often, they will later report that carrying out the hypnotist's suggestions seemed to happen by itself. The action seems to take place outside the hypnotized person's will or volition.

Sensory and Perceptual Changes

Some of the most dramatic effects that can be produced with hypnosis are alterations in sensation and perception. Sensory changes that can be induced through hypnosis include temporary blindness, deafness, or a complete loss of sensation in some part of the body (Hilgard, 1986a). For example, when the suggestion is made to a highly responsive subject that her arm is numb and cannot feel pain, she will not consciously experience the pain of a pinprick or of having her arm immersed in ice water. This property of hypnosis has led to its use as a technique in pain control (Montgomery & others, 2000). Painful dental and medical procedures, including surgery, have been successfully performed with hypnosis as the only anesthesia (Hilgard & others, 1994).

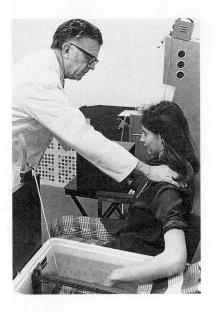

Hypnotic Suppression of Pain In this classic photo taken at the Stanford Laboratory of Hypnosis Research, psychologist Ernest Hilgard (1904–2001) instructs this hypnotized young woman that she will feel no pain in her arm. Her arm is then immersed in circulating ice water for several minutes, and she reports that she does not experience any pain. In contrast, a nonhypnotized subject perceives the same experience as extremely painful and can keep his arm in the ice water for no more than a few seconds.

People can experience hallucinations under hypnosis. If a highly responsive hypnotic subject is told that a close friend is sitting in a chair on the other side of the room, she will not only report seeing the friend in vivid detail but will walk over and "touch" the other person. Under hypnosis, people can also *not* perceive something that *is* there. For example, if the suggestion is made that a jar of rotten eggs has no smell, a highly suggestible person will not consciously perceive any odor.

Hypnosis can also influence behavior *outside* the hypnotic state. When a **posthypnotic suggestion** is given, the person will carry out that specific suggestion after the hypnotic session is over. For example, under hypnosis, a student was given the posthypnotic suggestion that the number 5 no longer existed. He was brought out of hypnosis and then asked to count his fingers. He counted 11 fingers! Counting again, the baffled young man was at a loss to explain his results.

Some posthypnotic suggestions have been reported to last for months, but most last only a few hours or days (Barnier & McConkey, 1998). So, even if the hypnotist does not include some posthypnotic signal to cancel the posthypnotic suggestion, the suggestion will eventually wear off.

Hypnosis and Memory

Memory can be significantly affected by hypnosis. In **posthypnotic amnesia,** a subject is unable to recall specific information or events that occurred before or during hypnosis. Posthypnotic amnesia is produced by a hypnotic suggestion that suppresses the memory of specific information, such as the subject's street address. The effects of posthypnotic amnesia are usually temporary, disappearing either spontaneously or when a posthypnotic signal is suggested by the hypnotist. When the signal is given, the information floods back into the subject's mind.

The opposite effect is called **hypermnesia,** which is enhancement of memory for past events through hypnotic suggestion. Police investigators sometimes use hypnosis in an attempt to enhance the memories of crime victims and witnesses. Despite the common belief that you can "zoom in" on briefly seen crime details under hypnosis, such claims are extremely exaggerated (Smith, 1983). Compared with regular police interview methods, hypnosis does *not* significantly enhance memory or improve the accuracy of memories (Nash, 2001; Register & Kihlstrom, 1987).

Many studies have shown that efforts to enhance memories hypnotically can lead to distortions and inaccuracies (Burgess & Kirsch, 1999). In fact, hypnosis can greatly increase confidence in memories that are actually incorrect (Kihlstrom & Barnhardt, 1993). False memories, also called *pseudomemories,* can be inadvertently created when hypnosis is used to aid recall (Lynn & Nash, 1994; Yapko, 1994a).

Age Regression through Hypnosis? Some people believe that hypnosis can allow you to re-experience an earlier stage of your life—a phenomenon called *age regression* (J. Green, 1999b). Under hypnosis, some adults *do* appear to relive experiences from their childhood, confidently displaying childlike speech patterns and behaviors. However, when attempts are made to verify specific details of the experiences, the details are usually inaccurate (Spanos, 1987–1988). Just as actual deafness and blindness are not produced by hypnotic suggestion, neither is a true return to childhood. Instead, hypnotic subjects combine fragments of actual memories with fantasies and ideas about how children of a particular age should behave.

Is Hypnosis a Special State of Consciousness?

One of the great debates in modern psychology comes down to this question: Are the changes in perception, thinking, and behaviors that occur during hypnosis the result of a "special" or "altered" state of consciousness? Here, we'll touch on some of the evidence for three competing points of view on this issue.

The State View: Hypnosis Involves a Special State of Consciousness

Considered the traditional viewpoint, the "state" explanation contends that hypnosis is a unique state of consciousness, distinctly different from our normal waking consciousness (Kosslyn & others, 2000). The state view is perhaps best represented by Hilgard's *neodissociation theory of hypnosis.* According to this view, consciousness is split into two simultaneous streams of mental activity during hypnosis. One stream of mental activity remains conscious, but a second stream of mental activity—the one responding to the hypnotist's suggestions—is "dissociated" from awareness. So according to the neodissociation explanation, the hypnotized young woman shown on page 151, whose hand is immersed in ice water, reported no pain because the painful sensations were dissociated from awareness.

The Non-State View: Ordinary Social Psychological Processes Can Explain Hypnosis

Some psychologists flatly reject the notion that hypnotically induced changes involve a "special" state of consciousness. According to the *social-cognitive view of hypnosis,* subjects are responding to the *social demands* of the hypnosis situation. They act the way they think good hypnotic subjects are supposed to act, conforming to the expectations of the hypnotist, their own expectations, and situational cues. In this view, the "hypnotized" young woman on page 151 reported no pain because that's what she expected to happen during the hypnosis session.

To back up the social-cognitive theory of hypnosis, Nicholas Spanos (1991, 1994, 1996) and his colleagues have amassed an impressive array of evidence showing that highly motivated people often perform just as well as hypnotized subjects in demonstrating pain reduction, amnesia, age regression, and hallucinations. Studies of people who simply *pretended* to be hypnotized have shown similar results. On the basis of such findings, non-state theorists contend that hypnosis can be explained in terms of rather ordinary psychological processes, including imagination, situational expectations, role enactment, compliance, and conformity (Wagstaff, 1999).

PET Scans During Hypnosis: Does the Brain Respond Differently?

Trying to reconcile the state and non-state explanations of hypnosis, researcher Stephen Kosslyn and his colleagues (2000) conducted a brain-imaging study. Highly hypnotizable volunteers viewed two images of rectangles, one in bright colors and one in shades of gray, while lying in a PET scanner. The researchers measured activity in brain regions known to be involved in color perception. While hypnotized, the participants were instructed to perform three tasks: to see the images as they were; to mentally "drain" color from the colored rectangles in order to see them in shades of gray; and to mentally "add" color to the gray rectangles. Essentially, these last two tasks were hypnosis-induced hallucinations.

What did the PET scans reveal? In contrast to what might be expected if the participants were merely playing the role of hypnotic subject, hypnosis produced distinct effects on brain activity. When the hypnotized participants were instructed to perceive colored rectangles, color regions in the brain activated, *regardless* of whether the participants were shown colored or gray rectangles. When participants were instructed to perceive gray rectangles, color regions in the brain deactivated, *regardless* of whether the participants were shown colored or gray rectangles. In other words, brain activity reflected the hypnosis-induced hallucinations—not the actual images that were shown to the participants. On the basis of these findings, Kosslyn (2001) concluded, "Hypnosis is not simply 'role playing,' but does in fact reflect the existence of a distinct mental brain state."

The Imaginative Suggestibility View: Some People Are Highly Suggestible

Psychologists Irving Kirsch and Wayne Braffman (2001) dismiss the idea that hypnotic subjects are merely acting. But they also contend that brain-imaging studies don't necessarily prove that hypnosis is a unique or distinct state. Rather, Kirsch and

The Limits of Hypnosis

Although the effects of hypnosis can be dramatic, there are limits to the behaviors that can be influenced by hypnosis. First, contrary to popular belief, you cannot be hypnotized against your will. Second, hypnosis cannot make you perform behaviors that are contrary to your morals and values. Thus, you're very unlikely to commit criminal or immoral acts under the influence of hypnosis—unless, of course, you find such actions acceptable (Hilgard, 1986b).

Third, hypnosis cannot make you stronger than your physical capabilities or bestow new talents. However, hypnosis *can* enhance physical skills or athletic ability by increasing motivation and concentration (Morgan, 1993). Table 4.4 on page 154 provides additional examples of how hypnosis can be used to help people.

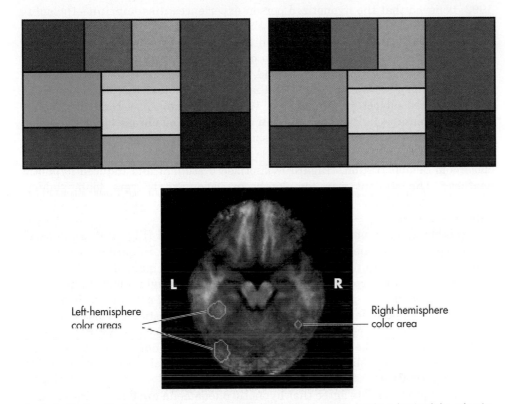

concluded that the effects of hypnosis are due to neither a unique psychological state nor role-playing. "Hypnotic responses reveal an astounding capacity that some people have to alter their experience in profound ways," Kirsch and Braffman (2001) write. "Hypnosis is only one of the ways in which this capacity is revealed. It can also be evoked—and almost to the same extent—without inducing hypnosis."

Psychologists continue to debate the essential nature of hypnosis and the best explanation of hypnotic effects (Kihlstrom, 2001). Despite the controversy over how best to explain hypnotic effects, psychologists do agree that hypnosis can be a highly effective therapeutic technique (Kirsch & others, 1995; Montgomery & others, 2000).

Brain Activation During Hypnosis The rectangles shown here—one in bright colors and the other in shades of gray—were used as stimuli to test brain activity during hypnosis. When hypnotized participants were asked to mentally add color to the gray rectangles, activity in brain regions involved in color perception sharply increased, as this PET scan shows. Conversely, when hypnotized participants were instructed to mentally drain color from the colored rectangles, the brain's color-perception regions deactivated. In other words, brain activity reflected the participants' subjective experience of the hypnosis-induced hallucinations—not the actual stimuli that were shown. According to the researchers, such findings contradict the notion that hypnosis is merely role playing (Kosslyn & others, 2001).

Braffman maintain that such studies emphasize individual differences in *imaginative suggestibility*—the degree to which a person is able to experience an imaginary state of affairs as if it were real.

In previous research, Braffman and Kirsch (1999) found that many participants were just as responsive to suggestions when they had *not* been hypnotized as when they had been hypnotized. They

Critical Thinking Questions

- Does the fact that highly motivated subjects can "fake" hypnotic effects invalidate the notion of hypnosis as a unique state of consciousness?

- Do individual differences in "imaginative suggestibility" provide a simpler explanation than "dissociation" in explaining responsiveness to hypnotic suggestions?

- What kinds of evidence could prove or disprove the notion that hypnosis is a unique state of consciousness?

Can hypnosis be used to help you lose weight, stop smoking, or stop biting your nails? The effectiveness of hypnosis in modifying habitual behaviors varies. For example, research provides little evidence to support the notion that hypnosis is more effective than other methods in controlling smoking behavior (Green & Lynn, 2000). In study after study, hypnosis has failed to produce long-term cessation of smoking (Spanos & others, 1995b). In contrast, hypnosis coupled with cognitive-behavioral therapy does enhance the effectiveness of weight-loss programs (J. Green, 1999a; Kirsch, 1996). In Chapter 14, on therapies, we'll explore cognitive and behavior therapy techniques in detail.

Table 4.4

Help Through Hypnosis

Research has demonstrated that hypnosis can effectively:

- Reduce pain and discomfort associated with cancer, rheumatoid arthritis, burn wounds, and other chronic conditions
- Reduce pain and discomfort associated with childbirth
- Reduce the use of narcotics to relieve postoperative pain
- Improve the concentration, motivation, and performance of athletes
- Lessen the severity and frequency of asthma attacks
- Eliminate recurring nightmares
- Enhance the effectiveness of psychotherapy in the treatment of obesity, hypertension, and anxiety
- Remove warts
- Eliminate or reduce stuttering
- Suppress the gag reflex during dental procedures

dissociation
The splitting of consciousness into two or more simultaneous streams of mental activity.

neodissociation theory of hypnosis
Theory proposed by Ernest Hilgard that explains hypnotic effects as being due to the splitting of consciousness into two simultaneous streams of mental activity, only one of which the hypnotic participant is consciously aware of during hypnosis.

hidden observer
Hilgard's term for the hidden, or dissociated, stream of mental activity that continues during hypnosis.

meditation
Any one of a number of sustained concentration techniques that focus attention and heighten awareness.

Explaining Hypnosis

Consciousness Divided?

How can hypnosis be explained? Psychologist **Ernest R. Hilgard** (1986a, 1991, 1992) believed that the hypnotized person experiences **dissociation**—the splitting of consciousness into two or more simultaneous streams of mental activity. According to Hilgard's **neodissociation theory of hypnosis,** a hypnotized person consciously experiences one stream of mental activity that is responding to the hypnotist's suggestions. But a second, dissociated stream of mental activity is also operating, processing information that is unavailable to the consciousness of the hypnotized subject. Hilgard (1986a, 1992) referred to this second, dissociated stream of mental activity as the **hidden observer.** (The phrase *hidden observer* does *not* mean that the hypnotized person has multiple personalities.)

Hilgard accidentally discovered the "hidden observer" while conducting a classroom demonstration. Hilgard hypnotized a student and induced hypnotic deafness. The student was completely unresponsive to very loud, sudden sounds, such as the sound of a starter pistol firing or of wooden blocks being banged together.

Another student, observing the demonstration, asked Hilgard if "some part" of the hypnotized person was actually aware of the sounds. Hilgard instructed the hypnotized student to raise his right index finger if some part of him could still hear. To Hilgard's surprise, the hypnotized student's right index finger rose! When brought out of hypnosis, the student had no recall of any sounds during the hypnotically induced deafness, *including* Hilgard's suggestion to raise his index finger. Hypnosis, it seems, had produced a split in consciousness. A conscious segment complied with the hypnotic suggestion of deafness, but a separate, dissociated segment unavailable to consciousness—the hidden observer—continued to process information.

Not all psychologists agree that hypnotic phenomena are due to dissociation, divided consciousness, or a hidden observer. In Critical Thinking Box 4.3 on pages 152–153, we examine this controversy more fully.

Meditation

Key Theme
- Meditation involves using one of various techniques to deliberately change conscious experience, inducing a state of focused attention and awareness.

Key Questions
- What are two general types of meditation?
- What are the effects of meditation?

Meditation refers to a group of techniques that induce an altered state of focused attention and heightened awareness. Meditation takes many forms and has been used for thousands of years as part of religious practices throughout the world. Virtually every major religion—Hinduism, Taoism, Buddhism, Judaism, Christianity, and Islam—has a rich tradition of meditative practices (Nelson, 2001). However, many people practice meditation independently of any religious tradition or spiritual context. Some forms of psychotherapy also include meditative practice as a component of the overall therapy (Epstein, 1995; Segal & others, 2002).

Common to all forms of meditation is the goal of controlling or retraining attention. Although meditation techniques vary a great deal, they can be divided into two general categories. *Concentration techniques* involve focusing awareness on a visual image, your breathing, a word, or a phrase. When a sound is used, it is typically a short word or a religious phrase, called a *mantra,* that is repeated mentally. *Opening-up techniques* involve a present-centered awareness of the passing moment, without mental judgment (Tart, 1994). Rather than concentrating on an object, sound, or activity, the meditator engages in quiet awareness of the "here and now" without distracting thoughts. The *zazen,* or "just sitting," technique of Zen Buddhism is a form of opening-up meditation (Austin, 1998).

Some meditative traditions, such as Zen Buddhism and mindfulness techniques, also stress the attainment of emotional control. This aspect of meditation has led to investigations of its effectiveness in programs to relieve anxiety and improve physical health and psychological well-being (Baer, 2003; Davidson & others, 2003).

Effects of Meditation

Much of the early research on meditation focused on its use as a relaxation technique that relieved stress and improved cardiovascular health. The meditation technique that was most widely used in this research was a from of concentrative meditation called *transcendental meditation* or *TM.* From a research standpoint, TM had many advantages. It can be quickly mastered and does not require any changes in lifestyle or beliefs. Practitioners follow a standardized, simple format. Meditators sit quietly with eyes closed and mentally repeat the mantra they have been given. Rather than struggling to clear the mind of thoughts, meditators are taught to allow distracting thoughts to simply "fall away" while they focus their attention on their mantra.

Numerous studies showed that even beginning meditators practicing TM experience a state of lowered physiological arousal, including a decrease in heart rate, lowered blood pressure, and changes in brain waves (C. N. Alexander & others, 1994; Dillbeck & Orme-Johnson, 1987). Advocates of TM claimed that such physical changes produce a unique state of consciousness with a wide variety of benefits, including stress reduction.

While much of the early research on meditation focused on short-term effects and meditation's health benefits, contemporary research on meditation is much more wide-ranging. One approach involves using sophisticated brain-imaging technology to study how the brain changes during meditation (Newberg & Iversen, 2003). Another approach involves the ongoing research collaboration among neuroscientists, psychologists, and a group of Tibetan Buddhist monks who

If you want to learn how to meditate, you can find the instructions for a simple but effective meditation technique on page 501.

Meditation in Different Cultures Meditation is an important part of many cultures. Tai chi is a form of meditation that involves a structured series of slow, smooth movements. Throughout China, many people begin their day with tai chi, often meeting in parks and other public places.

Studying the Well-Trained Mind Psychologist Richard Davidson talks with Buddhist monk Matthieu Ricard after a brain-imaging study. Tenzin Gyatso, the 14th Dalai Lama, has been instrumental in encouraging such collaborations between Western scientists and Tibetan Buddhists. As Gyatso (2003) wrote, "Buddhists have a 2,500-year history of investigating the workings of the mind. . . . Using imaging devices that show what occurs in the brain during meditation, Dr. Davidson has been able to study the effects of Buddhist practice for cultivating compassion, equanimity, or mindfulness."

have devoted decades to intensive study and meditative practice (Barinaga, 2003; Davidson, 2002). Because Tibetan Buddhism represents a rigorous system of mental training, researchers hope to learn more about conscious experience as well as meditation's effects on attention, emotional control, personality, and the brain (Houshmand & others, 2002; Lutz & others, 2004).

Many studies have shown that regular meditation can enhance physical and psychological functioning beyond that provided by relaxation alone (Andresen, 2000; Austin, 1998, 2003). Meditation and hypnosis are similar in that both involve the deliberate use of mental techniques to change the experience of consciousness. In the final section of this chapter, we'll consider one of the oldest strategies for deliberately altering conscious awareness—psychoactive drugs.

Psychoactive Drugs

Key Theme
- Psychoactive drugs alter consciousness by changing arousal, mood, thinking, sensations, and perceptions.

Key Questions
- What are four broad categories of psychoactive drugs?
- What are some common properties of psychoactive drugs?
- What factors influence the effects, use, and abuse of drugs?

Psychoactive drugs are chemical substances that can alter arousal, mood, thinking, sensation, and perception. In this section, we will look at the characteristics of four broad categories of psychoactive drugs:

1. *Depressants*—drugs that depress, or inhibit, brain activity
2. *Opiates*—drugs that are chemically similar to morphine and that relieve pain and produce euphoria
3. *Stimulants*—drugs that stimulate, or excite, brain activity
4. *Psychedelic drugs*—drugs that distort sensory perceptions

Common Properties of Psychoactive Drugs

Addiction is a broad term that refers to a condition in which a person feels psychologically and physically compelled to take a specific drug. People experience **physical dependence** when their body and brain chemistry have physically adapted to a drug. Many physically addictive drugs gradually produce **drug tolerance,** which means that increasing amounts of the drug are needed to gain the original, desired effect.

For people who are physically dependent on a drug, abstaining from the drug produces withdrawal symptoms. **Withdrawal symptoms** are unpleasant physical reactions to the lack of the drug, plus an intense craving for it. Withdrawal symptoms are alleviated by taking the drug again. Often, the withdrawal symptoms are opposite to the drug's action, a phenomenon called the **drug rebound effect.** For example, withdrawing from stimulating drugs, like the caffeine in coffee, may produce depression and fatigue. Withdrawal from depressant drugs, such as alcohol, may produce excitability.

Each psychoactive drug has a distinct biological effect. Psychoactive drugs may influence many different bodily systems, but their consciousness-altering effects are primarily due to their effect on the brain. Typically, these drugs influence brain activity by altering synaptic transmission among neurons. As we discussed in

psychoactive drug
A drug that alters consciousness, perception, mood, and behavior.

physical dependence
A condition in which a person has physically adapted to a drug so that he or she must take the drug regularly in order to avoid withdrawal symptoms.

drug tolerance
A condition in which increasing amounts of a physically addictive drug are needed to produce the original, desired effect.

withdrawal symptoms
Unpleasant physical reactions, combined with intense drug cravings, that occur when a person abstains from a drug on which he or she is physically dependent.

drug rebound effect
Withdrawal symptoms that are the opposite of a physically addictive drug's action.

drug abuse
Recurrent drug use that results in disruptions in academic, social, or occupational functioning or in legal or psychological problems.

Chapter 2, drugs affect synaptic transmission by increasing or decreasing neurotransmitter amounts or by blocking, mimicking, or influencing a particular neurotransmitter's effects (see Figure 2.6, page 47). Chronic drug use can also produce long-term changes in brain structures and functions, as discussed in the Focus on Neuroscience on page 158.

The biological effects of a given drug vary somewhat from one person to another. The person's weight, gender, and age may influence the intensity of the drug's effects. Whether the drug is taken on a full or empty stomach or in combination with other drugs also plays a role. Racial and ethnic differences may affect how a drug is metabolized. For example, African-Americans seem to absorb more nicotine from cigarettes than do European-Americans or Mexican-Americans, and they metabolize the nicotine more slowly (Caraballo & others, 1998; Pérez-Stable & others, 1998).

Psychological and environmental factors can also influence the effects of a drug. The response to a drug can be significantly affected by personality characteristics, mood, expectations, experience with the drug, and the setting in which the drug is taken (Marlatt & others, 1988; Stacy & others, 1990).

Why do people abuse drugs? There is no easy answer to that question. It's difficult to draw a hard-and-fast line between drug *use* and drug *abuse,* especially when the drug in question is legal, such as alcohol. Most people would not consider having a cold beer or two at a summer picnic an instance of drug abuse. Chug-a-lugging a six-pack, however, is a different matter.

In contrast to drug use, **drug abuse** refers to recurrent drug use that results in the disruption of academic, social, or occupational functioning or in legal or psychological problems (American Psychiatric Association, 2000a). Some authorities widen the definition of drug abuse to refer to *any* form of drug taking that results in harmful effects.

Many factors influence what is considered drug abuse. For example, determining what level of alcohol use constitutes "abuse" varies from one culture to another (Tanaka-Matsumi & Draguns, 1997). Even in the United States, different ethnic groups have very different norms regarding the use of alcohol. Jewish-, Italian-, Greek-, and Chinese-Americans have a tradition of moderate drinking. Drinking alcohol may be restricted to particular social occasions, such as weddings and other formal celebrations. Some U.S. religious groups, such as Mormons, Amish, and Muslims, forbid drinking alcohol under any circumstances. Asian-Americans and African-Americans have the lowest rates of alcohol use (Substance Abuse and Mental Health Services Administration, 2002).

Psychoactive Drugs As they take a break in a Jerusalem café, these students talk and relax—with the help of beer, coffee, Coca-Cola, and cigarettes. Although not used in every culture, caffeine, nicotine, and alcohol are three of the most widely used psychoactive substances in the world.

Dangerous Drugs, Tragic Deaths Former baseball star Ken Caminiti was only 41 when he died of an accidental drug overdose—a lethal combination of cocaine and opiate painkillers. His heart had been weakened by years of drug abuse that included steroids, alcohol, and crack cocaine. Once voted baseball's Most Valuable Player, Caminiti was on probation for cocaine possession at the time of his death.

The Depressants
Alcohol, Barbiturates, and Tranquilizers

Key Theme
■ Depressants inhibit central nervous system activity, while opiates are addictive drugs that relieve pain and produce euphoria.

Key Questions
■ What are the physical and psychological effects of alcohol?
■ How do barbiturates and tranquilizers affect the body?
■ What are the effects of opiates, and how do they affect the brain?

The **depressants** are a class of drugs that depress or inhibit central nervous system activity. In general, depressants produce drowsiness, sedation, or sleep. Depressants also relieve anxiety and lower inhibitions. All depressant drugs are potentially physically addictive. Further, the effects of depressant drugs are *additive,* meaning that the sedative effects are increased when depressants are combined.

Neuroscience: The Addicted Brain: Diminishing Rewards

focus on

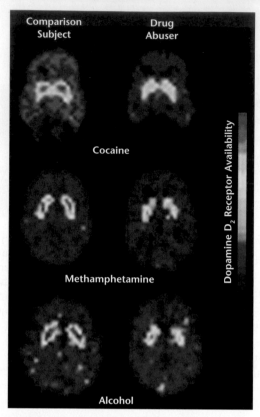

Comparison Subject | Drug Abuser

Cocaine

Methamphetamine

Alcohol

Dopamine D$_2$ Receptor Availability

Common Effects of Abused Drugs Different abused drugs initially produce their intoxicating effects in the same way—by increasing dopamine levels in the brain's reward system. But as the brain adjusts to the effects of drug abuse, long-term changes occur in the brain's reward circuitry. In the brain scans shown here, orange and yellow areas indicate the greatest number of dopamine receptors. As you compare the scans, you can see that regardless of the specific drug, drug abuse sharply reduces the number of dopamine receptors in the brain's reward system.

Addictive drugs include alcohol, cocaine, heroin, nicotine, and the amphetamines. Although their effects are diverse, these addictive drugs share one thing in common: They all activate dopamine-producing neurons in the brain's reward system. The initial dopamine surge in response to drug use is the internal reinforcing reward, prompting the person to repeat the drug-taking behavior (Self, 2005).

The brain's reward system evolved to reinforce behaviors that promote survival, such as eating and sexuality. A wide range of pleasurable activities can cause a temporary increase in dopamine levels, including exercising, listening to music, eating a delicious dessert, and even looking at an attractive person.

But in contrast to such naturally rewarding activities and substances, the artificially intense rewards of addictive drugs hijack the brain's reward system. Initially, the drug produces the intense dopamine-induced feelings of euphoria. But with repeated drug use, the brain's reward pathways *adapt* to the high dopamine levels. One result is that the availability of dopamine receptors is greatly reduced (Goldstein & Volkow, 2002). Along with decreased dopamine activity, other biochemical changes dampen or inhibit the brain's reward circuits, reducing the pleasurable effects of the abused substance. These adaptations create the conditions for *drug tolerance*—more of the substance is now needed to produce the same effect on mood and concentration (Nestler & Malenka, 2004).

As the brain's reward circuits are diminished, another change occurs. The normally reinforcing experiences in everyday life are no longer satisfying. Emotionally, depression and other negative emotional states become dominant (Little & others, 2003).

When the addictive drug is not taken, withdrawal symptoms occur, accompanied by intense craving for the abused substance. What causes the craving? One explanation is that the neurons in the brain's reward circuits have become hypersensitive to the abused substance (Nestler, 2001). Because the neurons physically change, this sensitization can be long-lasting, persisting for months and even years after drug use has ended. This is also why relapse can occur long after someone has stopped abusing drugs. Simply being exposed to drug-related stimuli or stressful life events can trigger craving—and relapse (Volkow & others, 2003).

With advanced imaging techniques, researchers are pinpointing the structural and functional changes in the brain's reward system in response to drug abuse (Lu & others, 2005). By identifying the common biochemical and physical changes that occur, scientists may one day be able to create more effective treatments to counteract the destructive effects of addictive drugs.

Alcohol

A staple of the human diet for thousands of years, alcoholic beverages provide a good example of the potential for a psychoactive drug to be misused (Vallee, 1998). Used in small amounts, alcohol reduces tension and anxiety. Evidence exists that light drinking reduces the risk of heart disease, probably because of its beneficial effects on cholesterol levels. Weddings, parties, and other social gatherings often include alcohol, a tribute to its relaxing and social lubricating properties.

But even though alcohol is a legal and readily available drug for adults, it's also a dangerous drug with a high potential for abuse. Consider these facts:

- Many drug experts believe that alcohol abuse has the highest social cost of all drug addictions.

- Alcohol is involved in at least 50 percent of all homicides, assaults, and highway fatalities (American Psychiatric Association, 2000a; Caetano & others, 2001).

- Approximately two-thirds of all cases of spousal abuse and violent child abuse involve alcohol use (Steele & Josephs, 1990).

- Drinking by pregnant women is the leading cause of birth defects and mental retardation—and the only preventable one (National Organization on Fetal Alcohol Syndrome, 2002).

depressants
A category of psychoactive drugs that depress or inhibit brain activity.

More than half of all Americans who are old enough to drink legally do so at least occasionally. An estimated 14 million Americans have serious alcohol problems. They drink excessively on a regular basis and suffer social, occupational, and health problems as a result of their drinking (Rosenberg, 1993). How many Americans are *alcoholics*—that is, physically addicted to alcohol? Estimates vary, but a recent survey conducted by the Substance Abuse and Mental Health Services Administration (2002) found that some 11 million people aged 12 and older were dependent upon or abused alcohol. Another 2 million people abused alcohol *and* one or more illegal drugs.

How Does Alcohol Affect the Body?   Generally, it takes about one hour to metabolize the alcohol in one drink, which is defined as 1 ounce of 80-proof whiskey, 4 ounces of wine, or 12 ounces of beer. All three drinks contain the same amount of alcohol; the alcohol is simply more diluted in beer than in hard liquor.

Factors such as body weight, gender, food consumption, and the rate of alcohol consumption also affect blood alcohol levels. A slender person who quickly consumes three drinks on an empty stomach will become more than twice as intoxicated as a heavier person who consumes three drinks with food. Women metabolize alcohol more slowly than do men. If a man and a woman of equal weight consume the same number of drinks, the woman will become more intoxicated.

Alcohol depresses the activity of neurons throughout the brain. Alcohol impairs cognitive abilities, such as concentration, memory, and speech, and physical abilities, such as muscle coordination and balance. As blood levels of alcohol rise, more brain activity is impaired, until the person loses consciousness. If blood alcohol levels continue to rise, death can occur because the brain's respiratory center can no longer function. For this reason, drinking contests are potentially lethal.

Binge drinking is a particularly risky practice. *Binge drinking* is defined as five or more drinks in a row for men, or four or more drinks in a row for women. Every year, several college students die of alcohol poisoning after ingesting large amounts of liquor in a short amount of time. Less well publicized are the other negative effects associated with binge drinking, including aggressive behavior, sexual assault, accidents, and property damage (Hingson & others, 2002; Wechsler & others, 2002).

A national survey of college students at 119 colleges found that close to 50 percent of all male students and 40 percent of all female students were binge drinkers (Wechsler & others, 2002). White students were most likely to binge-drink, while African-American students were least likely. While close to half of dormitory residents binged at least occasionally, more than 75 percent of fraternity and sorority house residents were binge drinkers. Table 4.5 shows the behavioral and physical effects of blood alcohol levels.

Because alcohol is physically addictive, the person with alcoholism who stops drinking may suffer from physical withdrawal symptoms. Alcohol withdrawal

The Dangers of Driving Under the Influence
Intoxicated drivers have impaired perceptual ability and psychomotor functions, delayed reaction time, and poor coordination. They are also likely to display impaired judgment, poor impulse control, and an inflated self-image. This deadly combination results in more than 25,000 U.S. traffic deaths each year.

Table 4.5

Behavioral Effects of Blood Alcohol Levels

Blood Alcohol Level	Behavioral Effects
0.05%	Lowered alertness; release of inhibitions; impaired judgment
0.10%	Slowed reaction times; impaired motor function; less caution
0.15%	Large, consistent increases in reaction time
0.20%	Marked depression in sensory and motor capability; obvious intoxication
0.25%	Severe motor disturbance; staggering; sensory perceptions greatly impaired
0.30%	Stuporous but conscious; no comprehension of the world around them
0.35%	Surgical anesthesia; minimal level causing death
0.40%	About half of those at this level die

This Is Fun? According to a national survey of college students, more than half "drank to get drunk" in the previous year (Wechsler & others, 2002). Approximately 75 percent of students who are members of fraternities and sororities admit to binge drinking. Despite the deaths from alcohol poisoning of several college students each year, binge drinking and public drunkenness remain common at spring break celebrations.

barbiturates
(barb-ITCH-yer-ets) A category of depressant drugs that reduce anxiety and produce sleepiness.

tranquilizers
Depressant drugs that relieve anxiety.

opiates
(OH-pee-ets) A category of psychoactive drugs that are chemically similar to morphine and have strong pain-relieving properties.

stimulants
A category of psychoactive drugs that increase brain activity, arouse behavior, and increase mental alertness.

caffeine
(kaff-EEN) A stimulant drug found in coffee, tea, cola drinks, chocolate, and many over-the-counter medications.

causes rebound hyperexcitability in the brain. The severity of the withdrawal symptoms depends on the level of physical dependence (Schuckit & others, 1998). With a low level of dependence, withdrawal may involve disrupted sleep, anxiety, and mild tremors ("the shakes"). At higher levels of physical dependence on alcohol, withdrawal may involve confusion, hallucinations, and severe tremors or seizures. Collectively, these severe symptoms are sometimes called *delirium tremens,* or the *DTs.* In cases of extreme physical dependence, withdrawal can cause seizures, convulsions, and even death in the absence of medical supervision (O'Brien, 1997).

What Are Alcohol's Psychological Effects? People are often surprised that alcohol is classified as a depressant. Initially, alcohol produces a mild euphoria, talkativeness, and feelings of good humor and friendliness, leading many people to think of alcohol as a stimulant. But these subjective experiences occur because alcohol *lessens inhibitions* by depressing the brain centers responsible for judgment and self-control. Reduced inhibitions and self-control contribute to the aggressive and violent behavior sometimes associated with alcohol abuse. But the loss of inhibitions affects individuals differently, depending on their environment and expectations regarding alcohol's effects (Bushman, 1993).

Barbiturates and Tranquilizers

Barbiturates are powerful depressant drugs that reduce anxiety and promote sleep, which is why they are sometimes called "downers." Barbiturates depress activity in the brain centers that control arousal, wakefulness, and alertness. They also depress the brain's respiratory centers.

Like alcohol, barbiturates at low doses cause relaxation, mild euphoria, and reduced inhibitions. Larger doses produce a loss of coordination, impaired mental functioning, and depression. High doses can produce unconsciousness, coma, and death. Barbiturates produce a very deep but abnormal sleep in which REM sleep is greatly reduced. Because of the additive effect of depressants, barbiturates combined with alcohol are particularly dangerous.

Common barbiturates include the prescription sedatives *Seconal* and *Nembutal.* The illegal drug *methaqualone* (street name *quaalude*) is almost identical chemically to barbiturates and has similar effects.

Barbiturates produce both physical and psychological dependence. Withdrawal from low doses of barbiturates produces irritability and REM rebound nightmares. Withdrawal from high doses of barbiturates can produce hallucinations, disorientation, restlessness, and life-threatening convulsions.

Tranquilizers are depressants that relieve anxiety. Commonly prescribed tranquilizers include *Xanax, Valium, Librium,* and *Ativan.* Chemically different from barbiturates, tranquilizers produce similar, although less powerful, effects. We will discuss these drugs in more detail in Chapter 14, on therapies.

The Opiates
From Poppies to Demerol

Often called *narcotics,* the **opiates** are a group of addictive drugs that relieve pain and produce feelings of euphoria. Natural opiates include *opium,* which is derived from the opium poppy; *morphine,* the active ingredient in opium; and *codeine,* which can be derived from either opium or morphine. Synthetic and semisynthetic opiates include *heroin, methadone,* and the prescription painkillers *OxyContin, Percodan,* and *Demerol.*

Opiates produce their powerful effects by mimicking the brain's own natural painkillers, called *endorphins.* Opiates occupy endorphin receptor sites in the brain. As you may recall from Chapter 2, the word *endorphin* literally means "the morphine within."

When used medically, opiates alter an individual's reaction to pain not by acting at the pain site but by reducing the brain's perception of pain. Many people recovering from surgery experience a wave of pain relief after receiving narcotics such as morphine, Demerol, or Percodan. People who take opiates in such circumstances rarely develop drug tolerance or dependence (Jacox & others, 1994).

The most frequently abused opiate is *heroin*. When injected into a vein, heroin reaches the brain in seconds, creating an intense rush of euphoria that is followed by feelings of contentment, peacefulness, and warmth. Withdrawing from heroin is not life threatening, but it does produce unpleasant drug rebound symptoms. Withdrawal symptoms include an intense craving for heroin, fever, chills, muscle cramps, and gastrointestinal problems.

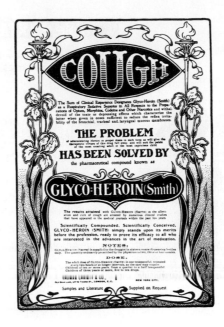

Heroin Cough Syrup Opium and its derivatives, including heroin, morphine, and codeine, were legal in the United States until 1914. In the late nineteenth and early twentieth centuries, opiates were commonly used in over-the-counter medications for a variety of ailments, from sleeplessness to "female problems" (Musto, 1991). This ad for "Glyco-Heroin" cough syrup appeared in 1904. Codeine is still used in some prescription cough syrups.

The Stimulants
Caffeine, Nicotine, Amphetamines, and Cocaine

Key Theme
■ Stimulant drugs increase brain activity, while the psychedelic drugs create perceptual distortions, alter mood, and affect thinking.

Key Questions
■ What are the general effects of stimulants and the specific effects of caffeine, nicotine, amphetamines, and cocaine?
■ What are the effects of mescaline, LSD, and marijuana?
■ What are the "club drugs," and what are their effects?

Stimulants vary in the strength of their effects, legal status, and the manner in which they are taken. All stimulant drugs, however, are at least mildly addicting, and all tend to increase brain activity. We'll first look at the most widely used and legal stimulants, caffeine and nicotine. Then we'll examine much more potent stimulants, cocaine and the amphetamines.

Caffeine and Nicotine

Caffeine is the most widely used psychoactive drug in the world. It is found in coffee, tea, cola drinks, chocolate, and many over-the-counter medications (see Table 4.6 on page 162). It's not surprising, then, that most Americans consume caffeine in some form every day.

Caffeine stimulates the cerebral cortex in the brain, resulting in an increase in mental alertness and wakefulness. Even a single cup of coffee has a noticeable effect on the cerebral cortex.

Yes, coffee drinkers, caffeine *is* physically addictive (Juliano & Griffiths, 2004). Regular coffee, tea, or cola drinkers will experience withdrawal symptoms if they abruptly stop their caffeine intake. Headaches, irritability, drowsiness, and fatigue may last up to a week. Even just a few hours of caffeine deprivation can produce noticeable withdrawal symptoms of sleepiness and fatigue. At high doses, caffeine can produce anxiety, restlessness, insomnia, and increased heart rate—symptoms that are collectively called "coffee nerves."

"Nowadays, Hal is ninety-nine percent caffeine-free"

Caffeine and Conversation Caffeine is the most widely used psychoactive drug in the world (Juliano & Griffiths, 2004). These French college students are enjoying a cup of espresso at an outdoor café.

Table 4.6

Common Sources of Caffeine

Item	Milligrams Caffeine
Coffee (short, 8 ounces)	85–250
Coffee (grande, 16 ounces)	220–550
Tea (8 ounces)	16–60
Chocolate (semisweet, baking; 1 ounce)	25
Soft drinks (12 ounces)	35–70
Energy drinks (8 ounces, Red Bull, Jolt)	40–80
Caffeinated waters (8 ounces, Water Joe, Java Water)	25–60
Over-the-counter stimulants (Nō–Dōz, Vivarin)	100–200
Over-the-counter analgesics (Anacin, Midol)	25–130
Over-the-counter cold remedies (Triaminicin, Coryban-D)	30

SOURCE: National Sleep Foundation (2004).

When Mike, in the Prologue, lit up a cigarette, he did so under the mistaken impression that smoking would help him relax and fall asleep. But cigarettes contain **nicotine,** an extremely addictive stimulant. Nicotine is found in all tobacco products, including pipe tobacco, cigars, cigarettes, and smokeless tobacco. About 25 percent of American adults use tobacco regularly. The proportion of smokers is much higher in Japan, many European countries, and developing countries (Bartecchi & others, 1995).

Like coffee, nicotine increases mental alertness and reduces fatigue or drowsiness. Brain-imaging studies show that nicotine increases neural activity in many areas of the brain, including the frontal lobes, thalamus, hippocampus, and amygdala (Rose & others, 2003; Stein & others, 1998). Thus, it's not surprising that smokers report that tobacco enhances mood, attention, arousal, and vigilance.

When cigarette smoke is inhaled, nicotine reaches the brain in seconds. But within 30 minutes or so, nicotine has left the brain. Thus, the addicted pack-a-day smoker will light a cigarette every 30 to 40 minutes to maintain a relatively constant nicotine level in the brain. Over the course of a year, that averages out to 70,000 "hits" of nicotine. Nicotine is highly addictive, both physically and psychologically (Laviolette & van der Kooy, 2004). People who start smoking for nicotine's stimulating properties often continue smoking to avoid the withdrawal symptoms. Along with an intense craving for cigarettes, withdrawal symptoms include jumpiness, irritability, tremors, headaches, drowsiness, "brain fog," and lightheadedness.

nicotine
A stimulant drug found in tobacco products.

amphetamines
(am-FET-uh-meens) A class of stimulant drugs that arouse the central nervous system and suppress appetite.

FOR BETTER OR FOR WORSE

Amphetamines and Cocaine

Like caffeine and nicotine, amphetamines and cocaine are addictive substances that stimulate brain activity, increasing mental alertness and reducing fatigue. However, amphetamines and cocaine also elevate mood and produce a sense of euphoria. When abused, both drugs can produce severe psychological and physical problems.

Sometimes called "speed" or "uppers," **amphetamines** suppress appetite and were once widely prescribed as diet pills. Tolerance to the appetite-suppressant effects occurs quickly, so progressive increases in amphetamine dosage are required to maintain the effect. Consequently, amphetamines are rarely prescribed today for weight control.

Using any type of amphetamines for an extended period of time is followed by "crashing"—withdrawal symptoms of fatigue, deep sleep, intense mental depression, and increased appetite. This is another example of a drug rebound effect. Users also become psychologically dependent on the drug for the euphoric state, or "rush," that it produces, especially when injected.

Benzedrine and *dexedrine* are prescription amphetamines. *Methamphetamine,* also known as *meth,* is an illegal drug that can be easily manufactured in home or street laboratories. Providing an intense high that is longer-lasting and less expensive than that of cocaine, methamphetamine use has spread from the western United States to the rest of the country, including small towns in the rural Midwest and South.

Methamphetamine is not only highly addictive but it also causes extensive brain damage and tissue loss (see Focus on Neuroscience). PET scans of former meth users showed a significant reduction in the number of dopamine receptors and transporters even after several months of abstinence (Volkow & others, 2001a). Dopamine transporters help transport "used" dopamine back into the neurons that produce it. Some former methamphetamine users had lost up to 24 percent of the normal level of dopamine transporters. Memory and motor skill problems were common in the former abusers and were most severe in those with the greatest loss of dopamine transporters (Volkow & others, 2001b).

Cocaine Toothache Drops? Prior to 1914, cocaine was legal in the United States and, like the opiates, was widely used as an ingredient in over-the-counter medicines (Jonnes, 1999). From this 1885 advertisement for Cocaine Toothache Drops, it's clear that cocaine was used to treat children as well as adults. Cocaine derivatives, such as novocaine and lidocaine, are still used medically as anesthetics. Cocaine was also part of Coca-Cola's original formula in 1888. It was replaced in 1903 with another stimulant, caffeine. Coca leaves, with the cocaine extracted for medical purposes, are still used for flavoring cola drinks.

focus on Neuroscience: How Methamphetamines Erode the Brain

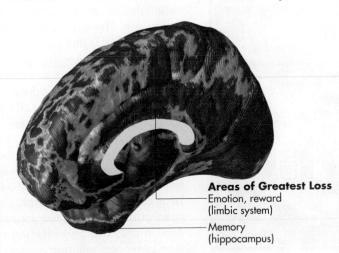

Areas of Greatest Loss
— Emotion, reward (limbic system)
— Memory (hippocampus)

Researcher Paul Thompson and his colleagues (2004) used MRI scans to compare the brains of chronic methamphetamine users to those of healthy adults. In the composite scan shown here, red indicates areas with tissue loss from 5 to 10 percent. Green indicates 3 to 5 percent tissue loss, and blue indicates relatively intact brain regions. Thompson found that meth abusers experienced up to 10 percent tissue loss in limbic system areas involved in emotion and reward. Significant tissue loss also occurred in hippocampal regions involved in learning and memory. "We expected some brain changes, but we didn't expect so much brain tissue to be destroyed," Thompson said. Not surprisingly, methamphetamine abusers performed more poorly on memory tests as compared to healthy people the same age (Thompson & others, 2004).

cocaine
A stimulant drug derived from the coca tree.

stimulant-induced psychosis
Schizophrenia-like symptoms that can occur as the result of prolonged amphetamine or cocaine use; also called *amphetamine psychosis* or *cocaine psychosis*.

psychedelic drugs
(*sy*-kuh-DEL-ick) A category of psychoactive drugs that create sensory and perceptual distortions, alter mood, and affect thinking.

mescaline
(MESS-kuh-*lin*) A psychedelic drug derived from the peyote cactus.

LSD
A synthetic psychedelic drug.

Cocaine is an illegal stimulant derived from the leaves of the coca tree, which is found in South America. (The coca plant is not the source of cocoa or chocolate, which is made from the beans of the *cacao* plant.) When inhaled, or "snorted," in purified, powdered form, cocaine reaches the brain within a few minutes. Inhaling cocaine produces intense euphoria, mental alertness, and self-confidence, which lasts for several minutes. A more concentrated form of cocaine, called *crack,* is smoked rather than inhaled.

Prolonged use of amphetamines or cocaine can result in **stimulant-induced psychosis,** also called *amphetamine psychosis* or *cocaine psychosis*. Schizophrenia-like symptoms develop, including auditory hallucinations of voices and bizarrely paranoid ideas.

Psychedelic Drugs
Mescaline, LSD, and Marijuana

The term **psychedelic drug** was coined in the 1950s to describe a group of drugs that create profound perceptual distortions, alter mood, and affect thinking. *Psychedelic* literally means "mind manifesting" (Tart, 1990).

Mescaline and LSD

Naturally occurring psychedelic drugs have been used for thousands of years. **Mescaline,** which is derived from the peyote cactus, has been used for centuries in the religious ceremonies of Mexican Indians. Another psychedelic drug, called *psilocybin,* is derived from *Psilocybe* mushrooms, sometimes called "magic mushrooms." Psilocybin has been used since 500 B.C. in religious rites in Mexico and Central America.

In contrast to these naturally occurring psychedelics, **LSD** (*lysergic acid diethylamide*) is a powerful psychedelic drug that was first synthesized in the late 1930s. LSD is far more potent than mescaline or psilocybin. Just 25 micrograms, or one-millionth of an ounce, of LSD can produce profound psychological effects with relatively few physiological changes.

LSD and psilocybin are very similar chemically to the neurotransmitter *serotonin,* which is involved in regulating moods and sensations (see Chapter 2). LSD and psilocybin mimic serotonin in the brain, stimulating serotonin receptor sites (Aghajanian, 1994).

The effects of a psychedelic experience vary greatly, depending on an individual's personality, current emotional state, surroundings, and the other people present. A "bad trip" can produce extreme anxiety, panic, and even psychotic episodes. Tolerance to psychedelic drugs may occur after heavy use. However, even heavy users of LSD do not develop physical dependence, nor do they experience withdrawal symptoms if the drug is not taken.

Adverse reactions to LSD include flashbacks (recurrences of the drug's effects), depression, long-term psychological instability, and prolonged psychotic reactions (Smith & Seymour, 1994). In a psychologically unstable or susceptible person, even a single dose of LSD can precipitate a severe psychotic reaction.

Peyote-Inspired Visions The Huichol Indians of Mexico have used peyote in religious ceremonies for hundreds of years. Huichol yarn paintings, like the one shown here, often depict imagery and scenes inspired by traditional peyote visions. These visions resemble the geometric shapes and radiating patterns of hallucinations induced by psychedelic drugs. Today, peyote continues to be used as a sacrament in the religious ceremonies of the Native American Church, a religion with more than 300,000 members (Swan & Big Bow, 1995). According to a recent study, the use of peyote as a sacrament in the context of church ritual was not associated with either psychological or cognitive problems in Navajo members of the Native American Church (Halpern & others, 2005).

Marijuana

The common hemp plant, *Cannabis sativa,* is used to make rope and cloth. But when its leaves, stems, flowers, and seeds are dried and crushed, the mixture is called **marijuana,** one of the most widely used illegal drugs. Marijuana's active ingredient is the chemical *tetrahydrocannabinol,* abbreviated *THC.* When marijuana is smoked, THC reaches the brain in less than 30 seconds. One potent form of marijuana, *hashish,* is made from the resin of the hemp plant. Hashish is sometimes eaten.

To lump marijuana with the highly psychedelic drugs mescaline and LSD is somewhat misleading. At high doses, marijuana can sometimes produce sensory distortions that resemble a mild psychedelic experience. Low to moderate doses of THC typically produce a sense of well-being, mild euphoria, and a dreamy state of relaxation. Senses become more focused and sensations more vivid. Taste, touch, and smell may be enhanced; time perception may be altered.

A little more than a decade ago, researchers discovered receptor sites in the brain that are specific for THC. They've also discovered a naturally occurring brain chemical, called *anandamide,* that is structurally similar to THC and that binds to the THC receptors in the brain (Devane & others, 1992). Anandamide appears to be involved in regulating the transmission of pain signals and may reduce painful sensations (Calignano & others, 1998; Walker & others, 1999). Researchers also suspect that anandamide may be involved in mood and memory.

There are very few THC receptors in the brainstem, the part of the brain that controls such life-support functions as breathing and heartbeat. Thus, high doses of THC do not interfere with respiratory and cardiac functions as depressants and opiates do (Piomelli, 2003).

Most marijuana users do not develop tolerance or physical dependence. Chronic users of extremely high doses can develop some tolerance to THC and may experience withdrawal symptoms when its use is discontinued (de Fonseca & others, 1997). Such symptoms include irritability, restlessness, insomnia, tremors, and decreased appetite.

Marijuana and its active ingredient, THC, have been shown to be helpful in the treatment of pain, epilepsy, hypertension, nausea, glaucoma, and asthma (Piomelli, 2003). In cancer patients, THC can prevent the nausea and vomiting caused by chemotherapy. However, the medical use of marijuana is limited and politically controversial.

On the negative side, marijuana interferes with muscle coordination and perception and may impair driving ability. When marijuana and alcohol use are combined, marijuana's effects are intensified—a dangerous combination for drivers. Marijuana has also been shown to interfere with learning, memory, and cognitive functioning (Pope & others, 2001).

Designer "Club" Drugs
Ecstasy and the Dissociative Anesthetic Drugs

Some drugs don't fit into neat categories. The "club drugs" are a loose collection of psychoactive drugs that are popular at dance clubs, parties, and the all-night dance parties called "raves." Many of these drugs are *designer drugs,* meaning that they were synthesized in a laboratory rather than derived from naturally occurring compounds. In this section, we'll take a look at three of the most popular club drugs—*ecstasy, ketamine,* and *PCP.*

The initials **MDMA** stand for the long chemical name of the quintessential club drug better known as **ecstasy.** Other street names are *X, XTC, Adam,* and the "love drug." Ecstasy was developed by a German pharmaceutical company in 1912 for possible use as an appetite suppressant, but it was not tested on humans until the 1970s. Structurally similar to both mescaline and amphetamine, MDMA

marijuana
A psychoactive drug derived from the hemp plant.

MDMA or ecstasy
Synthetic club drug that combines stimulant and mild psychedelic effects.

Rave Culture All-night dance parties, called raves, originated in Great Britain and quickly spread to other European countries and to the United States. Raves may draw anywhere from a few hundred to few thousand people or more. Highly caffeinated "energy drinks," amphetamines, methamphetamine and other stimulants may be consumed to maintain the energy needed to dance all night. Rave culture helped popularize the use of ecstasy, a synthetic drug. Ecstasy users may suck on baby pacifiers to cope with the drug's side-effects, which include jaw clenching and tooth grinding.

has stimulant and psychedelic effects. While the use of other illegal drugs has remained stable or declined over the past decade, the use of ecstasy has sharply increased in western Europe and the United States (Zickler, 2001).

At low doses, MDMA acts as a stimulant, but at high doses it has mild psychedelic effects. Its popularity, however, results from its emotional effects: Feelings of euphoria and increased well-being are common. People who have taken ecstasy also say that the drug makes them feel loving, open, and closer to others—effects that led to its use in psychotherapy for a brief time until its adverse effects became apparent (Braun, 2001). Ecstasy's side effects hint at the problems that can be associated with its use: dehydration, rapid heartbeat, tremors, muscle tension and involuntary teeth-clenching, and hyperthermia (abnormally high body temperature). Rave partygoers who take MDMA in crowded, hot surroundings are particularly at risk for collapse or death from dehydration and hyperthermia.

The "love drug" effects of ecstasy may result from its unique effect on serotonin in the brain. Along with causing neurons to release serotonin, MDMA also blocks serotonin reuptake, amplifying and prolonging serotonin effects (Braun, 2001). While flooding the brain with serotonin may temporarily enhance feelings of emotional well-being, there are adverse trade-offs.

First, the "high" of ecstasy is often followed by depression when the drug wears off. More ominously, animal studies have shown that moderate or heavy use of ecstasy can lead to long-term, potentially irreversible damage to serotonin nerve endings in the brain (Ricaurte & McCann, 2001). Several studies have shown similar damage to serotonin neurons in the human brain (Croft & others, 2001; Reneman & others, 2001a). Evidence suggests that female users are more susceptible to brain damage than male users (see Figure 4.6).

FIGURE 4.6 Effects of Ecstasy on the Brain The "ecstasy" of an MDMA trip takes a heavy toll on the brain, especially in women. These brain-scan images show serotonin activity (red) in the brains of **(a)** a normal female volunteer who had never taken ecstasy, **(b)** a moderate ecstasy user, and **(c)** a heavy ecstasy user. The study by Dutch scientist Liesbeth Reneman and her colleagues (2001a) included both male and female participants. Reneman found that the female participants were more susceptible to brain damage from ecstasy use than men were.

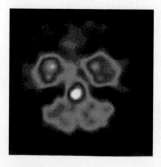

(a) Control, no MDMA use

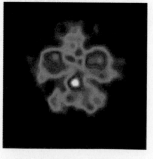

(b) Moderate MDMA use

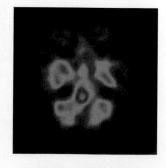

(c) Heavy MDMA use

Other studies have shown that serotonin levels become severely depleted after long-term use, possibly causing the depression that follows when the drug wears off (Kuhn & Wilson, 2001). Equally troubling are cognitive effects: In one study, memory and verbal reasoning problems persisted up to a year after the last dose was taken (Reneman & others, 2001b).

Another class of drugs found at dance clubs and raves are the **dissociative anesthetics,** including phencyclidine, better known as *PCP* or *angel dust,* and *ketamine* (street name *Special K*). Originally developed as anesthetics for surgery in the late 1950s, both PCP and ketamine deaden pain and, at high doses, can induce a stupor or coma. Because of their psychological effects, these drugs were largely abandoned for surgical use in humans.

Rather than producing actual hallucinations, PCP and ketamine produce marked feelings of dissociation and depersonalization. Feelings of detachment from reality—including distortions of space, time, and body image—are common. Generally, PCP has more intense and longer effects than ketamine does.

PCP can be eaten, snorted, or injected, but it is most often smoked or sprinkled on tobacco or marijuana. The effects are unpredictable, and a PCP trip can last for several days. Some users of PCP report feelings of invulnerability and exaggerated strength. PCP users can become severely disoriented, violent, aggressive, or suicidal. High doses of PCP can cause hyperthermia, convulsions, and death. PCP affects levels of the neurotransmitter *glutamate,* indirectly stimulating the release of dopamine in the brain. Thus, PCP is highly addictive. Memory problems and depression are common effects of long-term use.

dissociative anesthetics
Class of drugs that reduce sensitivity to pain and produce feelings of detachment and dissociation; includes the club drugs phencyclidine (PCP) and ketamine.

Closing Thoughts

As the great psychologist William James pointed out, consciousness is an ever-changing experience, difficult to pin down. In our survey of the many different aspects of consciousness, we've described our daily cycles of sleep, dreams, and wakefulness, along with the internal and external factors that influence the ebb and flow of our awareness. We've also looked at ways in which consciousness can be deliberately altered, whether by mental techniques, like hypnosis and meditation, or by taking psychoactive drugs.

In the Prologue, you read about the experiences of Mike and Nina. Some aspects of their nighttime experience are universal. All humans experience similar stages of wakefulness, drowsiness, deep sleep, and dreaming sleep. Other experiences, like Nina's sporadic episodes of night terrors and Mike's anxiety-driven bouts of insomnia, represent disruptions in the daily cycle of sleep and wakefulness.

Our survey should have also made it clear that consciousness can be influenced by many different factors, several of which are under your control. (Did someone say Starbucks?!!) Some personal choices, such as maintaining healthy sleep habits, can be beneficial. Others, such as drinking, smoking, or swallowing dangerous drugs, can have long-lasting negative effects. In the chapter Application, we'll suggest some ways in which you can use psychological research to improve the quality of *your* consciousness.

In this section we'll give you some research-based, practical suggestions to help you wake up in the morning, improve the quality of your sleep, and minimize the mental and physical disruptions that can occur when your body clock is out of sync with environmental time cues.

Dealing with Morning Brain Fog

There is surprisingly little research on how to deal with **sleep inertia**—sleepiness on awakening that interferes with your ability to perform mental or physical tasks. For some people, "morning brain fog" can last an hour or more before they feel fully alert (Jewett & others, 1999).

People who have trouble getting up in the morning tend to stay in bed until the last possible moment. This strategy, of course, only intensifies their disorientation, because they are forced to hustle out the door before they are fully awake.

The simplest antidote for sleep inertia seems to be the passage of time. So if you suffer from sleep inertia, try setting your alarm clock (and possibly a second one in the next room) to wake you 15 minutes *earlier* than usual. Resolve to hit the floor when the alarm goes off. The extra 15 minutes will help give your mind time to clear.

During that 15 minutes, sip a cup of coffee or tea, which promotes wakefulness. It takes approximately half an hour to feel the full effects of the caffeine. If the sun is up, sit near a window. If it's not, turn on the lights. Bright light, especially sunlight, helps brain fog dissipate by reducing blood levels of the hormone melatonin. To help engage your brain, glance at the newspaper or start a list of what you want to accomplish for the day. Though simple, these suggestions really do help, as your night-owl authors, neither of whom exactly greets the morning with enthusiasm, have discovered.

Improving the Quality of Your Sleep

Sleep researchers have identified many ways to improve the quality of your sleep:

- Timing is more important than you probably realize. In the early-evening hours, usually between 8:00 and 10:00 P.M.,

we normally experience a period of increased wakefulness that occurs prior to sleepiness. Sleep researchers call this presleep burst of wakefulness the "forbidden zone for sleep" (Lavie, 1989). So to avoid suddenly feeling wide awake in bed, you should go to bed after the forbidden zone, when your brain has begun to gear down to sleepiness.

- Monitor your caffeine intake, and don't drink caffeine-containing beverages or eat chocolate for at least three or four hours before going to bed. Look again at Table 4.6 on page 162, which lists some common sources of caffeine. Many over-the-counter medications include caffeine. Check the label if you take such medications before bedtime.

- Going to bed very hungry or very full will disrupt sleep, but a light snack will help reduce nighttime restlessness and increase total sleep time.

- Moderate exercise during the day seems to promote deep sleep, but exercise in the evening or shortly before going to bed may keep you awake.

- Soaking in a very warm bath shortly before bed promotes deep sleep by raising your core body temperature.

- A consistent bedtime routine and familiar surroundings enhance the quality of sleep. Try to go to bed about the same time each night and get up at approximately the same time every morning so that you stay in sync with your own pattern of circadian rhythms.

- Depressant drugs, such as alcohol and barbiturates, may produce drowsiness, but they also reduce REM sleep, disrupting the quality of your sleep. Hence, they should be avoided.

Finally, you may be pleased to discover that sex promotes sleep. For example, rabbits tend to sleep very little—with the exception of quickly nodding off into REM sleep after some amorous activity in the old rabbit hutch. The same phenomenon also seems to occur in humans, which is why sleep so often follows sexual interaction. As sleep researcher J. Allan Hobson (1995) put it, sex "not only

leads to muscle relaxation, but also clears the cerebral circuits of tedious humdrum."

Almost everyone occasionally has trouble falling asleep or staying asleep. Often this occurs because we're fretting about some problem or conflict. One strategy to help you let go of the problem for the night is to write down your concerns and what you plan to do about them the next day. Another strategy is to redirect your thoughts. Try vividly imagining yourself exploring a tranquil landscape or walking along a familiar route.

If you still can't fall asleep or stay asleep, don't overreact. Instead, get up and read in a comfortable chair until you feel drowsy, and then return to bed. If your sleeping problems persist for a week or more, ask your family doctor for advice or a referral to a sleep specialist.

Coping with the Night Shift

People vary in the ease with which they develop tolerance for working the night shift or rotating shifts. Here are some suggestions for minimizing the negative effects of night work:

- If you have a choice in your work schedule, the longer you can stay with one shift, the better. Frequent shift changes increase jet lag symptoms.

- If you work rotating shifts, try to make your schedule changes more compatible with circadian rhythms. Because of our natural tendency to drift toward longer days, it is easier to lengthen our days than to shorten them. Therefore, try to arrange your shift changes to progress from the morning to evening to night shifts.

- If you work the midnight shift, bright lights in the workplace, especially during the early part of the shift, will help your circadian cycles adjust to the night schedule (Dawson & Campbell, 1991).

- To promote sleep during the daytime, ask your doctor about taking melatonin. Melatonin supplements can help induce daytime sleep, improving mental alertness during night shifts (Dawson, 1995).

sleep inertia
(in-ER-shuh) Feeling of grogginess on awakening that interferes with the ability to perform mental or physical tasks.

Chapter Review
Consciousness and Its Variations

Key Points

Introduction: Consciousness: *Experiencing the "Private I"*

■ **Consciousness** refers to the immediate awareness of internal and external stimuli. Most psychologists today consider consciousness an important area of research, as did early psychologists.

Biological and Environmental "Clocks" That Regulate Consciousness

■ **Circadian rhythms** are regulated by the **suprachiasmatic nucleus (SCN),** the "master clock" located in the hypothalamus of the brain. In response to light detected by special photoreceptors, the SCN reduces the production of **melatonin** by the pineal gland. Increased melatonin makes you sleepy.

■ Under free-running conditions, human circadian rhythms drift toward a 25-hour day. Circadian rhythms become disrupted when environmental time cues are out of sync with the body clock. Symptoms of jet lag can be produced by travel across time zones or by rotating shift work.

Sleep

■ The invention of the **electroencephalograph,** which produces an **EEG** or **electroencephalogram,** and the discovery of rapid eye movements (REM) changed scientific views about sleep. The two basic types of sleep are **REM sleep** and **NREM sleep.**

■ When we are awake and alert, the brain generates **beta brain waves.** As brain activity gears down and drowsiness sets in, **alpha brain waves** are generated. **Hypnagogic hallucinations** can occur during this drowsy, presleep phase.

■ Each sleep stage is characterized by a specific pattern of brain activity. In the first 90 minutes of sleep, four different stages of NREM sleep are followed by a brief episode of REM sleep. Stage 2 of sleep is defined by the appearance of **sleep spindles** and **K complexes.** Throughout the night, episodes of REM sleep become progressively longer and NREM episodes become shorter.

■ As people age, periods of REM sleep and deep sleep become shorter, and more sleep time is spent in stage 2 NREM.

■ Sleep deprivation studies and the phenomenon of **REM rebound** demonstrate the biological need to sleep. The **restorative theory** and the **adaptive theory** offer different explanations for the function of sleep.

■ **Sleep disorders** are serious disturbances in the normal sleep pattern that interfere with daytime functioning and cause subjective distress.

■ The most common sleep disorder is **insomnia;** the next most common is **sleep apnea.** For many, insomnia is related to a condition called **restless legs syndrome (RLS).** The **parasomnias** include **sleepwalking, night terrors,** sleep bruxism, sleep-related eating disorder, and **REM sleep behavior disorder.** The symptoms of **narcolepsy,** including **cataplexy,** are experienced during the day.

Dreams and Mental Activity During Sleep

■ **Sleep thinking** occurs during NREM sleep. A **dream** is a storylike, unfolding episode of mental images that typically occurs during REM sleep.

■ During REM sleep, the brain is cut off from external stimuli. The frontal lobes and primary visual cortex are inactivated, but the hippocampus, amygdala, and other visual centers are highly active. REM sleep is needed for the consolidation of certain types of memories.

■ Most dreams reflect everyday concerns and include familiar people and settings. Changes in brain chemistry and functioning that occur during sleep probably contribute to the inability to remember dreams. There are individual differences in dream recall. **Nightmares** are unpleasant anxiety dreams.

■ Sigmund Freud believed that dream images are symbols of unconscious wishes. According to Freud, dreams are composed of **manifest content** and **latent content.** The **activation–synthesis model of dreaming** proposes that dreams reflect our subjective awareness of brain activation during sleep. Some researchers believe that dreaming consciousness is similar in its functions to waking consciousness.

Hypnosis

■ **Hypnosis** is an unusual state of awareness, defined as a cooperative social interaction in which the hypnotic participant responds to suggestions made by the hypnotist. Changes in perception, memory, and behavior may be produced. People vary in hypnotic susceptibility.

■ Under hypnosis, profound sensory and perceptual changes may be experienced, including pain reduction and hallucinations. **Posthypnotic suggestions** influence behavior outside the hypnotic state. Hypnosis is used in habit control, but its effectiveness varies. Hypnosis can produce **posthypnotic amnesia,** but not **hypermnesia.** Although hypnosis does not increase the accuracy of memories, it does increase confidence in memories and can produce false memories. Hypnosis cannot be used to make people perform behaviors that are contrary to their morals or values.

■ The **neodissociation theory** of Ernest Hilgard explains hypnosis as involving **dissociation** and a **hidden observer.** Some psychologists believe that hypnosis is not a special state of consciousness but can be explained by social and cognitive processes.

Meditation

- **Meditation** refers to techniques used to control attention so as to induce an altered state of focused attention and awareness.

- Research suggests that regular meditation enhances physical and psychological functioning.

Psychoactive Drugs

- **Psychoactive drugs** can alter arousal, mood, thinking, sensation, and perception. Many psychoactive drugs are addictive, producing **physical dependence** and **drug tolerance.** The physically dependent person who stops taking a drug experiences **withdrawal symptoms,** which often include the **drug rebound effect.**

- Psychoactive drugs affect brain activity by influencing synaptic transmission. Drug effects can be influenced by the person's weight, gender, race, metabolic rate, and the presence of other drugs. Personality characteristics, mood, expectations, experience with the drug, and the setting in which the drug is taken also affect the drug response.

- **Drug abuse** refers to recurrent drug use that leads to disruptions in academic, social, or occupational functioning and to legal or psychological problems. Many factors contribute to drug abuse, including social and cultural influences.

- **Depressants** are physically addictive drugs that inhibit central nervous system activity. Depressants include alcohol, **barbiturates,** and **tranquilizers.** Psychologically, alcohol lessens inhibitions, but its effects vary, depending on the person's environment and expectations. Barbiturates and tranquilizers produce relaxation and reduce inhibitions.

- **Opiates** are addictive drugs that relieve pain and produce feelings of euphoria. The opiates include opium, morphine, codeine, heroin, methadone, and prescription painkillers. Opiates relieve pain by mimicking the effect of endorphins in the brain.

- **Stimulants** include **caffeine, nicotine, amphetamines,** and **cocaine.** The stimulants increase brain activity, and all stimulants are addictive. Prolonged use of amphetamines or cocaine can lead to **stimulant-induced psychosis.**

- **Psychedelic drugs** include **mescaline, LSD,** and **marijuana.** The psychedelics create perceptual distortions, alter mood, and affect thinking. Although psychedelic drugs are not physically addictive, they can cause a variety of harmful effects.

- The "club drugs" are synthetic drugs used at dance clubs, parties, and "raves." These drugs include **MDMA (ecstasy)** and the **dissociative anesthetics** PCP and ketamine.

Key Terms

consciousness, p. 128

circadian rhythm, p. 130

suprachiasmatic nucleus (SCN), p. 131

melatonin, p. 131

electroencephalograph, p. 133

EEG (electroencephalogram), p. 133

REM sleep, p. 133

NREM sleep, p. 133

beta brain waves, p. 134

alpha brain waves, p. 134

hypnagogic hallucinations, p. 134

sleep spindles, p. 135

K complex, p. 135

sleep paralysis, p. 136

REM rebound, p. 138

restorative theory of sleep, p. 139

adaptive theory of sleep, p. 139

sleep disorders, p. 139

insomnia, p. 140

restless legs syndrome (RLS), p. 140

sleep apnea, p. 141

sleepwalking, p. 141

night terrors, p. 141

parasomnias, p. 142

REM sleep behavior disorder, p. 142

narcolepsy, p. 142

cataplexy, p. 142

sleep thinking, p. 143

dream, p. 143

nightmare, p. 147

manifest content, p. 148

latent content, p. 148

activation–synthesis model of dreaming, p. 148

hypnosis, p. 150

posthypnotic suggestion, p. 151

posthypnotic amnesia, p. 151

hypermnesia, p. 151

dissociation, p. 154

neodissociation theory of hypnosis, p. 154

hidden observer, p. 154

meditation, p. 154

psychoactive drug, p. 156

physical dependence, p. 156

drug tolerance, p. 156

withdrawal symptoms, p. 156

drug rebound effect, p. 156

drug abuse, p. 157

depressants, p. 157

barbiturates, p. 160

tranquilizers, p. 160

opiates, p. 160

stimulants, p. 161

caffeine, p. 161

nicotine, p. 162

amphetamines, p. 163

cocaine, p. 164

stimulant-induced psychosis, p. 164

psychedelic drugs, p. 164

mescaline, p. 164

LSD, p. 164

marijuana, p. 165

MDMA (ecstasy), p. 165

dissociative anesthetics, p. 167

sleep inertia, p. 168

Key People

Sigmund Freud (1856–1939) Austrian physician and founder of psychoanalysis; proposed that dream images are disguised and symbolic expressions of unconscious wishes and urges. (p. 148)

Ernest R. Hilgard (1904–2001) American psychologist who extensively studied hypnosis and advanced the *neodissociation theory of hypnosis.* (p. 154)

J. Allan Hobson (b. 1933) Contemporary American psychiatrist and neurobiologist who has extensively researched sleep and dreaming; proposed the *activation–synthesis model of dreaming.* (p. 148)

William James (1842–1910) American psychologist and philosopher who proposed that the subjective experience of consciousness is not episodic, but an ongoing stream of mental activity. (p. 129)

Web Companion Review Activities

You can find additional review activities by going to **www.DiscoveringPsychology.com** and clicking on the *Discovering Psychology* 4th Edition text cover. At the Discovering Psychology Web Companion you'll find the chapter learning objectives, flashcards for key terms and key people, interactive crossword puzzles, self-scoring practice quizzes, and other materials to help you master the information in this chapter.

We're More Alike

Learning

Prologue The Killer Attic

Sandy's parents, Erv and Fern, recently celebrated their fifty-fifth wedding anniversary. Sometimes it seems truly amazing that they've managed to stay together for so long, as you'll see from this true story.

It was a warm summer morning in Chicago. Erv and Fern drank their coffee and made plans for the day. The lawn needed mowing, the garage needed cleaning, and someone had to go to the post office to buy stamps. Fern, who doesn't like driving, said that she would mow the lawn if Erv would go to the post office. Erv, who doesn't like yard work, readily agreed to the deal.

As Erv left for the post office, Fern started cutting the grass in the backyard. When Erv returned, he parked the car around the corner under some large shade trees so that it would stay cool while he puttered around in the garage. Walking through the front door to drop off the stamps, he noticed that the attic fan was squeaking loudly. Switching it off, Erv decided to oil the fan before he tackled the garage. He retrieved the stepladder and oil from the basement, propped the ladder under the attic's trapdoor, and gingerly crawled up into the attic, leaving the trapdoor open.

Meanwhile, Fern was getting thirsty. As she walked past the garage on the way into the house, she noticed the car was still gone. "Why isn't Erv back yet? He must have stopped somewhere on the way back from the post office," she thought. As she got a glass of water, she noticed the stepladder and the open attic door. Muttering that Erv never put anything away, Fern latched the trapdoor shut and dragged the ladder back down to the basement.

Erv, who had crawled to the other side of the attic to oil the fan, never heard the attic trapdoor shut. It was very hot in the well-insulated, airless attic, so he tried to work fast. After oiling the fan, he crawled back to the trapdoor—only to discover that it was latched shut from the outside! "Fern," he hollered, "open the door!" But Fern was already back outside, mowing away, and couldn't hear Erv over the noise of the lawn mower. Erv, dripping with sweat, kept yelling and pounding on the trapdoor.

Outside, Fern was getting hot, too. She stopped to talk to a neighbor, leaving the lawn mower idling. He offered Fern a cold beer, and the two of them leaned over the fence, laughing and talking. From a small, sealed attic window, Erv watched the whole scene. Jealousy was now added to his list of discomforts. He was also seriously beginning to think that he might sweat to death in the attic heat. He could already see the tabloid headlines in the supermarket checkout line: LAUGHING WIFE DRINKS BEER WHILE HUSBAND COOKS IN ATTIC!

Finally, Fern went back to mowing, wondering what in the world had happened to Erv. Meanwhile, up in the attic, Erv was drenched with sweat and his heart was racing. He promised God he'd never complain about Chicago winters again. At last, Fern finished the lawn and walked back to the house. Hearing the back door open, Erv began to yell and pound on the trapdoor again.

"Hey, Fern! Fern!"

Fern froze in her tracks.

"Fern, let me out! I'm going to suffocate up here!"

"Erv! Is that you? Where are you?" she called, looking around.

"I'm in the attic! Let me out!"

"What are you doing in the attic? I thought you were at the store!"

"What do you *think* I'm doing? Let me out of here! Hurry!"

Once Fern was reassured that Erv had suffered no ill effects from being trapped in the attic, she burst out laughing. Later that day, still grumbling about Fern's hare-brained sense of humor, Erv removed the latch from the attic door. Ever since, when-ever Erv goes up into the attic, he posts a sign on the ladder that reads MAN IN THE ATTIC! And, even today, Erv gets a little anxious whenever he has to go up in the attic.

For her part, Fern is careful to check on Erv's whereabouts before she closes the attic door. But she still laughs when she tells the story of the "killer attic"—which she does frequently, as it never fails to crack up her listeners. Luckily, Erv is a good sport and is used to Fern's sense of humor.

Erv and Fern have both learned from their experience, as is reflected in the changes in their behavior. Learning new behaviors can occur in many ways, but it al-most always helps us adapt to changing circumstances, as you'll see in this chapter.

Introduction

What Is Learning?

Key Theme
- Learning refers to a relatively enduring change in behavior or knowledge as a result of experience.

Key Questions
- What is conditioning?
- What are three basic types of learning?

What do we mean when we say that Fern and Erv have "learned" from their ex-perience with the killer attic? In the everyday sense, *learning* often refers to for-mal methods of acquiring new knowledge or skills, such as learning in the classroom or learning to play the flute.

In psychology, however, the topic of learning is much broader. Psychologists formally define **learning** as a process that produces a relatively enduring change in behavior or knowledge as a result of an individual's experience. For example, Erv has learned to feel anxious and uncomfortable whenever he needs to enter the attic. He's also learned to take simple precautions, such as posting his MAN IN THE ATTIC! sign, to avoid getting locked in the attic again. As Erv's behavior demonstrates, the learning of new behaviors often reflects adapting to your envi-ronment. As the result of experience, you acquire new behaviors or modify old be-haviors so as to better cope with your surroundings.

learning
A process that produces a relatively enduring change in behavior or knowledge as a result of past experience.

conditioning
The process of learning associations between environmental events and behavioral responses.

In this broad sense of the word, learning occurs in every setting, not just in classrooms. And learning takes place at every age. Further, the psychological study of learning is not limited to humans. From alligators to zebras, learning is an important aspect of the behavior of virtually all animals.

Psychologists have often studied learning by observing and recording the learning experiences of animals in carefully controlled laboratory situations. Using animal subjects, researchers can precisely control the conditions under which a particular behavior is learned. The goal of much of this research has been to identify the general principles of learning that apply across a wide range of species, including humans.

Much of this chapter will focus on a very basic form of learning, called *conditioning*. **Conditioning** is the process of learning associations between environmental events and behavioral responses. This description may make you think conditioning has only a limited application to your life. In fact, however, conditioning is reflected in most of your everyday behavior, from simple habits to emotional reactions and complex skills.

In this chapter, we'll look at basic types of conditioning—classical conditioning and operant conditioning. As you'll see in the next section, *classical conditioning* explains how certain stimuli can trigger an automatic response, as the attic now triggers mild anxiety in Erv. And, as you'll see in a later section, *operant conditioning* is useful in understanding how we acquire new, voluntary actions, such as Erv's posting his sign whenever he climbs into the attic. Finally, toward the end of the chapter, we'll consider the process of *observational learning*, or how we acquire new behaviors by observing the actions of others.

Conditioning, Learning, and Behavior Through different kinds of experiences, people and animals acquire enduring changes in their behaviors. Psychologists have identified general principles of learning that explain how we acquire new behaviors—from simple responses to complex skills. As other members of their troop look on, these Scouts are learning how to build a campfire.

Classical Conditioning
Associating Stimuli

Key Theme
■ Classical conditioning is a process of learning associations between stimuli.

Key Questions
■ How did Pavlov discover and investigate classical conditioning?
■ How does classical conditioning occur?
■ What factors can affect the strength of a classically conditioned response?

One of the major contributors to the study of learning was not a psychologist but a Russian physiologist who was awarded a Nobel Prize for his work on digestion. **Ivan Pavlov** was a brilliant scientist who directed several research laboratories in St. Petersburg, Russia, at the turn of the twentieth century. Pavlov's involvement with psychology began as a result of an observation he made while investigating the role of saliva in digestion, using dogs as his experimental subjects.

In order to get a dog to produce saliva, Pavlov (1904) put food on the dog's tongue. After he had worked with the same dog for several days in a row, Pavlov noticed something curious. The dog began salivating *before* Pavlov put the food on its tongue. In fact, the dog began salivating when Pavlov entered the room or even at the sound of his approaching footsteps. But salivating is a *reflex*—a largely involuntary, automatic response to an external stimulus. (As we've noted in previous chapters, a *stimulus* is anything perceptible to the senses, such as a sight, sound, smell, touch, or taste.) The dog should salivate only *after* the food is presented, not before. Why would the reflex occur before the stimulus was presented? What was causing this unexpected behavior?

Ivan Pavlov (1849–1936) In his laboratory, Pavlov was known for his meticulous organization, keen memory, and attention to details (Windholz, 1990). But outside his lab, Pavlov was absentminded, forgetful, and impractical, especially regarding money. He often forgot to pick up his paycheck, and he sometimes lent money to people with hard luck stories who couldn't possibly pay him back (Fancher, 1996). On a trip to New York City, Pavlov carried his money so carelessly that he had his pocket picked in the subway, and his American hosts had to take up a collection to pay his expenses (Skinner, 1966).

Life in Pavlov's Laboratories During Pavlov's four decades of research, more than 140 scientists and students worked in the two laboratories under his direction. Twenty of his co-researchers were women, including his daughter, V. I. Pavlova. Pavlov, who had an extraordinary memory for details, carefully supervised the procedures of dozens of ongoing research projects. Nevertheless, he acknowledged that the scholarly achievements produced by his laboratories represented the collective effort of himself and his co-workers (Windholz, 1990).

classical conditioning
The basic learning process that involves repeatedly pairing a neutral stimulus with a response-producing stimulus until the neutral stimulus elicits the same response; also called *respondent conditioning* or *Pavlovian conditioning*.

unconditioned stimulus (UCS)
The natural stimulus that reflexively elicits a response without the need for prior learning.

unconditioned response (UCR)
The unlearned, reflexive response that is elicited by an unconditioned stimulus.

conditioned stimulus (CS)
A formerly neutral stimulus that acquires the capacity to elicit a reflexive response.

conditioned response (CR)
The learned, reflexive response to a conditioned stimulus.

If you own a dog, you've probably observed the same basic phenomenon. Your dog gets excited and begins to slobber when you shake a box of dog biscuits, even before you've given him a doggie treat. In everyday language, your pet has learned to anticipate food in association with some signal—namely, the sound of dog biscuits rattling in a box.

Pavlov's extraordinary gifts as a researcher enabled him to recognize the important implications of what had at first seemed a problem—a reflex (salivation) that occurred *before* the appropriate stimulus (food) was presented. He also had the discipline to systematically study how such associations are formed. In fact, Pavlov abandoned his research on digestion and devoted the remaining 30 years of his life to investigating different aspects of this phenomenon. Let's look at what he discovered in more detail.

Principles of Classical Conditioning

The process of conditioning that Pavlov discovered was the first to be extensively studied in psychology. Thus, it's called *classical conditioning* (Hilgard & Marquis, 1940). Also called *respondent conditioning* or *Pavlovian conditioning*, **classical conditioning** deals with behaviors that are elicited automatically by some stimulus. *Elicit* means "draw out" or "bring forth." That is, the stimulus doesn't produce a new behavior but rather *causes an existing behavior to occur.*

Classical conditioning always involves some kind of reflexive behavior. Remember, a reflex is a relatively simple, unlearned behavior, governed by the nervous system, that occurs *automatically* when the appropriate stimulus is presented. In Pavlov's (1904) original studies of digestion, the dogs salivated reflexively when food was placed on their tongues. But when the dogs began salivating in response to the sight of Pavlov or to the sound of his footsteps, a new, *learned* stimulus elicited the salivary response. Thus, in classical conditioning, a *new* stimulus–response sequence is learned.

How does this kind of learning take place? Essentially, classical conditioning is a process of learning an *association between two stimuli.* Classical conditioning involves pairing a *neutral* stimulus (e.g., the sight of Pavlov) with an *unlearned, natural* stimulus (food in the mouth) that automatically elicits a reflexive response (the dog salivates). If the two stimuli (Pavlov + food) are repeatedly paired, eventually the neutral stimulus (Pavlov) elicits the same basic reflexive response as the natural stimulus (food)—even in the absence of the natural stimulus. So, when the dog in the laboratory started salivating at the sight of Pavlov *before* the food was placed on its tongue, it was because the dog had formed a new, *learned association* between the sight of Pavlov and the food.

Pavlov used special terms to describe each element of the classical conditioning process. The natural stimulus that reflexively produces a response without prior learning is called the **unconditioned stimulus** (abbreviated **UCS**). In this example, the unconditioned stimulus is the food in the dog's mouth. The unlearned, reflexive response is called the **unconditioned response** (or **UCR**). The unconditioned response is the dog's salivation.

To learn more about his discovery, Pavlov (1927) controlled the stimuli that preceded the presentation of food. For example, in one set of experiments, he used a bell as a neutral stimulus—neutral because dogs don't normally salivate to the sound of a ringing bell. Pavlov first rang the bell and then gave the dog food. After this procedure was repeated several times, the dog began to salivate when the bell was rung, before the food was put in its mouth. At that point, the dog was *classically conditioned* to salivate to the sound of a bell alone. That is, the dog had *learned a new association* between the sound of the bell and the presentation of food.

Pavlov called the sound of the bell the *conditioned stimulus*. The **conditioned stimulus** (or **CS**) is the stimulus that is originally neutral but comes to elicit a reflexive response. He called the dog's salivation to the sound of the bell the **conditioned response** (or **CR**), which is the *learned* reflexive response to a previously neutral stimulus. The steps of Pavlov's conditioning process are outlined in Figure 5.1.

Classical conditioning terminology can be confusing. You may find it helpful to think of the word *conditioned* as having the same meaning as "learned." Thus, the "conditioned stimulus" refers to the "learned stimulus," the "unconditioned response" refers to the "unlearned response," and so forth.

It's also important to note that in this case the unconditioned response and the conditioned response describe essentially the same behavior—the dog's salivating. Which label is applied depends on which stimulus elicits the response. If the dog is salivating in response to a *natural* stimulus that was not acquired through learning, the salivation is an *unconditioned* response. If, however, the dog has learned to salivate to a *neutral* stimulus that doesn't normally produce the automatic response, the salivation is a *conditioned* response.

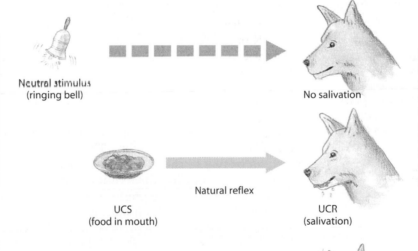

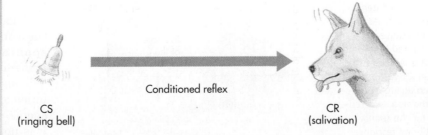

Before Conditioning
Prior to conditioning, the dog notices the bell ringing, but does not salivate. Here, the bell is a neutral stimulus. Food placed in the dog's mouth (the UCS) naturally produces the salivation reflex (the UCR).

Neutral stimulus
(ringing bell)

No salivation

UCS
(food in mouth)

Natural reflex

UCR
(salivation)

During Conditioning
In the conditioning phase, the neutral stimulus (the ringing bell) is repeatedly sounded immediately before food is placed in the dog's mouth (the UCS), which produces the natural reflex of salivation (the UCR).

Neutral stimulus
(ringing bell)

+

UCS
(food in mouth)

Natural reflex

UCR
(salivation)

After Conditioning
The ringing bell is no longer neutral. It is now called a CS because, when the bell is rung, the dog reacts with a conditioned reflex: It salivates even though no food is present. The salivation response is now called a CR.

CS
(ringing bell)

Conditioned reflex

CR
(salivation)

FIGURE 5.1 The Process of Classical Conditioning The diagram shows Pavlov's classical conditioning procedure. As you can see, classical conditioning involves the learning of an association between a neutral stimulus (the ringing bell) and a natural stimulus (food).

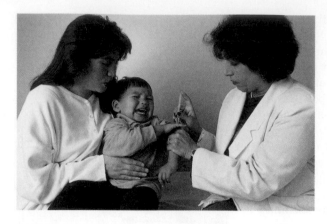

Stimulus Generalization: *Any* White Jacket Like most babies, our daughter Laura received several rounds of immunizations when she was an infant. And, like the infant in the photo, each painful injection (the UCS) elicited fear and made her cry (the UCR). After only the *second* vaccination, Laura developed a strong classically conditioned response—just the sight of a nurse's white uniform (a CS) triggered an emotional outburst of fear and crying (a CR). Interestingly, Laura's conditioned fear generalized to a wide range of white uniforms. As a toddler, Laura burst into tears in response to a pharmacist's white smock, a cosmetic saleswoman's white jacket, a butcher's white coat, and a veterinarian's white lab coat. These conditioned responses persisted until Laura was almost 4 years old.

Factors That Affect Conditioning

Over the three decades that Pavlov (1928) spent studying classical conditioning, he discovered many factors that could affect the strength of the conditioned response. For example, he discovered that the more frequently the conditioned stimulus and the unconditioned stimulus were paired, the stronger was the association between the two.

Pavlov also discovered that the *timing* of stimulus presentations affected the strength of the conditioned response. He found that conditioning was most effective when the conditioned stimulus was presented immediately *before* the unconditioned stimulus. In his early studies, Pavlov found that a half-second was the optimal time interval between the onset of the conditioned stimulus and the beginning of the unconditioned stimulus. Later, Pavlov and other researchers found that the optimal time interval could vary in different conditioning situations but was rarely more than a few seconds.

Pavlov (1927) noticed that once a dog was conditioned to salivate to a particular stimulus, new stimuli that were similar to the original conditioned stimulus could also elicit the conditioned salivary response. For example, Pavlov conditioned a dog to salivate to a low-pitched tone. When he sounded a slightly higher-pitched tone, the conditioned salivary response would also be elicited. Pavlov called this phenomenon *stimulus generalization.* **Stimulus generalization** occurs when stimuli that are similar to the original conditioned stimulus also elicit the conditioned response, even though they have never been paired with the unconditioned stimulus.

Just as a dog can learn to respond to similar stimuli, so it can learn the opposite—to *distinguish* between similar stimuli. For example, Pavlov repeatedly gave a dog some food following a high-pitched tone but did not give the dog any food following a low-pitched tone. The dog learned to distinguish between the two tones, salivating to the high-pitched tone but not to the low-pitched tone. This phenomenon, **stimulus discrimination,** occurs when a particular conditioned response is made to one stimulus but not to other, similar stimuli.

Once learned, can conditioned responses be eliminated? Pavlov (1927) found that conditioned responses could be gradually weakened. If the conditioned stimulus (the ringing bell) was repeatedly presented *without* being paired with the unconditioned stimulus (the food), the conditioned response seemed to gradually disappear. Pavlov called this process of decline and eventual disappearance of the conditioned response **extinction.**

Pavlov also found that the dog did not simply return to its unconditioned state following extinction (see Figure 5.2). If the animal was allowed a period of rest (such as a few hours) after the response was extinguished, the conditioned response would reappear when the conditioned stimulus was again presented. This reappearance of a previously extinguished conditioned response after a period of time without exposure to the conditioned stimulus is called **spontaneous recovery.** The phenomenon of spontaneous recovery demonstrates that extinction is not unlearning. That is, the learned response may seem to disappear, but it is not eliminated or erased (Bouton, 2000; Rescorla, 2001).

FIGURE 5.2 Extinction and Spontaneous Recovery in Pavlov's Laboratory This demonstration involved a dog that had already been conditioned to salivate (the CR) to just the sight of the meat powder (the CS). During the extinction phase, the CS was repeatedly presented at three-minute intervals and held just out of the dog's reach. As you can see in the graph, over the course of six trials the amount of saliva secreted by the dog quickly decreased to zero. This indicates that *extinction* had occurred. After a two-hour rest period, the CS was presented again. At the sight of the meat powder, the dog secreted saliva once more, evidence for the *spontaneous recovery* of the conditioned response.

SOURCE: Data adapted from Pavlov (1927).

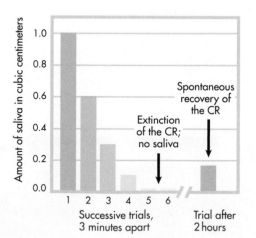

Amount of saliva in cubic centimeters

Spontaneous recovery of the CR

Extinction of the CR; no saliva

1 2 3 4 5 6

Successive trials, 3 minutes apart

Trial after 2 hours

From Pavlov to Watson
The Founding of Behaviorism

Key Theme
■ Behaviorism was founded by John Watson, who redefined psychology as the scientific study of behavior.

Key Questions
■ What were the fundamental assumptions of behaviorism?
■ How did Watson use classical conditioning to explain and produce conditioned emotional responses?
■ How did Watson apply classical conditioning techniques to advertising?

Over the course of three decades, Pavlov systematically investigated different aspects of classical conditioning. Throughout this process, he used dogs almost exclusively as his experimental subjects. Since Pavlov believed he had discovered the mechanism by which all learning occurs, it seems ironic that he had very little to say about applications of classical conditioning to human behavior. This irony is less puzzling when you understand that Pavlov wanted nothing to do with the newly established science of psychology. Why?

At the beginning of the twentieth century, psychology's early founders had defined the field as *the scientific study of the mind* (see Chapter 1). They advocated the use of introspective self-reports to achieve two fundamental goals: describing and explaining conscious thought and perceptions. Because the early psychologists wanted to study subjective conscious experiences, Pavlov did not see psychology as an exact or precise science, like physiology or chemistry. As Pavlov (1927) wrote, "It is still open to discussion whether psychology is a natural science, or whether it can be regarded as a science at all."

At about the same time Pavlov was conducting his systematic studies of classical conditioning in the early 1900s, a young psychologist named **John B. Watson** was attracting attention in the United States. Watson, like Pavlov, believed that psychology was following the wrong path by focusing on the study of subjective mental processes. In 1913, Watson directly challenged the early founders of psychology when he published a landmark article entitled "Psychology as the Behaviorist Views It." Watson's famous article opened with these sentences:

> Psychology as the behaviorist views it is a purely objective experimental branch of natural science. Its theoretical goal is the prediction and control of behavior. Introspection forms no essential part of its methods, nor is the scientific value of its data dependent upon the readiness with which they lend themselves to interpretation in terms of consciousness.

With the publication of this article, Watson founded a new school, or approach, in psychology, called **behaviorism.** Watson strongly advocated that psychology should be redefined as *the scientific study of behavior.* As he later (1924) wrote, "Let us limit ourselves to things that can be observed, and formulate laws concerning only those things. Now what can we observe? We can observe *behavior—what the organism does or says.*"

But having soundly rejected the methods of introspection and the study of consciousness, the young Watson was somewhat at a loss for a new method to replace them (Fancher, 1996). By 1915, when Watson was elected president of the American Psychological Association, he had learned of Pavlov's research. Watson (1916) embraced the idea of the conditioned reflex as the model he had been seeking to investigate and explain human behavior (Evans & Rilling, 2000).

stimulus generalization
The occurrence of a learned response not only to the original stimulus but to other, similar stimuli as well.

stimulus discrimination
The occurrence of a learned response to a specific stimulus but not to other, similar stimuli.

extinction (in classical conditioning)
The gradual weakening and apparent disappearance of conditioned behavior. In classical conditioning, extinction occurs when the conditioned stimulus is repeatedly presented without the unconditioned stimulus.

spontaneous recovery
The reappearance of a previously extinguished conditioned response after a period of time without exposure to the conditioned stimulus.

behaviorism
School of psychology and theoretical viewpoint that emphasize the scientific study of observable behaviors, especially as they pertain to the process of learning.

John Broadus Watson (1878–1958) Watson founded behaviorism in the early 1900s, emphasizing the scientific study of observable behaviors rather than the study of subjective mental processes. His influence spread far beyond the academic world. He wrote many books and articles for the general public on child rearing and other topics, popularizing the findings of the "new" science of psychology (Rilling, 2000).

Watson believed that virtually *all* human behavior is a result of conditioning and learning—that is, due to past experience and environmental influences. In championing behaviorism, Watson took his views to an extreme, claiming that neither talent, personality, nor intelligence was inherited. In a characteristically bold statement, Watson (1924) proclaimed:

> I should like to go one step further now and say, "Give me a dozen healthy infants, well-formed, and my own specified world to bring them up in and I'll guarantee to take any one at random and train him to become any type of specialist I might select—doctor, lawyer, artist, merchant-chief and yes, even beggar-man and thief, regardless of his talents, penchants, tendencies, abilities, vocations, and race of his ancestors." I am going beyond my facts and I admit it, but so have the advocates of the contrary and they have been doing it for many thousands of years.

Needless to say, Watson never actually carried out such an experiment, and his boast clearly exaggerated the role of the environment to make his point. Nevertheless, Watson's influence on psychology cannot be overemphasized. Behaviorism was to dominate psychology in the United States for more than 50 years. And, as you'll see in the next section, Watson did carry out a famous and controversial experiment to demonstrate how human behavior could be classically conditioned.

Conditioned Emotional Reactions
The Famous Case of Little Albert

Watson believed that, much as Pavlov's dogs reflexively salivated to food, human emotions could be thought of as reflexive responses involving the muscles and glands. In studies with infants, Watson (1919) identified three emotions that he believed represented inborn and natural unconditioned reflexes—fear, rage, and love. According to Watson, each of these innate emotions could be reflexively triggered by a small number of specific stimuli. For example, he found two stimuli that could trigger the reflexive fear response in infants: a sudden loud noise and a sudden dropping motion.

Watson's interest in the role of classical conditioning in emotions set the stage for one of the most famous and controversial experiments in the history of psychology. In 1920, Watson and a graduate student named Rosalie Rayner set out to demonstrate that classical conditioning could be used to deliberately establish a conditioned emotional response in a human subject. Their subject was a baby, whom they called "Albert B.," but who is now more popularly known as "Little Albert." Little Albert lived with his mother in the Harriet Lane Hospital in Baltimore, where his mother was employed.

Watson and Rayner (1920) first assessed Little Albert when he was only 9 months old. Little Albert was a healthy, unusually calm baby who showed no fear when presented with a tame white rat, a rabbit, a dog, and a monkey. He was also unafraid of cotton, masks, and even burning newspapers! But, as with other infants whom Watson had studied, fear could be triggered in Little Albert by a sudden loud sound—clanging a steel bar behind his head. In this case, the sudden clanging noise is the unconditioned stimulus, and the unconditioned response is fear.

Two months after their initial assessment, Watson and Rayner attempted to condition Little Albert to fear the tame white rat (the conditioned stimulus). Watson stood behind Little Albert. Whenever Little Albert reached toward the rat, Watson clanged the steel bar with a hammer. Just as before, of course, the unexpected loud CLANG! (the unconditioned stimulus) startled and scared the daylights out of Little Albert (the unconditioned response).

During the first conditioning session, Little Albert experienced two pairings of the white rat with the loud clanging sound. A week later, he experienced five more pairings of the two stimuli. After only these seven pairings of the loud noise and the white rat, the white rat alone triggered the conditioned response—extreme fear—in Little Albert (see Figure 5.3). As Watson and Rayner (1920) described:

> The instant the rat was shown, the baby began to cry. Almost instantly he turned sharply to the left, fell over on [his] left side, raised himself on all fours and began to crawl away so rapidly that he was caught with difficulty before reaching the edge of the table.

Watson and Rayner also found that stimulus generalization had taken place. Along with fearing the rat, Little Albert was now afraid of other furry animals, including a dog and a rabbit. He had even developed a classically conditioned fear response to a variety of fuzzy objects—a sealskin coat, cotton, Watson's hair, and a white-bearded Santa Claus mask!

Although the Little Albert study has achieved legendary status in psychology, it had several problems (Harris, 1979; Paul & Blumenthal, 1989). One criticism is that the experiment was not carefully designed or conducted. For example, Albert's fear and distress were not objectively measured but were subjectively evaluated by Watson and Rayner.

The experiment is also open to criticism on ethical grounds. Watson and Rayner (1920) did not extinguish Little Albert's fear of furry animals and objects, even though they believed that such conditioned emotional responses would "persist and modify personality throughout life." Whether they had originally intended to extinguish the fear is not completely clear (see Paul & Blumenthal, 1989). Little Albert left the hospital shortly after the completion of the experiment. Watson (1930) later wrote that he and Rayner could not try to eliminate Albert's fear response because the infant had been adopted by a family in another city shortly after the experiment had concluded. Today, conducting such an experiment would be considered unethical.

You can probably think of situations, objects, or people that evoke a strong classically conditioned emotional reaction in you, such as fear or anger. One example

FIGURE 5.3 A Classically Conditioned Fear Response In the photograph below, Rosalie Rayner holds Little Albert as John Watson looks on. Little Albert is petting the tame white rat, clearly not afraid of it. But, after being repeatedly paired with the UCS (a sudden, loud noise), the white rat becomes a CS. After conditioning, Little Albert is terrified of the tame rat. His fear generalized to other furry objects, including rabbits, cotton, Rayner's fur coat, and Watson in a Santa Claus beard.

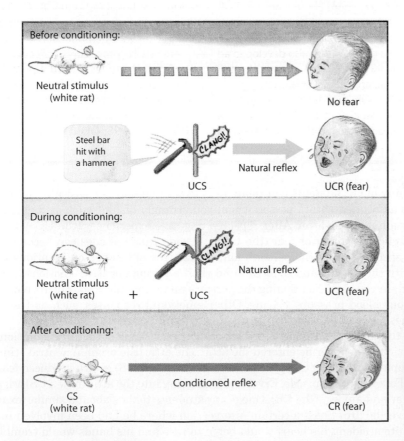

Before conditioning:

Neutral stimulus (white rat) → No fear

Steel bar hit with a hammer → UCS → Natural reflex → UCR (fear)

During conditioning:

Neutral stimulus (white rat) + UCS → Natural reflex → UCR (fear)

After conditioning:

CS (white rat) → Conditioned reflex → CR (fear)

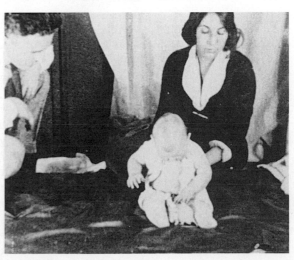

Watson, Classical Conditioning, and Advertising

From shampoos to soft drinks, advertising campaigns often use sexy models to promote their products. Today, we take this advertising tactic for granted. But it's actually yet another example of Watson's influence.

Shortly after the Little Albert experiment, Watson's wife discovered that he was having an affair with his graduate student Rosalie Rayner. Following a scandalous and highly publicized divorce, Watson was fired from his academic position. Despite his international fame as a scientist, no other university would hire him. Banned from academia, Watson married Rayner and joined the J. Walter Thompson advertising agency (Buckley, 1989).

Watson was a pioneer in the application of classical conditioning principles to advertising. "To make your consumer react," Watson told his colleagues at the ad agency, "tell him something that will tie up with fear, something that will stir up a mild rage, that will call out an affectionate or love response, or strike at a deep psychological or habit need" (quoted in Buckley, 1982).

Watson applied this technique to ad campaigns for Johnson & Johnson Baby Powder and Pebeco toothpaste in the 1920s. For the baby powder ad, Watson intentionally tried to stimulate an anxiety response in young mothers by creating doubts about their ability to care for their infants.

The Pebeco toothpaste campaign targeted the newly independent young woman who smoked. The ad raised the fear that attractiveness might be diminished by the effects of smoking—and Pebeco toothpaste was promoted as a way of increasing sexual attractiveness. One ad read, "Girls! Don't worry any more about smoke-stained teeth or tobacco-tainted breath. You can smoke and still be lovely if you'll just use Pebeco twice a day." Watson also developed ad campaigns for Pond's cold cream, Maxwell House coffee, and Camel cigarettes.

While Watson may have pioneered the strategy of associating products with "sex appeal," modern advertising has taken this technique to an extreme. Similarly, some ad campaigns pair products with images of adorable babies, cuddly kittens, happy families, or other "natural" stimuli that elicit warm, emotional responses. If classical conditioning occurs, the product by itself will also elicit a warm emotional response.

Are such procedures effective? In a word, yes. Attitudes toward a product or a particular brand can be influenced by advertising and marketing campaigns that use classical conditioning methods (see Grossman & Till, 1998; Olson & Fazio, 2001).

that many of our students can relate to is that of becoming classically conditioned to cues associated with a person whom you strongly dislike, such as a demeaning boss or a hateful ex-lover. After repeated negative experiences (the UCS) with the person eliciting anger or fear (the UCR), a wide range of cues can become conditioned stimuli (CSs)—the person's name, the sight of the person, locations associated with the person, and so forth—and elicit a strong negative emotional reaction (the CR) in you. Just mentioning the person's name can make your heart pound and send your blood pressure soaring. Other emotional responses, such as feelings of happiness or sadness, can also be classically conditioned.

In this chapter's Prologue, we saw that Erv became classically conditioned to feel anxious whenever he entered the attic. The attic (the original neutral stimulus) was coupled with being trapped in extreme heat (the UCS), which produced fear (the UCR). Following the episode, Erv found that going into the attic (now a CS) triggered mild fear and anxiety (the CR). One of our students told us about a similar example. Whenever he drove past a certain intersection where he had been involved in a serious auto accident, his heart would begin to race and his hands would tremble.

cathy®   **by Cathy Guisewite**

Aspects of sexual responses involve reflexive elements that also can be subject to classical conditioning, sometimes inadvertently. To illustrate, suppose that a neutral stimulus, such as the scent of a particular cologne, is regularly paired with the person with whom you are romantically involved. In other words, your romantic partner almost always wears his or her "signature" cologne. You, of course, are most aware of the scent when you are physically close to your partner in sexually arousing situations. After repeated pairings, the initially neutral stimulus—the particular cologne scent—can become a conditioned stimulus. Now, the scent of the cologne evokes feelings of romantic excitement or mild sexual arousal even in the absence of your lover or, in some cases, long after the relationship has ended. And, in fact, a wide variety of stimuli can become "sexual turn-ons" through classical conditioning.

Classically Conditioned Drug Effects

If you're a regular coffee drinker like both of your authors, you may have noticed that you begin to feel more awake and alert after just a few groggy sips of your first cup of coffee in the morning. However, it takes at least 20 minutes for the caffeine from the coffee to reach significant levels in your bloodstream. If you're feeling more awake *before* blood levels of caffeine rise, it's probably because you've developed a classically conditioned response to the sight, smell, and taste of coffee. Confirming that everyday experience, such conditioned responses to caffeine-associated stimuli have also been demonstrated experimentally (e.g., Flaten & Blumenthal, 1999; Mikalsen & others, 2001).

Figure 5.4 shows how regular coffee drinkers might acquire such a classically conditioned response. Think of each episode of coffee drinking as a classical conditioning trial. The UCS is the drug caffeine, which automatically triggers increased arousal and alertness, the UCR. The sight, smell, and taste of coffee are the originally neutral stimuli that eventually become conditioned stimuli by being repeatedly paired with caffeine's arousing effect.

Once this classically conditioned drug effect becomes well established, the smell or taste of coffee—even decaffeinated coffee—can trigger the conditioned response of increased arousal and alertness (Knowles, 1963; A. W. Smith & others, 1997). For

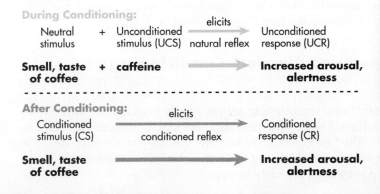

FIGURE 5.4 Classically Conditioned Drug Effects: Does Just the Smell of a Starbucks Coffee Grande Perk You Up? If it does, classical conditioning is at work! In his pioneering classical conditioning studies, Pavlov (1927) suggested that administering a drug could be viewed as a conditioning trial. Just like pairing the sound of a bell with the presentation of food, if specific environmental cues are repeatedly paired with a drug's administration, they can become conditioned stimuli that eventually elicit the drug's effect.

some habitual coffee drinkers, the conditioned response to caffeine-associated cues is so strong that a cup or two of decaffeinated coffee after a late evening meal can cause trouble sleeping.

Interestingly, conditioned drug effects seem to be involved in at least some instances of placebo response. Also called *placebo effect,* a **placebo response** occurs when an individual has a psychological and physiological reaction to what is actually a fake treatment or drug.

For example, in one study patients with hypertension (high blood pressure) were repeatedly given an antihypertensive medication in a particular environment. The effect of the antihypertensive medication was to reduce blood pressure. When given a placebo in the same environment, the fake pill also reduced their blood pressure. Why? Because a classically conditioned drug effect had occurred: The particular situational cues, including the act of taking what was believed to be the medication, elicited a drop in blood pressure. In contrast, other hypertension patients who had *no* prior experience with the medication did *not* experience reduced blood pressure when given the same placebo in the same environment (Suchman & Ader, 1992).

Contemporary Views of Classical Conditioning

Key Theme

- Contemporary learning researchers acknowledge the importance of both mental factors and evolutionary influences in classical conditioning.

Key Questions

- How has the involvement of cognitive processes in classical conditioning been demonstrated experimentally?
- What is meant by the phrase "the animal behaves like a scientist" in classical conditioning?
- How do taste aversions challenge the basic conditioning principles, and what is biological preparedness?

The traditional behavioral perspective holds that classical conditioning results from a simple association of the conditioned stimulus and the unconditioned stimulus. According to the behaviorists, mental processes such as thinking, anticipating, or deciding were not needed to explain the conditioning process.

However, not all psychologists were convinced that mental processes were so uninvolved in learning. Some wondered whether conditioning procedures did more than simply change how an organism responded. Could conditioning procedures change what the organism *knows* as well as what it *does*? According to the *cognitive perspective* (see Chapter 1), mental processes as well as external events are an important component in the learning of new behaviors. In the next section, we'll look at the role cognitive processes seem to play in classical conditioning. As you'll see, today's psychologists view the classical conditioning process very differently than Pavlov or Watson did (see Pearce & Bouton, 2001).

Cognitive Aspects of Classical Conditioning
Reliable Signals

According to Pavlov, classical conditioning occurs simply because two stimuli are associated closely in time. The conditioned stimulus (the bell) precedes the unconditioned stimulus (the food) usually by no more than a few seconds. But is it possible that Pavlov's dogs were learning more than the mere association of two stimuli that occurred very close together in time?

placebo response
An individual's psychological and physiological response to what is actually a fake treatment or drug; also called *placebo effect.*

To answer that question, let's begin with an analogy. Suppose that on your way to class you have to go through a railroad crossing. Every time a train approaches the crossing, warning lights flash. Being rather intelligent for your species, after a few weeks you conclude that the flashing lights will be quickly followed by a freight train barreling down the railroad tracks. You've learned an association between the flashing lights and an oncoming train, because the lights are a *reliable signal* that predict the presence of the train.

Now imagine that a friend of yours also has to cross train tracks but at a different location. The railroad has had nothing but problems with the warning lights at that crossing. Sometimes the warning lights flash before a train roars through, but sometimes they don't. And sometimes they flash when no train is coming. Does your friend learn an association between the flashing lights and oncoming trains? No, because here the flashing lights are an *unreliable signal*—they seem to have no relationship to a train's arrival.

Psychologist **Robert A. Rescorla** demonstrated that classically conditioned rats also assess the reliability of signals, much like you and your friend did at the different railroad crossings. In Rescorla's 1968 experiment, one group of rats heard a tone (the conditioned stimulus) that was paired 20 times with a brief electric shock (the unconditioned stimulus). A second group of rats experienced the *same* number of tone–shock pairings, but this group also experienced an *additional* 20 shocks with *no* tone (see Figure 5.5).

Then Rescorla tested for the conditioned fear response by presenting the tone alone to each group of rats. According to the traditional classical conditioning model, both groups of rats should have displayed the same levels of conditioned fear. After all, each group had received 20 tone–shock pairings. However, this is not what Rescorla found. The rats in the first group displayed a much stronger fear response to the tone than did the rats in the second group. Why?

According to Rescorla (1988), classical conditioning depends on the *information* the conditioned stimulus provides about the unconditioned stimulus. For learning to occur, the conditioned stimulus must be a *reliable signal* that predicts the presentations of the unconditioned stimulus. For the first group of rats, that was certainly the situation. Every time the tone sounded, a shock followed. But for the second group, the tone was an unreliable signal. Sometimes the tone preceded the shock, and sometimes the shock occurred without warning.

Rescorla concluded that the rats in both groups were *actively processing information* about the reliability of the signals they encountered. Rather than merely associating two closely paired stimuli, as Pavlov suggested, the animals assess the *predictive value* of stimuli. Applying this interpretation to classical conditioning, we can conclude that Pavlov's dogs learned that the bell was a signal that *reliably predicted* that food would follow.

According to this view, animals use cognitive processes to draw inferences about the signals they encounter in their environments. To Rescorla (1988), classical conditioning "is not a stupid process by which the organism willy-nilly forms

Pavlovian conditioning is a sophisticated and sensible mechanism by which organisms represent the world. Our current understanding of Pavlovian conditioning leads to its characterization as a mechanism by which the organism encodes relationships between events in the world. The conditioned stimulus and the unconditioned stimulus are simply two events and the organism can be seen as trying to determine the relationship between them.

Robert A. Rescorla (1997)

FIGURE 5.5 Reliable and Unreliable Signals
In Rescorla's experiment, both groups of rats experienced the same number of tone–shock pairings. However, the rats in group 1 received a shock only when the tone was sounded, while the rats in group 2 experienced additional shocks that were not paired with the tone. Subsequently, the rats in group 1 displayed a conditioned fear response to the tone and the rats in group 2 did not. Why did only the rats in group 1 become conditioned to display fear when they heard the tone?

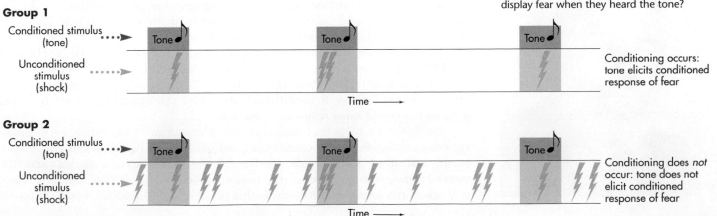

Classical Conditioning and Survival Animals quickly learn the signals that predict the approach of a predator. In classical conditioning terms, they learn to associate the approach of a predator (the unconditioned stimuli) with particular sounds, smells, or sights (the originally neutral stimuli that become conditioned stimuli). To survive, animals that are vulnerable to predators, such as this frightened deer, must be able to use environmental signals to predict events in their environment. Thus, a rustle in the underbrush, the faint whiff of a mountain lion, or a glimpse of a human tells the animal that it's time to flee.

John Garcia (b. 1917) John Garcia grew up working on farms in northern California. In his late twenties, Garcia enrolled at a community college. At the age of 48, Garcia earned his PhD in psychology from the University of California, Berkeley (Garcia, 1997). Garcia was one of the first researchers to experimentally demonstrate the existence of taste aversions and other "exceptions" to the general laws of classical conditioning. His research emphasized the importance of the evolutionary forces that shape the learning process.

associations between any two stimuli that happen to co-occur." Rather, his research suggests that "the animal behaves like a scientist, detecting causal relations among events and using a range of information about those events to make the relevant inferences" (Rescorla, 1980).

Because of studies by Rescorla and other researchers, today's understanding of how learning occurs in classical conditioning is very different from the explanations offered by Pavlov and Watson. Simply pairing events in time may not be enough for classical conditioning to occur. Instead, a conditioned stimulus must *reliably signal* that the unconditioned stimulus will follow. Put simply, classical conditioning seems to involve *learning the relationships between events* (Klein & Mowrer, 1989; Rescorla, 1988).

Evolutionary Aspects of Classical Conditioning
Biological Predispositions to Learn

According to Darwin's *theory of evolution by natural selection*, both the physical characteristics and the natural behavior patterns of any species have been shaped by evolution to maximize adaptation to the environment. Thus, just as physical characteristics vary from one species to another, so do natural behavior patterns. Some psychologists wondered whether an animal's natural behavior patterns, as shaped by evolution, would also affect how it learned new behaviors, especially behaviors important to its survival.

According to traditional behaviorists, the general principles of learning applied to virtually all animal species and all learning situations. Thus, they argued that the general learning principles of classical conditioning would be the same regardless of the species or the response being conditioned. However, in the 1960s, some researchers began to report "exceptions" to the well-established principles of classical conditioning (Lockard, 1971; Seligman, 1970). As you'll see in this section, one important exception involved a phenomenon known as a *taste aversion*. The study of taste aversions contributed to a new awareness of the importance of the organism's natural behavior patterns in classical conditioning.

Taste Aversions and Classical Conditioning: Spaghetti? No, Thank You!

A few years ago, Sandy made a pot of super spaghetti, with lots of mushrooms, herbs, spices, and some extra-spicy sausage. Being very fond of Sandy's spaghetti, Don ate two platefuls. Several hours later, in the middle of the night, Don came down with a nasty stomach virus. Predictably, Sandy's super spaghetti came back up—a colorful spectacle, to say the least. As a result, Don developed a **taste aversion**—he avoided eating spaghetti and felt queasy whenever he smelled spaghetti sauce. Don's taste aversion to spaghetti persisted for more than a year.

Such learned taste aversions are relatively common. Our students have told us about episodes of motion sickness, morning sickness, or illness that resulted in taste aversions to foods as varied as cotton candy, strawberries, and chicken soup. In some cases, a taste aversion can persist for years.

At first glance, it seems as if taste aversions can be explained by classical conditioning. In Don's case, a neutral stimulus (spaghetti) was paired with an unconditioned stimulus (a stomach virus), which produced an unconditioned response (nausea). Now a conditioned stimulus, the spaghetti sauce by itself elicited the conditioned response of nausea.

But notice that this explanation seems to violate two basic principles of classical conditioning. First, the conditioning did not require repeated pairings. Conditioning occurred in a *single pairing* of the conditioned stimulus and the unconditioned stimulus. Second, the time span between these two stimuli was *several hours*, not a matter of seconds. Is this possible? The anecdotal reports of people who develop specific taste aversions seem to suggest it is. But such reports lack the objectivity and systematic control that a scientific explanation of behavior requires.

Enter psychologist **John Garcia,** who demonstrated that taste aversions could be produced in laboratory rats under controlled conditions (Garcia & others, 1966). Garcia's procedure was straightforward. Rats first drank saccharin-flavored water (the neutral stimulus). Hours later, the rats were injected with a drug (the unconditioned stimulus) that produced gastrointestinal distress (the unconditioned response). After the rats recovered from their illness, they refused to drink the flavored water again. The rats had developed a taste aversion to the saccharin-flavored water, which had become a conditioned stimulus.

At first, many psychologists were skeptical of Garcia's findings because they seemed to violate the basic principles of classical conditioning. Several leading psychological journals refused to publish Garcia's research, saying the results were unconvincing or downright impossible (Garcia, 1981). But Garcia's results have been replicated many times. In fact, later research showed that taste aversions could develop even when a full 24 hours separated the presentation of the flavored water and the drug that produced illness (Etscorn & Stephens, 1973).

Conditioned taste aversions also challenged the notion that virtually any stimulus can become a conditioned stimulus. As Pavlov (1928) wrote, "Any natural phenomenon chosen at will may be converted into a conditioned stimulus . . . any visual stimulus, any desired sound, any odor, and the stimulation of any part of the skin." After all, Pavlov had demonstrated that dogs could be classically conditioned to salivate to a ringing bell, a ticking metronome, and even the sight of geometric figures.

But if this were the case, then why didn't Don develop an aversion to other stimuli he encountered between the time he ate the spaghetti and when he got sick? Why was it that only the spaghetti sauce became a conditioned stimulus that triggered nausea, not the dinner table, the silverware—or even Sandy, for that matter?

Contrary to what Pavlov suggested, Garcia and his colleagues demonstrated that the particular conditioned stimulus that is used *does* make a difference in classical conditioning (Garcia & Koelling, 1966). In another series of experiments, Garcia found that rats did *not* learn to associate a taste with a painful event, such as a shock. Nor did they learn to associate a flashing light and noise with illness. Instead, rats were much more likely to associate a *painful stimulus,* such as a shock, with *external stimuli,* such as flashing lights and noise. And rats were much more likely to associate a *taste stimulus* with *internal stimuli*—the physical discomfort of illness. Garcia and Koelling (1966) humorously suggested that a sick rat, like a sick person, speculates, "It must have been something I ate."

Why is it that certain stimuli are more easy to associate than others? One factor that helps explain Garcia's results is **biological preparedness**—the idea that an organism is innately predisposed to form associations between certain stimuli and responses. If the particular stimulus and response combination is *not* one that an animal is biologically prepared to associate, then the association may not occur or may occur only with great difficulty (see In Focus 5.2).

When this concept is applied to taste aversions, rats (and people) seem to be biologically prepared to associate an illness with a taste rather than with a location, a person, or an object. Hence, Don developed an aversion to the spaghetti sauce and not to the fork he had used to eat it. Apparently, both humans and rats are biologically prepared to learn taste aversions relatively easily. Thus, taste aversions can be classically conditioned more readily than can more arbitrary associations, such as that between a ringing bell and a plate of food.

Associations that are easily learned may reflect the evolutionary history and survival mechanisms of the particular animal species. For example, rats in the wild eat a wide variety of foods. If a rat eats a new food and gets sick several hours later, it's likely to survive longer if it learns from this experience to avoid that food in the future (Kalat, 1985; Seligman, 1970).

taste aversion
A classically conditioned dislike for and avoidance of a particular food that develops when an organism becomes ill after eating the food.

biological preparedness
In learning theory, the idea that an organism is innately predisposed to form associations between certain stimuli and responses.

Conditioning Taste Aversions in Coyotes
The fact that coyotes readily form taste aversions has been used to prevent them from preying on livestock (Bower, 1997; Garcia & Gustavson, 1997). To stop coyotes from killing lambs on sheep ranches, sheep carcasses are injected with a drug (lithium chloride) that produces extreme nausea. In the top photo, the coyote has discovered the carcass and is eating it. In the bottom photo, the nauseous coyote is writhing on the ground. In one study, captive coyotes were fed lithium-tainted rabbit and sheep carcasses. When later placed in a pen with live rabbits and sheep, the coyotes avoided them rather than attack them. In fact, some of the coyotes threw up at the sight of a live rabbit (Gustavson & others, 1976).

IN FOCUS 5.2

Biological Preparedness and Conditioned Fears: What Gives You the Creeps?

Do these photographs make you somewhat uncomfortable?

A *phobia* is an extreme, irrational fear of a specific object, animal, or situation. It was once believed that all phobias were acquired through classical conditioning, as was Little Albert's fear of the rat and other furry objects. But many people develop phobias without having experienced a traumatic event in association with the object of their fear (Merckelbach & others, 1992). Obviously, other forms of learning, such as observational learning, are involved in the development of some fears.

When people do develop conditioned fears as a result of traumatic events, they are more likely to associate fear with certain stimuli rather than others. Erv, not surprisingly, has acquired a conditioned fear response to the "killer attic." But why doesn't Erv shudder every time he hears a lawn mower or sees a ladder, the clothes he was wearing when he got trapped, or his can of oil?

Psychologist Martin Seligman (1971) noticed that phobias seem to be quite selective. Extreme, irrational fears of snakes, spiders, heights, and small enclosed places (like Erv and Fern's attic) are relatively common. But very few people have phobias of stairs, ladders, electrical outlets or appliances, or sharp objects, even though these things are far more likely to be associated with traumatic experiences or accidents.

Seligman proposed that humans are biologically prepared to develop fears of

objects or situations—such as snakes, spiders, and heights—that may once have posed a threat to humans' evolutionary ancestors. As Seligman (1971) put it, "The great majority of phobias are about objects of natural importance to the survival of the species." According to this view, people don't commonly develop phobias of knives, stoves, or cars because they're not biologically prepared to do so.

Support for this view is provided by early studies that tried to replicate Watson's Little Albert research. Elsie Bregman (1934) was unable to produce a conditioned fear response to wooden blocks and curtains, although she followed Watson's procedure carefully. And Horace English (1929) was unable to produce a conditioned fear of a wooden duck. Perhaps we're more biologically prepared to learn a fear of furry animals than of wooden ducks, blocks, or curtains!

More recently, psychologists Arne Öhman and Susan Mineka (2001, 2003) have accumulated experimental evidence that supports the biological preparedness hypothesis of phobias. For example, people more readily acquire conditioned fear responses to pictures of snakes and spiders paired with an electric shock than they do to pictures of mushrooms and flowers. Furthermore, the conditioned fears of spiders and snakes are much more resistant to extinction. Öhman and Mineka (2003) suggest that because poisonous snakes, reptiles, and insects have been associated with danger throughout the evolution of mammals, there is an evolved "fear module" in the brain that is highly sensitized to such evolutionarily relevant stimuli. For another view on how evolved brain mechanisms might be involved in fearful responses, see the discussion on pages 332–334.

That different species form some associations more easily than others also probably reflects the unique sensory capabilities and feeding habits that have evolved as a matter of environmental adaptation. Bobwhite quail, for instance, rely primarily on vision for identifying potential meals. In contrast, rats have relatively poor eyesight and rely primarily on taste and odor cues to identify food. Given these species differences, it shouldn't surprise you that quail, but not rats, can easily be conditioned to develop an aversion to blue-colored water—a *visual* stimulus. On the other hand, rats learn more readily than quail to associate illness with sour water—a *taste* stimulus (Wilcoxon & others, 1971). In effect, quail are biologically prepared to associate visual cues with illness, while rats are biologically prepared to associate taste cues with illness.

Taste aversion research emphasizes that the study of learning must consider the unique behavior patterns and capabilities of different species. As the result of evolution, animals have developed unique forms of behavior to adapt to their natural environments (Bolles, 1985). These natural behavior patterns and unique characteristics ultimately influence what an animal is capable of learning—and how easily it can be conditioned to learn a new behavior.

Operant Conditioning
Associating Behaviors and Consequences

Key Theme
■ Operant conditioning deals with the learning of active, voluntary behaviors that are shaped and maintained by their consequences.

Key Questions
■ How did Edward Thorndike study the acquisition of new behaviors, and what conclusions did he reach?
■ What were B. F. Skinner's key assumptions?
■ How are positive and negative reinforcement similar, and how are they different?

Classical conditioning can help explain the acquisition of many learned behaviors, including emotional and physiological responses. However, recall that classical conditioning involves reflexive behaviors that are automatically elicited by a specific stimulus. Most everyday behaviors don't fall into this category. Instead, they involve nonreflexive, or *voluntary,* actions that can't be explained with classical conditioning.

The investigation of how voluntary behaviors are acquired began with a young American psychology student named Edward L. Thorndike. A few years before Pavlov began his extensive studies of classical conditioning, Thorndike was using cats, chicks, and dogs to investigate how voluntary behaviors are acquired. Thorndike's pioneering studies helped set the stage for the later work of another American psychologist named B. F. Skinner. It was Skinner who developed *operant conditioning,* another form of conditioning that explains how we acquire and maintain voluntary behaviors.

Thorndike and the Law of Effect

Edward L. Thorndike was the first psychologist to systematically investigate animal learning and how voluntary behaviors are influenced by their consequences. At the time, Thorndike was only in his early twenties and a psychology graduate student. He conducted his pioneering studies to complete his dissertation and earn his doctorate in psychology. Published in 1898, Thorndike's dissertation, titled *Animal Intelligence: An Experimental Study of the Associative Processes in Animals,* is the most famous dissertation ever published in psychology (Chance, 1999). When Pavlov later learned of Thorndike's studies, he expressed admiration and credited Thorndike with having started objective animal research well before his own studies of classical conditioning (Hearst, 1999).

Thorndike's dissertation focused on the issue of whether animals, like humans, use reasoning to solve problems (Dewsbury, 1998). In an important series of experiments, Thorndike (1898) put hungry cats in specially constructed cages that he called "puzzle boxes." A cat could escape the cage by a simple act, such as pulling a loop or pressing a lever that would unlatch the cage door. A plate of food was placed just outside the cage, where the hungry cat could see and smell it.

Thorndike found that when the cat was first put into the puzzle box, it would engage in many different, seemingly random behaviors to escape. For example, the cat would scratch at the cage door, claw at the ceiling, and try to squeeze through the wooden slats (not to mention complain at the top of

Edward Lee Thorndike (1874–1949) As a graduate student, Thorndike became fascinated by psychology after taking a class taught by William James at Harvard University. Interested in the study of animal behavior, Thorndike conducted his first experiments with baby chicks. When his landlady protested about the chickens in his room, Thorndike moved his experiments, chicks and all, to the cellar of William James's home—much to the delight of the James children. Following these initial experiments, Thorndike constructed his famous "puzzle boxes" to study learning in cats. Later in life, Thorndike focused his attention on improving educational materials. Among his contributions was the Thorndike Barnhart Student Dictionary for children, which is still published today (R. L. Thorndike, 1991).

Thorndike's Puzzle Box Shown here is one of Thorndike's puzzle boxes, which were made mostly out of wood slats and wire mesh. Thorndike constructed a total of 15 different puzzle boxes, which varied in how difficult they were for a cat to escape from. In a simple box like this one, a cat merely had to pull on a loop of string at the back of the cage to escape. More complex boxes required the cat to perform a chain of three responses—step on a treadle, pull on a string, and push a bar up or down (Chance, 1999).

its lungs). Eventually, however, the cat would accidentally pull on the loop or step on the lever, opening the door latch and escaping the box. After several trials in the same puzzle box, a cat could get the cage door open very quickly.

Thorndike (1898) concluded that the cats did *not* display any humanlike insight or reasoning in unlatching the puzzle box door. Instead, he explained the cats' learning as a process of *trial and error* (Chance, 1999). The cats gradually learned to associate certain responses with successfully escaping the box and gaining the food reward. According to Thorndike, these successful behaviors became "stamped in," so that a cat was more likely to repeat these behaviors when placed in the puzzle box again. Unsuccessful behaviors were gradually eliminated.

Thorndike's observations led him to formulate the **law of effect:** Responses followed by a "satisfying state of affairs" are "strengthened" and more likely to occur again in the same situation. Conversely, responses followed by an unpleasant or "annoying state of affairs" are "weakened" and less likely to occur again.

Thorndike's description of the law of effect was an important first step in understanding how active, voluntary behaviors can be modified by their consequences. Thorndike, however, never developed his ideas on learning into a formal model or system (Hearst, 1999). Instead, he applied his findings to education, publishing many books on educational psychology (Beatty, 1998). Some 30 years after Thorndike's famous puzzle-box studies, the task of further investigating how voluntary behaviors are acquired and maintained would be taken up by another American psychologist, B. F. Skinner.

Burrhus Frederick Skinner (1904–1990) As a young adult, Skinner had hoped to become a writer. When he graduated from college, he set up a study in the attic of his parents' home and waited for inspiration to strike. After a year of "frittering" away his time, he decided that there were other ways to learn about human nature. As Skinner (1967) later wrote, "A writer might portray human behavior accurately, but he did not understand it. I was to remain interested in human behavior, but the literary method had failed me; I would turn to the scientific. . . . The relevant science appeared to be psychology, though I had only the vaguest idea of what that meant."

B. F. Skinner and the Search for "Order in Behavior"

From the time he was a graduate student in psychology until his death, the famous American psychologist **B. F. Skinner** searched for the "lawful processes" that would explain "order in behavior" (Skinner, 1956, 1967). Skinner was a staunch behaviorist. Like John Watson, Skinner strongly believed that psychology should restrict itself to studying only phenomena that could be objectively measured and verified—outwardly observable behavior and environmental events.

Skinner (1974) acknowledged the existence of what he called "internal factors," such as thoughts, expectations, and perceptions (Delprato & Midgley, 1992). However, Skinner believed that internal thoughts, beliefs, emotions, or motives could *not* be used to explain behavior. These fell into the category of "private events" that defy direct scientific observation and should not be included in an objective, scientific explanation of behavior (Baum & Heath, 1992).

Along with being influenced by Watson's writings, Skinner greatly admired Ivan Pavlov's work. Prominently displayed in Skinner's university office was one of his most prized possessions—an autographed photo of Pavlov (Catania & Laties, 1999). Skinner acknowledged that Pavlov's classical conditioning could explain the learned association of stimuli in certain reflexive responses (Iversen, 1992). But classical conditioning was limited to existing behaviors that were reflexively elicited. Skinner (1979) was convinced that he had "found a process of conditioning that was different from Pavlov's and much more like most learning in daily life." To Skinner, the most important form of learning was demonstrated by *new* behaviors that were *actively emitted* by the organism, such as the active behaviors produced by Thorndike's cats in trying to escape the puzzle boxes.

Skinner (1953) coined the term **operant** to describe any "active behavior that operates upon the environment to generate consequences." In everyday language, Skinner's principles of operant conditioning explain how we acquire the wide range of *voluntary* behaviors that we perform in daily life. But as a behaviorist who rejected mentalistic explanations, Skinner avoided the term *voluntary* because it would imply that behavior was due to a conscious choice or intention.

Skinner defined operant conditioning concepts in very objective terms and he avoided explanations based on subjective mental states. We'll closely follow Skinner's original terminology and definitions.

Reinforcement

Increasing Future Behavior

In a nutshell, Skinner's **operant conditioning,** also called *Skinnerian conditioning,* explains learning as a process in which behavior is shaped and maintained by its consequences. One possible consequence of a behavior is reinforcement. **Reinforcement** is said to occur when a stimulus or an event follows an operant and increases the likelihood of the operant being repeated. Notice that reinforcement is defined by the effect it produces—increasing or strengthening the occurrence of a behavior in the future.

Let's look at reinforcement in action. Suppose you put your money into a soft-drink vending machine and push the button. Nothing happens. You push the button again. Nothing. You try the coin-return lever. Still nothing. Frustrated, you slam the machine with your hand. Yes! Your can of soda rolls down the chute. In the future, if another vending machine swallows your money without giving you what you want, what are you likely to do? Hit the machine, right?

In this example, slamming the vending machine with your hand is the *operant*—the active response you emitted. The soft drink is the *reinforcing stimulus,* or *reinforcer*—the stimulus or event that is sought in a particular situation. In everyday language, a reinforcing stimulus is typically something desirable, satisfying, or pleasant. Skinner, of course, avoided such terms because they reflected subjective emotional states.

Positive and Negative Reinforcement

There are two forms of reinforcement: *positive reinforcement* and *negative reinforcement.* Both affect future behavior, but they do so in different ways (see Table 5.1). It's easier to understand these differences if you note at the outset that Skinner did not use the terms *positive* and *negative* in their everyday sense of meaning "good" and "bad" or "desirable" and "undesirable." Instead, think of the words *positive* and *negative* in terms of their mathematical meanings. *Positive* is the equivalent of a plus sign (+), meaning that something is added. *Negative* is the equivalent of a minus sign (−), meaning that something is subtracted or removed. If you keep that distinction in mind, the principles of positive and negative reinforcement should be easier to understand.

Positive reinforcement involves following an operant with the addition of a reinforcing stimulus. In positive reinforcement situations, a response is strengthened because something is *added* or presented. Everyday examples of positive reinforcement in action are easy to identify. Here are some examples:

- Your backhand return of the tennis ball (the operant) is low and fast, and your tennis coach yells "Excellent!" (the reinforcing stimulus).
- You watch a student production of *Hamlet* and write a short paper about it (the operant) for 10 bonus points (the reinforcing stimulus) in your literature class.
- You reach your sales quota at work (the operant) and you get a bonus check (the reinforcing stimulus).

In each example, if the addition of the reinforcing stimulus has the effect of making you more likely to repeat the operant in similar situations in the future, then positive reinforcement has occurred.

It's important to point out that what constitutes a *reinforcing stimulus* can vary from person to person, species to species, and situation to situation. While gold stars and stickers may be reinforcing to a third-grader, they would probably have little reinforcing value to your average high school student. As Skinner (1953)

law of effect
Learning principle proposed by Thorndike that responses followed by a satisfying effect become strengthened and are more likely to recur in a particular situation, while responses followed by a dissatisfying effect are weakened and less likely to recur in a particular situation.

operant
Skinner's term for an actively emitted (or voluntary) behavior that operates on the environment to produce consequences.

operant conditioning
The basic learning process that involves changing the probability that a response will be repeated by manipulating the consequences of that response; also called *Skinnerian conditioning.*

reinforcement
The occurrence of a stimulus or event following a response that increases the likelihood of that response being repeated.

positive reinforcement
A situation in which a response is followed by the addition of a reinforcing stimulus, increasing the likelihood that the response will be repeated in similar situations.

Both positive and negative reinforcement increase the likelihood of a behavior being repeated. Positive reinforcement involves a behavior that leads to a reinforcing or rewarding event. In contrast, negative reinforcement involves behavior that leads to the avoidance of or escape from an aversive or punishing event. Ultimately, both positive and negative reinforcement involve outcomes that strengthen future behavior.

Table 5.1

Comparing Positive and Negative Reinforcement

Process	Operant	Consequence	Effect on Behavior
Positive reinforcement	Studying to make dean's list	Make dean's list	Increase studying in the future
Negative reinforcement	Studying to avoid losing academic scholarship	Avoid loss of academic scholarship	Increase studying in the future

explained, "The only way to tell whether or not a given event or stimulus is reinforcing to a given organism under given conditions is to make a direct test."

It's also important to note that the reinforcing stimulus is not necessarily something we usually consider positive or desirable. For example, most teachers would not think of a scolding as being a reinforcing stimulus to children. But to children, adult attention can be a powerful reinforcing stimulus. If a child receives attention from the teacher only when he misbehaves, then the teacher may unwittingly be reinforcing misbehavior. The child may actually increase disruptive behavior in order to get the sought-after reinforcing stimulus—adult attention—even if it's in the form of being scolded. To reduce the child's disruptive behavior, the teacher would do better to reinforce the child's appropriate behavior by paying attention to him when he's *not* being disruptive, such as when he is working quietly.

Negative reinforcement involves an operant that is followed by the removal of an aversive stimulus. In negative reinforcement situations, a response is strengthened because something is being *subtracted* or removed. Remember that the word *negative* in the phrase *negative reinforcement* is used like a mathematical minus sign (−). For example, you take two aspirin (the operant) to remove a headache (the aversive stimulus). Thirty minutes later, the headache is gone. Are you now more likely to take aspirin to deal with bodily aches and pain in the future? If you are, then negative reinforcement has occurred.

Aversive stimuli typically involve physical or psychological discomfort that an organism seeks to escape or avoid. Consequently, behaviors are said to be negatively reinforced when they let you either (1) *escape* aversive stimuli that are already present or (2) *avoid* aversive stimuli before they occur. That is, we're more likely to repeat the same escape or avoidance behaviors in similar situations in the future. The headache example illustrates the negative reinforcement of *escape behavior.* By taking two aspirin, you "escaped" the headache. Paying your electric bill on time to avoid a late charge illustrates the negative reinforcement of *avoidance behavior.* Here are some more examples of negative reinforcement involving escape or avoidance behavior:

Types of Reinforcers Primary reinforcers, like warm hugs on a cold day, are naturally reinforcing—you don't have to learn their value. In contrast, the value of conditioned reinforcers, like grades and awards, has to be learned through their association with primary reinforcers. But conditioned reinforcers can be just as reinforcing as primary reinforcers. As proof, a beaming Lisa Leslie holds the gold medal she earned at the 2004 Olympic Games in Athens. The highest-scoring member of the U.S. women's basketball team, Leslie plays professional basketball for the Los Angeles Sparks.

- You make backup copies of important computer files (the operant) to avoid losing the data if the computer's hard drive should fail (the aversive stimulus).

- You dab some hydrocortisone cream on an insect bite (the operant) to escape the itching (the aversive stimulus).

- You get a flu shot in November (the operant) to avoid catching the flu (the aversive stimulus).

In each example, if escaping or avoiding the aversive event has the effect of making you more likely to repeat the operant in similar situations in the future, then negative reinforcement has taken place.

Primary and Conditioned Reinforcers

Skinner also distinguished two kinds of reinforcing stimuli: primary and conditioned. A **primary reinforcer** is one that is *naturally* reinforcing for a given species. That is, even if an individual has not had prior experience with the particular stimulus, the stimulus or event still has reinforcing properties. For example, food, water, adequate warmth, and sexual contact are primary reinforcers for most animals, including humans.

A **conditioned reinforcer,** also called a *secondary reinforcer,* is one that has acquired reinforcing value by being associated with a primary reinforcer. The classic example of a conditioned reinforcer is money. Money is reinforcing not because those flimsy bits of paper and little pieces of metal have value in and of themselves, but because we've learned that we can use them to acquire primary reinforcers and other conditioned reinforcers. Awards, frequent-flyer points, and college degrees are just a few other examples of conditioned reinforcers.

Conditioned reinforcers need not be as tangible as money or college degrees. The respect of your peers and the approval of your instructors or managers can be powerful conditioned reinforcers. Conditioned reinforcers can be as subtle as a smile, a touch, or a nod of recognition. Looking back at the Prologue, for example, Fern was reinforced by the laughter of her friends and relatives each time she told the "killer attic" tale—so she keeps telling the story!

Punishment
Using Aversive Consequences to Decrease Behavior

Key Theme
- Punishment is a process that decreases the future occurrence of a behavior.

Key Questions
- What factors influence the effectiveness of punishment?
- What effects are associated with the use of punishment to control behavior, and what are some alternative ways to change behavior?
- What are discriminative stimuli?

Positive and negative reinforcement are processes that *increase* the frequency of a particular behavior. The opposite effect is produced by punishment. **Punishment** is a process in which a behavior is followed by an aversive consequence that *decreases* the likelihood of the behavior's being repeated. Many people tend to confuse punishment and negative reinforcement, but these two processes produce entirely different effects on behavior (see Table 5.2). Negative reinforcement *always increases* the likelihood that an operant will be repeated in the future. Punishment *always decreases* the future performance of an operant.

Skinner (1953) identified two types of aversive events that can act as punishment. **Punishment by application,** also called *positive punishment,* involves a response being followed by the presentation of an aversive stimulus. The word *positive* in the phrase *positive punishment* signifies that something is added or presented in the situation. In this case, it's an aversive stimulus. Here are some everyday examples of punishment by application:

- An employee wears jeans to work (the operant) and is reprimanded by his supervisor for dressing inappropriately (the punishing stimulus).

- You make a comment (the operant) in your workgroup meetings, and a co-worker responds with a sarcastic remark (the punishing stimulus).

In each of these examples, if the presentation of the punishing stimulus has the effect of decreasing the behavior it follows, then punishment has occurred.

negative reinforcement
A situation in which a response results in the removal of, avoidance of, or escape from a punishing stimulus, increasing the likelihood that the response will be repeated in similar situations.

primary reinforcer
A stimulus or event that is naturally or inherently reinforcing for a given species, such as food, water, or other biological necessities.

conditioned reinforcer
A stimulus or event that has acquired reinforcing value by being associated with a primary reinforcer; also called a *secondary reinforcer.*

punishment
The presentation of a stimulus or event following a behavior that acts to decrease the likelihood of the behavior's being repeated.

punishment by application
A situation in which an operant is followed by the presentation or addition of an aversive stimulus; also called *positive punishment.*

Table 5.2

Comparing Punishment and Negative Reinforcement

Process	Operant	Consequence	Effect on Behavior
Punishment	Using radar detector	Receive speeding ticket and fine for illegal use of radar detector	Decrease use of radar detector in the future
Negative reinforcement	Using radar detector	Avoid speeding ticket and fine	Increase use of radar detector in the future

Punishment and negative reinforcement are two different processes that produce *opposite* effects on a given behavior. Punishment *decreases* the future performance of the behavior, while negative reinforcement *increases* it.

punishment by removal
A situation in which an operant is followed by the removal or subtraction of a reinforcing stimulus; also called *negative punishment*.

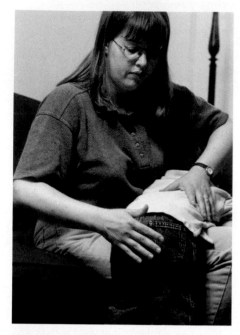

The Effects of Spanking Defined as hitting a child on the buttocks with an open hand without causing a bruise or physical harm, *spanking* is a common form of discipline in the United States. Some three-quarters of U.S. parents spank their children (Kazdin & Benjet, 2003; Straus & Stewart, 1999). Some researchers believe that mild and occasional spanking is not necessarily harmful, especially when used as a backup for other forms of discipline (Baumrind & others, 2002).

However, in a wide-ranging meta-analysis, psychologist Elizabeth Gershoff (2002) concluded that physical punishment is associated with increased aggressiveness, delinquency, and antisocial behavior in the child. Other negative effects include poor parent–child relationships and an increased risk that parental disciplinary tactics might escalate into physical abuse. As Skinner (1974) pointed out, gaining immediate compliance through punishment must be weighed against punishment's negative long-term effects.

This table provides a simple way of identifying the type of reinforcement or punishment based on whether a reinforcing or an aversive stimulus is presented or removed following an operant.

Although the punishing stimuli in these examples were administered by other people, punishing stimuli also occur as natural consequences for some behaviors. Inadvertently touching a hot iron, a live electrical wire, or a sharp object (the operant) can result in a painful injury (the punishing stimulus).

The second type of punishment is **punishment by removal,** also called *negative punishment*. The word *negative* indicates that some stimulus is subtracted or removed from the situation (see Table 5.3). In this case, it is the loss or withdrawal of a reinforcing stimulus following a behavior. That is, the behavior's consequence is the loss of some privilege, possession, or other desirable object or activity. Here are some everyday examples of punishment by removal:

- After she buys stock (the operant) in a "hot" new start-up company, the company fails and the investor loses all of her money (loss of reinforcing stimulus).

- Because he was flirting with another woman (the operant), a guy gets dumped by his girlfriend (loss of reinforcing stimulus).

In each example, if the behavior decreases in response to the removal of the reinforcing stimulus, then punishment has occurred. It's important to stress that, like reinforcement, punishment is defined by the effect it produces. In everyday usage, people often refer to a particular consequence as a punishment when, strictly speaking, it's not. Why? Because the consequence has *not* reduced future occurrences of the behavior. Hence, many consequences commonly thought of as punishments—being sent to prison, fined, reprimanded, ridiculed, or fired from a job—fail to reduce a particular behavior.

Why is it that aversive consequences don't always function as effective punishments? Skinner (1953) as well as other researchers have noted that several factors influence the effectiveness of punishment (see Axelrod & Apsche, 1983; Kazdin, 2001). For example, punishment is more effective if it immediately follows a response than if it is delayed. Punishment is also more effective if it consistently, rather than occasionally, follows a response. Though speeding tickets and prison sentences are commonly referred to as punishments, these aversive consequences are inconsistently applied and often administered only after a long delay. Thus, they don't always effectively decrease specific behaviors.

Even when punishment works, its use has several drawbacks. First, punishment may decrease a specific response, but it doesn't necessarily teach or promote a more appropriate response to take its place. Second, punishment that is intense may produce undesirable results, such as complete passivity, fear, anxiety, or hostility (Skinner, 1974). Finally, the effects of punishment are likely to be temporary (Estes & Skinner, 1941; Skinner, 1938). A child who is sent to her room for teasing her little brother may well repeat the behavior when her mother's back is turned. As Skinner (1971) noted, "Punished behavior is likely to reappear after the punitive consequences are withdrawn." For some suggestions on how to change behavior without using a punishing stimulus, see In Focus Box 5.3.

Table 5.3

Types of Reinforcement and Punishment

	Reinforcing stimulus	Aversive stimulus
Stimulus presented	Positive reinforcement	Positive punishment
Stimulus removed	Negative punishment	Negative reinforcement

IN FOCUS 5.3

Changing the Behavior of Others: Alternatives to Punishment

Although punishment may temporarily decrease the occurrence of a problem behavior, it doesn't promote more desirable or appropriate behaviors in its place. Throughout his life, Skinner remained strongly opposed to the use of punishment. Instead, he advocated the greater use of positive reinforcement to strengthen desirable behaviors (Dinsmoor, 1992; Skinner, 1971). Here are four strategies that can be used to reduce undesirable behaviors without resorting to punishment.

Strategy 1: Reinforce an Incompatible Behavior

The best method to reduce a problem behavior is to reinforce an *alternative* behavior that is both constructive and incompatible with the problem behavior. For example, if you're trying to decrease a child's whining, respond to her requests (the reinforcer) only when she talks in a normal tone of voice.

Strategy 2: Stop Reinforcing the Problem Behavior

Technically, this strategy is called *extinction*. The first step in effectively applying extinction is to observe the behavior carefully and identify the reinforcer that is maintaining the problem behavior. Then eliminate the reinforcer.

Suppose a co-worker is wasting your time with gossip. You want to extinguish his behavior of interrupting your work with needless chitchat. In the past, trying to be polite, you've responded to his behavior by acting interested (a reinforcer). You could eliminate the reinforcer by acting uninterested and continuing to work while he talks.

Using Reinforcement in the Classroom
Teachers at all levels use positive reinforcement to increase desired behaviors. Often, conditioned reinforcers, like stickers or gold stars, can be exchanged for other, more tangible rewards, like a new pencil.

It's important to note that when the extinction process is initiated, the problem behavior often *temporarily* increases. This situation is more likely to occur if the problem behavior has only occasionally been reinforced in the past. Thus, once you begin, be consistent in nonreinforcement of the problem behavior.

Strategy 3: Reinforce the Nonoccurrence of the Problem Behavior

This strategy involves setting a specific time period after which the individual is reinforced if the unwanted behavior has *not* occurred. For example, if you're trying to reduce bickering between your children, set an appropriate time limit, and then provide positive reinforcement if they have *not* squabbled during that interval.

Strategy 4: Remove the Opportunity to Obtain Positive Reinforcement

It's not always possible to identify and eliminate all the reinforcers that maintain a behavior. For example, a child's obnoxious behavior might be reinforced by the social attention of siblings or classmates.

In a procedure called *time-out from positive reinforcement,* the child is removed from the reinforcing situation for a short time, so that the access to reinforcers is eliminated. When the undesirable behavior occurs, the child is immediately sent to a time-out area that is free of distractions and social contact. The time-out period begins as soon as the child's behavior is under control. For children, a good rule of thumb is one minute of time-out per year of age.

Enhancing the Effectiveness of Positive Reinforcement

Often, these four strategies are used in combination. However, remember the most important behavioral principle: *Positively reinforce the behaviors that you want to increase.* There are several ways in which you can enhance the effectiveness of positive reinforcement:

- Make sure that the reinforcer is *strongly* reinforcing to the individual whose behavior you're trying to modify.

- The positive reinforcer should be delivered *immediately* after the preferred behavior occurs.

- The positive reinforcer should initially be given *every* time the preferred behavior occurs. When the desired behavior is well established, *gradually reduce the frequency of reinforcement.*

- Use a *variety* of positive reinforcers, such as tangible items, praise, special privileges, recognition, and so on. Minimize the use of food as a positive reinforcer.

- Capitalize on what is known as the *Premack principle*—a more preferred activity (e.g., painting) can be used to reinforce a less preferred activity (e.g., picking up toys).

- Encourage the individual to engage in *self-reinforcement* in the form of pride, a sense of accomplishment, and feelings of self-control.

©Baby Blues Partnership. Reprinted with special permission of King Features Syndicate.

CRITICAL THINKING 5.4

Is Human Freedom Just an Illusion?

Skinner's most famous invention was the *operant chamber*, more popularly known as a *Skinner box*, in which rats or pigeons were conditioned to perform simple behaviors, such as pressing a lever or pecking at a disk, to receive a food reward (see page 198). Had Skinner been content to confine his observations to the behavior of rats or pigeons in a Skinner box, his career might have been relatively uncontroversial. But Skinner was intensely interested in human behavior and social problems (Bjork, 1997a). He believed that operant conditioning principles could, and *should,* be applied on a broad scale to help solve society's problems.

Skinner's most radical—and controversial—belief was that such ideas as free will, self-determination, and individual choice are just an illusion. Skinner (1971) argued that behavior is not simply influenced by the environment but is *determined* by it. Control the environment, he said, and you will control human behavior. As he bluntly asserted in his controversial best-seller, *Beyond Freedom and Dignity* (1971), "A person does not act upon the world, the world acts upon him."

Such views did not sit well with the American public. Following the publication of *Beyond Freedom and Dignity,* one member of Congress denounced Skinner for "advancing ideas which threaten the future of our system of government by denigrating the American tradition of individualism, human dignity, and self-reliance" (quoted in Rutherford, 2000). Why the uproar?

Skinner's ideas clashed with the traditional American ideals of personal responsibility, individual freedom, and self-determination. Such ideals are based on the assumption that behavior arises from causes that are *within* the individual. All individuals are held responsible for their conduct and given credit for their achievements. Skinner labeled such notions the "traditional prescientific view" of human behavior.

According to Skinner, "A scientific analysis [of behavior] shifts both the responsibility and the achievement to the environment." Applying his ideas to social problems, such as alcoholism and crime, Skinner (1971) wrote, "It is the environment which is 'responsible' for objectionable behavior, and it is the environment, not some attribute of the individual, which must be changed."

To understand Skinner's point of view, it helps to think of society as a massive, sophisticated Skinner box. From the moment of birth, the environment shapes and determines your behavior through reinforcing or punishing consequences. Taking this view, you are no more personally responsible for your behavior than is a rat in a Skinner box pressing a lever to obtain a food

Discriminative Stimuli
Setting the Occasion for Responding

Another component of operant conditioning is the **discriminative stimulus**—the specific stimulus in the presence of which a particular operant is more likely to be reinforced. For example, a ringing phone is a discriminative stimulus that sets the occasion for a particular response—picking up the telephone and speaking.

This example illustrates how we've learned from experience to associate certain environmental cues or signals with particular operant responses. We've learned that we're more likely to be reinforced for performing a particular operant response when we do so in the presence of the appropriate discriminative stimulus. Thus, you've learned that you're more likely to be reinforced for screaming at the top of your lungs at a football game (one discriminative stimulus) than in the middle of class (a different discriminative stimulus).

In this way, according to Skinner (1974), behavior is determined and controlled by the stimuli that are present in a given situation. In Skinner's view, an individual's behavior is *not* determined by a personal choice or a conscious decision. Instead, individual behavior is determined by environmental stimuli and the person's reinforcement history in that environment. Skinner's views on this point have some very controversial implications, which are discussed in Critical Thinking Box 5.4.

We have now discussed all three fundamental components of operant conditioning (see Table 5.4). In the presence of a specific environmental stimulus (the

discriminative stimulus
A specific stimulus in the presence of which a particular response is more likely to be reinforced, and in the absence of which a particular response is not reinforced.

Time for Skinner's Ideas? The impact of the publication of *Beyond Freedom and Dignity* can be measured by Skinner's appearance on the cover of *Time* on September 20, 1971, shortly after the book was published. Skinner is shown in the middle of some of his most famous creations. Clockwise from upper left: pigeons trained to peck at a Ping-Pong ball; a rat pressing a lever in an operant chamber; an idealized rural scene representing the fictional utopia described in Skinner's novel, *Walden Two* (1948a); and a teaching machine, an early mechanical device for programmed instruction based on operant conditioning principles.

pellet. Just like the rat's behavior, your behavior is simply a response to the unique patterns of environmental consequences to which you have been exposed.

Skinner (1971) proposed that "a technology of behavior" be developed, one based on a scientific analysis of behavior. He believed that society could be redesigned using operant conditioning principles to produce more socially desirable behaviors—and happier citizens. He described such an ideal, utopian society in *Walden Two*, a novel he published in 1948. Critics charged Skinner with advocating a totalitarian state. They asked who would determine which behaviors were shaped and maintained (Rutherford, 2000; Todd & Morris, 1992).

As Skinner pointed out, however, human behavior is *already* controlled by various authorities: parents, teachers, politicians, religious leaders, employers, and so forth. Such authorities regularly use reinforcing and punishing consequences to shape and control the behavior of others. Skinner insisted that it is better to control behavior in a rational, humane fashion than to leave the control of behavior to the whims and often selfish aims of those in power. Skinner himself was adamantly opposed to the use of

punishment and other aversive stimuli to control behavior. Instead, he repeatedly advocated the greater use of positive reinforcement (Dinsmoor, 1992).

On the one hand, it may seem convenient to blame your history of environmental consequences for your failures and misdeeds. On the other hand, that means you can't take any credit for your accomplishments and good deeds, either!

Critical Thinking Questions

- If Skinner's vision of a socially engineered society using operant conditioning principles were implemented, would such changes be good or bad for society?

- Are human freedom and personal responsibility illusions? Or is human behavior fundamentally different from a rat's behavior in a Skinner box? If so, how?

- Is your behavior almost entirely the product of environmental conditioning? Think about your answer carefully. After all, exactly *why* are you reading this box?

Table 5.4

Components of Operant Conditioning

The examples given here illustrate the three key components involved in operant conditioning. The basic operant conditioning process works like this: In the presence of a specific discriminative stimulus, an operant response is emitted, which is followed by a consequence. Depending on the consequence, we are either more or less likely to repeat the operant when we encounter the same or a similar discriminative stimulus in the future.

	Discriminative Stimulus	Operant Response	Consequence	Effect on Future Behavior
Definition	The environmental stimulus that precedes an operant response	The actively emitted or voluntary behavior	The environmental stimulus or event that follows the operant response	Reinforcement increases the likelihood of operant being repeated; punishment or lack of reinforcement decreases the likelihood of operant being repeated.
Examples	Wallet on college sidewalk	Give wallet to security	$50 reward from wallet's owner	Positive reinforcement: More likely to turn in lost items to authorities
	Gas gauge almost on "empty"	Fill car with gas	Avoid running out of gas	Negative reinforcement: More likely to fill car when gas gauge shows empty
	Informal social situation at work	Tell an off-color, sexist joke	Formally reprimanded for sexism and inappropriate workplace behavior	Positive punishment: Less likely to tell off-color, sexist jokes in workplace
	Soft-drink vending machine	Put in quarters	Get no soft drink and lose money	Negative punishment: Less likely to use that vending machine

The Skinner Box Popularly called a Skinner box, after its inventor, an operant chamber is used to experimentally study operant conditioning in laboratory animals.

discriminative stimulus), we emit a particular behavior (the *operant*), which is followed by a consequence (*reinforcement* or *punishment*). If the consequence is either positive or negative reinforcement, we are *more* likely to repeat the operant when we encounter the same or similar discriminative stimuli in the future. If the consequence is some form of punishment, we are *less* likely to repeat the operant when we encounter the same or similar discriminative stimuli in the future.

Next, we'll build on the basics of operant conditioning by considering how Skinner explained the acquisition of complex behaviors.

Shaping and Maintaining Behavior

Key Theme
- New behaviors are acquired through shaping and can be maintained through different patterns of reinforcement.

Key Questions
- How does shaping work?
- What is the partial reinforcement effect, and how do the four schedules of reinforcement differ in their effects?
- What is behavior modification?

To scientifically study the relationship between behavior and its consequences in the laboratory, Skinner invented the **operant chamber,** more popularly known as the **Skinner box.** An operant chamber is a small cage with a food dispenser. Attached to the cage is a device that automatically records the number of operants made by an experimental animal, usually a rat or pigeon. For a rat, the typical operant is pressing a bar; for a pigeon, it is pecking at a small disk. Food pellets are usually used for positive reinforcement. Often, a light in the cage functions as a discriminative stimulus. When the light is on, pressing the bar or pecking the disk is reinforced with a food pellet. When the light is off, these responses do not result in reinforcement.

When a rat is first placed in a Skinner box, it typically explores its new environment, occasionally nudging or pressing the bar in the process. The researcher can accelerate the rat's bar-pressing behavior through a process called shaping. **Shaping** involves reinforcing successively closer approximations of a behavior until the correct behavior is displayed. For example, the researcher might first reinforce the rat with a food pellet whenever it moves to the half of the Skinner box in which the bar is located. Other responses would be ignored. Once that response has been learned, reinforcement is withheld until the rat moves even closer to the bar. Then the rat might be reinforced only when it touches the bar. Step by step, the rat is reinforced for behaviors that correspond ever more closely to the final goal behavior—pressing the bar.

Skinner believed that shaping could explain how people acquire a wide variety of abilities and skills—everything from tying shoes to operating sophisticated computer programs. Athletic coaches, teachers, parents, and child-care workers all use shaping techniques.

The Partial Reinforcement Effect: Building Resistance to Extinction

Once a rat had acquired a bar-pressing behavior, Skinner found that the most efficient way to strengthen the response was to immediately reinforce *every* occurrence of bar pressing. This pattern of reinforcement is called **continuous reinforcement.** In everyday life, of course, it's common for responses to be reinforced only sometimes—a pattern called **partial reinforcement.** For example, practicing your basketball skills isn't followed by putting the ball through the hoop on every shot. Sometimes you're reinforced by making a basket, and sometimes you're not.

---

operant chamber or **Skinner box**
The experimental apparatus invented by B. F. Skinner to study the relationship between environmental events and active behaviors.

shaping
The operant conditioning procedure of selectively reinforcing successively closer approximations of a goal behavior until the goal behavior is displayed.

continuous reinforcement
A schedule of reinforcement in which every occurrence of a particular response is reinforced.

partial reinforcement
A situation in which the occurrence of a particular response is only sometimes followed by a reinforcer.

extinction (in operant conditioning)
The gradual weakening and disappearance of conditioned behavior. In operant conditioning, extinction occurs when an emitted behavior is no longer followed by a reinforcer.

partial reinforcement effect
The phenomenon in which behaviors that are conditioned using partial reinforcement are more resistant to extinction than behaviors that are conditioned using continuous reinforcement.

(a)

(b)

(c)

Operant Conditioning at SeaWorld This sequence shows a SeaWorld trainer using operant conditioning principles with a dolphin that has already been shaped to perform somersaults. **(a)** The trainer gives the dolphin two discriminative stimuli—a distinct vocal sound and a specific hand gesture. **(b)** The dolphin quickly responds with the correct operant—a perfect somersault in the air. **(c)** The operant is positively reinforced with a piece of fish. The same basic techniques are also used to teach seals, sea lions, walruses, and killer whales to perform different tricks on cue.

Now suppose that despite all your hard work, your basketball skills are dismal. If practicing free throws was *never* reinforced by making a basket, what would you do? You'd probably eventually quit playing basketball. This is an example of **extinction.** In operant conditioning, when a learned response no longer results in reinforcement, the likelihood of the behavior's being repeated gradually declines.

Skinner (1956) first noticed the effects of partial reinforcement when he began running low on food pellets one day. Rather than reinforcing every bar press, Skinner tried to stretch out his supply of pellets by rewarding responses only periodically. He found that the rats not only continued to respond, but actually increased their rate of bar pressing.

One important consequence of partially reinforcing behavior is that partially reinforced behaviors tend to be more resistant to extinction than are behaviors conditioned using continuous reinforcement. This phenomenon is called the **partial reinforcement effect.** For example, when Skinner shut off the food-dispensing mechanism, a pigeon conditioned using continuous reinforcement would continue pecking at the disk 100 times or so before the behavior decreased significantly, indicating extinction. In contrast, a pigeon conditioned with partial reinforcement continued to peck at the disk thousands of times! If you think about it, this is not surprising. When pigeons, rats, or humans have experienced partial reinforcement, they've learned that reinforcement may yet occur, despite delays and nonreinforced responses, if persistent responses are made.

In everyday life, the partial reinforcement effect is reflected in behaviors that persist despite the lack of reinforcement. Gamblers may persist despite a string of losses, writers will persevere in the face of repeated rejection slips, and the family dog will continue begging for the scraps of food that it has only occasionally received at the dinner table in the past.

Superstitious Behavior and Accidental Reinforcement Like these New York Mets baseball players, professional athletes sometimes develop quirky superstitious rituals (Burger & Lynn, 2005). Skinner (1948b) pointed out that superstitions may result when a behavior is *accidentally* reinforced—that is, when reinforcement is just a coincidence. If you win a lottery when you play your "lucky" number, will you be more likely to play that number again?

The Schedules of Reinforcement

Skinner (1956) found that specific preset arrangements of partial reinforcement produced different patterns and rates of responding. Collectively, these different reinforcement arrangements are called **schedules of reinforcement.** As we describe the four basic schedules of reinforcement, it will be helpful to refer to Figure 5.6 on page 200, which shows the typical pattern of responses produced by each schedule.

With a **fixed-ratio (FR) schedule,** reinforcement occurs after a fixed number of responses. A rat on a 10-to-1 fixed-ratio schedule (abbreviated

FIGURE 5.6 Schedules of Reinforcement and Response Patterns Different patterns of responding are produced by the four basic schedules of reinforcement. The predictable nature of a *fixed-ratio schedule* (the blue line at far left) produces a high rate of responding, with a pause after the reinforcer is delivered. The unpredictable nature of *variable-ratio schedules* (red) also produces high, steady rates of responding, but with hardly any pausing between reinforcers. *Fixed-interval schedules* (purple) produce a scallop-shaped pattern of responding. The unpredictable nature of *variable-interval schedules* (orange) produces a moderate but steady rate of responding. (Based on Skinner, 1961.)

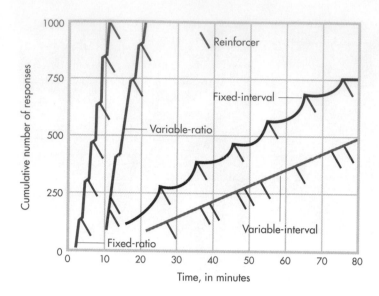

schedule of reinforcement
The delivery of a reinforcer according to a preset pattern based on the number of responses or the time interval between responses.

fixed-ratio (FR) schedule
A reinforcement schedule in which a reinforcer is delivered after a fixed number of responses has occurred.

variable-ratio (VR) schedule
A reinforcement schedule in which a reinforcer is delivered after an average number of responses, which varies unpredictably from trial to trial.

fixed-interval (FI) schedule
A reinforcement schedule in which a reinforcer is delivered for the first response that occurs after a preset time interval has elapsed.

variable-interval (VI) schedule
A reinforcement schedule in which a reinforcer is delivered for the first response that occurs after an average time interval, which varies unpredictably from trial to trial.

FR-10) would have to press the bar 10 times in order to receive one food pellet. Fixed-ratio schedules typically produce a high rate of responding that follows a burst–pause–burst pattern. In everyday life, the fixed-ratio schedule is reflected in any activity that requires a precise number of responses in order to obtain reinforcement. Piecework—work for which you are paid for producing a specific number of items, such as being paid $1 for every 100 envelopes you stuff—is an example of an FR-100 schedule.

With a **variable-ratio (VR) schedule,** reinforcement occurs after an *average* number of responses, which *varies* from trial to trial. A rat on a variable-ratio-20 schedule (abbreviated VR-20) might have to press the bar 25 times on the first trial before being reinforced and only 15 times on the second trial before reinforcement. Although the number of responses required on any specific trial is *unpredictable,* over repeated trials the ratio of responses to reinforcers works out to the predetermined average.

Variable-ratio schedules of reinforcement produce high, steady rates of responding with hardly any pausing between trials or after reinforcement. Gambling is the classic example of a variable-ratio schedule in real life. Each spin of the roulette wheel, toss of the dice, or purchase of a lottery ticket could be the big one, and the more often you gamble, the more opportunities you have to win (and lose, as casino owners are well aware).

On a **fixed-interval (FI) schedule,** a reinforcer is delivered for the first response emitted *after* the preset time interval has elapsed. A rat on a two-minute fixed-interval schedule (abbreviated FI-2 minutes) would receive no food pellets for any bar presses made during the first two minutes. But the first bar press *after* the two-minute interval had elapsed would be reinforced.

Fixed-interval schedules typically produce a scallop-shaped pattern of responding in which the number of responses tends to increase as the time for the next reinforcer draws near. For example, if your instructor gives you a test every four weeks, your studying behavior would probably follow the same scallop-shaped pattern of responding as the rat's bar-pressing behavior. As the end of the four-week interval draws near, studying behavior increases. After the test, studying behavior drops off until the end of the next four-week interval approaches.

On a **variable-interval (VI) schedule,** reinforcement occurs for the first response emitted after an *average* amount of time has elapsed, but the interval varies from trial to trial. Hence, a rat on a VI-30 seconds schedule might be reinforced for the first bar press after only 10 seconds have elapsed on the first trial, for the first bar press after 50 seconds have elapsed on the second

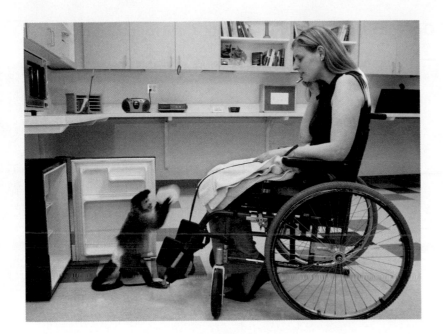

Creating "Helping Hands" with Operant Conditioning Founded by behavioral psychologist Mary Joan Willard, "Helping Hands" is a nonprofit organization that uses operant conditioning to train capuchin monkeys to provide live-in help to people who are paralyzed or otherwise severely disabled. Capuchins are used because of their high intelligence, dexterity, and ability to form a close bond with their human companions. At the Helping Hands "monkey college" near Boston, capuchins are trained to perform a wide range of helping behaviors, such as turning on lights, combing a person's hair, and loading a CD or videotape. Training can take up to two years. Shown is Toby, a 10-year-old capuchin monkey, as he retrieves a bottle from inside a closed refrigerator for his trainer.

trial, and for the first bar press after 30 seconds have elapsed on the third trial. This works out to an average of one reinforcer every 30 seconds.

Generally, the unpredictable nature of variable-interval schedules tends to produce moderate but steady rates of responding, especially when the average interval is relatively short. In daily life, we experience variable-interval schedules when we have to wait for events that follow an approximate, rather than a precise, schedule. Trying to connect to the Internet via a dial up modem during peak usage hours is one example. When you get a busy signal, you periodically try redialing (the operant) because you know that at some point you'll connect and be able to access the Internet (the reinforcer).

Applications of Operant Conditioning

In Focus Box 5.3 (on page 195) described how operant conditioning principles can be applied to reduce and eliminate problem behaviors. These examples illustrate **behavior modification,** the application of learning principles to help people develop more effective or adaptive behaviors. Most often, behavior modification involves applying the principles of operant conditioning to bring about changes in behavior.

Behavior modification has been used in such diverse situations as improving worker performance, increasing social skills in schoolchildren, promoting sleep at night, and increasing the use of automobile seatbelts (e.g., Kamps & others, 1992; Lilie & Rosenberg, 1990; Martens & others, 1992; Stajkovic & Luthans, 1997). Behavior modification has even been used to reduce "goofing off" by competitive athletes during practice sessions (Hume & Crossman, 1992). When swimmers were reinforced with music for focusing on practicing their skills, productive behavior increased dramatically. In each of these situations, the systematic use of reinforcement and shaping resulted in the increased occurrence of desirable behaviors. In Chapter 14, on therapies, we'll look at behavior modification techniques in more detail.

The principles of operant conditioning have also been used in the specialized training of animals, such as the capuchin monkey in the photo above, to help people who are physically challenged. Other examples are Seeing Eye dogs and dogs who assist people who are hearing-impaired. In the Focus on Neuroscience on page 202, we discuss how operant conditioning may someday be used to train rats for search-and-rescue missions.

behavior modification
The application of learning principles to help people develop more effective or adaptive behaviors.

Neuroscience: Virtual Operant Conditioning: Remote-Controlled "Ratbots"

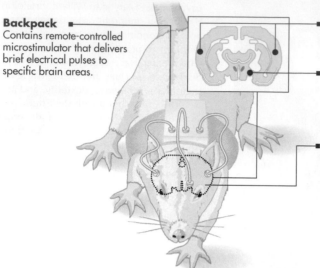

Backpack
Contains remote-controlled microstimulator that delivers brief electrical pulses to specific brain areas.

Brain sensory areas that process whisker sensations.

Brain area called *medial forebrain bundle* produces rewarding or pleasurable sensations.

Operantly Conditioned Movements
By electrically stimulating whisker sensory areas, the rat learns to turn left or right, which is reinforced by electrically stimulating a pleasure center in the rat's brain—the medial forebrain bundle.

Could trapped victims of earthquakes and other disasters someday be located by remote-controlled search-and-rescue rats? In a clever application of operant conditioning principles, researcher Sanjiv Talwar and his colleagues (2002) implanted electrodes into the brains of five rats. In each rat, one electrode stimulated the *medial forebrain bundle* (MFB), a brain area that has long been known to produce pleasurable sensations. A brief jolt to the MFB provides direct brain reward, reinforcing whatever behavior the rat is performing at that moment. Two more electrodes stimulated the brain areas involved in processing sensory signals from the rat's left and right whiskers. After some initial training, activation of one of the whisker electrodes functioned as a discriminative stimulus, signaling the rat to turn left or right. Each rat was

also fitted with a little backpack containing a wireless receiver that enabled the researchers to activate the electrodes from up to a quarter of a mile away.

Using radio signals transmitted from a laptop computer, the researchers commanded the rats to run, turn, jump, and climb through pipes, through concrete rubble, on elevated runways, off ledges, and up trees. Because the remote-controlled rats functioned much like robots—very agile robots—they were dubbed "ratbots."

Talwar and his colleagues (2002) believe that by using virtual reinforcement, rats could be trained to search for landmines or buried victims of earthquakes. As Talwar explains, "It would be a relatively simple matter to train rescue rats to recognize and home in on the smell of a human trapped under rubble."

Contemporary Views of Operant Conditioning

Key Theme

- In contrast to Skinner, today's psychologists acknowledge the importance of both cognitive and evolutionary factors in operant conditioning.

Key Questions

- How did Tolman's research demonstrate the involvement of cognitive processes in learning?
- What are cognitive maps, latent learning, and learned helplessness?
- How do an animal's natural behavior patterns affect the conditioning of operant behaviors?

In our discussion of classical conditioning, we noted that contemporary psychologists acknowledge the important roles played by cognitive factors and biological predispositions in classical conditioning. The situation is much the same with operant conditioning. The basic principles of operant conditioning have been confirmed in thousands of studies. However, our understanding of operant conditioning has been broadened by the consideration of cognitive factors and the recognition of the importance of natural behavior patterns.

Cognitive Aspects of Operant Conditioning

Rats! I Thought *You* Had the Map!

In Skinner's view, operant conditioning did not need to invoke cognitive factors to explain the acquisition of operant behaviors. Words such as *expect, prefer, choose,* and *decide* could not be used to explain how behaviors were acquired, maintained, or extinguished. Similarly, Thorndike and other early behaviorists believed that complex, active behaviors were no more than a chain of stimulus–response connections that had been "stamped in" by their effects.

However, not all learning researchers agreed with Skinner and Thorndike. **Edward C. Tolman** firmly believed that cognitive processes played an important role in the learning of complex behaviors—even in the lowly laboratory rat. According to Tolman, although such cognitive processes could not be observed directly, they could still be experimentally verified and inferred by careful observation of outward behavior (Tolman, 1932).

Much of Tolman's research involved rats in mazes. When Tolman began his research in the 1920s, many studies of rats in mazes had been done. In a typical experiment, a rat would be placed in the "start" box. A food reward would be put in the "goal" box at the end of the maze. The rat would initially make many mistakes in running the maze. After several trials, it would eventually learn to run the maze quickly and with very few errors.

But what had the rats learned? According to traditional behaviorists, the rats had learned a *sequence of responses,* such as "first corner—turn left; second corner—turn left; third corner—turn right," and so on. Each response was associated with the "stimulus" of the rat's position in the maze. And the entire sequence of responses was "stamped in" by the food reward at the end of the maze.

Tolman (1948) disagreed with that view. He noted that several investigators had reported as incidental findings that their maze-running rats had occasionally taken their own shortcuts to the food box. In one case, an enterprising rat had knocked the cover off the maze, climbed over the maze wall and out of the maze, and scampered directly to the food box (Lashley, 1929; Tolman & others, 1946). To Tolman, such reports indicated that the rats had learned more than simply the sequence of responses required to get to the food. Tolman believed instead that the rats eventually built up, through experience, a **cognitive map** of the maze—a mental representation of its layout.

As an analogy, think of the route you typically take to get to your psychology classroom. If a hallway along the way were blocked off for repairs, you would use your cognitive map of the building to come up with an alternative route to class. Tolman showed experimentally that rats, like people, seem to form cognitive maps (Tolman, 1948). And, like us, rats can use their cognitive maps to come up with an alternative route to a goal when the customary route is blocked (Tolman & Honzik, 1930a).

Tolman challenged the prevailing behaviorist model on another important point. According to Thorndike, for example, learning would not occur unless the behavior was "strengthened," or "stamped in," by a rewarding consequence. But Tolman showed that this was not necessarily the case. In a classic experiment, three groups of rats were put in the same maze once a day for several days (Tolman & Honzik, 1930b). For group 1, a food reward awaited the rats at the end of the maze. Their performance in the maze steadily improved; the number of errors and the time it took the rats to reach the goal box showed a steady decline with each trial. The rats in group 2 were placed in the maze each day with *no* food reward. They consistently made many errors, and their performance showed only slight improvement. The performance of the rats in groups 1 and 2 was exactly what the traditional behaviorist model would have predicted.

Now consider the behavior of the rats in group 3. These rats were placed in the maze with no food reward for the first 10 days of the experiment. Like the rats in group 2, they made many errors as they wandered about the maze. But,

cognitive map
Tolman's term for the mental representation of the layout of a familiar environment.

Edward Chace Tolman (1898–1956)
Although he looks rather solemn in this photo, Tolman was known for his openness to new ideas, energetic teaching style, and playful sense of humor. During an important speech, he showed a film of a rat in a maze with a short clip from a Mickey Mouse cartoon spliced in at the end (Gleitman, 1991). Tolman's research demonstrated that cognitive processes are an important part of learning, even in the rat.

FIGURE 5.7 Latent Learning Beginning with day 1, the rats in group 1 received a food reward at the end of the maze, and the number of errors they made steadily decreased each day. The rats in group 2 never received a food reward; they made many errors as they wandered about in the maze. The rats in group 3 did not receive a food reward on days 1 through 10. Beginning on day 11, they received a food reward at the end of the maze. Notice the sharp decrease in errors on day 12 and thereafter. According to Tolman, the rats in group 3 had formed a cognitive map of the maze during the first 11 days of the experiment. Learning had taken place, but this learning was not demonstrated until reinforcement was present—a phenomenon that Tolman called latent learning.

SOURCE: Tolman & Honzik (1930b).

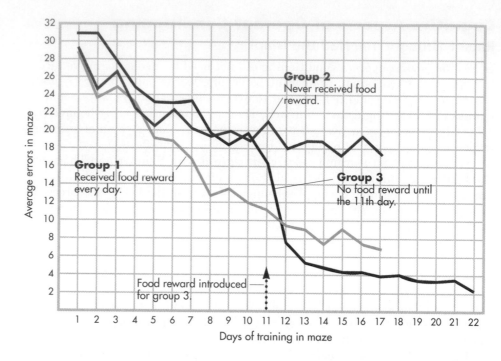

beginning on day 11, they received a food reward at the end of the maze. As you can see in Figure 5.7, there was a dramatic improvement in group 3's performance from day 11 to day 12. Once the rats had discovered that food awaited them at the end of the maze, they made a beeline for the goal. On day 12, the rats in group 3 ran the maze with very few errors, improving their performance to the level of the rats in group 1 that had been rewarded on every trial!

Tolman concluded that *reward*—or reinforcement—is *not necessary* for learning to take place (Tolman & Honzik, 1930b). The rats in group 3 had learned the layout of the maze and formed a cognitive map of the maze simply by exploring it for 10 days. However, they had not been motivated to *demonstrate* that learning until a reward was introduced. Rewards, then, seem to affect the *performance* of what has been learned rather than learning itself. To describe learning that is not immediately demonstrated in overt behavior, Tolman used the term **latent learning.**

From these and other experiments, Tolman concluded that learning involves the acquisition of knowledge rather than simply changes in outward behavior. According to Tolman (1932), an organism essentially learns "what leads to what." It learns to "expect" that a certain behavior will lead to a particular outcome in a specific situation.

Tolman is now recognized as an important forerunner of modern cognitive learning theorists (Gleitman, 1991; Olton, 1992). Many contemporary cognitive learning theorists follow Tolman in their belief that operant conditioning involves the *cognitive representation* of the relationship between a behavior and its consequence. Today, operant conditioning is seen as involving the cognitive *expectancy* that a given consequence will follow a given behavior (Bolles, 1972; Dickinson, 1997; Dickinson & Balleine, 2000).

Learned Helplessness
Expectations of Failure and Learning to Quit

Cognitive factors, particularly the role of expectation, are involved in another learning phenomenon, called *learned helplessness*. Learned helplessness was discovered by accident. Psychologists were trying to find out if classically conditioned

"Well, you don't look like an experimental psychologist to me."

latent learning
Tolman's term for learning that occurs in the absence of reinforcement but is not behaviorally demonstrated until a reinforcer becomes available.

responses would affect the process of operant conditioning in dogs. The dogs were strapped into harnesses and then exposed to a tone (the neutral stimulus) paired with an unpleasant but harmless electric shock (the UCS), which elicited fear (the UCR). After conditioning, the tone alone—now a CS—elicited the conditioned response of fear.

In the classical conditioning setup, the dogs were unable to escape or avoid the shock. But the next part of the experiment involved an operant conditioning procedure in which the dogs *could* escape the shock. The dogs were transferred to a special kind of operant chamber called a *shuttlebox,* which has a low barrier in the middle that divides the chamber in half. In the operant conditioning setup, the floor on one side of the cage became electrified. To escape the shock, all the dogs had to do was learn a simple escape behavior: Jump over the barrier when the floor was electrified. Normally, dogs learn this simple operant very quickly.

However, when the classically conditioned dogs were placed in the shuttlebox and one side became electrified, the dogs did *not* try to jump over the barrier. Rather than perform the operant to escape the shock, they just lay down and whined. Why?

To Steven F. Maier and Martin Seligman, two young psychology graduate students at the time, the explanation of the dogs' passive behavior seemed obvious. During the tone–shock pairings in the classical conditioning setup, the dogs *had learned that shocks were inescapable.* No active behavior that they engaged in—whether whining, barking, or struggling in the harness—would allow them to avoid or escape the shock. In other words, the dogs had "learned" to be helpless: They had developed the *cognitive expectation* that their behavior would have no effect on the environment.

To test this idea, Seligman and Maier (1967) designed a simple experiment. Dogs were arranged in groups of three. The first dog received shocks that it could escape by pushing a panel with its nose. The second dog was "yoked" to the first and received the same number of shocks. However, nothing the second dog did could stop the shock—they stopped only if the first dog pushed the panel. The third dog was the control and got no shocks at all.

After this initial training, the dogs were transferred to the shuttlebox. As Seligman and Maier had predicted, the first and third dogs quickly learned to jump over the barrier when the floor became electrified. But the second dog, the one that had learned that nothing it did would stop the shock, made no effort to jump over the barrier. Because the dog had developed the cognitive expectation that its behavior would have no effect on the environment, it had become passive (Seligman & Maier, 1967). The name of this phenomenon is **learned helplessness**—a phenomenon in which exposure to inescapable and uncontrollable aversive events produces passive behavior (Maier & others, 1969).

Since these early experiments, learned helplessness has been demonstrated in many different species, including primates, cats, rats, and fish (LoLordo, 2001). Even cockroaches demonstrate learned helplessness in a cockroach-sized shuttlebox after being exposed to inescapable shock (G. E. Brown & others, 1999).

In humans, numerous studies have found that exposure to uncontrollable, aversive events can produce passivity and learned helplessness. For example, college students who have experienced failure in previous academic settings may feel that academic tasks and setbacks are beyond their control. Thus, when faced with the demands of exams, papers, and studying, rather than rising to the challenge, they may experience feelings of learned helplessness (McKean, 1994). If a student believes that academic tasks are unpleasant, unavoidable, and beyond her control, even the slightest setback can trigger a sense of helpless passivity. Such students may be prone to engage in self-defeating responses, such as procrastinating or giving up prematurely.

How can learned helplessness be overcome? In their early experiments, Seligman and Maier discovered that if they forcibly dragged the dogs over the shuttlebox barrier when the floor on one side became electrified, the dogs would eventually overcome their passivity and begin to jump over the barrier on their

Learned Helplessness on the Football Field
Groups of people—even highly motivated people—can succumb to learned helplessness, as a study of National Football League teams showed (Reisel & Kopelman, 1995). A survey of three years of NFL records showed that teams that were badly beaten in one game tended to perform even worse than expected in the next game. Because the experience of being creamed by an opponent was so demoralizing, the team members stopped trying to succeed and simply "gave up" the next time they took the field.

learned helplessness
A phenomenon in which exposure to inescapable and uncontrollable aversive events produces passive behavior.

instinctive drift
The tendency of an animal to revert to instinctive behaviors that can interfere with the performance of an operantly conditioned response.

observational learning
Learning that occurs through observing the actions of others.

own (LoLordo, 2001; Seligman, 1992). For students who experience academic learned helplessness, establishing a sense of control over their schoolwork is the first step. Seeking knowledge about course requirements and assignments and setting goals, however modest, that can be successfully met can help students begin to acquire a sense of mastery over environmental challenges (McKean, 1994).

Since the early demonstrations of learned helplessness in dogs, the notion of learned helplessness has undergone several revisions and refinements (Abramson & others, 1978; Gillham & others, 2001). Learned helplessness has been shown to play a role in psychological disorders, particularly depression, and in the ways that people respond to stressful events. Learned helplessness has also been applied in such diverse fields as management, sales, and health psychology (Peterson & others, 1993). In Chapter 12, on stress, health, and coping, we will take up the topic of learned helplessness again.

Operant Conditioning and Biological Predispositions
Misbehaving Chickens

Skinner and other behaviorists firmly believed that the general laws of operant conditioning applied to all animal species—whether they were pecking pigeons or bar-pressing rats. As Skinner (1956) wrote:

> Pigeon, rat, monkey, which is which? It doesn't matter. Of course, these species have behavioral repertoires which are as different as their anatomies. But once you have allowed for differences in the ways in which they make contact with the environment, and in the ways in which they act upon the environment, what remains of their behavior shows astonishingly similar properties.

However, psychologists studying operant conditioning, like those studying classical conditioning, found that an animal's natural behavior patterns *could* influence the learning of new behaviors. Consider the experiences of Keller and Marian Breland, two of Skinner's students. The Brelands established a successful business training animals for television commercials, trade shows, fairs, and even displays in department stores (Bailey & Bailey, 1993; Breland & Breland, 1961). Using operant conditioning, the Brelands trained thousands of animals of many different species to perform all sorts of complex tricks.

But the Brelands weren't always successful in training the animals. For example, they tried to train a chicken to play baseball. The chicken learned to pull a loop that activated a swinging bat. After hitting the ball, the chicken was supposed to run to first base. The chicken had little trouble learning to pull the loop, but instead of running to first base, the chicken would chase the ball.

The Brelands also tried to train a raccoon to pick up two coins and deposit them into a metal box. The raccoon easily learned to pick up the coins but seemed to resist putting them into the box. Like a furry little miser, it would rub the coins together. And rather than dropping the coins in the box, it would dip the coins in the box and take them out again. As time went on, this behavior became more persistent, even though the raccoon was not being reinforced for it. In fact, the raccoon's "misbehavior" was actually *preventing* it from getting reinforced for correct behavior.

The Brelands noted that such nonreinforced behaviors seemed to reflect innate, instinctive responses. The chicken chasing the ball was behaving like a chicken chasing a bug. Raccoons in the wild instinctively clean and moisten their food by dipping it in streams or rubbing it between their forepaws. These natural behaviors interfered with the operant behaviors the Brelands were attempting to condition—a phenomenon called **instinctive drift.**

The biological predisposition to perform such natural behaviors was strong enough to overcome the lack of reinforcement. These instinctual behaviors also prevented the animals from engaging in the learned behaviors that would result in reinforcement. Clearly, reinforcement is not the sole determinant of behavior.

Animal Behavior and Misbehavior Marian and Keller Breland used the operant conditioning principles of shaping and reinforcement to train animals to perform all sorts of behaviors. For example, this cat has been trained to "play" the piano—a difficult feat, since pressing keys to obtain food is not a natural food-seeking behavior pattern for cats. The Brelands discovered that an animal's natural behavior patterns, even though they were not reinforced, can sometimes interfere with the learning of arbitrary responses.

And, inborn or instinctive behavior patterns can interfere with the operant conditioning of arbitrary responses.

Before you go on to the next section, take a few minutes to review Table 5.5 and make sure you understand the differences between classical and operant conditioning.

Table 5.5

Comparing Classical and Operant Conditioning

	Classical Conditioning	Operant Conditioning
Type of behavior	Reflexive, involuntary behaviors	Nonreflexive, voluntary behaviors
Source of behavior	Elicited by stimulus	Emitted by organism
Basis of learning	Associating two stimuli: CS + UCS	Associating a response and the consequence that follows it
Responses conditioned	Physiological and emotional responses	Active behaviors that operate on the environment
Extinction process	Conditioned response decreases when conditioned stimulus is repeatedly presented alone	Responding decreases with elimination of reinforcing consequences
Cognitive aspects	Expectation that CS reliably predicts the UCS	Performance of behavior influenced by the expectation of reinforcement or punishment
Biological predispositions	Innate predispositions influence how easily an association is formed between a particular stimulus and response	Behaviors similar to natural or instinctive behaviors are more readily conditioned

Observational Learning
Imitating the Actions of Others

Key Theme
- In observational learning, we learn through watching and imitating the behaviors of others.

Key Questions
- How did Albert Bandura demonstrate the principles of observational learning?
- What four mental processes are involved in observational learning?
- How has observational learning been shown in nonhuman animals?

Classical conditioning and operant conditioning emphasize the role of direct experiences in learning, such as directly experiencing a reinforcing or punishing stimulus following a particular behavior. But much human learning occurs *indirectly,* by watching what others do, then imitating it. In **observational learning,** learning takes place through observing the actions of others.

Humans develop the capacity to learn through observation at a very early age. Studies of 21-day-old infants have shown that they will imitate a variety of actions, including opening their mouths, sticking out their tongues, and making other facial expressions (Field & others, 1982; Meltzoff & Moore, 1977, 1983).

Albert Bandura is the psychologist most strongly identified with observational learning. Bandura (1974) believes that observational learning is the result of cognitive processes that are "actively judgmental and constructive," not merely "mechanical copying." To illustrate his theory, let's consider his famous experiment involving the imitation of aggressive behaviors (Bandura, 1965). In the experiment, 4-year-old children separately watched a short film showing an adult playing aggressively with a Bobo doll—a large, inflated balloon doll that stands upright because the bottom is weighted with sand. All the children saw the adult hit, kick, and punch the Bobo doll in the film.

Albert Bandura (b. 1925) Bandura contends that most human behavior is acquired through observational learning rather than through trial and error or direct experience of the consequences of our actions. Watching and processing information about the actions of others, including the consequences that occur, influence the likelihood that behavior will be imitated.

The Classic Bobo Doll Experiment Bandura demonstrated the powerful influence of observational learning in a series of experiments conducted in the early 1960s. Children watched a film showing an adult playing aggressively with an inflated Bobo doll. If they saw the adult rewarded with candy for the aggressive behavior or experience no consequences, the children were much more likely to imitate the behavior than if they saw the adult punished for the aggressive behavior (Bandura, 1965; Bandura & others, 1963).

However, there were three different versions of the film, each with a different ending. Some children saw the adult *reinforced* with soft drinks, candy, and snacks after performing the aggressive actions. Other children saw a version in which the aggressive adult was *punished* for the actions with a scolding and a spanking by another adult. Finally, some children watched a version of the film in which the aggressive adult experienced *no consequences*.

After seeing the film, each child was allowed to play alone in a room with several toys, including a Bobo doll. The playroom was equipped with a one-way window so that the child's behavior could be observed. Bandura found that the consequences the children observed in the film made a difference. Children who watched the film in which the adult was punished were much less likely to imitate the aggressive behaviors than were children who watched either of the other two film endings.

Then Bandura added an interesting twist to the experiment. Each child was asked to show the experimenter what the adult did in the film. For every behavior they could imitate, the child was rewarded with snacks and stickers. Virtually all the children imitated the adult's behaviors they had observed in the film, including the aggressive behaviors. The particular version of the film the children had seen made no difference.

Bandura (1965) explained these results much as Tolman explained latent learning. Reinforcement is *not* essential for learning to occur. Rather, the *expectation of reinforcement* affects the *performance* of what has been learned.

Bandura (1986) suggests that four cognitive processes interact to determine whether imitation will occur. First, you must pay *attention* to the other person's behavior. Second, you must *remember* the other person's behavior so that you can perform it at a later time. That is, you must form and store a mental representation of the behavior to be imitated. Third, you must be able to transform this mental representation into *actions that you are capable of reproducing*. These three factors—attention, memory, and motor skills—are necessary for learning to take place through observation.

Fourth, there must be some *motivation* for you to imitate the behavior. This factor is crucial to the actual performance of the learned behavior. You are more likely to imitate a behavior if there is some expectation that doing so will produce reinforcement or reward. Thus, all the children were capable of imitating the adult's aggressive behavior. But the children who saw the aggressive adult being rewarded were much more likely to imitate the aggressive behavior than were the children who saw the adult punished. Table 5.6 summarizes other factors that increase the likelihood of imitation.

Table 5.6
Factors That Increase Imitation
You're more likely to imitate:
• People who are rewarded for their behavior
• Warm, nurturing people
• People who have control over you or have the power to influence your life
• People who are similar to you in terms of age, sex, and interests
• People you perceive as having higher social status
• When the task to be imitated is not extremely easy or difficult
• If you lack confidence in your own abilities in a particular situation
• If the situation is unfamiliar or ambiguous
• If you've been rewarded for imitating the same behavior in the past
SOURCE: Based on research summarized in Bandura (1977, 1986, 1997).

Applications of Observational Learning

Bandura's finding that children will imitate film footage of aggressive behavior has more than just theoretical importance. One obvious implication has to do with the effects of negative behaviors that are depicted in films and television shows. Is there any evidence that television and other media can increase negative or destructive behaviors in viewers?

One recent study conducted by psychologist Rebecca Collins and her colleagues (2004) examined the impact of television portrayals of sexual activity on the behavior of U.S. adolescents between the ages of 12 and 17. Over the two-year period of the study, researchers found that adolescents who watched large amounts of television containing sexual content were twice as likely to begin engaging in sexual intercourse in the following year as adolescents who were the same age but watched the least amount of sexually oriented programming.

Are we talking about X-rated cable programs or sexually suggestive music videos? No. Among the programs that the researchers rated as high in sexual content were such popular shows as *Friends* and *That '70s Show*. In fact, researchers found that exposure to TV shows that simply *talked* about sex was associated with the same risks as exposure to TV that depicted sexual behavior. Although other factors contributed to the likelihood that adolescents would become sexually active, the impact of TV programming was substantial. "The 12-year-olds who watched a lot of television with sexual content behaved like the 14- or 15-year-olds who watched the least amount of sexual television," Collins (2004) pointed out.

Another important implication of Bandura's research relates to the effects of media depictions of violence on behavior. In Critical Thinking Box 5.5, we take an in-depth look at research on the relationship between "reel" and "real-world" violence.

Given the potential impact of negative media images, let's look at the flip side. Is there any evidence that television and other media can encourage socially desirable behavior?

A remarkably effective application of observational learning has been the use of television and radio dramas to promote social change and healthy behaviors in Asia, Latin America, and Africa (Population Communications International, 2004). Pioneered by Mexican television executive Miguel Sabido, the first such attempt was a long-running serial drama that used observational learning principles to promote literacy among adults. The main storyline centered on the experiences of a group of people in a literacy self-instruction group. Millions of viewers faithfully watched the series. In the year before the televised series, about 90,000 people were enrolled in such literacy groups. In the year during the series, enrollment jumped to 840,000 people (Bandura, 1997).

Since the success of this program, the nonprofit group Population Communications International (2004) has developed many such "entertainment-education programs" based on Bandura's observational learning paradigm. Each series is developed with the input of local advisers and is written, produced, and performed by creative talent in the country of the intended audience. These serial dramas motivate individuals to adopt new attitudes and behavior by modeling behaviors that promote family health, stable communities, and a sustainable environment. Among the most popular radio and television serial dramas:

- Culturally sensitive programs encouraging family planning and reproductive health in India, Brazil, and Tanzania
- Radio serials aimed at preventing the transmission of HIV/AIDS in Kenya and Peru
- An award-winning dramatic series set in a rural Chinese village, starring a young female protagonist, that emphasized the value of female children and economic independence for women.

One popular series in India focused on motivating villagers to improve sanitation, adopt fuel-conservation practices to reduce pollution, and launch a tree-planting campaign (Papa & others, 2000).

"Ordinary People" Population Communications International is a nonprofit group that develops television and radio dramatic series that are based on the principles of observational learning. This scene is from the Chinese television series *Bai Xing*, which means "Ordinary People." Set in a small village on the banks of the Yellow River in China, this award-winning dramatic series centers on the experiences of Lüye, a young woman who struggles against the rigidity of traditional beliefs and customs. Among the series' goals are to show the importance of economic independence for women and the need to overcome the traditional Chinese preference for sons over daughters. In this scene, Lüye is distraught over her impending marriage to a man she does not love, and is being comforted by her mother.

CRITICAL THINKING 5.5

Does "Reel" Violence Cause Real Aggressive Behavior?

Bandura's early observational learning studies showing preschoolers mimicking the movie actions of an adult and pummeling a Bobo doll provided a powerful paradigm to study the effects of "entertainment" violence. Bandura found that observed actions were most likely to be imitated when:

■ The model is attractive, of high status, and/or a dominant member of the viewer's social group.

■ The model is rewarded for his or her behavior.

■ The model is not punished for his or her actions.

Over the past four decades, more than 1,000 studies have investigated the relationship between media depictions of violence and increases in aggressive behavior in the real world (C. A. Anderson & others, 2003; Cantor, 2000). We'll highlight some key findings here.

How Prevalent Is Violence on American Television?

The amount of violence depicted on American television is truly staggering. One major research project, the National Television Violence Study (NTVS), (1996, 1997, 1998), measured depictions of violence in more than 8,000 hours of cable and network programming. Some of the NTVS findings:

■ Television programs that contain violence: 60 percent

■ Violent interactions that did *not* include any expression of pain: 55 percent

■ Violent programs that did *not* show any

long-term negative consequences of the violence: 80 percent

■ Violent scenes in which aggression is *not* punished: 58 percent

■ Violent scenes perpetrated by the "good guys" in their roles as heroes: 40 percent

■ Number of violent incidents a preschooler would observe by watching two hours of cartoons a day for a year: 10,000

Clearly, depictions of violence on television fulfill the criteria that are most likely to lead to imitation, especially by children.

The context in which television violence is typically presented—attractive characters performing unpunished violence that produces no pain—is destined to promote children's imitation of aggression and the acquisition of violent attitudes and behaviors.

Joanne Cantor, 1999

Isn't There Only a "Modest" Correlation Between Media Violence and Aggressive Behavior?

A large-scale meta-analysis pooled the results of more than 200 studies on the effects of violent media (Paik & Comstock, 1994). The meta-analysis found a positive and statistically significant overall correlation of +.31 between media violence and aggressive behavior. In other words, the greater the exposure to media violence, the greater the likelihood that

someone will behave aggressively. This finding held true regardless of the age of the participants—preschool, elementary school, high school, college, or adults.

Dissenters, many of whom are in the entertainment or media industry, argue that the +.31 correlation is only a "modest" correlation (e.g., Rhodes, 2000). But is it? Not when you compare the magnitude of the relationship between media violence and aggressive behavior with other known correlations, such as those shown in the accompanying graph. For example, the +.09 correlation between asbestos and cancer is much lower than the +.31 correlation between media violence and aggressive behavior. Nevertheless, it led to a massive national effort to remove asbestos from schools and other buildings.

How Is Exposure to Media Violence Linked to Aggressive Behavior?

The American Psychological Association, American Academy of Pediatrics, and four other public health organizations recently issued a joint statement on the impact of entertainment violence on children (Congressional Public Health Summit, 2000). The joint statement noted that well over 1,000 studies "point overwhelmingly to a causal connection between media violence and aggressive behavior in some children." The essence of that causal connection includes the following:

■ Children who see a lot of violence are more likely to view violence as an effective way of settling conflicts and are more likely to assume that violence is acceptable behavior.

■ Viewing violence can lead to emotional desensitization in real life and can decrease the likelihood that people will help a victim of violence in real life.

Are There Long-Term Effects? Do Kids Who Watch Lots of Media Violence Grow Up to Behave More Aggressively as Adults?

That's the basic conclusion of several longitudinal studies that have been conducted since the 1960s (C. A. Anderson &

CALVIN AND HOBBES   BILL WATTERSON

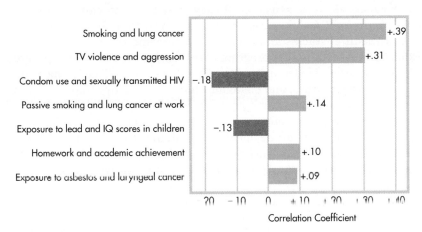

Smoking and lung cancer	+.39
TV violence and aggression	+.31
Condom use and sexually transmitted HIV	−.18
Passive smoking and lung cancer at work	+.14
Exposure to lead and IQ scores in children	−.13
Homework and academic achievement	+.10
Exposure to asbestos and laryngeal cancer	+.09

Correlation Coefficient

Comparing the Effect of Violent Media on Aggression with Other Known Effects

SOURCE: Adapted from data presented in Bushman & Anderson (2001).

others, 2003). For example, psychologist L. Rowell Huesmann and his colleagues (2003) conducted a 15-year longitudinal study that began with more than 500 boys and girls, ages 6 to 10, growing up in the Chicago area. When these individuals reached their early twenties, the researchers were able track down and resurvey 329 of them. The researchers also interviewed the participants' spouses or friends, and they obtained court records of criminal convictions.

The results showed that men who watched the most television violence as children were significantly more likely to have pushed, grabbed, or shoved their spouses and to have shoved another person in response to an insult. They were also three times more likely to have been convicted of a crime.

A similar pattern emerged with women who viewed high levels of TV violence as children. They were more likely to have thrown something at their spouses and to have shoved, punched, or choked another person who made them mad. Such women reported having punched, beaten, or choked another adult at more than four times the rate of other women. Women who viewed high levels of TV violence as children were also more likely

to have committed some type of criminal act.

Can Reduced Television Exposure Reduce Aggressive Behavior in the Real World?

Yes. Consider what happened in two California schools when third- and fourth-graders were encouraged to turn off the TV, VCR, and video games completely for ten days and then follow a media diet of no more than seven hours per week for six months. The actual violent content of the abandoned television, videos, or video games was not measured, although it's safe to assume that some were violent. At the end of the study, aggressive behavior in the children in the intervention school dropped by 25 percent as compared to aggressive behavior in the control group of students who did not reduce their video exposure (Robinson & others, 2001).

But What About the Fact That Most People Who Watch Violent Scenes on Television Don't Commit Crimes?

As Brad Bushman and Colleen Phillips (2001) point out, "The fact that TV violence does not noticeably increase vio-

lence in everybody does not mean that TV does not increase violence in anybody." *Some* people *are* affected by media violence. Laboratory experiments have shown that viewing just 15 minutes of a program featuring relatively mild violence increases the aggressiveness of more than one-quarter of the viewers (Bushman, 1995). Further, highly aggressive people are more likely to be drawn to violent media. After watching a violent movie, their levels of aggression increased to even higher levels (Black & Bevan, 1992).

In other words, even if *you* are not likely to be affected by the violent images that permeate our media culture, there is a substantial minority of other people who probably *are* susceptible to such influences. Because so many people are exposed to violent media, the effect on society can be immense even if only a small percentage of people are affected by them (Bushman & Anderson, 2001). Remember, the average prime-time television show has millions of viewers. Suppose just 5 percent of people become more aggressive after viewing a violent TV show. That's a potential influence on *hundreds of thousands* of viewers.

Critical Thinking Questions

■ Given the evidence summarized here, what conclusions can you draw about the effect of violent media images on aggressive behavior?

■ What, if anything, should be done to curb media depictions of violence? What about depictions of violence in cartoons?

■ How would you respond to the claim that "no direct, causal link between exposure to mock violence in the media and subsequent violent behavior has ever been demonstrated" (Rhodes, 2000)?

These long-running programs feature characters with whom the average viewer can easily identify. While the storylines are dramatic, they also reflect everyday challenges. As Bandura (2002) notes, "Seeing people similar to themselves change their lives for the better not only conveys strategies for how to do it but raises viewers' sense of efficacy that they too can succeed. Viewers come to admire and are inspired by characters in their likenesses who struggle with difficult obstacles and eventually overcome them."

Education-entertainment programs are designed to fulfill the optimal conditions for observational learning to occur (Bandura, 2002). The dramatic intensity, highly involving plot lines, and engaging characters ensure that viewers will become involved in the dramas and pay *attention*. To ensure that the modeled messages are *remembered*, an epilogue at the conclusion of each episode summarizes the key points and issues of the episode. To enhance the viewers' *ability* to carry out the modeled behaviors, a variety of support programs and groups are put in place when the series airs. And *motivating* people to change their behaviors in line with the modeled behaviors is accomplished by depicting the benefits of doing so. Research studies have confirmed the highly successful impact of these extremely popular dramas (see Singhal & others, 2004; Sood & others, 2004).

Beyond the effects of media depictions on behavior, observational learning has been applied in a wide variety of settings. The fields of education, vocational and job training, psychotherapy, and counseling use observational learning to help teach appropriate behaviors.

> *The serials dramatize the everyday problems people struggle with, and model functional strategies and solutions to them. This approach succeeds because it informs, enables, motivates and guides people for personal and social changes that improve their lives.*
>
> Albert Bandura (2004a)

Closing Thoughts

One theme throughout this chapter has been the quest to discover general laws of learning that would apply across virtually all species and situations. Watson was convinced that these laws were contained in the principles of classical conditioning. Skinner contended that they were to be found in the principles of operant conditioning. In a sense, they were both right. Thousands of experiments have shown that behavior can be reliably and predictably influenced by classical and operant conditioning procedures. By and large, the general principles of classical and operant conditioning hold up quite well across a wide range of species and situations.

But you've also seen that the general principles of classical and operant conditioning are just that—general, not absolute. Such researchers as John Garcia and Marian and Keller Breland recognized the importance of a species' evolutionary and biological heritage in acquiring new behaviors. Other researchers, such as Edward Tolman and Robert Rescorla, drew attention to the important role played by cognitive processes in learning. And Albert Bandura's investigations of observational learning underscored that classical and operant conditioning principles could not account for all learning.

Another prominent theme has been the adaptive nature of learning. Faced with an ever-changing environment, an organism's capacity to learn is critical to adaptation and survival. Clearly, there are survival advantages in being able to learn that a neutral stimulus can signal an important upcoming event, as in classical conditioning. An organism also enhances its odds of survival by being responsive to the consequences of its actions, as in operant conditioning. And, by observing the actions and consequences experienced by others, behaviors can be acquired through imitation. Thus, it is probably because these abilities are so useful in so many environments that the basic principles of learning are demonstrated with such consistency across so many species.

In the final analysis, it's probably safe to say that the most important consequence of learning is that it promotes the adaptation of many species, including humans, to their unique environments. Were it not for the adaptive nature of learning, Erv would probably get trapped in the attic again!

Self-control often involves choosing between two reinforcers: (1) a *long-term reinforcer* that will provide gratification at some point in the future or (2) a *short-term reinforcer* that provides immediate gratification but gets in the way of obtaining a long-term reinforcer. Objectively, the benefits of the long-term reinforcer far outweigh the benefits associated with the short-term, immediate reinforcer. Yet despite our commitment to the long-term goal, sometimes we choose a short-term reinforcer that conflicts with it. Why?

The Shifting Value of Reinforcers

The key is that *the relative value of reinforcers can shift over time* (Ainslie, 1975, 1992; Rachlin, 1974, 2000). Let's use an example to illustrate this principle. Suppose you sign up for an 8:00 A.M. class that meets every Tuesday morning. On Monday night, the short-term reinforcer (getting extra sleep on Tuesday morning) and the long-term reinforcer (getting a good course grade at the end of the semester) are both potential future reinforcers. Neither reinforcer is immediately available. So, when you compare these two future reinforcers, the value of making a good grade easily outweighs the value of getting extra sleep on Tuesday morning. That's why you duly set the alarm clock for 6:00 A.M. so you will get to class on time.

However, as the availability of a reinforcer gets closer, the subjective value of the reinforcer increases. Consequently, when your alarm goes off on Tuesday morning, the situation is fundamentally different. The short-term reinforcer is now immediately available: staying in that warm, comfy bed. Compared with Monday night when you set the alarm, the subjective value of extra sleep has increased significantly. Although making a good grade in the course is still important to you, its subjective value has not increased on Tuesday morning. After all, that long-term reinforcer is still in the distant future.

At the moment you make your decision, you choose whichever reinforcer has the greatest apparent value to you. At that moment, if the subjective value of the short-term reinforcer outweighs that of the long-term reinforcer, you're very likely to choose the short-term reinforcer (Rachlin, 1995, 2000). In other words, you'll probably stay in bed.

When you understand how the subjective values of reinforcers shift over time, the tendency to impulsively cave in to available short-term reinforcers starts to make more sense. The availability of an immediate, short-term reinforcer can temporarily outweigh the subjective value of a long-term reinforcer in the distant future. How can you counteract these momentary surges in the subjective value of short-term reinforcers? Fortunately, there are several strategies that can help you overcome the temptation of short-term reinforcers and improve self-control (Trope & Fishbach, 2000).

Strategy 1: Precommitment

Precommitment involves making an advance commitment to your long-term goal, one that will be difficult to change when a conflicting reinforcer becomes available (Green & Rachlin, 1996). In the case of getting to class on time, a precommitment could involve setting multiple alarms and putting them far enough away that you will be forced to get out of bed to shut each of them off. Or you could ask an early-rising friend to call you on the phone and make sure you're awake.

Strategy 2: Self-Reinforcement

Sometimes long-term goals seem so far away that your sense of potential future reinforcement seems weak compared with immediate reinforcers. One strategy to increase the subjective value of the long-term reinforcer is to use self-reinforcement for current behaviors related to your long-term goal. For example, promise yourself that if you spend two hours studying in the library, you'll reward yourself by watching a favorite television show.

It's important, however, to reward yourself only *after* you perform the desired behavior. If you say to yourself, "Rather than study tonight, I'll go to this party and make up for it by studying tomorrow," you've blown it. You've just reinforced yourself for *not* studying! This would be akin to trying to increase bar-pressing behavior in a rat by giving the rat a pellet of food *before* it pressed the bar. Obviously, this contradicts the basic principle of positive reinforcement in which behavior is *followed* by the reinforcing stimulus.

Strategy 3: Stimulus Control

Remember, environmental stimuli can act as discriminative stimuli that "set the occasion" for a particular response. In effect, the environmental cues that precede a be-havior can acquire some control over future occurrences of that behavior. So be aware of the environmental cues that are likely to trigger unwanted behaviors, such as studying in the kitchen (a cue for eating) or in an easy chair in the living room (a cue for watching television). Then replace those cues with others that will help you achieve your long-term goals.

For example, always study in a specific location, whether it's the library, in an empty classroom, or at a table or desk in a certain corner of your apartment. Over time, these environmental cues will become associated with the behavior of studying.

Strategy 4: Focus on the Delayed Reinforcer

The cognitive aspects of learning also play a role in choosing behaviors associated with long-term reinforcers (Metcalfe & Mischel, 1999; Mischel, 1996). When faced with a choice between an immediate and a delayed reinforcer, focus your attention on the delayed reinforcer. You'll be less likely to impulsively choose the short-term reinforcer (Ainslie, 1975).

Practically speaking, this means that if your goal is to save money for school, don't fantasize about a new stereo system or expensive running shoes. Focus instead on the delayed reinforcement of achieving your long-term goal (see Mischel & others, 1989). Imagine yourself proudly walking across the stage and receiving your college degree. Visualize yourself fulfilling your long-term career goals. The idea in selectively focusing on the delayed reinforcer is to mentally bridge the gap between the present and the ultimate attainment of your future goal. One of our students, a biology major, put a picture of a famous woman biologist next to her desk to help inspire her to study.

Strategy 5: Observe Good Role Models

Observational learning is another strategy you can use to improve self-control. Psychologist Walter Mischel (1966) found that children who observed others choose a delayed reinforcer over an immediate reinforcer were more likely to choose the delayed reinforcer themselves. So look for good role models. Observing others who are currently behaving in ways that will ultimately help them realize their long-term goals can make it easier for you to do the same.

Chapter Review

Key Points

Introduction: What Is Learning?

- **Learning** is defined as a relatively enduring change in behavior or knowledge that is due to past experience. Learning often reflects adaptation to the environment. **Conditioning** is the process of learning associations between environmental events and behavioral responses. Classical conditioning, operant conditioning, and observational learning are three types of learning.

Classical Conditioning: *Associating Stimuli*

- Ivan Pavlov, a Russian physiologist, discovered the principles of classical conditioning while studying the digestive system of dogs.

- **Classical conditioning** deals with reflexive behaviors that are elicited by a stimulus and results from learning an association between two stimuli. A neutral stimulus is repeatedly paired with an unlearned, natural stimulus (the **unconditioned stimulus, or UCS**), producing a reflexive response (the **unconditioned response, or UCR**). Eventually, the neutral stimulus (now called a **conditioned stimulus, or CS**) elicits the same reflexive response (the **conditioned response, or CR**) that was initially elicited by the natural stimulus.

- Factors that affect the strength of the conditioned response include the frequency with which the conditioned and unconditioned stimuli are paired and the timing of the stimulus presentations.

- In **stimulus generalization,** a new stimulus that is similar to the conditioned stimulus produces the conditioned response. In **stimulus discrimination,** one stimulus elicits the conditioned response but another, similar stimulus does not.

- In classical conditioning, **extinction** occurs when the conditioned stimulus no longer elicits the conditioned response. However, extinction is not unlearning. **Spontaneous recovery** of the conditioned response may occur.

- John B. Watson defined psychology as the scientific study of behavior and founded **behaviorism.** According to Watson, all human behavior is a result of conditioning and learning.

- As Watson demonstrated in his famous Little Albert study, emotional responses can be classically conditioned.

- Classical conditioning can also contribute to the **placebo response** and other drug effects.

Contemporary Views of Classical Conditioning

- Modern learning researchers acknowledge that mental processes and natural behavior patterns influence the learning process. Robert Rescorla demonstrated that classical conditioning involves *learning the relations between events* and assessing the reliability of signals.

- John Garcia's research showed that **taste aversions** violate key principles of classical conditioning, which is af-fected by **biological preparedness.** For a given species, some stimuli are more readily associated than others.

Operant Conditioning: *Associating Behaviors and Consequences*

- Edward Thorndike investigated the learning of active behaviors and formulated the **law of effect.** B. F. Skinner's operant conditioning principles explain how **operants,** or new, voluntary behaviors, are acquired.

- **Operant conditioning** explains learning as a process in which behavior is shaped and modified by its consequences. **Reinforcement** increases the likelihood of an operant's being repeated. In **positive reinforcement,** a response is strengthened because a reinforcing stimulus is added or presented. In **negative reinforcement,** a response is strengthened because an aversive stimulus is subtracted or removed. Reinforcers may be **primary reinforcers** or **conditioned reinforcers.**

- **Punishment** decreases the likelihood of an operant's being repeated. Two forms of punishment are **punishment by application** and **punishment by removal.** Aversive consequences do not always function as effective punishments. As a method of controlling behavior, punishment has many drawbacks.

- The **discriminative stimulus** is the stimulus in the presence of which a particular operant is likely to be reinforced; it sets the occasion for a particular response.

- New behaviors can be acquired through the process of **shaping.** An **operant chamber,** or **Skinner box,** is often used to study the acquisition of new behaviors by laboratory animals. Shaping is frequently used in everyday life to teach new behaviors.

- Once acquired, behaviors are maintained through **continuous reinforcement** or **partial reinforcement.** Behaviors on a partial reinforcement schedule are more resistant to **extinction** than are behaviors on a continuous reinforcement schedule. This phenomenon is known as the **partial reinforcement effect. Schedules of reinforcement** include the **fixed-ratio (FR), variable-ratio (VR), fixed-interval (FI),** and **variable-interval (VI) schedules.**

- In **behavior modification,** the principles of operant conditioning are applied to help people develop more adaptive behaviors.

Contemporary Views of Operant Conditioning

- Modern learning researchers acknowledge that operant conditioning involves cognitive processes and is influenced by natural behavior patterns. Edward Tolman's research on **cognitive maps** and **latent learning** demonstrated the involvement of cognitive processes in learning active behaviors. **Learned helplessness** may result when a person or an animal develops the cognitive expectation that aversive stimuli are unavoidable or uncontrollable.

- The phenomenon of **instinctive drift** refers to the fact that an animal's natural behavior patterns can affect operant conditioning by influencing what it is capable of learning.

Observational Learning: *Imitating the Actions of Others*

- Albert Bandura systematically investigated how new behaviors could be acquired through **observational learning.** Observational learning involves the cognitive processes of attention, memory, motor skills, and motivation.

Key Terms

learning, p. 174

conditioning, p. 175

classical conditioning, p. 176

unconditioned stimulus (UCS), p. 176

unconditioned response (UCR), p. 176

conditioned stimulus (CS), p. 177

conditioned response (CR), p. 177

stimulus generalization, p. 178

stimulus discrimination, p. 178

extinction (in classical conditioning), p. 178

spontaneous recovery, p. 178

behaviorism, p. 179

placebo response, p. 184

taste aversion, p. 186

biological preparedness, p. 187

law of effect, p. 190

operant, p. 190

operant conditioning, p. 191

reinforcement, p. 191

positive reinforcement, p. 191

negative reinforcement, p. 192

primary reinforcer, p. 192

conditioned reinforcer, p. 192

punishment, p. 193

punishment by application, p. 193

punishment by removal, p. 194

discriminative stimulus, p. 196

operant chamber (Skinner box), p. 198

shaping, p. 198

continuous reinforcement, p. 198

partial reinforcement, p. 198

extinction (in operant conditioning), p. 199

partial reinforcement effect, p. 199

schedule of reinforcement, p. 199

fixed-ratio (FR) schedule, p. 199

variable-ratio (VR) schedule, p. 200

fixed-interval (FI) schedule, p. 200

variable-interval (VI) schedule, p. 200

behavior modification, p. 201

cognitive map, p. 203

latent learning, p. 204

learned helplessness, p. 206

instinctive drift, p. 206

observational learning, p. 207

Key People

Albert Bandura (b. 1925) American psychologist who experimentally investigated observational learning, emphasizing the role of cognitive factors. (p. 207)

John Garcia (b. 1917) American psychologist who experimentally demonstrated the learning of taste aversions in animals, a finding that challenged several basic assumptions of classical conditioning. (p. 187)

Ivan Pavlov (1849–1936) Russian physiologist who first described the basic learning process of associating stimuli that is now called classical conditioning. (p. 175)

Robert A. Rescorla (b. 1940) American psychologist who experimentally demonstrated the involvement of cognitive processes in classical conditioning. (p. 185)

B. F. Skinner (1904–1990) American psychologist who developed the operant conditioning model of learning; em-

phasized studying the relationship between environmental factors and observable actions, not mental processes, in trying to achieve a scientific explanation of behavior. (p. 190)

Edward L. Thorndike (1874–1949) American psychologist who was the first to experimentally study animal behavior and document how active behaviors are influenced by their consequences; postulated the law of effect. (p. 189)

Edward C. Tolman (1898–1956) American psychologist who used the terms *cognitive map* and *latent learning* to describe experimental findings that strongly suggested that cognitive factors play a role in animal learning. (p. 203)

John B. Watson (1878–1958) American psychologist who, in the early 1900s, founded behaviorism, an approach that emphasizes the scientific study of outwardly observable behavior rather than subjective mental states. (p. 179)

Web Companion   Review Activities

You can find additional review activities by going to **www.DiscoveringPsychology.com** and clicking on the *Discovering Psychology* 4th Edition text cover. At the Discovering Psychology Web Companion you'll find the chapter learning objectives, flashcards for key terms and key people, interactive crossword puzzles, self-scoring practice quizzes, and other materials to help you master the information in this chapter.

Freeze Frame Memories

Memory

Prologue

The Drowning

Elizabeth was only 14 years old when her mother drowned. Although Elizabeth remembered many things about visiting her Uncle Joe's home in Pennsylvania that summer, her memory of the details surrounding her mother's death had always been hazy. As she explained:

> In my mind I've returned to that scene many times, and each time the memory gains weight and substance. I can see the cool pine trees, smell their fresh tarry breath, feel the lake's algae-green water on my skin, taste Uncle Joe's iced tea with fresh-squeezed lemon. But the death itself was always vague and unfocused. I never saw my mother's body, and I could not imagine her dead. The last memory I have of my mother was her tiptoed visit the evening before her death, the quick hug, the whispered, "I love you."

Some 30 years later, Elizabeth began to remember the details of her mother's death. While at her Uncle Joe's 90th birthday party, Elizabeth learned from a relative that she had been the one to discover her mother's body in Uncle Joe's swimming pool. With this realization, memories that had eluded Elizabeth for decades began to come back.

> The memories began to drift back, slow and unpredictable, like the crisp piney smoke from the evening campfires. I could see myself, a thin, dark-haired girl, looking into the flickering blue-and-white pool. My mother, dressed in her nightgown, is floating face down. "Mom? Mom?" I ask the question several times, my voice rising in terror. I start screaming. I remember the police cars, their lights flashing, and the stretcher with the clean, white blanket tucked in around the edges of the body. The memory had been there all along, but I just couldn't reach it.

As the memory crystallized, it suddenly made sense to Elizabeth why she had always felt haunted by her vague memories of the circumstances surrounding her mother's death. And it also seemed to explain, in part, why she had always been so fascinated by the topic of memory.

However, several days later, Elizabeth learned that the relative had been wrong—it was *not* Elizabeth who discovered her mother's body, but her Aunt Pearl. Other relatives confirmed that Aunt Pearl had been the one who found Elizabeth's mother in the swimming pool. Yet Elizabeth's memory had seemed so real.

memory
The mental processes that enable us to retain and use information over time.

encoding
The process of transforming information into a form that can be entered into and retained by the memory system.

storage
The process of retaining information in memory so that it can be used at a later time.

retrieval
The process of recovering information stored in memory so that we are consciously aware of it.

The Elizabeth in this true story is Elizabeth Loftus, a psychologist who is nationally recognized as the leading expert on the distortions that can occur in the memories of eyewitnesses. Loftus shares this personal story in her book *The Myth of Repressed Memory: False Memories and Allegations of Sexual Abuse,* which she co-wrote with science writer Katherine Ketcham in 1994.

Even though she is an expert on memory distortions and false memories, Loftus herself wasn't immune to the phenomenon. She experienced firsthand just how convincing a false memory can be. In retrospect, Loftus could see how she actively created information in her own mind that corresponded to the inaccurate information that she had been the one to discover her mother's body. She wrote, "That elaborate but completely fabricated memory confronted me with its detail and precision, its utter lack of ambiguity" (Loftus & Ketcham, 1994).

In this chapter, we'll consider the psychological and biological processes that underlie how memories are formed and forgotten. As you'll see, memory distortions such as the one Elizabeth Loftus experienced are relatively common. By the end of this chapter, you'll have a much better understanding of the memory process, including the reason that Elizabeth's "memory" of finding her mother's body seemed so real.

Introduction

What Is Memory?

Key Theme
■ Memory is a group of related mental processes that are involved in acquiring, storing, and retrieving information.

Key Questions
■ What are encoding, storage, and retrieval?
■ What is the stage model of memory?
■ What are the nature and function of sensory memory?

Memories Can Involve All Your Senses Think back to a particularly memorable experience from your high school years. Can you conjure up vivid memories of smells, tastes, sounds, or emotions associated with that experience? In the years to come, these teenagers may remember many sensory details associated with this impromptu football game on a crisp autumn afternoon.

Like Elizabeth's memories of her uncle's home, memories can be vivid and evoke intense emotions. We can conjure up distinct memories that involve all our senses, including smells, sounds, and even tactile sensations. For example, close your eyes and try to recall the feeling of rain-soaked clothes against your skin, the smell of popcorn, and the sound of the half-time buzzer during a high school basketball game.

Memory refers to the mental processes that enable us to acquire, retain, and retrieve information. Rather than being a single process, memory involves three fundamental processes: *encoding, storage,* and *retrieval.*

Encoding refers to the process of transforming information into a form that can be entered and retained by the memory system. For example, to memorize the definition of a key term that appears on a text page, you would visually *encode* the patterns of lines and dots on the page as meaningful words that could be retained by your memory. **Storage** is the process of retaining information in memory so that it can be used at a later time. **Retrieval** involves recovering the stored information so that we are consciously aware of it.

The Stage Model of Memory

No single model has been shown to capture all aspects of human memory (Tulving, 1997). However, one very influential model, the **stage model of memory,** is useful in explaining the basic workings of memory. In this model, shown in Figure 6.1, memory involves three distinct stages: *sensory memory, short-term memory,* and *long-term memory* (Atkinson & Shiffrin, 1968). The stage model is based on the idea that information is *transferred* from one memory stage to another.

The first stage of memory is called *sensory memory.* **Sensory memory** registers a great deal of information from the environment and holds it for a very brief period of time. After three seconds or less, the information fades. Think of your sensory memory as an internal camera that continuously takes "snapshots" of your surroundings. With each snapshot, you momentarily focus your attention on specific details. Almost instantly, the snapshot fades, only to be replaced by another.

During the very brief time the information is held in sensory memory, you "select," or pay *attention* to, just a few aspects of all the environmental information that's being registered. While studying, for example, you focus your attention on one page of your textbook, ignoring other environmental stimuli. The information you select from sensory memory is important, because this information is transferred to the second stage of memory, *short-term memory.*

stage model of memory
A model describing memory as consisting of three distinct stages: sensory memory, short-term memory, and long-term memory.

sensory memory
The stage of memory that registers information from the environment and holds it for a very brief period of time.

short-term memory
The active stage of memory in which information is stored for up to about 20 seconds.

long-term memory
The stage of memory that represents the long-term storage of information.

FIGURE 6.1 Overview of the Stage Model of Memory

Sensory Memory		Short-Term (Working) Memory		Long-Term Memory
• Environmental information is registered		• New information is transferred from sensory memory	Encoding and Storage	• Information that has been encoded in short-term memory is stored
• Large capacity for information	Attention	• Old information is retrieved from long-term memory		• Unlimited capacity for information
• Duration: 1/4 second to 3 seconds		• Limited capacity for information	Retrieval	• Duration: potentially permanent
		• Duration: approx. 20 seconds		

Short-term memory refers to the active, working memory system. Your short-term memory temporarily holds all the information you are currently thinking about or consciously aware of. That information is stored briefly in short-term memory—for up to about 20 seconds. Because you use your short-term memory to actively process conscious information in a variety of ways, short-term memory is often referred to as *working memory* (Baddeley, 1995, 2003). Imagining, remembering, and problem solving all take place in short-term memory.

Over the course of any given day, vast amounts of information flow through your short-term memory. Most of this information quickly fades and is forgotten in a matter of seconds. However, some of the information that is actively processed in short-term memory may be encoded for storage in long-term memory.

Long-term memory, the third memory stage, represents what most people typically think of as memory—the long-term storage of information, potentially for a lifetime. It's important to note that the transfer of information between short-term and long-term memory goes two ways. Not only does information flow from short-term memory to long-term memory, but much information also flows in the other direction, from long-term memory to short-term memory (Shiffrin & Nosofsky, 1994).

If you think about it, this makes a great deal of sense. Consider a routine cognitive task, such as carrying on a conversation. Such tasks involve processing current sensory data and retrieving relevant stored information, such as the meaning of individual words. In the next few sections, we'll describe each of the stages of memory in more detail.

The Interaction of Memory Stages in Everyday Life Imagine driving on a busy street in pouring rain. How might each of your memory stages be involved in successfully navigating the wet streets? What kinds of information would be transferred from sensory memory and retrieved from long-term memory?

George Sperling Sperling carried out his research on the duration of sensory memory while still a graduate student at Harvard. Now at the University of California–Irvine, he continues to study perception, attention, and cognition.

Sensory Memory
Fleeting Impressions of the World

Has something like this ever happened to you? You're engrossed in a suspenseful movie video. From another room, a family member calls out, "Where'd you put the phone book?" You respond with, "What?" Then, a split second later, the question registers in your mind. Before the other person can repeat the question, you reply, "Oh. It's on the kitchen counter."

You were able to answer the question because your *sensory memory* registered and preserved the other person's words for a few fleeting seconds—just long enough for you to recall what had been said to you while your attention was focused on the movie. Sensory memory stores a detailed record of a sensory experience, but only for a few seconds at the most.

The Duration of Sensory Memory
It Was There Just a Split Second Ago!

The characteristics of visual sensory memory were first identified largely through the research of psychologist **George Sperling** in 1960. In his experiment, Sperling flashed the images of 12 letters on a screen for one-twentieth of a second. The letters were arranged in four rows of three letters each. Subjects focused their attention on the screen and, immediately after the screen went blank, reported as many letters as they could remember.

On average, subjects could report only 4 or 5 of the 12 letters. However, several subjects claimed that they had actually seen *all* the letters but that the complete image had faded from their memory as they spoke, disappearing before they could verbally report more than 4 or 5 letters.

On the basis of this information, Sperling tried a simple variation on the original experiment (see Figure 6.2). He arranged the 12 letters in three rows of 4 letters each. Then, immediately *after* the screen went blank, he sounded a high-pitched, medium-pitched, or low-pitched tone. If the subjects heard the high-pitched tone, they were to report the letters in the top row; the medium-pitched tone signaled the middle row; and the low-pitched tone signaled the bottom row. If the subjects actually did see all the letters, Sperling reasoned, then they should be able to report the letters in a given row by focusing their attention on the indicated row *before* their visual sensory memory faded.

This is exactly what happened. If the tone followed the letter display in under one-third of a second, subjects could accurately report about three of the four letters in whichever row was indicated by the tone. However, if the interval between the screen going blank and the sound of the tone was more than one-third of a second, the accuracy of the reports decreased dramatically. By the time one second had elapsed, the image in the subject's visual sensory memory had already faded beyond recall.

FIGURE 6.2 Sperling's Experiment Demonstrating the Duration of Sensory Memory In George Sperling's (1960) classic experiment, (1) subjects stared at a screen on which rows of letters were projected for just one-twentieth of a second, then the screen then went blank. (2) After intervals varying up to one second, a tone was sounded that indicated the row of letters the subject should report. (3) If the tone was sounded within about one-third of a second, subjects were able to report the letters in the indicated row because the image of *all* the letters was still in sensory memory.

1. Letters are displayed on a screen for 1/20 of a second, then screen goes blank.

Length of time varies up to one second.

2. Tone is sounded, indicating row.

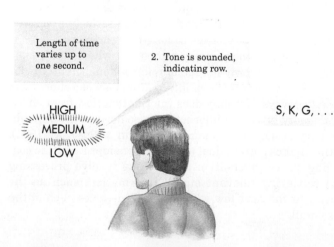

3. Subject reports letters in row indicated by tone.

S, K, G, . . .

Sperling's classic experiment demonstrated that our visual sensory memory holds a great deal of information very briefly, for about half a second. This information is available just long enough for us to pay attention to specific elements that are significant to us at that moment. This meaningful information is then transferred from the very brief storage of sensory memory to the somewhat longer storage of short-term memory.

Types of Sensory Memory
Pick a Sense, Any Sense!

Memory researchers believe there is a separate sensory memory for each sense—vision, hearing, touch, smell, and so on. Of the different senses, however, visual and auditory sensory memories have been the most thoroughly studied. *Visual sensory memory* is sometimes referred to as *iconic memory,* because it is the brief memory of an image, or icon. *Auditory sensory memory* is sometimes referred to as *echoic memory,* meaning a brief memory that is like an *echo.*

Researchers have found slight differences in the duration of sensory memory for visual and auditory information. Your visual sensory memory typically holds an image of your environment for about one-quarter to one-half second before it is replaced by yet another overlapping "snapshot." This is easy to demonstrate. Quickly wave a pencil back and forth in front of your face. Do you see the fading image of the pencil trailing behind it? That's your visual sensory memory at work. It momentarily holds the snapshot of the environmental image you see before it is almost instantly replaced by another overlapping image.

Your auditory sensory memory holds sound information a little longer, up to three or four seconds. This brief auditory sensory trace for sound allows you to hear speech as continuous words, or a series of musical notes as a melody, rather than as disjointed sounds. It also explains why you are able to "remember" something that you momentarily don't "hear," as in the example of the family member asking you where the phone book is.

An important function of sensory memory is to very briefly store sensory impressions so that they overlap slightly with one another. Thus, we perceive the world around us as continuous, rather than as a series of disconnected visual images or disjointed sounds.

Perception and Sensory Memory Traces Because your visual sensory memory holds information for a fraction of a second before it fades, rapidly presented stimuli overlap and appear continuous. Thus, you perceive the separate blades of a rapidly spinning windmill as a smooth blur of motion. Similarly, you perceive a lightning bolt streaking across the sky as continuous even though it is actually three or more separate bolts of electricity.

Short-Term, Working Memory
The Workshop of Consciousness

Key Theme
■ Short-term memory provides temporary storage for information transferred from sensory and long-term memory.

Key Questions
■ What are the duration and capacity of short-term memory?
■ How can you overcome the limitations of short-term memory?

You can think of *short-term memory,* or *working memory,* as the "workshop" of consciousness. It is the stage of memory in which information transferred from sensory memory *and* information retrieved from long-term memory become conscious (Ericsson & Kintsch, 1995). When you recall a past event or mentally add two numbers, the information is temporarily held and processed in your short-term memory. Your short-term memory also allows you to make sense out of this sentence by holding the beginning of the sentence in active memory while you read the rest of the sentence. Thus, working memory provides temporary storage for information that is currently being used in some conscious cognitive activity (Baddeley, 1995, 1998).

maintenance rehearsal
The mental or verbal repetition of information in order to maintain it beyond the usual 20-second duration of short-term memory.

chunking
Increasing the amount of information that can be held in short-term memory by grouping related items together into a single unit, or *chunk*.

The Duration of Short-Term Memory
Going, Going, Gone!

Information in short-term memory lasts longer than information in sensory memory, but its duration is still very short. Estimates vary, but generally you can hold most types of information in short-term memory up to about 20 seconds before it's forgotten (Peterson & Peterson, 1959). However, information can be maintained in short-term memory if it is *rehearsed,* or repeated, over and over. Because consciously rehearsing information will maintain it in short-term memory, this process is called **maintenance rehearsal.** For example, suppose that you decide to order a pizza for yourself and some friends. You look up the number in the phone book and mentally rehearse it until you can dial the phone.

Information that is *not* actively rehearsed is rapidly lost. Why? One possible explanation is that information that is not maintained by rehearsal simply fades away, or *decays,* with the passage of time. Another potential cause of forgetting in short-term memory is *interference* from new or competing information (Baddeley, 2002; Nairne, 2002). For example, if you are distracted by one of your friends asking you a question before you dial the pizza place, your memory of the phone number will quickly evaporate. Interference may also explain the irritating experience of forgetting someone's name just moments after you're introduced to him. If you engage the new acquaintance in conversation without rehearsing his name, the conversation may "bump" his name out of your short-term memory.

Demonstration of Short-Term Memory Capacity

Row 1 — 8 7 4 6
Row 2 — 3 4 9 6 2
Row 3 — 4 2 7 7 1 6
Row 4 — 5 1 4 0 8 1 3
Row 5 — 1 8 3 9 5 5 2 1
Row 6 — 2 1 4 9 7 5 2 4 8
Row 7 — 9 3 7 1 0 4 2 8 9 7
Row 8 — 7 1 9 0 4 2 6 0 4 1 8

The Capacity of Short-Term Memory
So That's Why There Were Seven Dwarfs!

Along with having a relatively short duration, short-term memory also has a relatively limited capacity. This is easy to demonstrate. Take a look at the numbers in the margin. If you've got a friend handy who's willing to serve as your research subject, simply read the numbers out loud, one row at a time, and ask your friend to repeat them back to you in the same order. Try to read the numbers at a steady rate, about one per second. Note each row that he correctly remembers.

How many numbers could your friend repeat accurately? Most likely, he could correctly repeat between five and nine numbers. That's what psychologist George Miller (1956) described as the limits of short-term memory in a classic paper entitled "The Magical Number Seven, Plus or Minus Two." Miller found that the capacity of short-term memory is limited to about seven items, or bits of information, at one time. So it's no accident that local telephone numbers are seven digits long (Cowan & others, 2004). And had Snow White met more than seven dwarfs, it would be even more difficult to remember all their names.

So what happens when your short-term memory store is filled to capacity? New information *displaces,* or bumps out, currently held information. Maintenance rehearsal is one way to avoid the loss of information from short-term memory. By consciously repeating the information you want to remember, you keep it active in short-term memory and prevent it from being displaced by new information.

U V A F D I C D B S A I

Although the capacity of your short-term memory is limited, there are ways to increase the amount of information you can hold in short-term memory at any given moment. To illustrate this point, let's try another short-term memory demonstration. Read the sequence of letters in the margin, then close your eyes and try to repeat the letters out loud in the same order.

How many letters were you able to remember? Unless you have an exceptional short-term memory, you probably could not repeat the whole sequence correctly. Now try this sequence of letters: D V D F B I U S A C I A.

You probably managed the second sequence with no trouble at all, even though it is made up of exactly the same letters as the first sequence. The ease with which you handled the second sequence demonstrates **chunking**—the grouping of related items together into a single unit. The first letter sequence was perceived as 12 separate items and probably exceeded your short-term memory's capacity. But the second letter sequence was perceived as only four "chunks" of information, which you easily remembered: DVD, FBI, USA, and CIA. Thus, chunking can increase the amount of information held in short-term memory. But to do so, chunking also often involves the retrieval of meaningful information from *long-term memory,* such as the meaning of the initials FBI (Ericsson & Kintsch, 1995).

The basic principle of chunking is incorporated into many numbers that we need to remember. Long strings of identification numbers, such as Social Security numbers or bank account numbers, are usually broken up by hyphens so that you can chunk them easily. Notice, however, that short-term memory is still limited to seven chunks. It's as if short-term memory has about seven mental slots for information. Each slot can hold a simple message or a complex message, but only about seven slots are available.

From Short-Term Memory to Working Memory

Our discussion of the short-term memory store has so far focused on just one type of information—verbal or acoustic codes, that is, speechlike stimuli that we can mentally recite. Lists of numbers, letters, words, or other items fall into this category. However, if you think about it, we also use our short-term memory to temporarily store and manipulate other types of stimuli, such as visual images. For example, suppose you're out shopping with a close friend who asks you whether you think a particular chair will match her living room furniture. Before you respond, you need to call up and hold a mental image of her living room. You are surely using your short-term memory as you consider her question, but how?

Earlier in the chapter, we mentioned that short-term memory is sometimes referred to as *working memory* because of its involvement in many mental activities, including reading, reasoning, mental imagery, and problem solving. For example, try solving the following arithmetic problem mentally, without writing anything down:

$$\frac{(7 \times 4) + 2}{(9 - 6) \times 2}$$

The difficulty lies not in the math, but in the mental juggling that is required as you multiply, add, subtract, and divide. To solve the problem, you must retrieve factual information from long-term memory ("What is 7×4?") and hold those facts in short-term memory while you perform other operations on the information. To do so, you are using what is called **working memory.**

The best-known model of working memory is that developed by British psychologist and memory researcher Alan Baddeley (1992, 2003). In Baddeley's model of working memory, there are three main components, each of which can function independently. One component, called the *phonological loop,* is specialized for verbal material, such as lists of numbers or words. This is the aspect of working memory that is often tested by standard memory

working memory
Short-term memory system involved in the temporary storage and active manipulation of information; in Baddeley's model, includes the *phonological loop, visuospatial sketchpad,* and *central executive* components.

FIGURE 6.3
Baddeley's Model of Working Memory: How Do I Get to Marty's House? Suppose you are trying to figure out the fastest way to get to a friend's house. In Baddeley's model of working memory, you would use the *phonological loop* to verbally recite the directions. Maintenance rehearsal helps keep the information active in the phonological loop. You would use the *visuospatial sketchpad* to imagine your route and any landmarks along the way. The *central executive* is the conscious part of your mind, which actively processes and integrates information from the phonological loop, the visuospatial sketchpad, and long-term memory.

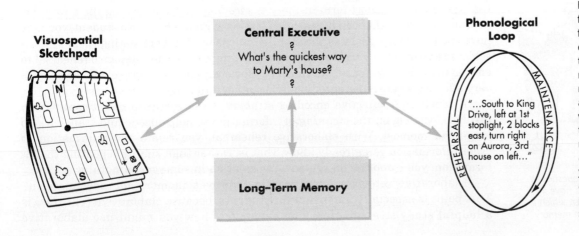

tasks (Mueller & others, 2003). The second component, called the *visuospatial sketchpad,* is specialized for spatial or visual material, such as remembering the layout of a room or city. The third component is the *central executive,* which controls attention, integrates information, and manages the activities of the phonological loop and the visuospatial sketchpad. The central executive also initiates retrieval and decision processes as necessary and integrates information coming into the system.

How do short-term memory and working memory differ? Although some researchers use the terms interchangeably, they have different connotations. The term *working memory* is generally used when the focus is on active, conscious mental "work," such as language comprehension, problem solving, or reasoning. The term *short-term memory* is more likely to be used when the focus is on simpler memory processes, such as the rehearsal of lists of syllables, words, or numbers.

Long-Term Memory

Key Theme
- Once encoded, an unlimited amount of information can be stored in long-term memory, which has different memory systems.

Key Questions
- What are ways to improve the effectiveness of encoding?
- How do procedural, episodic, and semantic memories differ, and what are implicit and explicit memory?
- How does the semantic network model explain the organization of long-term memory?

Long-term memory refers to the storage of information over extended periods of time. Technically, any information stored longer than the roughly 20-second duration of short-term memory is considered to be stored in long-term memory. In terms of maximum duration, some long-term memories last a lifetime.

In contrast to the limited capacities of sensory and short-term memory, the amount of information that can be held in long-term memory is limitless. Granted, it doesn't always feel limitless, but consider this: Every day, you remember the directions to your college; the names of hundreds of friends, relatives, and acquaintances; and how to start your car. Retrieving information from long-term memory happens quickly and with little effort—most of the time.

Encoding Long-Term Memories

How does information get "into" long-term memory? One very important function that takes place in short-term memory is *encoding,* or transforming the new information into a form that can be retrieved later (see Figure 6.4). As a student, you may have tried to memorize dates, facts, or definitions by simply repeating them to yourself over and over. This strategy reflects an attempt to use maintenance rehearsal to encode material into long-term memory. However, maintenance rehearsal is *not* a very effective strategy for encoding information into long-term memory.

A much more effective encoding strategy is **elaborative rehearsal,** which involves focusing on the *meaning* of information to help encode and transfer it to long-term memory. With elaborative rehearsal, you relate the information to other information you already know. That is, rather than simply repeating the information, you *elaborate* on the new information in some meaningful way.

Elaborative rehearsal significantly improves memory for new material. This point is especially important for students, because elaborative rehearsal is a helpful study strategy. Here's an example of how you might use elaborative

"The matters about which I'm being questioned, Your Honor, are all things I should have included in my long-term memory but which I mistakenly inserted in my short-term memory."

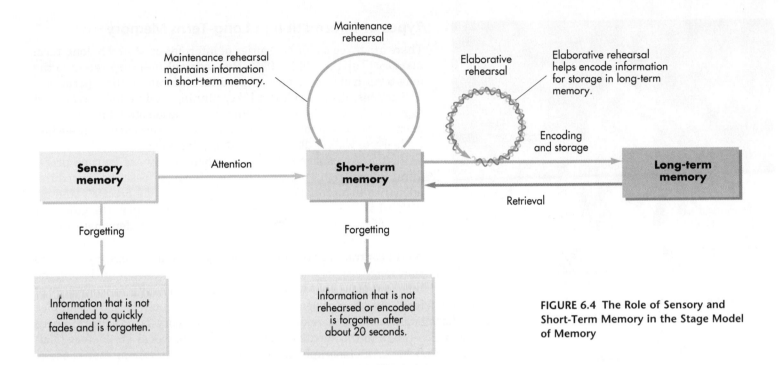

Maintenance rehearsal

Maintenance rehearsal maintains information in short-term memory.

Elaborative rehearsal

Elaborative rehearsal helps encode information for storage in long-term memory.

Encoding and storage

Sensory memory

Attention

Short-term memory

Long-term memory

Retrieval

Forgetting

Forgetting

Information that is not attended to quickly fades and is forgotten.

Information that is not rehearsed or encoded is forgotten after about 20 seconds.

FIGURE 6.4 The Role of Sensory and Short-Term Memory in the Stage Model of Memory

rehearsal to improve your memory for new information. In Chapter 2 we discussed three brain structures that are part of the limbic system: the *hypothalamus,* the *hippocampus,* and the *amygdala.* If you tried to memorize the definitions of these structures by reciting them over and over to yourself, you engaged in the not-so-effective memory strategy of maintenance rehearsal.

But if you elaborated on the information in some meaningful way, you would be more likely to recall it. For example, you could think about the limbic system's involvement in emotions, memory, and motivation by constructing a simple story. "I knew it was lunchtime because my hypothalamus told me I was *hungry, thirsty,* and cold. My hippocampus helped me remember a new restaurant that opened on *campus,* but when I got there I had to wait in line and my amygdala reacted with *anger.*" The story may be a bit silly, but many studies have shown that elaborative rehearsal leads to better retention (Lockhart & Craik, 1990).

Creating this simple story to help you remember the limbic system illustrates two additional factors that enhance encoding. First, applying information to yourself, called the *self-reference effect,* improves your memory for information. Second, the use of *visual imagery,* especially vivid images, also enhances encoding (Czienskowski & Giljohann, 2002; Paivio, 1995).

The fact that elaborative rehearsal results in more effective encoding and better memory of new information has many practical applications for students. As you study:

- Make sure you understand the new information by restating it in your own words.

- Actively question new information.

- Think about the potential applications and implications of the material.

- Relate the new material to information you already know, searching for connections that make the new information more meaningful.

- Generate your own examples of the concept, especially examples from your own experiences.

In the chapter Application, we'll give you more suggestions for strategies you can use to improve your memory.

elaborative rehearsal
Rehearsal that involves focusing on the meaning of information to help encode and transfer it to long-term memory.

Types of Information Stored in Long-Term Memory A memorable bicycle ride involves all three types of long-term memory. Remembering how to steer, brake, and balance on a bike are examples of *procedural memory*. Knowing the names of the different parts of a bicycle and how a bicycle differs from other forms of transportation would be examples of *semantic memory*. And, if this girl forms a vivid memory of the day she gave a young neighbor child a ride home from school on her bike, it will be an example of an *episodic memory*.

Types of Information in Long-Term Memory

There are three major categories of information stored in long-term memory (Tulving, 1985, 1995). **Procedural memory** refers to the long-term memory of how to perform different skills, operations, and actions. Typing, riding a bike, running, and making scrambled eggs are all examples of procedural information stored in long-term memory. We begin forming procedural memories early in life when we learn to walk, talk, feed ourselves, and so on.

Often, we can't recall exactly when or how we learned procedural information. And usually it's difficult to describe procedural memories in words. For example, try to describe *precisely* and *exactly* what you do when you blow-dry your hair, play the guitar, or ride a bicycle. A particular skill may be easy to demonstrate but very difficult to describe.

In contrast to procedural memory, **episodic memory** refers to your long-term memory of specific events or episodes, including the time and place that they occurred (Tulving, 2002). Your memory of attending a friend's wedding or your first day at college would both be examples of episodic memories. Closely related to episodic memory is *autobiographical memory*, which refers to the events of your life—your personal life history (Nelson & Fivush, 2004). Autobiographical memory plays a key role in your sense of self. Does culture affect autobiographical memory? In Culture and Human Behavior Box 6.1, we examine the impact of culture on people's earliest memories.

The third category of long-term memory is **semantic memory**—general knowledge that includes facts, names, definitions, concepts, and ideas. Semantic memory represents your personal encyclopedia of accumulated data and trivia stored in your long-term memory. Typically, you store semantic memories in long-term memory *without* remembering when or where you originally acquired the information. For example, can you remember when or where you learned that there are different time zones across the United States? Or when you learned that there are nine innings in a baseball game?

Implicit and Explicit Memory
Two Dimensions of Long-Term Memory

Studies with patients who have suffered different types of amnesia as a result of damage to particular brain areas have led memory researchers to recognize that long-term memory is *not* a simple, unitary system. Instead, long-term memory appears to be composed of separate but interacting subsystems and abilities.

What are these subsystems? One basic distinction that has been made is between *explicit memory* and *implicit memory*. **Explicit memory** is *memory with awareness*—information or knowledge that can be consciously recollected, including episodic and semantic information. Thus, remembering what you did last New Year's Day or the topics discussed in your last psychology class are both examples of explicit memory. Explicit memories are also called *declarative memories,* because, if asked, you can "declare" the information.

In contrast, **implicit memory** is *memory without awareness*. Implicit memories cannot be consciously recollected, but they still affect your behavior, knowledge, or performance of some task. For example, let's assume that you are a pretty good typist. Imagine that we asked you to type the following phrase with your eyes closed: "most zebras cannot be extravagant." Easy, right? Now, without looking at a typewriter or computer keyboard, try reciting, from left to right, the seven letters of the alphabet that appear on the bottom row of a keyboard. Can you do it? Your authors are both expert typists, and neither one of us could do this. Chances are, you can't either. (In case you're wondering, the letters are *ZXCVBNM.*)

procedural memory
Category of long-term memory that includes memories of different skills, operations, and actions.

episodic memory
Category of long-term memory that includes memories of particular events.

semantic memory
Category of long-term memory that includes memories of general knowledge of facts, names, and concepts.

explicit memory
Information or knowledge that can be consciously recollected; also called *declarative memory*.

implicit memory
Information or knowledge that affects behavior or task performance but cannot be consciously recollected; also called *nondeclarative memory*.

CULTURE AND HUMAN BEHAVIOR 6.1

Cultural Differences in Early Memories

For most adults, earliest memories are for events that occurred between the ages of 2 and 4. These early memories mark the beginning of autobiographical memory, which provides the basis for the development of an enduring sense of self (Howe, 2003). Cross-cultural research has shown how culture helps shape one's sense of self (Wang, 2004). As described in Chapter 1 (see page 12), in individualistic cultures the self is construed as *independent,* autonomous, and separate from other people or social contexts. In contrast, in collectivistic cultures the self is construed as *interdependent* and defined in terms of social relationships, roles, and responsibilities. Do cultural differences in the sense of self influence the content of our earliest memories?

Comparing the earliest memories of American college students and Chinese college students in Beijing, developmental psychologist Qi (pronounced "chee") Wang (2001) found a number of significant differences. First, the average age for earliest memory was about 3½ for the U.S.-born students and 4 for the China-born students. This finding confirmed earlier research that the age of earliest memory for Asian adults tends to be about six months later than for Americans (Mullen, 1994).

Wang also found striking differences in the content of the students' early memories. The Americans' memories were more likely

Culture and Earliest Memories Psychologist Qi Wang (2001) found that the earliest memories of Chinese adults tended to focus on routine activities that they shared with other members of their family or social group. Perhaps years from now, these children will remember eating meals or playing with their friends in this child-care center in Beijing.

to be discrete, one-point-in-time events focused on individual experiences or feelings, such as "I remember getting stung by a bee when I was 3 years old." The Chinese students' memories were more likely to be of general, routine activities that were centered on group activities with family or community members, such as "I remember walking to school every day with my friends."

For Americans, Wang notes, the past is like a drama in which the self plays the lead role. Themes of self-awareness and individual autonomy were more common in the American students' memories, which tended to focus on their own experiences, emotions, and thoughts. In contrast, Chinese students were more likely to include other people in their memories. Rather than focusing exclusively on their own behavior and thoughts, their earliest memories were typically brief accounts that centered on collective activities. For the Chinese students, the self is not easily separated from its social context.

Wang (2004) believes that cultural differences in autobiographical memory are formed in very early childhood, through interaction with family members. For example, *shared reminiscing*—the way that mothers talk to their children about their past experiences—has been shown to differ in Eastern and Western cultures (Fivush & Nelson, 2004). When Asian mothers reminisce with their children, they tend to talk about group settings or situations, and to de-emphasize emotions, such as anger, that might separate the child from the group. In contrast, Western mothers tend to focus more on the child's individual activities, accomplishments, and emotional reactions. As Katherine Nelson and Robyn Fivush (2004) observe, such conversations about the personal past "provide children with information about how to be a 'self' in their culture."

Here's the point of this simple demonstration. Your ability to type the phrase "most zebras cannot be extravagant" without looking demonstrates that you *do* know the location of the letters *Z, X, C, V, B, N,* and *M.* But your inability to recite that knowledge demonstrates that your memory of each key's location cannot be consciously recollected. Even though you're not consciously aware of the memory, it still affects your behavior. Implicit memories are also called *nondeclarative memories,* because you're unable to "declare" the information. Procedural memories, including skills and habits, typically reflect implicit memory processes. Figure 6.5, on page 228, summarizes the different types of long-term memory.

Although much of the memory research covered in this chapter centers on explicit memory, psychologists and neuroscientists have become increasingly interested in implicit memory. As we'll see in a later section, there is growing evidence that implicit memory and explicit memory involve different brain regions

FIGURE 6.5 Types of Long-Term Memory

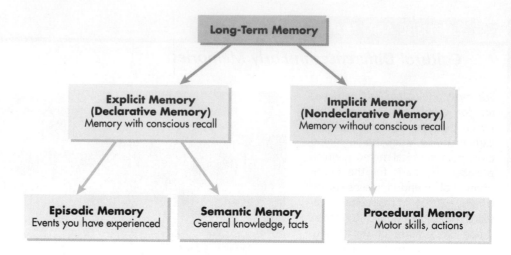

(Thompson, 2005). Some memory theorists believe that implicit memory and explicit memory are two distinct memory systems (Schacter & others, 1993; Squire & Kandel, 1999). Other researchers are more inclined to think that implicit and explicit memory simply involve the use of different types of encoding and retrieval processes (Roediger, 1990).

The Organization of Information in Long-Term Memory

Exactly *how* information is organized in long-term memory is not completely understood by memory researchers. Nonetheless, memory researchers know that information in long-term memory is *clustered* and *associated*.

FIGURE 6.6 Clustering Demonstration
Study the words on this list for one minute. Then count backward by threes from 108 to 0. When you've completed that task, write down as many of the words from the list as you can remember.

chair	apple
boat	car
footstool	airplane
orange	lamp
pear	banana
peach	dresser
bed	sofa
bus	bookcase
train	truck
plum	table
grapes	strawberry
motorcycle	bicycle

Clustering means organizing items into related groups, or *clusters,* during recall. You can experience clustering firsthand by trying the demonstration in Figure 6.6. Even though the words are presented in random order, you probably recalled groups of vehicles, fruits, and furniture. In other words, you organized the bits of information by clustering them into related categories.

Different bits and pieces of information in long-term memory are also logically linked, or associated. For example, what's the first word that comes to your mind in response to the word *red*? When we asked our students that same question, their top five responses were "blue," "apple," "color," "green," and "rose." Even if you didn't answer with one of the same associations, your response was based on some kind of logical association that you could explain if asked.

Memory researchers have developed several models to show how information is organized in long-term memory (Ratcliff & McKoon, 1994). One of the best-known models is called the **semantic network model** (Collins & Loftus, 1975). When one concept is activated in the semantic network, it can *spread* in any number of directions, *activating* other associations in the semantic network. For example, the word *red* might activate "blue" (another color), "apple" or "fire truck" (objects that are red), or "alert" (as in the phrase, "red alert"). In turn, these associations can activate other concepts in the network.

The semantic network model is a useful way of conceptualizing how information is organized in long-term memory. However, keep in mind that it is just a metaphor, not a physical structure in the brain. Nevertheless, the fact that information *is* organized in long-term memory has important implications for the retrieval process, as you'll see in the next section.

Retrieval
Getting Information from Long-Term Memory

clustering
Organizing items into related groups during recall from long-term memory.

semantic network model
A model that describes units of information in long-term memory as being organized in a complex network of associations.

retrieval
The process of accessing stored information.

retrieval cue
A clue, prompt, or hint that helps trigger recall of a given piece of information stored in long-term memory.

retrieval cue failure
The inability to recall long-term memories because of inadequate or missing retrieval cues.

Key Theme
■ Retrieval refers to the process of accessing and retrieving stored information in long-term memory.

Key Questions
■ What are retrieval cues and how do they work?

■ What do tip-of-the-tongue experiences tell us about the nature of memory?

■ How is retrieval tested, and what is the serial position effect?

So far, we've discussed some of the important factors that affect encoding and storing information in memory. In this section, we will consider factors that influence the retrieval process. Before you read any further, try the demonstration in Figure 6.7. After completing part (a) on this page, go to page 230 and try part (b). We'll refer to this demonstration throughout this section, so please take a shot at it. After you've completed both parts of the demonstration, continue reading.

Instructions: Spend 3 to 5 seconds reading each of the following sentences, and read through the list only once. As soon as you are finished, cover the list and write down as many of the sentences as you can remember (you need not write ca n be used" each time). Please begin now.

A brick can be used as a doorstop.
A ladder can be used as a bookshelf.
A wine bottle can be used as a candleholder.
A pan can be used as a drum.
A record can be used to serve potato chips.
A guitar can be used as a canoe paddle.
A leaf can be used as a bookmark.
An orange can be used to play catch.
A newspaper can be used to swat flies.
A TV antenna can be used as a clothes rack.
A sheet can be used as a sail.
A boat can be used as a shelter.
A bathtub can be used as a punch bowl.

A flashlight can be used to hold water.
A rock can be used as a paperweight.
A knife can be used to stir paint.
A pen can be used as an arrow.
A barrel can be used as a chair.
A rug can be used as a bedspread.
A telephone can be used as an alarm clock.
A scissors can be used to cut grass.
A board can be used as a ruler.
A balloon can be used as a pillow.
A shoe can be used to pound nails.
A dime can be used as a screwdriver.
A lampshade can be used as a hat.

Now that you've recalled as many sentences as you can, turn to Figure 6.7(b) on page 230.

FIGURE 6.7(a) Demonstration of Retrieval Cues

SOURCE: Bransford & Stein (1993).

The Importance of Retrieval Cues

Retrieval refers to the process of accessing, or *retrieving,* stored information. There's a vast difference between what is stored in our long-term memory and what we can actually access. In many instances, our ability to retrieve stored memories hinges on having an appropriate retrieval cue. A **retrieval cue** is a clue, prompt, or hint that can help trigger recall of a stored memory. If your performance on the demonstration experiment in Figure 6.7 was like ours, the importance of retrieval cues should have been vividly illustrated.

Let's compare results. How did you do on the first part of the demonstration, in Figure 6.7(a)? Don remembered 12 pairs of items. Sandy blew Don out of the water on the first part—she remembered 19 pairs of items. Like us, you undoubtedly reached a point at which you were unable to remember any more pairs. At that point, you experienced **retrieval cue failure,** which refers to the inability to recall long-term memories because of inadequate or missing retrieval cues.

Your authors both did much better on the demonstration in Figure 6.7(b), and you probably did, too. (Sandy got 24 of 26, and Don got 26 of 26 words, except that he remembered "clothes rack" as "clothesline.") Why the improvement? In part (b) you were presented with retrieval cues that helped you access your stored memories.

This exercise demonstrates the difference between information that is *stored* in long-term memory versus the information that you can *access*. Many of the items on the list that you could not recall in part (a) were not forgotten. They were simply inaccessible—until you had a retrieval cue to help jog your memory. This exercise illustrates that many memories only *appear* to be forgotten. With the right retrieval cue, you can often access stored information that seemed to be completely unavailable.

Common Retrieval Glitches
The Tip-of-the-Tongue Experience

Quick—can you remember the name of the one substance that can kill the comic book hero Superman? How about the name of Spiderman's uncle, who was killed in a robbery? If comic books aren't your thing, maybe you can answer this question: Who wrote the words to "The Star-Spangled Banner"?

Did any of these questions leave you feeling as if you knew the answer but just couldn't quite recall it? If so, you've just experienced one of the most common, and most frustrating, forms of retrieval failure, called the **tip-of-the-tongue (TOT) experience.** The TOT experience refers to the inability to get at a bit of information that you're absolutely certain is stored in your memory. Subjectively, it feels as though the information is very close, but just out of reach—or on the tip of your tongue (B. Schwartz, 2002).

TOT experiences appear to be universal, and the "tongue" metaphor is used to describe the experience in many cultures (B. Schwartz, 1999). On average, people have about one TOT experience per week. Although people of all ages experience such word-finding memory glitches, TOT experiences tend to be more common among older adults than younger adults (Burke & Shafto, 2004; James & Burke, 2000).

When experiencing this sort of retrieval failure, people can almost always dredge up partial responses or related bits of information from their memory. About half the time, people can accurately identify the first letter of the target word and the number of syllables in it. They can also often produce words with similar meanings or sounds (A. S. Brown, 1991). While momentarily frustrating, about 90 percent of TOT experiences are eventually resolved, often within a few minutes (Heine & others, 1999).

Tip-of-the-tongue experiences illustrate that retrieving information is not an all-or-nothing process. Often, we remember bits and pieces of what we want to remember. In many instances, information is stored in memory, but not accessible without the right retrieval cues. TOT experiences also emphasize a point that we made earlier. Information stored in memory is *organized* and connected in relatively logical ways. As you mentally struggle to retrieve the blocked information, logically connected bits of information are frequently triggered. In many instances, these related tidbits of information act as additional retrieval cues, helping you access the desired memory.

Testing Retrieval
Recall, Cued Recall, and Recognition

The first part of the demonstration in Figure 6.7 illustrated the use of recall as a strategy to measure memory. **Recall,** also called *free recall,* involves producing information using no retrieval cues. This is the memory measure that's used on essay tests. Other than the questions themselves, an essay test provides no retrieval cues to help jog your memory.

The second part of the demonstration used a different memory measurement, called **cued recall.** Cued recall involves remembering an item of information in response to a retrieval cue. Fill-in-the-blank and matching questions are examples of cued-recall tests.

A third memory measurement is **recognition,** which involves identifying the correct information from several possible choices. Multiple-choice tests involve recognition as a measure of long-term memory. The multiple-choice question provides you

---

> *Tip-of-the-tongue experiences (TOTs) are one of those illusive oddities of human cognition. Like slips of the tongue, déjà vu, and visual illusions, TOTs dazzle us with their subjective strength, yet at the same time, puzzle us with our frustrating inability to retrieve the desired word.*
>
> Bennett L. Schwartz (2002)

FIGURE 6.7(b) Demonstration of Retrieval Cues

SOURCE: Bransford & Stein (1993).

Instructions: *Do not* look back at the list of sentences in Figure 6.7(a). Use the following list as retrieval cues, and now write as many sentences as you can. Be sure to keep track of how many you can write down.

flashlight	lampshade
sheet	shoe
rock	guitar
telephone	scissors
boat	leaf
dime	brick
wine bottle	knife
board	newspaper
pen	pan
balloon	barrel
ladder	rug
record	orange
TV antenna	bathtub

with one correct answer and several wrong answers. If you have stored the information in your long-term memory, you should be able to recognize the correct answer.

Cued-recall and recognition tests are clearly to the student's advantage. Because these kinds of tests provide retrieval cues, the likelihood that you will be able to access stored information is increased.

The Serial Position Effect

Notice that the first part of the demonstration in Figure 6.7 did not ask you to recall the sentences in any particular order. Instead, the demonstration tested *free recall*—you could recall the items in any order. Take another look at your answers to Figure 6.7(a). Do you notice any sort of pattern to the items that you did recall?

Both your authors were least likely to recall items from the middle of the list. This pattern of responses is called the **serial position effect,** which refers to the tendency to retrieve information more easily from the beginning and the end of a list rather than from the middle. There are two parts to the serial position effect. The tendency to recall the first items in a list is called the *primacy effect,* and the tendency to recall the final items in a list is called the *recency effect.*

The primacy effect is especially prominent when you have to engage in *serial recall,* that is, when you need to remember a list of items in their original order. Remembering speeches, telephone numbers, and directions are a few examples of serial recall.

A Demonstration of the Serial Position Effect
Without singing them, try to recite the words of "The Star-Spangled Banner." If you're like most people, you'll correctly remember the words at the beginning and the end of "The Star-Spangled Banner" but have difficulty recalling the words and phrases in the middle—the essence of the serial position effect.

The Encoding Specificity Principle

Key Theme
■ According to the encoding specificity principle, re-creating the original learning conditions makes retrieval easier.

Key Questions
■ How can context and mood affect retrieval?
■ What role does distinctiveness play in retrieval, and how accurate are flashbulb memories?

One of the best ways to increase access to information in memory is to re-create the original learning conditions. This simple idea is formally called the **encoding specificity principle** (Tulving, 1983). As a general rule, the more closely retrieval cues match the original learning conditions, the more likely it is that retrieval will occur. The encoding specificity principle can take several forms. Examples include the context effect and mood congruence.

The Context Effect

The encoding specificity principle can explain some common experiences. Have you ever had trouble remembering some bit of information during a test but immediately recalled it as you entered the library where you normally study?

When you intentionally try to remember some bit of information, such as the definition of a term, you often encode into memory much more than just that isolated bit of information. As you study in the library, for example, at some level you're aware of all kinds of environmental cues. These cues might include the sights, sounds, and aromas within that particular situation. *The environmental*

tip-of-the-tongue (TOT) experience
A memory phenomenon that involves the sensation of knowing that specific information is stored in long-term memory, but being temporarily unable to retrieve it.

recall
A test of long-term memory that involves retrieving information without the aid of retrieval cues; also called *free recall.*

cued recall
A test of long-term memory that involves remembering an item of information in response to a retrieval cue.

recognition
A test of long-term memory that involves identifying correct information out of several possible choices.

serial position effect
The tendency to remember items at the beginning and end of a list better than items in the middle.

encoding specificity principle
The principle that when the conditions of information retrieval are similar to the conditions of information encoding, retrieval is more likely to be successful.

context effect

The tendency to recover information more easily when the retrieval occurs in the same setting as the original learning of the information.

mood congruence

An encoding specificity phenomenon in which a given mood tends to evoke memories that are consistent with that mood.

flashbulb memory

The recall of very specific images or details surrounding a vivid, rare, or significant personal event; details may or may not be accurate.

forgetting

The inability to recall information that was previously available.

cues in a particular context can become encoded as part of the unique memories you form while in that context. These same environmental cues can act as retrieval cues to help you access the memories formed in that context. This particular form of encoding specificity is called the context effect. The **context effect** is the tendency to remember information more easily when the retrieval occurs in the same setting in which you originally learned the information.

Thus, the environmental cues in the library where you normally study act as additional retrieval cues that help jog your memory. Of course, it's too late to help your test score, but the memory *was* there. Just for the record, studies have confirmed that when students are tested in the same room in which they learned the material, they perform better (e.g., Saufley & others, 1985).

Mood Congruence

Mood congruence refers to the idea that a given mood tends to evoke memories that are consistent with that mood. Research has consistently shown that your current mood influences the kinds of memories you recall (Eich & Forgas, 2003; Knight & others, 2002). A specific emotional state can act as a retrieval cue that evokes memories of events involving the same emotion. So, when you're in a positive mood, you're more likely to recall positive memories. When you're feeling blue, you're more likely to recall negative or unpleasant memories.

In seriously depressed individuals, the mood-congruence effect can actually prolong depression (Eich & others, 1997; Mineka & Nugent, 1995). The depressed mood enhances memory retrieval of sad experiences, such as personal failures or losses. In turn, dwelling on negative memories can intensify or prolong the depression.

Flashbulb Memories
Vivid Events, Accurate Memories?

If you rummage around your own memories, you'll quickly discover that highly unusual, surprising, or even bizarre experiences are easier to retrieve from memory than are routine events (Pillemer, 1998). Such memories are said to be characterized by a high degree of *distinctiveness*. That is, the encoded information represents a unique, different, or unusual memory. For example, if you were more likely to remember the unusual combinations than the ordinary combinations in the retrieval cue demonstration in Figure 6.7, distinctiveness probably played a role.

A wide variety of significant events can create vivid, distinctive, and long-lasting memories that are sometimes referred to as *flashbulb memories* (Brown & Kulik, 1982). Just as a camera flash captures the specific details of a scene, a **flashbulb memory** is thought to involve the recall of very specific details or images surrounding a significant, rare, or vivid event. Do flashbulb memories literally capture specific details, like the details of a photograph, that are unaffected by the passage of time?

Emotionally charged national events have provided a unique opportunity to study flashbulb memories. On September 12, 2001, psychologists Jennifer Talarico and David Rubin (2003) had Duke University students complete questionnaires about the terrorist attacks on the United States that had occurred the previous day. The students were asked such questions as: "Where were you when you first heard the news?" "Were there others present, and if so, who?" "What were you doing immediately before you first heard the news?" For comparison, the students also described some ordinary, everyday event that had occurred in their lives at about the same time, such as attending a sporting event or party.

Students were randomly assigned to a follow-up session either 1 week, 6 weeks, or 32 weeks later. At the follow-up sessions, they were asked to describe their memories of the ordinary event as well as their memory of the 9/11 attacks. They were also asked to evaluate the accuracy and vividness of their memories. Then, the researchers compared these accounts to their reports on September 12, 2001.

How did the flashbulb memories compare to the ordinary memories? Were the flashbulb memories more likely to be preserved unchanged over time? Not at

Flashbulb Memories? Can you remember where you were when you heard about the attacks on the World Trade Center and the Pentagon? The Oklahoma City bombing? Emotionally charged national events can supposedly trigger highly accurate, long-term flashbulb memories. Along with significant national tragedies, meaningful personal events, such as your high school graduation or your wedding day, can also supposedly produce vivid flashbulb memories. But are flashbulb memories more accurate than ordinary memories?

all. Both the flashbulb and everyday memories gradually decayed over time: The number of consistent details *decreased* and the number of inconsistent details *increased*. However, when the students rated the memory's vividness, their ability to recall the memory, and their belief in the memory's accuracy, only the ratings for the ordinary memory declined. In other words, despite having the same level of inconsistencies as the ordinary memories, the students *perceived* their flashbulb memories of 9/11 as being vivid and accurate.

Although flashbulb memories can seem incredibly vivid, they appear to function just as normal, everyday memories do. We remember some details, forget some details, and *think* we remember some details (Curci & others, 2001; Squire & others, 2001). What does seem to distinguish flashbulb memories from ordinary memories is the high degree of confidence the person has in the accuracy of these memories (Weaver, 1993). But clearly, confidence in a memory is no guarantee of accuracy. We'll come back to that important point shortly.

> *Flashbulb memories are not immune to forgetting, nor are they uncommonly consistent over time. Instead, exaggerated belief in memory's accuracy at long delays is what may have led to the conviction that flashbulb memories are more accurate than everyday memories.*
>
> Jennifer Talarico and David Rubin (2003)

Forgetting
When Retrieval Fails

Key Theme
■ Forgetting is the inability to retrieve information that was once available.

Key Questions
■ What discoveries were made by Hermann Ebbinghaus?

■ How do encoding failure, interference, and decay contribute to forgetting, and how can prospective memory be improved?

■ What is repression and why is the topic controversial?

Forgetting is so common that life is filled with reminders to safeguard against forgetting important information. Cars are equipped with buzzers so you don't forget to fasten your seatbelt or turn off your headlights. Dentists thoughtfully send brightly colored postcards and call you the day before so that your scheduled appointment doesn't slip your mind.

Although forgetting can be annoying, it does have adaptive value. Our minds would be cluttered with mountains of useless information if we remembered the name of every person we'd ever met, or every word of every conversation we'd ever had.

Psychologists define **forgetting** as the inability to remember information that was previously available. Note that this definition does not refer to the "loss" or "absence" of once-remembered information. While it's tempting to think of forgetting as simply the gradual loss of information from long-term memory over time, you'll see that this intuitively compelling view of forgetting is much too simplistic. And although psychologists have identified several factors that are involved in forgetting, exactly how—and why—forgetting occurs is still being actively researched (Dudai, 2004; Wixted, 2004).

Hermann Ebbinghaus
The Forgetting Curve

German psychologist **Hermann Ebbinghaus** began the scientific study of forgetting over a century ago. Because there was a seven-year gap between his completion of college and his first university teaching position, Ebbinghaus couldn't use university students for experimental subjects (Fancher, 1996). So to study forgetting, Ebbinghaus had to rely on the only available research subject: himself.

Ebbinghaus's goal was to determine how much information was forgotten after different lengths of time. But he wanted to make sure that he was studying

Hermann Ebbinghaus (1850–1909) After earning his Ph.D. in philosophy in 1873, Ebbinghaus worked as a private tutor for several years. It was during this time that he conducted his famous research on the memory of nonsense syllables. In 1885, he published his results in *Memory: A Contribution to Experimental Psychology*. In that text, Ebbinghaus observed, "Left to itself, every mental content gradually loses its capacity for being revived. Facts crammed at examination time soon vanish, if they were not sufficiently grounded by other study and later subjected to a sufficient review." Among his other notable contributions, he developed an early intelligence test, called the *Ebbinghaus Completion Test* (Lander, 1997).

the memory and forgetting of completely new material, rather than information that had preexisting associations in his memory. To solve this problem, Ebbinghaus (1885) created new material to memorize: thousands of nonsense syllables. A *nonsense syllable* is a three-letter combination, made up of two consonants and a vowel, such as WIB or MEP. It almost sounds like a word, but it is meaningless.

Ebbinghaus carefully noted how many times he had to repeat a list of 13 nonsense syllables before he could recall the list perfectly. To give you a feeling for this task, here's a typical list:

ROH, LEZ, SUW, QOV, XAR, KUF, WEP, BIW, CUL, TIX, QAP, WEJ, ZOD

Once he had learned the nonsense syllables, Ebbinghaus tested his recall of them after varying amounts of time, ranging from 20 minutes to 31 days. He plotted his results in the now-famous Ebbinghaus *forgetting curve,* shown in Figure 6.8.

The Ebbinghaus forgetting curve reveals two distinct patterns in the relationship between forgetting and the passage of time. First, much of what we forget is lost relatively soon after we originally learned it. How quickly we forget material depends on several factors, such as how well the material was encoded in the first place, how deeply it was processed, and how often it was rehearsed.

In general, if you learn something in a matter of minutes on just one occasion, most forgetting will occur very soon after the original learning—also in a matter of minutes. However, if you spend many sessions over days or weeks encoding new information into memory, the period of most rapid forgetting will be the first several weeks or months after such learning.

Second, the Ebbinghaus forgetting curve shows that the amount of forgetting eventually levels off. As you can see in Figure 6.8, there's very little difference between how much Ebbinghaus forgot eight hours later and a month later. The information that is *not* quickly forgotten seems to be remarkably stable in memory over long periods of time.

FIGURE 6.8 The Ebbinghaus Forgetting Curve Ebbinghaus's research demonstrated the basic pattern of forgetting: relatively rapid loss of some information, followed by stable memories of the remaining information.

SOURCE: Adapted from Ebbinghaus (1885).

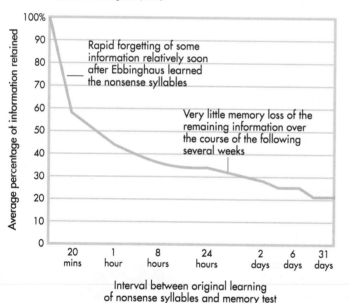

Why Do We Forget?

Ebbinghaus was a pioneer in the study of memory. His major contribution was to identify the basic pattern of forgetting: rapid forgetting of some information relatively soon after the original learning, followed by stability of the memories that remain. But what causes forgetting? Psychologists have identified several factors that contribute to forgetting, including encoding failure, decay, interference, and motivated forgetting.

Encoding Failure
It Never Got to Long-Term Memory

Without rummaging through your loose change, take a look at Figure 6.9. Circle the drawing that accurately depicts the face of a U.S. penny. Now, check your answer against a real penny. Were you correct?

When this task was presented to participants in one study, fewer than half of them picked the correct drawing (Nickerson & Adams, 1982). The explanation? Unless you're a coin collector, you've probably never looked carefully at a penny. Even though you may have handled thousands of pennies, chances are that you've only encoded the most superficial characteristics of a penny—its size, color, and texture—into your long-term memory.

In a follow-up study, William Marmie and Alice Healy (2004) allowed participants to study an unfamiliar coin for short periods of time, ranging from 15 seconds to 60 seconds. Even with only 15 seconds devoted to focusing on the coin's appearance, participants were better able to remember the details of the

encoding failure
The inability to recall specific information because of insufficient encoding of the information for storage in long-term memory.

prospective memory
Remembering to do something in the future.

unfamiliar coin than the all-too-familiar penny. In effect, Marmie and Healy (2004) confirmed that lack of attention at the time of encoding was responsible for the failure to accurately remember the appearance of a penny.

As these simple demonstrations illustrate, one of the most common reasons for forgetting is called **encoding failure**—we never encoded the information into long-term memory in the first place. Encoding failure explains why you forget a person's name three minutes after being introduced to her: The information was momentarily present in your short-term memory, but was never encoded into long-term memory.

Encoding failure can also help explain everyday memory failures due to *absent-mindedness*. Absent-mindedness occurs because you don't pay enough attention to a bit of information at the time when you should be encoding it, such as in which aisle you parked your car at the airport. Absent-minded memory failures often occur because your attention is *divided*. Rather than focusing your full attention on what you're doing, you're also thinking about other matters (Schacter, 2001).

Research has shown that divided attention at the time of encoding tends to result in poor memory for the information (Craik & others, 1996). Such absent-minded memory lapses are especially common when you're performing habitual actions that don't require much thought, such as parking your car in a familiar parking lot or setting down your cell phone, wallet, and keys when you come home. In some situations, divided attention might even contribute to déjà vu experiences, as we discuss in In Focus Box 6.2, on page 236.

Absent-mindedness is also implicated in another annoying memory problem—forgetting to do something in the future, such as returning a library book or taking a medication on schedule. Remembering to do something in the future is called **prospective memory.** In contrast to other types of memories, the crucial component of a prospective memory is *when* something needs to be remembered, rather than *what*.

Rather than encoding failure, prospective memory failures are due to *retrieval cue failure*—the inability to recall a memory because of missing or inadequate retrieval cues (see page 229). For example, you forget to mail your credit card payment on time and incur a late fee. The problem with this sort of scenario is that there is no strong, distinctive retrieval cue embedded in the situation. This is why ovens are equipped with timers that buzz and why your authors' kitchen calendar looks like a multicolored Post-it notes decoupage. Such strategies provide distinctive retrieval cues that will (hopefully) trigger those prospective memories at the appropriate moment. Table 6.1 lists additional suggestions to minimize prospective memory failures.

FIGURE 6.9 Test for Memory of Details of a Common Object Which of these drawings is an accurate picture of a real penny?

Table 6.1

Ten Suggestions for Avoiding Prospective Memory Failure

1 Make reminder cues DISTINCTIVE and make sure that they tell you *what* you are supposed to remember to do.

2 Make reminder cues obvious by posting them where you will definitely see them.

3 Be proactive! Create the reminder at the moment you realize that you need to do something in the future.

4 Put a notepad or Post-it notes and a pencil in lots of convenient places (e.g., your dresser, your car, the kitchen counter, etc.).

5 For things you need to remember to do in the very near future, buy small battery-operated kitchen timers. (Yes, it's true. We have seven timers scattered throughout our home offices.)

6 Leave yourself a voicemail message with the reminder at home or at work.

7 Buy a pocket calendar or daily planner and use it!

8 Use the calendar reminder and follow-up features on your computer or use a free Internet reminder service (e.g., www.memotome.com).

9 If your computer plays a central role in your life, you can download and use the free 3M Post-it Notes Lite software by going to the Chapter 6 Web Links at the *Discovering Psychology* Web companion.

10 Get in the habit of making and updating a to-do list.

Déjà Vu: An Illusion of Memory

The term **déjà vu** is French for "already seen." It involves the brief but intense feeling of having experienced something before but being unable to recall exactly when or where. Déjà vu experiences have been described in detail for well over a century (James, 1890). They can involve all of the senses, and there are a number of variations.

Déjà Vu Characteristics

How common are déjà vu experiences? Analyzing the results of more than 30 surveys, psychologist Alan Brown (2004) discovered that about two-thirds of individuals (68 percent) reported having had one or more déjà vu experiences in their life. One consistent finding is that the incidence of déjà vu steadily decreases over the lifespan. Young adults in the 20–24 age range tend to have the highest yearly incidence, averaging almost three déjà vu experiences per year. By the time people reach their early forties, they are averaging less than one déjà vu per year. However, a small minority of people seem to be especially prone to déjà vu experiences: About 16 percent claim to have a déjà vu experience about once a month.

A typical déjà vu experience is triggered by some kind of visual scene, and the intense feelings of familiarity last for just a few seconds. Déjà vu experiences are most common when people are feeling fatigued or emotionally distressed, in the evening, and in the company of others rather than alone. Well-educated people and people who travel frequently tend to have a higher incidence of déjà vu experiences (Brown, 2003).

Explaining Déjà Vu

Because déjà vu experiences can be so weird, some people immediately assume it must involve a paranormal explanation, such as being produced by precognition, clairvoyance, telepathy, or a past-life experience. Although a definitive scientific explanation of déjà vu has yet to be agreed upon, most psychologists do *not* believe that déjà vu experiences are paranormal in origin.

Neurological explanations of déjà vu are based on the notion that some brief brain dysfunction is responsible. One account holds that déjà vu occurs when there is a millisecond time lag in which information is sent to one cerebral hemisphere a split second before it is sent to the other hemisphere.

Some of the most useful explanations involve basic memory concepts, such as a disruption in *source memory*. **Source memory**, also termed **source monitoring**, refers to our ability to remember the original details or features of a memory, including when, where, and how we acquired the information.

To illustrate, let's say that you have an inexplicable déjà vu experience as you start up the walkway to enter Chicago's Shedd Aquarium. You know you've never visited the Shedd before, so you can't identify the source of the intense feeling of recognition. However, it's possible that you've simply *forgotten* the source of your memory (*source amnesia*). Magazine photos, a Web site, or a travel brochure are just a few possibilities. Of course, if you *could* identify the source of the familiarity (e.g., a documentary on the Discovery channel), then you probably would *not* have had a déjà vu experience.

Encoding failure may also be implicated in déjà vu experiences. According to the *inattentional blindness* explanation, déjà vu experiences can be produced when you're not really paying attention to your surroundings (Brown 2005). When you *do* focus your attention on the situation a split second later, those surroundings are perceived as suddenly—and inexplicably—familiar.

So, suppose you're talking on your cell phone as you stand in line in front of the Shedd Aquarium and are only minimally focused on your surroundings. As you end the phone call, you glance up at the entrance to the aquarium and suddenly . . . Voila! A déjà vu experience! (In this case, of course, the feeling that you have been there before is due to the fact that you really *have* been there before—a split second ago.)

Source amnesia and inattentional blindness are just two of the many scientific explanations for déjà vu. To learn more about déjà vu, check out Alan Brown's (2004) scholarly compilation of the research in his book *The Déjà Vu Experience*.

Decay Theory

Fading with the Passage of Time

According to **decay theory** we forget memories because we don't use them and they fade away over time as a matter of normal brain processes. The idea is that when a new memory is formed, it creates a *memory trace*—a distinct structural or chemical change in the brain. Over time, the normal metabolic processes of the brain are thought to erode the memory trace, especially if it is not "refreshed" by frequent rehearsal. The gradual fading of memories, then, would be similar to the fading of letters on billboards or newsprint exposed to environmental elements, such as sunlight.

Although decay theory makes sense intuitively, too much evidence contradicts it. Look again at the Ebbinghaus forgetting curve. If memories simply faded over time, you would expect to see a steady decline in the amount of information remembered with the passage of time. Instead, once the information held in memory stabilizes, it changes very little over time. In other words, the rate of forgetting actually *decreases* over time (Wixted, 2004).

Beyond that point, many studies have shown that information can be remembered decades after it was originally learned, even though it has not been rehearsed or recalled since the original memory was formed (Bahrick & Hall, 1991; Bahrick & Phelps, 1987). As we discussed earlier, the ability to access memories is strongly influenced by the kinds of retrieval cues provided when memory is tested (Slamecka, 1992). If the memory trace simply decayed over time, the presentation of potent retrieval cues should have no effect on the retrieval of information or events experienced long ago—but they do!

So have contemporary memory researchers abandoned decay theory as an explanation of forgetting? Not completely. Although decay is not regarded as the primary cause of forgetting, many of today's memory researchers believe that it contributes to forgetting (Altmann & Gray, 2002; Schacter, 2001).

Interference Theory
Memories Interfering with Memories

According to the **interference theory** of forgetting, forgetting is caused by one memory competing with or replacing another memory. The most critical factor is the similarity of the information. The more similar the information is in two memories, the more likely it is that interference will be produced.

There are two basic types of interference. **Retroactive interference** occurs when a *new* memory (the combination for the new lock you just bought for your bicycle) interferes with remembering an *old* memory (the combination for the lock you've been using at the gym). That is, retroactive interference involves information that is learned *after* the target learning.

Proactive interference occurs when an *old* memory (your previous zip code) interferes with remembering a *new* memory (your new zip code). Thus, proactive interference involves information that was learned *before* the target information was memorized. A rather embarrassing example of proactive interference occurs when someone refers to a current partner by a previous partner's name. Such momentary memory glitches seem to occur spontaneously, often in the thralls of passion or anger.

Motivated Forgetting
Forgetting Unpleasant Memories

Motivated forgetting refers to the idea that we forget because we are motivated to forget, usually because a memory is unpleasant or disturbing. One form of motivated forgetting, called **suppression,** involves the deliberate, conscious effort to forget information. For example, after seeing a disturbing report of a horrendous crime or massacre on the evening news, you consciously avoid thinking about it, turning your attention to other matters. According to some researchers, over time and with repeated effort, pushing an unwanted memory out of awareness may make the memory less accessible (M.C. Anderson & others, 2004; Levy & Anderson, 2002).

déjà vu
A brief but intense feeling of remembering a scene or an event that is actually being experienced for the first time; French for "already seen."

source memory or **source monitoring**
Memory for when, where, and how a particular piece of information was acquired.

decay theory
The view that forgetting is due to normal metabolic processes that occur in the brain over time.

interference theory
The theory that forgetting is caused by one memory competing with or replacing another.

retroactive interference
Forgetting in which a new memory interferes with remembering an old memory; backward-acting memory interference.

proactive interference
Forgetting in which an old memory interferes with remembering a new memory; forward-acting memory interference.

suppression
Motivated forgetting that occurs consciously.

DOONESBURY　　　BY GARRY TRUDEAU

repression
Motivated forgetting that occurs unconsciously.

Eyewitness Misidentification: Convicting the Wrong Man Four months after being attacked, kidnapped, and raped, an Oklahoma woman picked Arvin McGee out of a photographic line-up and identified him as the attacker. She claimed he had tied her up and carried her over his shoulders to a car. Then, she said, he drove her to a secluded area where he raped her. Based solely on the victim's eyewitness identification, McGee was arrested for the brutal crime. His first trial was declared a mistrial. His second ended in a hung jury. His third trial resulted in a guilty verdict. Despite the fact that McGee had an alibi and was also suffering from an abdominal hernia that would have made it virtually impossible for him to commit the crime, he was convicted and sentenced to 365 years in jail. Thirteen years after his conviction, DNA testing finally proved what McGee had maintained throughout his trials and years in prison—that he was innocent of the crime. Scores of studies have shown that eyewitness *mis*identification is the leading cause of wrongful convictions (Gross & others, 2004; Wells & Loftus, 2003).

Another form of motivated forgetting is fundamentally different and much more controversial. **Repression** is motivated forgetting that occurs unconsciously (Wilson & Dunn, 2004). With repression, all memory of a distressing event or experience is blocked from conscious awareness.

As we'll discuss in greater detail in Chapters 10 (Personality) and 14 (Therapies), the idea of repression is a cornerstone of *psychoanalysis,* Sigmund Freud's famous theory of personality and psychotherapy. Freud (1904) believed that psychologically threatening emotions, feelings, conflicts, and memories, especially those that originated in early childhood, become repressed. Even though they are blocked and unavailable to consciousness, the repressed conflicts continue to unconsciously influence the person's behavior, thoughts, and personality, often in maladaptive or unhealthy ways.

Among clinical psychologists who work with psychologically troubled people, the notion that behavior can be influenced by repressed memories is widely, but certainly not universally, accepted (Gleaves & others, 2004; Yapko, 1994a, 1994b). Among the general public, many people believe that we are capable of repressing memories of unpleasant events (Loftus & others, 1994). However, trying to scientifically confirm and study the influence of memories that a person does not remember is tricky, if not impossible.

One obvious problem is determining whether a memory has been "repressed" or simply forgotten. For example, several studies have found that people are better able to remember positive life experiences than negative life experiences (Lindsay, Wade, & others, 2004). Is that because unhappy experiences have been "repressed"? Or is it simply that people are less likely to think about, talk about, dwell on, or rehearse unhappy memories?

Among psychologists, repression is an extremely controversial topic (Kihlstrom, 2004; McNally, 2004). At one extreme are those who do not believe that true repression *ever* occurs (Holmes, 1990). At the other extreme are those who are convinced that repressed memories are at the root of many psychological problems, particularly repressed memories of childhood sexual abuse (Briere & Conte, 1993; Gleaves & others, 2004). This belief gave rise to a form of psychotherapy involving the recovery of repressed memories. Later in the chapter, we'll explore this controversy in Critical Thinking Box 6.3, "The Memory Wars: Recovered or False Memories?" on pages 244–245.

Imperfect Memories
Errors, Distortions, and False Memories

Key Theme
- Memories can be easily distorted, which can produce inaccuracies in eyewitness testimony.

Key Questions
- What is the misinformation effect?
- What is source confusion, and how can it distort memories?
- What are schemas and scripts, and how can they contribute to memory distortions?

Although people usually remember the general gist of what they experience, the fallibility of human memory is disturbing. Human memory does *not* function like a camera or tape recorder that captures a perfect copy of visual or auditory information. Instead, memory details can change over time. Without your awareness, details can be added, subtracted, exaggerated, or downplayed (Koriat & others, 2000). In fact, each of us has the potential to confidently and vividly remember the details of some event—and be completely *wrong*. Confidence in a memory is no guarantee that the memory is accurate.

How do errors and distortions creep into memories? A new memory is not simply recorded, but *actively constructed*. To form a new memory, you actively organize and encode different types of information—visual, auditory, tactile, and so on. When you later attempt to retrieve those details, you actively *reconstruct,* or rebuild, the details of the memory (Bartlett, 1932; Schacter & others, 1998). In the process of actively constructing or reconstructing a memory, various factors can contribute to errors and distortions in what you remember. Or, more accurately, what you *think* you remember.

At the forefront of research on memory distortions is **Elizabeth Loftus,** whose story we told in the Prologue. Loftus is one of the most widely recognized authorities on eyewitness memory and the different ways it can go awry. Not only has she conducted extensive research on this topic, but she has also testified as an expert witness in many high-profile cases (Loftus, 1996; Loftus & Ketcham, 1991).

The Misinformation Effect
The Influence of Postevent Information on Misremembering

Let's start by considering a Loftus study that has become a classic piece of research. Loftus and co-researcher John C. Palmer (1974) had subjects watch a film of an automobile accident, write a description of what they saw, and then answer a series of questions. There was one critical question in the series: "About how fast were the cars going when they contacted each other?" Different subjects were given different versions of that question. For some subjects, the word *contacted* was replaced with *hit*. Other subjects were given the words *bumped, collided,* or *smashed*.

Depending on the specific word used in the question, subjects provided very different estimates of the speed at which the cars in the film were traveling. As shown in Table 6.2, the subjects who gave the highest speed estimates got *smashed* (so to speak). Clearly, how a question is worded can influence what is remembered.

A week after seeing the film, the subjects were asked another series of questions. This time, the critical question was "Did you see any broken glass?" Although *no* broken glass was shown in the film, the majority of the subjects whose question had used the word *smashed* a week earlier said "yes." Notice what happened: Following the initial memory (the film of the automobile accident), new information (the word *smashed*) distorted the reconstruction of the memory (remembering broken glass that wasn't really there).

The use of suggestive questions is but one example of how the information a person gets *after* an event can change what the person later remembers about the event. Literally hundreds of studies have demonstrated the different ways that the **misinformation effect** can be produced (Loftus, 1996; Wells & Loftus, 2003). Basically, the research procedure involves three steps. First, participants are exposed to a simulated event, such as an automobile accident or a crime. Next, after a delay, half of the participants receive misinformation, while the other half receive no misinformation. In the final step, all of the participants try to remember the details of the original event.

In study after study, Loftus as well as other researchers have confirmed that postevent exposure to misinformation can distort the recollection of the original event by eyewitnesses (see Gerrie & others, 2004). People have recalled stop signs as yield signs, normal headlights as broken, barns along empty country roads, a blue vehicle as being white, and Minnie Mouse when they really saw Mickey Mouse! Whether it is in the form of suggestive questions, misinformation, or other exposure to conflicting details, such postevent experiences can distort eyewitness memories (Loftus, 2002; Wells & others, 2000).

misinformation effect

A memory-distortion phenomenon in which a person's existing memories can be altered if the person is exposed to misleading information.

Table | **6.2**

Estimated Speeds	
Word Used in Question	**Average Speed Estimate**
smashed	41 m.p.h.
collided	39 m.p.h.
bumped	38 m.p.h.
hit	34 m.p.h.
contacted	32 m.p.h.

SOURCE: After Loftus & Palmer (1974).

Psychological studies have shown that it is virtually impossible to tell the difference between a real memory and one that is a product of imagination or some other process. Our job as researchers in this area is to understand how it is that pieces of experience are combined to produce what we experience as "memory."

Elizabeth Loftus (2002)

The Misinformation Effect in Action In October 2002, the Washington, D.C., area was terrorized by a series of random sniper attacks. Early on, the police issued an alert that an eyewitness reported a white van speeding from the scene of a shooting. Later attacks brought more eyewitness reports of a white van or truck. Hundreds of white vans were pulled over and searched by the police. In reality, the killers, John Alan Muhammed and John Lee Malvo, were traveling in a dark blue Chevrolet Caprice. Ironically, several people had reported seeing a blue Caprice near different shooting scenes, but these reports were largely ignored because of the misinformed fixation on a white van.

source confusion
A memory distortion that occurs when the true source of the memory is forgotten.

false memory
A distorted or fabricated recollection of something that did not actually occur.

schema
(SKEE-muh) An organized cluster of information about a particular topic.

script
A schema for the typical sequence of an everyday event.

Source Confusion
Misremembering the Source of a Memory

Have you ever confidently remembered hearing something on television only to discover that it was really a friend who told you the information? Or mistakenly remembered doing something that you actually only *imagined* doing? Or confidently remembered that an event happened at one time and place only to learn later that it really happened at a *different* time and place?

If so, you can blame your faulty memories on a phenomenon called **source confusion.** Source confusion arises when the true source of the memory is forgotten or when a memory is attributed to the wrong source (Johnson & others, 1993; Leichtman & Ceci, 1995). The notion of source confusion can help explain the misinformation effect: False details provided *after* the event become confused with the details of the original memory.

Elizabeth's story in the Prologue also demonstrated how confusion about the source of a memory can give rise to an extremely vivid, but inaccurate, recollection. Vivid and accurate memories of her uncle's home, such as the smell of the pine trees and the feel of the lake water, became blended with Elizabeth's fantasy of finding her mother's body. The result was a **false memory,** which is a distorted or fabricated recollection of something that did not actually happen. Nonetheless, the false memory subjectively feels authentic and is often accompanied by all the emotional impact of a real memory.

Schemas, Scripts, and Memory Distortions
The Influence of Existing Knowledge on What Is Remembered

Given that information presented after a memory is formed can change the contents of that memory, let's consider the opposite effect: Can the knowledge you had *before* an event occurred influence your later memory of the event? If so, how?

Since you were a child, you have been actively forming mental representations called **schemas**—organized clusters of knowledge and information about particular topics. The topic can be almost anything—an object (e.g., a wind chime), a setting (e.g., a movie theater), or a concept (e.g., freedom). One kind of schema, called a **script,** involves the typical sequence of actions and behaviors at a common event, such eating in a restaurant or taking a plane trip.

Schemas are useful in organizing and forming new memories. Using the schemas you already have stored in long-term memory allows you to quickly integrate new experiences into your knowledge base. For example, consider your schema for "telephone." No longer just a utilitarian communication device, phones can be used to flirt, play games, or make a fashion statement. As the capabilities and functions of phones have expanded, your schema has changed to incorporate these new attributes. Your schema for "telephone" now includes cordless, wireless, and cellular phones, including devices that can transmit photos and text messages. So now, when you hear about a new cell phone that can download e-mail and stock quotes from the Internet, you can quickly integrate that information into your existing schema for "telephone."

Although useful, schemas can also contribute to memory distortions. In the classic "psychology professor's office" study described in the photo caption on the next page, students erroneously remembered objects that were not actually present but were consistent with their schema of a professor's office (Brewer & Treyens, 1981). The schemas we have developed can promote memory errors by prompting us to fill in missing details with schema-consistent information.

But what if a situation contains elements that are *inconsistent* with our schemas or scripts for that situation? Are inconsistent items more likely to stand out in our minds and be better remembered? In a word, yes. Numerous studies have demonstrated that items that are inconsistent with our expectations tend to be better recalled and recognized than items that are consistent with our expectations (e.g., Lampinen & others, 2001; Pezdek & others, 1989).

For example, University of Arkansas psychologist James Lampinen and his colleagues (2000) had participants listen to a story about a guy named Jack who performed some everyday activities, like washing his car and taking his dog to the veterinarian for shots. In each scene, Jack performed some actions that would have been consistent with the script (e.g., filling a bucket with soapy water, filling out forms at the vet's office) and some behaviors that were *not* part of a typical script for the activity (e.g., spraying the neighbor's kid with the hose, flirting with the vet's receptionist). When tested for details of the story, participants were more likely to recognize and remember the atypical actions than the consistent actions.

Much like the subjects in the professor's office study, participants in Lampinen's study also experienced compelling *false memories*. Almost always, the false memories were for actions that would have been consistent with the script—if they had actually happened in the story. For example, some participants vividly remembered that Jack rinsed the car off with a hose or that he put a leash on the dog before taking him to the vet's office. Neither of those actions occurred in the story.

False Memories of a Psychology Professor's Office After briefly waiting in the psychology professor's office shown above, participants were taken to another room and asked to recall details of the office—the real purpose of the study. Many participants falsely remembered objects that were not actually in the office, such as books, a filing cabinet, a telephone, a lamp, pens, pencils, and a coffee cup. Why? The details that the participants erroneously remembered were all items that would be consistent with a typical professor's office (Brewer & Treyens, 1981). Clearly, our schemas can cause memory errors bt prompting us to fill in missing detail with schema-consistent information.

Forming False Memories
From the Plausible to the Impossible

Key Theme
- A variety of techniques can create false memories for events that never happened.

Key Questions
- What is the *lost-in-the-mall* technique, and how does it produce false memories?
- What is imagination inflation, and how has it been demonstrated?
- What factors contribute to the formation of false memories?

Up to this point, we've talked about how misinformation, source confusion, and the mental schemas and scripts we've developed can change or add details to a memory that already exists. However, memory researchers have gone beyond changing a few details here and there. Since the mid-1990s, an impressive body of research has accumulated showing how false memories can be created for events that *never* happened (Loftus, 2003). We'll begin with another Loftus study that has become famous—the *lost-in-the-mall* study.

Imagination Inflation
Remembering Being Lost in the Mall

Loftus and Jacqueline Pickrell (1995) gave each of 24 participants written descriptions of four childhood events that had been provided by a parent or other older relative. Three of the events had really happened, but the fourth was a *pseudoevent*—a false story about the participant getting lost in a shopping mall. Here's the gist of the story: At about the age of 5 or 6, the person got lost for an extended period of time in a shopping mall, became very upset and cried, was rescued by an elderly person, and ultimately was reunited with the family. (Family members verified that the participant had never actually been lost in a shopping mall or department store as a child.)

After reading the four event descriptions, the participants wrote down as many details as they could remember about each event. About two weeks later, participants were interviewed and asked to recall as many details as they could about

WATERS SCHOOL   GRADE IA & 2B   207

Can Real Photos Create False Memories?
Psychologist Stephen Lindsay and his colleagues (2004a, 2004b) had participants look at their first-grade class photo and read a description of a prank that they were led to believe had occurred in the first grade—putting Slime in their teacher's desk. After a week of trying to remember the prank, two-thirds of the participants—65%—reported vivid, detailed memories of the prank. In contrast, only about a quarter (23%) of participants who tried to remember the prank but did *not* view a school photo developed false memories of the pseudoevent. Viewing an actual school photo, Lindsay believes, added to the legitimacy of the pseudoevent, making it seem more probable. It also provided vivid sensory details that blended with the imagined details to create elaborate and subjectively compelling false memories.

each of the four events. Approximately one to two weeks after that, participants were interviewed a second time and asked once again what they could remember about the four events.

By the final interview, 6 of the 24 participants had created either full or partial memories of being lost in the shopping mall. How entrenched were the false memories for those who experienced them? Even after being debriefed at the end of the study, some of the participants continued to struggled with the vividness of the false memory. "I totally remember walking around in those dressing rooms and my mom not being in the section she said she'd be in," one participant said (Loftus & Pickrell, 1995).

The research strategy of using information from family members to help create or induce false memories of childhood experiences has been dubbed the *lost-in-the-mall technique* (Loftus, 2003). By having participants remember real events along with imagining pseudoevents, researchers have created false memories for a wide variety of events. For example, participants have been led to believe that as a child they had been saved from nearly drowning by a lifeguard (Heaps & Nash, 2001). Or that they had knocked over a punch bowl on the bride's parents at a wedding reception (Hyman & Pentland, 1996).

Clearly, then, research has demonstrated that people can develop beliefs and memories for events that definitely did not happen to them. One key factor in the creation of false memories is the power of imagination. Put simply, *imagining the past as different from what it was can change the way you remember it*. Several studies have shown that vividly imagining an event markedly increases confidence that the event actually occurred in childhood, an effect called **imagination inflation** (Garry & Polaschek, 2000; Thomas & others, 2003).

How does imagining an event—even one that never took place—help create a memory that is so subjectively compelling? Several factors seem to be involved. First, repeatedly imagining an event makes the event seem increasingly *familiar*. People then misinterpret the sense of familiarity as an indication that the event really happened (Sharman & others, 2004).

Second, coupled with the sense of increased familiarity, people experience *source confusion*. That is, subtle confusion can occur as to whether a retrieved "memory" has a real event or an imagined event as its source. Over time people may come to misattribute their memory of *imagining* the pseudoevent as being a memory of the *actual occurrence* of the event.

Third, the more vivid and detailed the imaginative experience, the more likely it is that people will confuse the imagined event with a real occurrence (Thomas & others, 2003). Vivid sensory and perceptual details can make the imagined events "feel" more like "real" events.

Clearly, then, simple manipulations as suggestions and imagination exercises can increase the incidence and realism of false memories. So can vivid memory cues and family photos. The ease with which false memories can be implanted is more than just an academic question. It also has some powerful real-world implications. In Critical Thinking Box 6.3, on pages 244–245, we explore the highly charged controversy that has been dubbed "the memory wars."

Finally, we don't want to leave you with the impression that it's astonishing that anybody remembers *anything* accurately. In reality, people's memories tend to be quite accurate for the gist of what occurred. When memory distortions occur spontaneously in everyday life, they usually involve limited bits of information.

Still, the surprising ease with which memory details can become distorted is unnerving. The distorted memories can ring true and feel just as real as accurate memories. In the chapter Prologue, you saw how easily Elizabeth Loftus created a false memory. You also saw how quickly she became convinced of the false memory's authenticity and the strong emotional impact it had on her. Rather than being set in stone, human memories are more like clay: They can change shape with just a little bit of pressure.

imagination inflation
A memory phenomenon in which vividly imagining an event markedly increases confidence that the event actually occurred.

memory trace
The brain changes associated with a particular stored memory.

Table 6.3

Factors Contributing to False Memories

Factor	Description
Misinformation effect	When erroneous information received after an event leads to distorted or false memories of the event
Source confusion	Forgetting or misremembering the true source of a memory
Schema distortion	False or distorted memories caused by the tendency to fill in missing memory details with information that is consistent with existing knowledge about a topic
Imagination inflation	Unfounded confidence in a false or distorted memory caused by vividly imagining the pseudoevent
False familiarity	Increased feelings of familiarity due to repeatedly imagining an event
Blending fact and fiction	Using vivid, authentic details to add to the legitimacy and believability of a pseudoevent
Suggestion	Hypnosis, guided imagery, or other highly suggestive techniques that can inadvertently or intentionally create vivid false memories

The Search for the Biological Basis of Memory

Key Theme

■ Early researchers believed that memory was associated with physical changes in the brain, but these changes were only discovered in the last few decades.

Key Questions

■ How are memories both localized and distributed in the brain?

■ How do neurons change when a memory is formed?

Does the name *Ivan Pavlov* ring a bell? We hope so. As you should recall from Chapter 5, Pavlov was the Russian physiologist who classically conditioned dogs to salivate to the sound of a bell and other neutral stimuli. Without question, learning and memory are intimately connected. Learning an adaptive response depends on our ability to form new memories in which we associate environmental stimuli, behaviors, and consequences.

Pavlov (1927) believed that the memory involved in learning a classically conditioned response would ultimately be explained as a matter of changes in the brain. However, he only speculated about the kinds of brain changes that would produce the memories needed for classical conditioning to occur. Other researchers would take up the search for the physical changes associated with learning and memory. In this section, we look at some of the key discoveries that have been made in trying to understand the biological basis of memory.

The Search for the Elusive Memory Trace

An American physiological psychologist named **Karl Lashley** set out to find evidence for Pavlov's speculations. In the 1920s, Lashley began the search for the **memory trace,** or *engram*—the brain changes associated with the formation of a long-term memory. Guiding Lashley's research was his belief that memory was *localized,* meaning that a particular memory was stored in a specific brain area.

Karl S. Lashley (1890–1958) Lashley was trained as a zoologist but turned to psychology after he became friends with John B. Watson, the founder of behaviorism. Interested in discovering the physical basis of the conditioned reflex, Lashley focused his research on how learning and memory were represented in the brain. After years of frustrating research, Lashley (1950) humorously concluded, "This series of experiments has yielded a good bit of information about what and where memory is not. It has discovered nothing directly of the real nature of the engram. I sometimes feel in reviewing the evidence on the localization of the memory trace, that the necessary conclusion is that learning just is not possible."

CRITICAL THINKING 6.3

The Memory Wars: Recovered or False Memories?

Repressed memory therapy, recovered memory therapy, trauma therapy—these are some of the names of a new therapy that was embraced by many psychotherapists, counselors, social workers, and other mental health workers in the 1990s. Proponents claimed that they had identified the root cause of a wide assortment of psychological problems: buried memories of sexual abuse in childhood.

This therapeutic approach was based on the assumption that incidents of sexual and physical abuse experienced in childhood, especially when perpetrated by a trusted caregiver, were so psychologically threatening that the victims repressed all memories of the experience (Gleaves & others, 2004). Despite being repressed, these buried memories of unspeakable traumas continued to cause psychological and physical problems, ranging from low self-esteem to eating disorders, substance abuse, and depression.

The goal of repressed memory therapy was to help adult incest survivors "recover" their repressed memories of childhood sexual abuse. Reliving these painful experiences would help them begin "the healing process" of working through their anger and other intense emotions (Bass & Davis, 1994). Survivors were encouraged to confront their abusers and, if necessary, break all ties with their abusive families.

The Controversy: Methods Used to "Recover" Repressed Memories

The validity of the memories recovered in therapy became the center of a highly charged public controversy that has been dubbed "the memory wars" (Baker, 1998; Brenneis, 2000). A key issue was the methods used to help people unblock, or recover, repressed memories. Some recovered memory therapists used hypnosis, dream analysis, guided imagery, intensive group therapy, and other highly suggestive techniques to recover the long-repressed memories (Brown & others, 1998).

For example, recovery therapist Wendy Maltz (1991) advised those who could not recall abuse memories to "spend time imagining that you were sexually abused, without worrying about accuracy, proving anything, or having your ideas make sense. As you give rein to your imagination, let your intuition guide your thoughts."

Many patients supposedly recovered memories of repeated incidents of physical and sexual abuse, sometimes beginning in early infancy, ongoing for years, and involving multiple victimizers (Pendergrast, 1996). Even more disturbing, some patients recovered vivid memories of years of alleged ritual satanic abuse involving secret cults practicing cannibalism, torture, and ritual murder (Sakheim & Devine, 1992).

The Critical Issue: Recovered Memories or False Memories?

Are traumatic memories likely to be repressed? It is well established that in documented cases of trauma, most survivors are troubled by the *opposite* problem—they cannot forget their traumatic memories (Kihlstrom, 2004; McNally, 2004). Rather than being unable to remember the experience, trauma survivors suffer from recurring flashbacks, intrusive thoughts and memories of the trauma, and nightmares.

The controversy concerning repressed and recovered memories of childhood sexual abuse has been deeply divisive in psychology and psychiatry. Some scholars argue that there is no convincing evidence that people can banish and then recover memories of horrific experiences, whereas others proclaim overwhelming scientific support for the existence of repressed or dissociated memory.

Richard McNally (2003)

While it is relatively common for a person to be unable to remember *some* of the specific details of a traumatic event or to be troubled by memory problems after the traumatic event, such memory problems do *not* typically include difficulty in

---

Lashley searched for the specific location of the memory that a rat forms for running a maze. Lashley (1929) suspected that the specific memory was localized at a specific site in the *cerebral cortex,* the outermost covering of the brain that contains the most sophisticated brain areas. Once a rat had learned to run the maze, Lashley surgically removed tiny portions of the rat's cortex. After the rat recovered, Lashley tested the rat in the maze again. Obviously, if the rat could still run the maze, then the portion of the brain removed did not contain the memory.

Over the course of 30 years, Lashley systematically removed different sections of the cortex in trained rats. The result of Lashley's painstaking research? No matter which part of the cortex he removed, the rats were still able to run the maze (Lashley, 1929, 1950). At the end of his professional career, Karl Lashley concluded that memories are not localized in specific locations but instead are *distributed,* or stored, throughout the brain.

Lashley was wrong, but not completely wrong. Some memories *do* seem to be localized at specific spots in the brain. Some 20 years after Lashley's death, psychologist **Richard F. Thompson** and his colleagues resumed the search for the location of the memory trace that would confirm Pavlov's speculations.

remembering the trauma itself (McNally, 2004). Memory researchers agree that people might experience amnesia for a single traumatic incident but are skeptical that anyone could repress *all* memories of *repeated* incidents of abuse, especially when those incidents occurred over a period of several years (Loftus, 2001; Schacter, 1995).

Critics of recovery therapy contend that many of the supposedly "recovered" memories are actually *false memories* that are produced by the well-intentioned but misguided use of suggestive therapeutic techniques (de Rivera, 2000). Memory experts have many objections to the use of hypnosis and other highly suggestive techniques to recover repressed memories (Ceci & Loftus, 1994; Gerrie & others, 2004; Lindsay & Read, 1994; Lynn & others, 1997).

As you've seen in this chapter, compelling evidence shows the power of misinformation, suggestion, and imagination in the creation of vivid, but false, memories. As Elizabeth Loftus (2002) writes, "In more than twenty-five years of doing several hundred studies involving perhaps 20,000 people, we had distorted a significant portion of the subjects' memories. And the mechanism by which we can convince people they were lost, frightened, and crying in a mall is not so different than the mechanism by which therapists might unwittingly encourage memories of sexual abuse."

What Conclusions Can Be Drawn?

After years of debate, some areas of consensus have emerged (Knapp & Vande-Creek, 2000). First, there is no question that physical and sexual abuse in childhood is a serious social problem that also contributes to psychological problems in adulthood (Kendler, Bulik, & others, 2000; Nelson & others, 2002).

Second, some psychologists believe it is *possible* for memories of childhood abuse to be completely forgotten, only to surface many years later in adulthood (Brenneis, 2000; Schooler, 2001). Nevertheless, it's clear that repressed memories that have been recovered in psychotherapy need to be regarded with caution (Bowers & Favolden, 1996; Cloitre, 2004).

Third, as we've seen in this chapter, the details of memories can be distorted with disturbing ease. Consequently, the use of highly suggestive techniques to recover memories of abuse raises serious concerns about the accuracy of such memories. As we have noted repeatedly in this chapter, a person's confidence in a memory is no guarantee that the memory is indeed accurate. False or fabricated memories can seem just as detailed, vivid, and real as accurate ones (Gerrie & others, 2004; Payne & others, 1997).

Fourth, keep in mind that every act of remembering involves reconstructing a memory. The human memory system does not function like a video camera, perfectly preserving the details of an experience. Remembering an experience is not like popping a videotape into your VCR. Memories can change over time. Without our awareness, memories can grow and evolve, sometimes in unexpected ways. Finally, psychologists and other therapists have become more aware of the possibility of inadvertently creating false memories in therapy (Palm & Gibson, 1998). Guidelines have been developed to help mental health professionals avoid unintentionally creating false memories in clients (American Psychological Association Working Group, 1998; Ornstein & others, 1998; Pope & Brown, 1996).

Critical Thinking Questions

- Why is it difficult to determine the accuracy of a "memory" that is recovered in therapy?
- How could the phenomenon of source confusion be used to explain the production of false memories?

Thompson classically conditioned rabbits to perform a very simple behavior—an eye blink. By repeatedly pairing a tone with a puff of air administered to the rabbit's eye, he classically conditioned rabbits to blink reflexively in response to the tone alone (Thompson, 1994, 2000).

Thompson discovered that after a rabbit had learned this simple behavior, there was a change in the brain activity in a small area of the rabbit's *cerebellum,* a lower brain structure involved in physical movements. When this tiny area of the cerebellum was removed, the rabbit's memory of the learned response disappeared. It no longer blinked at the sound of the tone. However, the puff of air still caused the rabbit to blink reflexively, so the reflex itself had not been destroyed.

Richard F. Thompson (b. 1930) Like Karl Lashley, Richard Thompson, an American psychologist and neuroscientist, sought to discover the neurobiological basis for learning and memory. But, unlike Lashley, Thompson decided to use a very simple behavior—a classically conditioned eye blink—as a model system to locate a memory trace in the brain. He succeeded, identifying the critical region in the cerebellum where the memory of the learned behavior was stored.

focus on

Neuroscience: Assembling Memories: Echoes and Reflections of Perception

Perception   **Recall**

Picture

(a)   (b)

Sound

(c)   (d)

Retrieving the Memory of a Sensory Experience
Top row: (**a**) Perceiving a picture activates areas of the visual cortex.
(**b**) When the memory of the picture is recalled, it reactivates some of
the same areas of the visual cortex *(arrow)* that were involved in the
initial perception of the picture. Bottom row: (**c**) Perceiving a sound
activates areas of the auditory cortex. (**d**) When the memory of the
sound is recalled, it reactivates some of the same areas of the auditory
cortex *(arrow)* that were involved in the initial perception of the sound.

SOURCE: Wheeler & others (2000).

If we asked you to remember Paul McCartney's rendition of "Yesterday" or the theme from *Star Wars,* you would "hear" the song in your head. Conjure up a memory of your elementary school, and you "see" it in your mind. Vivid memories can include a great deal of sensory information—sounds, sights, and even odors and tastes. How are such rich sensory aspects of an experience incorporated into the memory that is retrieved?

Psychologists Mark Wheeler, Steven Petersen, and Randy Buckner (2000) set out to investigate this question using a simple memory task and fMRI. First, the participants spent two days studying labels for common objects that were paired with either a picture or a sound. For example, half of the participants memorized the word *dog* paired with a picture of a dog, and half memorized the word *dog* paired with the sound of a dog barking. The researchers then used fMRI to measure brain activity in the volunteers under two conditions: (1) a *perception* condition, in which the participants simply reviewed the pairings that they had learned, and (2) a *recall* condition, in which the volunteers were given the label and told to retrieve the memory and indicate whether the word was associated with a picture or a sound.

The results? Retrieving the memory activated a subset of the same brain areas that were involved in perceiving the sensory stimulus. Participants who had memorized the word *dog* with a *picture* of a dog showed a high level of activation in the *visual cortex* when they retrieved the memory. And participants who had memorized the word *dog* with the *sound* of a barking dog showed a high level of activation in the *auditory cortex* when they retrieved the memory.

Of course, many of our memories are highly complex, involving not just sensations but also thoughts and emotions. Neuroscientists assume that such complex memories involve traces that are widely distributed throughout the brain. However, they still don't understand how all these neural records are bound together and interrelated to form a single, highly elaborate memory (Buckner & Wheeler, 2001).

Thompson and his colleagues had confirmed Pavlov's speculations. The long-term memory trace of the classically conditioned eye blink was formed and stored in a very localized region of the cerebellum. So why had Karl Lashley failed? Unlike Thompson, Lashley was working with a relatively complex behavior. Running a maze involves the use of several senses, including vision, smell, and touch. In contrast, Thompson's rabbits had learned a very simple reflexive behavior—a classically conditioned eye blink.

Thus, part of the reason Lashley failed to find a specific location for a rat's memory of a maze was that the memory was not a single memory. Instead, the rat had developed a complex set of *interrelated memories* involving information from multiple senses. These interrelated memories were processed and stored in different brain areas. As a result, the rat's memories were *distributed* and stored across multiple brain locations. Hence, no matter which small brain area Lashley removed, the rat could still run the maze. So Lashley seems to have been right in suggesting that some memories are distributed throughout the brain.

When you combine the findings of Lashley and Thompson, they suggest that memories have the potential to be *both localized and distributed* (Squire & Kandel, 1999). Very simple memories may be localized in a specific area, whereas more complex memories seem to be distributed throughout the brain. A complex memory involves clusters of information, and each part of the memory may be stored in the brain area that originally processed the information (Greenberg & Rubin, 2003).

More recently, researchers have used brain imaging technology to confirm that many kinds of memories are distributed in the human brain. When we are performing a relatively complex memory task, multiple brain regions are activated—evidence of the distribution of memories involved in complex tasks (Frankland & Bontempi, 2005).

If multiple brain areas are involved when we form a new memory, are they also involved when we retrieve an existing memory? The Focus on Neuroscience on page 246 describes a clever study that investigated this question.

The Role of Neurons in Long-Term Memory

What exactly is it that is localized or distributed? Memories don't just float around in your brain. The notion of a memory trace suggests that some change must occur in the workings of the brain when a new long-term memory is stored. Logically, two possible changes could occur. First, the *functioning* of the neurons in the brain could somehow change. Second, the *structure* of the neurons could somehow change.

Given those two possibilities, the challenge for memory researchers has been to identify the specific neurons involved in a given memory, a task that is virtually impossible with the human brain because of its enormous complexity. What this task requires is a creature with a limited number of neurons that is also capable of learning new memories.

Enter *Aplysia*, a gentle, seaweed-munching sea snail that resides off the California coast. The study of *Aplysia* in the last 30 years has given memory researchers important clues to the brain changes involved in memory. *Aplysia* has only about 20,000 good-sized neurons. Thus, memory researchers, such as **Eric Kandel** (2001) at Columbia University, have been able to study the neuronal changes that occur when *Aplysia* forms a new memory for a simple classically conditioned response.

If you give *Aplysia* a gentle squirt with a WaterPik, followed by a mild electric shock to its tail, the snail reflexively withdraws its gill flap. When the process is repeated several times, *Aplysia* wises up and acquires a new memory of a classically conditioned response—it withdraws its gill when squirted with the WaterPik alone. This learned gill-withdrawal reflex seems to involve a circuit of just three neurons: one that detects the water squirt, one that detects the tail shock, and one that signals the gill-withdrawal reflex (see Figure 6.10).

When *Aplysia* acquires this new memory through repeated training trials, significant changes occur in the three-neuron circuit (Kandel, 2001). First, the *function* of the neurons is altered: There is an increase in the amount of the neurotransmitters produced by the neurons. Second, the *structure* of the snail's

Aplysia, the Supersnail of Memory Research Eric Kandel holds *Aplysia*, the sea snail that is used to study how neurons change when simple behaviors are learned and remembered. Kandel was awarded the Nobel Prize in 2000 for his discoveries on the neural basis of memory.

FIGURE 6.10 How Neurons Change as Aplysia Forms a New Memory When *Aplysia* is repeatedly squirted with water, and each squirt is followed by a mild shock to its tail, the snail learns to withdraw its gill flap if squirted with the water alone. Conditioning leads to structural and functional changes in the three neurons involved in the memory circuit.

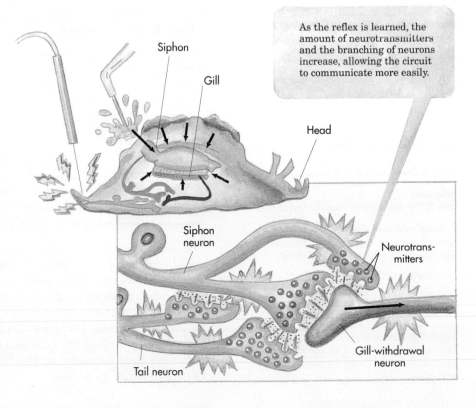

As the reflex is learned, the amount of neurotransmitters and the branching of neurons increase, allowing the circuit to communicate more easily.

Siphon

Gill

Head

Siphon neuron

Neurotransmitters

Gill-withdrawal neuron

Tail neuron

Creating New Synaptic Connections
Forming new memories involves strengthening existing synaptic connections and creating new synaptic connections between neurons in the brain. Neuroscientist Michael Colicos and his colleagues at the University of California–San Diego (2001) photographed structural changes in a single hippocampus neuron that occurred in response to repeated electrical stimulation. The spidery blue lines in the photo are physical changes in the neuron's structure that represent the first steps toward the formation of new synaptic connections with other neurons.

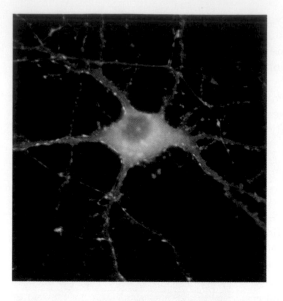

neurons changes: The number of interconnecting branches between the neurons increases, as does the number of synapses, or communication points, on each branch. These changes allow the neurons involved in the particular memory circuit to communicate more easily. Collectively, these changes are called **long-term potentiation,** which refers to a long-lasting increase in synaptic strength (Lamprecht & LeDoux, 2004; Malenka, 2003).

The same kinds of brain changes have been observed in more sophisticated mammals. Chicks, rats, and rabbits also show structural and functional neuron changes associated with new learning experiences and memories (Martin & others, 2000; Rioult-Pedotti & others, 2000). And, as you may recall from the Chapter 2 Application, there is evidence that the same kinds of changes occur in the human brain (e.g., Draganski & others, 2004).

In terms of our understanding of the memory trace, what do these findings suggest? Although there are vast differences between the nervous system of a simple creature such as *Aplysia* and the enormously complex human brain, some tentative generalizations are possible. Forming a memory seems to produce distinct functional and structural changes in specific neurons (Tsien, 2000). These changes create a memory circuit. Each time the memory is recalled, the neurons in this circuit are activated. As the structural and functional changes in the neurons strengthen the communication links in this circuit, the memory becomes established as a long-term memory (Kandel, 2001).

Processing Memories in the Brain
Clues from Amnesia

Key Theme
- Important insights into the brain structures involved in normal memory have been provided by case studies of people with amnesia caused by damaged brain tissue.

Key Questions
- Who is H.M. and what does his case reveal about normal memory processes?
- What brain structures are involved in normal memory?
- What are dementia and Alzheimer's disease?

long-term potentiation
A long-lasting increase in synaptic strength between two neurons.

amnesia
(am-NEE-zha) Severe memory loss.

retrograde amnesia
Loss of memory, especially for episodic information; backward-acting amnesia.

memory consolidation
The gradual, physical process of converting new long-term memories to stable, enduring long-term memory codes.

anterograde amnesia
Loss of memory caused by the inability to store new memories; forward-acting amnesia.

The complexity and inaccessibility of the human brain have made it virtually impossible to study the role of individual neurons in human memory. However, memory researchers have been able to study the role of specific brain structures in processing memories. Much of this research has involved studying individuals who have sustained a brain injury or had part of their brain surgically removed for medical reasons. Often, such individuals experience **amnesia,** or severe memory loss. By relating the type and extent of amnesia to the specific brain areas that have been damaged, researchers have uncovered clues as to how the human brain processes memories.

Retrograde Amnesia
Disrupting Memory Consolidation

One type of amnesia is **retrograde amnesia.** *Retrograde* means "backward moving." People who have retrograde amnesia are unable to remember some or all of their past, especially episodic memories for recent events. Retrograde amnesia often results from a blow to the head. Boxers sometimes suffer such memory losses after years of fighting. Head injuries from automobile and motorcycle accidents are another common cause of retrograde amnesia. Typically, memories of the events that immediately preceded the injury are completely lost, as in the case of accident victims who cannot remember details about what led up to the accident.

Apparently, establishing a long-term memory is like creating a Jell-O mold—it needs time to "set" before it becomes solid. This process of "setting" a new memory permanently in the brain is called memory consolidation (McGaugh, 2000). More specifically, **memory consolidation** is the gradual, physical process of converting new long-term memories to stable, enduring memory codes. If memory consolidation is disrupted before the process is complete, the vulnerable memory may be lost (Dudai, 2004).

In humans, memory consolidation can be disrupted by brain trauma, such as a sudden blow, concussion, electric shock, or encephalitis (Riccio & others, 2003). Similarly, many drugs, such as alcohol and the benzodiazepines, interfere with memory consolidation. In contrast, stimulants and the stress hormones that are released during emotional arousal tend to *enhance* memory consolidation (McGaugh, 2000).

Anterograde Amnesia
Disrupting Explicit Memory Formation

Another form of amnesia is **anterograde amnesia**—the inability to form *new* memories. *Anterograde* means "forward moving." The most famous case of anterograde amnesia is that of a man identified only by the initials H.M. to protect his identity.

In 1953, H.M. was 27 years old and had a history of severe, untreatable epileptic seizures. H.M.'s doctors located the brain area where the seizures seemed to originate. In desperation, they surgically removed portions of the medial (inner) temporal lobe on each side of H.M.'s brain, including the brain structure called the *hippocampus*.

After the experimental surgery, the frequency and severity of H.M.'s seizures were greatly reduced. However, another effect was quickly discovered. H.M.'s ability to form new memories of events and information had been destroyed. Although intended to treat H.M.'s seizures, the surgery had dramatically revealed the role of the hippocampus in forming new explicit memories for episodic and semantic information.

Psychologists **Brenda Milner** and **Suzanne Corkin** have studied H.M. extensively over the last 50 years (Corkin, 1984; Milner, 1970; Scoville & Milner, 1957). Today, H.M. is approaching his 80th birthday. If you were to meet H.M., he would appear normal enough. He has a good vocabulary and social skills, normal intelligence, and a delightful sense of humor. And he is well aware of his memory problem. When neuroscientist Suzanne Corkin (2002) asked him, "What do you do to try to remember?" he replied, "Well, that I don't know because I don't remember (chuckle) what I tried."

But H.M. lives in the eternal present. If you left his room and returned five minutes later, he wouldn't remember your name or having seen you before. He must be reintroduced to his doctors each time he sees them, even though some of them have been treating him for years (Ogden & Corkin, 1991).

For the most part, H.M.'s short-term memory seems to work just fine. If he actively repeats or rehearses information, he can hold it in short-term memory for an hour or more. However, he forgets the information if he switches his attention to something else and stops rehearsing it. H.M.'s long-term memory is also partially intact. He can retrieve long-term memories from before the time he was 16 years old, when the severe epileptic seizures began.

Disrupting the Consolidation of Memories Head injuries are common in football and many other sports. In one study, football players who were questioned immediately after a concussion or other head injury could remember how they were injured and the name of the play just performed. But if questioned 30 minutes later for the same information, they could not. Because the head injury had disrupted the memory consolidation process, the memories were permanently lost (Yarnell & Lynch, 1970).

Brenda Milner Born in England in 1918, Milner studied at Cambridge and immigrated to Canada shortly after World War II. Her groundbreaking research at the Montreal Neurological Institute—including the decades she spent working with the famous patient, H.M.—helped establish the field of neuropsychology.

Suzanne Corkin Since the mid-1960s, MIT neuropsychologist Suzanne Corkin has evaluated different aspects of H.M.'s memory abilities. In looking back on H.M.'s life, Corkin (2002) commented, "We all understand the rare opportunity we have had to work with him, and we are grateful for his dedication to research. He has taught us a great deal about the cognitive and neural organization of memory. We are in his debt."

In general, H.M. is unable to acquire new long-term memories of events (episodic information) or general knowledge (semantic information). However, every now and then, H.M. surprises his doctors and visitors with some bit of knowledge that he acquired after the surgery (see In Focus Box 6.4).

H.M.'s case suggests that the hippocampus is not involved in most short-term memory tasks, nor is it the storage site for already established long-term memories. Instead, the critical role played by the hippocampus seems to be the *encoding* of new memories for events and information and the *transfer* of them from short-term to long-term memory.

Implicit and Explicit Memory in Anterograde Amnesia The case of H.M. and those of other patients with anterograde amnesia have also contributed to our understanding of the distinction between implicit and explicit memory. As discussed earlier in the chapter, *implicit memories* are memories without conscious awareness. In contrast, *explicit memories* are memories with conscious awareness.

H.M. cannot readily form new episodic or semantic memories, which reflect the explicit memory system. But it turns out that H.M. *can* form new procedural memories, which reflect the implicit memory system. For example, when H.M. was given the same logical puzzle to solve several days in a row, he was able to solve it more quickly each day. This improvement showed that at some level he implicitly "remembered" the procedure involved in solving the puzzle. But if you asked H.M. if he had ever seen the puzzle before, he would answer "no" because he could not consciously (or explicitly) remember having learned how to solve the puzzle. Apparently, the hippocampus is less crucial to the formation of new implicit memories, such as procedural memories, than it is to the formation of new explicit memories.

Is H.M. an exception? No. Many studies have been conducted with other amnesia patients who have experienced damage to the hippocampus and related brain structures (e.g., Bayley & Squire, 2002). Like H.M., these patients are unable to form new explicit memories, but their performances on implicit memory tasks, which do not require conscious recollection of the new information, are much closer to normal (Schacter, 1998). Such findings suggest that implicit and explicit memory processes involve different brain regions.

Brain Structures Involved in Memory

FIGURE 6.11 Brain Structures Involved in Human Memory Shown here are some of the key brain structures involved in encoding and storing memories.

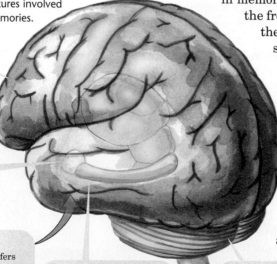

Prefrontal Cortex
Memory involving the sequence of events, but not the events themselves

Amygdala
Encodes emotional aspects of memories

Medial Temporal Lobe
(not visible) Encodes and transfers new explicit memories to long-term memory

Hippocampus
Encodes and transfers new explicit memories to long-term memory

Cerebellum
Memories involving movement

Along with the hippocampus, several other brain regions are involved in memory tasks, including the amygdala, the cerebellum, and the frontal cortex (see Figure 6.11). As you saw on page 245, the *cerebellum* is involved in classically conditioning simple reflexes, such as the eye-blink reflex. The cerebellum is also involved in procedural memories and other motor skill memories.

The *amygdala,* which is situated very close to the hippocampus, is involved in encoding and storing the emotional qualities associated with particular memories, such as fear or anger (McGaugh, 2004). For example, normal monkeys are afraid of snakes. But if the amygdala is damaged, a monkey loses its fear of snakes and other natural predators. The amygdala is also involved in encoding memories of sensory stimuli that are associated with rewards and punishments (Rolls, 2000).

The *frontal lobes* are involved in retrieving and organizing information that is associated with autobiographical and episodic memories (Greenberg & Rubin, 2003). The *prefrontal cortex* seems to play

IN FOCUS 6.4

H.M. and Famous People

When his hippocampus was removed, H.M. lost the ability to quickly encode new semantic and episodic memories. For example, he is unable to learn new vocabulary words or remember people he has met. But is the hippocampus necessary for *all* semantic learning? Or is it possible that other brain areas might support some limited learning of new knowledge?

To test this idea, psychologists Gail O'Kane, Elizabeth Kensinger, and Suzanne Corkin (2004) evaluated H.M. for his knowledge of people who became famous after his surgery in 1953. On the first day, H.M. was given the famous person's first name as a cue and asked to say the last name that came to his mind. Examples were "Elvis_____ (Presley)" and "Fidel _____ (Castro)," who first became famous during the 1950s; "Lyndon _____ (Johnson)" and "Ray _____ (Charles)" from the 1960s; "Sophia _____ (Loren)" from the 1970s; and "Ronald _____ (Reagan)" from the 1980s. H.M. was able to correctly supply the last name of 12 out of 35 famous people including Martin Luther King, Sophia Loren, and Ronald Reagan.

In a second test on the next day, H.M. was able to generate the last names for an additional 11 famous people after being given background information about them. For example, provided with the details "famous artist, born in Spain, formulated Cubism, works include *Guernica*," H.M. responded "Picasso" to the cue "first name is Pablo."

H.M.'s ability to generate the last names of well-known people indicates that he has acquired some declarative semantic knowledge. O'Kane and her colleagues (2004) wondered whether H.M. could go beyond this superficial knowledge and provide specific details. In a different test, H.M. was able to provide two or more pieces of information about 12 people who had become prominent after the onset of his amnesia. For example, after correctly identifying John F. Kennedy as a famous person, H.M. indicated that Kennedy was Catholic, had become president, that somebody shot him, and that he didn't survive. H.M. was also able to provide details about John Glenn, Ray Charles, Woody Allen, Liza Minelli, and Sophia Loren.

According to O'Kane and her colleagues (2004), "These results provide robust, unambiguous evidence that at least some semantic learning can be supported by structures beyond the hippocampus." However, the limitations of H.M.'s semantic learning must also be stressed. H.M. is still unable to quickly acquire new semantic or episodic memories. It was only after years of extended repetitions of information that H.M. acquired limited bits and pieces of new knowledge about some famous people.

---

an important role in memory as well, especially in the ability to remember the order of information.

The *medial temporal lobes*, like the frontal lobes, do not actually store the information that comprises our autobiographical memories. Rather, they are involved in encoding complex memories, by forming links among the information stored in multiple brain regions (Greenberg & Rubin, 2003). As we described in the Focus on Neuroscience on page 246, retrieving a memory can activate multiple brain regions.

Alzheimer's Disease
Gradually Losing the Ability to Remember

Understanding how the brain processes and stores memories has important implications. **Dementia** is a broad term that refers to the decline and impairment of memory, reasoning, language, and other cognitive functions. These cognitive disruptions occur to such an extent that they interfere with daily activities. Dementia is not a disease itself. Rather, it describes a group of symptoms that often accompanies a disease or a condition.

The most common cause of dementia is **Alzheimer's disease (AD).** It is estimated that about 4.5 million Americans suffer from AD. That number is expected

dementia
Progressive deterioration and impairment of memory, reasoning, and other cognitive functions occurring as the result of a disease or a condition.

Alzheimer's disease (AD)
A progressive disease that destroys the brain's neurons, gradually impairing memory, thinking, language, and other cognitive functions, resulting in the complete inability to care for oneself; the most common form of *dementia*.

focus on

Neuroscience: Mapping Brain Changes in Alzheimer's Disease

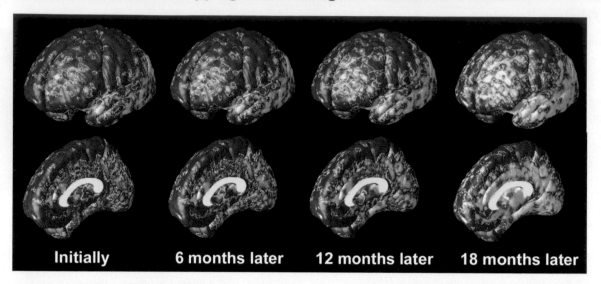

| Initially | 6 months later | 12 months later | 18 months later |

The hallmark of Alzheimer's disease is its relentless, progressive destruction of neurons in the brain, turning once-healthy tissue into a tangled, atrophied mass. This progressive loss of brain tissue is dramatically revealed in the MRI images shown here. Created by neuroscientist Paul Thompson and his colleagues (2003), these high-resolution "brain maps" represent composite images of the progressive effects of Alzheimer's disease (AD) in 12 patients over the course of two years. In these color-coded images, blue corresponds to normal tissue (no loss), red indicates up to 10 percent tissue loss, and white indicates up to 20 percent tissue loss.

Thompson likens the progression of AD to that of molten lava flowing around rocks—the disease leaves islands of brain tissue unscathed. The disease first attacks the temporal lobes, affecting areas involved in memory, especially short-term memory. Next affected are the frontal areas, which are involved in thinking, reasoning, self-control, and planning ahead. You can also see significant internal loss in limbic areas, which are involved in regulating emotion. At this point in the progression of AD, there is very little loss in sensory and visual brain areas. Eventually, however, the disease engulfs the entire brain.

to dramatically escalate as the "baby boomers" reach age 65 and beyond. The disease usually doesn't begin until after age 60, but the risk goes up with age. About 5 percent of men and women in the 65–74 age group have AD. Among adults age 85 and older, about half may have Alzheimer's disease (Hebert & others, 2003).

In the last 30 years, researchers have made enormous strides in understanding AD. Today it is known that the brains of AD patients develop an abundance of two abnormal structures—*beta-amyloid plaques* and *neurofibrillary tangles* (Shoghi-Jadid & others, 2002). The plaques are dense deposits of protein and other cell materials outside and around neurons. The tangles are twisted fibers that build up inside the neuron. Although most older people develop some plaques and tangles in their brains, the brains of AD patients have them to a much greater extent (Petersen, 2002). In the Focus on Neuroscience, you can vividly see the progressive loss of neurons that is the root cause of Alzheimer's disease.

In the early stages of AD, the symptoms of memory impairment are often mild, such as forgetting the names of familiar people, forgetting the location of familiar places, or forgetting to do things (Huppert & others, 2000). But as the disease progresses, memory loss and confusion become more pervasive. The person becomes unable to remember what month it is or the names of family members. Frustrated and disoriented by the inability to retrieve even simple information, the person can become agitated and moody. In the last stage of AD, brain damage is widespread. The person no longer recognizes loved ones and is unable to communicate in any meaningful way. All sense of self and identity has vanished. At the closing stages, the person becomes completely incapacitated and dies (National Institute on Aging, 2002).

Researchers still don't know what causes Alzheimer's disease. But what is known is that the disease extracts an enormous toll on both the person with AD and the family and caregivers who provide long-term daily care for that person. Not only is there a financial toll, but families and caregivers struggle with great physical and emotional stress as they try to cope with the mental and physical changes occurring in their loved one.

Today, there are many more resources available to help support families and other caregivers, such as the Alzheimer's Disease Education & Referral Center (www.alzheimers.org). On the horizon, there is hope as researchers learn more about treating and preventing Alzheimer's disease, including the possibility of a vaccine (see Raskind & others, 2004; Zandi & others, 2004).

Closing Thoughts

Human memory is at once both perfectly ordinary and quite extraordinary. With next to no mental effort, you form and recall countless memories as you go through daily life. Psychologists have made enormous progress in explaining how those memories are encoded, stored, retrieved, and forgotten.

Perhaps the most fascinating aspect of human memory is its fallibility. Memory is surprisingly susceptible to errors and distortions. Under some conditions, completely false memories can be experienced, such as Elizabeth Loftus's memory of discovering her mother's body in the swimming pool. Such false memories can be so subjectively compelling that they feel like authentic memories, yet confidence in a memory is not proof of the memory's truth.

Many mysteries of human memory remain, including exactly how memories are stored in and retrieved from the brain. Nevertheless, reliable ways of improving memory in everyday life have been discovered. In the Application we provide several suggestions to enhance your memory for new information.

APPLICATION	Superpower Memory in Minutes per Day!

Yes, that's what many memory self-help programs promise you. But after you cut through all the hype, what you are left with? Mostly what we're going to give you in this application—some well-established and effective but less-than-magical strategies to help boost your memory for important information.

1. Focus your attention.

Problems in absorbing new information arise when distracting thoughts, background noise, and other interruptions sidetrack your attention. Television is one common culprit (Armstrong & Sopory, 1997). Rather than studying in front of the tube, locate a quiet study space that's free from distractions so you can focus your attention. If distracting thoughts are competing for your attention, start your study session by reading aloud part of what you need to study (Hertel & Rude, 1991).

2. Commit the necessary time.

The more time you spend learning material, the better you will understand it and the longer you will remember it. Budget enough time to read the assigned material carefully. If you read material faster than you can comprehend it, you not only won't understand the material, you also won't remember it.

3. Space your study sessions.

Distributed practice means that you learn information over several sessions, which gives you time to mentally process and incorporate the information (Bjork, 2001; Son, 2004). Students who take the distributed-practice approach to learning retain significantly more information than students who use cramming, or *massed practice*.

4. Organize the information.

We have a strong natural tendency to organize information in long-term memory into categories. You can capitalize on this tendency by actively organizing information you want to remember. One way to

NON SEQUITUR

accomplish this is by outlining chapters or your lecture notes. Use the chapter headings and subheadings as categories, or, better yet, create your own categories. Under each category, list and describe the relevant terms, concepts, and ideas. This strategy can double the amount of information you can recall.

5. Elaborate on the material.

You've probably noticed that virtually every term or concept in this text is formally defined in just a sentence or two. But we also spend a paragraph or more explaining what the concept means. In order to remember the information you read, you have to do the same thing—engage in *elaborative rehearsal* and actively process the information for meaning (see page 224). Actively question new information and think about its implications. Form memory associations by relating the material to what you already know. Try to come up with examples that relate to your own life.

6. Use visual imagery.

Two memory codes are better than one (Paivio, 1986). Rather than merely encoding the information verbally, use mental imagery (Tindall-Ford & others, 1997). Much of the information in this text easily lends itself to visual imagery. Use the photographs and other illustrations to help form visual memories of the information. A simple way to make text information visually distinct is to highlight different concepts in different colors.

7. Use a mnemonic device.

A *mnemonic device* is a method or strategy to aid memory. Some of the most effective mnemonic devices use visual imagery. For example, the *method of loci* is a mnemonic device in which you remember items by visualizing them at specific locations in a familiar setting, such as the different rooms in your house or at specific locations on your way to work or school. To recall the items, mentally revisit the locations and imagine the specific item at that location.

Another mnemonic that involves creating visual associations is the *peg-word method*. First, you learn an easily remembered list containing the peg words, such as: 1 is bun, 2 is shoe, 3 is tree, 4 is door, 5 is hive, 6 is sticks, 7 is heaven, 8 is gate, 9 is vine, 10 is a hen, and you can keep going as needed. Then, you create a vivid mental image associating the first item you want to remember with the first peg word, the next item with the next peg word, and so on. To recall the list, use each successive peg word to help retrieve the mental image.

8. Explain it to a friend.

Memory research clearly supports the benefits of explaining new material out loud (Muth & others, 1988). After you read a section of material, stop. Summarize what you have read in your mind. When you think you understand it, try to explain the information to a friend or a family member.

9. Reduce interference within a topic.

If you occasionally confuse related terms and concepts, it may be because you're experiencing *interference* in your memories for similar information. To minimize memory interference for related information, first break the chapter into manageable sections, then learn the key information one section at a time. As you encounter new concepts, compare them with previously learned concepts, looking for differences and similarities. By building distinct memories for important information as you progress through a topic, you're more likely to distinguish between concepts so they don't get confused in your memory.

10. Counteract the serial position effect.

The *serial position effect* is our tendency to remember information at the beginning and end of a sequence. To counteract it, spend extra time with the information that falls in the middle. Once you've mastered a sequence of material, start at a different point each time you review the information.

11. Use contextual cues to jog memories.

Ideally, study in the setting in which you're going to be tested. If that's not possible, when you're taking a test and a specific memory gets blocked, imagine that your books and notes are in front of you and that you're sitting where you normally study. Simply imagining the surroundings where you learned the material can help jog those memories.

12. Sleep on it to help consolidate those memories.

It's been shown that sleep helps consolidate new memories. (Don't try this as an excuse in class.) Non-REM sleep (non-dreaming) seems to help consolidate declarative memories, while dreaming REM sleep seems to help consolidate procedural memories (Karni & others, 1994; Wixted, 2004). All-night cram sessions just before an exam are one of the *least* effective ways to learn new material.

13. Forget the ginkgo biloba.

Think you can supercharge the memory banks by taking the herb *ginkgo biloba*? If only it were that easy! Researcher Paul R. Solomon and his colleagues (2002) pitted ginkgo against a placebo in a randomized, double-blind study for six weeks involving over 200 participants who were mentally healthy. The bottom line? No effect. The ginkgo biloba did not improve performance on tests of learning, memory, attention, or concentration.

Chapter Review

Key Points

Introduction: What Is Memory?

- **Memory** refers to the mental processes that enable us to acquire, retain, and retrieve information. Key memory processes are **encoding, storage,** and **retrieval.**

The Stage Model of Memory

- The **stage model of memory** describes human memory as the process of transferring information from one memory stage to another. The three stages of memory are sensory memory, short-term memory, and long-term memory.

- **Sensory memory** briefly stores information about the environment. Information that we attend to is transferred from sensory memory to short-term memory; other information fades quickly.

- George Sperling discovered that visual sensory memory holds information for about half a second before the information fades.

- There is a separate sensory memory for each sense. Visual and auditory sensory memory are the most thoroughly studied. Auditory sensory memory lasts up to a few seconds.

- **Short-term memory** provides temporary storage for information transferred from sensory memory and information recalled from **long-term memory. Maintenance rehearsal** keeps information active in short-term memory. Either because of decay or interference, information that is not rehearsed is lost within about 20 seconds.

- The capacity of short-term memory is limited to about seven items, plus or minus two. **Chunking** can be used to increase the amount of information held in short-term memory.

- Alan Baddeley's model of **working memory** has three components: the phonological loop, visuospatial sketchpad, and central executive. Working memory is the short-term memory system that involves the active, conscious manipulation of verbal or spatial information.

- Long-term memory stores a limitless amount of information for extended periods of time.

- Encoding transforms information into a form that can be stored and retrieved later. The most effective encoding strategies involve **elaborative rehearsal.**

- Long-term memory includes **procedural, episodic,** and **semantic memory. Explicit memories** can be consciously recalled. **Implicit memories** cannot be consciously recalled, but affect behavior or performance. Information in long-term memory is **clustered** into related groups during recall. The **semantic network model** describes the organization of long-term memory.

Retrieval: *Getting Information from Long-Term Memory*

- **Retrieval** refers to the process of accessing information stored in long-term memory.

- **Retrieval cues** are hints that help us retrieve stored memories. Sometimes stored memories cannot be retrieved because of **retrieval cue failure,** such as in **tip-of-the-tongue (TOT) experiences.**

- Retrieval can be tested using **recall, cued recall,** and **recognition** measures. The **serial position effect** is our tendency to remember best the first and last items in a series.

- According to the **encoding specificity principle,** recreating aspects of the original learning conditions is one way to increase retrieval effectiveness. Examples of the encoding specificity principle include the **context effect** and **mood congruence.**

- Memories that are highly unusual tend to be easier to retrieve from long-term memory. **Flashbulb memories** can be extremely vivid, but, like normal memories, they are not always accurate.

Forgetting: *When Retrieval Fails*

- **Forgetting** refers to the inability to recall information that was previously available.

- The general pattern of forgetting is reflected in the forgetting curve, which is based on the classic research of Hermann Ebbinghaus.

- Psychologists have identified several factors that contribute to forgetting. **Encoding failure,** one cause of forgetting, is especially common when attention is divided. Divided attention may contribute to **déjà vu** experiences. Retrieval cue failure is implicated in **prospective memory** failures. **Decay theory** makes sense intuitively but has little research support. According to **interference theory,** forgetting results from **retroactive** and **proactive interference** with other information. Motivated forgetting can result from **suppression** or **repression.** Research support for repression is mixed.

Imperfect Memories: *Errors, Distortions, and False Memories*

- Misidentification by eyewitnesses is the leading cause of false conviction in rape and murder cases. Because retrieval involves the reconstruction of memories, memory details can become distorted. The **misinformation effect** and **source confusion** are both potential causes of eyewitness error and **false memories. Schemas** and **scripts** also contribute to memory errors.

- **Imagination inflation** helps explain how false memories of childhood experiences can be created. Being lost in a shopping mall and putting Slime in the teacher's desk in elementary school are some examples of false memory studies. Imagining vivid sensory details adds greatly to confidence in false memories.

The Search for the Biological Basis of Memory

- After extensive research, Karl Lashley concluded that memories are distributed rather than localized as a **memory trace.** Richard Thompson showed the physical changes that are associated with a simple conditioned reflex in rabbits. Today, it is believed that memories are both localized and distributed. Complex memories involve interrelated changes among many different brain areas.

- Eric Kandel showed that functional and structural changes in neurons are associated with acquiring a conditioned reflex in the sea snail *Aplysia.* Enduring memories are believed to be stored through **long-term potentiation,** a long-lasting increase in synaptic strength.

- **Retrograde amnesia** results when **memory consolidation** is disrupted. **Anterograde amnesia** results when the hippocampus is damaged, as in the case of H.M. **Amnesia** affects episodic memories rather than procedural memories and explicit memory rather than implicit memory. Brain structures involved in memory include the hippocampus, the amygdala, the cerebellum, the frontal lobes, the medial temporal lobes, and the prefrontal cortex. Impaired memory is a symptom of senile dementia and Alzheimer's disease.

- **Alzheimer's disease (AD)** is the most common cause of **dementia,** which refers to impairment in memory, reasoning, language, and other cognitive functions.

Key Terms

memory, p. 218

encoding, p. 218

storage, p. 218

retrieval, p. 218

stage model of memory, p. 219

sensory memory, p. 219

short-term memory, p. 219

long-term memory, p. 219

maintenance rehearsal, p. 222

chunking, p. 222

working memory, p. 223

elaborative rehearsal, p. 224

procedural memory, p. 226

episodic memory, p. 226

semantic memory, p. 226

explicit memory, p. 226

implicit memory, p. 226

clustering, p. 228

semantic network model, p. 228

retrieval, p. 229

retrieval cue, p. 229

retrieval cue failure, p. 229

tip-of-the-tongue (TOT) experience, p. 230

recall, p. 230

cued recall, p. 230

recognition, p. 230

serial position effect, p. 231

encoding specificity principle, p. 231

context effect, p. 232

mood congruence, p. 232

flashbulb memory, p. 232

forgetting, p. 233

encoding failure, p. 235

prospective memory, p. 235

déjà vu, p. 236

source memory (source monitoring), p. 236

decay theory, p. 236

interference theory, p. 237

retroactive interference, p. 237

proactive interference, p. 237

suppression, p. 237

repression, p. 238

misinformation effect, p. 239

source confusion, p. 240

false memory, p. 240

schema, p. 240

script, p. 240

imagination inflation, p. 242

memory trace, p. 243

long-term potentiation, p. 247

amnesia, p. 248

retrograde amnesia, p. 249

memory consolidation, p. 249

anterograde amnesia, p. 249

dementia, p. 251

Alzheimer's disease (AD), p. 251

Key People

Suzanne Corkin (b. 1937)   American neuropsychologist who has extensively investigated the neural basis of memory, including several investigations of the famous amnesia patient H.M. (p. 249)

Hermann Ebbinghaus (1850–1909)   German psychologist who originated the scientific study of forgetting; plotted the first forgetting curve, which describes the basic pattern of forgetting learned information over time. (p. 233)

Eric Kandel (b. 1929)   American neurobiologist, born in Austria, who won a Nobel Prize in 2000 for his work on the neural basis of learning and memory in the sea snail *Aplysia*. (p. 247)

Karl Lashley (1890–1958)   American physiological psychologist who attempted to find the specific brain location of particular memories. (p. 243)

Elizabeth F. Loftus (b. 1944)   American psychologist who has conducted extensive research on the memory distortions that can occur in eyewitness testimony. (p. 239)

Brenda Milner (b. 1918)   Canadian neuropsychologist whose groundbreaking research on the role of brain structures and functions in cognitive processes helped establish neuropsychology as a field; extensively studied the famous amnesia patient H.M. (p. 249).

George Sperling (b. 1934)   American psychologist who identified the duration of visual sensory memory in a series of classic experiments in 1960. (p. 220)

Richard F. Thompson (b. 1930)   American psychologist and neuroscientist who has conducted extensive research on the neurobiological foundations of learning and memory. (p. 244)

Web Companion   Review Activities

You can find additional review activities by going to **www.DiscoveringPsychology.com** and clicking on the *Discovering Psychology* 4th Edition text cover. At the Discovering Psychology Web Companion you'll find the chapter learning objectives, flashcards for key terms and key people, interactive crossword puzzles, self-scoring practice quizzes, and other materials to help you master the information in this chapter.

Judgment Day

Thinking, Language, and Intelligence

Prologue Mr. and Ms. Fix-It

"I found it! The rubber gasket between the sink and faucet is leaking!" Don yelled from under the kitchen sink.

"The *basket* is leaking!" our then-3-year-old daughter, Laura, who was holding the flashlight, enthusiastically relayed to Sandy.

"The *basket* is leaking?" Sandy asked. "What basket?"

"No, it's called a *gasket,* not a *basket,* honey," Don explained to Laura.

"Can you fix it?" Sandy asked.

"Piece of cake," Don replied as he crawled out from under the sink. "Laura and I will run down to the hardware store and just buy a new gasket."

Of course, the solution would not be that simple. "They don't sell *just* the gasket," the clerk at the hardware store explained. "You have to buy a whole new faucet."

"What's that going to run me?"

"Kitchen faucets start at $39.95 plus tax," the hardware guy said, smiling. "Then you'll need some replacement tubing for when you weld the new faucet in place. You have a welding torch, don't you? If you don't, a plumber probably wouldn't charge more than $150 or so to install it, not including the cost of the parts."

"Let me think about it," Don replied, frowning.

"Why didn't we buy a new basket?" Laura asked as she and Don walked out of the hardware store.

"It's called a *gasket,* Laura," Don explained. "It's just a piece of rubber that fits between two pieces of metal. It keeps the water that splashes around the faucet from dripping under the sink. Does that make sense?"

"I think so," Laura said thoughtfully. "Why didn't we buy one?"

"Because they want too much money for it," Don answered as he buckled Laura into her car seat.

As Laura chattered away on the drive home, Don mulled over calling a plumber. *A couple hundred bucks to replace a lousy piece of rubber. That's ridiculous.*

"We'll make one!" Don suddenly exclaimed.

"Make what, Daddy?" Laura responded, slightly startled.

"A new gasket! And best of all, Laura, it won't cost a cent!"

Less than five minutes later, Don and Laura were at a General Tire store. "Help yourself," the manager replied when Don asked if he could have a discarded inner tube. An hour later, the new "gasket" was in place—a piece of black rubber inner tube that Don had cut to the same shape as the original gasket. It worked like a charm. No drips.

"You missed your calling in life," Sandy quipped as Don stood basking in the glory of the moment.

cognition
The mental activities involved in acquiring, retaining, and using knowledge.

thinking
The manipulation of mental representations of information in order to draw inferences and conclusions.

mental image
A mental representation of objects or events that are not physically present.

"Hey, you just have to think creatively," Don replied, smiling.

Unfortunately, creative thinking is not always the answer. A few weeks later, when the upstairs toilet wouldn't flush properly, Mr. Fix-It spent almost two hours dismantling and lifting the entire toilet off the floor drain in search of the cause.

"You're sure you didn't flush one of your toys down the toilet?" Don asked Laura again.

"No, Daddy," Laura said solemnly, shaking her head, as she peered down the ominous-looking drain in the floor with her Barney flashlight.

"Well, I don't know what the hell is wrong with it," Don announced in frustration, wiping the sweat from his brow.

Sitting on the floor in the corner of the bathroom, Sandy flipped through the pages of a book called *The Complete Home Fix-It-Yourself Manual.* "Did you look at this book? There's a troubleshooting guide for toilets on this page."

"No, I did *not* look at it," Don huffed cynically. "I *know* how to unblock a toilet. First, you try a plunger. If that doesn't work, then you take the toilet off to find whatever is blocking the drain."

"That's what it lists to try *third* in this book," Sandy pointed out calmly. "What was the water level inside the tank?"

"It was a couple inches down from the fill line," Don answered.

"Well, it says here that if the water level is too low, the toilet bowl will drain sluggishly," Sandy explained matter-of-factly, then glanced up. "Did you try raising the water level to the fill line *before* you took the toilet apart?"

Silence loomed in the bathroom.

Well over an hour later Laura excitedly called downstairs to Sandy, "Mama! Mama! Come see! Daddy fixed the toilet."

"What was wrong with it?" Sandy innocently asked as she watched the toilet flush perfectly.

"The water level was just too low," Don replied, then cleared his throat.

"You're kidding!" Sandy feigned disbelief. "That must have been why it was listed as the *first* thing to check in that troubleshooting guide."

"I think you missed your calling in life," Don muttered.

"Well, you know what I always say, 'When in doubt, look it up!'" Sandy smiled.

All of us rely on a variety of cognitive processes to imagine, think, make decisions, and solve problems in daily life. In this chapter, we'll look at the broad issue of how we think, including how we solve problems, make decisions, and occasionally arrive at creative solutions. In the process, we'll come back to this story of Mr. and Ms. Fix-It to illustrate several important concepts and ideas.

Introduction

Thinking, Language, and Intelligence

Key Theme
- *Thinking* is a broad term that refers to how we use knowledge to analyze situations, solve problems, and make decisions.

Key Questions
- What are some of the basic characteristics of mental images?
- How do we manipulate mental images?
- What are concepts, and how are they formed?

Cognition is a general term that refers to the mental activities involved in acquiring, retaining, and using knowledge. In previous chapters, we've looked at fundamental cognitive processes such as perception, learning, and memory. These processes are critical in order for us to acquire and retain new knowledge.

In this chapter, we will focus on how we *use* that knowledge to analyze situations, solve problems, make decisions, and use language. As you'll see, such cognitive abilities are widely regarded as key dimensions of *intelligence*—a concept that we will also explore.

The Building Blocks of Thought
Mental Imagery and Concepts

In the most general sense, *thinking* is involved in all conscious mental activity, whether it is acquiring new knowledge, remembering, planning ahead, or daydreaming (Holyoak & Spellman, 1993). More narrowly, we can say that **thinking** involves manipulating mental representations of information in order to draw inferences and conclusions. Thinking, then, involves active mental processes and is often directed toward some goal, purpose, or conclusion.

What exactly is it that we think *with*? Thinking often involves the manipulation of two forms of mental representations: *mental images* and *concepts*. We'll look first at mental images.

Mental Images

When you read the Prologue, did you form a mental picture of a little girl peering down a cavernous floor drain with her Barney flashlight? Or Sandy sitting in the corner of the bathroom, looking at the home repair manual? The stories we tell in our prologues typically lend themselves to the creation of mental images. Formally, a **mental image** is a mental representation of objects or events that are not physically present.

We often rely on mental images to accomplish some cognitive task (Farah, 1995). For example, try reciting the letters of the alphabet that consist of only curved lines. To accomplish this task, you have to mentally visualize and then inspect an image of each letter of the alphabet.

Note that mental imagery is not strictly limited to visual "pictures." Most people are able to form images that involve senses other than vision (McKellar, 1972; Djordjevic & others, 2004). For example, you can probably easily create a mental representation for the taste and texture of a chocolate milk shake or the feel of wet clothing sticking to your skin. Nonetheless, most research on mental images has looked at how we manipulate visual images, and we'll focus on visual images in our discussion here.

Do people manipulate mental images in the same way that they manipulate their visual images of actual objects? Suppose we gave you a map of the United States and asked you to visually locate San Francisco. Then suppose we asked you to fix your gaze on another city. If the other city was far away from San Francisco (like New York), it would take you longer to visually locate it than if it was close by (like Los Angeles). If you were scanning a *mental* image rather than an actual map, would it also take you longer to scan across a greater distance?

In a classic study by Stephen Kosslyn and his colleagues (1978), participants first viewed and memorized a map of a fictitious island with distinct locations, such as a lake, a hut, and grass (see Figure 7.1). After the map was removed, participants were asked to imagine a specific location on the island, such as the sandy beach. Then a second location, such as the rock, was named. The participants mentally scanned across their mental image of the map and pushed a button when they reached the rock.

The researchers found that the amount of time it took to mentally scan to the new location was directly related to the distance between the two points. The greater the distance between the two points, the longer it took to scan the mental image of the map (Kosslyn & others, 1978). It seems, then, that we tend to scan a mental image in much the same way that we visually scan an actual image (Kosslyn & Thompson, 2000).

Thinking What types of cognitive activities might be involved in planning and executing a new line in the fashion industry? Drawing on existing knowledge and analyzing information about current trends would be required, as would forming mental images, solving problems, and making decisions. All of these mental activities would be involved in launching a new clothing line, just as they would be in any successful business venture.

FIGURE 7.1 Mentally Scanning Images This is a reduced version of the map used by Stephen Kosslyn and his colleagues (1978) to study the scanning of mental images. After subjects memorized the map, the map was removed. Subjects then mentally visualized the map and scanned from one location to another. As you can see by the average scanning times, it took subjects longer to scan greater distances on their mental images of the map, just as it takes longer to scan greater distances on an actual map.

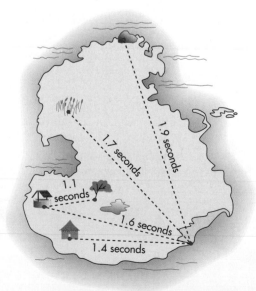

Neuroscience: Seeing Faces and Places in the Mind's Eye

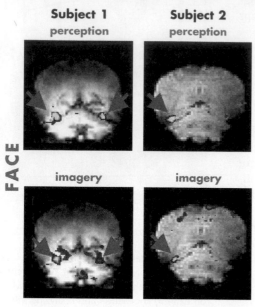

FACE

Subject 1 — perception
Subject 2 — perception

imagery   imagery

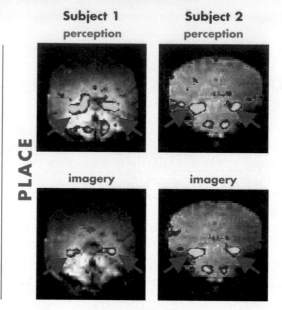

PLACE

Subject 1 — perception
Subject 2 — perception

imagery   imagery

Brain Activation During Perception and Mental Imagery

Shown here are the fMRIs of two participants in O'Craven and Kanwisher's (2000) study. Notice that the same brain areas are activated while perceiving or imagining a familiar face. Likewise, the same brain areas are activated while perceiving or imagining a familiar place. Also notice that the brain activation is slightly stronger in the perception condition than in the mental imagery condition.

Until the advent of sophisticated brain-scanning techniques, studying mental imagery relied on cognitive tasks, such as measuring how long participants reported it took to scan a mental image (see Kosslyn & others, 2001). Today, however, psychologists are using brain-imaging techniques to study mental imagery. One important issue is whether mental images activate the same brain areas that are involved in perception. Remember, perception takes place when the brain registers information that is received directly from sensory organs.

Previously, researchers have found that perceiving certain types of scenes or objects activates specific brain areas. For example, when we look at *faces,* a brain area dubbed the *fusiform facial area (FFA)* is activated. When we look at pictures of *places,* a different brain area, called the *parahippocampal place area,* or *PPA,* is activated (Epstein & Kanwisher, 1998; Kanwisher, 2001). Given these findings, the critical question is this: If we simply *imagine* faces or places, will the same brain areas be activated?

To answer that question, psychologists Kathleen O'Craven and Nancy Kanwisher (2000) used functional magnetic resonance imaging (fMRI) to compare brain activity during perception and imagery. Study participants underwent fMRI scans while they looked at photographs of familiar faces and places (scenes from their college campus). Next, the participants were asked to close their eyes and form a vivid mental image of each of the photographs that they had just viewed.

Three key findings emerged from the study. First, as you can see from the fMRI scans of two participants shown here, *imagining* a face or place activated the same brain region that is activated when *perceiving* a face or a place. More specifically, forming a mental image of a place activated the parahippocampal place area. And, forming a mental image of a face activated the fusiform facial area.

Second, compared to imagining a face or place, actually perceiving a face or place evoked a stronger brain response, as indicated by the slightly larger red and yellow areas in the perception fMRIs (upper row). Third, because the brain responses between the two conditions were so distinctive, O'Craven and Kanwisher could determine what the participants were imagining—faces or places—simply from looking at the fMRI scans.

Other neuroscientists have confirmed that there is considerable overlap in the brain areas involved in visual perception and mental images (Ganis & others, 2004). Clearly, perception and imagination share common brain mechanisms. So, at least as far as the brain is concerned, "the next best thing to being there" might just be closing your eyes . . . and going there in your mind's eye.

However, we don't simply look at mental images in our minds. Sometimes thinking involves the *manipulation* of mental images before we can arrive at an answer. For example, try the problem in Figure 7.2.

It probably took you longer to determine that the 3 in the middle was backward than to determine that the 3 on the far left was backward. Determining which 3s were backward required you to mentally *rotate* each one to an upright position. Just as it takes time to rotate a physical object, it takes time to mentally rotate an image. Furthermore, the greater the degree of rotation required, the longer it takes you to rotate the image mentally (Wohlschläger & Wohlschläger, 1998). Thus, it probably took you longer to mentally rotate the 3 in the middle, which you had to rotate 180 degrees, than it did to mentally rotate the 3 on the far left, which you only had to rotate 60 degrees.

FIGURE 7.2 Manipulating Mental Images Two of these threes are backward. Which ones?

Collectively, research seems to indicate that we manipulate mental images much as we manipulate the actual objects they represent (Rosenbaum & others, 2001). However, mental images are not perfect duplicates of our actual sensory experience. The mental images we use in thinking have some features in common with actual visual images, but they are not like photographs. Instead, they are *memories* of visual images. And, like memories, visual images are actively constructed and potentially subject to error (Reisberg & Chambers, 1991).

Concepts

Along with mental images, thinking also involves the use of concepts. A **concept** is a mental category we have formed to group objects, events, or situations that share similar features or characteristics. Concepts provide a kind of mental shorthand, economizing the cognitive effort required for thinking and communication.

Using concepts makes it easier to communicate with others, remember information, and learn new information. For example, the concept "food" might include anything from a sardine to a rutabaga. Although very different, we can still group rutabagas and sardines together because they share the central feature of being edible. If someone introduces us to a new delicacy and tells us it is *food,* we immediately know that it is something to eat—even if it is something we've never seen before.

Adding to the efficiency of our thinking is our tendency to organize the concepts we hold into orderly hierarchies composed of main categories and subcategories (Markman & Gentner, 2001). Thus a very general concept, such as "furniture," can be mentally divided into a variety of subcategories: tables, chairs, lamps, and so forth. As we learn the key properties that define general concepts, we also learn how members of the concept are related to one another.

How are concepts formed? When we form a concept by learning the *rules* or *features* that define the particular concept, it is called a **formal concept.** Children are taught the specific rules or features that define many simple formal concepts, such as geometric shapes. These defining rules or features can be simple or complex. In either case, the rules are logical but rigid. If the defining features, or *attributes,* are present, then the object is included as a member or example of that concept. For some formal concepts, this rigid all-or-nothing categorization procedure works well. For example, a substance can be categorized as a solid, liquid, or gas. The rules defining these formal concepts are very clear-cut.

However, as psychologist Eleanor Rosch (1973) pointed out, the features that define categories of natural objects and events in everyday life are seldom as clear-cut as the features that define formal concepts. A **natural concept** is a concept formed as a result of everyday experience rather than by logically determining whether an object or event fits a specific set of rules. Rosch suggested that, unlike formal concepts, natural concepts have "fuzzy boundaries." That is, the rules or attributes that define natural concepts are not always sharply defined.

Because natural concepts have fuzzy boundaries, it's often easier to classify some members of natural concepts than others (Rosch & Mervis, 1975). To illustrate this point, think about the defining features or rules that you usually associate with the natural concept "vehicle." With virtually no hesitation, you can say that a car, truck, and bus are all examples of this natural concept. How about a sled? Wheelbarrow? Raft? Elevator? It probably took you a few seconds to determine whether these objects are also vehicles. Why are some members of natural concepts easier to classify than others?

According to Rosch (1978), some members are better representatives of a natural concept than are others. The "best," or most typical, instance of a particular concept is called a **prototype**

concept
A mental category of objects or ideas based on properties they share.

formal concept
A mental category that is formed by learning the rules or features that define it.

natural concept
A mental category that is formed as a result of everyday experience.

prototype
The most typical instance of a particular concept.

Are These Mammals? The more closely an item matches the prototype of a concept, the more quickly we can identify the item as being an example of that concept. Because bats and dolphins don't fit our prototype for a mammal, it takes us longer to decide whether they belong to the category "mammal" than it does to classify animals that are closer to the prototype.

CULTURE AND HUMAN BEHAVIOR 7.2

The Effect of Language on Perception

Professionally, Benjamin Whorf (1897–1941) was an insurance company inspector. But his passion was the study of languages, particularly Native American languages. In the 1950s, Whorf proposed an intriguing theory that became known as the *Whorfian hypothesis.*

Whorf (1956) believed that a person's language determines the very structure of his or her thought and perception. Your language, he claimed, determines how you perceive and "carve up" the phenomena of your world. He argued that people who speak very different languages have completely different worldviews. More formally, the Whorfian hypothesis is called the **linguistic relativity hypothesis**—the notion that differences among languages cause differences in the thoughts of their speakers (Pinker, 1994).

To illustrate his hypothesis, Whorf contended that the Eskimos had many different words for "snow." But English, he pointed out, has only the word *snow.* According to Whorf (1956):

> We have the same word for falling snow, snow on the ground, snow packed hard like ice, slushy snow, wind-driven flying snow—whatever the situation may be. To an Eskimo, this all-inclusive word would be almost unthinkable; he would say that falling snow, slushy snow, and so on are

sensuously and operationally different, different things to contend with; he uses different words for them and for other kinds of snow.

Whorf's example would be compelling except for one problem: The Eskimos do *not* have dozens of different words for "snow." Rather, they have just a few words for "snow" (Martin, 1986; Pullum, 1991). Beyond that minor sticking point, think carefully about Whorf's example. Is it really true that English-speaking people have a limited capacity to describe snow? Or do not discriminate between different types of snow? The English language includes *snowflake, snowfall, slush, sleet, flurry, blizzard,* and *avalanche.* Avid skiers have many additional words to describe snow, from *powder* to *mogul* to *hardpack.*

More generally, people with expertise in a particular area tend to perceive and make finer distinctions than nonexperts do. Experts are also more likely to know the specialized terms that reflect those distinctions (Pinker, 1994). To the knowledgeable birdwatcher, for example, there are distinct differences between a cedar waxwing and a bohemian waxwing. To the nonexpert, they're just two brownish birds with yellow tail feathers.

Despite expert/nonexpert differences in noticing and naming details, we don't claim that the expert "sees" a different reality than a nonexpert. In other words, our perceptions and thought processes influence the language we use to describe those perceptions (Rosch, 1987). Notice that this conclusion is the exact *opposite* of the linguistic relativity hypothesis.

Whorf also pointed out that many languages have different color-naming systems. English has names for 11 basic colors: *black, white, red, green, yellow, blue, brown, purple, pink, orange,* and *gray.* However, some languages have only a few color terms. Navajo, for example, has only one word to describe both blue and green, but two different words for black (Fishman, 1960). Would people who had just a few words for colors "carve up" and perceive the electromagnetic spectrum differently?

Eleanor Rosch set out to answer this question (Heider & Olivier, 1972). The Dani-speaking people of New Guinea have words for only two colors. *Mili* is used for the dark, cool colors of black, green, and blue. *Mola* is used for light, warm colors, such as white, red, and yellow. According to the Whorfian hypothesis, the people of New Guinea, with names for only two classes of colors, should perceive color dif-

---

Further, language is a highly structured system that follows specific rules. Every language has its own unique *syntax,* or set of rules for combining words. Although you're usually unaware of these rules as you're speaking or writing, you immediately notice when a rule has been violated.

The rules of language help determine the meaning that is being communicated. For example, word-order rules are very important in determining the meaning of an English phrase. "The boy ate the giant pumpkin" has an entirely different meaning from "The giant pumpkin ate the boy." In other languages, meaning may be conveyed by different rule-based distinctions, such as specific pronouns, the class or category of word, or word endings (Hunt & Agnoli, 1991).

Another important characteristic of language is that it is creative, or *generative.* That is, you can generate an infinite number of new and different phrases and sentences.

A final important characteristic of human language is called *displacement.* You can communicate meaningfully about ideas, objects, and activities that are not physically present. You can refer to activities that will take place in the future, that took place in the past, or that will take place only if certain conditions are met ("If you get that promotion, maybe we can afford a new car"). You can also

linguistic relativity hypothesis
The hypothesis that differences among languages cause differences in the thoughts of their speakers.

ferently than English-speaking people, with names for 11 basic colors.

Rosch showed Dani speakers a brightly colored chip and then, 30 seconds later, asked them to pick out the color they had seen from an array of other colors. Despite their lack of specific words for the colors they had seen, the Dani did as well as English speakers on the test. The Dani people used the same word to label red and yellow, but they still distinguished between the two. Rosch concluded that the Dani people perceived colors in much the same way as English-speaking people.

Other research on color-naming in different languages has arrived at similar conclusions: Although color *names* may vary, color *perception* does not appear to depend on the language used (Lindsey & Brown, 2004; Delgado, 2004; Kay & Regier, 2003).

The bottom line? Whorf's strong contention that language *determines* perception and the structure of thought has not been supported. However, cultural and cognitive psychologists today are actively investigating the ways in which language can *influence* perception and thought

Can You Count Without Number Words?
Psychologist Peter Gordon (2004) traveled to the remote Amazon. In the test shown here, Gordon has lined up familiar objects on a tray in front of a Pirahã man, whose language does not have a counting system or words for specific quantities above the number two. Gordon asked Pirahã participants to match the arrangement of objects with objects from their own pile. Their accuracy plunged when he used more than three objects.

(Gentner & Goldin-Meadow, 2003; Majid & others, 2004).

A striking demonstration of the influence of language comes from recent studies of two remote indigenous peoples living in the Amazon region of Brazil. The language of the Pirahã people, an isolated tribe of less than 200 members, has words for only three quantities: "one," "two," and "many" (Gordon, 2004). Similarly, the Mundurukú language, spoken by another small Amazon tribe, has words only for quantities one through five (Pica & others, 2004). Above that number, they used such expressions as "some," "many," or "a small quantity." In both cases, individuals were unable to complete simple arithmetical tasks. For example, when shown arrangements of objects in different configurations, the Pirahã were unable to match the configuration of more than three objects. In another test, they could not reliably tell the difference between four and five objects placed in a row.

Such findings do not, by any means, confirm Whorf's belief that language *determines* thinking or perception (Gelman & Gallistel, 2004). Rather, they demonstrate how language categories can affect *how* individuals think about particular concepts.

carry on a vivid conversation about abstract ideas ("What is justice?") or strictly imaginary topics ("If you were going to spend a year in a space station orbiting Neptune, what would you bring along?").

How Language Influences Thinking

All your cognitive abilities are involved in understanding and producing language. Using learning and memory, you acquire and remember the meaning of words. You interpret the words you hear or read (or see, in the case of American Sign Language) through the use of perception. You use language to help you reason, represent and solve problems, and make decisions (Polk & Newell, 1995).

Language can influence thinking in several ways. For example, when you hear about a course titled "Man and His Environment," what image comes to mind? Do you visualize a group of men tromping through the forest, or do you imagine a mixed group of men and women?

The word *man* or the pronouns *he* and *his* can refer to either a male or a female in English, because English has no gender-neutral pronoun. So, according to the rules of the English language, the course title "Man and His Environment" technically refers to both men and women.

"People used to think of Miriam as zany. Later, she was generally perceived as kooky. Now, I'm afraid, the consensus is that she's flaky."

Giving Birth to a New Language In 1977, a special school for deaf children opened in Managua, Nicaragua. For the first time, deaf children had extensive contact with one another, and they quickly developed a system of gestures for communicating with one another. Over the past 30 years, the system of gestures has evolved into a unique new language with its own grammar and syntax (Senghas & others, 2004; Siegal, 2004). Today, *Idioma de Signos Nicaragense* (Nicaraguan Sign Language) is spoken by more than 800 deaf signers, ranging in age from 4 to 45 years old. According to psychologist Ann Senghas (2004), the evolution of Nicaraguan Sign Language demonstrates that humans are innately predisposed to learn the rules of language.

However, several studies have shown that using the masculine pronoun tends to produce images of males and exclude females (Foertsch & Gernsbacher, 1997; Gastil, 1990). In a classic study by Nancy Henley (1989), participants were given identical sentence fragments to complete. Examples included "If a writer expects to get a book published . . ." and "If an employee wants a raise . . ." Participants in the first group were given the masculine generic *he* to use in finishing the sentences. Participants in the second group were given either *they* or *he or she* to use in completing the sentences.

After completing the sentences, the subjects were asked to describe their mental imagery for each sentence and to provide a first name for the person they visualized. When the word *he* was used, subjects were much more likely to produce a male image and name than a female image and name. When the phrase *he or she* was used, subjects were only slightly more likely to use a male rather than a female image and name.

Using the masculine generic pronoun influences people to visualize a male, even when they "know" that *he* supposedly includes both men and women (Hamilton, 1988, 1991). Thus, using *he* to refer to both men and women in speech and writing tends to increase male bias.

Animal Communication

Can Animals Learn Language?

Without question, animals communicate. Chimpanzees "chutter" to warn of snakes, "rraup" to warn of an eagle, and "chirp" to let the others know that a leopard is nearby (Marler, 1967). Each of the warning calls of the vervet monkey of East Africa triggers specific behaviors for a particular danger, such as scurrying for cover in the bushes when the warning for an airborne predator is sounded (Cheney & Seyfarth, 1990). Even insects have complex communication systems. For example, honeybees perform a "dance" to report information about the distance, location, and quality of a pollen source to their hive mates (Esch & others, 2001; Gould & Gould, 1994).

Clearly, animals communicate with one another, but are they capable of mastering language? Some of the most promising results have come from the research of psychologists Sue Savage-Rumbaugh, Duane Rumbaugh, and their co-workers.

Vervet Monkeys Vervet monkeys sound different alarm calls for different kinds of predators. The "leopard" call sends the troop into the trees to avoid leopards and other ground predators. In response to the "eagle" call, the monkeys look up and take cover in bushes to hide from aerial predators.

These researchers are working with a rare chimpanzee species called the *bonobo*. In the mid-1980s, they taught a female bonobo, named Matata, to press symbols on a computer keyboard. Although Matata did not learn many symbols, her infant son, Kanzi, appeared to learn how to use the keyboard simply from watching his mother and her caretakers (Savage-Rumbaugh & Lewin, 1994).

Along with learning symbols, Kanzi also comprehends spoken English. Altogether, Kanzi understands more than 500 spoken English words. And, Kanzi can respond to new, complex spoken commands, such as "Put the ball on the pine needles," and "Can you go scare Matata with the mask?" (Savage-Rumbaugh & others, 1998; Segerdahl & others, 2006). Because these spoken commands are made by an assistant out of Kanzi's view, he cannot be responding to nonverbal cues.

Sue Savage-Rumbaugh with Kanzi Kanzi, a bonobo, communicates by pressing symbols on a computer keyboard. Kanzi uses the symbols to communicate requests and intentions—and even, when alone, to "talk" to himself. Kanzi now resides at the Great Ape Trust in Des Moines, Iowa, in a colony with seven other bonobos, where study of primate cognition continues in a natural environment (Segerdahl & others, 2006). To learn more about the Great Ape Trust sanctuary and the orangutans, bonobos, and research psychologists—including Savage-Rumbaugh—who live and work there, visit the Web site at www.GreatApeTrust.org.

Kanzi also seems to demonstrate an elementary understanding of syntax. He is able to respond correctly to commands whose meaning is determined by word order. For example, using a toy dog and toy snake, he responds appropriately to such commands as "Make the dog bite the snake" and "Make the snake bite the dog" (Savage-Rumbaugh & others, 1998). Kanzi seems to demonstrate a level of language comprehension that is roughly equivalent to that of a 2½-year-old human child.

Research evidence suggests that nonprimates also can acquire limited aspects of language. For example, Louis Herman and his coworkers (1993, 2002) have trained bottle-nosed dolphins to respond to sounds and gestures, each of which stands for a word. This artificial language incorporates syntax rules, such as those that govern word order.

Finally, consider Alex, an African gray parrot. Trained by Irene Pepperberg (1993, 2000), Alex can answer spoken questions with spoken words. After two decades of training, Alex has about a 100-word vocabulary, which includes words for objects, names, shapes, numbers, and simple phrases, such as "Come here," "How many?" and "Want to go." Alex can accurately answer questions about the color and number of objects. He can also categorize objects by color, shape, and material, which suggests that he comprehends simple concepts (Pepperberg & Gordon, 2005).

Irene Pepperberg with Alex Along with his language abilities, Alex displays an understanding of simple concepts. He can categorize objects in terms of their color, shape, size, or material. He also understands the concepts of bigger and smaller, sameness and difference. Shown a green block and a green ball and asked "What's the same?" Alex responds, "Color." Alex can even accurately label quantities up to the number six (Pepperberg & Gordon, 2005). For example, when shown an array of differently colored objects and asked, "How many green block?" Alex responds with the correct number, "Six." Pepperberg's research with Alex and other grey parrots has revolutionized our understanding of avian intelligence. To learn more about Alex and Pepperberg's ongoing research, visit Alex's home page at www.alexfoundation.org.

When animal language research began in the 1960s and 1970s, some critics contended that primates were simply producing learned responses to their trainers' nonverbal cues rather than demonstrating true language skills (Terrace, 1985). Over the last two decades, however studies conducted under more carefully controlled conditions have produced some compelling demonstrations of animal language learning. Nevertheless, even the performance of primate superstars such as Kanzi pales in comparison with the language learning demonstrated by a 3-year-old child (Pinker, 1994).

Collectively, animal language research reflects an active area of psychological research that is referred to as **animal cognition** or *comparative cognition* (Boysen & Hines, 1999; Papini, 2002). Although the results of these studies are fascinating, a great deal remains to be discovered about the potential of different species of animals to communicate, produce language, and solve problems—and their limitations in doing so. Many psychologists caution against jumping to the conclusion that animals can "think" or that they possess self-awareness, because such conclusions are far from proven (Blumberg & Wasserman, 1995).

animal cognition
The study of animal learning, memory, thinking, and language; also called *comparative cognition*.

intelligence
The global capacity to think rationally, act purposefully, and deal effectively with the environment.

intelligence
The global capacity to think rationally, act purposefully, and deal effectively with the environment.

mental age
A measurement of intelligence in which an individual's mental level is expressed in terms of the average abilities of a given age group.

intelligence quotient (IQ)
A measure of general intelligence derived by comparing an individual's score with the scores of others in the same age group.

> *To judge well, to comprehend well, to reason well, these are the essential activities of intelligence.*
>
> Alfred Binet and Théodore Simon (1905)

Alfred Binet French psychologist Alfred Binet (1857–1911) is shown here with an unidentified child and an instrument from his laboratory that was used to measure his young subjects' breathing rates while they performed different tasks (Cunningham, 1997). Although Binet developed the first systematic intelligence tests, he did not believe that he was measuring innate ability. Instead, he believed that his tests could identify schoolchildren who could benefit from special help.

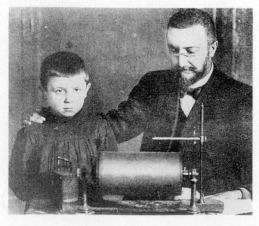

Measuring Intelligence

Key Theme
- *Intelligence* is defined as the global capacity to think rationally, act purposefully, and deal effectively with the environment.

Key Questions
- What roles did Binet, Terman, and Wechsler play in the development of intelligence tests?
- How did Binet, Terman, and Wechsler differ in their beliefs about intelligence and its measurement?
- Why are standardization, validity, and reliability important components of psychological tests?

Up to this point, we have talked about a broad range of cognitive abilities—the use of mental images and concepts, problem solving and decision making, and the use of language. All these mental abilities are aspects of what we commonly call *intelligence*.

What exactly is intelligence? We will rely on a formal definition developed by psychologist David Wechsler. Wechsler (1944, 1977) defined **intelligence** as the global capacity to think rationally, act purposefully, and deal effectively with the environment. Although many people commonly equate intelligence with "book smarts," notice that Wechsler's definition is much broader. To Wechsler, intelligence is reflected in effective, rational, and goal-directed behavior.

The Development of Intelligence Tests

Can intelligence be measured? If so, how? Intelligence tests attempt to measure general mental abilities, rather than accumulated knowledge or aptitude for a specific subject or area. In the next several sections, we will describe the evolution of intelligence tests, including the qualities that make any psychological test scientifically acceptable.

Alfred Binet
Identifying Students Who Needed Special Help

In the early 1900s, the French government passed a law requiring all children to attend school. Faced with the need to educate children from a wide variety of backgrounds, the French government commissioned psychologist **Alfred Binet** to develop procedures to identify students who might require special help.

With the help of French psychiatrist Théodore Simon, Binet devised a series of tests to measure different mental abilities. Binet deliberately did not test abilities, such as reading or mathematics, that the students might have been taught. Instead, he focused on elementary mental abilities, such as memory, attention, and the ability to understand similarities and differences.

Binet arranged the questions on his test in order of difficulty, with the simplest tasks first. He found that brighter children performed like older children. That is, a bright 7-year-old might be able to answer the same number of questions as an average 9-year-old, while a less capable 7-year-old might only do as well as an average 5-year-old.

This observation led Binet to the idea of a mental level, or **mental age,** that was different from a child's chronological age. An "advanced" 7-year-old might have a mental age of 9, while a "slow" 7-year-old might demonstrate a mental age of 5.

It is somewhat ironic that Binet's early tests became the basis for modern intelligence tests. First, Binet did *not* believe that he was measuring an inborn or permanent level of intelligence (Kamin, 1995). Rather, he believed that his tests could help identify "slow" children who could benefit from special help.

Second, Binet believed that intelligence was too complex a quality to describe with a single number (Siegler, 1992). He steadfastly refused to rank "normal" children on the basis of their scores, believing that such rankings would be unfair. He recognized that many individual factors, such as a child's level of motivation, might affect the child's score. Finally, Binet noted that an individual's score could vary from time to time (Fancher, 1996; Gould, 1993).

Lewis Terman and the Stanford-Binet Intelligence Test

There was enormous interest in Binet's test in the United States. The test was translated and adapted by Stanford University psychologist **Lewis Terman.** Terman's revision was called the *Stanford-Binet Intelligence Scale.* First published in 1916, the Stanford-Binet was for many years the standard for intelligence tests in the United States.

Terman adopted the suggestion of a German psychologist that scores on the Stanford-Binet test be expressed in terms of a single number, called the **intelligence quotient,** or **IQ.** This number was derived by dividing the individual's mental age by the chronological age and multiplying the result by 100. Thus, a child of average intelligence, whose mental age and chronological age were the same, would have an IQ score of 100. A "bright" 10-year-old child with a mental age of 13 would have an IQ of 130 ($^{13}/_{10}$ × 100). A "slow" child with a chronological age of 10 and a mental age of 7 would have an IQ of 70 ($^{7}/_{10}$ × 100). It was Terman's use of the intelligence quotient that resulted in the popularization of the phrase "IQ test."

World War I and Group Intelligence Testing

When the United States entered World War I in 1917, the U.S. military was faced with the need to rapidly screen 2 million army recruits. Using a group intelligence test designed by one of Terman's students, army psychologists developed the Army Alpha and Beta tests. The *Army Alpha* test was administered in writing, and the *Army Beta* test was administered orally to recruits and draftees who could not read.

After World War I ended, the Army Alpha and Army Beta group intelligence tests were adapted for civilian use. The result was a tremendous surge in the intelligence-testing movement. Group intelligence tests were designed to test virtually all ages and types of people, including preschool children, prisoners, and newly arriving immigrants (Anastasi, 1988; Kamin, 1995). However, the indiscriminate use of the tests also resulted in skepticism and hostility.

For example, newly arriving immigrants were screened as they arrived at Ellis Island. The result was sweeping generalizations about the intelligence of different nationalities and races. During the 1920s, a few intelligence testing experts even urged the U.S. Congress to severely limit the immigration of certain nationalities to keep the country from being "overrun with a horde of the unfit" (see Kamin, 1995).

Despite concerns about the misuse of the so-called IQ tests, the tests quickly became very popular. Lost was Binet's belief that intelligence tests were useful only to identify those who might benefit from special educational help. Contrary to Binet's contention, it soon came to be believed that the IQ score was a fixed, inborn characteristic that was resistant to change (Gould, 1993).

Terman and other American psychologists also believed that a high IQ predicted more than success in school. To investigate the relationship between IQ and success in life, Terman (1926) identified 1,500 California schoolchildren with "genius" IQ scores. He set up a longitudinal research study to follow their careers throughout their lives. Some of the findings of this landmark study are described in In Focus Box 7.3, "Does a High IQ Score Predict Success in Life?"

Testing Immigrants at Ellis Island This photograph, taken in 1917, shows an examiner administering a mental test to a newly arrived immigrant at the U.S. immigration center on Ellis Island. According to one intelligence "expert" of the time, 80 percent of the Hungarians, 79 percent of the Italians, and 87 percent of the Russians were "feeble-minded" (see Kamin, 1995). The new science of "mental testing" was used to argue for restrictions on immigration.

IN FOCUS 7.3

Does a High IQ Score Predict Success in Life?

Starting in 1921, Lewis M. Terman set out to investigate the common notion that genius-level intelligence is related to social and personal maladjustment, physical weakness, and mental instability. Terman identified 1,500 California children between the ages of 8 and 12 who had IQs above 140, the minimum IQ score for genius-level intelligence. The average IQ of the children was 150, and 80 children had scores above 170. Terman's goal was to track these children by conducting periodic surveys and interviews to see how genius-level intelligence would affect the course of their lives.

Within a few years, Terman (1926) showed that the highly intelligent children were far from being socially and physically inept. In fact, his findings indicated just the opposite. Those children tended to be socially well-adjusted. They were also taller, stronger, and healthier than average children, with fewer illnesses and accidents. Not surprisingly, those children performed exceptionally well in school.

Since Terman's death in 1956, the study has been continued by other psychologists, most notably Melita Oden, Robert Sears,

With the exception of moral character, there is nothing as significant for a child's future as his grade of intelligence.

Lewis M. Terman (1916)

and Pauline Sears. These collaborators in Terman's study kept track of the subjects, by then well into adulthood. Today, more than 70 years after the study began, psychologists continue to assess the professional and personal accomplishments of the surviving original subjects (Holahan & Sears, 1995).

How did Terman's "gifted" children fare in the real world as adults? As a group, they showed an astonishing range of accomplishments (Terman & Oden, 1947, 1959). In 1955, when average income was $5,000 a year, the average income for the group was $33,000. Two-thirds had graduated from college, and a sizable proportion had earned advanced academic or professional degrees. There were no "creative geniuses"—no Picassos, Einsteins, or Mozarts—but there were many doctors, lawyers, scientists, university professors, business executives, and other professionals in the group. Collectively, the gifted group had produced 2,200 scientific articles, 92 books, 235 patents, and 38 novels (Goleman, 1980). One individual had become a famous science fiction writer, and another was an Oscar-winning movie director.

However, not all of Terman's subjects were so successful. To find out why, Terman's colleague Melita Oden compared the 100 most successful men (the "A" group) and the 100 least successful men (the "C" group) in Terman's sample. Despite their high IQ scores, only a handful of the C group were professionals, and none was doing exceptionally well. Whereas the Cs were earning slightly above the national average income, the As were earning almost five times the national income and better than three times the average C-group income. In terms of their personal lives, the Cs were less healthy, had higher rates of alcoholism, and were three times more likely to be divorced than the As (Terman & Oden, 1959).

Given that the IQ scores of the A and C groups were essentially the same, what accounted for the difference in their levels of accomplishment? Terman noted that, as children, the As were much more likely to display "prudence and forethought, will power, perseverance, and the desire to

excel." As adults, the As were rated differently from the Cs on only three traits: They were more goal oriented, had greater perseverance, and had greater self-confidence. Overall, the As seemed to have greater ambition and a greater drive to achieve. In other words, *personality factors* seemed to account for the differences in level of accomplishment between the A group and the C group (Terman & Oden, 1959).

As the general success of Terman's gifted children demonstrates, high intelligence can certainly contribute to success in life. But intelligence alone is not enough. Although IQ scores do reliably predict academic success, success in school is no guarantee of success beyond school. Many different personality factors are involved in achieving success, such as motivation, emotional maturity, commitment to goals, creativity, and—perhaps most important—a willingness to work hard (Goleman, 1995; Renzulli, 1986). None of these attributes are measured by traditional IQ tests.

Terman's findings may have been overly optimistic about the relationship between high IQ scores and social and personal adjustment. Why? The children in Terman's study were first nominated by their teachers before having their IQ tested. Thus, it's possible that the teachers were more likely to select well-adjusted bright children over children who were just as intelligent but less socially adept. And, subsequent research has found that children with exceptionally high academic abilities are somewhat more likely to suffer personal problems, such as social isolation, than their less gifted peers (Winner, 1998).

Intelligence researchers continue to debate the degree to which IQ relates to success in life (Brody, 1997; Sternberg, 1997). However, contemporary research on IQ and professional eminence seems to confirm the essential findings of the original Terman study (Winner, 1997). Although intelligence is necessary for success in any field, the kind of intelligence that is reflected by high scores on traditional IQ tests is no guarantee of vocational success or professional eminence.

David Wechsler and the Wechsler Intelligence Scales

The next major advance in intelligence testing came as a result of a young psychologist's dissatisfaction with the Stanford-Binet and other intelligence tests in widespread use. **David Wechsler** was in charge of testing adults of widely varying cultural and socioeconomic backgrounds and ages at a large hospital in New York City. He designed a new intelligence test, called the *Wechsler Adult Intelligence Scale (WAIS),* which was first published in 1955.

The WAIS had two advantages over the Stanford-Binet. First, the WAIS was specifically designed for adults, rather than for children. Second, Wechsler's test provided scores on 11 subtests measuring different abilities. The subtest scores were grouped to provide an overall verbal score and performance score. The *verbal score* represented scores on subtests of vocabulary, comprehension, knowledge of general information, and other verbal tasks. The *performance score* reflected scores on largely nonverbal subtests, such as identifying the missing part in incomplete pictures, arranging pictures to tell a story, or arranging blocks to match a given pattern.

The design of the WAIS reflected Wechsler's belief that intelligence involves a variety of mental abilities. Because the WAIS provided an individualized profile of the subject's strengths and weaknesses on specific tasks, it marked a return to the attitudes and goals of Alfred Binet (Fancher, 1996; Sternberg, 1990).

The subtest scores on the WAIS also proved to have practical and clinical value. For example, a pattern of low scores on some subtests combined with high scores on other subtests might indicate a specific learning disability (Kaufman, 1990). Or someone who did well on the performance subtests but poorly on the verbal subtests might be unfamiliar with the culture rather than deficient in these skills (Aiken, 1997). That's because many items included on the verbal subtests draw on cultural knowledge.

Wechsler's test also provided an overall, global IQ score, but he changed the way that the IQ score was calculated. On the Stanford-Binet and other early tests, the IQ represented the mental age divided by chronological age. But this approach makes little sense when applied to adult subjects. Although a 12-year-old is typically able to answer more questions than an 8-year-old because of developmental differences, such year-by-year age differences lose their meaning in adulthood.

Instead, Wechsler calculated the IQ by comparing an individual's score with the scores of others in the same general age group, such as young adults. The average score for a particular age group was statistically fixed at 100. The range of scores is statistically defined so that two-thirds of all scores fall between 85 and 115—the range considered to indicate "normal" or "average" intelligence. This procedure proved so successful that it was adopted by the administrators of other tests, including the current version of the Stanford-Binet. Today, IQ scores continue to be calculated by this method.

The WAIS was revised in 1981 and again in 1997. Today the third edition of the WAIS is known as the WAIS-III. Since the 1960s, the WAIS has remained the most commonly administered intelligence test. Wechsler also developed two tests for children: the *Wechsler Intelligence Scale for Children (WISC)* and the *Wechsler Preschool and Primary Scale of Intelligence (WPPSI).*

Principles of Test Construction
What Makes a Good Test?

Many kinds of psychological tests measure various aspects of intelligence or mental ability. **Achievement tests** are designed to measure a person's level of knowledge, skill, or

David Wechsler Born in Romania, David Wechsler (1896–1981) emigrated with his family to New York when he was 6 years old. Like Binet, Wechsler believed that intelligence involved a variety of mental abilities. He also strongly believed that IQ scores could be influenced by personality, motivation, and cultural factors (Matarazzo, 1981).

achievement test
A test designed to measure a person's level of knowledge, skill, or accomplishment in a particular area.

The Wechsler Intelligence Scale for Children (WISC) Revised and updated in 1991, the WISC-III is designed to assess the intelligence of children ages 6 to 16. This psychologist is administering the WISC-III picture completion subtest to a 6-year-old girl. Other WISC-III subtests include vocabulary, arithmetic, arranging blocks to match a design, and arranging pictures so that they logically tell a story.

aptitude test
A test designed to assess a person's capacity to benefit from education or training.

standardization
The administration of a test to a large, representative sample of people under uniform conditions for the purpose of establishing norms.

normal curve or **normal distribution**
A bell-shaped distribution of individual differences in a normal population in which most scores cluster around the average score.

reliability
The ability of a test to produce consistent results when administered on repeated occasions under similar conditions.

validity
The ability of a test to measure what it is intended to measure.

***g* factor** or **general intelligence**
The notion of a general intelligence factor that is responsible for a person's overall performance on tests of mental ability.

accomplishment in a particular area, such as mathematics or a foreign language. In contrast, **aptitude tests** are designed to assess a person's capacity to benefit from education or training. The overall goal of an aptitude test is to predict your ability to learn certain types of information or perform certain skills.

Any psychological test must fulfill certain requirements to be considered scientifically acceptable. The three basic requirements of good test design are standardization, reliability, and validity. Let's briefly look at what each of those requirements entails.

Standardization

If you answer 75 of 100 questions correctly, what does that score mean? Is it high, low, or average? For an individual's test score to be interpreted, it has to be compared against some sort of standard of performance.

Standardization means that the test is given to a large number of subjects who are representative of the group of people for whom the test is designed. All the subjects take the same version of the test under uniform conditions. The scores of this group establish the *norms*, or the standards against which an individual score is compared and interpreted.

For IQ tests, such norms closely follow a pattern of individual differences called the **normal curve**, or **normal distribution**. In this bell-shaped pattern, most scores cluster around the average score. As scores become more extreme, fewer instances of the scores occur. In Figure 7.5, you can see the normal distribution of IQ scores on the WAIS-III. About 68 percent of subjects taking the WAIS-III will score between 85 and 115, the IQ range for "normal" intelligence. Less than 1 percent of the population have extreme scores that are above 145 or below 55.

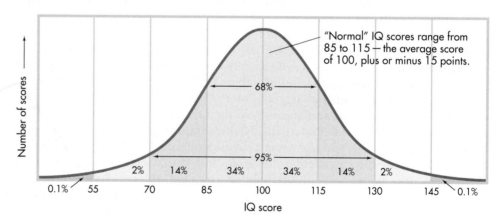

FIGURE 7.5 The Normal Curve of Distribution of IQ Scores The distribution of IQ scores on the WAIS-III in the general population tends to follow a bell-shaped normal curve, with the average score defined as 100. Notice that 68 percent of the scores fall within the "normal" IQ range of 85 to 115. Ninety-five percent of the general population score between 70 and 130, while only one-tenth of 1 percent score lower than 55 or higher than 145.

Reliability

A good test must also have **reliability.** That is, it must consistently produce similar scores on different occasions. How do psychologists determine whether a psychological test is reliable? One method is to administer two similar, but not identical, versions of the test at different times. Another procedure is to compare the scores on one half of the test with the scores on the other half of the test. A test is considered reliable if the test and retest scores are highly similar when such strategies are used.

Validity

Finally, a good test must demonstrate **validity,** which means that the test measures what it is supposed to measure. One way to establish the validity of a test is by demonstrating its predictive value. For example, if a test is designed to measure mechanical aptitude, people who received high scores should ultimately prove more successful in mechanical jobs than people who received low scores.

The Nature of Intelligence

Key Theme
- Psychologists do not agree about the basic nature of intelligence, including whether it is a single, general ability and whether it includes skills and talents as well as mental aptitude.

Key Questions
- What is *g*, and how did Spearman and Thurstone view intelligence?
- What is Gardner's theory of multiple intelligences?
- What is Sternberg's triarchic theory of intelligence?

The Wechsler Adult Intelligence Scale and the Stanford-Binet Intelligence Scale are standardized, reliable, and valid. But do they adequately measure intelligence? The question is not as simple as it sounds. There is considerable disagreement among psychologists about the nature of intelligence, including how intelligence should best be defined and measured (Neisser & others, 1996; Shavinina, 2001).

For example, take another look at the Prologue to this chapter, which described solving two real problems: a leaking faucet and a malfunctioning toilet. Obviously, solving these problems required a certain level of intelligence. But could that intelligence be adequately measured by an IQ test? Does an IQ test measure the ingenuity that Don demonstrated? Or Sandy's enterprising ability to find a resource to supply the knowledge that she knew she didn't have?

Theories of Intelligence

Much of the controversy over the definition of *intelligence* centers on two key issues. First, is intelligence a single, general ability, or is it better described as a cluster of different mental abilities? And second, should the definition of intelligence be restricted to the mental abilities measured by IQ and other intelligence tests? Or should intelligence be defined more broadly?

Although these issues have been debated for decades, they are far from being resolved. In this section, we'll describe the views of four influential psychologists on both issues.

Charles Spearman
Intelligence Is a General Ability

Some psychologists believe that a common factor, or general mental capacity, is at the core of different mental abilities. This approach originated with British psychologist **Charles Spearman.** Although Spearman agreed that an individual's scores could vary on tests of different mental abilities, he found that the scores on different tests tended to be similar. That is, people who did well or poorly on a test of one mental ability, such as verbal ability, tended also to do well or poorly on the other tests.

Spearman recognized that particular individuals might excel in specific areas. However, Spearman (1904) believed that a factor he called **general intelligence,** or the ***g*** **factor,** was responsible for their overall performance on tests of mental ability. Psychologists who follow this approach today think that intelligence can be described as a single measure of general cognitive ability, or *g* factor (Gottfredson, 1998). Thus, general mental ability could accurately be expressed by a single number, such as the IQ score. Lewis Terman's approach to measuring and defining intelligence as a single, overall IQ score was in the tradition of Charles Spearman.

Charles Spearman (1863–1945) British psychologist Charles Spearman (1904) believed that a single factor, which he called the *g* factor, underlies many different kinds of mental abilities. To Spearman, a person's level of general intelligence was equivalent to his or her level of "mental energy."

Louis L. Thurstone (1887–1955) American psychologist Lewis Thurstone studied electrical engineering and was an assistant to Thomas Edison before he became interested in the psychology of learning. Thurstone was especially interested in the measurements of people's attitudes and intelligence, and was an early critic of the idea of "mental age," believing that intelligence was too diverse to be quantified in a single number or IQ score.

Louis L. Thurstone
Intelligence Is a Cluster of Abilities

Psychologist **Louis L. Thurstone** disagreed with Spearman's notion that intelligence is a single, general mental capacity. Instead, Thurstone believed that there were seven different "primary mental abilities," each a relatively independent element of intelligence. Abilities such as verbal comprehension, numerical ability, reasoning, and perceptual speed are examples Thurstone gave of independent "primary mental abilities."

To Thurstone, the so-called *g* factor was simply an overall average score of such independent abilities and consequently was less important than an individual's specific *pattern* of mental abilities (Thurstone, 1937). David Wechsler's approach to measuring and defining intelligence as a pattern of different abilities was very similar to Thurstone's approach.

Howard Gardner
"Multiple Intelligences"

More recently, **Howard Gardner** has expanded Thurstone's basic notion of intelligence as different mental abilities that operate independently. However, Gard-

ner has stretched the definition of intelligence (Gardner & Taub, 1999). Rather than analyzing intelligence test results, Gardner (1985, 1993) looked at the kinds of skills and products that are valued in different cultures. He also studied brain-damaged individuals, noting that some mental abilities are spared when others are lost. To Gardner, this phenomenon implies that different mental abilities are biologically distinct and controlled by different parts of the brain.

Howard Gardner and His Theory of Multiple Intelligences According to Howard Gardner (b. 1943), many mental abilities are not adequately measured by traditional intelligence tests. As Gardner (2003) explains, "Different tasks call on different intelligences or combinations of intelligence. To perform music intelligently involves a different set of intelligences than preparing a meal, planning a course, or resolving a quarrel." Examples might include the spatial intelligence shown by the complex designs of a Navajo weaver, the extraordinary bodily-kinesthetic intelligence of Tiger Woods, and the musical intelligence of U2 singer and songwriter Bono.

Like Thurstone, Gardner has suggested that such mental abilities are independent of each other and cannot be accurately reflected in a single measure of intelligence. Rather than one intelligence, Gardner (1993, 1998a) believes, there are "multiple intelligences." To Gardner, "an intelligence" is the ability to solve problems, or to create products, that are valued within one or more cultural settings. Thus, he believes that intelligence must be defined within the context of a particular culture. Gardner (1998b) has proposed eight distinct, independent intelligences, which are summarized in Figure 7.6.

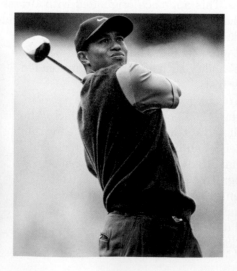

Linguistic intelligence	Adept use of language: poet, writer, public speaker, native storyteller
Logical-mathematical intelligence	Logical, mathematical, and scientific ability: scientist, mathematician, navigator, surveyor
Musical intelligence	Ability to create, synthesize, or perform music: Musician, composer, singer
Spatial intelligence	Ability to mentally visualize the relationships of objects or movements: sculptor, painter, expert chess player, architect
Bodily-kinesthetic intelligence	Control of bodily motions and capacity to handle objects skillfully: athlete, dancer, craftsperson
Interpersonal intelligence	Understanding of other people's emotions, motives, intentions: politician, salesperson, clinical psychologist
Intrapersonal intelligence	Understanding of one's own emotions, motives, and intentions: essayist, philosopher
Naturalist intelligence	Ability to discern patterns in nature: ecologist, zoologist, botanist

FIGURE 7.6 Gardner's Multiple Intelligences

Some of the abilities emphasized by Gardner, such as logical-mathematical intelligence, might be tapped by a standard intelligence test. However, other abilities, such as bodily-kinesthetic intelligence or musical intelligence, do not seem to be reflected on standard intelligence tests. Yet, as Gardner points out, such abilities are recognized and highly valued in many different cultures, including our own.

Robert Sternberg
Three Forms of Intelligence

Robert Sternberg agrees with Gardner that intelligence is a much broader quality than is reflected in the narrow range of mental abilities measured by a conventional IQ test. However, Sternberg (1988, 1995) disagrees with Gardner's notion of multiple, independent intelligences. He believes that some of Gardner's intelligences are more accurately described as specialized talents, whereas intelligence is a more general quality. Sternberg (1988) points out that you would be able to manage just fine if you were tone-deaf and lacked "musical intelligence" in most societies. However, if you didn't have the ability to reason and plan ahead, you would be unable to function in any culture.

Sternberg's **triarchic theory of intelligence** emphasizes both the universal aspects of intelligent behavior and the importance of adapting to a particular social and cultural environment. More specifically, Sternberg (1997) has proposed a different conception of intelligence, which he calls *successful intelligence*. Successful intelligence involves three distinct types of mental abilities: analytic, creative, and practical.

Analytic intelligence refers to the mental processes used in learning how to solve problems, such as picking a problem-solving strategy and applying it. Although conventional intelligence tests measure mental abilities, they do not evaluate the strategies used to solve problems, which Sternberg considers important in determining analytic intelligence. In the Prologue, Sandy's ability to review and select a problem-solving strategy from the "Fix-It" book reflected analytic intelligence.

Creative intelligence is the ability to deal with novel situations by drawing on existing skills and knowledge. The intelligent person effectively draws on past experiences to cope with new situations, which often involves finding an unusual way to relate old information to new. Don displayed creative intelligence when he came up with a novel way to fix the leaky kitchen faucet.

Practical intelligence involves the ability to adapt to the environment and often reflects what is commonly called "street smarts." Sternberg notes that what is required to adapt successfully in one particular situation or culture may be

"I don't have to be smart, because someday I'll just hire lots of smart people to work for me."

triarchic theory of intelligence
Sternberg's theory that there are three distinct forms of intelligence: analytic, creative, and practical.

very different from what is needed in another situation or culture. He stresses that the behaviors that reflect practical intelligence can vary depending on the particular situation, environment, or culture.

The exact nature of intelligence will no doubt be debated for some time. However, the intensity of this debate pales in comparison with the next issue we consider: the origins of intelligence.

The Roles of Genetics and Environment in Determining Intelligence

Key Theme

■ Both genes and environment contribute to intelligence, but the relationship is complex.

Key Questions

■ How are twin studies used to measure genetic and environmental influences on intelligence?

■ What is a heritability estimate, and why can't it be used to explain differences between groups?

■ What social and cultural factors affect performance on intelligence tests?

> *The nature-versus-nurture debate is now informed by current research on molecular biology that moves the question from which factor is more important to how and when expression of the human genome is triggered and maintained. The basic behavior genetics issue has become how environment influences gene expression.*
>
> Bernard Brown (1999)

Given that psychologists do not agree on the definition or nature of intelligence, it probably won't surprise you to learn that psychologists also do not agree on the *origin of intelligence*. On the surface, the debate comes down to this: Do we essentially *inherit* our intellectual potential from our parents, grandparents, and great-grandparents? Or is our intellectual potential primarily determined by our *environment* and upbringing?

The simple answer to both these questions is "yes." In a nutshell, virtually all psychologists agree that *both* heredity and environment are important in determining intelligence level. Where psychologists disagree is in identifying how much of intelligence is determined by heredity, how much by environment. The implications of this debate have provoked some of the most heated arguments in the history of psychology. In this section, we'll try to clarify some of the critical issues involved in this ongoing controversy.

To make sense of the IQ controversy, let's start with some basic points about the relationship between genes and the environment. At one time, it was commonly believed that genes provided the blueprint for human potential and development. Today, the "genes as blueprint" metaphor has been replaced by a "genes as data bank" metaphor (Brown, 1999; Marcus, 2004). It's now known that environmental factors influence *which* of the many genes we inherit are actually switched on, or activated. As psychologist Bernard Brown (1999) writes, "Genes are not destiny. There are many places along the gene–behavior pathway where genetic expression can be regulated."

Take the example of height. You inherit a potential *range* for height, rather than an absolute number of inches. Environmental factors influence how close you come to realizing that genetic potential. If you are healthy and well-nourished, you may reach the maximum of your genetic height potential. But if you are poorly nourished and not healthy, you probably won't.

To underscore the interplay between heredity and environment, consider the fact that in the last 50 years, the average height of Americans has increased by several inches. The explanation for this increase is that nutritional and health standards have steadily improved, not that the genetic heritage of Americans has fundamentally changed. However, heredity does play a role in establishing *limits* on height. If you're born with "short" genes (like your authors), you're unlikely to reach six foot four, no matter how good your nutrition (for more on genetics see pages 352–355).

The roles of heredity and environment in determining intelligence and personality factors are much more complex than the simple examples of height or eye color (Plomin, 2003). However narrowly intelligence is defined, the genetic range of intellectual potential is influenced by *many* genes, not by one single gene (Plomin & Spinath, 2004). No one knows how many genes might be involved. Given the complexity of genetic and environmental influences, how do scientists estimate how much of intelligence is due to genetics, how much to environment?

Twin Studies
Sorting Out the Influence of Genetics Versus Environment

One way this issue has been explored is by comparing the IQ scores of individuals who are genetically related to different degrees. *Identical twins* share exactly the same genes, because they developed from a single fertilized egg that split into two. Hence, any dissimilarities between them must be due to environmental factors rather than hereditary differences. *Fraternal twins* are like any other pair of siblings, because they develop from two different fertilized eggs.

As you can see in Figure 7.7, comparing IQ scores in this way shows the effects of both heredity and environment. Identical twins raised together have very similar IQ scores, whereas fraternal twins raised together have IQs that are less similar (McClearn & others, 1997; Plomin & Spinath, 2004).

However, notice that identical twins raised in separate homes have IQs that are slightly less similar, indicating the effect of different environments. And, although fraternal twins raised together have less similar IQ scores than do identical twins, they show more similarity in IQs than do nontwin siblings. Recall that the degree of genetic relatedness between fraternal twins and nontwin siblings is essentially the same. But because fraternal twins are the same age, their environmental experiences are likely to be more similar than are those of siblings who are of different ages.

Genetics or Environment? These identical twins have a lot in common—including a beautiful smile. Twins are often used in studies of the relative contributions that heredity and environment make to personality and other characteristics.

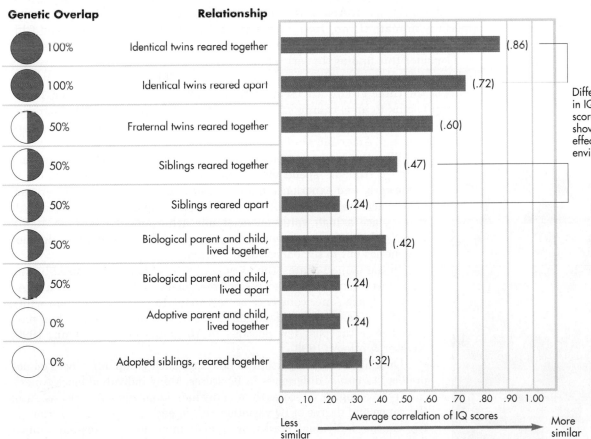

FIGURE 7.7 Genetics, Environment, and IQ Scores This graph shows the average correlations of IQ scores for individuals who are genetically related to different degrees. The graph is based on research by psychologists Thomas Bouchard and Matt McGue, who summarized the results from more than 100 separate studies on over 100,000 pairs of relatives (McGue & others, 1993). The data show that both genetics and environment have an effect on IQ scores. The more closely two individuals are related genetically, the more similar their IQ scores: Identical twins reared together are more alike than are fraternal twins reared together. However, the same data also show the importance of environmental influences: Identical twins reared together are more alike than are identical twins reared apart, and siblings who are reared together are more alike than are siblings reared in different homes.

heritability

The percentage of variation within a given population that is due to heredity.

Thus, *both* genetic *and* environmental influences are important. Genetic influence is shown by the fact that the closer the genetic relationship, the more similar the IQ scores. Environmental influences are demonstrated by two findings: First, two people who are genetically identical but are raised in different homes have different IQ scores. And second, two people who are genetically unrelated but are raised in the same home have IQs that are much more similar than are those of two unrelated people from randomly selected homes.

Using studies based on degree of genetic relatedness and using sophisticated statistical techniques to analyze the data, researchers have scientifically estimated **heritability**—the percentage of variation within a given population that is due to heredity. The currently accepted *heritability estimate* is about 50 percent for the general population (see Plomin, 2003; Plomin & Spinath, 2004).

In other words, approximately 50 percent of the difference in IQ scores *within* a given population is due to genetic factors. But there is disagreement even over this figure, depending on the statistical techniques and data sources used (Turkheimer & others, 2003).

It is important to stress that the 50 percent figure does *not* apply to a single individual's IQ score. If Mike's IQ is 120, it does not mean that 60 IQ points are due to Mike's environment and 60 points are genetically inherited. Instead, the 50 percent heritability estimate means that approximately 50 percent of the difference in IQ scores *within a specific group of people* is due to differences in their genetic makeup. More on this key point shortly.

Group Differences in IQ Scores

If the contributions of heredity and environment are roughly equal, why all the fuss? Much of the controversy over the role of heredity in intelligence is due to attempts to explain the differences in average IQ scores for different racial groups.

In comparing the *average IQ* for various racial groups, several studies have shown differences. For example, Japanese and Chinese schoolchildren tend to score above European-American children on intelligence and achievement tests, especially in math (Lynn, 1987; Stevenson & Lee, 1990). Are Japanese and Chinese children genetically more intelligent than European-American children?

Consider this finding: In early childhood, there are *no* significant differences in IQ among European-American, Japanese, and Chinese schoolchildren. The scores of the three groups are essentially the same (Stevenson & Stigler, 1992). The gap begins to appear only after the children start school, and it increases with every year of school attended. By middle school, Asian students tend to score much higher than American students on both math and reading tests.

Culture and Educational Achievement
These children attend kindergarten in Kawasaki, Japan. Children in Japan attend school six days a week. Along with spending more time in school each year than American children, Japanese children grow up in a culture that places a strong emphasis on academic success as the key to occupational success.

Why the increasing gap once children enter school? Japanese and Chinese students spend more time in school, spend more time doing homework, and experience more pressure and support from their parents to achieve academically. In addition, the Japanese and Chinese cultures place a high value on academic achievement (Gardner, 1995). Clearly, the difference between American and Asian students is due not to genetics but to the educational system.

In the United States, the most controversy has been caused by the differences in average IQ scores between black and white Americans. *As a group,* black Americans once scored about 15 points lower than white Americans *as a group* (MacKenzie, 1984). However, this gap has narrowed over the past few decades to 10 points or less (Flynn, 1999; Neisser & others, 1996).

Once again, it is important to note that such group differences do not predict *individual* differences in IQ scores. Many individual black Americans receive higher IQ scores than many individual white Americans. Also, the range and degree of IQ variation *within* each group—the variation of IQs among individual blacks or among individual whites—are much greater than the 10-point average difference *between* the two groups.

Differences *Within* Groups Versus Differences *Between* Groups

Some group differences in average IQ scores do exist. But heritability cannot be used to explain group differences. Although it is possible to estimate the degree of difference *within* a specific group that is due to genetics, it makes no sense to apply this estimate to the differences *between* groups (Rutter, 1997). Why? An analogy provided by geneticist Richard Lewontin (1970) may help you understand this important point.

Suppose you have a 50-pound bag of corn seeds and two pots. A handful of seeds is scooped out and planted in pot A, which has rich, well-fertilized soil. A second handful is scooped out and planted in pot B, which has poor soil with few nutrients (see Figure 7.8).

Because the seeds are not genetically identical, the plants *within group A* will vary in height. So will the plants *within group B*. Given that the environment (the soil) is the same for all the plants in one particular pot, this variation within each group of seeds is *completely* due to heredity—nothing differs but the plants' genes.

However, when we compare the average height of the corn plants in the two pots, pot A's plants have a higher average height than pot B's. Can the difference in these average heights be explained in terms of overall genetic differences between the seeds in each pot? No. The overall differences can be attributed to the two different environments, the good soil and the poor soil. In fact, because the environments are so different, it is impossible to estimate what the overall genetic differences are between the two groups of seeds.

Note also that even though, on the average, the plants in pot A are taller than the plants in pot B, some of the plants in pot B are taller than some of the plants in pot A. In other words, the average differences *within a group* of plants tell us nothing about whether an *individual* member of that group is likely to be tall or short.

The same point can be extended to the issue of average IQ differences between racial groups. Unless the environmental conditions of two racial groups are virtually identical, it is impossible to estimate the overall genetic differences between the two groups. Even if intelligence were *primarily* determined by heredity, which is not the case, IQ differences between groups could still be due entirely to the environment.

In the United States, black children, like members of many other minority groups, are more likely than white children to be raised in poverty and to have fewer educational opportunities. Environmental factors associated with poverty, such as poor nutrition and lack of prenatal care, can have a negative impact on intelligence. And, even when their socioeconomic status is roughly equal to that of white Americans, black Americans experience many forms of overt and subtle social discrimination (Steele & Aronson, 1995).

A classic study by psychologists Sandra Scarr and Richard Weinberg (1976) explored the relationship between racial IQ differences and the environment in which children are raised. Scarr and Weinberg looked at the IQ scores of black children who had been adopted by white families that were highly educated and above average in occupational status and income. When tested, the black children's IQ scores were several points higher than the average scores of *both* black and white children.

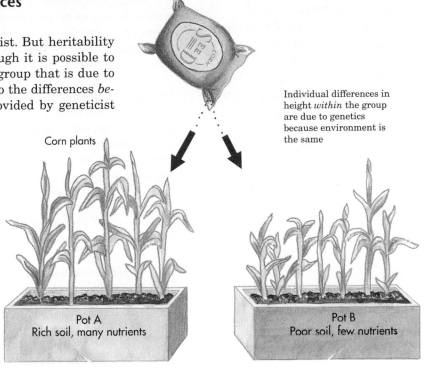

Corn plants

Individual differences in height *within* the group are due to genetics because environment is the same

Pot A
Rich soil, many nutrients

Pot B
Poor soil, few nutrients

Difference in average height *between* groups is due to environment

FIGURE 7.8 The Two Pots Analogy Because the two environments are very different, no conclusions can be drawn about possible overall genetic differences between the plants in pot A and the plants in pot B.

> *We need to appreciate that all human behavior is based on biology and, hence, will involve some degree of genetic influence. But, equally, all social behavior is bound to be affected by social context and, hence, will involve an important environmental influence.*
>
> Michael R. Rutter (1997)

Scarr and Weinberg concluded that IQ differences are due not to race but rather to the socioeconomic conditions and cultural values to which children are exposed. According to Weinberg (1989), the adopted black children performed well above average because they were provided with home environments in which they were taught the vocabulary and cognitive skills that IQ and achievement tests reward. A follow-up study of the children a decade later demonstrated the "persisting beneficial effects [on IQ scores] of being reared in the culture of the school and tests" (Weinberg & others, 1992; see also Waldman & others, 1994).

Other evidence for the importance of the environment in determining IQ scores derives from the improvement in average IQ scores that has occurred in several cultures and countries during the last few generations (Flynn, 1999; Neisser & others, 1996). For example, average IQ scores in Japan have risen dramatically since World War II.

In a survey of intelligence test scores around the world, 14 nations were found to have shown significant gains in average IQ scores in just one generation (Flynn, 1994, 1999). The average IQ score in the United States has also steadily increased over the past century (Kaufman, 1990). Such changes in a population can be accounted for only by environmental changes, because the amount of time involved is far too short for genetically influenced changes to have occurred.

Cross-Cultural Studies of Group Discrimination and IQ Differences

The effect of social discrimination on intelligence test scores has been shown in numerous cross-cultural studies (see Ogbu, 1986). In many different societies, average IQ is lower for members of a discriminated-against minority group, even when that group is not racially different from the dominant group.

Take the case of the Burakumin people of Japan. Americans typically think of Japan as relatively homogeneous, and indeed the Burakumin are not racially different from other Japanese. They look the same and speak the same language. However, the Burakumin are the descendants of an outcast group that for generations worked as tanners and butchers. Because they handled dead bodies and killed animals, the Burakumin were long considered unclean and unfit for social contact. For centuries, they were forced to live in isolated enclaves, apart from the rest of Japanese society (DeVos, 1992; DeVos & Wagatsuma, 1967).

Today, there are about 3 million Burakumin in Japan. Although the Burakumin were legally emancipated from their outcast status many years ago, substantial social discrimination against them persists (Payton, 1992). Because there is no way to tell if a Japanese citizen is of Burakumin descent, there are dozens of private detective agencies in Tokyo and other Japanese cities that openly specialize in tracking Burakumin who are trying to "pass" and hide their background. Corporations in Japan routinely consult computer databanks to identify Burakumin who apply for jobs, as do individuals who wish to investigate the ancestral background of prospective marriage partners.

The Burakumin are the poorest people in Japan. They are only half as likely as other Japanese to graduate from high school or attend college. Although there are no racial differences between the Burakumin and other Japanese, the average IQ scores of the Burakumin in Japan are well below those of other Japanese. As shown in Table 7.2, their average IQ scores are about 10

The Burakumin of Japan are not racially different from other Japanese, but they have suffered from generations of discrimination. Their average IQ scores are about 10 to 15 points below those of mainstream Japanese (Ogbu, 1986). In many other cultures, a similar gap in IQ scores exists between the discriminated-against minority and the dominant group.

Table 7.2

The Effects of Discrimination on IQ Scores in Japan

Range of IQ Scores	Non-Burakumin	Burakumin
Above 125	23.3	2.6
124–109	31.8	19.5
108–93	23.3	22.1
92–77	11.7	18.2
Below 76	9.9	37.6

Percentage of Children Scoring in a Given Range

SOURCE: Adapted from De Vos & Wagatsuma (1967), Table 2, p. 261.

to 15 points below those of mainstream Japanese. But, when Burakumin families immigrate to the United States, they are treated like any other Japanese. The children do just as well in school—and on IQ tests—as any other Japanese-Americans (Ogbu, 1986).

Of course, Japan is not the only society that discriminates against a particular social group. Many societies discriminate against specific minority groups, such as the Harijans in India (formerly called the untouchables), West Indians in Great Britain, Maoris in New Zealand, and Jews of non-European descent in Israel.

The Burakumin Protest Centuries of Discrimination Members of the Burakumin Emancipation Alliance protest discrimination in a peaceful demonstration in Tokyo. Their vests proclaim their demand for basic human rights for the Burakumin people. Today, the Burakumin are the poorest group in Japan. Compared to the general population of Japan, only about half as many Burakumin graduate from high school or attend college.

Children belonging to these minority groups score 10 to 15 points lower on intelligence tests than do children belonging to the dominant group in their societies. Children of the minority groups are often one or two years behind dominant-group children in basic reading skills and mathematical skills. Minority-group children are overrepresented in remedial programs and in school dropout rates. They are also underrepresented in higher education. The impact of discrimination on group differences in IQ remains even when the minority-group and dominant-group members are of similar socioeconomic backgrounds (Ogbu, 1986). In many ways, the educational experiences of these minority groups seem to parallel those of black Americans, providing a cross-cultural perspective on the consistent effects of discrimination in many different societies.

Culture and Human Behavior Box 7.4, "Stereotype Threat: Performing When There's a 'Threat in the Air,'" discusses another way that belonging to a stigmatized group can affect test performance.

Are IQ Tests Culturally Biased?

Another approach to explaining group differences in IQ scores has been to look at cultural bias in the tests themselves. If standardized intelligence tests reflect white, middle-class cultural knowledge and values, minority-group members might do poorly on the tests not because of lower intelligence but because of unfamiliarity with the white, middle-class culture.

Testing, Testing, Testing . . . Virtually all college students will be evaluated with standardized tests at some point in their college careers. Although great pains are taken to make tests as unbiased and objective as possible, many factors, both personal and situational, can affect performance on tests. Cultural factors, familiarity with the testing process, and anxiety or nervousness are just a few of the factors that can skew test results. So perhaps the best way to view standardized tests is as just one of many possible indicators of a student's level of knowledge—and of his or her potential to learn.

CULTURE AND HUMAN BEHAVIOR 7.4

Stereotype Threat: Performing When There's a "Threat in the Air"

Tests such as the Wechsler Adult Intelligence Scale (WAIS), SAT, and the American College Test (ACT) are *standardized*. That means that every individual experiences the same testing conditions, instructions, materials, and test questions. Obviously, one goal of standardization is to help ensure that such tests are as fair and unbiased as possible. However, it is impossible to standardize all conditions, including the expectations that we think other people might have about our performance in a particular situation.

As psychologist Claude Steele has discovered, if those expectations are negative, they can cause us to perform below our actual ability level. Steele coined the term **stereotype threat** to describe this phenomenon, which occurs when members of a particular group fear that they will be evaluated in terms of a negative stereotype about their group. As Steele (1997) explains, "It's a situational threat—a threat in the air—that, in general form, can affect the members of any group about whom a negative stereotype exists, whether it's skateboarders, older adults, white men, or gang members. Where bad stereotypes about these groups apply, members of these groups can fear being reduced to that stereotype."

Stanford Psychologist Claude Steele As Claude Steele has discovered, the awareness of threatening stereotypes can affect performance. The anxiety and self-doubt caused by stereotype threat may help explain group differences in intelligence, math, and other test scores.

To illustrate, consider the gender stereotype that females are poor at math, especially advanced mathematics. In one study, when female students took a difficult math test that was described in advance as producing gender differences, their scores were much lower than that of male students taking the same test. But when a matched group of female students took the same test but were told that it did *not* produce gender differences, their scores were equal to those of the male students (Spencer & others, 1999). Simply reminding the female students of the stereotype that women are less skilled in mathematics than men was enough to lower their scores.

Now consider a study by Margaret Shih and her colleagues (1999) showing just how easily stereotype awareness can be manipulated to affect test performance. Mathematically gifted Asian-American female college students were randomly assigned to two groups. One group filled out a questionnaire asking them several questions that were likely to remind them of their Asian background and activate the cultural stereotype that Asian-Americans have superior math abilities. The other group filled out a questionnaire asking them questions that were likely to remind them of their gender identity as females and activate the gender stereotype that women are not good at math. Then each group took a challenging math test.

The results? Those students who were reminded of their racial identity as Asians scored significantly higher on the exam than the students who were reminded of their gender identity as women. A control group of students, who filled out a neutral questionnaire, had scores in the middle of the two groups.

Why would being reminded of a negative stereotype undermine your performance on a test? Fear that you might confirm the negative stereotype creates stress, self-doubt, and anxiety (Ben-Zeev & others, 2005; Blascovich & others, 2001). In turn, anxiety, apprehension, and nervousness interfere with memory and problem-solving abilities (Quinn & Spencer, 2001; Schmader & Johns, 2003). Perhaps not sur-

prisingly, those students who are most highly motivated to perform well are most likely to be affected by stereotype threat (Wheeler & Petty, 2001).

The influence of stereotype threats is not confined to Asian-American or female students taking math tests or, for that matter, limited to tests of academic ability. Consider these additional examples:

- When told that a test was simply a laboratory task that investigated problem-solving strategies but did not measure intellectual ability, black and white students scored equally well. But when a matched group of students were given the same test and told that it was a test of intellectual ability, black students did much more poorly than white students (Steele & Aronson, 1995).

- When reminded of the *negative* stereotype of the elderly being forgetful, senior adults scored lower on memory tests than when they were not reminded of the stereotype. And, when reminded of the *positive* stereotype that elderly people are wise, older individuals scored higher on the same memory tests (Levy, 1996).

- After completing questionnaires about their social and economic background, French students from a low socioeconomic background who took a test described as a measure of intellectual ability performed worse than students from a wealthy background. But when the test was presented as *not* reflecting intellectual ability, the students performed just as well as the wealthier students (Croizet & Claire, 1998).

The key point here is that performance on tests, even tests that are carefully designed to be fair and objective, is surprisingly susceptible to social and cultural influences. How can the influence of stereotype threats be overcome? One way is for the test-giver to tackle the issue head-on: Simply saying that a particular test is racially fair or gender-neutral has been shown to reduce the effects of stereotype threat (Johns & others, 2005; Spencer & others, 1999).

Researchers have attempted to create tests that are "culture-fair" or "culture-free." However, it is now generally recognized that it is virtually impossible to design a test that is completely culture-free. As cross-cultural psychologist Patricia Greenfield (1997) argues, ability tests "reflect the values, knowledge, and communication strategies of their culture of origin." Within that culture, the intelligence test may be a valid measure. Thus, a test will tend to favor the people from the culture in which it was developed.

Cultural differences may also be involved in *test-taking behavior* (Sternberg, 1995). People from different cultural backgrounds may use strategies in solving problems or organizing information that are different from those required on standard intelligence tests (Miller-Jones, 1989). In addition, such cultural factors as motivation, attitudes toward test taking, and previous experiences with tests can affect performance and scores on tests.

stereotype threat
A psychological predicament in which fear that you will be evaluated in terms of a negative stereotype about a group to which you belong creates anxiety and self-doubt, lowering performance in a particular domain that is important to you.

Closing Thoughts

So what conclusions can we draw about the debates surrounding intelligence, including the role of heredity in mental ability?

First, it's clear that the IQ score of any individual—regardless of his or her racial, social, or economic group—is the result of a complex interaction among genetic and environmental factors. Second, environmental factors are much more likely than genetic factors to account for average IQ differences among distinct groups of people (Neisser & others, 1996). Third, within *any* given group of people, IQ differences among people are due at least as much to environmental influences as they are to genetic influences (Plomin & Spinath, 2004). And finally, IQ scores reflect what IQ tests are designed to measure—a particular group of mental abilities.

As we've seen throughout this chapter, we draw on *many* different types of mental abilities to solve problems, adapt to our environment, and communicate with others. As the story of Mr. and Ms. Fix-It in the Prologue illustrated, solving even the most mundane problems of life often involves flexible and creative thinking. In the chapter Application, we invite you attend a Workshop on Creativity, where you will learn several strategies that will help you become a more creative problem solver.

Creativity can be defined as a group of cognitive processes used to generate useful, original, and novel ideas or solutions to problems (Amabile & Tighe, 1993; Ochse, 1990). Notice that usefulness, along with originality, is involved in judging creativity. An idea can be highly original, but if it lacks usefulness it is not regarded as creative.

Although we typically think of creativity in terms of artistic expression, the act of creativity is almost always linked to the process of solving some problem. In that sense, creativity can occur in virtually any area of life.

Can you learn to be more creative? In general, creativity experts agree that you can. Although there is no simple formula that guarantees creative success, a few basic ingredients are central to the process of creative thinking. Here are several suggestions that can enhance your ability to think creatively.

1. Choose the goal of creativity.

Psychologists have found that virtually everyone possesses the intelligence and cognitive processes needed to be creative (Weisberg, 1988, 1993). But the creative individual values creativity as a personal goal. Without the personal goal of creativity, the likelihood of doing something creative is slim.

2. Reinforce creative behavior.

People are most creative when motivated by their own interest, the enjoyment of a challenge, and a personal sense of satisfaction and fulfillment (Amabile, 1996, 2001). This is called *intrinsic motivation*. In contrast, when people are motivated by external rewards, such as money or grades, they are displaying *extrinsic motivation*.

Researchers used to believe that extrinsic rewards made creative behavior much less likely. New research, however, seems to demonstrate that rewards can increase creative behavior in a person who has some training in generating creative solutions to problems (Eisenberger & others, 1998). When people know that creative behavior will be rewarded, they are more likely to behave in a creative way (Eisenberger & Cameron, 1996).

CALVIN AND HOBBS

3. Engage in problem finding.

In many cases, the real creative leap involves recognizing that a problem exists. This is referred to as *problem finding*. We often overlook creative opportunities by dismissing trivial annoyances rather than recognizing them as potential problems to be solved.

For example, consider the minor annoyance experienced by a man named Art Fry. Fry, a researcher for 3M Corporation, regularly sang in his church choir. In order to locate the hymns quickly during the Sunday service, Fry used little scraps of paper to mark their places. But the scraps of paper would sometimes fall out when Fry stood up to sing, and he'd have to fumble to find the right page (Kaplan, 1990).

While sitting in church, Fry recognized the "problem" and came up with a relatively simple solution. If you put a substance that is sticky, but not *too* sticky, on the scraps of paper, they'll stay on the page and you can take them off when they are not needed anymore.

If you haven't already guessed, Art Fry invented Post-it notes. The formula for the adhesive had been discovered years earlier at 3M, but nobody could imagine a use for a glue that did not bond permanently. The mental set of the 3M researchers was to find *stronger* glues, not weaker ones. Fry's story demonstrates the creative value of recognizing problems instead of simply dismissing them.

A technique called *bug listing* is one useful strategy to identify potential problems. Bug listing involves creating a list of things that annoy, irritate, or bug you. Such everyday annoyances are problems in need of creative solutions.

4. Acquire relevant knowledge.

Creativity requires a good deal of preparation (Weisberg, 1993). Acquiring a solid knowledge base increases your potential for recognizing how to creatively extend your knowledge or apply it in a new way. For example, if Don did not understand how the faucet in the kitchen functioned, he would never have been able to come up with a creative way to repair it. As the famous French chemist Louis Pasteur said, "Chance favors the prepared mind."

5. Try different approaches.

Creative people are flexible in their thinking. They step back from problems, turn them over, and mentally play with possibilities. By being flexible and imaginative, people seeking creative solutions generate many different responses. This is called *divergent thinking,* because it involves moving away (or diverging) from the problem and considering it from a variety of perspectives (Baer, 1993).

Looking for analogies is one technique to encourage divergent thinking. In problem solving, an *analogy* is the recognition of some similarity or parallel between two objects or events that are not usually compared. Similarities can be drawn in terms of the objects' operation, function, purpose, materials, or other characteristics.

For example, consider inventor Dean Kamen's ingenious "self-balancing human transporter," the *Segway,* which is modeled on the human body. As Kamen (2001) explains, "There's a gyroscope that acts like your inner ear, a computer that acts like your brain, motors that act like your muscles, and wheels that act like your feet." Rather than brakes, engine, or steering wheel, sophisticated sensors detect subtle shifts in body weight to maintain direction, speed, and balance. Designed for riding on sidewalks, the Segway can move at speeds up to 17 mph and can carry the average rider for a full day.

6. Exert effort and expect setbacks.

Flashes of insight or inspiration can play a role in creativity, but they usually occur only after a great deal of work. Whether you're trying to write a brilliant term paper or design the next Beanie Baby, creativity requires effort and persistence.

Finally, the creative process is typically filled with obstacles and setbacks. The best-

selling novelist Stephen King endured years of rejection of his manuscripts before his first book was published. Thomas Edison tried thousands of filaments before he created the first working light bulb. In the face of obstacles and setbacks, the creative person perseveres.

To summarize our workshop on creativity, we'll use the letters of the word *create* as an acronym. Thus, the basic ingredients of creativity are:

- **C**hoose the goal of creativity.
- **R**einforce creative behavior.
- **E**ngage in problem finding.
- **A**cquire relevant knowledge.
- **T**ry different approaches.
- **E**xert effort and expect setbacks.

Chapter Review
Thinking, Language, and Intelligence

Key Points

Introduction: Thinking, Language, and Intelligence

- **Cognition** refers to the mental activities involved in acquiring, retaining, and using knowledge.

- **Thinking** involves manipulating internal, mental representations of information in order to draw inferences and conclusions. Thinking often involves the manipulation of two kinds of mental representations: **mental images** and **concepts.**

- Most research has been done on visual mental images. We seem to treat mental images much as we do actual visual images or physical objects.

- Thinking also involves the use of concepts. **Formal concepts** are defined by logical rules. **Natural concepts** are likely to have fuzzy rather than rigid boundaries. We determine membership in natural concepts by comparing an object with our **prototype** for the natural concept or by comparing it to **exemplars** that we have stored in memory.

Solving Problems and Making Decisions

- **Problem solving** refers to thinking and behavior directed toward attaining a goal that is not readily available.

- Strategies commonly used in problem solving include **trial and error, algorithms,** and **heuristics.** Heuristics include breaking a problem into a series of subgoals and working backward from the goal. Sometimes problems are resolved through **insight** or **intuition.**

- **Functional fixedness** and **mental set** are two common obstacles to problem solving.

- Decision-making models include the single-feature model, the additive model, and the elimination by aspects model. Different strategies may be most helpful in different situations.

- When making risky decisions, we often use the **availability heuristic** and the **representativeness heuristic** to help us estimate the likelihood of events.

Language and Thought

- **Language** is a system for combining arbitrary symbols to produce an infinite number of meaningful statements.

- Language has the following characteristics: Meaning is conveyed by arbitrary symbols whose meaning is shared by speakers of the same language; language is a rule-based system; language is generative; and language involves displacement. Language influences thinking by affecting our perceptions of others.

- Animals communicate with members of their own species, sometimes in a complex fashion. Some can also be taught to communicate with humans. Bonobos and dolphins seem to have demonstrated an elementary grasp of the rules of syntax. **Animal cognition** is an active field of research in comparative psychology.

Measuring Intelligence

- **Intelligence** can be defined as the global capacity to think rationally, act purposefully, and deal effectively with the environment. Intelligence tests are designed to measure general mental abilities.

- Alfred Binet developed the first widely accepted intelligence test, which incorporated the idea of a **mental age** that was different from chronological age. Binet did not believe that intelligence was inborn or fixed or that it could be described by a single number.

- Lewis Terman adapted Binet's test for use in the United States and developed the concept of the **intelligence quotient,** or **IQ** score. Terman believed that success in life was primarily determined by IQ.

- Group intelligence tests were developed for screening military recruits during World War I.

- David Wechsler developed the Wechsler Adult Intelligence Scale (WAIS), which included scores on subtests that measured different mental abilities. Wechsler also changed the method of calculating overall IQ scores.

- **Achievement tests** and **aptitude tests** are two types of psychological tests. Psychological tests must meet the requirements of **standardization, reliability,** and **validity.** The norms, or standards, for intelligence tests follow the **normal curve,** or **normal distribution,** of scores.

The Nature of Intelligence

- Debate over the nature of intelligence centers on two key issues: (1) whether intelligence is a single factor or a cluster of different abilities and (2) how narrowly intelligence should be defined.

- Charles Spearman believed that intelligence could be described as a single factor, called **general intelligence,** or the **g factor.**

- Louis L. Thurstone believed that there were seven primary mental abilities.

- Howard Gardner believes that there are multiple intelligences. He defines *intelligence* as the ability to solve problems or create products that are valued within a cultural setting.

- Robert Sternberg's **triarchic theory of intelligence** emphasizes both the universal aspects of intelligence and the importance of adapting to a particular cultural environment. He identifies three forms of intelligence: analytic, creative, and practical intelligence.

- The IQ of any individual is the result of a complex interaction between heredity and environment. Intelligence is not determined by a single gene, but by the interaction of multiple genes.

- Twin studies are used to determine the degree to which genetics contributes to complex characteristics such as intelligence. **Heritability** refers to the percentage of variation within a given population that is due to heredity. Within a given racial group, the effects of environment and genetics are roughly equal.

- There are differences in the average IQ scores for different racial groups. However, there is more variation within a particular group than there is between groups.

- Although it is possible to calculate the differences within a given group that are due to heredity, it is not possible to calculate the differences between groups that are due to heredity. Unless the environments are identical, no comparisons can be drawn. Rather than genetic factors, environmental factors are more likely to be the cause of average IQ differences among groups.

- Cross-cultural studies have demonstrated that the average IQ scores of groups subject to social discrimination are frequently lower than the average IQ scores of the dominant social group, even when the groups are not racially different.

- Intelligence tests can be culturally biased. All intelligence tests reflect the culture in which they are developed. Cultural factors may also influence test-taking behavior and individual performance. IQ scores reflect only selected aspects of intelligence.

Key Terms

cognition, p. 260

thinking, p. 261

mental image, p. 261

concept, p. 263

formal concept, p. 263

natural concept, p. 263

prototype, p. 263

exemplars, p. 264

problem solving, p. 264

trial and error, p. 265

algorithm, p. 265

heuristic, p. 265

insight, p. 266

intuition, p. 266

functional fixedness, p. 266

mental set, p. 267

availability heuristic, p. 269

representativeness heuristic, p. 269

language, p. 271

linguistic relativity hypothesis, p. 272

animal cognition, p. 275

intelligence, p. 276

mental age, p. 276

intelligence quotient (IQ), p. 276

achievement test, p. 279

aptitude test, p. 280

standardization, p. 280

normal curve (normal distribution), p. 280

reliability, p. 280

validity, p. 280

g factor (general intelligence), p. 281

triarchic theory of intelligence, p. 283

heritability, p. 286

stereotype threat, p. 290

creativity, p. 292

Key People

Alfred Binet (1857–1911) French psychologist who, along with French psychiatrist Théodore Simon, developed the first widely used intelligence test. (p. 276)

Howard Gardner (b. 1943) Contemporary American psychologist whose theory of intelligence states that there is not one intelligence, but multiple independent intelligences. (p. 282)

Charles Spearman (1863–1945) British psychologist who advanced the theory that a general intelligence factor, called the g factor, is responsible for overall intellectual functioning. (p. 281)

Robert Sternberg (b. 1949) Contemporary American psychologist whose *triarchic theory of intelligence* identifies three forms of intelligence (analytic, creative, and practical). (p. 283)

Lewis Terman (1877–1956) American psychologist who translated and adapted the Binet-Simon intelligence test for use in the United States; he also began a major longitudinal study of the lives of gifted children in 1921. (p. 277)

Louis L. Thurstone (1887–1955) American psychologist who advanced the theory that intelligence is composed of several primary mental abilities and cannot be accurately described by an overall general or g factor measure. (p. 282)

David Wechsler (1896–1981) American psychologist who developed the Wechsler Adult Intelligence Scale, the most widely used intelligence test. (p. 279)

Web Companion | Review Activities

You can find additional review activities by going to **www.DiscoveringPsychology.com** and clicking on the *Discovering Psychology* 4th Edition text cover. At the Discovering Psychology Web Companion you'll find the chapter learning objectives, flashcards for key terms and key people, interactive crossword puzzles, self-scoring practice quizzes, and other materials to help you master the information in this chapter.

chapter

8

Motivation and Emotion

Prologue

Soaring with Angels

Richard and I had been best friends since our paths first crossed at Central High School in Sioux City, Iowa. Even then, Richard was extraordinary. He was good-looking and liked by everyone. He maintained almost a straight-A average in his classes. In our senior year, he was elected student body president. (To be perfectly honest, he beat me in the race for student body president.) And his talent as a diver had attracted the attention of college swimming coaches. Coming from a family of very modest means, Richard hoped for an athletic scholarship to attend college. He got one: The University of Arkansas awarded him a four-year athletic scholarship.

Richard met Becky when they were freshmen at the University of Arkansas. They seemed like a good match. Becky was smart, pretty, athletic, and had a wonderful sense of humor. They were also both Catholic, which greatly pleased Becky's parents. So it came as no surprise when Richard and Becky announced their plans to marry after graduating. But, in retrospect, I can't help thinking that Richard's timing was deliberate when he asked me, in front of Becky, to be his best man.

"You're *sure* you want to marry this guy?" I half-jokingly asked Becky.

"Only if he takes nationals on the three-meter board," Becky quipped. As it turned out, Richard did place third on the three-meter board the following spring at the national collegiate swimming competition. Then, three months before their wedding, Richard and I had the only argument we've ever had.

"I don't need to tell Becky about the past," Richard insisted.

"That's bull, Richard," I shouted. "This woman loves you and if you don't tell her about your homosexual urges, then you are marrying her under false pretenses."

"I do *not* have those feelings anymore!" Richard yelled back.

"If that's true, then tell her!" I demanded.

But it wasn't true, of course. Although Richard would not admit it to himself, he had only become adept at suppressing his sexual attraction to other men. At the time we had that argument, I was still the only person who knew that Richard harbored what he called "homosexual urges." Richard had first told me when we were juniors in high school. I was stunned. But Richard did not want to feel the way he did. In fact, he felt ashamed and guilty. Back then, being homosexual carried a much greater social stigma than it does today.

So when Richard and I were still in high school, we scraped up enough money to secretly send him to a psychologist for a few sessions. Despite our naive hopes for a quick "cure," Richard's troubling feelings remained. When he got to the University of Arkansas, Richard saw a counselor on a regular basis. After months of counseling, Richard believed he was capable of leading a heterosexual life.

Richard and Becky's wedding was magnificent. And, yes, I was the best man. After the wedding, they decided to stay in Fayetteville so that Richard could start graduate school. The inevitable happened less than a year later. Becky called me.

"I'm driving to Tulsa tonight. Don, you've *got* to tell me what's going on," she said, her voice strained, shaking. And I did, as gently as I could.

Richard and Becky's marriage was annulled. In time, Becky recovered psychologically, remarried, and had two children. Her bitterness toward Richard softened over the years. The last time we talked, she seemed genuinely forgiving of Richard.

For his part, Richard gave up trying to be something he was not. Instead, he came to grips with his sexual orientation, moved to San Francisco, and became a co-owner of two health clubs. True to form, Richard quickly became a respected and well-liked member of San Francisco's large gay community. He eventually met John, an accountant, with whom he formed a long-term relationship. But after Richard's move to San Francisco, our friendship faded.

It was our 20-year high school reunion that triggered Richard's unexpected call. When I told him I simply did not have the time to attend, he suggested stopping in Tulsa on his way to the reunion to meet Sandy and our daughter, Laura.

So on a warm May evening, Richard, Sandy, and I drank some margaritas, ate Chinese carryout, and talked until midnight. Just as I had expected, Sandy was quite taken with Richard. Indeed, Richard *was* a wonderful man—smart, funny, thoughtful, and sensitive. Laura, who was not quite 2 years old, was also enchanted by Richard. My only regret about that evening is that I did not take a picture of Richard sitting on our back deck as Laura brought him first one toy, then another, then another. As it turned out, it would be the last time I saw Richard.

About a year after he visited us in Tulsa, Richard was killed in a hang-gliding accident. As he was soaring over the rocky California coast, Richard swerved to miss an inexperienced flyer who crossed his path in the air. Richard lost control of his hang glider and was killed on impact when he plummeted into the rocky coastline.

A week later, more than 300 people crowded into St. Mary's Catholic Church in Sioux City, where Richard had been an altar boy in his youth. The outpouring of love and respect for Richard at the memorial service was a testament to the remarkable man he was.

What Richard's story illustrates is that who we are in this life—our identity—is not determined by any single characteristic or quality. Yes, Richard was gay, but that's not all Richard was, just as your sexual orientation is not the only characteristic that defines you or motivates your behavior. In this chapter we'll look at a wide variety of factors that motivate our behavior, including sexuality, striving to achieve, and the emotions we experience. In the process, we'll come back to Richard's story.

Introduction

Motivation and Emotion

Key Theme
■ Motivation refers to the forces acting on or within an organism to initiate and direct behavior.

Key Questions
■ What three characteristics are associated with motivation?
■ How is emotion related to the topic of motivation?

If you think about it, "something" inspired you to pick up this text, so that you are reading these words right now. Going a step further, "something" moved us to write these words. That "something" is what the topic of **motivation** is about—the biological, emotional, cognitive, or social forces that act on or within you, initiating and directing your behavior. Typically, psychologists don't measure motivation directly. Instead, some type of motivation is *inferred* when an organism performs a particular behavior, as when curiosity motivates exploratory behavior or hunger motivates eating behavior.

As an explanatory concept, motivation is very useful in both the scientific sense and the everyday sense. In conversations, people routinely use the word *motivation* to understand or explain the "why" behind the behavior of others. "And what motivated you to take up hang-gliding?" "She is so motivated to get into law school that she goes to the library every night to study for the law school entrance exam." Everyday statements like these reflect three basic characteristics commonly associated with motivation: activation, persistence, and intensity.

Activation is demonstrated by the initiation or production of behavior, such as Richard's decision to pursue competitive diving in high school. *Persistence* is demonstrated by continued efforts or the determination to achieve a particular goal, often in the face of obstacles. Day after day, Richard spent hours at the swimming pool honing the precision of his dives. Finally, *intensity* is seen in the greater vigor of responding that usually accompanies motivated behavior.

Motivation is closely tied to emotional processes, and vice versa. Often we are motivated to experience a particular emotion, such as feeling proud. In turn, the experience of an emotion—such as love, fear, or dissatisfaction—can motivate us to take action. Many forms of motivation have an emotional component, which is involved in the initiation and persistence of behavior. One reflection of the emotional intensity of Richard's motivation was the exhilaration he experienced when he placed third at a national collegiate swimming competition. In the second half of the chapter, we'll take a detailed look at emotion. As you'll see, *emotion* is a psychological state involving three distinct components: subjective experience, a physiological response, and a behavioral or expressive component.

"Could you give me a little push?"

Motivational Concepts and Theories

Key Theme
- Over the past century, instinct, drive, incentive, arousal, and humanistic theories were proposed to explain the general principles of motivation.

Key Questions
- How does each theory explain motivation?
- What were the limitations of each theory?
- What lasting ideas did each theory contribute to the study of motivation?

During the twentieth century, several broad theories of motivation were proposed. Each model eventually proved to be limited, explaining only certain aspects of motivation. However, key ideas and concepts from each model became essential to a complete understanding of motivation and were incorporated into newer theories. As you'll see in this section, the concepts used to explain motivation have become progressively more diverse.

Instinct Theories
Inborn Behaviors as Motivators

In the late 1800s, the fledgling science of psychology initially embraced instinct theories to explain motivation. According to **instinct theories,** people are motivated to engage in certain behaviors because of evolutionary programming. Just as animals display automatic and innate instinctual behavior patterns called *fixed action patterns,* such as migration or mating rituals, human behavior was also thought to be motivated by inborn instinctual behavior patterns.

motivation
The biological, emotional, cognitive, or social forces that activate and direct behavior.

instinct theories
The view that certain human behaviors are innate and due to evolutionary programming.

Table 8.1

James's List of Human Instincts

Attachment	Resentment
Fear	Curiosity
Disgust	Shyness
Rivalry	Sociability
Greediness	Bashfulness
Suspicion	Secretiveness
Hunting	Cleanliness
Play	Modesty
Shame	Love
Anger	Parental Love

In his famous text, *Principles of Psychology,* William James (1890) devoted a lengthy chapter to the topic of instinct. With an air of superiority, James noted that "no other mammal, not even the monkey, shows so large an array of instincts" as humans. The table shows some of the human instincts identified by James.

Motivation and Drive Theories According to drive theories of motivation, behavior is motivated by biological drives to maintain *homeostasis,* or an optimal internal balance. After a long soccer practice on a hot day, these high school students are motivated to rest, cool off, and drink water. Drive theories of motivation are useful in explaining biological motives like hunger, thirst, and fatigue, but are less useful in explaining psychological motives. For example, how could we explain their motivation to play competitive soccer? To practice long and hard on a hot summer day?

Inspired by Charles Darwin's (1859, 1871) landmark theory of evolution, early psychologists like William James and William McDougall (1908) devised lists of human instincts. Table 8.1 is a collection of the human instincts that William James (1890) included in his famous text, *Principles of Psychology.*

By the early 1900s, thousands of instincts had been proposed in one expert's list or another to account for just about every conceivable human behavior (Bernard, 1924). (The early instinct theorists were, no doubt, motivated by a "listing instinct.") But what does it mean to say that an assertive person has a "self-assertion instinct"? Or to say that our friend Richard had a "diving instinct"? The obvious problem with the early instinct theories was that merely describing and labeling behaviors did not explain them.

By the 1920s, instinct theories had fallen out of favor as an explanation of human motivation, primarily because of their lack of explanatory power. But the more general idea that some human behaviors are innate and genetically influenced remained an important element in the overall understanding of motivation. Today, psychologists taking the *evolutionary perspective* consider how our evolutionary heritage may influence patterns of human behaviors, such as eating behaviors or the expression of emotions. We'll consider what the evolutionary perspective has to say about both of those examples later in the chapter.

Drive Theories
Biological Needs as Motivators

Beginning in the 1920s, instinct theories were replaced by drive theories. In general, **drive theories** asserted that behavior is motivated by the desire to reduce internal tension caused by unmet biological needs, such as hunger or thirst. The basic idea was that these unmet biological needs "drive" or "push" us to behave in certain ways that will lead to a reduction in the drive. When a particular behavior successfully reduces a drive, the behavior becomes more likely to be repeated when the same need state arises again.

Leading drive theorists, including psychologists Robert S. Woodworth (1918, 1921) and Clark L. Hull (1943, 1952), believed that drives are triggered by the internal mechanisms of homeostasis. The principle of **homeostasis** states that the body monitors and maintains relatively constant levels of internal states, such as body temperature, fluid levels, and energy supplies. If any of these internal conditions deviates very far from the optimal level, the body initiates processes to bring the condition back to the normal or optimal range. Thus, the body automatically tries to maintain a "steady state," which is what *homeostasis* means.

According to drive theorists, when an internal imbalance is detected by homeostatic mechanisms, a **drive** to restore balance is produced. The drive activates behavior to reduce the need and to reestablish the balance of internal conditions. For example, after you have not eaten anything for several hours, this unmet biological need creates a *drive state—* hunger—that motivates or energizes your behavior. And how might the drive of hunger energize you to behave? You might make your way to the kitchen and forage in the refrigerator for some leftover guacamole dip or chocolate cake.

Today, the drive concept remains useful in explaining motivated behaviors that clearly have biological components, such as hunger, thirst, and sexuality. However, drive theories also have limitations. Let's consider hunger again. Is the motivation of eating behavior strictly a matter of physiological need? Obviously not. People often eat when they're not hungry and don't eat when they are hungry. And how could drive theories account for the motivation to buy a lottery ticket or run a marathon?

Incentive Motivation
Goal Objects as Motivators

Building on the base established by drive theories, incentive theories emerged in the 1940s and 1950s. **Incentive theories** proposed that behavior is motivated by the "pull" of external goals, such as rewards, money, or recognition. It's easy to think of many situations in which a particular goal, such as a promotion at work, can serve as an external incentive that helps activate particular behaviors.

Incentive theories drew heavily from well-established learning principles, such as *reinforcement,* and the work of influential learning theorists, such as Pavlov, Watson, Skinner, and Tolman (see Chapter 5). Edward Tolman (1932) also stressed the importance of cognitive factors in learning and motivation, especially the *expectation* that a particular behavior will lead to a particular goal.

When combined, drive and incentive theories account for a broad range of the "pushes" and "pulls" motivating many of our behaviors. But even in combination, drive and incentive explanations of motivation still had limitations. In some situations, such as playing a rapid-response video game, our behavior seems to be directed toward *increasing* tension and physiological arousal. If you think about it, our friend Richard's decision to take up diving was not motivated by either an internal, biological drive or an external incentive.

drive theories
The view that behavior is motivated by the desire to reduce internal tension caused by unmet biological needs.

homeostasis
(home-ee-oh-STAY-sis) The idea that the body monitors and maintains internal states, such as body temperature and energy supplies, at relatively constant levels; in general, the tendency to reach or maintain equilibrium.

drive
A need or internal motivational state that activates behavior to reduce the need and restore homeostasis.

incentive theories
The view that behavior is motivated by the pull of external goals, such as rewards.

arousal theory
The view that people are motivated to maintain a level of arousal that is optimal—neither too high nor too low.

sensation seeking
The degree to which an individual is motivated to experience high levels of sensory and physical arousal associated with varied and novel activities.

Arousal Theory
Optimal Stimulation as a Motivator

Racing your car down a barren stretch of highway, going to a suspenseful movie, shooting down the Super Slide at a water park—none of these activities seem to involve tension reduction, the satisfaction of some biological need, or the lure of some reward. Rather, performing the activity itself seems to motivate us. Why?

Arousal theory is based on the observation that people find both very high levels of arousal and very low levels of arousal quite unpleasant. When arousal is too low, we experience boredom and become motivated to *increase* arousal by seeking out stimulating experiences (Berlyne, 1960, 1971). But when arousal is too high, we seek to *reduce* arousal in a less stimulating environment. Thus, people are motivated to maintain an *optimal* level of arousal, one that is neither too high nor too low (Hebb, 1955). This optimal level of arousal varies from person to person, from time to time, and from one situation to another.

That the optimal level of arousal varies from person to person is especially evident in people dubbed *sensation seekers.* Sensation seekers find the heightened arousal of novel experiences very pleasurable. According to psychologist Marvin Zuckerman (1979, 1994), people who rank high on the dimension of **sensation seeking** have a need for varied, complex, and unique sensory experiences. No doubt Don ranks high on this dimension, since he has tried skydiving, aerobatic flying, and white-water rafting. (He also once ate a handful of biodegradable packing peanuts, much to the horror of a college secretary.) Although such experiences can sometimes involve physical or social risks, sensation seekers aren't necessarily drawn to danger—but rather to the novel experience itself. For example, college students who study abroad score significantly higher on sensation seeking than college students who stay in their country of origin (Schroth & McCormack, 2000).

Motivated to an Extreme They are aptly called "extreme sports," and they include such diverse activities as hang gliding, ice climbing, white-water kayaking, bungee jumping, and parachuting from mountain cliffs and radio towers. People who enjoy such high-risk activities are usually sensation seekers. For them, the rush of adrenaline that they experience when they push the outer limit is an exhilarating and rewarding experience.

Seeking Stimulation Like humans, animals are also motivated to seek out stimulation and explore novel environments. In his research with monkeys, Harry Harlow (1953c) found that arousal was a powerful motive. These young monkeys are trying to open a complicated lock, despite the lack of an incentive or reward for their behavior.

Like people, animals also seem to seek out novel environmental stimulation. Rats, cats, dogs, and other animals actively explore a new environment. In a series of classic studies, psychologist Harry Harlow (1953a, 1953b) showed that a monkey will spend hours trying to open a complicated lock, even when there is no incentive or reward for doing so. And, when kept in a boring cage, a monkey will "work" for the opportunity to open a window to peek into another monkey's cage or to watch an electric train run (Butler & Harlow, 1954).

Humanistic Theory
Human Potential as a Motivator

In the late 1950s, **humanistic theories of motivation** were championed by psychologists Carl Rogers and Abraham Maslow. Although not discounting the role of biological and external motivators, humanistic theories emphasized psychological and cognitive components in human motivation. Motivation was thought to be affected by how we perceive the world, how we think about ourselves and others, and our beliefs about our abilities and skills (Rogers, 1961, 1977).

According to the humanistic perspective, people are motivated to realize their highest personal potential. Although the motivation to strive for a positive self-concept and personal potential was thought to be inborn, humanistic theories also recognized the importance of the environment (Maslow, 1970). Without a supportive and encouraging environment—personal, social, and cultural—the motivation to strive toward one's highest potential could be jeopardized. Later in the chapter, we'll consider the most famous humanistic model of motivation, Maslow's *hierarchy of needs*.

We'll begin our survey of motivation by providing a description of basic motives that are strongly influenced by biological factors—hunger and sexuality. In later sections, we'll look at psychological motives, including competence and achievement motivation.

humanistic theories of motivation
The view that emphasizes the importance of psychological and cognitive factors in motivation, especially the notion that people are motivated to realize their personal potential.

glucose
Simple sugar that provides energy and is primarily produced by the conversion of carbohydrates and fats; commonly called *blood sugar*.

insulin
Hormone produced by the pancreas that regulates blood levels of glucose and signals the hypothalamus, regulating hunger and eating behavior.

basal metabolic rate (BMR)
When the body is at rest, the rate at which it uses energy for vital functions, such as heartbeat and respiration.

adipose tissue
Body fat that is the main source of stored, or reserve, energy.

energy homeostasis
The long-term matching of food intake to energy expenditure.

Biological Motivation
Hunger and Eating

Key Theme

- Hunger is a biological motive, but eating behavior is motivated by a complex interaction of biological, social, and psychological factors.

Key Questions

- What is energy homeostasis, and how does it relate to energy balance?
- What are the short-term signals that regulate eating behavior?
- What chemical signals are involved in the long-term regulation of a stable body weight?
- How do set-point and settling-point theories differ?

It seems simple: You're hungry, so you eat. But even a moment's reflection will tell you that eating behavior is not that straightforward. When, what, how much, and how often you eat is influenced by an array of psychological, biological, social, and cultural factors. Over the next several pages, we'll look at what researchers have learned about the motivational factors that trigger hunger and eating behavior. These research efforts have focused on answering several key questions:

- What signals regulate the motivation to start and stop eating?
- How do people maintain a stable body weight over time?
- Why do people become overweight or obese?
- What causes eating disorders?

Delicious or Disgusting? The need to eat is a universal human motive. However, culture influences *what* we eat, *when* we eat, and *how* we eat (Rozin, 1996). At a market in Beijing, China, this 8-year-old is about to enjoy a tasty treat—deep-fried grasshopper kabob. While not a feature at your typical U.S. restaurant, insects are standard fare in many countries. For example, grasshoppers, ant and fly larvae, and worms can be purchased as snacks in traditional markets in Mexico, where they have been a staple of the diet for thousands of years.

Energy Homeostasis
Calories Consumed = Calories Expended

In order to understand the regulation of hunger and eating behavior, we need to begin with some basics on how food is converted to energy in the body. The food that you eat is broken down by enzymes and gradually absorbed in your intestines. As part of this process, food is converted into amino acids, fatty acids, and simple sugars, providing "fuel" for your body. The simple sugar **glucose,** commonly called *blood sugar,* provides the main source of energy for all mammals, including humans. In the liver, glucose is converted to and stored as *glycogen,* which can be easily converted back to glucose for energy. The hormone **insulin,** secreted by the pancreas, helps control blood levels of glucose and promotes the uptake of glucose by the muscles and other body tissues. Insulin also helps in regulating eating behavior and maintaining a stable body weight.

About one-third of your body's energy is expended for the routine physical activities of daily life, such as walking, lifting objects, brushing your teeth, and digesting the food you eat. The remaining two-thirds of your body's energy is used for continuous bodily functions that are essential to life, such as generating body heat, heartbeat, respiration, and brain activity. When you are lying down and resting, the rate at which your body uses energy for vital body functions is referred to as your **basal metabolic rate (BMR).**

Obviously, you have to eat in order to have sufficient immediate energy for vital body functions and to survive. But another reason you eat is to maintain a reserve of stored energy. **Adipose tissue,** or body fat, is the main source of stored calories. Your liver, which monitors glucose levels in your bloodstream, can utilize this stored energy if necessary.

Positive Versus Negative Energy Balance

For most of us there is considerable daily variation in what, when, how often, and how much we eat (de Castro & others, 2000; Marcelino & others, 2001). Yet despite this day-to-day variability in eating behavior, our body weight, including our stores of body fat, tends to stay relatively constant over the course of weeks, months, and even years (Keesey & Hirvonen, 1997). Your typical or average body weight is called your *baseline body weight.*

A regulatory process called **energy homeostasis** helps you maintain your baseline body weight. Over time, most people experience *energy balance* (see Figure 8.1). This means that the number of calories you consume almost exactly matches the number of calories you expend for energy. The result is that your body weight, including body fat stores, tends to remain stable.

However, energy balance can become disrupted if you eat more or less food than you need. If your caloric intake exceeds the amount of calories expended for

Not one man in a billion, when taking his dinner, ever thinks of utility. He eats because the food tastes good and makes him want more.

William James, *Principles of Psychology* (1890)

FIGURE 8.1 Energy Balance The tendency of our bodies to maintain a stable body weight is well documented (Schwartz & others, 2000). Maintaining a stable body weight occurs when you experience *energy balance*— that is, when the calories you take in almost exactly match the calories you expend for physical activity and metabolism.

SOURCE: Adapted from Ravussin & Danforth (1999).

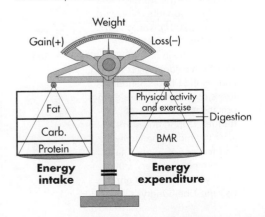

energy, you experience *positive energy balance*. When there is more glucose than your body needs for its energy requirements, the excess glucose is converted into reserve energy—fat. If positive energy balance persists over time, the size and number of the body fat cells that make up the adipose tissue increase. Conversely, if you diet or fast, *negative energy balance* occurs: Caloric intake falls short of the calories expended for energy. If this imbalance continues, body fat stores shrink as the reserve energy in fat cells is used for physical activity and metabolic functions.

These findings imply that energy homeostasis and a stable body weight are actively regulated by internal signals and mechanisms that influence eating behavior. But what exactly are these signals or mechanisms?

Short-Term Signals That Regulate Eating

Consuming food is so routine in our lives that most of us don't really think about what motivates us to stop what we're doing and begin eating. Psychologists and other researchers, however, are very motivated to answer that question. In the last few years they've made important new discoveries about the physiological and psychological factors involved in the motivation to eat (Strubbe & Woods, 2004).

Physiological Changes That Predict Eating

The idea that some internal, biochemical factor triggers our desire to eat makes intuitive sense. But what? Many people believe that eating is triggered by a drastic drop in blood glucose levels, which are rapidly restored by food consumption. This popular belief is *not* accurate. Actually, your blood levels of glucose and fats fluctuate very little over the course of a typical day. However, about 30 minutes before you eat, you experience a *slight* increase in blood levels of insulin and a *slight* decrease in blood levels of glucose (see Figure 8.2) (Campfield & others, 1996; Melanson & others, 1999).

A more important internal signal is a new hormone discovered by Japanese researcher Masayasu Kojima and his colleagues in 1999. **Ghrelin** (pronounced GRELL-in) is primarily manufactured by cells lining the stomach.

Ghrelin was quickly dubbed "the hunger hormone" when research showed that it strongly stimulates appetite. When rats were deprived of food, ghrelin levels increased sharply (Inui, 2001). More directly, rats whose brains were continuously infused with ghrelin ate voraciously and gained weight. When ghrelin receptors were blocked, their eating behavior subsided (Nakazato & others, 2001; Tschöp & others, 2000).

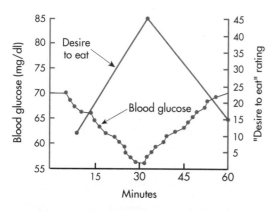

FIGURE 8.2 Blood Glucose and the Motivation to Eat The red dots depict the effects of insulin, which triggers a small decline in blood glucose over the course of about 30 minutes. As blood glucose decreases, the subjective desire to eat increases sharply, depicted by the blue line. If you do not eat, blood glucose level returns to normal within the hour and the desire to eat diminishes. A small decline in blood glucose level is one factor that reliably predicts the motivation to eat (Campfield & others, 1996).

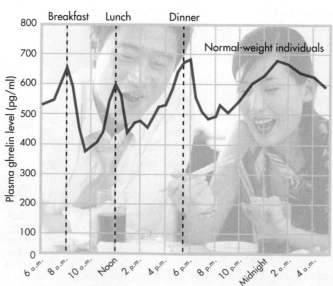

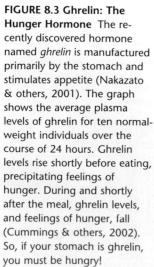

FIGURE 8.3 Ghrelin: The Hunger Hormone The recently discovered hormone named *ghrelin* is manufactured primarily by the stomach and stimulates appetite (Nakazato & others, 2001). The graph shows the average plasma levels of ghrelin for ten normal-weight individuals over the course of 24 hours. Ghrelin levels rise shortly before eating, precipitating feelings of hunger. During and shortly after the meal, ghrelin levels, and feelings of hunger, fall (Cummings & others, 2002). So, if your stomach is ghrelin, you must be hungry!

What about people? Researcher Donald Cummings and his colleagues (2002, 2001) showed that ghrelin is involved in the short-term regulation of eating behavior. As you can see in Figure 8.3, blood levels of ghrelin rise sharply before and fall abruptly after meals. Cummings also found that ghrelin seems to be involved in the long-term regulation of energy balance and weight. When participants in one of his studies lost weight by dieting, their overall plasma levels of ghrelin—and feelings of hunger—increased.

Two other internal factors are correlated with meal onset—

body temperature and metabolism rate. Prior to eating, body temperature increases and metabolism decreases. As the meal is consumed, this internal physiological pattern reverses: body temperature decreases and metabolism increases (De Vries & others, 1993; LeBlanc, 2000). This slight decrease in body temperature might explain why some people, including about a third of our students, occasionally feel cold after eating a meal.

Psychological Factors That Trigger Eating

In Chapter 5, we described *classical conditioning* and *operant conditioning*. Both forms of conditioning can affect eating behavior. For example, much as Pavlov's dogs were conditioned to salivate at the sound of a bell, your eating behavior has probably been influenced by years of classical conditioning. The time of day at which you normally eat (the *conditioned stimulus*) elicits reflexive internal physiological changes (the *conditioned response*), such as the changes in blood levels of insulin, glucose, and ghrelin, increased body temperature, and decreased metabolism. In turn, these internal physiological changes increase your sense of hunger. Other stimuli, such as the setting in which you normally eat or just the sight of food utensils, can also become associated with the anticipation of eating (T. L. Davidson, 2000; Nederkoorn & others, 2000; Tuomisto & others, 1998).

Operant conditioning and positive reinforcement play a role in eating, too. Voluntary eating behaviors are followed by a *reinforcing stimulus*—the taste of food. Granted, not all foods are equally reinforcing. Because of prior reinforcement experiences, people develop preferences for certain tastes, especially sweet, salty, and fatty tastes (Capaldi, 1996; Mennella & Beauchamp, 1996). In other words, foods with one of these tastes hold greater **positive incentive value** for some people. Hence, your motivation to eat is influenced by prior learning experiences that have shaped your expectations, especially the anticipated pleasure of eating certain foods.

Is Your Mouth Watering? Does the sight of this freshly baked chocolate chip cookie make you feel hungry? Some foods—like chocolate chip cookies—have a strong positive incentive value. Even if you've just eaten a large meal, the reinforcing value of a chocolate chip cookie might tempt you to keep eating. Although you might not have been particularly hungry before you read this page, looking at this photograph might send you to the kitchen in search of a sweet snack—which is exactly what happened to your authors!

Satiation Signals
Sensing When to Stop Eating

The feeling of fullness and diminished desire to eat that accompanies eating a meal is termed **satiation.** Several signals combine to help trigger satiation. One satiation signal involves *stretch receptors* in the stomach that communicate sensory information to the brainstem (Furness & others, 1999). The sensitivity of the stomach stretch receptors is increased by a hormone called **cholecystokinin,** thankfully abbreviated **CCK.** During meals, cholecystokinin is secreted by the small intestines and enters the bloodstream. In the brain, CCK acts as a neurotransmitter. Many studies have shown that CCK promotes satiation and reduces or stops eating (G. P. Smith & Gibbs, 1998). CCK also magnifies the satiety-producing effects of food in the stomach by slowing the rate at which the stomach empties (Liddle, 1997).

Psychological factors play a role in satiation, too. As you eat a meal, there is a decline in the positive incentive value of any available food, but especially the specific foods you are eating. So, after you have wolfed down four slices of pizza, the pizza's appeal begins to diminish. This phenomenon is termed **sensory-specific satiety** (Guinard & Brun, 1998; Hetherington & Rolls, 1996). Of course, if a *different* appealing food becomes available, your willingness to eat might return. Restaurants are well aware of this, which is why servers will bring a tempting platter of scrumptious desserts to your table after you've finished a large and otherwise satisfying dinner.

Long-Term Signals That Regulate Body Weight

In the last decade, researchers have discovered more than 20 different chemical messengers that monitor and help us maintain a stable body weight over time (see Schwartz & others, 2000; Woods & others, 2000). Three of the best-documented internal signals are *leptin, insulin,* and *neuropeptide Y.*

ghrelin
(GRELL-in) Hormone manufactured primarily by the stomach that stimulates appetite and the secretion of growth hormone by the pituitary gland.

positive incentive value
In eating behavior, the anticipated pleasure of consuming a particular food; in general, the expectation of pleasure or satisfaction in performing a particular behavior.

satiation
(say-she-AY-shun) In eating behavior, the feeling of fullness and diminished desire to eat that accompanies eating a meal; in general, the sensation of having an appetite or desire fully or excessively satisfied.

cholecystokinin (CCK)
(kola-sis-tow-KINE-in) Hormone secreted primarily by the small intestine that promotes satiation; also found in the brain.

sensory-specific satiety
(sah-TIE-it-tee) The reduced desire to continue consuming a particular food.

Ob/ob **Mice, Before and After Leptin** Leptin is a hormone produced by body fat. Because of a genetic mutation, these mice, dubbed *ob/ob* mice, lack the ability to produce leptin. Consequently, *ob/ob* mice behave as though their brain were telling them that their body fat reserves are completely depleted and that they are starving. *Ob/ob* mice have voracious appetites and five times as much body fat as normal-weight mice. Yet they display the characteristics of starving animals, including decreased immune system functioning, low body temperatures, and lack of energy. When the *ob/ob* mouse on the right was given supplemental leptin, it lost the excess fat and began eating normally. Its body temperature, immune system, and metabolism also became normal (Friedman & Halaas, 1998). Unfortunately, what worked for obese mice has not worked as easily for obese people, although researchers remain hopeful.

leptin
Hormone produced by fat cells that signals the hypothalamus, regulating hunger and eating behavior.

neuropeptide Y (NPY)
Neurotransmitter found in several brain areas, most notably the hypothalamus, that stimulates eating behavior and reduces metabolism, promoting positive energy balance and weight gain.

Leptin is a hormone secreted by the body's adipose tissue into the bloodstream (Halaas & others, 1995). The amount of leptin that is secreted is directly correlated with the amount of body fat. The brain receptor sites for leptin are located in several areas of the hypothalamus (Friedman & Halaas, 1998). Neurons in the stomach and the gut also have leptin receptor sites (Kirchgessner & Liu, 1999).

Leptin is a key element in the feedback loop that regulates energy homeostasis. If positive energy balance occurs, the body's fat stores increase, and so do blood levels of leptin. When the leptin level in the brain increases, food intake is reduced and the body's fat stores shrink over time (Ahima & Osei, 2004). Increased leptin levels also intensify the satiety-producing effects of CCK, further decreasing the amount of food consumed (Matson & others, 2000). Should negative energy balance occur, fat stores shrink and there is a corresponding decrease in leptin blood levels, which triggers eating behavior.

The hormone *insulin* is also involved in brain mechanisms controlling food intake and body weight. Like leptin, the amount of insulin secreted by the pancreas is directly proportional to the amount of body fat. In the brain, insulin receptors are located in the same hypothalamus areas as leptin receptors (Brüning & others, 2000). Increased brain levels of insulin are also associated with a reduction in food intake and body weight (Baskin & others, 1999). So in much the same way as leptin, insulin levels vary in response to positive or negative energy balance, triggering an increase or decrease in eating.

Abbreviated **NPY, neuropeptide Y** is a neurotransmitter manufactured throughout the brain, including the hypothalamus. During periods of negative energy balance and weight loss, decreased leptin and insulin levels promote the secretion of NPY by the hypothalamus. In turn, increased brain levels of neuropeptide Y trigger eating behavior, reduce body metabolism, and promote fat storage. Conversely, if positive energy balance and weight gain occur, neuropeptide Y activity decreases (A. Levine & Billington, 1997; Naveilhan & others, 1999).

In combination, the long-term and short-term eating-related signals we've discussed provide a feedback loop that is monitored by the hypothalamus (see Figure 8.4). As the hypothalamus detects changes in leptin, insulin, neuropeptide Y, ghrelin, CCK, and other internal signals, food intake and BMR are adjusted to promote or reduce weight gain. The end result? Over the course of time, energy balance is achieved. Your average body weight stays stable because the number of calories you consume closely matches the number of calories you expend for energy. Or, at least, that's how it's supposed to work.

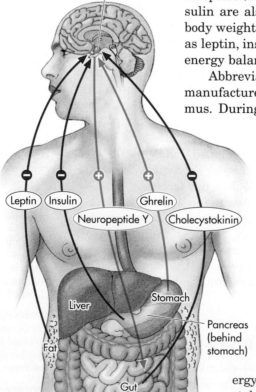

FIGURE 8.4 Regulating Appetite and Body Weight
Multiple signals interact to regulate your appetite and energy expenditure so that you maintain a stable body weight over time. As summarized in this drawing, your appetite is stimulated (⊕) by increased levels of ghrelin and neuropeptide Y. On the other hand, your appetite is suppressed (⊖) by increased levels of leptin, insulin, and CCK.

Eating and Body Weight over the Lifespan
Set Point or Settling Point?

So far we've discussed the regulation of eating in terms of the energy balance model, which is the essence of a popular theory called *set-point theory.* According to **set-point theory,** the body has a natural or optimal weight, called the *set-point weight,* that it is set to maintain. Much like a thermostat set to a particular temperature, your body vigorously defends this set-point weight from becoming lower or higher by regulating feelings of hunger and body metabolism (Keesey & Hirvonen, 1997; Keesey & Powley, 1986).

Although body weight tends to stay stable over extended periods of time, that does not necessarily mean that your baseline body weight is fixed at an optimal level throughout the lifespan. Instead, many people experience a strong tendency to drift to a heavier average body weight throughout adulthood. Why?

Settling-point models of weight regulation provide an alternate view that seems to better explain this tendency (see Pinel & others, 2000). According to settling-point models of weight regulation, your body weight tends to "settle" around the point at which equilibrium is achieved between energy expenditure and food consumption. Your *settling-point weight* will stay relatively stable as long as the factors influencing food consumption and energy expenditure don't change. However, if these factors do change, creating positive or negative energy balance, you will drift to a higher or lower settling-point body weight. In the next few sections, we'll consider some of the factors that contribute to the upward drift of body weight.

"Is this a good shoe for sitting?"

set-point theory
Theory that proposes that humans and other animals have a natural or optimal body weight, called the *set-point weight,* that the body defends from becoming higher or lower by regulating feelings of hunger and body metabolism.

settling-point models of weight regulation
General model of weight regulation suggesting that body weight settles, or stabilizes, around the point at which there is balance between the factors influencing energy intake and energy expenditure.

Excess Weight and Obesity
The Epidemic

Key Theme
- Overweight, obesity, and eating disorders are characterized by unhealthy body weight and maladaptive patterns of eating behavior.

Key Questions
- What is BMI, and why do people become overweight?
- What are the symptoms, characteristics, and causes of anorexia and bulimia nervosa?

In the United States today, 64 percent of adults—more than 115 million people—are either overweight or obese (National Center for Health Statistics, 2002a, 2002b). As Table 8.2 shows, some other countries also face the problem of an overweight population. As Figure 8.5 reveals, the percentage of overweight Americans escalates throughout adulthood, peaking in the fifth and sixth decades of life. But even early in life, 15 percent of children and adolescents are overweight. More unsettling, 1 of every 10 children in the preschool crowd (ages 2 to 5) is overweight (National Center for Health Statistics, 2002c).

The national trend toward excessive weight gain contrasts sharply with our cultural ideal of beauty and physical attractiveness—a very slender body (Wilfley & Rodin, 1995). Not surprisingly, at any given time one out of three women *and* one out of four men are trying to lose weight. Annually, Americans spend $33 *billion* on weight-reduction programs and diet foods (National Institutes of Health, 2000). Along with considerations of physical appearance, the motivation to lose weight often reflects health concerns.

Table 8.2

Percentages of Overweight People Around the World

United States	64%
Australia	56%
Russian Federation	54%
Great Britain	51%
Germany	50%
Canada	48%
Colombia	41%
Italy	39%
France	38%
Spain	37%
Brazil	36%
Japan	18%
China	15%

SOURCES: Australian Institute of Health and Welfare (1999); Heart and Stroke Foundation of Canada (1999); National Center for Health Statistics (2002a, 2002b, 2002c).

FIGURE 8.5 An Epidemic of Overweight and Obese Americans As you can see in this graph, the problem of being overweight escalates during young and middle adulthood. In each age group, more males than females are overweight. However, although the data are not shown here, more women than men are obese in each age group.

SOURCE: Adapted from National Center for Health Statistics (2002a, 2002b).

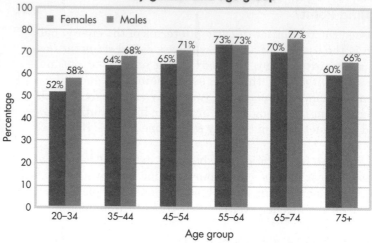

Percentage of overweight U.S. adults by gender and age group

■ Females ■ Males

Age group	Females	Males
20–34	52%	58%
35–44	64%	68%
45–54	65%	71%
55–64	73%	73%
65–74	70%	77%
75+	60%	66%

FIGURE 8.6 Calculating Your BMI: Where Do You Weigh In?

The **body mass index**, or **BMI**, provides a single numerical value that represents your height in relation to your weight. To determine your BMI, follow these steps:

Step 1. Multiply your weight in pounds by 703 _____

Step 2. Square your height in inches _____

Step 3. Divide step 1 by step 2 _____
This is your BMI.

If your BMI is:	You are:
18.4 or below	Underweight
18.5 to 24.9	Healthy weight
25.0 to 29.9	Overweight
30.0 and above	Obese

SOURCE: Centers for Disease Control and Prevention (2002).

How do you know if you are at a healthy weight? The most widely used method to determine weight status is the **body mass index,** abbreviated **BMI.** For adults, the body mass index provides a single numerical value that reflects your weight in relation to your height (see Figure 8.6).

Note that some people with a high BMI have excess weight that is attributable to muscle, bone, or body water, rather than fat. Thus, it is possible to be overweight and still be very healthy, as are bodybuilders or athletes who have developed their muscle mass. In contrast, someone who is **obese** has a BMI of 30 or greater—and an abnormally high proportion of body fat.

Factors Involved in Becoming Overweight

At the simplest level, the only way you can become overweight is if your caloric intake consistently exceeds your energy expenditure—the essence of *positive energy balance.* So the critical question is this: What kinds of factors are creating positive energy balance for so many people?

Too Little Sleep: Disrupting Hunger Hormones Multiple studies have shown that going without adequate sleep disrupts the hunger-related hormones leptin and ghrelin (e.g., Taheri & others, 2004). In one study, the sleep of healthy young men was restricted to just four hours a night for two nights. In response, blood levels of the appetite-suppressing hormone leptin fell by 18 percent and the appetite-increasing hormone ghrelin soared by 24 percent. This significantly increased feelings of hunger, especially for foods with high carbohydrate content (Spiegel & others, 2004). Other research has shown that adults who get by on about five hours of sleep a night are 50 percent more likely to be obese (Gangwisch, 2004).

Positive Incentive Value: Highly Palatable Foods Rather than hunger, we are often enticed to eat by the *positive incentive value* of the available foods and the anticipated pleasures of consuming those highly palatable foods. Did someone say *Godiva chocolate*?

GEECH, reprinted by permission of United Feature Syndicate, Inc.

CRITICAL THINKING 8.1

Has Evolution Programmed Us to Overeat?

Consider this fact. Numerous correlational studies of humans and experiments with rodents and Rhesus monkeys have consistently come to the same conclusion: Eating a restricted but balanced diet produces a variety of health benefits and promotes longevity (e.g., Barzilai & Gupta, 1999; Cefalu & others, 1997; Weindruch, 1996). So if eating a calorically restricted but balanced diet confers numerous health benefits and promotes longevity, *why* do so many people overeat?

University of British Columbia psychologists John P. J. Pinel, Sunaina Assanand, and Darrin R. Lehman (2000) believe that the evolutionary perspective provides several insights. For animals in the wild, food sources are often sporadic and unpredictable. When animals do find food, competition for it can be fierce, even deadly. If an animal waited to eat until it was hungry and its energy reserves were significantly diminished, it would run the risk of starving or falling prey to another animal.

Thus, the eating patterns of many animals have evolved so that they readily eat even if not hungry. Overeating when food is available ensures ample energy reserves to survive times when food is *not* available.

For most people living in food-abundant Western societies, foraging for your next meal is usually about as life-threatening as waiting your turn in the Taco Bell drive-

through lane. According to Pinel and his colleagues, people in food-rich societies do *not* eat because they are hungry or because their bodies are suffering from depleted energy resources. Rather, we are enticed by the anticipated pleasure of devouring that SuperSize burrito or calzone. In other words, we are motivated to eat by the *positive incentive value* of highly palatable foods.

When a food with a high positive incentive value is readily available, we eat, and often overeat, until we are satiated by that specific taste, which is termed *sensory-specific satiety*. Should another food with high positive incentive value become available, we continue eating and overconsume (Raynor & Epstein, 2001). As noted in the text, this is referred to as the *cafeteria diet effect*. From the evolutionary perspective, there is adaptive pressure to consume a

variety of foods. Why? Because consuming a varied diet helps promote survival by ensuring that essential nutrients, vitamins, and minerals are obtained.

But unlike our ancient ancestors scrounging through the woods for seeds, fruits, and vegetables to survive, today's humans are confronted with foraging for burgers, cheese fries, and Oreo McFlurries. Therein lies the crux of the problem. As Pinel and his colleagues (2000) explain, "The increases in the availability of high positive-incentive value foods that have occurred over the past few decades in industrialized nations—increases that have been much too rapid to produce adaptive evolutionary change—have promoted levels of ad libitum consumption that are far higher than those that are compatible with optimal health and long life."

Critical Thinking Questions

- Look back at the section on motivation theories. How might each theory (instinct, drive, incentive, arousal, and humanistic) explain the behavior of overeating?

- How might the insights provided by the evolutionary explanation be used to resist the temptation to overeat?

The "SuperSize It" Syndrome: Overeating   In the last two decades, average daily caloric intake has increased nearly 10 percent for men and 7 percent for women (Koplan & Dietz, 1999). Every day, we are faced with the opportunity to overeat at all-you-can-eat brunches, pizza buffets, and fast-food restaurants that offer to "SuperSize" your portions for only a few cents more.

The Cafeteria Diet Effect: Variety = More Consumed   If variety is the spice of life, it's also a sure-fire formula to pack on the pounds. Offered just one choice or the same old choice for a meal, we consume less. But when offered a variety of highly palatable foods, such as at a cafeteria or an all-you-can-eat buffet, we consume more (Zandstra & others, 2000). This is sometimes called the **cafeteria diet effect** (Raynor & Epstein, 2001).

Sedentary Lifestyles   Four out of ten American adults report that they *never* exercise, play sports, or engage in physically active hobbies like gardening or walking the dog. Both men and women tend to become more sedentary with age. When the averages are broken down by gender, more women (43 percent) than men (37 percent) lead sedentary lifestyles (National Center for Health Statistics, 2000b).

body mass index (BMI)
A numerical scale indicating adult height in relation to weight; calculated as (703 × weight in pounds)/(height in inches)^2.

obese
Condition characterized by excessive body fat and a body mass index equal to or greater than 30.0.

cafeteria diet effect
The tendency to eat more when a wide variety of palatable foods is available.

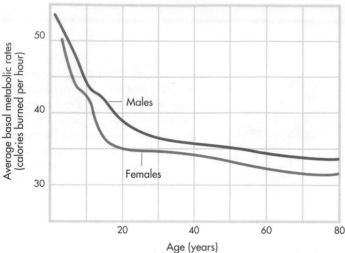

FIGURE 8.7 Age and Gender Differences in Metabolism From infancy through adolescence, there is a steep decline in the rate at which your body uses energy for vital functions, such as heartbeat, breathing, and body heat. Your BMR continues to decrease by about 2 to 3 percent during each decade of adulthood. At all points in the lifespan, women's metabolic rate is 3 to 5 percent lower than men's (Arciero & others, 1993).

SOURCE: Stuart & Davis (1972).

BMR: Individual Differences and Lifespan Changes Not everyone who overeats gains excess weight. One reason is that people vary greatly in their basal metabolic rate, which accounts for about two-thirds of your energy expenditure. On average, women have a metabolic rate that is 3 to 5 percent lower than men's (Arciero & others, 1993). Metabolism also decreases with age (Pannemans & Westerterp, 1995). Body metabolism is highest during growth periods early in the life-span (see Figure 8.7). After declining sharply between infancy and early adulthood, BMR decreases more slowly, by about 2 to 3 percent per decade of life (Poehlman & Horton, 1995). As your BMR decreases with age, less food is required to meet your basic energy needs. Consequently, it's not surprising that many people, upon reaching early adulthood, must begin to watch how much they eat.

Leptin Resistance Having greater fat stores, most obese people have high blood levels of leptin. So why don't these high blood levels of the leptin hormone reduce eating behavior and induce weight loss? Many obese people experience **leptin resistance,** in which the normal mechanisms through which leptin regulates body weight and energy balance are disrupted. Although leptin levels are high in the blood, they are often low in the obese person's cerebrospinal fluid (Caro & others, 1996). This suggests that leptin is not sufficiently transported from the blood to the brain. One possibility is that the obese person's high blood levels of leptin are overwhelming the transport system to the brain (Schwartz & others, 2000).

Dieting: BMR Resistance to Maintaining Weight Loss Any diet that reduces caloric intake will result in weight loss. The difficult challenge is to maintain the weight loss. Many overweight or obese dieters experience **weight cycling,** or *yo-yo dieting*—the weight lost through dieting is regained in weeks or months and maintained until the next attempt at dieting.

One reason this occurs is because the human body is much more effective at vigorously defending against weight *loss* than it is at protecting against weight *gain*. As caloric intake is reduced and fat cells begin to shrink, the person's body actively defends against weight loss by decreasing metabolism rate and energy

leptin resistance
A condition in which higher-than-normal blood levels of the hormone leptin do not produce the expected physiological response.

weight cycling
Repeated cycles of dieting, weight loss, and weight regain; also called *yo-yo dieting*.

eating disorder
A category of mental disorders characterized by severe disturbances in eating behavior.

anorexia nervosa
An eating disorder characterized by excessive weight loss, an irrational fear of gaining weight, and distorted body self-perception.

bulimia nervosa
An eating disorder characterized by binges of extreme overeating followed by self-induced vomiting, misuse of laxatives, or other inappropriate methods to purge the excessive food and prevent weight gain.

focus on

Neuroscience Dopamine Receptors and Obesity

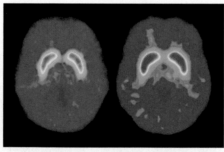

Obese   **Normal**

Eating to Stimulate Brain Reward? In Chapter 2, we noted that dopamine brain pathways are involved in the reinforcing feelings of pleasure and satisfaction. In Chapter 4, we also noted that many addictive drugs produce their pleasurable effects by increasing brain dopamine levels. These pleasurable effects are most reinforcing in people who have a low level of dopamine brain receptors (Volkow & others, 1999a, 1999b). Given that eating can be highly reinforcing and produces pleasurable sensations, could the same mechanisms also play a role in obesity?

In a recent study, researchers injected obese and normal weight individuals with a slightly radioactive chemical "tag" that binds to brain dopamine receptors. Positron emission tomography (PET) scans detected where the chemical tag bound with dopamine receptors, shown in red. The two PET scans reveal significantly fewer dopamine receptors for obese individuals (left) as compared to the normal weight control subjects (right). And, among the obese people in the study, the number of dopamine receptors decreased as BMI increased (Wang & others, 2001).

Researchers don't know yet whether the reduced number of dopamine receptors is a cause or a consequence of obesity. Nevertheless, the finding tentatively suggests that compulsive or binge eating might stimulate the brain's reward system and compensate for reduced dopamine signaling.

level. With energy expenditure reduced, far fewer calories are needed to maintain the excess weight. In effect, the body is using energy much more efficiently. If the person continues to restrict caloric intake, weight loss will plateau in a matter of weeks. When they go off the diet, their now more energy-efficient bodies quickly utilize the additional calories, and they regain the weight they lost.

Eating Disorders
Anorexia and Bulimia

Eating disorders involve serious and maladaptive disturbances in eating behavior. These disturbances can include extreme reduction of food intake, severe bouts of overeating, and obsessive concerns about body shape or weight (American Psychiatric Association, 2000a). The two main types of eating disorders are *anorexia nervosa* and *bulimia nervosa,* which usually begin during adolescence or early adulthood. Ninety to 95 percent of the people who experience an eating disorder are female (Kaye & others, 2000). Despite the 10-to-1 gender-difference ratio, the central features of eating disorders are similar for males and females (Andersen, 2002; Crosscope-Happel & others, 2000).

Anorexia Nervosa
Life-Threatening Weight Loss

Four key features define **anorexia nervosa.** First, the person refuses to maintain a minimally normal body weight. With a body weight that is 15 percent or more below normal, body mass index can drop to 12 or lower. Second, despite being dangerously underweight, the person with anorexia is intensely afraid of gaining weight or becoming fat. Third, she has a distorted perception about the size of her body. Although emaciated, she looks in the mirror and sees herself as fat or obese. And fourth, she denies the seriousness of her weight loss (American Psychiatric Association, 2000b).

The severe malnutrition caused by anorexia disrupts body chemistry in ways that are very similar to those caused by starvation (Fairburn, 1995). The person's basal metabolic rate decreases, as do blood levels of glucose, insulin, and leptin. Other hormonal levels drop, including the level of reproductive hormones. In women, reduced estrogen results in the menstrual cycle stopping. In males, decreased testosterone disrupts sex drive and sexual function (Crosscope-Happel & others, 2000). Because the ability to retain body heat is greatly diminished, people with severe anorexia often develop a soft, fine body hair called *lanugo* (Beumont, 2002).

Perfectionism and rigid thinking, poor peer relations, social isolation, and low self-esteem are common (Halmi & others, 2000). Although estimates vary, approximately 10 percent of people with anorexia nervosa die from starvation, suicide, or physical complications accompanying extreme weight loss (American Psychiatric Association, 2000b; Kaye & others, 2000).

Bulimia Nervosa
Bingeing and Purging

Like people with anorexia, people with **bulimia nervosa** fear gaining weight. Intense preoccupation and dissatisfaction with their bodies are also apparent. However, people with bulimia stay within a normal weight range or may even be slightly overweight. Another difference is that people with bulimia usually recognize that they have an eating disorder.

Is Anorexia Glamorous? There is enormous pressure on girls and women to be thin—a pressure that is even more intense in the entertainment world. Not surprisingly, there was a flurry of media attention when Mary-Kate Olsen, one half of the famed Olsen twins, was admitted to a treatment center for anorexia shortly after her 18th birthday. Despite the expressions of concern, the barrage of photos of the wafer-thin Mary-Kate posing in designer clothing tended to glamorize her condition. But there is nothing glamorous about a disorder that can result in heart or kidney failure, osteoporosis (reduced bone density), physical weakness, chronic fatigue, and loss of muscle, hair, and teeth. For more information or help in dealing with an eating disorder, you can visit the National Eating Disorders Association Web site at www.nationaleatingdisorders.org or you can call 1-800-931-2237.

Barbie, the American Ideal? If a normal-sized woman *(left)* was proportioned like a Barbie doll, she would look like the photograph on the right. Yale psychologist Kelly Brownell calculated that if a woman's hips stayed the same size, she would have to gain nearly a foot in height, add four inches to her chest, and lose five inches from her waist to meet the impossible standard set by Barbie. Many psychologists believe that such unrealistic standards contribute to the incidence of eating disorders in Western cultures.

People with bulimia nervosa experience extreme episodes of binge eating, consuming as many as 50,000 calories in a single binge. Binges typically occur twice a week and are often triggered by negative feelings or hunger (Agras & Apple, 1997). During the binge, the person usually consumes sweet, high-calorie foods that can be swallowed quickly, such as ice cream, cake, and candy. Binges typically occur in secrecy, leaving the person feeling ashamed, guilty, and disgusted by his own behavior. After bingeing, he compensates by purging himself of the excessive food by self-induced vomiting or by misuse of laxatives or enemas. Once he purges, he often feels psychologically relieved. Some people with bulimia don't purge themselves of the excess food. Rather, they use fasting and excessive exercise to keep their body weight within the normal range (American Psychiatric Association, 2000b).

Causes of Eating Disorders
A Complex Picture

Family and twin studies point to the role of genetic factors in both anorexia and bulimia, suggesting that some people are at greater risk to develop an eating disorder (e.g., Strober & others, 2001; Walters & Kendler, 1995). Researchers have also identified specific genes that are involved in eating disorders (Fumeron & others, 2001; Vink & others, 2001).

Both anorexia and bulimia involve decreases in brain activity of the neurotransmitter *serotonin* (Fumeron & others, 2001). Disrupted brain chemistry probably also contributes to the fact that eating disorders frequently co-occur with other psychiatric disorders, such as depression, substance abuse, personality disorders, and anxiety disorders, including obsessive–compulsive disorder (Bulik & others, 2000; Herzog & others, 1996).

The chemical signals that normally regulate eating behavior are also disrupted in the eating disorders. For example, we noted earlier that the hormone CCK helps trigger satiation. As compared to healthy volunteers, people with bulimia have *reduced* levels of CCK after a meal. This may partly explain why people with bulimia don't feel satiated until they have eaten extreme amounts (Pirke, 1995).

Although anorexia and bulimia have been documented for at least 150 years, contemporary Western cultural attitudes toward thinness and dieting probably contribute to the increased incidence of eating disorders today. This seems to be especially true with anorexia, which occurs predominantly in developed countries (Wilfley & Rodin, 1995). Still, it's important to remember that the vast majority of people who diet to lose weight do *not* develop an eating disorder.

Sexual Motivation and Behavior

Key Theme
■ Multiple factors are involved in human sexual motivation and behavior.

Key Questions
■ What biological factors are involved in sexual motivation and behavior?
■ What are the four stages of human sexual response?
■ What factors have been found to be associated with sexual orientation?

Psychologists consider the drive to have sex a basic human motive. But what exactly motivates that drive? Obviously, there are differences between sex and other basic motives, such as hunger. Engaging in sexual intercourse is essential to the survival of the human species, but it is not essential to the survival of any specific person. In other words, you'll die if you don't eat, but you won't die if you don't have sex (you may just *think* you will).

What Motivates Sexual Behavior?

In most animals, sexual behavior is biologically determined and triggered by hormonal changes in the female. During the cyclical period known as *estrus,* a female animal is fertile and receptive to male sexual advances. Roughly translated, the Greek word *estrus* means "frantic desire." Indeed, the female animal will often actively signal her willingness to engage in sexual activity—as any owner of an unneutered female cat or dog that's "in heat" can testify. In many, but not all, species, sexual activity takes place only when the female is in estrus.

As you go up the evolutionary scale, moving from relatively simple to more sophisticated animals, sexual behavior becomes less biologically determined and more subject to learning and environmental influences. Sexual behavior also becomes less limited to the goal of reproduction. For example, in some primate species, such as monkeys and apes, sexual activity can occur at any time, not just when the female is fertile. In these species, sexual interaction serves important social functions, defining and cementing relationships among the members of the primate group.

One rare species of chimplike apes, the bonobos of the Democratic Republic of the Congo, exhibits a surprising variety of sexual behaviors (de Waal & Lanting, 1998). Although most animals *copulate,* or have sex, with the male mounting the female from behind, bonobos often copulate face to face. Bonobos also engage in oral sex and intense tongue kissing. And bonobos seem to like variety. Along with having frequent heterosexual activity, whether the female is fertile or not, bonobos also engage in homosexual and group sex.

Emory University psychology professor Frans de Waal (1995), who has extensively studied bonobos, observes that their frequent and varied sexual behavior seems to serve important social functions. Sexual behavior is not limited to fulfilling the purpose of reproduction. Among the bonobos, sexual interaction is used to increase group cohesion, avoid conflict, and decrease tension that might be caused by competition for food. According to de Waal (1995), the bonobos' motto seems to be "Make love, not war."

In humans, of course, sexual behavior is not limited to a female's fertile period. Nor is the motivational goal of sex limited to reproduction. Although a woman's fertility is regulated by monthly hormonal cycles, these hormonal changes seem to have little effect on a female's sexual motivation (Davidson & Myers, 1988). Even when a woman's ovaries, which produce the female sex hormone *estrogen,* are surgically removed or stop functioning during menopause, there is little or no drop in sexual interest. In many nonhuman female mammals, however, removal of the ovaries results in a complete loss of interest in sexual activity. If injections of estrogen and other female sex hormones are given, the female animals' sexual interest returns.

In male animals, removal of the testes (castration) typically causes a steep drop in sexual activity and interest, although the decline is more gradual in sexually experienced animals. Castration causes a significant decrease in levels of *testosterone,* the hormone responsible for male sexual development. When human males experience lowered levels of testosterone because of illness or castration, a similar drop in sexual interest tends to occur, although the effects vary among individuals. Some men continue to lead a normal sex life for years, but others quickly lose all interest in sexual activity. In castrated men who experience a loss of sexual interest, injections of testosterone restore the sexual drive.

Testosterone is also involved in female sexual motivation (Davis, 2000). Most of the testosterone in a woman's body is produced by her adrenal glands. If these glands are removed or malfunction, causing testosterone levels to become abnormally low, sexual interest often wanes. When supplemental testosterone is administered, the woman's sex drive returns. Thus, in *both* men and women, sexual motivation is biologically influenced by the levels of the hormone testosterone in the body.

Of course, sexual behavior is greatly influenced by many cultural and social factors. We consider one aspect of sexual behavior in Culture and Human Behavior Box 8.2, "Evolution and Mate Preferences."

The Bonobos of the Congo Bonobos demonstrate a wide variety of sexual interactions, including face-to-face copulation, kissing, and sexual interaction among same-sex pairs (de Waal & Lanting, 1998). Sexual behavior is not limited to reproduction; it seems to play an important role in maintaining peaceful relations among members of the bonobo group. As Frans de Waal (1995) wrote, "For these animals, sexual behavior is indistinguishable from social behavior."

CULTURE AND HUMAN BEHAVIOR 8.2

Evolution and Mate Preferences

Did the cartoon make you smile? If it did, it's because you recognized a cultural pattern—the belief that men seek a beautiful, youthful partner, while women are more likely to value financial security and wealth. Cartoons and jokes aside, is there any merit to this observation? *Do* men and women differ in what they look for in a mate?

To investigate mate preferences, psychologist David Buss (1989, 1994) coordinated a large-scale survey of more than 10,000 people in 37 different cultures.

Across all cultures, Buss found, men were more likely than women to value youth and physical attractiveness in a potential mate. In contrast, women were more likely than men to value financial security, access to material resources, high status and education, and good financial prospects. Buss, an evolutionary psychologist, interprets these gender differences as reflecting the different "mating strategies" of men and women.

According to evolutionary psychology, mating behavior is adaptive to the degree that it furthers the reproductive success of transmitting one's genes to the next generation and beyond. And when it comes to reproductive success, Buss (1995a) contends that men and women face very different "adaptive problems" in selecting a mate.

According to Buss (1995b, 1996), the adaptive problem for men is to identify and mate with women who are fertile and likely to be successful at bearing their children. Thus, men are more likely to place a high value on youth, because it is associated with fertility and because younger women have a greater number of childbearing years ahead of them than older women. And, men value physical attractiveness because it signals that the woman is probably physically healthy and has high-quality genes.

Buss sees the adaptive problem for women as very different. Women also seek "good" genes, and thus they value men who are healthy and attractive. But they have a more pressing need: making sure that the children they do bear survive to

BIZARRO

ONE SECOND BEFORE THE BLIND DATE

BIZARRO © by Dan Piraro. Reprinted with permission of Universal Press Syndicate.

carry their genes into future generations. Pregnancy, lactation, and caring for infants, says Buss, leave women unable to acquire the resources needed to protect and feed themselves and their children. Thus, women look for a mate who will be a "good provider." They seek men who possess the resources that the women and their offspring will need to survive.

In most cultures, Buss (1995a) points out, men of high status and wealth are more able to marry younger and more attractive women than poor, low-status men are. In other words, older successful men, whether they are tribal chiefs, corporate CEOs, or aging rock superstars, have the greatest access to young, attractive women—the so-called "trophy wife." On the other side of the coin, physically attractive women can, and often do, marry men with more resources and higher status than do unattractive women.

Not surprisingly, this evolutionary explanation of sex differences is controversial. Some psychologists argue that it is overly deterministic and does not sufficiently acknowledge the role of culture, gender-role socialization, and other social factors (Caporael & Brewer, 1995; Hyde, 1996; Pratto, 1996).

Other psychologists interpret Buss's data in a different way. Tim Kasser and Yadika Sharma (1999) analyzed the mate preference data in terms of women's reproductive freedom and educational opportunity in each culture. They found that women who live in cultures that are low in both female reproductive freedom and educational equality between the sexes placed a higher value on a prospective mate's resources.

According to Kasser and Sharma (1999), "When a female is provided with opportunities to fend for herself, she can become less concerned with finding a mate who will provide resources for her, but when she has few opportunities to educate herself or control her own fertility, she will be more concerned with finding a mate who can provide her with the resources needed to support her and her children."

For his part, Buss (1996) is careful to point out that this theory does *not* claim that personal preferences have no effect on mate preferences. In fact, his extensive survey also found that men and women in all 37 cultures agreed that the *most* important factor in choosing a mate was mutual attraction and love. And, here's a finding that will probably be reassuring to those singles who have neither fabulous wealth nor heart-stopping beauty: Both sexes rated kindness, intelligence, emotional stability, health, and a pleasing personality as more important than a prospective mate's financial resources or good looks.

Finally, Buss and other evolutionary psychologists reject the idea that people, cultures, or societies are powerless to overcome tendencies that evolved over hundreds of thousands of years. Buss also flatly states that explaining some of the reasons that might underlie sexual inequality does *not* mean that sexual inequality is natural, correct, or justified. Rather, evolutionary psychologists believe that we must understand the conditions that foster sexual inequality in order to overcome or change those conditions (Smuts, 1996).

The Stages of Human Sexual Response

The human sexual response cycle was first mapped by sex research pioneers **William Masters** and **Virginia Johnson** during the 1950s and 1960s. Until the 1950s, information about sexual response had been gathered by observing the behavior of different animal species. Masters and Johnson felt that a more direct approach was needed to further the understanding of human sexual anatomy and physiology. Thus, in the name of science, Masters and Johnson observed hundreds of people engage in more than 10,000 episodes of sexual activity in their laboratory. Their findings, published in 1966, indicated that the human sexual response could be described as a cycle with four stages (see Figure 8.8).

As you read the descriptions of these stages, keep in mind that the transitions between stages are not as precise or abrupt as the descriptions might lead you to believe. Moreover, the duration of time spent in any particular stage can vary on different occasions of sexual interaction.

1. **Stage 1: Excitement** The *excitement phase* marks the beginning of sexual arousal. Sexual arousal can occur in response to sexual fantasies or other sexually arousing stimuli, physical contact with another person, or masturbation. In both sexes, the excitement stage is accompanied by a variety of bodily changes in anticipation of sexual interaction. There is a rapid rise in pulse rate and blood pressure. The rate of breathing increases. Blood shifts to the genitals, producing an erect penis in the male and swelling of the clitoris in the female. The female's vaginal lips expand and open up, and her vagina becomes lubricated in preparation for intercourse. Her nipples and breasts may also become enlarged, and the nipples become erect and more sensitive.

2. **Stage 2: Plateau** In the second phase, the *plateau phase*, physical arousal builds as pulse and breathing rates continue to increase. The penis becomes fully erect and sometimes secretes a few drops of fluid, which may contain active sperm. The testes increase in size. The clitoris withdraws under the clitoral hood but remains very sensitive to stimulation. The vaginal entrance tightens, putting pressure on the penis during intercourse. Vaginal lubrication continues. During the excitement and plateau stages, the degree of arousal may fluctuate up and down (Masters & others, 1995). During the plateau stage, the firmness of the male's erection may increase and decrease, and so may the female's degree of vaginal lubrication.

Pioneers of Sex Research: William Masters (1915–2001) and Virginia Johnson (b. 1925) In 1966 Masters and Johnson broke new ground in the scientific study of sexual behavior when they published *Human Sexual Response*. In that book they provided the first extensive laboratory data on the anatomy and physiology of the male and female sexual response. Although intended for clinicians, the book became a best-seller that was translated into over thirty languages. Some critics felt the Masters and Johnson research had violated "sacred ground" and dehumanized sexuality. But others applauded *Human Sexual Response* for advancing the understanding of human sexuality and dispelling misconceptions.

After opening a clinic for treatment of sexual problems, Masters and Johnson were featured on the cover of *Time* magazine in 1970. They also published *Human Sexual Inadequacy*, in which they described their innovative therapy techniques for treating sexual problems, including the use of male and female therapist teams to work with couples. The techniques they developed are still widely used in sex therapy today. Ultimately, Masters and Johnson promoted a view of human sexuality as a healthy and natural activity, one that could be a meaningful source of intimacy and fulfillment.

FIGURE 8.8 The Male and Female Sexual Response Cycles The figure on the left depicts the three basic variations of the female sexual response. Pattern 1 shows multiple orgasms. Pattern 2 shows sexual arousal that reaches the plateau stage but not orgasm, followed by a slow resolution. Pattern 3 depicts brief reductions in arousal during the excitement stage, followed by rapid orgasm and resolution. The figure on the right depicts the most typical male sexual response, in which orgasm is followed by a refractory period.

SOURCE: Masters & Johnson (1966).

Female Sexual Responses: Three Basic Variations

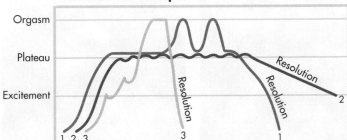

Typical Male Sexual Response

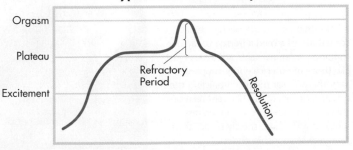

sexual orientation
The direction of a person's emotional and erotic attraction toward members of the opposite sex, the same sex, or both sexes.

3. **Stage 3: Orgasm** is the third and shortest phase of the sexual response cycle. During orgasm, blood pressure and heart rate reach their peak. The muscles in the vaginal walls and the uterus contract rhythmically, as do the muscles in and around the penis as the male ejaculates. Other muscles may contract as well, such as those in the face, arms, and legs. Both men and women describe the subjective experience of orgasm in similar—and very positive—terms.

The vast majority of men experience one intense orgasm. But many women are capable of experiencing multiple orgasms. If sexual stimulation continues following orgasm, women may experience additional orgasms within a short period of time.

4. **Stage 4: Resolution** Following orgasm, both sexes tend to experience a warm physical "glow" and a sense of well-being. Arousal slowly subsides and returns to normal levels in the *resolution phase.* The male experiences a *refractory period,* during which he is incapable of having another erection or orgasm. The duration of the male's refractory period varies. For one man it may last a matter of minutes, for another several hours. As men age, the duration of the refractory period tends to increase.

Sexual Orientation
The Elusive Search for an Explanation

Given that biological factors seem to play an important role in motivating sexual desire, it seems only reasonable to ask whether biological factors also play a role in sexual orientation. **Sexual orientation** refers to whether a person is sexually aroused by members of the same sex, the opposite sex, or both sexes. A *heterosexual* person is sexually attracted to individuals of the other sex, a *homosexual* person to individuals of the same sex, and a *bisexual* person to individuals of both sexes. Technically, the term *homosexual* can be applied to either males or females. However, female homosexuals are usually called *lesbians.* Male homosexuals typically use the term *gay* to describe their sexual orientation.

Sexual orientation is not nearly as cut and dried as many people believe. Some people *are* exclusively heterosexual or homosexual, but others are less easy to categorize. Many people who consider themselves heterosexual have had a homosexual experience at some point in their lives. In the same vein, many homosexuals have had heterosexual experiences (Rieger & others, 2005). Other people, like our friend Richard in the chapter Prologue, consider themselves to be homosexual but have had heterosexual relationships. The key point is that there is not always a perfect correspondence between a particular person's sexual identity, sexual desires, and sexual behaviors (Laumann & others, 1994).

Famous Gay Couples Legendary singer, songwriter, and musician Elton John spent years claiming to be bisexual, even marrying German sound engineer Renata Blauel in 1984. But when that marriage ended four years later, Elton admitted publicly what he said he had known privately for years—that he was homosexual. Since 1993, John's companion has been Canadian film producer David Furnish. In the photo, John and Furnish are shown leaving Guildhall in Windsor, England, after their civil partnership ceremony on December 21, 2005. "We love each other just as much as any other two human beings love each other," John (2005) explained. "In the twenty-first century, tolerance should be something that we promote a little more."

Comedian and popular talk show host Ellen DeGeneres struggled privately and in therapy for many years to come to grips with her sexual orientation before publicly coming out as a lesbian. As DeGeneres (2005) recalled, "To be 37 years old and be feeling this sense of shame, that nobody would like me if they found out I was gay, it was a pretty emotional thing to expose yourself to." In 1997, she made television history when she "outed" herself and her character in her television series *Ellen.* Although Ellen's first public relationship with Anne Heche created something of a media frenzy, today her romantic entanglements are treated just like those of other celebrity couples, with the popular media chronicling the ups and downs of her different relationships. She's shown here with actress Alexandra Hedison, shortly before their four-year relationship ended.

Determining the number of people who are homosexual or heterosexual is problematic for several reasons. First, survey results vary depending on how the researchers define the terms *homosexual, heterosexual,* and *bisexual.* Second, gays and lesbians are not distributed evenly throughout the population. In rural areas and small towns, gays, lesbians, and bisexuals make up about 1 percent of the population. But in the largest U.S. cities, approximately one of eight people (or 12 percent) consider themselves gay, lesbian, or bisexual (Michael & others, 1994). Thus, estimates of the size of the gay and lesbian population can vary, depending on:

- How researchers structure survey questions
- How they define the criteria for inclusion in gay, lesbian, or bisexual categories
- Where the survey is conducted
- How survey participants are selected

More important than the exact number of gays and lesbians is the recognition that gays and lesbians constitute a significant segment of the adult population in the United States. According to the most reasonable estimates, it's safe to say that between 7 million and 15 million American men and women are gay or lesbian (Patterson, 1995).

What Determines Sexual Orientation?

Despite considerable research on this question, psychologists and other researchers cannot say with certainty why people become homosexual or bisexual. For that matter, psychologists don't know exactly why people become *heterosexual* either. Still, research on sexual orientation has pointed toward several general conclusions, especially with regard to homosexuality.

Evidence from twin studies suggests that genetics plays a role in determining a homosexual orientation. For example, psychologists Michael Bailey and Richard Pillard (1991) compared the incidence of male homosexuality among pairs of identical twins (who have identical genes), fraternal twins (who are genetically as similar as any two nontwin siblings), and adoptive brothers (who have no common genetic heritage but shared the same upbringing). The researchers found that the closer the degree of genetic relationship, the more likely it was that when one brother was homosexual, the other brother would also be homosexual. Specifically, both brothers were homosexual in 52 percent of the identical twins, 22 percent of the fraternal twins, and 11 percent of the adoptive brothers.

Bailey and his colleagues (1993) discovered very similar results in twin studies of lesbians. In 48 percent of identical twins and 16 percent of fraternal twins, when one sister was lesbian, so was the other sister, compared with only 6 percent of adoptive sisters. Although intriguing, such genetic studies are subject to criticisms about methodology and other issues (Byne, 1994; Byne & Parsons, 1993). Furthermore, since the identical twins were both homosexual in only half of the twin pairs, it's clear that genetic predisposition alone cannot explain sexual orientation. Nevertheless, these studies and others support the notion that sexual orientation is at least partly influenced by genetics (Kendler, Thornton, & others, 2000).

Another biological factor that has been investigated is differences in brain structure between heterosexuals and homosexuals (LeVay & Hamer, 1994). Neurobiologist Simon LeVay (1991) discovered a small but significant difference between male heterosexuals and male homosexuals in a tiny cluster of neurons in the *hypothalamus,* which is known to be involved in sexual behavior. In male homosexuals and heterosexual women, the cluster was only half the size of the cluster in heterosexual men.

LeVay speculates that this tiny structure may be involved in determining sexual orientation (LeVay & Hamer, 1994). However, LeVay also carefully points out that there is no way of knowing whether this difference in brain structure *causes* homosexual behavior in men. Conceivably, it might be the other way around—homosexual behavior might cause the difference in brain structure.

U.S. Congressman Barney Frank: "You Can't Make Yourself a Different Person." One of the first openly gay politicians, Frank has been a member of the U.S. Congress since 1981. Frank first realized he was gay in his early teenage years. When asked if heterosexuality was ever an option for him, Frank (1996) responded, "I wished it was. But it wasn't. I can't imagine that anybody believes that a 13-year-old in 1953 thinks, 'Boy, it would really be great to be part of this minority that everybody hates and to have a really restricted life.' You can't make yourself a different person. I am who I am. I have no idea why."

In general, the only conclusion we can draw from these studies is that some biological factors are *correlated* with a homosexual orientation (Mustanski & others, 2002). As we've stressed, correlation does not necessarily indicate causality, only that two factors *seem* to occur together. So stronger conclusions about the role of genetic and biological factors in determining sexual orientation await more definitive research findings.

What about early life experiences? Is homosexuality due to abnormal parenting or early homosexual experiences? Alan Bell and his colleagues (1981) conducted an early comprehensive study investigating these and other popular beliefs regarding the causes of homosexual orientation. On the basis of in-depth interviews of almost 1,000 homosexual men and women, and a comparison group of about 500 heterosexual men and women, they came to the following conclusions:

- Homosexuality is *not* due to an unpleasant early heterosexual experience, such as being sexually abused during childhood by a member of the opposite sex.

- Homosexuality is *not* the result of an abnormal relationship between the parents and the child, such as having a father who is an inadequate male role model or having an overly dominant mother.

Bell and his colleagues (1981) also found that sexual orientation was determined before adolescence and long before the beginning of sexual activity. Gay men and lesbians typically became aware of homosexual feelings about three years before they engaged in any such sexual activity. In this regard, the pattern was very similar to that of heterosexual children, in whom heterosexual feelings are aroused long before the child expresses them in some form of sexual behavior.

Several researchers now believe that sexual orientation is established as early as age 6 (Strickland, 1995). Do children who later grow up to be homosexuals differ from children who later grow up to be heterosexuals? In at least one respect, there seems to be a difference.

Especially in early and middle childhood, boys and girls differ in their choice of toys, playmates, and play activities (Knafo & others, 2005). Evidence suggests that male and female homosexuals are less likely to have followed the typical pattern of gender-specific behaviors in childhood (Bailey & others, 2000; Bailey & Zucker, 1995). Compared to heterosexual men, gay men recall engaging in more cross-sex-typed behavior during childhood. For example, they remembered playing more with girls than with other boys, preferring girls' toys over boys' toys, and disliking rough-and-tumble play. Lesbians are also more likely to recall cross-gender behavior in childhood, but to a lesser degree than gay men.

A potential problem with such *retrospective studies* is that the participants may be biased in their recall of childhood events. One way to avoid that problem is by conducting a prospective study. A *prospective study* involves systematically observing a group of people over time to discover what factors are associated with the development of a particular trait, characteristic, or behavior.

One influential prospective study was conducted by Richard Green (1985, 1987). Green followed the development of sexual orientation in two groups of boys. The first group of boys had been referred to a mental health clinic because of their "feminine" behavior. He compared the development of these boys to a matched control group of boys who displayed typically "masculine" behavior in childhood. When all the boys were in their late teens, Green compared the two groups. He found that approximately 75 percent of the previously feminine boys were either bisexual or homosexual, as compared to only 4 percent of the control group.

As researchers J. Michael Bailey and Kenneth J. Zucker (1995) summarized, "There is clear evidence of a relation between patterns of childhood sex-typed behavior and later sexual orientation." However, these researchers and others note that this conclusion is more applicable to the development of sexual orientation in males than in females (L. Diamond, 1998; Carver & others, 2004).

Lesbian Parents According to data drawn from the 2000 U.S. Census, same-sex couples account for about 1 in 9 of the 5.5 million couples who are living together but not married. About a third of households headed by female same-sex couples include children below the age of 18, as do about 20% of households headed by male same-sex couples (Kurdek, 2005). Are the children of gay or lesbian parents likely to become homosexual themselves? Apparently the children of homosexual parents are no more likely to be gay or lesbian in adulthood than are children raised by heterosexual parents (Bailey & others, 1995; Golombok & Tasker, 1996). Research studies to date show few differences among the children of gay, lesbian, or heterosexual parents (Bos & others, 2004).

Once sexual orientation is established, whether heterosexual or homosexual, it is highly resistant to change (American Psychiatric Association, 2000a). The vast majority of homosexuals would be unable to change their orientation even if they wished to, just as the majority of heterosexuals would be unable to change their orientation if *they* wished to. Thus, it's a mistake to assume that homosexuals have deliberately chosen their sexual orientation any more than heterosexuals have. Indeed, when Richard was in high school, he would gladly have "chosen" to be heterosexual if the matter had been that simple.

It seems clear that no single factor determines whether people identify themselves as homosexual, heterosexual, or bisexual (Golombok & Tasker, 1996). Psychological, biological, social, and cultural factors are undoubtedly involved in determining sexual orientation. However, researchers are still unable to pinpoint exactly what those factors are and how they interact. As psychologist Bonnie Strickland (1995) has pointed out, "Sexual identity and orientation appear to be shaped by a complexity of biological, psychological, and social events. Gender identity and sexual orientation, at least for most people, especially gay men, occur early, are relatively fixed, and are difficult to change." As Richard learned, changing his sexual orientation was simply not possible.

Sexual Behavior

Key Theme
- Intimate, committed relationships are typically established during early adulthood, but they remain important throughout the lifespan.

Key Questions
- What characterizes the sexual behavior patterns of adulthood?
- How prevalent are sexual problems?

Perhaps because sexual behavior tends to be a private matter, it's understandable that people (psychologists included) are curious about what other people do—and don't do—sexually. The mass media tend to offer overheated images of people's sexual activity. If you believe the not-so-subtle media messages, everyone (except you) has such an active, steamy, and varied sex life that you can't help wondering how anyone (except you) ever finds the time to get their laundry done. Are the media images of sex in America accurate?

Researchers Robert T. Michael, Edward O. Laumann, and their colleagues at the University of Chicago will help answer that and other questions about adult sexual behavior in this section. They are the authors of the *National Health and Social Life Survey* (NHSLS)—a state-of-the-art, scientifically constructed national survey of adult sexual behavior in America. Throughout this section, we'll rely on this landmark survey to help us accurately answer the "Who's doing what, when, how often, and with whom" questions about human sexuality.

Looking for Mr. or Ms. Right Although people today are marrying at a later average age than they did in previous generations, most young adults are involved in an intimate, long-term relationship by the time they reach their mid-twenties. People are most likely to form an intimate relationship with someone who is similar to them and who is part of their existing social network (Michael & others, 1994).

How Many Sex Partners Do People Have?

For most Americans, the onset of adulthood marks a commitment to the task of establishing long-term, intimate relationships. During their twenties, most men and women develop an intimate relationship with another adult. By the age of 30, most Americans are part of a couple—either married or living with someone (Laumann & Youm, 2001).

The notion that people today, especially younger people, have more sex partners than people did 20 or 30 years ago is fundamentally accurate. Among people aged 30 to 50, about half have had five or more sexual partners. In contrast, only

focus on

Neuroscience: Romantic Love and the Brain

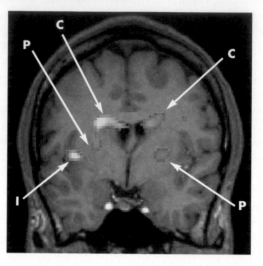

Feelings of euphoria are just one of the many sensations, thoughts, and emotions that accompany moments of impassioned, romantic love. As is shown in the fMRI scan, romantic love also produces a unique pattern of activation in the brain.

When it comes to love, it's been said that the brain is the most erotic organ in your body. Indeed, being head over heels in love is an emotionally intoxicating brain state. Do the overpowering feelings of romantic love involve a unique pattern of brain activity?

Using functional magnetic resonance imaging (fMRI) to detect brain activity, researchers Andreas Bartels and Semir Zeki (2000) investigated that idea with 17 love-struck young adults, all professing to be "truly, deeply, madly in love" with their romantic partner. Each participant was scanned several times while gazing at a photo of the romantic partner. Alternating with the "love" scans were "friendship" scans taken while the participant looked at a photo of a good friend who was of the same sex as the loved one.

Bartels and Zeki's (2000) results suggest that romantic love activates brain areas that are involved in other positive emotions, such as happiness, but in a way that represents a unique pattern. Shown here is a side-to-side fMRI brain scan depicting some of the brain areas activated by romantic love. Compared to looking at a photo of a close friend, looking at a photo of one's romantic partner produced heightened activity in four brain areas associated with emotion, including the *anterior cingulate cortex* (not shown), *caudate nucleus* (C), *putamen* (P), and *insula* (I).

Given the complexity of the sentiment of romantic love, the researchers were surprised that the brain areas activated were so small and limited to so few regions. (Perhaps this lack of extensive brain activation explains why love-struck individuals are sometimes oblivious to everything except the object of their infatuation.) Nonetheless, the four activated brain areas offer some insight into the intoxicating effects of romantic love. Why? Because these are the same brain areas that are activated in response to euphoria-producing drugs, such as opiates and cocaine. Clearly, there seem to be some close neural links between romantic love and euphoric states.

Table 8.3

Number of Sex Partners During the Previous Year

	0	1	2–4	5+
Total	12%	71%	14%	3%
By Gender				
Men	10	67	18	5
Women	14	75	10	2
By Age				
18–24	11	57	24	9
25–29	6	72	17	6
30–34	9	73	16	2
35–39	10	77	11	2
40–44	11	75	13	1
45–49	15	75	9	1
50–54	15	79	5	0
55–59	32	65	4	0

SOURCE: Adapted from data in Michael and others (1994), Table 6, pp. 102–103.

As shown in the data reported here, you can see that regardless of age or gender, about 80 percent of the survey respondents reported having had one or no sexual partners during the previous year.

about a third of those over age 50 have had five or more sexual partners (Laumann & others, 1994).

Why the difference between age groups in the number of sexual partners? The vast majority of adults who were in the 50–59 age range at the time of the NHSLS survey had their first sexual experience in the context of marriage. In contrast, only about a third of today's young adults had their first sexual experience in the context of marriage (Michael & others, 1994). Young adults today tend to become sexually active at an earlier age and are marrying at a later average age. Hence, younger people today tend to have more sexual partners than members of older generations.

Now consider a slightly different issue, the number of sexual partners in the past year. The majority of people—about 80 percent—had either *one* sexual partner or *none* in the previous year (see Table 8.3). Why so few sexual partners in the last year? In a word, marriage. Marriage continues to be a cornerstone of American society as well as a major developmental milestone for most people on the trek through adulthood. As people become adults, they experience considerable social pressure to find a partner and marry. Doing so confers numerous benefits, not the least of which is the social, legal, and moral acceptance of the sexual partnership.

By the age of 30, about 90 percent of Americans have married. Regardless of age or number of previous partners, once most couples marry or start cohabiting, they feel strongly committed to being faithful to each other. As Michael and his colleagues (1994) explained:

> Marriage regulates sexual behavior with remarkable precision. No matter what they did before they wed, no matter how many partners they had, the sexual lives of married people are similar. Despite the popular myth that there is a great deal of adultery in marriage, our data and other reliable studies do not find it. Instead, the vast majority are faithful while the marriage is intact.

Intimacy, Love, and Sexuality in Adulthood
Forming a long-term, committed relationship with another person is a key task of early adulthood. For many couples, the bonds of love and intimacy established in early adulthood last a lifetime.

How Often Do People Have Sex?

Perhaps the widest disparity between the media images and the NHSLS results involves the issue of how often people have sex. Here's what the NHSLS found. One-third of American adults have sex with a partner two or more times per week; one-third have sex a few times per month; and one-third have sex a few times a year or not at all. When the data are combined for all adults between ages 18 and 59, men have sex an average of about seven times per month, and women have sex an average of about six times per month (Laumann & others, 1994; Laumann & Youm, 2001). So, any way you look at it, the most frequent activity in America's bedrooms is sleep, not sex.

Which Americans have the most active sex lives? Those young, attractive, footloose, swinging singles, right? Wrong. The fact is that married or cohabiting couples have the most active sex lives (Laumann & Youm, 2001). If you think about it, this finding makes sense. Sexual activity is strongly regulated by the availability of a sex partner. Being a member of a stable couple is the social arrangement most likely to produce a readily accessible sexual partner.

Are people happy with their sex lives? The vast majority of the NHSLS respondents—about 85 percent—reported that they were physically and emotionally satisfied with their sexual relationships (Laumann & others, 1994). A higher proportion of married men and women than of single or cohabiting men and women reported being extremely emotionally satisfied with their sexual relationships (Waite & Joyner, 2001). Part of the explanation for this high percentage is that in today's society there is considerably less social pressure to endure an unhappy marriage "until death do you part" than there used to be. Hence, those who are sexually dissatisfied with their relationship are likely to separate or get divorced—and try again with someone else. The net result is that most Americans are happily married or cohabiting.

What Do People Do When They Have Sex?

Vaginal intercourse is nearly universal as the most widely practiced sexual activity among heterosexual couples (Laumann & others, 1994). What about other practices? More than two-thirds of Americans have either given or received *oral sex* at some point in their lives. Fewer men (26 percent) and women (20 percent) have ever engaged in *anal* sex (that is, a penis inserted in the partner's anus).

Given that most Americans seem to be having pretty traditional sex, you may be wondering whether they'd like to be a little more adventurous. So what do most people find appealing, and is that any different from what they actually do?

Although the list of potential sexual practices is varied, people prefer to stick with the tried and true. In descending order for both sexes, the most preferred sexual activities are (1) having vaginal intercourse; (2) watching the partner undress; (3) receiving oral sex; and (4) giving oral sex.

In some ways, the flip side of the coin is more revealing. What do people find *unappealing*? Regardless of age, at least 90 percent of women found no appeal in

In real life, the unheralded, seldom discussed world of married sex is actually the one that satisfies people the most. It may not be an exciting picture of sex in America, but if we look at the social forces that push us toward married life, it is an understandable, if not predicted, picture.

Robert T. Michael (1994)

Sexuality in Late Adulthood Sexual interest and activity are important dimensions of the lives of many senior adults. In a recent survey of older Americans, nearly half reported that they engage in sexual activity at least once a month. The survey also found that more than 70 percent of sexually active seniors said they were as satisfied or more satisfied with their sex lives compared to when they were in their forties (National Council on Aging, 1998; 2000).

(1) being forced to do something sexual; (2) forcing someone to do something sexual; (3) receiving anal intercourse; (4) having a same-gender sex partner; and (5) having sex with a stranger. With the exception of sex with a stranger, at least 90 percent of men also found these sexual practices unappealing. Other sexual practices that the majority of people do not find appealing include having group sex, using a vibrator or dildo (an object used as a substitute for an erect penis), and watching other people engage in sexual activity (Michael & others, 1994).

How Common Are Sexual Problems?

Sexual dysfunctions are consistent disturbances in sexual desire, arousal, or orgasm that cause psychological distress and interpersonal difficulties (American Psychiatric Association, 2000a).

Until recently, researchers did not have reliable data on the prevalence of many sexual dysfunctions. This situation changed, however, with the publication of additional results from the National Health and Social Life Survey. After analyzing the data, Edward Laumann and his colleagues (1999, 2001) found that the incidence of sexual dysfunction among adult Americans was much higher than previously believed: 43 percent of women and 31 percent of men suffered from sexual problems.

For women, the most common sexual problems were low sexual desire and arousal problems, including **female orgasmic disorder,** which is the consistent inability to achieve orgasm. For men, the most common sexual dysfunctions were **premature ejaculation** and **male erectile disorder,** which is characterized by consistent problems achieving or maintaining an erection. Overall, married and college-educated men and women had a much lower incidence of sexual problems than unmarried people or people with less education.

Gentlemen, start your engines! Any way you size it up, *male erectile disorder* is big business. From NASCAR to the NFL, it's hard to escape the advertising pitches for Viagra and its more recent rivals, Cialis and Levitra. Advertising for the three drugs topped $400 million in the U.S. in 2004. Since 1998, when Viagra became the first drug approved for the treatment of male erectile problems, including impotence, it has been tried by more than 16 million American men. Viagra, Cialis, and Levitra all treat erectile dysfunction by increasing blood flow to the penis. Although most people think of impotence as being a disorder associated with aging, less than a third of Viagra prescriptions go to men who are 60 and older (Schmit, 2005).

One interesting finding was that sexual problems were most common among young women and men older than age 50. The older men tended to report sexual problems related to the aging process: erection difficulties and lack of interest in sex. But what about the younger women? According to Laumann and his colleagues (1999), "Since young women are more likely to be single, their sexual activities involve higher rates of partner turnover as well as periodic spells of sexual inactivity. This instability, coupled with inexperience, generates stressful sexual encounters, providing the basis for sexual pain and anxiety."

The researchers also note that in women, sexual problems *declined* with age, except for problems with lubrication, which tended to increase after age 50. Finally, Laumann and Michael (2001) found that stress and emotional problems were associated with sexual difficulties. And, especially for women, sexual problems tended to produce unhappiness and emotional distress.

So what can we conclude? First, the picture that emerges of sexuality over the lifespan does not seem to match the typical media images. Upon reaching adulthood, the majority of Americans follow very traditional patterns of sexual behavior. Second, most people spend almost all their adult years involved in a stable sexual relationship with a single partner. Compared with single people, married or cohabiting couples have more active—and more fulfilling—sex lives. In fact, most Americans are fundamentally happy with the relationship they have with their partner. Finally, some people experience sexual dysfunctions that create psychological distress and interpersonal difficulties. Fortunately, many sexual dysfunctions can be successfully treated by psychologists or physicians who have received specialized training in sex therapy.

Psychological Needs as Motivators

Key Theme
■ According to the motivation theories of Maslow and of Deci and Ryan, psychological needs must be fulfilled for optimal human functioning.

Key Questions
■ How does Maslow's hierarchy of needs explain human motivation?
■ What are some important criticisms of Maslow's theory?
■ What are the basic premises of self-determination theory?

In studying the idea that we are motivated to satisfy fundamental psychological needs, psychologists have grappled with several key questions:

■ Are there universal psychological needs?

■ Are we internally or externally motivated to satisfy psychological needs?

■ What psychological needs must be satisfied for optimal human functioning?

In this section, we'll first consider two theories that have tried to answer those questions: Abraham Maslow's famous *hierarchy of needs* and the more recent *self-determination theory* of Edward L. Deci and Richard M. Ryan.

Maslow's Hierarchy of Needs

A major turning point in the discussion of human needs occurred when humanistic psychologist **Abraham Maslow** developed his model of human motivation in the 1940s and 1950s. Maslow acknowledged the importance of biological needs as motivators. But once basic biological needs are satisfied, he believed, "higher" psychological needs emerge to motivate human behavior.

The centerpiece of Maslow's (1954, 1968) model of motivation was his famous **hierarchy of needs,** summarized in Figure 8.9. Maslow believed that people are motivated to satisfy the needs at each level of the hierarchy before moving up to the next level. As people progressively move up the hierarchy, they are ultimately motivated by the desire to achieve self-actualization. The lowest levels of Maslow's hierarchy emphasize fundamental biological and safety needs. At the higher levels, the needs become more social and psychologically growth-oriented, culminating in the need to achieve *self-actualization.*

What exactly is self-actualization? Maslow (1970) himself had trouble defining the term, saying that self-actualization is "a difficult syndrome to describe accurately." Nonetheless, Maslow defined **self-actualization** in the following way:

It may be loosely described as the full use and exploitation of talents, capacities, potentialities, etc. Such people seem to be fulfilling themselves and to be doing the best that they are capable of doing. . . . They are people who have developed or are developing to the full stature of which they are capable.

sexual dysfunction
A consistent disturbance in sexual desire, arousal, or orgasm that causes psychological distress and interpersonal difficulties.

female orgasmic disorder
In females, sexual dysfunction characterized by consistent delays in achieving orgasm or the inability to achieve orgasm.

premature ejaculation
In males, sexual dysfunction characterized by orgasm occurring before it is desired, often immediately or shortly after sexual stimulation or penetration.

male erectile disorder
In males, sexual dysfunction characterized by a recurring inability to achieve or maintain an erect penis.

hierarchy of needs
Maslow's hierarchical division of motivation into levels that progress from basic physical needs to psychological needs to self-fulfillment needs.

self-actualization
Defined by Maslow as a person's "full use and exploitation of talents, capacities, and potentialities."

FIGURE 8.9 **Maslow's Hierarchy of Needs** Abraham Maslow believed that people are innately motivated to satisfy a progression of needs, beginning with the most basic physiological needs. Once the needs at a particular level are satisfied, the individual is motivated to satisfy the needs at the next level, steadily progressing upward. The ultimate goal is self-actualization, the realization of personal potential.

SOURCE: Based on Maslow (1970).

self-determination theory (SDT)
Edward Deci and Richard Ryan's theory that optimal human functioning can occur only if the psychological needs for autonomy, competence, and relatedness are satisfied.

intrinsic motivation
The desire to engage in tasks that the person finds inherently satisfying and enjoyable, novel, or optimally challenging; the desire to do something for its own sake.

extrinsic motivation
External factors or influences on behavior, such as rewards, consequences, or social expectations.

competence motivation
The desire to direct one's behavior toward demonstrating competence and exercising control in a situation.

achievement motivation
The desire to direct one's behavior toward excelling, succeeding, or outperforming others at some task.

Table 8.4	
Maslow's Characteristics of Self-Actualized People	
Realism and acceptance	Self-actualized people have accurate perceptions of themselves, others, and external reality. They easily accept themselves and others as they are.
Spontaneity	Self-actualized people are spontaneous, natural, and open in their behavior and thoughts. However, they can easily conform to conventional rules and expectations when situations demand such behavior.
Problem centering	Self-actualized people focus on problems outside themselves. They often dedicate themselves to a larger purpose in life, which is based on ethics or a sense of personal responsibility.
Autonomy	Although they accept and enjoy other people, self-actualized individuals have a strong need for privacy and independence. They focus on their own potential and development rather than on the opinions of others.
Continued freshness of appreciation	Self-actualized people continue to appreciate the simple pleasures of life with awe and wonder.
Peak experiences	Self-actualized people commonly have *peak experiences*, or moments of intense ecstasy, wonder, and awe during which their sense of self is lost or transcended. The self-actualized person may feel transformed and strengthened by these peak experiences.

SOURCE: Based on Maslow (1970).

" *It is quite true that man lives by bread alone—where there is no bread. But what happens to man's desires when there is plenty of bread and when his belly is chronically filled? At once other (and "higher") needs emerge and these, rather than physiological hungers, dominate the organism. And when these in turn are satisfied, again new (and still "higher") needs emerge, and so on. That is what we mean by saying that the basic human needs are organized into a hierarchy of relative prepotency.* "

Abraham Maslow (1943)

Beyond that general description, Maslow's research identified several characteristics of self-actualized people, which are summarized in Table 8.4.

Maslow's model of motivation generated considerable research, especially during the 1970s and 1980s. Some studies found support for Maslow's ideas (e.g., Graham & Balloun, 1973). Others, however, criticized his hierarchy of needs on several points (e.g., Fox, 1982; Neher, 1991; Wahba & Bridwell, 1976). Maslow's concept of self-actualization is very vague and almost impossible to define in a way that would allow it to be tested scientifically. And Maslow's initial studies on self-actualization were based on limited samples with questionable reliability. For example, Maslow (1970) often relied on the life stories of acquaintances whose identities were never revealed. He also studied the biographies and autobiographies of famous historical figures he believed had achieved self-actualization, such as Eleanor Roosevelt, Abraham Lincoln, and Albert Einstein.

There is a more important criticism. Despite the claim that self-actualization is an inborn motivational goal toward which all people supposedly strive, most people do *not* experience or achieve self-actualization. Maslow (1970) himself wrote that self-actualization "can seem like a miracle, so improbable an event as to be awe-inspiring." Maslow explained this basic contradiction in a number of different ways. For instance, he suggested that few people experience the supportive environment that is required to achieve self-actualization.

Although interest in Maslow's theory has waned, it continues to generate occasional research (e.g., Hagerty, 1999; Sumerlin & Bundrick, 1996). But in general, Maslow's notion that we must satisfy needs at one level before moving to the next level has not stood up (Sheldon & others, 2001). Perhaps Maslow's most important contribution was to encourage psychology to focus on the motivation and development of psychologically healthy people. In advocating that idea, he helped focus attention on psychological needs as motivators.

Deci and Ryan's Self-Determination Theory

University of Rochester psychologists **Edward L. Deci** and **Richard M. Ryan** (1985, 2000) have developed **self-determination theory**, abbreviated **SDT**. Much like Maslow's theory, SDT's premise is that people are actively growth-oriented and that they move toward a unified sense of self and integration with others. To realize optimal psychological functioning and growth throughout the lifespan, Ryan and Deci contend that three innate and universal psychological needs must be satisfied:

- *Autonomy*—the need to determine, control, and organize one's own behavior and goals so that they are in harmony with one's own interests and values.

- *Competence*—the need to effectively learn and master appropriately challenging tasks.

- *Relatedness*—the need to feel attached to others and experience a sense of belongingness, security, and intimacy.

How does a person satisfy the needs for autonomy, competence, and relatedness? In a supportive social, psychological, and physical environment, an individual will pursue interests, goals, and relationships that tend to satisfy these psychological needs. In turn, this enhances the person's psychological growth and intrinsic motivation. **Intrinsic motivation** is the desire to engage in tasks that the person finds inherently satisfying and enjoyable, novel, or optimally challenging.

Of course, much of our behavior in daily life is driven by extrinsic motivation (Ryan & La Guardia, 2000). **Extrinsic motivation** consists of external influences on behavior, such as rewards, social evaluations, rules, and responsibilities. According to Ryan and Deci, the person who has satisfied the needs for competence, autonomy, and relatedness actively *internalizes* and *integrates* different external motivators as part of his or her identity and values. In effect, the person incorporates societal expectations, rules, and regulations as values or rules that he or she personally endorses.

In support of self-determination theory, Deci and Ryan have compiled an impressive array of studies, including cross-cultural studies (see Deci & Ryan, 2000; Ryan & Deci, 2000, 2001). Taking the evolutionary perspective, they also contend that the needs for autonomy, competence, and relatedness have adaptive advantages. For example, the need for relatedness promotes resource sharing, mutual protection, and the division of work, increasing the likelihood that both the individual and the group will survive.

Extraordinary Achievement Motivation
The U.S. women's soccer team thrilled onlookers at the Rose Bowl stadium with their overtime win against China in the Women's World Cup Final. Some of the team members had been playing competitive soccer for more than a decade. Here, team captain Carla Overbeck holds the trophy after Brandi Chastain's winning penalty kick.

Competence and Achievement Motivation

Key Theme
- Competence and achievement motivation are important psychological motives.

Key Questions
- How does competence motivation differ from achievement motivation, and how is achievement motivation measured?
- What characteristics are associated with a high level of achievement motivation, and how does culture affect achievement motivation?

In self-determination theory, Deci and Ryan identified *competence* as a universal motive. You are displaying **competence motivation** when you strive to use your cognitive, social, and behavioral skills to be capable and exercise control in a situation (R. White, 1959). Competence motivation provides much of the motivational "push" to prove to yourself that you can successfully tackle new challenges, such as striving to do well in this class.

A step beyond competence motivation is **achievement motivation**—the drive to excel, succeed, or outperform others at some task. In the chapter Prologue, Richard clearly displayed a high level of achievement motivation. Running for student body president, competing as a diver at the national level of collegiate competition, and striving to maintain a straight-A average are all examples of Richard's drive to achieve.

basic emotions
The most fundamental set of emotion categories, which are biologically innate, evolutionarily determined, and culturally universal.

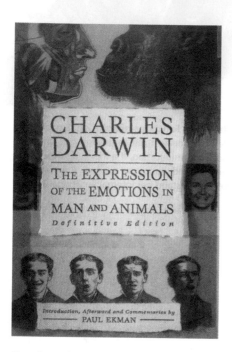

Darwin and Emotion *The Expression of the Emotions in Man and Animals* was a bestseller when it was first published in 1872. It was also the first scientific book to take advantage of the new technology of photography. Charles Darwin was one of the first scientists to systematically study emotional expressions. His purpose was to show the continuity of emotional expressions among nonhuman animals and humans—additional evidence for his evolutionary theory.

Table	8.5

The Basic Emotions	
Fear	Disgust
Surprise	Happiness
Anger	Sadness

Although there is some disagreement as to exactly which emotions best represent the universal set of basic emotions, most emotion researchers today agree on the six emotions shown above. Other possible candidates are contempt or disdain, pride, and excitement.

Mayer & Salovey, 1993). Why? Because they lack the ability to manage their own emotions, comprehend the emotional responses of others, and respond appropriately to the emotions of other people. In contrast, people who are high in emotional intelligence possess these abilities, and they are able to understand and use their emotions to help motivate themselves (Mayer & Salovey, 1997).

Evolutionary Explanations of Emotion

One of the earliest scientists to systematically study emotions was **Charles Darwin.** Darwin published *The Expression of the Emotions in Man and Animals* in 1872, 13 years after he had laid out his general theory of evolution in *On the Origin of Species by Means of Natural Selection* and only a year after his book on the evolution of humans, *The Descent of Man* (1871). Darwin (1872) described the facial expressions, body movements, and postures used to express specific emotions in animals and humans. He argued that emotions reflect evolutionary adaptations to the problems of survival and reproduction.

Like Darwin, today's evolutionary psychologists believe that emotions are the product of evolution (Tooby & Cosmides, 2000). Emotions help us solve adaptive problems posed by our environment. They "move" us toward potential resources, and they move us away from potential dangers. Fear prompts us to flee an attacker or evade a threat. Anger moves us to turn and fight a rival. Love propels us to seek out a mate and care for our offspring. Disgust prompts us to avoid a sickening stimulus. Obviously, the capacity to feel and be moved by emotion has adaptive value: An organism that is able to quickly respond to rewards or threats is more likely to survive and successfully reproduce.

Darwin (1872) also pointed out that emotional displays serve the important function of informing other organisms about an individual's internal state. When facing an aggressive rival, the snarl of a baboon signals its readiness to fight. A wolf rolling submissively on its back telegraphs its willingness to back down and avoid a fight.

Emotions are also important in situations that go well beyond physical survival. Virtually all human relationships are heavily influenced by emotions. Our emotional experience and expression, as well as our ability to understand the emotions of others, are crucial to the maintenance of social relationships (Reis & others, 2000).

In the next several sections, we'll consider each of the components of emotion in turn, beginning with the component that is most familiar: the subjective experience of emotion.

The Subjective Experience of Emotion

Most emotion researchers today agree that there are a limited number of **basic emotions** that all humans, in every culture, experience. These basic emotions are thought to be biologically determined, the products of evolution. And what are these basic emotions? As shown in Table 8.5, fear, disgust, surprise, happiness, anger, and sadness are most commonly cited as the basic emotions (Ekman, 1992a; Matsumoto, 2000).

Many psychologists contend that each basic emotion represents a sequence of responses that is innate and hard-wired in the brain (Tooby & Cosmides, 2000). But your emotional experience is not limited to pure forms of each basic emotion. Rather, each basic emotion represents a family of related emotional states (Ekman, 1994a, 1994b). For example, consider the many types of angry feelings, which can range from mild annoyance to bitter resentment or fierce rage.

Further, psychologists recognize that emotional experience can be complex and multifaceted (Cacioppo & Gardner, 1999). People often experience a *blend* of emotions. In more complex situations people may experience *mixed emotions,* in which very different emotions are experienced simultaneously or in rapid succession.

A common belief is that women are "naturally" more emotional than men. We explore this question in Critical Thinking Box 8.4. In fact, *both* men and women tend to view women as the more emotional sex (Hess & others, 2000). But are they? We explore this question in Critical Thinking Box 8.3.

CRITICAL THINKING 8.3

Are Women Really *More Emotional Than Men?*

"You never talk about your feelings!!" *she* said in exasperation. "And you *never* stop talking about yours!!" *he* shot back, frowning. Is this scene familiar?

One of our culture's most pervasive gender stereotypes is that women express their emotions more frequently and intensely than men do. In contrast, men supposedly are calmer and possess greater emotional control (Plant & others, 2000). Women, it's thought, cry easily. *Real* men don't cry at all.

Studies have shown that *both* men and women view women as the more emotional sex (Robinson & Clore, 2002). Women also place a higher value on emotional expressiveness than do men (Shields, 2002).

Women display more emotional awareness than do men (Feldman Barrett & others, 2000). Women are more accurate than men in deciphering the emotional meaning of nonverbal cues, such as facial expressions (Hall & Matsumoto, 2004). And they tend to be more sensitive and responsive to the emotional exchanges in a relationship, often playing the role of the "emotion specialist" (Gottman, 1994). But do such widely held stereotypes reflect actual gender differences in emotional experience?

Consider a study by Ann Kring and Albert Gordon (1998), in which participants separately watched film clips that typically evoke happiness, fear, or sadness. For example, a fear-evoking film clip depicted a man almost falling off the ledge of a tall building. During the film, the participants' facial expressions were secretly videotaped from behind a one-way mirror. Galvanic skin response was also monitored as an index of physiological arousal. *Galvanic skin response* (GSR) measures the skin's electrical conductivity, which changes in response to sweating and increased blood flow. After the film clip, the participants rated the extent to which they experienced different emotions.

Kring and Gordon found that men and women did *not* differ in their self-ratings of the emotions they experienced in response to the film clips. However, the women *were* more emotionally expressive than men. Women displayed more positive facial expressions in response to happy film clips and more negative facial expressions in response to the sad or fearful scenes. In terms of physiological arousal, the sexes did *not*

ZITS

© Zits Partnership. Reprinted with special permission of King Features Syndicate.

differ in their reactions to the happy or sad films. But when it came to the frightening film clips, the men reacted much more strongly than the women.

In a similar study, electrodes monitored facial muscle activity of male and female participants as they looked at fear-evoking pictures (Thunberg & Dimberg, 2000). Even though men and women rated the pictures as equally unpleasant, the women's facial muscles reacted much more strongly to the fearful images.

These and similar findings suggest that men and women are fairly similar in the *experience* of emotions, but that they do differ in the *expression* of emotions. How can we account for the gender differences in emotional expression?

First, psychologists have consistently found differences in the *types* of emotions expressed by men and women (see Shields, 2002). Analyzing cross-cultural data from 37 countries around the world, Agneta Fischer and her colleagues (2004) found this consistent pattern: Women report experiencing and expressing more sadness, fear, and guilt, while men report experiencing and expressing more anger and hostility.

Fischer and her colleagues (2004) argue that the male role encourages the expression of emotions that emphasize power and assertiveness. These *powerful emotions*—anger, hostility, and contempt—are emotions that confirm the person's autonomy and status. In contrast, the female role encourages the expression of emotions that imply vulnerability, self-blame, and helplessness. These *powerless emotions*—fear, sadness, shame, and guilt—are emotions that help maintain social harmony with others by minimizing conflict and hostility.

For both men and women, the expression of emotions is strongly influenced by *culturally determined display rules,* or societal norms of appropriate behavior in different situations. In many cultures, including the United States, women are allowed a wider range of emotional expressiveness and responsiveness than men. For men, it's considered "unmasculine" to be too open in expressing certain emotions. Crying is especially taboo (Vingerhoets & others, 2000). Thus, there are strong cultural and gender-role expectations concerning emotional expressiveness and sensitivity.

Like so many stereotypes, the gender stereotypes of emotions are not completely accurate. As psychologists Michael Robinson and Gerald Clore (2002) point out, men and women believe that their emotions differ far more than they actually do. Men and women differ less in their *experience* of emotion than they do in their *expression* of those emotions. However, women *are* the more emotional sex in terms of the ease with which they express their emotions, think about emotions, and recall emotional experiences (Feldman Barrett & others, 2000).

Critical Thinking Questions

- How are emotionally expressive males generally regarded in your social group? Emotionally expressive females? Does it make you uncomfortable when gender display rules are violated by either sex? Why?

- What kinds of consequences might occur if gender display rules were violated in a business environment? On a sports team? In a classroom?

Say "Cheese!" Her
simple test of the fa
back hypothesis. In
study by Fritz Strack
his colleagues (1988
participants who he
between their teeth
thought that cartoo
funnier than particip
held a pen between
(right). How does th
support the facial fee
hypothesis?

money or course credit. Just before the students left for the holidays, they were instructed to write an essay describing how they spent Christmas Eve. The essay had to be written and mailed within two days after Christmas Eve.

Half of the participants were instructed to write out specific implementation intentions describing exactly when and where they would write the report during the critical 48-hour period. They were also instructed to visualize the chosen opportunity and mentally commit themselves to it.

The other half of the participants were not asked to identify a specific time or place, but just instructed to write and mail the report within the 48 hours. The results? Of those in the implementation intention group, 71 percent wrote and mailed the report by the deadline. Only 32 percent of the other group did so (Gollwitzer & Brandstätter, 1997).

Mental Rehearsal: Visualize the Process

The mental images you create in anticipation of a situation can strongly influence your sense of self-efficacy and self-control as well as the effectiveness of your implementation intentions (Gollwitzer, 1999; Ozer & Bandura, 1990). For example, students sometimes undermine their own performance by vividly imagining their worst fears, such as becoming overwhelmed by anxiety during a class presentation or going completely blank during a test. However, the opposite is also possible. Mentally visualizing yourself dealing *effectively* with a situation can enhance your performance (Rivkin & Taylor, 1999; Sanna, 1999, 2000). Athletes, in particular, are aware of this and mentally rehearse their performance prior to competition.

So strive to control your thoughts in an optimistic way by mentally focusing on your capabilities and a positive outcome, not your limitations and worst fears. The key here is not just imagining a positive outcome. Instead, imagine and mentally rehearse the *process*—the skills you will effectively use and the steps you will take—to achieve the outcome *you* want (Pham & Taylor, 1999). Go for it!

Chapter Review
Motivation and Emotion

Key Points

Introduction: Motivation and Emotion

- **Motivation** refers to the forces that act on or within an organism to initiate and direct behavior. Three characteristics associated with motivation are activation, persistence, and intensity. Motivation is closely tied to emotion—we may be motivated to achieve certain emotions, and emotions may motivate us to take action.

Motivational Concepts and Theories

- During the twentieth century, many psychologists tried to develop general theories of motivation, but each model was too limited to explain all motivated behavior.

- **Instinct theories** of motivation, inspired by evolutionary theory, were limited in that they described and labeled behaviors but did not explain them.

- According to **drive theories,** behavior is motivated by the need to maintain **homeostasis.** Drive theories could not account for psychological motives or motives that are not related to a **drive,** or unmet need.

- According to **incentive theories,** behavior is motivated by external rewards.

- **Arousal theory** is based on the notion that people are motivated to maintain an optimal level of arousal, which can vary from one person to another. People who are high in **sensation seeking** seek high levels of arousal.

- **Humanistic theories of motivation** were based on the idea that people are motivated to achieve their highest potential.

Biological Motivation: *Hunger and Eating*

- Hunger is a biological motive, but eating behavior is also influenced by psychological, social, and cultural factors.

- Food provides **glucose,** the main source of the body's energy, which is regulated by **insulin.** Excess glucose is stored in **adipose tissue.** The **basal metabolic rate (BMR)** is the rate at which your body uses energy for vital body functions. **Energy homeostasis** helps people maintain their baseline body weight, which tends to remain stable over time unless conditions of positive or negative energy balance occur.

- Physiological factors that are correlated with eating are changes in glucose, insulin, **ghrelin,** body temperature, and

facial feedback hyp
The view that express
emotion, especially fa
subjective experience

two-factor theory c
Schachter and Singer'
emotion is the interac
cal arousal and the co
we apply to explain th

metabolism. Psychological factors that trigger eating behavior include classically conditioned stimuli and foods that, through operant conditioning and reinforcement, have acquired a **positive incentive value**. **Satiation** signals include **cholecystokinin (CCK)** and other physiological signals, as well as **sensory-specific satiety.**

■ Chemical signals that regulate body weight and help maintain a stable body weight over time include **leptin,** insulin, **neuropeptide Y,** and ghrelin. These factors are part of a complex feedback loop that also involves the hypothalamus in the brain. In response to a positive or negative energy balance, these factors influence appetite and metabolism so that body weight remains largely stable over time. The energy balance model is based on **set-point theory.** An alternative view, **settling-point models of weight regulation,** helps explain why baseline body weight can change over time in response to positive or negative energy balance.

■ The number of overweight people in the United States and other developed countries has steadily increased in the past decades. **Body mass index (BMI)** is one way to calculate weight status. Someone who is **obese** has a high BMI and an abnormally high proportion of body fat. Factors involved in becoming overweight include inadequate sleep, the ready availability of foods with a positive incentive value, overeating, the **cafeteria diet effect,** individual differences in BMR, and sedentary lifestyles.

■ Obesity leads to many health problems, some of which are life threatening. Several factors contribute to obesity, including genetic susceptibility, **leptin resistance,** and frequent dieting, which may lead to **weight cycling.** Obese people tend to have fewer dopamine receptors in their brains than normal-weight individuals, which may lead to compulsive eating to stimulate brain reward centers.

■ **Eating disorders** include **anorexia nervosa** and **bulimia nervosa.** Eating disorders are more common in females. Factors that contribute to the development of eating disorders include genetics, disruptions in serotonin, and disruptions in the chemical signals that normally regulate eating behavior. Cultural attitudes also contribute to eating disorders.

Sexual Motivation and Behavior

■ In nonhuman animals, sexual behavior is biologically determined and is typically triggered by hormonal changes in the female. In higher animals, sexual behavior is influenced more strongly by learning and environmental factors than by biological factors.

■ The four stages of human sexual response are excitement, plateau, orgasm, and resolution. Women are capable of multiple orgasms. Men experience a refractory period following orgasm.

■ **Sexual orientation** is not as easily categorized as many people think. Many people who have had one or more same-sex sexual experiences do not identify themselves as homosexual. Although psychologists do not know exactly what determines sexual orientation, genetics and differences in brain structure may be involved. Cross-gender play patterns in childhood seem to be related to a later homosexual

orientation. Sexual orientation develops at a fairly early age and is difficult to change.

■ Most adults are involved in an intimate relationship by the age of 30. Young adults today tend to have more sexual partners than previous generations did. Married people tend to have more active sex lives and to be more satisfied with their sex lives than unmarried people. Vaginal intercourse is the most preferred sexual activity.

■ A **sexual dysfunction** is a consistent disturbance in sexual response that causes the person psychological distress. Sexual problems are relatively common in the United States. Sexual problems are most common among young adult women and older men.

Psychological Needs as Motivators

■ According to Abraham Maslow's **hierarchy of needs,** people must fulfill basic physiological needs before they can be motivated by higher psychological needs, such as **self-actualization.** Maslow's model has been very influential, but it lacks empirical support.

■ **Self-determination theory (SDT),** developed by Edward Deci and Richard Ryan, is based on the premise that people are motivated to achieve a unified sense of self and integration with others. SDT includes three innate, universal psychological needs: autonomy, competence, and relatedness. **Intrinsic motivation** and **extrinsic motivation** are important principles in SDT.

■ Competence motivation refers to striving to be capable and exercise control, while **achievement motivation** refers to striving to excel or outperform others. The **Thematic Apperception Test (TAT)** is one way to measure achievement motivation. Achievement motivation is expressed differently in individualistic and collectivistic cultures.

Emotion

■ An **emotion** has three basic components: subjective experience, a physiological response, and a behavioral or expressive response.

■ Emotions have many functions, including triggering motivated behavior, and contribute to rational decision making and purposeful behavior. **Emotional intelligence** is needed to succeed in life. According to evolutionary psychologists, emotions are the product of evolution and help us solve important adaptive problems.

■ The **basic emotions** are innate and the product of evolution. Women tend to be more emotionally expressive than men. Emotions can be classified in terms of their degree of activation and pleasantness, and, in collectivistic societies, their level of **interpersonal engagement.**

■ Some emotions, such as fear, anger, and happiness, involve arousal of the sympathetic nervous system. The **amygdala** is a key structure in the brain's fear circuit, which also involves the thalamus, the cortex, and the hypothalamus. The amygdala can be activated by threatening stimuli before we are consciously aware of the stimulus, an ability that has adaptive survival value.

■ Facial expressions of the basic emotions are biologically innate, culturally universal, and the result of evolution. However, emotional expression is controlled by cultural **display rules.** Display rules also vary by gender, with men more likely to mask their emotions than women.

Theories of Emotion: *Explaining Emotion*

- Emotion theories differ in terms of which emotion component is emphasized. The **James–Lange theory** holds that emotion results from our perception of biological and behavioral responses. Contemporary evidence supporting the James–Lange theory includes neuroscience research demonstrating that we "feel" emotions in our body and the **facial feedback hypothesis.**

- There are two main cognitive theories of emotion. The **two-factor theory,** proposed by Schachter and Singer, holds that emotion results from applying a cognitive label to feelings of arousal. The **cognitive-mediational theory,** developed by Richard Lazarus, states that emotions result from the cognitive appraisal of the personal meaning of an event or stimulus. Emotion researchers today tend to agree that emotions can be triggered in multiple ways and that instinctive emotional responses may not require a conscious cognitive appraisal.

Key Terms

motivation, p. 298

instinct theories, p. 299

drive theories, p. 300

homeostasis, p. 300

drive, p. 300

incentive theories, p. 301

arousal theory, p. 301

sensation seeking, p. 301

humanistic theories of motivation, p. 302

glucose, p. 303

insulin, p. 303

basal metabolic rate (BMR), p. 303

adipose tissue, p. 303

energy homeostasis, p. 303

ghrelin, p. 304

positive incentive value, p. 305

satiation, p. 305

cholecystokinin (CCK), p. 305

sensory-specific satiety, p. 305

leptin, p. 306

neuropeptide Y (NPY), p. 306

set-point theory, p. 307

settling-point models of weight regulation, p. 307

body mass index (BMI), p. 308

obese, p. 308

cafeteria diet effect, p. 309

leptin resistance, p. 310

weight cycling, p. 310

eating disorder, p. 311

anorexia nervosa, p. 311

bulimia nervosa, p. 311

sexual orientation, p. 316

sexual dysfunction, p. 322

female orgasmic disorder, p. 322

premature ejaculation, p. 322

male erectile disorder, p. 322

hierarchy of needs, p. 323

self-actualization, p. 323

self-determination theory (SDT), p. 324

intrinsic motivation, p 325

extrinsic motivation, p. 325

competence motivation, p. 325

achievement motivation, p. 325

Thematic Apperception Test (TAT), p. 326

emotion, p. 327

emotional intelligence, p. 327

basic emotions, p. 328

interpersonal engagement, p. 330

amygdala, p. 331

display rules, p. 335

anthropomorphism, p. 337

James–Lange theory of emotion, p. 338

facial feedback hypothesis, p. 340

two-factor theory of emotion, p. 340

cognitive-mediational theory of emotion, p. 341

self-efficacy, p. 343

Key People

Walter Cannon (1871–1945)   American physiologist who developed an influential theory of emotion called the Cannon–Bard theory of emotion. (p. 338)

Charles Darwin (1809–1882)   English naturalist and scientist (also see Chapter 1) whose theory of evolution through natural selection was first published in *On the Origin of Species by Means of Natural Selection* in 1859. (p. 328)

Edward L. Deci (b. 1942)   American psychologist who, along with Richard M. Ryan, developed self-determination theory, which contends that optimal psychological functioning and growth can occur only if the psychological needs of autonomy, competence, and relatedness are satisfied. (p. 324)

Paul Ekman (b. 1934)   American psychologist and emotion researcher who is best known for his work in classifying basic emotions, analyzing facial expressions, and demonstrating that basic emotions and facial expressions are culturally universal. (p. 335)

William James (1842–1910)   American psychologist (also see Chapters 1 and 4) who developed an influential theory of emotion called the James–Lange theory. (p. 338)

Virginia E. Johnson (b. 1925)   American behavioral scientist who, along with William H. Masters, conducted pioneering research in the field of human sexuality and sex therapy. (p. 315)

Richard Lazarus (1922–2002)   American psychologist who promoted the cognitive perspective in the study of emotion; proposed the cognitive-mediational theory of emotion. (p. 341)

Abraham Maslow (1908–1970)   American psychologist and a founder of humanistic psychology who developed a hierarchical model of human motivation in which basic needs must first be satisfied before people can strive for self-actualization. (p. 323)

William H. Masters (1915–2001)   American physician who, along with Virginia E. Johnson, conducted pioneering research in the field of human sexuality and sex therapy. (p. 315)

Richard M. Ryan (b. 1953)   American psychologist who, along with Edward L. Deci, developed self-determination theory, which contends that optimal psychological functioning and growth can occur only if the psychological needs of autonomy, competence, and relatedness are satisfied. (p. 324)

Web Companion   Review Activities

You can find additional review activities at **www.DiscoveringPsychology.com** and clicking on *Discovering Psychology* 4th Edition text cover. At the Discovering Psychology Web Companion you will find self-scoring practice quizzes, two interactive crossword puzzles, flashcards, PsychSim and PsychQuest Activities, the chapter learning objectives, and other materials to help you master the information in this chapter. Use these materials to your advantage!

Fine China

Lifespan Development

Prologue

The Cheerleader and the Skydiver

"Oh, wow! Your wedding pictures!" Laura exclaimed, the lid now off of the long wardrobe box containing albums and bundles of photos, most of which had been compulsively labeled and dated by Don. Instantly, Tom Cat and Bob Cat, brothers intrepid and inseparable, appeared beside Laura, ready to explore the mysteries of yet another new box.

"Laura, will you come on! We're never going to get this basement organized at this rate," Don grumbled, teetering slightly off balance as he tried to shift a large wobbly cardboard box in the sea of other boxes covering most of the basement floor.

"You guys look so young!" our 14-year-old daughter observed, as she continued to flip through our wedding photo album. "Oh, there's Grandma and Grandpa! Who's the baby?"

"That's your cousin, Jordon. He's a little bit taller now, don't you think?" Given that Jordon was now a junior in high school, he should be. "Hey look, there's Paul and Asha."

"Will you get back to work, *please*?" Don said with exasperation. "Tom Cat, get out of that box!"

"Mom, who is this guy? He looks like Hagrid," Laura said, referring to the character from the Harry Potter books, as she pointed at the image of a huge bearded man in a tuxedo.

"Let me see," Sandy said, carefully stepping around a stack of textbooks to peer over Laura's shoulder. "Oh, that's Richard Krause."

"Richard was the man who hired me to teach many, many years ago," Don explained. "Long before you were born. Even before I met Mom."

"You taught at Hogwarts?" Laura asked innocently.

"Yes, and if you don't want your iPod to magically disappear, I'd put those wedding photos back and help move these journals to Mom's office," Don replied. "Bob Cat, don't eat those packing peanuts!"

We had been ignoring the sea of boxes in the basement for the months since we had moved to the wonderful old house that we now occupy. It is a house with lots of character, including a basement. Most houses in Tulsa don't have basements, which you'd think would be mandatory for such a tornado-prone part of the planet. But at this particular moment, it looked like a tornado had been through our basement, what with the stacks of boxes, books, bookshelves, and hodgepodge of assorted stuff strewn everywhere.

The tornado, in this case, was the whirlwind of moving our home and, more importantly, our home offices, in just six weeks—from December 1st to January 15th. That was how much time we had between semesters. It was also how much time we could take off from our writing schedule.

Several of Don's students looking to make some extra money for the holidays helped us pack up the entire house in just a couple of days. At the time, we had what we thought was a brilliant strategy: Anything that was not absolutely critical to the day-to-day functioning of our home offices got moved to the basement. It turned out to be brilliant—with one minor flaw: We now had no idea what was *in* any of those 300+ boxes labeled "basement." So 10 months later on a rainy Saturday afternoon as we opened box after box, it felt a little like the Christmas we had missed because of the move.

"My Legos! And my Beanie Babies! I knew this stuff was here someplace."

Moving is one of those events that forces you to reflect on your past as bits and pieces of memories are unearthed from the corners of closets, attics, and basements, even if only to quickly find a new home in some other corner. But for a few moments, images, scenes, and mementos of earlier chapters in one's life briefly reappear.

"Hey, Laura, you want to see some pictures of me in my high school yearbook?" Sandy asked as she opened the book from her senior year, the spine cracking as she did so. "This was our school newspaper staff. I was the managing editor. There's Danny, my best friend."

"Look at that girl's big hair and those short skirts!"

"There's Mr. Insley, the world's greatest physics teacher. I was in the first AP class ever taught at Steinmetz, and he taught it."

It's interesting how the different chapters of one's life, especially the adolescent years, can seem so intense and complicated at the time you are living them. But looking back years later, there's a sense of both familiarity and distance in looking at the person you were—and comparing her to the person you've become.

"You were a *cheerleader* in high school?!" Laura said with astonishment.

"Hey, those were the bad old days before Title IX," Sandy replied. "They wouldn't let girls do much else."

"Can we *please* save the trip down memory lane for some other Saturday?" Don interrupted. "Can we just stay on task?"

The task of life is, of course, to move forward and experience fully all the different transitions—the physical, psychological, and social changes—that we encounter throughout the lifespan. Thankfully, you can prepare for many transitions, like marriage, moving, or retirement. But other transitions are unexpected or impossible to predict, like accidents or illnesses. And some transitions, like the death of a loved one, are no less devastating when expected than when unexpected. Often we don't recognize the impact of the turning points in our lives until long after they've occurred, having led us down a path that we never really planned or expected.

Transitions. That's what this chapter is about. It's about the transitions in your life—your family, your childhood, your friends, your life right now. No matter who you are, what your life has been, or where you hope to go, you will make many of the same transitions throughout your life that every other person who reads this chapter will also make. It is those commonalities that define the main themes of this chapter on lifespan development. But what will make this chapter completely different from the one that everyone else reads are the unique elements of your own individual life story.

"Dad, is this yours?" Laura asked, holding up a dog-eared book.

"My skydiving manual!"

"You were a *skydiver*?"

Introduction
Your Life Story

developmental psychology
The branch of psychology that studies how people change over the lifespan.

Key Theme
■ Developmental psychology is the study of how people change over the lifespan.

Key Questions
■ What are the eight basic stages of the lifespan?
■ What are some of the key themes in developmental psychology?

One way to look at the "big picture" of your life is to think of your life as a story. You, of course, are the main character. Your life story so far has had a distinct plot, occasional subplots, and a cast of supporting characters, including family, friends, and lovers.

Like every other person's life story, yours has been influenced by factors beyond your control. One such factor is the unique combination of genes you inherited from your biological mother and father. Another is the historical era during which you grew up. Your individual development has also been shaped by the cultural, social, and family contexts within which you were raised.

The patterns of your life story, and the life stories of countless other people, are the focus of **developmental psychology**—the study of how people change physically, mentally, and socially throughout the lifespan. At every age and stage of life, developmental psychologists investigate the influence of multiple factors on development, including biological, environmental, social, cultural, and behavioral factors.

However, the impact of these factors on individual development is greatly influenced by attitudes, perceptions, and personality characteristics. For example, the adjustment to middle school may be a breeze for one child, but a nightmare for another. So although we are influenced by the events we experience, we also shape the meaning and consequences of those events.

Along with studying common patterns of growth and change, developmental psychologists look at the ways in which people *differ* in their development and life stories. As the Prologue illustrates, there is considerable individual variation among adults in the timing of social, occupational, and interpersonal accomplishments. As we'll note several times in this chapter, the typical, or "normal," pattern of development can also vary among cultures.

Developmental psychologists often conceptualize the lifespan in terms of basic *stages* of development (see Table 9.1). Traditionally, the stages of the lifespan are defined by age, which implies that we experience relatively sudden, age-related changes as we move from one stage to the next. Indeed, some of life's transitions *are* rather abrupt, such as entering the workforce, becoming a parent, or retiring. And some aspects of development, such as prenatal development and language development, are closely tied to *critical periods,* which are periods during which a child is maximally sensitive to environmental influences.

Still, most of our physical, mental, and social changes occur gradually. As we trace the typical course of human development in this chapter, the theme of *gradually unfolding changes* throughout the ages and stages of life will become more evident.

Another important theme in developmental psychology is the *interaction between heredity and environment.* Traditionally, this is called the *nature–nurture* issue (see Chapter 1). Although we are born with a specific genetic potential that we inherit from our biological parents, our environment influences and shapes how that potential is expressed. In turn, our genetic inheritance influences the ways in which we experience and interact with the environment.

Table 9.1	
Major Stages of the Lifespan	
Stage	**Age Range**
Prenatal	Conception to birth
Infancy and toddlerhood	Birth to 2 years
Early childhood	2 to 6 years
Middle childhood	6 to 12 years
Adolescence	12 to 18 years
Young adulthood	18 to 40 years
Middle adulthood	40 to 65 years
Late adulthood	65 years to death

The Chapters in Your Life Story If you think of your life as an unfolding story, then the major stages of the human lifespan represent the different "chapters" of your life. Each chapter is characterized by fundamentally different physical, cognitive, and social transitions, challenges and opportunities, demands and adjustments. Comparing different life stories reveals many striking similarities in the developmental themes of any given stage. But beyond those similarities, every life story is also characterized by considerable variations in the timing of life events and the pathways that are ultimately followed. In that sense, every life story is unique.

Continuity and Change over the Lifespan The twin themes of continuity and change throughout the lifespan are evident in the changing nature of relationships. Childhood friendships center on sharing activities, while peer relationships in adolescence emphasize sharing thoughts and feelings. Early adulthood brings the challenge of forming intimate relationships and beginning a family. Close relationships with friends and family continue to contribute to psychological well-being in late adulthood.

Developmental psychology is a broad field, covering a wide range of topics from many different perspectives. Our goal in this chapter is not to try to survey the entire field of lifespan development. Rather, we'll focus on presenting some of the most influential theories in developmental psychology and the key themes that have guided research on each stage of the lifespan. As we do so, we'll describe the typical patterns of development while noting the importance of individual variation.

Genetic Contributions to Your Life Story

zygote
The single cell formed at conception from the union of the egg cell and sperm cell.

chromosome
A long, threadlike structure composed of twisted parallel strands of DNA; found in the cell nucleus.

deoxyribonucleic acid (DNA)
The double-stranded molecule that encodes genetic instructions; the chemical basis of heredity.

gene
A unit of DNA on a chromosome that encodes instructions for making a particular protein molecule; the basic unit of heredity.

genotype
(JEEN-oh-type) The genetic makeup of an individual organism.

Key Theme
■ Your genotype consists of the chromosomes inherited from your biological parents, but your phenotype—the actual characteristics you display—results from the interaction of genetics and environmental factors.

Key Questions
■ What are DNA, chromosomes, and genes?
■ How do genes guide the development of living organisms?
■ What role does the environment play in the relationship between genotype and phenotype?

You began your life as a **zygote,** a single cell no larger than the period at the end of this sentence. Packed in that tiny cell was the unique set of genetic instructions that you inherited from your biological parents. Today, that same set of genetic information is found in the nucleus of nearly every cell of your body.

What form does that genetic data take? The genetic data you inherited from your biological parents is encoded in the chemical structure of the **chromosomes** that are found in the cell nucleus. As depicted in Figure 9.1, each chromosome is

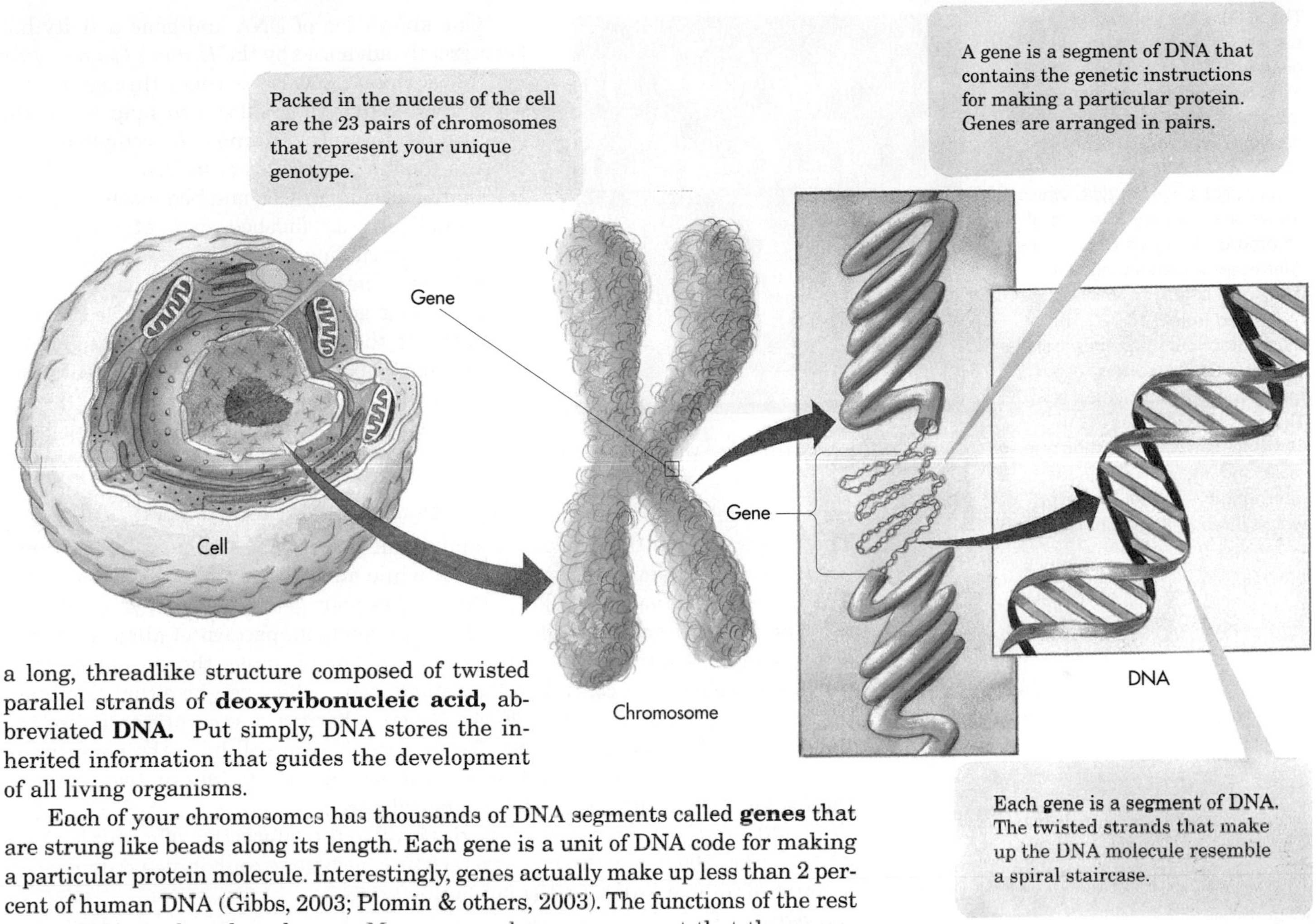

Packed in the nucleus of the cell are the 23 pairs of chromosomes that represent your unique genotype.

A gene is a segment of DNA that contains the genetic instructions for making a particular protein. Genes are arranged in pairs.

Gene

Cell

Chromosome

Gene

DNA

Each gene is a segment of DNA. The twisted strands that make up the DNA molecule resemble a spiral staircase.

a long, threadlike structure composed of twisted parallel strands of **deoxyribonucleic acid,** abbreviated **DNA.** Put simply, DNA stores the inherited information that guides the development of all living organisms.

Each of your chromosomes has thousands of DNA segments called **genes** that are strung like beads along its length. Each gene is a unit of DNA code for making a particular protein molecule. Interestingly, genes actually make up less than 2 percent of human DNA (Gibbs, 2003; Plomin & others, 2003). The functions of the rest of the DNA are largely unknown. Many researchers now suspect that these noncoding DNA regions act to regulate gene functioning (Mattick, 2004; Pennisi, 2004).

What do genes do? In a nutshell, your genes direct the manufacture of proteins. Proteins are used in virtually all of your body's functions—from building cells to manufacturing hormones to regulating brain activity. Your body requires hundreds of thousands of different proteins to function (Marcus, 2004). Each protein is formed by a specific combination of amino acids, and that combination is encoded in a particular gene.

FIGURE 9.1 Chromosomes, Genes, and DNA Each chromosome contains thousands of genes, and each gene is a unit of DNA instructions. Incredibly fine, the strands of DNA in a single human cell would be more than three inches long if unraveled. Here's a great piece of trivia for you: If the DNA present in one person were unraveled, it would stretch from Earth to Pluto and back—*twice!*

Your Unique Genotype

At fertilization, your biological mother's egg cell and your biological father's sperm cell each contributed 23 chromosomes. This matched set of chromosomes provides you with two copies of each gene—one contributed from your father's sperm and one from your mother's egg. This set of 46 chromosomes represents your unique genetic makeup, or **genotype.** Other than the reproductive cells (sperm or eggs), every cell in your body contains a complete, identical copy of your genotype.

Why, then, are body cells so different? Or, put another way, how does the single-celled zygote develop into a multicellular organism with hair, teeth, eyes, lungs, and other tissues? The dramatic differences among the size, shape, and function of cells that develop into skin, lung, or brain cells are *not* due to their having different sets of genes. Rather, the differences are due to *which* genes are "expressed" or activated. In other words, different cells develop because different genes are activated at different times. Some genes are active for just a few hours, others for a lifetime. Some genes are *never* expressed. For example, humans carry the genes to develop a tail, but we don't develop a tail because those genes are never activated.

The 23 Pairs of Human Chromosomes Each person's unique genotype is represented in the 23 pairs of chromosomes that are found in the nucleus of almost all human body cells. This photograph, taken through a microscope, depicts a *karyotype*, which shows one cell's complete set of chromosomes. By convention, the chromosomes are arranged in pairs from largest to smallest, numbered from 1 to 22. The 23rd pair of chromosomes, called the **sex chromosomes**, determines a person's biological sex. The sex chromosomes in this karyotype are XX, indicating a female, and are labeled X in the photograph. A male karyotype would have an XY combination.

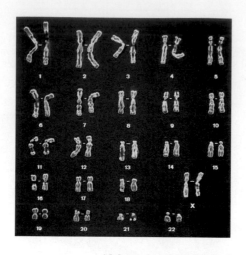

Our knowledge of DNA and gene activity has been greatly advanced by the *Human Genome Project*. More than 2,800 researchers throughout the world coordinated their efforts to map all of the genes in the **human genome**—the complete set of DNA in the human organism. In October 2004, the International Human Genome Sequencing Consortium published its finished map of the human genome (International Human Genome, 2004; Stein, 2004). One surprise involved the number of protein-coding genes that humans have. Previous estimates of the number of protein-coding genes ranged from 30,000 to as high as 100,000 genes. But more accurate techniques revealed that the human genome consists of only 20,000 to 25,000 genes.

Although all humans have the same basic set of genes, these genes can come in different versions, called **alleles.** Your genotype includes two copies of each gene—one inherited from each parent. These genes may be identical or different. The range of potential alleles for individual genes varies (Baker, 2004). Some genes have just a few different versions, while others have up to 50 or more. It is this unique combination of alleles that makes your genotype—and you—unique.

The best-known, although not the most common, pattern of allele variation is the simple dominant–recessive gene pair. For example, the development of freckles appears to be controlled by a single gene, which can be either dominant or recessive (Zhang & others, 2004). If you inherit a dominant version of the freckles gene from either or both of your parents, you will have the potential to display freckles. But to be freckle-free, you would have to inherit two recessive "no freckles" genes, one from each biological parent.

Unlike freckles, most characteristics involve the interaction of multiple genes (Grigorenko, 2003). For these characteristics, each gene contributes only a small amount of influence to a particular characteristic.

From Genotype to Phenotype

Whereas *genotype* refers to an organism's unique genetic makeup, the term **phenotype** refers to the characteristics that are actually observed in an organism. How does the information coded in your genotype translate into your phenotype?

In the past, a person's unique genotype was often described as a genetic "blueprint." The blueprint analogy implied that a person's genotype was a fixed, master plan that controlled virtually all aspects of development as it unfolded over the person's lifespan. But as science's understanding of genetic processes has advanced, it's become clear that the "blueprint" analogy is not an accurate one (Johnston & Edwards, 2002).

One problem with the blueprint analogy is that genes themselves don't actually control physical development or behavior. Rather, genes direct the synthesis and production of particular proteins. In turn, these proteins are the building blocks of all your body's tissues and functions, which ultimately *do* influence development and behavior (Marcus, 2004).

A more accurate analogy would be to describe a person's genotype as a massive *cookbook*. Like a cookbook, the genotype consists of an organized collection of recipes (genes) for building proteins for every conceivable occasion. Many of these recipes are the same for all living organisms—from mice to jellyfish (Pennisi, 2004). Other recipes are unique to one type of organism, such as bacteria, plants, or mammals.

A second problem with the genes-as-blueprint analogy is that genetic activity is far from fixed or inevitable. Instead, genes turn on and off. Gene activity may be triggered by the activity of *other* genes or by environmental factors. Thus,

human genome
The scientific description of the complete set of DNA in the human organism, including gene locations.

allele
(ah-LEEL) One of the different forms of a particular gene.

phenotype
(FEEN-oh-type) The observable traits or characteristics of an organism as determined by the interaction of genetics and environmental factors.

sex chromosomes
Chromosomes, designated as X or Y, that determine biological sex; the 23rd pair of chromosomes in humans.

prenatal stage
The stage of development before birth; divided into the germinal, embryonic, and fetal periods.

germinal period
The first two weeks of prenatal development.

gene expression is *flexible,* responding to fluctuations in the organism's internal state or external environment.

To illustrate how environmental factors can influence genetic expression, let's go back to the freckles example. Suppose that your genotype contains a copy of the dominant "freckles" gene. Will you develop freckles? Only if the freckles gene is triggered by a particular environmental factor—exposure to sunlight. In the case of freckles, the phenotype expression of the genetic potential takes place only under certain environmental conditions. On the other hand, if your genotype does not include the gene for freckles, you're unlikely to develop freckles, even if you spend a good deal of time in the sun.

The important point is this: *Different genotypes react differently to environmental factors* (Baker, 2004; Rowe, 2003). Your underlying genotype and environmental factors interact throughout your lifetime. Two people may have a very similar genotype, but if they live in very different environments, their phenotypes will also differ. Similarly, people with different genotypes will develop different phenotypes in response to similar environmental conditions.

Because genotypes react differently to environmental factors, psychologists and researchers will often speak of *genetic predispositions* to develop in a particular way (Parens, 2004). In other words, people with a particular genetic configuration are more or less sensitive to particular environmental factors. For example, think of people you know who have a genetic predisposition to sunburn easily, such as redheads or people with very fair skin. For such people, their genotype is especially sensitive to the effects of ultraviolet light.

Interactions among genes and between genotype and environment are not the only aspects that must be considered when we look at the relationship between genotype and phenotype. Genes can also *mutate,* or spontaneously change, from one generation to the next. Further, DNA itself can be damaged by environmental factors—such as ultraviolet light, radiation, or chemical toxins. Just as a typographical error in a complex recipe can ruin a favorite dish, errors in the genetic code can disrupt the production of the correct proteins and lead to birth defects or genetic disorders.

Prenatal Development

Key Theme
■ During the prenatal stage, the single-celled zygote develops into a full-term fetus.

Key Questions
■ What are the three stages of prenatal development?
■ What are teratogens, and what general principles seem to govern their impact on the fetus?

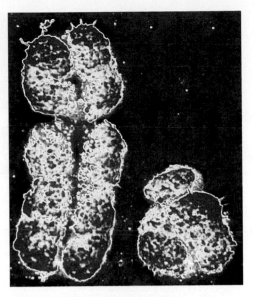

Human Sex Chromosomes: X and Y Biological sex is determined by the 23rd pair of chromosomes, the *sex chromosomes.* While every normal egg cell has one X chromosome, every normal sperm cell has either one X or one Y chromosome. Whether a zygote develops into a male or a female depends on whether the egg is fertilized by a sperm cell with a Y chromosome (XY, resulting in a male) or by a sperm cell with an X chromosome (XX, resulting in a female). Notice that the X chromosome (*left*) is larger and has more genes than the Y chromosome (*right*). This confers some protection against certain genetic disorders for females. Why? Because by having two X chromosomes, females are more likely to have a normal allele than a disease-producing allele. If a male has a disease-producing allele on his X chromosome, he is less likely to have a normal allele on his smaller Y chromosome to override it. This is why males are more likely to display various genetic disorders, such as red–green color blindness and hemophilia, which they inherit via the X chromosome contributed by their biological mother.

At conception, chromosomes from the biological mother and father combine to form a single cell—the fertilized egg, or *zygote.* Over the relatively brief span of nine months, that single cell develops into the estimated trillion cells that make up a newborn baby. This **prenatal stage** has three distinct phases: the germinal period, the embryonic period, and the fetal period.

The **germinal period,** also called the *zygotic period,* represents the first two weeks of prenatal development. During this time, the zygote undergoes rapid cell division before becoming implanted on the wall of the mother's uterus. Some of the zygote's cells will eventually form the structures that house and protect the developing fetus and will provide nourishment from the mother. By the end of the two-week germinal period, the single-celled zygote has developed into a cluster of cells called the *embryo.*

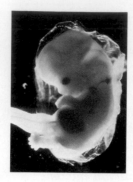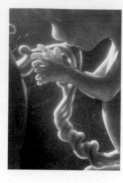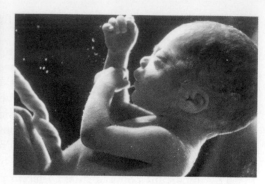

Prenatal Development Although it is less than an inch long, the beginnings of arms, legs, and fingers can already be distinguished in the 7-week-old embryo (*left*). The amniotic sac and the placenta can be clearly seen in this photograph. The fetus at 4 months (*center*) measures 6 to 10 inches long, and the mother may be able to feel the fetus's movements. Notice the well-formed umbilical cord. Near full term (*right*), the 8-month-old fetus gains body fat to help the newborn survive outside the mother's uterus.

The **embryonic period** begins with week 3 and extends through week 8. During this time of rapid growth and intensive cell differentiation, the organs and major systems of the body form. Genes on the sex chromosomes and hormonal influences also trigger the initial development of the sex organs.

Protectively housed in the fluid-filled *amniotic sac*, the embryo's lifeline is the umbilical cord. Extending from the placenta on the mother's uterine wall to the embryo's abdominal area, the *umbilical cord* delivers nourishment, oxygen, and water and carries away carbon dioxide and other wastes. The *placenta* is actually a disk-shaped, vascular organ that prevents the mother's blood from directly mingling with that of the developing embryo. Acting as a filter, the placenta prevents many harmful substances that might be present in the mother's blood from reaching the embryo.

The placenta cannot, however, filter out all harmful agents from the mother's blood. Harmful agents or substances that can cause abnormal development or birth defects are called **teratogens.** Generally, the greatest vulnerability to teratogens occurs during the embryonic stage, when major body systems are forming. Known teratogens include:

- Exposure to radiation
- Toxic chemicals and metals, such as mercury, PCBs, and lead
- Viruses and bacteria, such as German measles (rubella), syphilis, genital herpes, and human immunodeficiency virus (HIV)
- Drugs taken by the mother, such as alcohol, cocaine, and heroin

By the end of the embryonic period, the embryo has grown from a cluster of a few hundred cells no bigger than the head of a pin to over an inch in length. Now weighing about an ounce, the embryo looks distinctly human, even though its head accounts for about half its body size.

The third month heralds the beginning of the **fetal period**—the final and longest stage of prenatal development. The main task during the next seven months is for body systems to grow and reach maturity in preparation for life outside the mother's body. By the end of the third month, the *fetus* can move its arms, legs, mouth, and head. The fetus becomes capable of reflexive responses, such as fanning its toes if the sole of the foot is stroked and squinting if its eyelids are touched. During the fourth month, the mother experiences *quickening*—she can feel the fetus moving.

By the fifth month, all the brain cells the person will have at birth are present. After birth, the communication links between these brain cells continue to develop in complexity. The fetus has distinct sleep–wake cycles and periods of activity (see Figure 4.4 on page 138). During the sixth month, the fetus's brain activity becomes similar to that of a newborn baby.

During the final two months of this period, the fetus will double in weight, gaining an additional three to four pounds of body fat. This additional body fat will help the newborn adjust to changing temperatures outside the womb. It also contributes to the newborn's chubby appearance. As birth approaches, growth slows and the fetus's body systems become more active.

embryonic period
The second period of prenatal development, extending from the third week through the eighth week.

teratogens
Harmful agents or substances that can cause malformations or defects in an embryo or fetus.

fetal period
The third and longest period of prenatal development, extending from the ninth week until birth.

Development During Infancy and Childhood

Key Theme
■ Although physically helpless, newborn infants are equipped with reflexes and sensory capabilities that enhance their chances for survival.

Key Questions
■ How do the senses and the brain develop after birth?
■ What roles do temperament and attachment play in social and personality development?
■ What are the stages of language development?

The newly born infant enters the world with an impressive array of physical and sensory capabilities. Initially, his behavior is mostly limited to reflexes that enhance his chances for survival. Touching the newborn's cheek triggers the *rooting reflex*—the infant turns toward the source of the touch and opens his mouth. Touching the newborn's lips evokes the *sucking reflex*. If you put a finger on each of the newborn's palms, he will respond with the *grasping reflex*—the baby will grip your fingers so tightly that he can be lifted upright. As motor areas of the infant's brain develop over the first year of life, the rooting, sucking, and grasping reflexes are replaced by voluntary behaviors.

The newborn's senses—vision, hearing, smell, and touch—are keenly attuned to people. In a classic study, Robert Fantz (1961) demonstrated that the image of a human face holds the newborn's gaze longer than do other images. Other researchers have also confirmed the newborn's visual preference for the human face (Turati & others, 2002). Newborns only 10 *minutes* old will turn their heads to continue gazing at the image of a human face as it passes in front of them, but they will not visually follow other images (Johnson & others, 1991).

And, newborns quickly learn to differentiate between their mothers and strangers. Within just hours of their birth, newborns display a preference for their mother's voice and face over that of a stranger (Bushnell, 2001). For their part, mothers become keenly attuned to their infant's appearance, smell, and even skin texture (Kaitz & others, 1992). Fathers, too, are able to identify their newborn from a photograph after just minutes of exposure (Bader & Phillips, 2002).

Vision is the least developed sense at birth. A newborn infant is extremely nearsighted, meaning she can see close objects more clearly than distant objects. The optimal viewing distance for the newborn is about 6 to 12 inches, the perfect distance for a nursing baby to focus easily on her mother's face and make eye

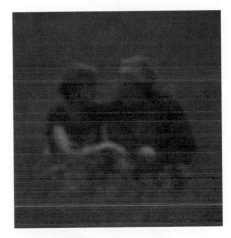

The Near-Sighted Newborn Classic research by psychologist Robert Fantz and his colleagues (1962) showed that the newborn comes into the world very near-sighted, having approximately 20/300 vision. The newborn's ability to detect the contrast of object edges and boundaries is also poorly developed (Stephens & Banks, 1987). As the above image illustrates, even by age three months, the infant's world is still pretty fuzzy.

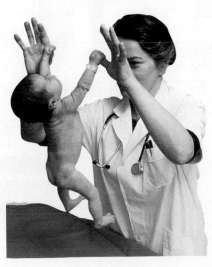

Newborn Reflexes When this 2-week-old baby (*left*) is held upright with her feet touching a flat surface, she displays the *stepping reflex*, moving her legs as if trying to walk. Another reflex that is present at birth is the *grasping reflex* (*right*). The infant's grip is so strong that he can support his own weight. Thought to enhance the newborn's chances for survival, these involuntary reflexes disappear after the first few months of life.

contact. Nevertheless, the infant's view of the world is pretty fuzzy for the first several months, even for objects that are within close range.

The interaction between adults and infants seems to compensate naturally for the newborn's poor vision. When adults interact with very young infants, they almost always position themselves so that their face is about 8 to 12 inches away from the baby's face. Adults also have a strong natural tendency to exaggerate head movements and facial expressions, such as smiles and frowns, again making it easier for the baby to see them.

Physical Development

By the time infants begin crawling, at around 7 to 8 months of age, their view of the world, including distant objects, will be as clear as that of their parents. The increasing maturation of the infant's visual system reflects the development of her brain. At birth, her brain is an impressive 25 percent of its adult weight. In contrast, her birth weight is only about 5 percent of her eventual adult weight. During infancy, her brain will grow to about 75 percent of its adult weight, while her body weight will reach only about 20 percent of her adult weight.

One outward reflection of the infant's developing brain is the attainment of more sophisticated motor skills. Figure 9.2 illustrates the sequence and average ages of motor skill development during infancy. The basic *sequence* of motor skill development is universal, but the *average ages* can be a little deceptive. Infants vary a great deal in the ages at which they master each skill. Although virtually all infants are walking well by 15 months of age, some infants will walk as early as 10 months. Each infant has his own genetically programmed timetable of physical maturation and developmental readiness to master different motor skills.

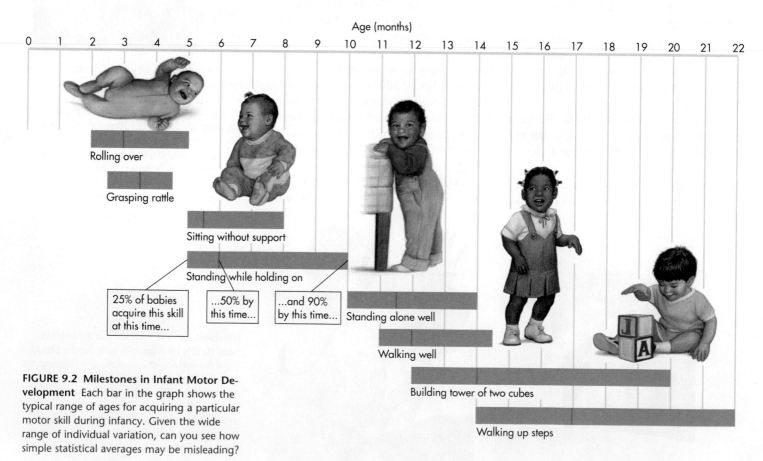

Age (months)

0 1 2 3 4 5 6 7 8 9 10 11 12 13 14 15 16 17 18 19 20 21 22

Rolling over

Grasping rattle

Sitting without support

Standing while holding on

25% of babies acquire this skill at this time...

...50% by this time...

...and 90% by this time...

Standing alone well

Walking well

Building tower of two cubes

Walking up steps

FIGURE 9.2 Milestones in Infant Motor Development Each bar in the graph shows the typical range of ages for acquiring a particular motor skill during infancy. Given the wide range of individual variation, can you see how simple statistical averages may be misleading?

Social and Personality Development

From birth, forming close social and emotional relationships with caregivers is essential to the infant's physical and psychological well-being. Although physically helpless, the young infant does not play a passive role in forming these relationships. As you'll see in this section, the infant's individual traits play an important role in the development of the relationship between infant and caregiver.

Temperamental Qualities: Babies Are Different!

Infants come into the world with very distinct and consistent behavioral styles. Some babies are consistently calm and easy to soothe. Other babies are fussy, irritable, and hard to comfort. Some babies are active and outgoing; others seem shy and wary of new experiences. Psychologists refer to these inborn predispositions to consistently behave and react in a certain way as an infant's **temperament.**

Interest in infant temperament was triggered by a classic longitudinal study launched in the 1950s by psychiatrists Alexander Thomas and Stella Chess. The focus of the study was on how temperamental qualities influence adjustment throughout life. Chess and Thomas rated young infants on a variety of characteristics, such as activity level, mood, regularity in sleeping and eating, and attention span. They found that about two-thirds of the babies could be classified into one of three broad temperamental patterns: *easy, difficult,* and *slow-to-warm-up.* About a third of the infants were characterized as *average* babies because they did not fit neatly into one of these three categories (Thomas & Chess, 1977).

Easy babies readily adapt to new experiences, generally display positive moods and emotions, and have regular sleeping and eating patterns. *Difficult* babies tend to be intensely emotional, are irritable and fussy, and cry a lot. They also tend to have irregular sleeping and eating patterns. *Slow-to-warm-up* babies have a low activity level, withdraw from new situations and people, and adapt to new experiences very gradually. After studying the same children from infancy through childhood, Thomas and Chess (1986) found that these broad patterns of temperamental qualities are remarkably stable.

Other temperamental patterns have been identified. For example, after decades of research, Jerome Kagan (2004; Kagan & Snidman, 2004) has classified temperament in terms of *reactivity. High-reactive* infants react intensely to new experiences, strangers, and novel objects. They tend to be tense, fearful, and inhibited. At the opposite pole are *low-reactive* infants, who tend to be calmer, uninhibited, and bolder. Sociable rather than shy, low-reactive infants are more likely to show interest than fear when exposed to new people, experiences, and objects.

Virtually all temperament researchers agree that individual differences in temperament have a genetic and biological basis (Kagan, 2004; Rothbart & others, 2000). However, researchers also agree that environmental experiences can modify a child's basic temperament (Pauli-Pott & others, 2004; Rothbart & Putnam, 2002). As Kagan (2004) points out, "Temperament is not destiny. Many experiences will affect high and low reactive infants as they grow up. Parents who encourage a more sociable, bold persona and discourage timidity will help their high reactive children develop a less-inhibited profile."

Because cultural attitudes affect child-rearing practices, infant temperament can also be affected by cultural beliefs. For example, cross-cultural studies of temperament have found that infants in the United States generally displayed more positive emotion than Russian or Asian infants (Gartstein & others, 2003). One explanation is that U.S. parents tend to value and encourage expressions of positive emotions, such as smiling and laughing, in their babies. In contrast, parents in other cultures, including those of Russia and many Asian countries, place a lesser emphasis on the importance of positive emotional expression. Thus, the development of temperamental qualities is yet another example of the complex interaction among genetic and environmental factors.

Hello, World! Some babies seem to be born wearing a smile. An "easy" baby is calm, easy to soothe, and usually cheerful. At the opposite extreme, "difficult" babies are more likely to be irritable and fussy. "Slow-to-warm-up" babies adapt to new experiences very slowly.

A temperamental bias can be likened to the basic form of the song of a particular species of bird. The animal's genome constrains the basic architecture of the song but does not determine all of its features; within broad limits, the adult song depends on exposure to the songs of other birds and the opportunity to hear its own vocalizations. A similar principle holds true for the effect of environmental influences on people.

Jerome Kagan (2004)

temperament
Inborn predispositions to consistently behave and react in a certain way.

Mary D. Salter Ainsworth (1913-1999) Although best known for her development of the "Strange Situation" technique to measure attachment, Mary D. Salter Ainsworth made many other contributions to developmental psychology. She originated the concept of the *secure base* and was the first researcher in the United States to make extensive, systematic, naturalistic observations of mother-infant interactions in their own homes. Her findings often surprised contemporary psychologists. For example, Ainsworth provided the first evidence demonstrating the importance of the caregiver's responsiveness to the infant's needs (Bretherton & Main, 2000).

Attachment: Forming Emotional Bonds

During the first year of life, the emotional bond that forms between the infant and her caregivers, especially her parents, is called **attachment**. As conceptualized by attachment theorist John Bowlby (1969, 1988) and psychologist **Mary D. Salter Ainsworth** (1979), attachment relationships serve important functions throughout infancy and, indeed, the lifespan. Ideally, the parent or caregiver functions as a *secure base* for the infant, providing a sense of comfort and security—a safe haven from which the infant can explore and learn about the environment. According to attachment theory, an infant's ability to thrive physically and psychologically depends in large part on the quality of attachment (Ainsworth & others, 1978).

In studying attachment, psychologists have typically focused on the infant's bond with the mother, since the mother is often the infant's primary caregiver. Still, it's important to note that most fathers are also directly involved with the basic care of their infants and children. In homes where both parents are present, children who are attached to one parent are also usually attached to the other (Fox & others, 1991; Furman & Simon, 2004). Infants are also capable of forming attachments to other consistent caregivers in their lives, such as relatives or workers at a day-care center. Thus, an infant can form *multiple* attachments (Field, 1996).

Generally, when parents are consistently warm, responsive, and sensitive to their infant's needs, the infant develops a *secure attachment* to her parents (Goldsmith & Harman, 1994; Koren-Karie & others, 2002). The infant's expectation that her needs will be met by her caregivers is the most essential ingredient to forming a secure attachment to them. And, cross-cultural studies have confirmed that sensitivity to the infant's needs is associated with secure attachment in diverse cultures (Posada & others, 2002, 2004).

In contrast, *insecure attachment* may develop when an infant's parents are neglectful, inconsistent, or insensitive to his moods or behaviors. Insecure attachment seems to reflect an ambivalent or detached emotional relationship between an infant and his parents (Ainsworth, 1979; Isabella & others, 1989).

How do researchers measure attachment? The most commonly used procedure, called the *Strange Situation,* was devised by Ainsworth. The Strange Situation is typically used with infants who are between 1 and 2 years old (Ainsworth & others, 1978). In this technique, the baby and his mother are brought into an unfamiliar room with a variety of toys. A few minutes later, a stranger enters the room. The mother stays with the child for a few moments, then departs, leaving the child alone with the stranger. After a few minutes, the mother returns, spends a few minutes in the room, leaves, and returns again. Through a one-way window, observers record the infant's behavior throughout this sequence of separations and reunions.

Psychologists assess attachment by observing the infant's behavior toward his mother during the Strange Situation procedure. When his mother is present, the *securely attached* infant will use her as a "secure base" from which to explore the new environment, periodically returning to her side. He will show distress when his mother leaves the room and will greet her warmly when she returns. A securely

The Importance of Attachment Secure attachment in infancy forms the basis for emotional bonds in later childhood. At one time, attachment researchers focused only on the relationship between mothers and infants. Today, the importance of the attachment relationship between fathers and children is also recognized (Grossman & others, 2002).

Where Does the Baby Sleep?

In most U.S. families, infants sleep in their own beds (Willinger & others, 2003). It may surprise you to discover that the United States is very unusual in this respect. In one survey of 100 societies, the United States was the *only* one in which babies slept in separate rooms. Another survey of 136 societies found that in two-thirds of the societies, infants slept in the same beds as their mothers. In the remainder, infants generally slept in the same room as their mothers (Morelli & others, 1992).

Gilda Morelli and her colleagues (1992) compared the sleeping arrangements of several middle-class U.S. families with those of Mayan families in a small town in Guatemala. They found that infants in the Mayan families slept with their mothers until they were 2 or 3, usually until another baby was about to be born. At that point, toddlers moved to the bed of another family member, usually the father or an older sibling. Children continued to sleep with other family members throughout childhood.

Mayan mothers were shocked when the American researchers told them that in-

fants in the United States slept alone and often in a different room from their parents. The Mayan mothers reacted with disapproval and pity for the infant. They believed that the practice was cruel and unnatural and would have negative effects on the infant's development.

When infants and toddlers sleep alone, bedtime marks a separation from their families. To ease the child's transition to sleeping, "putting the baby to bed" often involves lengthy bedtime rituals, including rocking, singing lullabies, or reading stories (Morrell & Steele, 2003). Small children take comforting items, such as a favorite blanket or teddy bear, to bed with them to ease the stressful transition to falling asleep alone. The child may also use his "security blanket" or "cuddly" to comfort himself when he wakes up in the night, as most small children do.

In contrast, the Mayan babies did not take cuddly items to bed, and no special routines marked the transition between wakefulness and sleep. Mayan parents were puzzled by the very idea. Instead, the Mayan babies simply went to bed when

their parents did or fell asleep in the middle of the family's social activities.

Morelli and her colleagues (1992) found that the different sleeping customs of the American and Mayan families reflect different cultural values. Some of the American babies slept in the same room as their parents when they were first born, which the parents felt helped foster feelings of closeness and emotional security in the newborns. Nonetheless, most of the American parents moved their babies to a separate room when they felt that the babies were ready to sleep alone, usually by the time they were 3 to 6 months of age. These parents explained their decision by saying that it was time for the baby to learn to be "independent" and "self-reliant."

In contrast, the Mayan parents felt that it was important to develop and encourage the infant's feelings of *interdependence* with other members of the family. Thus, in both Mayan and U.S. families, sleeping arrangements reflect cultural goals for child rearing and cultural values for relations among family members.

attached baby is easily soothed by his mother (Ainsworth & others, 1978; Lamb & others, 1985).

In contrast, an *insecurely attached* infant is less likely to explore the environment, even when her mother is present. In the Strange Situation, insecurely attached infants may appear either very anxious or completely indifferent. Such infants tend to ignore or avoid their mothers when they are present. Some insecurely attached infants become extremely distressed when their mothers leave the room. When insecurely attached infants are reunited with their mothers, they are hard to soothe and may resist their mothers' attempts to comfort them.

The quality of attachment during infancy is associated with a variety of long-term effects (Carlson & others, 2004; Goldsmith & Harman, 1994). Preschoolers with a history of being securely attached tend to be more prosocial, empathic, and socially competent than are preschoolers with a history of insecure attachment (Collins & Gunnar, 1990; Suess & others, 1992). In middle childhood, children with a history of secure attachment in infancy are better adjusted and have higher levels of social and cognitive development than do children who were insecurely attached in infancy (Stams & others, 2002). Adolescents who were securely attached in infancy have fewer problems, do better in school, and have more successful relationships with their peers than do adolescents who were insecurely attached in infancy (Sroufe, 1995, 2002).

Because attachment in infancy seems to be so important, psychologists have extensively investigated the impact of day care on attachment. In Critical Thinking Box 9.2 on the next page, we take a close look at this issue.

attachment
The emotional bond that forms between an infant and caregiver(s), especially his or her parents.

The Effects of Child Care on Attachment and Development

The majority of infants and toddlers in the United States routinely experience care by someone other than their mother or father (NICHD, 2003a). Given the importance of the emotional bond between infant and parent, should we be concerned that many young children experience daily separation from their parents?

High-Quality Day Care A high-quality day-care center offers a variety of age-appropriate activities and toys, and sometimes even a furry friend or two, as in this classroom. For toddlers and infants, consistency in caregivers is also extremely important.

Developmental psychologist Jay Belsky created considerable controversy when he published studies showing that infants under a year old were more likely to demonstrate insecure attachment if they experienced over 30 hours of day care per week (Belsky, 1986, 2001, 2002). Belsky (1992, 2002) concluded that children who entered full-time day care before their first birthday were "at risk" to be insecurely attached to their parents. He also claimed that extensive experience with nonmaternal care was linked to aggressive behavior in preschool and kindergarten.

Does extensive experience with day care during the first year of life create insecurely attached infants and toddlers? Does it produce negative effects in later childhood? Let's look at the evidence.

Belsky did not claim that *all* infants in day care were likely to experience insecure attachment. Reviewing the data in Belsky's studies and others, psychologist Alison Clarke-Stewart (1989, 1992) pointed out that the actual difference in attachment was quite small when infants experiencing day care were compared with infants cared for by a parent. The proportion of insecurely attached infants in day care is only

The Characteristics of High-Quality Day Care

- Whether care is in someone's home or in a day-care center, caregivers should be warm and responsive.

- Developmentally appropriate activities and a variety of play materials should be available.

- Caregivers should have some training and education in child development.

- Low staff turnover is essential, as consistency is especially important for infants and toddlers.

- The ratio of children to caregivers should be low. Two adults should care for no more than 8 infants, no more than 12 toddlers, or no more than 20 4- and 5-year olds.

SOURCE: National Association for the Education of Young Children (2005).

slightly higher than the proportion typically found in the general population (Lamb & others, 1992). In other words, *most* of the children who had started day

Language Development

Probably no other accomplishment in early life is as astounding as language development. By the time a child reaches 3 years of age, he will have learned approximately 3,000 words and the complex rules of his language.

According to linguist Noam Chomsky, every child is born with a biological predisposition to learn language—*any* language. In effect, children possess a "universal grammar"—a basic understanding of the common principles of language organization. Infants are innately equipped not only to understand language but also to extract grammatical rules from what they hear (Chomsky, 1965). The key task in the development of language is to learn a set of grammatical rules that allow the child to produce an unlimited number of sentences from a limited number of words.

At birth, infants can distinguish among the speech sounds of all the world's languages, no matter what language is spoken in their homes (Werker & Desjardins, 1995). Infants lose this ability by 10 months of age (Kuhl & others, 1992). Instead, they can distinguish only among the speech sounds that are present in the language to which they have been exposed. Thus, during the first year of life, infants begin to master the sound structure of their own native language.

care in infancy were securely attached, just like most of the children who had not experienced extensive day care during infancy. Similarly, a large, long-term study of the effects of child care on attachment found that spending more hours per week in day care was associated with insecure attachment only in preschoolers who also experienced less sensitive and less responsive maternal care (NICHD, 2001). Preschoolers whose mothers were sensitive and responsive showed no greater likelihood of being insecurely attached, regardless of the number of hours spent in day care.

So what about the long-term effects of day care? One study found that third-graders with extensive infant day-care experience were more likely to demonstrate a variety of social and academic problems (Vandell & Corasaniti, 1990). However, these children were not enrolled in high-quality day care, as defined in the accompanying table. Rather, they experienced average day-care conditions in a state with relatively low standards for day-care centers. But even in this case, it's difficult to assign the cause of these problems to day care itself. Why? Because developmental problems in the third-graders studied were

also associated with being raised exclusively by their mothers at home.

Psychologists and other child development researchers agree that the *quality* of child care is a key factor in facilitating secure attachment in early childhood and preventing problems in later childhood (NICHD, 2003a, 2003b). Yet child care is just one aspect of the child's developmental environment. Sensitive parenting and the quality of caregiving in the child's home have been found to have an even greater influence on social, emotional, and cognitive development than the quality of child care (Marshall, 2004; NICHD, 2002).

Many studies have found that children who experience high-quality care tend to be more sociable, better adjusted, and more academically competent than children who experience poor-quality care (Howes, 1991).

For example, Swedish psychologist Bengt-Erik Andersson (1989, 1992) studied children in Sweden who had experienced high-quality day care before age 1. As compared to children who had been cared for by a parent at home or who had started day care later in childhood, children who had started day care in infancy performed

better in school and were more socially and emotionally competent.

Clearly, then, day care in itself does not necessarily lead to undesirable outcomes. The critical factor is the *quality* of care (NICHD, 2002, 2003a). High-quality day care can potentially benefit children, even when it begins in early infancy. In contrast, low-quality care can potentially contribute to social and academic problems in later childhood (Sagi & others, 2002). Unfortunately, high quality day care is not readily available in many areas of the United States (Pope, 1997).

Critical Thinking Questions

- Why do you think there is so much controversy surrounding the issue of day care and mothers working outside the home?

- How can we best ensure that high-quality day care is available to those who need it

- Should the availability of affordable, high-quality daycare be a national priority?

Encouraging Language Development: Motherese

Just as infants seem to be biologically programmed to learn language, parents seem to be biologically programmed to encourage language development by the way they speak to infants and toddlers. People in every culture, especially parents, use a style of speech called *motherese*, or *infant-directed speech*, with babies (Kuhl & others, 1997).

Motherese is characterized by very distinct pronunciation, a simplified vocabulary, short sentences, high pitch, and exaggerated intonation and expression. Content is restricted to topics that are familiar to the child, and "baby talk" is often used—simplified words such as "go bye-bye" and "night-night." Questions are often asked, encouraging a response from the infant. Research by psychologist Ann Fernald (1985) has shown that infants prefer infant-directed speech to language spoken in an adult conversational style.

The adult use of infant-directed speech seems to be instinctive. Deaf mothers who use sign language modify their hand gestures when they communicate with infants and toddlers in a way that is very similar to the infant-directed speech of hearing mothers. Furthermore, as infants mature, the speech patterns of parents change to fit the child's developing language abilities (Deckner & others, 2003; Papoušek & others, 1985).

Deaf Babies Babble with Their Hands Deaf babies whose parents use American Sign Language (ASL) babble with their hands, rather than their voices (Petitto & others, 2001; Petitto & Marentette, 1991). Just as hearing babies repeat the same syllables over and over, deaf babies repeat the same simple hand gestures. Hearing babies born to deaf parents who are exposed only to sign language also babble with their hands (Petitto & others, 2004). The hand shapes represent basic components of ASL gestures, much like the syllables that make up the words of spoken language. Here, a baby repeats the sign for "A."

The Cooing and Babbling Stage of Language Development

As with many other aspects of development, the stages of language development appear to be universal. In virtually every culture, infants follow the same sequence of language development and at roughly similar ages (see Figure 9.3).

At about 3 months of age, infants begin to "coo," repeating vowel sounds such as *ahhhh* or *ooooo*, varying the pitch up or down. At about 5 months of age, infants begin to *babble*. They add consonants to the vowels and string the sounds together in sometimes long-winded productions of babbling, such as *ba-ba-ba-ba, de-de-de-de,* or *ma-ma-ma-ma.*

When infants babble, they are not simply imitating adult speech. Infants all over the world use the *same* sounds when they babble, including sounds that do not occur in the language of their parents and other caregivers. At around 9 months of age, babies begin to babble more in the sounds specific to their language. Babbling, then, seems to be a biologically programmed stage of language development (Petitto & others, 2004).

The One-Word Stage of Language Development

Long before babies become accomplished talkers, they understand much of what is said to them (Woodward & others, 1994). Before they are a year old, most infants can understand simple commands, such as "Bring Daddy the block," even though they cannot *say* the words *bring, Daddy,* or *block.* This reflects the fact that an infant's **comprehension vocabulary** (the words she understands) is much larger than her **production vocabulary** (the words she can say). Generally, infants acquire comprehension of words more than twice as fast as they learn to speak new words.

Somewhere around their first birthday, infants produce their first real words. First words usually refer to concrete objects or people that are important to the child, such as *mama, daddy,* or *ba-ba* (bottle). First words are also often made up of the syllables that were used in babbling.

FIGURE 9.3 Milestones in Language Comprehension and Production Approximate average age ranges for the first appearance of different stages of language development are shown here. Notice that language comprehension occurs much earlier than language production.

SOURCE: Based on Bornstein & Lamb (1992).

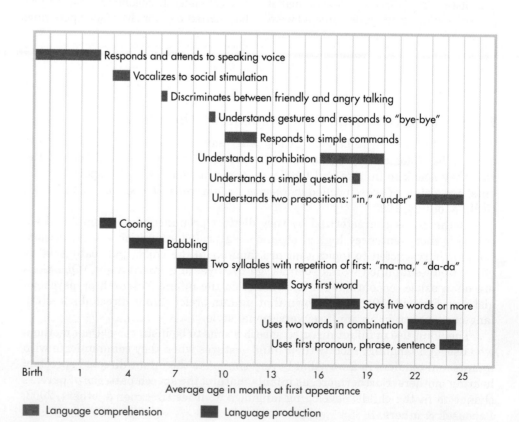

During the *one-word stage,* babies use a single word and vocal intonation to stand for an entire sentence. With the proper intonation and context, *baba* can mean "I want my bottle!" "There's my bottle!" or "Where's my bottle?"

The Two-Word Stage of Language Development

Around their second birthday, infants begin putting words together. During the *two-word stage,* infants combine two words to construct a simple "sentence," such as "Mama go," "Where kitty?" and "No potty!" During this stage, the words used are primarily content words—nouns, verbs, and sometimes adjectives or adverbs. Articles (*a, an, the*) and prepositions (*in, under, on*) are omitted. Two-word sentences reflect the first understandings of grammar. Although these utterances include only the most essential words, they basically follow a grammatically correct sequence.

At around 2½ years of age, children move beyond the two-word stage. They rapidly increase the length and grammatical complexity of their sentences. There is a dramatic increase in the number of words they can comprehend and produce. By the age of 3, the typical child has a production vocabulary of more than 3,000 words. Acquiring about a dozen new words per day, a child may have a production vocabulary of more than 10,000 words by school age (Bjorklund, 1995).

comprehension vocabulary
The words that are understood by an infant or child.

production vocabulary
The words that an infant or child understands and can speak.

gender
The cultural, social, and psychological meanings that are associated with masculinity or femininity.

gender roles
The behaviors, attitudes, and personality traits that are designated as either masculine or feminine in a given culture.

gender identity
A person's psychological sense of being male or female.

Gender-Role Development

Key Theme
■ Gender roles are the behaviors, attitudes, and traits that a given culture associates with masculinity and femininity.

Key Questions
■ What gender differences develop during childhood?
■ How do social learning theory and gender schema theory explain the development of gender roles?

Because the English language is less than precise in the arena of gender and sexuality, we need to clarify a couple of terms. **Gender** refers to the cultural and social meanings that are associated with maleness and femaleness (Eagly, 1995a). Think of "male" and "female" as designating the biological categories of sex. In contrast, a **gender role** consists of the behaviors, attitudes, and personality traits that a given culture designates as either "masculine" or "feminine" (Bailey & Zucker, 1995). Finally, **gender identity** refers to a person's psychological sense of being either male or female (Egan & Perry, 2001).

FAMILY CIRCUS

"That's the DOLL aisle, Daddy. Somebody might see us!"

© Bill Keane, Inc. Reprinted with special permission of King Features Syndicate.

Gender Differences in Childhood Behavior

Roughly between the ages of 2 and 3, children can identify themselves and other children as boys or girls, although the details are still a bit fuzzy to them (Egan & Perry, 2001). Preschoolers don't yet understand that sex is determined by physical characteristics. This is not surprising, considering that the biologically defining sex characteristics—the genitals—are hidden from view most of the time. Instead, young children identify the sexes in terms of external attributes, such as hairstyle, clothing, and activities.

From about the age of 18 months to the age of 2 years, sex differences in behavior begin to emerge. These differences become more pronounced throughout early childhood. Toddler girls play more with soft toys and dolls, and ask for help from adults more than toddler boys do. Toddler boys play more with blocks and

Separate Worlds? In childhood, boys tend to play in groups and prefer competitive games. In contrast, girls tend to establish close relationships with one or two other girls and to cement their friendship by sharing thoughts and feelings. How might such gender differences affect intimate relationships in adolescence and adulthood?

Are Girls Less Interested in Sports than Boys? As anyone who's watched a high school girls basketball game can confirm, girls can be just as competitive as boys. Contrary to what some people think, there is no evidence to support the notion that girls are inherently less interested in athletics than boys. During the middle childhood years, from ages 6 to 10, boys and girls are equally interested in sports (Women's Sports Foundation, 2005). Especially during adolescence, participation in sports enhances the self-esteem of girls (Pedersen & Seidman, 2004). Although boys are still provided with more opportunities to participate in sports, girls today receive much more encouragement to compete in sports than they used to.

transportation toys, such as trucks and wagons. They also play more actively than do girls (see Stern & Karraker, 1989). From the age of about 3 on, there are consistent gender differences in preferred toys and play activities. Children also develop a strong preference for playing with members of their own sex—girls with girls and boys with boys (Egan & Perry, 2001; Thorne, 1993). It's not uncommon to hear boys refer to girls as "icky" and girls refer to boys as "mean" or "rough." And, in fact, preschool boys *do* play more roughly than girls, cover more territory, and play in larger groups. Throughout the remainder of childhood, boys and girls play primarily with members of their own sex (Powlishta, 1995a, 1995b).

According to psychologist Carole Beal (1994), boys and girls almost seem to create separate "social worlds," each with its own style of interaction. They also learn particular ways of interacting that work well with peers of the same sex. For example, boys learn to assert themselves within a group of male friends. Girls tend to establish very close bonds with one or two friends. Girls learn to maintain their close friendships through compromise, conciliation, and verbal conflict resolution.

Children are far more rigid than adults in their beliefs in gender-role stereotypes. Children's strong adherence to gender stereotypes may be a necessary step in developing a gender identity (Powlishta, 1995b; Stangor & Ruble, 1987). Boys are far more rigid than girls in their preferences for toys associated with their own sex. Their attitudes about the sexes are also more rigid than are those held by girls. As girls grow older, they become even more flexible in their views of sex-appropriate activities and attributes, but boys become even less flexible (Katz & Ksansnak, 1994).

Explaining Gender Roles
Two Contemporary Theories

Based on the principles of learning, **social learning theory of gender-role development** contends that gender roles are learned through *reinforcement, punishment,* and *modeling.* From a very young age, children are reinforced or rewarded when they display gender-appropriate behavior and punished when they do not. For example, psychologists Beverly Fagot and Richard Hagan (1991) observed mothers and fathers interacting with their children in their homes. They found that 18-month-old boys received more positive reactions from their parents for playing with male-typed toys and for exhibiting aggressive or assertive behavior. In contrast, 18-month-old girls received more positive responses for attempts to communicate with their parents, while boys received more negative reactions for such attempts.

To what degree do such parental behaviors influence the development of gender differences? The effect is not as great as you might think. Psychologists Hugh

Lytton and David M. Romney (1991) conducted a meta-analysis of nearly 200 studies of parents' different treatment of boys and girls. They found that the actual effects of parental socialization in many areas of gender differences were relatively small. Yes, parents *do* tend to reinforce and encourage gender-appropriate play. But for the most part, parents treat their male and female children rather similarly.

If parents have only a minimal effect, how do children acquire their understanding of

Who wants to sleep, anyway?
Not us! We want to be
busy, busy, busy!

You've Come a Long Way, Baby? Children's books continue to reinforce gender stereotypes, sometimes in subtle ways. In this picture book for preschoolers, a little girl follows her big brother's lead. The boy is shown actively digging in the mud, happily getting dirty with his dog, bat and ball nearby. In contrast, the little girl, dressed in pink, stays clean as she daintily feeds and nurtures her kitten.

gender differences? Children are exposed to many other sources of information about gender roles, including television, books, and observation of same-sex adult role models. Hence, children also learn gender differences through *modeling*: They observe and then imitate the sex-typed behavior of significant adults and older children (Best & Williams, 1997). By observing and imitating such models—whether it's Mom cooking, Dad fixing things around the house, or a male superhero rescuing a helpless female on television—children come to understand that certain activities and attributes are considered more appropriate for one sex than for the other.

Gender schema theory, developed by **Sandra Bem,** incorporates some aspects of social learning theory. However, Bem (1981) approaches gender-role development from a more strongly cognitive perspective. In contrast to the relatively passive role played by children in social learning theory, **gender schema theory** contends that children *actively* develop mental categories (or *schemas*) for masculinity and femininity (Martin & Halverson, 1981; Martin & Ruble, 2004). That is, children actively organize information about other people and appropriate behavior, activities, and attributes into gender categories. Saying that "trucks are for boys and dolls are for girls" is an example of a gender schema.

According to gender schema theory, children, like many adults, look at the world through "gender lenses" (Bem, 1987). Gender schemas influence how people pay attention to, perceive, interpret, and remember gender-relevant behavior. Gender schemas also seem to lead children to perceive members of their own sex more favorably than members of the opposite sex (Martin & others, 2002, 2004).

Like schemas in general (see Chapter 6), children's gender schemas do seem to influence what they notice and remember. For example, 5-year-olds were shown pictures of children engaged in activities that violated common gender stereotypes, such as girls playing with trucks and boys playing with dolls (Martin & Halverson, 1981, 1983). A few days later, the 5-year-olds "remembered" that the *boys* had been playing with the trucks and the *girls* with the dolls!

Children also readily assimilate new information into their existing gender schemas. In a classic study, 4- to 9-year-olds were given boxes of gender-neutral gadgets, such as hole punches (Bradbard & others, 1986). But some gadgets were labeled as "girl toys" and some as "boy toys." The boys played more with the "boy" gadgets, and the girls played more with the "girl" gadgets. A week later, the children easily remembered which gadgets went with each sex. They also remembered more information about the gadgets that were associated with their own sex. Simply labeling the objects as belonging to boys or to girls had powerful consequences for the children's behavior and memory—evidence of the importance of gender schemas in learning and remembering new information.

Children are gender detectives who search for cues about gender—who should or should not engage in a particular activity, who can play with whom, and why girls and boys are different. Cognitive perspectives on gender development assume that children are actively searching for ways to find meaning in and make sense of the social world that surrounds them, and they do so by using the gender cues provided by society to help them interpret what they see and hear.

Carol Lynn Martin and Diane Ruble (2004)

social learning theory of gender-role development
The theory that gender roles are acquired through the basic processes of learning, including reinforcement, punishment, and modeling.

gender schema theory
The theory that gender-role development is influenced by the formation of schemas, or mental representations, of masculinity and femininity.

Cognitive Development

Key Theme
■ According to Piaget's theory, children progress through four distinct cognitive stages, and each stage marks a shift in how they think and understand the world.

Key Questions
■ What are Piaget's four stages of cognitive development?
■ What are three criticisms of Piaget's theory?
■ How do Vygotsky's ideas about cognitive development differ from Piaget's theory?

When Laura was almost 3, Sandy and Laura were investigating the tadpoles in the creek behind our home. "Do you know what tadpoles become when they grow up? They become frogs," Sandy explained. Laura looked very serious. After considering this new bit of information for a few moments, she asked, "Laura grow up to be a frog, too?"

Just as children advance in motor skill and language development, they also develop increasing sophistication in cognitive processes—thinking, remembering, and processing information. The most influential theory of cognitive development is that of Swiss psychologist **Jean Piaget.** Originally trained as a biologist, Piaget combined a boundless curiosity about the nature of the human mind with a gift for scientific observation (Brainerd, 1996).

Piaget (1952, 1972) believed that children *actively* try to make sense out of their environment rather than passively soaking up information about the world. To Piaget, many of the "cute" things children say actually reflect their sincere attempts to make sense of their world. In fact, Piaget carefully observed his own three children in developing his theory (Fischer & Hencke, 1996).

According to Piaget, children progress through four distinct cognitive stages: the sensorimotor stage, from birth to age 2; the preoperational stage, from age 2 to age 7; the concrete operational stage, from age 7 to age 11; and the formal operational stage, which begins during adolescence and continues into adulthood. As a child advances to a new stage, his thinking is *qualitatively different* from that of the previous stage. In other words, each new stage represents a fundamental shift in *how* the child thinks and understands the world.

Piaget saw this progression of cognitive development as a continuous, gradual process. As a child develops and matures, she does not simply acquire more information. Rather, she develops a new understanding of the world in each progressive stage, building on the understandings acquired in the previous stage (Siegler & Ellis, 1996). As the child *assimilates* new information and experiences, he eventually changes his way of thinking to *accommodate* new knowledge (Miller, 1993).

Piaget believed that these stages were biologically programmed to unfold at their respective ages (Flavell, 1996). He also believed that children in every culture progressed through the same sequence of stages at roughly similar ages. However, Piaget also recognized that hereditary and environmental differences could influence the rate at which a given child progressed through the stages (Fischer & Hencke, 1996; Wadsworth, 1996).

For example, a "bright" child may progress through the stages faster than a child who is less intellectually capable. A child whose environment provides ample and varied opportunities for exploration is likely to progress faster than a child who has limited environmental opportunities. Thus, even though the sequence of stages is universal, there can be individual variation in the rate of cognitive development.

Jean Piaget Swiss psychologist Jean Piaget (1896–1980) viewed the child as a little scientist, actively exploring his or her world. Much of Piaget's theory was based on his careful observation of individual children, especially his own children.

The Sensorimotor Stage

The **sensorimotor stage** extends from birth until about 2 years of age. During this stage, infants acquire knowledge about the world through actions that allow them to directly experience and manipulate objects. Infants discover a wealth of very practical sensory knowledge, such as what objects look like and how they taste, feel, smell, and sound.

Infants in this stage also expand their practical knowledge about motor actions—reaching, grasping, pushing, pulling, and pouring. In the process, they gain a basic understanding of the effects their own actions can produce, such as pushing a button to turn on the television or knocking over a pile of blocks to make them crash and tumble.

At the beginning of the sensorimotor stage, the infant's motto seems to be, "Out of sight, out of mind." An object exists only if she can directly sense it. For example, if a 4-month-old infant knocks a ball underneath the couch and it rolls out of sight, she will not look for it. Piaget interpreted this response to mean that to the infant, the ball no longer exists.

However, by the end of the sensorimotor stage, children acquire a new cognitive understanding, called object permanence. **Object permanence** is the understanding that an object continues to exist even if it can't be seen. Now the infant will actively search for a ball that she has watched roll out of sight. Infants gradually acquire an understanding of object permanence as they gain experience with objects, as their memory abilities improve, and as they develop mental representations of the world, which Piaget called *schemas* (Berthier & others, 2000).

The Preoperational Stage

The **preoperational stage** lasts from roughly age 2 to age 7. In Piaget's theory, the word *operations* refers to logical mental activities. Thus, the "preoperational" stage is a prelogical stage.

The hallmark of preoperational thought is the child's capacity to engage in symbolic thought. **Symbolic thought** refers to the ability to use words, images, and symbols to represent the world (DeLoache, 1995). One indication of the expanding capacity for symbolic thought is the child's impressive gains in language during this stage.

The child's increasing capacity for symbolic thought is also apparent in her use of fantasy and imagination while playing (Golomb & Galasso, 1995). A discarded box becomes a spaceship, a house, or a fort, as children imaginatively take on the roles of different characters. In doing so, children imitate (or try to imitate) actions they have mentally symbolized from situations observed days, or even weeks, earlier.

Still, the preoperational child's understanding of symbols remains immature. A 2-year-old shown a picture of a flower, for example, may try to smell it. A young child may be puzzled by the notion that a map symbolizes an actual location—as in the cartoon below. In short, preoperational children are still actively figuring out the relationship between symbols and the actual objects they represent (DeLoache, 1995).

This Feels Different! During the sensorimotor stage, infants and toddlers rely on sensory and motor skills to explore and make sense of the world around them.

sensorimotor stage
In Piaget's theory, the first stage of cognitive development, from birth to about age 2; the period during which the infant explores the environment and acquires knowledge through sensing and manipulating objects.

object permanence
The understanding that an object continues to exist even when it can no longer be seen.

preoperational stage
In Piaget's theory, the second stage of cognitive development, which lasts from about age 2 to age 7; characterized by increasing use of symbols and prelogical thought processes.

symbolic thought
The ability to use words, images, and symbols to represent the world.

FOR BETTER OR FOR WORSE

Preoperational Thinking: Manipulating Mental Symbols With a hodge-podge of toys, some fake fruit, a couple of scarves, and a firefighter's helmet, these two are having great fun. The preschool child's increasing capacity for symbolic thought is delightfully reflected in symbolic play and deferred imitation. In *symbolic play,* one object stands for another: a scarf can become a magic cape, a coat, a mask, or a tablecloth. *Deferred imitation* is the capacity to repeat an action observed earlier, such as the action of a checker in a store.

The thinking of preoperational children often displays **egocentrism.** By *egocentrism,* Piaget did not mean selfishness or conceit. Rather, egocentric children lack the ability to consider events from another person's point of view. Thus, the young child genuinely thinks that Grandma would like a new Beanie Baby or a Spiderman video for her upcoming birthday because that's what *he* wants. Egocentric thought is also operating when the child silently nods his head in answer to Grandpa's question on the telephone.

The preoperational child's thought is also characterized by irreversibility and centration. **Irreversibility** means that the child cannot mentally reverse a sequence of events or logical operations back to the starting point. For example, the child doesn't understand that adding "3 plus 1" and adding "1 plus 3" refer to the same logical operation. **Centration** refers to the tendency to focus, or center, on only one aspect of a situation, usually a perceptual aspect. In doing so, the child ignores other relevant aspects of the situation.

The classic demonstration of both irreversibility and centration involves a task devised by Piaget. When Laura was 5, we tried this task with her. First, we showed her two identical glasses, each containing exactly the same amount of liquid. Laura easily recognized the two amounts of liquid as being the same.

Then, while Laura watched intently, we poured the liquid from one of the glasses into a third container that was much taller and narrower than the others. "Which container," we asked, "holds more liquid?" Like any other preoperational child, Laura answered confidently, "The taller one!" Even when we repeated the procedure, reversing the steps over and over again, Laura remained convinced that the taller container held more liquid than did the shorter container.

This classic demonstration illustrates the preoperational child's inability to understand conservation. The principle of **conservation** holds that two equal physical quantities remain equal even if the appearance of one is changed, as long as nothing is added or subtracted (Piaget & Inhelder, 1974). Because of *centration,* the child cannot simultaneously consider the height and the width of the liquid in the container. Instead, the child focuses on only one aspect of the situation, the height of the liquid. And because of *irreversibility,* the child cannot cognitively reverse the series of events, mentally returning the poured liquid to its original container. Thus, she fails to understand that the two amounts of liquid are still the same.

egocentrism

In Piaget's theory, the inability to take another person's perspective or point of view.

irreversibility

In Piaget's theory, the inability to mentally reverse a sequence of events or logical operations.

centration

In Piaget's theory, the tendency to focus, or *center,* on only one aspect of a situation and ignore other important aspects of the situation.

conservation

In Piaget's theory, the understanding that two equal quantities remain equal even though the form or appearance is rearranged, as long as nothing is added or subtracted.

Piaget's Conservation Task Five-year-old Laura compares the liquid in the two short beakers, then watches as Sandy pours the liquid into a tall, narrow beaker. When asked which has more, she insists that there is more liquid in the tall beaker. As Piaget's classic task demonstrates, the average 5-year-old doesn't grasp this principle of conservation. Even though Laura repeated this demonstration several times for the photographer, she persisted in her belief that the tall beaker had more liquid. We tried the demonstration again when Laura was almost 7. Now in the concrete operational stage, Laura immediately understood that both beakers held the same amount of liquid—just as Piaget's theory predicts.

The Concrete Operational Stage

With the beginning of the **concrete operational stage,** at around age 7, children become capable of true logical thought. They are much less egocentric in their thinking, can reverse mental operations, and can focus simultaneously on two aspects of a problem. In short, they understand the principle of conservation. When presented with two rows of pennies, each row equally spaced, concrete operational children understand that the number of pennies in each row remains the same even when the spacing between the pennies in one row is increased.

As the name of this stage implies, thinking and use of logic tend to be limited to concrete reality—to tangible objects and events. Children in the concrete operational stage often have difficulty thinking logically about hypothetical situations or abstract ideas. For example, an 8-year-old will explain the concept of friendship in very tangible terms, such as, "Friendship is when someone plays with me." In effect, the concrete operational child's ability to deal with abstract ideas and hypothetical situations is limited to his or her personal experiences and actual events.

The Formal Operational Stage

At the beginning of adolescence, children enter the **formal operational stage.** In terms of problem solving, the formal operational adolescent is much more systematic and logical than the concrete operational child.

Formal operational thought reflects the ability to think logically even when dealing with abstract concepts or hypothetical situations (Piaget, 1972; Piaget & Inhelder, 1958). In contrast to the concrete operational child, the formal operational adolescent explains *friendship* by emphasizing more global and abstract characteristics, such as mutual trust, empathy, loyalty, consistency, and shared beliefs (Harter, 1990).

But, like the development of cognitive abilities during infancy and childhood, formal operational thought emerges only gradually. Formal operational thought continues to increase in sophistication throughout adolescence and adulthood. Although an adolescent may deal effectively with abstract ideas in one domain of knowledge, his thinking may not reflect the same degree of sophistication in other areas. Piaget (1973) acknowledged that even among many adults, formal operational thinking is often limited to areas in which they have developed expertise or a special interest.

Table 9.2 summarizes Piaget's stages of cognitive development.

From Concrete Operations to Formal Operations Logical thinking is evident during the concrete operational stage but develops more fully during the formal operational stage. At about the age of 12, the young person becomes capable of applying logical thinking to hypothetical situations and abstract concepts, such as the principles of molecular bonds in this chemistry class. But as is true of each of Piaget's stages, new cognitive abilities emerge gradually. Having a tangible model to manipulate helps these students grasp abstract chemistry concepts.

concrete operational stage
In Piaget's theory, the third stage of cognitive development, which lasts from about age 7 to adolescence; characterized by the ability to think logically about concrete objects and situations.

formal operational stage
In Piaget's theory, the fourth stage of cognitive development, which lasts from adolescence through adulthood; characterized by the ability to think logically about abstract principles and hypothetical situations.

Table 9.2

Piaget's Stages of Cognitive Development

Stage	Characteristics of the Stage	Major Change of the Stage
Sensorimotor (0–2 years)	Acquires understanding of object permanence. First understandings of cause-and-effect relationships.	Development proceeds from reflexes to active use of sensory and motor skills to explore the environment.
Preoperational (2–7 years)	Symbolic thought emerges. Language development occurs (2–4 years). Thought and language both tend to be egocentric. Cannot solve conservation problems.	Development proceeds from understanding simple cause-and-effect relationships to prelogical thought processes involving the use of imagination and symbols to represent objects, actions, and situations.
Concrete operations (7–11 years)	Reversibility attained. Can solve conservation problems. Logical thought develops and is applied to concrete problems. Cannot solve complex verbal problems and hypothetical problems.	Development proceeds from prelogical thought to logical solutions to concrete problems.
Formal operations (adolescence through adulthood)	Logically solves all types of problems. Thinks scientifically. Solves complex verbal and hypothetical problems. Is able to think in abstract terms.	Development proceeds from logical solving of concrete problems to logical solving of all classes of problems, including abstract problems.

> *As researchers continue to make progress in understanding how infants attain and use their physical knowledge, we come closer to unveiling the complex architecture that makes it possible for them to learn, so very rapidly, about the world around them.*

Renée Baillargeon (2004)

FIGURE 9.4 Testing Object Permanence in Babies How can you test object permanence in infants who are too young to reach for a hidden object? Three-and-a-half-month-old infants initially watched a possible event: The small carrot passes from one side of the panel to the other without appearing in the window. In the impossible event, the tall carrot does the same. Because the infants are surprised and look longer at the impossible event, Baillargeon and DeVos (1991) concluded that the infants had formed a mental representation of the existence, height, and path of each carrot as it moved behind the panel—the essence of object permanence (Baillargeon, 2004).

Criticisms of Piaget's Theory

Piaget's theory has inspired hundreds of research studies (Kessen, 1996). Generally, scientific research has supported Piaget's most fundamental idea: that infants, young children, and older children use distinctly different cognitive abilities to construct their understanding of the world. However, other aspects of Piaget's theory have been challenged.

Criticism 1: Piaget underestimated the cognitive abilities of infants and young children.   To test for object permanence, Piaget would show the infant an object, cover it with a cloth, and then observe whether the infant tried to reach under the cloth for the object. Obviously, such a response requires the infant to have a certain level of motor skill development. Using this procedure, Piaget found that it wasn't until an infant was about 9 months old that she behaved as if she understood that an object continued to exist after it was hidden. Even at this age, Piaget maintained, an infant's understanding of object permanence was immature and would not be fully developed for another year or so.

But what if the infant "knew" that the object was under the cloth but simply lacked the physical coordination to reach for it? How could you test this hypothesis? Rather than using manual tasks to assess object permanence and other cognitive abilities, psychologist **Renée Baillargeon** has used *visual* tasks. Baillargeon's research is based on the premise that infants, like adults, will look longer at "surprising" events that appear to contradict their understanding of the world.

In this research paradigm, the infant first watches an *expected event*, which is consistent with the understanding that is being tested. Then, the infant is shown an *unexpected event*. If the unexpected event violates the infant's understanding of physical principles, he should be surprised and look longer at the unexpected event than the expected event.

Figure 9.4 shows one of Baillargeon's classic tests of object permanence, conducted with Julie DeVos (Baillargeon & DeVos 1991). If the infant understands that objects continue to exist even when they are hidden, she will be surprised when the tall carrot unexpectedly does *not* appear in the window of the panel.

Using variations of this basic experimental procedure, Baillargeon and her colleagues have shown that infants as young as 2½ months of age display object permanence (Aguiar & Baillargeon, 1999; Luo & others, 2003). This is more than six months earlier than the age at which Piaget believed infants first showed evidence of object permanence.

Going beyond object permanence, Baillargeon and her colleagues have shown that infants at different ages acquire different expectations about how the physical world operates. They've found that infants develop *event-specific expectations*, rather than general principles (Baillargeon, 2002, 2004).

For example, the two events depicted in Figure 9.5 are similar in that both involve the disappearance of a tall object. However, 4½-month-old infants are surprised by one event – a tall object disappearing behind a short object—and not by the other—a tall object disappearing inside a short container (Hespos & Baillargeon, 2001). It's not until 7½ months of age that infants react with increased

Possible Event   Impossible Event

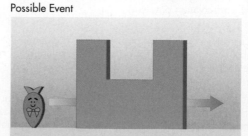 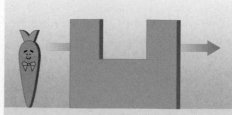

4.5 months

Behind Short Container

7.5 months

Inside Short Container

FIGURE 9.5 Infants Form Event-Specific Expectations About the World Susan Hespos and Renée Baillargeon (2001) found that 4½-month-old infants respond with increased attention when a tall object completely disappears when placed *behind* a shorter object (*left*) but not when a tall object disappears when placed *inside* a short container (*right*). It is not until the age of 7½ months that infants are also surprised by a tall container disappearing inside a short container. According to Baillargeon (2004), such findings demonstrate that infants form *event-specific expectations* about the physical world rather than general principles.

attention to the inside-container event. During infancy, it seems, each event is understood separately.

Piaget's discoveries laid the groundwork for our understanding of cognitive development. However, as developmental psychologists Jeanne Shinskey and Yuko Munakata (2005) observe, today's researchers recognize that "what infants appear to know depends heavily on how they are tested."

Criticism 2: Piaget underestimated the impact of the social and cultural environment on cognitive development.

In contrast to Piaget, the Russian psychologist **Lev Vygotsky** believed that cognitive development is strongly influenced by social and cultural factors. Vygotsky formulated his theory of cognitive development at about the same time as Piaget formulated his. However, Vygotsky's writings did not become available in the West until many years after his untimely death from tuberculosis in 1934 (Rowe & Wertsch, 2002; van Geert, 1998).

Vygotsky agreed with Piaget that children may be able to reach a particular cognitive level through their own efforts. However, Vygotsky (1978, 1987) argued that children are able to attain higher levels of cognitive development through the support and instruction that they receive from other people. Researchers have confirmed that social interactions, especially with older children and adults, play a significant role in a child's cognitive development (Gopnik, 1996; Wertsch & Tulviste, 1992).

One of Vygotsky's important ideas was his notion of the **zone of proximal development.** This refers to the gap between what children can accomplish on their own and what they can accomplish with the help of others who are more competent (Rowe & Wertsch, 2002). Note that the word *proximal* means "nearby," indicating that the assistance provided goes just slightly beyond the child's current abilities. Such guidance can help "stretch" the child's cognitive abilities to new levels.

Cross-cultural studies have shown that cognitive development is strongly influenced by the skills that are valued and encouraged in a particular environment, such as the ability to weave, hunt, or collaborate with others (Greenfield & others, 2003; Maynard & Greenfield, 2003). Such findings suggest that Piaget's stages are not as universal and culture-free as some researchers had once believed.

Criticism 3: Piaget overestimated the degree to which people achieve formal operational thought processes.

Researchers have found that many adults display abstract-hypothetical thinking only in limited areas of knowledge, and that some adults never display formal operational thought processes at all. College students, for example, may not display formal operational thinking when given problems outside their major, as when an English major is presented with a physics problem (DeLisi & Staudt, 1980). Late in his life, Piaget (1972, 1973) suggested that formal operational thinking might not be a universal phenomenon, but instead is the product of an individual's expertise in a specific area.

Rather than distinct stages of cognitive development, some developmental psychologists emphasize the **information-processing model of cognitive development** (Klahr, 1992; Siegler, 1996). This model focuses on the development

Lev Vygotsky Russian psychologist Lev Vygotsky was born in 1896, the same year as Piaget. He died in 1934 of tuberculosis. Recent decades have seen a resurgence of interest in Vygotsky's theoretical writings. Vygotsky emphasized the impact of social and cultural factors on cognitive development. According to Vygotsky, cognitive development always takes place within a social and cultural context.

zone of proximal development
In Vygotsky's theory of cognitive development, the difference between what children can accomplish on their own and what they can accomplish with the help of others who are more competent.

information-processing model of cognitive development
The model that views cognitive development as a process that is continuous over the lifespan and that studies the development of basic mental processes such as attention, memory, and problem solving.

of fundamental mental processes, like attention, memory, and problem solving (Halford, 2002). In this approach, cognitive development is viewed as a process of continuous change over the lifespan (Courage & Howe, 2002). Through life experiences, we continue to acquire new knowledge, including more sophisticated cognitive skills and strategies. In turn, this improves our ability to process, learn, and remember information.

With the exceptions that have been noted, Piaget's observations of the changes in children's cognitive abilities are fundamentally accurate. His description of the distinct cognitive changes that occur during infancy and childhood ranks as one of the most outstanding contributions to developmental psychology (Beilin, 1994).

Adolescence

Key Theme
- Adolescence is the stage that marks the transition from childhood to adulthood.

Key Questions
- What factors affect the timing of puberty?
- What characterizes adolescent relationships with parents and peers?
- What is Erikson's psychosocial theory of lifespan development?

Adolescence is the transitional stage between late childhood and the beginning of adulthood. Although it can vary by individual and gender, adolescence usually begins around age 11 or 12. It is a transition marked by sweeping physical, social, and cognitive changes as the individual moves toward independence and adult responsibilities. Outwardly, the most noticeable changes that occur during adolescence are the physical changes that accompany the development of sexual maturity. We'll begin by considering those changes, then turn to the aspects of social development during adolescence. Following that discussion, we'll consider some of the cognitive changes of adolescence, including identity formation.

Physical and Sexual Development

Nature seems to have a warped sense of humor when it comes to **puberty,** the physical process of attaining sexual maturation and reproductive capacity that begins during the early adolescent years. As you may well remember, physical development during adolescence sometimes proceeds unevenly. Feet and hands get bigger before legs and arms do. The torso typically develops last, so shirts and blouses sometimes don't fit quite right. And the left and right sides of the body can grow at different rates. The resulting lopsided effect can be quite distressing: One ear, foot, testicle, or breast may be noticeably larger than the other. Thankfully, such asymmetries tend to even out by the end of adolescence.

Although nature's game plan for physical change during adolescence may seem haphazard, puberty actually tends to follow a predictable sequence for each sex. These changes are summarized in Table 9.3 on the next page.

Primary and Secondary Sex Characteristics

The physical changes of puberty fall into two categories. Internally, puberty involves the development of the **primary sex characteristics,** which are the sex organs that are directly involved in reproduction. For example, the female's uterus and the male's testes enlarge in puberty. Externally, development of the **secondary sex characteristics,** which are not directly involved in reproduc-

Girls Get a Head Start These two eighth-graders are the same age! In terms of the progress of sexual and physical maturation, girls are usually about two years ahead of boys.

adolescence
The transitional stage between late childhood and the beginning of adulthood, during which sexual maturity is reached.

tion, signal increasing sexual maturity. Secondary sex characteristics include changes in height, weight, and body shape; the appearance of body hair and voice changes; and, in girls, breast development.

As you can see in Table 9.3, females are typically about two years ahead of males in terms of physical and sexual maturation. For example, the period of marked acceleration in weight and height gains, called the **adolescent growth spurt,** occurs about two years earlier in females than in males. Much to the chagrin of many sixth- and seventh-grade boys, it's not uncommon for their female classmates to be both heavier and taller than they are.

The statistical averages in Table 9.3 are informative, but—because they are only averages—they cannot convey the normal range of individual variation in the timing of pubertal events (see Ellis, 2004). For example, a female's first menstrual period, termed **menarche,** typically occurs around age 12 or 13, but menarche may take place as early as age 9 or 10 or as late as age 16 or 17. For boys, the testicles typically begin enlarging around age 11 or 12, but the process can begin before age 9 or after age 14. Thus, it's entirely possible for some adolescents to have already completed physical and sexual maturation before their classmates have even begun puberty. Yet they would all be considered well within the normal age range for puberty (Sun & others, 2002).

puberty
The stage of adolescence in which an individual reaches sexual maturity and becomes physiologically capable of sexual reproduction.

primary sex characteristics
Sexual organs that are directly involved in reproduction, such as the uterus, ovaries, penis, and testicles.

secondary sex characteristics
Sexual characteristics that develop during puberty and are not directly involved in reproduction but differentiate between the sexes, such as male facial hair and female breast development.

adolescent growth spurt
The period of accelerated growth during puberty, involving rapid increases in height and weight.

menarche
(meh-NAR-kee) A female's first menstrual period, which occurs during puberty.

Table 9.3

The Typical Sequence of Puberty

Girls	Average Age	Boys	Average Age
Ovaries increase production of estrogen and progesterone	9	Testes increase production of testosterone	10
Internal sex organs begin to grow larger	9½	External sex organs begin to grow larger	11
Breast development begins	10	Production of sperm and first ejaculation	13
Peak height spurt	12	Peak height spurt	14
Peak muscle and organ growth, including widening of hips	12½	Peak muscle and organ growth, including broadening of shoulders	14½
Menarche (first menstrual period)	12½	Voice lowers	15
First ovulation (release of fertile egg)	13½	Facial hair appears	16

SOURCE: Based on data in Brooks-Gunn & Reiter (1990).

Less obvious than the outward changes associated with puberty are the sweeping changes occurring in another realm of physical development: the adolescent's brain. We discuss these developments in the Focus on Neuroscience on page 377.

Factors Affecting the Timing of Puberty

Although you might be tempted to think that the onset of puberty is strictly a matter of biological programming, researchers have found that both genetics and environmental factors play a role in the timing of puberty. Genetic evidence includes the observation that girls usually experience menarche at about the same age as their mothers did (Brooks-Gunn & Reiter, 1990). And, not surprisingly, the timing of pubertal changes tends to be closer for identical twins than for nontwin siblings (Mustanski & others, 2004).

Environmental factors, such as nutrition and health, also influence the onset of puberty. Generally, well-nourished and healthy children begin puberty earlier than do children who have experienced serious health problems or inadequate nutrition. As living standards and health care have improved, the average age of puberty has steadily decreased in the United States over the last century.

For example, 150 years ago the average age of menarche in the United States was about 17 years old. Today it is about 12½ years old. The same downward trend is also evident in boys. Compared to the 1960s, boys today are beginning the physical changes of puberty about a year earlier (Herman-Giddens & others, 2001). In recent years, however, the trend toward earlier puberty seems to have slowed (see Parent & others, 2003).

Body size and degree of physical activity are also related to the timing of puberty. In general, stout or heavy children begin puberty earlier than do lean children. Girls who are involved in physically demanding athletic activities, such as gymnastics, figure skating, dancing, and competitive running, can experience delays in menarche of up to two years beyond the average age (Brooks-Gunn, 1988).

Interestingly, the timing of puberty is also influenced by the absence of the biological father in the home environment. Several studies have found that girls raised in homes in which the biological father is absent tend to experience puberty earlier than girls raised in homes with intact families (Ellis & Garber, 2000; Hoier, 2003). Researcher Brian Mustanski and his colleagues (2004) found similar results for both sexes in a large-scale study of more than 1,800 pairs of twins. In that study, both boys and girls raised in father-absent homes experienced accelerated physical development.

Other studies have revealed that the quality of family relationships is tied to the timing of puberty. The pattern that emerges is that negative and stressful family environments are associated with an earlier onset of puberty, including earlier menarche in girls. Why would such factors influence the timing of puberty? Although researchers are trying to pinpoint the exact mechanisms, part of the answer is that stressful family events increase many of the same hormones that are involved in activating puberty. On the other hand, positive family environments are associated with later physical development (see Ellis, 2004; Romans & others, 2003).

Early Versus Late Maturation

Adolescents tend to be keenly aware of the physical changes they are experiencing as well as of the *timing* of those changes compared with their peer group. Most adolescents are "on time," meaning that the maturational changes are occurring at roughly the same time for them as for others in their peer group.

However, some adolescents are "off time," experiencing maturation noticeably earlier or later than the majority of their peers. For girls, early maturation seems to carry a greater risk for a variety of negative health and psychological outcomes. For example, early-maturing girls tend to be more likely than late-maturing girls to have negative feelings about their body image and pubertal changes, such as menarche (Ge & others, 2003). Compared to late-maturing girls, early-maturing girls are less likely to have received factual information concerning development. They may also feel embarrassed by unwanted attention from older males (Brooks-Gunn & Reiter, 1990). Early-maturing girls also have higher rates of teenage pregnancy and are at greater risk for unhealthy weight gain later in life (Adair & Gordon-Larsen, 2001).

Early maturation can be advantageous for boys, but it is also associated with risks. Early-maturing boys tend to be popular with their peers. However, although they are more successful in athletics than late-maturing peers, they are also more susceptible to behaviors that put their health at risk, such as steroid use (McCabe & Ricciardelli, 2004). Early-maturing boys are also more prone to the symptoms of depression, problems at school, and engaging in drug or alcohol use (see Ge & others, 2001, 2003).

Effects of Early versus Late Maturation As any adult who remembers 7th grade gym class can attest, the timing of puberty varies widely. Early maturation can have different effects for boys and girls. Early-maturing boys tend to be successful in athletics and popular with their peers, but they are more susceptible to risky behaviors, such as drug, alcohol, or steroid use (McCabe & Ricciardelli, 2004). Early-maturing girls tend to have more negative feelings about the arrival of puberty and body changes, have higher rates of teenage pregnancy, and may be embarrassed or harassed by unwanted attention from older males (Ge & others, 2003; Adar & Gordon-Larsen, 2001).

Neuroscience: The Adolescent Brain: A Work in Progress

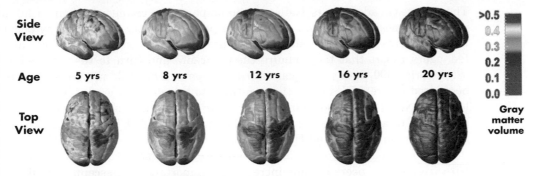

						Gray matter volume
Side View						>0.5 0.4 0.3 0.2 0.1 0.0
Age	5 yrs	8 yrs	12 yrs	16 yrs	20 yrs	
Top View						

For many adolescents, the teenage years, especially the early ones, seem to seesaw between moments of exhilaration and exasperation. Impressive instances of insightful behavior are counterbalanced by impulsive decisions made with no consideration of the potential risks or consequences. How can erratic adolescent behavior be explained?

For many years, the unpredictable behavior and mood swings of adolescents were explained as being due to "raging hormones." However, researchers have actually found little connection between hormone levels and adolescent behavior. As researcher Ronald Dahl (2003) explains, "High levels of sex hormones are not the cause of emotional problems in adolescents. Many adolescents with peak hormone levels experience no emotional difficulties at all." Rather than raging reproductive hormones, the explanation seems to lie within the adolescent brain.

To track changes in the developing brain, neuroscientists Jay Giedd, Elizabeth Sowell, Paul Thompson, and their colleagues have used magnetic resonance imaging (MRI) since the early 1990s to repeatedly scan the brains of normal kids and teenagers. One striking insight produced by their studies is that the human brain goes through not one but two distinct spurts of brain development—one during prenatal development and one during late childhood just prior to puberty (Giedd & others, 1999; Gogtay & others, 2004a).

In Chapter 2 we described how new neurons are produced at an astonishing rate during the first several months of prenatal development (see page 62)—so much so that by the sixth month of prenatal development, there is a vast overabundance of neurons in the fetal brain. During the final months of prenatal development, there is fierce competition among the neurons to make connections and survive. In the neuronal equivalent of "survival of the fittest," those neurons that don't make connections are eliminated. This process is called *pruning*.

During the years of infancy and early childhood, the brain's outer gray matter continues to develop and grow. The tapestry of interconnections between neurons becomes much more intricate as dendrites and axon terminals multiply and branch to extend their reach. White matter also increases as groups of neurons develop *myelin*, the white, fatty covering that insulates the axon and speeds communication between neurons.

Outwardly, these brain changes are reflected in the increasing cognitive and physical capabilities of the child. But in the brain itself, the "use-it-or-lose-it" principle is at work: Unused neuron circuits are being pruned. While it may seem counterintuitive, the loss of unused neurons and neuronal connections actually improves brain functioning by making the remaining neurons more efficient in processing information.

By 6 years of age, the child's brain is about 95 percent of its adult size. This well-documented fact led to the mistaken belief that brain development is essentially complete by late childhood. But the longitudinal MRI studies of normal kids and adolescents revealed something very surprising—a *second* wave of gray matter overproduction just prior to puberty, followed by a second round of neuronal pruning during the teenage years (Sowell & others, 2004).

Researchers are still not certain what causes this late childhood surge of cortical gray matter, but they know it is not due to a production of new neurons. Rather, the size, complexity, and connections among neurons all increase. This increase in gray matter peaks at about age 11 for girls and age 12 for boys (Durston & others, 2001).

Pruning Gray Matter from Back to Front

The color-coded series of brain images above shows the course of brain development from ages 5 to 20. Red indicates more gray matter, blue less gray matter. You can also watch four brief time-lapse "movies" of these brain changes courtesy of UCLA neuroscientist Paul Thompson and his colleagues (Gogtay & others, 2004b). The time-lapse movies are available at the *Discovering Psychology* 4th edition Web Companion site in the Chapter 9 Web Links: Internet Resources section.

The MRI images reveal that as the brain matures, neuronal connections are pruned and gray matter diminishes in a back-to-front wave. As pruning occurs, the connections that remain are strengthened and reinforced, and the amount of white matter in the brain steadily increases (Sowell & others, 2003).

More specifically, the first brain areas to mature are at the extreme front and back of the brain. These areas are involved with very basic functions, such as processing sensations and movement. The next brain areas to mature are the *parietal lobes*, which are involved in language and spatial skills.

The last brain area to experience pruning and maturity is the *prefrontal cortex*. This is significant because the prefrontal cortex plays a critical role in many advanced or "executive" cognitive functions, such as a person's ability to reason, plan ahead, organize, solve problems, and decide. And when does the prefrontal cortex reach full maturity? According to the MRI studies, not until a person reaches their mid-twenties (Gogtay & others, 2004a).

This suggests that an adolescent's occasional impulsive or immature behavior is at least partly a reflection of a brain that still has a long ways to go to reach full adult maturity. During adolescence, emotions and impulses can be intense and compelling. But the parts of the brain that are responsible for exercising judgment are still maturing. The result can be behavior that is immature, impulsive, unpredictable—or even risky.

Social Development

The changes in adolescents' bodies are accompanied by changes in their social interactions, most notably with parents and peers. Contrary to what many people think, parent–adolescent relationships are generally positive. In fact, most teenagers report that they admire their parents and turn to them for advice (Steinberg, 1990, 2001). As a general rule, when parent–child relationships have been good before adolescence, they continue to be relatively smooth during adolescence. Nevertheless, some friction seems to be inevitable as children make the transition to adolescence. We discuss the issue of conflict between adolescents and parents in Culture and Human Behavior Box 9.3.

Although parents remain influential throughout adolescence, relationships with friends and peers become increasingly important. Adolescents usually encounter greater diversity among their peers as they make the transitions to middle school and high school. To a much greater degree than during childhood, the adolescent's social network, social context, and community influence his or her values, norms, and expectations (Steinberg & others, 1995).

Parents often worry that peer influences will lead to undesirable behavior. Researchers have found, however, that peer relationships tend to *reinforce* the traits and goals that parents fostered during childhood (Steinberg, 2001). This finding is not as surprising as it might seem. Adolescents tend to form friendships with peers who are similar in age, social class, race, and beliefs about drinking, dating, church attendance, and educational goals.

Peer Relationships in Adolescence Although parents often worry about the negative impact of peers, peers can also have a positive influence on one another. These teenage volunteers are attending a leadership conference for Drug Free Youth in Town, a national community-based organization that works to prevent substance abuse in children and teens.

Friends often exert pressure on one another to study, make good grades, attend college, and engage in prosocial behaviors. So, although peer influence can lead to undesirable behaviors in some instances, peers can also influence one another in positive ways (Berndt, 1992; Mounts & Steinberg, 1995).

Romantic and sexual relationships also become increasingly important throughout the adolescent years. During early and middle adolescence, the physical changes of puberty prime the adolescent's interest in sexuality. One national survey showed that by the age of 12, about one-quarter of adolescents reported having had a "special romantic relationship." By age 15, that percentage increased to 50 percent, and reached 70 percent by the age of 17 (Carver & others, 2003).

Social and cultural factors also influence when, why, and how an adolescent initiates sexual behaviors. The beginning of dating, for example, coincides more strongly with cultural and social expectations and norms, such as when friends begin to date, than with an adolescent's degree of physical maturation (see Collins, 2003).

Far from being trivial, shallow, or transitory, romantic relationships can have a significant impact on the adolescent's psychological and social development (Furman, 2002). In terms of emotional impact, adolescents who are involved in a

ZITS

CULTURE AND HUMAN BEHAVIOR 9.3

Conflict Between Adolescents and Their Parents

Many people believe that relations between parents and their adolescent children are generally poor, marked by frequent and heated conflicts. Are the adolescent years a battleground?

Research on adolescents in the United States has shown that skirmishes between parents and their adolescent children *do* tend to increase, particularly during the early adolescent years (Buchanan & others, 1992; Laursen & Collins, 1994). Usually, conflicts focus on issues of control and authority and often revolve around parents' attempts to regulate everyday aspects of their children's lives.

As they enter adolescence, children are less willing to accept their parents' authority over their activities, choice of friends, and other aspects of their personal lives. In the same vein, they also tend to be more willing to disagree with their parents, argue with them, and challenge their authority. These tendencies naturally lead to an increase in bickering and sometimes even heated disputes.

Many developmental psychologists, however, view the increased conflict in early and middle adolescence as healthy, a necessary stage in the adolescent's development of increased independence and autonomy. After middle adolescence, conflicts with parents begin to decline and continue to do so throughout late adolescence (Laursen & Collins, 1994). As the adolescent matures, both parents and adolescent children become more comfortable with the adolescent's greater independence and autonomy.

Given the individualistic nature of U.S. culture, it's not surprising that developing

a separate, autonomous identity would be seen as a key developmental milestone on the path to adulthood (Greenfield & others, 2003). What about adolescents in collectivistic cultures? Is adolescence also marked by conflict in other cultures, especially collectivistic cultures?

To answer that question, psychologists have conducted research on adolescent development in non-Western collectivistic cultures and among adolescents of non-European descent (B. Schneider, 1998). Collectivistic cultures tend to be marked by a greater respect for authority, especially parental authority; a strong sense of family obligation; and a greater emphasis on harmony among family members. Is achieving identity as a separate individual as highly valued in these cultural contexts?

One study compared American adolescents of European descent with Chinese-American adolescents; Chinese adolescents living in Beijing, China; and Chinese adolescents living in Taipei, Taiwan (Chen & others, 1998). On the average, the European-American teenagers reported the *highest* level of conflict with their parents, while

the Chinese adolescents living in Beijing and Taipei reported the *lowest* levels. The Chinese-American teens fell between the European-Americans and the two Chinese groups. Although there was significantly more conflict in the European-American families, it's important to note that conflict between parents and adolescent children was present in *all* groups. This suggests that parent–adolescent conflict is a common dimension of family life in very different cultures.

Another perspective was provided by a wide-ranging study conducted by Andrew Fuligni (1998). Fuligni compared parent–adolescent conflict among different ethnic groups living in California: adolescents of Mexican, Chinese, Filipino, and European descent. The Filipino-, Chinese-, and Mexican-American adolescents generally demonstrated a greater respect for parental authority and less of an emphasis on individual autonomy.

Nevertheless, adolescents of all four ethnic groups reported very similar levels of conflict with their parents. As Fuligni (1998) observes, "Members of these different ethnic groups showed similar developmental trends in their ideas about authority and autonomy." As they progressed through adolescence, these teens became more willing to openly disagree with their parents. They also became increasingly more willing to challenge their parents' attempts to control various aspects of their personal lives. Thus, even within cultural and ethnic groups that traditionally emphasize parental authority, it seems that adolescents are motivated to assert their independence and developing autonomy.

---

romantic relationship are more prone to mood swings and, especially when the relationship is a stormy one, depression (Joyner & Udry, 2000). However, by late adolescence, romantic relationships can also lead to overall feelings of enhanced self-worth, feelings of competence, and enhanced relationships with friends and peers (Furman & Shaffer, 2003).

The physical and social developments we've discussed so far are the more obvious changes associated with the onset of puberty. No less important, however, are the cognitive changes that allow the adolescent to think and reason in new, more complex ways.

identity

A person's definition or description of himself or herself, including the values, beliefs, and ideals that guide the individual's behavior.

Identity Formation:
Erikson's Theory of Psychosocial Development

When psychologists talk about a person's **identity,** they are referring to the values, beliefs, and ideals that guide the individual's behavior (Erikson, 1964a; Marcia, 1991). Our sense of personal identity gives us an integrated and continuing sense of self over time. Identity formation is a process that continues throughout the lifespan. As we embrace new and different roles over the course of our lives, we define ourselves in new ways (Erikson & others, 1986; Grotevant, 1992).

For the first time in the lifespan, the adolescent possesses the cognitive skills necessary for dealing with identity issues in a meaningful way (Habermas & Bluck, 2000). Beginning in early adolescence, self-definition shifts. Preadolescent children tend to describe themselves in very concrete social and behavioral terms. An 8-year-old might describe himself by saying, "I play with Mark and I like to ride my bike." In contrast, adolescents use more abstract self-descriptions that reflect personal attributes, values, beliefs, and goals (Harter, 1990). Thus, a 14-year-old might say, "I have strong religious beliefs, love animals, and hope to become a veterinarian."

Some aspects of personal identity involve characteristics over which the adolescent really has no control, such as gender, race, ethnic background, and socioeconomic level. In effect, these identity characteristics are fixed and already internalized by the time an individual reaches the adolescent years.

Beyond such fixed characteristics, the adolescent begins to evaluate herself on several different dimensions. Social acceptance by peers, academic and athletic abilities, work abilities, personal appearance, and romantic appeal are some important aspects of self-definition. Another challenge facing the adolescent is to develop an identity that is independent of her parents while retaining a sense of connection to her family. Thus, the adolescent has not one but several self-concepts that she must integrate into a coherent and unified whole to answer the question "Who am I?"

The adolescent's task of achieving an integrated identity is one important aspect of psychoanalyst **Erik Erikson**'s influential theory of psychosocial development. Briefly, Erikson (1968) proposed that each of eight stages of life is associated with a particular psychosocial conflict that can be resolved in either a positive or a negative direction (see Table 9.4). Relationships with others play an important role in determining the outcome of each conflict. According to Erikson, the key psychosocial conflict facing adolescents is *identity versus role confusion.*

To successfully form an identity, adolescents not only must integrate various dimensions of their personality into a coherent whole, but they also must define the roles that they will adopt within the larger society on becoming an adult (Habermas & Bluck, 2000). To accomplish this, adolescents grapple with a wide variety of issues, such as selecting a potential career and formulating religious, moral, and political beliefs. They must also adopt social roles involving interpersonal relationships, sexuality, and long-term commitments such as marriage and parenthood.

In Erikson's (1968) theory, the adolescent's path to successful identity achievement begins with *role confusion,* which is characterized by little sense of commitment on any of these issues. This period is followed by a *moratorium period,* during which the adolescent experiments with different roles, values, and beliefs. Gradually, by choosing among the alternatives and making commitments, the adolescent arrives at an *integrated identity.*

Psychological research has generally supported Erikson's description of the process of identity formation (Grotevant, 1987; Marcia, 1991). However, it's important to keep in mind that identity continues to evolve over the entire lifespan, not just during the adolescent years (Grotevant, 1992). Adolescents and young adults seem to achieve a stable sense of identity in some areas earlier than in others. Far fewer adolescents and young adults have attained a stable sense of identity in the realm of religious and political beliefs than in the realm of vocational choice.

Psychoanalyst Erik Erikson Erikson (1902–1994) is shown here with his wife, Joan, in 1988. Erikson's landmark theory of psychosocial development stressed the importance of social and cultural influences on personality throughout the stages of life.

Table 9.4

Erik Erikson's Psychosocial Stages of Development

Life Stage	Psychosocial Conflict	Positive Resolution	Negative Resolution
Infancy (birth to 18 months)	Trust vs. mistrust	Reliance on consistent and warm caregivers produces a sense of predictability and trust in the environment.	Physical and psychological neglect by caregivers leads to fear, anxiety, and mistrust of the environment.
Toddlerhood (18 months to 3 years)	Autonomy vs. doubt	Caregivers encourage independence and self-sufficiency, promoting positive self-esteem.	Overly restrictive caregiving leads to self-doubt in abilities and low self-esteem.
Early childhood (3 to 6 years)	Initiative vs. guilt	The child learns to initiate activities and develops a sense of social responsibility concerning the rights of others; promotes self-confidence.	Parental overcontrol stifles the child's spontaneity, sense of purpose, and social learning; promotes guilt and fear of punishment.
Middle and late childhood (6 to 12 years)	Industry vs. inferiority	Through experiences with parents and "keeping up" with peers, the child develops a sense of pride and competence in schoolwork and home and social activities.	Negative experiences with parents or failure to "keep up" with peers leads to pervasive feelings of inferiority and inadequacy.
Adolescence	Identity vs. role confusion	Through experimentation with different roles, the adolescent develops an integrated and stable self-definition; forms commitments to future adult roles.	An apathetic adolescent or one who experiences pressures and demands from others may feel confusion about his or her identity and role in society.
Young adulthood	Intimacy vs. isolation	By establishing lasting and meaningful relationships, the young adult develops a sense of connectedness and intimacy with others.	Because of fear of rejection or excessive self-preoccupation, the young adult is unable to form close, meaningful relationships and becomes psychologically isolated.
Middle adulthood	Generativity vs. stagnation	Through child rearing, caring for others, productive work, and community involvement, the adult expresses unselfish concern for the welfare of the next generation.	Self-indulgence, self-absorption, and a preoccupation with one's own needs lead to a sense of stagnation, boredom, and a lack of meaningful accomplishments.
Late adulthood	Ego integrity vs. despair	In reviewing his or her life, the older adult experiences a strong sense of self-acceptance and meaningfulness in his or her accomplishments.	In looking back on his or her life, the older adult experiences regret, dissatisfaction, and disappointment about his or her life and accomplishments.

SOURCE: Adapted from Erikson (1964a).

Adult Development

Key Theme
■ Development during adulthood is marked by physical changes and the adoption of new social roles.

Key Question
■ What physical changes take place in adulthood?
■ What are some general patterns of adult social development?
■ What characterizes career paths in adulthood?

You can think of the developmental changes you experienced during infancy, childhood, and adolescence as early chapters in your life story. Those early life chapters helped set the tone and some of the themes for the primary focus of your life story—adulthood. During the half-century or more that constitutes

menopause
The natural cessation of menstruation and the end of reproductive capacity in women.

adulthood, predictable changes continue to occur. Self-definition evolves as people achieve independence and take on new roles and responsibilities. As you'll see in this section, the story of adulthood also reflects the increasing importance of individual variation. Although general patterns of aging exist, our life stories become more distinct and individualized with each passing decade of life (Schaie & Willis, 1996).

Physical Changes

Physical strength typically peaks in *early adulthood,* the twenties and thirties. By *middle adulthood,* roughly from the forties to the mid-sixties, physical strength and endurance gradually decline. Physical and mental reaction times also begin to slow during middle adulthood. During *late adulthood,* from the mid-sixties on, physical stamina and reaction time tend to decline further and faster.

Your unique genetic heritage greatly influences the unfolding of certain physical changes during adulthood, such as when your hair begins to thin, lose its color, and turn gray. Such genetically influenced changes can vary significantly from one person to another. For example, **menopause,** the cessation of menstruation that signals the end of reproductive capacity in women, may occur anywhere from the late thirties to the early fifties.

But your destiny is not completely ruled by genetics. Your lifestyle is one key environmental factor that can influence the aging process. Staying mentally and physically active and eating a proper diet can both slow and minimize the degree of physical decline associated with aging.

Another potent environmental force is simply the passage of time. Decades of use and environmental exposure take a toll on the body. Wrinkles begin to appear as we approach the age of 40, largely because of a loss of skin elasticity combined with years of making the same facial expressions. With each decade after age 20, the efficiency of various body organs declines. For example, lung capacity decreases, as does the amount of blood pumped by the heart.

Psychosocial Development in Young Adulthood Young adulthood brings many psychological challenges and transitions, not the least of which is choosing a life partner. According to psychoanalyst Erik Erikson (1968), the key psychosocial conflict of young adulthood is intimacy versus isolation. Erikson believed that the ability to establish a meaningful, intimate, and lasting relationship helps set the stage for healthy adult development.

Social Development

In his theory of psychosocial development, Erik Erikson (1982) described the two fundamental themes that dominate adulthood: love and work. According to Erikson (1964b, 1968), the primary psychosocial task of early adulthood is to form a committed, mutually enhancing, intimate relationship with another person. During middle adulthood, the primary psychosocial task becomes one of *generativity*—to contribute to future generations through your children, your career, and other meaningful activities. In this section, we'll consider the themes of love and work by examining adult friendships, marriage, family life, and careers.

Friends and Lovers in Adulthood

Largely because of competing demands on their time, adults typically have fewer friends than adolescents do. The focus of adult friendships is somewhat different for men and women. Female friends tend to confide in one another about their feelings, problems, and interpersonal relationships. In contrast, male friends typically minimize discussions about relationships or personal feelings or problems. Instead, male friends tend to do things together that they find mutually interesting, such as activities related to sports or hobbies (Norris & Tindale, 1994).

Beyond friendship, establishing a committed, intimate relationship takes on a new urgency in adulthood. Looking for Mr. or Ms. Right, getting married, and starting a family are the traditional tasks of early adulthood. However, in contrast to their parents, today's young adults are marrying at a later average age. As Figure 9.6 shows, in 1960 the median age for a first marriage was 23 for men and 20 for women. By 2003 those averages had increased to age 27 for men and age 25 for women. Many young adults postpone marriage until their late twenties or early thirties so they can finish their education and become established in a career. And, of course, it is a mistake to assume that the "traditional" family is the norm. There are many Americans who either never marry or don't remarry after they are widowed or divorced. In fact, the most recent U.S. Census found that some 60 million Americans had never married (U.S. Census Bureau, 2004b).

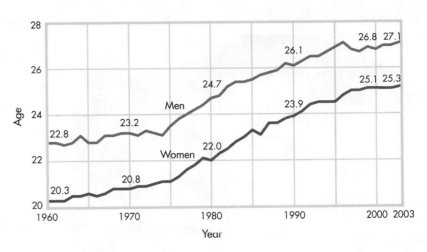

FIGURE 9.6 The Median Age at First Marriage The average age at first marriage is five years older for young adults today than it was in the 1960s. Part of the explanation for this trend is that more people are postponing marriage in order to get a college education. This is especially true for females. Between 1990 and 2004, the number of females enrolled in college increased by 16 percent compared to 8 percent for men. Currently, there are about 56 women enrolled in college for every 44 men. Among today's young adults, 25 percent of all men and women age 25 and older have a bachelor's degree.

SOURCES: Spraggins (2003); U.S. Census Bureau (2004a); National Center for Education Statistics (2005).

Whom is a person most likely to marry? As a general rule, the old adage "Birds of a feather flock together" seems to hold. People tend to be attracted to and marry others who are similar to them on a variety of dimensions, including physical attractiveness, social and educational status, ethnic background, attitudes, values, and beliefs (Brehm, 1992).

The Transition to Parenthood: Kids 'R' Us?

Although it is commonly believed that children strengthen the marital bond, marital satisfaction tends to decline after the birth of the first child (Twenge & others, 2003). For all the joy that can be derived from watching a child grow and experience the world, the first child's arrival creates a whole new set of responsibilities, pushes, and pulls on the marital relationship.

Without question, parenthood fundamentally alters your identity as an adult. With the birth or adoption of your first child, you take on a commitment to nurture the physical, emotional, social, and intellectual well-being of the next generation. This change in your identity can be a struggle, especially if the transition to parenthood was more of a surprise than a planned event (Mebert, 1991; Sandelowski & others, 1992).

Parenthood is further complicated by the fact that children are not born speaking fluently so that you can immediately enlighten them about the constraints of adult schedules, deadlines, finances, and physical energy. Instead, you must continually strive to adapt lovingly and patiently to your child's needs while managing all the other priorities in your life.

Not all couples experience a decline in marital satisfaction after the birth of a child. The hassles and headaches of child rearing can be minimized if the marital relationship is warm and positive and if both husband and wife share household and child-care responsibilities (Tsang & others, 2003). It also helps if you're blessed with a child who is born with a good disposition and an easy temperament. When infants are irritable, cry a lot, or are otherwise "difficult," parents find it harder to adjust to their new role (van den Boom & Hoeksma, 1994).

That many couples are marrying at a later age and waiting until their thirties to start a family also seems to be advantageous. Becoming a parent at an older age and waiting longer after marriage to start a family may ease the adjustment to parenthood. Why? Largely because the couple is more mature and the marital relationship is typically more stable.

Although marital satisfaction often declines when people first become parents, it rises again after children leave home (Norris & Tindale, 1994). Successfully

"Excuse me, but for some reason you have us traveling with our kids.'

Single-Parent Families Today, more than 30 percent of all children are being raised by a single parent. Many single parents provide their children with a warm, stable, and loving environment. In terms of school achievement and emotional stability, children in stable single-parent households do just as well as children with two parents living in the same home (Dawson, 1991).

FIGURE 9.7 The Changing Structure of American Families and Households Between 1970 and 2003, the number of American households increased from 63 million to 111 million. During that same period, however, the average size of the American household decreased from 3.14 to 2.57 persons. The two pie charts show how the structure of American households has undergone major shifts in the relatively short time span of three decades. Notice how the percentage of single-parent family groups has more than doubled, while the number of "traditional" families consisting of a married couple with children has dramatically decreased.

SOURCES: Fields (2004); U.S. Census Bureau (2004a).

launching your children into the adult world represents the attainment of the ultimate parental goal. It also means there is more time to spend in leisure activities with your spouse. Not surprisingly, then, marital satisfaction tends to increase steadily once children are out of the nest and flying on their own.

Variations in the Paths of Adult Social Development

Up to this point, we've described the "traditional" track of adult social development: finding a mate, getting married, starting and raising a family. However, there is enormous diversity in how the goal of intimacy is realized during adulthood (Edwards, 1995b). The nature of intimate relationships and family structures varies widely in the United States (see Figure 9.7).

For example, the number of unmarried couples living together increased dramatically at the end of the twentieth century—to well over 3 million couples. Currently, more than 30 percent of children are being raised by a single parent (Rawlings & Saluter, 1995). Given that more than half of all first marriages end in divorce, the phenomenon of remarrying and starting a "second family" later in life is not unusual (Karney & Bradbury, 1995). As divorce has become more common, the number of single parents and stepfamilies has also risen. And among married couples, some opt for a "child-free" life together. There are also gay and lesbian couples who, like many married couples, are committed to a long-term, monogamous relationship (Kurdek, 1995; Solomon & others, 2004).

Such diversity in adult relationships reflects the fact that adult social development does not always follow a predictable pattern. As you travel through adulthood, your life story may include many unanticipated twists in the plot and changes in the cast of characters. Just as the "traditional" family structure has its joys and heartaches, so do other configurations of intimate and family relationships. In the final analysis, *any* relationship that promotes the overall sense of happiness and well-being of the people involved is a successful one.

Careers in Adulthood

People follow a variety of routes in developing careers (Lachman, 2004). Most people explore different career options, narrow down those options, and tenta-

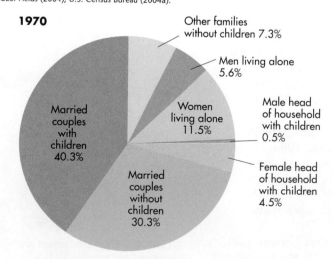

1970

Married couples with children 40.3%

Married couples without children 30.3%

Other families without children 7.3%

Men living alone 5.6%

Women living alone 11.5%

Male head of household with children 0.5%

Female head of household with children 4.5%

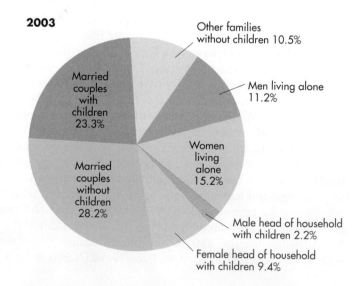

2003

Married couples with children 23.3%

Married couples without children 28.2%

Other families without children 10.5%

Men living alone 11.2%

Women living alone 15.2%

Male head of household with children 2.2%

Female head of household with children 9.4%

tively commit to a particular job in a particular field in young adulthood (Super, 1990). However, researchers have found that close to a third of people in their late twenties and early thirties do not just change jobs within a particular field—they completely switch occupational fields (Phillips & Blustein, 1994).

Dual-career families have become increasingly common. However, the career tracks of men and women often differ if they have children. Although today's fathers are more actively involved in child rearing than were fathers in previous generations, women still tend to have primary responsibility for child care (Wood & Repetti, 2004). Thus, married women with children are much more likely than are single women or childless women to interrupt their careers, leave their jobs, or switch to part-time work because of child-rearing responsibilities.

Do adults, particularly women, experience greater stress because of the conflicting demands of career, marriage, and family? Not necessarily. Generally, multiple roles seem to provide both men and women with a greater potential for increased feelings of self-esteem, happiness, and competence (Gilbert, 1994). The critical factor is not so much the number of roles that people take on but the *quality* of their experiences on the job, in marriage, and as a parent (Barnett & others, 1992). When experiences in these different roles are positive and satisfying, psychological well-being is enhanced. However, when work is dissatisfying, finding high-quality child care is difficult, and making ends meet is a never-ending struggle, stress can escalate and psychological well-being can plummet—for either sex (Schulz & others, 2004).

Late Adulthood and Aging

Key Theme
■ Late adulthood does not necessarily involve a steep decline in physical or cognitive capabilities.

Key Questions
■ What cognitive changes take place in late adulthood?
■ What factors influence social development in late adulthood?

The average life expectancy for men in the United States is about 75 years. For women, the average life expectancy is about 80 years. So the stage of late adulthood can easily last for a decade or longer. Although we experience many physical and sensory changes throughout adulthood, that's not to say that we completely fall apart when we reach our sixties, seventies, or even eighties. Some people in their nineties are healthier and more active than other people who are 20 years younger (Baltes & Mayer, 2001).

In American culture, but certainly not in all cultures, the phrase *old age* is often associated with images of poor health, inactivity, social isolation, and mental and physical incompetence. Are those images accurate? Far from it. The majority of older adults live healthy, active, and self-sufficient lives (Schaie & Willis, 1996).

In fact, the stereotypical image that most elderly people live in nursing homes is a major myth. In Table 9.5, you can see that of *all* American adults aged 65 and over, only 4.5 percent live in nursing homes. It's also interesting to note the downward trend that has occurred over the last decade in the percentages of senior adults who live in nursing homes. Even among those aged 85 and over, fewer than 20 percent live in nursing homes. Some older adults live with relatives, but most live in their own homes (U.S. Census Bureau, 2002).

Blended Families Approximately 17 percent of all children live in stepfamilies or *blended families,* sharing their home with children from an earlier marriage of their parent or stepparent (U.S. Census Bureau, 2004a). Sometimes, as is the case with this family, the children of the first marriage are much older than the children of the second marriage.

Although the term "blended families" is commonly used, not all stepfamilies agree with its use, pointing out that children in stepfamilies do not lose their identification or emotional attachment to the parent who is not part of the new household (Stepfamily Association of America, 2005).

"This next one is a hard-rockin', kick-ass, take-no-prisoners tune we wrote about turning sixty."

Table 9.5

U.S. Population Aged 65 and Older in Nursing Homes by Age: 1990 and 2000

	Percent of Age Group	
Age	1990	2000
65 years and over	**5.1**	**4.5**
65 to 74 years	1.4	1.1
75 to 84 years	6.1	4.7
85 years and over	24.5	18.2

SOURCE: Hetzel & Smith (2001).

Japan's Super-Seniors Despite the stereotypes held by many young people, old age doesn't necessarily involve infirmity or inactivity. Consider Tokyo resident Keizo Miura, shown doing part of his daily exercise routine. Miura, born in 1904, takes a 2-mile power walk at dawn each morning and is training for a mountain-climbing expedition to the Italian Alps. Miura celebrated his 100th birthday in 2004 by skiing with four generations of his family. Japan's elderly are not only the longest-lived but also the healthiest seniors in the world. Miura, like his fellow "super-seniors" in Japan, attributes his continued vigor to exercise and a healthy diet. Miura celebrated his 101st birthday on February 15, 2005.

Although they have more chronic medical conditions, elderly individuals tend to see themselves as relatively healthy, partly because they have fewer acute illnesses, such as colds and flu, than do younger people (National Center for Health Statistics, 2002). Even during the final year of life, the majority of older adults enjoy relatively good health, mental alertness, and self-sufficiency (Brock & others, 1994).

The number of older adults in the United States has been gradually increasing over the past several decades. At the beginning of the twentieth century, only about 1 American in 20 was 65 or older; today, 1 of every 8 Americans is. By the year 2030, 1 of 5 Americans will be an older adult (Kinsella & Velkoff, 2001).

Cognitive Changes

During which decade of life do you think people reach their intellectual peak? If you answered the twenties or thirties, you may be surprised by the results of longitudinal studies done by psychologist K. Warner Schaie. Since the 1950s, Schaie and his colleagues have followed some 5,000 people as they have aged to learn what happens to intellectual abilities.

Schaie (1995) found that general intellectual abilities gradually increase until one's early forties, then become relatively stable until about age 60. After age 60, a small but steadily increasing percentage of older adults experience slight declines on tests of general intellectual abilities, such as logical reasoning, math skills, word recall, and the ability to mentally manipulate images. But even after age 60, most older adults maintain these previous levels of abilities. A longitudinal study of adults in their seventies, eighties, and nineties found that there were slight but significant declines in memory, perceptual speed, and fluency. However, measures of knowledge, such as vocabulary, remained stable up to age 90 (Singer & others, 2003).

When declines in mental abilities occur during old age, Schaie found, the explanation is often simply a lack of practice or experience with the kinds of tasks used in mental ability tests. Even just a few hours of training on mental skills can improve test scores for most older adults (Schaie & Willis, 1986).

Is it possible to minimize declines in mental abilities in old age? In a word, "yes." Schaie (1994) found that those who are better educated and engage in physical and mental activities throughout older adulthood show the smallest declines in mental abilities. In contrast, the greatest intellectual declines tend to occur in older adults with unstimulating lifestyles, such as people who live alone, are dissatisfied with their lives, and engage in few activities.

Social Development

At one time it was believed that older adults gradually "disengage," or withdraw, from vocational, social, and relationship roles as they face the prospect of their lives ending (Cumming & Henry, 1961). But consider Sandy's father, Erv. Erv and about a dozen other retired men in their seventies and eighties belong to what they call the "Golden Agers' Club." They regularly get together to play cards, go out to lunch, and forage used bookstores and flea markets for treasures. About once a year, they take a fishing trip.

What Erv and his buddies epitomize is the activity theory of aging. According to the **activity theory of aging,** life satisfaction in late adulthood is highest when you maintain your previous level of activity, either by continuing old activities or by finding new ones (Benyamini & Lomranz, 2004).

Just like younger adults, older adults differ in the level of activity they find personally optimal. Some older adults pursue a busy lifestyle of social activities, travel, college classes, and volunteer work. Other older adults are happier with a quieter lifestyle, pursuing hobbies, reading, or simply puttering around their homes. Such individual preferences reflect lifelong temperamental and personality qualities that continue to be evident as a person ages (Costa & McCrae, 1989).

For many older adults, caregiving responsibilities can persist well into late adulthood. Sandy's parents, Fern and Erv, for example, spend a great deal of time helping out with their young grandchildren and caring for some of their older relatives. They're not unusual in that respect. Many older adults who are healthy and active find themselves taking care of other older adults who are sick or have physical limitations (Norris & Tindale, 1994).

Even for an older adult who is not very socially active, it's still important to have at least one confidant. Sometimes the confidant is simply a very close friend. For older men, the confidant is often the spouse. The social support provided by the confidant yields important psychological benefits for the older adult, such as higher morale, better mental health, and better psychological well-being (Rawlins, 1992). A confidant can also provide an important buffer for the older adult in coping with stressful events, such as health problems or the deaths of friends or family members.

Along with satisfying social relationships, the prescription for psychological well-being in old age includes achieving what Erik Erikson called *ego integrity*—the feeling that one's life has been meaningful (Erikson & others, 1986). Older adults experience ego integrity when they look back on their lives and feel satisfied with their accomplishments, accepting whatever mistakes or missteps they may have made.

In contrast, those who are filled with regrets or bitterness about past mistakes, missed opportunities, or bad decisions experience *despair*—a sense of disappointment in life. Often the theme of ego integrity versus despair emerges as older adults engage in a *life review*, thinking about or retelling their life story to others (Staudinger, 2001; Taft & Nehrke, 1990).

activity theory of aging
The psychosocial theory that life satisfaction in late adulthood is highest when people maintain the level of activity they displayed earlier in life.

A Lifetime of Experience to Share Like many other senior adults, Ettore Buonomo of New York City derives great personal satisfaction as a volunteer helping grade school students. Contributing to society, taking care of others, and helping people both younger and older than themselves often take on renewed importance to senior adults.

The Final Chapter
Dying and Death

Key Theme
■ Attitudes toward dying and death are as diverse in late adulthood as they are throughout the lifespan.

Key Questions
■ How did Kübler-Ross describe the stages of dying?
■ What are some individual variations in attitudes toward death and dying?

It is tempting to view death as the special province of the very old. Of course, death can occur at any point during the lifespan. It's also tempting to assume that older adults have come to a special understanding about death—that they view the prospect of dying with wisdom and serenity. In reality, attitudes toward death in old age show the same diversity that is reflected in other aspects of adult development. Not all older adults are resigned to death, even when poor health has severely restricted their activities (Kastenbaum, 1986, 1992).

As psychologist Robert Kastenbaum (1992) wrote, "Everyone lives in relationship to death at every point in the lifespan." In other words, long before encountering old age, each individual has a personal history of thinking about death. Some people are obsessed with issues of life and death from adolescence or early adulthood onward, while others, even in advanced old age, take more of a one-day-at-a-time approach to living.

In general, anxiety about death tends to peak in middle adulthood, then tends to *decrease* in late adulthood (Lonetto & Templer, 1986). At any age, people respond with a wide variety of emotions when faced with the prospect of imminent death, such as when they are diagnosed with a terminal illness.

Elisabeth Kübler-Ross (1969) interviewed more than 200 terminally ill patients and proposed that the dying go through five stages. First, they *deny* that death is imminent, perhaps insisting that their doctors are wrong or denying the seriousness of their illness. Second, they feel and express *anger* that they are dying. Third, they *bargain*—they try to "make a deal" with doctors, relatives, or God, promising to behave in a certain way if only they may be allowed to live. Fourth, they become *depressed*. Finally, they *accept* their fate.

Although Kübler-Ross's research did much to sensitize the public and the medical community to the emotional experience of dying, it now seems clear that dying individuals do *not* necessarily progress through the predictable sequence of stages that she described (Kastenbaum, 1992). Dying is as individual a process as living. People cope with the prospect of dying much as they have coped with other stresses in their lives.

Faced with impending death, some older adults react with passive resignation, others with bitterness and anger. Some people plunge into activity and focus their attention on external matters, such as making funeral arrangements, disposing of their property, or arranging for the care of other family members. And others turn inward, searching for the meaning of their life's story as the close of the final chapter draws near (Kastenbaum, 1992).

But even in dying, our life story doesn't just end. Each of us leaves behind a legacy of memories in the minds of those who survive us. As we live each day, we are building this legacy, through our words, our actions, and the choices we make.

Each of us began life being completely dependent on others for our survival. Over the course of our lifespan, others come to depend on us. It is those people whose lives we have touched in some way, whether for good or for ill, who will remember us. In this sense, the final chapter of our lives will be written not by us, but by those whose life stories have intersected with our own.

Closing Thoughts

Traditionally, development in childhood has received the most attention from developmental psychologists. Yet, as we have emphasized throughout this chapter, development is a lifelong process.

Throughout this chapter, you've seen that every life is a unique combination of universal and individualized patterns of development. Although some aspects of development unfold in a predictable fashion, every life story, including yours, is influenced by unexpected events and plot twists. Despite predictable changes, the wonderful thing about the developmental process is that you never *really* know what the next chapter of your life story may hold—as that former cheerleader from Chicago and skydiver from Iowa can testify.

authoritarian parenting style
Parenting style in which parents are demanding and unresponsive toward their children's needs or wishes.

permissive parenting style
Parenting style in which parents are extremely tolerant and not demanding; permissive-indulgent parents are more responsive to their children, whereas permissive-indifferent parents are not.

authoritative parenting style
Parenting style in which parents set clear standards for their children's behavior but are also responsive to their children's needs and wishes.

induction
A discipline technique that combines parental control with explaining why a behavior is prohibited.

Unfortunately, kids don't come with own-ers' manuals. Maybe that's why if you walk into any bookstore and head for the "par-enting" section, you'll see shelves of books offering advice on topics ranging from "how to toilet-train your toddler" to "how to talk to your teenager." We're not going to attempt to cover that range in this brief chapter Application. However, we will pre-sent some basic principles of parenting that have been shown to foster the devel-opment of children who are psychologi-cally well-adjusted, competent, and in control of their own behavior.

Basic Parenting Styles and Their Effects on Children

Psychologist Diana Baumrind (1971, 1991) has described three basic parenting styles: authoritarian, permissive, and authorita-tive. These parenting styles differ in terms of (1) *parental control* and (2) *parental re-sponsiveness* to the child's needs and wishes.

Parents with an **authoritarian par-enting style** are demanding but unre-sponsive to their children's needs or wishes. Authoritarian parents believe that they should shape and control the child's behavior so that it corresponds to an ab-solute set of standards. Put simply, they ex-pect children to obey the rules, no questions asked. Rules are made without input from the child, and they are enforced by punishment, often physical.

At the opposite extreme are two **per-missive parenting styles** (Maccoby & Martin, 1983). *Permissive-indulgent parents* are responsive, warm, and accepting of their children but impose few rules and rarely punish their children. *Permissive-in-different parents* are both unresponsive and uncontrolling. Establishing firm rules and consistently enforcing them is simply too much trouble for permissive-indifferent parents. If taken to an extreme, the lack of involvement of permissive-indifferent par-enting can amount to child neglect.

The third style is the **authoritative parenting style.** Authoritative parents are warm, responsive, and involved with their children. They set clear standards for mature, age-appropriate behavior and ex-pect their children to be responsive to parental demands. However, authoritative parents also feel a *reciprocal* responsibility to consider their children's reasonable de-mands and points of view. Thus, there is considerable give-and-take between parent and child. Rules are firm and consistently enforced, but the parents discuss the rea-sons for the rules with the child (Maccoby & Martin, 1983).

How do these different parenting styles affect young children? Baumrind (1971) found that the children of authoritarian parents are likely to be moody, unhappy, fearful, withdrawn, unspontaneous, and ir-ritable. The children of permissive parents tend to be more cheerful than the children of authoritarian parents, but they are more immature, impulsive, and aggressive. In contrast, the children of authoritative par-ents are likely to be cheerful, socially com-petent, energetic, and friendly. They show high levels of self-esteem, self-reliance, and self-control (Buri & others, 1988).

These different parenting styles also af-fect children's competence, adjustment, and delinquent behavior (Kaufmann & others, 2000; Palmer & Hollin, 2001). Au-thoritative parenting is associated with higher grades than authoritarian or permis-sive parenting (Kawamura & others, 2002). In one study of several hundred adoles-cents, this finding was consistent for virtu-ally all adolescents, regardless of ethnic or socioeconomic background (Dornbusch & others, 1987).

Adding to the evidence, psychologist Laurence Steinberg and his colleagues (1995) conducted a three-year longitudinal study involving more than 20,000 U.S. high school students. Steinberg found that authoritative parenting is associated with a broad range of beneficial effects for the adolescent, regardless of socioeconomic or ethnic background. As Steinberg summa-rized, "Adolescents raised in authoritative homes are better adjusted and more com-petent, they are confident about their abil-ities, competent in areas of achievement, and less likely than their peers to get into trouble" (Steinberg & others, 1995).

Why does an authoritative parenting style provide such clear advantages over other parenting styles? First, when children perceive their parents' requests as fair and reasonable, they are more likely to comply with the requests. Second, the children are more likely to *internalize* (or accept as their own) the reasons for behaving in a certain way and thus to achieve greater self-con-trol (Hoffman, 1977, 1994).

In contrast, authoritarian parenting pro-motes resentment and rebellion (Hoffman, 1977, 1988). Because compliance is based on external control and punishment, the child often learns to avoid the parent rather than independently control his or her own behavior (Gershoff, 2002). Finally, the child with permissive parents may never learn self-control. And because permissive par-ents have low expectations, the child may well live up to those expectations by failing

Situation: Nine-year-old Jeff wants to stay up late to watch a special program on television.

	Low responsiveness	High responsiveness
Low control	**Permissive-Indifferent** Doesn't notice that Jeff is up late; Jeff has no regular bedtime.	**Permissive-Indulgent** Says, "Fine, if it's that important to you."
High control	**Authoritarian** Says, "You know the rules. Bedtime is nine o'clock. No exceptions!"	**Authoritative** Asks why program is so important. Offers to record program so Jeff can watch it at a later time, or agrees that Jeff can stay up late tonight if he promises to go to bed early tomorrow.

Four Parenting Styles Researchers have identified four basic parenting styles, based on the dimen-sions of parental control and parental responsiveness.

ZITS

Zits cartoon, © Zits Partnership. Reprinted with special permission of King Features Syndicate.

to strive to fulfill his or her potential (Baumrind, 1971).

How to Be an Authoritative Parent: Some Practical Suggestions

Authoritative parents are high in both responsiveness and control. How can you successfully achieve that balance? Here are several suggestions based on psychological research.

1. Let your children know that you love them.

Attention, hugs, and other demonstrations of physical affection, coupled with a positive attitude toward your child, are some of the most important aspects of parenting, aspects that have enduring effects (Steinberg, 2001). Children who experience warm, positive relationships with their parents are more likely to become happy adults with stable marriages and good relationships with friends (Franz & others, 1991). So the question is simple: Have you hugged your kids today?

2. Listen to your children.

Let your children express their opinions, and respect their preferences when it's reasonable to do so. In making rules and decisions, ask for their input and give it genuine consideration. Strive to be fair and flexible, especially on issues that are less than earthshaking, such as which clothes they wear to school.

3. Use induction to teach as you discipline.

The most effective form of discipline is called **induction** because it *induces* understanding in the child. Induction combines controlling a child's behavior with *teaching* (Hoffman, 1977, 1994). Put simply, induction involves consistently explaining (a) the *reason* for prohibiting or performing certain behaviors; (b) the *consequences* of the action for the child; and (c) the *effect* of the child's behavior on others. When parents use induction, the child begins to understand that their actions are not completely arbitrary or unfair. The child is also more likely to internalize the reasoning and apply it in new situations (Schulman & Mekler, 1985).

4. Work with your child's temperamental qualities.

Think back to our earlier discussion of temperamental qualities. Be aware of your child's natural temperament and work with it, not against it. If your child is very active, for example, it is unrealistic to expect him to sit quietly during a four-hour plane or bus trip. Knowing that, you can increase the likelihood of positive experiences by planning ahead. Bring coloring books, picture books, or small toys to occupy the young child in a restaurant or at a family gathering. Take frequent "exercise stops" on a long car trip. If your child is unusually sensitive, shy, or "slow-to-warm-up," give her plenty of time to make the transition to new situations and provide lots of preparation so that she knows what to expect.

5. Understand your child's age-related cognitive abilities and limitations.

Some parents make the mistake of assuming that children think in the same way adults do. They may see a toddler or even an infant as purposely "misbehaving," "being naughty," or "rebelling," when the little one is simply doing what 1-year-olds or 3-year-olds do. Your expectations for appropriate behavior should be geared to the child's age and developmental stage (Barclay & Houts, 1995b). Having a thorough understanding of the information in this chapter is a good start. You might also consider taking a developmental psychology or child development class. Or go to your college library and check out some of the developmental psychology texts. By understanding your child's cognitive abilities and limitations at each stage of development, you're less likely to misinterpret behavior or to place inappropriate demands on him.

6. Don't expect perfection, and learn to go with the flow.

Accidents happen. Mistakes occur. Children get cranky or grumpy, especially when they're tired or hungry. Don't get too bent out of shape when your child's behavior is less than perfect. Be patient. Moments of conflict with children are a natural, inevitable, and healthy part of growing up. Look at those moments as part of the process by which a child achieves autonomy and a sense of self.

Finally, effective parenting is an ongoing process in which you, as the parent, should be regularly assessing your impact on your child. It's not always easy to combine responsiveness with control, or flexibility with an appropriate level of firmness. When you make a mistake, admit it not just to yourself, but also to your child. In doing so, you'll teach your child how to behave when she makes a mistake. As you'll discover, children are remarkably forgiving—and also resilient.

Chapter Review
Lifespan Development

Key Points

Introduction: Your Life Story

■ Developmental psychologists study the many ways in which people change over the lifespan. Key themes in **developmental psychology** include understanding the stages of lifespan development, the nature of change, and the interaction between heredity and environment.

Genetic Contributions to Your Life Story

■ At conception, the union of the sperm and egg result in the single-celled **zygote.** The zygote contains genetic instructions inherited from the biological parents, encoded in the **chromosomes.** Chromosomes are made of **deoxyribonucleic acid (DNA).** Each chromosome has thousands of DNA segments called **genes,** which encode instructions for making a particular protein.

■ An organism's unique **genotype** is found in almost every body cell. Cells differ not because they carry different genes but because they result from different genes being activated or expressed. Mapping of the **human genome** resulted in the discovery that humans have only 20,000–25,000 genes. Gene variations are called **alleles**. Some gene alleles are dominant or recessive. Most characteristics involve the interaction of multiple genes.

■ The **phenotype** results from the interaction of genes and environmental factors. Different genotypes respond differently to the same environmental factors.

Prenatal Development

■ During the nine months that make up the **prenatal stage,** the zygote develops into a full-term fetus. The prenatal stage includes the **germinal period,** the **embryonic period,** and the **fetal period.** The greatest vulnerability to **teratogens** occurs during the embryonic stage, when major bodily systems are forming.

Development During Infancy and Childhood

■ Newborns are equipped with reflexes and sensory capabilities that enhance their chances for survival. Vision, hearing, and smell are attuned to interaction with caregivers. The brain develops rapidly after birth. The sequence of motor skill development is generally universal, although there is individual variation in the rate of development.

■ Thomas and Chess demonstrated that infants seem to be born with different **temperaments.** They identified three basic temperamental patterns: easy, difficult, and slow-to-warm-up. According to Kagan, infants can be classified in terms of reactivity. Temperamental qualities seem to have a biological basis and persist through life, although they can be modified by environmental influences.

■ According to attachment theory, the infant's ability to thrive is dependent on the quality of his or her **attachment** to caregivers. Secure attachment develops when parents are sensitive and responsive to the infant's needs. Insecure attachment may develop when parents are insensitive to the infant's needs.

■ Infants are biologically predisposed to learn language. Adults encourage language development in infants by using motherese, also called infant-directed speech.

■ The stages of language development include cooing, babbling, the one-word stage, and the two-word stage. At every stage, **comprehension vocabulary** is larger than **production vocabulary.**

■ Each culture attaches its own significance to **gender. Gender roles** and **gender identity** begin to develop in early childhood. During childhood, boys and girls develop different toy preferences and play with members of their own sex.

■ Two contemporary theories that explain gender-role development are social learning theory and gender schema theory. **Social learning theory** is based on the principles of learning. Through reinforcement, punishment, and modeling, children learn the appropriate behaviors for each gender. **Gender schema theory** is based on the idea that children actively develop mental categories for each gender. Children's gender schemas influence what they learn and remember.

■ According to Jean Piaget's theory of cognitive development, children progress through distinct cognitive stages, each of which represents a shift in how they think and understand the world.

■ **Object permanence** is acquired during the **sensorimotor** stage. **Symbolic thought** is acquired during the **preoperational stage.** Preoperational thought is **egocentric** and characterized by **irreversibility** and **centration.** Thus, the preoperational child is unable to grasp the principles of **conservation.** Children become capable of logical thought during the **concrete operational stage,** but thinking is limited to tangible objects and events. During the **formal operational stage,** the adolescent can engage in logical mental operations involving abstract concepts and hypothetical situations.

■ Criticisms of Piaget's theory include the following: Piaget underestimated the cognitive abilities of infants and children; he underestimated the impact of the social and cultural environment on cognitive development; and he overestimated the degree to which people achieve formal operational thought processes. In contrast to Piaget's theory, Vygotsky's idea of the **zone of proximal development** emphasizes that children can progress to higher cognitive levels through the assistance of others who are more competent.

Two Generations

Personality

Prologue

The Secret Twin

The twins, Kenneth and Julian, were born a few years after the turn of the last century. At first, their parents, Gertrude and Henry, thought they were identical. Both had dark hair and deep brown eyes. Many years later, Kenneth's son, your author Don, would inherit these qualities.

But Gertrude and Henry quickly learned to tell the twins apart. Kenneth was slightly larger than Julian, and, even as infants, their personalities were distinctly different. In the photographs of Kenneth and Julian as children, Julian smiles broadly, almost merrily, his head cocked slightly. But Kenneth always looks straight at the camera, his expression thoughtful, serious, more intense.

We don't know much about Julian's childhood. Kenneth kept Julian's existence a closely guarded secret for more than 50 years. In fact, it was only a few years before his own death that Kenneth revealed that he had once had a twin brother named Julian.

Still, it's possible to get glimpses of Julian's early life from the letters the boys wrote home from summer camp in 1919 and 1920. Kenneth's letters to his mother were affectionate and respectful, telling her about their daily activities and reassuring her that he would look after his twin brother. "I reminded Julian about the boats and I will watch him <u>good</u>," Kenneth wrote in one letter. Julian's letters were equally affectionate, but shorter and filled with misspelled words. Julian's letters also revealed glimpses of his impulsive nature. He repeatedly promised his mother, "I will not go out in the boats alone again."

Julian's impulsive nature was to have a significant impact on his life. When he was 12 years old, Julian darted in front of a car and was seriously injured, sustaining a concussion. In retrospect, Kenneth believed that that was when Julian's problems began. Perhaps it was, because soon after the accident Julian first got into serious trouble: He was caught stealing money from the "poor box" at church.

Although Kenneth claimed that Julian had always been the smarter twin, Julian fell behind in high school and graduated a year later than Kenneth. After high school, Kenneth left the quiet farming community of Grinnell, Iowa, and moved to Minneapolis. He quickly became self-sufficient, taking a job managing newspaper carriers. Julian stayed in Grinnell and became apprenticed to learn typesetting. Given Julian's propensity for adventure, it's not surprising that he found typesetting monotonous. In the spring of 1928, Julian left Iowa, heading east to look for more interesting possibilities.

The Twins Julian *(left)* and Kenneth *(right),* with their father Henry, when they were about 10 years old. As boys, Kenneth and Julian were inseparable.

He found them in Tennessee. A few months after Julian left Iowa, Henry received word that Julian had been arrested for armed robbery and sentenced to 15 years in a Tennessee state prison. Though Kenneth was only 22 years old, Henry gave him a large sum of money and the family car and sent him to try to get Julian released.

Kenneth's conversation with the judge in Knoxville was the first of many times that he would deal with the judicial system on someone else's behalf. After much negotiation, the judge agreed: If Julian promised to leave Tennessee and never return, and Kenneth paid the cash "fines," Julian would be released from prison.

When Julian walked through the prison gates the next morning, Kenneth stood waiting with a fresh suit of clothes. "Mother and Father want you to come back to Grinnell," he told Julian. But Julian would not hear of it, saying that instead he wanted to go to California to seek his fortune.

"I can't let you do that, Julian," Kenneth said, looking hard at his twin brother.

"You can't stop me, brother," Julian responded, with a cocky smile. Reluctantly, Kenneth kept just enough money to buy himself a train ticket back to Iowa. He gave Julian the rest of the money and the family car.

Julian got as far as Phoenix, Arizona, before he met his destiny. In broad daylight, he robbed a drugstore at gunpoint. As he backed out of the store, a policeman spotted him. A gun battle followed, and Julian was shot twice. Somehow he managed to escape and holed up in a hotel room. Alone and untended, Julian died two days later from the bullet wounds. Once again, Kenneth was sent to retrieve his twin brother.

On a bitterly cold November morning in 1928, Julian's immediate family laid him to rest in the family plot in Grinnell. On the one hand, Kenneth felt largely responsible for Julian's misguided life. "I should have tried harder to help Julian," Kenneth later reflected. On the other hand, Julian had disgraced the family. From the day Julian was buried, the family never spoke of him again, not even in private.

Kenneth took it upon himself to atone for the failings of his twin brother. In the fall of 1929, Kenneth entered law school in Tennessee—the same state from which he had secured Julian's release from prison. Three years later, at the height of the Great Depression, Kenneth established himself as a lawyer in Sioux City, Iowa, where he would practice law for more than 50 years.

As an attorney, Kenneth Hockenbury was known for his integrity, his intensity in the courtroom, and his willingness to take cases regardless of the client's ability to pay. "Someone must defend the poor," he said repeatedly. In lieu of money, he often accepted labor from a working man or produce from farmers.

Sixty years after Julian's death, Kenneth died. But unlike the sparse gathering that had attended Julian's burial, scores of people came to pay their last respects to Kenneth Hockenbury. "Your father helped me so much," stranger after stranger told Don at Kenneth's funeral. Without question, Kenneth had devoted his life to helping others.

Why did Kenneth and Julian turn out so differently? Two boys, born on the same day into the same middle-class family. Kenneth the conscientious, serious one; Julian the laughing boy with mischief in his eyes. How can we explain the fundamental differences in their personalities?

No doubt your family, too, is made up of people with very different personalities. By the end of this chapter, you'll have a much greater appreciation for how psychologists explain such personality differences.

Introduction

What Is Personality?

Key Theme
■ Personality is defined as an individual's unique and relatively consistent patterns of thinking, feeling, and behaving.

Key Question
■ What are the four major theoretical perspectives on personality?

That you already have an intuitive understanding of the word *personality* is easy to demonstrate. Just from reading this chapter's Prologue, you could easily describe different aspects of Kenneth's and Julian's personalities. Indeed, we frequently toss around the word *personality* in everyday conversations. "He's very competent, but he has an abrasive personality." "She's got such a delightful personality, you can't help liking her."

Your intuitive understanding of personality is probably very similar to the way that psychologists define the concept. **Personality** is defined as an individual's unique and relatively consistent patterns of thinking, feeling, and behaving. A **personality theory** is an attempt to describe and explain how people are similar, how they are different, and why every individual is unique. In short, a personality theory ambitiously tries to explain the *whole person*. At the outset, it's important to stress that no single theory can adequately explain *all* of the aspects of human personality. Every personality theory has its unique strengths and limitations.

Personality theories often reflect the work of a single individual or of a few closely associated individuals. Thus, it's not surprising that many personality theories bear the distinct personal stamp of their creators to a much greater degree than do other kinds of psychological theories. Consequently, we've tried to let the personality theorists speak for themselves. Throughout this chapter, you'll encounter carefully chosen quotations from the theorists' own writings. These quotations will give you brief glimpses into the minds of some of the most influential thinkers in psychology.

There are many personality theories, but they can be roughly grouped under four basic perspectives: the psychoanalytic, humanistic, social cognitive, and trait perspectives. In a nutshell, here's what each perspective emphasizes:

■ The *psychoanalytic perspective* emphasizes the importance of unconscious processes and the influence of early childhood experience.

■ The *humanistic perspective* represents an optimistic look at human nature, emphasizing the self and the fulfillment of a person's unique potential.

■ The *social cognitive perspective* emphasizes learning and conscious cognitive processes, including the importance of beliefs about the self, goal setting, and self-regulation.

■ The *trait perspective* emphasizes the description and measurement of specific personality differences among individuals.

After looking at some of the major personality theories that reflect each perspective, we'll consider a closely related topic—how personality is measured and evaluated. And yes, we'll talk about the famous inkblots. But for the inkblots to make sense, we need to trace the evolution of modern personality theories. We'll begin with the tale of a bearded, cigar-smoking gentleman from Vienna of whom you just may have heard—Sigmund Freud.

Explaining Personality Some people are outgoing, expressive, and fun-loving, like the mother–daughter pair in this picture. Other people consistently display the opposite qualities. Are such personality differences due to early childhood experiences? Genetics? Social environment? Personality theories attempt to account for the individual differences that make each one of us unique.

personality
An individual's unique and relatively consistent patterns of thinking, feeling, and behaving.

personality theory
A theory that attempts to describe and explain similarities and differences in people's patterns of thinking, feeling, and behaving.

The Psychoanalytic Perspective on Personality

Key Theme
- Freud's psychoanalysis stresses the importance of unconscious forces, sexual and aggressive instincts, and early childhood experience.

Key Questions
- What were the key influences on Sigmund Freud's thinking?
- How are unconscious influences revealed?
- What are the three basic structures of personality, and what are the defense mechanisms?

Freud the Outsider Sigmund Freud (1856–1939) is shown with his wife, Martha, and youngest child, Anna, at their Vienna home in 1898. Freud always considered himself to be an outsider. First, he was a Jew at a time when anti-Semitism was strong in Europe. Second, Freud's belief that expressions of sexuality are reflected in the behavior of infants and young children was unconventional and shocking to many. To some degree, however, Freud enjoyed his role as the isolated scientist—it served him well in trying to set himself, and his ideas on personality, apart from other researchers.

Sigmund Freud, one of the most influential figures of the twentieth century, was the founder of psychoanalysis. **Psychoanalysis** is a theory of personality that stresses the influence of unconscious mental processes, the importance of sexual and aggressive instincts, and the enduring effects of early childhood experience on personality. Because so many of Freud's ideas have become part of our common culture, it is difficult to imagine just how radical a figure he appeared to his contemporaries. The following biographical sketch highlights some of the important influences that shaped Freud's ideas and theory.

The Life of Sigmund Freud

Sigmund Freud was born in 1856 in what is today Pribôr, Czech Republic. When he was 4 years old, his family moved to Vienna, where he lived until the last year of his life. Sigmund was the firstborn child of Jacob and Amalie Freud. By the time he was 10 years old, there were six more siblings in the household. Of the seven children, Sigmund was his mother's favorite. As Freud later wrote, "A man who has been the indisputable favorite of his mother keeps for life the feeling of being a conqueror, that confidence of success that often induces real success" (Jones, 1953).

Freud was extremely bright and intensely ambitious. He studied medicine, became a physician, and then proved himself an outstanding physiological researcher. Early in his career, Freud was among the first investigators of a new drug that had anesthetic and mood-altering properties—cocaine. However, one of Freud's colleagues received credit for the discovery of the anesthetic properties of cocaine, a matter that left Freud bitter. Adding to his disappointment, Freud's enthusiasm for the medical potential of cocaine quickly faded when he recognized that the drug was addictive (Fancher, 1973).

Prospects for an academic career in scientific research were very poor, especially for a Jew in Vienna, which was intensely anti-Semitic at that time. So when he married Martha Bernays in 1886, Freud reluctantly gave up physiological research for a private practice in neurology. The income from private practice would be needed: Sigmund and Martha had six children. One of Freud's daughters, Anna Freud, later became an important psychoanalytic theorist.

psychoanalysis
Sigmund Freud's theory of personality, which emphasizes unconscious determinants of behavior, sexual and aggressive instinctual drives, and the enduring effects of early childhood experiences on later personality development.

free association
A psychoanalytic technique in which the patient spontaneously reports all thoughts, feelings, and mental images as they come to mind.

Influences in the Development of Freud's Ideas

Freud's theory evolved gradually during his first 20 years of private practice. He based his theory on observations of his patients as well as on self-analysis. An early influence on Freud was Joseph Breuer, a highly respected physician. Breuer described to Freud the striking case of a young woman with an array of puzzling psychological and physical symptoms. Breuer found that if he first hypnotized this patient, then asked her to talk freely about a given symptom, forgotten memories of traumatic events emerged. After she freely expressed the pent-up emotions associated with the event, her symptom disappeared. Breuer called this phenomenon *catharsis* (Freud, 1925).

At first, Freud embraced Breuer's technique, but he found that not all of his patients could be hypnotized. Eventually, Freud dropped the use of hypnosis and developed his own technique of **free association** to help his patients uncover forgotten memories. Freud's patients would spontaneously report their uncensored thoughts, mental images, and feelings as they came to mind. From these "free associations," the thread that led to the crucial long-forgotten memories could be unraveled. Breuer and Freud described several of their case studies in their landmark book, *Studies on Hysteria*. Its publication in 1895 marked the beginning of psychoanalysis.

In 1900, Freud published what many consider his most important work, *The Interpretation of Dreams*. By the early 1900s, Freud had developed the basic tenets of his psychoanalytic theory and was no longer the isolated scientist. He was gaining international recognition and developing a following.

In 1904, Freud published what was to become one of his most popular books, *The Psychopathology of Everyday Life*. He described how unconscious thoughts, feelings, and wishes are often reflected in acts of forgetting, inadvertent slips of the tongue, accidents, and errors. By 1909, Freud's influence was also felt in the United States, when he and other psychoanalysts were invited to lecture at Clark University in Massachusetts. For the next 30 years, Freud continued to refine his theory, publishing many books, articles, and lectures.

The last two decades of Freud's life were filled with many personal tragedies. The terrible devastation of World War I weighed heavily on his mind. In 1920, one of his daughters died. In the early 1920s, Freud developed cancer of the jaw, a condition for which he would ultimately undergo more than 30 operations. And during the late 1920s and early 1930s, the Nazis were steadily gaining power in Germany.

Given the climate of the times, it's not surprising that Freud came to focus on humanity's destructive tendencies. For years he had asserted that sexuality was the fundamental human motive, but now he added aggression as a second powerful human instinct. During this period, Freud wrote *Civilization and Its Discontents* (1930), in which he applied his psychoanalytic perspective to civilization as a whole. The central theme of the book is that human nature and civilization are in basic conflict—a conflict that cannot be resolved.

Freud's extreme pessimism was undoubtedly a reflection of the destruction he saw all around him. By 1933, Adolf Hitler had seized power in Germany. Freud's books were banned and publicly burned in Berlin. Five years later, the Nazis marched into Austria, seizing control of Freud's homeland. Although Freud's life was clearly threatened, it was only after his youngest daughter, Anna, had been detained and questioned by the Gestapo that Freud reluctantly agreed to leave Vienna. Under great duress, Freud moved his family to the safety of England. A year later, his cancer returned. In 1939, Freud died in London at the age of 83 (Gay, 1988).

This brief sketch cannot do justice to the richness of Freud's life and the influence of his culture and society on his ideas. Today, Freud's legacy continues to influence psychology, philosophy, literature, and art (Gay, 1999).

Freud the Leader In 1909, Freud visited the United States to lecture on his ideas at Clark University in Massachusetts. A year later, Freud and his many followers founded the International Psychoanalytic Association.

Freud the Exile In the spring of 1938, Freud fled Nazi persecution for the safety of London on the eve of World War II. Four of Freud's sisters who remained behind later died in the Nazi extermination camps. He is shown arriving in England, his eldest daughter, Mathilde, at his side. Freud died in London on September 23, 1939.

unconscious

In Freud's theory, a term used to describe thoughts, feelings, wishes, and drives that are operating below the level of conscious awareness.

Freud's Dynamic Theory of Personality

Freud (1940) saw personality and behavior as the result of a constant interplay between conflicting psychological forces. These psychological forces operate at three different levels of awareness: the conscious, the preconscious, and the unconscious. All the thoughts, feelings, and sensations that you're aware of at this particular moment represent the *conscious* level. The *preconscious* contains information that you're not currently aware of but can easily bring to conscious awareness, such as memories of recent events or your street address.

However, the conscious and preconscious are merely the visible tip of the iceberg of the mind. The bulk of this psychological iceberg is made up of the **unconscious,** which lies submerged below the waterline of the preconscious and conscious (see Figure 10.1). You're not directly aware of these submerged thoughts, feelings, wishes, and drives, but the unconscious exerts an enormous influence on your conscious thoughts and behavior.

Although it is not directly accessible, Freud (1904) believed that unconscious material often seeps through to the conscious level in distorted, disguised, or symbolic forms. Like a detective searching for clues, Freud carefully analyzed his patients' reports of dreams and free associations for evidence of unconscious wishes, fantasies, and conflicts. Dream analysis was particularly important to Freud. "The interpretation of dreams is the royal road to a knowledge of the unconscious activities of the mind," he wrote in *The Interpretation of Dreams* (1900). Beneath the surface images, or *manifest content,* of a dream lies its *latent content*—the true, hidden, unconscious meaning that is disguised in the dream symbols (see Chapter 4).

Freud (1904, 1933) believed that the unconscious can also be revealed in unintentional actions, such as accidents, mistakes, instances of forgetting, and inadvertent slips of the tongue, which are often referred to as "Freudian slips." According to Freud, many seemingly accidental or unintentional actions are not accidental at all, but are determined by unconscious motives.

FIGURE 10.1 Levels of Awareness and the Structure of Personality Freud believed that personality is composed of three psychological processes—the id, the ego, and the superego—that operate at different levels of awareness. If you think of personality as being like an iceberg, the bulk of this psychological iceberg is represented by the irrational, impulsive id, which lies beneath the waterline of consciousness. Unlike the entirely unconscious id, the rational ego and the moralistic superego are at least partially conscious.

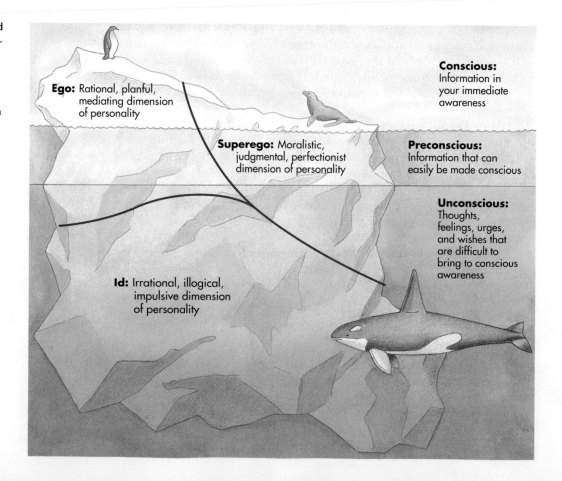

Ego: Rational, planful, mediating dimension of personality

Superego: Moralistic, judgmental, perfectionist dimension of personality

Id: Irrational, illogical, impulsive dimension of personality

Conscious: Information in your immediate awareness

Preconscious: Information that can easily be made conscious

Unconscious: Thoughts, feelings, urges, and wishes that are difficult to bring to conscious awareness

The Structure of Personality

According to Freud (1933), each person possesses a certain amount of psychological energy. This psychological energy evolves to form the three basic structures of personality—the id, the ego, and the superego (see Figure 10.1). Understand that these are not separate identities or brain structures. Rather, they are distinct psychological processes.

The **id,** the most primitive part of the personality, is entirely unconscious and present at birth. The id is completely immune to logic, values, morality, danger, and the demands of the external world. It is the original source of psychological energy, parts of which will later evolve into the ego and superego (Freud, 1933, 1940). The id is rather difficult to describe in words. "We come nearer to the id with images," Freud (1933) wrote, "and call it a chaos, a cauldron of seething excitement."

The id's reservoir of psychological energy is derived from two conflicting instinctual drives: the life instinct and the death instinct. The *life instinct,* which Freud called **Eros,** consists of biological urges that perpetuate the existence of the individual and the species—hunger, thirst, physical comfort, and, most important, sexuality. Freud (1915c) used the word **libido** to refer specifically to sexual energy or motivation. The *death instinct,* which Freud (1940) called **Thanatos,** is destructive energy that is reflected in aggressive, reckless, and life-threatening behaviors, including self-destructive actions.

The id is ruled by the **pleasure principle**—the relentless drive toward immediate satisfaction of the instinctual urges, especially sexual urges (Freud, 1920). Thus, the id strives to increase pleasure, reduce tension, and avoid pain. Even though it operates unconsciously, Freud saw the pleasure principle as the most fundamental human motive.

Equipped only with the id, the newborn infant is completely driven by the pleasure principle. When cold, wet, hungry, or uncomfortable, the newborn wants his needs addressed immediately. As the infant gains experience with the external world, however, he learns that his caretakers can't or won't always immediately satisfy those needs.

Thus, a new dimension of personality develops from part of the id's psychological energy—the **ego.** Partly conscious, the ego represents the organized, rational, and planning dimensions of personality (Freud, 1933). As the mediator between the id's instinctual demands and the restrictions of the outer world, the ego operates on the reality principle. The **reality principle** is the capacity to postpone gratification until the appropriate time or circumstances exist in the external world (Freud, 1940).

As the young child gains experience, she gradually learns acceptable ways to satisfy her desires and instincts, such as waiting her turn rather than pushing another child off a playground swing. Hence, the ego is the pragmatic part of the personality that learns various compromises to reduce the tension of the id's

Appealing to the Id How would Freud explain the appeal of this billboard? In Freud's theory, the id is ruled by the pleasure principle—the instinctual drive to increase pleasure, reduce tension, and avoid pain. Advertisements like this one, which encourage us to be hedonistic, appeal to the pleasure principle.

id
Latin for *the it*; in Freud's theory, the completely unconscious, irrational component of personality that seeks immediate satisfaction of instinctual urges and drives; ruled by the pleasure principle.

Eros
In Freud's theory, the self-preservation or life instinct, reflected in the expression of basic biological urges that perpetuate the existence of the individual and the species.

libido
In Freud's theory, the psychological and emotional energy associated with expressions of sexuality; the sex drive.

Thanatos
In Freud's theory, the death instinct, reflected in aggressive, destructive, and self-destructive actions.

pleasure principle
In Freud's theory, the motive to obtain pleasure and avoid tension or discomfort; the most fundamental human motive and the guiding principle of the id.

ego
Latin for *I*; in Freud's theory, the partly conscious rational component of personality that regulates thoughts and behavior and is most in touch with the demands of the external world.

reality principle
In Freud's theory, the capacity to accommodate external demands by postponing gratification until the appropriate time or circumstances exist.

cathy®   by Cathy Guisewite

Establishing the Superego "Don't take something without permission" is just one of the many rules and values we learn as children from parents and other authorities. The internalization of such values is what Freud called the superego—the inner voice that is our conscience. When we fail to live up to its moral ideals, the superego imposes feelings of guilt, shame, and inferiority.

superego
In Freud's theory, the partly conscious, self-evaluative, moralistic component of personality that is formed through the internalization of parental and societal rules.

ego defense mechanisms
In psychoanalytic theory, largely unconscious distortions of thoughts or perceptions that act to reduce anxiety.

repression
In psychoanalytic theory, the unconscious exclusion of anxiety-provoking thoughts, feelings, and memories from conscious awareness; the most fundamental ego defense mechanism.

displacement
In psychoanalytic theory, the ego defense mechanism that involves unconsciously shifting the target of an emotional urge to a substitute target that is less threatening or dangerous.

sublimation
In psychoanalytic theory, an ego defense mechanism that involves redirecting sexual urges toward productive, socially acceptable, nonsexual activities; a form of displacement.

instinctual urges. If the ego can't identify an acceptable compromise to satisfy an instinctual urge, such as a sexual urge, it can *repress* the impulse, or remove it from conscious awareness (Freud, 1915a).

In early childhood, the ego must deal with external parental demands and limitations. Implicit in those demands are the parents' values and morals, their ideas of the right and wrong ways to think, act, and feel. Eventually, the child encounters other advocates of society's values, such as teachers and religious and legal authorities (Freud, 1926). Gradually, these social values move from being externally imposed demands to being *internalized* rules and values.

By about age 5 or 6, the young child has developed an internal, parental voice that is partly conscious—the **superego.** As the internal representation of parental and societal values, the superego evaluates the acceptability of behavior and thoughts, then praises or admonishes. Put simply, your superego represents your conscience, issuing demands "like a strict father with a child" (Freud, 1926). It judges your own behavior as right or wrong, good or bad, acceptable or unacceptable. And, should you fail to live up to these morals, the superego can be harshly punitive, imposing feelings of inferiority, guilt, shame, self-doubt, and anxiety. If we apply Freud's terminology to the twins described in the chapter Prologue, Kenneth's superego was clearly stronger than Julian's.

The Ego Defense Mechanisms
Unconscious Self-Deceptions

The ego has a difficult task. It must be strong, flexible, and resourceful to successfully mediate conflicts among the instinctual demands of the id, the moral authority of the superego, and external restrictions. According to Freud (1923), everyone experiences an ongoing daily battle among these three warring personality processes.

When the demands of the id or superego threaten to overwhelm the ego, *anxiety* results (Freud, 1915b). If instinctual id impulses overpower the ego, a person may act impulsively and perhaps destructively. Using Freud's terminology, you could say that Julian's id was out of control when he stole from the church and tried to rob the drugstore. In contrast, if superego demands overwhelm the ego, an individual may suffer from guilt, self-reproach, or even suicidal impulses for failing to live up to the superego's moral standards (Freud, 1936). Using Freudian terminology again, it is probably safe to say that Kenneth's feelings of guilt over Julian were inspired by his superego.

If a realistic solution or compromise is not possible, the ego may temporarily reduce anxiety by *distorting* thoughts or perceptions of reality through processes that Freud called **ego defense mechanisms** (A. Freud, 1946; Freud, 1915c). By resorting to these largely unconscious self-deceptions, the ego can maintain an integrated sense of self while searching for a more acceptable and realistic solution to a conflict between the id and superego.

The most fundamental ego defense mechanism is **repression** (Freud, 1915a, 1936). To some degree, repression occurs in every ego defense mechanism. In simple terms, repression is unconscious forgetting. Unbeknownst to the person, anxiety-producing thoughts, feelings, or impulses are pushed out of conscious awareness into the unconscious. Common examples include traumatic events, past failures, embarrassments, disappointments, the names of disliked people, episodes of physical pain or illness, and unacceptable urges.

Repression, however, is not an all-or-nothing psychological process. As Freud (1939) explained, "The repressed material retains its impetus to penetrate into consciousness." In other words, if you encounter a situation that is very similar to one you've repressed, bits and pieces of memories of the previous situation may begin to resurface. In such instances, the ego may employ other defense mechanisms that allow the urge or information to remain partially conscious.

This is what occurs with the ego defense mechanism of displacement. **Displacement** occurs when emotional impulses are redirected to a substitute object or person, usually one less threatening or dangerous than the original source of conflict (A. Freud, 1946). For example, an employee angered by his supervisor's unfair treatment may displace his hostility onto family members when he comes home from work. He consciously experiences anger but directs it toward someone other than its true target, which remains unconscious.

Freud (1930) believed that a special form of displacement, called *sublimation,* is largely responsible for the productive and creative contributions of people and even of whole societies. **Sublimation** involves displacing sexual urges toward "an aim other than, and remote from, that of sexual gratification" (Freud, 1914). In effect, sublimation channels sexual urges into productive, socially acceptable, nonsexual activities.

The major defense mechanisms are summarized in Table 10.1. In Freud's view, the drawback to using any defense mechanism is that maintaining these self-deceptions requires psychological energy. As Freud (1936) pointed out regarding the most basic defense mechanism, repression does not take place "on a single occasion" but rather demands "a continuous expenditure of effort." Such effort depletes psychological energy that is needed to cope effectively with the demands of daily life.

The use of defense mechanisms is very common. Many psychologically healthy people temporarily use ego defense mechanisms to deal with stressful events. When ego defense mechanisms are used in limited areas and on a short-term basis, psychological energy is not seriously depleted. Ideally, we strive to maintain realistic perceptions of the world and our motives, and search for workable solutions to conflicts and problems. Using ego defense mechanisms is often a way of buying time

Sublimation In Freud's view, creative or productive behaviors represent the rechanneling of sexual energy, or libido—an ego defense mechanism he termed *sublimation.* Freud believed that civilization's greatest achievements are the result of the sublimation of instinctual energy into socially acceptable activities. Later personality theorists criticized Freud's refusal to consider creativity a drive in its own right.

Table 10.1

The Major Ego Defense Mechanisms

Defense	Description	Example
Repression	The complete exclusion from consciousness of anxiety-producing thoughts, feelings, or impulses; most basic defense mechanism.	Three years after being hospitalized for back surgery, the person can remember only vague details about the event.
Displacement	The redirection of emotional impulses toward a substitute person or object, usually one less threatening or dangerous than the original source of conflict.	Angered by a neighbor's hateful comment, a mother spanks her daughter for accidentally spilling her milk.
Sublimation	A form of displacement in which sexual urges are rechanneled into productive, nonsexual activities.	A graduate student works on her thesis 14 hours a day while her husband is on an extended business trip.
Rationalization	Justifying one's actions or feelings with socially acceptable explanations rather than consciously acknowledging one's true motives or desires.	After being rejected by a prestigious university, a student explains that he is glad, because he would be happier at a smaller, less competitive college.
Projection	The attribution of one's own unacceptable urges or qualities to others.	A married woman who is sexually attracted to a co-worker accuses him of flirting with her.
Reaction formation	Thinking or behaving in a way that is the extreme opposite of unacceptable urges or impulses.	Threatened by his awakening sexual attraction to girls, an adolescent boy goes out of his way to tease and torment adolescent girls.
Denial	The failure to recognize or acknowledge the existence of anxiety-provoking information.	Despite drinking five martinis every night, a man says he is not an alcoholic because he never drinks before 5 PM.
Undoing	A form of unconscious repentance that involves neutralizing or atoning for an unacceptable action or thought with a second action or thought.	A woman who gets a tax refund by cheating on her taxes makes a larger than usual donation to the church collection on the following Sunday.
Regression	Retreating to a behavior pattern characteristic of an earlier stage of development.	After her parents' bitter divorce, a 10-year-old girl refuses to sleep alone in her room, crawling into bed with her mother.

psychosexual stages
In Freud's theory, age-related developmental periods in which the child's sexual urges are focused on different areas of the body and are expressed through the activities associated with those areas.

Oedipus complex
In Freud's theory, a child's unconscious sexual desire for the opposite-sex parent, usually accompanied by hostile feelings toward the same-sex parent.

identification
In psychoanalytic theory, an ego defense mechanism that involves reducing anxiety by imitating the behavior and characteristics of another person.

while we consciously or unconsciously wrestle with more realistic solutions for whatever is troubling us. But when defense mechanisms delay or interfere with our use of more constructive coping strategies, they can be counterproductive.

Personality Development
The Psychosexual Stages

Key Theme
- ■ The psychosexual stages are age-related developmental periods, and each stage represents a different focus of the id's sexual energies.

Key Questions
- ■ What are the five psychosexual stages, and what are the core conflicts of each stage?
- ■ What is the consequence of fixation?
- ■ What role does the Oedipus complex play in personality development?

According to Freud (1905), people progress through five psychosexual stages of development. The foundations of adult personality are established during the first five years of life, as the child progresses through the *oral, anal,* and *phallic* psychosexual stages. The *latency stage* occurs during late childhood, and the fifth and final stage, the *genital stage,* begins in adolescence.

Each psychosexual stage represents a different focus of the id's sexual energies. Freud (1940) contended that "sexual life does not begin only at puberty, but starts with clear manifestations after birth." This statement is often misinterpreted. Freud was *not* saying that an infant experiences sexual urges in the same way that an adult does. Instead, Freud believed that the infant or young child expresses primitive sexual urges by seeking sensual pleasure from different areas of the body. Thus, the **psychosexual stages** are age-related developmental periods in which sexual impulses are focused on different bodily zones and are expressed through the activities associated with these areas.

Over the first five years of life, the expression of primitive sexual urges progresses from one bodily zone to another in a distinct order: the mouth, the anus, and the genitals. The first year of life is characterized as the *oral stage*. During this time the infant derives pleasure through the oral activities of sucking, chewing, and biting. During the next two years, pleasure is derived through elimination and acquiring control over elimination—the *anal stage*. In the *phallic stage*, pleasure seeking is focused on the genitals.

Fixation
Unresolved Developmental Conflicts

At each psychosexual stage, Freud (1905) believed, the infant or young child is faced with a developmental conflict that must be successfully resolved in order to move on to the next stage. The heart of this conflict is the degree to which parents either frustrate or overindulge the child's expression of pleasurable feelings. Hence, Freud (1940) believed that parental attitudes and the timing of specific child-rearing events, such as weaning or toilet training, leave a lasting influence on personality development.

If frustrated, the child will be left with feelings of unmet needs characteristic of that stage. If overindulged, the child may be reluctant to move on to the next stage. In either case, the result of an unresolved developmental conflict is *fixation* at a particular stage. The person continues to seek pleasure through behaviors that are similar to those associated with that psychosexual stage. For example, the adult who constantly chews gum, smokes, or bites her fingernails may have unresolved oral psychosexual conflicts.

"He has a few things to work through, but we're good together."

The Oedipus Complex
A Psychosexual Drama

The most critical conflict that the child must successfully resolve for healthy personality and sexual development occurs during the phallic stage (Freud, 1923, 1940). As the child becomes more aware of pleasure derived from the genital area, Freud believed, the child develops a sexual attraction to the opposite-sex parent and hostility toward the same-sex parent. This is the famous **Oedipus complex,** named after the protagonist of a Greek myth. Abandoned at birth, Oedipus does not know the identity of his parents. As an adult, Oedipus unknowingly kills his father and marries his mother.

According to Freud, this attraction to the opposite-sex parent plays out as a sexual drama in the child's mind, a drama with different plot twists for boys and for girls. For boys, the Oedipus complex unfolds as a confrontation with the father for the affections of the mother. The little boy feels hostility and jealousy toward his father, but he realizes that his father is more physically powerful. The boy experiences *castration anxiety,* or the fear that his father will punish him by castrating him (Freud, 1933).

To resolve the Oedipus complex and these anxieties, the little boy ultimately joins forces with his former enemy by resorting to the defense mechanism of **identification.** That is, he imitates and internalizes his father's values, attitudes, and mannerisms. There is, however, one strict limitation in identifying with the father. Only the father can enjoy the sexual affections of the mother. This limitation becomes internalized as a taboo against incestuous urges in the boy's developing superego, a taboo that is enforced by the superego's use of guilt and societal restrictions (Freud, 1905, 1923).

Girls also ultimately resolve the Oedipus complex by identifying with the same-sex parent and developing a strong superego taboo against incestuous urges. But the underlying sexual drama in girls follows different themes. The little girl discovers that little boys have a penis and that she does not. She feels a sense of deprivation and loss that Freud termed *penis envy.*

According to Freud (1940), the little girl blames her mother for "sending her into the world so insufficiently equipped." Thus, she develops contempt for and resentment toward her mother. However, in her attempt to take her mother's place with her father, she also *identifies* with her mother. Like the little boy, the little girl internalizes the attributes of the same-sex parent.

Freud's views on female sexuality, particularly the concept of penis envy, are among his most severely criticized ideas. Perhaps recognizing that his explanation of female psychosexual development rested on shaky ground, Freud (1926) admitted, "We know less about the sexual life of little girls than of boys. But we need not feel ashamed of this distinction. After all, the sexual life of adult women is a 'dark continent' for psychology."

Competing with Mom for Dad? According to Freud, the child identifies with the same-sex parent as a way of resolving sexual attraction toward the opposite-sex parent—the Oedipus complex. Freud believed that imitating the same-sex parent also plays an important role in the development of gender identity and, ultimately, of healthy sexual maturity.

The Latency and Genital Stages

Freud felt that because of the intense anxiety associated with the Oedipus complex, the sexual urges of boys and girls become repressed during the *latency stage* in late childhood. Outwardly, children in the latency stage express a strong desire to associate with same-sex peers, a preference that strengthens the child's sexual identity.

The final resolution of the Oedipus complex occurs in adolescence, during the *genital stage.* As incestuous urges start to resurface, they are prohibited by the moral ideals of the superego as well as by societal restrictions. Thus, the person directs sexual urges toward socially acceptable substitutes, who often resemble the person's opposite-sex parent (Freud, 1905).

It often happens that a young man falls in love seriously for the first time with a mature woman, or a girl with an elderly man in a position of authority; this is a clear echo of the [earlier] phase of development that we have been discussing, since these figures are able to re-animate pictures of their mother or father.

Sigmund Freud (1905)

In Freud's theory, a healthy personality and sense of sexuality result when conflicts are successfully resolved at each stage of psychosexual development (summarized in Table 10.2). Successfully negotiating the conflicts at each psychosexual stage results in the person's capacity to love and in expressions of productive living through one's life's work, child rearing, and other accomplishments.

Table 10.2

Freud's Psychosexual Stages

Age	Stage	Description
Birth to age 1	**Oral**	The mouth is the primary focus of pleasurable and gratifying sensations, which the infant achieves via feeding and exploring objects with his mouth.
Ages 1 to 3	**Anal**	The anus is the primary focus of pleasurable sensations, which the young child derives in developing control over elimination via toilet training.
Ages 3 to 6	**Phallic**	The genitals are the primary focus of pleasurable sensations, which the child derives through sexual curiosity, masturbation, and sexual attraction to the opposite-sex parent.
Ages 7 to 11	**Latency**	Sexual impulses become repressed and dormant as the child develops same-sex friendships with peers and focuses on school, sports, and other activities.
Adolescence	**Genital**	As the adolescent reaches physical sexual maturity, the genitals become the primary focus of pleasurable sensations, which the person seeks to satisfy in heterosexual relationships.

What we properly call instincts are physiological urges, and are perceived by the senses. But at the same time, they also manifest themselves in fantasies and often reveal their presence only by symbolic images. These manifestations are what I call the archetypes. They are without known origin; and they reproduce themselves in any time or in any part of the world.

Carl Jung (1964)

The Neo-Freudians
Freud's Descendants and Dissenters

Key Theme

■ The neo-Freudians followed Freud in stressing the importance of the unconscious and early childhood, but they developed their own personality theories.

Key Questions

■ How did the neo-Freudians generally depart from Freud's ideas?
■ What were the key ideas of Jung, Horney, and Adler?
■ What are three key criticisms of Freud's theory and of the psychoanalytic perspective?

Freud's ideas were always controversial. But by the early 1900s, he had attracted a number of followers, many of whom went to Vienna to study with him. Although these early followers developed their own personality theories, they still recognized the importance of many of Freud's basic notions, such as the influence of unconscious processes and early childhood experiences. In effect, they kept the foundations that Freud had established but offered new explanations for personality processes. Hence, these theorists are often called *neo-Freudians* (the prefix *neo* means "new"). The neo-Freudians and their theories are considered part of the psychoanalytic perspective on personality.

In general, the neo-Freudians disagreed with Freud on three key points. First, they took issue with Freud's belief that behavior was primarily motivated by sexual urges. Second, they disagreed with Freud's contention that personality is fundamentally determined by early childhood experiences. Instead, the neo-Freudians believed that personality can also be influenced by experiences throughout the lifespan. Third, the neo-Freudian theorists departed from Freud's generally pessimistic view of human nature and society.

In Chapter 9, on lifespan development, we described the psychosocial theory of one famous neo-Freudian, Erik Erikson. In this chapter, we'll look at the basic ideas of three other important neo-Freudians: Carl Jung, Karen Horney, and Alfred Adler.

Carl Jung
Archetypes and the Collective Unconscious

Born in a small town in Switzerland, **Carl Jung** (1875–1961) was fascinated by the myths, folktales, and religions of his own and other cultures. After studying medicine, Jung was drawn to the relatively new field of psychiatry because he believed it could provide deeper insights into the human mind (Jung, 1963).

Intrigued by Freud's ideas, Jung began a correspondence with him. At their first meeting, the two men were so compatible that they talked for 13 hours nonstop. Freud felt that his young disciple was so promising that he called him his "adopted son" and his "crown prince." It would be Jung, Freud decided, who would succeed him and lead the international psychoanalytic movement. However, Jung was too independent to relish his role as Freud's unquestioning disciple. As Jung continued to put forth his own ideas, his close friendship with Freud ultimately ended in bitterness (Solomon, 2003).

Jung rejected Freud's belief that human behavior is fueled by the instinctual drives of sex and aggression. Instead, Jung believed that people are motivated by a more general psychological energy that pushes them to achieve psychological growth, self-realization, and psychic wholeness and harmony. Jung (1963) also believed that personality continues to develop in significant ways throughout the lifespan.

In studying different cultures, Jung was struck by the universality of many images and themes, which also surfaced in his patients' dreams and preoccupations. These observations led to some of Jung's most intriguing ideas, the notions of the collective unconscious and archetypes.

Jung (1936) believed that the deepest part of the individual psyche is the **collective unconscious,** which is shared by all people and reflects humanity's collective evolutionary history. He described the collective unconscious as containing "the whole spiritual heritage of mankind's evolution, born anew in the brain structure of every individual" (Jung, 1931).

collective unconscious
In Jung's theory, the hypothesized part of the unconscious mind that is inherited from previous generations and that contains universally shared ancestral experiences and ideas.

The Mandala To Jung (1974), the mandala was the archetypal symbol of the self and psychic wholeness. Mandala images are found in cultures throughout the world. Shown here are a ceremonial buffalo robe of the Plains Indians *(left);* the Bhavacakra, or Buddhist Wheel of Life, from Tibet *(center);* and one of the many examples from the Christian tradition, a beautiful rose window in the main portal of the Notre Dame cathedral in Reims, France *(right).*

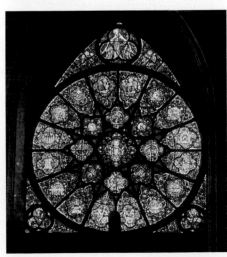

archetypes
(AR-kuh-types) In Jung's theory, the inherited mental images of universal human instincts, themes, and preoccupations that are the main components of the collective unconscious.

Contained in the collective unconscious are the **archetypes,** the mental images of universal human instincts, themes, and preoccupations (Jung, 1964). Common archetypal themes that are expressed in virtually every culture are the hero, the powerful father, the nurturing mother, the witch, the wise old man, the innocent child, and death and rebirth.

Two important archetypes that Jung (1951) described are the *anima* and the *animus*—the representations of feminine and masculine qualities. Jung believed that every man has a "feminine" side, represented by his anima, and that every woman has a "masculine" side, represented by her animus. To achieve psychological harmony, Jung believed, it is important for men to recognize and accept their feminine aspects and for women to recognize and accept the masculine side of their nature.

Not surprisingly, Jung's concepts of the collective unconscious and shared archetypes have been criticized as being unscientific or mystical. As far as we know, individual experiences cannot be genetically passed down from one generation to the next. Regardless, Jung's ideas make more sense if you think of the collective unconscious as reflecting shared human experiences. The archetypes, then, can be thought of as symbols that represent the common, universal themes of the human life cycle. These universal themes include birth, achieving a sense of self, parenthood, the spiritual search, and death.

Archetypes in Popular Culture According to Jung, archetypal images are often found in popular myths, novels, and even films. Consider the classic film *The Wizard of Oz.* The motherless child, Dorothy, is on a quest for self-knowledge and selfhood, symbolized by the circular Emerald City. She is accompanied by her symbolic helpers, the Cowardly Lion (seeking courage), the Tin Woodsman (seeking love), and the Scarecrow (seeking wisdom).

Although Jung's theory never became as influential as Freud's, some of his ideas have gained wide acceptance. For example, Jung (1923) was the first to describe two basic personality types: *introverts,* who focus their attention inward, and *extraverts,* who turn their attention and energy toward the outside world. We will encounter these two basic personality dimensions again, when we look at trait theories later in this chapter. Finally, Jung's emphasis on the drive toward psychological growth and self-realization anticipated some of the basic ideas of the humanistic perspective on personality, which we'll look at shortly.

Karen Horney
Basic Anxiety and "Womb Envy"

Trained as a Freudian psychoanalyst, **Karen Horney** (1885–1952) (pronounced HORN-eye) emigrated from Germany to the United States during the Great Depression in the 1930s. Horney noticed distinct differences between her American and her German patients. While Freud traced psychological problems to sexual conflicts, Horney found that her American patients were much more worried about their jobs and economic problems than their sex lives. Thus, Horney came to stress the importance of cultural and social factors in personality development—matters that Freud had largely ignored (Horney, 1945).

Horney also stressed the importance of social relationships, especially the parent–child relationship, in the development of personality. She believed that disturbances in human relationships, not sexual conflicts, were the cause of psychological problems. Such problems arise from the attempt to deal with *basic anxiety,* which Horney (1945) described as "the feeling a child has of being isolated and helpless in a potentially hostile world."

Horney (1945) described three patterns of behavior that the individual uses to defend against basic anxiety: moving toward, against, or away from other people. Those who move *toward* other people have an excessive need for approval and affection. Those who move *against* others have an excessive need for power, especially power over other people. They are often competitive, critical, and domineering, and they need to feel superior to others. Finally, those who move *away from* other people have an excessive need for independence and self-sufficiency, which often makes them aloof and detached from others.

Horney contended that people with a healthy personality are *flexible* in balancing these different needs, for there are times when each behavior pattern is appropriate. As Horney (1945) wrote, "One should be capable of giving in to others, of fighting, and keeping to oneself. The three can complement each other and make for a harmonious whole." But when one pattern becomes the predominant way of dealing with other people and the world, psychological conflict and problems can result.

Horney also sharply disagreed with Freud's interpretation of female development, especially his notion that women suffer from penis envy. What women envy in men, Horney (1926) claimed, is not their penis, but their superior status in society. In fact, Horney contended that men often suffer *womb envy,* envying women's capacity to bear children. Neatly standing Freud's view of feminine psychology on its head, Horney argued that *men* compensate for their relatively minor role in reproduction by constantly striving to make creative achievements in their work (Gilman, 2001). As Horney (1945) wrote, "Is not the tremendous strength in men of the impulse to creative work in every field precisely due to their feelings of playing a relatively small part in the creation of living beings, which constantly impels them to an overcompensation in achievement?"

Horney shared Jung's belief that people are not doomed to psychological conflict and problems. Also like Jung, Horney believed that the drive to grow psychologically and achieve one's potential is a basic human motive.

Alfred Adler
Feelings of Inferiority and Striving for Superiority

Born in Vienna, **Alfred Adler** (1870–1937) was an extremely sickly child. Yet through determination and hard work, he overcame his physical weaknesses. After studying medicine, he became associated with Freud. But from the beginning of Adler's interest in psychoanalysis, he disagreed with Freud on several issues. In particular, Adler placed much more emphasis on the importance of conscious thought processes and social motives. Eventually, Adler broke away from Freud to establish his own theory of personality.

Adler (1933b) believed that the most fundamental human motive is *striving for superiority*—the desire to improve oneself, master challenges, and move toward self-perfection and self-realization. Striving toward superiority arises from universal *feelings of inferiority* that are experienced during infancy and childhood, when the child is helpless and dependent on others. These feelings motivate people to *compensate* for their real or imagined weaknesses by emphasizing their talents and abilities and by working hard to improve themselves. Hence, Adler (1933a) saw the universal human feelings of inferiority as ultimately constructive and valuable.

However, when people are unable to compensate for specific weaknesses or when their feelings of inferiority are excessive, they can develop an *inferiority complex*—a general sense of inadequacy, weakness, and helplessness. People with an inferiority complex are often unable to strive for mastery and self-improvement.

At the other extreme, people can *overcompensate* for their feelings of inferiority and develop a *superiority complex.* Behaviors caused by a superiority complex might include exaggerating one's accomplishments and importance in an effort to cover up weaknesses and denying the reality of one's limitations (Adler, 1954).

Evaluating Freud and the Psychoanalytic Perspective on Personality

Like it or not, Sigmund Freud's ideas have had a profound and lasting impact on our culture and on our understanding of human nature. Today, opinions on Freud span the entire spectrum. Some see him as a genius who discovered brilliant,

Man, [Freud] postulated, is doomed to suffer or destroy. . . . My own belief is that man has the capacity as well as the desire to develop his potentialities and become a decent human being, and that these deteriorate if his relationship to others and hence to himself is, and continues to be, disturbed. I believe that man can change and go on changing as long as he lives.

Karen Horney (1945)

To be a human being means to have inferiority feelings. One recognizes one's own powerlessness in the face of nature. One sees death as the irrefutable consequence of existence. But in the mentally healthy person this inferiority feeling acts as a motive for productivity, as a motive for attempting to overcome obstacles, to maintain oneself in life.

Alfred Adler (1933a)

A Century of Influence One indicator of Freud's influence is that he appeared on the cover of *Time* magazine four different times—in 1924, just before his death in 1939, in 1993, and again in 1999. The 1999 cover shown here, a caricature of Freud psychoanalyzing Albert Einstein, was a special issue of *Time* commemorating the 100 greatest scientists and thinkers of the twentieth century.

> *For good or ill, Sigmund Freud, more than any other explorer of the psyche, has shaped the mind of the 20th century. The very fierceness and persistence of his detractors are a wry tribute to the staying power of Freud's ideas.*
>
> Peter Gay (1999)

> *Step by step, we are learning that Freud has been the most overrated figure in the entire history of science and medicine—one who wrought immense harm through the propagation of false etiologies, mistaken diagnoses, and fruitless lines of inquiry.*
>
> Frederick Crews (1995)

lasting insights into human nature. Others contend that Freud was a deeply neurotic, driven man who successfully foisted his twisted personal view of human nature onto an unsuspecting public (Crews, 1984, 1996).

The truth, as you might suspect, lies somewhere in between. Although Freud has had an enormous impact on psychology and on society, there are several valid criticisms of Freud's theory and, more generally, of the psychoanalytic perspective. We'll discuss three of the most important problems next.

Inadequacy of Evidence

Freud's theory relies wholly on data derived from his relatively small number of patients and from self-analysis. Most of Freud's patients were relatively well-to-do, well-educated members of the middle and upper classes in Vienna at the beginning of the twentieth century. Freud (1916, 1919, 1939) also analyzed the lives of famous historical figures, such as Leonardo da Vinci, and looked to myth, religion, literature, and evolutionary prehistory for confirmation of his ideas. Any way you look at it, this is a small and rather skewed sample from which to draw sweeping generalizations about human nature.

Furthermore, it is impossible to objectively assess Freud's "data." Freud did not take notes during his private therapy sessions. And, of course, when he did report a case in detail, it is still Freud's interpretation of the case that is recorded. For Freud, proof of the validity of his ideas depended on his uncovering similar patterns in different patients. So the critical question is this: Was Freud imposing his own ideas onto his patients, seeing only what he expected to see? Some critics think so (e.g., Crews, 1996; Masson, 1984a, 1984b; P. Robinson, 1993).

Lack of Testability

Many psychoanalytic concepts are so vague and ambiguous that they are impossible to objectively measure or confirm (Crews, 1996). For example, how might you go about proving the existence of the id or the superego? Or how could you operationally define and measure the effects of the pleasure principle, the life instinct, or the Oedipus complex?

Psychoanalytic "proof" often has a "heads I win, tails you lose" style to it. In other words, psychoanalytic concepts are often impossible to *dis*prove because even seemingly contradictory information can be used to support Freud's theory. For example, if your memory of childhood doesn't jibe with Freud's description of the psychosexual stages or the Oedipus complex, well, that's because you've repressed it. Freud himself was not immune to this form of reasoning (P. Robinson, 1993). When one of Freud's patients reported dreams that didn't seem to reveal a hidden wish, Freud interpreted the dreams as betraying the patient's hidden wish to disprove Freud's dream theory!

As Freud acknowledged, psychoanalysis is better at explaining *past* behavior than at predicting future behavior (Gay, 1989). Indeed, psychoanalytic interpretations are so flexible that a given behavior can be explained by any number of completely different motives. For example, a man who is extremely affectionate toward his wife might be exhibiting displacement of a repressed incestuous urge (he is displacing his repressed affection for his mother onto his wife), reaction formation (he actually hates his wife intensely, so he compensates by being overly affectionate), or fixation at the oral stage (he is overly dependent on his wife).

Nonetheless, several key psychoanalytic ideas *have* been substantiated by empirical research (Westen, 1990, 1998). Among these are the ideas that (1) much of mental life is unconscious; (2) early childhood experiences have a critical influence on interpersonal relationships and psychological adjustment; and (3) people differ significantly in the degree to which they are able to regulate their impulses, emotions, and thoughts toward adaptive and socially acceptable ends.

Sexism

Many people feel that Freud's theories reflect a sexist view of women. Because penis envy produces feelings of shame and inferiority, Freud (1925) claimed, women are more vain, masochistic, and jealous than men. He also believed that women are more influenced by their emotions and have a lesser ethical and moral sense than men.

As Horney and other female psychoanalysts have pointed out, Freud's theory uses male psychology as a prototype. Women are essentially viewed as a deviation from the norm of masculinity (Horney, 1926; Thompson, 1950). Perhaps, Horney suggested, psychoanalysis would have evolved an entirely different view of women if it were not dominated by the male point of view.

To Freud's credit, women were quite active in the early psychoanalytic movement. Several female analysts became close colleagues of Freud (Freeman & Strean, 1987; Roazen, 1999, 2000). And it was Freud's daughter Anna, rather than any of his sons, who followed in his footsteps as an eminent psychoanalyst. Ultimately, Anna Freud became her father's successor as leader of the international psychoanalytic movement.

The weaknesses in Freud's theory and in the psychoanalytic approach to personality are not minor problems. All the same, Freud made some extremely significant contributions to modern psychological thinking. Most important, he drew attention to the existence and influence of mental processes that occur outside conscious awareness, an idea that continues to be actively investigated by today's psychological researchers.

Anna Freud (1895–1982) Freud's youngest daughter, Anna, became his chief disciple and was herself the founder of a psychoanalytic school. Expanding on her father's theory, she applied psychoanalysis to therapy with children. She is shown here addressing a debate on psychoanalysis at the Sorbonne University in Paris in 1950.

The Humanistic Perspective on Personality

Key Theme

- The humanistic perspective emphasizes free will, self-awareness, and psychological growth.

Key Questions

- What role do the self-concept, actualizing tendency, and unconditional positive regard play in Rogers's personality theory?
- What are key strengths and weaknesses of the humanistic perspective?

By the 1950s, the field of personality was dominated by two completely different perspectives: Freudian psychoanalysis and B. F. Skinner's brand of behaviorism (see Chapter 5). While Freud's theory of personality proposed elaborate and complex internal states, Skinner believed that psychologists should focus on observable behaviors and on the environmental factors that shape and maintain those behaviors (see Rogers & Skinner, 1956). As Skinner (1971) wrote, "A person does not act upon the world, the world acts upon him."

The Emergence of the "Third Force"

Another group of psychologists had a fundamentally different view of human nature. In opposition to both psychoanalysis and behaviorism, they championed a "third force" in psychology, which they called humanistic psychology. **Humanistic psychology** is a view of personality that emphasizes human potential and such uniquely human characteristics as self-awareness and free will (Cain, 2002).

humanistic psychology
The theoretical viewpoint on personality that generally emphasizes the inherent goodness of people, human potential, self-actualization, the self-concept, and healthy personality development.

In contrast to Freud's pessimistic view of people as being motivated by unconscious sexual and destructive instincts, the humanistic psychologists saw people as being innately good. Humanistic psychologists also differed from psychoanalytic theorists by their focus on the *healthy* personality rather than on psychologically troubled people.

In contrast to the behaviorist view that human and animal behavior is due largely to environmental reinforcement and punishment, the humanistic psychologists believed that people are motivated by the need to grow psychologically. They also doubted that laboratory research with rats and pigeons accurately reflected the essence of human nature, as the behaviorists claimed. Instead, humanistic psychologists contended that the most important factor in personality is the individual's *conscious, subjective perception of his or her self* (Purkey & Stanley, 2002).

The two most important contributors to the humanistic perspective were Carl Rogers and Abraham Maslow. In Chapter 8, on motivation, we discussed **Abraham Maslow's** famous *hierarchy of needs* and his concept of self-actualization (see page 323). Like Maslow, Rogers placed considerable importance on the tendency of human beings to strive to fulfill their potential and capabilities.

Carl Rogers
On Becoming a Person

Carl Rogers (1902–1987) grew up in a large, close-knit family in Oak Park, Illinois, a suburb of Chicago. His parents were highly religious and instilled a moral and ethical atmosphere in the home, which no doubt influenced Rogers's early decision to become a minister. After studying theology, Rogers decided that the ministry was not for him. Instead, he turned to the study of psychology, ultimately enjoying a long, productive, and distinguished career as a psychotherapist, writer, and university professor.

Like Freud, Rogers developed his personality theory from his clinical experiences with his patients. Rogers referred to his patients as "clients" to emphasize their active and voluntary participation in therapy. In marked contrast to Freud, Rogers was continually impressed by his clients' drive to grow and develop their potential.

These observations convinced Rogers that the most basic human motive is the **actualizing tendency**—the innate drive to maintain and enhance the human organism. According to Rogers, all other human motives, whether biological or social, are secondary. He compared the actualizing tendency to a child's drive to learn to walk despite early frustration and falls. To get a sense of the vastly different views of Rogers and Freud, read Critical Thinking Box 10.1.

> *At bottom, each person is asking, "Who am I, really? How can I get in touch with this real self, underlying all my surface behavior? How can I become myself?"*
>
> Carl Rogers (1961)

The Self-Concept

Rogers (1959) was struck by how frequently his clients in therapy said, "I'm not really sure who I am" or "I just don't feel like myself." This observation helped form the cornerstone of Rogers's personality theory: the idea of the self-concept. The **self-concept** is the set of perceptions and beliefs that you have about yourself, including your nature, your personal qualities, and your typical behavior.

According to Rogers (1980), people are motivated to act in accordance with their self-concept. So strong is the need to maintain a consistent self-concept that people will deny or distort experiences that contradict their self-concept.

The self-concept begins evolving early in life. Because they are motivated by the actualizing tendency, infants and young children naturally gravitate toward self-enhancing experiences. But as children develop a greater sense of self-awareness, there is an increasing need for positive regard. *Positive regard* is the sense of being loved and valued by other people, especially one's parents.

actualizing tendency
In Rogers's theory, the innate drive to maintain and enhance the human organism.

self-concept
The set of perceptions and beliefs that you hold about yourself.

CRITICAL THINKING 10.1

Freud Versus Rogers on Human Nature

Freud's view of human nature was deeply pessimistic. He believed that the human aggressive instinct was innate, persistent, and pervasive. Were it not for internal superego restraints and external societal restraints, civilization as we know it would collapse: The destructive instincts of humans would be unleashed. As Freud (1930) wrote in *Civilization and Its Discontents:*

> Men are not gentle creatures who want to be loved, and who at the most can defend themselves if they are attacked; they are, on the contrary, creatures among whose instinctual endowments is to be reckoned a powerful share of aggressiveness. As a result, their neighbor is for them not only a potential helper or sexual object, but also someone who tempts them to satisfy their aggressiveness on him, to exploit his capacity for work without compensation, to use him sexually without his consent, to seize his possessions, to humiliate him, to cause him pain, to torture and to kill him. *Man is a wolf to man.* Who, in the face of all his experience of life and of history, will have the courage to dispute this assertion?

In Freud's view, then, the essence of human nature is destructive. Control of these destructive instincts is necessary. Yet societal, cultural, religious, and moral restraints also make people frustrated, neurotic, and unhappy. Why? Because the strivings of the id toward instinctual satisfaction *must* be frustrated if civilization and the human race are to survive. Hence, as the title of Freud's book emphasizes, civilization is inevitably accompanied by human "discontent."

A pretty gloomy picture, isn't it? Yet if you watch the evening news or read the newspaper, you may find it hard to disagree with Freud's negative image of human nature. People *are* often exceedingly cruel and selfish, committing horrifying acts of brutality against strangers and even against loved ones.

However, you might argue that people can also be extraordinarily kind, self-sacrificing, and loving toward others. Freud would agree with this observation. Yet according to his theory, "good" or "moral" behavior does not disprove the essentially destructive nature of people. Instead, he explains good or moral behavior

Are People Innately Good . . . or Innately Evil? These volunteers are members of Doctors Without Borders, an international group of medical workers that won the Nobel Peace Prize for its work in helping the victims of violence and disasters all over the world. Here, they carry a wounded survivor of a brutal massacre to safety in a refugee camp. On the one hand, killings motivated by political or ethnic hatred seem to support Freud's contentions about human nature. On the other hand, the selfless behavior of those who help others, often at a considerable cost to themselves, seems to support Rogers's view. Which viewpoint do you think more accurately describes the essence of human nature?

in terms of superego control, sublimation of the instincts, displacement, and so forth.

But is this truly the essence of human nature? Carl Rogers disagreed strongly. "I do not discover man to be well characterized in his basic nature by such terms as *fundamentally hostile, antisocial, destructive, evil,*" Rogers (1957a) wrote. Instead, Rogers believed that people are more accurately described as "*positive, forward-moving, constructive, realistic, trustworthy.*"

If this is so, how can Rogers account for the evil and cruelty in the world? Rogers didn't deny that people can behave destructively and cruelly. Yet throughout his life, Rogers insisted that people are innately good. Rogers (1981) explained the existence of evil in this way:

> My experience leads me to believe that it is cultural factors which are the major factor in our evil behaviors. The rough

manner of childbirth, the infant's mixed experience with the parents, the constricting, destructive influence of our educational system, the injustice of our distribution of wealth, our cultivated prejudices against individuals who are different—all these elements and many others warp the human organism in directions which are antisocial.

In sharp contrast to Freud, Rogers (1964) said we should *trust* the human organism, because the human who is truly free to choose will naturally gravitate toward behavior that serves to perpetuate the human race and improve society as a whole:

> I dare to believe that when the human being is inwardly free to choose whatever he deeply values, he tends to value those objects, experiences, and goals that will make for his own survival, growth, and development, and for the survival and development of others. . . . The psychologically mature person as I have described him has, I believe, the qualities which would cause him to value those experiences which would make for the survival and enhancement of the human race.

Two great thinkers, two diametrically opposing views of human nature. Now it's your turn to critically evaluate their views.

Critical Thinking Questions

- Are people inherently driven by aggressive instincts, as Freud claimed? Must the destructive urges of the id be restrained by parents, culture, religion, and society if civilization is to continue? Would an environment in which individuals were unrestrained inevitably lead to an unleashing of destructive instincts?

- Or are people naturally good, as Rogers claimed? If people existed in a truly free and nurturing environment, would they invariably make constructive choices that would benefit both themselves and society as a whole?

conditional positive regard
In Rogers's theory, the sense that you will be valued and loved only if you behave in a way that is acceptable to others; conditional love or acceptance.

unconditional positive regard
In Rogers's theory, the sense that you will be valued and loved even if you don't conform to the standards and expectations of others; unconditional love or acceptance.

Rogers (1959) maintained that most parents provide their children with **conditional positive regard**—the sense that the child is valued and loved only when she behaves in a way that is acceptable to others. The problem with conditional positive regard is that it causes the child to learn to deny or distort her genuine feelings. For example, if little Amy's parents scold and reject her when she expresses angry feelings, her strong need for positive regard will cause her to deny her anger, even when it's justified or appropriate. Eventually, Amy's self-concept will become so distorted that genuine feelings of anger are denied, because they are inconsistent with her self-concept as "a good girl who never gets angry." Because of the fear of losing positive regard, she cuts herself off from her true feelings.

Like Freud, Rogers believed that feelings and experiences could be driven from consciousness by being denied or distorted. But Rogers believed that feelings become denied or distorted not because they are threatening but because they contradict the self-concept. In this case, people are in a state of *incongruence:* Their self-concept conflicts with their actual experience (Rogers, 1959). Such a person is continually defending against genuine feelings and experiences that are inconsistent with his self-concept. As this process continues over time, a person progressively becomes more "out of touch" with his true feelings and his essential self, often experiencing psychological problems as a result.

How is incongruence to be avoided? In the ideal situation, a child experiences a great deal of unconditional positive regard from parents and other authority figures. **Unconditional positive regard** refers to the child's sense of being unconditionally loved and valued, even if she doesn't conform to the standards and expectations of others. In this way, the child's actualizing tendency is allowed its fullest expression. However, Rogers did *not* advocate permissive parenting. He thought that parents were responsible for controlling their children's behavior and for teaching them acceptable standards of behavior. Rogers maintained that parents can discipline their child without undermining the child's sense of self-worth.

Unconditional Positive Regard Rogers contended that healthy personality development is the result of being unconditionally valued and loved as a person. He advised parents and teachers to control a child's inappropriate behavior without rejecting the child himself. Such a style of discipline teaches acceptable behaviors without diminishing the child's sense of self-worth.

For example, parents can disapprove of a child's specific *behavior* without completely rejecting the *child herself.* In effect, the parent's message should be, "I do not value your behavior right now, but I still love and value *you.*" In this way, according to Rogers, the child's essential sense of self-worth can remain intact.

Rogers (1957b) believed that it is through consistent experiences of unconditional positive regard that one becomes a psychologically healthy, fully functioning person. The *fully functioning person* has a flexible, constantly evolving self-concept. She is realistic, open to new experiences, and capable of changing in response to new experiences.

Rather than defending against or distorting her own thoughts or feelings, the person experiences *congruence:* Her sense of self is consistent with her emotions and experiences. The actualizing tendency is fully operational in her, and she makes conscious choices that move her in the direction of greater growth and fulfillment of potential. Rogers (1957b, 1964) believed that the fully functioning person is likely to be creative and spontaneous and to enjoy harmonious relationships with others.

© 1994 The New Yorker Collection from Cartoonbank.com. Donald Reilly.

"To this day, I can hear my mother's voice— harsh, accusing. 'Lost your mittens? You naughty kittens! Then you shall have no pie!' "

Evaluating the Humanistic Perspective on Personality

The humanistic perspective has been criticized on two particular points. First, humanistic theories are hard to validate or test scientifically. Humanistic theories tend to be based on philosophical assumptions or clinical observations rather than on empirical research. For example, concepts like the self-concept, unconditional positive regard, and the actualizing tendency are very difficult to define or measure objectively.

Second, many psychologists believe that humanistic psychology's view of human nature is *too* optimistic. For example, if self-actualization is a universal human motive, why are self-actualized people so hard to find? And, critics claim, humanistic psychologists have minimized the darker, more destructive side of human nature. Can we really account for all the evil in the world by ascribing it to a restrictive upbringing or society?

The influence of humanistic psychology has waned since the 1960s and early 1970s (Cain, 2003). Nevertheless, it has made lasting contributions, especially in the realms of psychotherapy, counseling, education, and parenting (K. Schneider, 1998). The humanistic perspective has also promoted the scientific study of such topics as the healthy personality and creativity. Finally, the importance of subjective experience and the self-concept has become widely accepted in different areas of psychology (Markus & Cross, 1990; Markus & Kitayama, 1994).

> "*I am quite aware that out of defensiveness and inner fear individuals can and do behave in ways which are incredibly cruel, horribly destructive, immature, regressive, antisocial, and hurtful. Yet one of the most refreshing and invigorating parts of my experience is to work with such individuals and to discover the strongly positive directional tendencies which exist in them, as in all of us, at the deepest levels."*
>
> Carl Rogers (1961)

The Social Cognitive Perspective on Personality

Key Theme

■ The social cognitive perspective stresses conscious thought processes, self-regulation, and the importance of situational influences.

Key Questions

■ What is the principle of reciprocal determination?
■ What is the role of self-efficacy beliefs in personality?
■ What are key strengths and weaknesses of the social cognitive perspective?

Have you ever noticed how different your behavior and sense of self can be in different situations? Consider this example: You feel pretty confident as you enter your English composition class. After all, you're pulling an A, and your prof nods approvingly every time you participate in the class discussion, which you do frequently. In contrast, your college algebra class is a disaster. You're worried about passing the course, and you feel so shaky about your skills that you're afraid to even ask a question, much less participate in class. Even a casual observer would notice how differently you behave in the two different situations—speaking freely and confidently in one class, staring at your desk in hopes that your instructor won't notice you in the other.

The idea that a person's conscious thought processes in different situations strongly influence his or her actions is one important characteristic of the *social cognitive perspective* on personality (Cervone, 2004). According to the social cognitive perspective, people actively process information from their social experiences. This information influences their goals, expectations, beliefs, and behavior, as well as the specific environments they choose.

social cognitive theory
Albert Bandura's theory of personality, which emphasizes the importance of observational learning, conscious cognitive processes, social experiences, self-efficacy beliefs, and reciprocal determinism.

reciprocal determinism
A model proposed by psychologist Albert Bandura that explains human functioning and personality as caused by the interaction of behavioral, cognitive, and environmental factors.

self-efficacy
The beliefs that people have about their ability to meet the demands of a specific situation; feelings of self-confidence or self-doubt.

The capacity to exercise control over the nature and quality of life is the essence of humanness. Unless people believe they can produce desired results and forestall detrimental ones by their actions, they have little incentive to act or persevere in the face of difficulties.

Albert Bandura (2001)

FIGURE 10.2 Reciprocal Determinism

SOURCE: Bandura (1997).

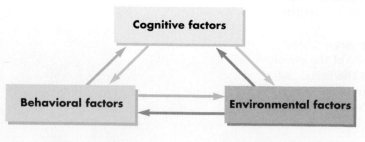

The social cognitive perspective differs from psychoanalytic and humanistic perspectives in several ways. First, rather than basing their approach on self-analysis or insights derived from psychotherapy, social cognitive personality theorists rely heavily on experimental findings. Second, the social cognitive perspective emphasizes conscious, self-regulated behavior rather than unconscious mental influences and instinctual drives. And third, as in our English-versus-algebra-class example, the social cognitive approach emphasizes that our sense of self can vary, depending on our thoughts, feelings, and behaviors in a given situation.

Albert Bandura and Social Cognitive Theory

Although several contemporary personality theorists have embraced the social cognitive approach to explaining personality, probably the most influential is **Albert Bandura** (b. 1925). We examined Bandura's now-classic research on *observational learning* in Chapter 5. In Chapter 8, we encountered Bandura's more recent research on self-efficacy. Here, you'll see how Bandura's ideas on both these topics are reflected in his personality theory, called social cognitive theory. **Social cognitive theory** emphasizes the social origins of thoughts and actions but also stresses active cognitive processes and the human capacity for *self-regulation* (Bandura, 2004).

As Bandura's early research demonstrated, we learn many behaviors by observing, and then imitating, the behavior of other people. But, as Bandura (1997) has pointed out, we don't merely observe people's actions. We also observe the *consequences* that follow people's actions, the *rules* and *standards* that apply to behavior in specific situations, and the ways in which people *regulate their own behavior*. Thus, environmental influences are important, but conscious, self-generated goals and standards also exert considerable control over thoughts, feelings, and actions (Bandura, 2001).

For example, consider your own goal of getting a college education. No doubt many social and environmental factors influenced your decision. In turn, your conscious decision to attend college determines many aspects of your current behavior, thoughts, and emotions. And your goal of attending college classes determines which environments you choose.

Bandura (1986, 1997) explains human behavior and personality as being caused by the interaction of behavioral, cognitive, and environmental factors. He calls this process **reciprocal determinism** (see Figure 10.2). According to this principle, each factor both influences the other factors and is influenced by the other factors. Thus, in Bandura's view, our environment influences our thoughts and actions, our thoughts influence our actions and the environments we choose, our actions influence our thoughts and the environments we choose, and so on in a circular fashion.

Beliefs of Self-Efficacy
Anybody Here Know How to Fix a Light Switch?

Collectively, a person's cognitive skills, abilities, and attitudes represent the person's *self-system*. According to Bandura (2001), it is our self-system that guides how we perceive, evaluate, and control our behavior in different situations. Bandura (2004) has found that the most critical elements influencing the self-system are our beliefs of self-efficacy. **Self-efficacy** refers to the degree to which you are subjectively convinced of your own capabilities and effectiveness in meeting the demands of a particular situation.

For example, your authors, Don and Sandy, are at opposite ends of the spectrum in their beliefs of self-efficacy when it comes to repairs around the house. Don thinks he can fix anything, whether he really can or not. Sandy likes to describe herself as "mechanically challenged." When a light switch recently broke in our house, it was obvious that Sandy had very little faith in her ability to fix or replace it: She instantly hollered for help. As Don was investigating the matter, he casually asked Sandy whether *she* could replace the light switch.

"Me? You must be kidding," Sandy immediately responded. "It would never occur to me to even *try* to replace a light switch."

Bandura would be quick to point out how Sandy's weak belief of self-efficacy about electrical repairs guides her behavior—it would prevent her from even attempting to fix a light switch on her own. When Don reassured Sandy that the directions were right on the light-switch package and that it was a very simple task, Sandy still expressed strong self-doubt about her abilities. "I'd probably blow up the house or burn it down or black out the whole neighborhood," she said.

Albert Bandura would, no doubt, smile at how readily Sandy's remark was an everyday confirmation of his research finding that our beliefs of self-efficacy help shape our imagination of future consequences (Bandura, 1992; Ozer & Bandura, 1990). In Sandy's case, her weak belief of self-efficacy contributed to her imagination of dire future consequences should she attempt this task.

Bandura's concept of self-efficacy makes it easier to understand why people often fail to perform optimally at certain tasks, even though they possess the necessary skills. Sandy has made presentations in front of hundreds of people, knows how to slab a geode with a diamond saw, can easily navigate Chicago's rush-hour traffic, and once single-handedly landed an eight-pound northern pike. In all these situations, she has strong feelings of self-efficacy. But hand her a package containing a light switch and she's intimidated.

Hence, our self-system is very flexible. How we regard ourselves and our abilities varies depending on the situations or tasks we're facing. In turn, our beliefs influence the tasks we are willing to try and how persistent we'll be in the face of obstacles (Bandura, 1996).

With the light switch, Don insisted on proving to Sandy that she was capable of changing it. "Well, maybe if I watched you install one, I might be willing to try it," Sandy finally offered. Sandy's suggestion illustrates how we acquire new behaviors and strengthen our beliefs of self-efficacy in particular situations—through observational learning and *mastery experiences* (Bandura, 2001, 2004). When we perform a task successfully, our sense of self-efficacy becomes stronger. When we fail to deal effectively with a particular task or situation, our sense of self-efficacy is undermined.

From very early in life, children develop feelings of self-efficacy from their experiences in dealing with different tasks and situations, such as athletic, social, and academic activities (Bandura & others, 2003). As Bandura (1992) has pointed out, developing self-efficacy begins in childhood, but it continues as a lifelong process. Each stage of the lifespan presents new challenges. And just for the record, Sandy *did* successfully replace the broken light switch. Now, about that dripping faucet . . .

Evaluating the Social Cognitive Perspective on Personality

A key strength of the social cognitive perspective on personality is its grounding in empirical, laboratory research (Bandura, 2004). The social cognitive perspective is built on research in learning, cognitive psychology, and social psychology, rather than on clinical impressions. And, unlike vague psychoanalytic and humanistic concepts, the concepts of social cognitive theory are scientifically testable—that is, they

> *The most effective way of developing a strong sense of efficacy is through* mastery experiences. *Successes build a robust belief in one's efficacy. Failures undermine it. A second way is through* social modeling. *If people see others like themselves succeed by sustained effort, they come to believe that they, too, have the capacity to do so.* Social persuasion *is a third way of strengthening people's beliefs in their efficacy. If people are persuaded that they have what it takes to succeed, they exert more effort than if they harbor self-doubts and dwell on personal deficiencies when problems arise.*
>
> Albert Bandura (2004)

Self-Efficacy We acquire a strong sense of self-efficacy by meeting challenges and mastering new skills specific to a particular situation. With her mother showing her how to ride her new bike, this 3-year-old is well on her way to developing a strong sense of self-efficacy in this domain. Self-efficacy beliefs begin to develop in early childhood but continue to evolve throughout the lifespan as we encounter new and different challenges.

can be operationally defined and measured. For example, psychologists can study beliefs of self-efficacy by comparing subjects who are low in self-efficacy in a given situation with subjects who are high in self-efficacy (e.g., Ozer & Bandura, 1990). Not surprisingly, then, the social cognitive perspective has had a major impact on the study of personality.

However, some psychologists feel that the social cognitive approach to personality applies *best* to laboratory research. In the typical laboratory study, the relationships among a limited number of very specific variables are studied. In everyday life, situations are far more complex, with multiple factors converging to affect behavior and personality. Thus, an argument can be made that clinical data, rather than laboratory data, may be more reflective of human personality.

The social cognitive perspective also ignores unconscious influences, emotions, or conflicts. Some psychologists argue that the social cognitive theory focuses on very limited areas of personality—learning, the effects of situations, and the effects of beliefs about the self. Thus, it seems to lack the richness of psychoanalytic and humanistic theories, which strive to explain the *whole* person, including the unconscious, irrational, and emotional aspects of personality (Westen, 1990).

Nevertheless, by emphasizing the reciprocal interaction of mental, behavioral, and situational factors, the social cognitive perspective recognizes the complex combination of factors that influence our everyday behavior. By emphasizing the important role of learning, especially observational learning, the social cognitive perspective offers a developmental explanation of human functioning that persists throughout one's lifetime. Finally, by emphasizing the self-regulation of behavior, the social cognitive perspective places most of the responsibility for our behavior—and for the consequences we experience—squarely on our own shoulders.

The Trait Perspective on Personality

Key Theme
■ Trait theories of personality focus on identifying, describing, and measuring individual differences.

Key Questions
■ What are traits, and how do surface and source traits differ?
■ What are three influential trait theories, and how might heredity affect personality?
■ What are key strengths and weaknesses of trait theories of personality?

"Oh, God! Here comes little Miss Perky."

Suppose we asked you to describe the personality of a close friend. How would you begin? Would you describe her personality in terms of her unconscious conflicts, the congruence of her self-concept, or her level of self-efficacy? Probably not. Instead, you'd probably generate a list of her personal characteristics, such as "outgoing," "cheerful," and "generous." This rather commonsense approach to personality is shared by the trait theories.

The trait approach to personality is very different from the theories we have encountered thus far. The psychoanalytic, humanistic, and social cognitive theories emphasize the *similarities* among people. They focus on discovering the universal processes of motivation and development that explain human personality (Revelle, 1995). Although these theories do deal with individual differences, they do so only indirectly. In contrast, the trait approach to personality *focuses primarily on describing individual differences* (Funder, 2001).

Trait theorists view the person as being a unique combination of personality characteristics or attributes, called *traits*. A **trait** is formally defined as a relatively stable, enduring predisposition to behave in a certain way. A **trait theory** of personality, then, is one that focuses on identifying, describing, and measuring individual differences in behavioral predispositions. Think back to our description of the twins, Kenneth and Julian, in the chapter Prologue. You can probably readily identify some of their personality traits. For example, Julian was described as impulsive, cocky, and adventurous, while Kenneth was serious, intense, and responsible.

People possess traits to different degrees. For example, a person might be extremely shy, somewhat shy, or not shy at all. Hence, a trait is typically described in terms of a range from one extreme to its opposite. Most people fall in the middle of the range (average shyness), while fewer people fall at opposite poles (extremely shy or extremely outgoing).

Surface Traits and Source Traits

Most of the terms that we use to describe people are **surface traits**—traits that lie on "the surface" and can be easily inferred from observable behaviors. Examples of surface traits include attributes like "happy," "exuberant," "spacey," and "gloomy." The list of potential surface traits is extremely long. Personality researcher Gordon Allport combed through an English-language dictionary and discovered more than 4,000 words that described specific personality traits (Allport & Odbert, 1936).

Source traits are thought to be more fundamental than surface traits. As the most basic dimension of personality, a source trait can potentially give rise to a vast number of surface traits. Trait theorists believe that there are relatively few source traits. Thus, one goal of trait theorists has been to identify the most basic set of universal source traits that can be used to describe all individual differences (Pervin, 1994).

Two Representative Trait Theories
Raymond Cattell and Hans Eysenck

How many source traits are there? Not surprisingly, trait theorists differ in their answers. Pioneer trait theorist **Raymond Cattell** reduced Allport's list of 4,000 terms to about 171 characteristics by eliminating terms that seemed to be redundant or uncommon (see John, 1990). Cattell collected data on a large sample of people, who were rated on each of the 171 terms. He then used a statistical technique called *factor analysis* to identify the traits that were most closely related to one another. After further research, Cattell eventually reduced his list to 16 key personality factors, which are listed in Table 10.3.

Cattell (1994) believed that these 16 personality factors represent the essential source traits of human personality. To measure these traits, Cattell developed what has become one of the most widely used personality tests, the *Sixteen Personality Factor Questionnaire* (abbreviated *16PF*). We'll discuss the 16PF in more detail later in the chapter.

An even simpler model of universal source traits was proposed by British psychologist **Hans Eysenck** (1916–1997). Eysenck's methods were similar to Cattell's, but his conception of personality includes just three dimensions. The first dimension is *introversion–extraversion,* which is the degree to which a person directs his energies outward toward the environment and other people versus inward toward his inner and self-focused experiences. A person who is high on the dimension of *introversion* might be quiet, solitary, and reserved, avoiding new experiences. A person high on the *extraversion* scale would be outgoing

trait
A relatively stable, enduring predisposition to consistently behave in a certain way.

trait theory
A theory of personality that focuses on identifying, describing, and measuring individual differences in behavioral predispositions.

surface traits
Personality characteristics or attributes that can easily be inferred from observable behavior.

source traits
The most fundamental dimensions of personality; the broad, basic traits that are hypothesized to be universal and relatively few in number.

Raymond Cattell (1905–1998) Cattell was a strong advocate of the trait approach to personality. His research led to the development of the Sixteen Personality Factor Questionnaire, one of the most widely used psychological tests for assessing personality.

Table 10.3

Cattell's 16 Personality Factors

1 Reserved, unsociable	⟷	Outgoing, sociable
2 Less intelligent, concrete	⟷	More intelligent, abstract
3 Affected by feelings	⟷	Emotionally stable
4 Submissive, humble	⟷	Dominant, assertive
5 Serious	⟷	Happy-go-lucky
6 Expedient	⟷	Conscientious
7 Timid	⟷	Venturesome
8 Tough-minded	⟷	Sensitive
9 Trusting	⟷	Suspicious
10 Practical	⟷	Imaginative
11 Forthright	⟷	Shrewd, calculating
12 Self-assured	⟷	Apprehensive
13 Conservative	⟷	Experimenting
14 Group-dependent	⟷	Self-sufficient
15 Undisciplined	⟷	Controlled
16 Relaxed	⟷	Tense

SOURCE: Adapted from Cattell (1973).

Raymond Cattell believed that personality could be described in terms of 16 source traits, or basic personality factors. Each factor represents a dimension that ranges between two extremes.

and sociable, enjoying new experiences and stimulating environments.

Eysenck's second major dimension is *neuroticism–emotional stability. Neuroticism* refers to a person's predisposition to become emotionally upset, while *stability* reflects a person's predisposition to be emotionally even. Surface traits associated with neuroticism are anxiety, tension, depression, and guilt. At the opposite end, emotional stability is associated with the surface traits of being calm, relaxed, and even-tempered.

Eysenck believed that by combining these two dimensions people can be classified into four basic types: introverted–neurotic, introverted–stable, extraverted–neurotic, and extraverted–stable. Each basic type is associated with a different combination of surface traits, as shown in Figure 10.3.

In later research, Eysenck identified a third personality dimension, called *psychoticism* (Eysenck, 1990; Eysenck & Eysenck, 1975). A person high on this trait is antisocial, cold, hostile, and unconcerned about others. A person who is low on psychoticism is warm and caring toward others. In the chapter Prologue, Julian might be described as above average on psychoticism, while Kenneth was extremely low on this trait.

Eysenck (1990) believed that individual differences in personality are due to biological differences among people. For example, Eysenck proposed that an introvert's nervous system is more easily aroused than is an extravert's nervous system. Assuming that people tend to seek out an optimal level of arousal (see Chapter 8), extraverts would seek stimulation from their environment more than introverts would. And, because introverts would be more uncomfortable than extraverts in a highly stimulating environment, introverts would be much less likely to seek out stimulation.

Do introverts and extraverts actually prefer different environments? In a clever study, John Campbell and Charles Hawley (1982) found that extraverted students tended to study in a relatively noisy, open area of a college library, where there were ample opportunities for socializing with other students. Introverted students preferred to study in a quiet section of the library, where individual carrels and small tables were separated by tall bookshelves. As Eysenck's theory predicts, the introverts preferred study areas that minimized stimulation, while the extraverts preferred studying in an area that provided stimulation.

Brain-imaging studies are providing a different line of evidence supporting Eysenck's idea that personality traits reflect biological differences (Canli, 2004; Canli & others, 2002, 2004). The Focus on Neuroscience describes a pioneer investigation of the association of particular personality traits with distinct patterns of brain activity.

FIGURE 10.3 Eysenck's Theory of Personality Types Hans Eysenck's representation of the four basic personality types. Each type represents a combination of two basic personality dimensions: extraversion–introversion and neuroticism–emotional stability. Note the different surface traits in each quadrant that are associated with each basic personality type.

SOURCE: Adapted from Eysenck (1982).

Neuroscience: Personality Traits and Patterns of Brain Activity

focus on

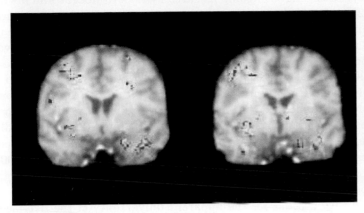 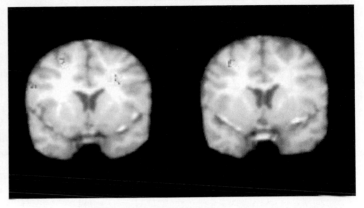

(a) Extraversion correlating with brain reactivity to positive pictures

(b) Neuroticism correlating with brain reactivity to negative pictures

People who rate high on the personality trait of extraversion tend to be upbeat, optimistic, and sociable. They also report experiencing more positive emotions on a daily basis than less extraverted people. In contrast, people who rate high on neuroticism tend to be anxious, worried, and socially insecure. And they report more negative emotions in everyday life than less neurotic people. Could these personality traits also influence how the brain responds to emotional situations?

To investigate this idea, psychologist Turhan Canli and his colleagues (2001) gave 14 healthy female volunteers a personality test to determine their level of extraversion or neuroticism. Then, each woman was placed in a functional magnetic resonance imaging (fMRI) scanner to record her brain's reaction to positive images (e.g., a happy couple, puppies, ice cream, sunsets) or negative images (e.g., angry or crying people, spiders, guns, or a cemetery).

The fMRI showed that the women who scored high on extraversion had greater brain reactivity to positive images than did the women who scored low on extraversion. In image (a), red locations show significant positive correlations between extraversion and reac-

tions to positive images. For the extraverted women, brain activity in response to the positive images was most strongly correlated with brain areas associated with emotion, including the frontal cortex and the amygdala.

In contrast, the women who scored high on neuroticism had more brain activation in response to negative images, but in fewer brain areas associated with emotions. In image (b), blue locations show significant positive correlations between neuroticism and reactions to negative images. These areas of activation were mostly in the left frontal and temporal cortical areas.

What this study shows is that specific personality traits are associated with individual differences in the brain's reaction to emotional stimuli. According to researcher John Gabrieli (2001), "Depending on personality traits, people's brains seem to amplify some aspects of experience over others. All of the participants in this study saw very positive and very negative scenes, but people's brain reactions were very different. One group saw the cup as being very full while the other group saw it as very empty."

Sixteen Are Too Many, Three Are Too Few

The Five-Factor Model

Many trait theorists felt that Cattell's trait model was too complex and that his 16 personality factors could be reduced to a smaller, more basic set of traits. Yet Eysenck's three-dimensional trait theory seemed too limited, failing to capture other important dimensions of human personality (see Block, 1995).

Today, the consensus among many trait researchers is that the essential building blocks of personality can be described in terms of five basic personality dimensions, which are sometimes called "the Big Five" (Funder, 2001). According to the **five-factor model of personality,** these five dimensions represent the structural organization of personality traits (McCrae & Costa, 1996).

What are the Big Five? Different trait researchers describe the five basic traits somewhat differently. However, the most commonly accepted five factors are extraversion, neuroticism, agreeableness, conscientiousness, and openness to experience. Table 10.4 summarizes the Big Five traits, as defined by personality theorists Robert McCrae and Paul Costa, Jr. Note that factor 1, neuroticism, and factor 2, extraversion, are essentially the same as Eysenck's first two personality dimensions.

five-factor model of personality
A trait theory of personality that identifies five basic source traits (extraversion, neuroticism, agreeableness, conscientiousness, and openness to experience) as the fundamental building blocks of personality.

Table 10.4

The Five-Factor Model of Personality

Factor 1: Neuroticism

Calm	←——→	Worrying
Even-tempered, unemotional	←——→	Temperamental, emotional
Hardy	←——→	Affectionate

Factor 2: Extraversion

Reserved	←——→	Affectionate
Loner	←——→	Joiner
Quiet	←——→	Talkative

Factor 3: Openness to Experience

Down-to-Earth	←——→	Imaginative
Unconventional, uncreative	←——→	Original, creative
Prefer routine	←——→	Prefer variety

Factor 4: Agreeableness

Antagonistic	←——→	Acquiescent
Ruthless	←——→	Softhearted
Suspicious	←——→	Trusting

Factor 5: Conscientiousness

Lazy	←——→	Hardworking
Aimless	←——→	Ambitious
Quitting	←——→	Persevering

SOURCE: Adapted from McCrae & Costa (1990).

This table shows the five major personality factors, according to Big Five theorists Robert McCrae and Paul Costa, Jr. Listed below each major personality factor are surface traits that are associated with it. Note that each factor represents a dimension or range between two extreme poles. Most people will fall somewhere in the middle between the two opposing poles.

The Continuity of Traits over the Lifespan Kenneth's conscientiousness was a trait that was evident throughout his life. Because he was too old to join the military when the United States entered World War II, Kenneth volunteered his legal expertise to the American Red Cross, providing them with legal services for the western half of the United States.

Does the five-factor model describe the universal structure of human personality? According to ongoing research by Robert McCrae and his colleagues (2004, 2005) the answer appears to be yes. In one wide-ranging study, trained observers rated the personality traits of representative individuals in fifty different cultures, including Arab cultures like Kuwait and Morocco and African cultures like Uganda and Ethiopia (McCrae & others, 2005). With few exceptions, people could be reliably described in terms of the five-factor structure of personality. Other research has shown that people in European, African, Arab, and Asian cultures describe personality using terms that are consistent with the five-factor model (Allik & McCrae, 2004; Rossier & others, 2005). Based upon abundant cross-cultural research, trait theorists Juri Allik and Robert McCrae (2002, 2004) now believe that the Big Five personality traits are basic features of the human species, universal and probably biologically based.

How can we account for the apparent universality of the five-factor structure? Psychologist David Buss (1991, 1995a) has one intriguing explanation. Buss thinks we should look at the utility of these factors from an evolutionary perspective. He believes that the Big Five traits reflect the personality dimensions that are the most important in the "social landscape" to which humans have had to adapt. Being able to identify who has social power (extraversion), who is likely to share resources (agreeableness), and who is trustworthy (conscientiousness) enhances our likelihood of survival.

Research has shown that traits are remarkably stable over time. A young adult who is very extraverted, emotionally stable, and relatively open to new experiences is likely to grow into an older adult who could be described in much the same way (McCrae & Costa, 1990; McCrae & others, 2000). However, this is not to say that personality traits don't change at all. Longitudinal data suggest that some general trends are evident over the lifespan. These include a slight decline in Neuroticism and Openness to Experience, an increase in Agreeableness and Conscientiousness, and stability in Extraversion from early to late adulthood (Terracciano & others, 2005). In other words, most people become more dominant, agreeable, conscientious, and emotionally stable as they mature psychologically (Caspi & others, 2005).

Traits are also generally consistent across different situations. However, situational influences may affect the expression of personality traits. Situations in which your behavior is limited by social "rules" or expectations may limit the expression of your personality characteristics. For example, even the most extraverted person may be subdued at a funeral. In general, behavior is most likely

to reflect personality traits in familiar, informal, or private situations with few social rules or expectations (A. H. Buss, 1989).

Keep in mind, however, that human behavior is the result of a complex *interaction* between traits and situations (Mischel, 2004). People *do* respond, sometimes dramatically, to the demands of a particular situation. But the situations that people choose, and the characteristic way in which they respond to similar situations, are likely to be consistent with their individual personality dispositions (Mischel & Shoda, 1995; Mischel & others, 2002).

Personality Traits and Behavioral Genetics
Just a Chip off the Old Block?

Do personality traits run in families? Are personality traits determined by genetics? Many trait theorists, such as Raymond Cattell and Hans Eysenck, believed that traits are at least partially genetic in origin. For example, our daughter Laura has always been outgoing and sociable, traits that she shares with both her parents. But is she outgoing because she inherited that trait from us? Or is she outgoing because we modeled and reinforced outgoing behavior? Is it even possible to sort out the relative influence that genetics and environmental experiences have on personality traits?

The field of **behavioral genetics** studies the effects of genes and heredity on behavior. Most behavioral genetics studies on humans involve measuring similarities and differences among members of a large group of people who are genetically related to different degrees. The basic research strategy is to compare the degree of difference among subjects to their degree of genetic relatedness. If a trait is genetically influenced, then the more closely two people are genetically related, the more you would expect them to be similar on that trait (see Chapter 7).

Such studies may involve comparisons between identical twins and fraternal twins or comparisons between twins reared apart and identical twins reared together (see In Focus Box 10.2). Adoption studies, in which adopted children are compared to their biological and adoptive relatives, are also used in behavioral genetics.

Evidence gathered from twin studies and adoption studies shows that certain personality traits *are* substantially influenced by genetics (see Caspi & others, 2005). The evidence for genetic influence is particularly strong for extraversion and neuroticism, two of the Big Five personality traits (Plomin & others, 1994, 2001). Twin studies have also found that openness to experience, conscientiousness, and agreeableness are also influenced by genetics, although to a lesser extent (Bouchard, 2004).

So is personality completely determined by genetics? Not at all. As behavioral geneticists Robert Plomin and Essi Colledge (2001) explain, "Individual differences in complex psychological traits are due at least as much to environmental influences as they are to genetic influences. Behavioral genetics research provides the best available evidence for the importance of the environment." In other words, the influence of environmental factors on personality traits is at least equal to the influence of genetic factors (Rowe, 2003). Some additional evidence that underscores this point is that identical twins are most alike in early life. As the twins grow up, leave home, and encounter different experiences and environments, their personalities become more different (Bouchard, 2004; McCartney & others, 1990).

Evaluating the Trait Perspective on Personality

Although psychologists continue to disagree on how many basic traits exist, they do generally agree that people can be described and compared in terms of basic personality traits. But like the other personality theories, the trait approach has its weaknesses (Block, 1995).

One criticism is that trait theories don't really explain human personality (Pervin, 1994). Instead, they simply label

behavioral genetics
An interdisciplinary field that studies the effects of genes and heredity on behavior.

> *Behavioral genetics has documented, without a shadow of a remaining doubt, that personality is to some degree genetically influenced: Identical twins reared apart have similar traits. The tabula rasa view of personality as a blank slate at birth that is written upon by experience, for many years a basic assumption of theories of all stripes, is wrong.*
>
> David C. Funder (2001)

> *Genes confer dispositions, not destinies.*
>
> Danielle Dick & Richard Rose (2002)

Why Are Siblings So Different? Although two children may grow up in the same home, they experience the home environment in very different ways. Even an event that affects the entire family, such as divorce, unemployment, or a family move, may be experienced quite differently by each child in the family (Dunn & Plomin, 1990). Children are also influenced by varied experiences outside the home, such as their relationships with teachers, classmates, and friends. Illness and accidents are other nonshared environmental influences. Of course, sibling relationships are themselves a potential source of influence on personality development.

IN FOCUS 10.2

Explaining Those Amazing Identical-Twin Similarities

As part of the ongoing "Minnesota Study of Twins Reared Apart" at the University of Minnesota, researchers David Lykken, Thomas Bouchard, and other psychologists have been studying a very unusual group of people: over 100 pairs of identical and fraternal twins who were separated at birth or in early childhood and raised in different homes. Shortly after the study began in 1980, the researchers were struck by some of the amazing similarities between identical twins (Lykken & others, 1992). Despite having been separated for most of their lives, many twins had similar personality traits, occupations, hobbies, and habits.

One of the most famous cases is that of the "Jim twins," who had been separated for close to 40 years. Like many of the other reunited twins, the two Jims had similar heights, postures, and voice and speech patterns. More strikingly, both Jims had married and divorced women named Linda, and then married women named Betty. One Jim named his son James Allan, while the other Jim named his son James Alan. Both Jims bit their nails, chain-smoked Salems, and enjoyed working in their basement workshops. And both Jims had vacationed at the same Florida beach, driving there in the same model Chevrolet (Lykken & others, 1992).

Granted, such similarities could simply be due to coincidence. Linda, Betty, James, and Alan are not exactly rare names in the United States. And literally thousands of people buy the same model car every year, just as thousands of people vacation in Florida. Besides, if you look closely at any two people of the same age, sex, and culture, there are bound to be similarities. It's probably a safe bet, for example, to say that most college students enjoy eating pizza and often wear jeans and T-shirts.

But it's difficult to dismiss as mere coincidences all the striking similarities between identical twins in the Minnesota study. Lykken and his colleagues (1992) have pointed out numerous quirky similarities that occurred in the identical twins they studied but did not occur in the fraternal-twin pairs. For example, in

Heredity or Environment? Along with sharing common genes, many identical twins share common interests and talents—like concert pianists Alvin (*left*) and Alan Chow. As students at the University of Maryland, they graduated with identical straight-A averages—and shared the stage as co-valedictorians. Both studied piano at Juilliard, and today they are both music professors with active performance schedules. In addition to performing solo, they frequently perform together in recital. Because the Chow twins were reared together, it would be difficult to determine the relative importance of environmental and genetic influences on their talents and career paths.

the entire sample of twins, there were only two subjects who had been married five times; two subjects who habitually wore seven rings; and two who left love notes around the house for their wives. In each case, the two were identical twins. And only two subjects independently (and correctly) diagnosed a problem with researcher Bouchard's car—a faulty wheel bearing. Again, the two were members of an identical-twin pair. While Lykken and his colleagues acknowledge that some identical-twin similarities are probably due to coincidence, such as the Jim twins marrying women with the same first names, others are probably genetically influenced.

So does this mean that there's a gene for

getting married five times or wearing seven rings? Not exactly. Although some physical characteristics and diseases are influenced by a single gene, complex psychological characteristics, such as your personality, are influenced by a large number of genes acting in combination (Caspi & others, 2005; Marcus, 2004). Unlike fraternal twins and regular siblings, identical twins share the same specific *configuration* of interacting genes. Lykken and his colleagues suggest that many complex psychological traits, including the strikingly similar idiosyncrasies of identical twins, may result from a unique configuration of interacting genes.

Lykken and his colleagues call certain traits *emergenic traits* because they appear (or *emerge*) only out of a unique configuration of many interacting genes. Although they are genetically influenced, emergenic traits do not run in families. To illustrate the idea of emergenic traits, consider the couple of average intelligence who give birth to an extraordinarily gifted child. By all predictions, this couple's offspring should have normal, average intelligence. But because of the unique configuration of the child's genes acting in combination, extraordinary giftedness emerges (Lykken & others, 1992).

David Lykken compares emergenic traits to a winning poker hand. All the members of the family are drawing from the same "deck," or pool of genes. But one member may come up with the special configuration of cards that produces a royal flush—the unique combination of genes that produces an Einstein or a Beethoven. History is filled with cases of people with exceptional talents and abilities in varied fields who grew up in average families.

Finally, it's important to point out that there were many differences, as well as similarities, between the identical twins in the Minnesota study. For example, one twin was prone to depression, while the other was not; one twin was an alcoholic, while the other did not drink. So, even with identical twins, it must be remembered that personality is only *partly* determined by genetics.

general predispositions to behave in a certain way. Second, trait theorists don't attempt to explain how or why individual differences develop. After all, saying that trait differences are due partly to genetics and partly to environmental influences doesn't say much.

A third criticism is that trait approaches generally fail to address other important personality issues, such as the basic motives that drive human personality, the role of unconscious mental processes, how beliefs about the self influence personality, or how psychological change and growth occur (McAdams, 1992). Conspicuously absent are the grand conclusions about the essence of human nature that characterize the psychoanalytic and humanistic theories. So, although trait theories are useful in describing individual differences and predicting behavior, there are limitations to their usefulness.

As you've seen, each of the major perspectives on personality has contributed to our understanding of human personality. The four perspectives are summarized in Table 10.5.

Our discussion of personality would not be complete without a description of how personality is formally evaluated and measured. In the next section, we'll briefly survey the tests that are used in personality assessment.

Assessing Personality
Psychological Tests

Key Theme
■ Tests to measure and evaluate personality fall into two basic categories: projective tests and self-report inventories.

Key Questions
■ What are the most widely used personality tests, and how are they administered and interpreted?
■ What are the strengths and weaknesses of projective tests and self-report inventories?

When we discussed intelligence tests in Chapter 7, we described what makes a good psychological test. Beyond intelligence tests, there are literally hundreds of **psychological tests** that can be used to assess abilities, aptitudes, interests, and personality (see Plake & Impara, 2001). Any psychological test is useful insofar as it achieves two basic goals:

1. It accurately and consistently reflects a person's characteristics on some dimension.

2. It predicts a person's future psychological functioning or behavior.

In this section, we'll look at the very different approaches used in the two basic types of personality tests—projective tests and self-report inventories. After looking at some of the most commonly used tests in each category, we'll evaluate the strengths and weaknesses of each approach.

Table	10.5

The Major Personality Perspectives

Perspective	Key Theorists	Key Themes and Ideas
Psychoanalytic	Sigmund Freud	Influence of unconscious psychological processes; importance of sexual and aggressive instincts; lasting effects of early childhood experiences
	Carl Jung	The collective unconscious, archetypes, and psychological harmony
	Karen Horney	Importance of parent–child relationship; defending against basic anxiety; womb envy
	Alfred Adler	Striving for superiority, compensating for feelings of inferiority
Humanistic	Carl Rogers	Emphasis on the self-concept, psychological growth, free will, and inherent goodness
	Abraham Maslow	Behavior as motivated by hierarchy of needs and striving for self-actualization
Social cognitive	Albert Bandura	Reciprocal interaction of behavioral, cognitive, and environmental factors; emphasis on conscious thoughts, self-efficacy beliefs, self-regulation, and goal setting
Trait	Raymond Cattell	Emphasis on measuring and describing individual differences; 16 source traits of personality
	Hans Eysenck	Three basic dimensions of personality: introversion–extraversion, neuroticism–emotional stability, and psychoticism
	Robert McCrae, Paul Costa, Jr.	Five-factor model: five basic dimensions of personality: neuroticism, extraversion, openness to experience, agreeableness, conscientiousness

psychological test
A test that assesses a person's abilities, aptitudes, interests, or personality, on the basis of a systematically obtained sample of behavior.

What Do You See in the Inkblot? Intrigued by Freud and Jung's theories, Swiss psychiatrist Hermann Rorschach (1884–1922) set out to develop a test that would reveal the contents of the unconscious. Rorschach believed that people were more likely to expose their unconscious conflicts, motives, and defenses in their descriptions of the ambiguous inkblots than they would be if the same topics were directly addressed. Rorschach published a series of ten inkblots with an accompanying manual in a monograph titled *Psychodiagnostics: A Diagnostic Test Based on Perception* in 1921. Because he died the following year, Rorschach never knew how popular his projective test would become. Although the validity of the test is questionable, the Rorschach Inkblot Test is still the icon most synonymous with psychological testing in the popular media.

Projective Tests
Like Seeing Things in the Clouds

Projective tests developed out of psychoanalytic approaches to personality. In the most commonly used projective tests, a person is presented with a vague image, such as an inkblot or an ambiguous scene, then asked to describe what she "sees" in the image. The person's response is thought to be a projection of her unconscious conflicts, motives, psychological defenses, and personality traits. Notice that this idea is related to the defense mechanism of *projection,* which was described in Table 10.1 (page 403). The first projective test was the famous **Rorschach Inkblot Test,** published by Swiss psychiatrist Hermann Rorschach in 1921 (Hertz, 1992).

The Rorschach test consists of 10 cards, 5 that show black-and-white inkblots and 5 that depict colored inkblots. One card at a time, the person describes whatever he sees in the inkblot. The examiner records the person's responses verbatim and also observes his behavior, gestures, and reactions.

Numerous scoring systems exist for the Rorschach. Interpretation is based on such criteria as whether the person reports seeing animate or inanimate objects, human or animal figures, and movement and whether the person deals with the whole blot or just fragments of it (Exner, 1993).

A more structured projective test is the **Thematic Apperception Test,** abbreviated **TAT,** which we discussed in Chapter 8. In the TAT, the person looks at a series of cards, each depicting an ambiguous scene. The person is asked to create a story about the scene, including what the characters are feeling and how the story turns out. The stories are scored for the motives, needs, anxieties, and conflicts of the main character and for how conflicts are resolved (Bellak, 1993). As with the Rorschach, interpreting the TAT involves the subjective judgment of the examiner.

Strengths and Limitations of Projective Tests

Although sometimes used in research, projective tests are mainly used in counseling and psychotherapy. According to many clinicians, the primary strength of projective tests is that they provide a wealth of qualitative information about an individual's psychological functioning, information that can be explored further in psychotherapy.

However, there are several drawbacks to projective tests. First, the testing situation or the examiner's behavior can influence a person's responses. Second, the scoring of projective tests is highly subjective, requiring the examiner to

projective test
A type of personality test that involves a person's interpreting an ambiguous image; used to assess unconscious motives, conflicts, psychological defenses, and personality traits.

Rorschach Inkblot Test
A projective test using inkblots, developed by Swiss psychiatrist Hermann Rorschach in 1921.

Graphology: The "Write" Way to Assess Personality?

Does the way that you shape your *d*'s, dot your *i*'s, and cross your *t*'s reveal your true inner nature? That's the basic premise of **graphology**, a pseudoscience that claims that your handwriting reveals your temperament, personality traits, intelligence, and reasoning ability. If that weren't enough, graphologists also claim that they can accurately evaluate a job applicant's honesty, reliability, leadership potential, ability to work with others, and so forth (Beyerstein & Beyerstein, 1992).

Handwriting analysis is very popular throughout North America and Europe. In the United States alone, there are over 30 graphology societies, each promoting its own specific methods of analyzing handwriting (Beyerstein, 1996). Many different types of agencies and institutions use graphology. For example, the FBI and the U.S. State Department have consulted graphologists to assess the handwriting of people who mail death threats to government officials (Scanlon & Mauro, 1992).

Graphology is especially popular in the business world. Thousands of American companies, including Sears, U.S. Steel, and Bendix, have used graphology to assist in hiring new employees (Basil, 1991; Taylor & Sackheim, 1988). The use of graphology in hiring and promotions is even more widespread in Europe. According to one estimate, over 80 percent of European companies use graphology in personnel matters (Greasley, 2000).

When subjected to scientific evaluation, how does graphology fare? Consider a study by Anthony Edwards and Peter Armitage (1992) that investigated graphologists' ability to distinguish between people in three different groups:

- Successful versus unsuccessful secretaries

- Successful business entrepreneurs versus librarians and bank clerks

- Actors and actresses versus monks and nuns

In designing their study, Edwards and Armitage enlisted the help of leading graphologists and incorporated their suggestions into the study design. The graphologists preapproved the study's format and indicated that they felt it was a fair test of graphology. The graphologists

DILBERT

also predicted they would have a high degree of success in discriminating between the people in each group. One graphologist stated that the graphologists would have close to a 100 percent success rate. Remember that prediction.

The three groups—successful/unsuccessful secretaries, entrepreneurs/librarians, and actors/monks—represented a combined total of 170 participants. As requested by the graphologists, all participants indicated their age, sex, and hand preference. Each person also produced 20 lines of spontaneous handwriting on a neutral topic.

Four leading graphologists independently evaluated the handwriting samples. For each group, the graphologists tried to assign each handwriting sample to one category or the other. Two control measures were built into the study: (1) The handwriting samples were also analyzed by four ordinary people with *no* formal training in graphology or psychology; and (2) a *typewritten* transcript of the handwriting samples was evaluated by four psychologists. The psychologists made their evaluations on the basis of the *content* of the transcripts rather than on the handwriting itself.

In the accompanying table, you can see how well the graphologists fared as com-

pared to the untrained evaluators and the psychologists. Clearly, the graphologists fell far short of the nearly perfect accuracy they predicted they would demonstrate. In fact, in one case, the *untrained* assessors actually *outperformed* the graphologists—they were slightly better at identifying successful versus unsuccessful secretaries.

Overall, the completely inexperienced judges achieved a success rate of 59 percent correct. The professional graphologists achieved a slightly better success rate of 65 percent. Obviously, this is not a great difference.

Hundreds of other studies have cast similar doubts on the ability of graphology to identify personality characteristics and to predict job performance from handwriting samples (see Dean, 1992; Furnham, 1991; Neter & Ben-Shakhar, 1989). In a global review of the evidence, psychologist Barry Beyerstein (1996) wrote, "Graphologists have unequivocally failed to demonstrate the validity or reliability of their art for predicting work performance, aptitudes, or personality. . . . If graphology cannot legitimately claim to be a scientific means of measuring human talents and leanings, what is it really? In short, it is a pseudoscience."

Success Rates by Type of Assessor

Group Assessed	Graphologists	Untrained Assessors	Psychologists
Good/bad secretaries	67%	70%	56%
Entrepreneurs/librarians	63%	53%	52%
Actors/monks	67%	58%	53%
Overall success rate	65%	59%	54%

The Thematic Apperception Test Developed by psychologists Christiana Morgan and Henry Murray (1935), the TAT involves creating a story about an ambiguous scene, like the one shown on the card this young man is holding. The person is thought to project his own motives, conflicts, and other personality characteristics into the story he creates. According to Murray (1943), "Before he knows it, he has said things about an invented character that apply to himself, things which he would have been reluctant to confess in response to a direct question."

make numerous judgments about the person's responses. Consequently, two examiners may test the same individual and arrive at different conclusions. Third, projective tests often fail to produce consistent results. If the same person takes a projective test on two separate occasions, very different results may be found. Finally, projective tests are poor at predicting future behavior.

The bottom line? Despite their widespread use, hundreds of studies of projective tests seriously question their *validity*—that the tests measure what they purport to measure—and their *reliability*—the consistency of test results (see Lilienfeld & others, 2000, 2001). Nonetheless, projective tests remain very popular, especially among clinical psychologists (Butcher & Rouse, 1996).

Self-Report Inventories
Does Anyone Have an Eraser?

Self-report inventories typically use a paper-and-pencil format and take a direct, structured approach to assessing personality. People answer specific questions or rate themselves on various dimensions of behavior or psychological functioning. Often called *objective personality tests,* self-report inventories contain items that have been shown by previous research to differentiate between people on a particular personality characteristic. Unlike projective tests, self-report inventories are objectively scored by comparing a person's answers to standardized norms collected on large groups of people.

The most widely used self-report inventory is the **Minnesota Multiphasic Personality Inventory (MMPI)** (Butcher & Rouse, 1996). First published in the 1940s and revised in the 1980s, the current version is referred to as the *MMPI-2.* The MMPI consists of over 500 statements. The person responds to each statement with "True," "False," or "Cannot say." Topics include social, political, religious, and sexual attitudes; physical and psychological health; interpersonal relationships; and abnormal thoughts and behaviors (Graham, 1993). Items similar to those used in the MMPI are shown in Table 10.6.

The MMPI is widely used by clinical psychologists and psychiatrists to assess patients. It is also used to evaluate the mental health of candidates for such occupations as police officers, doctors, nurses, and professional pilots. What keeps people from simply answering items in a way that makes them look psychologically healthy? Like many other self-report inventories, the MMPI has special scales to detect whether a person is answering honestly and consistently (Butcher, 1999). For example, if someone responds "True" to items such as "I *never* put off until tomorrow what I should do today" and "I *always* pick up after myself," it's probably a safe bet that she is inadvertently or intentionally distorting her other responses.

The MMPI was originally designed to assess mental health and detect psychological symptoms. In contrast, the California Personality Inventory and the Sixteen Personality Factor Questionnaire are personality inventories that were designed to assess normal populations. Of the 462 true–false items on the

graphology
A pseudoscience that claims to assess personality, social, and occupational attributes based on a person's distinctive handwriting, doodles, and drawing style.

Thematic Apperception Test (TAT)
A projective personality test that involves creating stories about each of a series of ambiguous scenes.

self-report inventory
A type of psychological test in which a person's responses to standardized questions are compared to established norms.

Minnesota Multiphasic Personality Inventory (MMPI)
A self-report inventory that assesses personality characteristics and psychological disorders; used to assess both normal and disturbed populations.

Table 10.6

Simulated MMPI-2 Items

Most people will use somewhat unfair means to gain profit or an advantage rather than lose it.

I am often very tense on the job.

The things that run through my head sometimes are horrible.

Sometimes there is a feeling like something is pressing in on my head.

Sometimes I think so fast I can't keep up.

I am worried about sex.

I believe I am being plotted against.

I wish I could do over some of the things I have done.

SOURCE: MMPI-2®.

California Personality Inventory (CPI)
A self-report inventory that assesses personality characteristics in normal populations.

Sixteen Personality Factor Questionnaire (16PF)
A self-report inventory developed by Raymond Cattell that generates a personality profile with ratings on 16 trait dimensions.

California Personality Inventory (CPI), nearly half are drawn from the MMPI. The CPI provides measures on such characteristics as interpersonal effectiveness, self-control, independence, and empathy. Profiles generated by the CPI are used to predict such things as high school and college grades, delinquency, and job performance (Gough, 1989).

The **Sixteen Personality Factor Questionnaire (16PF)** was originally developed by Raymond Cattell and is based on his trait theory. The 16PF uses a forced-choice format in which the person must respond to each item by choosing one of three alternatives. Just as the test's name implies, the results generate a profile on Cattell's 16 personality factors. Each personality factor is represented as a range, with a person's score falling somewhere along the continuum between the two extremes (see Figure 10.4). The 16PF is widely used for career counseling, marital counseling, and evaluating employees and executives (Karson & O'Dell, 1989).

Strengths and Limitations of Self-Report Inventories

The two most important strengths of self-report inventories are their *standardization* and their *use of established norms* (see Chapter 7). Each person receives the same instructions and responds to the same items. The results of self-report

FIGURE 10.4 The 16PF: Example Questions and Profiles The 16PF, developed by Raymond Cattell, is a self-report inventory that contains 185 items like those shown in part (a). When scored, the 16PF generates a personality profile. In part (b), personality profiles of airline pilots and writers are compared. Cattell (1973) found that pilots are more controlled, more relaxed, more self-assured, and less sensitive than writers.

SOURCE: Cattell & others (1993).

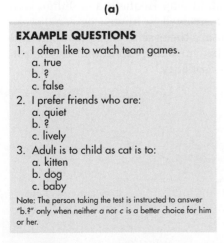

(a)

EXAMPLE QUESTIONS

1. I often like to watch team games.
   a. true
   b. ?
   c. false
2. I prefer friends who are:
   a. quiet
   b. ?
   c. lively
3. Adult is to child as cat is to:
   a. kitten
   b. dog
   c. baby

Note: The person taking the test is instructed to answer "b. ?" only when neither a nor c is a better choice for him or her.

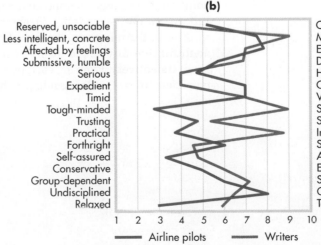

(b)

	1	2	3	4	5	6	7	8	9	10	
Reserved, unsociable											Outgoing, sociable
Less intelligent, concrete											More intelligent, abstract
Affected by feelings											Emotionally stable
Submissive, humble											Dominant, assertive
Serious											Happy-go-lucky
Expedient											Conscientious
Timid											Venturesome
Tough-minded											Sensitive
Trusting											Suspicious
Practical											Imaginative
Forthright											Shrewd, calculating
Self-assured											Apprehensive
Conservative											Experimenting
Group-dependent											Self-sufficient
Undisciplined											Controlled
Relaxed											Tense

—— Airline pilots   —— Writers

possible selves
The aspect of the self-concept that includes images of the selves that you hope, fear, or expect to become in the future.

inventories are objectively scored and compared to norms established by previous research. In fact, the MMPI, the CPI, and the 16PF can all be scored by computer.

As a general rule, the reliability and validity of self-report inventories are far greater than those of projective tests. Literally thousands of studies have demonstrated that the MMPI, the CPI, and the 16PF provide accurate, consistent results that can be used to generally predict behavior (Anastasi & Urbina, 1997).

However, self-report inventories also have their weaknesses. First, despite the inclusion of items designed to detect deliberate deception, there is considerable evidence that people can still successfully fake responses and answer in socially desirable ways (Anastasi & Urbina, 1997). Second, some people are prone to responding in a set way. They may consistently pick the first alternative or answer "True" whether the item is true for them or not. And some tests, such as the MMPI and CPI, include hundreds of items. Taking these tests can become quite tedious, and people may lose interest in carefully choosing the most appropriate response.

Third, people are not always accurate judges of their own behavior, attitudes, or attributes. And some people defensively deny their true feelings, needs, and attitudes, even to themselves (Shedler & others, 1993). For example, a person might indicate that she enjoys parties, even though she actually avoids social gatherings whenever possible.

To sum up, personality tests are generally useful strategies that can provide insights about the psychological makeup of people. But no personality test, by itself, is likely to provide a definitive description of a given individual. In practice, psychologists and other mental health professionals usually combine personality test results with behavioral observations and background information, including interviews with family members, co-workers, or other significant people in the person's life.

Finally, people can and often do change over time, especially when their life circumstances undergo a significant change. Hence, projective tests and self-report inventories provide a barometer of personality and psychological functioning only at the time of the test.

Closing Thoughts

Over the course of this chapter, you've encountered firsthand some of the most influential contributors to modern psychological thought. As you'll see in Chapter 14, the major personality perspectives provide the basis for many forms of psychotherapy. Clearly, the psychoanalytic, humanistic, social cognitive, and trait perspectives each provide a fundamentally different way of conceptualizing personality. That each perspective has strengths and limitations underscores the point that no single perspective can explain all aspects of human personality. Indeed, no one personality theory could explain why Kenneth and Julian were so different. And, given the complex factors involved in human personality, it's doubtful that any single theory ever will capture the essence of human personality in its entirety. Even so, each perspective has made important and lasting contributions to the understanding of human personality.

APPLICATION   Possible Selves: Imagine the Possibilities

Some psychologists believe that a person's self-concept is not a singular mental self-image, as Carl Rogers proposed, but a *multifaceted system* of related images and ideas (Hermans, 1996; Markus & Kunda, 1986). This collection of related images about yourself reflects your goals, values, emotions, and relationships (Markus & Cross, 1990; Markus & Wurf, 1987).

According to psychologist Hazel Markus and her colleagues, an important aspect of your self-concept has to do with your images of the selves that you *might* become— your **possible selves.** Possible selves are highly personalized, vivid, futuristic images of the self that reflect hopes, fears, and fantasies. As Markus and co-researcher Paula Nurius (1986) wrote, "The possible selves that are hoped for might include the successful self, the creative self, the rich self, the thin self, or the loved and admired self, whereas the dreaded possible selves could be the alone self, the depressed self, the incompetent self, the alcoholic self, the unemployed self, or the bag lady self."

The Influence of Hoped-For and Dreaded Possible Selves

Possible selves are more than just idle daydreams or wishful fantasies. In fact, possible selves influence our behavior in important ways (Markus & Nurius, 1986; Oyserman & others, 1995). We're often not aware of the possible selves that we have incorporated into our self-concepts. Nevertheless, they can serve as powerful forces that either activate or stall our efforts to reach important goals. Your incentive,

drive, and motivation are greatly influenced by your possible selves, and so are your decisions and choices about future behavior (Robinson & others, 2003).

Imagine that you harbor a hoped-for possible self of becoming a professional musician. You would probably practice with greater regularity and intensity than someone who does not hold a vivid mental picture of performing solo at Carnegie Hall or being named Performer of the Year at the American Country Music Awards.

Dreaded possible selves can also influence behavior, whether they are realistic or not. Consider Don's father, Kenneth. Although never wealthy, Kenneth was financially secure throughout his long life. Yet Kenneth had lived through the Great Depression and witnessed firsthand the financial devastation that occurred in the lives of countless people. Kenneth seems to have harbored a dreaded possible self of becoming penniless. When Kenneth died, the family found a $100 bill tucked safely under his mattress.

A positive possible self, even if it is not very realistic, can protect an individual's self-esteem in the face of failure (Markus & Nurius, 1986). A high school girl who thinks she is unpopular with her classmates may console herself with visions of a possible self as a famous scientist who snubs her intellectually inferior classmates at her 10-year class reunion. As Hazel Markus and Paul Nurius (1986) explained:

> Positive possible selves can be exceedingly liberating because they foster hope that the present self is not immutable. At the same time, negative

possible selves can be powerfully imprisoning because their [emotional impact] and expectations may stifle attempts to change or develop.

Possible Selves, Self-Efficacy Beliefs, and Motivation

Self-efficacy beliefs are closely connected to the idea of possible selves. Performing virtually any task involves the construction of a possible self that is capable and competent of performing the action required (Ruvolo & Markus, 1992).

Thus, people who vividly imagine possible selves as "successful because of hard work" persist longer and expend more effort on tasks than do people who imagine themselves as "unsuccessful despite hard work" (Ruvolo & Markus, 1992). The motivation to achieve academically increases when your possible selves include a future self who is successful because of academic achievement (Oyserman & others, 1995). To be most effective, possible selves should incorporate concrete strategies for attaining goals. For examples, students who visualized themselves taking specific steps to improve their grades—such as doing homework daily or signing up for tutoring— were more successful than students who simply imagined themselves doing better in school (Oyserman & others, 2004).

Applying the Research: Assessing Your Possible Selves

How can you apply these research findings to *your* life? First, it's important to stress again that we're often unaware of how

the possible selves we've mentally constructed influence our beliefs, actions, and self-evaluations. Thus, the first step is to consciously assess the role that your possible selves play in your life (Oyserman & others, 1995).

Take a few moments and jot down the "possible selves" that are active in your working self-concept. To help you in this task, write three responses to each of the following questions:

1. Next year, I expect to be . . .
2. Next year, I am afraid that I will be . . .
3. Next year, I want to avoid becoming . . .

After focusing on the short-term future, take these same questions and extend them to 5 years from now or even 10 years from now. Most likely, certain themes and goals will consistently emerge. Now the critical questions:

■ How are your possible selves affecting your *current* motivation, goals, feelings, and decisions?

■ Are your possible selves even remotely plausible?

■ Are they pessimistic and limiting?

■ Are they unrealistically optimistic?

Finally, ask yourself honestly: What realistic strategies are you using to try to become like the self that you want to become? To avoid becoming the selves that you dread?

To make sure that your possible selves go beyond the stage of fantasy or wishful thinking, it's important that you link your expectations and hopes to concrete strategies about how to behave to reach your desired possible self (Oyserman & others, 2004).

These questions should help you gain some insight into whether your possible selves are influencing your behavior in productive, constructive ways. If they are not, now is an excellent time to think about replacing or modifying the possible selves that operate most powerfully in your own self-concept. Why is this so important? Because to a large extent, who we become is guided by who we *imagine* we'll become. Just imagine the possibilities of who *you* could become!

Chapter Review

Personality

Key Points

Introduction: What Is Personality?

■ **Personality** is defined as an individual's unique and relatively consistent patterns of thinking, feeling, and behaving. **Personality theories** attempt to explain how people are similar in these patterns, why they are different, and why every individual is unique.

■ The four major theoretical perspectives on personality are the psychoanalytic, humanistic, social cognitive, and trait perspectives.

The Psychoanalytic Perspective on Personality

■ **Psychoanalysis** was founded by Sigmund Freud. It stresses the unconscious, the importance of sex and aggression, and the influence of early childhood experience. Freud's theory was extremely controversial throughout his lifetime and remains so today.

■ Freud believed that behavior is strongly influenced by the unconscious. The contents of the **unconscious** can surface in disguised form in **free associations,** dreams, slips of the tongue, and apparent accidents.

■ Personality consists of three psychological processes: id, ego, and superego. The **id** is fueled by instinctual energy and ruled by the **pleasure principle.** The two instinctual drives are **Eros,** the life instinct, and **Thanatos,** the death instinct. **Libido** is the psychological and emotional energy associated with the sex drive. The **ego** is partly conscious and is ruled by the **reality principle.** The **superego** is partly conscious and represents internalized moral values and rules.

■ Anxiety results when the demands of the id or the superego threaten to overwhelm the ego. **Ego defense mechanisms** reduce anxiety by distorting either thoughts or reality. **Repression** is involved in all ego defense mechanisms. **Displacement** is another defense mechanism involving the unconscious shifting of emotional impulses to a less threatening substitute target. **Sublimation** is a special form of displacement.

■ The **psychosexual stages** are age-related developmental periods in which sexual impulses are expressed through different bodily zones and activities associated with those areas. The foundations of adult personality are established during the first five years of life by the child's progression through the oral, anal, and phallic stages. One result of the **Oedipus complex** is that children come to imitate the behavior and characteristics of the same-sex parent, a process Freud called **identification.** Fixation at a particular stage may result if the developmental conflicts are not successfully resolved. The latency and genital stages occur during late childhood and adolescence.

- The neo-Freudians believed in the importance of the unconscious and early childhood experience but disagreed with other aspects of Freud's theory. Carl Jung emphasized psychological growth and proposed the existence of the **collective unconscious** and **archetypes.** Karen Horney emphasized the role of social relationships in protecting against basic anxiety. Horney objected to Freud's views on female development, particularly his idea of penis envy. Alfred Adler believed that the most fundamental human motive was to strive for superiority.

- Freud's theory has been criticized for resting on insufficient evidence, being difficult to test, and being sexist.

The Humanistic Perspective on Personality

- **Humanistic psychology** was championed as the "third force" in psychology. It emphasized human potential, psychological growth, self-awareness, and free will. Important humanistic theorists were Carl Rogers and Abraham Maslow.

- Rogers believed that the most basic human motive is the **actualizing tendency.** He viewed the **self-concept** as the most important aspect of personality. **Conditional positive regard** by parents or other caregivers causes a person to deny or distort aspects of experience, leading to a state of incongruence with regard to the self-concept. In contrast, **unconditional positive regard** leads to a state of congruence. The fully functioning person experiences congruence, the actualizing tendency, and psychological growth.

- The humanistic perspective on personality has been criticized for being difficult to validate or test scientifically and for being too optimistic.

The Social Cognitive Perspective on Personality

- Albert Bandura's **social cognitive theory** stresses the role of conscious thought processes, goals, and self-regulation. **Reciprocal determinism** emphasizes the interaction of behavioral, cognitive, and environmental factors in behavior and personality.

- **Self-efficacy** beliefs influence behavior, performance, motivation, and persistence.

- Social cognitive theories emphasize the interaction of multiple factors in determining personality and behavior. Although a key strength of this perspective is its grounding in empirical research, it has been criticized for its limited view of human personality, which ignores unconscious conflicts and emotions.

The Trait Perspective on Personality

- **Trait theories** focus on measuring and describing individual differences, or **traits. Surface traits** can be easily inferred from observable behaviors. **Source traits** are thought to represent the basic, fundamental dimensions of personality.

- Raymond Cattell believed that there are 16 basic personality factors. Hans Eysenck proposed that there are three basic personality dimensions. Eysenck believed that the extraversion–introversion dimension may reflect physiological differences.

- According to the **five-factor model,** there are five basic personality dimensions: extraversion, neuroticism, agreeableness, conscientiousness, and openness to experience.

- Traits are generally stable over time and across situations, although situations do influence how and whether traits are expressed.

- **Behavioral genetics** research uses twin and adoption studies to measure the relative influence of genetics and environment. Extraversion, neuroticism, openness to experience, and conscientiousness seem to have a significant genetic component.

- The trait perspective is useful in describing individual differences and in predicting behavior. Trait theories have been criticized for their failure to explain human personality and the development of individual differences.

Assessing Personality: Psychological Tests

- Valid **psychological tests** accurately reflect personal characteristics on some dimension and predict future psychological functioning or behavior. The two basic types of personality tests are projective tests and self-report inventories. **Projective tests** developed out of the psychoanalytic approach and include the **Rorschach Inkblot Test** and the **Thematic Apperception Test.**

- Projective tests provide qualitative information about an individual. They have some limitations: Responses may be affected by the examiner or the situation; scoring is very subjective; results may be inconsistent; and they do not predict behavior well.

- **Self-report inventories** are objectively scored and differentiate among people on particular personality characteristics. Self-report inventories include the **MMPI, CPI,** and **16PF.** The reliability, validity, and predictive value of self-report inventories are high. However, people do not always respond honestly or accurately to items in self-report inventories. Psychological tests provide just one measure of personality at a particular point in time.

High Life

Social Psychology

Prologue

The "Homeless" Man

Remember Erv and Fern, Sandy's parents, from Chapter 5? A few years ago, Fern and Erv got two free plane tickets when they were bumped from an overbooked flight. They decided to visit a city they had always wanted to see—San Francisco. Even though Fern was excited about the trip, she was also anxious about visiting the earthquake zone. Erv wasn't especially worried about earthquakes. Mostly, they both wanted to see the famous sights, eat seafood, wander through shops, and explore used bookstores, which is Erv's favorite hobby.

As it turned out, Fern and Erv were both quite taken by the beauty and charm of San Francisco. But they were also disturbed by the number of homeless people they saw on the city streets, sleeping in the doorways of expensive shops and restaurants. This was especially disturbing to Fern, who has a heart of gold and is known among her family and friends for her willingness to help others, even complete strangers.

On the third morning of their San Francisco visit, Erv and Fern were walking along one of the hilly San Francisco streets near the downtown area. That's when Fern saw a scruffy-looking man in faded jeans sitting on some steps, holding a cup. Surely this was one of San Francisco's less fortunate, Fern thought to herself. Without a moment's hesitation, Fern rummaged through her purse, walked over to the man, and dropped a handful of quarters in his cup.

"Hey, lady! What the hell d'ya think you're doing!?!" the man exclaimed.

"Oh, my! Aren't you homeless!?" Fern asked, mortified and turning bright red.

"Lady, this *is* my home," the man snapped, motioning with his thumb to the house behind him. "I live here! And that's my cup of coffee you just ruined!"

Fortunately, the "homeless" man also had a sense of humor. After fishing Fern's quarters out of his coffee, he chatted with the out-of-towners, enlightening them on the extraordinary cost of San Francisco real estate. As they parted, the not-so-homeless man ended up recommending a couple of his favorite seafood restaurants.

Like Fern, we all try to make sense out of our social environment. We constantly make judgments about the traits, motives, and goals of other people. And, like Fern, sometimes we make mistakes! In this chapter, we will look at how we interpret our social environment, including how we form impressions of other people. We'll explore how our behavior, including our willingness to help others, is influenced by the social environment and other people. In the process, we'll come back to Erv and Fern's incident with the "homeless" man to illustrate several important concepts.

Introduction

What Is Social Psychology?

Why did Fern think the man on the steps was homeless? How did the "homeless" man initially interpret Fern's efforts to help him? And in contrast to Fern, not everyone who feels compassion toward homeless people acts in accordance with that attitude. Why did Fern do so?

These are the kinds of issues social psychologists study. **Social psychology** is the scientific study of how individuals think, feel, and behave in social situations. In this chapter, we focus on two basic areas of social psychology. We'll begin by exploring different dimensions of social cognition. **Social cognition** refers to how we form impressions of other people, how we interpret the meaning of other people's behavior, and how our behavior is affected by our attitudes (Bodenhausen & others, 2003). Later in the chapter, we'll look at **social influence,** which focuses on how our behavior is affected by situational factors and other people. The study of social influence includes such questions as why we conform to group norms, what compels us to obey an authority figure, and under what circumstances people will help a stranger.

Person Perception
Forming Impressions of Other People

Key Theme
- Person perception refers to the mental processes we use to form judgments about other people.

Key Questions
- What four principles are followed in the person perception process?
- How do social categorization, implicit personality theories, and physical attractiveness affect person perception?

Consider the following scenario. You're attending a college in the middle of a big city and commute from your apartment to the campus via the subway. Today you stayed on campus a bit later than usual, so the rush hour is pretty much over. As a seasoned subway rider, you know you're safer when the subway is full of commuters. So as you step off the platform into the subway car, you're feeling just a bit anxious. The car is more than half full. If you want to sit down, you'll have to share a seat with some other passenger. You quickly survey your fellow passengers. In a matter of seconds, you must decide which stranger you'll share your ride home with, elbow to elbow, thigh to thigh. How will you decide?

Even if you've never ridden on a subway, it doesn't matter. You could just as easily imagine choosing a seat on a bus or in a crowded movie theater. What these situations have in common is a task that most of us confront almost every day: On the basis of very limited information, we must quickly draw conclusions about the nature of people who are complete strangers to us. We also have to make some rough predictions as to how those strangers are likely to behave. How do we arrive at these conclusions?

Person perception refers to the mental processes we use to form judgments and draw conclusions about the characteristics of others. Person perception is an active and

How Do We Form Impressions of Other People? Deciding where to sit in a subway car or on the bus involves making some quick decisions about other people. What kinds of factors do you consider when you make such judgments about others?

subjective process that always occurs in some *interpersonal context* (Jones, 1990). Every interpersonal context has three key components:

- The characteristics of the individual you are attempting to size up
- Your own characteristics as the perceiver
- The specific situation in which the process occurs

Each component influences the conclusions you reach about other people. As a psychological process, person perception follows some basic principles (see Fiske, 1993; Fiske & Neuberg, 1990; Jones, 1990). We'll illustrate these basic principles using the subway scenario.

Principle 1. Your reactions to others are determined by your perceptions of them, not by who or what they really are. Put simply, you treat others according to how you perceive them to be. So, as you step inside the subway car, you quickly choose not to sit next to the big, burly man with a scowl on his face. Why? Because *you* perceive Mr. Burly-Surly as potentially threatening. This guy's picture is probably on the FBI bulletin board at the post office for being an axe murderer, you think. Of course, he could just as easily be a burly florist who's surly because he's getting home late. It doesn't matter. Your behavior toward him is determined by your subjective perception of him as potentially threatening.

Principle 2. Your goals in a particular situation determine the amount and kinds of information you collect about others. Your goal in this situation is simple: You want to share a subway seat with someone who will basically leave you alone. Hence, you focus your attention on the characteristics of other people that seem to be relevant to your goal, ignoring details that are unrelated to it (Hilton & Darley, 1991; Swann, 1984). After all, you're not looking for a date for Saturday night, a plumber, or a lab partner for your biology class. If you were, you'd focus on very different aspects of the other people in the situation (Goodwin & others, 2002).

Principle 3. In every situation, you evaluate people partly in terms of how you expect them to act in that situation. Whether you're in a classroom, restaurant, or public restroom, your behavior is governed by **social norms**—the "rules," or expectations, for appropriate behavior in that social situation. Riding a subway is no exception to this principle (Milgram, 1992). For example, you don't sit next to someone else when empty seats are available, you don't try to borrow your seatmate's newspaper, and you avoid eye contact with others.

These "subway rules" aren't posted anywhere, of course. Nevertheless, violating these social norms will draw attention from others and probably make them uneasy. So as you size up your fellow subway passengers, you're partly evaluating their behavior in terms of how people-riding-the-subway-at-night-in-a-big-city should behave.

Principle 4. Your self-perception also influences how you perceive others and how you act on your perceptions. Your decision about where to sit is also influenced by how you perceive your *self.* For example, if you think of yourself as looking a bit threatening (even though you're really a mild-mannered biology major), you may choose to sit next to the 20-something guy with a briefcase rather than the anxious-looking middle-aged woman who's clutching her purse with both hands.

NEW IN TOWN

"Goodbye everybody."

social psychology
The branch of psychology that studies how people think, feel, and behave in social situations.

social cognition
The mental processes people use to make sense out of their social environment.

social influence
The effects of situational factors and other people on an individual's behavior.

person perception
The mental processes we use to form judgments and draw conclusions about the characteristics and motives of other people.

social norms
The "rules," or expectations, for appropriate behavior in a particular social situation.

social categorization
The mental process of categorizing people into groups (or *social categories*) on the basis of their shared characteristics.

implicit personality theory
A network of assumptions or beliefs about the relationships among various types of people, traits, and behaviors.

In combination, these four basic principles underscore the fact that person perception is not a one-way process in which we objectively survey other people and then logically evaluate their characteristics. Instead, the context, our self-perceptions, and the perceptions we have of others all interact. Each component plays a role in the judgments we form of others.

Social Categorization
Using Mental Shortcuts in Person Perception

Social categorization is the mental process of classifying people into groups on the basis of common characteristics. Much of this mental work is automatic and spontaneous, and it often occurs outside your conscious awareness (Bargh & others, 1996; Macrae & others, 1994).

When you have limited time to form your impressions and limited information about a person, such as another passenger in the subway car, you tend to rely on very broad social categories, such as the other person's gender, race, age, and occupation (Fiske, 1993; Fiske & Neuberg, 1990). You glance at a person and quickly categorize him as, for example, "Asian male, 20-something, probably a college student."

Using social categories has disadvantages and advantages. On the one hand, relegating someone to a social category on the basis of superficial information ignores that person's unique qualities. In effect, you're jumping to conclusions about a person on the basis of very limited information. Sometimes these conclusions are wrong, as Fern was when she categorized the man with a cup in his hand as "homeless."

On the other hand, relying on social categories is a natural, adaptive cognitive process. After all, social categories provide us with considerable basic information about other people. Using social categories allows us to mentally organize and remember information about others more efficiently and effectively (Macrae & others, 1994).

When it's important to your goals to perceive another person as accurately as possible, you're less likely to rely on automatic categorization (Macrae & Bodenhausen, 2001). Instead, you go into mental high gear, consciously and deliberately exerting mental effort to understand the other person better and to form a more accurate impression (Fiske, 1993; Kunda & Thagard, 1996). You might also check the impressions that you form by seeking additional information, such as calling a job applicant's previous employers.

Using Social Categories We often use superficial cues such as clothing and context to assign people to social categories and draw conclusions about their behavior. For example, you might characterize some people in this crowd as belonging to the category of "businessmen" because they are wearing suits and ties—and conclude that they are on their way to or from work. What other sorts of social categories are evident here?

Implicit Personality Theories
He's *Not* That Kind of Person!

Closely related to social categories are implicit personality theories. An **implicit personality theory** is a network of assumptions or beliefs about the relationships among various types of people, traits, and behaviors. Through previous social experiences, we form cognitive *schemas,* or mental frameworks, about the traits and behaviors associated with different "types" of people. When we perceive someone to be a particular "type," we often assume that the person will display those traits and behaviors (Sedikides & Anderson, 1994).

For example, your choice of a seatmate on the subway might well reflect some of your own implicit personality theories. You might feel comfortable sitting next to the silver-haired man who's reading the *Wall Street Journal,* wearing an expensive suit, and carrying a leather briefcase. Why? Because these

What Is Beautiful Is Good We are culturally conditioned to associate beauty with goodness and evil with ugliness—an implicit personality theory that has been dubbed the "what is beautiful is good" myth. One example of this cultural conditioning is the classic Disney film *Snow White*. In the scene shown, the wicked stepmother is disguised as an old woman, complete with a wart on her nose. She offers the poisoned apple to the innocent and virtuous heroine, Snow White. (The Walt Disney Co.)

superficial characteristics lead you to assume that he's a particular type of person—a conservative businessman. And on the basis of your implicit personality theory for a "conservative businessman," you conclude that he's a "law-abiding citizen" who is not likely to try to pick your pocket or whip out a gun and start shooting.

As the subway scenario illustrates, physical appearance cues play an important role in person perception. Particularly influential is physical attractiveness (Horton, 2003). From childhood, we are bombarded with the cultural message that "what is beautiful is good." In myths, fairy tales, cartoons, movies, and even computer games, heroes are handsome, heroines are beautiful, and the evil villains are ugly. As a result of such cultural conditioning, most people *do* associate physical attractiveness with a wide range of desirable characteristics. For example, good-looking people are perceived as being more intelligent, happier, and better adjusted than other people (Eagly & others, 1991). Are they?

After analyzing dozens of studies, psychologist Alan Feingold (1992) found very *few* personality differences between beautiful people and their plainer counterparts. Physical attractiveness is *not* correlated with intelligence, mental health, or even self-esteem. Overall, attractive people tend to be less lonely, more popular, and less anxious in social situations—all characteristics related to the advantage that their physical attractiveness seems to confer on them in social situations. As you'll read in the Focus on Neuroscience on page 442, there may be a brain-based explanation for the social success enjoyed by physically attractive people.

Like social categories, implicit personality theories can be useful as mental shortcuts in perceiving other people. But just like social categories, implicit personality theories are not always accurate. In some instances, they can even be dangerously misleading.

Consider a man named John, whom Sandy met when she was a research associate at a University of Chicago research institute. John was a divorced, slightly overweight, middle-aged businessman who had built up a successful contracting and remodeling business. He lived in a quiet suburban neighborhood, where he was well-liked. Every year John threw a block party for his neighbors, and he often helped them with minor home repairs. He was involved in local politics and civic organizations. And John regularly volunteered at a nearby hospital, where, dressed as Pogo the clown, he would perform magic tricks and pass out candy to sick and injured children.

Sounds like the kind of person you wouldn't mind knowing, doesn't he? Sandy met John under somewhat different circumstances. When John came to see Dr. Lawrence Freedman, the psychiatrist with whom Sandy worked, he was shackled in leg irons and handcuffs and flanked by three police officers. Freedman (1983) had been appointed by the courts to evaluate John's mental condition. Outside the clinic, a squadron of police had sealed off every possible escape route from the area. Stationed on the roofs of the nearby buildings were police sharpshooters.

Pogo the Clown Dressed as Pogo the clown, John would visit sick children in the hospital to cheer them up. He was also a successful building contractor and active in local politics. Given this information, what sorts of personal qualities would you expect him to display?

Neuroscience: Brain Reward When Making Eye Contact with Attractive People

Eye-Contact Face

Non–Eye-Contact Face

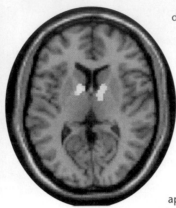

How does physical attractiveness contribute to social success? A study by neuroscientist Knut Kampe and his colleagues (2001) at University College London may offer some insights. In their functional magnetic resonance imaging (fMRI) study, participants were scanned while they looked at color photographs of 40 different faces, some looking directly at the viewer (eye-contact) and some glancing away (non–eye-contact). After the fMRI scanning session, participants rated the attractiveness of the faces they had seen.

The results showed that when we make direct eye contact with a physically attractive person, an area on each side of the brain called the *ventral striatum* is activated (yellow areas in fMRI scan).

When the attractive person's eye gaze is shifted away from the viewer, activity in the ventral striatum decreases. What makes this so interesting is that the ventral striatum is a brain area that predicts reward (Schultz & others, 1997). Neural activity in the ventral striatum increases when an unexpected reward, such as food or water, suddenly appears. Conversely, activity in the ventral striatum decreases when an expected reward fails to appear.

As Kampe (2001) explains, "What we've shown is that when we make eye contact with an attractive person, the brain area that predicts reward starts firing. If we see an attractive person but cannot make eye contact with that person, the activity in this region goes down, signaling disappointment. This is the first study to show that the brain's ventral striatum processes rewards in the context of human social interaction.

Why were so many police guarding a guy who dressed up as a clown and entertained sick children? Because this man was John Wayne Gacy, "the undisputed champion of American serial killers," as *Newsweek* described him (Holmes, 1994). Gacy was subsequently convicted of murdering 33 boys and young men, most of whom he had buried in a crawl space under his suburban home. After years of legal appeals, Gacy was executed in 1994.

One reason Gacy had escaped detection for so many years was that he contradicted the implicit personality theory most people have for a serial killer. Indeed, most of us find it difficult to believe that a ruthless murderer would also be well-liked by his neighbors and successful in business—or that he would be someone who compassionately visited sick children in the hospital.

Although they can lead us to inaccurate conclusions, implicit personality theories represent another important social cognition strategy in our efforts to make sense out of other people. Like social categories, implicit personality theories simplify information processing about other people and provide a mental framework that helps us organize observations, memories, and beliefs about people (Macrae & others, 1994).

cathy

by Cathy Guisewite

Attribution
Explaining Behavior

Key Theme
■ Attribution refers to the process of explaining your own behavior and the behavior of other people.

Key Questions
■ What are the fundamental attribution error, the actor–observer discrepancy, and the self-serving bias?
■ How do attributional biases affect our judgments about the causes of behavior?
■ How does culture affect attributional processes?

As you're studying in the college library, the activities of two workers catch your attention. The two men are trying to lift and move a large file cabinet. "Okay, let's lift it and tip it this way," one guy says with considerable authority. In unison, they heave and tip the file cabinet. When they do, all four file drawers come flying out, bonking the first guy on the head. As the file cabinet goes crashing to the floor, you bite your lip to keep from laughing and think to yourself, "Yeah, they're obviously a pair of 40-watt bulbs."

Why did you arrive at that conclusion? After all, it's completely possible that the workers were not dimwits. Maybe the lock on the file drawers broke. Or maybe there was some other explanation for their mishap.

Attribution is the process of inferring the cause of someone's behavior, including your own. Psychologists also use the word *attribution* to refer to the explanation you make for a particular behavior. The attributions you make have a strong influence on your thoughts and feelings about other people.

If your attribution for the file cabinet incident was that the workers were not very bright, you demonstrated a pattern that occurs consistently in explaining the behavior of other people. *We tend to spontaneously attribute the behavior of others to internal, personal characteristics, while ignoring or underestimating the effects of external, situational factors.* This bias is so common in individualistic cultures that it's called the **fundamental attribution error** (Ross, 1977). Even though it's entirely possible that situational forces are behind another person's behavior, we tend to automatically assume that the cause is an internal, personal characteristic (Van Boven & others, 1999).

The fundamental attribution error plays a role in a common explanatory pattern called **blaming the victim.** The innocent victim of a crime, disaster, or serious illness is blamed for having somehow caused the misfortune or for not having taken steps to prevent it. For example, many people blame the poor for their dire straits, the sick for bringing on their illnesses, and battered women and rape survivors for somehow "provoking" their attackers. Hindsight makes it seem as if the victim should have been able to predict and prevent what was going to happen (Goldinger & others, 2003).

Along with the fundamental attribution error, a second bias contributes to unfairly blaming the victim of misfortune. People have a strong need to believe that the world is fair—that "we get what we deserve and deserve what we get." Social psychologist Melvin Lerner (1980) calls this the **just-world hypothesis.** Blaming the victim reflects the belief that, because the world is just, the victim must have done *something* to deserve his or her fate.

attribution
The mental process of inferring the causes of people's behavior, including one's own. Also refers to the explanation made for a particular behavior.

fundamental attribution error
The tendency to attribute the behavior of others to internal, personal characteristics, while ignoring or underestimating the effects of external, situational factors; an attributional bias that is common in individualistic cultures.

blaming the victim
The tendency to blame an innocent victim of misfortune for having somehow caused the problem or for not having taken steps to avoid or prevent it.

just-world hypothesis
The assumption that the world is fair and that therefore people get what they deserve and deserve what they get.

Blaming the Victim Elizabeth Smart is reunited with her mother and father in March 2003. Kidnapped at knifepoint from her bedroom in the middle of the night, Elizabeth spent nine months in the company of Brian Mitchell, a drifter and self-styled prophet who called himself "Emmanuel," and his wife, Wanda Barzee. After being held at various campsites, sometimes chained to a tree, Elizabeth, wearing a veil, wandered with the Mitchells through Utah and California. When at last found by police, Elizabeth at first refused to identify herself, claiming to be Mitchell's daughter. As details of her captivity became public, some observers wondered why Elizabeth had never tried to escape, call the police, or reveal her identity to others. Why do some people "blame the victim" after crimes, accidents, or other tragedies?

When You Can't Blame the Victim

"Blaming the victim" is one way that people reestablish their belief that the world is just. But what about situations where it is impossible to justify the victim's fate, as in the case of people who died in the terrorist attacks against the United States in September 2001? Psychologist Cheryl Kaiser and her colleagues (2004) found that when people feel sympathy for the victim, they tend to use a different strategy to restore balance to the world: they advocate revenge against those who perpetrated the injustice. As Kaiser explains, "Punishing the people who perpetrated the injustice is a form of retributive justice: Although bad things happened to good people, if the bad people are punished, they will get what they deserve, which will restore justice."

Why do we have a psychological need to believe in a just world? Well, if you believe the world is unfair, then no one—including you—is safe from tragic twists of fate and chance, no matter how virtuous, careful, or conscientious you may be (Thornton, 1992). Thus, believing the just-world hypothesis provides a way to psychologically defend yourself against the threatening thought, "It could just as easily have been me.'"

The Actor–Observer Discrepancy
You're a Klutz, but *I* Slipped on Some Ice!

There is an interesting exception to the fundamental attribution error. When it comes to explaining our *own* behavior, we tend to be biased in the opposite direction. We're more likely to use an *external, situational* attribution than an *internal, personal* attribution. This common attributional bias is called the **actor–observer discrepancy** because there is a discrepancy between the attributions you make when you are the *actor* in a given situation and those you make when you are the *observer* of other people's behavior (Jones & Nisbett, 1971).

Once you become aware of the actor–observer discrepancy, it's almost embarrassing to admit how often you succumb to it. He dropped the file cabinet because he is a dimwit; you dropped the file cabinet because you didn't have room to tip it the other way. Some jerk pulled out in front of your car because she's a reckless, inconsiderate moron; you pulled out in front of her car because your view was blocked by a school bus. And so on.

How can we explain the strong tendency to commit the actor–observer discrepancy? One possible explanation is that we simply have more information about the potential causes of our own behavior than we do about the causes of other people's behavior. When you observe another driver turn directly into the path of your car, that's typically the only information you have on which to judge her behavior. But when *you* pull in front of another car, you perceive your own behavior in the context of the many situational factors that influenced your action. You're aware of such factors as visibility and road conditions. You also know what motivated your behavior and how differently you have behaved in similar situations in the past. Thus, you are much more aware of the extent to which *your* behavior has been influenced by situational factors (Fiske & Taylor, 1991; Jones, 1990).

actor–observer discrepancy
The tendency to attribute one's own behavior to external, situational causes, while attributing the behavior of others to internal, personal causes; especially likely to occur with regard to behaviors that lead to negative outcomes.

self-serving bias
The tendency to attribute successful outcomes of one's own behavior to internal causes and unsuccessful outcomes to external, situational causes.

CULTURE AND HUMAN BEHAVIOR 11.1

Explaining Failure and Murder: Culture and Attributional Biases

Although the self-serving bias is common in individualistic cultures such as Australia and the United States, it is far from universal. In collectivistic cultures, such as Asian cultures, an opposite attributional bias is often demonstrated (Bond, 1994; Moghaddam & others, 1993). Called the *self-effacing bias* or *modesty bias*, it involves blaming failure on internal, personal factors, while attributing success to external, situational factors.

For example, compared to American students, Japanese and Chinese students are more likely to attribute academic failure to personal factors, such as lack of effort, instead of situational factors (Dornbusch & others, 1996). Thus, a Japanese student who does poorly on an exam is likely to say, "I didn't study hard enough." When Japanese or Chinese students perform poorly in school, they are expected to study harder and longer (Stevenson & Stigler, 1992). In contrast, Japanese and Chinese students tend to attribute academic *success* to *situational* factors. For example, they might say, "The exam was very easy" or "There was very little competition this year" (Stevenson & others, 1986).

Psychologists Hazel Markus and Shinobu Kitayama (1991) believe that the self-effacing bias reflects the emphasis that interde-

pendent cultures place on fitting in with other members of the group. As the Japanese proverb goes, "The nail that sticks up gets pounded down." In collectivistic cultures, self-esteem does not rest on doing better than others in the group. Rather, standing out from the group is likely to produce psychological discomfort and tension.

Cross-cultural differences are also evident with the fundamental attribution error. In general, members of collectivistic cultures are less likely to commit the fundamental attribution error than are members of individualistic cultures (M. Bond & Smith, 1996; Choi & others, 1999). That is, collectivists are more likely to attribute the causes of another person's behavior to external, situational factors rather than to internal, personal factors—the exact *opposite* of the attributional bias that is demonstrated in individualistic cultures.

To test this idea in a naturally occurring context, psychologists Michael Morris and Kaiping Peng (1994) compared articles reporting the same mass murders in Chinese-language and English-language newspapers. In one case, the murderer was a Chinese graduate student attending a U.S. university. In the other case, the murderer was a U.S. postal worker. Regardless

> *Haughtiness invites ruin; humility receives benefits.*
>
> **Chinese proverb**

of whether the murderer was American or Chinese, the news accounts were fundamentally different depending on whether the *reporter* was American or Chinese.

The American reporters were more likely to explain the killings by making personal, internal attributions. For example, American reporters emphasized the murderers' personality traits, such as the graduate student's "bad temper" and the postal worker's "history of being mentally unstable."

In contrast, the Chinese reporters emphasized situational factors, such as the fact that the postal worker had recently been fired from his job and the fact that the graduate student had failed to receive an academic award. The Chinese reporters also cited social pressures and problems in U.S. society to account for the actions of the killers.

Clearly, then, how we account for our successes and failures, as well as how we account for the actions of others, is yet another example of how human behavior is influenced by cultural conditioning.

Not surprisingly, then, we're less susceptible to the actor–observer discrepancy with people whom we know well. Because we possess more information about the behavior of our friends and relatives in different situations, we're more aware of the possible situational influences on their behavior (Aron & others, 1992). We're also better at seeing situations from their point of view.

The Self-Serving Bias
Using Explanations That Meet Our Needs

If you've ever listened to other students react to their grades on an important exam, you've seen the **self-serving bias** in action. When students do well on a test, they tend to congratulate themselves and to attribute their success to how hard they studied, their intelligence, and so forth—all *internal* attributions. But when a student blows a test big time, the *external* attributions fly left and right: "They were all trick questions!" "I couldn't concentrate because the guy behind me kept coughing" (Kruger & Gilovich, 2004).

In a wide range of situations, people tend to credit themselves for their success and to blame their failures on external circumstances (Schlenker & Weigold, 1992). Psychologists explain the self-serving bias as resulting from an attempt to save face and protect self-esteem in the face of failure (Dunning & others, 1995).

Explaining Misfortune: The Self-Serving Bias Given the self-serving bias, is this bicyclist likely to explain his accident by listing internal factors such as carelessness or inexperience? Or is he more likely to blame external factors, such as faulty brakes or a mismarked trail?

Although common in many societies, the self-serving bias is far from universal, as cross-cultural psychologists have discovered (see Culture and Human Behavior Box 11.1 on page 445). The various attributional biases are summarized in Table 11.1.

Table 11.1

Some Common Attributional Biases

Bias	Description
Fundamental attribution error	We tend to explain the behavior of other people by attributing their behavior to internal, personal characteristics, while underestimating or ignoring the effects of external, situational factors.
Actor–observer discrepancy	When we are the *actor,* we tend to attribute our own behavior to external causes. When we are the *observer* of someone else's behavior, we tend to attribute their behavior to internal causes.
Blaming the victim	We tend to blame the victims of misfortune for causing their own misfortune or for not taking steps to prevent or avoid it. Partly due to the *just-world hypothesis.*
Self-serving bias	We have a tendency to take credit for our *successes* by attributing them to internal, personal causes, along with a tendency to distance ourselves from our *failures* by attributing them to external, situational causes. Most common in individualistic cultures.
Self-effacing (or modesty) bias	We tend to blame ourselves for our *failures,* attributing them to internal, personal causes, while downplaying our *successes* by attributing them to external, situational causes. Most common in collectivistic cultures.

The Social Psychology of Attitudes

Key Theme

- An attitude is a learned tendency to evaluate objects, people, or issues in a particular way.

Key Questions

- What are the three components of an attitude?
- Under what conditions are attitudes most likely to determine behavior?
- What is cognitive dissonance?

Who does a better job of leading the United States—the Republicans or the Democrats? Should the United States have national health care coverage for all of its citizens? How do you feel about the death penalty? Reinstating the military draft for both men and women? A woman as president? Smoking in public places? Reality television shows? Sex education in public schools?

On these and many other subjects, you've probably formed an attitude. Psychologists formally define an **attitude** as a learned tendency to evaluate some object, person, or issue in a particular way (Olson & Zanna, 1993; Zimbardo & Leippe, 1991). Attitudes are typically positive or negative, but they can also be *ambivalent,* as when you have mixed feelings about an issue or person (Ajzen, 2001).

attitude
A learned tendency to evaluate some object, person, or issue in a particular way; such evaluations may be positive, negative, or ambivalent.

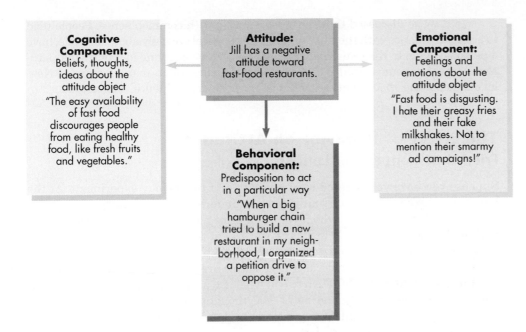

Cognitive Component:
Beliefs, thoughts, ideas about the attitude object

"The easy availability of fast food discourages people from eating healthy food, like fresh fruits and vegetables."

Attitude:
Jill has a negative attitude toward fast-food restaurants.

Emotional Component:
Feelings and emotions about the attitude object

"Fast food is disgusting. I hate their greasy fries and their fake milkshakes. Not to mention their smarmy ad campaigns!"

Behavioral Component:
Predisposition to act in a particular way

"When a big hamburger chain tried to build a new restaurant in my neighborhood, I organized a petition drive to oppose it."

FIGURE 11.1 The Components of Attitudes An attitude is a positive or negative evaluation of an object, person, or idea. An attitude may have cognitive, emotional, and behavioral components.

As shown in Figure 11.1, attitudes can include three components (Eagly & Chaiken, 1998). First, an attitude may have a *cognitive component:* your thoughts and conclusions about a given topic or object. For example, one of our colleagues, Aaron, is a staunch environmentalist. On more than one occasion, Aaron has said, "In my opinion, cars and trucks need to be much more fuel-efficient so that we can reduce or eliminate air pollution in our cities." Second, an attitude may have an emotional or *affective component,* as when Aaron starts ranting about drivers he sees on the highway: "It makes me furious to see people driving those huge SUVs to work, especially when they don't even have passengers!" Finally, an attitude may have a *behavioral component,* in which attitudes are reflected in action. In Aaron's case, he bought a hybrid gasoline/electric car that gets 60 miles to the gallon, even in the city. Even so, he frequently rides his bicycle to campus rather than drive.

Attitudes and Behavior
These Greenpeace activists have set up a symbolic wind turbine in front of the Castle Peak coal power station in Hong Kong. They are demonstrating their commitment to renewable energy and their opposition to coal plants in Asia that contribute to global warming. People who hold strong opinions and express them frequently, like these Greenpeace activists, are most likely to behave in accordance with their attitudes.

The Effect of Attitudes on Behavior

You may take it for granted that your attitudes tend to guide your behavior. But social psychologists have consistently found that people don't always act in accordance with their attitudes. For example, you might disapprove of cheating, yet find yourself sneaking a peek at a classmate's exam paper when the opportunity presents itself. Or you might favor a certain political candidate, yet not vote on election day.

Under what conditions are your attitudes most likely to influence or determine your behavior? Social psychologists have found that you're most likely to behave in accordance with your attitudes when any of the following conditions exist:

- Attitudes are extreme or are frequently expressed (Ajzen, 2001).
- Attitudes have been formed through direct experience (Fazio, 1990).
- You are very knowledgeable about the subject (Wood & others, 1995).
- You have a vested interest in the subject and personally stand to gain or lose something on a specific issue (Lehman & Crano, 2002).
- You anticipate a favorable outcome or response from others for doing so (Ajzen, 1991).

cognitive dissonance
An unpleasant state of psychological tension or arousal (*dissonance*) that occurs when two thoughts or perceptions (*cognitions*) are inconsistent; typically results from the awareness that attitudes and behavior are in conflict.

What we've discussed thus far meshes nicely with common sense. People tend to act in accordance with their attitudes when they feel strongly about an issue, have a personal stake in the issue, and anticipate a positive outcome in a particular situation. In short, your attitudes do influence your behavior in many instances. Now, let's consider the opposite question: Can your behavior influence your attitudes?

The Effect of Behavior on Attitudes
Fried Grasshoppers for Lunch?!

Suppose you have volunteered to participate in a psychology experiment. At the lab, you're asked to indicate your degree of preference for a variety of foods, including fried grasshoppers, which you rank pretty low on the list. During the experiment, the experimenter instructs you to eat some fried grasshoppers. You manage to swallow three of the crispy critters. At the end of the experiment, your attitudes toward grasshoppers as a food source are surveyed again.

Later in the day, you talk to a friend who also participated in the experiment. You mention how friendly and polite you thought the experimenter was. As it turns out, your friend had a very different experience. He thought the experimenter was an arrogant, rude jerk.

Here's the critical question: Whose attitude toward eating fried grasshoppers is more likely to change in a positive direction—yours or your friend's? Given that you interacted with a friendly experimenter, most people assume that *your* feelings about fried grasshoppers are more likely to have improved than your friend's attitude. In fact, it is your friend—who encountered the obnoxious experimenter—who is much more likely to hold a more positive attitude toward eating fried grasshoppers than you.

At first glance, this finding seems to go against the grain of common sense. So how can we explain this outcome? To begin with, the fried grasshoppers story represents the basic design of a classic experiment by psychologist **Philip Zimbardo** and his colleagues (1965). Zimbardo's experiment and other similar ones underscore the power of cognitive dissonance. **Cognitive dissonance** is an unpleasant state of psychological tension (*dissonance*) that occurs when there's an inconsistency between two thoughts or perceptions (*cognitions*). This state of dissonance is so unpleasant that we are strongly motivated to reduce it (Festinger, 1957, 1962).

Cognitive dissonance commonly occurs in situations in which you become uncomfortably aware that your behavior and your attitudes are in conflict. In these situations, you are simultaneously holding two conflicting cognitions: your original attitude versus the realization that you have behaved in a way that contradicts that attitude. If you can easily rationalize your behavior to make it consistent with your attitude, then any dissonance you might experience can be quickly and easily resolved. But when your behavior *cannot* be easily justified, how can you resolve the contradiction and eliminate the unpleasant state of dissonance? Since you can't go back and change the behavior, *you change your attitude to make it consistent with your behavior.*

Let's take another look at the results of the grasshopper study, this time from the perspective of cognitive dissonance theory. Your attitude toward eating grasshoppers did *not* change, because you could easily rationalize the conflict between your attitude ("Eating grasshoppers is disgusting") and your behavior (eating three grasshoppers). You probably justified your behavior by

Fried Grasshoppers—Tasty or Disgusting?
Most Americans do not rate fried grasshoppers as one of their favorite foods. Suppose you agreed to eat a handful of grasshoppers after being asked to do so by a rude, unfriendly research assistant. Do you think your attitude toward fried grasshoppers would improve more than a person who ate grasshoppers after being asked to do so by a friendly, polite experimenter?

saying something like, "I ate the grasshoppers because the experimenter was such a nice guy and I wanted to help him out."

However, your friend, who encountered the rude experimenter, can't easily explain the contradiction between disliking grasshoppers and voluntarily eating them. Thus, he experiences an uncomfortable state of cognitive dissonance. Since he can't go back and change his behavior, he is left with the only part of the equation that can be changed—his attitude (see

Figure 11.2). "You know, eating those grasshoppers wasn't *that* bad," your friend comments. "In fact, they were kind of crunchy." Notice how his change in attitude reduces the dissonance between his previous attitude and his behavior.

Attitude change due to cognitive dissonance is quite common in everyday life. For example, consider the person who impulsively buys a new leather coat that she really can't afford. "It was too good a bargain to pass up," she rationalizes.

Cognitive dissonance can also change the strength of an attitude to make it consistent with some behavior that has already been performed. For example, people tend to be much more favorably inclined toward a given political candidate *after* they have voted for him or her than just before (Beasley & Joslyn, 2001).

A similar example of cognitive dissonance in action involves choosing between two basically equal alternatives, especially if the decision is important and difficult to undo (Festinger, 1962). Suppose you had to choose between two colleges or two jobs. Each choice has desirable and undesirable features, creating dissonance. But once you actually make the choice, you immediately bring your attitudes more closely into line with your commitment, reducing cognitive dissonance. In other words, after you make the choice, you emphasize the negative features of the choice you've rejected, which is commonly called a "sour grapes" rationalization. You also emphasize the positive features of the choice to which you have committed yourself—a "sweet lemons" rationalization.

Philip G. Zimbardo
Phil Zimbardo (b. 1933) grew up in an immigrant family in a poor neighborhood in the South Bronx, an experience that sensitized him to the power of situational influences and the destructive nature of stereotypes and prejudice (Zimbardo, 2005). Much of Zimbardo's research has been focused on investigating what he has called "the subtle but pervasive power of situations to influence human behavior." Zimbardo's research has ranged from attitude change to shyness, prison reform, and the psychology of evil. As Zimbardo (2000b) observes, "The joy of being a psychologist is that almost everything in life is psychology, or should be, or could be. One can't live mindfully without being enmeshed in the psychological processes that are around us." Later in the chapter, we'll encounter the experiment for which Zimbardo is most famous—the Stanford Prison Experiment.

FIGURE 11.2 How Cognitive Dissonance Leads to Attitude Change When your behavior conflicts with your attitudes, an uncomfortable state of tension is produced. However, if you can rationalize or explain your behavior, the conflict (and the tension) is eliminated or avoided. If you *can't* explain your behavior, you may change your attitude so that it is in harmony with your behavior.

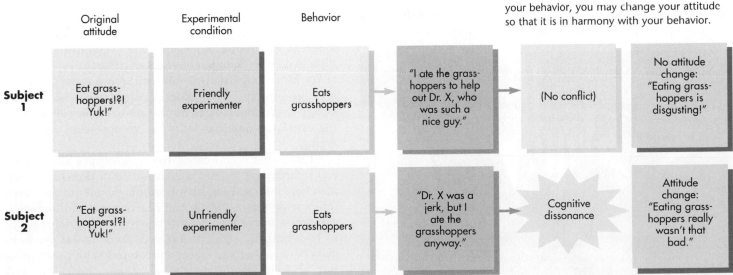

prejudice
A negative attitude toward people who belong to a specific social group.

stereotype
A cluster of characteristics that are associated with all members of a specific social group, often including qualities that are unrelated to the objective criteria that define the group.

Understanding Prejudice

Key Theme

- Prejudice refers to a negative attitude toward people who belong to a specific social group, while stereotypes are clusters of characteristics that are attributed to people who belong to specific social categories.

Key Questions

- What is the function of stereotypes, and how do they relate to prejudice?
- What are in-groups and out-groups, and how do they influence social judgments?
- What is ethnocentrism?

In this section, you'll see how person perception, attribution, and attitudes come together in explaining **prejudice**—a negative attitude toward people who belong to a specific social group.

Prejudice is ultimately based on the exaggerated notion that members of other social groups are very different from members of our own social group. So as you read this discussion, it's important for you to keep two well-established points in mind. First, *racial and ethnic groups are far more alike than they are different* (Jones, 1991). And second, any differences that may exist *between* members of different racial and ethnic groups are far smaller than differences *among* various members of the same group.

From Stereotypes to Prejudice: In-Groups and Out-Groups

As we noted earlier, using social categories to organize information about other people seems to be a natural cognitive tendency. Many social categories can be defined by relatively objective characteristics, such as age, language, religion, and skin color. A specific kind of social category is a **stereotype**—a cluster of characteristics that are attributed to members of a specific social group or category (Fiske, 1998; Hilton & von Hippel, 1996). In other words, stereotypes are based on the assumption that people have certain characteristics *because* of their membership in a particular group.

Stereotypes typically include qualities that are unrelated to the objective criteria that define a given category (Taylor & Porter, 1994). For example, we can objectively sort people into different categories by age. But our stereotypes for different age groups may include many qualities that have little to do with "number of years since birth." Associations of "reckless and irresponsible" with teenagers, "forgetful and incompetent" with elderly people, and "boring and stodgy" with middle-aged adults are examples of associating unrelated qualities with age groups—that is, stereotyping.

Like other social categories, stereotypes simplify social information so that we can sort out, process, and remember information about other people more easily (Macrae & others, 1994). And like our use of other social categories, our tendency to stereotype social groups seems to be a natural cognitive process. Some social psychologists believe that the use of stereotypes is an inescapable fact of social cognition (Lee & others, 1995; Taylor & Porter, 1994). However, relying on stereotypes can cause

Combating Prejudice and Stereotyping
The attacks on the United States by members of a radical Islamic terrorist group in September 2001 brought an increased awareness of religious differences among ethnic groups. But along with outbreaks of anger against members of certain religious groups, there were also many attempts to reach across racial, ethnic, and religious divisions to find a new sense of national unity. Here, clergy of different faiths join hands and sing during an interfaith prayer service in Detroit, Michigan, one of hundreds that took place in cities across the country in the days and weeks following the attacks on the World Trade Center and the Pentagon.

numerous problems (Stanger, 1995). Attributing a stereotypic cause for an outcome or event can blind us to the true causes of events (Sanbonmatsu & others, 1994). For example, a parent who assumes that a girl's poor computer skills are due to her gender rather than a lack of instruction might never encourage her to overcome her problem.

Research by psychologist Claude Steele (1997, 2003) has demonstrated an even more insidious effect of stereotypes, particularly derogatory stereotypes, called stereotype threat. As we discussed in Chapter 7 (see page 290), simply being aware that your social group is associated with a particular stereotype can negatively impact your performance on tests or tasks that measure abilities that are thought to be associated with that stereotype. For example, even mathematically gifted women scored lower on a difficult math test when told that the test tended to produce gender differences than when told that the test did not produce gender differences (Spencer & others, 1999).

Once they are formed, stereotypes are hard to shake. One reason for this is that stereotypes are not always completely false (Ottati & Lee, 1995). Sometimes they have a kernel of truth, making them easy to confirm, especially when you see only what you expect to see (Judd & Park, 1993; Swim, 1994). However, there's a vast difference between a kernel and the cornfield. When stereotypic beliefs become expectations that are applied to *all* members of a given group, stereotypes can be both misleading and damaging (Stangor & Lange, 1994).

Consider the stereotype that men are more assertive than women and that women are more nurturant than men. This stereotype does have some truth to it, but only in terms of the *average* difference between men and women (see Eagly, 1995b; Hyde, 2005). Thus, it would be inappropriate to automatically apply this stereotype to *every* individual man and woman. Doing so would be an example of prejudice.

Equally important, when confronted by evidence that contradicts a stereotype, people tend to discount that information in a variety of ways (Seta & Seta, 1993; Weisz & Jones, 1993). For example, suppose you are firmly convinced that all "Zeegs" are dishonest, sly, and untrustworthy. One day you absentmindedly leave your wallet on a store's checkout counter. As you walk into the parking lot, you hear a voice calling, "Hey, you forgot your wallet!" It's a Zeeg running after you and waving your wallet in the air. "I was behind you in line and thought you might need this," the Zeeg smiles, handing you your wallet.

Will this experience change your stereotype of Zeegs as dishonest, sly, and untrustworthy? Probably not. It's more likely that you'll conclude that this individual Zeeg is an *exception* to the stereotype. If you run into more than one honest Zeeg, you may create a mental subgroup for individuals who belong to the larger group but depart from the stereotype in some way (Stangor & Lange, 1994). By creating a subcategory of "honest, hardworking Zeegs," you can still maintain your more general stereotype of Zeegs as dishonest, sly, and untrustworthy.

Creating special cases, or exceptions, allows people to maintain stereotypes in the face of contradictory evidence. Typical of this exception-that-proves-the-rule approach is the person who says, "Hey, I'm not prejudiced! Why, some of my best friends are Zeegs."

Stereotypes are closely related to another tendency in person perception. People have a strong tendency to perceive others in terms of two very basic social categories: "us" and "them." More precisely, the **in-group** ("us") refers to the group or groups to which we belong, and **out-groups** ("them") refer to groups of which we are not a member. As you'll see, we're more likely to resort to negatively biased stereotypes to describe members of out-groups than to describe fellow members of our in-group (Hewstone & others, 2002).

In-groups and out-groups aren't necessarily limited to racial, ethnic, or religious boundaries. Sometimes, it seems, virtually any characteristic can be used to make in-group and out-group distinctions: Cubs versus White Sox fans, Northsiders versus Southsiders, math majors versus English majors, and so forth.

The Power of Stereotypes American movies have made the image of the cowboy almost universally recognizable. What kinds of qualities are associated with the stereotype of the cowboy? How might that stereotype be an inaccurate portrayal of a person working on a cattle ranch today?

in-group
A social group to which one belongs.

out-group
A social group to which one does not belong.

The Out-Group Homogeneity Effect
They're All the Same to Me

Two important patterns characterize our views of in-groups versus out-groups. First, when we describe the members of our *in-group,* we typically see them as being quite varied, despite having enough features in common to belong to the same group. In other words, we notice the diversity within our own group.

Second, we tend to see members of the *out-group* as much more similar to one another, even in areas that have little to do with the criteria for group membership (Hilton & von Hippel, 1996; Stangor & Lange, 1994). This tendency is called the **out-group homogeneity effect.** (The word *homogeneity* means "similarity" or "uniformity.")

For example, what qualities do you associate with the category of "engineering major"? If you're *not* an engineering major, you're likely to see engineering majors as a rather similar crew: male, logical, analytical, conservative, and so forth. However, if you *are* an engineering major, you're much more likely to see your in-group as quite *heterogeneous,* or varied (Park & others, 1992). You might even come up with several subgroups, such as studious engineering majors, party-animal engineering majors, and electrical engineering majors versus chemical engineering majors.

In-Group Bias
We're Tactful—*They're* Sneaky

In-group bias is our tendency to make favorable, positive attributions for behaviors by members of our in-group and unfavorable, negative attributions for behaviors by members of out-groups (Hewstone & others, 2002). We succeeded because we worked hard; they succeeded because they lucked out. We failed because of circumstances beyond our control; they failed because they're stupid and incompetent. We're thrifty; they're stingy. And so on.

One form of in-group bias is called **ethnocentrism**—the belief that one's culture or ethnic group is superior to others. You're engaging in ethnocentrism when you use your culture or ethnic group as the yardstick by which you judge other cultures or ethnic groups. Not surprisingly, ethnocentric thinking contributes to the formation of negative stereotypes about other cultures whose customs differ from our own (Smith, 1993; Triandis, 1994).

In combination, stereotypes and in-group/out-group bias form the *cognitive* basis for prejudicial attitudes (Hilton & von Hippel, 1996). But, as with many attitudes, prejudice also has a strong *emotional* component. In the case of prejudice, the emotions are intensely negative—hatred, contempt, fear, loathing. *Behaviorally,* prejudice can be displayed in the form of *discrimination*—behaviors ranging from privately sneering at to physically attacking members of the out-group.

How can we account for the extreme emotions that often characterize prejudice against out-group members? One theory holds that prejudice and intergroup hostility increase when different groups are competing for scarce resources, whether jobs, acreage, oil, water, or political power (Bobo, 1988a, 1988b). Prejudice and intergroup hostility are also likely to increase during times of social change (Brewer, 1994; Staub, 1996).

However, prejudice often exists in the absence of direct competition for resources, changing social conditions, or even contact with members of a particular out-group. What accounts for prejudice in such situations? Increasingly, social psychologists are examining the *emotional* basis of prejudice (see Mackie & Hamilton, 1993; Smith, 1993). Research by psychologist Victoria Esses and her colleagues (1993) has demonstrated that people are often prejudiced against groups that are perceived as threatening important in-group norms and values. For example, a person might be extremely prejudiced against gays and lesbians, because he feels that they threaten his in-group's cherished values, such as a strong commitment to traditional sex roles and family structure (Haddock & others, 1993).

out-group homogeneity effect
The tendency to see members of out-groups as very similar to one another.

in-group bias
The tendency to judge the behavior of in-group members favorably and out-group members unfavorably.

ethnocentrism
The belief that one's own culture or ethnic group is superior to all others and the related tendency to use one's own culture as a standard by which to judge other cultures.

Overcoming Prejudice

Key Theme
- Prejudice can be overcome when rival groups cooperate to achieve a common goal.

Key Questions
- How has this finding been applied in the educational system?
- What other conditions are essential to reducing tension between groups?
- How can prejudice be overcome at the individual level?

How can prejudice be combated at the group level? A classic series of studies headed by psychologist **Muzafer Sherif** helped clarify the conditions that produce intergroup conflict *and* harmony. Sherif and his colleagues (1961) studied a group of 11-year-old boys in an unlikely setting for a scientific experiment: a summer camp located at Robbers Cave State Park in Oklahoma.

The Robbers Cave Experiment

Pretending to be camp counselors and staff, the researchers observed the boys' behavior under carefully orchestrated conditions. The boys were randomly assigned to two groups. The groups arrived at camp in separate buses and were headquartered in different areas of the camp. One group of boys dubbed themselves the Eagles, the other the Rattlers. After a week of separation, the researchers arranged for the groups to meet in a series of competitive games. A fierce rivalry quickly developed, demonstrating the ease with which mutually hostile groups could be created.

The rivalry became increasingly bitter. The Eagles burned the Rattlers' flag. In response, the Rattlers trashed the Eagles' cabin. Somewhat alarmed, the researchers tried to diminish the hostility by bringing the two groups together under peaceful circumstances and on an equal basis—having them go to the movies together, eat in the same dining hall, and so forth. But contact alone did not mitigate the hostility. If anything, these situations only served as opportunities for the rival groups to berate and attack each other. For example, when the Rattlers and Eagles ate together in the same dining hall, a massive food fight erupted!

How could harmony between the groups be established? Sherif and his fellow researchers created a series of situations in which the two groups would need to *cooperate to achieve a common goal.* For example, the researchers secretly sabotaged the water supply. Working together, the Eagles and the Rattlers managed to fix it. On another occasion, the researchers sabotaged a truck that was to bring food to the campers. The hungry campers overcame their differences to join forces and restart the truck. After a series of such joint efforts, the rivalry diminished and the groups became good friends (Sherif, 1956; Sherif & others, 1961).

Creating Conflict Between Groups
Psychologist Muzafer Sherif and his colleagues demonstrated how easily hostility and distrust could be created between two groups. Competitive situations, like this tug-of-war, increased tension between the Rattlers and the Eagles.

Overcoming Group Conflict To decrease hostility between the Rattlers and the Eagles at Robbers Cave, the researchers created situations that required the joint efforts of both groups to achieve a common goal, such as fixing the water supply. These co-operative tasks helped the boys recognize their common interests and become friends.

Sherif successfully demonstrated how hostility between groups could be created and, more important, how that hostility could be overcome. However, other researchers questioned whether these results would apply to other inter-group situations. After all, these boys were very homogeneous: white, middle class, Protestant, and carefully selected for being healthy and well-adjusted (Fiske & Ruscher, 1993; Sherif, 1966). In other words, there were no *intrinsic* differences between the Rattlers and the Eagles; there was only the artificial distinction created by the researchers.

The Jigsaw Classroom
Promoting Cooperation

Social psychologist Elliot Aronson (1990, 1992) tried adapting the results of the Robbers Cave experiments to a very different group situation—a newly integrated elementary school. Realizing that mere contact between black and white children was not dissipating tension and prejudice, Aronson reasoned that perhaps the competitive schoolroom atmosphere was partly at fault. Perhaps tension between racial groups might decrease if cooperation replaced competition.

Aronson and his colleagues tried a teaching technique that stressed cooperative, rather than competitive, learning situations (see Aronson, 1990; Aronson & Bridgeman, 1979). Dubbed the *jigsaw classroom technique,* this approach brought together students in small, ethnically diverse groups to work on a mutual project. Like the pieces of a jigsaw puzzle, each student had a unique contribution to make toward the success of the group. Each student became an expert on one aspect of the overall project and had to teach it to the other members of the group. Thus, interdependence and cooperation replaced competition.

The results? Children in the jigsaw classrooms benefited. They had higher self-esteem and a greater liking for children in other ethnic groups than did children in traditional classrooms. They also demonstrated a lessening of negative stereotypes and prejudice and a reduction in intergroup hostility (see Aronson, 1987, 1995; Aronson & Bridgeman, 1979). As Aronson (1999) points out, "Cooperation changes our tendency to categorize the out-group from 'those people' to 'us people.'"

Conformity
Following the Crowd

Key Theme
■ Social influence involves the study of how behavior is influenced by other people and by the social environment.

Key Questions
■ What factors influence the degree to which people will conform?
■ Why do people conform?
■ How does culture affect conformity?

conformity
The tendency to adjust one's behavior, attitudes, or beliefs to group norms in response to real or imagined group pressure.

As we noted on page 438, *social influence* is the psychological study of how our behavior is influenced by the social environment and other people. For example, if you typically contribute to class discussions, you've probably felt the power of social influence in classes where nobody else said a word. No doubt you found yourself feeling at least slightly uncomfortable every time you ventured a comment or question.

If you changed your behavior to mesh with that of your classmates, you demonstrated conformity. **Conformity** occurs when we change our behavior, attitudes, or beliefs in response to real or imagined group pressure (Kiesler & Kiesler, 1969).

There's no question that all of us conform to group norms to some degree. The more critical issue is *how far* we'll go to adjust our perceptions and opinions so that they're in sync with the majority opinion—an issue that intrigued psychologist **Solomon Asch.** Asch (1951) posed a straightforward question: Would people still conform to the group if the group opinion was clearly wrong?

To study this question experimentally, Asch (1955) chose a simple, objective task with an obvious answer (Figure 11.3). A group of people sat at a table and looked at a series of cards. On one side of each card was a standard line. On the other side were three comparison lines. All each person had to do was publicly indicate which comparison line was the same length as the standard line.

Asch's experiment had a hidden catch. All the people sitting around the table were actually in cahoots with the experimenter, except for one—the real subject. Had you been the real subject in Asch's (1956) experiment, here's what you would have experienced. The first card is shown, and the five people ahead of you respond, one at a time, with the obvious answer: "Line B." Now it's your turn, and you respond the same. The second card is put up. Again, the answer is obvious and the group is unanimous. So far, so good.

Then the third card is shown, and the correct answer is just as obvious: Line C. But the first person confidently says, "Line A." And so does everyone else, one by one. Now it's your turn. To you it's clear that the correct answer is line C. But the five people ahead of you have already publicly chosen line A. How do you respond? You hesitate. Do you go with the flow or with what you know?

The real subject was faced with the uncomfortable situation of disagreeing with a unanimous majority on 12 of 18 trials in Asch's experiment. Notice, there was *no* direct pressure to conform—just the implicit, unspoken pressure of answering differently from the rest of the group.

Over a hundred subjects experienced Asch's experimental dilemma. Not surprisingly, participants differed in their degree of conformity. Nonetheless, the majority of Asch's subjects (76 percent) conformed with the group judgment on at least one of the critical trials. When the data for all subjects were combined, the subjects followed the majority and gave the wrong answer on *37 percent* of the critical trials (Asch, 1955, 1957). In comparison, a control group of subjects who responded alone instead of in a group accurately chose the matching line 99 percent of the time.

Although the majority opinion clearly exerted a strong influence, it's also important to stress the flip side of Asch's results. On almost two-thirds of the trials in which the majority named the wrong line, the subjects stuck to their guns and gave the correct answer, despite being in the minority (see Friend & others, 1990).

Life in society requires consensus as an indispensable condition. But consensus, to be productive, requires that each individual contribute independently out of his experience and insight. When consensus comes under the dominance of conformity, the social process is polluted and the individual at the same time surrenders the powers on which his functioning as a feeling and thinking being depends."

Solomon Asch (1955)

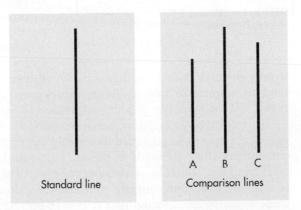

Standard line

Comparison lines

FIGURE 11.3 Sample Line Judgment Task Used in the Asch Conformity Studies In Asch's classic studies on conformity, subjects were asked to pick the comparison line that matched the standard line.

SOURCE: Asch (1957).

Adolescents and Conformity Conformity to group norms peaks in early adolescence, as the similar hairstyles and clothing of these friends show. Think back to your own adolescence. Do you remember how important it was to you to fit in with other adolescents, especially those in your peer group?

Factors Influencing Conformity

The basic model of Asch's classic experiment has been used in hundreds of studies exploring the dynamics of conformity (Hoffman & others, 2001; R. Bond & Smith, 1996). Why do we sometimes find ourselves conforming to the larger group? There are two basic reasons.

First is our desire to be liked and accepted by the group, which is referred to as **normative social influence.** If you've ever been ridiculed and rejected for going against the grain of a unanimous group, you've had firsthand experience with the pressure of normative social influence. Second is our desire to be right. When we're uncertain or doubt our own judgment, we may look to the group as a source of accurate information, which is called **informational social influence.**

Asch and other researchers identified several conditions that promote conformity, which are summarized in Table 11.2. But Asch also discovered that conformity *decreased* under certain circumstances. For example, having an ally seemed to counteract the social influence of the majority. Subjects were more likely to go against the majority view if just one other participant did so. Other researchers have found that any dissent increases resistance to the majority opinion, even if the other person's dissenting opinion is wrong (Allen & Levine, 1969). Conformity also lessens even if the other dissenter's competence is questionable, as in the case of a dissenter who wore thick glasses and complained that he could not see the lines very well (Allen & Levine, 1971).

Table 11.2

Factors That Promote Conformity

You're more likely to conform to group norms when:

- You are facing a unanimous group of at least four or five people
- You must give your response in front of the group
- You have not already expressed commitment to a different idea or opinion
- You find the task is ambiguous or difficult
- You doubt your abilities or knowledge in the situation
- You are strongly attracted to a group and want to be a member of it

SOURCES: Asch (1955); Campbell & Fairey (1989); Deutsch & Gerard (1955); Gerard & others (1968); Tanford & Penrod (1984).

normative social influence
Behavior that is motivated by the desire to gain social acceptance and approval.

informational social influence
Behavior that is motivated by the desire to be correct.

obedience
The performance of an action in response to the direct orders of an authority or person of higher status.

Culture and Conformity

Do patterns of conformity differ in other cultures? British psychologists Rod Bond and Peter Smith (1996) found in a wide-ranging meta-analysis that conformity is generally higher in collectivistic cultures than in individualistic cultures. Because individualistic cultures tend to emphasize independence, self-expression, and standing out from the crowd, the whole notion of conformity tends to carry a negative connotation.

In collectivistic cultures, however, publicly conforming while privately disagreeing tends to be regarded as socially appropriate tact or sensitivity. Publicly challenging the judgments of others, particularly the judgment of members of one's in-group, would be considered rude, tactless, and insensitive to the feelings of others. Thus, conformity in collectivistic cultures does not seem to carry the same negative connotation that it does in individualistic cultures.

Obedience
Just Following Orders

Key Theme
- Stanley Milgram conducted a series of controversial studies on obedience, which is behavior performed in direct response to the orders of an authority.

Key Questions
- What were the results of Milgram's original obedience experiments?
- What experimental factors were shown to increase the level of obedience?
- What experimental factors were shown to decrease the level of obedience?

Stanley Milgram was one of the most creative and innovative researchers that social psychology has known (Blass, 1992; Miller, 1986; Zimbardo, 1992). Sadly, Milgram died of a heart attack at the age of 51. Though Milgram made many contributions to social psychology, he is best known for his experimental investigations of obedience. **Obedience** is the performance of an action in response to the direct orders of an authority or person of higher status, such as a teacher or a supervisor.

Milgram was intrigued by Asch's discovery of how easily people could be swayed by group pressure. But Milgram wanted to investigate behavior that had greater personal significance than simply judging the lengths of lines on a card (Milgram, 1963, 1980). Thus, Milgram posed what he saw as the most critical question: Could a person be pressured by others into committing an immoral act, some action that violated his or her own conscience, such as hurting a stranger? In his efforts to answer that question, Milgram embarked on one of the most systematic and controversial investigations in the history of psychology: to determine how and why people obey the destructive dictates of an authority figure.

Social Psychologist Stanley Milgram (1933–1984) Milgram is best known for his obedience studies, but his creative research skills went far beyond the topic of obedience. To study the power of social norms, for example, Milgram sent his students out into New York City to intrude into waiting lines or ask subway passengers to give up their seats. Milgram often capitalized on the "texture of everyday life" to "examine the way in which the social world impinges on individual action and experience" (Milgram, 1974a).

Milgram's Original Obedience Experiment

Milgram was only 28 years old when he conducted his first obedience experiments. At the time, he was a new faculty member at Yale University in New Haven, Connecticut. He recruited participants through direct-mail solicitations and ads in the local paper. Collectively, Milgram's subjects represented a wide range of occupational and educational backgrounds. Postal workers, high school teachers, white-collar workers, engineers, and laborers participated in the study.

Outwardly, it appeared that two subjects showed up at Yale University to participate in each session of the psychology experiment, but the second subject was actually an accomplice working with Milgram. The role of the experimenter, complete with white lab coat, was played by a high school biology teacher. When both subjects arrived, the experimenter greeted them and gave them a plausible explanation of the study's purpose: to examine the effects of punishment on learning.

Both subjects drew slips of paper to determine who would be the "teacher" and who the "learner." However, the drawing was rigged so that the real subject was always the teacher and the accomplice was always the learner. The learner was actually a mild-mannered, 47-year-old accountant who had been carefully rehearsed for his part in the drama. Assigned to the role of the teacher, the real subject would be responsible for "punishing" the learner's mistakes by administering electric shocks.

Immediately after the drawing, the teacher and learner were taken to another room, where the learner was strapped into an "electric chair." The teacher was then taken to a different room, from which he could hear but not see the learner. Speaking into a microphone, the

The "Electric Chair" With the help of the real subject, who had been assigned to the role of "teacher," the experimenter straps the "learner" into the electric chair. Unbeknownst to the real subject, the learner was actually a 47-year-old accountant who had been carefully rehearsed for his part in the experimental deception. The experimenter told both subjects, "Although the shocks can be extremely painful, they cause no permanent tissue damage."

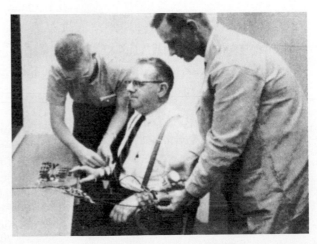

Milgram's "Shock Generator" Machine
A young Stanley Milgram sits next to his "shock generator." Milgram went to great lengths to make the shock generator look as authentic as possible. The front panel of the bogus shock generator had been engraved by professional industrial engravers. Whenever the teacher pressed a shock switch, the red light above the switch went on, a buzzing and clicking sound was heard, and the needle on the voltage meter swung to the right. Very convincing details. Do you think you would have been fooled into believing that this was a real shock generator?

This table shows examples of the learner's protests as different voltage levels. If the teacher administered shocks beyond the 330-volt level, the learner's agonized screams were replaced with an ominous silence.

teacher tested the learner on a simple word-pair memory task. In the other room, the learner pressed one of four switches to indicate with which alternative the word had previously been paired. The learner's response was registered in an answer box positioned on top of the "shock generator" in front of the teacher. Each time the learner answered incorrectly, the teacher was to deliver an electric shock.

Just in case there was any lingering doubt in the teacher's mind about the legitimacy of the shock generator, the *teacher* was given a sample jolt using the switch marked 45 volts. In fact, this sample shock was the only real shock given during the course of the staged experiment.

The first time the learner answered incorrectly, the teacher was to deliver an electric shock at the 15-volt level. With each subsequent error, the teacher was told to progress to the next level on the shock generator. The teacher was also told to announce the voltage level to the learner before delivering the shock.

At predetermined voltage levels, the learner vocalized first his discomfort, then his pain, and, finally, agonized screams. Some of the learner's vocalizations at the different voltage levels are shown in Table 11.3. After 330 volts, the learner's script called for him to fall silent. If the teacher protested that he wished to stop or that he was worried about the learner's safety, the experimenter would say, "The experiment requires that you continue" or "You have no other choice, you *must* continue."

Table 11.3

The Learner's Schedule of Protests in Milgram's Obedience Experiment

120 volts	→	Ugh! Hey, *this* really hurts.
150 volts	→	Ugh!!! Experimenter! That's all. Get me out of here. I told you I had heart trouble. My heart's starting to bother me now. Get me out of here, please. My heart's starting to bother me. I refuse to go on. Let me out.
210 volts	→	Ugh!! Experimenter! Get me out of here. I've had enough. I *won't* be in the experiment any more.
270 volts	→	(*Agonized scream.*) Let me out of here. Let me out of here. Let me out of here. Let me out. Do you hear? Let me out of here.
300 volts	→	(*Agonized scream.*) I absolutely refuse to answer any more. Get me out of here. You can't hold me here. Get me out. Get me out of here.
315 volts	→	(*Intensely agonized scream.*) I told you I refuse to answer. I'm no longer part of this experiment.
330 volts	→	(*Intense and prolonged agonized scream.*) Let me out of here. Let me out of here. My heart's bothering me. Let me out, I tell you. (*Hysterically*) Let me out of here. Let me out of here. You have no right to hold me here. Let me out! Let me out! Let me out! Let me out of here! Let me out! Let me out!

SOURCE: Milgram (1974a), pp. 56–57.

According to the script, the experiment would be halted when the teacher–subject refused to obey the experimenter's orders to continue. Alternatively, if the teacher–subject obeyed the experimenter, the experiment would be halted once the teacher had progressed all the way to the maximum shock level of 450 volts.

Either way, after the experiment the teacher was interviewed and it was explained that the learner had not actually received dangerous electric shocks.

To underscore this point, a "friendly reconciliation" was arranged between the teacher and the learner, and the true purpose of the study was explained to the subject.

The Results of Milgram's Original Experiment

Can you predict how Milgram's subjects behaved? Of the 40 subjects, how many obeyed the experimenter and went to the full 450-volt level? On a more personal level, how do you think *you* would have behaved had you had been one of Milgram's subjects?

Milgram himself asked psychiatrists, college students, and middle-class adults to predict how subjects would behave (see Milgram, 1974a). All three groups predicted that *all* of Milgram's subjects would refuse to obey at some point. They predicted that most subjects would refuse at the 150-volt level, the point at which the learner first protested. They also believed that only a few rare individuals would go as far as the 300-volt level. Finally, *none* of those surveyed thought that any of Milgram's subjects would go to the full 450 volts.

As it turned out, they were all wrong. *Two-thirds of Milgram's subjects—26 of the 40—went to the full 450-volt level.* And of those who defied the experimenter, *not one stopped before the 300-volt level.* The actual results of Milgram's original obedience study are shown in Table 11.4.

Surprised? Milgram himself was stunned by the results, never expecting that the majority of subjects would administer the maximum voltage. Were his results a fluke? Did Milgram inadvertently assemble a sadistic group of New Haven residents who were all too willing to inflict extremely painful, even life-threatening, shocks on a complete stranger?

The answer to both these questions is no. Milgram's obedience study has been repeated many times in the United States and other countries (see Blass, 2000). And, in fact, Milgram (1974a) replicated his own study on numerous occasions, using variations of his basic experimental procedure. In one replication, for instance, Milgram's subjects were 40 women. Were female subjects any less likely to inflict pain on a stranger? Not at all. The results were identical. Confirming Milgram's results since then, eight other studies also found no sex differences in obedience to an authority figure (see Blass, 2000).

Perhaps Milgram's subjects saw through his elaborate experimental hoax, as some critics have suggested (Orne & Holland, 1968). Was it possible that the subjects did not believe that they were really harming the learner? Again, the answer seems to be no. Milgram's subjects seemed totally convinced that the situation was authentic. And they did not behave in a cold-blooded, unfeeling way. Far from it. As the experiment progressed, many subjects showed signs of extreme tension and conflict. In describing the reaction of one subject, Milgram (1963) wrote, "I observed a mature and initially poised businessman enter the laboratory smiling and confident. Within 20 minutes he was reduced to a twitching, stuttering wreck, who was rapidly approaching a point of nervous collapse."

Table 11.4

The Results of Milgram's Original Study

Shock Level	Switch Labels and Voltage Levels	Number of Subjects Who Refused to Administer a Higher Voltage Level
	Slight Shock	
1	15	
2	30	
3	45	
4	60	
	Moderate Shock	
5	75	
6	90	
7	105	
8	120	
9	135	
10	150	
11	165	
12	180	
	Very Strong Shock	
13	195	
14	210	
15	225	
16	240	
	Intense Shock	
17	255	
18	270	
19	285	
20	300	
	Extreme Intensity Shock	
21	315	5
22	330	
23	345	4
24	360	2
	Danger: Severe Shock	1
25	375	1
26	390	
27	405	1
28	420	
	XXX	
29	435	
30	450	26*

*Number of subjects administered the full 450 volts to the learner.

Contrary to what psychiatrists, college students, and middle-class adults predicted, the majority of Milgram's subjects did not refuse to obey by the 150-volt level of shock. As this table shows, 14 of Milgram's 40 subjects (35 percent) refused to continue at some point after administering 300 volts to the learner. However, twenty-six of the 40 subjects (65 percent) remained obedient to the very end, administering the full 450 volts to the learner.

SOURCE: Milgram (1974a), p. 35.

The Aftereffects of Milgram's Study: Were Subjects Harmed? Milgram's findings were disturbing. But some psychologists found his methods equally upsetting. For example, in one experimental variation, participants were ordered to physically hold the learner's hand on a "shock plate." Thirty percent obeyed. To psychologist Diana Baumrind (1964), it was unethical for Milgram to subject his participants to that level of emotional stress, humiliation, and loss of dignity. But Milgram (1964) countered that he had not set out to create stress in his subjects. It was his unanticipated *results*, not his *methods*, that disturbed people. Who would object to his experiment, he asked, "if everyone had broken off at 'slight shock' or at the first sign of the learner's discomfort?"

Concerns were also expressed that participants would experience serious aftereffects from the experiment. However, in a follow-up questionnaire, 84% of participants in Milgram's experiment indicated that they were "glad to have taken part in the experiment," and only about 1 percent regretted participating (Milgram, 1974b).

Making Sense of Milgram's Findings
Multiple Influences

Milgram, along with other researchers, identified several aspects of the experimental situation that had a strong impact on the subjects (see Blass, 1992, 2000; Milgram, 1965). Here are some of the forces that influenced subjects to continue obeying the experimenter's orders:

- *A previously well-established mental framework to obey.* Having volunteered to participate in a psychology experiment, Milgram's subjects arrived at the lab with the mental expectation that they would obediently follow the directions of the person in charge—the experimenter. They also accepted compensation on their arrival, which may have increased their sense of having made a commitment to cooperate with the experimenter.

- *The situation, or context, in which the obedience occurred.* The subjects were familiar with the basic nature of scientific investigation, believed that scientific research was worthwhile, and were told that the goal of the experiment was to "advance the scientific understanding of learning and memory" (Milgram, 1974a). All these factors predisposed the subjects to trust and respect the experimenter's authority (Darley, 1992). Even when subjects protested, they were polite and respectful. Milgram suggested that subjects were afraid that defying the experimenter's orders would make them appear arrogant, rude, disrespectful, or uncooperative.

- *The gradual, repetitive escalation of the task.* At the beginning of the experiment, the subject administered a very low level of shock—15 volts. Subjects could easily justify using such low levels of electric shock in the service of science. The shocks, like the learner's protests, escalated only gradually. Each additional shock was only 15 volts stronger than the preceding one.

- *The experimenter's behavior and reassurances.* Many subjects asked the experimenter who was responsible for what might happen to the learner. In every case, the teacher was reassured that the *experimenter* was responsible for the learner's well-being. Thus, the subjects could believe that they were not responsible for the consequences of their actions. They could tell themselves that their behavior must be appropriate if the experimenter approved of it.

- *The physical and psychological separation from the learner.* Several "buffers" distanced the subject from the pain that he was inflicting on the learner. First, the learner was in a separate room and not visible. Only his voice could be heard. Second, punishment was depersonalized: The subject simply pushed a switch on the shock generator. Finally, the learner never appealed directly to the teacher to stop shocking him. The learner's pleas were always directed toward the *experimenter,* as in "Experimenter! Get me out of here!" Undoubtedly, this contributed to the subject's sense that the experimenter, rather than the subject, was ultimately in control of the situation, including the teacher's behavior.

Conditions That Undermine Obedience
Variations on a Theme

In a lengthy series of experiments, Milgram systematically varied the basic obedience paradigm. To give you some sense of the enormity of Milgram's undertaking, approximately *1,000* subjects, each tested individually, experienced some variation of Milgram's obedience experiment. Thus, Milgram's obedience research represents one of the largest and most integrated research programs in social psychology (Blass, 2000).

By varying his experiments, Milgram identified several conditions that decreased the likelihood of destructive obedience, which are summarized in Figure 11.4. For example, willingness to obey diminished sharply when the buffers that separated the teacher from the learner were lessened or removed, such as when both of them were put in the same room.

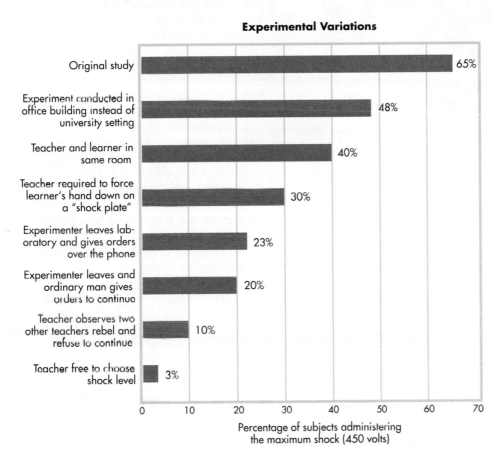

Experimental Variations

Variation	Percentage
Original study	65%
Experiment conducted in office building instead of university setting	48%
Teacher and learner in same room	40%
Teacher required to force learner's hand down on a "shock plate"	30%
Experimenter leaves laboratory and gives orders over the phone	23%
Experimenter leaves and ordinary man gives orders to continue	20%
Teacher observes two other teachers rebel and refuse to continue	10%
Teacher free to choose shock level	3%

Percentage of subjects administering
the maximum shock (450 volts)

FIGURE 11.4 Factors That Decrease Destructive Obedience By systematically varying his basic experimental design, Milgram identified several factors that diminish the likelihood of destructive obedience. In this graph, you can see the percentage of subjects who administered the maximum shock in different experimental variations. For example, when Milgram's subjects observed what they thought were two other subjects disobeying the experimenter, the real subjects followed their lead 90 percent of the time and refused to continue.

SOURCE: Adapted from data reported in Milgram (1974a).

If Milgram's findings seem to cast an unfavorable light on human nature, there are two reasons to take heart. First, when teachers were allowed to act as their own authority and freely choose the shock level, 95 percent of them did not venture beyond 150 volts—the first point at which the learner protested. Clearly, Milgram's subjects were not responding to their own aggressive or sadistic impulses, but rather to orders from an authority figure.

Second, Milgram found that people were more likely to muster up the courage to defy an authority when they saw others do so. When Milgram's subjects observed what they thought were two other subjects disobeying the experimenter, the real subjects followed their lead 90 percent of the time and refused to continue. Like the subjects in Asch's experiment, Milgram's subjects were more likely to stand by their convictions when they were not alone in expressing them.

Despite these encouraging notes, the overall results of Milgram's obedience research painted a bleak picture of human nature. And, more than forty years after the publication of Milgram's research, the moral issues that his findings highlighted are still with us. Should military personnel be prosecuted for obeying orders to commit an immoral or illegal act? Who should be held responsible? We discuss a contemporary instance of destructive obedience in Critical Thinking Box 11.2 on the next page.

The individual who is commanded by a legitimate authority ordinarily obeys. Obedience comes easily and often. It is a ubiquitous and indispensable feature of social life.

Stanley Milgram (1963)

CRITICAL THINKING 11.2

Abuse at Abu Ghraib: Why Do Ordinary People Commit Evil Acts?

Even the censored photos of Iraq's Abu Ghraib prison were shocking. Naked prisoners piled in a pyramid, threatened or bitten by guard dogs. A hooded prisoner standing on a box with wires dangling from his outstretched arms. Worse yet, images of smiling American soldiers posing behind the prisoners, giving the "thumbs up" sign for the camera. *American soldiers*? Aren't we supposed to be the *good guys*?

In the international uproar that followed, U.S. political leaders and Defense Department officials scrambled, damage control at the top of their lists. "A few bad apples," was the official pronouncement— just isolated incidents of over-zealous or sadistic soldiers run amok. The few "bad apples" were identified and arrested: nine members of an Army Reserve unit based in Cresaptown, Maryland.

Why would ordinary Americans mistreat people like that? How can normal people commit such cruel, immoral acts?

Unless we learn the dynamics of "why," we will never be able to counteract the powerful forces that can transform ordinary people into evil perpetrators.

Philip Zimbardo, 2004b

What actually happened at Abu Ghraib?

At its peak population in early 2004, the Abu Ghraib prison complex, some 20 miles west of Baghdad, housed more than 6,000 Iraqi detainees. These were Iraqis who had been detained during the American invasion and occupation of Iraq. The detainees ranged from petty thieves and other criminals to armed insurgents. But also swept up in the detention were many Iraqi civilians who seemed guilty only of being in the wrong place at the wrong time. The prison complex was short of food, water, and basic sanitary facilities, understaffed and poorly supervised (McGeary, 2004).

There had been numerous reports that prisoners were being mistreated at Abu Ghraib, including official complaints by the International Red Cross. However, most Americans had no knowledge of the prison

Would you have obeyed? "I was instructed by persons in higher rank to 'stand there, hold this leash, look at the camera'," Lynndie England (2005) said. Among those calling the shots was her then-lover, Corporal Charles Graner, the alleged ringleader who was sentenced to ten years in prison for his attacks on Iraqi detainees. Graner, England, and one other reservist were convicted of mistreatment and given prison sentences, while the other six reservists made plea deals. No officers were court-martialed or charged with any criminal offense, although some were fined, demoted, or relieved of their command.

conditions until late April, 2004, when the photographs documenting shocking incidents of abuse were shown on national television and featured in the *New Yorker* magazine (Hersh, 2004a, 2004b).

The worst incidents took place in a particular cell-block which was controlled by military intelligence personnel rather than regular Army military police. This cell-block held the prisoners that were thought to be most dangerous and who had been identified as potential "terrorists" or "insurgents" (Hersh, 2005). The Army Reserve soldiers assigned to guard these prisoners were told that their role was to assist military intelligence by "loosening up" the prisoners for later interrogation (Taguba, 2004).

What factors contributed to the events that occurred at Abu Ghraib prison?

Multiple elements combined to create the conditions for brutality, including *in-group versus out-group thinking*, *negative stereo-*

types, *dehumanization*, and *prejudice*. The Iraqi prisoners were of a different culture, ethnic group, and religion than the prison guards, none of whom spoke Arabic. To the American prison guards, the Arab prisoners represented a despised, dangerous, and threatening out-group. Categorizing the prisoners in this way allowed the guards to *dehumanize* the detainees, who were seen as subhuman (Fiske & others, 2004).

Because the detainees were presumed to be potential terrorists, the guards were led to believe that it was their duty to mistreat them in order to help extract useful information. In this way, aggression was transformed from being inexcusable and inhumane into a virtuous act of patriotism (Kelman, 2005). Thinking in this way also helped reduce any *cognitive dissonance* the soldiers might have been experiencing by *justifying* the aggression. "I was doing what I believed my superiors wanted me to do," said Army Reserve Private Lynndie England (2004), a file clerk from West Virginia.

Is what happened at Abu Ghraib similar to what happened in Milgram's studies?

Milgram's controversial studies showed that even ordinary citizens will obey an authority figure and commit immoral acts of destructive obedience. Some of the accused soldiers, like England, did claim that they were "just following orders." The photographs of England with naked prisoners, especially the one in which she was holding a naked male prisoner on a leash, created international outrage and revulsion. But England (2004) testified that her superiors praised the photos and told her, "Hey, you're doing great, keep it up."

But were the guards "just following orders"?

During the investigation and court-martials, soldiers who were called as witnesses for the prosecution testified that no *direct* orders were given to abuse or mistreat any prisoners (Zernike, 2004). However, as a classic and controversial experiment by

Stanford University psychologist **Philip Zimbardo** and his colleagues (1973) showed, *implied* social norms and roles can be just as powerful as explicit orders.

The **Stanford Prison Experiment** was conducted in 1971 (Haney & others, 1973). Twenty-four male college students were randomly assigned to be either prisoners or prison guards. They played their roles in a makeshift, but realistic, prison that had been set up in the basement of a Stanford University building. All of the participants had been evaluated and judged to be psychologically healthy, well-adjusted individuals.

The value of the Stanford Prison Experiment resides in demonstrating the evil that good people can be readily induced into doing to other good people within the context of socially approved roles, rules, and norms...

Philip Zimbardo, 2000a

Originally, the experiment was slated to run for two weeks. But after just six days, the situation was spinning out of control. As Zimbardo (2005) recalls, "Within a few days, [those] assigned to the guard role became abusive, red-necked prison guards. Every day the level of hostility, abuse, and degradation of the prisoners became worse and worse. Within 36 hours the first prisoner had an emotional breakdown, crying, screaming, and thinking irrationally." Prisoners who did not have extreme stress reactions became passive and depressed.

While Milgram's experiments showed the effects of *direct authority pressure,* the Stanford Prison Experiment demonstrated the powerful influence of *situational roles* and *conformity to implied social rules and norms.* These influences are especially pronounced in vague or novel situations (Zimbardo & others, 2000). In confusing or ambiguous situations, *normative social influence* is more likely to occur. When people are not certain what to do, they tend to rely on cues provided by others and to conform their behavior to those in their immediate social group (Fiske & others, 2004).

At Abu Ghraib, the accused soldiers received no special training and were ignorant of either international or Army regulations regarding the treatment of civilian detainees or enemy prisoners of war (Taguba, 2004). Lynndie England, for example, was trained as a file clerk, not a prison guard. In the chaotic cell-block, the guards apparently took their cues from one another and from the military intelligence personnel who encouraged them to "set the conditions" for interrogation (Taguba, 2004; Hersh, 2005).

Are people helpless to resist destructive obedience in a situation like Abu Ghraib prison?

No. As Milgram demonstrated, *people can and do resist pressure to perform evil actions.* Not all military personnel at Abu Ghraib went along with the pressure to mistreat prisoners (Hersh, 2005; Taguba, 2004). Consider these examples:

- National Guard 1st Lieutenant David Sutton stopped the abuse of a prisoner by other soldiers and immediately reported it to his commanding officer.

- Master-at-Arms William J. Kimbro, a Navy dog handler, adamantly refused to participate in improper interrogations using dogs to intimidate prisoners despite being pressured by the military intelligence personnel (Hersh, 2004b).

- When handed a CD filled with digital photographs depicting prisoners being abused and humiliated, Specialist Joseph M. Darby turned it over to the Army Criminal Investigation Division. It was Darby's conscientious action that finally prompted a formal investigation of the prison.

At the court-martials, army personnel called as prosecution witnesses testified that the abusive treatment shown in the photographs would *never* be allowed under any stretch of the normal rules for handling inmates in a military prison (Zernike, 2004).

In fact, as General Peter Pace, chairman of the Joint Chiefs of Staff stated forcefully in a November, 2005 press conference, "It is absolutely the responsibility of every U.S. service member, if they see inhumane treatment being conducted, to intervene to stop it... If they are physically present when inhumane treatment is taking place, they have an *obligation* to try to stop it."

Finally, it's important to point out that understanding the factors that contributed to the events at Abu Ghraib does *not* excuse the perpetrators' behavior or absolve them of individual responsibility. And, as Milgram's research shows, the action of even one outspoken dissenter can inspire others to resist unethical or illegal commands from an authority figure.

Critical Thinking Questions

- How might the fundamental attribution error lead people to blame "a few bad apples" rather than noticing situational factors that contributed to the Abu Ghraib prison abuse?

- Who should be held responsible for the inhumane conditions and abuse that occurred at Abu Ghraib prison?

Accepting responsibility
At her trial, Lynndie England, the file clerk from a small town in West Virginia, apologized for her actions. In an interview after her conviction, England (2005) said that she was still "haunted" by memories of events in the prison. She would always feel guilty, she said, "for doing the wrong thing, posing in pictures when I shouldn't have, degrading [the prisoners] and humiliating them—and not saying anything to anybody else to stop it."

Asch, Milgram, and the Real World

Implications of the Classic Social Influence Studies

Stanford Prison Experiment
Brief but controversial psychological study conducted in 1971 investigating the influence of social roles, rules, and norms in which Stanford University students were randomly assigned the roles of prison guards or prisoners in a make-shift prison created in the basement of a university building.

The scientific study of conformity and obedience has produced some important insights. The first is the degree to which our behavior is influenced by situational factors. Being at odds with the majority or with authority figures is very uncomfortable for most people—enough so that our judgment and perceptions can be distorted and we may act in ways that violate our conscience.

More important, perhaps, is the insight that each of us *does* have the capacity to resist group or authority pressure (Rochat & others, 2000). Because the central findings of these studies are so dramatic, it's easy to overlook the fact that some subjects refused to conform or obey despite considerable social and situational pressure. Consider the response of a subject in one of Milgram's later studies (Milgram, 1974a). A 32-year-old industrial engineer named Jan Rensaleer protested when he was commanded to continue at the 255-volt level:

> **EXPERIMENTER:** *It is absolutely essential that you continue.*
>
> **MR. RENSALEER:** *Well, I won't—not with the man screaming to get out.*
>
> **EXPERIMENTER:** *You have no other choice.*
>
> **MR. RENSALEER:** *I* do *have a choice.* (Incredulous and indignant) *Why don't I have a choice? I came here on my own free will. I thought I could help in a research project. But if I have to hurt somebody to do that, or if I was in his place, too, I wouldn't stay there. I can't continue. I'm very sorry. I think I've gone too far already, probably.*

Like some of the other participants in the obedience and conformity studies, Rensaleer effectively resisted the situational and social pressures that pushed him to obey. So did Sergeant Joseph M. Darby, the young man who turned over the CD with incriminating photos of Abu Ghraib abuse to authorities, triggering the investigation. As Darby later testified, the photos shocked him. "They violated everything that I personally believed in and everything that I had been taught about the rules of war." Another man who took a stand, stopping and then reporting an abusive incident in the prison was 1st Lieutenant David Sutton. As he put it, "The way I look at it, if I don't do something, I'm just as guilty." Table 11.5 summarizes several strategies that can help people resist the pressure to conform or obey in a destructive, dangerous, or morally questionable situation.

Destructive Obedience and Prejudice
Blind obedience to authority combined with ethnic prejudice in Germany during World War II led to the slaughter of millions of Jews in concentration camps (Saltzman, 2000). When questioned after the war, Nazi officials and soldiers claimed that they were "just following orders." More than a half-century after the end of World War II, ethnic hatred, genocide, and politically inspired mass killings continued in regions as far-flung as Bosnia, Croatia, Rwanda, and the Sudan.

Table 11.5

Resisting an Authority's Unacceptable Orders

- Verify your own discomfort by asking yourself, "Is this something I would do if I were controlling the situation?"

- Express your discomfort. It can be as simple as saying, "I'm really not comfortable with this."

- Resist even slightly objectionable commands so that the situation doesn't escalate into increasingly immoral or destructive obedience.

- If you realize you've already done something unacceptable, stop at that point rather than continuing to comply.

- Find or create an excuse to get out of the situation and validate your concerns with someone who is not involved with the situation.

- Question the legitimacy of the authority. Most authorities have legitimacy only in specific situations. If the authority is out of his or her legitimate context, they have no more authority in the situation than you.

- If it is a group situation, find an ally who also feels uncomfortable with the authority's orders. Two people expressing dissent in harmony can effectively resist conforming to the group's actions.

SOURCES: Milgram, 1963, 1974a; Asch, 1956, 1957; Haney & others, 1973; Zimbardo, 2000, 2004; Blass, 1991, 2004; American Psychological Association, 2005.

How are such people different from those who conform or obey? Unfortunately, there's no satisfying answer to that question. No specific personality trait consistently predicts conformity or obedience in experimental situations such as those Asch and Milgram created (see Blass, 1991; Burger, 1992). In other words, the social influences that Asch and Milgram created in their experimental situations can be compelling even to people who are normally quite independent.

Finally, we need to emphasize that conformity and obedience are not completely bad in and of themselves. Quite the contrary. Conformity and obedience are necessary for an orderly society, which is why such behaviors were instilled in all of us as children. The critical issue is not so much whether people conform or obey, because we all do so every day of our lives. Rather, the critical issue is whether the norms we conform to, or the orders we obey, reflect values that respect the rights, well-being, and dignity of others.

Helping Behavior
Coming to the Aid of Strangers

Key Theme
- Prosocial behavior describes any behavior that helps another person, including altruistic acts.

Key Questions
- What factors increase the likelihood that people will help a stranger?
- What factors decrease the likelihood that people will help a stranger?
- How can the lack of bystander response in the Genovese murder case be explained in light of psychological research on helping behavior?

It was about 3:20 A.M. on Friday, March 13, 1964, when 28-year-old Kitty Genovese returned home from her job managing a bar. Like other residents in her middle-class New York City neighborhood, she parked her car at an adjacent railroad station. Her apartment entrance was only 100 feet away.

Kitty Genovese

The Murder Scene At the end of the sidewalk you can see the railroad station where Genovese parked her car. Along the sidewalk are entrances to shops as well as stairways leading to apartments above the shops. After Genovese staggered to the entrance of her apartment, her attacker returned and stabbed her to death.

As she got out of her car, she noticed a man at the end of the parking lot. When the man moved in her direction, she began walking toward a nearby police call box, which was under a streetlight in front of a bookstore. On the opposite side of the street was a 10-story apartment building. As she neared the streetlight, the man grabbed her and she screamed. Across the street, lights went on in the apartment building. "Oh, my God! He stabbed me! Please help me! Please help me!" she screamed.

"Let that girl alone!" a man yelled from one of the upper apartment windows. The attacker looked up, then walked off, leaving Kitty on the ground, bleeding. The street became quiet. Minutes passed. One by one, lights went off. Struggling to her feet, Kitty made her way toward her apartment. As she rounded the corner of the building moments later, her assailant returned, stabbing her again. "I'm dying! I'm dying!" she screamed.

Again, lights went on. Windows opened and people looked out. This time, the assailant got into his car and drove off. It was now 3:35 A.M. Fifteen minutes had passed since Kitty's first screams for help. A New York City bus passed by. Staggering, then crawling, Kitty moved toward the entrance of her apartment. She never made it. Her attacker returned, searching the apartment entrance doors. At the second apartment entrance, he found her, slumped at the foot of the steps. This time, he stabbed her to death.

It was 3:50 A.M. when someone first called the police. The police took just two minutes to arrive at the scene. About half an hour later, an ambulance carried Kitty Genovese's body away. Only then did people come out of their apartments to talk to the police.

Over the next two weeks, police investigators learned that a total of 38 people had witnessed Kitty's murder—a murder that involved three separate attacks over a period of about 30 minutes. Why didn't anyone try to help her? Or call the police when she first screamed for help?

When *The New York Times* interviewed various experts, they seemed baffled, although one expert said it was a "typical" reaction (Mohr, 1964). If there was a common theme in their explanations, it seemed to be "apathy." The occurrence was simply representative of the alienation and depersonalization of life in a big city, people said (see Rosenthal, 1964a, 1964b).

Not everyone bought this pat explanation. In the first place, it wasn't true. As social psychologists **Bibb Latané** and **John Darley** (1970) later pointed out in their landmark book, *The Unresponsive Bystander: Why Doesn't He Help?*:

> People often help others, even at great personal risk to themselves. For every "apathy" story, one of outright heroism could be cited. . . . It is a mistake to get trapped by the wave of publicity and discussion surrounding incidents in which help was not forthcoming into believing that help never comes. People sometimes help and sometimes don't. What determines when help will be given?

That's the critical question, of course. When do people help others? And *why* do people help others?

Prosocial Behavior in Action Everyday life is filled with countless acts of prosocial behavior. Many people volunteer their time and energy to help others, like these teenagers serving Christmas dinner at a church soup kitchen in Minneapolis.

When we help another person with no expectation of personal reward or benefit, we're displaying **altruism** (Piliavin & others, 1981). An altruistic act is fundamentally selfless—the individual is motivated purely by the desire to help someone in need. Everyday life is filled with little acts of altruistic kindness, such as Fern giving the "homeless" man a handful of quarters or the stranger who thoughtfully holds a door open for you as you juggle an armful of packages.

Altruistic actions fall under the broader heading of **prosocial behavior,** which describes any behavior that helps another person, whatever the underlying motive. Note that prosocial behaviors are not necessarily altruistic. Sometimes we help others out of guilt. And sometimes we help others in order to gain something, such as recognition, rewards, increased self-esteem, or having the favor returned (Ames & others, 2004; Baumeister & others, 1994).

Factors That *Increase* the Likelihood of Bystanders Helping

Kitty Genovese's death triggered hundreds of investigations into the conditions under which people will help others (Dovidio, 1984). Those studies began in the 1960s with the pioneering efforts of Latané and Darley, who conducted a series of ingenious experiments in which people appeared to need help. Often, these studies were conducted using locations in and around New York City as a kind of open-air laboratory.

Other researchers joined the effort to understand what factors influence a person's decision to help another (see Eisenberg, 1991; Levy & others, 2002). Some of the most significant factors that have been found to increase the likelihood of helping behavior are noted below.

- *The "feel good, do good" effect.* People who feel good, successful, happy, or fortunate are more likely to help others (see Salovey & others, 1991; Schaller & Cialdini, 1990). Those good feelings can be due to virtually any positive event, such as receiving a gift, succeeding at a task, listening to pleasant music, finding a small amount of money, or even just enjoying a warm, sunny day.

- *Feeling guilty.* We tend to be more helpful when we're feeling guilty. For example, after telling a lie or inadvertently causing an accident, people were more likely to help others (Baumeister & others, 1994; Cialdini & others, 1973). Even guilt induced by surviving the 9/11 terrorist attacks spurred helping behavior in many people during the aftermath (Wayment, 2004).

- *Seeing others who are willing to help.* Whether it's donating blood, helping a stranded motorist change a flat tire, or dropping money in the Salvation Army kettle during the holiday season, we're more likely to help if we observe others do the same (Bryan & Test, 1967; Sarason & others, 1991).

- *Perceiving the other person as deserving help.* We're more likely to help people who are in need of help through no fault of their own. For example, people are twice as likely to give some change to a stranger if they believe the stranger's wallet has been stolen than if they believe the stranger has simply spent all his money (Latané & Darley, 1970).

- *Knowing how to help.* Research has confirmed that simply knowing what to do contributes greatly to the decision to help someone else (e.g., Clark & Word, 1974; Huston & others, 1981).

- *A personalized relationship.* When people have any sort of personal relationship with another person, they're more likely to help that person. Even minimal social interaction with each other, such as making eye contact or engaging in small talk, increases the likelihood that one person will help the other (Howard & Crano, 1974; Solomon & others, 1981).

altruism
Helping another person with no expectation of personal reward or benefit.

prosocial behavior
Any behavior that helps another, whether the underlying motive is self-serving or selfless.

Bystander Intervention In the situation shown here, bystanders are coming to the aid of a stranger injured in a car accident on a New York City street. What factors in this situation may have influenced their decision to help the accident victim?

Factors That *Decrease* the Likelihood of Bystanders Helping

It's equally important to consider influences that decrease the likelihood of helping behavior. As we look at some of the key findings, we'll also note how each factor might have played a role in the death of Kitty Genovese.

- *The presence of other people.* People are much more likely to help when they are alone (Latané & Nida, 1981). If other people are present or imagined (Garcia & others, 2002), helping behavior declines—a phenomenon called the **bystander effect.**

How can we account for this surprising finding? There seem to be two major reasons for the bystander effect. First, the presence of other people creates a **diffusion of responsibility.** The responsibility to intervene is *shared* (or *diffused*) among all the onlookers. Because no one person feels all the pressure to respond, each bystander becomes less likely to help.

Ironically, the sheer number of bystanders seemed to be the most significant factor working against Kitty Genovese. Remember that when she first screamed, a man yelled down, "Let that girl alone!" With that, each observer instantly knew that he

The Bystander Effect In contrast to the situation shown in the photograph on page 467, the people in this situation are obviously trying to ignore the heated argument between the man and the woman, even though the man has the woman pinned against a wall. What factors in this situation make it less likely that bystanders will intervene and try to help a stranger?

or she was not the only one watching the events on the street below. Hence, no single individual felt the full responsibility to help. Instead, there was a diffusion of responsibility among all the bystanders so that each individual's share of responsibility was small indeed.

Second, the bystander effect seems to occur because each of us is motivated to some extent by the desire to behave in a socially acceptable way (*normative social influence*) and to appear correct (*informational social influence*). Thus, we often rely on the reactions of others to help us define a situation and guide our response to it. In the case of Kitty Genovese, the lack of intervention by any of the witnesses may have signaled the others that intervention was not appropriate, wanted, or needed.

- *Being in a big city or a very small town.* Kitty Genovese was attacked late at night in one of the biggest cities in the world, New York. Are people less likely to help strangers in big cities? Researcher Nancy Steblay (1987) has confirmed that this common belief is true— but with a twist. People are less likely to help a stranger in very big cities (300,000 people or more) *or* in very small towns (5,000 people or less). Either extreme—very big or very small—seems to work against helping a stranger.

- *Vague or ambiguous situations.* When situations are ambiguous and people are not certain that help is needed, they're less likely to offer help (Solomon & others, 1978). The ambiguity of the situation may also have worked against Kitty Genovese. The people in the apartment building saw a man and a woman struggling on the street below but had no way of knowing whether the two were acquainted. "We thought it was a lovers' quarrel," some of the witnesses later said (Gansberg, 1964). Researchers have found that people are especially reluctant to intervene when the situation appears to be a domestic dispute or a "lovers' quarrel," because they are not certain that assistance is wanted (Shotland & Straw, 1976).

bystander effect
A phenomenon in which the greater the number of people present, the less likely each individual is to help someone in distress.

diffusion of responsibility
A phenomenon in which the presence of other people makes it less likely that any individual will help someone in distress because the obligation to intervene is shared among all the onlookers.

- *__When the personal costs for helping outweigh the benefits.__* As a general rule, we tend to weigh the costs as well as the benefits of helping in deciding whether to act. If the potential costs outweigh the benefits, it's less likely that people will help (Dovidio & others, 1991; Hedge & Yousif, 1992). The witnesses in the Genovese case may have felt that the benefits of helping Genovese were outweighed by the potential hassles and danger of becoming involved in the situation.

On a small yet universal scale, the murder of Kitty Genovese dramatically underscores the power of situational and social influences on our behavior. Although social psychological research has provided insights about the factors that influenced the behavior of those who witnessed the Genovese murder, it should not be construed as a justification for the inaction of the bystanders. After all, Kitty Genovese's death probably could have been prevented by a single phone call. If we understand the factors that decrease helping behavior, we can recognize and overcome those obstacles when we encounter someone who needs assistance. If *you* had been Kitty Genovese, how would *you* have hoped other people would react?

Closing Thoughts

We began this chapter with a Prologue about Fern trying to help a stranger in a strange city. As it turned out, Fern's social perceptions of the man were inaccurate: He was not a "homeless" person living on the streets of San Francisco. As simple as this incident was, it underscored a theme that was repeatedly echoed throughout our subsequent discussions of person perception, attribution, and attitudes. Our subjective impressions, whether they are accurate or not, play a pivotal role in how we perceive and think about other people.

A different theme emerged in our later discussions of conformity, obedience, and helping behavior. Social and situational factors, especially the behavior of others in the same situation, can have powerful effects on how we act at a given moment. But like Fern, each of us has the freedom to choose how we respond in a given situation. When we're aware of the social forces that influence us, it can be easier for us to choose wisely.

In the final analysis, we are social animals who often influence one another's thoughts, perceptions, and actions, sometimes in profound ways. In the chapter Application, we'll look at some of the ways that social psychological insights have been applied by professional persuaders—and how you can counteract attempts to persuade you.

APPLICATION	The Persuasion Game

Our daughter, Laura, was three-and-a-half years old, happily munching her Cheerios and doodling pictures in the butter on her bread. Don sat across from her at the kitchen table, reading a draft of this chapter. "Don't play with your food, Laura," Don said without looking up.

"Okay, Daddy," she chirped. "Daddy, are you in a happy mood?"

Don paused. "Yes, I'm in a happy mood, Laura," he said thoughtfully. "Are you in a happy mood?"

"Yes, Daddy," Laura replied as she made the banana peel dance around her placemat. "Daddy, will you get me a Mermaid Barbie doll for my birthday?"

Ah, so young and so clever! From very early in life, we learn the basics of **persuasion**—the deliberate attempt to influence the attitudes or behavior of another person in a situation in which that person has some freedom of choice. Clearly, Laura had figured out one basic rule: She's more likely to persuade Mom or Dad when they're in "a happy mood."

Professional persuaders often manipulate people's attitudes and behavior using techniques based on two fundamental social norms: the rule of reciprocity and the rule of commitment (Cody & Seiter, 2001). Here we'll provide you with some practical suggestions to avoid being taken in by persuasion techniques.

The Rule of Reciprocity

The *rule of reciprocity* is a simple but powerful social norm (Cialdini & Trost, 1998). If someone gives you something or does you a favor, you feel obligated to return the favor. That's why encyclopedia salespeople offer you a "free" dictionary for listening to their spiel and department stores that sell expensive cosmetics offer "free" makeovers. Technically, you are under "no obligation" to buy anything. Nonetheless, the tactic often creates an uncomfortable sense of obligation, so you *do* feel pressured to reciprocate by buying the product (Cialdini, 2000).

One strategy that uses the rule of reciprocity is called the *door-in-the-face technique* (Dillard, 1991; Perloff, 1993). First, the persuader makes a large request that you're certain to refuse. For example, Joe asks to borrow $500. You figuratively "slam the door in his face" by quickly turning him

down. But then Joe, apologetic, appears to back off and makes a much smaller request—to borrow $20. From your perspective, it appears that Joe has made a concession to you and is trying to be reasonable. This puts you in the position of reciprocating with a concession of your own. "Well, I can't lend you $500," you grumble, "but I guess I could lend you 20 bucks." Of course, the persuader's real goal was to persuade you to comply with the second, smaller request.

The rule of reciprocity is also operating in the *that's-not-all technique* (Zimbardo & Leippe, 1991). First, the persuader makes an offer. But before you can accept or reject it, the persuader appears to throw in something extra to make the deal even more attractive to you. So as you're standing there mulling over the price of the more expensive DVD player, the salesperson says, "Listen, I'm offering you a great price but that's not all I'll do—I'll throw in some headphones at no charge." From your perspective, it appears as though the salesperson has just done you a favor by making a concession you did not ask for. This creates a sense of obligation for you to reciprocate by buying the "better" package.

The Rule of Commitment

Another powerful social norm is the *rule of commitment*. Once you make a public commitment, there is psychological and interpersonal pressure on you to behave consistently with your earlier commitment. The *foot-in-the-door technique* is one strategy that capitalizes on the rule of commitment (Cialdini, 2000; Perloff, 1993). Here's how it works.

First, the persuader makes a small request that you're likely to agree to. For example, she might ask you to wear a lapel pin publicizing a fundraising drive for a charity (Pratkanis & Aronson, 1992). By agreeing to wear the lapel pin, you've made a *commitment* to the fundraising effort. At that point, she has gotten her "foot in the door." Later, the persuader asks you to comply with a second, larger request, such as donating money to the charity. Because of your earlier commitment, you feel psychologically pressured to behave consistently by now agreeing to the larger commitment (Gorassini &

Olson, 1995).

The rule of commitment is also operating in the *low-ball technique*. First, the persuader gets you to make a commitment by deliberately understating the cost of the product you want. He's thrown you a "low ball," one that is simply too good to turn down. In reality, the persuader has no intention of honoring the artificially low price.

Here's an example of the low-ball technique in action: You've negotiated an excellent price (the "low ball") on a used car and filled out the sales contract. The car salesman shakes your hand and beams, then takes your paperwork into his manager's office for approval. Ten minutes pass—enough time for you to convince yourself that you've made the right decision and solidify your commitment to it.

At that point, the salesman comes back from his manager's office looking dejected. "I'm terribly sorry," the car salesman says. "My manager won't let me sell the car at that price because we'd lose too much money on the deal. I told him I would even take a lower commission, but he won't budge."

Notice what has happened. The attractive low-ball price that originally prompted you to make the commitment has been pulled out from under your feet. What typically happens? Despite the loss of the original inducement to make the purchase—the low-ball price—people often feel compelled to keep their commitment to make the purchase even though it is at a higher price (Cialdini, 2000).

Defending Against Persuasion Techniques

How can you reduce the likelihood that you'll be manipulated into making a decision that is not in your best interest? Here are three practical suggestions.

1. Sleep on it.

Persuasive transactions typically occur quickly. Part of this is our own doing. We've finally decided to go look at a new computer, automobile, or whatever, so we're psychologically primed to buy the product. The persuader uses this psychological momentum to help coax you into signing on the dotted line right then and there. It's only later, of course, that you sometimes have second thoughts. So when you think you've got the deal you want, tell the persuader that you always sleep on important decisions before making a final commitment.

The sleep-on-it rule often provides an opportunity to discover whether the persuader is deliberately trying to pressure or manipulate you. If the persuader responds to your sleep-on-it suggestion by saying something like, "This offer is good for today only," then it's likely that he or she is afraid that your commitment to the deal will crumble if you think about it too carefully or look elsewhere.

2. Play devil's advocate.

List all of the reasons why you should *not* buy the product or make a particular commitment (Pratkanis & Aronson, 1992). Arguing *against* the decision will help activate your critical thinking skills. It's also helpful to discuss important decisions with a friend, who might be able to point out disadvantages that you have overlooked.

3. When in doubt, do nothing.

Learn to trust your gut feelings when something doesn't feel quite right. If you feel that you're being psychologically pressured or cornered, you probably are. As a general rule, if you feel any sense of hesitation, lean toward the conservative side and do nothing. If you take the time to think things over, you'll probably be able to identify the source of your reluctance.

Chapter Review Social Psychology

Key Points

Introduction: What Is Social Psychology?

■ **Social psychology** is the scientific study of how individuals think, feel, and behave in social situations. **Social cognition** and **social influence** are two important areas of research in social psychology.

Person Perception: *Forming Impressions of Other People*

■ **Person perception** is an active and subjective process that occurs in an interpersonal context. The interpersonal context includes the characteristics of the individual you are judging, your own characteristics, and the situation.

■ Person perception is influenced by subjective perceptions, personal goals, **social norms,** and self-perception.

■ People often rely on social categories when they evaluate others. **Social categorization** may be automatic or deliberate. Using social categories is cognitively efficient but can lead to inaccurate conclusions.

■ Because we expect certain traits and behaviors to go together, we often form and rely on implicit personality theories in person perception. **Implicit personality theories** provide a mental framework that organizes observations, memories, and beliefs about other people. One common implicit personality theory is "what is beautiful is good." However, there are few personality differences between attractive and less attractive people.

Attribution: *Explaining Behavior*

■ The **attribution** process refers to how we infer the cause of our own or another person's behavior. Attributions can strongly influence our opinions of other people, but the attribution process is susceptible to many biases.

■ Three important attributional biases are the **fundamental attribution error,** the **actor–observer discrepancy,** and the **self-serving bias.** The **just-world hypothesis,** along with the fundamental attribution error, contributes to

blaming the victim of a tragedy. In some collectivistic cultures, people display the modesty, or self-effacing, bias and are less prone to making the fundamental attribution error than are people in individualistic cultures.

The Social Psychology of Attitudes

- An **attitude** is a learned tendency to evaluate an object, person, or issue in a particular way. This evaluation is usually positive or negative, but may be ambivalent. Attitudes can have cognitive, emotional, and behavioral components.

- Attitudes are likely to determine behaviors when they are extreme or expressed frequently, when they have been formed through direct experience, when people are very knowledgeable about the attitude object, when people have a vested interest in the subject of the attitude, and when people expect a favorable outcome from acting in accordance with their attitude.

- When behavior conflicts with attitudes, **cognitive dissonance** may occur, and people may change their attitudes to conform to their behavior.

Understanding Prejudice

- **Prejudice** refers to a negative attitude toward people who belong to a specific social group. **Stereotypes** are characteristics associated with all members of particular social groups. Relying on stereotypes can have many negative consequences. Stereotyped thinking can distort perception and cause us to inaccurately prejudge individuals. Once formed, stereotypes resist change.

- Judgments of others are also influenced by whether they are members of the **in-group** or an **out-group.** We're more likely to use negative stereotypes to evaluate members of out-groups. The **out-group homogeneity effect, in-group bias,** and **ethnocentrism** are three forms of bias that can result from in-group/out-group thinking.

- Stereotypes form the cognitive basis for prejudicial attitudes. Prejudice also has emotional and behavioral components.

- Muzafer Sherif demonstrated that intergroup conflict can be decreased when groups engage in a cooperative effort. Cooperative learning is one way of reducing prejudice in classrooms.

Conformity: *Following the Crowd*

- **Social influence** is the psychological study of how behavior is influenced by the social environment and other people.

Conformity occurs when people change their behavior, attitudes, or beliefs in response to real or imagined group pressure. Sometimes people conform publicly but not privately.

- Research by Solomon Asch demonstrated the degree to which people will conform to a majority view and the conditions under which conformity is most likely. **Normative** and **informational social influence** both contribute to conformity.

- Conformity is generally higher in collectivistic cultures than in individualistic cultures. Conformity to group norms is viewed less negatively in many collectivistic cultures than it is in individualistic cultures.

Obedience: *Just Following Orders*

- **Obedience** was studied most extensively by Stanley Milgram. In Milgram's original obedience experiment, the subject (the "teacher") thought he was delivering ever-increasing levels of electric shock to another person (the "learner"). In contrast to predictions, most of the subjects obeyed the experimenter and progressed to the maximum shock level.

- Milgram identified several powerful aspects of the original experimental situation that influenced subjects to obey the experimenter and continue delivering electric shocks. In later experiments, Milgram also identified several situational factors that made people less likely to obey.

- Asch's research on conformity and Milgram's research on obedience demonstrate the degree to which behavior is influenced by situational factors.

Helping Behavior: *Coming to the Aid of Strangers*

- The scientific study of helping behavior—**altruism** and **prosocial behavior**—was spurred by the murder of Kitty Genovese in front of 38 witnesses. Although no one intervened to save Genovese, sometimes people do help strangers.

- Bibb Latané and John Darley extensively studied the circumstances under which people will help a stranger. Several factors have been identified that affect the likelihood of bystander intervention. **Diffusion of responsibility** is the most important factor that explains the **bystander effect.**

Key Terms

social psychology, p. 438

social cognition, p. 438

social influence, p. 438

person perception, p. 438

social norms, p. 439

social categorization, p. 440

implicit personality theory, p. 440

attribution, p. 443

fundamental attribution error, p. 443

blaming the victim, p. 443

just-world hypothesis, p. 443

actor–observer discrepancy, p. 444

self-serving bias, p. 445

attitude, p. 446

cognitive dissonance, p. 448

prejudice, p. 450

stereotype, p. 450

in-group, p. 451

out-group, p. 451

out-group homogeneity effect, p. 452

in-group bias, p. 452

ethnocentrism, p. 452

conformity, p. 455

normative social influence, p. 456

informational social influence, p. 456

obedience, p. 457

Stanford Prison Experiment, p. 453

altruism, p. 466

prosocial behavior, p. 466

bystander effect, p. 468

diffusion of responsibility, p. 468

persuasion, p. 470

Key People

Solomon Asch (1907–1996) American social psychologist who is best known for his pioneering studies of conformity. (p. 455)

John M. Darley (b. 1938) Contemporary American social psychologist who, along with co-researcher Bibb Latané, is best known for his pioneering studies of bystander intervention in emergency situations. (p. 466)

Bibb Latané (b. 1937) Contemporary American social psychologist who, along with co-researcher John Darley, is best known for his pioneering studies of bystander intervention in emergency situations. (p. 466)

Stanley Milgram (1933–1984) American social psychologist who is best known for his controversial series of studies investigating destructive obedience to an authority. (p. 457)

Muzafer Sherif (1906–1988) American social psychologist who is best known for his Robbers Cave experiments to study prejudice, conflict resolution, and group processes. (p. 453)

Philip G. Zimbardo (b. 1933) American social psychologist, known for his research on cognitive dissonance and social influence, and especially for the Stanford Prison Experiment, which demonstrated how situational forces can impact behavior. (p. 448)

Web Companion Review Activities

You can find additional review activities by going to **www.DiscoveringPsychology.com** and clicking on the *Discovering Psychology* 4th Edition text cover. At the Discovering Psychology Web Companion you'll find the chapter learning objectives, flashcards for key terms and key people, interactive crossword puzzles, self-scoring practice quizzes, and other materials to help you master the information in this chapter.

Buy One Get One Free

Stress, Health, and Coping

Prologue Katie's Story

A beautiful, crystal-clear New York morning. In her high-rise apartment at 1 West Street, our 20-year-old niece Katie was fixing herself some breakfast. From the street below, Katie could hear the muted sound of sirens, but she thought nothing of it. The phone rang. It was Lydia, her roommate, calling from her job in midtown Manhattan. "Katie, you're not going to believe this. A plane hit the World Trade Center. Go up on the roof and take a look!"

Katie hung up the phone and scurried up the fire escape stairwell, joining other residents already gathered on the roof. Down below, sirens were blaring and she could see emergency vehicles, fire engines, and people racing from all directions toward the World Trade Center, just a few blocks away. There was a gaping hole in the north tower. Thick black smoke was billowing out, drifting upward, and filling the sky. She thought she could see the flames. *What a freaky accident.*

After watching for a few minutes, Katie turned to go back downstairs and get ready for her dance class. Then, "Look at that plane!" someone yelled. Seconds later, a massive jet roared overhead and slammed into the World Trade Center's south tower, exploding into a huge fireball.

People screaming. Panic. Pushing and shoving at the stairwell door. *Get back to the apartment.* The television. Live views of the burning towers. Newscaster shouting: "Terrorist attack! New York is being attacked!" The TV went dead. *Don't panic. What am I going to do? Are we being bombed?*

Two thousand miles away. A sunny Colorado morning. Phone ringing. Judy was sound asleep. Ringing. Answer the phone. "Katie? What's wrong? Is someone in your apartment? Calm down, I can't understand . . . ."

"Mom, New York is being attacked! I don't know what to do! What should I do?" Katie sobbed uncontrollably.

Judy flipped on the television. Bizarre scenes of chaos in New York. *Oh my God, Katie's only a few blocks from the World Trade Center.* "Katie, stay in your apartment! Don't . . . ." The phone connection went dead.

Katie dropped the phone. *Worthless. Don't panic.* Lights flickered off, then on. Pounding on the door. "Evacuate the building! Get out!" a man's voice shouted. "Get out now! Use the stairwell!" *Gotta get out of here. Get out.*

Putting on her shoes and pulling a T-shirt over her pajamas, Katie grabbed her cell phone and raced out of her apartment toward the crowded stairwell. On the street was a scene of mass confusion. *Cross the street.* She joined a throng of people gathering in Battery Park. *Breathe. Stay calm.* As the crowd watched the towers burn, people shouted out more news. *Pentagon has been hit. White House is on fire. More planes in the air. President on Air Force One.*

Shaking, she couldn't take her eyes off the burning towers. *What's falling?* Figures falling from the windows of the Trade Center, a hundred stories high. *On fire. That person was on fire. Oh my God, they're jumping out of the buildings! Don't look!* Firefighters, EMT workers, police, media people swarming on the plaza at the base of the buildings. *This is not real. It's a movie. It's not real.*

Suddenly, unbelievably, the south tower crumbled. Onlookers screaming. *It's collapsing! It's coming down.* A vast ball of smoke formed, mushrooming in the sky. Like everyone else in the park, Katie turned and started running blindly. Behind her, a huge cloud of black smoke, ash, and debris followed, howling down West Street like a tornado.

Running. Cops shouting. "Go north! Don't go back! Get out of here!" *Don't go north. Go toward the ferry.* Choking on the smoke and dust, Katie covered her face with her T-shirt and stumbled down the street, moving toward the harbor. *I'm going to choke . . . can't breathe.* She saw a group of people near the Staten Island Ferry. *Get on the ferry, get out of Manhattan.* Another explosion. Panic. More people running.

Katie is still not certain how, dazed and disoriented, she ended up on a boat—a commuter ferry taking people to Atlantic Highlands, New Jersey. *Stop shaking. I'm safe. Stop shaking.* Covered with soot. Filthy. Standing in her pajamas amid stunned Wall Street workers in their suits and ties. Call anyone. Trying to call people. *Cell phone dead . . . no, please work!* "Here, Miss, use mine, it's working." Call anyone. Crying. *They're dead. Those firemen, the EMT workers on the plaza. They're all dead.* From the boat, she got a call through to her dance teacher, Pam, who lived in New Jersey. Pam would come and get her. She could stay with Pam.

Katie survived, but the next few weeks were difficult ones. Like the other residents of buildings near the World Trade Center, Katie wasn't allowed back into her apartment for many days. She had no money, no clothes, none of her possessions. And the reminders were everywhere. Fire station shrines, signs for the subway stop that didn't exist anymore, photographs of the missing on fences and walls. And the haunting memories—images of people jumping, falling, the faces of the rescue workers, the plane ripping through the building.

Eventually, like millions of other New Yorkers, Katie regained her equilibrium. "Are things back to normal?" Katie says, "No, things will never be normal again, not in a hundred years. But it's okay. I'm fine. And I'm not going to leave New York. This is where I am, this is where I live, this is where I can dance."

Introduction
What Is Stress?

Key Theme
■ When events are perceived as exceeding your ability to cope with them, you experience an unpleasant emotional and physical state called stress.

Key Questions
■ What is health psychology, and what is the biopsychosocial model?
■ How do life events, daily hassles, and conflict contribute to stress?
■ What are some social and cultural sources of stress?

When you think of the causes of psychological stress, your initial tendency is probably to think of events and issues directly related to yourself, such as school, work, or family pressures. And, indeed, we don't want to minimize those events as stressors. If you're like most of our students, you probably have ample first-hand experience with the stress of juggling the demands of college, work, and family responsibilities. Those pressures represent very real and personal concerns for many of us as we negotiate the challenges of daily life.

But as the terrorist attacks of September 11, 2001, unfolded, our entire nation was thrown into an extraordinary state of shared psychological stress as we watched, minute by minute, reeling in disbelief. It is impossible, of course, to convey the anguish, grief, and despair experienced by the thousands of people who lost loved ones as a result of the attacks. It is equally impossible to convey the sense of relief that thousands of other people felt when they eventually learned that their loved ones—like our niece Katie—had survived the attack.

What exactly is *stress*? It's one of those words that is frequently used but is hard to define precisely. Early stress researchers, who mostly studied animals, defined stress in terms of the physiological response to harmful or threatening events (e.g., Selye, 1956). However, people are far more complex than animals in their response to potentially stressful events. Two people may respond very differently to the same potentially stressful event.

Since the 1960s, psychologists have been studying the human response to stress, including the effects of stress on health and how people cope with stressful events. It has become clear that psychological and social factors, as well as biological factors, are involved in the stress experience and its effects.

Today, **stress** is widely defined as a negative emotional state occurring in response to events that are perceived as taxing or exceeding a person's resources or ability to cope. This definition emphasizes the important role played by a person's perception or appraisal of events in the experience of stress. Whether we experience stress depends largely on our *cognitive appraisal* of an event and the resources we have to deal with the event (Lazarus & Folkman, 1984; Tomaka & others, 1993).

If we think that we have adequate resources to deal with a situation, it will probably create little or no stress in our lives. But if we perceive our resources as being inadequate to deal with a situation we see as threatening, challenging, or even harmful, we'll experience the effects of stress. If our coping efforts are effective, stress will decrease. If they are ineffective, stress will increase.

The study of stress is a key topic in **health psychology,** one of the most rapidly growing specialty areas in psychology. Health psychology is also sometimes referred to as *behavioral medicine*. Health psychologists are interested in how biological, psychological, and social factors influence health, illness, and treatment. Along with developing strategies to foster emotional and physical well-being, they investigate issues such as the following:

■ How to promote health-enhancing behaviors

■ How people respond to being ill

How Do You Define Stress? From a ripped grocery bag to a life-threatening illness, stressors come in all sizes. Any event can produce stress—if you think you don't have the resources to cope with it.

stress
A negative emotional state occurring in response to events that are perceived as taxing or exceeding a person's resources or ability to cope.

health psychology
The branch of psychology that studies how biological, behavioral, and social factors influence health, illness, medical treatment, and health-related behaviors.

- How people respond in the patient–health practitioner relationship
- Why some people don't follow medical advice

Health psychologists work with many different health care professionals, including physicians, dentists, nurses, social workers, and occupational and physical therapists. In their research and clinical practice, health psychologists are guided by the **biopsychosocial model.** According to this model, health and illness are determined by the complex interaction of biological factors (e.g., genetic predispositions), psychological and behavioral factors (e.g., health beliefs and attitudes, lifestyle, stress), and social conditions (e.g., family relationships, social support, cultural influences). Throughout this chapter, we'll look closely at the roles that different biological, psychological, and social factors play in our experience of stress.

Sources of Stress

Life is filled with potential **stressors**—events or situations that produce stress. Virtually any event or situation can be a source of stress if you question your ability or resources to deal effectively with it (Lazarus & Folkman, 1984). In this section, we'll survey some of the most important and common sources of stress.

Life Events and Change
Is *Any* Change Stressful?

Early stress researchers Thomas Holmes and Richard Rahe (1967) believed that any change that required you to adjust your behavior and lifestyle would cause stress. In an attempt to measure the amount of stress people experienced, they developed the *Social Readjustment Rating Scale.* The scale included 43 life events that are likely to require some level of adaptation. Each life event was assigned a numerical rating that estimates its relative impact in terms of *life change units*. Sample items from the original Social Readjustment Rating Scale are shown in Table 12.1.

Life event ratings range from 100 life change units for the most stress-producing to 11 life change units for the least stress-producing events. Cross-cultural studies have shown that people in many different cultures tend to rank the magnitude of stressful events in a similar way (McAndrew & others, 1998). Notice that some of the life events are generally considered to be positive events, such as a vacation. According to the life events approach, *any* change, whether positive or negative, is inherently stress-producing.

To measure their level of stress, people simply check off the life events they have experienced in the past year and total the life change units. Holmes and Rahe found that people who had accumulated more than 150 life change units within a year had an increased rate of physical or psychological illness (Holmes & Masuda, 1974; Rahe, 1972).

Despite its initial popularity, several problems with the life events approach have been noted. First, the link between scores on the Social Readjustment Rating Scale and the development of physical and psychological problems is relatively weak. In general, scores on the Social Readjustment Rating Scale are *not* very good predictors of poor physical or mental health. Instead, researchers have found that most people weather major life events without developing serious physical or psychological problems (Coyne & Downey, 1991; Kessler & others, 1985).

Second, the Social Readjustment Rating Scale does not take into account a person's subjective appraisal of an event, response to that event, or ability to cope with the event (Hammen, 2005; Lazarus, 1999). Instead, the number of life change units on the scale is preassigned, reflecting the assumption that a given life event will have the same impact on virtually everyone. But clearly, the stress-producing potential of an event might vary widely from one person to another. For instance, if you are in a marriage that is filled with conflict, tension, and unhappiness, get-

Table 12.1

The Social Readjustment Rating Scale: Sample Items

Life Event	Life Change Units
Death of spouse	100
Divorce	73
Marital separation	65
Death of close family member	63
Major personal injury or illness	53
Marriage	50
Fired at work	47
Retirement	45
Pregnancy	40
Change in financial state	38
Death of close friend	37
Change to different line of work	36
Mortgage or loan for major purchase	31
Foreclosure on mortgage or loan	30
Change in work responsibilities	29
Outstanding personal achievement	28
Begin or end school	26
Trouble with boss	23
Change in work hours or conditions	20
Change in residence	20
Change in social activities	18
Change in sleeping habits	16
Vacation	13
Christmas	12
Minor violations of the law	11

SOURCE: Holmes & Rahe (1967).

The Social Readjustment Rating Scale, developed by Thomas Holmes and Richard Rahe (1967), was an early attempt to quantify the amount of stress experienced by people in a wide range of situations. Holmes and Rahe reasoned that any life event that required some sort of adaptation or change would create stress, whether the life event was pleasant or unpleasant.

ting divorced (73 life change units) might be significantly less stressful than remaining married.

Third, the life events approach assumes that change in itself, whether good or bad, produces stress. However, researchers have found that negative life events have greater adverse effects on health, especially when they're unexpected and uncontrollable (Dohrenwend & others, 1993). In contrast, positive or desirable events are much *less* likely to affect your health adversely. Today, most researchers agree that undesirable events are significant sources of stress but that change in itself is not necessarily stressful.

Nonetheless, the Social Readjustment Rating Scale is still often used in stress research (Lynch & others, 2005; Scully & others, 2000). Efforts have been made to revise and update the scale so that it more fully takes into account the influences of gender, age, marital status, and other characteristics (C. Hobson & Delunas, 2001).

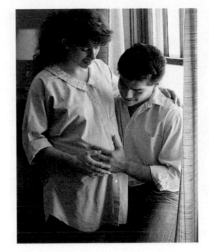

Major Life Events and Stress Would a welcome pregnancy or losing your home in a fire both produce damaging levels of stress? According to the life events approach, any event that required you to change or adjust your lifestyle would produce significant stress—whether the event was positive or negative, planned or unexpected. How was the life events approach modified by later research?

Daily Hassles
That's Not What I Ordered!

What made you feel "stressed out" in the last week? Chances are it was not a major life event. Instead, it was probably some unexpected but minor annoyance, such as splotching ketchup on your new white T-shirt, misplacing your keys, or discovering that you've been standing in the wrong line.

Stress researcher **Richard Lazarus** and his colleagues suspected that such ordinary irritations in daily life might be an important source of stress. To explore this idea, they developed a scale measuring **daily hassles**—everyday occurrences that annoy and upset people (DeLongis & others, 1982; Kanner & others, 1981). The *Daily Hassles Scale* measures the occurrence of everyday annoyances, such as losing something, getting stuck in traffic, and even being inconvenienced by lousy weather.

Are there gender differences in the frequency of daily hassles? One study measured the daily hassles experienced by married couples (Almeida & Kessler, 1998). The women experienced both more daily hassles and higher levels of psychological stress than their husbands did. For men, the most common sources of daily stress were financial and job-related problems. For women, family demands and interpersonal conflict were the most frequent causes of stress. However, when women *do* experience a stressful day in the workplace, the stress is more likely to spill over into their interactions with their husbands and other family members (Schulz & others, 2004). Men, on the other hand, are more likely to simply withdraw.

How important are daily hassles in producing stress? The frequency of daily hassles is linked to both psychological distress and physical symptoms, such as headaches and backaches (DeLongis & others, 1988). In fact, the number of daily hassles people experience is a better predictor of physical illness and symptoms than is the number of major life events experienced (Burks & Martin, 1985).

Why do daily hassles take such a toll? One explanation is that such minor stressors are *cumulative* (Repetti, 1993). Each hassle may be relatively unimportant in itself, but after a day filled with minor hassles, the effects add up. People feel drained, grumpy, and stressed out. Daily hassles also contribute to the stress produced by major life events. Any major life change, whether positive or negative, can create a ripple effect, generating a host of new daily hassles (Pillow & others, 1996).

For example, like many other New Yorkers, our niece Katie had to contend with a host of daily hassles after the terrorist attacks. She had no place to live, could not get access to her clothing or other possessions, and was unable to get money from the Red Cross because her roommate's father's name was on the lease. After pleading with the National Guardsmen patroling the area, Katie and her roommate, Lydia, were allowed to get some of their belongings out of their

Richard Lazarus (1922–2002) Psychologist Richard Lazarus has made several influential contributions to the study of stress and coping. His definition of stress emphasizes the importance of cognitive appraisal in the stress response. He also demonstrated the significance of everyday hassles in producing stress.

biopsychosocial model
The belief that physical health and illness are determined by the complex interaction of biological, psychological, and social factors.

stressors
Events or situations that are perceived as harmful, threatening, or challenging.

daily hassles
Everyday minor events that annoy and upset people.

Major Life Events, Daily Hassles, and Stress
After the collapse of the two World Trade Center towers, people who lived in nearby apartments were evacuated. More than a week after the disaster, these lower Manhattan residents are waiting to be escorted by members of the National Guard to retrieve some of their possessions. Even after people were allowed to return to their homes, they had to deal with damaged apartments, air filled with smoke and dust, and a lack of basic services, like telephone service. The daily hassles created by major disasters add to the level of stress felt by those affected.

apartment. They loaded as much as they could into a shopping cart, dragging and pushing the cart some 30 blocks north to a friend's home. Katie had to take a second waitress job to pay for the new, more expensive apartment.

Social and Cultural Sources of Stress

Social conditions can also be an important source of stress. Racism and discrimination, whether real or suspected, can create stress (Contrada & others, 2000). Crowding, crime, unemployment, poverty, inadequate health care, and substandard housing are all associated with increased stress (Gallo & Matthews, 2003). When people live in an environment that is inherently stressful, they often experience ongoing, or *chronic*, stress (Krantz & McCeney, 2002).

People in the lowest socioeconomic levels of society tend to have the highest levels of psychological distress, illness, and death (Cohen & Williamson, 1988). In a poverty-stricken neighborhood, people are likely to be exposed to more negative life events and to have fewer resources available to cope with those events. Daily hassles are also more common.

Stress can also result when cultures clash. For refugees, immigrants, and their children, adapting to a new culture can be extremely stress-producing (Berry, 2003; Chun & others, 2003). In Culture and Human Behavior Box 12.1, we describe the stress that can result from adapting to a different culture.

Conflict
Torn Between Two Choices

Another common source of stress is **conflict**—feeling pulled between two opposing desires, motives, or goals (Mellers, 2000). There are three basic types of conflict, each with a different potential to produce stress. These conflicts are described in terms of *approach* and *avoidance*. An individual is motivated to *approach* desirable or pleasant outcomes and to *avoid* undesirable or unpleasant outcomes.

An *approach–approach conflict* represents a win–win situation—you're faced with a choice between two equally appealing outcomes. Approach–approach conflicts are usually easy to resolve and don't produce much stress. More stressful are *avoidance–avoidance conflicts*—choosing between two unappealing or undesirable outcomes. A common response is to avoid both outcomes by delaying the decision (Tversky & Shafir, 1992).

Most stressful are *approach–avoidance conflicts*. Here, a goal has both desirable and undesirable aspects. When faced with an approach–avoidance conflict, people often *vacillate,* unable to decide whether to approach or avoid the goal. From a distance, the desirable aspects of the goal can exert a strong pull. But as you move toward or approach the goal, the negative aspects loom more vividly in your mind, and you pull back (Epstein, 1982). Not surprisingly, people facing approach–avoidance conflicts often find themselves "stuck"—unable to resolve the conflict but unable to stop thinking about it, either (Emmons & King, 1988). The result is a significant increase in feelings of stress and anxiety.

How can you get "unstuck"? There are several things you can do to resolve an approach–avoidance conflict. First, accept the reality that very few of life's major decisions are likely to be simple, with one alternative standing head and shoulders above the others. Second, see if you can adopt a *partial-approach strategy,* in which you test the waters but leave yourself an "out" before making a final decision or commitment.

Third, get as much information as you can about each option. Try to analyze objectively the pros and cons of every option. (We described this strategy of decision making in Chapter 7.) Finally, discuss the issue with a friend or someone outside the conflict. Doing so may help you see other possible rewards or pitfalls that your own analysis might have missed.

conflict
A situation in which a person feels pulled between two or more opposing desires, motives, or goals.

acculturative stress
(ah-KUL-chur-uh-tiv) The stress that results from the pressure of adapting to a new culture.

CULTURE AND HUMAN BEHAVIOR 12.1

The Stress of Adapting to a New Culture

Refugees and immigrants are often unprepared for the dramatically different values, language, food, customs, and climate that await them in their new land. Coping with a new culture can be extremely stress-producing (Johnson & others, 1995). The process of changing one's values and customs as a result of contact with another culture is referred to as *acculturation*. Thus, the term **acculturative stress** describes the stress that results from the pressure of adapting to a new culture (Berry, 1994, 2003).

Many factors can influence the degree of acculturative stress that a person experiences. For example, when the new society is one that accepts ethnic and cultural diversity, acculturative stress is reduced (Shuval, 1993). The ease of transition is also enhanced when the person has some familiarity with the new language and customs, advanced education, and social support from friends, family members, and cultural associations (Finch & Vega, 2003).

Cross-cultural psychologist John Berry has found that a person's attitudes are important in determining how much acculturative stress is experienced. When people encounter a new cultural environment, they are faced with two fundamental questions: (1) Should I seek positive relations with the dominant society? (2) Is my original cultural identity of value to me, and should I try to maintain it?

The answers to these questions result in one of four possible patterns of acculturation: integration, assimilation, separation, or marginalization (see the diagram). Each pattern represents a different way of cop-

		Question 1: Should I seek positive relations with the dominant society?	
		Yes	**No**
Question 2: Is my original cultural identity of value to me, and should I try to maintain it?	**Yes**	Integration	Separation
	No	Assimilation	Marginalization

Patterns of Adapting to a New Culture According to cross-cultural psychologist John Berry (1994, 2003), there are four basic patterns of adapting to a new culture. Which pattern is followed depends on how the person responds to the two key questions shown.

ing with the stress of adapting to a new culture (Berry, 1994, 2003).

Integrated individuals continue to value their original cultural customs but also seek to become part of the dominant society. Ideally, the integrated individual feels comfortable in both her culture of origin and the culture of the dominant society, moving easily from one to the other (LaFromboise, Coleman, & Gerton, 1993). The successfully integrated individual's level of acculturative stress will be low (Ward & Rana-Deuba, 1999).

Assimilated individuals give up their old cultural identity and try to become part of the new society. They may adopt the new clothing, religion, and social values of the new environment and abandon their old customs and language.

Assimilation usually involves a moderate level of stress, partly because it involves a psychological loss—one's previous cultural identity. People who follow this pattern also face the possibility of being rejected either by members of the majority culture or by members of their original culture (LaFromboise & others, 1993). The process of learning new behaviors and suppressing old behaviors can also be moderately stressful.

Individuals who follow the pattern of *separation* maintain their cultural identity and avoid contact with the new culture. They may refuse to learn the new language, live in a neighborhood that is primarily populated by others of the same ethnic background, and socialize only with members of their own ethnic group.

In some instances, such withdrawal from the larger society is self-imposed. However, separation can also be the result of discrimination by the dominant society, as when people of a particular ethnic group are discouraged from fully participating in the dominant society. Not surprisingly, the level of acculturative stress associated with separation is likely to be very high.

Finally, the *marginalized* person lacks cultural and psychological contact with *both* his traditional cultural group and the culture of his new society. By taking the path of marginalization, he has lost the important features of his traditional culture but has not replaced them with a new cultural identity.

Marginalized individuals are likely to experience the greatest degree of acculturative stress, feeling as if they don't really belong anywhere. Essentially, they are stuck in an unresolved conflict between the traditional culture and the new social environment. They are also likely to experience feelings of alienation and a loss of identity (Berry & Kim, 1988).

Acculturative Stress As this Sikh family crossing a busy street in Chicago has discovered, adapting to a new culture can be a stressful process. What factors can make the transition less stressful? How can the acculturation process be eased?

Physical Effects of Stress
The Mind–Body Connection

Key Theme
■ The effects of stress on physical health were demonstrated in research by Walter Cannon and Hans Selye.

Key Questions
■ What endocrine pathways are involved in the fight-or-flight response and the general adaptation syndrome?
■ What is psychoneuroimmunology, and how does the immune system interact with the nervous system?
■ What kinds of stressors affect immune system functioning?

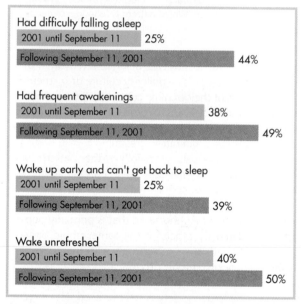

Had difficulty falling asleep

2001 until September 11	25%
Following September 11, 2001	44%

Had frequent awakenings

2001 until September 11	38%
Following September 11, 2001	49%

Wake up early and can't get back to sleep

2001 until September 11	25%
Following September 11, 2001	39%

Wake unrefreshed

2001 until September 11	40%
Following September 11, 2001	50%

Percent of American Adults Who Have Had Sleep Problems Prior to and Following September 11

FIGURE 12.1 Disrupted Sleep: One Indicator of Stress In the weeks immediately following the September 11, 2001, terrorist attacks, the psychological stress of those events was evident in the increased sleep disruptions experienced by millions of Americans. Almost a year after the attacks, hundreds of the firefighters and emergency medical workers who responded to the situation continued to experience sleep disruptions as the psychological stress lingered.

SOURCE: National Sleep Foundation (2002).

From headaches to heart attacks, stress contributes to a wide range of disorders, especially when it is long-term, or chronic (Krantz & McCeney, 2002). Basically, stress appears to undermine physical well-being in two ways: indirectly and directly (Schneiderman & others, 2005).

First, stress can *indirectly* affect a person's health by prompting behaviors that jeopardize physical well-being, such as not eating or sleeping properly (see Figure 12.1). For example, among residents of Manhattan, there was a sharp rise in substance abuse during the weeks after the September 11 attacks. Almost 30 percent of residents participating in a New York Academy of Medicine survey reported that they had increased their level of alcohol consumption, cigarette smoking, or marijuana use (Vlahov & others, 2002). High levels of stress can also interfere with cognitive abilities, such as attention, concentration, and memory (Mandler, 1993). In turn, such cognitive disruptions can increase the likelihood of accidents and injuries.

Second, stress can *directly* affect physical health by altering body functions, leading to symptoms, illness, or disease (Kiecolt-Glaser & others, 2002). Here's a very common example: When people are under a great deal of stress, their neck and head muscles can contract and tighten, resulting in stress-induced tension headaches. But exactly how do stressful events influence bodily processes, such as muscle contractions?

Stress and the Endocrine System

To explain the connection between stress and health, researchers have focused on how the nervous system, including the brain, interacts with two other important body systems: the endocrine and immune systems. We'll first consider the role of the endocrine system in our response to stressful events and then look at the connections between stress and the immune system.

Walter Cannon
Stress and the Fight-or-Flight Response

Any kind of immediate threat to your well-being is a stress-producing experience that triggers a cascade of changes in your body. As we've noted in previous chapters, this rapidly occurring chain of internal physical reactions is called the **fight-or-flight response.** Collectively, these changes prepare us either to fight or to take flight from an immediate threat.

The fight-or-flight response was first described by American physiologist **Walter Cannon,** one of the earliest contributors to stress research. Cannon (1932) found that the fight-or-flight response involved both the sympathetic nervous system and the endocrine system (see Chapter 2).

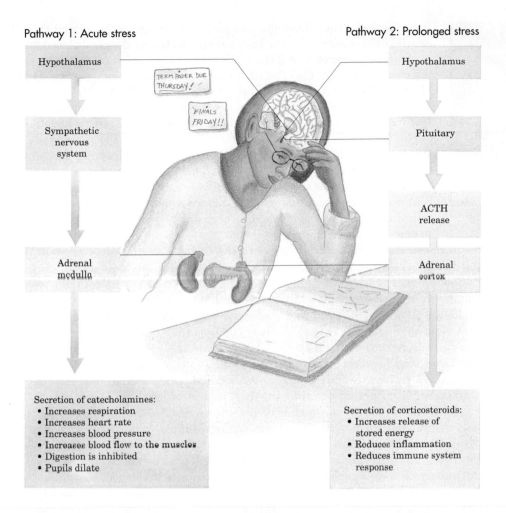

Pathway 1: Acute stress

Hypothalamus

↓

Sympathetic nervous system

↓

Adrenal medulla

↓

Secretion of catecholamines:
• Increases respiration
• Increases heart rate
• Increases blood pressure
• Increases blood flow to the muscles
• Digestion is inhibited
• Pupils dilate

Pathway 2: Prolonged stress

Hypothalamus

↓

Pituitary

↓

ACTH release

↓

Adrenal cortex

↓

Secretion of corticosteroids:
• Increases release of stored energy
• Reduces inflammation
• Reduces immune system response

FIGURE 12.2 Endocrine System Pathways in Stress Two different endocrine system pathways are involved in the response to stress. Walter Cannon identified the endocrine pathway shown on the left side of this diagram. This is the pathway involved in the fight-or-flight response to immediate threats. Hans Selye identified the endocrine pathway shown on the right. This second endocrine pathway plays an important role in dealing with prolonged, or chronic, stressors.

Walter B. Cannon (1875–1945) Cannon made many lasting contributions to psychology, including an influential theory of emotion, which we discussed in Chapter 8. During World War I, Cannon's research on the effects of stress and trauma led him to recognize the central role of the adrenal glands in mobilizing the body's resources in response to threatening circumstances—the essence of the *fight-or-flight response*. Cannon also coined the term *homeostasis,* which is the tendency of the body to maintain a steady internal state.

With the perception of a threat, the hypothalamus and lower brain structures activate the sympathetic nervous system (see left side of Figure 12.2). The sympathetic nervous system stimulates the adrenal medulla to secrete hormones called **catecholamines,** including *adrenaline* and *noradrenaline.* Circulating through the blood, catecholamines trigger the rapid and intense bodily changes associated with the fight-or-flight response. Once the threat is removed, the high level of bodily arousal subsides gradually, usually within about 20 to 60 minutes.

As a short-term reaction, the fight-or-flight response helps ensure survival by swiftly mobilizing internal physical resources to defensively attack or flee an immediate threat. Without question, the fight-or-flight response is very useful if you're suddenly faced with a life-threatening situation, such as a guy pointing a gun at you in a deserted parking lot. However, when exposure to an unavoidable threat is prolonged, the intense arousal of the fight-or-flight response can also become prolonged. Under these conditions, Cannon believed, the fight-or-flight response could prove harmful to physical health.

Hans Selye
Stress and the General Adaptation Syndrome

Cannon's suggestion that prolonged stress could be physically harmful was confirmed by Canadian endocrinologist **Hans Selye.** Most of Selye's pioneering research was done with rats that were exposed to prolonged stressors, such as electric shock, extreme heat or cold, or forced exercise. Regardless of the condition that Selye used to produce prolonged stress, he found the same pattern of physical changes in the rats. First, the adrenal glands became enlarged. Second, stomach ulcers and loss of weight occurred. And third, there was shrinkage of the thymus gland and lymph glands, two key components of the immune system.

fight-or-flight response
A rapidly occurring chain of internal physical reactions that prepare people either to fight or take flight from an immediate threat.

catecholamines
(*cat*-eh-COLE-uh-meens) Hormones secreted by the adrenal medulla that cause rapid physiological arousal; include adrenaline and noradrenaline.

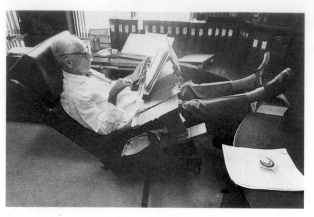

A Pioneer in Stress Research With his tie off and his feet up, Canadian endocrinologist Hans Selye (1907–1982) looks the very picture of relaxation. Selye's research at the University of Montreal documented the physical effects of exposure to prolonged stress. His popular book *The Stress of Life* (1956) helped make *stress* a household word.

general adaptation syndrome
Selye's term for the three-stage progression of physical changes that occur when an organism is exposed to intense and prolonged stress. The three stages are alarm, resistance, and exhaustion.

corticosteroids
(core-tick-oh-STAIR-oydz) Hormones released by the adrenal cortex that play a key role in the body's response to long-term stressors.

immune system
Body system that produces specialized white blood cells that protect the body from viruses, bacteria, and tumor cells.

lymphocytes
(LIMF-oh-sites) Specialized white blood cells that are responsible for immune defenses.

Selye believed that these distinct physical changes represented the essential effects of stress—the body's response to any demand placed on it.

Selye discovered that if the bodily "wear and tear" of the stress-producing event continued, the effects became evident in three progressive stages. He called these stages the **general adaptation syndrome.** During the initial *alarm stage,* intense arousal occurs as the body mobilizes internal physical resources to meet the demands of the stress-producing event. Selye (1976) found that the rapidly occurring changes during the alarm stage result from the release of catecholamines by the adrenal medulla, as Cannon had previously described.

In the *resistance stage,* the body actively tries to resist or adjust to the continuing stressful situation. The intense arousal of the alarm stage diminishes, but physiological arousal remains above normal and resistance to new stressors is impaired.

If the stress-producing event persists, the *exhaustion stage* may occur. In this third stage, the symptoms of the alarm stage reappear, only now irreversibly. As the body's energy reserves become depleted, adaptation begins to break down, leading to exhaustion, physical disorders, and, potentially, death.

Selye (1956, 1976) found that prolonged stress activates a second endocrine pathway (see Figure 12.2) that involves the hypothalamus, the pituitary gland, and the adrenal cortex. In response to a stressor, the hypothalamus signals the pituitary gland to secrete a hormone called *adrenocorticotropic hormone,* abbreviated *ACTH.* In turn, ACTH stimulates the adrenal cortex to release stress-related hormones called **corticosteroids,** the most important of which is *cortisol.*

In the short run, the corticosteroids provide several benefits, helping protect the body against the harm caused by stressors. For example, corticosteroids reduce inflammation of body tissues and enhance muscle tone in the heart and blood vessels. However, unlike the effects of catecholamines, which tend to diminish rather quickly, corticosteroids have long-lasting effects. If a stressor is prolonged, continued high levels of corticosteroids can weaken important body systems, lowering immunity and increasing susceptibility to physical symptoms and illness. There is mounting evidence that chronic stress can lead to increased vulnerability to acute and chronic diseases, including cardiovascular disease, and even to premature aging (Robles & others, 2005; Segerstrom & Miller, 2004). Chronic stress can also lead to depression and other psychological problems (Hammen, 2005).

Selye's pioneering studies are widely regarded as the cornerstone of modern stress research. His description of the general adaptation syndrome firmly established some of the critical biological links between stress-producing events and their potential impact on physical health. But as you'll see in the next section, the endocrine system is not the only body system affected by stress: The immune system, too, is part of the mind–body connection.

Stress and the Immune System

The **immune system** is your body's surveillance system. It detects and battles foreign invaders, such as bacteria, viruses, and tumor cells. Your immune system

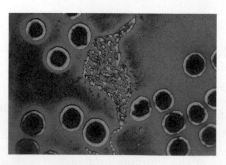

Lymphocytes in Action In this color-enhanced photo, you can see white blood cells, or lymphocytes, attacking and ingesting the bead-like chain of streptococcus bacteria, which can cause diseases such as pneumonia and scarlet fever.

comprises several organs, including bone marrow, the spleen, the thymus, and lymph nodes (see Figure 12.3). The most important elements of the immune system are **lymphocytes**—the specialized white blood cells that fight bacteria, viruses, and other foreign invaders. Lymphocytes are initially manufactured in the bone marrow. From the bone marrow, they migrate to other immune system organs, such as the thymus and spleen, where they develop more fully and are stored until needed.

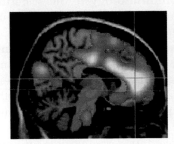

Received opiate painkiller

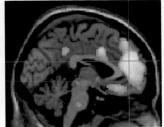

Received placebo

Neuroscience: The Mysterious Placebo Effect

The *placebo effect* is perhaps one of the most dramatic examples of how the mind influences the body. A *placebo* is an inactive substance with no known effects, like a sugar pill or an injection of sterile water. Placebos are often used in biomedical research to help gauge the effectiveness of an actual medication or treatment. But after being given a placebo, many research participants, including those suffering from pain or diseases, experience benefits from the placebo treatment. How can this be explained?

In Chapter 2 we noted that one possible way that placebos might reduce pain is by activating the brain's own natural painkillers—the *endorphins*. (The endorphins are structurally similar to opiate painkillers, like morphine.) One reason for believing this is that a drug called *naloxone*, which blocks the brain's endorphin response, also blocks the painkilling effects of placebos (Fields & Levine, 1984). Might placebos reduce pain by activating the brain's natural opioid network?

A brain-imaging study by Swedish neuroscientist Predrag Petrovic and his colleagues (2002) tackled this question. In the study, painfully hot metal was placed on the back of each volunteer's hand. Each volunteer was then given an injection of either an actual opioid painkiller or a saline solution placebo. About 30 seconds later, positron

emission tomography (PET) was used to scan the participants' brain activity.

Both the volunteers who received the painkilling drug *and* the volunteers who received the placebo treatment reported that the injection provided pain relief. In the two PET scans shown here, you can see that the genuine painkilling drug *(left)* and the placebo *(right)* activated the same brain area, called the *anterior cingulate cortex* (marked by the cross). The anterior cingulate cortex is known to contain many opioid receptors. Interestingly, the level of brain activity was directly correlated with the participants' subjective perception of pain relief. The PET scan on the right shows the brain activity of those participants who had strong placebo responses.

Many questions remain about exactly how placebos work, but the PET scan study by Petrovic and his colleagues (2002) vividly substantiates the biological reality of the placebo effect. In a recent study, Jon-Kar Zubieta and his colleagues (2005) showed that a placebo treatment activated opioid receptors in several brain regions associated with pain. Further, the greater the activation, the higher the level of pain individual volunteers were able to tolerate. As these studies show, cognitive expectations, learned associations, and emotional responses can have a profound effect on the perception of pain. Other studies have shown that placebos produce measurable effects on other types of brain processes, including those of people experiencing Parkinson's disease or major depression (Fuente-Fernández & others, 2001; Leuchter & others, 2002).

Psychoneuroimmunology

Until the 1970s, the immune system was thought to be completely independent of other body systems, including the nervous and endocrine systems. Thus, most scientists believed that psychological processes could not influence the immune system response.

That notion was challenged in the mid-1970s, when psychologist **Robert Ader** teamed up with immunologist Nicholas Cohen. Ader (1993) recalls, "As a psychologist, I was not aware of the general position of immunology that there were no connections between the brain and the immune system." But Ader and Cohen showed that the immune system response in rats could be classically conditioned (see Chapter 5). After repeatedly pairing flavored water with a drug that suppressed immune system functioning, Ader and Cohen (1975) demonstrated that the flavored water *alone* suppressed the immune system.

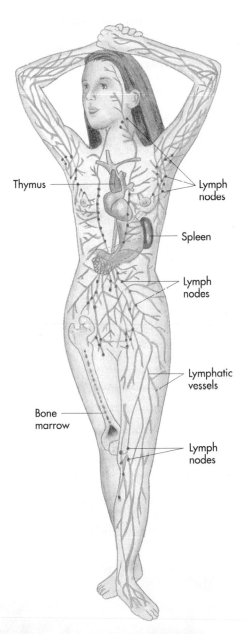

FIGURE 12.3 The Immune System Your immune system battles bacteria, viruses, and other foreign invaders that try to set up housekeeping in your body. The specialized white blood cells that fight infection are manufactured in the bone marrow and are stored in the thymus, spleen, and lymph nodes until needed.

Conditioning the Immune System
Psychologist Robert Ader *(left)* teamed with immunologist Nicholas Cohen *(right)* and demonstrated that immune system responses could be classically conditioned. Ader and Cohen's groundbreaking research helped lead to the new field of psychoneuroimmunology—the study of the connections among psychological processes, the nervous system, and the immune system.

psychoneuroimmunology
An interdisciplinary field that studies the interconnections among psychological processes, nervous and endocrine system functions, and the immune system.

Ader and Cohen's research helped establish a new interdisciplinary field called *psychoneuroimmunology*. **Psychoneuroimmunology** is the scientific study of the connections among psychological processes *(psycho-)*, the nervous system *(-neuro-)* and the immune system *(-immunology)*.

Today, it is known that there are many interconnections among the immune system, the endocrine system, and the nervous system, including the brain (Ader, 2001; Segerstrom & Miller, 2004). First, the central nervous system and the immune system are *directly* linked via sympathetic nervous system fibers, which influence the production and functioning of lymphocytes.

Second, the surfaces of lymphocytes contain receptor sites for neurotransmitters and hormones, including catecholamines and cortisol. Thus, rather than operating independently, the activities of lymphocytes and the immune system are directly influenced by neurotransmitters, hormones, and other chemical messengers from the nervous and endocrine systems.

Third, psychoneuroimmunologists have discovered that lymphocytes themselves *produce* neurotransmitters and hormones. These neurotransmitters and hormones, in turn, influence the nervous and endocrine systems. In other words, there is ongoing interaction and communication among the nervous system, the endocrine system, and the immune system. Each system influences *and* is influenced by the other systems (Ader, 2001).

Stressors That Can Influence the Immune System

When researchers began studying how stress affects the immune system, they initially focused on extremely stressful events (see Kiecolt-Glaser & Glaser, 1993). For example, researchers looked at how the immune system was affected by such intense stressors as the reentry and splashdown of returning *Skylab* astronauts, being forced to stay awake for days, and fasting for a week (Kimzey, 1975; Leach & Rambaut, 1974; Palmblad & others, 1979). Each of these highly stressful events, it turned out, was associated with reduced immune system functioning.

Could immune system functioning also be affected by more common negative life events, such as the death of a spouse, divorce, or marital separation? In a word, yes. Researchers consistently found that the stress caused by the end or disruption of important interpersonal relationships impairs immune function, putting people at greater risk for health problems (Kiecolt-Glaser, 1999; Kiecolt-Glaser & Newton, 2001). And perhaps not surprisingly, chronic stressors that continue for years, such as caring for a family member with Alzheimer's disease, also diminish immune system functioning (Robles & others, 2005).

What about the ordinary stressors of life, such as the pressure of school exams? Do they affect immune system functioning? Since 1982, psychologist **Janice Kiecolt-Glaser** and her husband, immunologist Ronald Glaser, have collected immunological and psychological data from medical students. Several times each academic year, the medical students face three-day examination periods. Kiecolt-Glaser and Glaser (1991, 1993) have consistently found that even the rather commonplace stress of exams adversely affects the immune system.

What are the practical implications of reduced immune system functioning? One consistent finding is that psychological stress can increase the length of time it takes for a wound to heal. In one study, dental students volunteered to receive two small puncture wounds on the roofs of their mouths (Marucha & others, 1998). To compare the impact of stress on wound healing, the students received the first wound when they were on summer vacation and the second wound three days before their first major exam during the fall term. The results? The wounds inflicted before the major test healed an average of 40 percent more slowly—an extra three days—than the wounds inflicted on the same volunteers during summer vacation. Other studies have shown similar findings (Glaser & Kiecolt-Glaser, 2005).

Ron Glaser and Janice Kiecolt-Glaser Two of the leading researchers in psychoneuroimmunology are psychologist Janice Kiecolt-Glaser and her husband, immunologist Ron Glaser. Their research has shown that the effectiveness of the immune system can be lowered by many common stressors—from marital arguments to caring for sick relatives (see Glaser & Kiecolt-Glaser, 2005).

What about the relationship between stress and infection? In a series of carefully controlled studies, psychologist Sheldon Cohen and his colleagues (1991, 1993, 1998) demonstrated that people who are experiencing high levels of stress are more susceptible to infection by a cold virus than people who are not under stress (see Figure 12.4). Subjects who experienced *chronic* stressors that lasted a month or longer were most likely to develop colds after being exposed to a cold virus. One reason may be that, as Selye showed, chronic stress triggers the secretion of corticosteroids, which influence immune system functioning (G. E. Miller & others, 2002). For example, one study showed that stress interfered with the long-term effectiveness of vaccinations against influenza in young adults (Burns & others, 2003). In the short term, stress was associated with a strong immune system response to the flu vaccine. But after five months, the stressed-out young adults were virtually unprotected against the flu.

Health psychologists have found that a wide variety of stressors are associated with diminished immune system functioning, increasing the risk of health problems and slowing recovery times (Kiecolt-Glaser & others, 2002; Robles & others, 2005). However, while stress-related decreases in immune system functioning may heighten our susceptibility to health problems, exposure to stressors does not automatically translate into poorer health. Physical health is affected by the interaction of many factors, including heredity, nutrition, health-related habits, and access to medical care. Also required, of course, is exposure to bacteria, viruses, and other sources of infection or disease.

Finally, the simple fact is that some people are more vulnerable to the negative effects of stress than others (Adler & Matthews, 1994). Why? As you'll see in the next section, researchers have found that a wide variety of psychological factors can influence people's reactions to stressors.

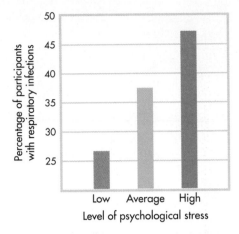

FIGURE 12.4 Stress and the Common Cold Are you more likely to catch a cold if you're under a great deal of stress? Sheldon Cohen and his colleagues (1991, 1993) measured levels of psychological stress in healthy volunteers, then exposed them to a cold virus. While quarantined in apartments for a week, the participants were monitored for signs of respiratory infection. The results? As shown in the graph, the researchers found an almost perfect relationship between the level of stress and the rate of infection. The higher the volunteers' psychological stress level, the higher the rate of respiratory infection.

Individual Factors That Influence the Response to Stress

Key Theme
- Psychologists have identified several psychological factors that can modify an individual's response to stress and affect physical health.

Key Questions
- How do feelings of control, explanatory style, and negative emotions influence stress and health?
- What is Type A behavior, and what role does hostility play in the relationship between Type A behavior and health?

People vary a great deal in the way they respond to a distressing event, whether it's a parking ticket or a pink slip. In part, individual differences in reacting to stressors result from how people appraise an event and their resources for coping with the event. However, psychologists and other researchers have identified several factors that influence an individual's response to stressful events. In this section, we'll take a look at some of the most important psychological and social factors that seem to affect an individual's response to stress.

Psychological Factors

It's easy to demonstrate the importance of psychological factors in the response to stressors. Sit in any airport waiting room during a busy holiday travel season and observe how differently people react to news of flight cancellations or delays.

Some people take the news calmly, while others become enraged and indignant. Psychologists have confirmed what common sense suggests: Psychological processes play a key role in determining the level of stress experienced.

Personal Control

Who is more likely to experience more stress, a person who has some control over a stressful experience or a person who has no control? Psychological research has consistently shown that having a sense of control over a stressful situation reduces the impact of stressors and decreases feelings of anxiety and depression (Dickerson & Kemeny, 2004; Taylor, Kemeny, & others, 2000). Those who can control a stress-producing event often show no more psychological distress or physical arousal than people who are not exposed to the stressor.

Psychologists Judith Rodin and Ellen Langer (1977) demonstrated the importance of a sense of control in a classic series of studies with nursing home residents. One group of residents—the "high-control" group—was given the opportunity to make choices about their daily activities and to exercise control over their environment. In contrast, residents assigned to the "low-control" group had little control over their daily activities. Decisions were made for them by the nursing home staff. Eighteen months later, the high-control residents were more active, alert, sociable, and healthier than the low-control residents. And, twice as many of the low-control residents had died (Langer & Rodin, 1976; Rodin & Langer, 1977).

How does a sense of control affect health? If you feel that you can control a stressor by taking steps to minimize or avoid it, you will experience less stress, both subjectively and physiologically (Heth & Somer, 2002; Thompson & Spacapan, 1991). Having a sense of personal control also works to our benefit by enhancing positive emotions, such as self-confidence and feelings of self-efficacy, autonomy, and self-reliance (Taylor, Kemeny, & others, 2000). In contrast, feeling a lack of control over events produces all the hallmarks of the stress response. Levels of catecholamines and corticosteroids increase, and the effectiveness of immune system functioning decreases (see Maier & Watkins, 2000; Rodin, 1986).

However, the perception of personal control in a stressful situation must be *realistic* to be adaptive (Heth & Somer, 2002). Studies of people with chronic diseases, like heart disease and arthritis, have shown that unrealistic perceptions of personal control contribute to stress and poor adjustment (Affleck, Tennen, & Croog, 1987; Affleck, Tennen, Pfeiffer, & others, 1987).

Uncontrollable Stressors There was nothing this man could do to protect his apartment, which faced the World Trade Center towers. A month after the terrorist attacks, he surveys his damaged neighborhood and sorts through the wreckage that was once his home. Psychological research has shown that stressors that are experienced as beyond your control can be especially damaging to physical and mental health.

Further, not everyone benefits from feelings of enhanced personal control. Cross-cultural studies have shown that a sense of control is more highly valued in individualistic, Western cultures than in collectivistic, Eastern cultures. Comparing Japanese and British participants, Darryl O'Connor and Mikiko Shimizu (2002) found that a heightened sense of personal control *was* associated with a lower level of perceived stress—but only among the British participants.

Explanatory Style
Optimism Versus Pessimism

We all experience defeat, rejection, or failure at some point in our lives. Yet despite repeated failures, rejections, or defeats, some people persist in their efforts. In contrast, some people give up in the face of failure and setbacks—the essence of *learned helplessness*, which we discussed in Chapter 5. What distinguishes between those who persist and those who give up?

According to psychologist **Martin Seligman** (1990, 1992), how people characteristically explain their failures and defeats makes the difference. People who have an **optimistic explanatory style** tend to use *external, unstable,* and *specific* explanations for negative events. In contrast, people who have a **pessimistic explanatory style** use *internal, stable,* and *global* explanations for negative events. Pessimists are also inclined to believe that no amount of personal effort will improve their situation. Not surprisingly, pessimists tend to experience more stress than optimists.

Let's look at these two explanatory styles in action. Optimistic Olive sees an attractive guy at a party and starts across the room to introduce herself and strike up a conversation. As she approaches him, the guy glances at her, then abruptly turns away. Hurt by the obvious snub, Optimistic Olive retreats to the buffet table. Munching on some fried zucchini, she mulls the matter over in her mind. At the same party, Pessimistic Pete sees an attractive female across the room and approaches her. He, too, gets a cold shoulder and retreats to the chips and clam dip. Standing at opposite ends of the buffet table, here is what each of them is thinking:

How Do You Explain Your Setbacks and Failures? Everyone experiences setbacks, rejection, and failure at some point. The way you explain your setbacks has a significant impact on motivation and on mental and physical health. If this store owner blames his business failure on temporary and external factors, such as a short-lived downturn in the economy, he may be more likely to try opening a new store in the future.

> **OPTIMISTIC OLIVE:** *What's his problem?* (External *explanation: The optimist blames other people or external circumstances.*)
>
> **PESSIMISTIC PETE:** *I must have said the wrong thing. She probably saw me stick my elbow in the clam dip before I walked over.* (Internal *explanation: The pessimist blames self.*)
>
> **OPTIMISTIC OLIVE:** *I'm really not looking my best tonight. I've just got to get more sleep.* (Unstable, temporary *explanation*)
>
> **PESSIMISTIC PETE:** *Let's face it, I'm a pretty boring guy and really not very good-looking.* (Stable, permanent *explanation*)
>
> **OPTIMISTIC OLIVE:** *He looks pretty preoccupied. Maybe he's waiting for his girlfriend to arrive. Or his boyfriend! Ha!* (Specific *explanations*)
>
> **PESSIMISTIC PETE:** *Women never give me a second look, probably because I dress like a nerd and I never know what to say to them.* (Global, pervasive *explanation*)
>
> **OPTIMISTIC OLIVE:** *Whoa! Who's that hunk over there?! Okay, Olive, turn on the charm! Here goes!* (Perseverance *after a rejection*)
>
> **PESSIMISTIC PETE:** *Maybe I'll just hold down this corner of the buffet table . . . or go home and soak up some TV.* (Passivity *and* withdrawal *after a rejection*)

Most people, of course, are neither as completely optimistic as Olive nor as totally pessimistic as Pete. Instead, they fall somewhere along the spectrum of optimism and pessimism, and their explanatory style may vary somewhat in different situations (Peterson & Bossio, 1993). Even so, a person's characteristic explanatory style, particularly for negative events, is relatively stable across the lifespan (Burns & Seligman, 1989).

Like personal control, explanatory style is related to health consequences (Gilham & others, 2001). One study showed that explanatory style in early adulthood predicted physical health status decades later. On the basis of interviews conducted at age 25, explanatory style was evaluated for a large group of Harvard graduates. At the time of the interviews, all the young men were in excellent physical and mental health. Thirty-five years later, however, those who had an optimistic explanatory style were significantly healthier than those with a pessimistic explanatory style (Peterson & others, 1988).

optimistic explanatory style
Accounting for negative events or situations with external, unstable, and specific explanations.

pessimistic explanatory style
Accounting for negative events or situations with internal, stable, and global explanations.

Type A behavior pattern
A behavioral and emotional style characterized by a sense of time urgency, hostility, and competitiveness.

Other studies have shown that a pessimistic explanatory style is associated with poorer physical health (Jackson & others, 2002; Peterson & Bossio, 2001). For example, first-year law school students who had an optimistic, confident, and generally positive outlook experienced fewer negative moods than did pessimistic students (Segerstrom & others, 1998). And, in terms of their immune system measures, the optimistic students had significantly higher levels of lymphocytes, T cells, and helper T cells. Explaining the positive relationship between optimists and good health, Suzanne Segerstrom and her colleagues (2003) suggest that optimists are more inclined to persevere in their efforts to overcome obstacles and challenges. Optimists are also more likely to cope effectively with stressful situations than pessimists, perhaps because they attribute their failures to their coping strategies and adjust them accordingly (Iwanaga & others, 2004).

Chronic Negative Emotions
The Hazards of Being Grouchy

Everyone experiences an occasional bad mood. However, some people almost always seem to be unhappy campers—they frequently experience bad moods and negative emotions (Marshall & others, 1992). Are people who are prone to chronic negative emotions more likely to suffer health problems?

Howard S. Friedman and Stephanie Booth-Kewley (1987) set out to answer this question. After systematically analyzing more than 100 studies investigating the potential links between personality factors and disease, they concluded that people who are habitually anxious, depressed, angry, or hostile *are* more likely to develop a chronic disease such as arthritis or heart disease.

How might chronic negative emotions predispose people to develop disease? Not surprisingly, tense, angry, and unhappy people experience more stress than do happier people. They also report more frequent and more intense daily hassles than people who are generally in a positive mood (Bolger & Schilling, 1991; Bolger & Zuckerman, 1995). And they react much more intensely, and with far greater distress, to stressful events (Marco & Suls, 1993).

Of course, everyone occasionally experiences bad moods. Are transient negative moods also associated with health risks? One series of studies investigated the relationship between daily mood and immune system functioning (Stone & others, 1987, 1994). For three months, participants recorded their moods every day. On the days on which they experienced negative events and moods, the effectiveness of their immune systems dipped. But their immune systems improved on the days on which they experienced positive events and good moods. And in fact, other studies have found that higher levels of hope and other positive emotions are associated with a decreased likelihood of developing health problems (Richman & others, 2005).

Type A Behavior and Hostility

The concept of Type A behavior originated about 30 years ago, when two cardiologists, Meyer Friedman and Ray Rosenman, noticed that many of their patients

Calvin and Hobbes by Bill Watterson

shared certain traits. The original formulation of the **Type A behavior pattern** included a cluster of three characteristics: (1) an exaggerated sense of time urgency, often trying to do more and more in less and less time; (2) a general sense of hostility, frequently displaying anger and irritation; and (3) intense ambition and competitiveness. In contrast, people who were more relaxed and laid back were classified as displaying the *Type B behavior pattern* (Janisse & Dyck, 1988; Rosenman & Chesney, 1982).

Friedman and Rosenman (1974) interviewed and classified more than 3,000 middle-aged, healthy men as either Type A or Type B. They tracked the health of these men for eight years and found that Type A men were twice as likely to develop heart disease as Type B men. This held true even when the Type A men did not display other known risk factors for heart disease, such as smoking, high blood pressure, and elevated levels of cholesterol in their blood. The conclusion seemed clear: The Type A behavior pattern was a significant risk factor for heart disease.

Although early results linking the Type A behavior pattern to heart disease were impressive, studies soon began to appear in which Type A behavior did *not* reliably predict the development of heart disease (see Krantz & McCeney, 2002). These findings led researchers to question whether the different components of the Type A behavior pattern were equally hazardous to health. After all, many people thrive on hard work, especially when they enjoy their jobs. And, high achievers don't necessarily suffer from health problems (Robbins & others, 1991).

When researchers focused on the association between heart disease and each separate component of the Type A behavior pattern—time urgency, hostility, and achievement striving—an important distinction began to emerge (Suls & Bunde, 2005). Feeling a sense of time urgency and being competitive or achievement oriented did *not* seem to be associated with the development of heart disease. Instead, the critical component that emerged as the strongest predictor of cardiac disease was hostility (Miller & others, 1996). *Hostility* refers to the tendency to feel anger, annoyance, resentment, and contempt and to hold cynical and negative beliefs about human nature in general. Hostile people are also prone to believing that the disagreeable behavior of others is intentionally directed against them. Thus, hostile people tend to be suspicious, mistrustful, cynical, and pessimistic (Barefoot, 1992).

Hostile people are much more likely than other people to develop heart disease, even when other risk factors are taken into account (Niaura & others, 2002). In one study that covered a 25-year span, hostile men were five times as likely to develop heart disease and nearly seven times as likely to die as nonhostile men (Barefoot & others, 1983). The results of this prospective study are shown in Figure 12.5. Subsequent research has found that high hostility levels increase the likelihood of dying from *all* natural causes, including cancer (Miller & others, 1996).

How does hostility predispose people to heart disease and other health problems? First, hostile Type As tend to react more intensely to a stressor than other people do (Lyness, 1993). They experience greater increases in blood pressure, heart rate, and the production of stress-related hormones. Because of their attitudes and behavior, hostile men and women also tend to *create* more stress in their own lives (Suls & Bunde, 2005). They experience more frequent, and more severe, negative life events and daily hassles than other people (Smith, 1992).

In general, the research evidence demonstrating the role of personality factors in the development of stress-related disease is impressive. Nevertheless, it's important to keep this evidence in perspective: Personality characteristics are just *some* of the many factors involved in the overall picture of health and disease. We look at this issue in more detail in Critical Thinking Box 12.2 on page 492. And, in the chapter Application, we describe some of the steps that you can take to help you minimize the effects of stress on your health.

The Type A Behavior Pattern The original formulation of the Type A behavior pattern included hostility, ambition, and a sense of time urgency. Type A people always seem to be in a hurry, hate wasting time, and often try to do two or more things at once. Do you think any of the people in this photograph might qualify as Type A?

FIGURE 12.5 Hostility and Mortality
Beginning when they were in medical school, more than 250 doctors were monitored for their health status for 25 years. In this prospective study, those who had scored high in hostility in medical school were seven times more likely to die by age 50 than were those who had scored low in hostility.

SOURCE: Based on Barefoot & others (1983), p. 61.

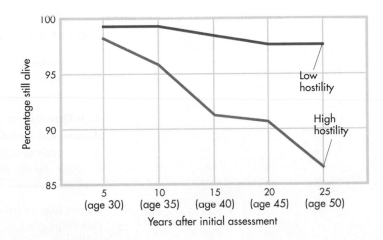

Do Personality Factors Cause Disease?

- You overhear a co-worker saying, "I'm not surprised he had a heart attack—the guy is a workaholic!"

- An acquaintance casually remarks, "She's been so depressed since her divorce. No wonder she got cancer."

- A tabloid headline hails, "New Scientific Findings: Use Your Mind to Cure Cancer!"

Statements like these make health psychologists, physicians, and psychoneuro-immunologists extremely uneasy. Why? Throughout this chapter, we've presented scientific evidence that emotional states can affect the functioning of the endocrine system and the immune system. Both systems play a significant role in the development of various physical disorders. We've also shown that personality factors, such as hostility and pessimism, are associated with an increased likelihood of developing poor health. But saying that "emotions affect the immune system" is a far cry from making such claims as "a positive attitude can cure cancer."

Psychologists and other scientists are cautious in the statements they make about the connections between personality and health for several reasons. First, many studies investigating the role of psychological factors in disease are *correlational.* That is, researchers have statistical evidence that two factors happen together so often that the presence of one factor reliably predicts the occurrence of the other. However, correlation does not necessarily indicate causality—it indicates only that two factors occur

"What do you mean, I have an ulcer? I give ulcers, I don't get them!"

© 2002 The New Yorker Collection from cartoonbank.com. Joseph Farris.

together. It's completely possible that some third, unidentified factor may have caused the other two factors to occur.

Second, personality factors might indirectly lead to disease via poor health habits. Low control, pessimism, chronic negative emotions, and hostility are each associated with poor health habits (Herbert & Cohen, 1993; Peterson, 2000). In turn, poor health habits are associated with higher rates of illness. That's why psychologists who study the role of personality factors in disease are typically careful to measure and consider the possible influence of the participants' health practices.

Third, it may be that the disease influences a person's emotions, rather than the other way around. After being diagnosed

with advanced cancer or heart disease, most people would probably find it difficult to feel cheerful, optimistic, or in control of their lives.

One way researchers try to disentangle the relationship between personality and health is to conduct carefully controlled prospective studies. A *prospective study* starts by assessing an initially healthy group of participants on variables thought to be risk factors, such as certain personality traits. Then the researchers track the health, personal habits, health habits, and other important dimensions of the participants' lives over a period of months, years, or decades. In analyzing the results, researchers can determine the extent to which each risk factor contributed to the health or illness of the participants. Thus, prospective studies provide more compelling evidence than do correlational studies that are based on people who are already in poor health.

Critical Thinking Questions

- Given that health professionals frequently advise people to change their health-related behaviors to improve physical health, should they also advise people to change their psychological attitudes, traits, and emotions? Why or why not?

- What are the advantages and disadvantages of prospective studies?

Social Factors: A Little Help from Your Friends

Key Theme

- Social support refers to the resources provided by other people.

Key Questions

- How has social support been shown to benefit health?
- How can relationships and social connections sometimes increase stress?
- What gender differences have been found in social support and its effects?

Psychologists have become increasingly aware of the importance that close relationships play in our ability to deal with stressors and, ultimately, in our physical health. Consider the following research evidence:

- Patients with advanced breast cancer who attended weekly support-group sessions survived twice as long as a matched group of patients with equally advanced cancer who did not attend support groups. Both groups of women received comparable medical treatment. The added survival time for those who attended support-group sessions was longer than that which could have been provided by any known medical treatment (Spiegel, 1993b; Spiegel & others, 1989).

- After monitoring the health of 2,800 people for seven years, researchers found that people who had no one to talk to about their problems were three times as likely to die after being hospitalized for a heart attack than were those who had at least one person to provide such support (Berkman & others, 1992).

- The health of nearly 7,000 adults was tracked for nine years. Those who had few social connections were twice as likely to die from all causes than were those who had numerous social contacts, even when risk factors such as cigarette smoking, obesity, and elevated cholesterol levels were taken into account (Berkman, 1995; Berkman & Syme, 1979).

- In a study begun in the 1950s, college students rated their parents' level of love and caring. More than 40 years later, 87 percent of those who had rated their parents as being "low" in love and caring had been diagnosed with a serious physical disease. In contrast, only 25 percent of those who had rated their parents as being "high" in love and caring had been diagnosed with a serious physical disease (Russek & Schwartz, 1997).

These are just a few of the hundreds of studies conducted in recent years exploring how interpersonal relationships influence our health and ability to tolerate stress. To investigate the role played by personal relationships in stress and health, psychologists measure the level of **social support**—the resources provided by other people in times of need (Hobfoll & Stephens, 1990). Repeatedly, researchers have found that socially isolated people have poorer health and higher death rates than people who have many social contacts or relationships (Southwick & others, 2005; Uchino & others, 1996). In fact, social isolation seems to be just as potent a health risk as smoking, high blood cholesterol, obesity, or physical inactivity (Cohen & others, 2000).

"A Sense of Being Loved by Our Community . . ." Author Philip Simmons had been an English professor for nine years when he learned that he had Lou Gehrig's disease, a fatal neuromuscular condition that usually kills its victims in two to five years. But Simmons beat those odds and lived an incredibly productive life for almost ten years, in part by learning to ask for—and accept—help from his friends. For several years, some thirty friends and neighbors helped the Simmons family with the routine chores of daily life, such as fixing dinner and chauffeuring kids. Said Philip's wife, Kathryn, "It gives us a sense of being loved by our community."

How Social Support Benefits Health

Social support may benefit our health and improve our ability to cope with stressors in several ways (Cohen & others, 2000). First, the social support of friends and relatives can modify our appraisal of a stressor's significance, including the degree to which we perceive it as threatening or harmful. Simply knowing that support and assistance are readily available may make the situation seem less threatening.

Second, the presence of supportive others seems to decrease the intensity of physical reactions to a stressor. Thus, when faced with a painful medical procedure or some other stressful situation, many people find the presence of a supportive friend to be calming.

Third, social support can influence our health by making us less likely to experience negative emotions (Cohen & Herbert, 1996). Given the well-established link between chronic negative emotions and poor health, a strong social support network can promote positive moods and emotions, enhance self-esteem, and increase feelings of personal control. In contrast, loneliness and depression are unpleasant emotional states that increase levels of stress hormones and adversely affect immune system functioning (Weisse, 1992).

The flip side of the coin is that relationships with others can also be a significant *source* of stress (Swickert & others, 2002). In fact, negative interactions

social support
The resources provided by other people in times of need.

The Health Benefits of Companionship
This married couple in their seventies are enjoying an afternoon of cross-country skiing. Numerous research studies have shown that married people and couples live longer than people who are single, divorced, or widowed (Burman & Margolin, 1992). How do close relationships benefit health?

Pets as a Source of Social Support Pets can provide both companionship and social support, especially for people with limited social contacts. Can the social support of pets buffer the negative effects of stress? One study showed that elderly people with pets had fewer doctor visits and reported feeling less stress than elderly people without pets (Siegel, 1990). Other studies have found that the presence of a pet cat or dog can lower blood pressure and lessen the cardiovascular response to acute stress (Allen & others, 2002).

with other people are often more effective at creating psychological distress than positive interactions are at improving well-being (Lepore, 1993; Rook, 1992). And, although married people tend to be healthier than unmarried people overall, marital conflict has been shown to have adverse effects on physical health, especially for women (Kiecolt-Glaser & Newton, 2001).

Clearly, the quality of interpersonal relationships is an important determinant of whether those relationships help or hinder our ability to cope with stressful events (Feeney & Kirkpatrick, 1996). When other people are perceived as being judgmental, their presence may increase the individual's physical reaction to a stressor. In two clever studies, psychologist Karen Allen and her colleagues (1991, 2002) demonstrated that the presence of a favorite dog or cat was more effective than the presence of a spouse or friend in lowering reactivity to a stressor. Why? Perhaps because the pet was perceived as being nonjudgmental, nonevaluative, and unconditionally supportive. Unfortunately, the same is not always true of friends, family members, and spouses.

Stress may also increase when well-meaning friends or family members offer unwanted or inappropriate social support. In Focus Box 12.3 offers some suggestions on how to provide helpful social support and avoid inappropriate support behaviors.

Gender Differences in the Effects of Social Support

Women may be particularly vulnerable to some of the problematic aspects of social support, for a couple of reasons. First, women are more likely than men to serve as providers of support, which can be a very stressful role (Hobfoll & Vaux, 1993; Shumaker & Hill, 1991). Consider the differences found in one study. When middle-aged male patients were discharged from the hospital after a heart attack, they went home and their wives took care of them. But when middle-aged female heart attack patients were discharged from the hospital, they went home and fell back into the routine of caring for their husbands (Coyne & others, 1990).

Second, women may be more likely to suffer from the *stress contagion effect*, becoming upset about negative life events that happen to other people whom they care about (Belle, 1991). Since women tend to have larger and more intimate social networks than men, they have more opportunities to become distressed by what happens to people who are close to them. And women are more likely than men to be upset about negative events that happen to their relatives and friends.

For example, when Judy was unable to reach her daughter Katie by phone on the morning of September 11, she quickly called two family members for advice and comfort: her mother, Fern, in Chicago, and her sister, your author Sandy, in Tulsa. Of course, there was nothing Sandy or Fern could do to help

IN FOCUS 12.3

Providing Effective Social Support

A close friend turns to you for help in a time of crisis or personal tragedy. What should you do or say? As we've noted in this chapter, appropriate social support can help people weather crises and can significantly reduce the amount of distress that they feel. Inappropriate support, in contrast, may only make matters worse.

Researchers generally agree that there are three broad categories of social support: emotional, tangible, and informational. Each provides different beneficial functions (Peirce & others, 1996; Taylor & Aspinwall, 1993).

Emotional support includes expressions of concern, empathy, and positive regard. *Tangible support* involves direct assistance, such as providing transportation, lending money, or helping with meals, child care, or household tasks. When people offer helpful suggestions, advice, or possible resources, they are providing *informational support*.

It's possible that all three kinds of social support might be provided by the same person, such as a relative, spouse, or very close friend. More commonly, we turn to different people for different kinds of support.

Research by psychologist Stevan Hobfoll and his colleagues (1992) has identified several support behaviors that are typically perceived as helpful by people under stress. In a nutshell, you're most likely to be perceived as helpful if you:

- are a good listener and show concern and interest

- ask questions that encourage the person under stress to express his or her feelings and emotions

- express understanding about why the person is upset

- express affection for the person, whether with a warm hug or simply a pat on the arm

- are willing to invest time and attention in helping

- can help the person with practical tasks, such as housework, transportation, or responsibilities at work or school

Just as important is knowing what *not* to do or say. Here are several behaviors that, however well intentioned, are often perceived as unhelpful:

- Giving advice that the person under stress has not requested

- Telling the person, "I know exactly how you feel"—it's a mistake to think that you have experienced distress identical to what the other person is experiencing

- Talking about yourself or your own problems

- Minimizing the importance of the person's problem by saying things like, "Hey, don't make such a big deal out of it; it could be a lot worse" or "Don't worry, everything will turn out okay"

- Pretending to be cheerful

- Offering your philosophical or religious interpretation of the stressful event by saying things like, "It's just fate," "It's God's will," or "It's your karma"

Finally, remember that although social support is helpful, it is *not* a substitute for counseling or psychotherapy. If a friend seems overwhelmed by problems or emotions, or is having serious difficulty handling the demands of everyday life, you should encourage him or her to seek professional help. Most college campuses have a counseling center or a health clinic that can provide referrals to qualified mental health workers. Sliding fee schedules, based on ability to pay, are usually available. Thus, you can assure the person that cost need not be an obstacle to getting help—or an additional source of stress!

Katie escape the chaos of lower Manhattan. Like Judy, Sandy and Fern became increasingly upset and worried as they watched the events of the day unfold from hundreds of miles away with no news of Katie's fate. When stressful events strike, women tend to reach out to one another for support and comfort (Taylor, Klein, & others, 2000).

In contrast, men are more likely to be distressed only by negative events that happen to their immediate family—their wives and children (Wethington & others, 1987). Men tend to rely heavily on a close relationship with their spouse, placing less importance on relationships with other people. Women, in contrast, are more likely to list close friends along with their spouse as confidants (Shumaker & Hill, 1991). Because men tend to have a much smaller network of intimate others, they may be particularly vulnerable to social isolation, especially if their spouse dies. Thus, it's not surprising that the health benefits of being married are more pronounced for men than for women (Kiecolt-Glaser & Newton, 2001).

Coping
How People Deal with Stress

Key Theme
- Coping refers to the ways in which we try to change circumstances, or our interpretation of circumstances, to make them less threatening.

Key Questions
- What are the two basic forms of coping, and when is each form typically used?
- What are some of the most common coping strategies?
- How does culture affect coping style?

Think about some of the stressful periods that have occurred in your life. What kinds of strategies did you use to deal with those distressing events? Which strategies seemed to work best? Did any of the strategies end up working against your ability to reduce the stressor? If you had to deal with the same events again today, would you do anything differently?

Katie survived a terrorist attack on her neighborhood by being resourceful and, as she would be the first to admit, through sheer good luck. But how did she survive the months following? Along with having a good support system—friends, relatives, and a dance teacher who could offer her emotional and tangible help—she used a number of different strategies to cope with the stress that she continued to experience.

Two Ways of Coping
Problem-Focused and Emotion-Focused Coping

Ways of Coping Like the stress response itself, adaptive coping is a dynamic and complex process. Imagine that you had lost your home and most of your possessions in a fire. What kinds of coping strategies might prove most helpful?

The strategies that you use to deal with distressing events are examples of coping. **Coping** refers to the ways in which we try to change circumstances, or our interpretation of circumstances, to make them more favorable and less threatening (Folkman & Lazarus, 1991; R. S. Lazarus, 1999, 2000).

Coping tends to be a dynamic, ongoing process. We may switch our coping strategies as we appraise the changing demands of a stressful situation and our available resources at any given moment. We also evaluate whether our efforts have made a stressful situation better or worse and adjust our coping strategies accordingly (see Cheng, 2003).

When coping is effective, we adapt to the situation and stress is reduced. Unfortunately, coping efforts do not always help us adapt. Maladaptive coping can involve thoughts and behaviors that intensify or prolong distress or that produce self-defeating outcomes (Bolger & Zuckerman, 1995). The rejected lover who continually dwells on her former companion, passing up opportunities to form new relationships and letting her studies slide, is demonstrating maladaptive coping.

Adaptive coping responses serve many functions. Most important, adaptive coping involves realistically evaluating the situation and determining what can be done to minimize the impact of the stressor. But adaptive coping also involves dealing with the emotional aspects of the situation. In other words, adaptive coping often includes developing emotional tolerance for negative life events, maintaining self-esteem, and keeping emotions in balance. Finally, adaptive coping efforts are directed toward preserving important relationships during stressful experiences (Lazarus, 1993; Lazarus & Folkman, 1984).

Psychologists Richard Lazarus and Susan Folkman (1984) have described two basic types of coping, each of which serves a different purpose. **Problem-**

focused coping is aimed at managing or changing a threatening or harmful stressor. Problem-focused coping strategies tend to be most effective when you can exercise some control over the stressful situation or circumstances (Park & others, 2004). But if you think that nothing can be done to alter a situation, you tend to rely on **emotion-focused coping:** You direct your efforts toward relieving or regulating the emotional impact of the stressful situation. Although emotion-focused coping doesn't change the problem, it can help you feel better about the situation. People are flexible in the coping styles they adopt, often relying on different coping strategies for different stressors (Park & others, 2004).

Problem-Focused Coping Strategies
Changing the Stressor

Problem-focused coping strategies represent actions that have the goal of changing or eliminating the stressor. When people use aggressive or risky efforts to change the situation, they are engaging in *confrontive coping*. Ideally, confrontive coping is direct and assertive without being hostile. When it is hostile or aggressive, confrontive coping may well generate negative emotions in the people being confronted, damaging future relations with them (Folkman & Lazarus, 1991).

In contrast, *planful problem solving* involves efforts to rationally analyze the situation, identify potential solutions, and then implement them. In effect, you take the attitude that the stressor represents a problem to be solved. Once you assume that mental stance, you follow the basic steps of problem solving (see Chapter 7).

Emotion-Focused Coping Strategies
Changing Your Reaction to the Stressor

When the stressor is one over which we can exert little or no control, we often focus on dimensions of the situation that we *can* control—the emotional impact of the stressor on us (Thompson & others, 1994). All the different forms of emotion-focused coping share the goal of reducing or regulating the emotional impact of a stressor.

When you shift your attention away from the stressor and toward other activities, you're engaging in the emotion-focused coping strategy called *escape–avoidance*. As the name implies, the basic goal is to escape or avoid the stressor and neutralize distressing emotions. Excessive sleeping and the use of drugs and alcohol are maladaptive forms of escape–avoidance, as are escaping into fantasy or wishful thinking. More constructive escape–avoidance strategies include exercising or immersing yourself in your studies, hobbies, or work.

For example, Katie found that returning to her daily dance class was the most helpful thing she did to cope with her feelings. During those two hours, Katie was able to let go of her memories of death and destruction. Doing what she loved, surrounded by people she loved, Katie began to feel whole again.

By focusing your attention on something other than the stressor, escape–avoidance tactics provide emotional relief in the short run. Thus, avoidance strategies can be helpful when you are facing a stressor that is brief and has limited consequences. But avoidance strategies such as wishful thinking tend to be counterproductive when the stressor is a severe or long-lasting one, like a serious or chronic disease (Stanton & Snider, 1993). Escape–avoidance strategies are also associated with increased psychological distress in facing other types of stressors, such as adjusting to college (Aspinwall & Taylor, 1992).

In the long run, escape–avoidance tactics are associated with poor adjustment and symptoms of depression and anxiety (Stanton & Snider, 1993). That's not surprising if you think about it. After all, the problem *is* still there. And if the problem is one that needs to be dealt with promptly, such as a pressing medical concern, the delays caused by escape–avoidance strategies can make the stressful situation worse.

Problem-Focused Coping People rely on different coping strategies at different times in dealing with the same stressor. After dealing with the emotional impact of losing their homes to a hurricane, these Florida neighbors engaged in problem-focused coping as they help clear the site before rebuilding.

coping
Behavioral and cognitive responses used to deal with stressors; involves our efforts to change circumstances, or our interpretation of circumstances, to make them more favorable and less threatening.

problem-focused coping
Coping efforts primarily aimed at directly changing or managing a threatening or harmful stressor.

emotion-focused coping
Coping efforts primarily aimed at relieving or regulating the emotional impact of a stressful situation.

IN FOCUS 12.4

Gender Differences in Responding to Stress: "Tend-and-Befriend" or "Fight-or-Flight"?

Physiologically, men and women show the same hormonal and sympathetic nervous system activation that Walter Cannon described as the "fight-or-flight" response to stress (1932). Yet *behaviorally,* the two sexes react very differently.

To illustrate, consider this finding: When fathers come home after a stressful day at work, they tend to withdraw from their families, wanting to be left alone—an example of the "flight" response (Schulz & others, 2004). If their workday was filled with a lot of interpersonal conflicts, they tend to initiate conflicts with family members— evidence of the "fight" response. In contrast, when mothers experience high levels of stress at work, they come home and are *more* nurturing toward their children (Repetti, 1989; Repetti & Wood, 1997).

As we have noted in this chapter, women tend to be much more involved in their social networks than men. And, as compared to men, women are much more likely to seek out and use social support when they are under stress (Belle, 1991; Glynn & others, 1999). Throughout their lives, women tend to mobilize social support—especially from other women—in times of stress (Taylor, Klein, & others, 2000). We saw this pattern in our story about Katie. Just as Katie called her mother, Judy, when her neighborhood came under attack, Judy called her sister, Sandy, and her *own* mother when she feared that her daughter's life was in danger.

Why the gender difference in coping with stress? Health psychologists Shelley Taylor, Laura Klein, and their colleagues (2000, 2002) believe that evolutionary theory offers some insight. According to the evolutionary perspective, the most adaptive response in virtually any situation is one that promotes the survival of both the individual *and* the individual's offspring.

"I'm somewhere between O. and K."

© 1994 The New Yorker Collection from cartoonbank.com. Edward Koren.

Given that premise, neither fighting nor fleeing is likely to have been an adaptive response for females, especially females who were pregnant, nursing, or caring for their offspring. According to Taylor and her colleagues (2000), "Stress responses that enabled the female to simultaneously protect herself and her offspring are likely to have resulted in more surviving offspring." Rather than fighting or fleeing, they argue, women developed a *tend-and-befriend* behavioral response to stress.

What is the "tend-and-befriend" pattern of responding? *Tending* refers to "quieting and caring for offspring and blending into the environment," Taylor and her colleagues (2000) write. That is, rather than confronting or running from the threat, females take cover and protect their young. Evidence supporting this behavior pattern includes studies of nonhuman animals showing that many female animals adopt a "tending" strategy when faced by a threat (Francis & others, 1999; Liu & others, 1997).

The "befriending" side of the equation relates to women's tendency to seek social support during stressful situations. Taylor

and her colleagues (2000) describe *befriending* as "the creation of networks of associations that provide resources and protection for the female and her offspring under conditions of stress."

However, both males and females show the same neuroendocrine responses to an acute stressor—the sympathetic nervous system activates, stress hormones pour into the bloodstream, and, as those hormones reach different organs, the body kicks into high gear. So why do women "tend and befriend" rather than "fight or flee," as men do? Taylor points to the effects of another hormone, *oxytocin.* Higher in females than in males, oxytocin is associated with maternal behaviors in all female mammals, including humans. Oxytocin also tends to have a calming effect on both males and females (see Southwick & others, 2005).

Taylor speculates that oxytocin might simultaneously help calm stressed females and promote affiliative behavior. Supporting this speculation is research showing that oxytocin increases affiliative behaviors and reduces stress in many mammals (Carter & DeVries, 1999; Light & others, 2000). For example, one study found that healthy men who received a dose of oxytocin before being subjected to a stressful procedure were less anxious and had lower cortisol levels than men who received a placebo (Heinrichs & others, 2003).

In humans, oxytocin is highest in nursing mothers. Pleasant physical contact, such as hugging, cuddling, and touching, stimulates the release of oxytocin. In combination, all of these oxytocin-related changes seem to help turn down the physiological intensity of the fight-or-flight response for women. And perhaps, Taylor and her colleagues suggest, they also promote the tend-and-befriend response.

Seeking social support is the coping strategy that involves turning to friends, relatives, or other people for emotional, tangible, or informational support. As we discussed earlier in the chapter, having a strong network of social support can help buffer the impact of stressors (Brissette & others, 2002; Finch & Vega, 2003). Confiding in a trusted friend gives you an opportunity to vent your emotions and better understand the stressful situation.

When you acknowledge the stressor but attempt to minimize or eliminate its emotional impact, you're engaging in the coping strategy called *distancing.*

Downplaying or joking about the stressful situation is one form of distancing (Abel, 2002). Sometimes people emotionally distance themselves from a stressor by discussing it in a detached, depersonalized, or intellectual way. Among Katie's circle of young friends, distancing was common. They joked about the soot, the dust, the National Guard troops guarding the subway stations.

In certain high-stress occupations, distancing can help workers cope with painful human problems. Clinical psychologists, social workers, rescue workers, police officers, and medical personnel often use distancing to some degree to help them deal with distressing situations without falling apart emotionally themselves.

In contrast to distancing, *denial* is a refusal to acknowledge that the problem even exists. Like escape–avoidance strategies, denial can compound problems in situations that require immediate attention.

Perhaps the most constructive emotion-focused coping strategy is *positive reappraisal*. When we use positive reappraisal, we not only try to minimize the negative emotional aspects of the situation, but we also try to create positive meaning by focusing on personal growth. Even in the midst of deeply disturbing situations, positive reappraisal can help people experience positive emotions and minimize the potential for negative aftereffects (Folkman & Moskowitz, 2000). For example, Katie noted that in the days following the collapse of the two towers, "It was really beautiful. Everyone was pulling together, New Yorkers were helping each other."

Similarly, a study by Barbara Fredrickson and her colleagues (2003) found that some college students "looked for the silver lining" after the September 11 terrorist attacks, reaching out to others and expressing gratitude for the safety of their loved ones. Those who found a positive meaning in the aftermath of the attacks were least likely to develop depressive symptoms and other problems in the following weeks. As Fredrickson and her colleagues (2003) observed, "Amidst the emotional turmoil generated by the September 11 terrorist attacks, subtle and fleeting experiences of gratitude, interest, love, and other positive emotions appeared to hold depressive symptoms at bay and fuel postcrisis growth."

Katie, too, was able to creatively transform the meaning of her experience. As part of her application to a college dance program, she choreographed and performed an original dance expressing sadness, fear, hope, and renewal—all the emotions that she experienced on that terrible day. Her ability to express her feelings artistically has helped her come to terms with her memories.

However, it's important to note that there is no single "best" coping strategy. In general, the most effective coping is flexible, meaning that we fine-tune our coping strategies to meet the demands of a particular stressor (Cheng, 2003; Park & others, 2004). And, people often use multiple coping strategies, combining problem-focused and emotion-focused forms of coping (Dunkel-Schetter & others, 1992; Lazarus, 1993). In the initial stages of a stressful experience, we may rely on emotion-focused strategies to help us step back emotionally from a problem. Once we've regained our equilibrium, we may use problem-focused coping strategies to identify potential solutions.

Culture and Coping Strategies

Culture seems to play an important role in the choice of coping strategies. Americans and other members of individualistic cultures tend to emphasize personal autonomy and personal responsibility in dealing with problems. Thus, they are *less* likely to seek social support in stressful situations than are members of collectivistic cultures, such as Asian cultures (Marsella & Dash-Scheuer, 1988). Members of collectivistic cultures tend to be more oriented toward their social group, family, or community and toward seeking help with their problems.

Individualists also tend to emphasize the importance and value of exerting control over their circumstances, especially circumstances that are threatening or stressful (O'Connor & Shimizu, 2002). Thus, they favor problem-focused strategies, such as confrontive coping and planful problem solving. These strategies

Transcending Personal Tragedy: Choosing Hope In the case of a few extraordinary people, like the late actor, director, and social activist Christopher Reeve, tragedy becomes the motivator for personal growth. After a horseback-riding accident in 1995 left him paralyzed from the shoulders down, Reeve established the nonprofit Christopher Reeve Paralysis Foundation and raised millions of dollars for research on spinal cord injuries. Refusing to accept the conventional scientific dogma that recovery of function was impossible, he also embarked on an intensive exercise program that eventually led to his recovering limited movement and sensation—revolutionizing the thinking on recovery from and treatment of spinal cord injury. As neurosurgeon Philip Steig (2004) said, "Christopher used his injury as an opportunity to help mankind." The title of his book, *Nothing Is Impossible: Reflections on a New Life*, reflects Reeve's personal philosophy. As he said, "When we have hope, we discover powers within ourselves we may have never known—the power to make sacrifices, to endure, to heal, and to love. Once we choose hope, everything is possible."

involve directly changing the situation to achieve a better fit with their wishes or goals (Markus & Kitayama, 1991).

In collectivistic cultures, however, a greater emphasis is placed on controlling your personal reactions to a stressful situation rather than trying to control the situation itself. This emotion-focused coping style emphasizes gaining control over inner feelings by accepting and accommodating yourself to existing realities (O'Connor & Shimizu, 2002; Thompson & others, 1994).

For example, the Japanese emphasize accepting difficult situations with maturity, serenity, and flexibility (Weisz & others, 1984). Common sayings in Japan are "The true tolerance is to tolerate the intolerable" and "Flexibility can control rigidity" (Azuma, 1984). Along with controlling inner feelings, many Asian cultures also stress the goal of controlling the outward expression of emotions, however distressing the situation (Johnson & others, 1995).

These cultural differences in coping underscore the point that there is no formula for effective coping in all situations. That we use multiple coping strategies throughout almost every stressful situation reflects our efforts to identify what will work best at a given moment in time. To the extent that any coping strategy helps us identify realistic alternatives, manage our emotions, and maintain important relationships, it is adaptive and effective.

Closing Thoughts

Katie's Dance

From national tragedies and major life events to the minor hassles and annoyances of daily life, stressors come in all sizes and shapes. Any way you look at it, stress is an unavoidable part of life. Stress that is prolonged or intense can adversely affect both our physical and psychological well-being. Fortunately, most of the time people deal effectively with the stresses in their lives. And as Katie's story demonstrates, the effects of even the most intense stressors can be minimized if we cope with them effectively.

Ultimately, the level of stress that we experience is due to a complex interaction of psychological, biological, and social factors. We hope that reading this chapter has given you a better understanding of how stress affects your life and of how you can reduce its impact on your physical and psychological well-being. In the chapter Application, we'll suggest some concrete steps that you can take to minimize the harmful impact of stress in *your* life.

APPLICATION   Minimizing the Effects of Stress

Sometimes stressful situations persist despite our best efforts to resolve them. Knowing that chronic stress can jeopardize your health, what can you do to minimize the adverse impact of stress on your physical well-being? Here are four practical suggestions.

Suggestion 1: Avoid or Minimize the Use of Stimulants

In dealing with stressful situations, people often turn to stimulants to help keep them going, such as coffee or caffeinated energy drinks. If you know someone who smokes, you've probably observed that most smokers

react to stress by increasing their smoking (Ng & Jeffery, 2003; Todd, 2004). The problem is that common stimulants like caffeine and nicotine actually work *against* you in coping with stress. They increase the physiological effects of stress by raising heart rate and blood pressure. In effect, users of stimulant drugs are already primed to respond with greater reactivity, exaggerating the physiological consequences of stress (B. Smith & others, 2001; Lovallo & others, 1996).

The best advice? Avoid stimulant drugs altogether. If that's not possible, make a conscious effort to monitor your use of stim-

ulants, especially when you're under stress. You'll find it easier to deal with stressors when your nervous system is not already in high gear because of caffeine, nicotine, or other stimulants. Minimizing your use of stimulants will also make it easier for you to implement the next suggestion.

Suggestion 2: Exercise Regularly

Numerous studies all point to the same conclusion: Regular exercise, particularly aerobic exercise like walking, swimming, or running, is one of the best ways to reduce the impact of stress (Bass & others, 2002;

Ensel & Lin, 2004). The key word here is *regular*. Try walking briskly for 20 minutes four or five times a week. It will improve your physical health and help you cope with stress. In fact, just about any kind of physical exercise helps buffer the negative effects of stress. (Rapidly right-clicking your computer mouse doesn't count.) Compared to sofa slugs, physically fit people are less physiologically reactive to stressors and produce lower levels of stress hormones (Rejeski & others, 1991, 1992). Psychologically, regular exercise reduces anxiety and depressed feelings and increases self-confidence and self-esteem (Sacks, 1993).

Suggestion 3: Get Enough Sleep

With the ongoing push to get more and more done, people often stretch their days by short-changing themselves on sleep. But sleep deprivation just adds to your feelings of stress. "Without sufficient sleep it is more difficult to concentrate, make careful decisions, and follow instructions," explains researcher Mark Rosekind (2003). "You are more likely to make mistakes or errors, and are more prone to being impatient and lethargic. And, your attention, memory and reaction time are all adversely affected."

by John Jonik

The stress–sleep connection also has the potential to become a vicious cycle. School, work, or family-related pressures contribute to reduced or disturbed sleep, leaving you less than adequately rested and making efforts to deal with the situation all the more taxing and distressful (Akerstedt & others, 2002). And, inadequate sleep, even for just a few nights, takes a physical toll on the body, leaving us more prone to health problems (National Sleep Foundation, 2002, 2004; Spiegel & others, 1999).

Fortunately, research indicates that the opposite is also true: Getting adequate sleep promotes resistance and helps buffer the effects of stress (Mohr & others, 2003). For some suggestions to help promote a good night's sleep, see the Application at the end of Chapter 4.

Suggestion 4: Practice a Relaxation Technique

You can significantly reduce stress-related symptoms by regularly using any one of a variety of relaxation techniques (Benson, 1993). One effective technique is *progressive muscle relaxation* (Pawlow & others, 2003). This technique involves systematically tensing and then relaxing the major muscle groups of your body while lying down or sitting in a comfortable chair.

You begin by tensing your facial and jaw muscles, paying careful attention to the feeling of muscle tightness. Then take a deep breath, hold it for a few seconds, and exhale slowly as you relax your facial and jaw muscles as completely as possible. As you do so, notice the difference between the sensations of tension and the warm feelings of relaxation. Progressively work your way down your body, tensing and then relaxing muscle groups.

A very effective relaxation technique is *meditation,* which we discussed in Chapter 4. Meditation involves focusing your attention on an object, word, or phrase. Shown in the list below are the instructions for a simple meditation technique that we encourage you to try. Numerous studies have demonstrated the physical and psychological benefits of meditation (Barnes & others, 2001; Waelde & others, 2004; Walton & others, 2002).

How to Meditate

Here is a simple but effective meditation technique developed by British psychologist and meditation researcher Michael A. West. Practice the technique for 15 to 20 minutes twice a day for at least two weeks.

1 Sit quietly in an upright position in a room where you are not likely to be disturbed.

2 Close your eyes and relax your body. Sit quietly for about half a minute.

3 Begin to repeat the word *one* easily and silently to yourself, or choose some other simple word, such as *peace* or *calm*.

4 Don't concentrate too hard on the sound. The word need only be a faint idea at times—you don't have to keep repeating it clearly.

5 Think the word easily. It may change by getting louder or softer, longer or shorter, or it may not change at all. In every case, just take it as it comes.

6 Remember, the word has no special meaning or special significance. It is a simple device that helps in meditation.

7 Continue the meditation in this way for about 15 minutes. Don't worry about achieving a deep level of meditation or about whether you are concentrating on the sound.

8 Don't try to control thoughts. If thoughts come during meditation, don't worry about it. When you become aware that you have slipped into a train of thought, just go very easily back to the sound. Don't make great efforts to exclude thoughts—just favor the sound.

9 If you become aware of outside noises or other distracting sounds, go easily back to the word; don't fight to exclude those distractions. Do the same as you would with thoughts. Accept them, but favor the sound.

10 Above all, you are meant to enjoy the meditation, so don't try too hard; just take it easily as it comes.

SOURCE: West (1987).

Chapter Review
Stress, Health, and Coping

Key Points

Introduction: What Is Stress?

■ **Stress** can be defined as a negative emotional state that occurs in response to events that are appraised as taxing or exceeding a person's resources.

■ **Health psychologists** study stress and other psychological factors that influence health, illness, and treatment. Health psychologists are guided by the **biopsychosocial model.**

■ **Stressors** are events or situations that produce stress. According to the life events approach, any event that requires adaptation produces stress. The Social Readjustment Rating Scale is one way to measure the impact of life events. The life events approach does not take into account a person's subjective appraisal of an event. It also assumes that any change, whether good or bad, produces stress.

■ **Daily hassles** are a significant source of stress and also contribute to the stress produced by major life events.

■ Stress can also be caused by approach–approach, avoidance–avoidance, or approach–avoidance **conflicts.** Approach–avoidance conflicts tend to create the most stress.

■ Social factors, such as unemployment, crime, and racism, can be significant sources of stress, often producing chronic stress. Stress can also result when people encounter different cultural values.

Physical Effects of Stress: The Mind–Body Connection

■ Stress can affect health indirectly, by influencing health-related behaviors, and directly, by influencing the body's functioning.

■ Walter Cannon identified the endocrine pathway involved in the **fight-or-flight response.** This endocrine pathway includes the sympathetic nervous system, the adrenal medulla, and the release of **catecholamines.**

■ In studying the physical effects of prolonged stressors, Hans Selye identified the three-stage **general adaptation syndrome,** which includes the alarm, resistance, and exhaustion stages. Selye found that prolonged stress involves a second endocrine pathway, which includes the hypothalamus, the pituitary gland, the adrenal cortex, and the release of **corticosteroids.**

■ Stress affects the functioning of the **immune system**. The most important elements of the immune system are **lymphocytes.** Ader and Cohen's discovery that the immune system could be classically conditioned helped launch the new field of **psychoneuroimmunology.** Subsequent research has discovered that the nervous, endocrine, and immune systems are directly linked and continually influence one another.

■ Stressors that affect immune system functioning include both unusual and common life events, along with everyday pressures. Although stress may increase susceptibility to infection and illness, many other factors are involved in physical health.

Individual Factors That Influence the Response to Stress

■ The impact of stressors is reduced when people feel a sense of control over the stressful situation. Feelings of control have both physical and psychological benefits.

■ The way people explain negative events often determines whether they will persist or give up after failure. People with an **optimistic explanatory style** use external, unstable, and specific explanations for negative events. People with a **pessimistic explanatory style** use internal, stable, and global explanations for negative events. A pessimistic explanatory style contributes to stress and undermines health.

■ Chronic negative emotions are related to the development of some chronic diseases. People who frequently experience negative emotions experience more stress than other people. Transient negative moods have also been shown to diminish immune system functioning.

■ The **Type A behavior pattern** can predict the development of heart disease. The most critical health-compromising component of Type A behavior is hostility. Hostile people react more intensely to stressors and experience stress more frequently than do nonhostile people.

■ Social isolation contributes to poor health. **Social support** improves the ability to deal with stressors by modifying the appraisal of a stressor, decreasing the physical reaction to a stressor, and making people less likely to experience negative emotions. When the quality of relationships is poor, or when social support is inappropriate or unwanted, relationships may increase stress.

■ Women are more likely than men to be the providers of social support and tend to be more vulnerable to the stress contagion effect. Men are less likely to be upset by negative events that happen to people outside their immediate family.

Coping: How People Deal with Stress

■ **Coping** refers to the way in which people try to change either their circumstances or their interpretations of circumstances in order to make them more favorable and less threatening. Coping may be either maladaptive or adaptive.

■ When people think that something can be done to change a situation, they tend to use **problem-focused coping** strategies, which involve changing a harmful stressor.

■ When people think that a situation cannot be changed, they tend to rely on **emotion-focused coping** strategies, which involve changing their emotional reactions to the stressor.

■ Problem-focused coping strategies include confrontive coping and planful problem solving.

■ Emotion-focused coping strategies include escape–avoidance, seeking social support, distancing, denial, and positive reappraisal. Effective coping is flexible, and people often rely on multiple coping strategies in stressful situations.

■ Culture affects the choice of coping strategies. People in individualistic cultures tend to favor problem-focused strategies. People in collectivistic cultures are more likely to seek social support, and they emphasize emotion-focused coping strategies more.

Key Terms

stress, p. 477

health psychology, p. 477

biopsychosocial model, p. 478

stressors, p. 478

daily hassles, p. 479

conflict, p. 480

acculturative stress, p. 481

fight-or-flight response, p. 482

catecholamines, p. 483

general adaptation syndrome, p. 484

corticosteroids, p. 484

immune system, p. 484

lymphocytes, p. 484

psychoneuroimmunology, p. 486

optimistic explanatory style, p. 489

pessimistic explanatory style, p. 489

Type A behavior pattern, p. 491

social support, p. 493

coping, p. 496

problem-focused coping, p. 496

emotion-focused coping, p. 497

Key People

Robert Ader (b. 1932) American psychologist who, with immunologist Nicholas Cohen, first demonstrated that immune system responses could be classically conditioned; helped establish the new interdisciplinary field of psychoneuroimmunology. (p. 485)

Walter B. Cannon (1871–1945) American physiologist who made several important contributions to psychology, especially in the study of emotions. Described the fight-or-flight response, which involves the sympathetic nervous system and the endocrine system (also see Chapter 8). (p. 482)

Janice Kiecolt-Glaser (b. 1951) American psychologist who, with immunologist Ronald Glaser, has conducted extensive research on the effects of stress on the immune system. (p. 486)

Richard Lazarus (1922–2002) American psychologist who helped promote the cognitive perspective on emotion and stress; developed the cognitive appraisal model of stress and coping with co-researcher Susan Folkman (also see Chapter 8). (p. 479)

Martin Seligman (b. 1942) American psychologist who conducted research on explanatory style and the role it plays in stress, health, and illness. (p. 489)

Hans Selye (1907–1982) Canadian endocrinologist who was a pioneer in stress research; defined stress as "the nonspecific response of the body to any demand placed on it" and described a three-stage response to prolonged stress that he termed the *general adaptation syndrome.* (p. 483)

Web Companion | Review Activities

You can find additional review activities by going to **www.DiscoveringPsychology.com** and clicking on the *Discovering Psychology* 4th Edition text cover. At the Discovering Psychology Web Companion you'll find the chapter learning objectives, flashcards for key terms and key people, interactive crossword puzzles, self-scoring practice quizzes, and other materials to help you master the information in this chapter.

Life Walk

chapter

13

Psychological Disorders

Prologue Behind the Steel Door

I had just turned 13 when my dad was hospitalized. At the time, I didn't realize just how sick he was. He nearly died before a diseased kidney was removed, saving his life. Because my junior high was only three blocks from the hospital, I visited him every day after school before going to my paper route. It was one of those visits that defined the course of my life.

Lost in my thoughts as I walked through the maze of dim hospital hallways, I took a wrong turn. When I got near the end of the hallway, I realized it was a dead end and started to turn around. That's when her voice pierced the silence, screaming in agony.

"*Help me! Fire! Fire! Fire! Please* help me!"

At first I was confused about the direction from which the voice was coming. Then I saw a panic-stricken face against the small window of a steel door. I ran to the door and tried to open it, but it was locked.

"Help me, *somebody!* Fire! Fire! Fire!" she screamed again.

"I'll get help!" I yelled back to her, but she didn't seem to see or hear me. My heart racing, I ran back down the dim hallway to a nurses' station.

"There's a woman who needs help! There's a fire!" I quickly explained to a nurse.

But instead of summoning help, the nurse looked at me with what can only be described as disdain. "Which hallway?" she said flatly, and I pointed in the direction from which I had come. "That's the psychiatric ward down there," she explained. "Those people are crazy."

I stared at her for a moment, feeling confused. *Crazy?* "But she needs help," I finally blurted out.

"That's why she's on the psychiatric ward," the nurse replied calmly. "Which room are you trying to find?"

I didn't answer her. Instead, I walked back down the hallway. I took a deep breath and tried to slow my heart down. As I approached the steel door, the woman was still there, screaming. Standing at the door, I watched her through the wire-reinforced glass. She was completely oblivious to my presence.

"There's fire! I see fire! Fire! Fire! *Fire!*"

She was probably about 25 years old. Her faced looked gaunt, dirty, her hair stringy and unkempt. I remember the dark circles under her deep-set eyes, her pupils dilated with sheer, raw panic.

"Listen to me, there's *no* fire," I said loudly, tapping on the glass, trying to get her attention.

"Help me, *please*," she sobbed, laying her cheek against the glass.

"My name is Don," I said, tapping on the glass again. "Listen to me, there's no fire."

That's when the attendants came, dressed in white hospital garb. The young woman slapped at their hands as they tried to pull her away from the door. I pressed my face to the glass, trying to see what was happening. *Don't hurt her!* For just an instant I saw her face again, and she looked directly into my eyes.

"It's okay, there's *no* fire!" I yelled, then she was gone.

I stood by the steel door, my mind racing. *What was wrong with her? Where did they take her? Why did she think there was a fire? Did she really see flames?*

When I finally got to my father's hospital room, we talked the entire time about the woman. Although my dad knew something about mental disorders, he wasn't able to answer the most important questions that I wanted answered: What was wrong with the woman? And what caused her to be that way? "If you'd like," my dad finally said, "I can arrange for you to talk to a psychiatrist that I know. He can probably answer your questions about that better than I can."

A few weeks later, I spent about 30 minutes with the psychiatrist. In very general terms, he talked to me about mental disorders and their treatment. He also explained how psychiatrists usually take a medical approach, typically prescribing different kinds of medication. In contrast, clinical psychologists use different kinds of psychotherapy to help people with psychological disorders. It was at that moment that I knew I wanted to be a clinical psychologist and help people like the woman I had seen.

I never saw that young woman again, nor did I ever find out what happened to her. But I will never forget her face or the sound of her terrified voice. Since that fateful day, I've spent many years of my life working on psychiatric wards, often trying to help people who were just as confused as that young woman.

In this chapter, we'll look at the symptoms that characterize some of the most common psychological disorders, including the one that was being experienced by the young woman I saw that day. As we do, you'll come to better understand how the symptoms of a psychological disorder can seriously impair a person's ability to function. We'll also talk about what researchers have learned about some of the underlying causes of psychological disorders. As you'll see, biological, psychological, and social factors have been implicated as contributing to many psychological disorders.

Introduction

Understanding Psychological Disorders

Key Theme
- Understanding psychological disorders includes considerations of their origins, symptoms, and development, as well as how behavior relates to cultural and social norms.

Key Questions
- What is a psychological disorder, and what differentiates abnormal behavior from normal behavior?
- What is DSM-IV-TR, and how was it developed?
- How prevalent are psychological disorders?

Does *The Far Side* cartoon on the facing page make you smile? The cartoon is humorous, but it's actually intended to make some serious points. It reflects several common misconceptions about psychological disorders that we hope will be dispelled by this chapter.

First, there's the belief that "crazy" behavior is very different from "normal" behavior. Granted, sometimes it is, like the behavior of the young woman who was screaming "Fire!" when there was no fire. But as you'll see throughout this chapter, the line that divides "normal" and "crazy" behavior is often not as sharply defined as most people think. In many instances, the difference between normal and abnormal behavior is a matter of degree. For example, as you leave your apartment or house, it's normal to check or even double-check that the door is securely locked. However, if you feel compelled to go back and check the lock 50 times, it would be considered abnormal behavior.

The dividing line between normal and abnormal behavior is also often determined by the social or cultural context in which a particular behavior occurs (Foulks, 1991). For example, among traditional Hindus in India, certain dietary restrictions are followed as part of the mourning process. It would be a serious breach of social norms if an Indian widow ate fish, meat, onions, garlic, or any other "hot" foods within six months of her husband's death (see Shweder & others, 1990). A Catholic widow in the United States would consider such restrictions absurd.

Second, when we encounter people whose behavior strikes us as weird, unpredictable, or baffling, it's easy to simply dismiss them as "just plain nuts," as in *The Far Side* cartoon, or "crazy," as in the nurse's insensitive response in the Prologue. Although convenient, such a response is too simplistic. It could also be wrong. Sometimes, unconventional people are labeled as crazy when they're actually just creatively challenging the conventional wisdom with new ideas.

Even if a person's responses are seriously disturbed, labeling that person as "crazy" or "just plain nuts" tells us nothing meaningful. What are the person's specific symptoms? What might be the cause of the symptoms? How did they develop? How long can they be expected to last? And how might the person be helped? The area of psychology and medicine that focuses on these questions is called **psychopathology**—the scientific study of the origins, symptoms, and development of psychological disorders. In this chapter and the next, we'll take a closer look at psychological disorders and their treatment.

The Far Side cartoon reflects a third troubling issue. There is still a strong social stigma attached to suffering from a psychological disorder (Hinshaw & Cicchetti, 2000; Read & Harré, 2001). Because of the social stigma that can be associated with psychological disorders, people are often reluctant to seek the help of mental health professionals (Kessler & others, 2004; Sirey & others, 2001). People who *are* under the care of a mental health professional often hide the fact, telling only their closest friends—and understandably so. Being labeled "crazy" carries all kinds of implications, most of which reflect negative stereotypes about people with mental illness (see Corrigan, 1998). In Critical Thinking Box 13.1, we discuss the accuracy of such stereotypes in more detail.

THE FAR SIDE® BY GARY LARSON

> *The mentally ill are not some distinct set of "them" out there who are completely different from "us" sane people. Instead, the vast majority of us have been touched by some form of mental illness at some time in our lives either through personal experience or through the illness of a close loved one.*
>
> Ronald C. Kessler (2003a)

What Is a Psychological Disorder?

Up to this point, we've used the terms *psychological disorder* and *mental disorder* interchangeably. Psychologists generally prefer the term *psychological disorder,* whereas psychiatrists tend to prefer the term *mental disorder.* Both terms are widely used in the research literature. But what exactly are we talking about when we say that someone has a psychological or mental disorder?

A **psychological disorder** or **mental disorder** can be defined as a pattern of behavioral or psychological symptoms that causes significant personal distress, impairs the ability to function in one or more important areas of life, or both (DSM-IV-TR, 2000). An important qualification is that the pattern of behavioral or psychological symptoms must represent a serious departure from the prevailing social and cultural norms. Hence, the behavior of a traditional Hindu woman who refuses to eat onions, garlic, or other "hot" foods following the death of her husband is perfectly normal because that norm is part of the Hindu culture (see Triandis, 1994).

What determines whether a given pattern of symptoms or behaviors qualifies as a psychological disorder? Throughout this chapter, you'll notice numerous references to DSM-IV-TR. **DSM-IV-TR** stands for the *Diagnostic and Statistical Manual of Mental Disorders,* Fourth Edition, Text Revision, which was published by the

psychopathology
The scientific study of the origins, symptoms, and development of psychological disorders.

psychological disorder or **mental disorder**
A pattern of behavioral and psychological symptoms that causes significant personal distress, impairs the ability to function in one or more important areas of daily life, or both.

DSM-IV-TR
Abbreviation for the *Diagnostic and Statistical Manual of Mental Disorders,* Fourth Edition, Text Revision; the book published by the American Psychiatric Association that describes the specific symptoms and diagnostic guidelines for different psychological disorders.

CRITICAL THINKING 13.1

Are People with a Mental Illness as Violent as the Media Portray Them?

A recent children's show on public television presented a retelling of the classic novel *Tom Sawyer* by Mark Twain. However, unlike the original story, the name of the chief villain had been changed: Twain's "Indian Joe" was renamed "Crazy Joe."

As this example illustrates, writers for television are well aware that it is no longer considered acceptable to portray negative stereotypes of particular racial or ethnic groups, including Native Americans. Unfortunately, it also illustrates that another stigmatized group is still fair game: the mentally ill.

In analyzing U.S. television programming, researcher George Gerbner (1993, 1998) found that people with mental disorders are the most stigmatized group portrayed on television. People with mental disorders are depicted in two highly negative, stereotypical ways. One stereotype is that of the mentally disturbed person as a helpless victim. The other stereotype is that of the mentally disordered person as an evil villain who is unpredictable, dangerous, and violent.

Gerbner found that although 5 percent of "normal" television characters are murderers, 20 percent of "mentally ill" characters are killers. About 40 percent of normal characters are violent, but 70 percent of characters labeled as mentally ill are violent. This media stereotype reflects and reinforces the widespread belief among Americans that people with mental illness are violent and threatening (Link & Stueve, 1998; Monahan, 1992). Further reinforcing that belief is selective media reporting that sensationalizes violent acts by people with mental disorders (Angermeyer & Matschinger, 1996).

Are people with mental disorders more violent than other people? A study by psychologist Henry Steadman and his colleagues (1998) monitored the behavior of more than 1,000 former mental patients in the year after they were discharged from psychiatric facilities. As a control group, they also monitored the behavior of a matched group of people who were not former mental patients but were living in the same neighborhood.

Hollywood Versus Reality A deranged, evil killer on the loose is a standard plot in many television dramas and movie thrillers, such as the *Halloween* and *Friday the 13th* films (W. Wilson, 1999). In *The Silence of the Lambs* and *Red Dragon* (as shown here), Anthony Hopkins portrayed Hannibal Lecter, a psychopathic serial killer who helps the FBI catch other psychopathic serial killers. Such media depictions foster the stereotype that people with a mental illness are prone to violence. Does research on this issue support that conclusion?

The researchers found that, overall, the former mental patients did *not* have a higher rate of violence than the comparison group. Former mental patients who demonstrated symptoms of substance abuse were the most likely to engage in violent behavior. However, the same was also true of the control group. In other words, substance abuse was associated with more violent behavior in *all* the participants, whether they had a history of mental illness or not. The study also found that the violent behavior that did occur was most frequently aimed at friends and family members, not at strangers.

Other research has found that people with severe mental disorders who are experiencing extreme psychological symptoms, such as bizarre delusional ideas and hallucinated voices, do display a *slightly* higher level of violent and illegal behavior than do

"normal" people (Link & others, 1992; Malla & Payne, 2005). However, the person with a mental disorder who is not suffering from such symptoms is no more likely than the average person to be involved in violent or illegal behavior. Other factors, such as living in impoverished neighborhoods and abusing drugs or alcohol, are stronger predictors of violence (Eronen & others, 1998; Silver & others, 1999).

Clearly, the incidence of violent behavior among current or former mental patients is grossly exaggerated in media portrayals. In 1999, the U.S. Department of Health and Human Services published a comprehensive report titled *Mental Health: A Report of the Surgeon General*. The report emphasized that fear of violence from people with a mental disorder contributes to the stigma of mental illness. The report also emphasized that such fears are largely unfounded. In reviewing the research, the report summarized it this way: "The overall contribution of mental disorders to the total level of violence in society is exceptionally small. In fact, there is very little risk of violence or harm to a stranger from casual contact with an individual who has a mental disorder."

Critical Thinking Questions

- Can you think of any reasons why people with psychological disorders are more likely to be depicted as villains than members of other social groups?

- Can you think of any television shows or movies in which characters with a severe psychological disorder were shown in a sympathetic light? If so, are such depictions more or less common than depictions of people with a mental illness as dangerous or violent?

- What evidence could you cite to challenge the notion that people with psychological disorders are dangerous?

Diagnostic criteria for 301.7 Antisocial Personality Disorder

A. There is a pervasive pattern of disregard for and violation of the rights of others occurring since age 15 years, as indicated by three (or more) of the following:

    (1) failure to conform to social norms with respect to lawful behaviors as indicated by repeatedly performing acts that are grounds for arrest

    (2) deceitfulness, as indicated by repeated lying, use of aliases, or conning others for personal profit or pleasure

    (3) impulsivity or failure to plan ahead

    (4) irritability and aggressiveness, as indicated by repeated physical fights or assaults

    (5) reckless disregard for safety of self or others

    (6) consistent irresponsibility, as indicated by repeated failure to sustain consistent work behavior or honor financial obligations

    (7) lack of remorse, as indicated by being indifferent to or rationalizing having hurt, mistreated, or stolen from another

B. The individual is at least age 18 years.

C. There is evidence of Conduct Disorder with onset before age 15 years.

D. The occurrence of antisocial behavior is not exclusively during the course of Schizophrenia or a Manic Episode.

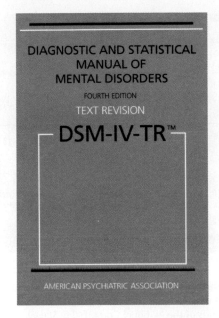

FIGURE 13.1 Sample DSM-IV-TR Diagnostic Criteria Each of the more than 250 psychological disorders described in DSM-IV-TR has specific criteria that must be met in order for a person to be diagnosed with that disorder. Shown above are the DSM-IV-TR criteria for antisocial personality disorder, which is also referred to as *psychopathy, sociopathy,* or *dyssocial personality disorder.* The number 301.7 identifies the specific disorder according to an international code developed by the World Health Organization. The code helps researchers make statistical comparisons of the prevalence of mental disorders in different countries and cultures.

SOURCE: DSM-IV-TR (2000), p. 706.

American Psychiatric Association in 2000. (The original DSM-IV was published in 1994. The updated "text revision" of DSM-IV was published in 2000 to incorporate new research and information.)

DSM-IV-TR is a book that describes approximately 250 specific psychological disorders. It includes the symptoms, the exact criteria that must be met to make a diagnosis, and the typical course for each mental disorder. An example of the diagnostic criteria for one mental disorder is shown in Figure 13.1. DSM-IV-TR provides mental health professionals with both a common language for labeling mental disorders and comprehensive guidelines for diagnosing mental disorders.

It's important to understand that DSM-IV-TR was not written by a single person or even a single organization. Rather, DSM-IV-TR represents the *consensus* of a wide range of mental health professionals and organizations. In developing DSM-IV-TR, teams of mental health professionals conducted extensive reviews of the research findings for each category of mental disorder. More than 1,000 mental health experts, mostly psychiatrists and clinical psychologists, participated in the development of DSM-IV-TR. More than 60 professional organizations, including the American Psychological Association and the American Psychological Society, reviewed early drafts of DSM-IV-TR. Despite these efforts, the *Diagnostic and Statistical Manual of Mental Disorders* has its critics as well as those who would suggest fundamental changes (e.g., Dell, 2001; Tsuang & others, 2000; Widiger & Clark, 2000). Nevertheless, DSM-IV-TR is still the most comprehensive and authoritative set of guidelines available for diagnosing psychological disorders. Thus, we'll refer to it often in this chapter.

The Prevalence of Psychological Disorders
A 50–50 Chance?

Just how common are psychological disorders? A team headed by Ronald Kessler and his colleagues (1994) undertook a comprehensive survey, called the National Comorbidity Survey (NCS), to investigate the question. A representative sample of more than 8,000 Americans, aged 5 to 54, were asked about the symptoms of psychological disorders that they had experienced (1) during the previous 12 months and (2) at any point in their lives. A replication of the NCS survey, using

How Prevalent Are Psychological Disorders?
Psychological disorders are far more common than most people think. According to the findings of the National Comorbidity Survey, every year about one in three American adults experiences the symptoms of some type of psychological disorder. However, most people who experience such symptoms do not seek treatment or help (Kessler & others, 2004).

updated DSM-IV criteria, is currently underway (Kessler & Merikangas, 2004; Kessler & others, 2004).

The NCS results were surprising. First, the researchers found that psychological disorders were much more prevalent than previously thought. Thirty percent, or roughly one in three respondents, had experienced the symptoms of a psychological disorder during the previous 12 months. Even more startling, almost one in two adults—48 percent—had experienced the symptoms of a psychological disorder at some point during their lifetime.

Lead researcher Ronald C. Kessler (2003b) helps put these findings into perspective. As he points out, "It wouldn't surprise anyone if I said that 99.9% of the population had been physically ill at some time in their life. Why, then, should it surprise anyone that 50% of the population has been mentally ill at some time in their life? The reason, of course, is that we invest the term 'mentally ill' with excess meaning. A number of common mental illnesses, like adjustment disorders and brief episodes of depression, are usually mild and self-limiting. Many people experience these kinds of disorders at some time in their life."

Another striking finding was that 80 percent of those who had suffered from the symptoms of a mental disorder in the previous year had *not* sought any type of treatment or help for their symptoms. Although that finding may surprise you, it's consistent with other research (see Kessler & others, 2004).

There are two ways to look at this finding. On the one hand, it's clear that many people who could benefit from mental health treatment do not seek it. This may reflect a lack of awareness about psychological disorders or the fact that a stigma still exists when it comes to seeking treatment for psychological symptoms. Also, many people lack access to mental health services or lack the financial resources to pay for treatment.

On the other hand, even though the incidence of mental disorders is much higher than previously believed, *most* people seem to weather the symptoms without becoming completely debilitated and without professional intervention (Narrow & others, 2002). As NCS director Ronald Kessler (1994) explained, "Really serious conditions that demanded immediate treatment affected 3% to 5% of our sample. These people typically had developed several mental disorders over time, not just one disorder that suddenly appeared."

The NCS also found that the prevalence of certain mental disorders differed for men and women. As you can see in Figure 13.2, women had a higher prevalence of anxiety and depression, and men had a higher prevalence of substance abuse disorders and antisocial personality disorder (Kessler, 2003a; Kessler & others, 1994). In trying to explain these gender differences, researchers are investigating differences in exposure to negative life events, willingness to seek help, genetics, and coping styles (Nolen-Hoeksema, 2001).

For the remainder of this chapter, we'll focus on the mental disorders in five DSM-IV-TR categories: anxiety disorders, mood disorders, personality disorders, dissociative disorders, and schizophrenia. The psychological disorders in these five categories are some of the most common disorders encountered by mental health professionals. They're also the ones that our students ask us about most often. And to help you distinguish between normal and maladaptive behaviors, we'll start the discussion of each mental disorder category by describing behavior that falls within the normal range of psychological functioning, such as normal mood variations or feelings of anxiety.

Table 13.1 describes other categories of mental disorders contained in DSM-IV-TR. Some of these disorders have been discussed in previous chapters. In the chapter Application, we'll look at what you can do to help prevent one of the most disturbing consequences of psychological problems—suicide.

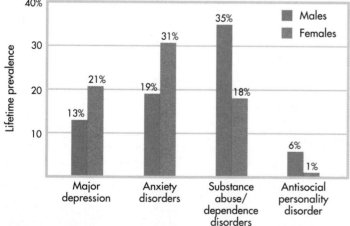

FIGURE 13.2 Gender Differences in the Lifetime Prevalence of Selected Psychological Disorders in the National Comorbidity Survey

SOURCE: Adapted from Kessler & others (1994), p. 12.

Table 13.1

Some Key Diagnostic Categories in DSM-IV-TR

Diagnostic Category	Core Features	Examples of Specific Disorders
Infancy, childhood, or adolescent disorders	Includes a wide range of developmental, behavioral, learning, and communication disorders that are usually first diagnosed in infancy, childhood, or adolescence. Symptoms of a particular disorder may vary depending on a child's age and development level.	**Autistic disorder:** Onset of symptoms prior to age of 3. Characterized by severely impaired social and communication skills, including delayed or a complete lack of language development. Symptoms often include repetitive behaviors, such as body rocking, and abnormal interests, such as intense preoccupation with mechanical toys. **Tourette's disorder:** Onset prior to age of 18. Characterized by motor tics, such as recurring spasmodic movements of the head or arms, and vocal tics, such as recurring and sudden clicking, grunting, or snorting sounds. Sometimes involves uncontrollable utterances of profane or obscene words.
Substance-related disorders (see Chapter 4)	Occurrence of adverse social, behavioral, psychological, and physical effects from seeking or using substances such as alcohol, amphetamines, cocaine, marijuana, hallucinogens, and other drugs.	**Substance abuse:** A recurring pattern of impaired ability to function at work, school, or home due to repeated substance use. **Substance dependence:** A maladaptive pattern of substance use usually resulting in drug tolerance, withdrawal symptoms when the drug is discontinued, and compulsive drug-taking behavior that seriously impairs occupational and social functioning.
Somatoform disorders	Persistent, recurring complaints of bodily (or *somatic*) symptoms that have no physical or medical basis.	**Body dysmorphic disorder:** Exaggerated concern and preoccupation about minor or imagined defects in appearance. **Hypochondriasis:** Preoccupation with imagined diseases based on the person's misinterpretation of bodily symptoms or functions.
Sexual and gender identity disorders	Difficulty in the expression of normal sexuality, including confusion about gender identity, decreased sexual desire or arousal, difficulty having or in timing of orgasm, pain or discomfort during sex, or the use of inappropriate objects to produce sexual arousal.	**Fetishism:** Recurrent, intense, sexually arousing fantasies, urges, or behaviors, usually involving nonliving objects, such as female undergarments, shoes, boots, or other articles of clothing. **Gender identity disorder:** The strong and persistent desire to be the other sex.
Eating disorders (see Chapter 8)	Disturbances in eating behavior that involve obsessive concerns about becoming overweight, a distorted body image, and the inability to maintain a healthy body weight.	**Anorexia nervosa:** Severe restriction of eating and the failure to maintain a normal body weight due to the intense fear of gaining weight. **Bulimia nervosa:** Repeated episodes of binge eating followed by self-induced vomiting, misuse of laxatives, fasting, or excessive exercise.
Sleep disorders (see Chapter 4)	Disruptions in the amount, quality, or timing of sleep. Includes difficulty initiating or maintaining sleep, excessive sleepiness, or abnormal behavioral or psychological events during sleep or sleep–wake transitions.	**Narcolepsy:** Recurrent episodes of unintended sleep in inappropriate situations, such as while driving a car or attending a meeting. **Sleep terror disorder:** Repeated episodes of abruptly awakening from sleep, usually beginning with a panicky scream or cry. Intense fear, rapid heartbeat and breathing, sweating, and other signs of autonomic arousal are evident. Also called *night terror* disorder.
Impulse-control disorders	Inability to resist an impulse, urge, or temptation to perform an act that is harmful to the self or others.	**Kleptomania:** The impulse to steal objects not needed for personal use or monetary value. **Pyromania:** The urge to set fires for pleasure, gratification, or relief of tension.

SOURCE: DSM-IV-TR (2000).

anxiety
An unpleasant emotional state characterized by physical arousal and feelings of tension, apprehension, and worry.

anxiety disorders
A category of psychological disorders in which extreme anxiety is the main diagnostic feature and causes significant disruptions in the person's cognitive, behavioral, or interpersonal functioning.

generalized anxiety disorder (GAD)
An anxiety disorder characterized by excessive, global, and persistent symptoms of anxiety; also called *free-floating anxiety.*

Anxiety Disorders
Intense Apprehension and Worry

Key Theme
■ The main symptom of anxiety disorders is intense anxiety that disrupts normal functioning.

Key Questions
■ How does pathological anxiety differ from normal anxiety?
■ What characterizes generalized anxiety disorder and panic disorder?
■ What are the phobias, and how have they been explained?

Anxiety is a familiar emotion to all of us—that feeling of tension, apprehension, and worry that often hits during personal crises and everyday conflicts. Although it is unpleasant, anxiety is sometimes helpful. Think of anxiety as your personal, internal alarm system that tells you that something is not quite right. When it alerts you to a realistic threat, anxiety is adaptive and normal. For example, anxiety about your grades may motivate you to study harder.

Anxiety has both physical and mental effects. As your internal alarm system, anxiety puts you on *physical alert,* preparing you to defensively "fight" or "flee" potential dangers. Anxiety also puts you on *mental alert,* making you focus your attention squarely on the threatening situation. You become extremely vigilant, scanning the environment for potential threats. When the threat has passed, your alarm system shuts off and you calm down. But even if the problem persists, you can normally put your anxious thoughts aside temporarily and attend to other matters.

In the **anxiety disorders,** however, the anxiety is *maladaptive,* disrupting everyday activities, moods, and thought processes. It's as if you're dealing with a faulty car alarm that activates at the slightest touch and has a broken "off" switch.

Three features distinguish normal anxiety from pathological anxiety. First, pathological anxiety is *irrational.* The anxiety is provoked by perceived threats that are exaggerated or nonexistent, and the anxiety response is out of proportion to the actual importance of the situation. Second, pathological anxiety is *uncontrollable.* The person can't shut off the alarm reaction, even when he or she knows it's unrealistic. And third, pathological anxiety is *disruptive.* It interferes with relationships, job or academic performance, or everyday activities (Mendlowicz & Stein, 2000). In short, pathological anxiety is unreasonably intense, frequent, persistent, and disruptive.

As a symptom, anxiety occurs in many different psychological disorders. In the anxiety disorders, however, anxiety is the *main* symptom, although it is manifested differently in each of the disorders.

Generalized Anxiety Disorder
Worrying About Anything and Everything
Global, persistent, chronic, and excessive apprehension is the main feature of **generalized anxiety disorder,** abbreviated **GAD.** People with this disorder are constantly tense and anxious, and their anxiety is pervasive. They feel anxious about a wide range of life circumstances, sometimes with little or no apparent justification (Craske & Waters, 2005). The more issues about which a person worries excessively, the more likely it is that he or she suffers from generalized anxiety disorder (DSM-IV-TR, 2000).

Normally, anxiety quickly dissipates when a threatening situation is resolved. In generalized anxiety disorder, however, when one source of worry is removed, another quickly moves in to take its place. The anxiety can be attached to virtually any object or to none at all. Because of this, generalized anxiety disorder is sometimes referred to as *free-floating anxiety.*

Panic Attacks and Panic Disorders
Sudden Episodes of Extreme Anxiety

Generalized anxiety disorder is like the dull ache of a sore tooth—a constant, ongoing sense of uneasiness, distress, and apprehension. In contrast, a **panic attack** is a sudden episode of extreme anxiety that rapidly escalates in intensity. The most common symptoms of a panic attack are a pounding heart, rapid breathing, breathlessness, and a choking sensation. The person may also sweat, tremble, and experience lightheaded-ness, chills, or hot flashes. Accompanying the intense, escalat-ing surge of physical arousal are feelings of terror and the belief that one is about to die, go crazy, or completely lose con-trol. A panic attack typically peaks within 10 minutes of onset and then gradually subsides. Nevertheless, the physical symp-toms of a panic attack are so severe and frightening that it's not unusual for people to rush to an emergency room, convinced that they are hav-ing a heart attack, stroke, or seizure (Shulman & others, 1994).

Panic Attack!
The rapidly escalating physical arousal of a panic attack results in a constellation of frighten-ing symptoms: pounding heart, breathlessness, sweating, trembling, and choking sensations. In panic disorder, panic at-tacks are frequent and unpredictable, often seeming to happen for no apparent reason. How do psychologists explain the development of panic disorder?

When panic attacks occur *frequently* and *unexpectedly,* the person is said to be suffering from **panic disorder.** In this disorder, the frequency of panic attacks is highly variable and quite unpredictable. One person may have panic attacks several times a month. Another person may go for months without an attack and then experience panic attacks for several days in a row. Understandably, people with panic disorder are quite apprehensive about when and where the next panic attack will hit (Craske & Waters, 2005).

Sometimes the first panic attack occurs after a stressful experience, such as an injury or illness, or during a stressful period of life, such as while changing jobs or during a period of marital conflict (Craske & others, 1990). In other cases, however, the first panic attack seems to come from nowhere. In a survey of panic disorder pa-tients, 40 percent could not identify any stressful event or negative life experience that might have precipitated the initial panic attack (Shulman & others, 1994).

Explaining Panic Disorder

Both biological and psychological causes seem to be implicated in panic disorder. On the biological side, family and twin studies have found that panic disorder tends to run in families (Hettema & others, 2001). This finding suggests that some individuals may inherit a greater vulnerability to develop panic disorder. However, many panic disorder patients do not have relatives with the disorder (DSM-IV-TR, 2000). So genetics alone does not provide a complete explanation.

Psychologically, people with panic disorder are unusually sensitive to the signs of physical arousal (Antony & others, 1992; Ehlers & Breuer, 1992). The fluttering heartbeat or momentary dizziness that the average person barely no-tices signals disaster to the panic-prone. For example, when normal subjects and panic disorder patients are given a substance, like caffeine, that triggers physio-logical arousal, only the panic disorder patients react with a full-blown panic attack (Margraf & Ehlers, 1989). Why?

According to the *cognitive-behavioral theory of panic disorder,* people with panic disorder tend to misinterpret the physical signs of arousal as catastrophic and dangerous (Rapee & others, 1992; Zinbarg & others, 1992). When their heart starts to pound and their breathing escalates, they interpret their physical symp-toms as frightening or dangerous. This interpretation adds to their physiological arousal and, in a vicious cycle, intensifies the symptoms.

After a frightening initial attack, the person becomes extremely apprehen-sive about suffering another panic attack. In turn, he becomes even more keenly attuned to physical changes that might signal the onset of another frightening at-tack. Ironically, this sensitivity simply increases the likelihood that another panic attack will occur.

panic attack
A sudden episode of extreme anxiety that rapidly escalates in intensity.

panic disorder
An anxiety disorder in which the person experiences frequent and unexpected panic attacks.

Table 13.2

Some Unusual Phobias

Amathophobia	Fear of dust
Anemophobia	Fear of wind
Aphephobia	Fear of being touched by another person
Bibliophobia	Fear of books
Catotrophobia	Fear of breaking a mirror
Ergophobia	Fear of work or responsibility
Erythrophobia	Fear of red objects
Gamophobia	Fear of marriage
Hypertrichophobia	Fear of growing excessive amounts of body hair
Levophobia	Fear of things being on the left side of your body
Phobophobia	Fear of acquiring a phobia
Phonophobia	Fear of the sound of your own voice
Triskaidekaphobia	Fear of the number 13

The result? After a series of panic attacks, the person becomes behaviorally conditioned to respond with fear to the physical symptoms of arousal (Bouton & others, 2001). Once established, such a conditioned response, combined with catastrophic thoughts, can act as a springboard for repeated panic attacks, leading to panic disorder.

Syndromes resembling panic disorder have been reported in many cultures. For example, the Spanish phrase *ataque de nervios* literally means "attack of nerves." It's a disorder reported in many Latin American cultures, in Puerto Rico, and among Latinos in the United States. *Ataque de nervios* has many symptoms in common with panic disorder—heart palpitations, dizziness, and the fear of dying, going crazy, or losing control. However, the person experiencing *ataque de nervios* also becomes hysterical. She may scream, swear, strike out at others, and break things (Salmán & others, 1997). *Ataque de nervios* typically follows a severe stressor, especially one involving a family member. Funerals, accidents, or family conflicts often trigger such attacks (Guarnaccia, 1993). Because *ataque de nervios* tends to elicit immediate social support from others, it seems to be a culturally shaped, acceptable way to respond to severe stress (Liebowitz & others, 1994).

The Phobias
Fear and Loathing

A **phobia** is a strong or irrational fear of something, usually a specific object or situation. Having a phobia does not necessarily mean that a person has a psychological disorder. In the general population, *mild* phobias that don't significantly interfere with a person's ability to function are very common. Many people are fearful of certain animals, such as dogs or snakes, or moderately uncomfortable in particular situations, such as flying in a plane or riding in an elevator. Nonetheless, many people cope with such fears without being overwhelmed with anxiety.

In comparison, people with **specific phobia,** formerly called *simple phobia,* are terrified of a particular object or situation. Encountering the feared situation or object can provoke a full-fledged panic attack in some people. The incapacitating terror and anxiety interfere with the ability to function in daily life. Even though he knows that his fear is excessive and irrational, the person will go to great lengths to avoid the feared object or situation.

About 10 percent of the general population will experience a specific phobia at some point in their lives (Kessler & others, 1994). More than twice as many women as men suffer from specific phobia. Occasionally, people have unusual phobias, such as the elderly woman that Don knew who was terrified of household cleaning supplies (see Table 13.2). Generally, the objects or situations that produce specific phobias tend to fall into four categories:

- *Fear of particular situations,* such as flying, driving, tunnels, bridges, elevators, crowds, or enclosed places
- *Fear of features of the natural environment,* such as heights, water, thunderstorms, or lightning
- *Fear of injury or blood,* including the fear of injections, needles, and medical or dental procedures
- *Fear of animals and insects,* such as snakes, spiders, dogs, cats, slugs, or bats

Agoraphobia
Fear of Panic Attacks in Public Places

One type of phobia deserves special mention—agoraphobia. Compared to the specific phobias, agoraphobia is both more disabling and more complex. Literally, *agoraphobia* means "fear of the marketplace." But rather than fearing public places per se, a person with **agoraphobia** fears having a panic attack in a public place from which it might be difficult to escape or where it might be difficult to get help (McNally & Luoro, 1992). Consequently, people with agoraphobia avoid (1) situations that they think might provoke a panic attack and (2) situations in which they would be unable to escape or get help if they *did* suffer a panic attack.

Although both agoraphobia and panic disorder are characterized by panic attacks, not everyone with panic disorder develops agoraphobia (Swoboda & others, 2003). People who do seem to be especially worried that they will embarrass themselves in public or that others will evaluate them in a negative way. Crowds, standing in line, stores or elevators, public transportation, and traveling in a car may all be avoided because of the fear of suffering a panic attack and being unable to escape the situation. Consequently, many people with agoraphobia become prisoners in their own homes, unable to go beyond the front door.

Social Phobia
Fear of Social Situations

A second type of phobia also deserves additional comment—**social phobia.** Also called **social anxiety disorder,** social phobia is the most prevalent anxiety disorder, and is more prevalent among women than men (Craske & Waters, 2005; Yonkers & others, 2001). Social phobia goes well beyond the shyness that everyone sometimes feels at social gatherings. Rather, the person with social phobia is paralyzed by fear of social situations, especially if the situation involves performing even routine behaviors in front of others. Eating a meal in public, making small talk at a party, or using a public restroom can be agonizing for the person with social phobia.

The core of social phobia seems to be an irrational fear of being embarrassed, judged, or critically evaluated by others. People with social phobia recognize that their fear is excessive and unreasonable, but they still approach social situations with tremendous anxiety (Alden & others, 2004). In severe cases, they may even suffer a panic attack in social situations. When the fear of being embarrassed or failing in public significantly interferes with daily life, it qualifies as social phobia (DSM-IV-TR, 2000).

As with panic attacks, cultural influences can add some novel twists to social phobia. Consider the Japanese disorder called *taijin kyofusho. Taijin kyofusho* usually affects young Japanese males. It has several features in common with social phobia, including extreme social anxiety and avoidance of social situations. However, the person with *taijin kyofusho* is not worried about being embarrassed in public. Rather, reflecting the cultural emphasis of concern for others, the person with *taijin kyofusho* fears that his appearance or smell, facial expression, or body language will offend, insult, or embarrass other people (Iwamasa, 1997).

phobia
A strong or irrational fear of something, usually a specific object or situation, that does not necessarily interfere with the ability to function in daily life.

specific phobia
An anxiety disorder characterized by an extreme and irrational fear of a specific object or situation that interferes with the ability to function in daily life; formerly called *simple phobia.*

agoraphobia
An anxiety disorder involving the extreme and irrational fear of experiencing a panic attack in a public situation and being unable to escape or get help.

social phobia or **social anxiety disorder**
An anxiety disorder involving the extreme and irrational fear of being embarrassed, judged, or scrutinized by others in social situations.

Social Phobia Social phobia is far more debilitating than everyday shyness. This pleasant scene shows a happy bride dancing with her mother as the wedding guests look on. For those who suffer from social phobia, dancing in public would be impossible, and even attending the wedding as a guest might cause overwhelming anxiety.

Yuck! It's hard to suppress a shudder of disgust at the sight of a slug sliming its way across the sidewalk . . . or a cockroach scuttling across the kitchen floor. Are such responses instinctive? Why are people more likely to develop phobias for slugs, maggots, and cockroaches than for mosquitoes or grasshoppers?

Explaining Phobias
Learning Theories

The development of some phobias can be explained in terms of basic learning principles (Craske & Waters, 2005). *Classical conditioning* may well be involved in the development of a specific phobia that can be traced back to some sort of traumatic event. In Chapter 5, on learning, we saw how psychologist John Watson classically conditioned "Little Albert" to fear a tame lab rat that had been paired with loud noise. Following the conditioning, the infant's fear generalized to other furry objects. In much the same way, our neighbor Michelle has been extremely phobic of dogs ever since she was bitten by a German shepherd when she was 4 years old. In effect, Michelle developed a *conditioned response* (fear) to a *conditioned stimulus* (the German shepherd) that has *generalized* to similar stimuli—any dog.

Operant conditioning can also be involved in the avoidance behavior that characterizes phobias. In Michelle's case, she quickly learned that she could reduce her anxiety and fear by avoiding dogs altogether. To use operant conditioning terms, her *operant response* of avoiding dogs is *negatively reinforced* by the relief from anxiety and fear that she experiences.

Observational learning can also be involved in the development of phobias. Some people learn to be phobic of certain objects or situations by observing the fearful reactions of someone else who acts as a *model* in the situation. The child who observes a parent react with sheer panic to the sight of a spider or mouse may imitate the same behavioral response. People can also develop phobias from observing vivid media accounts of disasters, as when some people become afraid to fly after watching graphic TV coverage of a plane crash.

We also noted in Chapter 5 that humans seem *biologically prepared* to acquire fears of certain animals or situations, such as snakes or heights, that were survival threats in human evolutionary history (McNally, 1987). People also seem to be predisposed to develop phobias toward creatures that arouse disgust, like slugs, maggots, or cockroaches (Webb & Davey, 1993). Instinctively, it seems, many people find such creatures repulsive, possibly because they are associated with disease, infection, or filth. Such phobias may reflect a fear of contamination or infection that is also based on human evolutionary history (Davey, 1993; Ware & others, 1994).

Posttraumatic Stress Disorder
Reexperiencing the Trauma

Key Theme
- Extreme anxiety and intrusive thoughts are symptoms of both posttraumatic stress disorder (PTSD) and obsessive–compulsive disorder (OCD).

Key Questions
- What is PTSD, and what causes it?
- What is obsessive–compulsive disorder?
- What are the most common types of obsessions and compulsions?

A Half-Century of Psychological Pain The symptoms of posttraumatic stress disorder can apparently last a lifetime. More than 60 years after the close of World War II, thousands of veterans, now in their eighties, still suffer from nightmares, anxiety, and other PTSD symptoms (Lee & others, 1995). Some experts estimate that as many as 200,000 World War II veterans may continue to suffer from the symptoms of posttraumatic stress disorder.

Posttraumatic stress disorder, abbreviated **PTSD,** is a long-lasting anxiety disorder that develops in response to an extreme physical or psychological trauma. Extreme traumas are events that produce intense feelings of horror and helplessness, such as a serious physical injury or threat of injury to yourself or to loved ones.

Originally, posttraumatic stress disorder was primarily associated with direct experiences of military combat. However, it's now known that PTSD can also develop in survivors of other sorts of extreme traumas, such as natural disasters, physical or sexual assault, random shooting sprees, or terrorist attacks (McNally, 2003). Rescue workers, relief workers, and emergency service personnel can also develop PTSD symptoms (Eriksson & others, 2001). Simply witnessing the injury or death of others can be sufficiently traumatic for PTSD to occur.

In any given year, it's estimated that more than 5 million American adults experience PTSD. There is also a significant gender difference—more than twice as many women as men experience PTSD after exposure to trauma (J. R. Davidson, 2001; Fullerton & others, 2001). Children can also experience the symptoms of PTSD, both during childhood and later, upon reaching adulthood (Margolin & Gordis, 2000).

Three core symptoms characterize posttraumatic stress disorder (DSM-IV-TR, 2000). First, the person *frequently recalls the event,* replaying it in her mind. Such recollections are often *intrusive,* meaning that they are unwanted and interfere with normal thoughts. Second, the person *avoids stimuli or situations* that tend to trigger memories of the experience and undergoes a general *numbing of emotional responsiveness.* Third, the person experiences the *increased physical arousal* associated with anxiety. He may be easily startled, experience sleep disturbances, have problems concentrating and remembering, and be prone to irritability or angry outbursts (Tucker & Trautman, 2000).

Posttraumatic stress disorder is somewhat unusual in that the source of the disorder is the traumatic event itself, rather than a cause that lies within the individual. Even well-adjusted and psychologically healthy people may develop PTSD when exposed to an extremely traumatic event (Ozer & others, 2003).

Terrorist attacks, because of their suddenness and intensity, are particularly likely to produce posttraumatic stress disorder in survivors, rescue workers, and observers (Njenga & others, 2004; North & Pfefferbaum, 2002). For example, four years after the bombing of the Murrah Building in Oklahoma City, more than a third of the survivors suffered from posttraumatic stress disorder. Almost all the survivors had some PTSD symptoms, such as flashbacks, nightmares, intrusive thoughts, and anxiety (North & others, 1999). Even so, people with a prior history of trauma tended to fare worse in follow-up studies a few years after the bombing (Trautman & others, 2002).

However, it's also important to note that no stressor, no matter how extreme, produces posttraumatic stress disorder in everyone. Why is it that some people develop PTSD while others don't? Several factors influence the likelihood of developing posttraumatic stress disorder. First, people with a personal or family history of psychological disorders are more likely to develop PTSD when exposed to an extreme trauma (Leonardo & Hen, 2005). Second, the magnitude of the trauma plays an important role. More extreme stressors are more likely to produce PTSD. Finally, when people undergo *multiple* traumas, the incidence of PTSD can be quite high (Tomb, 1994).

The Aftermath of Terror Surveys of Manhattan residents have found that up to 20 percent suffered symptoms of posttraumatic stress disorder in the months following the terrorist attacks of September 11, 2001 (DeLisi & others, 2003; Galea & others, 2002). People who lived near the World Trade Center or lost a family member or friend had the highest rates of trauma-related symptoms. However, people across the United States experienced symptoms of PTSD, especially those who spent a great deal of time viewing television images of the attacks and their aftermath (Ahern & others, 2004; Blanchard & others, 2004).

Obsessive–Compulsive Disorder
Checking It Again . . . and Again

When you leave your home, you probably check to make sure all the doors are locked. You may even double-check just to be on the safe side. But once you're confident that the door is locked, you don't think about it again.

Now imagine you've checked the door *30* times. Yet you're still not quite sure that the door is really locked. You know the feeling is irrational, but you feel compelled to check again and again. Imagine you've *also* had to repeatedly check that the coffeepot was unplugged, that the stove was turned off, and so forth. Finally, imagine that you only got two blocks away from home before you felt compelled to turn back and check *again*—because you still were not certain.

Sound agonizing? This is the psychological world of the person who suffers from one form of obsessive–compulsive disorder. **Obsessive–compulsive disorder (OCD)** is an anxiety disorder in which a person's life is dominated by repetitive thoughts *(obsessions)* and behaviors *(compulsions).*

posttraumatic stress disorder (PTSD) An anxiety disorder in which chronic and persistent symptoms of anxiety develop in response to an extreme physical or psychological trauma.

obsessive–compulsive disorder (OCD) An anxiety disorder in which the symptoms of anxiety are triggered by intrusive, repetitive thoughts and urges to perform certain actions.

People with paranoid personality disorder are just as distrustful of people who are close to them, even when there is no evidence to support their suspicious beliefs. Not surprisingly, people with paranoid personality disorder are very reluctant to form close attachments or confide in others. Doing so, they believe, leaves them vulnerable, because the other person could use that information against them. In routine social situations, they often misinterpret the innocent comments or actions of others. Playful teasing from a co-worker is seen as a deliberate insult, an attack on their character or reputation (DSM-IV-TR, 2000).

Getting along with the person with a paranoid personality disorder is like trying to walk on eggshells. Inappropriate outbursts of anger can occur when the person feels as though he has been wronged by some kind of slight, insult, or injustice—which happens frequently. Even a minor criticism or constructive suggestion can trigger a hostile reaction.

They also have a strong tendency to blame others for their own shortcomings. They are often harshly critical of what they perceive as the shortcomings of colleagues, friends, or family members. Though they may superficially present themselves as being objective and unemotional, their underlying hostility is evident in sarcastic comments and put-downs. If another person responds in kind, it only confirms their belief that other people are out to attack them.

Pathological jealousy commonly characterizes the intimate relationships of the person with a paranoid personality disorder. Although his spouse or sexual partner may never have given any indication of unfaithfulness, he still suspects and accuses his mate of harboring feelings of infidelity. When his partner is 10 minutes late, makes casual social conversation with other people, or inadvertently rushes out of the house without her wedding ring, the individual with paranoid personality disorder seizes on this behavior as "evidence" of the intent to be unfaithful. The goal of this pathological jealousy is to dominate and maintain complete control of his partner. In doing so, the person thinks he can keep his partner from betraying him and hurting him emotionally.

Unfortunately, there's not a great deal of research on what causes paranoid personality disorder (Bernstein & others, 1995). However, the disorder also tends to co-occur with schizotypal and avoidant personality disorders (Thompson-Pope & Turkat, 1993).

Antisocial Personality Disorder
Violating the Rights of Others

Often referred to as a *psychopath* or *sociopath,* the individual with **antisocial personality disorder** has the ability to lie, cheat, steal, and otherwise manipulate and harm other people. And, when caught, the person shows little or no remorse for having caused pain, damage, or loss to others (Lykken, 1995). It's as though the person has no conscience or sense of guilt. This pattern of blatantly disregarding and violating the rights of others is the central feature of antisocial personality disorder (DSM-IV-TR, 2000). In the general population, approximately 6 percent of men and 1 percent of women display the characteristics of antisocial personality disorder (Kessler & others, 1994).

Evidence of this maladaptive personality pattern is often seen in childhood or early adolescence (Lynam & Gudonis, 2005). In many cases, the child has repeated run-ins with the law or school authorities. Behaviors that draw the attention of authorities can include cruelty to animals, attacking or harming adults or other

antisocial personality disorder
A personality disorder characterized by a pervasive pattern of disregarding and violating the rights of others; such individuals are also often referred to as *psychopaths* or *sociopaths.*

borderline personality disorder
A personality disorder characterized by instability of interpersonal relationships, self-image, and emotions, and marked impulsivity.

children, theft, setting fires, and destroying property. During childhood and adolescence, this pattern of behavior is typically diagnosed as *conduct disorder*. The habitual failure to conform to social norms and rules often becomes the person's predominant life theme, which continues into adulthood (Myers & others, 1998).

Deceiving and manipulating others for their own personal gain is another hallmark of individuals with antisocial personality disorder. With an uncanny ability to look you directly in the eye and speak with complete confidence and sincerity, they will lie in order to gain money, sex, or whatever their goal may be. When confronted with their actions, they respond with indifference or offer some superficial rationalization to justify their behavior. Often, they are contemptuous about the feelings or rights of others, blaming the victim for his or her stupidity.

Because they are consistently irresponsible, individuals with antisocial personality disorder often fail to hold a job or meet financial obligations. Losing or quitting one job after another, defaulting on loans, and failing to make child support payments are common occurrences. Their past is often checkered with arrests and jail sentences. High rates of alcoholism and other forms of substance abuse are also strongly associated with antisocial personality disorder (Bahlmann & others, 2002; Ladd & Petry, 2003). However, by middle to late adulthood, the antisocial tendencies of such individuals tend to diminish (Black & others, 1997).

Borderline Personality Disorder
Chaos and Emptiness

Of all the personality disorders, the chaotic disorder called **borderline personality disorder** is the most commonly diagnosed. Of the estimated 10 million Americans with borderline personality disorder, about 75 percent are women. Borderline personality disorder is primarily characterized by chronic instability in emotions, self-image, and relationships. Moods are uncontrollable, intense, and fluctuate quickly. The person unpredictably swings from one mood extreme to another. Angry, sarcastic outbursts are common (DSM-IV-TR, 2000).

The person with borderline personality disorder often has a pervasive feeling of emptiness and is desperately afraid of abandonment. Her sense of self is unstable and just as chaotic as her external world. Partly because her identity is so fragile, she constantly seeks reassurance and definition from others, and then erupts in anger when it is not forthcoming.

Relationships careen out of control as the person shifts from inappropriately idealizing the newfound lover or friend to complete contempt or hostility. This is someone who sees herself, and everyone else, in absolutes: perfect or worthless, ecstatic or miserable (Mason & Kreger, 1998).

Borderline personality disorder is also characterized by self-destructiveness (Bohus & others, 2004; Morgenstern & others, 1997). Self-mutilation, threats of suicide, and suicide attempts are common, especially in response to perceived rejection or abandonment. People with borderline personality disorder are also likely to lack control over their impulses, including self-damaging impulses. They may gamble, drive recklessly, abuse drugs, or be sexually promiscuous. Depression, substance abuse, and eating disorders are commonly present (Trull & others, 2003).

What causes borderline personality disorder? As with the other personality disorders, multiple factors have been implicated. Because people with borderline personality disorder have such intense and chronic fears of abandonment and are terrified of being alone, some researchers believe that a disruption in attachment relationships in early childhood is an important cause (Gunderson, 1997).

Other researchers have noted that many borderline patients report having experienced physical, sexual, or emotional abuse in childhood (Bailey & Shriver, 1999). One study of hospitalized patients found that a disrupted childhood was common in borderline patients, particularly experiences of neglect by both parents (Zanarini & others, 1997).

An Ordinary Family Man: The Dangers of Antisocial Personality Disorder President of his church council, and a very active church member, Dennis Rader had been a Scout leader and worked for the Wichita, Kansas, animal control department. Married for 34 years, Rader had been very involved in the lives of his two children. But Rader was also the serial killer BTK. In court, Rader shocked even seasoned police officers with his matter-of-fact, emotionless recital of the details of his ten murders. Like Rader, people with antisocial personality disorder wear a "mask of sanity" (Lynam & Gudonis, 2005). Because they are socially skilled, their crimes often escape detection. Because they lack empathy, they see other people only as objects for their gratification.

dissociative experience
A break or disruption in consciousness during which awareness, memory, and personal identity become separated or divided.

dissociative disorders
A category of psychological disorders in which extreme and frequent disruptions of awareness, memory, and personal identity impair the ability to function.

The Dissociative Disorders
Fragmentation of the Self

Key Theme

■ In the dissociative disorders, disruptions in awareness, memory, and identity interfere with the ability to function in everyday life.

Key Questions

■ What is dissociation, and how do normal dissociative experiences differ from the symptoms of dissociative disorders?

■ What are dissociative amnesia, dissociative fugue, and dissociative identity disorder (DID)?

■ What is thought to cause DID?

Despite the many changes you've experienced throughout your lifetime, you have a pretty consistent sense of identity. You're aware of your surroundings and can easily recall memories from the recent and distant past. In other words, a normal personality is one in which *awareness, memory,* and *personal identity* are associated and well integrated.

In contrast, a **dissociative experience** is one in which a person's awareness, memory, and personal identity become separated or divided. While that may sound weird, dissociative experiences are not inherently pathological. Mild dissociative experiences are quite common and completely normal (Kihlstrom & others, 1994). For example, you become so absorbed in a book or movie that you lose all track of time. Or, you're so preoccupied with your thoughts while driving that when you arrive at your destination, you remember next to nothing about the trip. In each of these cases, you've experienced a temporary "break" or "separation" in your memory or awareness—a mild form of dissociation.

Clearly, then, dissociative experiences are not necessarily abnormal. But in the **dissociative disorders,** the dissociative experiences are more extreme and frequent and severely disrupt everyday functioning. Awareness, or recognition of familiar surroundings, may be completely obstructed. Memories of pertinent personal information may be unavailable to consciousness. Identity may be lost, confused, or fragmented (Spiegel & Cardeña, 1991).

The category of dissociative disorders consists of three basic disorders: *dissociative amnesia, dissociative fugue,* and *dissociative identity disorder,* which was previously called *multiple personality disorder.* Until recently, the dissociative disorders were thought to be extremely rare. How rare? An extensive review conducted in the 1940s uncovered a grand total of 76 reported cases of dissociative disorders since the beginnings of modern medicine in the 1700s (Taylor & Martin, 1944). Although a few more cases were reported during the 1950s and 1960s, the clinical picture changed dramatically in the 1970s when a surge of dissociative disorder diagnoses occurred (Kihlstrom, 2005). Later in this discussion we'll explore some of the possible reasons as well as the controversy surrounding the "epidemic" of dissociative disorders that began in the 1970s.

Dissociation and Possession A Candomble priestess in Brazil holds a woman who is "possessed" by a Christian saint during a religious ceremony. Such dissociative trance and possession states are common in religions around the world (Krippner, 1994). When dissociative experiences take place within a religious ritual context, they are not considered abnormal. In fact, such experiences may be highly valued (Mulhern, 1991).

Dissociative Amnesia and Fugue
Forgetting and Wandering

Dissociative amnesia refers to the partial or total inability to recall important information that is not due to a medical condition, such as an illness, an injury, or a drug. Usually the person develops amnesia for personal events and information, rather than for general knowledge or skills. That is, the person may not be able to remember his wife's name but does remember how to read and who Martin Luther King Jr. was. In most cases, dissociative amnesia is a response to stress, trauma, or an extremely distressing situation, such as combat, marital problems, or physical abuse (Spiegel & Cardeña, 1991).

A closely related disorder is dissociative fugue. In **dissociative fugue,** the person outwardly appears completely normal. However, the person has extensive amnesia and is confused about his identity. While in the fugue state, he suddenly and inexplicably travels away from his home, wandering to other cities or even countries. In some cases, people in a fugue state adopt a completely new identity.

Like dissociative amnesia, dissociative fugues are thought to be associated with traumatic events or stressful periods (Loewenstein, 1993). Interestingly, when the person "awakens" from the fugue state, he may remember his past history but have amnesia for what occurred *during* the fugue state (DSM-IV-TR, 2000).

Dissociative Identity Disorder
Multiple Personalities

Among the dissociative disorders, none is more fascinating—or controversial—than dissociative identity disorder, formerly known as *multiple personality disorder.* **Dissociative identity disorder,** abbreviated **DID,** involves extensive memory disruptions for personal information along with the presence of two or more distinct identities, or "personalities," within a single person.

Typically, each personality has its own name and is experienced as if it has its own personal history and self-image. These alternate personalities, often called *alters* or *alter egos,* may be of widely varying ages and different genders. Alters are not really separate people. Rather, they constitute a "system of mind" (Kluft, 1993). That is, the alters seem to embody different aspects of the individual's personality that, for some reason, cannot be integrated into the primary personality. The alternate personalities hold memories, emotions, and motives that are not admissible to the individual's conscious mind.

At different times, different alter egos take control of the person's experience, thoughts, and behavior (Kihlstrom, 1992). Typically, the primary personality is unaware of the existence of the alternate personalities. However, the alter egos may have knowledge of each other's existence and share memories (Kihlstrom & others, 1994). Sometimes the experiences of one alter are accessible to another alter but not vice versa.

Symptoms of amnesia and memory problems are reported in virtually all cases of DID (Allen & Iacono, 2001; Huntjens & others, 2003). There are frequent gaps in memory for both recent and childhood experiences. Commonly, the person with dissociative identity disorder "loses time" and is unable to recall her behavior or whereabouts during specific time periods. In addition to their memory problems, people with DID typically have numerous psychiatric and physical symptoms, along with a chaotic personal history (Saxe & others, 1994). Symptoms of major depression, anxiety, posttraumatic stress disorder, substance abuse, sleep disorders, and self-destructive behavior are also very common. Often, the DID patient has been diagnosed with a variety of other psychological disorders before the DID diagnosis is made (Gleaves & others, 1999, 2003).

Not all mental health professionals are convinced that dissociative identity disorder is a genuine psychological disorder. For example, a survey by Justine

dissociative amnesia
A dissociative disorder involving the partial or total inability to recall important personal information.

dissociative fugue
(fyoog) A dissociative disorder involving sudden and unexpected travel away from home, extensive amnesia, and identity confusion.

dissociative identity disorder (DID)
A dissociative disorder involving extensive memory disruptions along with the presence of two or more distinct identities, or "personalities"; formerly called *multiple personality disorder.*

"Tell me more about these nine separate and distinct personalities."

Lalonde and his colleagues (2001) found that fewer than 1 in 7 American and Canadian psychiatrists felt that diagnoses of dissociative disorders were supported by strong scientific evidence. Much of such skepticism is related to the fact that the number of cases of DID has surged in last few decades. As psychologist John Kihlstrom (2005) notes:

> An interesting feature of the DID "epidemic" is an increase not just in the number of cases but also in the number of alter egos reported per case. The proliferation of alter egos within cases, as well as the proliferation of cases, has been one of the factors leading to skepticism about the disorder itself.

To some psychologists, this suggests that DID patients have learned "how to behave like a multiple" from media portrayals of sensational cases or by responding to their therapists' suggestions (Gee & others, 2003; Spanos, 1994). Another possible explanation is that symptoms of the different dissociative disorders can be difficult to distinguish from bipolar disorder, borderline personality disorder, and schizophrenia (Kihlstrom, 2005).

It must be noted that DID is not the only psychological disorder in which prevalence rates have increased over time. For example, rates of both obsessive–compulsive disorder and PTSD have also increased, primarily because mental health professionals have become more aware of these disorders and more likely to screen for symptoms (Gleaves, 1996). The dissociative disorders are summarized in Table 13.6.

Explaining Dissociative Identity Disorder

According to one explanation, dissociative identity disorder represents an extreme form of dissociative coping (Gleaves, 1996). A very high percentage of DID patients report having suffered extreme physical or sexual abuse in childhood—over 90 percent in most surveys (Coons, 1994). According to this explanation, in order to cope with the trauma, the child "dissociates" himself or herself from it, creating alternate personalities to experience the trauma.

Over time, alternate personalities are created to deal with the memories and emotions associated with intolerably painful experiences. Feelings of anger, rage, fear, and guilt that are too powerful for the child to consciously integrate can be dissociated into these alternate personalities. In effect, dissociation becomes a pathological defense mechanism that the person uses to cope with overwhelming experiences (Spiegel, 1993a).

Although widely accepted among therapists who work with dissociative identity disorder patients, the dissociative coping theory is difficult to test empirically. One problem is that memories of childhood are notoriously unreliable (Loftus, 1993). Since DID is usually diagnosed in adulthood, it is very difficult, and often impossible, to determine whether the reports of childhood abuse are real or imaginary. Despite the difficulties of objective verification, a few researchers have confirmed memories of childhood abuse with independent evidence, such as medical records and court testimony by family members and social workers (see Gleaves & others, 1999).

Another problem with the "traumatic memory" explanation of dissociative identity disorder is that just the *opposite* effect occurs to most trauma victims— they are bothered by recurring and intrusive memories of the traumatic event. For example, in a study by Gail Goodman and her colleagues (2003), more than 80% of young adults with a documented history of childhood sexual abuse remembered the abuse. Of those who didn't report the abuse, reluctance to disclose the abuse and being too young to remember the abuse seemed to be the most likely explanations.

Although the scientific debate about the validity of the dissociative disorders is likely to continue for some time, the dissociative disorders are fundamentally different from the last major category of disorders we'll consider—schizophrenia.

Table	13.6

Dissociative Disorders

Dissociative Amnesia
- Inability to remember important personal information, too extensive to be explained by ordinary forgetfulness

Dissociative Fugue
- Sudden, unexpected travel away from home
- Amnesia
- Confusion about personal identity or assumption of new identity

Dissociative Identity Disorder
- Presence of two or more distinct identities, each with consistent patterns of personality traits and behavior
- Behavior that is controlled by two or more distinct, recurring identities
- Amnesia; frequent memory gaps

Schizophrenia
A Different Reality

Key Theme
■ One of the most serious psychological disorders is schizophrenia, which involves severely distorted beliefs, perceptions, and thought processes.

Key Questions
■ What are the major symptoms of schizophrenia, and how do positive and negative symptoms differ?
■ What are the main subtypes of schizophrenia?
■ What factors have been implicated in the development of schizophrenia?

Normally, you've got a pretty good grip on reality. You can easily distinguish between external reality and the different kinds of mental states that you routinely experience, such as dreams or daydreams. But as we negotiate life's many twists and turns, the ability to stay firmly anchored in reality is not a given. Rather, we're engaged in an ongoing process of verifying the accuracy of our thoughts, beliefs, and perceptions.

If any mental disorder demonstrates the potential for losing touch with reality, it's schizophrenia. **Schizophrenia** is a psychological disorder that involves severely distorted beliefs, perceptions, and thought processes. During a schizophrenic episode, people lose their grip on reality, like the woman screaming "Fire!" in the chapter Prologue. They experience an entirely different inner world, one that is often characterized by mental chaos, disorientation, and frustration.

Symptoms of Schizophrenia

The characteristic symptoms of schizophrenia can be described in terms of two broad categories: positive and negative symptoms. **Positive symptoms** reflect an excess or distortion of normal functioning. Positive symptoms include (1) *delusions,* or false beliefs; (2) *hallucinations,* or false perceptions; and (3) severely disorganized thought processes, speech, and behavior. In contrast, **negative symptoms** reflect an absence or reduction of normal functions, such as greatly reduced motivation, emotional expressiveness, or speech.

According to DSM-IV-TR, schizophrenia is diagnosed when two or more of these characteristic symptoms are actively present for a month or longer. Usually, schizophrenia also involves a longer personal history, typically six months or more, of odd behaviors, beliefs, perceptual experiences, and other less severe signs of mental disturbance (Malla & Payne, 2005).

Positive Symptoms
Delusions, Hallucinations, and Disturbances in Sensation, Thinking, and Speech

A **delusion** is a false belief that persists in spite of compelling contradictory evidence. Schizophrenic delusions are not simply unconventional or inaccurate beliefs. Rather, they are bizarre and farfetched notions. The person may believe that secret agents are poisoning his food or that the next-door neighbors are actually aliens from outer space who are trying to transform him into a remote-controlled robot. The delusional person often becomes preoccupied with his erroneous beliefs and ignores any evidence that contradicts them.

Certain themes consistently appear in schizophrenic delusions. When *delusions of reference* occur, the person is convinced that other people are constantly talking about her or that everything that happens is somehow related to her. Billboards and advertisements contain cryptic messages directed at her. The radio

Glimpses of Schizophrenia This drawing was made by a young man hospitalized for schizophrenia. At the time the picture was drawn, he was hallucinating and extremely paranoid. The drawing provides glimpses of the distorted perceptions and thoughts that are characteristic of a schizophrenic episode. Notice the smaller face that is superimposed on the larger face, which might represent the hallucinated voices that are often heard in schizophrenic episodes.

schizophrenia
A psychological disorder in which the ability to function is impaired by severely distorted beliefs, perceptions, and thought processes.

positive symptoms
In schizophrenia, symptoms that reflect excesses or distortions of normal functioning, including delusions, hallucinations, and disorganized thoughts and behavior.

negative symptoms
In schizophrenia, symptoms that reflect defects or deficits in normal functioning, including flat affect, alogia, and avolition.

delusion
A falsely held belief that persists in spite of compelling contradictory evidence.

FIGURE 13.4 Incidence of Different Types of Hallucinations in Schizophrenia Schizophrenia-related hallucinations can occur in any sensory modality. Auditory hallucinations, usually in the form of voices, are the most common type of hallucinations that occur in schizophrenia, followed by visual hallucinations.

SOURCE: Adapted from data in Mueser & others (1990) and Bracha & others (1989).

hallucination
A false or distorted perception that seems vividly real to the person experiencing it.

announcer is talking to her specifically, not to listeners in general. In contrast, *delusions of grandeur* involve the belief that the person is extremely powerful, important, or wealthy. In *delusions of persecution*, the basic theme is that others are plotting against or trying to harm the person or someone close to her.

Schizophrenic delusions are often so convincing that they can provoke inappropriate or bizarre behavior. Delusional thinking may lead to dangerous behaviors, as when a person responds to his delusional ideas by hurting himself or attacking others.

Among the most disturbing experiences in schizophrenia are **hallucinations**, which are false or distorted perceptions that seem vividly real (see Figure 13.4). The content of hallucinations is often tied to the person's delusional beliefs. For example, if she harbors delusions of grandeur, hallucinated voices may reinforce her grandiose ideas by communicating instructions from God, the devil, or angels. If the person harbors delusions of persecution, hallucinated voices or images may be extremely frightening, threatening, or accusing. The content of hallucinations and delusions may also be influenced by culture and religiosity, as described in Culture and Human Behavior Box 13.3.

When a schizophrenic episode is severe, hallucinations can be virtually impossible to distinguish from objective reality. For example, the young woman in the Prologue probably did see vivid but hallucinated images of fire. When schizophrenic symptoms are less severe, the person may recognize that the hallucination is a product of his own mind. As one young man confided to your author Don, "I know the voices aren't real, but I can't make them stop talking to me." As this young man got better, the hallucinated voices did eventually stop.

Other positive symptoms of schizophrenia include disturbances in sensation, thinking, and speech. Visual, auditory, and tactile experiences may seem distorted or unreal. For example, one woman described the sensory distortions in this way:

> Looking around the room, I found that things had lost their emotional meaning. They were larger than life, tense, and suspenseful. They were flat, and colored as if in artificial light. I felt my body to be first giant, then minuscule. My arms seemed to be several inches longer than before and did not feel as though they belonged to me. (Anonymous, 1990)

Along with sensory distortions, the person may experience severely disorganized thinking. It becomes enormously difficult to concentrate, remember, and integrate important information while ignoring irrelevant information (Barch, 2005). The person's mind drifts from topic to topic in an unpredictable, illogical manner. Such disorganized thinking is often reflected in the person's speech (Barch & Berenbaum, 1996). Ideas, words, and images are sometimes strung together in ways that seem nonsensical to the listener.

Negative Symptoms
Flat Affect, Alogia, and Avolition

Negative symptoms consist of marked deficits or decreases in behavioral or emotional functioning. One commonly seen negative symptom is referred to as *flat affect,* or *affective flattening.* Regardless of the situation, the person responds in an emotionally "flat" way, showing a dramatic reduction in emotional responsiveness and facial expressions. Speech is slow and monotonous, lacking normal vocal inflections. A closely related negative symptom is *alogia,* or greatly reduced production of speech. In alogia, verbal responses are limited to brief, empty comments.

Finally, *avolition* refers to the inability to initiate or persist in even simple forms of goal-directed behaviors, such as dressing, bathing, or engaging in social activities. Instead, the person seems to be completely apathetic, sometimes sitting still for hours at a time.

focus on

Neuroscience

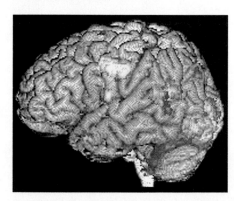

The Hallucinating Brain Researcher David Silbersweig and his colleagues (1995) used PET scans to take a "snapshot" of brain activity during schizophrenic hallucinations. The scan shown here was recorded at the exact instant a schizophrenic patient hallucinated disembodied heads yelling orders at him. The bright orange areas reveal activity in the left auditory and visual areas of his brain, but not in the frontal lobe, which normally is involved in organized thought processes.

CULTURE AND HUMAN BEHAVIOR 13.3

Travel Advisory: The Jerusalem Syndrome

Whether it occurs in Baltimore or Beijing, Minneapolis or Moscow, schizophrenia is usually characterized by delusions and hallucinations. However, the *content* of the person's delusions and hallucinations is often influenced by cultural factors, including that culture's dominant religious beliefs. Consider one interesting example: the *Jerusalem syndrome,* which has been described by psychiatrist Yair Bar-El and his colleagues (2000) at Kfar Shaul Mental Health Center in Israel.

Christians, Jews, and Muslims regard the city of Jerusalem as a richly historical and holy city. Annually, about 2 million tourists from around the world visit the city. But for about 100 visitors every year, arriving in the famous holy city triggers a psychotic break that involves religious delusions and hallucinations—the essence of the *Jerusalem syndrome.* About half of these people require psychiatric hospitalization (Fastovsky & others, 2000). The disorder occurs frequently enough that Jerusalem tour guides and hotel personnel are familiar with it and will notify authorities when they spot someone displaying the symptoms.

Identifying with biblical characters is a common feature of the Jerusalem syndrome. As a general rule, Christians tend to believe that they are Jesus Christ, the Virgin Mary,

A Pilgrimage Gone Awry Being in the presence of a historic religious site like the Wailing Wall in Jerusalem is an overwhelming emotional experience for many tourists. In some vulnerable people, such experiences trigger a temporary episode of psychological instability and religious delusions.

or John the Baptist. In contrast, Jews tend to gravitate toward a Hebrew hero like Moses, Samson, or King David. And Muslims simply tend to say that they're the Mahdi (Messiah).

Usually, the person has a history of serious mental disorders, such as previous episodes of schizophrenia or bipolar disorder. But in about 10 percent of Jerusalem syndrome cases, the person has *no* history of mental disorders. Instead, the person spontaneously experiences a psychotic episode while in Jerusalem.

For example, a Swiss lawyer was on a three-week group tour of Greece, Israel, and Egypt. Everything was fine until the tour visited Jerusalem. On the first night in Jerusalem, the man became nervous and agitated, withdrew from the group, and became obsessed with becoming clean and pure, taking many showers. Then, using the white hotel linen to make a biblical-style, toga-like gown, he marched to one of Jerusalem's holy sites and delivered a rambling "sermon" about how humanity should adopt a more moral and simple way of life. Fortunately, within a matter of days, the syndrome passed and the man's symptoms abated.

What causes the Jerusalem syndrome? One possible explanation is that the disruptions of travel temporarily influence a person's mental state. According to Bar-El and his colleagues (2000), factors such as time-zone changes, unfamiliar surroundings, and exposure to strangers and foreigners probably contribute to the transient psychological instability. In a vulnerable person, encountering cultural differences in behavior combined with being on a spiritual pilgrimage to one of the world's great holy cities can trigger an acute psychotic episode.

Types of Schizophrenia

Figure 13.5 shows the frequency of positive and negative symptoms at the time of hospitalization for schizophrenia. These symptoms are used in diagnosing the particular subtype of schizophrenia. DSM-IV-TR includes three basic subtypes of schizophrenia: *paranoid, catatonic,* and *disorganized* (see Table 13.7).

The *paranoid type* of schizophrenia is characterized by the presence of delusions, hallucinations, or both. However, people with paranoid schizophrenia show virtually no cognitive impairment, disorganized behavior, or negative symptoms. Instead, well-organized delusions of persecution or grandeur are operating. Auditory hallucinations in the form of voices talking about the delusional ideas are also often evident. Convinced that others are plotting against them, these people react with extreme distrust of others. Or they may assume an air of superiority, confident in the delusional belief that they have "special powers." The paranoid type is the most common type of schizophrenia.

The *catatonic type* of schizophrenia is marked by highly disturbed movements or actions. These may include bizarre postures or grimaces, extremely

People with schizophrenia might hear the roars of Satan or the whispers of children. They might move armies with their thoughts and receive instructions from other worlds. They might feel penetrated by scheming parasites, stalked by enemies, or praised by guardian angels. People with schizophrenia might also speak nonsensically, their language at once intricate and impenetrable. And many would push, or be pushed, to the edge of the social landscape, overcome by solitude.

K. Walter Heinrichs, 2005

FIGURE 13.5 Presence of Symptoms in Schizophrenia This graph shows how often specific positive and negative symptoms were present in a study of over 100 individuals at the time they were hospitalized for schizophrenia. Delusions were the most common positive symptom, and avolition, or apathy, was the most common negative symptom.

SOURCE: Based on data reported in Andreasen & Flaum (1991).

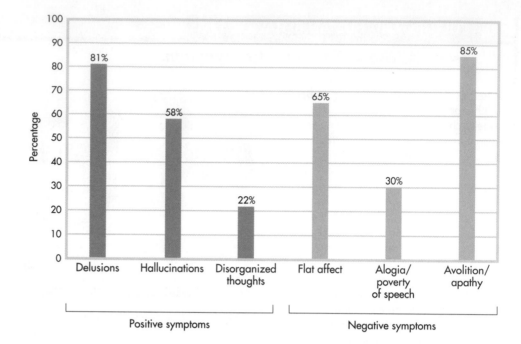

Table 13.7

Types of Schizophrenia

Paranoid Type
- Well-organized delusional beliefs reflecting persecutory or grandiose ideas
- Frequent auditory hallucinations, usually voices
- Little or no disorganized behavior, speech, or flat affect

Catatonic Type
- Highly disturbed movements or actions, such as extreme excitement, bizarre postures or grimaces, or being completely immobile
- Echoing of words spoken by others, or imitation of movements of others

Disorganized Type
- Flat or inappropriate emotional expressions
- Severely disorganized speech and behavior
- Fragmented delusional ideas and hallucinations

Undifferentiated Type
- Display of characteristic symptoms of schizophrenia but not in a way that fits the pattern for paranoid, catatonic, or disorganized type

agitated behavior, complete immobility, the echoing of words just spoken by another person, or imitation of the movements of others. People with this form of schizophrenia will resist direction from others and may also assume rigid postures to resist being moved. Catatonic schizophrenia is often characterized by another unusual symptom, called *waxy flexibility*. Like a wax figure, the person can be "molded" into any position and will hold that position indefinitely. The catatonic type of schizophrenia is very rare.

The prominent features of the *disorganized type* of schizophrenia are extremely disorganized behavior, disorganized speech, and flat affect. Delusions and hallucinations are sometimes present, but they are not well organized and integrated, like those that characterize paranoid schizophrenia. Instead, people with the disorganized type experience delusions and hallucinations that contain fragmented, shifting themes. Silliness, laughing, and giggling may occur for no apparent reason. In short, the person's behavior is very peculiar. This type of schizophrenia was formerly called *hebephrenic schizophrenia*, and that term is still sometimes used.

Finally, the label *undifferentiated type* is used when an individual displays some combination of positive and negative symptoms that does not clearly fit the criteria for the paranoid, catatonic, or disorganized types.

The Prevalence and Course of Schizophrenia

Every year, about 200,000 new cases of schizophrenia are diagnosed in the United States. The onset of schizophrenia typically occurs during young adulthood (Beratis & others, 1994). Annually, approximately 1 million Americans are treated for schizophrenia. All told, about 1 percent of the U.S. population will experience at least one episode of schizophrenia at some point in life (Regier & others, 1993). Worldwide, no society or culture is immune to this mental disorder. Most cultures correspond very closely to the 1 percent rate of schizophrenia seen in the United States (Gottesman, 1991).

The course of schizophrenia is marked by enormous individual variability. Even so, a few global generalizations are possible (Krausz & Müller-Thomsen, 1993; Malla & Payne, 2005; Walker & others, 2004). The good news is that about one-quarter of those who experience an episode of schizophrenia recover completely and never experience another episode. Another one-quarter experience recurrent episodes of schizophrenia, but often with only minimal impairment in the ability to function.

Now the bad news. For the rest of those who have experienced an episode of schizophrenia—about one-half of the total—schizophrenia becomes a chronic mental illness, and the ability to function may be severely impaired. The people in this last category face the prospect of repeated hospitalizations and extended treatment. Thus, chronic schizophrenia places a heavy emotional, financial, and psychological burden on people with the disorder, their families, and society.

Explaining Schizophrenia

Schizophrenia is an extremely complex disorder. There is enormous individual variability in the onset, symptoms, duration, and recovery from schizophrenia. So it shouldn't come as a surprise that the causes of schizophrenia seem to be equally complex. In this section, we'll survey some of the factors that have been implicated in the development of schizophrenia.

Genetic Factors
Family, Twin, Adoption, and Gene Studies

Studies of families, twins, and adopted individuals have firmly established that genetic factors play a significant role in many cases of schizophrenia. First, family studies have consistently shown that schizophrenia tends to cluster in certain families (Kendler & Diehl, 1993; Prescott & Gottesman, 1993). Second, family and twin studies have consistently shown that the more closely related a person is to someone who has schizophrenia, the greater the risk that she will be diagnosed with schizophrenia at some point in her lifetime (see Figure 13.6). Third, adoption studies have consistently shown that if either *biological* parent of an adopted individual had schizophrenia, the adopted individual is at greater risk to

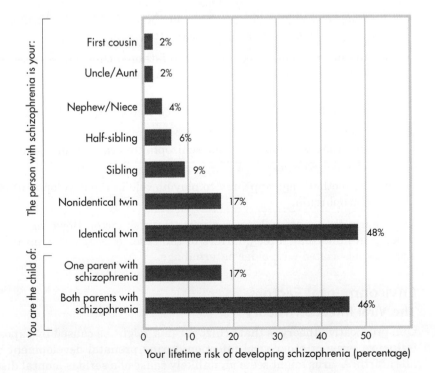

FIGURE 13.6 The Risk of Developing Schizophrenia Among Blood Relatives The risk percentages shown here reflect the collective results of about 40 studies investigating the likelihood of developing schizophrenia among blood relatives. As you can see, the greatest risk occurs if you have an identical twin who has schizophrenia (48 percent lifetime risk) or if both of your biological parents have schizophrenia (46 percent lifetime risk). However, environmental factors, as well as genetic ones, are involved in the development of schizophrenia.

SOURCE: Gottesman (1991), p. 96.

develop schizophrenia (Tienari & others, 1994). And fourth, by studying families that display a high rate of schizophrenia, researchers have consistently found that the presence of certain genetic variations seems to increase susceptibility to the disorder (Fanous & others, 2005; Williams & others, 2005)

Ironically, the strongest evidence that points to genetic involvement in schizophrenia—the almost 50 percent risk rate for a person whose identical twin has schizophrenia—is the same evidence that underscores the importance of environmental factors (Torrey, 1992). If schizophrenia were purely a matter of inherited maladaptive genes, then you would expect a risk rate much closer to 100 percent for monozygotic twins. Obviously, nongenetic factors must play a role in explaining why half of identical twins with a schizophrenic twin do *not* develop schizophrenia.

Paternal Age
Older Fathers and the Risk of Schizophrenia

Despite the fact that family and twin studies point to the role of genetic factors in the risk of developing schizophrenia, no genetic model thus far explains all of the patterns of schizophrenia occurrence within families (Kendler & Diehl, 1993). Adding to the perplexity is the fact that schizophrenia often occurs in individuals with *no* family history of mental disorders.

One explanation for these anomalies is that for each generation, new cases of schizophrenia arise from genetic mutations carried in the sperm of the biological fathers, especially older fathers. As men age, their sperm cells continue to reproduce by dividing. By the time a male is 20, his sperm cells have undergone about 200 divisions; by the time he is 40, about 660 divisions. As the number of divisions increases over time, the sperm cells accumulate genetic mutations that can then be passed on to that man's offspring. Hence, the theory goes, as paternal age increases, the risk of offspring developing schizophrenia also increases.

Researcher Dolores Malaspina and her colleagues (2001) explored this notion by reviewing data on more than 87,000 people born in Jerusalem from 1964 to 1976. Of this group, 658 people had been diagnosed with schizophrenia by 1998. After controlling for various risk factors, the researchers found that paternal age was a strong and significant predictor of the schizophrenia diagnoses. Specifically, Malaspina and her colleagues (2001) found that:

- Men in the 45-to-49 age group who fathered children were twice as likely to have offspring with schizophrenia as compared to fathers age 25 and under.

- Men in the 50+ age range were three times more likely to produce offspring with schizophrenia.

- More than one-quarter of the schizophrenia cases could be attributed to the father's age.

- The mother's age appeared to play *no* role in the development of schizophrenia.

Clearly, then, paternal age is a potential risk factor. However, it's important to keep in mind that three-quarters of the cases of schizophrenia in this study were *not* associated with older paternal age.

Environmental Factors
The Viral Infection Theory

One provocative theory is that schizophrenia might be caused by exposure to an influenza virus or other viral infection during prenatal development or shortly after birth. A virus might seem an unlikely cause of a serious mental disorder, but viruses *can* spread to the brain and spinal cord by traveling along nerves. According to this theory, exposure to a viral infection during prenatal development or early infancy affects the developing brain, producing changes that make the individual more vulnerable to schizophrenia later in life.

There is growing evidence to support the viral infection theory. In one compelling study, psychiatrist Alan S. Brown and his colleagues (2004) compared stored blood samples of 64 mothers of people who later developed schizophrenia with a matched set of blood samples from women whose children did not develop schizophrenia. Both sets of blood samples had been collected years earlier during the women's pregnancies. After analyzing the blood samples for the presence of influenza antibodies, Brown and his colleagues (2004) found that women who had been exposed to the flu virus during the first trimester had a sevenfold increased risk of bearing a child who later developed schizophrenia.

Previous studies using maternal recall and the dates of influenza epidemics have demonstrated similar findings: Children whose mothers were exposed to a flu virus during pregnancy, especially during the first or second trimester, show an increased rate of schizophrenia (A. Brown & others, 2000; Huttunen & others, 1994; Venables, 1996). A related finding is that schizophrenia occurs more often in people who were born in the winter and spring months, when upper respiratory infections are most common (Torrey & others, 1993, 1997).

Abnormal Brain Structures
Loss of Gray Matter

Researchers have found that about half of the people with schizophrenia show some type of brain structure abnormality (Cannon & Marco, 1994). The most consistent finding has been the enlargement of the fluid-filled cavities, called *ventricles*, located deep within the brain (Gaser & others, 2004). However, researchers are not certain how enlarged ventricles might be related to schizophrenia. Another difference that has been found is a loss of gray matter tissue (Paillère-Martinot & others, 2001). As we discussed in Chapter 2 (see page 65), *gray matter* refers to the glial cells, neuron cell bodies, and unmyelinated axons that compose the quarter-inch-thick cerebral cortex.

To investigate the neurological development of schizophrenia, neuroscientist Paul M. Thompson and his colleagues (2001) undertook a prospective study of brain structure changes in 12 adolescents with early-onset childhood schizophrenia. The 6 females and 6 males had all experienced schizophrenic symptoms, including psychotic symptoms, before the age of 12. The intent of the study was to provide a visual picture of the timing, rates, and anatomical distribution of brain structure changes in adolescents with schizophrenia.

Each of the 12 adolescents was scanned repeatedly with high-resolution MRIs over a five-year period, beginning when the teenagers were about 14. The adolescents were carefully matched with healthy teens of the same gender, age, socioeconomic background, and height. The findings of this important study are featured in the Focus on Neuroscience on page 540.

Although there is evidence that brain abnormalities are found in schizophrenia, such findings do not prove that brain abnormalities are the sole cause of schizophrenia. First, some people with schizophrenia do *not* show brain structure abnormalities. Second, the evidence is correlational. Researchers are still investigating whether differences in brain structures and activity are the cause or the consequence of schizophrenia. Third, the kinds of brain abnormalities seen in schizophrenia are also seen in other mental disorders. Rather than specifically causing schizophrenia, it's quite possible that brain abnormalities might contribute to psychological disorders in general.

Identical Twins but Not Identical Brains David and Steven Elmore are identical twins, but they differ in one important respect—Steven *(right)* has schizophrenia. Behind each is a CAT scan, which reveals that Steven's brain is slightly smaller, with less area devoted to the cortex at the top of the brain. Steven also has larger fluid-filled ventricles, which are circled in red on his brain scan. As researcher Daniel Weinberger (1995) commented, "The part of the cortex that Steven is missing serves as perhaps the most evolved part of the human brain. It performs complicated tasks such as thinking organized thoughts. This might help explain why paranoid delusions and hallucinations are characteristic of schizophrenia."

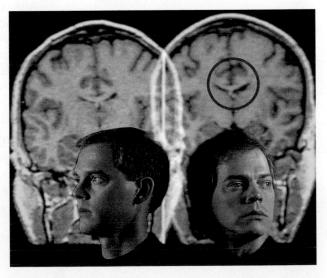

Neuroscience: Schizophrenia: A Wildfire in the Brain

Rate of Gray Matter Loss

Normal Adolescents | Schizophrenic Subjects

Average Annual Loss

-2%
-3%
-4%
-5%

In a five-year prospective study, neuroscientist Paul Thompson and his colleagues (2001) used high-resolution brain scans to map brain structure changes in normal adolescents and adolescents with early-onset schizophrenia. Thompson found marked differences in the brain development of normal teens and teens with schizophrenia. As expected, the healthy teenagers showed a gradual, small loss of gray matter—about 1 percent—over the five-year study. This loss is due to the normal pruning of unused brain connections that takes place during adolescence (see Chapter 9, page 377).

But in sharp contrast to the normal teens, the teenagers with schizophrenia showed a severe loss of gray matter that developed in a specific, wavelike pattern. The loss began in the parietal lobes and, over the five years of the study, progressively spread forward to the temporal and frontal regions. As Thompson (2001) noted, "We were stunned to see a spreading wave of tissue loss that began in a small region of the brain. It moved across the brain like a forest fire, destroying more tissue as the disease progressed."

The brain images show the average rate of gray matter loss over the five-year period. Gray matter loss ranged from about 1 percent (blue) in the normal teens to more than 5 percent (pink) in the schizophrenic teens. One fascinating finding was that the amount of gray matter loss was directly correlated to the teenage patients' clinical symptoms. Psychotic symptoms increased the most in the participants who lost the greatest quantity of gray matter.

Also, the *pattern* of loss mirrored the progression of neurological and cognitive deficits associated with schizophrenia. For example, more rapid gray matter loss in the *temporal lobes* was associated with more severe *positive* symptoms, such as hallucinations and delusions. More rapid loss of gray matter in the *frontal lobes* was strongly correlated with the severity of *negative* symptoms, including flat affect and poverty of speech. When the participants were 18 to 19 years old and the final brain scans were taken, the patterns of gray matter loss were similar to those found in the brains of adult patients with schizophrenia.

Despite the wealth of information generated by Thompson's study, the critical question remains unanswered: What sparks the cerebral forest fire in the schizophrenic brain?

Abnormal Brain Chemistry
The Dopamine Hypothesis

According to the **dopamine hypothesis,** schizophrenia is related to excessive activity of the neurotransmitter dopamine in the brain. Two pieces of indirect evidence support this notion. First, antipsychotic drugs, such as Haldol, Thorazine, and Stelazine, *reduce or block dopamine activity in the brain.* These drugs reduce schizophrenic symptoms in many people. Second, drugs that enhance dopamine activity in the brain, such as amphetamines and cocaine, can produce schizophrenia-like symptoms in normal adults or increase symptoms in people who already have schizophrenia (see Walker & others, 2004).

Although the dopamine hypothesis is compelling, there are inconsistencies. Not all individuals who have schizophrenia experience a reduction of symptoms in response to the antipsychotic drugs that reduce dopamine activity in the brain. And for many patients, these drugs reduce some but not all schizophrenic symptoms (Heinrichs, 1993). So although it seems likely that dopamine is somehow involved in schizophrenia, its exact role is far from clear.

Psychological Factors
Unhealthy Families

Researchers have investigated such factors as dysfunctional parenting, disturbed family communication styles, and critical or guilt-inducing parental styles as possible contributors to schizophrenia (J. Johnson & others, 2001; Miklowitz, 1994). However, no single psychological factor seems to emerge consistently as causing schizophrenia. Rather, it seems that those who are genetically predisposed to develop schizophrenia may be more vulnerable to the effects of disturbed family environments (Fowles, 1992).

dopamine hypothesis
The view that schizophrenia is related to, and may be caused by, excessive activity of the neurotransmitter dopamine in the brain.

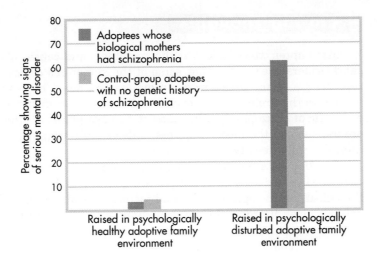

FIGURE 13.7 The Finnish Adoptive Family Study of Schizophrenia In the Finnish Adoptive Family Study, psychiatrist Pekka Tienari and his colleagues (1994) tracked the mental health of two groups of adopted individuals: one group with biological mothers who had schizophrenia and a control group whose biological mothers did not have schizophrenia. This graph shows the strong influence of the adoptive family environment on the development of serious mental disorders.

Strong support for this view comes from a landmark study conducted by Finnish psychiatrist Pekka Tienari and his colleagues (1987, 1994). In the Finnish Adoptive Family Study of Schizophrenia, researchers followed about 150 adopted individuals whose biological mothers had schizophrenia. As part of their study, the researchers assessed the adoptive family's degree of psychological adjustment, including the mental health of the adoptive parents. The study also included a control group of about 180 adopted individuals whose biological mothers did *not* have schizophrenia.

Tienari and his colleagues (1994) found that adopted children with a schizophrenic biological mother had a much higher rate of schizophrenia than did the children in the control group. However, this was true *only* when the children were raised in a psychologically disturbed adoptive home. As you can see in Figure 13.7, when children with a genetic background of schizophrenia were raised in a psychologically healthy adoptive family, they were *no more likely* than the control-group children to develop schizophrenia.

Although adopted children with no genetic history of schizophrenia were less vulnerable to the psychological stresses of a disturbed family environment, they were by no means completely immune to such influences. As Figure 13.7 shows, one-third of the control-group adoptees developed symptoms of a serious psychological disorder if they were raised in a disturbed family environment.

Tienari's study underscores the complex interaction of genetic and environmental factors. Clearly, children who were genetically at risk to develop schizophrenia benefited from being raised in a healthy psychological environment. Put simply, a healthy psychological environment may counteract a person's inherited vulnerability for schizophrenia. Conversely, a psychologically unhealthy family environment can act as a catalyst for the onset of schizophrenia, especially for those individuals with a genetic history of schizophrenia.

After more than a century of intensive research, schizophrenia remains a baffling disorder. Thus far no single biological, psychological, or social factor has emerged as the causal agent in schizophrenia. Nevertheless, researchers are expressing greater confidence that the pieces of the schizophrenia puzzle are beginning to form a more coherent picture.

Even if the exact causes of schizophrenia remain elusive, there is still reason for optimism. In the last few years, new antipsychotic drugs have been developed that are much more effective in treating both the positive and negative symptoms of schizophrenia. In the next chapter, we'll take a detailed look at the different treatments and therapies for schizophrenia and other psychological disorders.

Closing Thoughts

In this chapter, we've looked at the symptoms and causes of several psychological disorders. We've seen that some of the symptoms of psychological disorders represent a sharp break from normal experience. The behavior of the young woman in the Prologue is an example of the severely disrupted functioning characteristic of schizophrenia. In contrast, the symptoms of other psychological disorders, such as the mood disorders, differ from normal experience primarily in their degree, intensity, and duration.

Psychologists are only beginning to understand the causes of many psychological disorders. The broad picture that emerges reflects a familiar theme: Biological, psychological, and social factors all contribute to the development of psychological disorders. In the next chapter, we'll look at how psychological disorders are treated.

In the chapter Application, we'll explore one of the most serious consequences of psychological problems—suicide. Since people who are contemplating suicide often turn to their friends before they seek help from a mental health professional, we'll also suggest several ways in which you can help a friend who expresses suicidal intentions.

APPLICATION   Understanding and Helping to Prevent Suicide

Who Commits Suicide?

Suicide and attempted suicide are all too common. Each year in the United States about 30,000 people take their own lives. For every death by suicide, it's estimated that 25 people have attempted suicide (American Association of Suicidology, 2004). In any given year, some 500,000 people require emergency room treatment as a result of attempted suicide (McCaig & Burt, 2004).

Most people don't realize that close to twice as many Americans die each year from suicide as from homicide. In 2002, suicide was the 11th leading cause of death, while homicide ranked as 14th (National Center for Health Statistics, 2004).

Women outnumber men by three to one in the number of suicide attempts. However, men outnumber women by better than four to one in suicide deaths, primarily because men tend to use more lethal methods, such as shooting and hanging (Kochanek & Smith, 2004).

Suicide is the third leading cause of death for young people aged 15 to 24. Over the last four decades, the suicide rate

How to Help a Friend The majority of those who attempt suicide communicate their intentions to friends or family members (Shneidman, 1998). When a friend is despondent and desperate, you can help by listening, expressing your understanding and compassion, and, if necessary, referring him or her to a professional counselor or suicide prevention specialist.

for adolescents and young adults has increased by almost 300 percent (U.S. Public Health Service, 1999). Although this trend has received considerable media attention,

the suicide rate of adolescents and young adults is still below that of older adults. In fact, the highest suicide rate consistently occurs in the oldest segments of our population—among those age 75 and above (Kochanek & Smith, 2004).

A notion that is often perpetuated in the popular press is that there is a significant increase in the number of suicides during the winter holidays. This claim is a myth, plain and simple. However, there are consistent seasonal variations in suicide deaths. In the United States, suicide rates are lowest during the winter months and highest in the spring (Romer & others, 2003).

On average, someone commits suicide in the United States every 17 minutes. It is estimated that each suicide affects the lives of at least six other people.

What Risk Factors Are Associated with Suicidal Behavior?

Hundreds of studies have identified psychosocial and environmental factors that are associated with an increased risk of suicidal behavior (e.g., L. Brown & others, 2004; Gould & others, 2003; Joiner & others, 2005; Lieb & others, 2005). Some of the factors that increase the risk of suicidal behavior include:

- Feelings of hopelessness and social isolation
- Recent relationship problems or a lack of significant relationships
- Poor coping and problem-solving skills
- Poor impulse control and impaired judgment
- Rigid thinking or irrational beliefs
- A major psychological disorder, especially depression, bipolar disorder, or schizophrenia
- Alcohol or other substance abuse
- Childhood physical or sexual abuse
- Prior self-destructive behavior
- A family history of suicide
- Presence of a firearm in the home

Why Do People Attempt or Commit Suicide?

The suicidal person's view of life has become progressively more pessimistic and negative. At the same time, his view of self-inflicted death as an alternative to life becomes progressively more acceptable and positive (Shneidman, 1998, 2004).

Some people choose suicide in order to escape the pain of a chronic illness or the slow, agonizing death of a terminal disease. Others commit suicide because of feelings of hopelessness, depression, guilt, rejection, failure, humiliation, or shame (Lester, 1997). The common denominator is that they see suicide as the only escape from their own unbearably painful emotions (Jamison, 2000). Ann, for example, was deeply despondent over the fact that she had failed to live up to her own expectations of becoming a highly acclaimed, successful painter.

When faced with a dilemma, the average person tends to see a range of possible solutions, accepting the fact that none of the solutions may be ideal. In contrast, the suicidal person's thinking and perceptions have become rigid and constricted. She can see only two ways to solve her problems: a magical resolution or suicide. Because she cannot imagine a realistic way of solving

her problems, death seems to be the only logical option (Shneidman, 1998, 2004).

How Can You Help Prevent Suicide?

If someone is truly intent on taking his or her own life, it may be impossible to prevent them from doing so. But that does not mean that you can't try to help a friend who is expressing suicidal intentions. People often turn to their friends rather than to mental health professionals. If a friend confides that he or she is feeling hopeless and suicidal, these guidelines may help you help your friend.

It's important to stress, however, that these guidelines are meant only to help you provide "psychological first aid" in a crisis situation. They do *not* qualify you as a suicide prevention expert. Your goal is to help your friend weather the immediate crisis so that he or she can be directed to a mental health professional.

So ubiquitous is the impulse to commit suicide that one out of every two Americans has at some time considered, threatened, or actually attempted suicide.

David Lester, 1997

Guideline 1: Actively listen as the person talks and vents her feelings.

The suicidal person often feels isolated or lonely, with few sources of social support. Let the person talk, and try to genuinely empathize with your friend's feelings. An understanding friend who is willing to take the time to listen patiently without passing judgment may provide just the support the person needs to overcome the immediate suicidal feelings. Hearing themselves talk can also help suicidal individuals identify and better understand their own feelings.

Guideline 2: Don't deny or minimize the person's suicidal intentions.

Brushing aside suicidal statements with platitudes, like "Don't be silly, you've got everything to live for," or clichés, like "Every cloud has a silver lining," is not a helpful response. This is *not* the time to be glib, patronizing, or superficial. Instead, ask your friend if she wants to talk about her feelings. Try to be matter-of-fact and confirm that she is indeed seriously suicidal,

rather than simply exaggerating her frustration or disappointment.

How can you confirm that the person is suicidal? Simply ask her, "Are you really thinking about killing yourself?" Talking about specific suicide plans (how, when, and where), giving away valued possessions, and putting her affairs in order are some indications that a person's suicidal intentions are serious.

Guideline 3: Identify other potential solutions.

The suicidal person is operating with psychological blinders that prevent him from seeing alternative courses of action or other ways of looking at his problems. How can you remove those blinders? Simply saying, "Here are some options you may not have thought about" is a good starting point. You might list alternative solutions to the person's problems, helping him to understand that other potential solutions do exist, even though none may be perfect (Shneidman, 1998).

Guideline 4: Ask the person to delay his decision.

Most suicidal people are ambivalent about wanting to die. If your friend did not have mixed feelings about committing suicide, he probably wouldn't be talking to you. If he is still intent on suicide after talking about other alternatives, ask him to *delay* his decision. Even a few days' delay may give the person enough time to psychologically regroup, consider alternatives, or seek help.

Guideline 5: Encourage the person to seek professional help.

If the person is seriously suicidal and may harm herself in the near future, do *not* leave her alone. The most important thing you can do is help to get the person referred to a mental health professional for evaluation and treatment. If you don't feel you can do this alone, find another person to help you.

There are any number of resources you can suggest, including local suicide hotlines or mental health associations, the college counseling service, and the person's family doctor or religious adviser. You can also suggest calling 1-800-SUICIDE (1-800-784-2433), which will connect you with a crisis center in your area.

Chapter Review

Key Points

Introduction: Understanding Psychological Disorders

- Distinguishing "normal" from "abnormal" behavior involves consideration of many different factors, including cultural norms. **Psychopathology** refers to the scientific study of the origins, symptoms, and development of psychological disorders.

- A **psychological disorder,** or **mental disorder,** is a pattern of behavioral or psychological symptoms that causes significant personal distress and/or impairs the ability to function. The diagnostic criteria for specific psychological disorders are described in **DSM-IV-TR.**

- The prevalence of psychological disorders is much higher than had previously been thought. According to one comprehensive survey, approximately one in two Americans will experience a psychological disorder at some point in their lifetime, and approximately one in three Americans has experienced the symptoms of a psychological disorder in the previous year.

Anxiety Disorders: Intense Apprehension and Worry

- In contrast to normal **anxiety**, **anxiety disorders** consist of irrational and uncontrollable feelings that are unreasonably intense, frequent, persistent, and disruptive.

- **Generalized anxiety disorder (GAD)** and **panic disorder** are characterized by intense anxiety that is not triggered by a specific stimulus. Generalized anxiety disorder involves a constant, persistent state of anxiety. Panic disorder involves sudden episodes of extreme, intense anxiety, which are called **panic attacks.**

- The **phobias** involve intense, irrational fear and avoidance of the feared object or situation. Important forms of phobias include **specific phobia, social phobia (social anxiety disorder),** and **agoraphobia,** which is fear of having a panic attack in a public or inescapable situation. Learning theories and evolved biological predispositions have been offered as explanations of the development of phobias.

- **Posttraumatic stress disorder (PTSD)** develops in response to an extreme psychological or physical trauma. Symptoms include frequent intrusive memories of the trauma, avoidance, emotional numbness, and increased physical arousal.

- **Obsessive–compulsive disorder** is an anxiety disorder in which a person's life is dominated by repetitive thoughts **(obsessions)** and actions **(compulsions).** Biological factors that have been implicated in obsessive–compulsive disorder include serotonin deficiency and brain dysfunction.

Mood Disorders: Emotions Gone Awry

- **Mood disorders**, also called *affective disorders,* involve serious, persistent disturbances in emotions that cause psychological discomfort and/or impair the ability to function.

- The symptoms of **major depression** include negative emotions, extreme pessimism, thoughts of suicide, cognitive impairment, lack of motivation, and sleep disruption for a period of two weeks or longer. **Dysthymic disorder** is a milder but chronic form of depression.

- Major depression is the most common psychological disorder. Left untreated, depression may recur and become progressively more severe. **Seasonal affective disorder (SAD)** generally occurs with the onset of the fall and winter months, and is associated with lesser amounts of sunlight.

- **Bipolar disorder** usually involves periods of depression alternating with **manic episodes.** A milder form of bipolar disorder is **cyclothymic disorder.** Bipolar disorder is less common than major depression.

- Genetics, brain chemistry, and stress have all been implicated in mood disorders. The neurotransmitters serotonin and norepinephrine have been implicated in depression. Another neurotransmitter, glutamate, may be involved in bipolar disorder.

Personality Disorders: Maladaptive Traits

- **Personality disorders** are characterized by inflexible, maladaptive patterns of thoughts, emotions, behavior, and interpersonal functioning. These traits are stable over time and across situations, and deviate from the social and behavioral expectations of the individual's culture.

- Personality disorders are grouped into three clusters: the odd, eccentric cluster; the dramatic, emotional, erratic cluster; and the anxious, fearful cluster.

- **Paranoid personality disorder** is characterized by a pervasive distrust and suspiciousness of the motives of others. Others are perceived as trying to exploit or deceive the person. Inappropriate outbursts of anger, blaming others for the person's own inadequacies, and pathological jealousy are common features of this disorder.

- **Antisocial personality disorder** is characterized by a pervasive pattern of disregarding and violating the rights of others. People with this personality disorder habitually deceive and manipulate others for their own gain. A history of substance abuse, arrests, and other irresponsible behaviors is common. Multiple factors seem to be involved in the development of antisocial personality disorder.

- **Borderline personality disorder** is characterized by instability of interpersonal relationships, self-image, and emotions. Mood swings, impulsive actions, self-destructive tendencies, and substance abuse are common features. Factors that seem to contribute to the development of this disorder include parental neglect or abuse during childhood.

The Dissociative Disorders: Fragmentation of the Self

■ **Dissociative experiences** involve a disruption in awareness, memory, and personal identity. In the **dissociative disorders,** however, dissociative experiences are extreme, frequent, and disruptive.

■ **Dissociative amnesia** refers to the inability to recall important information that is not due to a medical condition and cannot be explained by ordinary forgetfulness. **Dissociative fugue** involves amnesia and sudden, unexplained travel away from home.

■ **Dissociative identity disorder (DID)** involves memory gaps and the presence of two or more distinct identities. Some psychologists are skeptical of dissociative identity disorder. According to one theory, DID is caused by trauma in childhood and represents an extreme form of coping through dissociation.

Schizophrenia: A Different Reality

■ **Schizophrenia** is a psychological disorder that involves severely distorted beliefs, perceptions, and thought processes.

■ The **positive symptoms** of schizophrenia represent excesses in normal functioning. They include **delusions, hallucinations,** and severely disorganized thought processes, speech, and behavior. **Negative symptoms** reflect deficits or decreases in normal functioning. They include flat affect, alogia, and avolition.

■ Three subtypes of schizophrenia are the paranoid type, the catatonic type, and the disorganized type, each of which is distinguished by a particular combination of symptoms. When the pattern of symptoms does not match any of these three subtypes, the diagnosis of undifferentiated type is made.

■ The course of schizophrenia is highly variable. Schizophrenia becomes chronic in about one-half of the people who experience a schizophrenic episode. About one-quarter recover completely, and about one-quarter experience recurrent episodes but are able to function with minimal impairment.

■ Family, twin, and adoption studies have shown that genetics contributes to the development of schizophrenia. However, studies of identical twins demonstrate that nongenetic factors play at least an equal role in the development of schizophrenia. The risk of schizophrenia is higher in the offspring of older fathers.

■ Excess dopamine—the **dopamine hypothesis**—and abnormalities in brain structure and function have been identified as factors associated with schizophrenia.

■ Environmental factors that may be involved in schizophrenia include exposure to a virus during prenatal development and a psychologically unhealthy family environment. Adopted children who were genetically at risk to develop schizophrenia were found to be less likely to develop the disorder when raised in a psychologically healthy family.

Key Terms

psychopathology, p. 507

psychological disorder (mental disorder), p. 507

DSM-IV-TR, p. 507

anxiety, p. 512

anxiety disorders, p. 512

generalized anxiety disorder (GAD), p. 512

panic attack, p. 513

panic disorder, p. 513

phobia, p. 514

specific phobia, p. 514

agoraphobia, p. 515

social phobia (social anxiety disorder), p. 515

posttraumatic stress disorder (PTSD), p. 516

obsessive–compulsive disorder (OCD), p. 517

obsessions, p. 518

compulsions, p. 518

mood disorders, p. 520

major depression, p. 520

dysthymic disorder, p. 521

seasonal affective disorder (SAD), p. 522

bipolar disorder, p. 523

manic episode, p. 523

cyclothymic disorder, p. 523

personality disorder, p. 527

paranoid personality disorder, p. 527

antisocial personality disorder, p. 528

borderline personality disorder, p. 529

dissociative experience, p. 530

dissociative disorders, p. 530

dissociative amnesia, p. 531

dissociative fugue, p. 531

dissociative identity disorder (DID), p. 531

schizophrenia, p. 533

positive symptoms, p. 533

negative symptoms, p. 533

delusion, p. 533

hallucination, p. 534

dopamine hypothesis, p. 540

Web Companion | Review Activities

You can find additional review activities by going to **www.DiscoveringPsychology.com** and clicking on the *Discovering Psychology* 4th Edition text cover. At the Discovering Psychology Web Companion you'll find the chapter learning objectives, flashcards for key terms and key people, interactive crossword puzzles, self-scoring practice quizzes, and other materials to help you master the information in this chapter.

Training Ground

Therapies

Prologue

"A Clear Sense of Being Heard . . ."

How would we describe Marcia? She's an extraordinarily kind, intelligent woman. Her thoughtfulness and sensitivity are tempered by a ready laugh and a good sense of humor. She's happily married, has a good job as a feature writer for a large suburban newspaper, and has two young children, who only occasionally drive her crazy. If Marcia has a flaw, it's that she tends to judge herself much too harshly. She's too quick to blame herself when anything goes wrong.

Juggling a full-time career, marriage, and parenting is a challenge for anyone, but Marcia always makes it look easy. The last time we had dinner at Bill and Marcia's home, the meal featured home-grown vegetables, made-from-scratch bread, and fresh seasonings from the herb pots in the kitchen. Outwardly, Marcia appears to have it all. But a few years ago, she began to experience a pervasive sense of dread and unease—feelings that gradually escalated into a full-scale depression. Marcia describes the onset of her feelings in this way:

> Physically I began to feel as if I were fraying around the edges. I had a constant sense of anxiety and a recurring sense of being a failure. My daughter, Maggie, was going through a rather difficult stage. Andy was still a baby. I felt worn out. I started worrying constantly about my children. Are they safe? Are they sick? What's going to happen? Are my kids going to get hurt? I knew that I really didn't have any reason to worry that much, but I did. It finally struck me that my worrying and my anxiety and my feelings of being a failure were not going to go away on their own.

Marcia decided to seek help. She made an appointment with her therapist, a psychiatrist whom Marcia had last seen 10 years earlier, when she had helped Marcia cope with a very difficult time in her life. Marcia summarizes her experience this way:

> How has therapy helped me? My feelings before a therapy session may vary greatly, depending on the issue under discussion. However, I always find the sessions cathartic and I invariably feel great relief. I feel a sense of being understood by someone who knows me but who is detached from me. I have a clear sense of being heard, as though my therapist has given me a gift of listening and of allowing me to see myself as the worthwhile and capable person I am. It is as though therapy allows me to see more clearly into a mirror that my problems have obscured.

psychotherapy
The treatment of emotional, behavioral, and interpersonal problems through the use of psychological techniques designed to encourage understanding of problems and modify troubling feelings, behaviors, or relationships.

biomedical therapies
The use of medications, electroconvulsive therapy, or other medical treatments to treat the symptoms associated with psychological disorders.

Over the course of several months, Marcia gradually began to feel better. Today, Marcia is calmer, more confident, and feels much more in control of her emotions and her life. As Marcia's mental health improved, so did her relationships with her children and her husband.

Psychotherapy has also helped me communicate more clearly. It has enabled me to become more resilient after some emotional conflict. It has had a preventive effect in helping me to ignore or manage situations that might under certain circumstances trigger depression, anxiety, or obsessive worry. And it makes me a better parent and marriage partner.

Therapy's negative effects? I'm poorer; it costs money. And therapy poses the risk of becoming an end in itself. Psychotherapy has the attraction of being a safe harbor from the petty assaults of everyday life. There's always the danger of losing sight of the goal of becoming a healthier and more productive person, and becoming stuck in the therapy process.

Marcia's experience with psychotherapy reflects many of the themes we will touch on in this chapter. We'll look at different forms of therapy that psychologists and other mental health professionals use to help people cope with psychological problems. We'll also consider the popularity of self-help groups and how they differ from more structured forms of therapy. Toward the end of the chapter, we'll discuss biomedical approaches to the treatment of psychological disorders. Over the course of the chapter, we'll come back to Marcia's story.

Psychotherapy and Biomedical Therapy

Key Theme
- Two forms of therapy are used to treat psychological disorders and personal problems—psychotherapy and the biomedical therapies.

Key Questions
- What is psychotherapy, and what is its basic assumption?
- What is biomedical therapy, and how does it differ from psychotherapy?

Seeking Help People enter psychotherapy for many different reasons. Some people seek to overcome severe psychological disorders, while others want to learn how to cope better with everyday challenges or relationship problems. And, for some people, the goal of therapy is to attain greater self-knowledge or personal fulfillment.

People seek help from mental health professionals for a variety of reasons. Like Marcia, many people seek help because they are suffering from some form of a *psychological disorder*—troubling thoughts, feelings, or behaviors that cause psychological discomfort or interfere with a person's ability to function.

But not everyone who seeks professional help is suffering from a psychological disorder. Many people seek help in dealing with troubled relationships, such as parent–child conflicts or an unhappy marriage. And sometimes people need help with life's transitions, such as coping with the death of a loved one, dissolving a marriage, or adjusting to retirement.

In this chapter, we'll look at the two broad forms of therapy that mental health professionals use to help people: *psychotherapy* and *biomedical therapy*. **Psychotherapy** refers to the use of psychological techniques to treat emotional, behavioral, and interpersonal problems. While there are many different types of psychotherapy, they all share the assumption that psychological factors play a significant role in a person's troubling feelings, behaviors, or relationships. Table 14.1 summarizes the diverse range of mental health professionals who use psychotherapy techniques to help people.

Table 14.1

Who's Who Among Mental Health Professionals

Clinical psychologist	Holds an academic doctorate (PhD, PsyD, or EdD) and is required to be licensed to practice. Assesses and treats mental, emotional, and behavioral disorders. Has expertise in psychological testing and evaluation, diagnosis, psychotherapy, research, and prevention of mental and emotional disorders. May work in private practice, hospitals, or community mental health centers.
Psychiatrist	Holds a medical degree (MD or DO) and is required to be licensed to practice. Has expertise in the diagnosis, treatment, and prevention of mental and emotional disorders. Often has training in psychotherapy. May prescribe medications, electroconvulsive therapy, or other medical procedures.
Psychoanalyst	Usually a psychiatrist or clinical psychologist who has received additional training in the specific techniques of psychoanalysis, the form of psychotherapy originated by Sigmund Freud.
Licensed professional counselor	Holds at least a master's degree in counseling, with extensive supervised training in assessment, counseling, and therapy techniques. May be certified in specialty areas. Most states require licensure or certification.
Psychiatric social worker	Holds a master's degree in social work (MSW). Training includes an internship in a social service agency or mental health center. Most states require certification or licensing. May or may not have training in psychotherapy.
Marriage and family therapist	Usually holds a master's degree, with extensive supervised experience in couple or family therapy. May also have training in individual therapy. Many states require licensing.
Psychiatric nurse	Holds an RN degree and has selected psychiatry or mental health nursing as a specialty area. Typically works on a hospital psychiatric unit or in a community mental health center. May or may not have training in psychotherapy.

In contrast to psychotherapy, the **biomedical therapies** involve the use of medication or other medical treatments to treat the symptoms associated with psychological disorders. Drugs that are used to treat psychological or mental disorders are termed *psychotropic medications*. The biomedical therapies are based on the assumption that the symptoms of many psychological disorders involve biological factors, such as abnormal brain chemistry. As we saw in Chapter 13, the involvement of biological factors in many psychological disorders is well documented. Treating psychological disorders with a combination of psychotherapy and biomedical therapy, especially psychotropic medications, has become increasingly common (Keller & others, 2000; Thase & Jindal, 2004).

Until very recently, only licensed physicians, such as psychiatrists, were legally allowed to prescribe the different forms of biomedical therapy. However, that tradition is changing (Foxhall, 2001a, 2001b). In the 1990s the U.S. Department of Defense conducted a very successful program involving 10 licensed psychologists in the military. The psychologists were given additional intensive training in prescribing psychotropic medications to treat psychological disorders (Dunivin, 2003a; Laskow & Grill, 2003).

The success of the Department of Defense program was one of the factors that persuaded New Mexico lawmakers to enact legislation in 2002 that permitted licensed psychologists to acquire additional training to prescribe psychotropic medications (Dittman, 2003). In 2004, Louisiana became the second state to grant prescription-writing privileges to properly trained psychologists (Holloway, 2004a). Similar legislation is pending in several other states. And, a recent survey of psychology professionals in Canada found that a majority favored

Prescription Privileges for Military Psychologists Lieutenant Colonel Debra Dunivin, a licensed psychologist, was one of the graduates of the Department of Defense's Psychopharmacology Demonstration Project. In the project, Dunivin and other military psychologists underwent intensive postdoctoral training so that they could independently prescribe psychotropic medications for the treatment of psychological disorders. Today, she continues to prescribe medications in her work at Walter Reed Army Medical Center in Washington, D.C. As Dunivin (2003b) explains, "I've learned new intervention skills in pharmacotherapy that enable me to treat a wider range of conditions without splitting the treatment among different providers."

Sigmund Freud and Psychoanalytic Therapy At the beginning of the twentieth century, Sigmund Freud (1856–1939) developed an influential form of psychotherapy called psychoanalysis. Traditional psychoanalysis is not widely practiced today, partly because it is too lengthy and expensive. However, many of the techniques that Freud pioneered, such as free association, dream analysis, and transference, are still commonly used in different forms of psychotherapy.

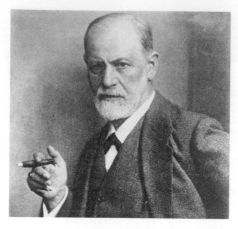

psychoanalysis

A type of psychotherapy originated by Sigmund Freud in which free association, dream interpretation, and analysis of resistance and transference are used to explore repressed or unconscious impulses, anxieties, and internal conflicts.

extending prescription privileges to Canadian clinical psychologists who were properly trained (St-Pierre & Melnyk, 2004).

However, not all psychologists favor the idea of extending prescription privileges to qualified psychologists (see Heiby & others, 2004; Long, 2005). Some argue that clinical psychologists should focus on what they do best: providing psychological interventions and treatments that help people acquire more effective patterns of thinking and behaving. Others are concerned that the safety and well-being of patients could be at risk if psychologists receive inadequate training to prescribe psychotropic medications (Robiner & others, 2003). It remains to be seen if those concerns are valid.

We'll begin this chapter by surveying some of the most influential approaches in psychotherapy: psychoanalytic, humanistic, behavioral, and cognitive. Each approach is based on different assumptions about the underlying causes of psychological problems. And each approach uses different strategies to produce beneficial changes in the way a person thinks, feels, and behaves—the ultimate goal of all forms of psychotherapy. After discussing the effectiveness of psychotherapy, we'll look at the most commonly used biomedical treatments for psychological disorders.

Psychoanalytic Therapy

Key Theme

■ Psychoanalysis is a form of therapy developed by Sigmund Freud and is based on his theory of personality.

Key Questions

■ What are the key assumptions and techniques of psychoanalytic therapy?
■ How do short-term dynamic therapies differ from psychoanalysis, and what is interpersonal therapy?

When cartoonists portray a psychotherapy session, they often draw a person lying on a couch and talking while a bearded gentleman sits behind the patient, passively listening. This stereotype reflects some of the key ingredients of traditional **psychoanalysis,** a form of psychotherapy originally developed by **Sigmund Freud** in the early 1900s. Although psychoanalysis was developed a century ago, its assumptions and techniques continue to influence many psychotherapies today (Luborsky & Barrett, 2006).

Sigmund Freud and Psychoanalysis

As a therapy, traditional psychoanalysis is closely interwoven with Freud's theory of personality. As you may recall from Chapter 10, on personality, Freud stressed that early childhood experiences provided the foundation for later personality development. When early experiences result in unresolved conflicts and frustrated urges, these emotionally charged memories are *repressed,* or pushed out of conscious awareness. Although unconscious, these

Freud's Famous Couch During psychoanalytic sessions, Freud's patients would lie on the couch. Freud himself sat at the head of the couch, out of the patient's view. Freud believed that this arrangement encouraged the patient's free flow of thoughts, feelings, and images. Although some traditional psychoanalysts still have the patient lie on a couch, many psychoanalysts today favor comfortable chairs on which analyst and patient sit, facing each other.

repressed conflicts continue to influence a person's thoughts and behavior, including the dynamics of his relationships with others.

Psychoanalysis is designed to help unearth unconscious conflicts so the patient attains *insight* as to the real source of her problems. Through the intense relationship that develops between the psychoanalyst and the patient, longstanding psychological conflicts are recognized and re-experienced. If the analytic treatment is successful, the conflicts are resolved.

Freud developed several techniques to coax long-repressed memories, impulses, and conflicts to a patient's consciousness (Liff, 1992). In the famous technique called **free association,** the patient spontaneously reports all her thoughts, mental images, and feelings while lying on a couch. The psychoanalyst usually sits out of view, occasionally asking questions to encourage the flow of associations.

Blocks in free association, such as a sudden silence or an abrupt change of topic, were thought to be signs of resistance. **Resistance** is the patient's conscious or unconscious attempts to block the process of revealing repressed memories and conflicts (Luborsky & Barrett, 2006). Resistance is a sign that the patient is uncomfortably close to uncovering psychologically threatening material.

Dream interpretation is another important psychoanalytic technique. Because psychological defenses are reduced during sleep, Freud (1911) believed that unconscious conflicts and repressed impulses were expressed symbolically in dream images. Often, the dream images were used to trigger free associations that might shed light on the dream's symbolic meaning.

More directly, the psychoanalyst sometimes makes carefully timed **interpretations,** explanations of the unconscious meaning of the patient's behavior, thoughts, feelings, or dreams. The timing of such interpretations is important. If an interpretation is offered before the patient is psychologically ready to confront an issue, she may reject the interpretation or respond defensively, increasing resistance (Henry & others, 1994).

One of the most important processes that occurs in the relationship between the patient and the psychoanalyst is called transference. **Transference** occurs when the patient unconsciously responds to the therapist as though the therapist were a significant person in the patient's life, often a parent. As Freud (1940) explained, "The patient sees in his analyst the return—the reincarnation—of some important figure out of his childhood or past, and consequently transfers on to him the feelings and reactions that undoubtedly applied to this model."

The psychoanalyst encourages transference by purposely remaining as neutral as possible. In other words, the psychoanalyst does not reveal personal feelings, take sides, make judgments, or actively advise the patient. This therapeutic neutrality is designed to produce "optimal frustration" so that the patient transfers and projects unresolved conflicts onto the psychoanalyst (Eagle & Wolitzky, 1992).

As the transference become more intense, the patient relives unconscious emotional conflicts that have been repressed since childhood. Only now, these conflicts are being relived and played out in the context of the relationship between the psychoanalyst and the patient.

All these psychoanalytic techniques are designed to help the patient see how past conflicts influence her current behavior and relationships, including her relationship with the psychoanalyst. Once these kinds of insights are achieved, the psychoanalyst helps the patient work through and resolve long-standing conflicts. As resolutions occur, maladaptive behavior patterns that were previously driven by unconscious conflicts can be replaced with more adaptive emotional and behavioral patterns.

The intensive relationship between the patient and the psychoanalyst takes time to develop. On average, the traditional psychoanalyst sees the patient four or five times a week over the course of four years or longer (Garfield & Bergin, 1994). Freud's patients were on the couch six days a week (Liff, 1992). Obviously, traditional psychoanalysis is a slow, expensive process that few people can afford. For those who have the time and the money, traditional psychoanalysis is still available.

> *The resistance accompanies the treatment step by step. Every single association, every act of the person under treatment must reckon with the resistance and represents a compromise between the forces that are striving towards recovery and opposing ones.*
>
> Sigmund Freud (1912)

free association
A technique used in psychoanalysis in which the patient spontaneously reports all thoughts, feelings, and mental images as they come to mind, as a way of revealing unconscious thoughts and emotions.

resistance
In psychoanalysis, the patient's unconscious attempts to block the revelation of repressed memories and conflicts.

dream interpretation
A technique used in psychoanalysis in which the content of dreams is analyzed for disguised or symbolic wishes, meanings, and motivations.

interpretation
A technique used in psychoanalysis in which the psychoanalyst offers a carefully timed explanation of the patient's dreams, free associations, or behaviors to facilitate the recognition of unconscious conflicts or motivations.

transference
In psychoanalysis, the process by which emotions and desires originally associated with a significant person in the patient's life, such as a parent, are unconsciously transferred to the psychoanalyst.

short-term dynamic therapies
Type of psychotherapy that is based on psychoanalytic theory but differs in that it is typically time-limited, has specific goals, and involves an active, rather than neutral, role for the therapist.

interpersonal therapy (IPT)
A brief, psychodynamic psychotherapy that focuses on current relationships and is based on the assumption that symptoms are caused and maintained by interpersonal problems.

client-centered therapy
A type of psychotherapy developed by humanistic psychologist Carl Rogers in which the therapist is nondirective and reflective, and the client directs the focus of each therapy session; also called *person-centered therapy.*

Short-Term Dynamic Therapies

Most people entering psychotherapy today are not seeking the kind of major personality overhaul that traditional psychoanalysis is designed to produce. Instead, people come to therapy expecting help with specific problems. People also expect therapy to provide beneficial changes in a matter of weeks or months, not years.

Many different forms of **short-term dynamic therapies** based on traditional psychoanalytic notions are now available (Binder & others, 1995; Levenson, 2003). These short-term dynamic therapies have several features in common (Koss & Shiang, 1994). Therapeutic contact lasts for no more than a few months. The patient's problems are quickly assessed at the beginning of therapy. The therapist and patient agree on specific, concrete, and attainable goals. In the actual sessions, most psychodynamic therapists are more directive than are traditional psychoanalysts, actively engaging the patient in a dialogue.

As in traditional psychoanalysis, the therapist uses interpretations to help the patient recognize hidden feelings and transferences that may be occurring in important relationships in her life (Liff, 1992).

One particularly influential short-term psychodynamic therapy is **interpersonal therapy,** abbreviated **IPT.** In contrast to other psychodynamic therapies, interpersonal therapy focuses on *current* relationships and social interactions rather than on past relationships. Originally developed as a brief treatment for depression, interpersonal therapy is based on the assumption that psychological symptoms are caused and maintained by interpersonal problems (Klerman & others, 1984; Weissman & others, 2000).

Interpersonal therapy may be brief or long-term, but it is highly structured (Klerman & Weissman, 1993). In the first phase of treatment, the therapist identifies the interpersonal problem that is causing difficulties. In the interpersonal therapy model, there are four categories of personal problems: unresolved grief, role disputes, role transitions, and interpersonal deficits. *Unresolved grief* refers to problems dealing with the death of significant others, while *role disputes* refer to repetitive conflicts with significant others, such as the person's partner, family members, friends, or co-workers. *Role transitions* include problems involving major life changes, such as going away to college, becoming a parent, getting married or divorced, or retiring. *Interpersonal deficits* refer to absent or faulty social skills that limit the ability to start or maintain healthy relationships with others (Mallinckrodt, 2001). During treatment, the therapist helps the person understand his particular interpersonal problem and develop strategies to resolve it.

IPT is used to treat eating disorders and substance abuse as well as depression. It is also effective in helping people deal with interpersonal problems, such as marital conflict, parenting issues, and conflicts at work (Weissman & others, 2000; Whisman, 2001). In one innovative application, IPT was successfully used to treat symptoms of depression in villagers in Uganda, demonstrating its effectiveness in a non-Western culture (Bolton & others, 2003).

Were Sigmund Freud alive today, would he be upset by these departures from traditional psychoanalysis? Not at all. In fact, Freud himself treated some of his patients using short-term psychodynamic therapy that sometimes lasted for only one lengthy session. Several of Freud's patients completed psychoanalysis in as little as two months (Magnavita, 1993).

Even though traditional, lengthy psychoanalysis is uncommon today, Freud's basic assumptions and techniques continue to be influential. Although contemporary research has challenged some of Freud's original ideas, modern researchers are also studying the specific factors that seem to influence the effectiveness of basic Freudian techniques, such as dream analysis, interpretation, transference, and the role of insight in reducing psychological symptoms (Glucksman & Kramer, 2004; Luborsky & Barrett, 2006).

BIZARRO

AT THE RISK OF SOUNDING CLICHE, DOCTOR, LET ME SAY THAT I HAVE CERTAIN UNRESOLVED ISSUES REGARDING MY PARENTS.

Humanistic Therapy

Key Theme
- The most influential humanistic psychotherapy is client-centered therapy, which was developed by Carl Rogers.

Key Questions
- What are the key assumptions of humanistic therapy, including client-centered therapy?
- What therapeutic techniques and conditions are important in client-centered therapy?
- How do client-centered therapy and psychoanalysis differ?

The *humanistic perspective* in psychology emphasizes human potential, self-awareness, and freedom of choice (see Chapter 10). Humanistic psychologists contend that the most important factor in personality is the individual's conscious, subjective perception of his or her self. They see people as being innately good and motivated by the need to grow psychologically. If people are raised in a genuinely accepting atmosphere and given freedom to make choices, they will develop healthy self-concepts and strive to fulfill their unique potential as human beings (Cain, 2002; Rice & Greenberg, 1992).

Carl Rogers and Client-Centered Therapy

The humanistic perspective has exerted a strong influence on psychotherapy (Cain, 2002, 2003). Probably the most influential of the humanistic psychotherapies is **client-centered therapy,** also called *person-centered therapy,* developed by **Carl Rogers.** In naming his therapy, Rogers (1951) deliberately used the word *client* rather than *patient*. He believed that the medical term *patient* implied that people in therapy were "sick" and were seeking treatment from an all-knowing authority figure who could "heal" or "cure" them. Instead of stressing the therapist's expertise or perceptions of the patient, client-centered therapy emphasizes the *client's* subjective perception of himself and his environment (Zimring & Raskin, 1992).

Like Freud, Rogers saw the therapeutic relationship as the catalyst that leads to insight and lasting personality change. But Rogers viewed the nature of this relationship very differently from Freud. According to Rogers (1977), the therapist should not exert power by offering carefully timed "interpretations" of the patient's unconscious conflicts. Advocating just the opposite, Rogers believed that the therapist should be *nondirective*. That is, the therapist must not direct the client, make decisions for the client, offer solutions, or pass judgment on the client's thoughts or feelings. Instead, Rogers believed, change in therapy must be chosen and directed by the client (Bozarth & others, 2002). The therapist's role is to create the conditions that allow the client, not the therapist, to direct the focus of therapy.

What are the therapeutic conditions that promote self-awareness, psychological growth, and self-directed change? Rogers (1957c, 1980) believed that three qualities of the therapist are necessary: *genuineness, unconditional positive regard,* and *empathic understanding*. First, *genuineness* means that the therapist honestly and openly shares her thoughts and feelings with the client. By modeling genuineness, the therapist indirectly encourages the client to exercise this capability more fully in himself.

Carl Rogers (1902–1987) Shown on the far right, Rogers contended that human potential would flourish in an atmosphere of genuineness, unconditional positive regard, and empathic understanding. Rogers filmed many of his therapy sessions as part of a research program to identify the most helpful aspects of client-centered therapy.

Client-Centered Therapy The client-centered therapist strives to create a warm, accepting climate that allows the client the freedom to explore troubling issues. The therapist engages in active listening, reflecting both the content and the personal meaning of what the client is saying. In doing so, the therapist helps the client develop a clearer perception and understanding of her own feelings and motives.

Second, the therapist must value, accept, and care for the client, whatever her problems or behavior. Rogers called this quality *unconditional positive regard.* Rogers believed that people develop psychological problems largely because they have consistently experienced only *conditional acceptance.* That is, parents, teachers, and others have communicated this message to the client: "I will accept you only *if* you conform to my expectations." Because acceptance by significant others has been conditional, the person has cut off or denied unacceptable aspects of herself, distorting her self-concept. In turn, these distorted perceptions affect her thoughts and behaviors in unhealthy, unproductive ways.

The therapist who successfully creates a climate of unconditional positive regard fosters the person's natural tendency to move toward self-fulfilling decisions without fear of evaluation or rejection. Rogers (1977) described this important aspect of therapy in this way:

> Unconditional positive regard means that when the therapist is experiencing a positive, acceptant attitude toward whatever the client *is* at that moment, therapeutic movement or change is more likely. It involves the therapist's willingness for the client to be whatever feeling is going on at that moment— confusion, resentment, fear, anger, courage, love, or pride. . . . The therapist prizes the client in a total rather than a conditional way.

Third, the therapist must communicate *empathic understanding* by reflecting the content and personal meaning of the feelings being experienced by the client. In effect, the therapist creates a psychological mirror, reflecting the client's thoughts and feelings as they exist in the client's private inner world. The goal is to help the client explore and clarify his feelings, thoughts, and perceptions. In the process, the client begins to see himself, and his problems, more clearly (Egan, 1994).

Empathic understanding requires the therapist to listen *actively* for the personal meaning beneath the surface of what the client is saying (Watson, 2002). Rogers believed that when the therapeutic atmosphere contains genuineness, unconditional positive regard, and empathic understanding, change is more likely to occur. Such conditions foster feelings of being psychologically safe, accepted, and valued. In this therapeutic atmosphere, change occurs as the person's self-concept and worldview gradually become healthier and less distorted. According to Rogers (1977), "As the client becomes more self-aware, more self-acceptant, less defensive and more open, she finds at last some of the freedom to grow and change in directions natural to the human organism." In effect, the client is moving in the direction of *self-actualization*—the realization of his or her unique potentials and talents.

A large number of studies have generally supported the importance of genuineness, unconditional positive regard, and empathic understanding (Asay &

An empathic way of being with another person has several facets. It means entering the private perceptual world of the other and becoming thoroughly at home in it. It involves being sensitive, moment by moment, to the changing felt meanings which flow in this other person, to the fear or rage or tenderness or confusion or whatever that he or she is experiencing.

Carl Rogers (1980)

PEANUTS

Lambert, 2002). Such factors promote trust and self-exploration in therapy. However, these conditions, by themselves, may not be sufficient to help clients change (Cain & Seeman, 2002; Sachse & Elliott, 2002).

Motivational Interviewing: Helping Clients Commit to Change

Carl Rogers and his client-centered therapy have had an enormous impact (Kirschenbaum, 2004). The client-centered approach continues to be developed by therapists, teachers, social workers, and counselors (Elliott & Greenberg, 2002). Of particular note has been the development of motivational interviewing. *Motivational interviewing (MI)* is designed to help clients overcome the mixed feelings or reluctance they might have about committing to change. Usually lasting only a session or two, MI is more directive than traditional client-centered therapy (Hettema & others, 2005).

The main goal of MI is to encourage and strengthen the client's self-motivating statements or "change talk." These are expressions of the client's need, desire, and reasons for change. Using client-centered techniques, the therapist responds with empathic understanding and reflective listening, helping the client explore his or her own values and motivations for change. When the client expresses reluctance, the therapist acknowledges the mixed feelings and redirects the emphasis toward change. As Jennifer Hettema and her colleagues (2005) explain:

> The counselor seeks to evoke the client's own motivation, with confidence in the human desire and capacity to grow in positive directions. Instead of implying that "I have what you need," MI communicates, "You have what you need." In this way, MI falls squarely within the humanistic "third force" in the history of psychotherapy.

Along with being influential in individual psychotherapy, the client-centered approach has been applied to marital counseling, parenting, education, business, and even community and international relations (Criswell, 2003; K. Schneider, 1998). Table 14.2 compares some aspects of psychoanalysis and client-centered therapy.

Table 14.2

Comparing Psychodynamic and Humanistic Therapies

Type of Therapy	Founder	Source of Problems	Treatment Techniques	Goals of Therapy
Psychoanalysis	Sigmund Freud	Repressed, unconscious conflicts stemming from early childhood experiences	Free association, analysis of dream content, interpretation, and transference	To recognize, work through, and resolve long-standing conflicts
Client-centered therapy	Carl Rogers	Conditional acceptance that causes the person to develop a distorted self-concept and worldview	Nondirective therapist who displays unconditional positive regard, genuineness, and empathic understanding	To develop self-awareness, self-acceptance, and self-determination

Behavior Therapy—From Bad Habits to Severe Psychological Disorders Nail biting and cigarette smoking are examples of the kinds of everyday maladaptive behaviors that can be successfully treated with behavior therapy. Behavioral techniques can also be used to treat more severe psychological problems, such as phobias, and to improve functioning in people with severe mental disorders such as schizophrenia and autism.

behavior therapy
A type of psychotherapy that focuses on directly changing maladaptive behavior patterns by using basic learning principles and techniques; also called *behavior modification.*

counterconditioning
A behavior therapy technique based on classical conditioning that involves modifying behavior by conditioning a new response that is incompatible with a previously learned response.

systematic desensitization
A type of behavior therapy in which phobic responses are reduced by pairing relaxation with a series of mental images or real-life situations that the person finds progressively more fear-provoking; based on the principle of counterconditioning.

Behavior Therapy

Key Theme
- Behavior therapy uses learning principles to directly change problem behaviors.

Key Questions
- What are the key assumptions of behavior therapy?
- What therapeutic techniques are based on classical conditioning, and how are they used to treat psychological disorders and problems?
- What therapy treatments are based on operant conditioning, and how are they used to treat psychological disorders and problems?

Psychoanalysis, client-centered therapy, and other insight-oriented therapies maintain that the road to psychologically healthier behavior is through increased self-understanding of motives and conflicts. As insights are acquired through therapy, problem behaviors and feelings presumably will give way to more adaptive behaviors and emotional reactions.

However, gaining insight into the source of problems does not necessarily result in desirable changes in behavior and emotions. Even though you fully understand *why* you are behaving in counterproductive ways, your maladaptive or self-defeating behaviors may continue. For instance, an adult who is extremely anxious about public speaking may understand that he feels that way because he was raised by a critical and demanding parent. But having this insight into the underlying cause of his anxiety may do little, if anything, to reduce his anxiety or change his avoidance of public speaking.

In sharp contrast to the insight-oriented therapies we discussed in the preceding sections, the goal of **behavior therapy,** also called *behavior modification,* is to modify specific problem behaviors, not to change the entire personality. And, rather than focusing on the past, behavior therapists focus on current behaviors.

Behavior therapists assume that maladaptive behaviors are *learned,* just as adaptive behaviors are. Thus, the basic strategy in behavior therapy involves unlearning maladaptive behaviors and learning more adaptive behaviors in their place. Behavior therapists employ techniques that are based on the learning principles of classical conditioning, operant conditioning, and observational learning to modify the problem behavior.

Techniques Based on Classical Conditioning

Just as Pavlov's dogs learned to salivate to a ringing bell that had become associated with food, learned associations can be at the core of some maladaptive behaviors, including strong negative emotional reactions. In the 1920s, psychologist John Watson demonstrated this phenomenon with his famous "Little Albert" study. In Chapter 5, we described how Watson classically conditioned an infant known as Little Albert to fear a tame lab rat by repeatedly pairing the rat with a loud clanging sound. Over time, Albert's conditioned fear generalized to other furry objects, including a fur coat, cotton, and a Santa Claus mask (Watson & Rayner, 1920).

Mary Cover Jones
The First Behavior Therapist

Watson himself never tried to eliminate Little Albert's fears. But Watson's research inspired one of his students, **Mary Cover Jones,** to explore ways of reversing conditioned fears. With Watson acting as a consultant, Jones (1924a) treated a 3-year-old named Peter who "seemed almost to be Albert grown a bit older." Like Little Albert, Peter was fearful of various furry objects, including a tame rat, a fur coat, cotton, and wool. Because Peter was especially afraid of a tame rabbit, Jones focused on eliminating the rabbit fear. She used a procedure that has come to be known as **counterconditioning**—the learning of a new conditioned response that is incompatible with a previously learned response.

Jones's procedure was very simple (Jones, 1924b; Watson, 1924). The caged rabbit was brought into Peter's view but kept far enough away to avoid eliciting fear (the original conditioned response). With the rabbit visible at a tolerable distance, Peter sat in a high chair and happily munched his favorite snack, milk and crackers. Peter's favorite food was used because, presumably, the enjoyment of eating would naturally elicit a positive response (the desired conditioned response). Such a positive response would be incompatible with the negative response of fear.

Every day for almost two months, the rabbit was inched closer and closer to Peter as he ate his milk and crackers. As Peter's tolerance for the rabbit's presence gradually increased, he was eventually able to hold the rabbit in his lap, petting it with one hand while happily eating with his other hand (Jones, 1924a, 1924b). Not only was Peter's fear of the rabbit eliminated, but he also stopped being afraid of other furry objects, including the rat, cotton, and the fur coat (Watson, 1924).

Along with counterconditioning, Jones (1924a) used social imitation, or *observational learning,* techniques to help eliminate Peter's fear of rabbits (Kornfeld, 1989). As part of the treatment, Peter observed other children petting or holding the tame rabbit. Eventually, Peter imitated the actions of the nonfearful children. For her pioneering efforts in the treatment of children's fears, Jones is widely regarded as the first behavior therapist (Gieser, 1993; Reiss, 1990).

Systematic Desensitization

Mary Cover Jones's pioneering studies in treating children's fears laid the groundwork for the later development of a more standardized procedure to treat phobias and other anxiety disorders. Developed by South African psychiatrist Joseph Wolpe in the 1950s, the procedure is called *systematic desensitization* (Wolpe, 1958, 1982). Based on the same premise as counterconditioning, **systematic desensitization** involves learning a new conditioned response (relaxation) that is incompatible with or inhibits the old conditioned response (fear and anxiety).

Three basic steps are involved in systematic desensitization (Morris, 1991). First, the patient learns *progressive relaxation,* which involves successively relaxing one muscle group after another until a deep state of relaxation is achieved. Second, the behavior therapist helps the patient construct an *anxiety hierarchy,* which is a list of anxiety-provoking images associated with the feared situation, arranged in a hierarchy from least to most anxiety-producing (see Figure 14.1). The patient also develops an image of a relaxing *control scene,* such as walking on a secluded beach on a sunny day.

The third step involves the actual process of desensitization. While deeply relaxed, the patient imagines the least threatening scene on the anxiety hierarchy. After he can maintain complete relaxation while imagining this scene, he moves to the next. If the patient begins to feel anxiety or tension, the behavior therapist guides him back to imagining the previous scene or the control scene. If necessary, the therapist helps the patient relax again, using the progressive relaxation technique.

Over several sessions, the patient gradually and systematically works his way up the hierarchy, imagining each scene while maintaining complete relaxation. Very systematically, each imagined scene becomes paired with a conditioned response of relaxation rather than anxiety, and desensitization to the feared situation takes place. Once mastered with mental images, the desensitization procedure may be continued in the actual feared situation. If the technique is successful, the feared situation no longer produces a conditioned response of fear and anxiety. In practice, systematic desensitization is often combined with other techniques, such as *observational learning* (Bandura, 2004b). For example, as part of a treatment program for people who were phobic of dental treatment, participants watched videotapes of

Mary Cover Jones (1896–1987) This photograph, taken around 1919, shows Mary Cover Jones as a college student in her early twenties. Although Jones pioneered the use of behavioral techniques in therapy, she did not consider herself a "behaviorist" and ultimately came to disagree with many of Watson's views. Fifty years after she treated Peter, Jones (1975) wrote, "Now I would be less satisfied to treat the fears of a three-year-old . . . in isolation from him as a tantalizingly complex person with unique potentials for stability and change."

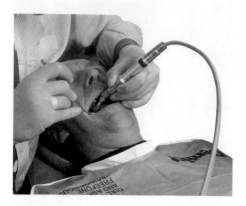

FIGURE 14.1 A Sample Anxiety Hierarchy Used in Systematic Desensitization As part of systematic desensitization, the therapist helps the client develop an anxiety hierarchy. The sample anxiety hierarchy shown here illustrates the kinds of scenes that might be listed by a person who is phobic of dental treatment (Getka & Glass, 1992). Starting at the bottom of the hierarchy, relaxation is paired with each scene until the client can calmly visualize the image. Only then does he move to the next scene in the hierarchy.

Degree of Fear	Imagined Scene
100	Holding mouth open, eyes closed, listening to the sound of the dental drill as a cavity is repaired
95	Holding mouth open in preparation for an oral injection
90	Lying back in dental chair, eyes closed, as dentist examines teeth
85	Lying back in dental chair, mouth open, listening to the sounds of dental equipment, as dental technician cleans teeth
80	Lying in dental chair, watching dental technician unwrap sterilized dental tools
75	Being greeted by the dental technician and walking back to dental examination chair
70	Sitting in dentist's waiting room
60	Driving to dentist's office for appointment
50	Looking at the bright yellow reminder postcard on the refrigerator and thinking about dental appointment
40	Listening to a family member talk about her last dental visit
30	Looking at television or magazine advertisements depicting people in a dentist's chair
25	Calling dentist's office to make an appointment
20	Thinking about calling dentist's office to set up an appointment
15	Driving past dentist's office on a workday
10	Driving past dentist's office on a Sunday afternoon

patients calmly receiving routine dental care (Getka & Glass, 1992). In another example, medical students who suffered from test anxiety combined systematic desensitization with exercise, rehearsal of test-taking behaviors, and actual practice using study guides and practice tests (Powell, 2004). Finally, Box 14.1 describes how computer technology is used to treat phobias and other anxiety disorders.

The Bell and Pad Treatment

Another problem that has been effectively treated by techniques based on classical conditioning is bedwetting by children over the age of 6. (Occasional bedwetting by children under the age of 6 is not considered a clinical problem.) Children who are bedwetters tend to be very deep sleepers. Behavior therapy is based on the assumption that the child who wets the bed has not learned to wake up when his bladder is full. The **bell and pad treatment** uses classical conditioning to pair arousal with the sensation of a full bladder.

A special insulated pad is placed under the bottom bedsheet. When the child starts to wet the bed, a loud bell goes off, waking the child. After shutting off the alarm, the child uses the bathroom and then changes the sheet. Before going back to bed, he resets the alarm.

Over the course of a few weeks, the child becomes conditioned so that the sensation of a full bladder (the conditioned stimulus) triggers waking arousal (the desired conditioned response). In the process, the child's sleeping cycles are also modified so that the child is not such a heavy sleeper. In use since the 1930s, the bell and pad treatment is highly effective, with a success rate of about 75 percent. Pharmacological treatments for bedwetting are also available, but the bell and pad approach has many advantages over drug treatment (Mikkelson, 2001). Along with being less expensive than drug treatments, its effects are longer lasting, with a much lower rate of relapse when treatment ends.

Aversive Conditioning

The psychologist John Garcia first demonstrated how taste aversions could be classically conditioned (see Chapter 5). After rats drank a sweet-flavored water, Garcia injected them with a drug that made them ill. The rats developed a strong taste aversion for the sweet-flavored water, avoiding it altogether (Garcia & others, 1966). In much the same way, **aversive conditioning** attempts to create an unpleasant conditioned response to a harmful stimulus, such as cigarette smoking or alcohol consumption. For substance abuse and addiction, taste aversions are commonly induced with the use of nausea-inducing drugs. For example, a medication called *Antabuse* is used in aversion therapy for alcoholism. If a person taking

bell and pad treatment
A behavior therapy technique used to treat nighttime bedwetting by conditioning arousal from sleep in response to bodily signals of a full bladder.

aversive conditioning
A relatively ineffective type of behavior therapy that involves repeatedly pairing an aversive stimulus with the occurrence of undesirable behaviors or thoughts.

IN FOCUS 14.1

Using Virtual Reality to Conquer Phobias

Virtual reality (VR) therapy consists of computer-generated scenes that you view using a special motion-sensitive helmet, as shown in the photograph. Move your head in any direction and an electromagnetic sensor in the helmet detects the movement, and the computer-generated scene you see changes accordingly. Turning a handgrip lets you move forward or backward to explore your artificial world. You can also use a virtual hand to reach out and touch objects, such as an elevator button or a spider.

VR technology is now being used in the treatment of specific phobias, including fear of flying, heights, spiders, and enclosed places (Garcia-Palacios & others, 2002; Rothbaum & others, 2002). In the virtual reality scene, patients are progressively exposed to the feared object or situation. For example, psychologist Ralph Lamson used virtual reality as a form of computer-assisted systematic desensitization to help more than 60 patients conquer their fear of heights. Rather than mental images, the person experiences computer-generated images that seem almost real. Once the helmet is donned, patients begin a 40-minute journey that starts in a café and progresses to a narrow wooden plank that leads to a bridge.

Although computer-generated and cartoonlike, the scenes of being high above the ground on the plank or bridge are real enough to trigger the physiological indicators of anxiety. Lamson encourages the person to stay in the same spot until the anxiety diminishes. Once relaxed, the person continues the

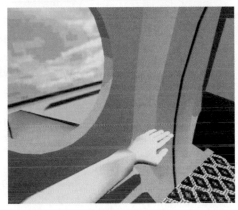

VR journey. By the time the person makes the return journey back over the plank, heart rate and blood pressure are close to normal. After virtual reality therapy, over 90 percent of Lamson's patients successfully rode a glass elevator up to the 15th floor.

Once experimental, virtual reality therapy has become an accepted treatment for specific phobias and is now being extended to other anxiety disorders, such as social phobia, panic disorder, and acrophobia (Anderson & others, 2003; Botella & others, 2004; Krijn & others, 2004). One innovative application of VR therapy is in the treatment of posttraumatic stress disorder (PTSD) in Vietnam War veterans and others (Rothbaum & Schwartz, 2002). Many PTSD patients are unable or unwilling to mentally re-create the traumatic events that caused their disorder, but the vivid sensory details of the "virtual world" encourage the patient to relive the experience in a controlled fashion.

For example, a young woman who suffered from severe PTSD after witnessing and barely escaping the attack on the World Trade Center was finally able to relive the events of the day through controlled, graduated exposure to a virtual reenactment of the events (Difede & Hoffman, 2002). Similarly, war veterans can be exposed to the sights and sounds of combat in a way that could not be accomplished in the "real world" of a therapist's office or busy downtown street.

VR therapy is easier and less expensive to administer than graduated exposure to the actual feared object or situation. Another advantage is that the availability of VR may make people who are extremely phobic more willing to seek treatment. In one survey of people who were phobic of spiders, more than 80 percent preferred virtual reality treatment over graduated exposure to real spiders (Garcia-Palacios & others, 2001).

Antabuse consumes any amount of alcohol, he or she will experience extreme nausea (Owen-Howard, 2001). For some behavioral problems, such as sexual deviance or compulsive self-injury, mild electric shocks are used.

Aversive conditioning techniques have been used to treat cigarette smoking and other substance abuse, sexual deviance, self-injurious behavior, and compulsive gambling (see Emmelkamp, 2004). The effectiveness of aversive conditioning in treating substance abuse is enhanced when clients are very motivated and when it is combined with other forms of therapy (Bordnick & others, 2004; Carroll & others, 2000). In general, however, aversive conditioning is not very effective and its use is not widespread (Emmelkamp, 2004).

The Bell and Pad Treatment for Bedwetting On the bedside table is an electronic device that monitors a moisture-sensitive pad that is placed below the bottom sheet of the bed. If the child wets the bed, a loud buzzer and a bright light are activated, waking the child. Over the course of several weeks, the bell and pad device conditions arousal from sleep in response to bodily signals of a full bladder.

token economy
A form of behavior therapy in which the therapeutic environment is structured to reward desired behaviors with tokens or points that may eventually be exchanged for tangible rewards.

cognitive therapies
A group of psychotherapies based on the assumption that psychological problems are due to maladaptive patterns of thinking; treatment techniques focus on recognizing and altering these unhealthy thinking patterns.

Techniques Based on Operant Conditioning

B. F. Skinner's *operant conditioning* model of learning is based on the simple principle that behavior is shaped and maintained by its consequences (see Chapter 5). Behavior therapists have developed several treatment techniques that are derived from operant conditioning. *Shaping* involves reinforcing successive approximations of a desired behavior. Shaping is often used to teach appropriate behaviors to patients who are mentally disabled by autism, mental retardation, or severe mental illness. For example, shaping has been used to increase the attention span of hospitalized patients with severe schizophrenia (Silverstein & others, 2001).

Other operant conditioning techniques involve controlling the consequences that follow behaviors. *Positive* and *negative reinforcement* are used to increase the incidence of desired behaviors. *Extinction,* or the absence of reinforcement, is used to reduce the occurrence of undesired behaviors.

Let's illustrate how operant techniques are used in therapy by describing a behavioral program to treat a 4-year-old girl's sleeping problems (Ronen, 1991). The first step in the treatment program was to identify specific problem behaviors and determine their *baseline rate,* or how often each problem occurred before treatment began. After measuring the baseline rate, the therapist could target each problem behavior individually and objectively measure the child's progress. The parents next identified several very specific behavioral goals for their daughter. These goals included not crying when she was put to bed, not crying if she woke up in the night, not getting into her parents' bed, and staying in her own bed throughout the night.

The parents were taught operant techniques to decrease the undesirable behaviors and increase desirable ones. For example, to *extinguish* the girl's screaming and crying, the parents were taught to ignore the behavior rather than continue to reinforce it with parental attention. In contrast, desirable behaviors were to be *positively reinforced* with abundant praise, encouragement, social attention, and other rewards. Figure 14.2 shows the little girl's progress for three specific problem behaviors.

Operant conditioning techniques have been applied to many different kinds of psychological problems, from habit and weight control to helping autistic children learn to speak and behave more adaptively. Techniques based on operant conditioning have also been successfully used to modify the behavior of people who are severely disabled by retardation or mental disorders (O'Leary & Wilson, 1987).

The **token economy** is an example of the use of operant conditioning techniques to modify the behavior of groups of people (Bloxham & others, 1993). A token economy is a very structured environment, a system for strengthening deisred behaviors through positive reinforcement. Basically, tokens or points are awarded as positive reinforcers for desirable behaviors and withheld or taken away for undesirable behaviors. The tokens can be exchanged for other reinforcers, such as special privileges.

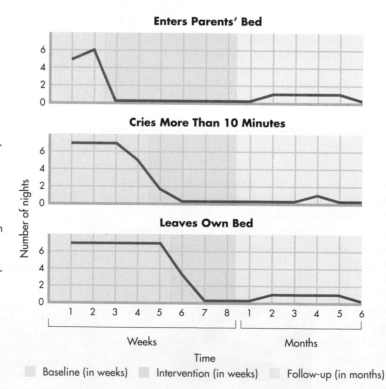

FIGURE 14.2 The Effect of Operant Conditioning Techniques These graphs depict the changes in three specific sleep-related problem behaviors of a 4-year-old girl over the course of behavioral therapy. The intervention for each problem behavior was introduced separately over several weeks. As you can see, behavior therapy produced a rapid reduction in the rate of each problem behavior. The green area shows the maintenance of desired behavior changes over a six-month follow-up.

SOURCE: Adapted from Ronen (1991).

Token economies have been used in prisons, classrooms, and juvenile correction institutions, as well as with people diagnosed with psychiatric disorders or mental retardation in hospitals and group homes (Field & others, 2004; Glenn, 1990; Kazdin, 1982). They have been shown to be effective even with severely disturbed patients who have been hospitalized for many years (Paul & Menditto, 1992). However, token economies proved difficult to implement, especially in community-based outpatient clinics, so they are not in wide use today (R. Lieberman, 2000).

A modified version of the token economy has been used with outpatients in a treatment program called *contingency management interventions*. Like the token economy, a contingency management intervention involves carefully specified behaviors, a target group of clients or patients, and the use of vouchers or other conditioned reinforcers that can be exchanged for prizes, cash, or other rewards. Contingency management interventions have proven to be especially effective in the outpatient treatment of people who are dependent on heroin, cocaine, alcohol, or multiple drugs (Lamb & others, 2004; Petry & others, 2004). In some cases, the contingency management interventions significantly reduced substance abuse in patients for whom other forms of treatment had failed.

Table 14.3 briefly summarizes key points about behavior therapy.

Table 14.3

Behavior Therapy

Type of Therapy	Foundation	Source of Problems	Treatment Techniques	Goals of Therapy
Behavior therapy	Based on classical conditioning, operant conditioning, and observational learning	Learned maladaptive behavior patterns	Systematic desensitization, virtual reality, bell and pad treatment, aversive conditioning, reinforcement and extinction, token economy, contingency management interventions, observational learning	To unlearn maladaptive behaviors and replace them with adaptive, appropriate behaviors

Cognitive Therapies

Key Theme
- Cognitive therapies are based on the assumption that psychological problems are due to maladaptive thinking.

Key Questions
- What are rational-emotive therapy and cognitive therapy, and how do they differ?
- What is cognitive-behavioral therapy?

Whereas behavior therapy assumes that faulty learning is at the core of problem behaviors and emotions, the **cognitive therapies** assume that the culprit is *faulty thinking*. The key assumption of the cognitive therapies could be put like this: Most people blame their unhappiness and problems on external events and situations, but the real cause of unhappiness is the way the person *thinks* about the events, not the events themselves. Thus, cognitive therapists zero in on the faulty patterns of thinking that they believe are causing the psychological problems. Once faulty patterns of thinking have been identified, the next step is to *change* them to more adaptive, healthy patterns of thinking. In this section, we'll look at how this change is accomplished in two influential forms of cognitive therapy: Ellis's *rational-emotive therapy* (RET) and Beck's *cognitive therapy* (CT).

There is nothing either good or bad, but thinking makes it so.

William Shakespeare, *Hamlet*

Albert Ellis (b. 1913) A colorful and sometimes controversial figure, Albert Ellis developed rational-emotive therapy (RET). Rational-emotive therapy promotes psychologically healthier thought processes by disputing irrational beliefs and replacing them with more rational interpretations of events.

Albert Ellis and Rational-Emotive Therapy

Shakespeare said it more eloquently, but psychologist **Albert Ellis** has expressed the same sentiment: "You largely feel the way you think." Ellis was trained as both a clinical psychologist and a psychoanalyst. As a practicing psychoanalyst, Ellis became increasingly disappointed with the psychoanalytic approach to solving human problems. Psychoanalysis simply didn't seem to work: His patients would have insight after insight, yet never get any better.

In the 1950s, Ellis began to take a more active, directive role in his therapy sessions. He developed **rational-emotive therapy,** abbreviated **RET** in the 1950s. RET is based on the assumption that "people are not disturbed by things but rather by their view of things" (Ellis, 1991). The key premise of RET is that people's difficulties are caused by their faulty expectations and irrational beliefs. Rational-emotive therapy focuses on changing the patterns of irrational thinking that are believed to be the primary cause of the client's emotional distress and psychological problems.

Ellis points out that most people mistakenly believe that they become upset and unhappy because of external events. But Ellis (1993) would argue that it's not external events that make people miserable—it's their *interpretation* of those events. It's not David's behavior that's really making Carrie miserable—it's Carrie's *interpretation* of the meaning of David's behavior. In rational-emotive therapy, psychological problems are explained by the "ABC" model, as shown in Figure 14.3. According to this model, when an *Activating event* (**A**) occurs, it is the person's *Beliefs* (**B**) about the event that cause emotional *Consequences* (**C**). Notice how this differs from the commonsense view that it is the event (A) that causes the emotional and behavioral consequences (C).

Identifying the core irrational beliefs that underlie personal distress is the first step in rational-emotive therapy. Often, irrational beliefs reflect "musts" and "shoulds" that are absolutes, such as the notion that "I should be competent at everything I do." Other common irrational beliefs are listed in Table 14.4.

The consequences of such thinking are unhealthy negative emotions, like extreme anger, despair, resentment, and feelings of worthlessness. Not only does the person feel miserable, but she also feels that she is unable to control or cope with an upsetting situation. These kinds of irrational cognitive and emotional responses interfere with constructive attempts to change disturbing situations (Ellis & Harper, 1975). According to RET, the result is self-defeating behaviors, anxiety disorders, depression, and other psychological problems.

FIGURE 14.3 The "ABC" Model in Rational-Emotive Therapy Common sense tells us that unhappiness and other unpleasant emotions are caused by unpleasant or disturbing events. This view is shown in the top part of the figure. But Albert Ellis (1993) points out that it is really our *beliefs* about the events, not the events themselves, that make us miserable, as diagrammed in the bottom part of the figure.

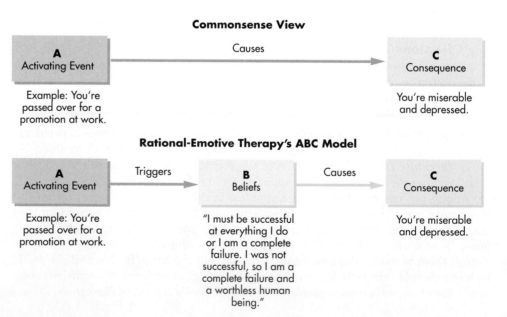

Table 14.4

Irrational Beliefs

1 It is a dire necessity for you to be loved or approved by virtually everyone in your community.

2 You must be thoroughly competent, adequate, and achieving in all possible respects if you are to consider yourself worthwhile.

3 Certain people are bad, wicked, or villainous, and they should be severely blamed and punished for their villainy. You should become extremely upset over other people's wrongdoings.

4 It is awful and catastrophic when things are not the way you would very much like them to be.

5 Human unhappiness is externally caused, and you have little or no ability to control your bad feelings and emotions.

6 It is easier to avoid than to face difficulties and responsibilities. Avoiding difficulties whenever possible is more likely to lead to happiness than facing difficulties.

7 You need to rely on someone stronger than yourself.

8 Your past history is an all-important determinant of your present behavior. Because something once strongly affected your life, it should indefinitely have a similar effect.

9 You should become extremely upset over other people's problems.

10 There is a single perfect solution to all human problems, and it is catastrophic if this perfect solution is not found.

SOURCE: Based on Ellis (1991).

According to rational-emotive therapy, unhappiness and psychological problems can often be traced to people's irrational beliefs. Becoming aware of these irrational beliefs is the first step toward replacing them with more rational alternatives. Some of the most common irrational beliefs are listed here.

Promotional Rational Living Along with hundreds of professional journal articles, Ellis has published more than 75 self-help books. One of his most popular titles is his classic text, *A Guide to Rational Living,* which has gone through several editions since it was first published in 1961. His other bestsellers include *Sex Without Guilt* and *How to Stubbornly Refuse to Make Yourself Miserable About Anything—Yes, Anything.* Ellis has also tried his hand at song-writing. One of his most famous songs, called "Whine, Whine, Whine," includes these lyrics: "Life really owes me the things that I miss, Fate has to grant me eternal bliss! And since I must settle for less than this—Whine, whine, whine!"

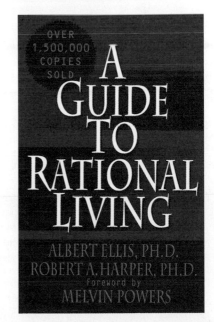

The second step in rational-emotive therapy is for the therapist to vigorously *dispute and challenge the irrational beliefs.* In doing so, rational-emotive therapists tend to be very direct and even confrontational (Haaga & Davison, 1991). Rather than trying to establish a warm, supportive atmosphere, rational-emotive therapists rely on logical persuasion and reason to push the client toward recognizing and surrendering his irrational beliefs (Hollon & Beck, 2004). According to Ellis (1991), blunt, harsh language is sometimes needed to push people into helping themselves.

From the client's perspective, rational-emotive therapy requires considerable effort. First, the person must admit her irrational beliefs and accept the fact that those beliefs are irrational and unhealthy, which is not as easy as it sounds. Old mental habits don't always yield easily. Equally challenging, the client must radically change her way of interpreting and responding to stressful events (Haaga & Davison, 1991).

The long-term therapeutic goal of RET is to teach clients to recognize and dispute their own irrational beliefs in a wide range of situations. However, responding "rationally" to unpleasant situations does not mean denying your feelings (Ellis & Bernard, 1985). Ellis believes that it is perfectly appropriate and rational to feel sad when you are rejected, or regretful when you make a mistake. Appropriate emotions are the consequences of rational beliefs, such as "I would prefer that everyone like me, but that's not likely to happen" or "It would be nice if I never failed at anything, but it's unlikely that I will always succeed in everything I do." Such healthy mental and emotional responses encourage people to work toward constructively changing or coping with difficult situations (Ellis & Harper, 1975).

Albert Ellis is a colorful figure whose ideas have been extremely influential in psychotherapy (Haaga & Davison, 1993). Rational-emotive therapy is a popular approach in clinical practice, partly because it is straightforward and simple (Arnkoff & Glass, 1992). It has been shown to be generally effective in the treatment of

rational-emotive therapy (RET)
A type of cognitive therapy, developed by psychologist Albert Ellis, that focuses on changing the client's irrational beliefs.

Aaron T. Beck (b. 1921) In Aaron Beck's cognitive therapy, called CT, clients learn to identify and change their automatic negative thoughts. Originally developed to treat depression, CT has also been applied to other psychological problems, such as anxiety disorders, phobias, and eating disorders.

According to Aaron Beck, depressed people perceive and interpret experience in very negative terms. They are prone to systematic errors in logic, or cognitive biases, which shape their negative interpretation of events. The table shows the most common cognitive biases in depression.

depression, social phobia, and certain anxiety disorders. Rational-emotive therapy is also useful in helping people overcome self-defeating behaviors, such as an excessive need for approval, extreme shyness, and chronic procrastination.

Aaron Beck and Cognitive Therapy

Psychiatrist **Aaron T. Beck** was initially trained as a psychoanalyst. Beck's development of **cognitive therapy,** abbreviated **CT,** grew out of his research on depression (Beck, 2004; Beck & others, 1979). Seeking to scientifically validate the psychoanalytic assumption that depressed patients "have a need to suffer," Beck began collecting data on the free associations and dreams of his depressed patients. What he found, however, was that his depressed patients did *not* have a need to suffer. In fact, his depressed patients often went to great lengths to avoid being rejected by others.

Instead, Beck discovered that depressed people have an extremely negative view of the past, present, and future (Beck & others, 1979). Rather than realistically evaluating their situation, depressed patients have developed a *negative cognitive bias*, consistently distorting their experiences in a negative way. Their negative perceptions of events and situations are shaped by deep-seated, self-deprecating beliefs, such as "I can't do anything right," "I'm worthless," or "I'm unlovable" (Beck, 1991). Beck's cognitive therapy essentially focuses on correcting the cognitive biases that underlie depression and other psychological disorders (see Table 14.5).

Beck's CT has much in common with Ellis's rational-emotive therapy. Like Ellis, Beck believes that what people think creates their moods and emotions. And like RET, CT involves helping clients identify faulty thinking and replace unhealthy patterns of thinking with healthier ones.

Table 14.5

Cognitive Biases in Depression

Cognitive Bias (Error)	Description	Example
Arbitrary inference	Drawing a negative conclusion when there is little or no evidence to support it.	When Joan calls Jim to cancel their lunch date because she has an important meeting at work, Jim concludes that she is probably going out to lunch with another man.
Selective abstraction	Focusing on a single negative detail taken out of context, ignoring the more important aspects of the situation.	During Jacqueline's annual review, her manager praises her job performance but notes that she could be a little more confident when she deals with customers over the phone. Jacqueline leaves her manager's office thinking that he is on the verge of firing her because of her poor telephone skills.
Overgeneralization	Drawing a sweeping, global conclusion based on an isolated incident and applying that conclusion to other unrelated areas of life.	Tony spills coffee on his final exam. He apologizes to his instructor but can't stop thinking about the incident. He concludes that he is a klutz who will never be able to succeed in a professional career.
Magnification and minimization	Grossly overestimating the impact of negative events and grossly underestimating the impact of positive events so that small, bad events are magnified, but good, large events are minimized.	One week after Emily aces all her midterms, she worries about flunking out of college when she gets a B on an in-class quiz.
Personalization	Taking responsibility, blaming oneself, or applying external events to oneself when there is no basis or evidence for making the connection.	Richard becomes extremely upset when his instructor warns the class about plagiarism. He thinks the instructor's warning was aimed at him, and he concludes that the instructor suspects him of plagiarizing parts of his term paper.

SOURCE: Based on Beck & others (1979), p. 14.

But in contrast with Ellis's emphasis on "irrational" thinking, Beck believes that depression and other psychological problems are caused by *distorted thinking* and *unrealistic beliefs* (Arnkoff & Glass, 1992; Hollon & Beck, 2004). Rather than logically debating the "irrationality" of a client's beliefs, the CT therapist encourages the client to *empirically test the accuracy of his or her assumptions and beliefs.* Let's look at how this occurs in Beck's CT.

The first step in CT is to help the client learn to recognize and monitor the automatic thoughts that occur without conscious effort or control (Beck, 1991). Whether negative or positive, automatic thoughts can control your mood and shape your emotional and behavioral reactions to events (Robins & Hayes, 1993). Because their perceptions are shaped by their negative cognitive biases, depressed people usually have automatic thoughts that reflect very negative interpretations of experience. Not surprisingly, the result of such negative automatic thoughts is a deepened sense of depression, hopelessness, and helplessness.

In the second step of CT, the therapist helps the client learn how to *empirically test* the reality of the automatic thoughts that are so upsetting. For example, to test the belief that "I always say the wrong thing," the therapist might assign the person the task of initiating a conversation with three acquaintances and noting how often he actually said the wrong thing.

Initially, the CT therapist acts as a model, showing the client how to evaluate the accuracy of automatic thoughts. By modeling techniques for evaluating the accuracy of automatic thoughts, the therapist hopes to eventually teach the client to do the same on her own. The CT therapist also strives to create a therapeutic climate of *collaboration* that encourages the client to contribute to the evaluation of the logic and accuracy of automatic thoughts (Beck & others, 1979; Robins & Hayes, 1993). This approach contrasts with the confrontational approach used by the RET therapist, who directly challenges the client's thoughts and beliefs.

Beck's cognitive therapy has been shown to be effective in treating depression and other psychological disorders, including anxiety disorders, borderline personality disorders, eating disorders, posttraumatic stress disorder, and relationship problems (G. K. Brown & others, 2004; Hollon & Beck, 2004). Along with effectively treating depression, cognitive therapy may also help *prevent* depression from recurring, especially if clients learn and then use the skills they have learned in therapy. In one recent study, high-risk patients who had experienced several episodes of depression in the past were much less likely to relapse when they continued cognitive therapy after their depression had lifted (Jarrett & others, 2001). Beck's cognitive therapy techniques have even been adapted to help treat psychotic symptoms, such as the delusions and disorganized thought processes that often characterize schizophrenia (Alford & Correia, 1994; Chadwick & others, 1994).

Table 14.6 summarizes the key characteristics of the two cognitive therapies presented here.

cognitive therapy (CT)
A type of cognitive therapy, developed by psychiatrist Aaron T. Beck, that focuses on changing the client's unrealistic beliefs.

Table 14.6

Comparing Cognitive Therapies

Type of Therapy	Founder	Source of Problems	Treatment Techniques	Goals of Therapy
Rational-emotive therapy (RET)	Albert Ellis	Irrational beliefs	Very directive: Identify, logically dispute, and challenge irrational beliefs	Surrender of irrational beliefs and absolutist demands
Cognitive therapy (CT)	Aaron T. Beck	Unrealistic, distorted perceptions and interpretations of events due to cognitive biases	Directive collaboration: Teach client to monitor automatic thoughts; test accuracy of conclusions; correct distorted thinking and perception	Accurate and realistic perception of self, others, and external events

cognitive-behavioral therapy (CBT)
Therapy that integrates cognitive and behavioral techniques and that is based on the assumption that thoughts, moods, and behaviors are interrelated.

group therapy
A form of psychotherapy that involves one or more therapists working simultaneously with a small group of clients.

family therapy
A form of psychotherapy that is based on the assumption that the family is a system and that treats the family as a unit.

Cognitive-Behavioral Therapy

Although we've presented cognitive and behavioral therapies in separate sections, it's important to note that cognitive and behavioral techniques are often combined in therapy. **Cognitive-behavioral therapy** (abbreviated **CBT**) refers to a group of psychotherapies that incorporate techniques from *both* approaches. CBT is based on the assumption that cognitions, behaviors, and emotional responses are interrelated (Brewin, 1996; Hollon & Beck, 2004). Thus, changes in thought patterns will affect moods and behaviors, and changes in behaviors will affect thoughts and moods. Along with challenging maladaptive beliefs and substituting more adaptive cognitions, the therapist uses behavior modification, shaping, reinforcement, and modeling to teach problem solving and to change unhealthy behavior patterns.

The hallmark of cognitive-behavioral therapy is its pragmatic approach. Therapists design an integrated treatment plan, utilizing the techniques that are most appropriate for specific problems.

Cognitive-behavioral therapy has been used in the treatment of children, adolescents, and the elderly (Kazdin, 2003; Wetherell & others, 2003). Studies have shown that cognitive-behavioral therapy is a very effective treatment for many disorders, including depression, eating disorders, substance abuse, and anxiety disorders (Chambless & Ollendick, 2001). Cognitive-behavioral therapy can also help decrease the incidence of delusions and hallucinations in patients with schizophrenia and psychotic symptoms (Garety & others, 2000; Lecomte & Lecomte, 2002). In part, the treatment involves offering patients alternative explanations for their delusions and hallucinations, and teaching them how to test the reality of their mistaken beliefs and perceptions.

Group and Family Therapy

Key Theme
- Group therapy involves one or more therapists working with several clients simultaneously.

Key Questions
- What are some key advantages of group therapy?
- What is family therapy, and how do its assumptions and techniques differ from those of individual therapy?

Individual psychotherapy offers a personal relationship between a client and a therapist, one that is focused on a single client's problems, thoughts, and emotions. But individual psychotherapy has certain limitations (Feldman & Powell, 1992). The therapist sees the client in isolation, rather than within the context of the client's interactions with others. Hence, the therapist must rely on the client's interpretation of reality and the client's description of relationships with others.

Group Therapy

Group therapy involves one or more therapists working with several people simultaneously. Group therapy may be provided by a therapist in private practice or at a community mental health clinic. Often, group therapy is an important part of the treatment program for hospital inpatients (Kibel, 1993). Groups may be as small as 3 or 4 people or as large as 10 or more people.

"So, would anyone in the group care to respond to what Clifford has just shared with us?"

Virtually any approach—psychodynamic, client-centered, behavioral, or cognitive—can be used in group therapy (Alonso & Swiller, 1993a). And just about any problem that can be handled individually can be dealt with in group therapy.

Group therapy has a number of advantages over individual psychotherapy (Dies, 1993). First, group therapy is very cost-effective: A single therapist can work simultaneously with several people. Thus, it is less expensive for the client and less time-consuming for the therapist. Second, rather than relying on a client's self-perceptions about how she relates to other people, the therapist can observe her actual interactions with others. Observing the way clients interact with others in a group may provide unique insights into their personalities and behavior patterns (Alonso & Swiller, 1993b; Porter, 1993).

Third, the support and encouragement provided by the other group members may help a person feel less alone and understand that his or her problems are not unique. For example, a team of family therapists set up group meetings with family members and co-workers of people who had died in the attacks on the World Trade Center (Boss & others, 2003). The therapists' goals included helping the families come to terms with their loss, especially in cases where the bodies of their loved ones had not been recovered. One woman, who had lost dozens of co-workers, some of them close friends, explained the impact of the group sessions in this way:

A Family Therapy Session Family therapists typically work with all the members of a family at the same time, including young children. The family therapist can then directly observe how family members interact, resolve differences, and exert control over one another. As unhealthy patterns of family interactions are identified, they can often be replaced with new patterns that promote the psychological well-being of the family as a whole.

> As I saw the widows dealing with their loss, and believing it a bit more, it helped me to accept it even more. It was easier with sharing together. Strength in numbers. It makes you feel less alone. Out of the thousands of people you bump into, not everyone can understand what you've been through. If I am with any one of the families, I know they will understand what I am going through. We comfort each other. Even a blood sister might not understand as well.

Fourth, group members may provide each other with helpful, practical advice for solving common problems and can act as models for successfully overcoming difficulties. Finally, working within a group gives people an opportunity to try out new behaviors in a safe, supportive environment. For instance, someone who is very shy and submissive can practice more assertive behaviors and receive honest feedback from other group members.

Group therapy is typically conducted by a mental health professional. In contrast, *self-help groups* and *support groups* are typically conducted by nonprofessionals. Self-help groups and support groups have become increasingly popular in the United States. As discussed in Focus Box 14.2 on page 568, the potential of these groups to promote mental health should not be underestimated.

Couple Therapy Couple therapy focuses on helping people who are in a committed relationship. Couple therapy usually emphasizes improving communication, increasing intimacy, and strengthening the relationship bond. On the basis of this couple's body language, does the therapist seem to be succeeding at achieving those goals?

Family and Couple Therapy

Most forms of psychotherapy, including most group therapies, tend to see a person's problems—and the solutions to those problems—as primarily originating within the individual himself. **Family therapy** operates on a different premise, focusing on the whole family rather than on an individual. The major goal of family therapy is to alter and improve the ongoing interactions among family members. Typically, family therapy involves every member of the family, even young children, and may also include important members of the extended family, such as grandparents or in-laws (Sexton & others, 2004).

IN FOCUS 14.2

Self-Help Groups: Helping Yourself by Helping Others

Every month our local newspaper publishes a list of more than 300 self-help and support groups that meet in our area. These groups range from the familiar (Alcoholics Anonymous, Tough-Love) to the obscure (Abused by Religion, Cult Awareness Group, Cross-Dressers of Green County), and from the general (Parents of Adolescents, Effective Black Parenting) to the specific (Multiple Sclerosis—Newly Diagnosed). There are also groups for people dealing with life's transitions and crises, such as divorce, retirement, or bereavement.

What this bewildering array of groups have in common is that all of them are organized and led by nonprofessionals. Typically, such groups are made up of members who have a common problem and meet for the purpose of exchanging psychological support. Some groups are focused on psychological growth and change. Other groups have a more practical emphasis, providing information and advice (Carroll, 1993). The groups either are free or charge nominal fees to cover the cost of materials.

The format of self-help groups varies enormously. Some groups are quite freewheeling, but others are highly structured (McFadden & others, 1992). Meetings may follow a prescribed format, and there may be rules regulating contacts among group members outside the meetings. For example, our friend Marcia attends weekly meetings of a self-help group called Emotions Anonymous. In Marcia's group, each person takes a turn speaking for five minutes. Interruptions are not allowed, and other members simply listen without responding to the speaker's comments.

Many self-help groups follow a 12-step approach, patterned after the famous 12-step program of Alcoholics Anonymous (AA). The 12 steps of AA include themes of admitting that you have a problem, seeking help from a "higher power," confessing your shortcomings, repairing your relationships with others, and helping other people who have the same problem. These 12 steps have been adapted by many different groups to fit their particular problem.

Some psychologists criticize the 12-step approach for its emphasis on the idea that people are "powerless" to cope with their problems on their own and must depend on a higher power and on other group members (Kasl, 1992).

Just how helpful are self-help groups? Research has shown that self-help groups can be as effective as therapy provided by a mental health professional, at least for some psychological problems (Christensen & Jacobson, 1994). Given that many people cannot afford professional counseling, self-help groups may be a cost-effective alternative to psychotherapy for some people.

What is not known is *why* self-help groups are effective. Support and encouragement from others are undoubtedly important. So may be the "helper therapy" principle on which all self-help groups are based: People who help other people are themselves helped. But more research is needed to clarify the elements that contribute most to a successful outcome.

Research is also needed to identify the kinds of people and problems that are most likely to benefit from a self-help approach (Christensen & Jacobson, 1994). One study suggests that 12-step attendees who find sponsors and who have a high motivation to change are more likely to stay involved in a program (Kelly & Moos, 2003).

An Alcoholics Anonymous Meeting Founded in 1935, Alcoholics Anonymous has more than 2 million members worldwide. People from all walks of life attend AA, and many credit AA for turning their lives around. Because AA group members are guaranteed anonymity, their faces cannot be shown in the photograph. Many other kinds of self-help groups are modeled on the AA program.

Family therapy is based on the assumption that the family is a *system*, an interdependent unit, not just a collection of separate individuals. The family is seen as a dynamic structure in which each member plays a unique role. According to this view, every family has certain unspoken "rules" of interaction and communication. Some of these tacit rules revolve around issues such as which family members exercise power and how, who makes decisions, who keeps the peace, and what kinds of alliances members have formed among themselves. As such issues are explored, unhealthy patterns of family interaction can be identified and replaced with new "rules" that promote the psychological health of the family as a unit.

Family therapy is often used to enhance the effectiveness of individual psychotherapy. For example, patients with schizophrenia are less likely to experience relapses when family members are involved in therapy (Pitschel-Walz & others, 2001). In many cases, the therapist realizes that the individual client's problems reflect conflict and disturbance in the entire family system (Lebow & Gurman, 1995). In order for the client to make significant improvements, the family as a whole must become psychologically healthier. Family therapy is also indicated when there is conflict among family members or when younger children are being treated for behavior problems, such as truancy or aggressive behavior (Kazdin, 1994).

Many family therapists also provide *marital* or *couple therapy*. The term *couple therapy* is preferred today because such therapy is conducted with any couple in a committed relationship, whether they are married or unmarried, heterosexual or homosexual (Lebow & Gurman, 1995). As is the case with family therapy, there are many different approaches to couple therapy (Sexton & others, 2004). For example, *behavioral couple therapy* is based on the assumption that couples are satisfied when they experience more reinforcement than punishment in their relationship. Thus, it focuses on increasing caring behaviors and teaching couples how to constructively resolve conflicts and problems. In general, most couple therapies have the goal of improving communication, reducing negative communication, and increasing intimacy between the pair (Christensen & Heavey, 1999).

BIZARRO

Evaluating the Effectiveness of Psychotherapy

Key Themes
■ Decades of research demonstrate that psychotherapy is effective in helping people with psychological disorders.

Key Questions
■ What are the common factors that contribute to successful outcomes in psychotherapy?
■ What is eclecticism?

Let's start with a simple fact: Most people with psychological symptoms do *not* seek help from mental health professionals (Kessler & others, 1994, 2004). This suggests that most people eventually weather their psychological problems without professional intervention. Some people cope with psychological difficulties with the help and support of friends and family. And some people eventually improve simply with the passage of time, a phenomenon called *spontaneous remission* (see Eysenck, 1952, 1994). Does psychotherapy offer significant benefits over just waiting for the possible "spontaneous remission" of symptoms?

The basic strategy for investigating this issue is to compare people who enter psychotherapy with a carefully selected, matched control group of people who do not receive psychotherapy (Kendall & others, 2004). During the past half-century, hundreds of such studies have investigated the effectiveness of the major forms of psychotherapy (Chambless & Ollendick, 2001; Orlinsky & others, 2004). To combine and interpret the results of such large numbers of studies, researchers have used a statistical technique called *meta-analysis*. Meta-analysis involves pooling the results of several studies into a single analysis, essentially creating one large study that can reveal overall trends in the data.

When meta-analysis is used to summarize studies that compare people who receive psychotherapy treatment to no-treatment controls, researchers consistently arrive at the same conclusion: *Psychotherapy is significantly more effective than no*

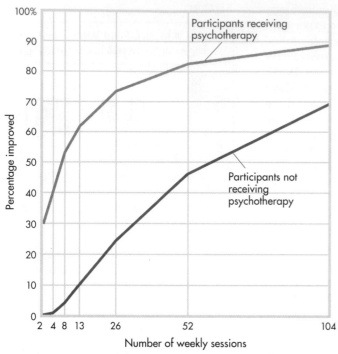

FIGURE 14.4 Psychotherapy Versus No Treatment This graph depicts the rates of improvement for more than 2,000 people in weekly psychotherapy and for 500 people who did not receive psychotherapy. As you can see, after only eight weekly sessions, better than 50 percent of participants receiving psychotherapy were significantly improved. After the same length of time, only 4 percent of participants not receiving psychotherapy showed "spontaneous remission" of symptoms. Clearly, psychotherapy accelerates both the rate and degree of improvement for those experiencing psychological problems.

SOURCE: Adapted from McNeilly & Howard (1991). Reprinted by permission of Guilford Press.

treatment. On the average, the person who completes psychotherapy treatment is better off than about 80 percent of those in the untreated control group (Asay & Lambert, 1999).

The benefits of psychotherapy usually become apparent in a relatively short time. As shown in Figure 14.4, approximately 50 percent of people show significant improvement by the eighth weekly session of psychotherapy. By the end of six months of weekly psychotherapy sessions, about 75 percent are significantly improved (McNeilly & Howard, 1991).

The gains that people make as a result of psychotherapy also tend to endure long after the therapy has ended, sometimes for years (Lambert & Ogles, 2004). Even brief forms of psychotherapy tend to produce beneficial and long-lasting changes (Koss & Shiang, 1994). And, multiple meta-analyses have found that both individual and group therapy are equally effective in producing significant gains in psychological functioning (Burlingame & others, 2004).

Brain-imaging technologies are providing another line of evidence demonstrating the power of psychotherapy to bring about change. In one study, PET scans were used to measure brain activity before and after 10 weeks of therapy for obsessive–compulsive disorder (Schwartz & others, 1996). The psychotherapy patients who improved showed the same changes in brain function that are associated with effective drug therapy for this disorder (see page 519 in Chapter 13).

Similarly, as we'll show you later in this chapter, PET scans of patients with depression show changes in brain functioning toward more normal levels after 12 weeks of interpersonal therapy (Martin & others, 2001). In other words, psychotherapy alone produces distinct physiological changes in the brain—changes that are associated with a reduction in symptoms.

Nevertheless, it's important to note that psychotherapy is *not* a miracle cure. While most people experience significant benefits from psychotherapy, not everyone benefits to the same degree. Some people who enter psychotherapy improve only slightly or not at all. And in some cases, people get worse despite therapeutic intervention. Having more severe problems and numerous interpersonal difficulties contribute to negative therapy outcomes (Lambert & Ogles, 2004; Mohr, 1995).

Is One Form of Psychotherapy Superior?

Given that the major types of psychotherapy use different assumptions and techniques, does one type of psychotherapy stand out as more effective than the others? In some cases, one type of psychotherapy is more effective than another in treating a particular problem. For example, cognitive therapy and interpersonal therapy are effective in treating depression (Elkin & others, 1989, 1996). Cognitive, cognitive-behaviorial, and behavior therapies tend to be more successful than insight-oriented therapies in helping people who are experiencing panic disorder, obsessive–compulsive disorder, and phobias (Chambless & Ollendick, 2001; Clark & others, 2003). Insight-oriented therapies are also less effective than other therapies in the treatment of disorders characterized by severe psychotic symptoms, such as schizophrenia (Mueser & Glynn, 1993).

However, when meta-analysis techniques are used to assess the collective results of treatment outcome studies, a surprising but consistent finding emerges: *In general, there is little or no difference in the effectiveness of different psychotherapies.* Despite sometimes dramatic differences in psychotherapy techniques, all of the standard psychotherapies have very similar success rates (Kopta & others, 1999; Nathan & others, 2000).

One important qualification must be made at this point. In this chapter, we've devoted considerable time to explaining four major approaches to therapy: psychoanalytic and psychodynamic therapy; humanistic therapy; behavior therapy; and cognitive and cognitive-behavioral therapies. While distinct, all of these psychotherapy approaches have in common the fact that they are *empirically supported treatments*. In other words, they are based on known psychological principles, have been subjected to controlled scientific trials, and have demonstrated their effectiveness in helping people with psychological problems (Chambless & Ollendick, 2001).

In contrast, one ongoing issue in contemporary psychotherapy is the proliferation of *untested* psychotherapies (Beutler, 2000; Lilienfeld, 1998). The fact that there is little difference in outcome among the empirically supported therapies does *not* mean that any and every form of psychotherapy is equally effective (Herbert & others, 2000). Too often, untested therapy techniques are heavily marketed and promoted, promising miraculous cures with little or no empirical research to back up their claims (A. A. Lazarus, 2000).

We examine the empirical evidence for one heavily promoted new therapy in Science Versus Pseudoscience Box 14.3.

Therapeutic Sensitivity to Cultural Differences A therapist's sensitivity to a client's cultural values can affect the ability to form a good working relationship and, ultimately, the success of psychotherapy (V. L. S. Thompson & others, 2004). Thus, some clients prefer to see therapists who are from the same ethnic or cultural background, as is the case with the Korean-American therapist and client shown. In general, therapists have become more attuned to the important role played by culture in effective psychotherapy.

What Factors Contribute to Effective Psychotherapy?

How can we explain the fact that different forms of psychotherapy are basically equivalent in producing positive results? One possible explanation is that the factors that are crucial to producing improvement are present in *all* effective therapies. Researchers have identified a number of common factors that are related to a positive therapy outcome (see Hubble & others, 1999).

First and most important is the quality of the *therapeutic relationship* (Bachelor & Horvath, 1999). In effective psychotherapies, the therapist–client relationship is characterized by mutual respect, trust, and hope. Working in a cooperative alliance, both people are actively trying to achieve the same goals.

Second, certain *therapist characteristics* are associated with successful therapy. Effective therapists have a caring attitude and the ability to listen empathically. They are genuinely committed to their clients' welfare (Strupp, 1996). Regardless of orientation, effective therapists tend to be warm, sensitive, and responsive people, and they are perceived as sincere and genuine (Beutler & others, 1994, 2004).

Effective therapists are also sensitive to the *cultural differences* that may exist between themselves and their clients (Pope-Davis & others, 2001). As described in Culture and Human Behavior Box 14.4 on page 574, cultural differences can be a barrier to effective psychotherapy. Increasingly, training in cultural sensitivity and multicultural issues is being incorporated into psychological training programs in the United States (G. Hall, 2001).

Third, *client characteristics* are important (Clarkin & Levy, 2004). If the client is motivated, committed to therapy, and actively involved in the process, a successful outcome is much more likely (Tallman & Bohart, 1999). Emotional and social maturity and the ability to express thoughts and feelings are important. Clients who are optimistic, who expect psychotherapy to help them with their problems, and who don't have a previous history of psychological disorders are more likely to benefit from therapy (Leon & others, 1999). Finally, *external circumstances,* such as a stable living situation and supportive family members, can enhance the effectiveness of therapy.

© 1999 Sidney Harris

"I UTILIZE THE BEST FROM FREUD, THE BEST FROM JUNG AND THE BEST FROM MY UNCLE MARTY, A VERY SMART FELLOW."

SCIENCE VERSUS PSEUDOSCIENCE 14.3

EMDR: Can You Wave Your Fears Away?

In the late 1980s, a psychology graduate student named Francine Shapiro was walking alone in a park, grappling with some troubling thoughts. According to Shapiro, "I noticed that when a disturbing thought entered my mind, my eyes spontaneously started moving back and forth. At the same time, I noticed that my disturbing thought had shifted from consciousness, and when I brought it back to mind, it no longer bothered me as much" (Shapiro & Forrest, 1997). Speculating that her back-and-forth eye movements were simulating the rapid eye movements (REM) of dreaming sleep, Shapiro developed a treatment technique in which patients suffering from traumatic memories visually followed her waving finger while simultaneously holding a mental image of disturbing memories, events, or situations.

Ultimately, Shapiro earned her doctorate in psychology by treating 22 patients with posttraumatic stress disorder (PTSD) with her new therapy, which she dubbed **eye movement desensitization reprocessing,** abbreviated **EMDR.** In two published papers, Shapiro (1989a, 1989b) reported that almost all of her patients experienced significant relief from their symptoms after just *one* EMDR therapy session.

This was the beginning of what was to become one of the fastest-growing—and most lucrative—therapeutic techniques of the last 15 years (Herbert & others, 2000). How popular is EMDR? Since Shapiro established her EMDR Institute in 1990, more than 40,000 therapists have been trained in EMDR. Close to a million patients have been treated with the new therapy (EMDR Institute, 2001).

Since its launch, the claims, techniques, and jargon of EMDR have undergone some changes. While originally touted as a one-session treatment for the distress associated with traumatic memories in PTSD (Shapiro, 1989a), EMDR therapy today frequently

Eye Movement Desensitization Reprocessing (EMDR) In EMDR therapy, the client visually follows the therapist's moving finger while mentally focusing on a traumatic memory or vivid mental image of a troubling situation. Supposedly, the rhythmic eye movements help the client to "release" and "integrate" the trauma.

involves multiple sessions. According to Shapiro (1995), comprehensive EMDR treatment involves eight phases, which combine elements of psychodynamic, behavioral, and cognitive therapies. Along with the eye movements, other forms of "bilateral stimulation" may be used, such as tones in alternating ears or taps on different sides of the body.

Along with posttraumatic stress disorder, EMDR has been used to treat panic disorder and other anxiety disorders, addiction, substance abuse, and sleep disorders. Proponents claim that EMDR is also effective in overcoming depression, phobias, pathological gambling, and self-esteem problems, as well as helping athletes and workers achieve "peak performance" (see EMDR Institute, 2001; Shapiro & Forrest, 1997).

Originally, Shapiro (1989b) contended that the eye movements simulated brain processes during sleep, "releasing" and "integrating" traumatic memories. More recently, Shapiro (1995) has proposed that EMDR facilitates what she calls "Accelerated Information Processing," in which "dysfunc-

tionally stored information can be properly assimilated through a dynamically activated processing system." Supposedly, EMDR "accelerates a natural information processing" that helps heal the nervous system.

Is EMDR "the breakthrough therapy for overcoming anxiety, stress, and trauma," as is claimed on the cover of Shapiro's 1997 book? Does it represent a "paradigm shift" in psychotherapy, as its founder (Shapiro, 1995) claims? Let's consider the evidence.

Does EMDR Provide Therapeutic Benefits Compared to *No* Treatment?

Yes, numerous studies have shown that patients experience relief from symptoms of anxiety after EMDR. In a meta-analysis of dozens of studies examining EMDR, Canadian psychologists Paul Davidson and Kevin Parker (2001) concluded the following: "When outcomes of EMDR treatment are compared with no treatment, and when outcomes are compared with pretreatment status, clients are better off with EMDR treatment than without." Other researchers have also found that patients benefit from EMDR and that EMDR is more effective than no treatment at all (DeBell & Jones, 1997; Goldstein & others, 2000).

Is EMDR *More* Effective Than Other Standard Therapies?

The alert reader will have noticed that EMDR has many elements in common with other treatment techniques, some of them well established and based on well-documented psychological principles. For example, **exposure therapy** is one technique that has long been recognized as an effective treatment for PTSD and phobias. Exposure therapy is related to systematic desensitization: The person gradually and repeatedly relives the frightening experience under controlled conditions to help him overcome his fear of the dreaded object or situation and establish

---

eye movement desensitization reprocessing (EMDR)
Therapy technique in which the client holds a vivid mental image of a troubling event or situation while rapidly moving his or her eyes back and forth in response to the therapist's waving finger or while the therapist administers some other form of bilateral stimulation, such as sounding tones in alternate ears.

Notice that none of these factors are specific to any particular brand of psychotherapy. However, this does not mean that differences between psychotherapy techniques are completely irrelevant. Rather, it's important that there be a good "match" between the person seeking help and the specific psychotherapy techniques used. One person may be very comfortable with psychodynamic techniques, such as exploring childhood memories and free association. Another person might be more open to behavioral techniques, like systematic desensitization. For therapy to be optimally effective, the individual should feel comfortable with both the therapist and the therapist's approach to therapy.

more adaptive beliefs and cognitions. Using a combination of behavioral and cognitive techniques, exposure therapy has a high rate of success in the treatment of anxiety disorders (Foa & Meadows, 1997).

Is EMDR more effective than exposure therapy or other cognitive-behavioral treatments? No. When Davidson and Parker (2001) compared the effectiveness of EMDR to other exposure treatments, no difference was found. EMDR was no more effective than standard treatments for anxiety disorders, including PTSD. Other researchers have found that EMDR is *less* effective than exposure therapy for PTSD (Taylor & others, 2003).

Are the Eye Movements Necessary?

Several research studies have compared standard EMDR with other treatments that duplicate all aspects of the treatment *except* the eye-movement component. For example, some studies have compared treatment effects between an eye-movement condition (EMDR) and "sham" EMDR, a kind of placebo condition in which the participants fixed their eyes on a bright light that did not move or engaged in finger tapping with alternate hands. All these studies found *no difference* between "real" EMDR and sham EMDR (DeBell & Jones, 1997; Feske &

Goldstein, 1997; Goldstein & others, 2000). In their meta-analysis, Davidson and Parker (2001) agreed with other researchers: There was *no difference* in outcome between treatments that incorporated eye movements and the "sham" EMDR that did not.

So if you remove the eye movements from the EMDR treatment protocol, what is left? Harvard psychologist Richard McNally (1998), an expert in the treatment of anxiety disorders, puts it succinctly: "What is effective in EMDR is not new, and what is new is not effective." Psychologists Gerald Rosen and Jeffrey Lohr (1997) are more blunt:

> Shapiro took existing elements from cognitive-behavior therapies, added the unnecessary ingredient of finger waving, and then took the technique on the road before science could catch up.

Is EMDR a Pseudoscience?

Some psychologists argue that EMDR is just that—a pseudoscience (Lilienfeld, 1998; G. Rosen & others, 1999). Psychologist James D. Herbert and his colleagues (2000) note several ways in which EMDR displays the fundamental characteristics of a pseudoscience, which were discussed in Chapter 1:

> EMDR appears to possess the outward form of science but little of its substance.

The appearance of science, such as case studies reported in peer reviewed journals, selective publicity of weak tests of effectiveness, [and] scientific-sounding jargon . . . serve to obscure EMDR's lack of scientific substance and have persuaded many of its scientific legitimacy. Although there is little evidence to support the strong claims of EMDR's proponents, this treatment has resulted in a significant financial return.

The case of EMDR highlights an ongoing problem in contemporary psychotherapy. Too often, "revolutionary" new therapies are developed, advertised, and marketed directly to the public—and to therapists—*before* controlled scientific studies of their effectiveness have been conducted (A. Lazarus, 2000). Many of the untested therapies are ineffective or, as in the case of EMDR, no more effective than established therapies (Lilienfeld & others, 2003; Lohr & others, 2003). Others are downright dangerous, such as the "rebirthing" technique that resulted in the death of a young girl in Colorado in April 2000. Ten-year-old Candace Newmaker suffocated after being wrapped in a blanket, covered with pillows, and restrained by four adult "therapists" who taunted her when she cried, pleaded for air, and repeatedly told them she could not breathe.

Like many pseudosciences, such fringe therapies rely on anecdotes and testimonials to persuade others of their efficacy. Their proponents often resort to vague, scientific-sounding explanations of their mechanisms rather than established—and testable—scientific principles (Lilienfeld, 1998). James Herbert and his colleagues (2000) argue that new therapeutic techniques should be tested *before* they are put into widespread use, not after. The conditions that new therapies should meet are summarized in the table at left.

The Burden of Proof

Psychologist James D. Herbert and his colleagues (2000) argue that before being put into widespread use, new therapies should provide empirically based answers to the following questions:

- Does the treatment work better than no treatment?
- Does the treatment work better than a placebo?
- Does the treatment work better than standard treatments?
- Does the treatment work through the processes that its proponents claim?

SOURCE: Herbert & others (2000).

Increasingly, such a personalized approach to therapy is being facilitated by the movement of mental health professionals toward **eclecticism**—the pragmatic and integrated use of diverse psychotherapy techniques (Lambert & others, 2004). Today, therapists identify themselves as eclectic more often than any other orientation (Lambert & Ogles, 2004). *Eclectic psychotherapists* carefully tailor the therapy approach to the problems and characteristics of the person seeking help. For example, an eclectic therapist might integrate insight-oriented techniques with specific behavioral techniques to help someone suffering from extreme shyness.

exposure therapy
Behavioral therapy for phobias, panic disorder, posttraumatic stress disorder, or related anxiety disorders in which the person is repeatedly exposed to the disturbing object or situation under controlled conditions.

eclecticism
(eh-KLEK-tuh-*sizz*-um) The pragmatic and integrated use of techniques from different psychotherapies.

CULTURE AND HUMAN BEHAVIOR 14.4

Cultural Values and Psychotherapy

The goals and techniques of many established approaches to psychotherapy tend to reflect European and North American cultural values. In this box, we'll look at how those cultural values can clash with the values of clients from other cultures, diminishing the effectiveness of psychotherapy.

A Focus on the Individual

In Western psychotherapy, the client is usually encouraged to become more assertive, more self-sufficient, and less dependent on others in making decisions. Problems are assumed to have an internal cause and are expected to be solved by the client alone. Therapy emphasizes meeting the client's individual needs, even if those needs conflict with the demands of significant others. In collectivistic cultures, however, the needs of the individual are much more strongly identified with the needs of the group to which he or she belongs (Triandis, 1996).

For example, traditional Native Americans are less likely than European-Americans to believe that personal problems are due to an internal cause within the individual (Sue & others, 1994). Instead, one person's problems may be seen as a problem for the entire community to resolve.

In traditional forms of Native American healing, family members, friends, and other members of the community may be asked to participate in the treatment or healing rituals. One type of therapy, called *network therapy,* is conducted in the person's home and can involve as many as 70 members of the individual's community or tribe (LaFromboise, Trimble, & others, 1993b).

Latino cultures, too, emphasize interdependence over independence. In particular, they stress the value of *familismo*—the importance of the extended family network. Because the sense of family is so central to Latino culture, psychologist Lilian Comas-Diaz (1993) recommends that members of the client's extended family, such as grand-

Cultural Values Even after immigrating to the United States, many people maintain strong ties with their cultural heritage. Here, Arab-American children attend an Islamic school. Notice that the young female students as well as the teacher are wearing the traditional *chador,* or veil. The traditional beliefs of some cultures, such as the Islamic belief that women should be modest and obedient to their husbands, may conflict with the values inherent in Western psychotherapies.

parents and in-laws, be actively involved in psychological treatment.

Many collectivistic Asian cultures also emphasize a respect for the needs of others. The Japanese psychotherapy called *Naikan therapy* is a good example of how such cultural values affect the goals of psychotherapy (Reynolds, 1990). According to Naikan therapy, being self-absorbed is the surest path to psychological suffering. Thus, the goal of Naikan therapy is to replace the focus on the self with a sense of gratitude and obligation toward others. Rather than talking about how his own needs were not met by family members, the Naikan client is asked to meditate on how he has failed to meet the needs of others.

The Importance of Insight

Psychodynamic, humanistic, and cognitive therapies all stress the importance of insight or awareness of an individual's thoughts and feelings. But many cultures do *not* emphasize the importance of exploring painful thoughts and feelings in re-

solving psychological problems. For example, Asian cultures stress that mental health is enhanced by the avoidance of negative thinking. Hence, a depressed or anxious person in China and many other Asian countries would be encouraged to *avoid* focusing on upsetting thoughts (Sue & others, 1994).

Intimate Disclosure Between Therapist and Client

Many Western psychotherapies are based on the assumption that the clients will disclose their deepest feelings and most private thoughts to their therapists. But in some cultures, intimate details of one's personal life would never be discussed with a stranger. Asians are taught to disclose intimate details only to very close friends. For example, a young Vietnamese student of ours vowed never to return to see a psychologist she had consulted about her struggles with depression. The counselor, she complained, was too "nosy" and asked too many personal questions. In many cultures, people are far more likely to turn to family members or friends than they are to mental health professionals (Nishio & Bilmes, 1993).

The demands for emotional openness may also clash with cultural values. In Asian cultures, people tend to avoid the public expression of emotions and often express thoughts and feelings nonverbally. Native American cultures tend to value the restraint of emotions rather than the open expression of emotions (LaFromboise, Trimble, & others, 1993b).

Recognizing the need for psychotherapists to become more culturally sensitive, the American Psychological Association has recommended formal training in multicultural awareness for all psychologists (Edwards, 1995a; Hall, 1997). The APA (2003) has also published extensive guidelines for psychologists who provide psychological help to culturally diverse populations. Interested students can download a copy of the APA guidelines at: www.apa.org/pi/multiculturalguidelines.pdf

Biomedical Therapies

Key Theme

■ The biomedical therapies are medical treatments for the symptoms of psychological disorders and include medication and electroconvulsive therapy.

Key Questions

■ What medications are used to treat the symptoms of schizophrenia, anxiety, bipolar disorder, and depression, and how do they achieve their effects?

■ What is electroconvulsive therapy, and what are its advantages and disadvantages?

psychotropic medications
(sy-ko-TRO-pick) Drugs that alter mental functions, alleviate psychological symptoms, and are used to treat psychological or mental disorders.

Medical treatments for psychological disorders actually predate modern psychotherapy by hundreds of years. In past centuries, patients were whirled, soothed, drenched, restrained, and isolated—all in an attempt to alleviate symptoms of psychological disorders. Today, such "treatments" seem cruel, inhumane, and useless (see images below). Keep in mind, however, that these early treatments were based on the limited medical knowledge of the time. As you'll see in this section, some of the early efforts to treat psychological disorders did eventually evolve into treatments that are widely used today.

For the most part, it was not until the twentieth century that effective biomedical therapies were developed to treat the symptoms of mental disorders. Today, the most common biomedical therapy is the use of **psychotropic medications**—prescription drugs that alter mental functions and alleviate psychological symptoms. Although often used alone, psychotropic medications are increasingly combined with psychotherapy (Thase & Jindal, 2004; Kupfer & Frank, 2001).

In 2005, psychotropic medications outsold all other categories of medicines in the United States, accounting for $28.7 billion dollars in sales

Source: NDCHealth, 2005

Antipsychotic Medications

For more than 2,000 years, traditional practitioners of medicine in India used an herb derived from the snakeroot plant to diminish the psychotic symptoms commonly associated with schizophrenia: hallucinations, delusions, and

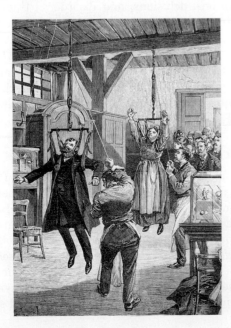

Historical Treatments for Mental Illness
Left: Found in Peru, this pre-Columbian skull shows the results of primitive surgery on the brain, called *trephining,* presumably as a treatment to allow evil spirits to leave the body. *Center:* A "tranquilizing chair" was developed in the early 1800s to restrain and sedate unmanageable patients. *Right:* An early treatment apparatus called the "circulating swing" involved spinning patients.

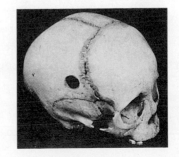

The First Antipsychotic Drug More than 2,000 years ago, ancient Hindu medical texts prescribed the use of an herb derived from *Rauwolfia serpentina,* or snakeroot plant, to treat epilepsy, insomnia, and other ailments. But its primary use was to treat *oonmaad*—a Sanskrit term for an abnormal mental condition that included disruptions in "wisdom, perception, knowledge, character, creativity, conduct, and behavior" (Bhatara & others, 1997). Today it is known that the herb has a high affinity for dopamine receptors in the brain.

disordered thought processes (Bhatara & others, 1997). The same plant was used in traditional Japanese medicine to treat anxiety and restlessness (Jilek, 1993). In the 1930s, Indian physicians discovered that the herb was also helpful in the treatment of high blood pressure. They developed a synthetic version of the herb's active ingredient, called *reserpine.*

Reserpine first came to the attention of American researchers as a potential treatment for high blood pressure. But it wasn't until the early 1950s that American researchers became aware of research in India demonstrating the effectiveness of reserpine in treating schizophrenia (Frankenburg, 1994).

It was also during the 1950s that French scientists began investigating the psychoactive properties of another drug, called *chlorpromazine.* Like reserpine, chlorpromazine diminished the psychotic symptoms commonly seen in schizophrenia. Hence, reserpine and chlorpromazine were dubbed **antipsychotic medications.** Because chlorpromazine had fewer side effects than reserpine, it nudged out reserpine as the preferred medication for treating schizophrenia-related symptoms. Since then, chlorpromazine has been better known by its trade name, *Thorazine,* and is still used to treat psychotic symptoms. The antipsychotic drugs are also referred to as *neuroleptic medications* or simply *neuroleptics.*

How do these drugs diminish psychotic symptoms? Reserpine and chlorpromazine act differently on the brain, but both drugs reduce levels of the neurotransmitter called *dopamine.* Since the development of these early drugs, more than 30 other antipsychotic medications have been developed (see Table 14.7). These antipsychotic medications also act on dopamine receptors in the brain (Abi-Dargham, 2004; Laruelle & others, 2003).

The first antipsychotics effectively reduced the *positive symptoms* of schizophrenia—hallucinations, delusions, and disordered thinking (see Chapter 13). This therapeutic effect had a revolutionary impact on the number of people hospitalized for schizophrenia. Until the 1950s, patients with schizophrenia were thought to be incurable. These chronic patients formed the bulk of the population on the "back wards" of psychiatric hospitals. With the introduction of the antipsychotic medications, however, the number of patients in mental hospitals decreased dramatically (see Figure 14.5).

Drawbacks of Antipsychotic Medications

Even though the early antipsychotic drugs allowed thousands of patients to be discharged from hospitals, these drugs had a number of drawbacks. First, they didn't actually *cure* schizophrenia. Psychotic symptoms often returned if a person stopped taking the medication.

Second, the early antipsychotic medications were not very effective in eliminating the *negative symptoms* of schizophrenia—social withdrawal, apathy, and lack of emotional expressiveness (Marder & others, 1993). In some cases, the drugs even made negative symptoms worse. Third, the antipsychotics often produced unwanted side

Table 14.7		
Antipsychotic Medications		
	Generic Name	**Trade Name**
Typical Antipsychotics	Chlorpromazine	Thorazine
	Fluphenazine	Prolixin
	Trifluoperazine	Stelazine
	Thioridazine	Mellaril
	Thiothixene	Navane
	Haloperidol	Haldol
Atypical Antipsychotics	Clozapine	Clozaril
	Risperidone	Risperdal
	Olanzapine	Zyprexa
	Sertindole	Serlect
	Quetiapine	Seroquel
Third Generation Antipsychotics	Aripiprazole	Abilify

SOURCE: Adapted from Julien (2005).

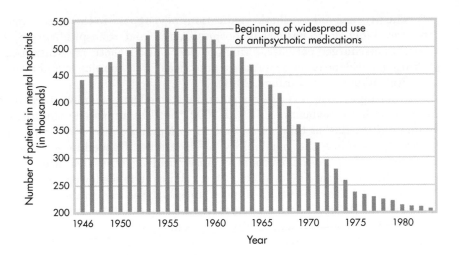

FIGURE 14.5 Change in the Number of Patients Hospitalized for Mental Disorders, 1946–1983 When the first antipsychotic drugs came into wide use in the late 1950s, the number of people hospitalized for mental disorders began to drop sharply.

SOURCE: Adapted from Julien (2005).

effects, such as dry mouth, weight gain, constipation, sleepiness, and poor concentration (Gerlach & Peacock, 1994).

Fourth, the fact that the early antipsychotics *globally* altered brain levels of dopamine turned out to be a double-edged sword. Dopamine pathways in the brain are involved not only in psychotic symptoms, but also in normal motor movements. Consequently, the early antipsychotic medications could produce motor-related side effects—muscle tremors, rigid movements, a shuffling gait, and a masklike facial expression (Barondes, 1993). This collection of side effects occurred so commonly that mental hospital staff members sometimes informally referred to it as the "Thorazine shuffle."

Even more disturbing, the long-term use of antipsychotic medications causes a small percentage of people to develop a potentially irreversible motor disorder called *tardive dyskinesia.* Tardive dyskinesia is characterized by severe, uncontrollable facial tics and grimaces, chewing movements, and other involuntary movements of the lips, jaw, and tongue.

Closely tied to the various side effects of the first antipsychotic drugs is a fifth problem: the "revolving door" pattern of hospitalization, discharge, and rehospitalization. Schizophrenic patients, once stabilized by antipsychotic medication, were released from hospitals into the community. But because of the medication's unpleasant side effects, inadequate medical follow-up, or both, many patients eventually stopped taking the medication. When psychotic symptoms returned, the patients were rehospitalized.

The Atypical Antipsychotics

During the past decade, a second generation of antipsychotic drugs has been introduced. Called **atypical antipsychotic medications,** these drugs affect brain levels of dopamine and *serotonin.* The first atypical antipsychotics were *clozapine* and *risperidone.* More recent atypical antipsychotics include *olanzapine, sertindole,* and *quietapine.*

The atypical antipsychotics have several advantages over the older antipsychotic drugs (see Barnes & Joyce, 2001). First, the new drugs are less likely to cause movement-related side effects. That's because they do not block dopamine receptors in the movement areas of the brain. Instead, they more selectively target dopamine receptors in brain areas associated with psychotic symptoms (Rivas-Vasquez, 2003). The atypical antipsychotics are also much more effective in treating the negative symptoms of schizophrenia—apathy, social withdrawal, and flat emotions. Some patients who have not responded to the older antipsychotic drugs improve dramatically with the new medications (Marder & Meibach, 1994).

antipsychotic medications
(*an*-tee-sy-KOT-ick or antī-sī-KOT-ick) Prescription drugs that are used to reduce psychotic symptoms; frequently used in the treatment of schizophrenia; also called *neuroleptics.*

atypical antipsychotic medications
Newer antipsychotic medications that, in contrast to the early antipsychotic drugs, block dopamine receptors in brain regions associated with psychotic symptoms rather than more globally throughout the brain, resulting in fewer side effects.

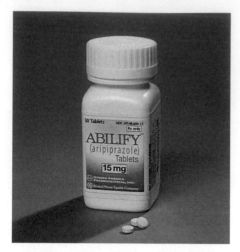

A New Generation of Antipsychotic Medications Released in 2003, *Abilify* represents a new, third generation of antipsychotic medications. Like the traditional and the atypical antipsychotic medications, Abilify affects dopamine levels in the brain. However, Abilify seems to regulate the availability of dopamine by blocking dopamine receptors when levels are too high and mimicking dopamine when levels are too low. Ability also affects brain levels of serotonin. Clinical trials indicate that Abilify is just as effective as the second-generation antipsychotic medications while seeming to produce fewer side effects—which means that patients are less likely to discontinue taking the medication (Rivas-Vasquez, 2003).

The atypical antipsychotic medications also appear to lessen the incidence of the "revolving door" pattern of hospitalization and rehospitalization. As compared to discharged patients taking the older antipsychotic medications, patients taking risperidone or olanzapine are much less likely to relapse and return to the hospital (Rabinowitz & others, 2001).

Offering hope for even fewer potential side effects is a new, third generation of antipsychotic medications. In late 2002, the FDA approved *aripiprazole*, trade name *Abilify*. Rather than merely blocking dopamine receptors, aripiprazole appears to stabilize the availability of dopamine. Depending on the level of dopamine present in the neuronal synapse, the drug either increases or decreases the amount of dopamine available. Early clinical trials showed that aripiprazole was as effective as the other atypical antipsychotic medications but had fewer side effects (DeLeon & others, 2004; Rivas-Vasquez, 2003). Adding to the potential of this new medication, Abilify also seems to be effective in the treatment of manic episodes associated with bipolar disorder (Keck & others, 2003).

Antianxiety Medications

Anxiety that is intense and persistent can be disabling, interfering with a person's ability to eat, sleep, and function. **Antianxiety medications** are prescribed to help people deal with the problems and symptoms associated with pathological anxiety (see Table 14.8).

The best-known antianxiety drugs are the *benzodiazepines,* which include the trade-name drugs *Valium* and *Xanax*. These antianxiety medications calm jittery feelings, relax the muscles, and promote sleep. They take effect rapidly, usually within an hour or so. In general, the benzodiazepines produce their effects by increasing the level of *GABA,* a neurotransmitter that inhibits the transmission of nerve impulses in the brain and slows brain activity (see Chapter 2).

Taken for a week or two, and in therapeutic doses, the benzodiazepines can effectively reduce anxiety levels. However, the benzodiazepines have several potentially dangerous side effects. First, they can reduce coordination, alertness, and reaction time. Second, their effects can be intensified when they are combined with alcohol and many other drugs, including over-the-counter antihistamines. Such a combination can produce severe drug intoxication, even death.

Third, the benzodiazepines are physically addictive if taken in large quantities or over a long period of time. If physical dependence occurs, the person must withdraw from the drug gradually, as abrupt withdrawal can produce life-threatening symptoms. Because of their addictive potential, the benzodiazepines are less widely prescribed today.

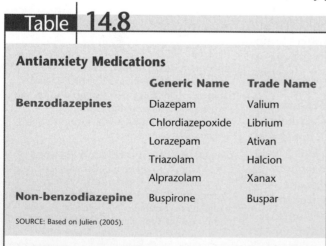

Table 14.8		
Antianxiety Medications		
	Generic Name	**Trade Name**
Benzodiazepines	Diazepam	Valium
	Chlordiazepoxide	Librium
	Lorazepam	Ativan
	Triazolam	Halcion
	Alprazolam	Xanax
Non-benzodiazepine	Buspirone	Buspar

SOURCE: Based on Julien (2005).

A newer antianxiety drug with the trade name *Buspar* has fewer side effects. Buspar is not a benzodiazepine, and it does not affect the neurotransmitter GABA. In fact, exactly how Buspar works is unclear, but it is believed to affect brain dopamine and serotonin levels (Mahmood & Sahajwalla, 1999). Regardless, Buspar relieves anxiety while allowing the individual to maintain normal alertness. It does not cause the drowsiness, sedation, and cognitive impairment that are associated with the benzodiazepines. And Buspar seems to have a very low risk of dependency and physical addiction.

However, Buspar has one major drawback: It must be taken for two to three *weeks* before anxiety is reduced. While this decreases Buspar's potential for abuse, it also decreases its effectiveness for treating acute anxiety. For immediate, short-term relief from anxiety, the benzodiazepines are still regarded as the most effective medications currently available.

Lithium

In Chapter 13, on psychological disorders, we described *bipolar disorder,* previously known as *manic depression.* The medication most commonly used to treat bipolar disorder is **lithium,** a naturally occurring substance. Lithium counteracts both manic and depressive symptoms in bipolar patients. Its effectiveness in treating bipolar disorder has been well established since the 1960s (Shou, 1993).

As a treatment for bipolar disorder, lithium stops acute manic episodes over the course of a week or two. Once an acute manic episode is under control, the long-term use of lithium can help prevent relapses into either mania or depression. The majority of patients with bipolar disorder respond well to lithium therapy (Keck & McElroy, 1993). However, lithium doesn't help everyone. Some people on lithium therapy experience relapses (Sachs & others, 1994).

Like all other medications, lithium has potential side effects. If the lithium level is too low, manic symptoms persist. If it is too high, lithium poisoning may occur, with symptoms such as vomiting, muscle weakness, and reduced muscle coordination. Consequently, the patient's lithium blood level must be carefully monitored.

How lithium works was once a complete mystery. Lithium's action was especially puzzling because it prevented mood disturbances at both ends of the emotional spectrum—mania *and* depression. It turns out that lithium affects levels of an excitatory neurotransmitter called *glutamate,* which is found in many areas of the brain. Apparently, lithium stabilizes the availability of glutamate within a narrow, normal range, preventing both abnormal highs and abnormal lows (Dixon & Hokin, 1998).

Bipolar disorder can also be treated with an anticonvulsant medicine called *Depakote.* Originally used to prevent epileptic seizures, Depakote seems to be especially helpful in treating those who rapidly cycle through bouts of bipolar disorder several times a year. It's also useful for treating bipolar patients who do not respond to lithium (Jefferson, 1995).

Antidepressant Medications

The **antidepressant medications** counteract the classic symptoms of depression—hopelessness, guilt, dejection, suicidal thoughts, difficulty concentrating, and disruptions in sleep, energy, appetite, and sexual desire. The first generation of antidepressants consists of two classes of drugs, called *tricyclics* and *MAO inhibitors* (see Table 14.9 on page 580). Tricyclics and MAO inhibitors affect multiple neurotransmitter pathways in the brain. Evidence suggests that these medications alleviate depression by increasing the availability of two key brain neurotransmitters, *norepinephrine* and *serotonin.* However, even though brain levels of norepinephrine and serotonin begin to rise within *hours* of taking a tricyclic or MAO inhibitor, it can take up to six *weeks* before depressive symptoms begin to lift (Richelson, 1993).

In about 75 percent of patients with depression, tricyclics and MAO inhibitors effectively eliminate depressive symptoms (Fawcett, 1994; Hornig-Rohan & Amsterdam, 1994). But these drugs can also produce numerous side effects. Tricyclic antidepressants can cause weight gain, dizziness, dry mouth and eyes, and sedation. And, because tricyclics affect the cardiovascular system, an overdose can be fatal. As for the MAO inhibitors, they can interact with a chemical found in many foods, including cheese, smoked meats, and red wine. Eating these foods while taking an MAO inhibitor can result in dangerously high blood pressure, leading to stroke or even death.

The search for antidepressants with fewer side effects led to the development of the second generation of antidepressants. Second-generation antidepressants include *trazodone* and *bupropion.* Although chemically different from the tricyclics, the second-generation antidepressants were generally no more

Lithium Water Lithium salt, a naturally occurring substance, was used in many over-the-counter medicines before it was discovered to be helpful in the treatment of mania. As this late-nineteenth-century ad shows, small amounts of lithium salt were also added to bottled water. An early version of the soft drink 7-Up included small amounts of lithium (Maxmen & Ward, 1995). Marketed as "lithium soda," the ad campaign claimed that it was the drink that took "the ouch out of the grouch!"

antianxiety medications
Prescription drugs that are used to alleviate the symptoms of anxiety.

lithium
A naturally occurring substance that is used in the treatment of bipolar disorder.

antidepressant medications
Prescription drugs that are used to reduce the symptoms associated with depression.

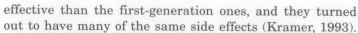

Table 14.9

Antidepressant Medications

	Generic Name	Trade Name
First-Generation Antidepressants		
Tricyclic antidepressants	Imipramine	Tofranil
	Desipramine	Norpramin
	Amitriptyline	Elavil
MAO inhibitors	Phenelzine	Nardil
	Tranylcypromine	Parnate
Second-Generation Antidepressants	Trazodone	Desyrel
	Bupropion	Wellbutrin
Selective Serotonin Reuptake Inhibitors (SSRIs)	Fluoxetine	Prozac
	Sertraline	Zoloft
	Paroxetine	Paxil
	Fluvoxamine	Luvox
Dual-Action Antidepressants	Nefazodone	Serzone
	Mirtazapine	Remeron
	Citalopram	Celexa
Dual-Reuptake Inhibitors	Venlafaxine	Effexor
	Duloxetine	Cymbalta

SOURCE: Based on Julien (2005).

effective than the first-generation ones, and they turned out to have many of the same side effects (Kramer, 1993).

In 1987, the picture changed dramatically with the introduction of a third group of antidepressants, the **selective serotonin reuptake inhibitors,** abbreviated **SSRIs.** Rather than acting on multiple neurotransmitter pathways, the SSRIs primarily affect the availability of a single neurotransmitter—serotonin. Compared with the earlier antidepressants, the new antidepressants act much more selectively in targeting specific serotonin pathways in the brain. The first SSRI to be released was *fluoxetine,* which is better known by its trade name, *Prozac.* Prozac was quickly followed by its chemical cousins, *Zoloft* and *Paxil.*

Prozac was specifically designed to alleviate depressive symptoms with fewer side effects than earlier antidepressants. It achieved that goal with considerable success. Although no more effective than tricyclics or MAO inhibitors, Prozac and the other SSRI antidepressants tend to produce fewer, and milder, side effects. But no medication is risk-free. Among Prozac's potential side effects are headaches, nervousness, difficulty sleeping, loss of appetite, and sexual dysfunction (Michelson & others, 2000).

Because of its overall effectiveness and relatively mild side-effects profile, Prozac quickly became very popular. By the early 1990s, an estimated *1 million prescriptions per month* were being written for Prozac. By the late 1990s, Prozac had become the best-selling antidepressant in the world. Today, Prozac is available in generic form, greatly reducing its cost. But even so, the antidepressants Prozac and Zoloft account for more than $4 billion a year in sales in just the United States (*NOCHealth,* 2005).

Since the original SSRIs were released, new antidepressants have been developed, including *Serzone, Remeron,* and *Celexa.* These antidepressants, called *dual-action antidepressants,* also affect serotonin levels, but their mechanism is somewhat different from that of the SSRIs. They are as effective as the SSRIs but have different side effects.

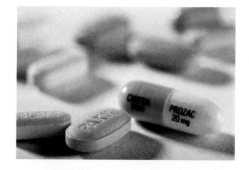

Finally, *Effexor* and *Cymbalta* are two newer antidepressants that are best classified as dual-reuptake inhibitors, affecting levels of both serotonin and norepinephrine. Possibly because of its dual action, Effexor seems to be somewhat more effective than the SSRIs in alleviating the symptoms of depression (Thase & others, 2001). However, Effexor's potential side effects include diminished sexual interest and weight gain. In contrast, Cymbalta was approved by the FDA in late 2004. However, the effectiveness of Cymbalta as an antidepressant has yet to be demonstrated beyond clinical trials.

Electroconvulsive Therapy

As we have just seen, millions of prescriptions are written for antidepressant medications in the United States every year. In contrast, about 100,000 patients a year receive **electroconvulsive therapy,** or **ECT,** as a medical treatment for severe depression. Also known as *electroshock therapy* or *shock therapy,* electroconvulsive therapy involves using a brief burst of electric current to induce a seizure in the brain, much like an epileptic seizure. Although ECT is most commonly used to treat depression, it is occasionally used to treat mania, catatonia, and other severe mental disorders (Glass, 2001).

ECT is a relatively simple and quick medical procedure, usually performed in a hospital. The patient lies on a table. Electrodes are placed on one or both of

Neuroscience: Comparing Psychotherapy and Antidepressant Medication

Prefrontal cortex

Prefrontal cortex

Prefrontal cortex

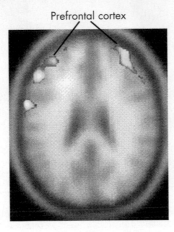

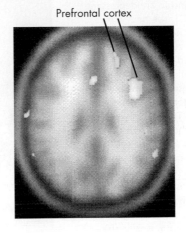

(a)
Baseline—before treatment

(b)
Decrease in activity after 12 weeks
of treatment with Paxil

(c)
Decrease in activity after 12 weeks of
treatment with interpersonal therapy

Both antidepressant medication and psychotherapy have been used to treat major depression. As we discussed in Chapter 14, major depression is characterized by a variety of physical symptoms, including changes in brain activity (Sackeim, 2001; Thase, 2001). Antidepressants are assumed to work their effect by changing brain chemistry and activity. Does psychotherapy have the same effect?

In a recent study, PET scans were done on 24 people with major depression and compared to a matched group of normal control subjects who were *not* depressed (Brody & others, 2001). Compared with the nondepressed adults, the depressed individuals showed increased activity in three areas of the brain: the *prefrontal cortex,* the *caudate nucleus,* and the *thalamus.* The day after the first scan, 10 of the 24 depressed individuals started taking the antidepressant Paxil, an SSRI. The remaining 14 individuals with depression started interpersonal therapy (discussed earlier in this chapter), a psychodynamic therapy that has been shown to be effective in the treatment of depression. Twelve weeks after beginning treatment, the participants' depressive symptoms were measured, and all 24 study participants underwent PET scans again.

Following *either* treatment, patients' depressive symptoms improved. And, the PET scans revealed that patients in *both* groups showed a trend toward more normalized brain functioning. Activity declined significantly in brain regions that had shown abnormally high activity before treatment began.

The PET scans shown here depict changes in the prefrontal cortex, one of the regions that showed a significant change toward more normal metabolic levels. Scan **(a)** shows activity levels in the prefrontal cortex before treatment. Scans **(b)** and **(c)** show the metabolic *decrease* in activity following treatment with Paxil **(b)** or interpersonal therapy **(c)**. In this comparison, note that **(b)** and **(c)** show the amount of change from the baseline condition, rather than the actual level of metabolic activity.

As these findings emphasize, *both* psychotherapy and antidepressant medication affect brain chemistry and functioning. In another study, both patients who were treated with interpersonal therapy and patients who were treated with the antidepressant Effexor showed improvement and similar changes in brain functioning (Martin & others, 2001).

SOURCE: Brody & others (2001).

the patient's temples, and the patient is given a short-term, light anesthetic and muscle-relaxing drugs. To ensure adequate airflow, a breathing tube is placed in the patient's throat.

While the patient is unconscious, a split-second burst of electricity induces a seizure. The seizure lasts for about a minute. Outwardly, the seizure typically produces mild muscle tremors. After the anesthesia wears off and the patient wakes up, confusion and disorientation may be present for a few hours. It is common for the patient to experience a temporary or permanent memory loss for the events leading up to the treatment. To treat major depression, a series of 6 to 10 ECT treatments are usually spaced over a few weeks.

In the short term, ECT is a very effective treatment for severe depression: About 80 percent of depressed patients improve (Glass, 2001). ECT also relieves the symptoms of depression very quickly, typically within days. Because of its rapid therapeutic effects, ECT can be a lifesaving procedure for extremely suicidal or severely depressed patients. Such patients may not survive for the several weeks it takes for antidepressant drugs to alleviate symptoms. In fact, it is not difficult to find former ECT patients who will flatly say that ECT saved their lives.

selective serotonin reuptake inhibitors (SSRIs)
Class of antidepressant medications that increase the availability of serotonin in the brain and cause fewer side effects than earlier antidepressants; they include Prozac, Paxil, and Zoloft.

electroconvulsive therapy (ECT)
A biomedical therapy used primarily in the treatment of depression that involves electrically inducing a brief brain seizure; also called *electroshock therapy* or *shock therapy.*

Electroconvulsive Therapy ECT is still used in the treatment of depression, especially in people who do not respond to antidepressant medication. In modern ECT, the person is given a short-acting anesthetic and muscle relaxants. A mild brain seizure, which lasts about a minute, is induced by a brief pulse of electricity. In the photo, the man standing at the head of the hospital gurney is the anesthesiologist, who is monitoring the patient's breathing and vital signs. The woman on the right is a surgical nurse who is assisting the anesthesiologist. The woman on the left is a psychiatric nurse, who is making clinical observations of the patient's response. The man on the left is the psychiatrist. He is watching the electroencephalograph readout of the patient's brain waves, which indicates the beginning and end of the seizure. Finally, the black object in the patient's mouth is an intubator tube, which helps ensure that the patient gets adequate oxygen during the procedure.

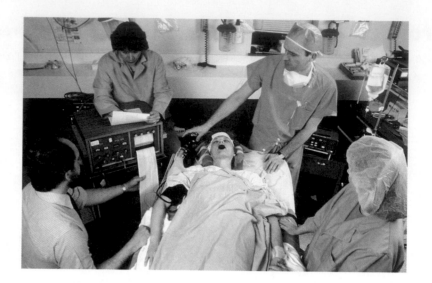

ECT may also be considered when patients are not helped by antidepressant medications or psychotherapy or when they cannot tolerate the side effects of medications. For some people, such as elderly individuals, ECT may be less dangerous than antidepressant drugs. In general, the complication rate from ECT is very low.

Nevertheless, inducing a brain seizure is not a matter to be taken lightly. ECT has potential dangers. Serious cognitive impairments can occur, such as extensive amnesia and disturbances in language and verbal abilities. However, fears that ECT might produce brain damage have not been confirmed by research (Devanand & others, 1994).

ECT's biggest drawback is that its antidepressive effects can be short-lived. Relapses within four months are relatively common (Glass, 2001). About half the patients treated for major depression experience a relapse within six months. Today, patients are often treated with long-term antidepressant medication following ECT, which reduces the relapse rate (Sackeim & others, 2001). In cases of severe, recurrent depression, ECT may also be periodically readministered to prevent the return of depressive symptoms (Gagné & others, 2000).

At this point, you may be wondering why ECT is not in wider use. The reason is that ECT is the most controversial medical treatment for psychological disorders (Glass, 2001). Not everyone agrees that ECT is either safe or effective (Breggin, 1991). For example, ECT has been banned in some countries, like Japan, because of concerns about its safety. Furthermore, not all patients benefit from ECT. Many patients report mixed feelings about their ECT experiences (Koopowitz & others, 2003).

How does ECT work? Despite more than 50 years of research, it's still not known why electrically inducing a convulsion relieves the symptoms of depression (Glass, 2001). Brain-imaging studies suggest that ECT reduces activity in brain regions involved in depression (Nobler & others, 2001).

Closing Thoughts

As you've seen throughout this chapter, a wide range of therapies are available to help people who are troubled by psychological symptoms and disorders. Like our friend Marcia, whose story we told in the Prologue, many people benefit psychologically from psychotherapy. As the first part of the chapter showed, psychotherapy can help people by providing insight, developing more effective behaviors and coping strategies, and changing thought patterns.

The biomedical therapies, discussed in the second part of the chapter, can also help people with psychological problems. This was also true in Marcia's case, when she reluctantly agreed to try an antidepressant medication. For almost a year, Marcia took a low dose of one of the SSRI antidepressant medications. It helped in the short term, lessening the feelings of depression and anxiety and giving her time to work through various issues in therapy and develop greater psychological resilience. Today, people are increasingly being helped by a combination of psychotherapy and one of the psychotropic medications.

As our discussion of the effectiveness of psychotherapy has shown, characteristics of both the therapist and the client are important to the success of psychotherapy. In the chapter Application, we describe the attitudes that should be brought to the therapeutic relationship, discuss some general ground rules of psychotherapy, and dispel some common misunderstandings. The Application will help you understand the nature of the therapeutic relationship and provide information useful to anyone who may be considering entering psychotherapy.

APPLICATION   What to Expect in Psychotherapy

The cornerstone of psychotherapy is the relationship between the therapist and the person seeking help. But the therapy relationship is different from all other close relationships. On the one hand, the therapist–client relationship is characterized by intimacy and the disclosure of very private, personal experiences. On the other hand, there are distinct boundaries to the therapist–client relationship. To a therapy client, especially one who is undertaking psychotherapy for the first time, the therapy relationship may sometimes seem confusing and contradictory.

The following guidelines should help you understand the special nature of the therapy relationship and develop realistic expectations about the process of psychotherapy.

1. Strengthen your commitment to change.

Therapy is not about maintaining the status quo. It is about making changes in terms of how you think, feel, act, and respond. For many people, the idea of change produces mixed feelings. You can strengthen your commitment and readiness to change by thinking about the reasons you want to change, the psychological abilities you already possess, and your willingness to try (Hettema & others, 2005).

NON SEQUITUR   by Wiley Miller

2. Therapy is a collaborative effort.

Don't expect your therapist to do all the work for you. If you are going to benefit from psychotherapy, you must actively participate in the therapeutic process. Often, therapy requires effort not only during the therapy sessions but also *outside* them. Many therapists assign "homework" to be completed between sessions. You may be asked to keep a diary of your thoughts and behaviors, read assigned material, rehearse skills that you've learned in therapy, and so forth. Such exercises are important components of the overall therapy process.

3. Don't confuse catharsis with change.

In the chapter Prologue, Marcia mentions the cathartic effect of therapy. *Catharsis* refers to the emotional release that people experience from the simple act of talking about their problems. Although it usually produces short-term emotional relief, catharsis in itself does not resolve the problem. Even so, catharsis is an important element of psychotherapy. Discussing emotionally charged issues with a therapist can lessen your sense of psychological tension and urgency and can help you explore the problem more rationally and objectively.

4. Don't confuse insight with change.

Despite what you've seen in the movies, developing insight into the sources or nature of your psychological problems does not magically resolve them. Nor does insight automatically translate into healthier thoughts and behaviors. Instead, insight allows you to look at and understand your problems in a new light. The opportunity for change occurs when your therapist helps you use these insights to redefine past experiences, resolve psychological conflicts, and explore more adaptive forms of behavior. Even with the benefit of insight, it takes effort to change how you think, behave, and react to other people.

5. Don't expect your therapist to make decisions for you.

One of the most common misunderstandings about psychotherapy is that your therapist is going to tell you how to run your life. Not so. Virtually all forms of therapy are designed to increase a person's sense of responsibility, confidence, and mastery in dealing with life's problems. Your therapist won't make your decisions for you, but he or she *will* help you explore your feelings about important decisions—including ambivalence or fear. Some people find this frustrating because they want the therapist to tell them what to do. But if your therapist made decisions for you, it would only foster dependency and undermine your ability to be responsible for your own life.

6. Expect therapy to challenge how you think and act.

As you confront issues that you've never discussed before or even admitted to yourself, you may find therapy very anxiety-provoking. Moments of psychological discomfort are a normal, even expected, part of the therapy process.

Think of therapy as a psychological magnifying glass. Therapy tends to magnify both your strengths and your weaknesses. Such intense self-scrutiny is not always flattering. Examining how you habitually deal with failure and success, conflict and resolution, disappointment and joy can be disturbing. You may become aware of the psychological games you play or of how you use ego defense mechanisms to distort reality. You may have to acknowledge your own immature, maladaptive, or destructive behavior patterns. Although it can be painful, becoming aware that changes are needed is a necessary step toward developing healthier forms of thinking and behavior.

7. Your therapist is not a substitute friend.

Unlike friendship, which is characterized by a mutual give-and-take, psychotherapy is focused solely on *you*. Rather than thinking of your therapist as a friend, think of him or her as an expert consultant—someone you've hired to help you deal better with your problems. The fact that your therapist is not socially or personally involved with you allows him or her to respond objectively and honestly. Part of what allows you to trust your therapist and "open up" emotionally is the knowledge that your therapist is ethically and legally bound to safeguard the confidentiality of what you say.

8. Therapeutic intimacy does not include sexual intimacy.

It's very common for clients to have strong feelings of affection, love, and even sexual attraction toward their therapists (Pope & Tabachnick, 1993). After all, the most effective therapists tend to be warm, empathic people who are genuinely caring and supportive (Beutler & others, 2004).

However, *it is never ethical or appropriate for a therapist to have any form of sexual contact with a client.* There are *no* exceptions to that statement. Sexual contact between a therapist and a client violates the ethical standards of all mental health professionals.

How often does sexual contact occur? About 7 percent of male and 2 percent of female therapists admit that they have had sexual contact with clients (Davis & others, 1995; Williams, 1992).

Sexual involvement between client and therapist can be enormously damaging (Pope, 1990). Not only does it destroy the therapist's professional objectivity, but it also destroys the trust the client has invested in the therapist. When a therapist becomes sexually involved with a client, regardless of who initiated the sexual contact, the client is being exploited.

Rather than exploiting a client's feelings of sexual attraction, an ethical therapist will help the client understand and work through such feelings. Therapy should ultimately help you develop closer, more loving relationships with other people—but *not* with your therapist.

9. Don't expect change to happen overnight.

Change occurs in psychotherapy at different rates for different people. How quickly change occurs depends on many factors, such as the seriousness of your problems, the degree to which you are psychologically ready to make needed changes, and the therapist's skill in helping you implement those changes. As a general rule, most people make significant progress in a few months of weekly therapy sessions (McNeilly & Howard, 1991). You can help create the climate for change by choosing a therapist you feel comfortable working with and by genuinely investing yourself in the therapy process.

Chapter Review

Therapies

Key Points

Introduction: Psychotherapy and Biomedical Therapy

- Psychological disorders can be treated with psychotherapy or biomedical therapy. **Psychotherapy** is based on the assumption that psychological factors play an important role in psychological disorders and symptoms. The **biomedical therapies** are based on the assumption that biological factors play an important role in psychological disorders and symptoms.

Psychoanalytic Therapy

- **Psychoanalysis** is a form of therapy developed by Sigmund Freud and based on his theory of personality. The goal of psychoanalysis is to unearth repressed conflicts and resolve them in therapy.

- Psychoanalytic techniques and processes include **free association, resistance, dream interpretation, interpretation,** and **transference.** Traditional psychoanalysis involves an intense, long-term relationship between the patient and the psychoanalyst.

- **Short-term dynamic therapies** are based on psychoanalytic ideas but are more problem-focused and of shorter duration than traditional psychoanalysis. Therapists play a more directive role than traditional psychoanalysts, but they still use psychoanalytic techniques to help the patient resolve unconscious conflicts. **Interpersonal therapy (IPT)** is based on the premise that interpersonal problems are the cause of psychological disorders.

Humanistic Therapy

- **Client-centered therapy** was developed by Carl Rogers. Important aspects of client-centered therapy include a client who directs the focus of therapy sessions and a therapist who is genuine, demonstrates unconditional positive regard, and communicates empathic understanding.

- According to Rogers, clients change and grow when their self-concept becomes healthier as a result of these therapeutic conditions.

Behavior Therapy

- **Behavior therapy** assumes that maladaptive behaviors are learned and uses learning principles to directly change problem behaviors.

- Mary Cover Jones was the first behavior therapist, using the procedure of **counterconditioning** to extinguish phobic behavior in a child.

- Classical conditioning principles are involved in the use of **systematic desensitization** to treat phobias, the **bell and pad treatment** to treat bedwetting, and **aversive conditioning** to treat harmful behaviors such as smoking and alcohol addiction.

- Operant conditioning techniques include using positive reinforcement for desired behaviors and extinction for undesired behaviors. The **token economy** represents the application of operant conditioning to modify the behavior of groups of people who live in a hospital or other institution. Contingency management interventions are one application of the token economy, typically used in outpatient treatment.

Cognitive Therapies

- The **cognitive therapies** are based on the assumption that psychological problems are caused by maladaptive patterns of thinking. Treatment focuses on changing unhealthy thinking patterns to healthier ones.

- **Rational-emotive therapy (RET)** was developed by Albert Ellis. RET focuses on changing the irrational thinking that is assumed to be the cause of emotional distress and psychological problems. Therapy involves identifying and challenging core irrational beliefs.

- **Cognitive therapy (CT)** was developed by Aaron T. Beck. CT is based on the assumption that psychological problems are caused by unrealistic and distorted thinking. Therapy involves teaching the client to recognize negative automatic thoughts and cognitive biases, and to empirically test the reality of the upsetting automatic thoughts.

- **Cognitive-behavioral therapy (CBT)** is based on the assumption that thoughts, moods, and behaviors are functionally interrelated. CBT combines cognitive and behavioral techniques in an integrated but flexible treatment plan.

Group and Family Therapy

- **Group therapy** involves one or more therapists working with several people simultaneously. Group therapy has these advantages: It is cost-effective; therapists can observe clients interacting with other group members; clients benefit from the support, encouragement, and practical suggestions provided by other group members; and people can try out new behaviors in a safe, supportive environment.

- **Family therapy** focuses on the family rather than on the individual and is based on the assumption that the family is an interdependent system. Marital or couple therapy focuses on improving communication, problem-solving skills, and intimacy between members of a couple.

Evaluating the Effectiveness of Psychotherapy

- Meta-analysis has been used to combine the findings of many different studies on the effectiveness of psychotherapy. In general, psychotherapy has been shown to be significantly more effective than no treatment.

- Among the standard psychotherapies, no particular form of therapy is superior to the others. However, particular forms of therapy are more effective than others for treating some specific problems.

- Factors identified as crucial to therapy's effectiveness include the quality of the therapeutic relationship; the therapist's characteristics; the therapist's sensitivity to cultural differences; the client's characteristics; and supportive, stable external circumstances.

- Most psychotherapists today identify their orientation as **eclectic,** meaning that they integrate the techniques of more than one form of psychotherapy, tailoring their approach to the individual client's needs.

Biomedical Therapies

- The most common biomedical therapy is **psychotropic medications.**

- **Antipsychotic medications** include reserpine and chlorpromazine, which alter dopamine levels throughout the brain. Although these drugs reduce positive symptoms of schizophrenia, they have little effect on negative symptoms. Serious side effects can include the development of tardive dyskinesia after long-term use.

- The newer, second-generation **atypical antipsychotic medications** affect both serotonin and dopamine levels in the brain. The atypical antipsychotics have fewer side effects and more effectively treat the positive and negative symptoms of schizophrenia.

- **Antianxiety medications** include the benzodiazepines, such as diazepam (Valium). The benzodiazepines are effective in the treatment of anxiety but are potentially addictive and have many side effects. Buspirone (Buspar) is a newer antianxiety medication that is apparently nonaddictive.

- **Lithium** effectively treats bipolar disorder by regulating glutamate levels in the brain. Depakote, an anticonvulsant, is also used to treat bipolar disorder.

- **Antidepressant medications** include the tricyclics, the MAO inhibitors, and the second-generation antidepressants. New antidepressants, including the **selective serotonin reuptake inhibitors (SSRIs),** the dual-action antidepressants, and the dual-reuptake inhibitors, tend to produce fewer side effects than the first- and second-generation antidepressants.

- **Electroconvulsive therapy (ECT),** which involves delivering a brief electric shock to the brain, is sometimes used in treating severe depression. The therapeutic effects of ECT tend to be short-lived, lasting no more than a few months. Partly because it is controversial, ECT is used far less frequently than antidepressant medication in the treatment of depression.

Key Terms

Key People

Aaron T. Beck (b. 1921) American psychiatrist who founded cognitive therapy (CT), a psychotherapy based on the assumption that depression and other psychological problems are caused by biased perceptions, distorted thinking, and inaccurate beliefs. (p. 564)

Albert Ellis (b. 1913) American psychologist who founded the cognitive psychotherapy called rational-emotive therapy (RET), which emphasizes recognizing and changing irrational beliefs. (p. 562)

Sigmund Freud (1856–1939) Austrian physician and founder of psychoanalysis who theorized that psychological symptoms are the result of unconscious and unresolved conflicts stemming from early childhood (also see Chapter 10). (p. 550)

Mary Cover Jones (1896–1987) American psychologist who conducted the first clinical demonstrations of behavior therapy. (p. 556)

Carl Rogers (1902–1987) American psychologist who helped found humanistic psychology and developed client-centered therapy (also see Chapter 10). (p. 553)

Web Companion Review Activities

You can find additional review activities by going to **www.DiscoveringPsychology.com** and clicking on the *Discovering Psychology* 4th Edition text cover. At the Discovering Psychology Web Companion you'll find the chapter learning objectives, flashcards for key terms and key people, interactive crossword puzzles, self-scoring practice quizzes, and other materials to help you master the information in this chapter.

Statistics: Understanding Data

Marie D. Thomas *California State University, San Marcos*

Prologue The Tables Are Turned: A Psychologist Becomes a Research Subject

For 12 months I was a participant in a research project that was designed to compare the effects of "traditional" and "alternative" diet, exercise, and stress-reduction programs (Riegel & others, 1996). Volunteers who were randomly assigned to the *traditional* program were taught to eat a high-fiber, low-fat diet; do regular aerobic exercise; and practice a progressive muscle relaxation technique. Participants who were randomly assigned to the *alternative* program received instruction in yoga and in a meditation technique, along with a diet based on body type and tastes. I was randomly assigned to the *no-treatment* control group, which was monitored throughout the year for weight and general health but received no diet, exercise, or stress-reduction intervention.

The participants in the study were drawn from a large medical group. Invitations to participate in the study were sent to 15,000 members of the medical group. Out of that initial pool, 124 volunteers were recruited, and about 40 were randomly selected for each group—the *traditional, alternative,* and *no-treatment control groups.* The participants included men and women between the ages of 20 and 56. A total of 88 subjects lasted the full year. The researchers were pleased that so many of us stayed with the project; it isn't easy to get people to commit to a year-long study!

Data collection began even before participants found out the group to which they had been randomly assigned. We were mailed a thick packet of questionnaires covering a wide range of topics. One questionnaire asked about our current health status, use of prescription and over-the-counter medications, use of vitamins, and visits to both physicians and alternative health care practitioners. Another questionnaire focused on self-perceptions of health and well-being. Here we rated our mood, energy level, physical symptoms, and health in general. A lifestyle survey requested information about diet (how often did we eat red meat? how many servings of fruits and vegetables did we consume a day?), exercise (how many times per week did we do aerobic exercise?), and behavior (such as cigarette smoking and consumption of alcoholic beverages). The lifestyle survey also assessed psychological variables such as levels of stress and happiness and how well we felt we were coping.

At our first meeting with the researchers, we handed in the questionnaires and were told which of the three groups we had been assigned to. We returned early the next morning to have our blood pressure and weight measured and to have blood drawn for tests of our levels of cholesterol, triglycerides, and glucose. The two intervention groups also received a weekend of training in their respective programs. In addition to daily practice of the techniques they had been taught, people in the *traditional* and *alternative* groups were expected to maintain a "compliance diary"—a daily record of their exercise, diet, and relaxation/meditation activities. The purpose of this diary was to determine whether health outcomes were better for people who practiced the techniques regularly. At first I was disappointed when I was randomly assigned to the control group because I was especially interested in learning the alternative techniques. However, I was relieved later when I found out how much detailed record keeping the intervention groups had to do!

The researchers accumulated even more data over the yearlong period. Every 3 months, our blood pressure and weight were measured. At 6 and 12 months, the researchers performed blood tests and asked us to fill out questionnaires identical to those we'd completed at the beginning of the project.

The study included many variables. The most important independent variable (the variable that the researcher manipulates) was group assignment: *traditional* program, *alternative* program, or *no-treatment* control. The dependent variables (variables that are not directly manipulated by the researcher but that may change in response to manipulations of the independent variable) included weight, blood pressure, cholesterol level, self-perceptions regarding health, and mood. Since the dependent variables were measured several times, the researchers could study changes in them over the course of the year.

This study can help to answer important questions about the kinds of programs that tend to promote health. But the purpose of describing it here is not just to tell you whether the two intervention programs were effective and whether one worked better than the other. In the next couple of sections, I will use this study to help explain how researchers use **statistics** to (1) summarize the data they have collected and (2) draw conclusions about the data. The job of assessing what conclusions can be drawn from the research findings is the domain of *inferential statistics,* which I'll discuss later in this appendix. We'll begin by exploring how research findings can be summarized in ways that are brief yet meaningful and easy to understand. For this, researchers use *descriptive statistics.*

This pie chart shows how much pie I ate while making this chart.

© Dan Piraro. Reprinted with special permission of King Features Syndicate.

statistics
A branch of mathematics used by researchers to organize, summarize, and interpret data.

descriptive statistics
Mathematical methods used to organize and summarize data.

frequency distribution
A summary of how often various scores occur in a sample of scores. Score values are arranged in order of magnitude, and the number of times each score occurs is recorded.

histogram
A way of graphically representing a frequency distribution; a type of bar chart that uses vertical bars that touch.

Descriptive Statistics

The study of programs to promote health generated a large amount of data. How did the researchers make sense of such a mass of information? How did they summarize it in meaningful ways? The answer lies in descriptive statistics. **Descriptive statistics** do just what their name suggests—they describe data. There are many ways to describe information. This appendix will examine four of the most common: frequency distributions, measures of central tendency, measures of variability, and measures of relationships. Since I don't have access to all the data that the health-promotion researchers gathered, I'll use hypothetical numbers to illustrate these statistical concepts.

Frequency Distribution

Suppose that at the start of the health-promotion study 30 people in the *traditional* group reported getting the following number of hours of aerobic exercise each week:

2, 5, 0, 1, 2, 2, 7, 0, 6, 2, 3, 1, 4, 5, 2,
1, 1, 3, 2, 1, 0, 4, 2, 3, 0, 1, 2, 3, 4, 1

Even with only 30 cases, it is difficult to make much sense of these data. Researchers need a way to organize such *raw scores* so that the information makes sense at a glance. One way to organize the data is to determine how many participants reported exercising 0 hours per week, how many reported exercising 1 hour, and so on, until all the reported amounts are accounted for. If the data were put into a table, the table would look like Table A.1.

This table is one way of presenting a **frequency distribution**—a summary of how often various scores occur. Categories are set up (in this case, the number of hours of aerobic exercise per week), and occurrences of each category are tallied to give the frequency of each one.

What information can be gathered from this frequency distribution table? We know immediately that most of the participants did aerobic exercise less than 3 hours per week. The number of hours per week peaked at 2 and declined steadily thereafter. According to the table, the most diligent exerciser worked out about an hour per day.

Some frequency distribution tables include an extra column that shows the percentage of cases in each category. For example, what percentage of participants reported 2 hours of aerobic exercise per week? The percentage is calculated by dividing the category frequency (8) by the total number of people (30), which yields about 27 percent.

While a table is good for summarizing data, it is often useful to present a frequency distribution visually, with graphs. One type of graph is the **histogram** (Figure A.1). A histogram is like a bar chart with two special features: The bars are always vertical, and they always touch. Categories (in our example, the number of hours of aerobic exercise per week) are placed on the

Table A.1

A Frequency Distribution Table

Hours of Aerobic Exercise per Week	Frequency
0	4
1	7
2	8
3	4
4	3
5	2
6	1
7	1
	30

A table like this is one way of presenting a frequency distribution. It shows at a glance that most of the people in our hypothetical group of 30 were not zealous exercisers before they began their traditional health-promotion program. Nearly two-thirds of them (19 people) engaged in vigorous exercise for 2 hours or less each week.

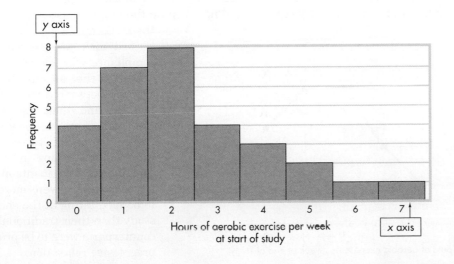

FIGURE A.1 A Histogram This histogram is another way of presenting the data given in Table A.1. Like the table, the histogram shows that most people do, at best, only a moderate amount of aerobic exercise (2 hours or less each week). This is immediately clear from the fact that the highest bars on the chart are on the left, where the hours of exercise are lowest.

FIGURE A.2 A Frequency Polygon (Positive Skew) Like Table A.1 and Figure A.1, this frequency polygon shows at a glance that the number of hours of aerobic exercise weekly is not great for most people. The high points come at 1 and 2 hours, which doesn't amount to much more than 10 or 15 minutes of exercise daily. An asymmetrical distribution like this one, which includes mostly low scores, is said to be positively skewed.

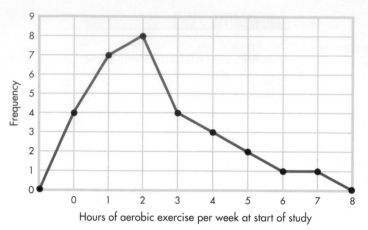

Hours of aerobic exercise per week at start of study

x (horizontal) axis, and the y (vertical) axis shows the frequency of each category. The resulting graph looks something like a city skyline, with buildings of different heights.

Another way of graphing the same data is with a **frequency polygon,** shown in Figure A.2. A mark is made above each category at the point representing its frequency. These marks are then connected by straight lines. In our example, the polygon begins before the "0" category and ends at a category of "8," even though both these categories have no cases in them. This is traditionally done so that the polygon is a closed figure.

Frequency polygons are good for showing the shape of a distribution. The polygon in Figure A.2 looks like a mountain, rising sharply over the first two categories, peaking at 2, and gradually diminishing from there. Such a distribution is asymmetrical, or a **skewed distribution,** meaning that if we drew a line through the middle of the x axis (halfway between 3 and 4 hours), more scores would be piled up on one side of the line than on the other. More specifically, the polygon in Figure A.2 represents a *positively skewed* distribution, indicating that most people had low scores. A *negatively skewed* distribution would have mostly high scores, with fewer scores at the low end of the distribution. For example, if the traditional diet and exercise intervention worked, the 30 participants should, as a group, be exercising more at the end of the study than they had been at the beginning. Perhaps the distribution of hours of aerobic exercise per week at the end of the study would look something like Figure A.3—a distribution with a slight negative skew.

In contrast to skewed distributions, a **symmetrical distribution** is one in which scores fall equally on both halves of the graph. A special case of a symmetrical distribution, the normal curve, is discussed in a later section.

A useful feature of frequency polygons is that more than one distribution can be graphed on the same set of axes. For example, the end-of-study hours of aerobic exercise per week for the *traditional* and *alternative* groups could be compared on a single graph. Doing so would make it possible to see at a glance whether one group was exercising more than the other after a year of their respective programs.

By the way, Figure A.3 is actually a figment of my imagination. According to the diaries kept by the traditional- and alternative-program participants, compliance with the exercise portion of the program decreased over time. This does not necessarily mean that these subjects were exercising *less* at the end of the study than at the beginning, but they certainly did not keep up the program as it was taught to them. Compliance with the prescribed diets was steadier than compliance with exercise; compliance by the alternative group dropped between 3 months and 6 months, and then rose steadily over time. There was, however, one major difference between the two intervention groups in terms of compliance. Participants in the alternative group were more likely to be meditating at the end of the study than their traditional-group counterparts were to be practicing progressive relaxation.

FIGURE A.3 A Frequency Polygon (Negative Skew) When more scores fall at the high end of a distribution than at the low end, the distribution is said to be negatively skewed. We would expect a negatively skewed distribution if a health-promotion program worked and encouraged more hours of aerobic exercise. The more effective the program, the greater the skew.

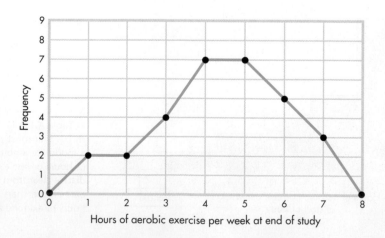

Hours of aerobic exercise per week at end of study

Measures of Central Tendency

Frequency distributions can be used to organize a set of data and tell us how scores are generally distributed. But researchers often want to put this information into a more compact form. They want to be able to summarize a distribution with a single score that is "typical." To do this, they use a **measure of central tendency.**

The Mode

The **mode** is the easiest measure of central tendency to calculate. The mode is simply the score or category that occurs most frequently in a set of raw scores or in a frequency distribution. The mode in the frequency distribution shown in Table A.1 is 2; more participants reported exercising 2 hours per week than any other category. In this example, the mode is an accurate representation of central tendency, but this is not always the case. In the distribution 1, 1, 1, 10, 20, 30, the mode is 1, yet half the scores are 10 and above. This type of distortion is the reason measures of central tendency other than the mode are needed.

The Median

Another way of describing central tendency is to determine the **median,** or the score that falls in the middle of a distribution. If the exercise scores were laid out from lowest to highest, they would look like this:

0, 0, 0, 0, 1, 1, 1, 1, 1, 1, 1, 2, 2, 2, 2, 2, 2, 2, 2, 3, 3, 3, 3, 4, 4, 4, 5, 5, 6, 7

↑

What would the middle score be? Since there are 30 scores, look for the point that divides the distribution in half, with 15 scores on each side of this point. The median can be found between the 15th and 16th scores (indicated by the arrow). In this distribution, the answer is easy: A score of 2 is the median as well as the mode.

The Mean

A problem with the mode and the median is that both measures reflect only one score in the distribution. For the mode, the score of importance is the most frequent one; for the median it is the middle score. A better measure of central tendency is usually one that reflects *all* scores. For this reason the most commonly used measure of central tendency is the **mean,** or arithmetic average. You have calculated the mean many times. It is computed by summing a set of scores and then dividing by the number of scores that went into the sum. In our example, adding together the exercise distribution scores gives a total of 70; the number of scores is 30, so 70 divided by 30 gives a mean of 2.33.

Formulas are used to express how a statistic is calculated. The formula for the mean is

$$\overline{X} = \frac{\Sigma X}{N}$$

In this formula, each letter and symbol has a specific meaning:

$\overline{X}$ is the symbol for the mean.

Σ is sigma, the Greek letter for capital S, and it stands for "sum." (Taking a course in statistics is one way to learn the Greek alphabet!)

X represents the scores in the distribution, so the numerator of the equation says, "Sum up all the scores."

N is the total number of scores in the distribution.

frequency polygon
A way of graphically representing a frequency distribution; frequency is marked above each score category on the graph's horizontal axis, and the marks are connected by straight lines.

skewed distribution
An asymmetrical distribution; more scores occur on one side of the distribution than on the other. In a *positively* skewed distribution, most of the scores are low scores; in a *negatively* skewed distribution, most of the scores are high scores.

symmetrical distribution
A distribution in which scores fall equally on both sides of the graph. The normal curve is an example of a symmetrical distribution.

measure of central tendency
A single number that presents some information about the "center" of a frequency distribution.

mode
The most frequently occurring score in a distribution.

median
The score that divides a frequency distribution exactly in half, so that the same number of scores lie on each side of it.

mean
The sum of a set of scores in a distribution divided by the number of scores; the mean is usually the most representative measure of central tendency.

Therefore, the formula says, "The mean equals the sum of all the scores divided by the total number of scores."

Although the mean is usually the most representative measure of central tendency because each score in a distribution enters into its computation, it is particularly susceptible to the effect of extreme scores. Any unusually high or low score will pull the mean in its direction. Suppose, for example, that in our frequency distribution for aerobic exercise one exercise zealot worked out 70 hours per week. The mean number of aerobic exercise hours would jump from 2.33 to 4.43. This new mean is deceptively high, given that most of the scores in the distribution are 2 and below. Because of just that one extreme score, the mean has become less representative of the distribution. Frequency tables and graphs are important tools for helping us identify extreme scores *before* we start computing statistics.

Measures of Variability

In addition to identifying the central tendency in a distribution, researchers may want to know how much the scores in that distribution differ from one another. Are they grouped closely together or widely spread out? To answer this question, we need some **measure of variability.** Figure A.4 shows two distributions with the same mean but with different variability.

A simple way to measure variability is with the **range,** which is computed by subtracting the lowest score in the distribution from the highest score. Let's say that there are 15 participants in the traditional diet and exercise group and that their weights at the beginning of the study varied from a low of 95 pounds to a high of 155 pounds. The range of weights in this group would be 155 − 95 = 60 pounds.

As a measure of variability, the range provides a limited amount of information because it depends on only the two most extreme scores in a distribution (the highest and lowest scores). A more useful measure of variability would give some idea of the average amount of variation in a distribution. But variation from what? The most common way to measure variability is to determine how far scores in a distribution vary from the distribution's mean. We saw earlier that the mean is usually the best way to represent the "center" of the distribution, so the mean seems like an appropriate reference point.

What if we subtract the mean from each score in a distribution to get a general idea of how far each score is from the center? When the mean is subtracted from a score, the result is a *deviation* from the mean. Scores that are above the mean would have positive deviations, and scores that are below the mean would have negative deviations. To get an average deviation, we would need to sum the deviations and divide by the number of deviations that went into the sum. There is a problem with this procedure, however. If deviations from the mean are added together, the sum will be 0 because the negative and positive deviations will cancel each other out. In fact, the real definition of the mean is "the only point in a distribution where all the scores' deviations from it add up to 0."

We need to somehow "get rid of" the negative deviations. In mathematics, such a problem is solved by squaring. If a negative number is squared, it becomes positive. So instead of simply adding up the deviations and dividing by the number of scores (N), we first square each deviation, then add together the *squared* deviations and divide by N. Finally, we need to compensate for the squaring operation. To do this, we take the square root of the number just calculated. This leaves us with the **standard deviation.** The larger the standard deviation, the more spread out are the scores in a distribution.

Let's look at an example to make this clearer. Table A.2 lists the hypothetical weights of the 15 participants in the traditional group at the beginning of the study. The mean, which is the sum of the weights divided by 15, is calculated to

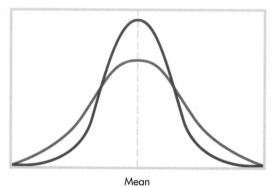

Mean

FIGURE A.4 Distributions with Different Variability Two distributions with the same mean can have very different variability, or spread, as shown in these two curves. Notice how one is more spread out than the other; its scores are distributed more widely.

Table A.2

Calculating the Standard Deviation

Weight	Mean	Weight − Mean	(Weight − Mean) Squared
X	$\overline{X}$	$X - \overline{X}$	$(X - \overline{X})^2$
155	124	31	961
149	124	25	625
142	124	18	324
138	124	14	196
134	124	10	100
131	124	7	49
127	124	3	9
125	124	1	1
120	124	−4	16
115	124	−9	81
112	124	−12	144
110	124	−14	196
105	124	−19	361
102	124	−22	484
95	124	−29	841

Sum (Σ) = 1,860 $\Sigma = 0$ $\Sigma = 4,388$

Mean $(\overline{X})$ = 124

$$SD = \sqrt{\frac{\Sigma(X - \overline{X})^2}{N}} = \sqrt{\frac{4,388}{15}} = 17.10$$

To calculate the standard deviation, you simply add all the scores in a distribution (the left-hand column in this example) and divide by the total number of scores to get the mean. Then you subtract the mean from each score to get a list of deviations from the mean (third column). Next you square each deviation (fourth column), add the squared deviations together, divide by the total number of cases, and take the square root.

measure of variability
A single number that presents information about the spread of scores in a distribution.

range
A measure of variability; the highest score in a distribution minus the lowest score.

standard deviation
A measure of variability; expressed as the square root of the sum of the squared deviations around the mean divided by the number of scores in the distribution.

be 124 pounds, as shown at the bottom of the left-hand column. The first step in computing the standard deviation is to subtract the mean from each score, which gives that score's deviation from the mean. These deviations are listed in the third column of the table. The next step is to square each of the deviations (done in the fourth column), then add the squared deviations ($\Sigma = 4,388$) and divide that total by the number of participants ($N = 15$). Finally, we take the square root to obtain the standard deviation ($SD = 17.10$). The formula for the standard deviation (SD) incorporates these instructions:

$$SD = \sqrt{\frac{\Sigma(X - \overline{X})^2}{N}}$$

Notice that when scores have large deviations from the mean, the *standard deviation* is also large.

z Scores and the Normal Curve

The mean and the standard deviation provide useful descriptive information about an entire set of scores. But researchers can also describe the relative position of any individual score in a distribution. This is done by locating how far away from the mean the score is in terms of standard deviation units. A statistic called a **z score** gives us this information:

$$z = \frac{X - \bar{X}}{SD}$$

This equation says that to compute a z score, we subtract the mean from the score we are interested in (that is, we calculate its deviation from the mean) and divide this quantity by the standard deviation. A positive z score indicates that the score is above the mean, and a negative z score shows that the score is below the mean. The larger the z score, the farther away from the mean the score is.

Let's take an example from the distribution found in Table A.2. What is the z score of a weight of 149 pounds? To find out, you simply subtract the mean from 149 and divide by the standard deviation.

$$z = \frac{149 - 124}{17.10} = 1.46$$

A z score of +1.46 tells us that a person weighing 149 pounds falls about one and a half standard deviations above the mean. In contrast, a person weighing 115 pounds has a weight below the mean and would have a negative z score. If you calculate this z score you will find it is −.53. This means that a weight of 115 is a little more than one-half a standard deviation below the mean.

Some variables, such as height, weight, and IQ, if graphed for large numbers of people, fall into a characteristic pattern. Figure A.5 shows this pattern, which is called the **standard normal curve** or the **standard normal distribution.** The normal curve is symmetrical (that is, if a line is drawn down its center, one side of the curve is a mirror image of the other side), and the mean, median, and mode fall exactly in the middle. The x axis of Figure A.5 is marked off in standard deviation units, which, conveniently, are also z scores. Notice that most of the cases fall between −1 and +1 *SD*s, with the number of cases sharply tapering off at either end. This pattern is the reason the normal curve is often described as "bell shaped."

The great thing about the normal curve is that we know exactly what percentage of the distribution falls between any two points on the curve. Figure A.5 shows the percentages of cases between major standard deviation units. For example, 34.13 percent of the distribution falls between 0 and +1. That means that 84.13 percent of the distribution falls *below* one standard deviation (the 34.13 percent that is between 0 and +1, plus the 50 percent that falls below 0). A person who obtains a z score of +1 on some normally distributed variable has scored better than 84 percent of the other people in the distribution. If a variable is normally distributed (that is, if it has the standard bell-shaped pattern), a person's z score can tell us exactly where that person stands relative to everyone else in the distribution.

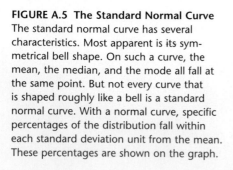

FIGURE A.5 The Standard Normal Curve
The standard normal curve has several characteristics. Most apparent is its symmetrical bell shape. On such a curve, the mean, the median, and the mode all fall at the same point. But not every curve that is shaped roughly like a bell is a standard normal curve. With a normal curve, specific percentages of the distribution fall within each standard deviation unit from the mean. These percentages are shown on the graph.

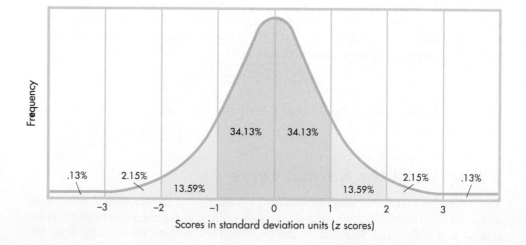

Correlation

So far, the statistical techniques we've looked at focus on one variable at a time, such as hours of aerobic exercise weekly or pounds of weight. Other techniques allow us to look at the relationship, or **correlation,** between two variables. Statistically, the magnitude and direction of the relationship between two variables can be expressed by a single number called a **correlation coefficient**.

To compute a correlation coefficient, we need two sets of measurements from the same individuals or from pairs of people who are similar in some way. To take a simple example, let's determine the correlation between height (we'll call this the x variable) and weight (the y variable). We start by obtaining height and weight measurements for each individual in a group. The idea is to combine all these measurements into one number that expresses something about the relationship between the two variables, height and weight. However, we are immediately confronted with a problem: The two variables are measured in different ways. Height is measured in inches, and weight is measured in pounds. We need some way to place both variables on a single scale.

Think back to our discussion of the normal curve and z scores. What do z scores do? They take data of any form and put them into a standard scale. Remember, too, that a high score in a distribution always has a positive z score, and a low score in a distribution always has a negative z score. To compute a correlation coefficient, the data from both variables of interest can be converted to z scores. Therefore, each individual will have two z scores: one for height (the x variable) and one for weight (the y variable).

Then, to compute the correlation coefficient, each person's two z scores are multiplied together. All these "cross-products" are added up, and this sum is divided by the number of individuals. In other words, a correlation coefficient is the average (or mean) of the z-score cross-products of the two variables being studied:

$$\text{correlation coefficient} = \frac{\sum z_x z_y}{N}$$

A correlation coefficient can range from +1.00 to −1.00. The exact number provides two pieces of information: It tells us about the *magnitude* of the relationship being measured, and it tells us about its *direction*. The magnitude, or degree, of relationship is indicated by the size of the number. A number close to 1 (whether positive or negative) indicates a strong relationship, while a number close to 0 indicates a weak relationship. The sign (+ or −) of the correlation coefficient tells us about the relationship's direction.

A **positive correlation** means that as one variable increases in size, the second variable also increases. For example, height and weight are positively correlated: As height increases, weight tends to increase also. In terms of z scores, a positive correlation means that high z scores on one variable tend to be multiplied by high z scores on the other variable and that low z scores on one variable tend to be multiplied by low z scores on the other. Remember that just as two positive numbers multiplied together result in a positive number, so two negative numbers multiplied together also result in a positive number. When the cross-products are added together, the sum in both cases is positive.

A **negative correlation,** in contrast, means that two variables are *inversely* related. As one variable increases in size, the other variable decreases. For example, professors like to believe that the more hours students study, the fewer errors they will make on exams. In z-score language, high z scores (which are positive) on one variable (more hours of study) tend to be multiplied by low z scores (which are negative) on the other variable (fewer errors on exams), and vice versa, making negative cross-products. When the cross-products are summed and divided by the number of cases, the result is a negative correlation coefficient.

FIGURE A.6 Scatter Plot of a Positive Correlation A correlation (or the lack of one) can be clearly shown on a scatter diagram. This one shows a moderately strong positive correlation between subjects' compliance with the yoga component of the alternative health-promotion program and their energy level. The positive direction of the correlation is indicated by the upward-sloping pattern of the dots, from bottom left to top right. This means that if one variable is high, the other tends to be high, too, and vice versa. That the strength of the relationship is only moderate is indicated by the fact that the data points (each indicating an individual subject's score) are not all positioned along a straight diagonal line.

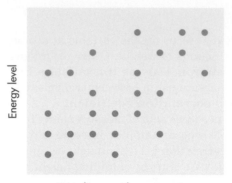

Energy level

Compliance with yoga routine

An easy way to show different correlations is with graphs. Plotting two variables together creates a **scatter diagram** or **scatter plot,** like the ones in Figures A.6, A.7, and A.8. These figures show the relationship between complying with some component of the alternative health-promotion program and some other variable related to health. Although the figures describe relationships actually found in the study, I have made up the specific correlations to illustrate key points.

Figure A.6 shows a moderately strong positive relationship between compliance with the yoga part of the alternative program and a person's energy level. You can see this just by looking at the pattern of the data points. They generally form a line running from lower left to upper right. When calculated, this particular correlation coefficient is +.59, which indicates a correlation roughly in the middle between 0 and +1.00. In other words, people who did more yoga tended to have higher energy levels. The "tended to" part is important. Some people who did not comply well with the yoga routine still had high energy levels, while the reverse was also true. A +1.00 correlation, or a *perfect* positive correlation, would indicate that frequent yoga sessions were *always* accompanied by high levels of energy, and vice versa. What would a scatter diagram of a perfect +1.00 correlation look like? It would be a straight diagonal line starting in the lower left-hand corner of the graph and progressing to the upper right-hand corner.

Several other positive correlations were found in this study. Compliance with the alternative diet was positively associated with increases in energy and positive health perceptions. In addition, following the high-fiber, low-fat traditional diet was associated with a higher level of coping and high vitamin intake.

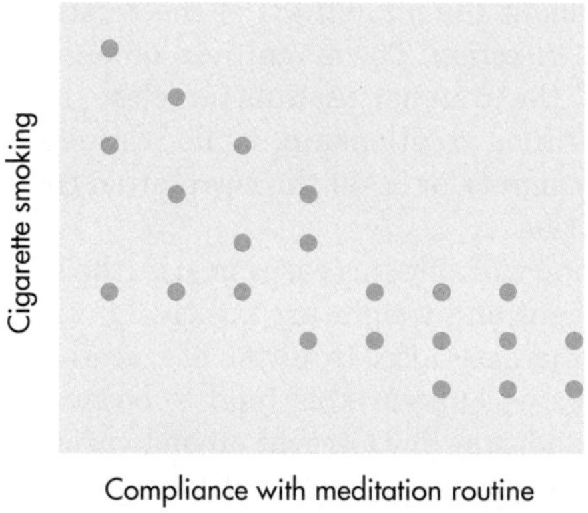

FIGURE A.7 Scatter Plot of a Negative Correlation In general, people who engage in meditation more often tend to smoke less. This negative correlation is indicated by the downward-sloping pattern of dots, from upper left to lower right. Because these dots are clustered somewhat closer together than those in Figure A.6, we can tell at a glance that the relationship here is somewhat stronger.

Cigarette smoking

Compliance with meditation routine

The study also found some negative correlations. Figure A.7 illustrates a *negative* correlation between compliance with the meditation part of the alternative program and cigarette smoking. This correlation coefficient is −.77. Note that the data points fall in the opposite direction from those in Figure A.6, indicating that as the frequency of meditation increased, cigarette smoking decreased. The pattern of points in Figure A.7 is closer to a straight line than is the

pattern of points in Figure A.6. A correlation of −.77 shows a relationship of greater magnitude than does a correlation of +.59. But though −.77 is a relatively high correlation, it is not a perfect relationship. A *perfect* negative relationship would be illustrated by a straight diagonal line starting in the upper left-hand corner of the graph and ending at the lower right-hand corner.

Finally, Figure A.8 shows two variables that are not related to each other. The hypothetical correlation coefficient between compliance with the aerobic exercise part of the traditional program and a person's level of coping is +.03, barely above 0. In the scatter diagram, data points fall randomly, with no general direction to them. From a *z*-score point of view, when two variables are not related, the cross-products are mixed—that is, some are positive and some are negative.

Sometimes high z scores on one variable go with high z scores on the other, and low z scores on one variable go with low z scores on the other. In both cases, positive cross-products result. In other pairs of scores, high z scores on one variable go with low z scores on the other variable (and vice versa), producing negative cross-products. When the cross-products for the two variables are summed, the positive and negative numbers cancel each other out, resulting in a 0 (or close to 0) correlation.

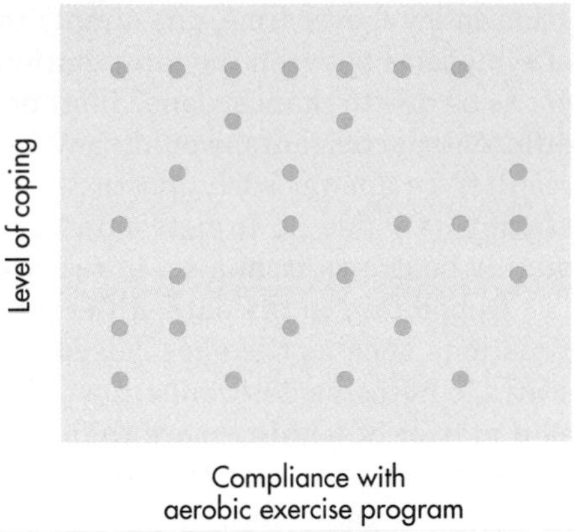

In addition to describing the relationship between two variables, correlation coefficients are useful for another purpose: prediction. If we know a person's score on one of two related variables, we can predict how he or she will perform on the other variable. For example, in a recent issue of a magazine I found a quiz to rate my risk of heart disease. I assigned myself points depending on my age, HDL ("good") and total cholesterol levels, systolic blood pressure, and other risk factors, such as cigarette smoking and diabetes. My total points (-2) indicated that I had less than a 1 percent risk of developing heart disease in the next five years. How could such a quiz be developed? Each of the factors I rated is correlated to some degree with heart disease. The older you are and the higher your cholesterol and blood pressure, the greater your chance of developing heart disease. Statistical techniques are used to determine the relative importance of each of these factors and to calculate the points that should be assigned to each level of a factor. Combining these factors provides a better prediction than any single factor because none of the individual risk factors correlate perfectly with the development of heart disease.

One thing you cannot conclude from a correlation coefficient is *causality*. In other words, the fact that two variables are highly correlated does not necessarily mean that one variable directly causes the other. Take the meditation and cigarette-smoking correlation. This negative correlation tells us that people in the study who diligently practiced meditation tended to smoke less than those who seldom meditated. Regular meditation may have had a direct effect on the desire to smoke cigarettes, but it is also possible that one or more other variables affected both meditation and smoking. For example, perhaps participation in the study convinced some people that they needed to change their lifestyles completely. Both compliance with the meditation routine and a decreased level of cigarette smoking may have been "caused" by this change in lifestyle. As discussed in Chapter 1, the *experimental method* is the only method that can provide compelling scientific evidence of a cause-and-effect relationship between two or more variables. Can you think of a way to test the hypothesis that regularly practicing meditation causes a reduction in the desire to smoke cigarettes?

Level of coping

Compliance with
aerobic exercise program

FIGURE A.8 Scatter Plot of No Correlation
You may be surprised to learn that in this study, compliance with the aerobic exercise portion of the traditional program was not related to level of coping. This scatter diagram shows that lack of relationship. The points fall randomly, revealing no general direction or trend and thus indicating the absence of a correlation.

Inferential Statistics

Let's say that the mean number of physical symptoms (like pain) experienced by the participants in each of the three groups was about the same at the beginning of the health-promotion study. A year later, the number of symptoms had decreased in the two intervention groups but had remained stable in the control group. This may or may not be a meaningful result. We would expect the average number of symptoms to be somewhat different for each of the three groups because each group consisted of different people. And we would expect some fluctu-

scatter diagram or **scatter plot**
A graph that represents the relationship between two variables.

inferential statistics
Mathematical methods used to determine how likely it is that a study's outcome is due to chance and whether the outcome can be legitimately generalized to a larger population.

population
A complete set of something—people, nonhuman animals, objects, or events.

sample
A subset of a population.

ation in level over time, due simply to chance. But are the differences in number of symptoms between the intervention groups and the control group large enough *not* to be due to chance alone? If other researchers conducted the same study with different participants, would they be likely to get the same general pattern of results? To answer such questions, we turn to inferential statistics. **Inferential statistics** guide us in determining what inferences, or conclusions, can legitimately be drawn from a set of research findings.

Depending on the data, different inferential statistics can be used to answer questions such as the ones raised in the preceding paragraph. Each inferential statistic helps us determine how likely a particular finding is to have occurred as a matter of nothing more than chance or random variation. If the inferential statistic indicates that the odds of a particular finding occurring are considerably greater than mere chance, we can conclude that our results are *statistically significant.* In other words, we can conclude with a high degree of confidence that the manipulation of the independent variable, rather than simply chance, is the reason for the results.

To see how this works, let's go back to the normal curve for a moment. Remember that we know exactly what percentage of a normal curve falls between any two z scores. If we choose one person at random out of a normal distribution, what is the chance that this person's z score is above +2? If you look again at Figure A.5, you will see that 2.28 percent of the curve lies above a z score (or standard deviation unit) of +2. Therefore, the chance, or *probability,* that the person we choose will have a z score above +2 is .0228 (or 2.28 chances out of 100). That's a pretty small chance. If you study the normal curve, you will see that the majority of cases (95.44 percent of the cases, to be exact) fall between −2 and +2 SDs, so in choosing a person at random, that person is not likely to fall above a z score of +2.

When researchers test for statistical significance, they usually employ statistics other than z scores, and they may use distributions that differ in shape from the normal curve. The logic, however, is the same. They compute some kind of inferential statistic that they compare to the appropriate distribution. This comparison tells them the likelihood of obtaining their results if chance alone is operating.

The problem is that no test exists that will tell us for sure whether our intervention or manipulation "worked"; we always have to deal with probabilities, not certainties. Researchers have developed some conventions to guide them in their decisions about whether or not their study results are statistically significant. Generally, when the probability of obtaining a particular result if random factors alone are operating is less than .05 (5 chances out of 100), the results are considered statistically significant. Researchers who want to be even more sure set their probability value at .01 (1 chance out of 100).

Because researchers deal with probabilities, there is a small but real possibility of *erroneously* concluding that study results are significant. The results of one study, therefore, should never be completely trusted. In order to have greater confidence in a particular effect or result, the study should be repeated, or *replicated.* If the same results are obtained in different studies, then we can be more certain that our conclusions about a particular intervention or effect are correct.

One final point about inferential statistics. Are the researchers interested only in the changes that might have occurred in the small groups of people participating in the health-promotion study, or do they really want to know whether the interventions would be effective for people in general? This question focuses on the difference between a population and a sample. A **population** is a complete set of something—people, nonhuman animals, objects, or events. The researchers who designed this study wanted to know whether the interventions they developed would benefit *all* people (or, more precisely, all people between the ages of 20 and 56). Obviously, they could not conduct a study on this entire population. The best they could do was choose some portion of that population to serve as subjects; in other words, they selected a **sample.** The study was conducted on this sample. The researchers analyzed the sample results, using inferential statistics to make guesses about what they would have found had they studied the entire population. Inferential statistics allow researchers to take the findings they obtain from a sample and apply them to a population.

So what did the health-promotion study find? Did the interventions work? The answer is "yes," sort of. The traditional- and alternative-treatment groups, when combined, improved more than did the no-treatment control group. At the end of the study, participants in the two intervention programs had better self-perceptions regarding health, better mood, more energy, and fewer physical symptoms. Compared with the traditional and the no-treatment groups, the alternative group showed greater improvement in health perceptions and a significant decrease in depression and the use of prescription drugs. Interestingly, participation in the treatment groups did not generally result in changes in health risk, such as lowered blood pressure or decreased weight. The researchers believe that little change occurred because the people who volunteered for the study were basically healthy individuals. The study needs to be replicated with a less healthy sample. In sum, the intervention programs had a greater effect on health perceptions and psychological variables than on physical variables. The researchers concluded that a health-promotion regimen (either traditional or alternative) is helpful. I'm sure other studies will be conducted to explore these issues further!

It's my fervent hope, Fernbaugh, that these are meaningless statistics.

Endnote

Although I briefly saw other study participants at each three-month data-collection point, I never spoke to anyone. The last measurement session, however, was also a celebration for our year-long participation in the project. Approximately 30 people attended my session, and participants from each of the three groups were present. After our blood was drawn and our blood pressure and weight readings were taken, we were treated to breakfast. Then one of the principal researchers *debriefed* us: She gave us some background on the study and told us what she hoped to learn. At this point, participants were given the opportunity to talk about how the study had affected their lives. It was fascinating to hear members of the intervention groups describe the changes they had made over the past year. One woman said that a year ago she could never imagine getting up early to meditate, yet now she looks forward to awakening each morning at 4:00 A.M. for her first meditation session. Other people described the modifications they had made in their diet and exercise patterns and how much better they felt. Although I did not experience either of the interventions, I know that simply being a subject in the study made me more conscious of what I ate and how much I exercised. This could have been a confounding factor; that is, it could have inadvertently changed my behavior even though I was in the control group. In fact, my weight decreased and my level of "good" cholesterol increased over the course of the year.

We were not paid for our participation in this study, but we received small gifts as tokens of the researchers' appreciation. In addition, we were all given the option of taking any or all of the intervention training at no cost (and some courses in alternative techniques could be quite expensive). The most important thing for me was the satisfaction of participation—the fact that I had stayed with the study for an entire year and, in a small way, had made a contribution to science.

growth is the greater reliance of private companies and government agencies on outside expertise to improve productivity (U. S. Bureau of Labor Statistics, 2000).

Employment interviewer is a third I/O-related career open to those with bachelor's degrees. Employment interviewers typically work for personnel supply firms, matching employers with job applicants and job applicants with employers. An employment interviewer needs sales ability because he or she is expected to attract clients and job applicants to the personnel supply firm. Self-confidence is needed, too, as are strong oral and interpersonal skills.

Demand for employment interviewers is expected to grow at an average rate. Some of the demand is being curtailed by the increased use of computerized job matches and information systems (U.S. Bureau of Labor Statistics, 2000).

If you would like to learn more about career opportunities in I/O psychology, visit some of the Web sites listed in Table B.1. For information that every employee should know, read In Focus Box B.1.

Table B.1

Below is a list of Web sites that relate to working in the field of industrial/organizational psychology.

www.aomonline.org	Academy of Management
www.dol.gov	The U.S. Department of Labor Job Information Site
www.shrm.org	The Society for Human Resource Management
www.siop.org	The Society for Industrial and Organizational Psychology

IN FOCUS B.1

What Every Employee Should Know

Getting the Boss to Like You

Employees who are good citizens (e.g., who help other employees, volunteer to do extra work, don't complain, and help their supervisors without being asked) are valuable to organizations, and as a result they may be recognized by their supervisors with better performance evaluations and bigger pay raises. In contrast, employees who are viewed as ingratiating (who are "political," seeking only to further their personal interests) do not reap these same benefits. In comparing the concept of being a good citizen with that of being ingratiating, Kenneth Eastman (1994) concluded that even though two employees might behave in similar ways, the motives that supervisors attributed to these behaviors were important to whether an employee was considered a good citizen or ingratiating. On a practical note, employees should become aware of how others, especially their supervisors, are interpreting their behavior (Eastman, 1994). Sincerity, consistency, and loyalty are likely to positively influence supervisors as they evaluate their employees.

Dispute Resolution

Imagine that you have been clearly and repeatedly sexually harassed by your supervisor or a co-worker. To address this problem, you may choose to use either (1) formal administrative and legal channels by filing a complaint with the Equal Employment Opportunity Commission (EEOC) or (2) the organization's system for resolving internal disputes. Organizations cannot forbid employees to use formal, legal channels, but they can encourage employees to use internal complaint procedures. In fact, the vast majority of complaints are handled internally, never reaching the courts or administrative agencies (Miller & Sarat, 1981). Internal complaint procedures should involve a neutral third-party mediator or arbitrator who helps to resolve the issue. Because internal dispute resolution often provides greater flexibility in solving problems, this process may be more likely to result in outcomes that are satisfactory for both parties in the dispute (Bush, 1989). However, it may be difficult for the third-party arbitrator or mediator to be truly neutral. The third party not only works for the organization but also would likely be involved in assisting or representing the organization should the employee file an external complaint (Edelman & others, 1993).

Getting Fired: Your Rights

In the absence of a specific contract, the relationship between employer and employee is an "at-will" one. Employment-at-will means that either the employer or the employee may terminate the relationship at any time, for any reason, without prior warning (Bakaly & Grossman, 1995). However, there are some restrictions on this doctrine. Specifically, employers are prohibited from discharging employees on the basis of legally protected characteristics (e.g., sex, race, religion), for exercising rights guaranteed by law (e.g., filing a discrimination charge against the employer), or for refusing to engage in illegal, immoral, or unethical acts on behalf of the employer. In addition, some discharged employees have been successful in suing the organization on the basis that an implied contract was violated. (You may have noticed that most employee handbooks state clearly that they are not contracts. This is to prevent discharged employees from arguing in court that the handbook was a contract.) Clearly, the power relationship between employer and employee is asymmetrical, with employees being more likely than employers to suffer if the relationship ends with discharge.

Personnel Psychology

Industrial or personnel psychology, as you have seen, focuses on the measurement of human knowledge, skills, and abilities; the measurement of job performance; the matching of people and jobs; and the training of workers.

Three major goals of personnel psychologists are: (1) selecting the best applicants for jobs, (2) training employees so that they perform their jobs effectively, and (3) accurately evaluating employee performance. The first step in attaining each of these goals is to perform a job analysis.

job analysis
An assessment of the major responsibilities of a particular job and the human characteristics needed to fill it.

The First Step
Job Analysis

Job analysis is a technique in which the major responsibilities of a job, along with the human characteristics needed to fill it, are determined. Information about the job is usually collected from employees who currently hold the job or from their supervisors. These people may be observed at their work, interviewed, or asked to complete surveys. Figure B.2 presents a job analysis for the position of job analyst itself.

Once a job's requirements are determined and written down in a job analysis, it is easier to achieve the goal of selecting an appropriate person for the position. Selection devices, such as tests and interviews, are used to determine which applicants have the knowledge, skills, and abilities specified in a job analysis. For example, a job analysis might reveal that as a salesperson, a dominant, extraverted personality is important. Applicants' personality traits might therefore be measured to screen for those who have these characteristics.

After appropriate applicants have been selected, the job of training them begins. Here, too, the key is to have a clear view of the job procedures, knowledge, and skills needed for effective job performance—that is, to have a good job analysis. Training program developers might begin by comparing the current work procedures, knowledge, and skills of employees with the information obtained from a job analysis. They would then design training programs to eliminate gaps between what currently exists and what is optimal.

Job analysis is also the first step in the design of performance appraisal systems. Before actual performance can be measured, expected performance must be defined. Job analysis defines and clarifies what effective performance is so that performance appraisal instruments may be developed.

JOB ANALYST alternate titles: personnel analyst

Collects, analyzes, and prepares occupational information to facilitate personnel, administration, and management functions of organization; consults with management to determine type, scope, and purpose of study. Studies current organizational occupational data and compiles distribution reports, organization and flow charts, and other background information required for study. Observes jobs and interviews workers and supervisory personnel to determine job and worker requirements. Analyzes occupational data, such as physical, mental, and training requirements of jobs and workers, and develops written summaries, such as job descriptions, job specifications, and lines of career movement. Utilizes developed occupational data to evaluate or improve methods and techniques for recruiting, selecting, promoting, evaluating, and training workers, and administration of related personnel programs. May specialize in classifying positions according to regulated guidelines to meet job classification requirements of civil service system, a specialty known as Position Classifier.

FIGURE B.2 A Sample Job Analysis The job analysis is a crucial tool in personnel psychology. A thorough job analysis is the first step not only in selecting among job applicants but also in training employees for specific positions and in evaluating their performance. This job analysis is for the job of job analyst itself.

SOURCE: *Dictionary of Occupational Titles* (1991).

A Closer Look at Personnel Selection

Have you ever applied for a job and not been hired? If so, you probably wondered what happened. Did you lose the job because of something you said or did in the interview or, perhaps, because of your responses on an application test? In this section, you'll learn about the applicant selection process. While you won't necessarily discover why you weren't picked for a particular job, you will get a better understanding of the selection processes that many companies use. This knowledge may help you to feel better prepared and more relaxed the next time you apply for a job.

The goal in personnel selection is to hire only those applicants who will perform the job effectively. A variety of selection devices are used to choose among applicants. The effectiveness of each device depends, in part, on its appropriateness

BIZZARO

THE MODERN JOB INTERVIEW —

...ONE FINAL QUESTION: WITH WHICH CHARACTER IN *DILBERT* DO YOU IDENTIFY MOST CLOSELY?

PERSONNEL DIRECTOR

selection device validity
The extent to which a personnel selection device is successful in distinguishing between those who will become high performers at a certain job and those who will not.

for a particular job. For example, a test of visual acuity may be a good selection device for the job of airline pilot but a poor selection device for the job of sewing-machine operator (some sewing-machine operators are able to sew with their eyes closed!). Personnel psychologists are concerned with the degree to which selection devices are valid. **Selection device validity** refers to the extent to which a selection device is successful in distinguishing between those applicants who will become high performers and those who will not. If a personality measure is used to select salespeople, it is considered valid if those whom it singles out as potential high performers do, indeed, become high performers.

Psychological Tests

Psychological tests are one kind of selection device that employers often use. Such tests are usually classified on the basis of what they measure. Common types of psychological tests are cognitive ability tests, mechanical aptitude tests, motor and sensory ability tests, and personality tests.

Cognitive ability tests measure general intelligence or specific cognitive skills, such as mathematical or verbal ability. Some items from two cognitive ability tests are presented in Figure B.3. *Mechanical ability tests* measure mechanical reasoning and may be used to predict job performance for engineering, carpentry, and assembly work. Figure B.4 presents sample items from the Bennett Test of Mechanical Comprehension. *Motor ability tests* include measures of fine dexterity in fingers and hands (for jobs that require the assembly of products with tiny parts), accuracy and speed of arm and hand movements, and eye–hand coordination. *Sensory ability tests* include measures of visual acuity, color vision, and hearing.

Personality tests may be designed to measure either abnormal or normal personality characteristics. An assessment of abnormal personality characteristics might be appropriate for selecting people for sensitive jobs, such as nuclear power plant operator, police officer, and airline pilot. Recently, tests designed to measure normal personality traits, such as conscientiousness, extraversion, and agreeableness, have become more popular for the selection of employees (e.g., Barrick & Mount, 1991, 1993; Tett & others, 1991).

(a) 1. RESENT/RESERVE — Do these words
       1 have similar meanings
       2 have contradictory meanings
       3 mean neither the same nor opposite
   2. Paper sells for 21 cents per pad. What will 4 pads cost?

(b)

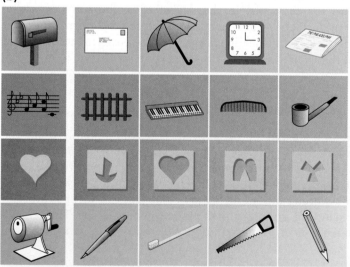

FIGURE B.3 Sample Items from Two Cognitive Ability Tests Cognitive ability tests can measure either general intelligence or specific cognitive skills, such as mathematical ability. **(a)** These two items are from the Wonderlic Personnel Test, which is designed to assess general cognitive ability. Employers assume that people who cannot answer most such questions correctly would not be good candidates for jobs that require general knowledge and reasoning skills. **(b)** The chart is from the Non-Verbal Reasoning Test. It assesses reasoning skills apart from the potentially confounding factor of skill with the English language.

SOURCES: Corsini (1957); Wonderlic (1998).

For each item find the picture that goes best with the picture in the first box. Draw a dark line from the upper right corner to the lower left corner in the proper box to show the right answer.

Because of legal restrictions on the use of polygraph tests in the workplace, honesty tests have also become more widely used in recent years. Honesty tests attempt to assess an applicant's level of honesty by asking about past behaviors involving theft or dishonesty, attitudes about theft and the punishment of it, and perceptions about the prevalence of theft. Honesty tests are used primarily in retail situations—and with good reason. Research indicates that dishonest employees steal $10.37 worth of merchandise for every dollar's worth stolen by shoplifters (Washburn, 1997). Furthermore, according to one study (Wimbush & Dalton, 1997), half of employees with access to cash steal from their employers. Many honesty tests are available to employers, some of which do a good job of predicting admissions of theft (i.e., comparing honesty test responses with anonymous admissions of theft) and polygraph results (i.e., comparing honesty test responses with polygraph operators' judgments about an individual's truthfulness) (Ones & others, 1993; Snyman & others, 1991).

Work Samples and Situational Exercises

Two other kinds of personnel selection devices are work samples and situational exercises. Work samples are typically used for jobs involving the manipulation of objects, while situational exercises are usually used for jobs involving managerial or professional skills. Work samples provide a high degree of realism in that they require applicants to complete work-related problems. They have been called "high-fidelity simulations" in that they require applicants to complete tasks as if they were on the job (Motowidlo & others, 1997). A high degree of realism is important because it may serve as a realistic job preview (RJP) (Phillips, 1998; Premack & Wanous, 1985). RJPs give applicants a realistic view of the job so that they have more information to help them to decide whether or not to accept the job. This technique may reduce turnover by preventing people who would have quit early on from taking the job in the first place.

One work-sample test for the job of mechanic, for instance, required the applicant to perform tasks such as taking apart and repairing a gearbox and installing pulleys and belts. Successful performance on the work-sample test did, in fact, predict successful performance on the job (Campion, 1972). A common situational exercise is the in-basket test, which requires the applicant to sort through a series of memos, directives, reports, letters, and phone messages in a limited amount of time (Frederickson, 1968). The employer evaluates the way in which the applicant organizes and deals with the items.

Selection Interviews

Although the general interview is one of the most commonly used selection devices, it typically possesses low validity. That is, assessments of applicants in general interviews are not strongly related to the applicants' subsequent job performance (Hunter & Hunter, 1984). The reason for the low validity of interviews is that they are often unstructured. The questions asked may be vague and unrelated to job performance, such as "Tell me about yourself" and "Why do you want this job?" In addition, different questions are sometimes asked of different applicants; as a result, it is difficult to compare their responses, and employers are forced to evaluate them on the basis of different information. Consider how unfair it would be if some students in your class were graded on their exam performance, others on their class attendance, and still others on their physical attractiveness (Berry & Houston, 1993).

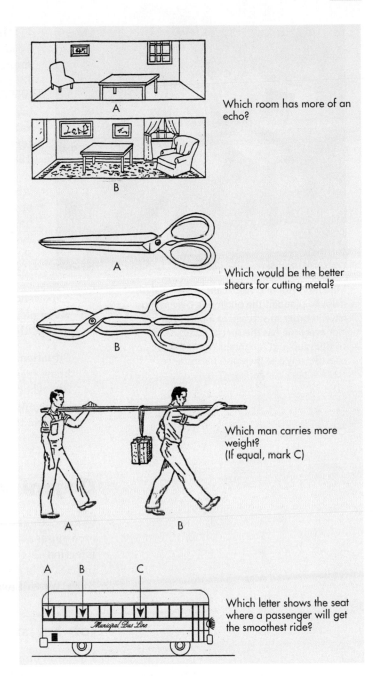

Which room has more of an echo?

Which would be the better shears for cutting metal?

Which man carries more weight?
(If equal, mark C)

Which letter shows the seat where a passenger will get the smoothest ride?

FIGURE B.4 Sample Items from a Mechanical Ability Test Questions such as these from the Bennett Test of Mechanical Comprehension are designed to assess a person's ability to figure out the physical properties of things. Such a test might be used to predict job performance for carpenters or assembly-line workers.

SOURCE: Bennett (1940).

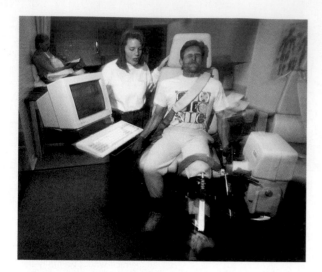

Matching Job and Applicant A job analysis helps to pinpoint the qualities a person must have in order to succeed at a particular job. Not everyone has the special combination of compassion and toughness needed to be an effective physical therapist, for instance.

In contrast to unstructured interviews, structured ones, if developed and conducted properly, are adequate predictors of job performance. A structured interview should (1) be based on a job analysis, (2) include questions that elicit job-related information about the applicant, (3) ask the same questions of all applicants and in the same order, and (4) be evaluated by a panel of interviewers who record and rate the applicant's responses. When these criteria are met, the interview is likely to be an effective selection tool (Campion & others, 1988).

A situational interview is a type of structured interview in which an applicant is presented with a situation and asked how he or she would respond to it. Situational interviews may be experience-based, with applicants being asked how they have handled past work situations, or they may be based on hypothetical situations. Pulakos and Schmitt (1995) give these examples of each type of interview item:

Experience-based question: Think about a time when you had to motivate an employee to perform a job task that he or she disliked but that you needed the individual to do. How did you handle that situation?

Situational question: Suppose you were working with an employee who you knew greatly disliked performing a particular job task. You were in a situation where you needed this task completed, and this employee was the only one available to assist you. What would you do to motivate the employee to perform the task? (p. 292)

Organizational Behavior

Organizational behavior (OB) focuses on how the organization and the social environment in which people work affect their attitudes and behaviors. Job satisfaction is the attitude most thoroughly researched by I/O psychologists. The impact of leadership on attitudes and behaviors is another well-researched OB topic. We will examine both of these topics here.

Job Satisfaction

Lucy and Jane are both engineers who work in the same department of the same company. Lucy is almost always eager to get to work in the morning. She feels that her work is interesting and that she has plenty of opportunities to learn new skills. In contrast, Jane is unhappy because she feels that she doesn't get the recognition she deserves at work. She also complains that the company doesn't give enough vacation time to employees and that it provides inadequate benefits. Jane can't think of many good things about her job. She's even beginning to feel that her job is negatively affecting her personal life.

Fortunately, Lucy is more typical of American workers than Jane is. In a Gallup poll conducted in August 2001, 80 percent of the U.S. workers sampled indicated that they were satisfied with their jobs. Employees tended to be more satisfied with their relations with co-workers and with the physical safety of the work environment. They were less satisfied with levels of on-the-job stress and pay.

Several approaches have been used to explain differences in job satisfaction. One approach is based on a **discrepancy hypothesis,** which consists of three ideas: (1) that people differ in what they want from a job, (2) that people differ in how they evaluate what they experience at work, and (3) that level of satisfaction is based on the difference between what is desired and what is experienced (Lawler, 1973; Locke, 1976). Lucy and Jane, for instance, may not only want different things from their jobs; they may also make different assessments of the same events at work. Although their supervisor may treat them in the same encouraging manner, Lucy may see the boss's encouragement as supportive while Jane may view it as condescending. As a result, one perceives a discrepancy between desires and experiences, whereas the other does not.

A significant amount of research supports the discrepancy hypothesis. For example, negative discrepancies (getting less than desired) have been related to dissatisfaction. Interestingly, positive discrepancies (getting more than desired) have also been related to dissatisfaction in some cases (Rice & others, 1989). As an example, you might be dissatisfied with a job because it involves more contact with customers than you wanted or expected.

Another hypothesis to explain job satisfaction is the **social influence hypothesis,** which is based on the idea that people interpret their situations in part according to the reactions of others (Salancik & Pfeffer, 1977). For instance, when listening to a comedian, some people will make sure others are laughing before they laugh themselves. Similarly, when evaluating their own job satisfaction, people may be influenced by the attitudes of their co-workers regarding the degree to which the job is satisfying. After hearing Jane complain about the job, Lucy might report a lower level of satisfaction than she would have without Jane's influence. In a laboratory study, people who heard others evaluate a task positively were also likely to evaluate the task positively when they performed it later. Similarly, people who heard others evaluate a task negatively were later likely to evaluate the task negatively (Weiss & Shaw, 1979).

The **dispositional factors hypothesis** has also been used to explain differences in job satisfaction. Some researchers believe that "job attitudes may reflect a biologically based trait that predisposes individuals to see positive or negative content in their lives" (Staw & Ross, 1985, p. 471). In other words, some people may be prone to negative perceptions and feelings (such as suspicion, fear, worry, and dissatisfaction), whereas others may be prone to positive ones (such as trust, enthusiasm, and satisfaction). In one study, researchers who examined identical twins raised apart found support for the idea that a tendency toward a positive or negative outlook may be biologically based. They found that sets of twins had similar levels of job satisfaction and concluded that job satisfaction may be explained in part by genetic factors (Arvey & others, 1989).

Each of these three hypotheses—discrepancy between desires and experiences, social influence, and inherited dispositions—explains some of the differences in job satisfaction among people. But as is true with most psychological research into human behavior, none of these approaches by itself can completely explain differences in job satisfaction.

Whatever its causes, job satisfaction or the lack of it can affect a person's general level of contentment. Job satisfaction has been found to be related to overall life satisfaction (see, for example, Judge & Watanabe, 1993; Lancer & others, 1989; Weaver, 1978). In general, satisfaction (or dissatisfaction) in one area of life has been found to spill over into others; feelings of happiness or unhappiness tend to pervade all aspects of our lives (Weaver, 1978). This is one reason why high job satisfaction among employees should be a goal of all organizations. In addition to reducing absenteeism and turnover, it contributes to employees' overall level of happiness. Companies might also provide resources to help employees cope with personal problems—again, because of the spillover effect: Happiness in one's personal life is likely to spill over into one's work life.

An interesting line of research examines situations in which job dissatisfaction results in employees actively trying to improve their working conditions. Dissatisfied employees may act creatively by proposing new ways of doing things or making suggestions on how to improve the work situation. Jing Zhou and Jennifer George (2001) have found that dissatisfied employees are more likely to behave creatively when they are committed to staying with the organization, when they have supportive co-workers or co-workers who provide them with useful feedback, or when they perceive the organization as being supportive of creativity.

discrepancy hypothesis
An approach to explaining job satisfaction that focuses on the discrepancy, if any, between what a person wants from a job and how that person evaluates what is actually experienced at work.

social influence hypothesis
The view that a person's level of job satisfaction is influenced by the job satisfaction levels of other people.

dispositional factors hypothesis
The view that a person's level of job satisfaction may be due in part to a genetically based disposition toward a positive or negative outlook.

IN FOCUS B.2

Differences Between Male and Female Managers

My friend Janice has on occasion called me to complain about her supervisor (who happens to be female) and say that she would much rather work for a man than a woman. I also know a number of people who say that they prefer female to male supervisors. Although employees sometimes have strong preferences regarding the gender of their supervisors, research indicates that there are actually few differences between male and female managers.

For example, in one study that examined the conflict-management style of supervisors (Korabik & others, 1993), few personality or behavioral differences were found between male and female managers. However, the gender of the manager influenced how people reacted to the manager. Specifically, female managers who were viewed as dominating were more strongly criticized than males who

were viewed as dominating. In addition, female managers who were viewed as obliging received more positive ratings than males who were obliging.

Another study examined the conflict-resolution style of male and female managers at work and at home (Chusmir & Mills, 1989). Again, male and female managers behaved very similarly both at work and at home as they dealt with conflict. Both genders tended to handle conflict more competitively at work than at home and to be more accommodating at home than at work. Interestingly, the rank of the manager in the organizational hierarchy was a strong predictor of how the manager would handle conflict at home as well as at work.

Although male and female managers tend to be similar in personality and behavior, they may tend to talk about their

jobs differently and delegate work differently. When male and female managers were interviewed, women were found to talk about how they accomplished their work, whereas men tended to talk about the importance of their work (Statham, 1987). When delegating work, female managers tended to delegate work and then set up checkpoints and time lines to ensure that the work was completed properly. In contrast, male managers tended to delegate and then assume that the work was getting done.

What may be most important to managerial effectiveness is the congruence between managerial style and the preferences and needs of subordinates. For example, an employee who is still learning and developing might welcome a supervisor who is more involved, whereas an employee with a great deal of task experience might prefer to be left to work independently.

Leadership

Leadership is one of the most widely researched topics in I/O psychology, having been investigated in thousands of studies. "Leaders" are those who have the ability to direct groups toward the attainment of goals. According to this definition of leadership, one of the functions of a manager is to lead. Keep in mind, though, that managers act not only as leaders but also as negotiators, disturbance handlers, resource allocators, and decision makers (Mintzberg, 1973). Being a good leader is only one aspect of being a good manager. In Focus Box B.2 discusses the differences between male and female managers.

Leader Effectiveness

What Makes a Leader? Nelson Mandela is an extraordinarily charismatic leader. Not only did he keep his political organization, the African National Congress, functioning during his 27 years of imprisonment, but he also guided South Africa out of its racist apartheid system with a minimum of violence and turmoil.

I/O psychologists have spent a great deal of time trying to determine what makes someone an effective leader. The **trait approach to leader effectiveness,** one of the earliest approaches to the study of leadership, is based on the idea that leaders are born, not made. According to this view, some people possess certain qualities or characteristics that make them natural leaders. Examples are John F. Kennedy, Martin Luther King Jr., Colin Powell, and Bill Clinton. These people presumably shared certain characteristics that made them good leaders, and these characteristics would have made them good leaders in practically any situation. A large number of traits—such as height, physical attractiveness, dominance, flexibility, and intelligence—have been examined to see whether they determine how effective a leader will be. However, after a substantial amount of research, little connection has been found between personal traits and leader effectiveness (Hollander & Julian, 1970; Stogdill, 1948).

After the trait approach failed to identify characteristics of effective leaders, researchers began to examine the *behaviors* of leaders in the hope of verifying

behavioral theories of leader effectiveness. They reasoned that the behaviors of effective and ineffective leaders must differ. One of the most influential studies of leadership behavior was conducted at Ohio State University. The researchers identified two major types of leadership behavior: consideration and initiating structure (Fleishman & Harris, 1962). *Consideration* describes leaders who are deeply concerned about their followers and who spend time building trust, respect, and warmth between themselves and their followers. *Initiating structure* describes leaders who are task-oriented, who structure tasks for their followers, and who push for things to get done. Initiating structure has been related to high productivity, but also to low job satisfaction and high personnel turnover. In contrast, consideration has been related to high job satisfaction, but also to low productivity in some situations (Bass, 1981; Locke & Schweiger, 1979).

Additional research on initiating structure and consideration behaviors has led researchers to conclude that the *situation* might have an impact on the effectiveness of a leader's behavior. In some situations, initiating structure might be best; in other situations, consideration might be more effective. The theories that developed from this view are called **situational** (or **contingency**) **theories of leadership.** These theories tend to be complicated, but they seem to do a better job of explaining leader effectiveness than either the trait approach or behavioral theories.

In the last 20 years or so, researchers have once again become interested in leadership traits. In particular, the trait of charisma has received a lot of attention. Typically, charismatic leaders have a high need for power, are extremely self-confident, and believe strongly in a particular cause. Thanks to their compelling personalities and highly developed interpersonal skills, charismatic leaders have extraordinary effects on their followers (House, 1977). For example, a study of U.S. presidents from George Washington to Ronald Reagan revealed that the more charismatic the president, the greater his success with domestic issues (House & others, 1991).

Charismatic leaders are able to change the attitudes and beliefs of their followers and may even be able to evoke strong compliance from them. The followers are motivated by love, enthusiasm, and devotion to their leader. In some cases, compliance to the wishes of a charismatic leader may be so strong that followers are willing to engage in unethical or illegal behavior.

Much of the research on leadership has emphasized the impact of leaders on followers. This ignores the fact that followers also influence leaders. In contrast, the **leader–member exchange model** emphasizes the interaction between supervisor and subordinates (Dansereau & others, 1975; Graen & Cashman, 1975), recognizing that the relationship between leader and followers is unique to each leader–follower dyad—that is, supervisors have unique relationships with each of their subordinates. Supervisors may even create distinct "in-groups" (i.e., subordinates who are treated like partners because they are thought to be motivated and capable) and "out-groups" (subordinates who are viewed as less valuable than in-group members). Some research indicates that in-group members are more likely to be extraverts and to have attitudes similar to those of their supervisors (Phillips & Bedeian, 1994).

The existence of clearly defined in-groups is likely to foster resentment from those who are excluded (Yukl, 1989). Therefore, it is likely that effective leaders manage to develop a special relationship with each subordinate such that subordinates are not treated exactly the same, but each is made to feel valued for his or her unique contributions.

Research on upward influence (i.e., subordinates' influence on supervisors) has examined two types of goals that subordinates try to attain when influencing leaders: organizational goals (e.g., obtaining adequate resources to perform a task) and personal goals (e.g., recognition, approval, pay raises) (Yukl & others, 1995). Upward-influence tactics such as assertiveness and ingratiation have been found to be ineffective, whereas rational persuasion seems to enhance the leader's impression of the persuader's potential for promotion (Thacker & Wayne, 1995).

trait approach to leader effectiveness
An approach to determining what makes an effective leader that focuses on the personal characteristics displayed by successful leaders.

behavioral theories of leader effectiveness
Theories of leader effectiveness that focus on differences in the behaviors of effective and ineffective leaders.

situational (contingency) theories of leadership
Theories that focus on how a particular situation influences a leader's effectiveness.

leader–member exchange model
A model of leadership emphasizing that the quality of the interactions between supervisors and subordinates varies depending on the unique characteristics of both.

Leader Emergence

Research on the emergence of leaders examines who in a group is likely to become the group leader. This topic differs from that of leader effectiveness because not everyone who emerges as a leader is a good leader. For example, in a discussion with your classmates, you might find that a particular person dominates the conversation and directs the group's efforts. This person is clearly the group's leader, but the effect of his or her behavior on group productivity and satisfaction may be either positive or negative. Using a technique called *leaderless group discussion,* in which a group is given a problem to solve or a topic to discuss, researchers study the group to see who emerges as the leader. Intelligence, aggressiveness, decisiveness, and dominance are personal qualities that have been related to leader emergence (Lord & others, 1986).

Workplace Trends and Issues

Both technological advances and social trends can have a major impact on employment conditions and practices. For example, many organizations have become much more accepting of *telecommuting,* in which employees work from home and communicate with the organization via e-mail, telephone, and fax transmissions. Other trends driven by technological advances include employers' use of the Internet to recruit new employees and of software to secretly monitor the electronic communications of their current workers. One social trend that has influenced workplace conditions is an awareness of the need for employees to better balance the demands of work, personal needs, and family life. These developments have implications for the work of I/O psychologists. Let's take a closer look at each of them.

Telecommuting or Telework   Organizations such as AT&T, Merrill-Lynch, American Express, Ford Motor Company, and Coca-Cola—along with many others—have telework programs in place (Schilling, 1999). These programs offer such advantages to employees as flexible work schedules, more freedom at work, and less time wasted commuting. From the employer's point of view, telecommuting may reduce costs associated with renting office space and increase the ability to attract and retain talented employees (Howard, 2000; Peltin & Crowder, 2000). However, telework is not for everyone. The characteristics of the position and the employee should be considered.

Telecommuting employees should be self-motivated and flexible, possess a high level of job knowledge and skills, have strong communication and organizational skills, and have a low need for social interaction. They should enjoy responsibility and be trustworthy and reliable (Schilling, 1999). In other words, telecommuters are people who work well with little supervision.

To manage from a distance, supervisors of teleworkers should set measurable performance goals, have clear standards to assess performance, give specific performance feedback, and set timetables (Schilling, 1999). Industrial psychologists might develop specialized selection and performance evaluation systems to predict and then measure the performance of teleworkers.

Internet Recruiting   Internet job-search services, such as Monster.com and Wetfeet.com, and company Web sites have changed the way in which employees are recruited. For example, in a study reported in HRFocus Newsbriefs (2000), university students were found to spend about four hours on a company's Web site

Telework or Telecommuting: Working at Home   As telecommunication technology has become more widespread, so has the number of employees who *telecommute* or work from home. For the individual who is self-motivated and has good communication skills, telecommuting offers the advantages of greater autonomy and flexible time management. On the down side, teleworkers are more likely to work in the evenings and on the weekends (Steward, 2000). Men and women vary in their reasons for telecommuting. Being able to earn money and care for their children at the same time is a motivating factor for many women (Sullivan & Lewis, 2001).

during a job search. In addition to the time spent on company Web pages, job applicants electronically search for articles on prospective employers, post résumés on job boards, and seek career advice.

In a study comparing *Fortune*'s 100 Best Companies with *Fortune*'s 500 Biggest Companies, the 100 Best Companies were found to be more proactive in using their Web sites on the Internet to attract job applicants (Brice & Waung, 2001). Those companies were more likely than the 500 Biggest Companies to include corporate mission statements, make references to community outreach programs, and describe policies affecting work–life balance on their Web pages. Given that *Fortune*'s 100 Best Companies tend to be more progressive and proactive, it is no surprise that they have been the first to use the Internet to communicate effectively with job applicants.

Industrial psychologists might examine the usefulness of Internet recruiting. Does this type of recruiting attract better employees? Does it make a positive impression on job applicants? How realistic are the descriptions of jobs and organizations on the Internet compared to other recruitment sources?

Privacy In the Workplace   Employees have fewer rights in the workplace than they may realize. For example, although the federal Wire Tapping Act (Title I of the Electronic Communications Privacy Act of 1986) bars the interception of electronic communications without the consent of at least one of the parties involved in the communication, businesses are exempt from this restriction. That is, employers may legally intercept communications in the ordinary course of business (Katz, 1999). To complicate matters, state wire-tapping laws vary and may differ a great deal from the federal Wire Tapping Act. In general, organizations are free to monitor employees' Internet use. Organizations that do so should have clear policies that are communicated to employees regarding such monitoring. Industrial psychologists might examine the impact of such monitoring on employee behavior and morale.

Work–Life Balance   Many employees report that they are seeking a better balance between their jobs and their personal lives, and some organizations promise to make this possible. These employers believe that policies affecting work–life balance will attract and retain better employees and will even improve the bottom line. For example, the SAS Institute has generous policies affecting work–life balance. The resulting low turnover is estimated to save the organization $75 million a year (Fishman, 2000). Flexible work schedules, telecommuting, job sharing, sabbaticals, and more vacation and leave time are some of the benefits that many organizations offer to retain employees. Some employers even offer concierge services (e.g., pickup and delivery of dry cleaning, on-site hair styling) and on-site health clubs to help employees balance personal activities and work. Critics argue that such services tend to be offered by organizations in which long hours are required. Similarly, while cell phones, pagers, and laptop computers might be seen as perks by their recipients, these devices further blur the distinction between home and work, resulting in employees who are constantly "on call."

In the future, I/O psychologists will continue to have a significant role in the workplace. To keep pace with the changing needs of employees and rapid technological advances, I/O psychologists will continue to adjust the focus of their research and its applications to improve the experiences of people at work.

Appendix Review
Industrial/Organizational Psychology

Key Points

What Is Industrial/Organizational Psychology?

- **Industrial/organizational (I/O) psychology** is a broad field that examines human behavior in the workplace. I/O psychologists spend their time working in these six content areas: (1) selection and placement, which focuses on developing assessment techniques to select people for jobs; (2) training and development, which focuses on determining what types of skills need to be enhanced and on evaluating the effectiveness of training programs; (3) performance management, which involves identifying performance standards and developing ways to measure performance; (4) **organizational development (OD),** which seeks to bring about positive change in an organization by examining organizational structure and the social systems within the organization; (5) quality of work life, which emphasizes the importance of maintaining a healthy and productive workforce; and (6) **ergonomics,** which focuses on the design of equipment and procedures in light of human capabilities and limitations. The "industrial," or "I," side of I/O psychology is also called **personnel psychology.** In contrast, the "organizational," or "O," side is sometimes called **organizational behavior.**

Work Settings, Type of Training, and Employment Outlook

- A doctorate or master's degree is required to work as an I/O psychologist. The employment outlook has been good over the years, with consistently less than 1 percent unemployment among I/O psychologists surveyed by the American Psychological Association.

- I/O psychologists may work in colleges or universities or as consultants to organizations. They may also work for large private corporations or for public institutions, such as government agencies.

- In certain fields related to I/O psychology, jobs are sometimes available for people with bachelor's degrees. These fields include personnel, training, and labor-relations specialists and managers; management analysts and consultants; and employment interviewers.

Personnel Psychology

- A first step in the work of personnel psychologists is to perform a **job analysis**—a determination of the major responsibilities of a certain job and the human characteristics needed to fill it. A good job analysis is key to successful personnel selection, effective job-training programs, and accurate evaluation of job performance.

- Personnel psychologists use many devices to help them with their goal of selecting the best applicants for jobs. These include psychological tests, work samples and situational exercises, and selection interviews. Personnel psychologists are concerned about **selection device validity**—the extent to which the device succeeds in distinguishing between those applicants who will become high performers and those who will not.

Organizational Behavior

- One topic extensively studied in the field of organizational behavior is job satisfaction. Researchers have tried to explain different levels of job satisfaction in three ways: the **discrepancy hypothesis,** which focuses on gaps between what a person wants from a job and what he or she actually experiences; the **social influence hypothesis,** which looks at how people interpret their situations in relation to others' reactions; and the **dispositional factors hypothesis,** which links job satisfaction to inherited dispositions. New research examines the situations in which dissatisfied employees are likely to act to improve the workplace.

- Leadership is also a widely studied topic in the field of organizational behavior. Researchers have tried to explain leadership effectiveness through the **trait approach to leader effectiveness, behavioral theories of leader effectiveness,** and **situational (contingency) theories of leadership.** Of these three approaches, situational theories seem to do the best job. Research also examines how supervisors and subordinates interact (the **leader–member exchange model**), how followers affect leaders' behavior, and how leaders emerge in a group.

Workplace Trends and Issues

- The workplace of today has been influenced greatly by technological advances. The Internet has affected the ways in which employers seek job candidates and the ways in which job candidates learn about potential employers. It has also affected the social organization of the workplace, allowing some employees to work from home. Technological advances have also made it easier for employers to spy on their employees. Finally, many employees are concerned about work–life balance, and many employers are changing their policies in that area in an attempt to attract and retain good employees.

Key Terms

industrial/organizational (I/O) psychology, p. B-1

personnel psychology, p. B-1

organizational behavior, p. B-1

organizational development (OD), p. B-2

ergonomics, p. B-2

job analysis, p. B-5

selection device validity, p. B-6

discrepancy hypothesis, p. B-8

social influence hypothesis, p. B-9

dispositional factors hypothesis, p. B-9

trait approach to leader effectiveness, p. B-10

behavioral theories of leader effectiveness, p. B-11

situational (contingency) theories of leadership, p. B-11

leader–member exchange model, p. B-11

Web Companion   Review Activities

You can find additional review activities at **www.worthpublishers.com/hockenbury.** The *Psychology* 4th edition Web Companion has a self-scoring practice quiz, flashcards, two interactive crossword puzzles, and other activities to help you master the material in this chapter.

Glossary

A

absolute threshold The smallest possible strength of a stimulus that can be detected half the time. (p. 86)

accommodation The process by which the lens changes shape to focus incoming light so that it falls on the retina. (p. 89)

acculturative stress (ah-KUL-chur-uh-tiv) The stress that results from the pressure of adapting to a new culture. (p. 481)

acetylcholine (uh-*seet*-ull-KO-leen) Neuro-transmitter that causes muscle contraction and is involved in memory function. (p. 48)

achievement motivation The desire to direct one's behavior toward excelling, succeeding, or outperforming others at some task. (p. 325)

achievement test A test designed to measure a person's level of knowledge, skill, or accomplishment in a particular area. (p. 279)

action potential A brief electrical impulse by which information is transmitted along the axon of a neuron. (p. 43)

activation–synthesis model of dreaming The theory that brain activity during sleep produces dream images (*activation*), which are combined by the brain into a dream story (*synthesis*). (p. 148)

activity theory of aging The psychosocial theory that life satisfaction in late adulthood is highest when people maintain the level of activity they displayed earlier in life. (p. 386)

actor–observer discrepancy The tendency to attribute one's own behavior to external, situational causes, while attributing the behavior of others to internal, personal causes; especially likely to occur with regard to behaviors that lead to negative outcomes. (p. 444)

actualizing tendency In Rogers's theory, the innate drive to maintain and enhance the human organism. (p. 412)

acupuncture Ancient Chinese medical procedure involving the insertion and manipulation of fine needles into specific locations on the body to alleviate pain and treat illness; modern acupuncture may involve sending electrical current through the needles rather than manipulating them. (p. 122)

adaptive theory of sleep The view that the unique sleep patterns of different animals evolved over time to help promote survival and environmental adaptation; also called the *evolutionary theory of sleep*. (p. 139)

adipose tissue Body fat that is the main source of stored, or reserve, energy. (p. 303)

adolescence The transitional stage between late childhood and the beginning of adulthood, during which sexual maturity is reached. (p. 374)

adolescent growth spurt The period of accelerated growth during puberty, involving rapid increases in height and weight. (p. 375)

adrenal cortex The outer portion of the adrenal glands. (p. 56)

adrenal glands Pair of endocrine glands that are involved in the human stress response. (p. 56)

adrenal medulla The inner portion of the adrenal glands; secretes epinephrine and nor-epinephrine. (p. 56)

afterimage A visual experience that occurs after the original source of stimulation is no longer present. (p. 95)

agoraphobia An anxiety disorder involving the extreme and irrational fear of experiencing a panic attack in a public situation and being unable to escape or get help. (p. 515)

algorithm A problem-solving strategy that involves following a specific rule, procedure, or method that inevitably produces the correct solution. (p. 265)

allele (ah-LEEL) One of the different forms of a particular gene. (p. 354)

all-or-none law The principle that either a neuron is sufficiently stimulated and an action potential occurs or a neuron is not sufficiently stimulated and an action potential does not occur. (p. 45)

alpha brain waves Brain-wave pattern associated with relaxed wakefulness and drowsiness. (p. 134)

altruism Helping another person with no expectation of personal reward or benefit. (p. 466)

Alzheimer's disease (AD) A progressive disease that destroys the brain's neurons, gradually impairing memory, thinking, language, and other cognitive functions, resulting in the complete inability to care for oneself; the most common form of *dementia*. (p. 251)

amnesia (am-NEE-zha) Severe memory loss. (p. 248)

amphetamines (am-FET-uh-meens) A class of stimulant drugs that arouse the central nervous system and suppress appetite. (p. 163)

amplitude The intensity or amount of energy of a wave, reflected in the height of the wave; the amplitude of a sound wave determines a sound's loudness. (p. 97)

amygdala (uh-MIG-dull-uh) Almond-shaped cluster of neurons in the brain's temporal lobe, involved in memory and emotional responses, especially fear. (pp. 69, 331)

animal cognition The study of animal learning, memory, thinking, and language. (p. 275)

anorexia nervosa An eating disorder characterized by excessive weight loss, an irrational fear of gaining weight, and distorted body self-perception. (p. 311)

anterograde amnesia Loss of memory caused by the inability to store new memories; forward-acting amnesia. (p. 249)

anthropomorphism The attribution of human traits, motives, emotions, or behaviors to nonhuman animals or inanimate objects. (p. 337)

antianxiety medications Prescription drugs that are used to alleviate the symptoms of anxiety. (p. 578)

antidepressant medications Prescription drugs that are used to reduce the symptoms associated with depression. (p. 579)

antipsychotic medications (an-tee-sy-KOT-ick) Prescription drugs that are used to reduce psychotic symptoms; frequently used in the treatment of schizophrenia; also called *neuroleptics*. (p. 576)

antisocial personality disorder A personality disorder characterized by a pervasive pattern of disregarding and violating the rights of others; such individuals are also often referred to as *psychopaths* or *sociopaths*. (p. 528)

anxiety An unpleasant emotional state characterized by physical arousal and feelings of tension, apprehension, and worry. (p. 512)

anxiety disorders A category of psychological disorders in which extreme anxiety is the main diagnostic feature and causes significant disruptions in the person's cognitive, behavioral, or interpersonal functioning. (p. 512)

aphasia (uh-FAZE-yuh) The partial or complete inability to articulate ideas or understand spoken or written language because of brain injury or damage. (p. 71)

aptitude test A test designed to assess a person's capacity to benefit from education or training. (p. 280)

archetypes (AR-kuh-types) In Jung's theory, the inherited mental images of universal human instincts, themes, and preoccupations that are the main components of the collective unconscious. (p. 408)

arousal theory The view that people are motivated to maintain a level of arousal that is optimal—neither too high nor too low. (p. 301)

attachment The emotional bond that forms between an infant and caregiver(s), especially his or her parents. (p. 360)

attitude A learned tendency to evaluate some object, person, or issue in a particular way; such evaluations may be positive, negative, or ambivalent. (p. 446)

attribution The mental process of inferring the causes of people's behavior, including one's own. Also refers to the explanation made for a particular behavior. (p. 443)

atypical antipsychotic medications Newer antipsychotic medications that, in contrast to the early antipsychotic drugs, block dopamine receptors in brain regions associated with psychotic symptoms rather than more globally throughout the brain, resulting in fewer side effects. (p. 577)

audition The technical term for the sense of hearing. (p. 96)

authoritarian parenting style Parenting style in which parents are demanding and unresponsive toward their children's needs or wishes. (p. 389)

authoritative parenting style Parenting style in which parents set clear standards for their children's behavior but are also responsive to their children's needs and wishes. (p. 389)

autonomic nervous system (aw-toe-NOM-ick) Subdivision of the peripheral nervous system that regulates involuntary functions. (p. 52)

availability heuristic A strategy in which the likelihood of an event is estimated on the basis of how readily available other instances of the event are in memory. (p. 269)

aversive conditioning A relatively ineffective type of behavior therapy that involves repeatedly pairing an aversive stimulus with the occurrence of undesirable behaviors or thoughts. (p. 558)

axon The long, fluid-filled tube that carries a neuron's messages to other body areas. (p. 42)

axon terminals Branches at the end of the axon that contain tiny pouches, or sacs, called synaptic vesicles. (p. 46)

B

barbiturates (barb-ITCH-yer-ets) A category of depressant drugs that reduce anxiety and produce sleepiness. (p. 160)

basal metabolic rate (BMR) When the body is at rest, the rate at which it uses energy for vital functions, such as heartbeat and respiration. (p. 303)

basic emotions The most fundamental set of emotion categories, which are biologically innate, evolutionarily determined, and culturally universal. (p. 328)

basilar membrane (BAZ-uh-ler or BAZE-uh-ler) The membrane within the cochlea of the ear that contains the hair cells. (p. 98)

behavior modification The application of learning principles to help people develop more effective or adaptive behaviors. (p. 201)

behavior therapy A type of psychotherapy that focuses on directly changing maladaptive behavior patterns by using basic learning principles and techniques; also called *behavior modification*. (p. 556)

behavioral genetics An interdisciplinary field that studies the effects of genes and heredity on behavior. (p. 423)

behavioral theories of leader effectiveness Theories of leader effectiveness that focus on differences in the behaviors of effective and ineffective leaders. (p. B-11)

behaviorism School of psychology and theoretical viewpoint that emphasize the study of observable behaviors, especially as they pertain to the process of learning. (pp. 7, 179)

bell and pad treatment A behavior therapy technique used to treat nighttime bedwetting by conditioning arousal from sleep in response to bodily signals of a full bladder. (p. 558)

beta brain waves Brain-wave pattern associated with alert wakefulness. (p. 134)

binocular cues (by-NOCK-you-ler) Distance or depth cues that require the use of both eyes. (p. 112)

biofeedback Technique that involves using auditory or visual feedback to learn to exert voluntary control over involuntary body functions, such as heart rate, blood pressure, blood flow, and muscle tension. (p. 122)

biological preparedness In learning theory, the idea that an organism is innately predisposed to form associations between certain stimuli and responses. (p. 187)

biological psychology Specialized branch of psychology that studies the relationship between behavior and bodily processes and systems; also called *biopsychology* or *psychobiology*. (p. 40)

biomedical therapies The use of medications, electroconvulsive therapy, or other medical treatments to treat the symptoms associated with psychological disorders. (p. 549)

biopsychosocial model The belief that physical health and illness are determined by the complex interaction of biological, psychological, and social factors. (p. 478)

bipolar cells In the retina, the specialized neurons that connect the rods and cones with the ganglion cells. (p. 92)

bipolar disorder A mood disorder involving periods of incapacitating depression alternating with periods of extreme euphoria and excitement; formerly called *manic depression*. (p. 523)

blaming the victim The tendency to blame an innocent victim of misfortune for having somehow caused the problem or for not having taken steps to avoid or prevent it. (p. 443)

blind spot The point at which the optic nerve leaves the eye, producing a small gap in the field of vision. (p. 91)

body mass index (BMI) A numerical scale indicating adult height in relation to weight; calculated as $(703 \times$ weight in pounds$)/($height in inches$)^2$. (p. 308)

borderline personality disorder A personality disorder characterized by instability of interpersonal relationships, self-image, and emotions, and marked impulsivity. (p. 529)

bottom-up processing Information processing that emphasizes the importance of the sensory receptors in detecting the basic features of a stimulus in the process of recognizing a whole pattern; analysis that moves from the parts to the whole; also called *data-driven processing*. (p. 106)

brainstem A region of the brain made up of the hindbrain and the midbrain. (p. 63)

brightness The perceived intensity of a color, which corresponds to the amplitude of the light wave. (p. 94)

bulimia nervosa An eating disorder characterized by binges of extreme overeating followed by self-induced vomiting, misuse of laxatives, or other inappropriate methods to purge the excessive food and prevent weight gain. (p. 311)

bystander effect A phenomenon in which the greater the number of people present, the less likely each individual is to help someone in distress. (p. 467)

C

cafeteria diet effect The tendency to eat more when a wide variety of palatable foods is available. (p. 309)

caffeine (kaff-EEN) A stimulant drug found in coffee, tea, cola drinks, chocolate, and many over-the-counter medications. (p. 161)

California Personality Inventory (CPI) A self-report inventory that assesses personality characteristics in normal populations. (p. 429)

case study An intensive study of a single individual or small group of individuals. (p. 21)

cataplexy A sudden loss of voluntary muscle strength and control that is usually triggered by an intense emotion. (p. 142)

catecholamines (cat-eh-COLE-uh-meens) Hormones secreted by the adrenal medulla that cause rapid physiological arousal; include adrenaline and noradrenaline. (p. 483)

cell body Processes nutrients and provides energy for the neuron to function; contains the cell's nucleus; also called the *soma*. (p. 42)

central nervous system (CNS) Division of the nervous system that consists of the brain and spinal cord. (p. 51)

centration In Piaget's theory, the tendency to focus, or *center,* on only one aspect of a situation and ignore other important aspects of the situation. (p. 370)

cerebellum (sare-uh-BELL-um) A large, two-sided hindbrain structure at the back of the brain; responsible for muscle coordination and maintaining posture and equilibrium. (p. 64)

cerebral cortex (suh-REE-brull or SARE-uh-brull) The wrinkled outer portion of the forebrain, which contains the most sophisticated brain centers. (p. 65)

cerebral hemispheres The nearly symmetrical left and right halves of the cerebral cortex. (p. 65)

cholecystokinin (CCK) (kola-sis-tow-KINE-in) Hormone secreted primarily by the small intestine that promotes satiation; also found in the brain. (p. 305)

chromosome A long, threadlike structure composed of twisted parallel strands of DNA; found in the cell nucleus. (p. 352)

chunking Increasing the amount of information that can be held in short-term memory by grouping related items together into a single unit, or *chunk.* (p. 222)

circadian rhythm (ser-KADE-ee-en) A cycle or rhythm that is roughly 24 hours long; the cyclical daily fluctuations in biological and psychological processes. (p. 130)

classical conditioning The basic learning process that involves repeatedly pairing a neutral stimulus with a response-producing stimulus until the neutral stimulus elicits the same response; also called *respondent conditioning* or *Pavlovian conditioning.* (p. 176)

client-centered therapy A type of psychotherapy developed by humanistic psychologist Carl Rogers in which the therapist is nondirective and reflective, and the client directs the focus of each therapy session; also called *person-centered therapy.* (p. 553)

clustering Organizing items into related groups during recall from long-term memory. (p. 228)

cocaine A stimulant drug derived from the coca tree. (p. 164)

cochlea (COCK-lee-uh) The coiled, fluid-filled inner-ear structure that contains the basilar membrane and hair cells. (p. 97)

cognition The mental activities involved in acquiring, retaining, and using knowledge. (p. 260)

cognitive dissonance An unpleasant state of psychological tension or arousal (*dissonance*) that occurs when two thoughts or perceptions (*cognitions*) are inconsistent; typically results from the awareness that attitudes and behavior are in conflict. (p. 448)

cognitive map Tolman's term for the mental representation of the layout of a familiar environment. (p. 203)

cognitive neuroscience The study of the neural basis of cognitive process that integrates contributions from psychology, neuroscience, and computer science. (p. 60)

cognitive therapies A group of psychotherapies based on the assumption that psychological problems are due to maladaptive patterns of thinking; treatment techniques focus on recognizing and altering these unhealthy thinking patterns. (p. 561)

cognitive therapy (CT) A type of cognitive therapy, developed by psychiatrist Aaron T. Beck, that focuses on changing the client's unrealistic beliefs. (p. 564)

cognitive-behavioral therapy (CBT) Therapy that integrates cognitive and behavioral techniques and that is based on the assumption that thoughts, moods, and behaviors are interrelated. (p. 566)

cognitive-mediational theory of emotion Lazarus's theory that emotions result from the cognitive appraisal of a situation's effect on personal well-being. (p. 341)

collective unconscious In Jung's theory, the hypothesized part of the unconscious mind that is inherited from previous generations and that contains universally shared ancestral experiences and ideas. (p. 407)

collectivistic cultures Cultures that emphasize the needs and goals of the group over the needs and goals of the individual. (p. 12)

color The perceptual experience of different wavelengths of light, involving hue, saturation (purity), and brightness (intensity). (p. 94)

color blindness One of several inherited forms of color deficiency or weakness in which an individual cannot distinguish between certain colors. (p. 95)

comparative psychology Branch of psychology that studies the behavior of different animal species. (p. 32)

competence motivation The desire to direct one's behavior toward demonstrating competence and exercising control in a situation. (p. 325)

comprehension vocabulary The words that are understood by an infant or child. (p. 364)

compulsions Repetitive behaviors or mental acts that are performed to prevent or reduce anxiety. (p. 518)

concept A mental category of objects or ideas based on properties they share. (p. 263)

concrete operational stage In Piaget's theory, the third stage of cognitive development, which lasts from about age 7 to adolescence; characterized by the ability to think logically about concrete objects and situations. (p. 371)

conditional positive regard In Rogers's theory, the sense that you will be valued and loved only if you behave in a way that is acceptable to others; conditional love or acceptance. (p. 414)

conditioned reinforcer A stimulus or event that has acquired reinforcing value by being associated with a primary reinforcer; also called a *secondary reinforcer.* (p. 192)

conditioned response (CR) The learned, reflexive response to a conditioned stimulus. (p. 177)

conditioned stimulus (CS) A formerly neutral stimulus that acquires the capacity to elicit a reflexive response. (p. 177)

conditioning The process of learning associations between environmental events and behavioral responses. (p. 175)

cones The short, thick, pointed sensory receptors of the eye that detect color and are responsible for color vision and visual acuity. (p. 90)

conflict A situation in which a person feels pulled between two or more opposing desires, motives, or goals. (p. 480)

conformity The tendency to adjust one's behavior, attitudes, or beliefs to group norms in response to real or imagined group pressure. (p. 455)

consciousness Personal awareness of mental activities, internal sensations, and the external environment. (p. 128)

conservation In Piaget's theory, the understanding that two equal quantities remain equal even though the form or appearance is rearranged, as long as nothing is added or subtracted. (p. 370)

context effect The tendency to recover information more easily when the retrieval occurs in the same setting as the original learning of the information. (p. 232)

continuous reinforcement A schedule of reinforcement in which every occurrence of a particular response is reinforced. (p. 198)

control group or **control condition** In an experiment, the group of participants who are exposed to all experimental conditions, except the independent variable or treatment of interest; the group against which changes in the experimental group are compared. (p. 26)

coping Behavioral and cognitive responses used to deal with stressors; involves our efforts to change circumstances, or our interpretation of circumstances, to make them more favorable and less threatening. (p. 496)

cornea (CORE-nee-uh) A clear membrane covering the visible part of the eye that helps gather and direct incoming light. (p. 89)

corpus callosum A thick band of axons that connects the two cerebral hemispheres and acts as a communication link between them. (p. 65)

correlation The relationship between two variables. (p. A-9)

correlation coefficient A numerical indication of the magnitude and direction of the relationship (the correlation) between two variables. (pp. 23, A-9)

correlational study A research strategy that allows the precise calculation of how strongly related two factors are to each other. (p. 23)

cortical localization The notion that different functions are located or localized in different areas of the brain; also called *localization of function*. (pp. 59, 70)

corticosteroids (core-tick-oh-STAIR-oydz) Hormones released by the adrenal cortex that play a key role in the body's response to long-term stressors. (p. 484)

counterconditioning A behavior therapy technique based on classical conditioning that involves modifying behavior by conditioning a new response that is incompatible with a previously learned response. (p. 557)

creativity A group of cognitive processes used to generate useful, original, and novel ideas or solutions to problems. (p. 292)

critical thinking The active process of trying to minimize the influence of preconceptions and biases while rationally evaluating evidence, determining the conclusions that can be drawn from evidence, and considering alternative explanations. (p. 16)

cross-cultural psychology Branch of psychology that studies the effects of culture on behavior and mental processes. (p. 12)

cued recall A test of long-term memory that involves remembering an item of information in response to a retrieval cue. (p. 230)

culture The attitudes, values, beliefs, and behaviors shared by a group of people and communicated from one generation to another. (p. 13)

cyclothymic disorder (sī-klo-THY-mick) A mood disorder characterized by moderate but frequent mood swings that are not severe enough to qualify as bipolar disorder. (p. 523)

D

daily hassles Everyday minor events that annoy and upset people. (p. 479)

decay theory The view that forgetting is due to normal metabolic processes that occur in the brain over time. (p. 236)

decibel (DESS-uh-bell) The unit of measurement for loudness. (p. 97)

déjà vu A brief but intense feeling of remembering a scene or an event that is actually being experienced for the first time; French for "already seen." (p. 236)

delusion A falsely held belief that persists in spite of compelling contradictory evidence. (p. 533)

demand characteristics In a research study, subtle cues or signals expressed by the researcher that communicate the kind of response or behavior that is expected from the participant. (p. 31)

dementia Progressive deterioration and impairment of memory, reasoning, and other cognitive functions occurring as the result of a disease or a condition. (p. 251)

dendrites Multiple short fibers that extend from the neuron's cell body and receive information from other neurons or from sensory receptor cells. (p. 42)

deoxyribonucleic acid (DNA) The double-stranded molecule that encodes genetic instructions; the chemical basis of heredity. (p. 353)

dependent variable The factor that is observed and measured for change in an experiment; thought to be influenced by the independent variable. (p. 25)

depressants A category of psychoactive drugs that depress or inhibit brain activity. (p. 157)

depth perception The use of visual cues to perceive the distance or three-dimensional characteristics of objects. (p. 111)

descriptive research methods Scientific procedures that involve systematically observing behavior in order to describe the relationship among behaviors and events. (p. 19)

descriptive statistics Mathematical methods used to organize and summarize data. (p. A-2)

developmental psychology The branch of psychology that studies how people change over the lifespan. (p. 351)

difference threshold The smallest possible difference between two stimuli that can be detected half the time; also called *just noticeable difference*. (p. 86)

diffusion of responsibility A phenomenon in which the presence of other people makes it less likely that any individual will help someone in distress because the obligation to intervene is shared among all the onlookers. (p. 468)

discrepancy hypothesis An approach to explaining job satisfaction that focuses on the discrepancy, if any, between what a person wants from a job and how that person evaluates what is actually experienced at work. (p. B-8)

discriminative stimulus A specific stimulus in the presence of which a particular response is more likely to be reinforced, and in the absence of which a particular response is not reinforced. (p. 196)

displacement In psychoanalytic theory, the ego defense mechanism that involves unconsciously shifting the target of an emotional urge to a substitute target that is less threatening or dangerous. (p. 403)

display rules Social and cultural regulations governing emotional expression, especially facial expressions. (p. 335)

dispositional factors hypothesis The view that a person's level of job satisfaction may be due in part to a genetically based disposition toward a positive or negative outlook. (p. B-9)

dissociation The splitting of consciousness into two or more simultaneous streams of mental activity. (p. 154)

dissociative amnesia A dissociative disorder involving the partial or total inability to recall important personal information. (p. 531)

dissociative anesthetics Class of drugs that reduce sensitivity to pain and produce feelings of detachment and dissociation; includes the club drugs phencyclidine (PCP) and ketamine. (p. 167)

dissociative disorders A category of psychological disorders in which extreme and frequent disruptions of awareness, memory, and personal identity impair the ability to function. (p. 530)

dissociative experience A break or disruption in consciousness during which awareness, memory, and personal identity become separated or divided. (p. 530)

dissociative fugue (fyoog) A dissociative disorder involving sudden and unexpected travel away from home, extensive amnesia, and identity confusion. (p. 531)

dissociative identity disorder (DID) A dissociative disorder involving extensive memory disruptions along with the presence of two or more distinct identities, or "personalities"; formerly called *multiple personality disorder*. (p. 531)

dopamine (DOPE-uh-meen) Neurotransmitter involved in the regulation of bodily movement, thought processes, and rewarding sensations. (p. 48)

dopamine hypothesis The view that schizophrenia is related to, and may be caused by, excessive activity of the neurotransmitter dopamine in the brain. (p. 540)

double-blind study Experimental technique in which neither the participants nor the researcher interacting with the participants is aware of the group or condition to which the participants have been assigned. (p. 31)

dream A storylike episode of unfolding mental imagery during sleep. (p. 143)

dream interpretation A technique used in psychoanalysis in which the content of dreams is analyzed for disguised or symbolic wishes, meanings, and motivations. (p. 551)

drive A need or internal motivational state that activates behavior to reduce the need and restore homeostasis. (p. 300)

drive theories The view that behavior is motivated by the desire to reduce internal tension caused by unmet biological needs. (p. 300)

drug abuse Recurrent drug use that results in disruptions in academic, social, or occupational functioning or in legal or psychological problems. (p. 157)

drug rebound effect Withdrawal symptoms that are the opposite of a physically addictive drug's action. (p. 156)

drug tolerance A condition in which increasing amounts of a physically addictive drug are needed to produce the original, desired effect. (p. 156)

DSM-IV-TR Abbreviation for the *Diagnostic and Statistical Manual of Mental Disorders,* Fourth Edition, Text Revision; the book published by the American Psychiatric Association that describes the specific symptoms and diagnostic guidelines for different psychological disorders. (p. 507)

dysthymic disorder (dis-THY-mick) A mood disorder involving chronic, low-grade feelings of depression that produce subjective discomfort but do not seriously impair the ability to function. (p. 521)

E

eardrum A tightly stretched membrane at the end of the ear canal that vibrates when hit by sound waves. (p. 97)

eating disorder A category of mental disorders characterized by severe disturbances in eating behavior. (p. 311)

eclecticism (ee-KLEK-tuh-*sizz*-um) The pragmatic and integrated use of techniques from different psychotherapies. (p. 573)

EEG (electroencephalogram) The graphic record of brain activity produced by an electroencephalograph. (p. 133)

ego Latin for *I*; in Freud's theory, the partly conscious rational component of personality that regulates thoughts and behavior and is most in touch with the demands of the external world. (p. 401)

ego defense mechanisms In psychoanalytic theory, largely unconscious distortions of thoughts or perceptions that act to reduce anxiety. (p. 402)

egocentrism In Piaget's theory, the inability to take another person's perspective or point of view. (p. 370)

elaborative rehearsal Rehearsal that involves focusing on the meaning of information to help encode and transfer it to long-term memory. (p. 224)

electroconvulsive therapy (ECT) A biomedical therapy used primarily in the treatment of depression that involves electrically inducing a brief brain seizure; also called *electroshock therapy* or *shock therapy*. (p. 580)

electroencephalograph (e-lec-tro-en-SEFF-uh-low-graph) An instrument that uses electrodes placed on the scalp to measure and record the brain's electrical activity. (pp. 59, 133)

embryonic period The second period of prenatal development, extending from the third week through the eighth week. (p. 356)

emotion A complex psychological state that involves subjective experience, a physiological response, and a behavioral or expressive response. (p. 327)

emotional intelligence The capacity to understand and manage your own emotional experiences and to perceive, comprehend, and respond appropriately to the emotional responses of others. (p. 327)

emotion-focused coping Coping efforts primarily aimed at relieving or regulating the emotional impact of a stressful situation. (p. 497)

empirical evidence Evidence that is based on objective observation, measurement, and/or experimentation. (p. 15)

encoding The process of transforming information into a form that can be entered into and retained by the memory system. (p. 218)

encoding failure The inability to recall specific information because of insufficient encoding of the information for storage in long-term memory. (p. 235)

encoding specificity principle The principle that when the conditions of information retrieval are similar to the conditions of information encoding, retrieval is more likely to be successful. (p. 231)

endocrine system (EN-doe-krin) System of glands located throughout the body that secrete hormones into the bloodstream. (p. 54)

endorphins (en-DORF-ins) Neurotransmitters that regulate pain perceptions. (p. 48)

energy homeostasis The long-term matching of food intake to energy expenditure. (p. 303)

episodic memory Category of long-term memory that includes memories of particular events. (p. 226)

ergonomics A subarea of I/O psychology that focuses on the design of equipment and the development of work procedures in accordance with human capabilities and limitations. (p. B-2)

Eros In Freud's theory, the self-preservation or life instinct, reflected in the expression of basic biological urges that perpetuate the existence of the individual and the species. (p. 401)

ESP (extrasensory perception) Perception of information by some means other than through the normal processes of sensation. (p. 108)

ethnocentrism The belief that one's own culture or ethnic group is superior to all others and the related tendency to use one's own culture as a standard by which to judge other cultures. (p. 452)

evolutionary psychology The application of principles of evolution, including natural selection, to explain psychological processes and phenomena. (p. 11)

exemplars Individual instances of a concept or category, held in memory. (p. 264)

expectancy effects Changes in a subject's behavior produced by the subject's belief that change should happen; also called *placebo effects*. (p. 31)

experimental group or experimental condition In an experiment, the group of participants who are exposed to all experimental conditions, including the independent variable or treatment of interest. (p. 26)

experimental method A method of investigation used to demonstrate cause-and-effect relationships by purposely manipulating one factor thought to produce change in another factor. (p. 25)

explicit memory Information or knowledge that can be consciously recollected; also called *declarative memory*. (p. 226)

exposure therapy Behavioral therapy for phobias, panic disorder, posttraumatic stress disorder, or related anxiety disorders in which the person is repeatedly exposed to the disturbing object or situation under controlled conditions. (p. 572)

extinction (in classical conditioning) The gradual weakening and apparent disappearance of conditioned behavior. In classical conditioning, extinction occurs when the conditioned stimulus is repeatedly presented without the unconditioned stimulus. (p. 178)

extinction (in operant conditioning) The gradual weakening and disappearance of conditioned behavior. In operant conditioning, extinction occurs when an emitted behavior is no longer followed by a reinforcer. (p. 199)

extrinsic motivation External factors or influences on behavior, such as rewards, consequences, or social expectations. (p. 325)

eye movement desensitization reprocessing (EMDR) Therapy technique in which the client holds a vivid mental image of a troubling event or situation while rapidly moving his or her eyes back and forth in response to the therapist's waving finger or while the therapist administers some other form of bilateral stimulation, such as sounding tones in alternate ears. (p. 572)

F

facial feedback hypothesis The view that expressing a specific emotion, especially facially, causes the subjective experience of that emotion. (p. 340)

false memory A distorted or fabricated recollection of something that did not actually occur. (p. 240)

family therapy A form of psychotherapy that is based on the assumption that the family is a system and that treats the family as a unit. (p. 567)

female orgasmic disorder In females, sexual dysfunction characterized by consistent delays in achieving orgasm or the inability to achieve orgasm. (p. 322)

fetal period The third and longest period of prenatal development, extending from the ninth week until birth. (p. 356)

fight-or-flight response A rapidly occurring chain of internal physical reactions that prepare people either to fight or take flight from an immediate threat. (p. 482)

figure–ground relationship A Gestalt principle of perceptual organization that states that we automatically separate the elements of a perception into the feature that clearly stands out (the figure) and its less distinct background (the ground). (p. 107)

five-factor model of personality A trait theory of personality that identifies five basic source traits (extraversion, neuroticism, agreeableness, conscientiousness, and openness to experience) as the fundamental building blocks of personality. (p. 421)

fixed-interval (FI) schedule A reinforcement schedule in which a reinforcer is delivered for the first response that occurs after a preset time interval has elapsed. (p. 199)

fixed-ratio (FR) schedule A reinforcement schedule in which a reinforcer is delivered after a fixed number of responses has occurred. (p. 199)

flashbulb memory The recall of very specific images or details surrounding a vivid, rare, or significant personal event; details may or may not be accurate. (p. 232)

forebrain The largest and most complex brain region, which contains centers for complex behaviors and mental processes; also called the *cerebrum*. (p. 65)

forgetting The inability to recall information that was previously available. (p. 233)

formal concept A mental category that is formed by learning the rules or features that define it. (p. 263)

formal operational stage In Piaget's theory, the fourth stage of cognitive development, which lasts from adolescence through adulthood; characterized by the ability to think logically about abstract principles and hypothetical situations. (p. 371)

fovea (FO-vee-uh) A small area in the center of the retina, composed entirely of cones, where visual information is most sharply focused. (p. 91)

free association A technique used in psychoanalysis in which the patient spontaneously reports all thoughts, feelings, and mental images as they come to mind, as a way of revealing unconscious thoughts and emotions. (pp. 399, 551)

frequency The rate of vibration, or the number of sound waves per second. (p. 97)

frequency distribution A summary of how often various scores occur in a sample of scores. Score values are arranged in order of magnitude, and the number of times each score occurs is recorded. (p. A-3)

frequency polygon A way of graphically representing a frequency distribution; frequency is marked above each score category on the graph's horizontal axis, and the marks are connected by straight lines. (p. A-4)

frontal lobe The largest lobe of each cerebral hemisphere; processes voluntary muscle movements and is involved in thinking, planning, and emotional control. (p. 66)

functional fixedness The tendency to view objects as functioning only in their usual or customary way. (p. 266)

functional magnetic resonance imaging (fMRI) A noninvasive imaging technique that uses magnetic fields to map brain activity by measuring changes in the brain's blood flow and oxygen levels. (p. 60)

functional plasticity The brain's ability to shift functions from damaged to undamaged brain areas. (p. 76)

functionalism Early school of psychology that emphasized studying the purpose, or function, of behavior and mental experiences. (p. 5)

fundamental attribution error The tendency to attribute the behavior of others to internal, personal characteristics, while ignoring or underestimating the effects of external, situational factors; an attributional bias that is common in individualistic cultures. (p. 443)

G

g factor or **general intelligence** The notion of a general intelligence factor that is responsible for a person's overall performance on tests of mental ability. (p. 281)

GABA (gamma-aminobutyric acid) Neurotransmitter that usually communicates an inhibitory message. (p. 48)

ganglion cells In the retina, the specialized neurons that connect to the bipolar cells; the bundled axons of the ganglion cells form the optic nerve. (p. 91)

gate-control theory of pain The theory that pain is a product of both physiological and psychological factors that cause spinal gates to open and relay patterns of intense stimulation to the brain, which perceives them as pain. (p. 104)

gender The cultural, social, and psychological meanings that are associated with masculinity or femininity. (p. 365)

gender identity A person's psychological sense of being male or female. (p. 365)

gender roles The behaviors, attitudes, and personality traits that are designated as either masculine or feminine in a given culture. (p. 365)

gender schema theory The theory that gender-role development is influenced by the formation of schemas, or mental representations, of masculinity and femininity. (p. 367)

gene A unit of DNA on a chromosome that encodes instructions for making a particular protein molecule; the basic unit of heredity. (p. 353)

general adaptation syndrome Selye's term for the three-stage progression of physical changes that occur when an organism is exposed to intense and prolonged stress. The three stages are alarm, resistance, and exhaustion. (p. 484)

generalized anxiety disorder (GAD) An anxiety disorder characterized by excessive, global, and persistent symptoms of anxiety; also called *free-floating anxiety*. (p. 512)

genotype (JEEN-oh-type) The genetic makeup of an individual organism. (p. 353)

germinal period The first two weeks of prenatal development. (p. 355)

Gestalt psychology (geh-SHTALT) A school of psychology founded in Germany in the early 1900s that maintained that our sensations are actively processed according to consistent perceptual rules that result in meaningful whole perceptions, or *gestalts*. (p. 107)

ghrelin (GRELL-in) Hormone manufactured primarily by the stomach that stimulates appetite and the secretion of growth hormone by the pituitary gland. (p. 304)

glial cells (GLEE-ull) Support cells that assist neurons by providing structural support, nutrition, and removal of cell wastes; manufacture myelin. (p. 41)

glucose Simple sugar that provides energy and is primarily produced by the conversion of carbohydrates and fats; commonly called *blood sugar*. (p. 303)

gonads The endocrine glands that secrete hormones that regulate sexual characteristics and reproductive processes; ovaries in females and testes in males. (p. 56)

graphology A pseudoscience that claims to assess personality, social, and occupational attributes based on a person's distinctive handwriting, doodles, and drawing styles. (p. 427)

group therapy A form of psychotherapy that involves one or more therapists working simultaneously with a small group of clients. (p. 566)

gustation Technical name for the sense of taste. (p. 99)

H

hair cells The hairlike sensory receptors for sound, which are embedded in the basilar membrane of the cochlea. (p. 98)

hallucination A false or distorted perception that seems vividly real to the person experiencing it. (p. 534)

health psychology The branch of psychology that studies how biological, behavioral, and social factors influence health, illness, medical treatment, and health-related behaviors. (p. 477)

heritability The percentage of variation within a given population that is due to heredity. (p. 286)

heuristic A problem-solving strategy that involves following a general rule of thumb to reduce the number of possible solutions. (p. 265)

hidden observer Hilgard's term for the hidden, or dissociated, stream of mental activity that continues during hypnosis. (p. 154)

hierarchy of needs Maslow's hierarchical division of motivation into levels that progress from basic physical needs to psychological needs to self-fulfillment needs. (p. 323)

hippocampus A curved forebrain structure that is part of the limbic system and is involved in learning and forming new memories. (p. 68)

histogram A way of graphically representing a frequency distribution; a type of bar chart that uses vertical bars that touch. (p. A-3)

homeostasis (home-ee-oh-STAY-sis) The idea that the body monitors and maintains internal states, such as body temperature and energy supplies, at relatively constant levels; in general, the tendency to reach or maintain equilibrium. (p. 300)

hormones Chemical messengers secreted into the bloodstream primarily by endocrine glands. (p. 54)

hue The property of wavelengths of light known as color; different wavelengths correspond to our subjective experience of different colors. (p. 94)

human genome The scientific description of the complete set of DNA in the human organism, including gene locations. (p. 354)

humanistic psychology The theoretical viewpoint on personality that generally emphasizes the inherent goodness of people, human potential, self-actualization, the self-concept, and healthy personality development. (pp. 8, 411)

humanistic theories of motivation The view that emphasizes the importance of psychological and cognitive factors in motivation, especially the notion that people are motivated to realize their personal potential. (p. 302)

hypermnesia (high-perm-NEE-zha) The supposed enhancement of a person's memory for past events through a hypnotic suggestion. (p. 151)

hypnagogic hallucinations (hip-na-GAH-jick) Vivid sensory phenomena that occur during the onset of sleep. (p. 134)

hypnosis (hip-NO-sis) A cooperative social interaction in which the hypnotized person responds to the hypnotist's suggestions with changes in perception, memory, and behavior. (p. 150)

hypothalamus (hi-poe-THAL-uh-muss) A peanut-sized forebrain structure that is part of the limbic system and regulates behaviors related to survival, such as eating, drinking, and sexual activity. (p. 68)

hypothesis (high-POTH-eh-sis) A tentative statement about the relationship between two or more variables. (p. 15)

I

id Latin for *the it*; in Freud's theory, the completely unconscious, irrational component of personality that seeks immediate satisfaction of instinctual urges and drives; ruled by the pleasure principle. (p. 401)

identification In psychoanalytic theory, an ego defense mechanism that involves reducing anxiety by imitating the behavior and characteristics of another person. (p. 405)

identity A person's definition or description of himself or herself, including the values, beliefs, and ideals that guide the individual's behavior. (p. 380)

illusory correlation The mistaken belief that two factors or events are related when they are not. (p. 20)

imagination inflation A memory phenomenon in which vividly imagining an event markedly increases confidence that the event actually occurred. (p. 242)

immune system Body system that produces specialized white blood cells that protect the body from viruses, bacteria, and tumor cells. (p. 484)

implicit memory Information or knowledge that affects behavior or task performance but cannot be consciously recollected; also called *nondeclarative memory*. (p. 226)

implicit personality theory A network of assumptions or beliefs about the relationships among various types of people, traits, and behaviors. (p. 440)

incentive theories The view that behavior is motivated by the pull of external goals, such as rewards. (p. 301)

independent variable The purposely manipulated factor thought to produce change in an experiment; also called the *treatment of interest*. (p. 25)

individualistic cultures Cultures that emphasize the needs and goals of the individual over the needs and goals of the group. (p. 12)

induction A discipline technique that combines parental control with explaining why a behavior is prohibited. (p. 390)

industrial/organizational (I/O) psychology The branch of psychology that focuses on the study of human behavior at work. (p. B-1)

inferential statistics Mathematical methods used to determine how likely it is that a study's outcome is due to chance and whether the outcome can be legitimately generalized to a larger population. (p. A-12)

informational social influence Behavior that is motivated by the desire to be correct. (p. 456)

information-processing model of cognitive development The model that views cognitive development as a process that is continuous over the lifespan and that studies the development of basic mental processes such as attention, memory, and problem solving. (p. 373)

in-group A social group to which one belongs. (p. 451)

in-group bias The tendency to judge the behavior of in-group members favorably and out-group members unfavorably. (p. 452)

inner ear The part of the ear where sound is transduced into neural impulses; consists of the cochlea and semicircular canals. (p. 97)

insight The sudden realization of how a problem can be solved. (p. 266)

insomnia A condition in which a person regularly experiences an inability to fall asleep, to stay asleep, or to feel adequately rested by sleep. (p. 140)

instinct theories The view that certain human behaviors are innate and due to evolutionary programming. (p. 299)

instinctive drift The tendency of an animal to revert to instinctive behaviors that can interfere with the performance of an operantly conditioned response. (p. 206)

insulin Hormone produced by the pancreas that regulates blood levels of glucose and signals the hypothalamus, regulating hunger and eating behavior. (p. 303)

intelligence The global capacity to think rationally, act purposefully, and deal effectively with the environment. (p. 276)

intelligence quotient (IQ) A measure of general intelligence derived by comparing an individual's score with the scores of others in the same age group. (p. 276)

interference theory The theory that forgetting is caused by one memory competing with or replacing another. (p. 237)

interneuron Type of neuron that communicates information from one neuron to the next. (p. 41)

interpersonal engagement Emotion dimension reflecting the degree to which emotions involve a relationship with another person or other people. (p. 330)

interpersonal therapy (IPT) A brief, psychodynamic psychotherapy that focuses on current relationships and is based on the assumption that symptoms are caused and maintained by interpersonal problems. (p. 544)

interpretation A technique used in psychoanalysis in which the psychoanalyst offers a carefully timed explanation of the patient's dreams, free associations, or behaviors to facilitate the recognition of unconscious conflicts or motivations. (p. 551)

intrinsic motivation The desire to engage in tasks that the person finds inherently satisfying and enjoyable, novel, or optimally challenging; the desire to do something for its own sake. (p. 325)

intuition Coming to a conclusion or making a judgment without conscious awareness of the thought processes involved. (p. 266)

iris (EYE-riss) The colored part of the eye, which is the muscle that controls the size of the pupil. (p. 89)

irreversibility In Piaget's theory, the inability to mentally reverse a sequence of events or logical operations. (p. 370)

J

James–Lange theory of emotion The theory that emotions arise from the perception of body changes. (p. 338)

job analysis An assessment of the major responsibilities of a particular job and the human characteristics needed to fill it. (p. B-5)

just-world hypothesis The assumption that the world is fair and that therefore people get what they deserve and deserve what they get. (p. 443)

K

K complexes Single but large high-voltage spikes of brain activity that characterize stage 2 NREM sleep. (p. 135)

kinesthetic sense (kin-ess-THET-ick) The technical name for the sense of location and position of body parts in relation to one another. (p. 105)

L

language A system for combining arbitrary symbols to produce an infinite number of meaningful statements. (p. 271)

latent content In Freud's psychoanalytic theory, the unconscious wishes, thoughts, and urges that are concealed in the manifest content of a dream. (p. 148)

latent learning Tolman's term for learning that occurs in the absence of reinforcement but is not behaviorally demonstrated until a reinforcer becomes available. (p. 204)

lateralization of function The notion that specific psychological or cognitive functions are processed primarily on one side of the brain. (p. 71)

law of effect Learning principle proposed by Thorndike that responses followed by a satisfying effect become strengthened and are more likely to recur in a particular situation, while responses followed by a dissatisfying effect are weakened and less likely to recur in a particular situation. (p. 190)

leader–member exchange model A model of leadership emphasizing that the quality of the interactions between supervisors and subordinates varies depending on the unique characteristics of both. (p. B-11)

learned helplessness A phenomenon in which exposure to inescapable and uncontrollable aversive events produces passive behavior. (p. 205)

learning A process that produces a relatively enduring change in behavior or knowledge as a result of past experience. (p. 174)

lens A transparent structure located behind the pupil that actively focuses, or bends, light as it enters the eye. (p. 89)

leptin Hormone produced by fat cells that signals the hypothalamus, regulating hunger and eating behavior. (p. 306)

leptin resistance A condition in which higher-than-normal blood levels of the hormone leptin do not produce the expected physiological response. (p. 310)

libido In Freud's theory, the psychological and emotional energy associated with expressions of sexuality; the sex drive. (p. 401)

limbic system A group of forebrain structures that form a border around the brainstem and are involved in emotion, motivation, learning, and memory. (p. 67)

linguistic relativity hypothesis The hypothesis that differences among languages cause differences in the thoughts of their speakers. (p. 272)

lithium A naturally occurring substance that is used in the treatment of bipolar disorder. (p. 579)

long-term memory The stage of memory that represents the long-term storage of information. (p. 219)

long-term potentiation A long-lasting increase in synaptic strength between two neurons. (p. 247)

loudness The intensity (or amplitude) of a sound wave, measured in decibels. (p. 97)

LSD A synthetic psychedelic drug. (p. 164)

lymphocytes (LIMF-oh-sites) Specialized white blood cells that are responsible for immune defenses. (p. 484)

M

magnetic resonance imaging (MRI) A noninvasive imaging technique that produces highly detailed images of the brain using electromagnetic signals generated by the brain in response to magnetic fields. (p. 60)

maintenance rehearsal The mental or verbal repetition of information in order to maintain it beyond the usual 20-second duration of short-term memory. (p. 222)

major depression A mood disorder characterized by extreme and persistent feelings of despondency, worthlessness, and hopelessness, causing impaired emotional, cognitive, behavioral, and physical functioning. (p. 520)

male erectile disorder In males, sexual dysfunction characterized by a recurring inability to achieve or maintain an erect penis. (p. 322)

manic episode A sudden, rapidly escalating emotional state characterized by extreme euphoria, excitement, physical energy, and rapid thoughts and speech. (p. 523)

manifest content In Freud's psychoanalytic theory, the elements of a dream that are consciously experienced and remembered by the dreamer. (p. 148)

marijuana A psychoactive drug derived from the hemp plant. (p. 165)

MDMA or **ecstasy** Synthetic club drug that combines stimulant and mild psychedelic effects. (p. 165)

mean The sum of a set of scores in a distribution divided by the number of scores; the mean is usually the most representative measure of central tendency. (p. A-5)

measure of central tendency A single number that presents some information about the "center" of a frequency distribution. (p. A-5)

measure of variability A single number that presents information about the spread of scores in a distribution. (p. A-6)

median The score that divides a frequency distribution exactly in half, so that the same number of scores lie on each side of it. (p. A-5)

meditation Any one of a number of sustained concentration techniques that focus attention and heighten awareness. (p. 154)

medulla (meh-DOOL-uh) A hindbrain structure that controls vital life functions such as breathing and circulation. (p. 64)

melatonin (mel-ah-TONE-in) A hormone manufactured by the pineal gland that produces sleepiness. (p. 131)

memory The mental processes that enable us to retain and use information over time. (p. 218)

memory consolidation The gradual, physical process of converting new long-term memories to stable, enduring long-term memory codes. (p. 249)

memory trace The brain changes associated with a particular stored memory. (p. 243)

menarche (meh-NAR-kee) A female's first menstrual period, which occurs during puberty. (p. 375)

menopause The natural cessation of menstruation and the end of reproductive capacity in women. (p. 382)

mental age A measurement of intelligence in which an individual's mental level is expressed in terms of the average abilities of a given age group. (p. 276)

mental image A mental representation of objects or events that are not physically present. (p. 261)

mental set The tendency to persist in solving problems with solutions that have worked in the past. (p. 267)

mescaline (MESS-kuh-*lin*) A psychedelic drug derived from the peyote cactus. (p. 164)

meta-analysis A statistical technique that involves combining and analyzing the results of many research studies on a specific topic in order to identify overall trends. (p. 17)

midbrain The middle and smallest brain region, involved in processing auditory and visual sensory information. (p. 64)

middle ear The part of the ear that amplifies sound waves; consists of three small bones: the hammer, the anvil, and the stirrup. (p. 97)

Minnesota Multiphasic Personality Inventory (MMPI) A self-report inventory that assesses personality characteristics and psychological disorders; used to assess both normal and disturbed populations. (p. 428)

misinformation effect A memory-distortion phenomenon in which a person's existing memories can be altered if the person is exposed to misleading information. (p. 239)

mode The most frequently occurring score in a distribution. (p. A-5)

monocular cues (moe-NOCK-you-ler) Distance or depth cues that can be processed by either eye alone. (p. 111)

mood congruence An encoding specificity phenomenon in which a given mood tends to evoke memories that are consistent with that mood. (p. 232)

mood disorders A category of mental disorders in which significant and persistent disruptions in mood or emotions cause impaired cognitive, behavioral, and physical functioning; also called *affective disorders.* (p. 520)

moon illusion A visual illusion involving the misperception that the moon is larger when it is on the horizon than when it is directly overhead. (p. 117)

moral reasoning The aspect of cognitive development that has to do with how an individual reasons about moral decisions. (p. 376)

motivation The biological, emotional, cognitive, or social forces that activate and direct behavior. (p. 298)

motor neuron Type of neuron that signals muscles to relax or contract. (p. 41)

Müller-Lyer illusion A famous visual illusion involving the misperception of the identical length of two lines, one with arrows pointed inward, one with arrows pointed outward. (p. 116)

myelin sheath (MY-eh-lin) A white, fatty covering wrapped around the axons of some neurons that increases their communication speed. (p. 43)

N

narcolepsy (NAR-ko-lep-see) A sleep disorder characterized by excessive daytime sleepiness and brief lapses into sleep throughout the day. (p. 142)

natural concept A mental category that is formed as a result of everyday experience. (p. 263)

naturalistic observation The systematic observation and recording of behaviors as they occur in their natural setting. (p. 19)

negative correlation A finding that two factors vary systematically in opposite directions, one increasing as the other decreases. (pp. 24, A-9)

negative reinforcement A situation in which a response results in the removal of, avoidance of, or escape from a punishing stimulus, increasing the likelihood that the response will be repeated in similar situations. (p. 192)

negative symptoms In schizophrenia, symptoms that reflect defects or deficits in normal functioning, including flat affect, alogia, and avolition. (p. 533)

neodissociation theory of hypnosis Theory proposed by Ernest Hilgard that explains hypnotic effects as being due to the splitting of consciousness into two simultaneous streams of mental activity, only one of which the hypnotic participant is consciously aware of during hypnosis. (p. 154)

nerves Bundles of neuron axons that carry information in the peripheral nervous system. (p. 51)

nervous system The primary internal communication network of the body; divided into the central nervous system and the peripheral nervous system. (p. 51)

neurogenesis The development of new neurons. (p. 62)

neuron Highly specialized cell that communicates information in electrical and chemical form; a nerve cell. (p. 41)

neuroscience The study of the nervous system, especially the brain. (p. 40)

neurotransmitters Chemical messengers manufactured by a neuron. (p. 46)

nicotine A stimulant drug found in tobacco products. (p. 162)

night terrors A sleep disturbance characterized by an episode of increased physiological arousal, intense fear and panic, frightening hallucinations, and no recall of the episode the next morning; typically occurs during stage 3 or stage 4 NREM sleep; also called *sleep terrors.* (p. 141)

nightmare A frightening or unpleasant anxiety dream that occurs during REM sleep. (p. 147)

nociceptors Specialized sensory receptors for pain that are found in the skin, muscles, and internal organs. (p. 103)

norepinephrine (nor-ep-in-EF-rin) Neurotransmitter involved in learning and memory; also a hormone manufactured by adrenal glands. (p. 48)

normal curve or **normal distribution** A bell-shaped distribution of individual differences in a normal population in which most scores cluster around the average score. (p. 280)

normative social influence Behavior that is motivated by the desire to gain social acceptance and approval. (p. 456)

NREM sleep Quiet, typically dreamless sleep in which rapid eye movements are absent; divided into four stages; also called *quiet sleep.* (p. 133)

O

obedience The performance of an action in response to the direct orders of an authority or person of higher status. (p. 457)

obese Condition characterized by excessive body fat and a body mass index equal to or greater than 30.0. (p. 308)

object permanence The understanding that an object continues to exist even when it can no longer be seen. (p. 369)

observational learning Learning that occurs through observing the actions of others. (p. 207)

obsessions Repeated, intrusive, and uncontrollable irrational thoughts or mental images that cause extreme anxiety and distress. (p. 518)

obsessive-compulsive disorder (OCD) An anxiety disorder in which the symptoms of anxiety are triggered by intrusive, repetitive thoughts and urges to perform certain actions. (p. 517)

occipital lobe (ock-SIP-it-ull) An area at the back of each cerebral hemisphere that is the primary receiving area for visual information. (p. 66)

Oedipus complex In Freud's theory, a child's unconscious sexual desire for the opposite-sex parent, usually accompanied by hostile feelings toward the same-sex parent. (p. 405)

olfaction Technical name for the sense of smell. (p. 99)

olfactory bulb (ole-FACK-toe-ree) The enlarged ending of the olfactory cortex at the front of the brain where the sensation of smell is registered. (p. 100)

operant Skinner's term for an actively emitted (or voluntary) behavior that operates on the environment to produce consequences. (p. 190)

operant chamber or **Skinner box** The experimental apparatus invented by B. F. Skinner to study the relationship between environmental events and active behaviors. (p. 198)

operant conditioning The basic learning process that involves changing the probability that a response will be repeated by manipulating the consequences of that response; also called *Skinnerian conditioning.* (p. 191)

operational definition A precise description of how the variables in a study will be manipulated or measured. (p. 15)

opiates (OH-pee-ets) A category of psychoactive drugs that are chemically similar to morphine and have strong pain-relieving properties. (p. 160)

opponent-process theory of color vision The theory that color vision is the product of opposing pairs of color receptors, red-green, blue-yellow, and black-white; when one member of a color pair is stimulated, the other member is inhibited. (p. 95)

optic chiasm (KI-az-em) Point in the brain where the optic nerve fibers from each eye meet and partly cross over to the opposite side of the brain. (p. 92)

optic disk Area of the retina without rods or cones, where the optic nerve exits the back of the eye. (p. 91)

optic nerve The thick nerve that exits from the back of the eye and carries visual information to the visual cortex in the brain. (p. 92)

optimistic explanatory style Accounting for negative events or situations with external, unstable, and specific explanations. (p. 489)

organizational behavior A subarea of I/O psychology that focuses on how the organization and the social environment in which people work affect their attitudes and behaviors. (p. B-1)

organizational development (OD) A subarea of I/O psychology that focuses on bringing about positive change in an organization, such as increased profitability or improved products. (p. B-2)

outer ear The part of the ear that collects sound waves; consists of the pinna, the ear canal, and the eardrum. (p. 97)

out-group A social group to which one does not belong. (p. 451)

out-group homogeneity effect The tendency to see members of out-groups as very similar to one another. (p. 452)

P

pain The unpleasant sensation of physical discomfort or suffering that can occur in varying degrees of intensity. (p. 102)

panic attack A sudden episode of extreme anxiety that rapidly escalates in intensity. (p. 513)

panic disorder An anxiety disorder in which the person experiences frequent and unexpected panic attacks. (p. 513)

paranoid personality disorder A personality disorder characterized by a pervasive distrust and suspiciousness of the motives of others without sufficient basis. (p. 527)

paranormal phenomena Alleged abilities or events that fall outside the range of normal experience and established scientific explanations. (p. 20)

parapsychology The scientific investigation of claims of paranormal phenomena and abilities. (p. 108)

parasomnias (pare-uh-SOM-nee-uz) A category of sleep disorders characterized by arousal or activation during sleep or sleep transitions; includes *sleepwalking, night terrors, sleep bruxism, sleep-related eating disorder,* and *REM sleep behavior disorder.* (p. 142)

parasympathetic nervous system Branch of the autonomic nervous system that maintains normal bodily functions and conserves the body's physical resources. (p. 54)

parietal lobe (puh-RYE-et-ull) An area on each hemisphere of the cerebral cortex located above the temporal lobe that processes somatic sensations. (p. 66)

partial reinforcement A situation in which the occurrence of a particular response is only sometimes followed by a reinforcer. (p. 198)

partial reinforcement effect The phenomenon in which behaviors that are conditioned using partial reinforcement are more resistant to extinction than behaviors that are conditioned using continuous reinforcement. (p. 199)

perception The process of integrating, organizing, and interpreting sensations. (p. 85)

perceptual constancy The tendency to perceive objects, especially familiar objects, as constant and unchanging despite changes in sensory input. (p. 115)

perceptual illusion The misperception of the true characteristics of an object or an image. (p. 116)

perceptual set The influence of prior assumptions and expectations on perceptual interpretations. (p. 119)

peripheral nervous system (per-IF-er-ull) Division of the nervous system that includes all the nerves lying outside the central nervous system. (p. 52)

permissive parenting style Parenting style in which parents are extremely tolerant and not demanding; permissive-indulgent parents are more responsive to their children, whereas permissive-indifferent parents are not. (p. 389)

person perception The mental processes we use to form judgments and draw conclusions about the characteristics and motives of other people. (p. 438)

personality An individual's unique and relatively consistent patterns of thinking, feeling, and behaving. (p. 397)

personality disorder Inflexible, maladaptive patterns of thoughts, emotions, behavior, and interpersonal functioning that are stable over time and across situations, and deviate from the expectations of the individual's culture. (p. 527)

personality theory A theory that attempts to describe and explain similarities and differences in people's patterns of thinking, feeling, and behaving. (p. 397)

personnel psychology A subarea of I/O psychology that focuses on matching people's characteristics to job requirements, accurately measuring job performance, and assessing employee training needs. (p. B-1)

persuasion The deliberate attempt to influence the attitudes or behavior of another person in a situation in which that person has some freedom of choice. (p. 469)

pessimistic explanatory style Accounting for negative events or situations with internal, stable, and global explanations. (p. 489)

phenotype (FEEN-oh-type) The observable traits or characteristics of an organism as determined by the interaction of genetics and environmental factors. (p. 354)

pheromones Chemical signals released by an animal that communicate information and affect the behavior of other animals of the same species. (p. 100)

phobia A strong or irrational fear of something, usually a specific object or situation, that does not necessarily interfere with the ability to function in daily life. (p. 514)

phrenology (freh-NOL-uh-gee) A discredited pseudoscientific theory of the brain that claimed that personality characteristics, moral character, and intelligence could be determined by examining the bumps on a person's skull. (p. 59)

physical dependence A condition in which a person has physically adapted to a drug so that he or she must take the drug regularly in order to avoid withdrawal symptoms. (p. 156)

pitch The relative highness or lowness of a sound, determined by the frequency of a sound wave. (p. 97)

pituitary gland (pih-TOO-ih-tare-ee) Endocrine gland attached to the base of the brain that secretes hormones that affect the function of other glands as well as hormones that act directly on physical processes. (p. 56)

placebo control group (pluh-SEE-bo) In an experiment, a control group in which the participants are exposed to a fake independent variable, or placebo. The effects of the placebo are compared to the effects of the actual independent variable, or treatment of interest, on the experimental group. (p. 29)

placebo response An individual's psychological and physiological response to what is actually a fake treatment or drug; also called *placebo effect.* (p. 184)

pleasure principle In Freud's theory, the motive to obtain pleasure and avoid tension or discomfort; the most fundamental human motive and the guiding principle of the id. (p. 401)

pons A hindbrain structure that connects the medulla to the two sides of the cerebellum; helps coordinate and integrate movements on each side of the body. (p. 64)

population A complete set of something—people, nonhuman animals, objects, or events. (p. A-12)

positive correlation A finding that two factors vary systematically in the same direction, increasing or decreasing in size together. (pp. 24, A-9)

positive incentive value In eating behavior, the anticipated pleasure of consuming a particular food; in general, the expectation of pleasure or satisfaction in performing a particular behavior. (p. 305)

positive reinforcement A situation in which a response is followed by the addition of a reinforcing stimulus, increasing the likelihood that the response will be repeated in similar situations. (p. 191)

positive symptoms In schizophrenia, symptoms that reflect excesses or distortions of normal functioning, including delusions, hallucinations, and disorganized thoughts and behavior. (p. 533)

positron emission tomography (PET scan) An invasive imaging technique that provides color-coded images of brain activity by tracking the brain's use of a radioactively tagged compound, such as glucose, oxygen, or a drug. (p. 60)

possible selves The aspect of the self-concept that includes images of the selves that you hope, fear, or expect to become in the future. (p. 431)

posthypnotic amnesia The inability to recall specific information because of a hypnotic suggestion. (p. 151)

posthypnotic suggestion A suggestion made during hypnosis that the person should carry out a specific instruction following the hypnotic session. (p. 151)

posttraumatic stress disorder (PTSD) An anxiety disorder in which chronic and persistent symptoms of anxiety develop in response to an extreme physical or psychological trauma. (p. 516)

practice effect Any change in performance that results from mere repetition of a task. (p. 31)

prejudice A negative attitude toward people who belong to a specific social group. (p. 450)

premature ejaculation In males, sexual dysfunction characterized by orgasm occurring before it is desired, often immediately or shortly after sexual stimulation or penetration. (p. 322)

prenatal stage The stage of development before birth; divided into the germinal, embryonic, and fetal periods. (p. 355)

preoperational stage In Piaget's theory, the second stage of cognitive development, which lasts from about age 2 to age 7; characterized by increasing use of symbols and prelogical thought processes. (p. 369)

primary reinforcer A stimulus or event that is naturally or inherently reinforcing for a given species, such as food, water, or other biological necessities. (p. 192)

primary sex characteristics Sexual organs that are directly involved in reproduction, such as the uterus, ovaries, penis, and testicles. (p. 374)

proactive interference Forgetting in which an old memory interferes with remembering a new memory; forward-acting memory interference. (p. 237)

problem-focused coping Coping efforts primarily aimed at directly changing or managing a threatening or harmful stressor. (p. 496)

problem solving Thinking and behavior directed toward attaining a goal that is not readily available. (p. 264)

procedural memory Category of long-term memory that includes memories of different skills, operations, and actions. (p. 226)

production vocabulary The words that an infant or child understands and can speak. (p. 364)

projective test A type of personality test that involves a person's interpreting an ambiguous

image; used to assess unconscious motives, conflicts, psychological defenses, and personality traits. (p. 426)

proprioceptors (pro-pree-oh-SEP-ters) Sensory receptors, located in the muscles and joints, that provide information about body position and movement. (p. 105)

prosocial behavior Any behavior that helps another, whether the underlying motive is self-serving or selfless. (p. 466)

prospective memory Remembering to do something in the future. (p. 235)

prototype The most typical instance of a particular concept. (p. 263)

pseudoscience A fake or false science that makes claims based on little or no scientific evidence. (p. 20)

psychedelic drugs (sy-kuh-DEL-ick) A category of psychoactive drugs that create sensory and perceptual distortions, alter mood, and affect thinking. (p. 164)

psychoactive drug A drug that alters consciousness, perception, mood, and behavior. (p. 156)

psychoanalysis A type of psychotherapy originated by Sigmund Freud in which free association, dream interpretation, and analysis of resistance and transference are used to explore repressed or unconscious impulses, anxieties, and internal conflicts. (pp. 7, 398, 550)

psychological disorder or **mental disorder** A pattern of behavioral and psychological symptoms that causes significant personal distress, impairs the ability to function in one or more important areas of daily life, or both. (p. 507)

psychological test A test that assesses a person's abilities, aptitudes, interests, or personality, on the basis of a systematically obtained sample of behavior. (p. 425)

psychology The science of behavior and mental processes. (p. 3)

psychoneuroimmunology An interdisciplinary field that studies the interconnections among psychological processes, nervous- and endocrine-system functions, and the immune system. (p. 486)

psychopathology The scientific study of the origins, symptoms, and development of psychological disorders. (p. 507)

psychosexual stages In Freud's theory, age-related developmental periods in which the child's sexual urges are focused on different areas of the body and are expressed through the activities associated with those areas. (p. 404)

psychotherapy The treatment of emotional, behavioral, and interpersonal problems through the use of psychological techniques designed to encourage understanding of problems and modify troubling feelings, behaviors, or relationships. (p. 548)

psychotropic medications (sy-ko-TRO-pick) Drugs that alter mental functions, alleviate

psychological symptoms, and are used to treat psychological or mental disorders. (p. 575)

puberty The stage of adolescence in which an individual reaches sexual maturity and becomes physiologically capable of sexual reproduction. (p. 374)

punishment The presentation of a stimulus or event following a behavior that acts to decrease the likelihood of the behavior's being repeated. (p. 193)

punishment by application A situation in which an operant is followed by the presentation or addition of an aversive stimulus; also called *positive punishment*. (p. 193)

punishment by removal A situation in which an operant is followed by the removal or subtraction of a reinforcing stimulus; also called *negative punishment*. (p. 194)

pupil The opening in the middle of the iris that changes size to let in different amounts of light. (p. 89)

R

random assignment The process of assigning participants to experimental conditions so that all participants have an equal chance of being assigned to any of the conditions or groups in the study. (p. 26)

random selection Process in which subjects are selected randomly from a larger group such that every group member has an equal chance of being included in the study. (p. 22)

range A measure of variability; the highest score in a distribution minus the lowest score. (p. A-6)

rational-emotive therapy (RET) A type of cognitive therapy, developed by psychologist Albert Ellis, that focuses on changing the client's irrational beliefs. (p. 562)

reality principle In Freud's theory, the capacity to accommodate external demands by postponing gratification until the appropriate time or circumstances exist. (p. 401)

recall A test of long-term memory that involves retrieving information without the aid of retrieval cues; also called *free recall*. (p. 230)

reciprocal determinism A model proposed by psychologist Albert Bandura that explains human functioning and personality as caused by the interaction of behavioral, cognitive, and environmental factors. (p. 416)

recognition A test of long-term memory that involves identifying correct information out of several possible choices. (p. 230)

reinforcement The occurrence of a stimulus or event following a response that increases the likelihood of that response being repeated. (p. 191)

reliability The ability of a test to produce consistent results when administered on repeated occasions under similar conditions. (p. 280)

REM rebound A phenomenon in which a person who is deprived of REM sleep greatly increases the amount of time spent in REM sleep at the first opportunity to sleep uninterrupted. (p. 138)

REM sleep Type of sleep during which rapid eye movements (REM) and dreaming usually occur and voluntary muscle activity is suppressed; also called *active sleep* or *paradoxical sleep*. (p. 133)

REM sleep behavior disorder A sleep disorder in which the sleeper acts out his or her dreams. (p. 142)

replicate To repeat or duplicate a scientific study in order to increase confidence in the validity of the original findings. (p. 18)

representative sample A selected segment that very closely parallels the larger population being studied on relevant characteristics. (p. 22)

representativeness heuristic A strategy in which the likelihood of an event is estimated by comparing how similar it is to the prototype of the event. (p. 269)

repression In psychoanalytic theory, the unconscious exclusion of anxiety-provoking thoughts, feelings, and memories from conscious awareness; the most fundamental ego defense mechanism. (pp. 238, 402)

resistance In psychoanalysis, the patient's unconscious attempts to block the revelation of repressed memories and conflicts. (p. 551)

resting potential State in which a neuron is prepared to activate and communicate its message if it receives sufficient stimulation. (p. 43)

restless legs syndrome (RLS) A condition in which unpleasant sensations in the lower legs are accompanied by an irresistible urge to move the legs, temporarily relieving the unpleasant sensation but disrupting sleep. (p. 140)

restorative theory of sleep The view that sleep and dreaming are essential to normal physical and mental functioning. (p. 139)

reticular formation (reh-TICK-you-ler) A network of nerve fibers located in the center of the medulla that helps regulate attention, arousal, and sleep; also called the *reticular activating system*. (p. 64)

retina (RET-in-uh) A thin, light-sensitive membrane located at the back of the eye that contains the sensory receptors for vision. (p. 90)

retrieval The process of recovering information stored in memory so that we are consciously aware of it. (pp. 218, 229)

retrieval cue A clue, prompt, or hint that helps trigger recall of a given piece of information stored in long-term memory. (p. 229)

retrieval cue failure The inability to recall long-term memories because of inadequate or missing retrieval cues. (p. 229)

retroactive interference Forgetting in which a new memory interferes with remem-

bering an old memory; backward-acting memory interference. (p. 237)

retrograde amnesia Loss of memory, especially for episodic information; backward-acting amnesia. (p. 249)

reuptake The process by which neurotransmitter molecules detach from a postsynaptic neuron and are reabsorbed by a presynaptic neuron so they can be recycled and used again. (p. 46)

rods The long, thin, blunt sensory receptors of the eye that are highly sensitive to light, but not to color, and that are primarily responsible for peripheral vision and night vision. (p. 90)

Rorschach Inkblot Test A projective test using inkblots, developed by Swiss psychiatrist Hermann Rorschach in 1921. (p. 426)

rule of falsifiability In order for a claim to be scientifically tested and proved true, there must be identifiable evidence that could prove the claim false. (p. 20)

S

sample A selected segment of the population used to represent the group that is being studied (p. 22); a subset of a population. (p. A-12)

satiation (say-she-AY-shun) In eating behavior, the feeling of fullness and diminished desire to eat that accompanies eating a meal; in general, the sensation of having an appetite or desire fully or excessively satisfied. (p. 305)

saturation The property of color that corresponds to the purity of the light wave. (p. 94)

scatter diagram or **scatter plot** A graph that represents the relationship between two variables. (p. A-10)

schedule of reinforcement The delivery of a reinforcer according to a preset pattern based on the number of responses or the time interval between responses. (p. 199)

schema (SKEE-muh) An organized cluster of information about a particular topic. (p. 240)

schizophrenia A psychological disorder in which the ability to function is impaired by severely distorted beliefs, perceptions, and thought processes. (p. 533)

scientific method A set of assumptions, attitudes, and procedures that guide researchers in creating questions to investigate, in generating evidence, and in drawing conclusions. (p. 14)

script A schema for the typical sequence of an everyday event. (p. 240)

seasonal affective disorder (SAD) A mood disorder in which episodes of depression typically occur during the fall and winter and subside during the spring and summer. (p. 522)

secondary sex characteristics Sexual characteristics that develop during puberty and are not directly involved in reproduction but differentiate between the sexes, such as male facial hair and female breast development. (p. 374)

selection device validity The extent to which a personnel selection device is successful in distinguishing between those who will become high performers at a certain job and those who will not. (p. B-6)

selective serotonin reuptake inhibitors (SSRIs) Class of antidepressant medications that increase the availability of serotonin in the brain and cause fewer side effects than earlier antidepressants; they include Prozac, Paxil, and Zoloft. (p. 580)

self-actualization Defined by Maslow as a person's "full use and exploitation of talents, capacities, and potentialities." (p. 323)

self-concept The set of perceptions and beliefs that you hold about yourself. (p. 412)

self-determination theory (SDT) Edward Deci and Richard Ryan's theory that optimal human functioning can occur only if the psychological needs for autonomy, competence, and relatedness are satisfied. (p. 324)

self-efficacy The beliefs that people have about their ability to meet the demands of a specific situation; feelings of self-confidence or self-doubt. (pp. 343, 416)

self-report inventory A type of psychological test in which a person's responses to standardized questions are compared to established norms. (p. 428)

self-serving bias The tendency to attribute successful outcomes of one's own behavior to internal causes and unsuccessful outcomes to external, situational causes. (p. 444)

semantic memory Category of long-term memory that includes memories of general knowledge of facts, names, and concepts. (p. 226)

semantic network model A model that describes units of information in long-term memory as being organized in a complex network of associations. (p. 228)

sensation The process of detecting a physical stimulus, such as light, sound, heat, or pressure. (p. 85)

sensation seeking The degree to which an individual is motivated to experience high levels of sensory and physical arousal associated with varied and novel activities. (p. 301)

sensorimotor stage In Piaget's theory, the first stage of cognitive development, from birth to about age 2; the period during which the infant explores the environment and acquires knowledge through sensing and manipulating objects. (p. 369)

sensory adaptation The decline in sensitivity to a constant stimulus. (p. 88)

sensory memory The stage of memory that registers information from the environment and holds it for a very brief period of time. (p. 219)

sensory neuron Type of neuron that conveys information to the brain from specialized receptor cells in sense organs and internal organs. (p. 41)

sensory receptors Specialized cells unique to each sense organ that respond to a particular form of sensory stimulation. (p. 85)

sensory-specific satiety (sah-TIE-it-tee) The reduced desire to continue consuming a particular food. (p. 305)

serial position effect The tendency to remember items at the beginning and end of a list better than items in the middle. (p. 231)

serotonin (ser-ah-TONE-in) Neurotransmitter involved in sleep and emotions. (p. 48)

set-point theory Theory that proposes that humans and other animals have a natural or optimal body weight, called the *set-point weight,* that the body defends from becoming higher or lower by regulating feelings of hunger and body metabolism. (p. 307)

settling-point models of weight regulation General model of weight regulation suggesting that body weight settles, or stabilizes, around the point at which there is balance between the factors influencing energy intake and energy expenditure. (p. 307)

sex chromosomes Chromosomes, designated as X or Y, that determine biological sex; the 23rd pair of chromosomes in humans. (p. 354)

sexual dysfunction A consistent disturbance in sexual desire, arousal, or orgasm that causes psychological distress and interpersonal difficulties. (p. 322)

sexual orientation The direction of a person's emotional and erotic attraction toward members of the opposite sex, the same sex, or both sexes. (p. 316)

shape constancy The perception of a familiar object as maintaining the same shape regardless of the image produced on the retina. (p. 115)

shaping The operant conditioning procedure of selectively reinforcing successively closer approximations of a goal behavior until the goal behavior is displayed. (p. 198)

short-term dynamic therapies Type of psychotherapy that is based on psychoanalytic theory but differs in that it is typically time-limited, has specific goals, and involves an active, rather than neutral, role for the therapist. (p. 552)

short-term memory or **working memory** The active stage of memory in which information is stored for up to about 20 seconds. (p. 219)

situational (contingency) theories of leadership Theories that focus on how a particular situation influences a leader's effectiveness. (p. B-11)

Sixteen Personality Factor Questionnaire (16PF) A self-report inventory developed by Raymond Cattell that generates a personality profile with ratings on 16 trait dimensions. (p. 429)

size constancy The perception of an object as maintaining the same size despite changing images on the retina. (p. 115)

skewed distribution An asymmetrical distribution; more scores occur on one side of the distribution than on the other. In a positively skewed distribution, most of the scores are low

scores; in a negatively skewed distribution, most of the scores are high scores. (p. A-4)

sleep apnea (APP-nee-uh) A sleep disorder in which the person repeatedly stops breathing during sleep. (p. 141)

sleep disorders Serious disturbances in the normal sleep pattern that interfere with daytime functioning and cause subjective distress. (p. 139)

sleep inertia (in-ER-shuh) Feeling of grogginess on awakening that interferes with the ability to perform mental or physical tasks. (p. 168)

sleep paralysis A temporary condition in which a person is unable to move upon awakening in the morning or during the night. (p. 136)

sleep spindles Short bursts of brain activity that characterize stage 2 NREM sleep. (p. 135)

sleep thinking Repetitive, bland, and uncreative ruminations about real-life events during sleep. (p. 143)

sleepwalking A sleep disturbance characterized by an episode of walking or performing other actions during stage 3 or stage 4 NREM sleep; also called *somnambulism.* (p. 141)

social categorization The mental process of categorizing people into groups (or *social categories*) on the basis of their shared characteristics. (p. 440)

social cognition The mental processes people use to make sense out of their social environment. (p. 436)

social cognitive theory Albert Bandura's theory of personality, which emphasizes the importance of observational learning, conscious cognitive processes, social experiences, self-efficacy beliefs, and reciprocal determinism. (p. 416)

social influence The effects of situational factors and other people on an individual's behavior. (p. 438)

social influence hypothesis The view that a person's level of job satisfaction is influenced by the job satisfaction levels of other people. (p. B-9)

social learning theory of gender-role development The theory that gender roles are acquired through the basic processes of learning, including reinforcement, punishment, and modeling. (p. 366)

social norms The "rules," or expectations, for appropriate behavior in a particular social situation. (p. 439)

social phobia or social anxiety disorder An anxiety disorder involving the extreme and irrational fear of being embarrassed, judged, or scrutinized by others in social situations. (p. 515)

social psychology The branch of psychology that studies how people think, feel, and behave in social situations. (p. 438)

social support The resources provided by other people in times of need. (p. 493)

somatic nervous system Subdivision of the peripheral nervous system that communicates sensory information to the central nervous system and carries motor messages from the central nervous system to the muscles. (p. 52)

source confusion A memory distortion that occurs when the true source of the memory is forgotten. (p. 240)

source memory or **source monitoring** Memory for when, where, and how a particular piece of information was acquired. (p. 236)

source traits The most fundamental dimensions of personality; the broad, basic traits that are hypothesized to be universal and relatively few in number. (p. 419)

specific phobia An anxiety disorder characterized by an extreme and irrational fear of a specific object or situation that interferes with the ability to function in daily life; formerly called *simple phobia.* (p. 514)

spinal reflexes Simple, automatic behaviors that are processed in the spinal cord. (p. 51)

split-brain operation A surgical procedure that involves cutting the corpus callosum. (p. 73)

spontaneous recovery The reappearance of a previously extinguished conditioned response after a period of time without exposure to the conditioned stimulus. (p. 178)

stage model of memory A model describing memory as consisting of three distinct stages: sensory memory, short-term memory, and long-term memory. (p. 219)

standard deviation A measure of variability; expressed as the square root of the sum of the squared deviations around the mean divided by the number of scores in the distribution. (p. A-6)

standard normal curve or **standard normal distribution** A symmetrical distribution forming a bell-shaped curve in which the mean, median, and mode are all equal and fall in the exact middle. (p. A-8)

standardization The administration of a test to a large, representative sample of people under uniform conditions for the purpose of establishing norms. (p. 280)

Stanford Prison Experiment Brief but controversial psychological study conducted in 1971 investigating the influence of social roles, rules, and norms in which Stanford University students were randomly assigned the roles of prison guards or prisoners in a make-shift prison created in the basement of a university building. (p. 463)

statistically significant A mathematical indication that research results are not very likely to have occurred by chance. (p. 17)

statistics A branch of mathematics used by researchers to organize, summarize, and interpret data. (pp. 17, A-2)

stereotype A cluster of characteristics that are associated with all members of a specific social group, often including qualities that are unrelated to the objective criteria that define the group. (p. 450)

stereotype threat A psychological predicament in which fear that you will be evaluated in terms of a negative stereotype about a group to which you belong creates anxiety and self-doubt, lowering performance in a particular domain that is important to you. (p. 290)

stimulant-induced psychosis Schizophrenia-like symptoms that can occur as the result of prolonged amphetamine or cocaine use; also called *amphetamine psychosis* or *cocaine psychosis*. (p. 164)

stimulants A category of psychoactive drugs that increase brain activity, arouse behavior, and increase mental alertness. (p. 161)

stimulus discrimination The occurrence of a learned response to a specific stimulus but not to other, similar stimuli. (p. 178)

stimulus generalization The occurrence of a learned response not only to the original stimulus but to other, similar stimuli as well. (p. 178)

stimulus threshold The minimum level of stimulation required to activate a particular neuron. (p. 43)

storage The process of retaining information in memory so that it can be used at a later time. (p. 218)

stress A negative emotional state occurring in response to events that are perceived as taxing or exceeding a person's resources or ability to cope. (p. 477)

stressors Events or situations that are perceived as harmful, threatening, or challenging. (p. 478)

structural plasticity The brain's ability to change its physical structure in response to learning, active practice, or environmental influences. (p. 76)

structuralism Early school of psychology that emphasized studying the most basic components, or structures, of conscious experiences. (p. 4)

sublimation In psychoanalytic theory, an ego defense mechanism that involves redirecting sexual urges toward productive, socially acceptable, nonsexual activities; a form of displacement. (p. 403)

subliminal perception The perception of stimuli that are below the threshold of conscious awareness. (p. 87)

substance P A neurotransmitter that is involved in the transmission of pain messages to the brain. (p. 103)

substantia nigra (sub-STAN-she-uh NYE-gruh) An area of the midbrain that is involved in motor control and contains a large concentration of dopamine-producing neurons. (p. 64)

superego In Freud's theory, the partly conscious, self-evaluative, moralistic component of personality that is formed through the internalization of parental and societal rules. (p. 402)

suppression Motivated forgetting that occurs consciously. (p. 237)

suprachiasmatic nucleus (SCN) (soup-rah-*kye*-az-MAT-ick) A cluster of neurons in the hypothalamus in the brain that governs the timing of circadian rhythms. (p. 131)

surface traits Personality characteristics or attributes that can easily be inferred from observable behavior. (p. 419)

survey A questionnaire or interview designed to investigate the opinions, behaviors, or characteristics of a particular group. (p. 21)

symbolic thought The ability to use words, images, and symbols to represent the world. (p. 369)

symmetrical distribution A distribution in which scores fall equally on both sides of the graph. The normal curve is an example of a symmetrical distribution. (p. A-4)

sympathetic nervous system Branch of the autonomic nervous system that produces rapid physical arousal in response to perceived emergencies or threats. (p. 54)

synapse (SIN-aps) The point of communication between two neurons. (p. 45)

synaptic gap (sin-AP-tick) The tiny space between the axon terminal of one neuron and the dendrite of an adjoining neuron. (p. 45)

synaptic transmission (sin-AP-tick) The process through which neurotransmitters are released by one neuron, cross the synaptic gap, and affect adjoining neurons. (p. 46)

synaptic vesicles (sin-AP-tick VESS-ick-ulls) Tiny pouches or sacs in the axon terminals that contain chemicals called neurotransmitters. (p. 46)

systematic desensitization A type of behavior therapy in which phobic responses are reduced by pairing relaxation with a series of mental images or real-life situations that the person finds progressively more fear-provoking; based on the principle of counterconditioning. (p. 557)

T

taste aversion A classically conditioned dislike for and avoidance of a particular food that develops when an organism becomes ill after eating the food. (p. 186)

taste buds The specialized sensory receptors for taste that are located on the tongue and inside the mouth and throat. (p. 101)

temperament Inborn predispositions to consistently behave and react in a certain way. (p. 359)

temporal lobe An area on each hemisphere of the cerebral cortex near the temples that is the primary receiving area for auditory information. (p. 66)

teratogens Harmful agents or substances that can cause malformations or defects in an embryo or fetus. (p. 356)

thalamus (THAL-uh-muss) A forebrain structure that processes sensory information for all senses, except smell, and relays it to the cerebral cortex. (p. 68)

Thanatos In Freud's theory, the death instinct, reflected in aggressive, destructive, and self-destructive actions. (p. 401)

Thematic Apperception Test (TAT) A projective personality test that involves creating stories about each of a series of ambiguous scenes. (pp. 326, 426)

theory A tentative explanation that tries to integrate and account for the relationship of various findings and observations. (p. 19)

thinking The manipulation of mental representations of information in order to draw inferences and conclusions. (p. 261)

timbre (TAM-ber) The distinctive quality of a sound, determined by the complexity of the sound wave. (p. 97)

tip-of-the-tongue (TOT) experience A memory phenomenon that involves the sensation of knowing that specific information is stored in long-term memory but being temporarily unable to retrieve it. (p. 230)

token economy A form of behavior therapy in which the therapeutic environment is structured to reward desired behaviors with tokens or points that may eventually be exchanged for tangible rewards. (p. 560)

top-down processing Information processing that emphasizes the importance of the observer's knowledge, expectations, and other cognitive processes in arriving at meaningful perceptions; analysis that moves from the whole to the parts; also called *conceptually driven processing*. (p. 106)

trait A relatively stable, enduring predisposition to consistently behave in a certain way. (p. 419)

trait approach to leader effectiveness An approach to determining what makes an effective leader that focuses on the personal characteristics displayed by successful leaders. (p. B-10)

trait theory A theory of personality that focuses on identifying, describing, and measuring individual differences in behavioral predispositions. (p. 419)

tranquilizers Depressant drugs that relieve anxiety. (p. 160)

transduction The process by which a form of physical energy is converted into a coded neural signal that can be processed by the nervous system. (p. 85)

transference In psychoanalysis, the process by which emotions and desires originally associated with a significant person in the patient's life, such as a parent, are unconsciously transferred to the psychoanalyst. (p. 551)

trial and error A problem-solving strategy that involves attempting different solutions and eliminating those that do not work. (p. 265)

triarchic theory of intelligence Sternberg's theory that there are three distinct forms of intelligence: analytic, creative, and practical. (p. 283)

trichromatic theory of color vision The theory that the sensation of color results because cones in the retina are especially sensitive to red light (long wavelengths), green light (medium wavelengths), or blue light (short wavelengths). (p. 94)

two-factor theory of emotion Schachter and Singer's theory that emotion is the interaction of physiological arousal and the cognitive label that we apply to explain the arousal. (p. 340)

Type A behavior pattern A behavioral and emotional style characterized by a sense of time urgency, hostility, and competitiveness. (p. 491)

U

unconditional positive regard In Rogers's theory, the sense that you will be valued and loved even if you don't conform to the standards and expectations of others; unconditional love or acceptance. (p. 414)

unconditioned response (UCR) The unlearned, reflexive response that is elicited by an unconditioned stimulus. (p. 176)

unconditioned stimulus (UCS) The natural stimulus that reflexively elicits a response without the need for prior learning. (p. 176)

unconscious In Freud's theory, a term used to describe thoughts, feelings, wishes, and drives that are operating below the level of conscious awareness. (p. 400)

V

validity The ability of a test to measure what it is intended to measure. (p. 280)

variable A factor that can vary, or change, in ways that can be observed, measured, and verified. (p. 15)

variable-interval (VI) schedule A reinforcement schedule in which a reinforcer is delivered for the first response that occurs after an average time interval, which varies unpredictably from trial to trial. (p. 200)

variable-ratio (VR) schedule A reinforcement schedule in which a reinforcer is delivered after an average number of responses, which varies unpredictably from trial to trial. (p. 200)

vestibular sense (vess-TIB-you-ler) The technical name for the sense of balance, or equilibrium. (p. 105)

W

wavelength The distance from one wave peak to another. (p. 88)

Weber's law (VAY-berz) A principle of sensation that holds that the size of the just noticeable difference will vary depending on its relation to the strength of the original stimulus. (p. 86)

weight cycling Repeated cycles of dieting, weight loss, and weight regain; also called *yo-yo dieting*. (p. 310)

withdrawal symptoms Unpleasant physical reactions, combined with intense drug cravings, that occur when a person abstains from a drug on which he or she is physically dependent. (p. 156)

working memory Short-term memory system involved in the temporary storage and active manipulation of information; in Baddeley's model, includes the phonological loop, visuospatial sketchpad, and central executive components. (p. 223)

Z

z score A number, expressed in standard deviation units, that shows a score's deviation from the mean. (p. A-8)

zone of proximal development In Vygotsky's theory of cognitive development, the difference between what children can accomplish on their own and what they can accomplish with the help of others who are more competent. (p. 373)

zygote The single cell formed at conception from the union of the egg cell and sperm cell. (p. 352)

References

Aarts, Henk, & Dijksterhuis, Ap. (2000). Habits as knowledge structures: Automaticity in goal-directed behavior. *Journal of Personality and Social Psychology, 78,* 53–63.

Abad, Vivien C., & Guilleminault, Christian. (2004). Review of rapid eye movement behavior sleep disorders. *Current Science, 4,* 157–163.

Abel, Millicent H. (2002). Humor, stress, and coping strategies. *Humor, 15,* 365–381.

Abi-Dargham, Anissa. (2004). Do we still believe in the dopamine hypothesis? New data bring new evidence. *International Journal of Neuropsychopharmacology, 7*(Suppl.1), S1–S5.

Abramov, Israel, & Gordon, James. (1994). Color appearance: On seeing red—or yellow, or green, or blue. *Annual Review of Psychology, 45,* 451–485.

Abrams, Michael. (2002, June). Sight unseen. *Discover, 23,* 54–59.

Abramson, Lyn Y.; Seligman, Martin E. P.; & Teasdale, John D. (1978). Learned helplessness in humans: Critique and reformulation. *Journal of Abnormal Psychology, 87,* 49–74.

Ader, Robert. (1993). Conditioned responses. In Bill Moyers & Betty Sue Flowers (Eds.), *Healing and the mind*. New York: Doubleday.

Ader, Robert. (2001). Psychoneuroimmunology. *Current Directions in Psychological Science, 10,* 94–98.

Ader, Robert, & Cohen, Nicholas. (1975). Behaviorally conditioned immunosuppression. *Psychosomatic Medicine, 37,* 333–340.

Adler, Alfred. (1933a/1979). Advantages and disadvantages of the inferiority feeling. In Heinz L. Ansbacher & Rowena R. Ansbacher (Eds.), *Superiority and social interest: A collection of later writings*. New York: Norton.

Adler, Alfred. (1933b/1979). On the origin of the striving for superiority and of social interest. In Heinz L. Ansbacher & Rowena R. Ansbacher (Eds.), *Superiority and social interest: A collection of later writings*. New York: Norton.

Adler, Alfred. (1954). *Understanding human nature*. New York: Fawcett.

Adler, Nancy, & Matthews, Karen. (1994). Health psychology: Why do some people get sick and some stay well? *Annual Review of Psychology, 45,* 229–259.

Adolphs, Ralph; Tranel, Daniel; & Damasio, Antonio R. (1998). The human amygdala in social judgment. *Nature, 393,* 470–474.

Affleck, Glenn; Tennen, Howard; & Croog, Sydney. (1987). Causal attribution, perceived control, and recovery from a heart attack. *Journal of Social and Clinical Psychology, 5,* 399–355.

Affleck, Glenn; Tennen, Howard; Pfeiffer, Carol; & Fifield, Judith. (1987). Appraisals of control and predictability in reacting to a chronic disease. *Journal of Personality and Social Psychology, 53,* 273–279.

Aghajanian, George K. (1994). Serotonin and the action of LSD in the brain. *Psychiatric Annals, 24*(3), 137–141.

Agosta, William C. (1992). *Chemical communication: The language of pheromones*. New York: Scientific American Library.

Agras, W. Steward, & Apple, Robin F. (1997). *Overcoming eating disorders: A cognitive-behavioral treatment for bulimia nervosa and binge-eating*. San Antonio, TX: Harcourt Brace.

Aguiar, Andréa, & Baillargeon, Renée. (1999). 2.5-month-old infants' reasoning about when objects should and should not be occluded. *Cognitive Psychology, 39,* 116–157.

Ahern, Jennifer; Galea, Sandro; Resnick, Heidi; & Vlahov, David. (2004). Television images and probable posttraumatic stress disorder after September 11: The role of background characteristics, event exposures, and perievent panic. *Journal of Nervous and Mental Diseases, 192,* 217–226.

Ahima, Rexford S., & Osei, Suzette Y. (2004). Leptin and appetite control in lipodystrophy. *Journal of Clinical Endocrinology and Metabolism, 89,* 4254–4257.

Aiken, Lewis R. (1997). *Psychological testing and assessment* (9th ed.). Boston: Allyn & Bacon.

Ainslie, George. (1975). Specious reward: A behavioral theory of impulsiveness and impulse control. *Psychological Bulletin, 82,* 463–496.

Ainslie, George. (1992). *Picoeconomics: The strategic interaction of successive motivational states within the person*. Cambridge, England: Cambridge University Press.

Ainsworth, Mary D. Salter. (1979). Attachment as related to mother-infant interaction. In J. G. Rosenblatt, R. A. Hinde, C. Beer, & M. Busnel (Eds.), *Advances in the study of behavior* (Vol. 9). New York: Academic Press.

Ainsworth, Mary D. Salter; Blehar, Mary C.; Waters, Everett; & Wall, Sally. (1978). *Patterns of attachment: A psychological study of the Strange Situation*. Hillsdale, NJ: Erlbaum.

Ajzen, Icek. (1991). The theory of planned behavior. *Organizational Behavior and Human Decision Processes, 50,* 179–211.

Ajzen, Icek. (2001). Nature and operations of attitudes. *Annual Review of Psychology, 52*(1), 27–58.

Akerstedt, T.; Knutsson, A.; Westerholm, P.; Theorell, T.; Alfredsson, L.; & Kecklund, G. (2002). Sleep disturbances, work stress and work hours: A cross-sectional study. *Journal of Psychosomatic Research, 53,* 741–748.

Alden, Lynn E.; Mellings, Tanna M. B.; & Laposa, Judith M. (2004). Framing social information and generalized social phobia. *Behavior Research & Therapy, 42,* 585–600.

Alexander, Charles N.; Robinson, Pat; Orme-Johnson, David W.; & Schneider, Robert H. (1994). The effects of transcendental meditation compared to other methods of relaxation and meditation in reducing risk factors, morbidity, and mortality. *Homeostasis in Health and Disease, 35,* 243–263.

Alford, Brad A., & Correia, Christopher J. (1994). Cognitive therapy of schizophrenia: Theory and empirical status. *Behavior Therapy 25,* 17–33.

Allen, John J. B., & Iacono, William G. (2001). Assessing the validity of amnesia in dissociative identity disorder: A dilemma for the DSM and the courts. *Psychology, Public Policy, and Law, 7,* 311–344.

Allen, Karen M.; Blascovich, Jim; & Mendes, Wendy B. (2002). Cardiovascular reactivity and the presence of pets, friends, and spouses: The truth about cats and dogs. *Psychosomatic Medicine, 64,* 727–739.

Allen, Karen M.; Blascovich, Jim; Tomaka, Joe; & Kelsey, Robert M. (1991). Presence of human friends and pet dogs as moderators of autonomic responses to stress in women. *Journal of Personality and Social Psychology, 61,* 582–589.

Allen, Vernon L., & Levine, John M. (1969). Consensus and conformity. *Journal of Experimental Social Psychology, 5,* 389–399.

Allen, Vernon L., & Levine, John M. (1971). Social support and conformity: The role of independent assessment of reality. *Journal of Experimental Social Psychology, 7,* 48–58.

Allik, Jüri, & McCrae, Robert R. (2002). A five-factor theory perspective. In Robert R. McCrae & Jüri Allik (Eds.), *The five-factor model of personality across cultures*. New York: Kluwer Academic/Plenum Press.

Allik, Jüri, & McCrae, Robert R. (2004). Toward a geography of personality traits: Patterns of profiles across 36 cultures. *Journal of Cross-Cultural Psychology, 35,* 13–28.

Allport, Gordon W., & Odbert, Harold S. (1936). Trait-names: A psycho-lexical study. *Psychological Monographs, 47*(211).

Almeida, David M., & Kessler, Ronald C. (1998). Everyday stressors and gender differences in daily distress. *Journal of Personality and Social Psychology, 75,* 670–680.

Alonso, Anne, & Swiller, Hillel I. (Eds.). (1993a). *Group therapy in clinical practice.* Washington, DC: American Psychiatric Press.

Alonso, Anne, & Swiller, Hillel I. (1993b). Introduction: The case for group therapy. In Anne Alonso & Hillel I. Swiller (Eds.), *Group therapy in clinical practice.* Washington, DC: American Psychiatric Press.

Altmann, Erik M., & Gray, Wayne D. (2002). Forgetting to remember: The functional relationship of decay and interference. *Psychological Science, 13,* 27–33.

Amabile, Teresa. (1996). *Creativity in context.* Boulder, CO: Westview Press.

Amabile, Teresa. (2001). Beyond talent: John Irving and the passionate craft of creativity. *American Psychologist, 56,* 333–336.

Amabile, Teresa M., & Tighe, Elizabeth. (1993). Questions of creativity. In John Brockman (Ed.), *Creativity.* New York: Simon & Schuster.

American Association of Suicidology. (2004, December 1). *AAS fact sheets: Suicide in the U.S.* Washington, DC: American Association of Suicidology. Retrieved January 7, 2005, from http://www.suicidology.org/associations/1045/files/Suicide2002.pdf

American Psychiatric Association. (1994). *Diagnostic and statistical manual of mental disorders* (4th ed.). Washington, DC: American Psychiatric Association.

American Psychiatric Association. (2000a). *Diagnostic and statistical manual of mental disorders* (4th ed., Text Revision: DSM-IV-TR). Washington, DC: American Psychiatric Association.

American Psychiatric Association. (2000b). Practice guidelines for the treatment of patients with eating disorders [Revision]. *American Journal of Psychiatry, 157*(Suppl.).

American Psychological Association. (1992). *Guidelines for ethical conduct in the care and use of animals.* Washington, DC: American Psychological Association.

American Psychological Association. (2001). *Information on hypnosis: What is hypnosis? The Division 30 definition and description of hypnosis.* Washington, DC: American Psychological Association. Retrieved January 9, 2002, from http://www.apa.org/divisions/div30/hypnosis.html

American Psychological Association. (2002). Ethical principles of psychologists and code of conduct. *American Psychologist, 57,* 1060–1073.

American Psychological Association. (2003). Guidelines on multicultural education, training, research, practice, and organizational change for psychologists. *American Psychologist, 58,* 377–402. PDF of guidelines available at: www.apa.org/pi/multiculturalguidelines.pdf

American Psychological Association. (2005). Obeying and resisting malevolent orders. Accessed on November 28, 2005 from: http://www.psychologymatters.org/milgram.html

American Psychological Association Working Group on Investigation of Memories of Childhood Abuse. (1998). Final conclusions of the American Psychological Association Working Group on Investigation of Memories of Childhood Abuse. *Psychology, Public Policy, and Law, 4,* 933–940.

Ames, Daniel R.; Flynn, Francis J.; & Weber, Elke U. (2004). It's the thought that counts: On perceiving how helpers decide to lend a hand. *Personality and Social Psychology Bulletin, 30*(4), 461–474.

Anastasi, Anne. (1988). *Psychological testing* (6th ed.). New York: Macmillan.

Anastasi, Anne, & Urbina, Susana. (1997). *Psychological testing* (7th ed.). Upper Saddle River, NJ: Prentice Hall.

Anch, A. Michael; Browman, Carl P.; Mitler, Merrill M.; & Walsh, James K. (1988). *Sleep: A scientific perspective.* Englewood Cliffs, NJ: Prentice-Hall.

Ancoli-Israel, Sonia. (1997). The polysomnogram. In Mark R. Pressman & William C. Orr (Eds.), *Understanding sleep: The evaluation and treatment of sleep disorders.* Washington, DC: American Psychological Association.

Andersen, Arnold E. (2002). Rethinking the DSM-IV diagnosis of eating disorders. *Eating Disorders, 10,* 177–180.

Anderson, Craig A. (2004). An update on the effects of playing violent video games. *Journal of Adolescence, 27,* 113–122.

Anderson, Craig A.; Berkowitz, Leonard; Donnerstein, Edward; Huesmann, L. Rowell; Johnson, James D.; Linz, Daniel; Malamuth, Neil M.; & Wartella, Ellen. (2003, December). The influence of media violence on youth. *Psychological Science in the Public Interest, 4,* 81–110. Retrieved July 16, 2004, from http://www.psychologicalscience.org/pdf/pspi/pspi43.pdf

Anderson, Craig A.; Carnegey, Nicholas L.; Flanagan, Mindy; Benjamin, Arlin J., Jr., Eubanks, Janie; & Valentine, Jeffrey C. (2004). Violent video games: Specific effects of violent content on aggressive thoughts and behavior. In Mark P. Zanna (Ed.), *Advances in experimental social psychology* (Vol. 36). San Diego,CA: Academic Press.

Anderson, Craig A., & Dill, Karen E. (2000). Video games and aggressive thoughts, feelings, and behavior in the laboratory and in life. *Journal of Personality and Social Psychology, 78,* 772–790.

Anderson, James R., & Meno, Pauline. (2003). Psychological influences on yawning in children. *Current Psychology Letters: Behavior,* *Brain & Cognition, 11*(2), np. Retrieved August 19, 2004, from http://cpl.revues.org/document390.html

Anderson, James R.; Myowa-Yamakoshi, Masako; & Matsuzawa, Tetsuro. (2004). Contagious yawning in chimpanzees. *Proceedings of the Royal Society of London: Biology Letters.* Retrieved August 19, 2004, from http://www.pubs.royalsoc.ac.uk/biolethomelink7.shtml

Anderson, Karen E., & Savage, Cary R. (2004). Cognitive and neurobiological findings in obsessive-compulsive disorder. *Psychiatric Clinics of North America, 27,* 37–47.

Anderson, Michael C.; Ochsner, Kevin N.; Kuhl, Brice; Cooper, Jeffrey; Robertson, Elaine; Gabrieli, Susan W.; Glover, Gary H.; & Gabrieli, John D. E. (2004, January 9). Neural systems underlying the suppression of unwanted memories. *Science, 303,* 232–235.

Andersson, Bengt-Erik. (1989). Effects of day care: A longitudinal study. *Child Development, 60,* 857–866.

Andersson, Bengt-Erik. (1992). Effects of day care on cognitive and socioemotional competence of thirteen-year-old Swedish schoolchildren. *Child Development, 63,* 20–36.

Andreasen, Nancy C., & Flaum, Michael. (1991). Schizophrenia: The characteristic symptoms. *Schizophrenia Bulletin, 17,* 27–49.

Andresen, Jensine. (2000). Meditation meets behavioural medicine: The story of experimental research on meditation. *Journal of Consciousness Studies, 7,* 17–73.

Angermeyer, Matthias C., & Matschinger, Herbert. (1996). The effect of violent attacks by schizophrenic persons on the attitude of the public towards the mentally ill. *Social Science & Medicine, 43*(12), 1721–1728.

Angier, Natalie. (1995, February 14). Powerhouse of senses, smell, at last gets its due. *New York Times,* pp. C1, C6.

Anonymous. (1990). First person account: Birds of a psychic feather. *Schizophrenia Bulletin, 16,* 165–168.

Antony, Martin M.; Brown, Timothy A.; & Barlow, David H. (1992). Current perspectives on panic and panic disorder. *Current Directions in Psychological Science, 1,* 79–82.

APA Committee on Animal Research and Ethics. (2004). *Research with animals in psychology.* Washington, DC: American Psychological Association. Retrieved July 16, 2004, from http://www.apa.org/science/animal2.html

Arciero, Paul J.; Goran, Michael I.; & Poehlman, Eric T. (1993). Resting metabolic rate is lower in women than in men. *Journal of Applied Physiology, 75,* 2514–2520.

Arkin, Arthur M., & Antrobus, John S. (1991). The effects of external stimuli applied prior to and during sleep on sleep experience. In Steven J. Ellman & John S. Antrobus (Eds.), *The mind in sleep: Psychology and psychophysiology* (2nd ed.). New York: Wiley.

Armstrong, G. Blake, & Sopory, Pradeep. (1997). Effects of background television on phonological and visuo-spatial working memory. *Communication Research, 24,* 459–480.

Arnkoff, Diane B., & Glass, Carol R. (1992). Cognitive therapy and psychotherapy integration. In Donald K. Freedheim (Ed.), *History of psychotherapy: A century of change.* Washington, DC: American Psychological Association.

Aron, Arthur; Aron, Elaine N.; & Smollan, Danny. (1992). Inclusion of other in the self scale and the structure of interpersonal closeness. *Journal of Personality and Social Psychology, 63,* 596–612.

Aronson, Elliot. (1987). Teaching students what they think they already know about prejudice and desegregation. In Vivian Parker Makosky (Ed.), *G. Stanley Hall Lecture Series* (Vol. 7). Washington, DC: American Psychological Association.

Aronson, Elliot. (1990). Applying social psychology to desegregation and energy conservation. *Personality and Social Psychology Bulletin, 16,* 118–132.

Aronson, Elliot. (1992). The return of the repressed: Dissonance theory makes a comeback. *Psychological Inquiry, 3,* 303–311.

Aronson, Elliot. (1995). *The social animal* (7th ed). New York: Freeman

Aronson, Elliot. (1999). The power of self-persuasion. *American Psychologist, 54,* 875–883.

Aronson, Elliot, & Bridgeman, Diane. (1979). Jigsaw groups and the desegregated classroom: In pursuit of common goals. *Personality and Social Psychology Bulletin, 5,* 438–466.

Arvey, Richard D.; Bouchard, Thomas J.; Segal, Nancy L.; & Abraham, Lauren M. (1989). Job satisfaction: Environmental and genetic components. *Journal of Applied Psychology, 74,* 187–192.

Asay, Ted P., & Lambert, Michael J. (1999). The empirical case for the common factors in therapy: Quantitative findings. In Mark A. Hubble, Barry L. Duncan, & Scott D. Miller (Eds.), *The heart and soul of change: What works in therapy.* Washington, DC: American Psychological Association.

Asay, Ted P., & Lambert, Michael J. (2002). Therapist relational variables. In David J. Cain & Julius Seeman (Eds.), *Humanistic psychotherapies: Handbook of research and practice.* Washington, DC: American Psychological Association.

Asch, Solomon E. (1951). Effects of group pressure upon the modification and distortion of judgments. In Harold S. Guetzkow (Ed.), *Groups, leadership, and men: Research in human relations. Reports on research sponsored by the Human Relations and Morale Branch of the Office of Naval Research, 1945–1950.* Pittsburgh, PA: Carnegie Press.

Asch, Solomon E. (1955, November). Opinions and social pressure. *Scientific American, 193,* 31–35.

Asch, Solomon E. (1956). Studies of independence and conformity: A minority of one against a unanimous majority. *Psychological Monographs, 70*(9, Whole No. 416).

Asch, Solomon E. (1957). An experimental investigation of group influence. In *Symposium on preventive and social psychiatry.* Washington, DC: U.S. Government Printing Office, Walter Reed Army Institute of Research.

Aschoff, Jurgen. (1993). On the passage of subjective time in temporal isolation. *Psychologica Belgica, 33,* 147–157.

Aschoff, Jurgen. (1994). The timing of defecation within the sleep-wake cycle of humans during temporal isolation. *Journal of Biological Rhythms, 9,* 43–50.

Aserinsky, Eugene, & Kloitman, Nathaniel. (1953). Regularly occurring periods of eye motility and concomitant phenomena during sleep. *Science, 118,* 273–274.

Ashcraft, Mark H. (1994). *Human memory and cognition* (2nd ed.). New York: HarperCollins.

Aspinwall, Lisa G., & Taylor, Shelley E. (1992). Modeling cognitive adaptation: A longitudinal investigation of the impact of individual differences and coping on college adjustment and performance. *Journal of Personality and Social Psychology, 63,* 989–1003.

Astin, John A. (2004). Mind-body therapies for the management of pain. *Clinical Journal of Pain, 20,* 27–32.

Atkinson, Richard C., & Shiffrin, Richard M. (1968). Human memory: A proposed system and its control processes. In Kenneth W. Spence & Janet T. Spence (Eds.), *The psychology of learning and motivation: Advances in research and theory* (Vol. 2). New York: Academic Press.

Austin, James H. (1998). *Zen and the brain.* Cambridge, MA: MIT Press.

Austin, James H. (2003, Winter). Your self, your brain, and Zen. *Cerebrum, 5,* 47–66.

Australian Institute of Health and Welfare (AIHW). (1999). *Heart, stroke and vascular diseases: Australian facts* (AIHW Cat. No. CVD 7, Cardiovascular Disease Series No. 10). Canberra, Australia: AIHW and the Heart Foundation of Australia.

Axel, Richard. (1995, October). The molecular logic of smell. *Scientific American, 273,* 154–159.

Axelrod, Saul, & Apsche, Jack. (1983). *The effects of punishment on human behavior.* New York: Academic Press.

Azuma, Hiroshi. (1984). Secondary control as a heterogeneous category. *American Psychologist, 39,* 970–971.

Bachelor, Alexandra, & Horvath, Adam. (1999). The therapeutic relationship. In Mark A. Hubble, Barry L. Duncan, & Scott D. Miller (Eds.), *The heart and soul of change: What works in therapy.* Washington, DC: American Psychological Association.

Baddeley, Alan D. (1992, January 31). Working memory. *Science, 255,* 556–559.

Baddeley, Alan D. (1995). Working memory. In Michael S. Gazzaniga (Ed.), *The cognitive neurosciences.* Cambridge, MA: MIT Press.

Baddeley, Alan D. (1998). *Human memory: Theory and practice* (2nd ed.). Boston: Allyn & Bacon.

Baddeley, Alan D. (2002). Is working memory still working? *European Psychologist, 7,* 85–97.

Baddeley, Alan D. (2003). Working memory: Looking back and looking forward. *Nature Reviews Neuroscience, 4,* 829–839.

Bader, Alan P., & Phillips, Roger D. (2002). Fathers' recognition of their newborns by visual-facial and olfactory cues. *Psychology of Men and Masculinity, 3,* 79–84.

Baer, John. (1993). *Creativity and divergent thinking: A task-specific approach.* Hillsdale, NJ: Erlbaum.

Baer, Ruth A. (2003). Mindfulness training as a clinical intervention: A conceptual and empirical review. *Clinical Psychology: Science & Practice, 10,* 125–143.

Bahlmann, Miriam; Preuss, U. W.; & Soyka, M. (2002). Chronological relationship between antisocial personality disorder and alcohol dependence. *European Addiction Research, 8,* 195–200.

Bahrick, Harry P., & Hall, Lynda K. (1991). Lifetime maintenance of high school mathematics content. *Journal of Experimental Psychology: General, 120,* 20–33.

Bahrick, Harry P., & Phelps, Elizabeth. (1987). Retention of Spanish vocabulary over eight years. *Journal of Experimental Psychology: Learning, Memory, and Cognition, 13,* 344–349.

Bailey, J. Michael; Bobrow, David; Wolfe, Marilyn; & Mikach, Sarah. (1995). Sexual orientation of adult sons of gay fathers. *Developmental Psychology, 31,* 124–129.

Bailey, J. Michael; Dunne, Michael P.; & Martin, Nicholas G. (2000). Genetic and environmental influences on sexual orientation and its correlates in an Australian twin sample. *Journal of Personality and Social Psychology, 78,* 524–536.

Bailey, J. Michael, & Pillard, Richard C. (1991). A genetic study of male sexual orientation. *Archives of General Psychiatry, 48,* 1089–1096.

Bailey, J. Michael; Pillard, Richard C.; Neale, Michael C.; & Agyei, Yvonne. (1993). Heritable factors influence sexual orientation in women. *Archives of General Psychiatry, 50,* 217–223.

Bailey, J. Michael, & Shriver, Amy. (1999). Does childhood sexual abuse cause borderline personality disorder? *Journal of Sex and Marital Therapy, 25,* 45–57.

Bailey, J. Michael, & Zucker, Kenneth J. (1995). Childhood sex-typed behavior and sexual orientation: A conceptual analysis and quantitative review. *Developmental Psychology, 31,* 43–55.

Bailey, Marian Breland, & Bailey, Robert E. (1993). "Misbehavior": A case history. *American Psychologist, 48,* 1157–1158.

Baillargeon, Renée. (2002). The acquisition of physical knowledge in infancy: A summary in eight lessons. In U. Goswami (Ed.), *Handbook of childhood cognitive development*. Oxford, England: Blackwell.

Baillargeon, Renée. (2004). Infants' physical world. *Current Directions in Psychological Science, 13,* 89–94.

Baillargeon, Renée, & DeVos, Julie. (1991). Object permanence in young infants: Further evidence. *Child Development, 62,* 1227–1246.

Bakaly, Charles J., Jr., & Grossman, Joel M. (1995). *The modern law of employment relationships*. Upper Saddle River, NJ: Prentice Hall.

Baker, Catherine. (2004). *Behavioral genetics: An introduction to how genes and environments interact through development*. New York: American Association for the Advancement of Science.

Baker, Robert A. (Ed.). (1998). *Child sexual abuse and false memory syndrome*. Amherst, NY: Prometheus Books.

Ball, Thomas M.; Shapiro, Daniel E.; Monheim, Cynthia J.; & Weydert, Joy A. (2003). A pilot study of the use of guided imagery for the treatment of recurrent abdominal pain in children. *Clinical Pediatrics, 42,* 527–532.

Baltes, Paul B., & Mayer, Karl Ulrich. (2001). *The Berlin aging study: Aging from 70 to 100*. New York: Cambridge University Press.

Bandura, Albert. (1965). Influence of models' reinforcement contingencies on the acquisition of imitative behaviors. *Journal of Personality and Social Psychology, 1,* 589–595.

Bandura, Albert. (1974). Behavior theory and the models of man. *American Psychologist, 29,* 859–869.

Bandura, Albert. (1977). *Social learning theory*. Englewood Cliffs, NJ: Prentice-Hall.

Bandura, Albert. (1986). *Social foundations of thought and action: A social cognitive theory*. Englewood Cliffs, NJ: Prentice-Hall.

Bandura, Albert. (1989). Human agency in social cognitive theory. *American Psychologist, 44,* 1175–1184.

Bandura, Albert. (1990). Conclusion: Reflections on nonability determinants of competence. In Robert J. Sternberg & John Kolligian, Jr. (Eds.), *Competence considered*. New Haven, CT: Yale University Press.

Bandura, Albert. (1991). Self-regulation of motivation through anticipatory and self-reactive mechanisms. In Richard Dienstbier (Ed.), *Nebraska Symposium on Motivation 1990* (Vol. 38). Lincoln: University of Nebraska Press.

Bandura, Albert. (1992). Exercise of personal agency through the self-efficacy mechanism. In Ralf Schwarzer (Ed.), *Self-efficacy: Thought control of action*. Washington, DC: Hemisphere.

Bandura, Albert. (1996). Failures in self-regulation: Energy depletion or selective disengagement? *Psychological Inquiry, 7,* 20–24.

Bandura, Albert. (1997). *Self-efficacy: The exercise of control*. New York: Freeman.

Bandura, Albert. (2001). Social cognitive theory: An agentic perspective. *Annual Review of Psychology, 52,* 1–26.

Bandura, Albert. (2002). Environmental sustainability by sociocognitive deceleration of population growth. In Peter Schmuck & Wesley P. Schultz (Eds.), *The psychology of sustainable development*. Dordrecht, The Netherlands: Kluwer.

Bandura, Albert. (2004a). Quoted in Population Communications International: Telling stories, saving lives. Retrieved September 5, 2004, from http://www.population.org/index. shtml

Bandura, Albert. (2004b). Swimming against the mainstream: The early years from chilly tributary to transformative mainstream. *Behavior Research and Therapy, 42,* 613–630.

Bandura, Albert; Caprara, Gian Vittorio; Barbaranelli, Claudio; Gerbino, Maria; & Pastorelli, Concetta. (2003). Role of affective self-regulatory efficacy in diverse spheres of psychosocial functioning. *Child Development, 74,* 769–782.

Bandura, Albert; Ross, Dorothea; & Ross, Sheila A. (1963). Imitation of film-mediated aggressive models. *Journal of Abnormal and Social Psychology, 66,* 3–11.

Banich, Marie T. (1998). Integration of information between the cerebral hemispheres. *Current Directions in Psychological Science, 7,* 32–37.

Baranski, Joseph V.; Pigeau, Ross; Dinich, Peter; & Jacobs, Ira. (2004, July). Effects of modafinil on cognitive and meta-cognitive performance. *Human Psychopharmacology: Clinical & Experimental, 19*(5), 323–332.

Barch, Deanna M. (2005). The cognitive neuroscience of schizophrenia. *Annual Review of Clinical Psychology, 1,* 321-353.

Barch, Deanna M., & Berenbaum, Howard. (1996). Language production and thought disorder in schizophrenia. *Journal of Abnormal Psychology, 105,* 81–88.

Barclay, Deborah R., & Houts, Arthur C. (1995a). Childhood enuresis. In Charles E. Schaefer (Ed.), *Clinical handbook of sleep disorders in children*. Northvale, NJ: Aronson.

Barclay, Deborah R., & Houts, Arthur C. (1995b). Parenting skills: A review and developmental analysis of training content. In William O'Donohue & Leonard Krasner (Eds.), *Handbook of psychological skills training: Clinical techniques and applications*. Boston: Allyn & Bacon.

Barefoot, John C. (1992). Developments in the measurement of hostility. In Howard S. Friedman (Ed.), *Hostility, health, and coping*. Washington, DC: American Psychological Association.

Barefoot, John C.; Dahlstrom, W. Grant; & Williams, Redford B. (1983). Hostility, CHD incidence, and total mortality: A 25-year follow-up study of 255 physicians. *Psychosomatic Medicine, 45,* 59–63.

Bar-El, Yair; Durst, Rimona; Katz, Gregory; & others. (2000). Jerusalem syndrome. *British Journal of Psychiatry, 176,* 86–90.

Bargh, John A.; Chen, Mark; & Burrows, Lara. (1996). Automaticity of social behavior: Direct effects of trait construct and stereotype activation on action. *Journal of Personality and Social Psychology, 71,* 230–244.

Bargh, John A., & Churchland, Tanya L. (1999). The unbearable automaticity of being. *American Psychologist, 54,* 462–479.

Barinaga, Marcia. (2003). Buddhism and neuroscience: Studying the well-trained mind. *Science, 302,* 44–46.

Barnes, Thomas R. E., & Joyce, Eileen M. (2001). Antipsychotic drug treatment: Recent advances. *Current Opinion in Psychiatry, 14,* 25–37.

Barnes, Vernon A.; Treiber, Frank; & Davis, Harry. (2001). Impact of Transcendental Meditation® on cardiovascular function at rest and during acute stress in adolescents with high normal blood pressure. *Journal of Psychosomatic Research, 51,* 597–605.

Barnett, Rosalind C.; Marshall, Nancy L.; & Singer, Judith D. (1992). Job experiences over time, multiple roles, and women's mental health: A longitudinal study. *Journal of Personality and Social Psychology, 62,* 634–644.

Barnier, Amanda J., & McConkey, Kevin M. (1998). Posthypnotic responding away from the hypnotic setting. *Psychological Science, 9,* 256–262.

Barnier, Amanda J., & McConkey, Kevin M. (1999). Absorption, hypnotizability and context: Non-hypnotic contexts are not all the same. *Contemporary Hypnosis, 16,* 1–8.

Barondes, Samuel H. (1993). *Molecules and mental illness*. New York: Scientific American Library.

Barrick, Murray R., & Mount, Michael K. (1991). The Big Five personality dimensions and job performance: A meta-analysis. *Personnel Psychology, 44,* 1–26.

Barrick, Murray R., & Mount, Michael K. (1993). Autonomy as a moderator of the relationship between the Big Five personality dimensions and job performance. *Journal of Applied Psychology, 78,* 111–118.

Bartecchi, Carl E.; MacKenzie, Thomas D.; & Schrier, Robert W. (1995, May). The global tobacco epidemic. *Scientific American, 272,* 44–51.

Bartels, Andreas, & Zeki, Semir. (2000, November 27). The neural basis of romantic love. *NeuroReport, 11,* 3829–3834. Retrieved March 1, 2002, from http://www.vislab.ucl.ac.uk/pdf/ NeuralBasisOfLove.pdf

Bartlett, Frederic C. (1932). *Remembering*. Cambridge, England: Cambridge University Press.

Basford, J. R. (2001). A historical perspective of the popular use of electric and magnetic therapy. *Archives of Physical Medicine and Rehabilitation, 82,* 1261–1269.

Basil, Robert. (1991). Graphology and personality: Let the buyer beware. In Kendrick Frazier (Ed.), *The hundredth monkey and other paradigms of the paranormal.* Buffalo, NY: Prometheus Books.

Baskin, Denis G.; Lattemann, Dianne Figlewicz; Seeley, Randy J.; Woods, Stephen C.; Porte, Daniel, Jr.; & Schwartz, Michael W. (1999). Insulin and leptin: Dual adiposity signals to the brain for the regulation of food intake and body weight. *Brain Research, 848,* 114–123.

Bass, Bernard M. (1981). *Stogdill's handbook of leadership.* New York: Free Press.

Bass, Ellen, & Davis, Linda. (1994). *The courage to heal* (3rd ed.). New York: HarperPerennial.

Bass, Martha A.; Enochs, Wendy K.; & DiBrezzo, Ro. (2002). Comparison of two exercise programs on general well-being of college students. *Psychological Reports, 91,* 1195–1201.

Baum, William, & Heath, Jennifer L. (1992). Behavioral explanations and intentional explanations in psychology. *American Psychologist, 47,* 1312–1317.

Baumeister, Roy F.; Stillwell, Arlene M.; & Heatherton, Todd F. (1994). Guilt: An interpersonal approach. *Psychological Bulletin, 115,* 243–267.

Baumrind, Diana. (1964). Some thoughts on ethics of research: After reading Milgram's "Behavioral Study of Obedience." *American Psychologist, 19,* 421–423.

Baumrind, Diana. (1971). Current patterns of parental authority. *Developmental Psychology Monographs, 4,* 1–103.

Baumrind, Diana. (1991). The influence of parenting style on adolescent competence and substance abuse. *Journal of Early Adolescence, 11,* 56–95.

Baumrind, Diana; Larzelere, Robert E.; & Cowan, Philip A. (2002). Ordinary physical punishment: Is it harmful? Comment on Gershoff (2002). *Psychological Bulletin, 128,* 580–589.

Bayley, Peter J., & Squire, Larry R. (2002). Medial temporal lobe amnesia: Gradual acquisition of factual information by nondeclarative memory. *Journal of Neuroscience, 22,* 5741–5748.

Baylis, Gordon C., & Driver, Jon. (2001). Shape-coding in IT cells generalizes over contrast and mirror reversal, but not figure-ground reversal. *Nature Neuroscience, 4,* 937–942.

Beal, Carole R. (1994). *Boys and girls: The development of gender roles.* New York: McGraw-Hill.

Beasley, Ryan K., & Joslyn, Mark R. (2001). Cognitive dissonance and post-decision attitude change in six presidential elections. *Political Psychology, 22*(3), 521–540.

Beatty, Barbara. (1998). From laws of learning to a science of values: Efficiency and morality in Thorndike's educational psychology. *American Psychologist, 53,* 1145–1152.

Bechara, Antoine; Damasio, Hanna; Tranel, Daniel; & Damasio, Antonio. (1997). Deciding advantageously before knowing the advantageous strategy. *Science, 275,* 1293–1295.

Bechara, Antoine, & Naqvi, Nasir. (2004). Listening to your heart: Interoceptive awareness as a gateway to feeling. *Nature Neuroscience, 7,* 102–103.

Beck, Aaron T. (1991). Cognitive therapy: A 30-year retrospective. *American Psychologist, 46,* 368–375.

Beck, Aaron T. (2004, March). Quoted in Anita Bowles: Beck in action. *APS Observer, 17*(3), pp. 7–8.

Beck, Aaron T.; Rush, A. John; Shaw, Brian F.; & Emery, Gary. (1979). *Cognitive therapy of depression.* New York: Guilford Press.

Beck, Aaron T.; Steer, Robert A.; Beck, Judith S.; & Newman, Cory F. (1993). Hopelessness, depression, suicidal ideation, and clinical diagnosis of depression. *Suicide and Life Threatening Behavior, 23,* 139–145.

Begg, Ian M.; Needham, Douglas R.; & Bookbinder, Marc. (1993). Do backward messages unconsciously affect listeners? No. Canadian *Journal of Experimental Psychology, 47,* 1–14.

Beilin, Harry. (1994). Jean Piaget's enduring contribution to developmental psychology. In Ross D. Parke, Peter A. Ornstein, John J. Rieser, & Carolyn Zahn-Waxler (Eds.), *A century of developmental psychology.* Washington, DC: American Psychological Association.

Bell, Alan; Weinberg, Martin; & Hammersmith, Sue. (1981). *Sexual preference: Its development in men and women.* Bloomington: Indiana University Press.

Bellak, Leopold. (1993). *The Thematic Apperception Test, the Children's Apperception Test, and the Senior Apperception Technique in clinical use* (5th ed.). Boston: Allyn & Bacon.

Belle, Deborah. (1991). Gender differences in the social moderators of stress. In Alan Monat & Richard S. Lazarus (Eds.), *Stress and coping: An anthology* (3rd ed.). New York: Columbia University Press.

Belsky, Jay. (1986). Infant day care: A cause for concern. *Zero to Three, 6,* 1–7.

Belsky, Jay. (1992). Consequences of child care for children's development: A deconstructionist view. In Alan Booth (Ed.), *Child care in the 1990s: Trends and consequences.* Hillsdale, NJ: Erlbaum.

Belsky, Jay. (2001). Emanuel Miller Lecture: Developmental risks (still) associated with early child care. *Journal of Child Psychology, Psychiatry and Allied Disciplines, 42,* 845–859.

Belsky, Jay. (2002). Quantity counts: Amount of child care and children's socioemotional development. *Journal of Development & Behavioral Pediatrics, 23,* 167–170.

Bem, Daryl J., & Honorton, Charles. (1994). Does psi exist? Replicable evidence for an anomalous process of information transfer. *Psychological Bulletin, 115,* 4–18.

Bem, Sandra L. (1981). Gender schema theory: A cognitive account of sex typing. *Psychological Review, 88,* 354–364.

Bem, Sandra L. (1987). Gender schema theory and the romantic tradition. In P. Shaver & C. Hendrick (Eds.), *Sex and gender.* Beverly Hills, CA: Sage.

Benjamin, Ludy T., Jr. (1997). Wilhelm Wundt: The American connection. In Wolfgang G. Bringmann, Helmut E. Lück, Rudolf Miller, & Charles E. Early (Eds.), *A pictorial history of psychology.* Chicago: Quintessence.

Bennett, David A.; Wilson, Robert S.; Schneider, Julie A.; Evans, D. A.; Mendes de Leon, C. F.; Arnold, S. E; & others. (2003). Education modifies the relation of Alzheimer's disease pathology to level of cognitive function in older persons. *Neurology, 60,* 1909–1915.

Bennett, George K. (1940). *Bennett Test of Mechanical Comprehension.* New York: Psychological Corporation.

Benson, Etienne. (2002, October). Pheromones, in context. *APA Monitor on Psychology, 33,* 46–48.

Benson, Herbert. (1993). The relaxation response. In Daniel Goleman & Joel Gurin (Eds.), *Mind/body medicine: How to use your mind for better health.* Yonkers, NY: Consumer Reports Books.

Benyamini, Yael, & Lomranz, Jacob. (2004). The relationship of activity restriction and replacement with depressive symptoms among older adults. *Psychology and Aging, 19,* 362–366.

Ben-Zeev, Talia; Fein, Steven; & Inzlicht, Michael. (2005). Arousal and stereotype threat. *Journal of Experimental Social Psychology, 41,* 174–181.

Beratis, Stavroula; Gabriel, Joanna; & Holdas, Stavros. (1994). Age of onset in subtypes of schizophrenic disorders. *Schizophrenia Bulletin, 20,* 287–296.

Berkman, Lisa F. (1995). The role of social relations in health promotion. *Psychosomatic Medicine, 57,* 245–254.

Berkman, Lisa F.; Leo-Summers, Linda; & Horowitz, Ralph I. (1992). Emotional support and survival after myocardial infarction. *Annals of Internal Medicine, 117,* 1003–1009.

Berkman, Lisa F., & Syme, S. Leonard. (1979). Social networks, host resistance, and mortality: A nine-year follow-up study of Alameda County residents. *American Journal of Epidemiology, 109,* 186–204.

Berlyne, Daniel E. (1960). *Conflict, arousal, and curiosity.* New York: McGraw-Hill.

Berlyne, Daniel E. (1971). *Aesthetics and psychobiology*. New York: Appleton-Century-Crofts.

Berman, Brian M.; Lao, Lixing; Langenberg, Patricia; Lee, Wen Lin; Gilpin, Adele M. K.; & Hochberg, Marc C. (2004, December 21). Effectiveness of acupuncture as adjunctive therapy in osteoarthritis of the knee: A randomized, controlled trial. *Annals of Internal Medicine, 141,* 901–910.

Bermond, Bob; Fasotti, L.; Nieuwenhuyse, B.; & Schuerman, J. (1991). Spinal cord lesions, peripheral feedback and intensities of emotional feelings. *Cognition & Emotion, 5,* 201–220.

Bernard, Luther L. (1924). *Instinct: A study in social psychology*. New York: Holt.

Berndt, Thomas J. (1992). Friendship and friends' influence in adolescence. *Current Directions in Psychological Science, 1,* 156–159.

Bernstein, David P.; Useda, David; & Siever, Larry J. (1995). Paranoid personality disorder. In W. John Livesley (Ed.), *The DSM-IV personality disorders: Diagnosis and treatment of mental disorders*. New York: Guilford Press.

Berry, John W. (1994). Acculturative stress. In Walter J. Lonner & Roy Malpass (Eds.), *Psychology and culture*. Boston: Allyn & Bacon.

Berry, John W. (2003). Conceptual approaches to acculturation. In Kevin M. Chun, Pamela Balls Organista, & Gerardo Marín (Eds.), *Acculturation: Advances in theory, measurement and applied research*. Washington, DC: American Psychological Association.

Berry, John W., & Kim, Uichol. (1988). Acculturation and mental health. In Pierre R. Dasen, John W. Berry, & Norman Sartorius (Eds.), *Health and cross-cultural psychology: Toward applications* (Cross-cultural Research and Methodology Series, Vol. 10). Newbury Park, CA: Sage.

Berry, Lilly M., & Houston, John P. (1993). *Psychology at work*. Madison, WI: Brown & Benchmark.

Berthier, Neil E.; DeBlois, S.; Poirier, Christopher R.; Novak, Melinda A.; & Clifton, Rachel K. (2000). Where's the ball? Two- and three-year-olds reason about unseen events. *Developmental Psychology, 36,* 394–401.

Best, Deborah L., & Williams, John E. (1997). Sex, gender, and culture. In John W. Berry, Marshall H. Segall, & Cigdem Kagitçibasi (Eds.), *Handbook of cross-cultural psychology: Vol. 3. Social behavior and applications*. Boston: Allyn & Bacon.

Betancourt, Hector, & López, Steven Regeser. (1993). The study of culture, ethnicity, and race in American psychology. *American Psychologist, 48,* 629–637.

Beumont, Pierre J.V. (2002). Clinical presentation of anorexia and bulimia nervosa. In Kelly D. Brownell & C. G. Fairburn (Eds.), *Eating disorders and obesity: A comprehensive handbook* (2nd ed.). New York: Guilford Press.

Beutler, Larry E. (2000). Empirically based decision making in clinical practice. *Prevention and Treatment, 3*(Article 27). Available on the World Wide Web, http://journals.apa.org/prevention/volume3/pre0030027a.html

Beutler, Larry E.; Machado, Paulo P. P.; & Neufeldt, Susan Allstetter. (1994). Therapist variables. In Allen E. Bergin & Sol L. Garfield (Eds.), *Handbook of psychotherapy and behavior change* (4th ed.). New York: Wiley.

Beutler, Larry E.; Malik, Mary; Alimohamed, Shabia; Harwood, T. Mark; Talebi, Hani; Noble, Sharon; & Wong, Eunice. (2004). Therapist variables. In Michael J. Lambert (Ed.), *Bergin and Garfield's handbook of psychotherapy and behavior change* (5th ed.). New York: Wiley.

Beyerstein, Barry L. (1996). Graphology. In Gordon Stein (Ed.), *The encyclopedia of the paranormal*. Amherst, NY: Prometheus Books.

Beyerstein, Barry L. (1999). Whence cometh the myth that we only use 10% of our brains? In Sergio Della Sala (Ed.), *Mind myths: Exploring popular assumptions about the mind and brain*. Chichester, England: Wiley.

Beyerstein, Barry L., & Beyerstein, Dale (Eds.). (1992). *The write stuff: Evaluations of graphology—The study of handwriting analysis*. Amherst, NY: Prometheus Books.

Bhatara, Vinod S.; Sharma, J. N.; Gupta, Sanjay; & Gupta, Y. K. (1997). *Rauwolfia serpentina*: The first herbal antipsychotic. *American Journal of Psychiatry, 154,* 894.

Binder, Jeffrey L.; Strupp, Hans H.; & Henry, William P. (1995). Psychodynamic theories in practice: Time-limited dynamic psychotherapy. In Bruce Bongar & Larry E. Beutler (Eds.), *Comprehensive textbook of psychotherapy: Theory and practice*. New York: Oxford University Press.

Binet, Alfred, & Simon, Théodore. (1905). New methods for the diagnosis of the intellectual level of subnormals. *L'Année Psychologique, 11,* 191–244.

Bjork, Daniel W. (1997a). *B. F. Skinner: A life*. Washington, DC: American Psychological Association.

Bjork, Daniel W. (1997b). *William James: The center of his vision*. Washington, DC: American Psychological Association.

Bjork, Robert A. (2001, March). How to succeed in college: Learn how to learn. *APS Observer, 14*(3), 9.

Bjorklund, Barbara R. (1995). Language development and cognition. In David F. Bjorklund (Ed.), *Children's thinking: Developmental function and individual differences* (2nd ed.). Pacific Grove, CA: Brooks/Cole.

Black, Donald W.; Monahan, Patrick; Baumgard, Connie H.; & Bell, Sue E. (1997). Predictors of long-term outcome in 45 men with antisocial personality disorder. *Annals of Clinical Psychiatry, 9,* 211–217.

Black, Stephen L., & Bevan, Susan. (1992). At the movies with Buss and Durkee: A natural experiment on film violence. *Aggressive Behavior, 18,* 37–45.

Blackmore, Susan. (1985). Belief in the paranormal: Probability judgments, illusory control, and the chance baseline shift. *British Journal of Psychology, 76,* 459–468.

Blackmore, Susan. (1998). Lucid dreams. In Kendrick Frazier (Ed.), *Encounters with the paranormal: Science, knowledge, and belief*. Amherst, NY: Prometheus Books.

Blanchard, Edward B.; Kuhn, Eric; Rowell, Dianna L.; Hickling, Edward J.; Wittrock, David; Rogers, Rebecca L.; Johnson, Michelle R.; & Steckler, Debra C. (2004). Studies of the vicarious traumatization of college students by the September 11th attacks: Effects of proximity, exposure, and connectedness. *Behavior Research and Therapy, 42,* 191–205.

Blascovich, Jim; Spencer, Steven J.; Quinn, Diane; & Steele, Claude. (2001). African Americans and high blood pressure: The role of stereotype threat. *Psychological Science, 12,* 225–229.

Blass, Thomas. (1991). Understanding behavior in the Milgram obedience experiment. *Journal of Personality and Social Psychology, 60,* 398–413.

Blass, Thomas. (1992). The social psychology of Stanley Milgram. In Mark P. Zanna (Ed.), *Advances in experimental social psychology* (Vol. 25). San Diego, CA: Academic Press.

Blass, Thomas. (2000). The Milgram Paradigm after 35 years. Some things we now know about obedience to authority. In Thomas Blass (Ed.), *Obedience to authority: Current perspectives on the Milgram paradigm*. Mahwah, NJ: Erlbaum.

Bliwise, Donald L. (1997). Sleep and aging. In Mark R. Pressman & William C. Orr (Eds.), *Understanding sleep: The evaluation and treatment of sleep disorders*. Washington, DC: American Psychological Association.

Block, Jack. (1995). A contrarian view of the five-factor approach to personality description. *Psychological Bulletin, 117,* 187–215.

Bloxham, G.; Long, C. G.; Alderman, N.; & Hollin, C. R. (1993). The behavioral treatment of self-starvation and severe self-injury in a patient with borderline personality disorder. *Journal of Behavioral Therapy and Experimental Psychiatry, 24,* 251–267.

Blumberg, Mark S., & Sokoloff, Greta. (2001). Do infant rats cry? *Psychological Review, 108,* 83–95.

Blumberg, Mark S.; Sokoloff, Greta; Kirby, Robert F.; & Kent, Kristen J. (2000). Distress vocalizations in infant rats: What's all the fuss about? *Psychological Science, 11,* 78–81.

Blumberg, Mark S., & Wasserman, Edward A. (1995). Animal mind and the argument from design. *American Psychologist, 50,* 133–144.

Blumenthal, Arthur L. (1998). Leipzig, Wilhelm Wundt, and psychology's gilded age. In Gregory A. Kimble & Michael Wertheimer (Eds.), *Portraits of pioneers in psychology* (Vol. 3). Washington, DC: American Psychological Association.

Bobo, Lawrence. (1988a). Attitudes toward the black political movement: Trends, meaning, and effects on racial policy preferences. *Social Psychology Quarterly, 51,* 287–302.

Bobo, Lawrence. (1988b). Group conflict, prejudice, and the paradox of contemporary racial attitudes. In Phyllis A. Katz & Dalmas A. Taylor (Eds.), *Eliminating racism: Profiles in controversy.* New York: Plenum Press.

Bodenhausen, Galen V.; Macrae, C. Neil; & Hugenberg, Kurt. (2003). Social cognition. In T. Million & M. J. Lerner (Eds.), *Handbook of psychology: Personality and social psychology: Vol. 5* (pp. 257-282). New York: Wiley.

Bohus, Martin; Haaf, Brigitte; Simms, Timothy; Limberger, Matthias F.; Schmahl, Christian; Unckel, Christine; Lieb, Klaus; & Linehan, Marsha M. (2004). Effectiveness of inpatient dialectical behavioral therapy for borderline personality disorder: A controlled trial. *Behavior Research and Therapy, 42,* 487–499.

Bolger, Niall, & Schilling, Elizabeth A. (1991). Personality and problems of everyday life: The role of neuroticism in exposure and reactivity to stress. *Journal of Personality, 59,* 355–386.

Bolger, Niall, & Zuckerman, Adam. (1995). A framework for studying personality in the stress process. *Journal of Personality and Social Psychology, 69,* 890–902.

Bolles, Robert C. (1972). Reinforcement, expectancy, and learning. *Psychological Review, 79,* 394–409.

Bolles, Robert C. (1985). The slaying of Goliath: What happened to reinforcement theory? In Timothy D. Johnston & Alexandra T. Pietrewicz (Eds.), *Issues in the ecological study of learning.* Hillsdale, NJ: Erlbaum.

Bolton, Paul; Bass, Judith; Neugebauer, Richard; Verdeli, Helen; Clougherty, Kathleen F.; Wickramaratne, Priya; & others. (2003). Group interpersonal psychotherapy for depression in rural Uganda: A randomized controlled trial. *Journal of the American Medical Association, 289,* 3117–3124.

Bond, Michael Harris. (1986). *The psychology of the Chinese people.* New York: Oxford University Press.

Bond, Michael Harris. (1994). Continuing encounters with Hong Kong. In Walter J. Lonner & Roy Malpass (Eds.), *Psychology and culture.* Boston: Allyn & Bacon.

Bond, Michael Harris, & Smith, Peter B. (1996). Cross-cultural social and organizational psychology. *Annual Review of Psychology, 47,* 205–235.

Bond, Rod, & Smith, Peter B. (1996). Culture and conformity: A meta-analysis of studies using Asch's (1952b, 1956) line judgment task. *Psychological Bulletin, 119,* 111–137.

Bordnick, Patrick S.; Elkins, Ralph L.; Orr, T. Edward; Walters, Paul; & Thyer, Bruce A. (2004). Evaluating the relative effectiveness of three aversion therapies designed to reduce craving among cocaine users. *Behavioral Interventions, 18,* 1–24.

Bornstein, Marc H., & Lamb, Michael E. (1992). *Development in infancy: An introduction* (3rd ed.). New York: McGraw-Hill.

Bornstein, Marc H., & Marks, Lawrence E. (1982, January). Color revisionism. *Psychology Today, 16,* 64–73.

Bornstein, Robert F. (1989). Subliminal techniques as propaganda tools: Review and critique. *Journal of Mind and Behavior, 10,* 231–262.

Bornstein, Robert F. (1993). Subliminal mere exposure effects. In Robert F. Bornstein & Thane S. Pittman (Eds.), *Perception without awareness: Cognitive, clinical, and social perspectives.* New York: Guilford Press.

Bos, Henny M. W.; van Balen, Frank; & van den Boom, Dymphna. (2004). Experience of parenthood, couple relationship, social support, and child-rearing goals in planned lesbian mother families. *Journal of Child Psychology and Psychiatry, 45,* 755–764.

Boss, Pauline; Beaulieu, Lorraine; Wieling, Elizabeth; Turner, William; & LaCruz, Shulaika. (2003). Healing loss, ambiguity, and trauma: A community-based intervention with families of union workers missing after the 9/11 attack in New York City. *Journal of Marital and Family Therapy, 29,* 455–467.

Bouchard, Thomas J., Jr. (2004). Genetic influence on human psychological traits. *Psychological Science, 13,* 148–151.

Bouton, Mark E. (2000). A learning theory perspective on lapse, relapse, and the maintenance of behavior change. *Health Psychology, 19,* 57–63.

Bouton, Mark E.; Mineka, Susan; & Barlow, David H. (2001). A modern learning theory perspective on the etiology of panic disorder. *Psychological Review, 108,* 4–32.

Bower, Bruce. (1997, March 29). Forbidden flavors: Scientists consider how disgusting tastes can linger surreptitiously in memory. *Science News, 151,* 198–199.

Bower, Gordon H. (1993). The fragmentation of psychology? *American Psychologist, 48,* 905–907.

Bowers, Kenneth S., & Favolden, Peter. (1996). Revisiting a century-old Freudian slip—From suggestion disavowed to the truth repressed. *Psychological Bulletin, 119,* 355–380.

Bowers, Kenneth S.; Regehr, Glenn; Balthazard, Claude; & Parker, Kevin. (1990). Intuition in the context of discovery. *Cognitive Psychology, 22,* 72–110.

Bowlby, John. (1969). *Attachment and loss: Vol. 1. Attachment.* New York: Basic Books.

Bowlby, John. (1988). *A secure base.* New York: Basic Books.

Boysen, Sally T., & Hines, G. T. (1999). Current issues and emerging theories in animal cognition. *Annual Review of Psychology, 50,* 683–705.

Bozarth, Jerold D.; Zimring, Fred M.; & Tausch, Reinhard. (2002). Client-centered therapy: The evolution of a revolution. In David J. Cain & Julius Seeman (Eds.), *Humanistic psychotherapies: Handbook of research and practice.* Washington, DC: American Psychological Association.

Bracha, H. Stefan; Wolkowitz, Owen M.; Lohr, James B.; Karson, Craig N.; & Bigelow, Llewellyn B. (1989). High prevalence of visual hallucinations in research subjects with chronic schizophrenia. *American Journal of Psychiatry, 146,* 526–528.

Bradbard, Marilyn R.; Martin, Carol L.; Endsley, Richard C.; & Halverson, Charles F. (1986). Influence of sex stereotypes on children's exploration and memory: A competence versus performance distinction. *Developmental Psychology, 22,* 481–486.

Braffman, Wayne, & Kirsch, Irving. (1999). Imaginative suggestibility and hypnotizability: An empirical analysis. *Journal of Personality and Social Psychology, 77,* 578–587.

Brainard, George C.; Hanifin, John P.; Rollag, Mark D.; & others. (2001a). Action spectrum for melatonin regulation in humans: Evidence for a novel circadian photoreceptor. *Journal of Neuroscience, 21,* 6405–6412.

Brainard, George C.; Hanifin, John P.; Rollag, Mark D.; & others. (2001b). Human melatonin regulation is not mediated by the three cone photopic visual system. *Journal of Clinical Endocrinology and Metabolism, 86,* 433–436.

Brainerd, Charles J. (1996). Piaget: A centennial celebration. *Psychological Science, 7,* 191–195.

Bransford, John D., & Stein, Barry S. (1993). *The IDEAL problem solver: A guide for improving thinking, learning, and creativity* (2nd ed.). New York: Freeman.

Braun, Allen R.; Balkin, Thomas J.; Wesensten, Nancy J.; Gwadry, Fuad; Carson, Richard E.; Varga, Mary; & others. (1998, January 2). Dissociated patterns of activity in visual cortices and their projections during human rapid eye movement during sleep. *Science, 279,* 91–95.

Braun, Stephen. (2001, Spring). Ecstasy on trial: Seeking insight by prescription. *Cerebrum, 3,* 10–21.

Breggin, Peter R. (1991). *Toxic psychiatry.* New York: St. Martin's Press.

Bregman, Elsie O. (1934). An attempt to modify the emotional attitude of infants by the conditioned response technique. *Journal of Genetic Psychology, 45,* 169–198.

Brehm, Sharon S. (1992). *Intimate relationships* (2nd ed.). New York: McGraw-Hill.

Breland, Keller, & Breland, Marian. (1961). The misbehavior of organisms. *American Psychologist, 16,* 681–684.

Brenneis, C. Brooks. (2000). Evaluating the evidence: Can we find authenticated recovered memory? *Psychoanalytic Psychology, 17,* 61–77.

Breslau, Naomi; Kilbey, M. Marlyne; & Andreski, Patricia. (1993). Nicotine dependence and major depression: New evidence from a prospective investigation. *Archives of General Psychiatry, 50,* 31–35.

Breslau, Naomi; Novak, Scott P.; & Kessler, Ronald C. (2004). Psychiatric disorders and stages of smoking. *Biological Psychiatry, 55,* 69–76.

Breslau, Naomi; Peterson, Edward L.; Schultz, Lonni R.; & others. (1998). Major depression and stages of smoking: A longitudinal investigation. *Archives of General Psychiatry, 55,* 161–166.

Bretherton, Inge; & Main, Mary. (2000). Mary Dinsmore Salter Ainsworth (1913–1999), *American Psychologist, 55,* 1148–1149.

Breuer, Josef, & Freud, Sigmund. (1895/1957). *Studies on hysteria* (James Strachey, Ed. & Trans., in collaboration with Anna Freud). New York: Basic Books.

Brewer, Marilyn B. (1994). The social psychology of prejudice: Getting it all together. In Mark P. Zanna & James M. Olson (Eds.), *The psychology of prejudice: The Ontario Symposium* (Vol. 7). Hillsdale, NJ: Erlbaum.

Brewer, William F., & Treyens, James C. (1981). Role of schemata in memory for places. *Cognitive Psychology, 13,* 207–230.

Brewin, Chris R. (1996). Theoretical foundations of cognitive-behavior therapy for anxiety and depression. *Annual Review of Psychology, 47,* 33–57.

Brice, Thomas S., & Waung, M. (2001, April). *Web site recruitment characteristics: America's Best v. America's Biggest.* Presented at the Society for the Advancement of Management International Management Conference. Las Vegas, NV.

Briere, John, & Conte, Jon. (1993). Self-reported amnesia for abuse in adults molested as children. *Journal of Traumatic Stress, 6*(1), 21–31.

Bringmann, Wolfgang G.; Voss, Ursula; & Ungerer, Gustav A. (1997). Wundt's laboratories. In Wolfgang G. Bringmann, Helmut E. Lück, Rudolf Miller, & Charles E. Early (Eds.), *A pictorial history of psychology.* Chicago: Quintessence.

Brissette, Ian; Scheier, Michael F.; & Carver, Charles S. (2002). The role of optimism in social network development, coping, and psychological adjustment during a life transition. *Journal of Personality and Social Psychology, 82,* 102–111.

Brock, Dwight B.; Lemke, Jon H.; & Berkman, Lisa F. (1994). Mortality and physical functioning in epidemiologic studies of three older populations. *Journal of Aging and Social Policy, 6*(3), 21–32.

Broder, Michael S. (1999). So you want to work in the media? 21 things I wish I had known when I first asked myself that question. In Lita Linzer Schwartz (Ed.), *Psychology and the media: A second look.* Washington, DC: American Psychological Association.

Brody, Arthur L.; Saxena, Sajaya; Stoessel, Paula; Gillies, Laurie; Fairbanks, Lynn A.; Alborzian, Shervin; & others. (2001, July). Regional brain metabolic changes in patients with major depression treated with either paroxetine or interpersonal therapy. *Archives of General Psychiatry, 58,* 631–640.

Brody, Nathan. (1997). Intelligence, schooling, and society. *American Psychologist, 52,* 1046–1050.

Brooks-Gunn, Jeanne. (1988). Antecedents and consequences of variations of girls' maturational timing. In Melvin D. Levine & Elizabeth R. McAnarney (Eds.), *Early adolescent transitions.* Lexington, MA: Lexington Books.

Brooks-Gunn, Jeanne, & Reiter, Edward O. (1990). The role of pubertal processes. In S. Shirley Feldman & Glen R. Elliott (Eds.), *At the threshold: The developing adolescent.* Cambridge, MA: Harvard University Press.

Brown, Alan S. (1991). A review of the tip-of-the-tongue experience. *Psychological Bulletin, 109*(2), 204–223.

Brown, Alan S. (2003). A review of the déjà vu experience. *Psychological Bulletin, 129,* 394–413.

Brown, Alan S. (2004). *The déjà vu experience: Essays in cognitive psychology.* New York: Psychology Press.

Brown, Alan S. (2005, January 31). Looking at déjà vu for the first time. *The Scientist, 19*(2), 20–21.

Brown, Alan S.; Begg, Melissa D.; Gravenstein, Stefan; Schaefer, Catherine A.; Wyatt, Richard J.; Bresnahan, Michaeline; Babulas, Vicki P.; & Susser, Ezra S. (2004). Serological evidence of prenatal influenza in the etiology of schizophrenia. *Archives of General Psychiatry, 61,* 774–780.

Brown, Alan S.; Schaefer, Catherine A.; Wyatt, Richard J.; & others. (2000). Maternal exposure to respiratory infections and adult schizophrenia spectrum disorders: A prospective birth cohort study. *Schizophrenia Bulletin, 26,* 287–295.

Brown, Bernard. (1999, April). Optimizing expression of the common human genome for child development. *Current Directions in Psychological Science, 8,* 37–41.

Brown, Daniel; Scheflin, Alan W.; & Hammond, D. Corydon. (1998). *Memory, trauma treatment, and the law.* New York: Norton.

Brown, Gary E.; Davis, Eric; & Johnson, Amanda. (1999). Forced exercise blocks learned helplessness in the cockroach (Periplaneta americana). *Psychological Reports, 84,* 155–156.

Brown, Gregory K.; Newman, Cory F.; Charlesworth, Sarah E.; Crits-Christoph, Paul; & Beck, Aaron T. (2004). An open clinical trial of cognitive therapy for borderline personality disorder. *Journal of Personality Disorders, 18,* 257–271.

Brown, Lisa M.; Bongar, Bruce; & Cleary, Karin M. (2004). A profile of psychologists'

views of critical risk factors for completed suicide in older adults. *Professional Psychology: Research & Practice, 35,* 90–96.

Brown, Roger, & Kulik, James. (1982). Flashbulb memories. In Ulric Neisser (Ed.), *Memory observed: Remembering in natural contexts.* San Francisco: Freeman.

Browning, Caryl Ann. (2001). Music therapy in childbirth: Research in practice. *Music Therapy Perspectives, 19,* 74–81.

Brüning, Jens C.; Gautam, Dinesh; & others. (2000, September 22). Role of brain insulin receptor in control of body weight and reproduction. *Science, 289,* 2122–2125.

Bryan, James H., & Test, Mary Ann. (1967). Models and helping: Naturalistic studies in aiding behavior. *Journal of Personality and Social Psychology, 6,* 400–407.

Buchanan, Christy Miller; Eccles, Jacquelynne S.; & Becker, Jill B. (1992). Are adolescents the victims of raging hormones? Evidence for activational effects of hormones on moods and behavior at adolescence. *Psychological Bulletin, 111,* 62–107.

Buck, Linda B. (2000). The molecular architecture of odor and pheromone sensing in mammals. *Cell, 100,* 611–618.

Buckley, Kerry W. (1982). The selling of a psychologist: John Broadus Watson and the application of behavioral techniques to advertising. *Journal of the History of the Behavioral Sciences, 18,* 207–221.

Buckley, Kerry W. (1989). *Mechanical man: John Broadus Watson and the beginnings of behaviorism.* New York: Guilford Press.

Buckner, Randy L., & Wheeler, Mark E. (2001). The cognitive neuroscience of remembering. *Nature Reviews Neuroscience, 2,* 624–634.

Budai, Dénes. (2000). Neurotransmitters and receptors in the dorsal horn of the spinal cord. *Acta Biologica Szegediensis, 44,* 21–38.

Bulik, Cynthia M.; Sullivan, Patrick F.; & Kendler, Kenneth S. (2000). An empirical study of the classification of eating disorders. *American Journal of Psychiatry, 157,* 886–895.

Burger, Jerry M. (1992). *Desire for control: Personality, social, and clinical perspectives.* New York: Plenum Press.

Burger, Jerry M, & Lynn, Amy L. (2005). Superstitious behavior among American and Japanese professional baseball players. *Basic and Applied Social Psychology, 27,* 71–76.

Burgess, Cheryl A., & Kirsch, Irving. (1999). Expectancy information as a moderator of the effects of hypnosis on memory. *Contemporary Hypnosis, 16,* 22–31.

Buri, John R.; Louiselle, Peggy A.; Misukanis, Thomas M.; & Mueller, Rebecca A. (1988). Effects of parental authoritarianism and authoritativeness on self-esteem. *Personality and Social Psychology Bulletin, 14,* 271–282.

Burke, Deborah M., & Shafto, Meredith A. (2004). Aging and language production. *Current Directions in Psychological Science, 13,* 21–24.

Burks, Nancy, & Martin, Barclay. (1985). Everyday problems and life change events: Ongoing versus acute sources of stress. *Journal of Human Stress, 11*, 27–35.

Burlingame, Gary M.; MacKenzie, K. Roy; & Strauss, Bernhard. (2004). Small group treatment: Evidence for effectiveness and mechanisms of change. In Michael J. Lambert (Ed.), *Bergin and Garfield's handbook of psychotherapy and behavior change* (5th ed.). New York: Wiley.

Burman, Bonnie, & Margolin, Gayla. (1992). Analysis of the association between marital relationships and health problems: An interactional perspective. *Psychological Bulletin, 112*, 39–63.

Burnfield, Jennifer L., & Medsker, Gina J. (1999). Income and employment of SIOP Members in 1997. *The Industrial-Organizational Psychologist, 36*, 19–30.

Burns, Melanie, & Seligman, Martin E. P. (1989). Explanatory style across the lifespan: Evidence for stability over 52 years. *Journal of Personality and Social Psychology, 56*, 471–477.

Burns, Victoria E.; Carroll, Douglas; Drayson, Mark; Whitham, Martin; & Ring, Christopher. (2003). Life events, perceived stress and antibody response to influenza vaccination in young, healthy adults. *Journal of Psychosomatic Research, 55*, 569–572.

Burrell, Brian. (2005). *Postcards from the brain museum. The improbable search for meaning in the matter of famous minds.* New York: Broadway Books.

Bush, R. (1989). Defining quality in dispute resolution: Taxonomies and anti-taxonomies of quality arguments. *Denver University Law Review, 66*, 335.

Bushman, Brad J. (1993). Human aggression while under the influence of alcohol and other drugs: An integrative research review. *Current Directions in Psychological Science, 2*, 148–152.

Bushman, Brad J. (1995). Moderating role of trait aggressiveness in the effects of violent media on aggression. *Journal of Personality and Social Psychology, 69*, 950–960.

Bushman, Brad J., & Anderson, Craig J. (2001). Media violence and the American public: Scientific facts versus media misinformation. *American Psychologist, 56*, 477–489.

Bushman, Brad J., & Phillips, Colleen M. (2001). If the television program bleeds, memory for the advertisement recedes. *Current Directions in Psychological Science, 2*, 43–47.

Bushnell, I. W. R. (2001). Mother's face recognition in newborn infants: Learning and memory. *Infant and Child Development, 10*, 67–74.

Buss, Arnold H. (1989). Personality as traits. *American Psychologist, 44*, 1378–1388.

Buss, David M. (1989). Sex differences in human mate preferences: Evolutionary hypotheses tested in 37 cultures. *Behavioral and Brain Sciences, 12*, 1–49.

Buss, David M. (1991). Evolutionary personality psychology. *Annual Review of Psychology, 42*, 459–491.

Buss, David M. (1994). *The evolution of desire: Strategies of human mating.* New York: Basic Books.

Buss, David M. (1995a). Evolutionary psychology: A new paradigm for psychological science. *Psychological Inquiry, 6*, 1–31.

Buss, David M. (1995b). Psychological sex differences: Origins through sexual selection. *American Psychologist, 50*, 164–168.

Buss, David M. (1996). Sexual conflict: Evolutionary insights into feminism and the "Battle of the Sexes." In David M. Buss & Neil M. Malamuth (Eds.), *Sex, power, conflict: Evolutionary and feminist perspectives.* New York: Oxford University Press.

Buss, David M. (1999). *Evolutionary psychology: The new science of the mind.* Boston: Allyn & Bacon.

Butcher, James N. (1999). *A beginner's guide to the MMPI-2.* Washington, DC: American Psychological Association.

Butcher, James N., & Rouse, Steven V. (1996). Personality: Individual differences and clinical assessment. *Annual Review of Psychology, 47*, 87–111.

Butler, Robert A., & Harlow, Harry F. (1954). Persistence of visual exploration in monkeys. *Journal of Comparative and Physiological Psychology, 47*, 258–263.

Byne, William. (1994, May). The biological evidence challenged. *Scientific American, 270*, 50–55.

Byne, William, & Parsons, Bruce. (1993). Human sexual orientation: The biologic theories reappraised. *Archives of General Psychiatry, 50*, 228–239.

Cacioppo, John T., & Gardner, Wendi L. (1999). Emotion. *Annual Review of Psychology, 50*, 191–214.

Caetano, Raul; Schafer, John; & Cunradi, Carol B. (2001). Alcohol-related intimate partner violence among white, black, and Hispanic couples in the United States. *Alcohol Research and Health, 25*, 58–65.

Cain, David J. (2002). Defining characteristics, history, and evolution of humanistic psychotherapies. In David J. Cain & Julius Seeman (Eds.), *Humanistic psychotherapies: Handbook of research and practice.* Washington, DC: American Psychological Association.

Cain, David J. (2003). Advancing humanistic psychology and psychotherapy: Some challenges and proposed solutions. *Journal of Humanistic Psychology, 43*, 10–41.

Cain, David J., & Seeman, Julius (Eds.). (2002). *Humanistic psychotherapies: Handbook of research and practice.* Washington, DC: American Psychological Association.

Calignano, Antonio; La Rana, Giovanna; Giuffrida, Andrea; & Piomelli, Daniele. (1998, July 16). Control of pain initiation by endogenous cannabinoids. *Nature, 394*, 277.

Calkins, Mary W. (1893). Statistics of dreams. *American Journal of Psychology, 5*, 311–343.

Campbell, Jennifer D., & Fairey, Patricia J. (1989). Informational and normative routes to conformity: The effect of faction size as a function of norm extremity and attention to the stimulus. *Journal of Personality and Social Psychology, 57*, 457–458.

Campbell, John B., & Hawley, Charles W. (1982). Study habits and Eysenck's theory of extraversion-introversion. *Journal of Research in Personality, 16*, 139–146.

Campfield, L. Arthur; Smith, Françoise J.; Rosenbaum, Michael; & Hirsch, Jules. (1996). Human eating: Evidence for a physiological basis using a modified paradigm. *Neuroscience and Biobehavioral Reviews, 20*, 133–137.

Campion, James E. (1972). Work sampling for personnel selection. *Journal of Applied Psychology, 56*, 40–44.

Campion, Michael A.; Pursell, Elliot D.; & Brown, Barbara K. (1988). Structured interviewing: Raising the psychometric properties of the employment interview. *Personnel Psychology, 41*, 25–42.

Canli, Turhan. (2004). Functional brain-mapping of extraversion and neuroticism: Learning from individual differences in emotion processing. *Journal of Personality, 72*, 1105–1132.

Canli, Turhan; Amin, Zenab; Haas, Brian; Omura, Kazufumi; & Constable, R. Todd. (2004). A double dissociation between mood states and personality traits in the anterior cingulate. *Behavioral Neuroscience, 118*, 897–904.

Canli, Turhan; Sivers, Heidi; Whitfield, Susan L.; Gotlib, Ian H.; & Gabrieli, John D. E. (2002). Amygdala response to happy faces as a function of extraversion. *Science, 296*, 2191.

Canli, Turhan; Zhao, Zuo; Desmond, John E.; Kang, Eunjoo; Gross, James; & Gabrieli, John D. E. (2001). An fMRI study of personality influences on brain reactivity to emotional stimuli. *Behavioral Neuroscience, 115*, 33–42.

Cannon, Tyrone D., & Marco, Elysa. (1994). Structural brain abnormalities as indicators of vulnerability to schizophrenia. *Schizophrenia Bulletin, 20*, 89–102.

Cannon, Walter B. (1927). The James-Lange theory of emotion: A critical examination and an alternative theory. *American Journal of Psychology, 39*, 106–124.

Cannon, Walter B. (1932). *The wisdom of the body.* New York: Norton.

Cannon, Walter B.; Lewis, J. T.; & Britton, S. W. (1927). The dispensability of the sympathetic division of the autonomic nervous system. *Boston Medical and Surgical Journal, 197*, 514.

Cantor, Joanne. (2000, August 5). *Media violence and children's emotions: Beyond the "smoking gun."* Paper presented at the annual convention of the American Psychological Association, Washington, DC. Retrieved

September 29, 2001, from http://www.joannecantor.com/EMOTIONS2sgl.htm

Capaldi, Elizabeth D. (1996). Conditioned food preferences. In Elizabeth D. Capaldi (Ed.), *Why we eat what we eat: The psychology of eating*. Washington, DC: American Psychological Association.

Caporael, Linda R. (2001). Evolutionary psychology: Toward a unifying theory and a hybrid science. *Annual Review of Psychology, 52*, 607–628.

Caporael, Linda R., & Brewer, Marilynn B. (1995). Hierarchical evolutionary theory: There is an alternative, and it's not creationism. *Psychological Inquiry, 6*, 31–33.

Caraballo, Ralph S.; Giovino, Gary A.; Pechacek, Terry F.; Mowery, Paul D.; Richter, Patricia A.; Strauss, Warren J.; & others. (1998, July 8). Racial and ethnic differences in serum cotinine levels of cigarette smokers. *Journal of the American Medical Association, 280*, 135–139.

Carlson, Elizabeth A.; Sroufe, Alan L.; & Egelund, Byron. (2004). The construction of experience: A longitudinal study of representation and behavior. *Child Development, 75*, 66–83.

Caro, José F.; Kolaczynski, Jerzy W.; & others. (1996, July 20). Decreased cerebrospinal-fluid serum leptin ratio in obesity: A possible mechanism for leptin resistance. *Lancet, 348*, 159–161.

Carpenter, Ronda J. (1997). Margaret Floy Washburn. In Wolfgang G. Bringmann, Helmut E. Lück, Rudolf Miller, & Charles E. Early (Eds.), *A pictorial history of psychology*. Chicago: Quintessence.

Carroll, Kathleen M.; Nich, Charla; Ball, Samuel A.; McCance, Elinore; Frankforter, Tami L.; & Rounsaville, Bruce J. (2000). One-year follow-up of disulfiram and psychotherapy for cocaine-alcohol users: Sustained effects of treatment. *Addiction, 95*, 1335–1349.

Carroll, Kathleen Whiteman. (1993). Family support groups for medically ill patients and their families. In Anne Alonso & Hillel I. Swiller (Eds.), *Group therapy in clinical practice*. Washington, DC: American Psychiatric Press.

Carroll, Marilyn E., & Overmier, J. Bruce (Eds.). (2001). *Animal research and human health: Advancing human welfare through behavioral science*. Washington, DC: American Psychological Association.

Carskadon, Mary A., & Taylor, Jennifer F. (1997). Public policy and sleep disorders. In Mark R. Pressman & William C. Orr (Eds.), *Understanding sleep: The evaluation and treatment of sleep disorders*. Washington, DC: American Psychological Association.

Carter, C. Sue, & DeVries, A. Courtney. (1999). Stress and soothing: An endocrine perspective. In Michael Lewis & Douglas Ramsay (Eds.), *Soothing and stress*. Mahwah, NJ: Erlbaum.

Cartwright, Rosalind Dymond, & Kaszniak, Alfred. (1991). The social psychology of dream reporting. In Steven J. Ellman & John S. Antrobus (Eds.), *The mind in sleep: Psychology and psychophysiology* (2nd ed.). New York: Wiley.

Carver, Karen; Joyner, Kara; & Udry, J. Richard. (2003). National estimates of adolescent romantic relationships. In Paul Florsheim (Ed.), *Adolescent romantic relations and sexual behavior: Theory, research, and practical implications*. Mahwah, NJ: Erlbaum.

Carver, Priscilla R.; Egan, Susan K.; & Perry, David G. (2004). Children who question their heterosecuality. *Developmental Psychology, 40*, 43–53.

Caspi, Avshalom; Roberts, Brent W.; & Shiner, Rebecca L. (2005). Personality development: Stability and change. *Annual Review of Psychology, 56*, 453–484.

Catania, A. Charles, & Laties, Victor G. (1999). Pavlov and Skinner: Two lives in science (an introduction to B. F. Skinner's "Some responses to the stimulus 'Pavlov' "). *Journal of the Experimental Analysis of Behavior, 72*, 455–461.

Cattell, Raymond B. (1973, July). Personality pinned down. *Psychology Today*, pp. 40–46.

Cattell, Raymond B. (1994). A cross-validation of primary personality structure in the 16 P.F. by two parcelled factor analysis. *Multivariate Experimental Clinical Research, 10*(3), 181–191.

Cattell, Raymond B.; Cattell, A. Karen S.; & Cattell, Heather E. P. (1993). *16 PF questionnaire* (5th ed.). Champaign, IL: Institute for Personality and Ability Testing.

Ceci, Stephen J., & Loftus, Elizabeth F. (1994). "Memory work": A royal road to false memories? Special issue: Recovery of memories of childhood sexual abuse. *Applied Cognitive Psychology, 8*, 351–364.

Cefalu, William T.; Wagner, Janice D.; & others. (1997). A study of caloric restriction and cardiovascular aging in cynomolgus monkeys (Macaca fascicularis): A potential model for aging research. *Journal of Gerontology, Series A, 52*, B10–B21.

Celnik, Pablo, & Cohen, Leonardo G. (2003). Functional relevance of cortical plasticity. In Simon Boniface & Ulf Ziemann (Eds.), *Plasticity in the human nervous system: Investigation with transcranial magnetic stimulation*. New York: Cambridge University Press.

Centers for Desease Control and Prevention. (2002, April 29). BMI: Body mass index for adults. Retrieved January 3, 2003, from: http://www.cdc.gov/nccdphp/dnpa/bmi/bmi-adult.htm

Cervone, Daniel. (2004). The architecture of personality. *Psychological Review, 111*, 183–204.

Cervone, Daniel. (2005). Personality architecture: Within-person structures and processes. *Annual Review of Personality, 56*, 423–452.

Chadwick, P. D. J.; Lowe, C. F.; Horne, P. J.; & Higson, P. J. (1994). Modifying delusions: The role of empirical testing. *Behavior Therapy, 25*, 35–49.

Chambless, Dianne L., & Ollendick, Thomas H. (2001). Empirically supported psychological interventions: Controversies and evidence. *Annual Review of Psychology, 52*, 685–716.

Chance, Paul. (1999). Thorndike's puzzle boxes and the origins of the experimental analysis of behavior. *Journal of the Experimental Analysis of Behavior, 72*, 433–440.

Chaudhari, Nirupa; Landin, Ana Marie; & Roper, Stephen D. (2000). A metabotropic glutamate receptor variant functions as a taste receptor. *Nature Neuroscience, 3*, 113–119.

Chemelli, Richard M.; Willie, Jon T.; Sinton, Christopher M.; & others. (1999, August 20). Narcolepsy in orexin knockout mice: Molecular genetics of sleep regulation. *Cell, 98*, 409–412.

Chen, Chuansheng; Greenberger, Ellen; Lester, Julia; Dong, Qi; & Guo, Miaw-Sheue. (1998). A cross-cultural study of family and peer correlates of adolescent misconduct. *Developmental Psychology, 34*, 770–781.

Cheney, Dorothy L., & Seyfarth, Robert M. (1990). *How monkeys see the world*. Chicago: University of Chicago Press.

Cheng, Cecilia. (2003). Cognitive and motivational processs underlying coping flexibility: A dual-process model. *Journal of Personality and Social Psychology, 84*, 425–438.

Choi, Incheol; Nisbett, Richard E.; & Norenzayen, Ara. (1999). Causal attribution across cultures: Variation and universality. *Psychological Bulletin, 125*, 47–63.

Chomsky, Noam. (1965). *Aspects of a theory of syntax*. Cambridge, MA: MIT Press.

Christensen, Andrew, & Heavey, Christopher L. (1999). Interventions for couples. *Annual Review of Psychology, 50*, 165–190.

Christensen, Andrew, & Jacobson, Neil S. (1994). Who (or what) can do psychotherapy: The status and challenge of nonprofessional therapies. *Psychological Science, 5*, 8–14.

Chun, Kevin M.; Balls-Organista, Pamela; & Marin, Gerardo (Eds.). (2003). *Acculturation: Advances in theory, measurement and applied research*. Washington, DC: American Psychological Association.

Chusmir, L. H., & Mills, J. (1989). Gender differences in conflict resolution styles of managers: At work and at home. *Sex Roles, 20*, 149–163.

Chwalisz, Kathleen; Diener, Ed; & Gallagher, Dennis. (1988). Autonomic arousal feedback and emotional experience: Evidence from the spinal cord injured. *Journal of Personality and Social Psychology, 54*, 820–828.

Cialdini, Robert B. (2000). *Influence: Science and practice*. Boston: Allyn & Bacon.

Cialdini, Robert B.; Darby, Betty Lee; & Vincent, Joyce E. (1973). Transgression and altruism: A case for hedonism. *Journal of Experimental Social Psychology, 9*, 502–516.

Cialdini, Robert B., & Trost, Melanie R. (1998). Social influence, social norms, conformity, and compliance. In Daniel T. Gilbert, Susan T. Fiske, & Gardner Lindzey (Eds.), *The handbook of social psychology* (4th ed., Vol. 2). New York: McGraw-Hill.

Cioffi, Delia, & Holloway, James. (1993). Delayed costs of suppressed pain. *Journal of Personality and Social Psycyhology, 64,* 274–282.

Clark, Damon A.; Mitra, Partha P.; & Wang, Samuel S.-H. (2001). Scalable architecture in mammalian brains. *Nature, 411,* 189–193.

Clark, David M.; Ehlers, Anke; McManus, Freda; Hackman, Ann; Fennell, Melanie; Campbell, Helen; Flower, Teresa; Davenport, Clare; & Louis, Beverly. (2003). Cognitive therapy versus fluoxetine in generalized social phobia: A randomized placebo-controlled trial. *Journal of Counseling and Clinical Psychology, 71,* 1058–1067.

Clark, Russell D., III, & Word, Larry E. (1974). Where is the apathetic bystander? Situational characteristics of the emergency. *Journal of Personality and Social Psychology, 29,* 279–287.

Clarke-Stewart, K. Alison. (1989). Infant day care: Maligned or malignant? *American Psychologist, 44,* 266–273.

Clarke-Stewart, K. Alison. (1992). Consequences of child care for children's development. In Alan Booth (Ed.), *Child care in the 1990s: Trends and consequences.* Hillsdale, NJ: Erlbaum.

Clarkin, John F., & Levy, Kenneth N. (2004). The influence of client variables on psychotherapy. In Michael J. Lambert (Ed.), *Bergin and Garfield's handbook of psychotherapy and behavior change* (5th ed.). New York: Wiley.

Cloitre, Marylene. (2004). Aristotle revisited: The case of recovered memories. *Clinical Psychology: Science and Practice, 11,* 42–46.

Cobos, Pilar; Sánchez, María; Pérez, Nieves; & Vila, Jaime. (2004). Effects of spinal cord injuries on the subjective component of emotions. *Cognition & Emotion, 18,* 281–287.

Cody, Michael J., & Seiter, John S. (2001). Compliance principles in retail sales in the United States. In Wihelmina Wosinska, Robert B. Cialdini, Daniel W. Barrett, & Janusz Reykowski (Eds.), *The practice of social influence in multiple cultures.* Mahwah, NJ: Erlbaum.

Cohen, Hal. (2003). Creature comforts: Housing animals in complex environments. *The Scientist, 17*(9), 22–24.

Cohen, Jonathan D., & Tong, Frank. (2001, September 28). Perspectives. Neuroscience: The face of controversy. *Science, 293,* 2405–2407.

Cohen, Lindsey L. (2002). Reducing infant immunization distress through distraction. *Health Psychology, 21,* 207–211.

Cohen, Sheldon; Frank, Ellen; Doyle, William J.; Skoner, David P.; Rabin, Bruce; & Gwaltney, Jack M., Jr. (1998). Types of stressors that increase susceptibility to the common cold in healthy adults. *Health Psychology, 17,* 214–223.

Cohen, Sheldon; Gottlieb, Benjamin H.; & Underwood, Lynn G. (2000). Social relationships and health. In Sheldon Cohen, Lynn Underwood, & Benjamin H. Gottlieb (Eds.), *Social support measurement and intervention: A guide for health and social scientists.* New York: Oxford University Press.

Cohen, Sheldon, & Herbert, Tracy B. (1996). Health psychology: Psychological factors and physical disease from the perspective of human psychoneuroimmunology. *Annual Review of Psychology, 47,* 113–142.

Cohen, Sheldon; Tyrrell, David A. J.; & Smith, Andrew P. (1991). Psychological stress and susceptibility to the common cold. *New England Journal of Medicine, 325,* 606–612.

Cohen, Sheldon; Tyrrell, David A. J.; & Smith, Andrew P. (1993). Negative life events, perceived stress, negative affect, and susceptibility to the common cold. *Journal of Personality and Social Psychology, 64,* 131–140.

Cohen, Sheldon, & Williamson, Gail M. (1988). Perceived stress in a probability sample of the United States. In Shirlynn Spacapan & Stuart Oskamp (Eds.), *The social psychology of health: The Claremont Symposium on Applied Social Psychology* (4th ed.). Newbury Park, CA: Sage.

Cohn, D'Vera. (2002, January 24). For zoo denizens, a taste of the wild. *The Washington Post.* Retrieved January 25, 2002, from http://www.msnbc.com/news/693181.asp

Colcombe, Stanley; Erickson, Kirk I.; Raz, Naftali; Webb, Andrew G.; Cohen, Neal J.; McAuley, Edward; & Kramer, Arthur F. (2003). Aerobic fitness reduces brain tissue loss in aging humans. *Journal of Gerontology, Series A: Biological and Medical Sciences, 58,* 176–180.

Colicos, Michael A.; Collins, Boyce E.; Sailor, Michael J.; & Goda, Yukiko. (2001). Remodeling of synaptic actin induced by photoconductive stimulation. *Cell, 107,* 605–616.

Collier, R. M. (1940). An experimental study of the effects of subliminal stimuli. *Psychological Monographs, 52*(2), 1–59.

Collins, Allan M., & Loftus, Elizabeth F. (1975). A spreading activation theory of semantic processing. *Psychological Review, 82,* 407–428.

Collins, Rebecca L. (2004, September 7). Quoted in "Rand study finds adolescents who watch a lot of TV with sexual content have sex sooner." Retrieved September 8, 2004, from http://www.rand.org/news/press.04/09.07.html

Collins, Rebecca L.; Elliott, Marc N.; Berry, Sandra H.; Kanouse, David E.; Kunkel, Dale; Hunter, Sarah B.; & Miu, Angela. (2004). Watching sex on television predicts adolescent initiation of sexual behavior. *Pediatrics, 114,* 280–289.

Collins, W. Andrew. (2003). More than myth: The developmental significance of romantic relationships during adolescence. *Journal of Research on Adolescence, 13,* 1–24.

Collins, W. Andrew, & Gunnar, Megan. (1990). Social and personality development. *Annual Review of Psychology, 41,* 387–416.

Comas-Diaz, Lilian. (1993). Hispanic/Latino communities: Psychological implications. In Donald R. Atkinson, George Morten, & Derald Wing Sue (Eds.), *Counseling American minorities: A cross-cultural perspective* (4th ed.). Madison, WI: Brown & Benchmark.

Congressional Public Health Summit. (2000, July 26). Joint statement on the impact of entertainment violence on children. Retrieved September 29, 2001, from http://www.aap.org/advocacy/releases/jstmtevc.htm

Connor-Greene, Patricia A. (1993). From the laboratory to the headlines: Teaching critical evaluation of the press reports of research. *Teaching of Psychology, 20*(3), 167–169.

Contrada, Richard J.; Ashmore, Richard D.; Gary, Melvin L.; Coups, Elliot; Egeth, Jill D.; Sewell, Andrea; & others. (2000). Ethnicity-related sources of stress and their effects on well-being. *Current Directions of Psychological Science, 9,* 136–139.

Coons, Philip M. (1994). Confirmation of childhood abuse in child and adolescent cases of multiple personality disorder and dissociative disorder not otherwise specified. *Journal of Nervous and Mental Diseases, 182,* 461–464.

Cooper, Rosemary. (1994). Normal sleep. In Rosemary Cooper (Ed.), *Sleep.* New York: Chapman & Hall.

Cooper, Rosemary, & Bradbury, Sue. (1994). Techniques in sleep recording. In Rosemary Cooper (Ed.), *Sleep.* New York: Chapman & Hall.

Corballis, Michael C. (1999). Are we in our right minds? In Sergio Della Sala (Ed.), *Mind myths: Exploring popular assumptions about the mind and brain.* Chichester, England: Wiley.

Corballis, Paul M.; Funnell, Margaret G.; & Gazzaniga, Michael S. (2002). Hemispheric asymmetries for simple visual judgments in the split brain. *Neuropsychologia, 40,* 401–410.

Coren, Stanley. (1992). *The left-hander syndrome: The causes and consequences of left-handedness.* New York: Free Press.

Coren, Stanley. (1994). Twinning is associated with an increased risk of left-handedness and inverted writing hand posture. *Early Human Development, 40*(1), 23–27.

Corkin, Suzanne. (1984). Lasting consequences of bilateral medial temporal lobectomy: Clinical course and experimental findings in H.M. *Seminars in Neurology, 4,* 249–259.

Corkin, Suzanne. (2002). What's new with the amnesic patient H.M.? *Nature Reviews Neuroscience, 3,* 153–160.

Corrigan, Patrick W. (1998). The impact of stigma on severe mental illness. *Cognitive and Behavioral Practice, 5,* 201–222.

Corsini, Raymond J. (1957). *Non-verbal reasoning test*. Park Ridge, IL: London House Press.

Corvin, Aiden; O'Mahony, Ed; O'Regan, Myra; & others. (2001). Cigarette smoking and psychotic symptoms in bipolar affective disorder. *British Journal of Psychiatry, 179*, 35–38.

Coryell, William; Akiskal, Hagop S.; Leon, Andrew C.; Winokur, George; Maser, John D.; Mueller, Timothy I.; & Keller, Martin B. (1994). The time course of nonchronic major depressive disorder: Uniformity across episodes and samples. *Archives of General Psychiatry, 51*, 405–410.

Cosmides, Leda; Tooby, John; & Barkow, Jerome H. (1992). Introduction: Evolutionary psychology and conceptual integration. In Jerome H. Barkow, Leda Cosmides, & John Tooby (Eds.), *The adapted mind: Evolutionary psychology and the role of culture*. New York: Oxford University Press.

Costa, Paul T., Jr., & McCrae, Robert R. (1989). Personality continuity and the changes of adult life. In Martha Storandt & Gary R. VandenBos (Eds.), *The adult years: Continuity and change*. Washington, DC: American Psychological Association.

Courage, Mary L., & Howe, Mark L. (2002). From infant to child: The dynamics of cognitive change in the second year of life. *Psychological Bulletin, 128*, 250–277.

Cowan, Nelson; Chen, Zhijian; & Rouder, Jeffrey N. (2004). Constant capacity in an immediate serial-recall task: A logical sequel to Miller (1956). *Psychological Science, 15*, 634–640.

Coyne, James C., & Downey, Geraldine. (1991). Social factors and psychopathology: Stress, social support, and coping processes. *Annual Review of Psychology, 42*, 401–425.

Coyne, James C.; Ellard, John H.; & Smith, David A. F. (1990). Social support, interdependence, and the dilemmas of helping. In Barbara R. Sarason, Irwin G. Sarason, & Gregory R. Pierce (Eds.), *Social support: An interactional view*. New York: Wiley.

Crabtree, Steve. (2003, September 16). Grand theft of innocence? Teens and video games. The Gallup Organization. Retrieved July 16, 2004 from www.gallup.com/content/default.asp?ci=9253

Craik, Fergus I. M.; Govoni, Richard; Naveh-Benjamin, Moshe; & Anderson, Nicole D. (1996). The effects of divided attention on encoding and retrieval processes in human memory. *Journal of Experimental Psychology: General, 125*, 159–180.

Craske, Michelle G.; Miller, Patricia P.; Rotunda, Robert; & Barlow, David H. (1990). A descriptive report of initial unexpected panic attacks in minimal and extensive avoiders. *Behavior Research and Therapy, 28*, 395–400.

Craske, Michelle G., & Waters, Allison M. (2005). Panic disorder, phobias, and generalized anxiety disorder. *Annual Review of Clinical Psychology, 1*, 197–225.

Crews, Frederick. (1984/1986). The Freudian way of knowledge. In *Skeptical engagements*. New York: Oxford University Press.

Crews, Frederick. (1995). Confessions of a Freud basher. In Frederick Crews (Ed.), *The memory wars: Freud's legacy in dispute*. New York: New York Review of Books.

Crews, Frederick. (1996). The verdict on Freud. *Psychological Science, 7*, 63–68.

Criswell, Eleanor. (2003). A challenge to humanistic psychology in the 21st century. *Journal of Humanistic Psychology, 43*, 42–52.

Critchley, Hugo D.; Wiens, Stefan; Rotshtein, Pia; Ohman, Arne; & Dolan, Raymond J. (2004). Neural systems supporting interoceptive awareness. *Nature Neuroscience, 7*, 189–195.

Croft, Rodney J.; Klugman, Anthony; Baldeweg, Torsten; & Gruzelier, John H. (2001). Electrophysiological evidence of serotonergic impairment in long-term MDMA ("Ecstasy") users. *American Journal of Psychiatry, 158*, 1687–1692.

Croizet, Jean-Claude, & Claire, Theresa. (1998). Extending the concept of stereotype and threat to social class: The intellectual underperformance of students from low socioeconomic backgrounds. *Personality and Social Psychology Bulletin, 24*, 588–654.

Crosscope-Happel, Cindy; Hutchins, David E.; & others. (2000). Male anorexia nervosa: A new focus. *Journal of Mental Health Counseling, 22*, 365–370.

Cumming, Elaine, & Henry, William. (1961). *Growing old: The process of disengagement*. New York: Basic Books.

Cummings, Donald E.; Purnell, Jonathan Q.; Frayo, R. Scott; Schmidova, K.; Wisse, B. E.; & Weigle, David S. (2001). A preprandial rise in plasma ghrelin levels suggests a role in meal initiation in humans. *Diabetes, 50*, 1714–1719.

Cummings, Donald E.; Weigle, David S.; Frayo, R. Scott; Breen, Patricia A.; Ma, Marina K.; Dellinger, E. Patchen; & Purnell, Jonathan Q. (2002). Plasma ghrelin levels after diet-induced weight loss or gastric bypass surgery. *New England Journal of Medicine, 346*, 1623–1630.

Cunningham, Jacqueline L. (1997). Alfred Binet and the quest for testing higher mental functioning. In Wolfgang G. Bringmann, Helmut E. Lück, Rudolf Miller, & Charles E. Early (Eds.), *A pictorial history of psychology*. Chicago: Quintessence.

Curci, Antonietta; Luminet, Olivier; Finkenauer, Catrin; & Gisle, Lydia. (2001). Flashbulb memories in social groups: A comparative test-retest study of the memory of French President Mitterand's death in a French and a Belgian group. *Memory, 9*, 81–101.

Czeisler, Charles A.; Shanahan, Theresa L.; Klerman, Elizabeth B.; Martens, Heinz; Brotman, Daniel J.; Emens, Jonathan S.; & others. (1995). Suppression of melatonin secretion in some blind patients by exposure to bright light. *New England Journal of Medicine, 332*(1), 6–11.

Czienskowski, Uwe, & Giljohann, Stefanie. (2002). Intimacy, concreteness, and the "self-reference effect." *Experimental Psychology, 49*, 73–79.

Dahl, Ronald. (2003, Summer). Beyond raging hormones: The tinderbox in the teenage brain. *Cerebrum, 5*(3), 7–22.

Dalgleish, Tim. (2004). The emotional brain. *Nature Reviews Neuroscience, 5*, 582–589.

Damasio, Antonio R. (1994). *Descartes' error: Emotion, reason, and the human brain*. New York: Putnam.

Damasio, Antonio R.; Grabowski, Thomas J.; Bechara, Antoine; Damasio, Hanna; Ponto, Laura L. B.; Parvizi, Josef; & Hichwa, Richard D. (2000). Subcortical and cortical brain activity during the feeling of self-generated emotions. *Nature Neuroscience, 3*, 1049–1056.

Damasio, Hanna; Grabowski, Thomas; Frank, Randle; Galaburda, Albert M.; & Damasio, Antonio R. (1994, May 20). The return of Phineas Gage: Clues about the brain from the skull of a famous patient. *Science, 264*, 1102–1105.

Dansereau, Fred; Graen, George; & Haga, William. (1975). A vertical dyad linkage approach to leadership within formal organizations. *Organizational Behavior and Human Performance, 13*, 46–78.

Darley, John M. (1992). Social organization for the production of evil [Book review essay]. *Psychological Inquiry, 3*, 199–218.

Darwin, Charles R. (1859/1998). *On the origin of species by means of natural selection*. New York: Modern Library.

Darwin, Charles R. (1871/1981). *The descent of man, and selection in relation to sex* (Introductions by John T. Bonner & Robert M. May). Princeton, NJ: Princeton University Press.

Darwin, Charles. (1872/1998). *The expression of emotions in man and animals* (3rd ed.). New York: Appleton.

Davey, Graham C. L. (1993). Factors influencing self-rated fear to a novel animal. *Cognition & Emotion, 7*, 461–471.

Davidson, Jonathan R. T. (2001). Recognition and treatment of posttraumatic stress disorder. *Journal of the American Medical Association, 286*, 584–588.

Davidson, Julian M., & Myers, L. S. (1988). Endocrine factors in sexual psychophysiology. In Raymond C. Rosen & J. Gayle Beck (Eds.), *Patterns of sexual arousal: Psychophysiological processes and clinical applications*. New York: Guilford Press.

Davidson, Paul R., & Parker, Kevin C. H. (2001). Eye movement desensitization and reprocessing (EMDR): A meta-analysis. *Journal of Consulting and Clinical Psychology, 69*, 305–316.

Davidson, Richard J. (2002). Toward a biology of positive affect and compassion. In Richard J. Davidson & Anne Harrington (Eds.), *Visions of compassion: Western scientists and Tibetan*

Buddhists examine human nature. New York: Oxford University Press.

Davidson, Richard J.; Kabat-Zinn, Jon; Schumacher, Jessica; & others. (2003). Alterations in brain and immune function produced by mindfulness meditation. *Psychosomatic Medicine, 65,* 564–570.

Davidson, Terry L. (2000). Pavlovian occasion setting: A link between physiological change and appetitive behavior. *Appetite, 35,* 271–272.

Davis, Adrian, & Annett, Marian. (1994). Handedness as a function of twinning, age, and sex. *Cortex, 30*(1), 105–111.

Davis, Mary Helen; Drogin, Eric Y.; & Wright, Jesse H. (1995). Therapist-patient sexual intimacy: A guide for the subsequent therapist. *Journal of Psychotherapy Practice and Research, 4,* 140–149.

Davis, Michael, & Whalen, Paul J. (2001). The amygdala: Vigilance and emotion. *Molecular Psychiatry, 6,* 13–14.

Davis, Susan. (2000). Testosterone and sexual desire in women. *Journal of Sex Education and Therapy, 25,* 25–32.

Dawson, Deborah A. (1991). Family structure and children's health and well-being: Data from the 1988 national health interview study on child health. *Journal of Marriage and the Family, 53,* 573–584.

Dawson, Drew. (1995). Improving adaptation to simulated night shift: Timed exposure to bright light versus daytime melatonin administration. *Sleep, 18,* 11–18.

Dawson, Drew, & Campbell, Scott S. (1991). Time exposure to bright light improves sleep and alertness during simulated night shifts. *Sleep, 14,* 511–516.

Dean, Geoffrey. (1992). The bottom line: Effect size. In Barry Beyerstein & Dale Beyerstein (Eds.), *The write stuff: Evaluations of graphology—The study of handwriting analysis.* Amherst, NY: Prometheus Books.

Dean, Geoffrey; Mather, Arthur; & Kelly, Ivan W. (1996). Astrology. In Gordon Stein (Ed.), *The encyclopedia of the paranormal.* Buffalo, NY: Prometheus Books.

DeBell, Camille, & Jones, R. Deniece. (1997). As good as it seems? A review of EMDR experimental research. *Professional Psychology: Research and Practice, 28,* 153–163.

de Castro, John M.; Bellisle, France; Dalix, Anne-Marie; & Pearcey, Sharon M. (2000). Palatability and intake relationships in free-living humans: Characterization and independence of influence in North Americans. *Physiology and Behavior, 70,* 343–350.

Deci, Edward L., & Ryan, Richard M. (1985). *Intrinsic motivation and self-determination in human behavior.* New York: Plenum Press.

Deci, Edward L., & Ryan, Richard M. (2000). The "what" and "why" of goal pursuits: Human needs and the self-determination of behavior. *Psychological Inquiry, 11,* 227–268.

Deckner, Deborah F.; Adamson, Lauren B.; & Bakeman, Roger. (2003). Rhythm in mother–infant interactions. *Infancy, 4,* 201–217.

de Fonseca, Fernando Rodriguez; Carrera, M.; Rocío A.; Navarro, Miguel; Koob, George F.; & Weiss, Friedbert. (1997, June 27). Activation of corticotropin-releasing factor in the limbic system during cannabinoid withdrawal. *Science, 276,* 2050–2054.

DeGeneres, Ellen. (2005). Quote from interview: "The Real Ellen Story—Coming Out Party London." Retrieved February 27, 2005, from http://www.ellen-degeneres.com/

DeLeon, Anthony; Patel, Nick C.; & Crismon, M. Lynn. (2004). Aripiprazole: A comprehensive review of its pharmacology, clinical efficacy, and tolerability. *Clinical Therapeutics, 26,* 649–666.

Delgado, Ann R. (2004). Order in Spanish colour words: Evidence against linguistic relativity. *British Journal of Psychology, 95,* 81–90.

DeLisi, Lynn E.; Maurizio, Andrea; Yost, Marla; Papparozzi, Carey F.; Fulchino, Cindy; Katz, Craig L.; & others. (2003). A survey of New Yorkers after the Sept. 11, 2001, terrorist attacks. *American Journal of Psychiatry, 160,* 780–783.

DeLisi, Richard, & Staudt, Joanne. (1980). Individual differences in college students' performance on formal operations tasks. *Journal of Applied Developmental Psychology, 1,* 163–174.

Dell, Paul F. (2001). Why the diagnostic criteria for dissociative identity disorder should be changed. *Journal of Trauma and Dissociation, 2,* 7–37.

DeLoache, Judy S. (1995). Early symbol understanding and use. In Douglas L. Medin (Ed.), *The psychology of learning and motivation: Advances in research and theory* (Vol. 33). New York: Academic Press.

DeLongis, Anita; Coyne, James C.; Dakof, C.; Folkman, Susan; & Lazarus, Richard S. (1982). Relationship of daily hassles, uplifts, and major life events to health status. *Health Psychology, 1,* 119–136.

DeLongis, Anita; Folkman, Susan; & Lazarus, Richard S. (1988). The impact of stress on health and mood: Psychological and social resources as mediators. *Journal of Personality and Social Psychology, 54,* 486–495.

Delprato, Dennis J., & Midgley, Bryan D. (1992). Some fundamentals of B. F. Skinner's behaviorism. *American Psychologist, 47,* 1507–1520.

Dement, William C., & Pelayo, Rafael. (1997). Public health impact and treatment of insomnia. *European Psychiatry, 12,* 31s–39s.

de Rivera, Joseph. (2000). Understanding persons who repudiate memories recovered in therapy. *Professional Psychology: Research and Practice, 31,* 378–386.

Deutsch, Morton, & Gerard, Harold B. (1955). A study of normative and informational social influence upon individual judgment. *Journal of Abnormal and Social Psychology, 51,* 629–636.

DeValois, Russell L., & DeValois, Karen K. (1975). Neural coding of color. In E. C. Carterette & M. P. Friedman (Eds.), *Handbook of perception* (Vol. 5). New York: Academic Press.

Devanand, Davangere P.; Dwork, Andrew J.; Hutchinson, Edward R.; Bolwig, Tom G.; & Sackeim, Harold A. (1994). Does ECT alter brain structure? *American Journal of Psychiatry, 151,* 957–970.

Devane, William A.; Hanus, L.; Breuer, A.; Pertwee, R. G.; Stevenson, L. A.; Griffin, G.; & others. (1992). Isolation and structure of a brain constituent that binds to the cannabinoid receptor. *Science, 258,* 1946–1949.

De Vos, George Alphonse. (1992). *Social cohesion and alienation: Minorities in the United States and Japan.* Boulder, CO: Westview Press.

De Vos, George Alphonse, & Wagatsuma, Hiroshi. (1967). *Japan's invisible race: Caste in culture and personality.* Berkeley and Los Angeles: University of California Press.

De Vries, J.; Strubbe, J.H.; Wildering, W.C.; Gorter J. A.; & Prins A. J. (1993). Patterns of body temperature during feeding in rats under varying ambient temperatures. *Physiology and Behavior, 53,* 229–235.

de Waal, Frans B. M. (1995, March). Bonobo sex and society. *Scientific American, 271,* 82–88.

de Waal, Frans B. M., & Lanting, Frans. (1998). *Bonobo: The forgotten ape.* Berkeley: University of California Press.

Dewsbury, Donald A. (1998). Celebrating E. L. Thorndike a century after animal intelligence. *American Psychologist, 53,* 1121–1124.

Dewsbury, Donald A. (2000). Introduction: Snapshots of psychology circa 1900. *American Psychologist, 55,* 255–259.

Diamond, Lisa M. (1998). Development of sexual orientation among adolescent and young adult women. *Developmental Psychology, 34,* 1085–1095.

Diamond, Marian Cleeves; Scheibel, Arnold B.; Murphy, Greer M.; & Harvey, Thomas. (1985). On the brain of a scientist: Albert Einstein. *Experimental Neurology, 88,* 198–204.

Dick, Danielle M., & Rose, Richard J. (2002). Behavior genetics: What's new? What's next? *Current Directions in Psychological Science, 11,* 70–74.

Dickerson, Sally S., & Kemeny, Margaret E. (2004). Acute stressors and cortisol responses: A theoretical integration and synthesis of laboratory research. *Psychological Bulletin, 130,* 355–391.

Dickinson, Anthony. (1997). Bolles's psychological syllogism. In Mark E. Bouton & Michael S. Fanselow (Eds.), *Learning, motivation, and cognition: The functional behaviorism of*

Robert C. Bolles. Washington, DC: American Psychological Association.

Dickinson, Anthony, & Balleine, Bernard W. (2000). Causal cognition and goal-directed action. In Cecilia Heyes & Ludwig Huber (Eds.), *The evolution of cognition*. Cambridge, MA: MIT Press.

Dictionary of occupational titles. (1991). Washington, DC: U. S. Government Printing Office.

Dies, Robert R. (1993). Research on group psychotherapy: Overview and clinical applications. In Anne Alonso & Hillel I. Swiller (Eds.), *Group therapy in clinical practice*. Washington, DC: American Psychiatric Press.

Dillard, James Price. (1991). The current status of research on sequential-request compliance techniques. *Personality and Social Psychology Bulletin, 17*, 283–288.

Dillbeck, Michael C., & Orme-Johnson, David W. (1987). Physiological differences between transcendental meditation and rest. *American Psychologist, 42*, 879–881.

Dinsmoor, James A. (1992). Setting the record straight: The social views of B. F. Skinner. *American Psychologist, 47*, 1454–1463.

Dittman, Melissa. (2003, February). Psychology's first prescribers. *Monitor on Psychology, 34*, 36–39.

Dixon, John F., & Hokin, Lowell E. (1998, July 7). Lithium acutely inhibits and chronically up-regulates and stabilizes glutamate by presynaptic nerve endings in mouse cerebral cortex. *Proceedings of the National Academy of Sciences, USA, 95*, 8363–8368.

Djordjevic, Jelena; Zatorre, R. J.; Petrides, M.; & Jones-Gotman, M. (2004). The mind's nose: Effects of odor and visual imagery on odor detection. *Psychological Science, 15*, 143–148.

Dohrenwend, Bruce P.; Raphael, Karen G.; Schwartz, Sharon; Stueve, Ann; & Skodol, Andrew. (1993). The structured event probe and narrative rating method for measuring stressful life events. In Leo Goldberger & Shlomo Breznitz (Eds.), *Handbook of stress: Theoretical and clinical aspects* (2nd ed.). New York: Free Press.

Domhoff, G. William. (1993). The repetition of dreams and dream elements: A possible clue to a function of dreams. In Alan Moffitt, Milton Kramer, & Robert Hoffman (Eds.), *The functions of dreaming*. Albany: State University of New York Press.

Domhoff, G. William. (1996). *Finding meaning in dreams: A quantitative approach*. New York and London: Plenum Press.

Domhoff, G. William. (1999). Drawing theoretical implications from descriptive empirical findings on dream content. *Dreaming, 9*, 201–210.

Domhoff, G. William. (2003). *The scientific study of dreams: Neural networks, cognitive development, and content analysis*. Washington, DC: American Psychological Association.

Dornbusch, Sanford M.; Glasgow, Kristan L.; & Lin, I-Chun. (1996). The social structure of schooling. *Annual Review of Psychology, 47*, 401–429.

Dornbusch, Sanford M.; Ritter, Philip L.; Leiderman, P. Herbert; Roberts, Donald F.; & Fraleigh, Michael J. (1987). The relation of parenting style to adolescent school performance. *Child Development, 58*, 1244–1257.

Dovidio, John F. (1984). Helping behavior and altruism: An empirical and conceptual overview. *Advances in Experimental Social Psychology, 17*, 361–427.

Dovidio, John F.; Piliavin, Jane A.; Gaertner, Samuel L.; Schroeder, David A.; & Clark, Russell D., III. (1991). The arousal: Cost-reward model and the process of intervention: A review of the evidence. In Margaret S. Clark (Ed.), *Prosocial behavior: Vol. 12. Review of personality and social psychology*. Newbury Park, CA: Sage.

Draganski, Bogdan; Gaser, Christian; Busch, Volker; Schuierer, Gerhard; Bogdahn, Ulrich; & May, Arne. (2004). Neuroplasticity: Changes in grey matter induced by training. *Nature, 427*, 311–312.

DSM-IV-TR. (2000). *Diagnostic and statistical manual of mental disorders* (4th ed., Text Revision). Washington, DC: American Psychiatric Association.

Duclos, Sandra E.; Laird, James D.; Schneider, Eric; Sexter, Melissa; Stern, Lisa; & Van Lighten, Lisa. (1989). Emotion-specific effects of facial expressions and postures on emotional experience. *Journal of Personality and Social Psychology, 57*, 100–108.

Dudai, Yadin. (2004). The neurobiology of consolidations, or, How stable is the engram? *Annual Review of Psychology, 55*, 51–86.

Dufresne, Todd. (2003). *Killing Freud: Twentieth-century culture and the death of psychoanalysis*. New York: Continuum.

Dulac, Catherine, & Torello, A. Thomas. (2003). Molecular detection of pheromone signals in mammals: From genes to behaviour. *Nature Reviews Neuroscience, 4*, 551–562.

Duncker, Karl. (1929/1967). Induced motion. In Willis D. Ellis (Ed.), *Source book of Gestalt psychology*. New York: Humanities Press.

Duncker, Karl. (1945). On problem solving. *Psychological Monographs, 58*(Whole No. 270).

Dunivin, Debra. (2003a). Experiences of a DoD prescribing psychology: A personal experience. In Morgan T. Sammons, Ruth Ullmann Paige, & Ronald F. Levant (Eds.), *Prescriptive authority for psychologists: A history and guide*. Washington, DC: American Psychological Association.

Dunivin, Debra. (2003b). Quoted in Dittman, Melissa: "Psychology's first prescribers." *Monitor on Psychology, 34*, 38.

Dunkel-Schetter, Christine; Feinstein, Lawrence G.; Taylor, Shelley E.; & Falke, Roberta L. (1992). Patterns of coping with cancer. *Health Psychology, 11*, 79–87.

Dunn, Judy, & Plomin, Robert. (1990). *Separate Lives: Why siblings are so different*. New York: Basic Books.

Dunning, David; Leuenberger, Ann; & Sherman, David A. (1995). A new look at motivated inference: Are self-serving theories of success a product of motivational forces? *Journal of Personality and Social Psychology, 69*, 58–68.

Durston, Sarah; Hulshoff Pol, Hilleke E.; Casey, B.J.; Giedd, Jay N.; Buitelaar, Jan K.; & van Engeland, Herman. (2001). Anatomical MRI of the developing brain: What have we learned? *Journal of the American Academy of Child and Adolescent Psychiatry, 40*, 1012–1020.

Dusenberry, David B. (1992). *Sensory ecology: How organisms acquire and respond to information*. New York: Freeman.

Eagle, Morris, N. (1959). The effects of subliminal stimuli of aggressive content upon conscious cognition. *Journal of Personality, 23*, 48–52.

Eagle, Morris N., & Wolitzky, David L. (1992). Psychoanalytic theories of psychotherapy. In Donald K. Freedheim (Ed.), *History of psychotherapy: A century of change*. Washington, DC: American Psychological Association.

Eagly, Alice H. (1995a). The science and politics of comparing women and men. *American Psychologist, 50*, 145–158.

Eagly, Alice H. (1995b). Reflections on the commenters' views. *American Psychologist, 50*, 169–171.

Eagly, Alice H.; Ashmore, Richard D.; Makhijani, Mona G.; & Longo, Laura C. (1991). What is beautiful is good, but . . . : A meta-analytic review of research on the physical attractiveness stereotype. *Psychological Bulletin, 110*, 109–128.

Eagly, Alice H., & Chaiken, Shelly. (1998). Attitude structure and function. In Daniel T. Gilbert, Susan T. Fiske, & Gardner Lindzey (Eds.), *The handbook of social psychology* (4th ed., Vol. 1). New York: McGraw-Hill.

Eastman, Kenneth K. (1994). In the eyes of the beholder: An attributional approach to ingratiation and organizational citizenship behavior. *Academy of Management Journal, 37*, 1379–1391.

Ebbinghaus, Hermann. (1885/1987). *Memory: A contribution to experimental psychology* (Henry A. Ruger & Clara E. Bussenius, Trans.). New York: Dover.

Edelman, Lauren B.; Erlanger, Howard S.; & Lande, John. (1993). Informal dispute resolution: The transformation of civil rights in the workplace. *Law & Society Review, 27*, 497–534.

Edwards, Anthony G. P., & Armitage, Peter. (1992). An experiment to test the discriminating ability of graphologists. *Personality and Individual Differences, 13*, 69–74.

Edwards, Randall. (1995a, February). Future demands culturally diverse education. *APA Monitor, 26*, 43.

Edwards, Randall. (1995b, September). Psychologists foster the new definition of family. *APA Monitor, 26*, 38.

Egan, Gerard. (1994). *The skilled helper: A problem-management approach to helping* (5th ed.). Pacific Grove, CA: Brooks/Cole.

Egan, Susan K., & Perry, David G. (2001). Gender identity: A multidimensional analysis with implications for psychosocial adjustment. *Developmental Psychology, 37*, 451–463.

Ehlers, Anke, & Breuer, Peter. (1992). Increased cardiac awareness in panic disorder. *Journal of Abnormal Psychology, 101*, 371–382.

Eich, Eric, & Forgas, Joseph P. (2003). Mood, cognition, and memory. In Alice F. Healy & Robert W. Proctor (Eds.), *Handbook of psychology: Experimental psychology* (Vol. 4, pp. 61–83). New York: Wiley.

Eich, Eric; Macaulay, Dawn; & Lam, Raymond W. (1997). Mania, depression, and mood dependent memory. *Cognition & Emotion, 11*, 607–618.

Einstein, Danielle, & Menzies, Ross G. (2004). The presence of magical thinking in obsessive compulsive disorder. *Behavior Research and Therapy, 42*, 539–549.

Eisenberg, Nancy. (1991). Meta-analytic contributions to the literature on prosocial behavior. *Personality and Social Psychology Bulletin, 17*, 273–284.

Eisenberger, Robert; Armeli, Stephen; & Pretz, Jean. (1998). Can the promise of reward increase creativity? *Journal of Personality and Social Psychology, 74*, 704–714.

Eisenberger, Robert, & Cameron, Judy. (1996). Detrimental effects of reward: Reality or myth? *American Psychologist, 51*, 1153–1166.

Ekman, Paul. (1980). *The face of man.* New York: Garland.

Ekman, Paul. (1982). *Emotion in the human face* (2nd ed.). New York: Cambridge University Press.

Ekman, Paul. (1992a). Are there basic emotions? *Psychological Review, 99*, 550–553.

Ekman, Paul. (1992b). Facial expressions of emotion: New findings, new questions. *Psychological Science, 3*, 34–38.

Ekman, Paul. (1993). Facial expression and emotion. *American Psychologist, 48*, 384–392.

Ekman, Paul. (1994a). Are there basic emotions? In Paul Ekman & Richard J. Davidson (Eds.), *The nature of emotion: Fundamental questions.* New York: Oxford University Press.

Ekman, Paul. (1994b). Strong evidence for universals in facial expressions: A reply to Russell's mistaken critique. *Psychological Bulletin, 115*, 268–287.

Ekman, Paul. (1998). Afterword. In Darwin, Charles (1872/1998), *The expression of the emotions in man and animals.* New York: Oxford University Press.

Ekman, Paul. (2003). *Emotions revealed.* New York: Henry Holt.

Ekman, Paul, & Davidson, Richard J. (1993). Voluntary smiling changes regional brain activity. *Psychological Science, 4*, 342–345.

Ekman, Paul, & Friesen, Wallace V. (1978). *Facial action coding system: A technique for the measurement of facial movement.* Palo Alto, CA: Consulting Psychologists Press.

Ekman, Paul; Friesen, Wallace V.; O'Sullivan, Maureen; Chan, Anthony; Diacoyanni-Tarlatzis, Irene; Heider, Karl; & others. (1987). Universal and cultural differences in the judgments of facial expressions of emotion. *Journal of Personality and Social Psychology, 53*, 712–717.

Elfenbein, Hillary Anger, & Ambady, Nalini. (2002). On the universality and specificity of emotion recognition: A meta-analysis. *Psychological Bulletin, 128*, 203–235.

Elkin, Irene; Gibbons, Robert D.; Shea, M. Tracie; & Shaw, Brian F. (1996). Science is not a trial (but it can sometimes be a tribulation). *Journal of Consulting and Clinical Psychology, 64*, 92–103.

Elkin, Irene; Shea, M. Tracie; Watkins, John T.; Imber, Stanley D.; Sotsky, Stuart M.; Collins, Joseph F.; & others. (1989). National Institute of Mental Health Treatment of Depression Collaborative Research Program: General effectiveness of treatments. *Archives of General Psychiatry, 46*, 971–982.

Elliott, Robert, & Greenberg, Leslie S. (2002). Process—experiential psychotherapy. In David J. Cain & Julius Seeman (Eds.), *Humanistic psychotherapies: Handbook of research and practice.* Washington, DC: American Psychological Association.

Ellis, Albert. (1991). *Reason and emotion in psychotherapy.* New York: Carol.

Ellis, Albert. (1993). Reflections on rational-emotive therapy. *Journal of Consulting and Clinical Psychology, 61*, 199–201.

Ellis, Albert, & Bernard, Michael E. (1985). What is rational-emotive therapy (RET)? In Albert Ellis & Michael E. Bernard (Eds.), *Clinical applications of rational-emotive therapy.* New York: Plenum Press.

Ellis, Albert, & Harper, Robert A. (1975). *A new guide to rational living.* Hollywood, CA: Wilshire Book Company.

Ellis, Bruce J. (2004). Timing of pubertal maturation in girls: An integrated life history approach. *Psychological Bulletin, 130*, 920–958.

Ellis, Bruce J., & Garber, Judy. (2000). Psychosocial antecedents of variation in girls' pubertal timing: Maternal depression, stepfather presence, and marital and family stress. *Child Development, 71*, 485–501.

EMDR Institute. (2001). Overview and general description of EMDR. Retrieved October 15, 2001, from http://www.emdr.com/general.htm

Emmelkamp, Paul M. G. (2004). Behavior therapy with adults. In Michael J. Lambert (Ed.), *Bergin and Garfield's handbook of psychotherapy and behavior change* (5th ed.). New York: Wiley.

Emmons, Robert, & King, Laura. (1988). Conflict among personal strivings: Immediate and long-term implications for psychological and physical well-being. *Journal of Personality and Social Psychology, 54*, 1040–1048.

Empson, Jacob. (2002). *Sleep and dreaming* (3rd ed.). New York: Palgrave/St. Martin's Press.

Engel, Stephen A. (1999). Using neuroimaging to measure mental representations: Finding color-opponent neurons in visual cortex. *Current Directions in Psychological Science, 8*, 23–27.

England, Lynndie. (2004, May 12). Quoted in: "Army private 'ordered to pose'." *Cable News Network (CNN).* Accessed on 5/13/04 from http://www.cnn.com/2004/US/05/12/prisoner.abuse.england.ap/index.html

England, Lynndie. (2005, October 2). Quoted in: "Behind the Abu Ghraib photos." *Dateline NBC.* Accessed on November 30, 2005 from http://msnbc.msn.com/id/9532670/

English, Horace B. (1929). Three cases of the "conditioned fear response." *Journal of Abnormal and Social Psychology, 24*, 221–225.

Ensel, Walter M., & Lin, Nan. (2004). Physical fitness and the stress process. *Journal of Community Psychology, 32*, 81–101.

Epley, Nicholas; Savitsky, Kenneth; & Kachelski, Robert A. (1999, September/October). What every skeptic should know about subliminal persuasion. *Skeptical Inquirer, 23*(5), 40–45, 58.

Epstein, Mark. (1995). *Thoughts without a thinker: Psychotherapy from a Buddhist perspective.* New York: Basic Books.

Epstein, Russell, & Kanwisher, Nancy. (1998). A cortical representation of the local visual environment. *Nature, 392*, 598–601.

Epstein, Seymour. (1982). Conflict and stress. In Leo Goldberger & Shlomo Breznitz (Eds.), *Handbook of stress: Theoretical and clinical aspects.* New York: Free Press.

Ericsson, K. Anders, & Kintsch, Walter. (1995). Long-term working memory. *Psychological Review, 102*, 211–245.

Erikson, Erik H. (1964a). *Childhood and society* (Rev. ed.). New York: Norton.

Erikson, Erik H. (1964b). *Insight and responsibility.* New York: Norton.

Erikson, Erik H. (1968). *Identity: Youth and crisis.* New York: Norton.

Erikson, Erik H. (1982). *The life cycle completed: A review.* New York: Norton.

Erikson, Erik H.; Erikson, Joan M.; & Kivnick, Helen Q. (1986). *Vital involvement in old age: The experience of old age in our time.* New York: Norton.

Eriksson, Cynthia B.; Vande Kemp, Hendrika; & others. (2001). Trauma exposure and PTSD symptoms in international relief and development personnel. *Journal of Traumatic Stress, 14,* 205–219.

Eriksson, Peter S.; Perfilieva, Ekaterina; Björk-Eriksson, Thomas; Alborn, Ann-Marie; Nordborg, Claes; Peterson, Daniel A.; & Gage, Fred A. (1998). Neurogenesis in the adult hippocampus. *Nature Medicine, 4,* 1313–1317.

Eronen, Markku; Angermeyer, Matthias C.; & Schulze, Beate. (1998). The psychiatric epidemiology of violent behaviour. *Social Psychiatry and Psychiatric Epidemiology, 33*(Suppl. 1), S13–S23.

Esch, Harald E.; Zhang, Shaowu; Srinivasan, Mandyan V.; & Tautz, Juergen. (2001). Honeybee dances communicate distances measured by optic flow. *Nature, 411,* 581–583.

Esses, Victoria M.; Haddock, Geoffrey; & Zanna, Mark P. (1993). Values, stereotypes, and emotions as determinants of intergroup attitudes. In Diane M. Mackie & David L. Hamilton (Eds.), *Affect, cognition, and stereotyping: Interactive processes in group perception.* San Diego, CA: Academic Press.

Estes, William K., & Skinner, B. F. (1941). Some quantitative properties of anxiety. *Journal of Experimental Psychology, 29,* 390–400.

Etscorn, Frank, & Stephens, Ronald. (1973). Establishment of conditioned taste aversions with a 24-hour CS-US interval. *Physiological Psychology, 1,* 251–253.

Evans, Gary W.; Bullinger, Monika; & Hygge, Staffan. (1998). Chronic noise exposure and physiological response: A prospective study of children living under environmental stress. *Psychological Science, 9,* 75–77.

Evans, Rand B. (1991). E. B. Titchener on scientific psychology and technology. In Gregory A. Kimble, Michael Wertheimer, & Charlotte White (Eds.), *Portraits of pioneers in psychology* (Vol. 1). Washington, DC: American Psychological Association.

Evans, Rand B. (1999a, December). Psychology continues to redefine itself. *APA Monitor, 30*(11), 15.

Evans, Rand B. (1999b, December). Cognitive psychology sees a return to power. *APA Monitor, 30*(11), 20.

Evans, Rand B., & Rilling, Mark. (2000). How the challenge of explaining learning influenced the origins and development of John B. Watson's behaviorism. *American Journal of Psychology, 113,* 275–301.

Exner, John E., Jr. (1993). *The Rorschach: A comprehensive system* (3rd ed., Vol. 1). New York: Wiley.

Eysenck, Hans J. (1952). The effects of psychotherapy: An evaluation. *Journal of Consulting Psychology, 16,* 319–324.

Eysenck, Hans J. (1982). *Personality, genetics, and behavior.* New York: Praeger.

Eysenck, Hans J. (1985). *Decline and fall of the Freudian empire.* New York: Penguin Books.

Eysenck, Hans J. (1990). Biological dimensions of personality. In Lawrence A. Pervin (Ed.), *Handbook of personality: Theory and research.* New York: Guilford Press.

Eysenck, Hans J. (1994). The outcome problem in psychotherapy: What have we learned? *Behavior Research and Therapy, 32,* 447–495.

Eysenck, Hans J., & Eysenck, Sybil B. G. (1975). *Psychoticism as a dimension of personality.* London: Hodder & Stoughton.

Fagot, Beverly I., & Hagan, Richard. (1991). Observations of parent reactions to sex-stereotyped behaviors: Age and sex effects. *Child Development, 62,* 617–628.

Fairburn, Christopher G. (1995). Physiology of anorexia nervosa. In Kelly D. Brownell & Christopher G. Fairburn (Eds.), *Eating disorders and obesity: A comprehensive handbook.* New York: Guilford Press.

Fancher, Raymond E. (1973). *Psychoanalytic psychology: The development of Freud's thought.* New York: Norton.

Fancher, Raymond E. (1996). *Pioneers of psychology* (3rd ed.). New York: Norton.

Fanous, Ayman H.; van den Oord, Edwin J.; Riley, Brien P.; Aggen, Steven H.; Neale, Michael C.; O'Neill, F. Anthony; Walsh, Dermot; & Kendler, Kenneth S. (2005). Relationships between a high-risk haplotype in the *DTNBP1* (dysbindin) gene and clinical features of schizophrenia. *American Journal of Psychiatry, 162,* 1824–1832.

Fantz, Robert L. (1961, May). The origin of form perception. *Scientific American, 204,* 66–72.

Fantz, Robert L.; Ordy, J. M.; & Udelf, M. S. (1962). Maturation of pattern vision in infants during the first six months. *Journal of Comparative and Physiological Psychology, 55,* 907–917.

Farah, Martha J. (1995). The neural bases of mental imagery. In Michael S. Gazzaniga (Ed.), *The cognitive neurosciences.* Cambridge, MA: MIT Press.

Farberman, Rhea K. (1999). What the media needs from news sources. In Lita Linzer Schwartz (Ed.), *Psychology and the media: A second look.* Washington, DC: American Psychological Association.

Farberman, Rhea K. (2003). Strategies for successful interactions with the news media. In Mitchell J. Prinstein & Marcus D. Patterson (Eds.), *The portable mentor: Expert guide to a successful career in psychology.* New York: Kluwer Academic/Plenum Press.

Fastovsky, Natasha; Teitelbaum, Alexander; & others. (2000). The Jerusalem syndrome. *Psychiatric Services, 51,* 1052.

Fawcett, Jan. (1994). Antidepressants: Partial response in chronic depression. *British Journal of Psychiatry, 165*(Suppl. 26), 37–41.

Fazio, Russell H. (1990). Multiple processes by which attitudes guide behavior: The MODE model as an integrative framework. In Mark P. Zanna (Ed.), *Advances in experimental social psychology* (Vol. 23). San Diego, CA: Academic Press.

Feeney, Brooke C., & Kirkpatrick, Lee A. (1996). Effects of adult attachment and presence of romantic partners on physiological responses to stress. *Journal of Personality and Social Psychology, 70,* 255–270.

Feingold, Alan. (1992). Good-looking people are not what we think. *Psychological Bulletin, 111,* 304–341.

Feldman, Larry B., & Powell, Sandra L. (1992). Integrating therapeutic modalities. In John C. Norcross & Marvin R. Goldfried (Eds.), *Handbook of psychotherapy integration.* New York: Basic Books.

Feldman Barrett, Lisa; Lane, Richard D.; Sechrest, Lee; & Schwartz, Gary E. (2000). Sex differences in emotional awareness. *Personality and Social Psychology Bulletin, 26,* 1027–1035.

Feldman Barrett, Lisa, & Russell, James A. (1999). The structure of current affect: Controversies and emerging consensus. *Current Directions in Psychological Science, 8,* 10–14.

Fernald, Ann. (1985). Four-month-old infants prefer to listen to motherese. *Infant Behavior and Development, 8,* 181–182.

Feske, Ulrike, & Goldstein, Alan J. (1997). Eye movement desensitization and reprocessing treatment for panic disorder: A controlled outcome and partial dismantling study. *Journal of Clinical and Consulting Psychology, 65,* 1026–1035.

Festinger, Leon. (1957). *A theory of cognitive dissonance.* Stanford, CA: Stanford University Press.

Festinger, Leon. (1962). Cognitive dissonance. *Scientific American, 207,* 93–99. (Reprinted in *Contemporary psychology: Readings from Scientific American,* 1971, San Francisco: Freeman)

Field, Clinton E.; Nash, Heather M.; Handwerk, Michael L.; & Friman, Patrick C. (2004). A modification of the token economy for nonresponsive youth in family-style residential care. *Behavior Modification, 28,* 438–457.

Field, Tiffany. (1996). Attachment and separation in young children. *Annual Review of Psychology, 47,* 541–561.

Field, Tiffany M.; Woodson, Robert; Greenberg, Reena; & Cohen, Debra. (1982). Discrimination and imitation of facial expressions by neonates. *Science, 218,* 179–182.

Fields, Howard L., & Levine, Jon D. (1984). Placebo analgesia: A role for endorphins. *Trends in Neuroscience, 7,* 271–273.

Fields, Jason. (2004, November). *America's families and living arrangements: 2003* (Current Population Reports, P20–553). Washington, DC: U.S. Government Printing Office. Retrieved March 1, 2005, from http://www.census.gov/prod/2004pubs/p20-553.pdf

Fillingim, Roger B. (2000). *Sex, gender, and pain: Progress in pain research and management* (Vol. 17). Seattle, WA: International Association for the Study of Pain, IASP Press.

Finch, Brian Karl, & Vega, William A. (2003). Acculturation stress, social support, and self-rated health among Latinos in California. *Journal of Immigrant Health, 5*, 109–117.

Fine, Ione (2002). Quoted in *The man who learnt to see*. BB2 Documentary.

Fine, Ione; Wade, Alex R.; Brewer, Alyssa A.; May, Michael G.; Goodman, Daniel F.; Boynton, Geoffrey M.; Wandell, Brian A.; & MacLeod, Donald I. A. (2003). Long-term deprivation affects visual perception and cortex. *Nature Neuroscience, 6*, 915–916.

Fischer, Agneta H.; Rodriguez-Mosquera, Patricia M.; van Vianen, Annelies E. M.; & Manstead, Antony S. R. (2004). Gender and culture differences in emotion. *Emotion, 4*, 87–94.

Fischer, Kurt W., & Hencke, Rebecca W. (1996). Infants' construction of actions in context: Piaget's contribution to research on early development. *Psychological Science, 7*, 204–210.

Fisher, Carrie. (2001). In her own words: Carrie Fisher interviewed by Robert Epstein, Ph.D. *Psychology Today, 34*, 36–37.

Fisher, Seymour, & Greenberg, Roger. (1996). *Freud scientifically appraised*. New York: Wiley.

Fishman, C. (2000). Moving toward a balanced work life. *Workforce, 79*, 38–42.

Fishman, Joshua A. (1960/1974). A systematization of the Whorfian hypothesis. In John W. Berry & P. R. Dasen (Eds.), *Culture and cognition: Readings in cross-cultural psychology*. London: Methuen.

Fiske, Susan T. (1993). Social cognition and perception. *Annual Review of Psychology, 44*, 155–194.

Fiske, Susan T. (1998). Stereotyping, prejudice, and discrimination. In Daniel T. Gilbert, Susan T. Fiske, & Gardner Lindzey (Eds.), *The handbook of social psychology* (4th ed., Vol. 2). New York: McGraw-Hill.

Fiske, Susan T.; Harris, Lasana T.; & Cuddy, Amy J. C. (2004). Why ordinary people torture enemy prisoners. *Science, 306*, 1482–1483.

Fiske, Susan T., & Neuberg, Steven L. (1990). A continuum of impression formation, from category-based to individuating processes: Influences of information and motivation on attention and interpretation. In Mark P. Zanna (Ed.), *Advances in experimental social psychology* (Vol. 23). San Diego, CA: Academic Press/Harcourt.

Fiske, Susan T., & Ruscher, Janet B. (1993). Negative interdependence and prejudice: Whence the affect? In Diane M. Mackie & David L. Hamilton (Eds.), *Affect, cognition, and stereotyping: Interactive processes in group perception*. San Diego, CA: Academic Press.

Fiske, Susan T., & Taylor, Shelley E. (1991). *Social cognition* (2nd ed.). New York: McGraw-Hill.

Fivush, Robyn, & Nelson, Katherine. (2004). Culture and language in the emergence of autobiographical memory. *Psychological Science, 15*, 573–577.

Flack, William F.; Laird, James D.; & Cavallaro, Lorraine A. (1999). Separate and combined effects of facial expressions and bodily postures on emotional feelings. *European Journal of Social Psychology, 29*, 203–217.

Flaten, Magne Arve, & Blumenthal, Terry D. (1999). Caffeine-associated stimuli elicit conditioned responses: An experimental model of the placebo effect. *Psychopharmacology, 145*, 105–112.

Flavell, John H. (1996). Piaget's legacy. *Psychological Science, 7*, 200-203.

Fleishman, Edwin A., & Harris, Edwin F. (1962). Patterns of leadership behavior related to employee grievances and turnover. *Personnel Psychology, 15*, 43–56.

Flynn, James R. (1994). IQ gains over time. In Robert J. Sternberg (Ed.), *Encyclopedia of human intelligence*. New York: Macmillan.

Flynn, James R. (1999). Searching for justice: The discovery of IQ gains over time. *American Psychologist, 54*, 5–20.

Foa, Edna B., & Meadows, Elizabeth A. (1997). Psychosocial treatments for posttraumatic stress disorder: A critical review. *Annual Review of Psychology, 48*, 449–480.

Foertsch, Julie, & Gernsbacher, Morton Ann. (1997). In search of gender neutrality: Is singular they a cognitively efficient substitute for generic he? *Psychological Science, 8*, 106–111.

Folkman, Susan, & Lazarus, Richard S. (1991). Coping and emotion. In Alan Monat & Richard S. Lazarus (Eds.), *Stress and coping: An anthology* (3rd ed.). New York: Columbia University Press.

Folkman, Susan, & Moskowitz, Judith Tedlie. (2000). Positive affect and the other side of coping. *American Psychologist, 55*, 647–654.

Foulkes, David. (1993). Data constraints on theorizing about dream function. In Alan Moffitt, Milton Kramer, & Robert Hoffman (Eds.), *The functions of dreaming*. Albany: State University of New York Press.

Foulkes, David. (1997). A contemporary neurobiology of dreaming? *Sleep Research Society Bulletin, 3*(1), 2–4.

Foulks, Edward F. (1991). Transcultural psychiatry and normal behavior. In Daniel Offer & Melvin Sabshin (Eds.), *The diversity of normal behavior: Further contributions to normatology*. New York: Basic Books.

Fowles, Don C. (1992). Schizophrenia: Diathesis-stress revisited. *Annual Review of Psychology, 43*, 303–336.

Fox, Michael J. (1998, December 2). Interview with Todd Gold. *People Magazine*. http://www.pathfinder.com/people/weekly/features/interview.html

Fox, Nathan A.; Kimmerly, Nancy L.; & Schafer, William D. (1991). Attachment to mother/Attachment to father: A meta-analysis. *Child Development, 62*, 210–225.

Fox, William M. (1982). Why we should abandon Maslow's need hierarchy theory. *Journal of Humanistic Education and Development, 21*, 29–32.

Francis, Darlene; Diorio, Josie; Liu, Dong; & Meaney, Michael J. (1999). Nongenomic transmission across generations of maternal behavior and stress responses in the rat. *Science, 286*, 1155–1158.

Frank, Barney. (1996, February 4). Quoted in Claudia Dreifus: "And then there was Frank." *New York Times Magazine*, pp. 22–25.

Frank, Mark G., & Stennett, Janine. (2001). The forced-choice paradigm and the perception of facial expressions of emotion. *Journal of Personality and Social Psychology, 80*, 75–85.

Frankenburg, Frances R. (1994). History of the development of antipsychotic medication. *Psychiatric Clinics of North America, 17*, 531–540.

Frankland, Paul W., & Bontempi, Bruno. (2005). The organization of recent and remote memories. *Nature Reviews Neuroscience, 6*, 119–130.

Franz, Carol E.; McClelland, David C.; & Weinberger, Joel. (1991). Childhood antecedents of conventional social accomplishment in midlife adults: A 36-year prospective study. *Journal of Personality and Social Psychology, 60*, 586–595.

Frederickson, N. (1968). *Organization climates and administrative performance*. Princeton, NJ: Educational Testing Service.

Fredrickson, Barbara L.; Tugade, Michele M.; Waugh, Christian E.; & Larkin, Gregory R. (2003). How good are positive motions in crises? A prospective study of resilience and emotions following the terrorist attacks on the United States on September 11, 2001. *Journal of Personality and Social Psychology, 84*, 365–376.

Freedman, Lawrence Z. (1983). *By reason of insanity: Essays on psychiatry and the law*. Wilmington, DE: Scholarly Resources.

Freeman, Lucy, & Strean, Herbert S. (1987). *Freud and women*. New York: Continuum.

Freud, Anna. (1946). *The ego and mechanisms of defence* (Cecil Baines, Trans.). New York: International Universities Press.

Freud, Sigmund. (1900/1974). The interpretation of dreams. In James Strachey (Ed.), *The standard edition of the complete psychological works of Sigmund Freud* (Vols. 4 & 5). London: Hogarth Press.

Freud, Sigmund. (1904/1965). *The psychopathology of everyday life* (Alan Tyson, Trans. & James Strachey, Ed.). New York: Norton.

Freud, Sigmund. (1905/1975). *Three essays on the theory of sexuality* (James Strachey, Ed.). New York: Basic Books.

Freud, Sigmund. (1911/1989). On dreams. In Peter Gay (Ed.), *The Freud reader*. New York: Norton.

Freud, Sigmund. (1912/1958). The dynamics of resistance. *The standard edition of the complete psychological works of Sigmund Freud* (Vol. 12, pp. 97–108). London: Hogarth Press.

Freud, Sigmund. (1914/1948). On narcissism: An introduction. In Joan Riviere (Trans.), *Collected papers: Vol. 4. Papers on metapsychology and applied psychoanalysis*. London: Hogarth Press.

Freud, Sigmund. (1915a/1948). Repression. In Joan Riviere (Trans.), *Collected papers: Vol. 4. Papers on metapsychology and applied psychoanalysis*. London: Hogarth Press.

Freud, Sigmund. (1915b/1959). Analysis, terminable and interminable. In Joan Riviere (Trans.), *Collected papers: Vol. 5. Miscellaneous papers* (2nd ed.). London: Hogarth Press.

Freud, Sigmund. (1915c/1959). Libido theory. In Joan Riviere (Trans.), *Collected papers: Vol. 5. Miscellaneous papers* (2nd ed.). London: Hogarth Press.

Freud, Sigmund. (1916/1964). *Leonardo da Vinci and a memory of his childhood*. (James Strachey, Trans., in collaboration with Anna Freud). New York: Norton.

Freud, Sigmund. (1919/1989). *Totem and taboo: Some points of agreement between the mental lives of savages and neurotics* (James Strachey, Ed. & Trans., with a biographical introduction by Peter Gay). New York: Norton.

Freud, Sigmund. (1920/1961). *Beyond the pleasure principle* (James Strachey, Ed.). New York: Norton.

Freud, Sigmund. (1923/1962). *The ego and the id* (Joan Riviere, Trans., & James Strachey, Ed.). New York: Norton.

Freud, Sigmund. (1925/1989). Some psychical consequences of the anatomical distinction between the sexes. In Peter Gay (Ed.), *The Freud reader*. New York: Norton.

Freud, Sigmund. (1926/1947). *The question of lay analysis: An introduction to psychoanalysis* (Nancy Proctor-Gregg, Trans.). London: Imago.

Freud, Sigmund. (1930/1961). *Civilization and its discontents* (James Strachey, Ed. & Trans.). New York: Norton.

Freud, Sigmund. (1933). *New introductory lectures on psychoanalysis* (W. J. H. Sprott, Trans.). New York: Norton.

Freud, Sigmund. (1936). *The problem of anxiety* (Henry Alden Bunker, Trans.). New York: The Psychoanalytic Quarterly Press and Norton.

Freud, Sigmund. (1939/1967). *Moses and monotheism* (Katherine Jones, Trans.). New York: Vintage Books.

Freud, Sigmund. (1940/1949). *An outline of psychoanalysis* (James Strachey, Trans.). New York: Norton.

Friedland, Robert P.; Fritsch, Thomas; Smyth, Kathleen A.; Koss, Elisabeth; Lerner, Alan J.; Chen, Chien Hsiun; & others. (2001). Patients with Alzheimer's disease have reduced activities in mid-life compared with healthy control-group members. *Proceedings of the National Academy of Sciences, USA, 98*, 3440–3445.

Friedman, Howard S., & Booth-Kewley, Stephanie. (1987). The "disease-prone personality": A meta-analytic view of the construct. *American Psychologist, 42*, 539–555.

Friedman, Jeffrey M., & Halaas, Jeffrey L. (1998, October 22). Leptin and the regulation of body weight in mammals. *Nature, 395*, 763–770.

Friedman, Meyer, & Rosenman, Ray H. (1974). *Type A behavior and your heart*. New York: Knopf.

Friend, Ronald; Rafferty, Yvonne; & Bramel, Dana. (1990). A puzzling misinterpretation of the Asch "conformity" study. *European Journal of Social Psychology, 20*, 29–44.

Friesen, Wallace V. (1972). *Cultural differences in facial expressions in a social situation: An experimental test of the concept of display rules*. Unpublished doctoral dissertation, University of California, San Francisco.

Frijda, Nico H. (1994). Varieties of affect: Emotions and episodes, moods, and sentiments. In Paul Ekman & Richard J. Davidson (Eds.), *The nature of emotion: Fundamental questions*. New York: Oxford University Press.

Frincke, Jessica L., & Pate, William E., II. (2004, March). *Yesterday, today, and tomorrow: Careers in psychology: 2004: What students need to know*. Washington, DC: APA Research Office. Paper presented at the annual convention of the Southeastern Psychological Association, Atlanta. Retrieved July 17, 2004, from http://research.apa.org/sepa2004.pdf

Fuente-Fernández, Raúl de la; Ruth, Thomas J.; Sossi, Vesna; & others. (2001, August 10). Expectation and dopamine release: Mechanism of the placebo effect in Parkinson's disease. *Science, 293*, 1164–1166.

Fuligni, Andrew J. (1998). Authority, autonomy, and parent-adolescent conflict and cohesion: A study of adolescents from Mexican, Chinese, Filipino, and European backgrounds. *Developmental Psychology, 34*, 782–792.

Fullerton, Carol S.; Ursano, Robert J.; Epstein, Richard S.; & others. (2001). Gender differences in posttraumatic stress disorder after motor vehicle accidents. *American Journal of Psychiatry, 158*, 1486–1491.

Fumeron F.; Betoulle D.; Aubert R.; & others. (2001). Association of a functional 5-HT transporter gene polymorphism with anorexia nervosa and food intake. *Molecular Psychiatry, 6*, 9–10.

Funder, David C. (2001). Personality. *Annual Review of Psychology, 52*, 197–221.

Furman, Wyndol. (2002). The emerging field of adolescent romantic relationships. *Current Directions in Psychological Science, 11*, 177–180.

Furman, Wyndol, & Shaffer, Laura. (2003). National estimates of adolescent romantic relationships. In Paul Florsheim (Ed.), *Adolescent romantic relations and sexual behavior: Theory, research, and practical implications*. Mahwah, NJ: Erlbaum.

Furman, Wyndol, & Simon, Valerie A. (2004). Concordance in attachment states of mind and styles with respect to fathers and mothers. *Developmental Psychology, 40*, 1239–1247.

Furness, John B.; Kunze, Wolfgang A. A.; & Clerc, Nadine. (1999). Nutrient tasting and signaling mechanisms in the gut. II. The intestine as a sensory organ: Neural, endocrine, and immune responses. *American Journal of Physiology, 277*, G922–G928.

Furnham, Adrian. (1991). Write and wrong: The validity of graphological analysis. In Kendrick Frazier (Ed.), *The hundredth monkey and other paradigms of the paranormal*. Buffalo, NY: Prometheus Books.

Gabrieli, John D. E. (2001, February 4). Quoted in APA news release: Personality influences the brain's responses to emotional situations more than thought, according to new research. Retrieved November 9, 2001, from http://www.apa.org/releases/brain.html

Gage, Fred H. (2003, September). Brain, repair yourself. *Scientific American,* pp. 46–53.

Gagné, Gerard G., Jr.; Furman, Martin J.; Carpenter, Linda L.; & Price, Lawrence H. (2000). Efficacy of continuation ECT and antidepressant drugs compared to long-term antidepressants alone in depressed patients. *American Journal of Psychiatry, 157*, 1960–1965.

Galaburda, Albert M. (1999). Albert Einstein's brain. *Lancet, 354*, 1821.

Galanter, Eugene. (1962). Contemporary psychophysics. In R. Brown, E. Galanter, E. H. Hess, & G. Mandler (Eds.), *New directions in psychology*. New York: Holt, Rinehart & Winston.

Galati, Dario; Sini, Barbara; Schmidt, Susanne; & Tinti, Carla. (2003). Spontaneous facial expressions in congenitally blind and sighted children aged 8–11. *Journal of Visual Impairment and Blindness, 97*, 418–428.

Galea, Sandro; Ahern, Jennifer; Resnick, Heidi; Kilpatrick, Dean; Bucuvalas, Michael; & others. (2002). Psychological sequelae of the September 11 terrorist attacks in New York City. *New England Journal of Medicine, 346*, 982–987.

Gallo, Linda C., & Matthews, Karen A. (2003). Understanding the association between socioeconomic status and physical health: Do negative emotions play a role? *Psychological Bulletin, 129*, 10–51.

Gangwisch, James. (2004, November 16). *Lack of sleep may lead to excess weight*. Paper presented at the North American Association for the Study of Obesity (NAASO) annual scientific meeting, Las Vegas, NV. Summary retrieved December 17, 2004, from http://www.naaso.org/news/20041116.asp

Ganis, Giorgio; Thompson, William; & Kosslyn, Stephen. (2004). Brain areas underlying visual mental imagery and visual perception: An fMRI study. *Cognitive Brain Research, 20,* 226–241.

Gansberg, Martin. (1964, March 27). 37 who saw murder didn't call the police. *New York Times,* pp. 1, 38.

Garcia, John. (1981). Tilting at the paper mills of academe. *American Psychologist, 36,* 149–158.

Garcia, John. (1997). Foreword by Robert C. Bolles: From mathematics to motivation. In Mark E. Bouton & Michael S. Fanselow (Eds.), *Learning, motivation, and cognition: The functional behaviorism of Robert C. Bolles.* Washington, DC: American Psychological Association.

Garcia, John; Ervin, Frank R.; & Koelling, Robert A. (1966). Learning with prolonged delay of reinforcement. *Psychonomic Science, 5,* 121–122.

Garcia, John, & Gustavson, Andrew R. (1997, January). Carl R. Gustavson (1946–1996): Pioneering wildlife psychologist. *APS Observer, 10*(1), 34–35.

Garcia, John, & Koelling, Robert A. (1966). Relation of cue to consequence in avoidance learning. *Psychonomic Science, 4,* 123–124.

Garcia-Palacios, Azucena; Hoffman, Hunter G.; Carlin, Albert; Furness, Thomas A., III; & Botella, Cristina. (2002). Virtual reality in the treatment of spider phobia: A controlled study. *Behavior Research and Therapy, 40,* 983–993.

Garcia-Palacios, Azucena; Hoffman, Hunter G.; See, Sheer Kong; Tsai, Amy; & Botella, Cristina. (2001). Redefining therapeutic success with virtual reality exposure therapy. *CyberPsychology and Behavior, 4,* 341–348.

Gardner, Howard. (1985). *Frames of mind: The theory of multiple intelligences.* New York: Basic Books.

Gardner, Howard. (1993). *Frames of mind: The theory of multiple intelligences* (2nd ed.). New York: Basic Books.

Gardner, Howard. (1995). Cracking open the IQ box. In Steven Fraser (Ed.), *The Bell Curve wars: Race, intelligence, and the future of America.* New York: Basic Books.

Gardner, Howard. (1998a). Are there additional intelligences? The case for naturalist, spiritual, and existential intelligences. In J. Kane (Ed.), *Education, information, and transformation.* Upper Saddle River, NJ: Prentice Hall.

Gardner, Howard. (1998b, Winter). A multiplicity of intelligences. Scientific American presents: *Exploring Intelligence, 9,* 18–23.

Gardner, Howard. (2003). Three distinct meanings of intelligence. In Robert Sternberg, Jacques Lautrey, & Todd I. Lubert (Eds.), *Models of intelligence: International perspectives.* Washington, DC: American Psychological Association.

Gardner, Howard, & Taub, James. (1999, Fall). Debating "Multiple intelligences." *Cerebrum, 1,* 13–36.

Gardner, Sue, & Herbert, Camilla. (2002). The modern media—Avoiding pitfalls, advancing psychology. *The Psychologist, 15,* 342–345.

Garety, Philippa A.; Fowler, David; & Kuipers, Elizabeth. (2000). Cognitive-behavioral therapy for medication-resistant symptoms. *Schizophrenia Bulletin, 26,* 73–86.

Garfield, Sol L., & Bergin, Allen E. (1994). Introduction and historical overview. In Allen E. Bergin & Sol L. Garfield (Eds.), *Handbook of psychotherapy and behavior change* (4th ed.). New York: Wiley.

Garry, Maryanne, & Polaschek, Devon L. L. (2000). Imagination and memory. *Current Directions in Psychological Science, 9,* 6–10.

Gartstein, Maria A.; Slobodskaya, Helena R.; & Kinsht, Irina A. (2003). Cross-cultural differences in temperament in the first year of life: United States of America (US) and Russia. *International Journal of Behavioral Development, 27,* 316–328.

Gaser, Christian; Nenadic, Igor; Buchsbaum, Bradley R.; Hazlett, Erin A.; & Buchsbaum, Monte S. (2004). Ventricular enlargement in schizophrenia related to volume reduction of the thalamus, striatum, and superior temporal cortex. *American Journal of Psychiatry, 16,* 154–156.

Gastil, John. (1990). Generic pronouns and sexist language: The oxymoronic character of masculine generics. *Sex Roles, 23,* 629–642.

Gay, Peter. (1988). *Freud: A life for our time.* New York: Norton.

Gay, Peter (Ed.). (1989). *The Freud reader.* New York: Norton.

Gay, Peter. (1999, March 29). Psychoanalyst: Sigmund Freud. *Time 100 Special Issue: Scientists and Thinkers of the 20th Century, 153*(12), 66–69.

Gazzaniga, Michael S. (1995). Consciousness and the cerebral hemispheres. In Michael S. Gazzaniga (Ed.), *The cognitive neurosciences.* Cambridge, MA: MIT Press.

Gazzaniga, Michael S. (1998, July). The split brain revisited. *Scientific American, 279,* 50–55.

Gear, Robert W.; Miaskowski, Christine; Gordon, N. C.; Paul, S. M.; Heller, P. H.; & Levine, Jon D. (1996). Kappa-opioids produce significantly greater analgesia in women than in men. *Nature Medicine, 2,* 1248–1250.

Gee, Travis; Allen, Kelly; & Powell, Russell A. (2003). Questioning premorbid dissociative symptomatology in dissociative identity disorder: Comment on Gleaves, Hernandez, and Warner (1999). *Professional Psychology: Research and Practice, 34,* 114–116.

Geldard, Frank A. (1972). *The human senses* (2nd ed.). New York: Wiley.

Gelman, Rochel, & Gallistel, C. R. (2004). Language and the origin of numerical concepts. *Science, 306,* 441–443.

Gendolla, Guido H. E. (2000). On the impact of mood on behavior: An integrative theory and a review. *Review of General Psychology, 4,* 378–408.

Gentner, Dedre, & Goldin-Meadow, Susan. (Eds.). (2003). *Language in mind: Advances in the study of language and thought.* Cambridge, MA: MIT Press.

Gerard, Harold B.; Wilhelmy, Roland A.; & Conolley, Edward S. (1968). Conformity and group size. *Journal of Personality and Social Psychology, 8,* 79–82.

Gerbner, George. (1993). Images that hurt: Mental illness in the mass media. *Journal of the California Alliance for the Mentally Ill, 4*(1), 17–20.

Gerbner, George. (1998). Images of mental illness in the mass media. *Media Development, 2.* Retrieved February 14, 2003, from: http://www.wacc.org.uk/publications/md/md1998-2/gerbner.html

Gerlach, Jes, & Peacock, Linda. (1994). Motor and mental side effects of clozapine. *Journal of Clinical Psychiatry, 55*(9, Suppl. B), 107–109.

Gerrie, Matthew P.; Garry, Maryanne; & Loftus, Elizabeth F. (2004). False memories. In Neil Brewer & Kip Williams (Eds.), *Psychology and law: An empirical perspective.* New York: Guilford Press.

Gershoff, Elizabeth Thompson. (2002). Corporal punishment by parents and associated child behavior and experiences: A meta-analytic and theoretical review. *Psychological Bulletin, 128,* 539–579.

Getka, Eric J., & Glass, Carol R. (1992). Behavioral and cognitive-behavioral approaches to the reduction of dental anxiety. *Behavior Therapy, 23,* 433–448.

Gibbs, W. Wayt. (2003, December). The unseen genome: Beyond DNA. *Scientific American, 289*(6), 106–113.

Giedd, Jay N.; Blumenthal, Jonathan; Jeffries, Neal O.; Castellanos, F. X.; Liu, Hong; Rapoport, Judith L.; & others. (1999). Brain development during childhood and adolescence: A longitudinal MRI study. *Nature Neuroscience, 2,* 861–863.

Gieser, Marlon T. (1993). The first behavior therapist as I knew her. *Journal of Behavior Therapy and Experimental Psychiatry, 24,* 321–324.

Gigerenzer, Gerd. (2004). Dread risk, September 11, and fatal traffic accidents. *Psychological Sciences, 15,* 286–287.

Gilbert, Lucia Albino. (1994). Current perspectives on dual-career families. *Current Directions in Psychological Science, 3,* 101–105.

Gillham, Jane E.; Shatte, Andrew J.; Reivich, Karen J.; & Seligman, Martin E. P. (2001). Optimism, pessimism, and explanatory style. In Edward C. Chang (Ed.), *Optimism and pessimism: Implications for theory, research, and practice.* Washington, DC: American Psychological Association.

Gilman, Sander L. (2001). Images in psychiatry: Karen Horney, M.D., 1885–1952. *American Journal of Psychiatry, 158,* 1205.

Gilovich, Thomas. (1997, March/April). Some systematic biases of everyday judgment. *Skeptical Inquirer, 21,* 31–35.

Gitlin, Michael J.; Swendsen, Joel; Heller, Tracy L.; & Hammen, Constance. (1995). Relapse and impairment in bipolar disorder. *American Journal of Psychiatry, 152,* 1635–1640.

Glaser, Ronald, & Kiecolt-Glaser, Janice K. (2005). Stress-induced immune dysfunction: Implications for health. *Nature Reviews Immunology, 5,* 243-250.

Glass, Richard M. (2001). Electro convulsive therapy: Time to bring it out of the shadows. *Journal of the American Medical Association, 285,* 1346–1348.

Gleaves, David H. (1996). The sociocognitive model of dissociative identity disorder: A reexamination of the evidence. *Psychological Bulletin, 120,* 42–59.

Gleaves, David H.; Hernandez, Elsa; & Warner, Mark S. (1999). Corroborating premorbid dissociative symptomatology in dissociative identity disorder. *Professional Psychology: Research and Practice, 30,* 341–345.

Gleaves, David H.; Hernandez, Elsa; & Warner, Mark S. (2003). The etiology of dissociative identity disorder. Reply to Gee, Allen, and Powell (2003). *Professional Psychology: Research and Practice, 34,* 116–118.

Gleaves, David H.; Smith, Steven M.; Butler, Lisa D.; & Spiegel, David. (2004). False and recovered memories in the laboratory and clinic: A review of experimental and clinical evidence. *Clinical Psychology: Science and Practice, 11,* 3–28.

Gleitman, Henry. (1991). Edward Chace Tolman: A life of scientific and social purpose. In Gregory A. Kimble, Michael Wertheimer, & Charlotte White (Eds.), *Portraits of pioneers in psychology.* Washington, DC: American Psychological Association/Hillsdale, NJ: Erlbaum.

Glenn, S. M. (1990). Token economy approaches for psychiatric patients. *Behavior Modification, 14,* 383–407.

Glucksman, Myron L., & Kramer, Milton. (2004). Using dreams to assess clinical change during treatment. *Journal of the American Academy of Psychoanalysis and Dynamic Psychiatry, 32,* 345–358.

Glynn, Laura M.; Christenfeld, Nicholas; & Gerin, William. (1999). Gender, social support, and cardiovascular responses to stress. *Psychosomatic Medicine, 61,* 234–242.

Gogtay, Nitin; Giedd, Jay N.; Lusk, Leslie; Hayashi, Kiraless M.; Rapoport, Judith L.; Thompson, Paul M.; & others. (2004a, May 25). Dynamic mapping of human cortical development during childhood through early adulthood. *Proceedings of the National Academy of Sciences, USA, 101,* 8174–8179. Retrieved November 30, 2004, from http://www.pnas.org/cgi/reprint/101/21/8174

Gogtay, Nitin; Giedd, Jay N.; Lusk, Leslie; Hayashi, Kiraless M.; Rapoport, Judith L.; Thompson, Paul M.; & others. (2004b, May 25). Dynamic mapping of human cortical development during childhood through early adulthood: Supporting information: Movies 1–4. *Proceedings of the National Academy of Sciences, USA. 101,* 8174–8179. Retrieved November 30, 2004, from http://www.pnas.org/cgi/content/full/0402680101/DC1

Gökcebay, Nilgün; Cooper, Rosemary; Williams, Robert L.; Hirshkowitz, Max; & Moore, Constance A. (1994). Function of sleep. In Rosemary Cooper (Ed.), *Sleep.* New York: Chapman & Hall.

Gold, Paul E.; Cahill, Larry; & Wenk, Gary L. (2002). Gingko biloba: A cognitive enhancer? *Psychological Science in the Public Interest, 3,* 2–11.

Goldinger, Stephen D.; Kleider, Heather M.; Azuma, Tamiko; & Beike, Denise R. (2003). "Blame the victim" under memory load. *Psychological Science, 14*(1), 81–85.

Goldsmith, H. Hill, & Harman, Catherine. (1994). Temperament and attachment; individuals and relationships. *Current Directions in Psychological Science, 3,* 53–61.

Goldstein, Alan J.; de Beurs, Edwin; Chambless, Dianne L.; & Wilson, Kimberly A. (2000). EMDR for panic disorder with agoraphobia: Comparison with waiting list and credible attention-placebo control condition. *Journal of Consulting and Clinical Psychology, 68,* 947–956.

Goldstein, Daniel G., & Gigerenzer, Gerd (2002). Models of ecological rationality: The recognition heuristic. *Psychological Review, 109,* 75–90.

Goldstein, Rita Z., & Volkow, Nora D. (2002). Drug addiction and its underlying neurobiological basis: Neuroimaging evidence for the involvement of the frontal cortex. *American Journal of Psychiatry, 159,* 1642–1652.

Goleman, Daniel. (1980, February). 1,528 little geniuses and how they grew. *Psychology Today,* pp. 28–53.

Goleman, Daniel. (1995). *Emotional intelligence.* New York: Bantam Books.

Gollwitzer, Peter M. (1999). Implementation intentions: Strong effects of simple plans. *American Psychologist, 54,* 493–503.

Gollwitzer, Peter M., & Brandstätter, Veronika. (1997). Implementation intentions and effective goal pursuit. *Journal of Personality and Social Psychology, 73,* 186–199.

Golomb, Claire, & Galasso, Lisa. (1995). Make-believe and reality: Explorations of the imaginary realm. *Developmental Psychology, 31,* 800–810.

Golombok, Susan, & Tasker, Fiona. (1996). Do parents influence the sexual orientation of their children? Findings from a longitudinal study of lesbian families. *Developmental Psychology, 32,* 3–11.

Goodman, Elizabeth, & Capitman, John. (2000). Depressive symptoms and cigarette smoking among teens. *Pediatrics, 106,* 748–755.

Goodman, Gail S.; Ghetti, Simona; Quas, Jodi A.; Edelstein, Robin S.; Alexander, Kristen Weede; Redlich, Allison D.; Cordon, Ingrid M.; & Jones, David P. H. (2003). A prospective study of memory for child sexual abuse: New findings relevant to the repressed-memory controversy. *Psychological Science, 14,* 113–118.

Goodwin, Stephanie A.; Fiske, Susan T.; Rosen, Lee D.; & Rosenthal, Alisa M. (2002). The eye of the beholder: Romantic goals and impression biases. *Journal of Experimental Social Psychology, 38*(3), 232–241.

Gopnik, Alison. (1996). The post-Piaget era. *Psychological Science, 7,* 221–225.

Gorassini, Donald R., & Olson, James M. (1995). Does self-perception change explain the foot-in-the-door effect? *Journal of Personality and Social Psychology, 69,* 91–105.

Gordon, Peter. (2004, October 15). Numerical cognition without words: Evidence from Amazonia. *Science, 306,* 496–499.

Gottesman, Irving I. (1991). *Schizophrenia genesis: The origins of madness.* New York: Freeman.

Gottfredson, Linda S. (1998, Winter). The general intelligence factor. *Scientific American Presents: Exploring Intelligence, 9,* 24-29.

Gottman, John M. (1994). *Why marriages succeed or fail . . . And how you can make yours last.* New York: Simon & Schuster.

Gough, Harrison G. (1989). The California Personality Inventory. In Charles S. Newmark (Ed.), *Major psychological assessment instruments* (Vol. 2). Boston: Allyn & Bacon.

Gould, Elizabeth, & Gross, Charles G. (2002). Neurogenesis in adult mammals: Some progress and problems. *Journal of Neuroscience, 22,* 619–623.

Gould, Elizabeth; Reeves, Alison J.; Graziano, Michael S. A.; & Gross, Charles G. (1999, October 15). Neurogenesis in the neocortex of adult primates. *Science, 286,* 548–552.

Gould, Elizabeth; Vail, N.; Wagers, M.; & Gross, Charles G. (2001). Adult-generated hippocampal and neocortical neurons in macaques have a transient existence. *Proceedings of the National Academy of Sciences, USA, 98,* 10910–10917.

Gould, James L., & Gould, Carol Grant. (1994). *The animal mind.* New York: Freeman.

Gould, Madelyn S.; Greenberg, Ted; Velting, Drew M.; & Shaffer, David. (2003). Youth suicide risk and preventive interventions: A review of the past 10 years. *Journal of the American Academy of Child & Adolescent Psychiatry, 42,* 386–405.

Gould, Stephen Jay. (1993). *The mismeasure of man* (2nd ed.). New York: Norton.

Graen, George, & Cashman, James F. (1975). A role making model of leadership in formal organizations: A developmental approach. In J. G.

Hunt & L. L. Larson (Eds.), *Leadership frontiers*. Kent, OH: Kent State University Press.

Graham, John R. (1993). *MMPI-2: Assessing personality and psychopathology* (2nd ed.). New York: Oxford University Press.

Graham, William K., & Balloun, Joe. (1973). An empirical test of Maslow's need hierarchy theory. *Journal of Humanistic Psychology, 13,* 97–108.

Greasley, Peter. (2000). Handwriting analysis and personality assessment: The creative use of analogy, symbolism, and metaphor. *European Psychologist, 5,* 44–51.

Green, Joseph P. (1999a). Hypnosis and the treatment of smoking cessation and weight loss. In Irving Kirsch, Antonio Capafons, Etzel Cardena-Buelna, & Salvador Amigo (Eds.), *Clinical hypnosis and self-regulation: cognitive-behavior perspectives*. Washington, DC: American Psychological Association.

Green, Joseph P. (1999b). Hypnosis, context effects, and the recall of early autobiographical memories. *International Journal of Clinical and Experimental Hypnosis, 47,* 284–300.

Green, Joseph P., & Lynn, Steven Jay. (2000). Hypnosis and suggestion-based approaches to smoking cessation: An examination of the evidence. *International Journal of Clinical and Experimental Hypnosis, 48,* 195–224.

Green, Leonard, & Rachlin, Howard. (1996). Commitment using punishment. *Journal of the Experimental Analysis of Behavior, 65,* 593–601.

Green, Richard. (1985). Gender identity in childhood and later sexual orientation: Follow-up of 78 males. *American Journal of Psychiatry, 142,* 339–341.

Green, Richard. (1987). *The "sissy boy syndrome" and the development of homosexuality*. New Haven, CT: Yale University Press.

Greenberg, Daniel L., & Rubin, David C. (2003). The neuropsychology of autobiographical memory. *Cortex, 39,* 687–728.

Greenfield, Patricia M. (1997). You can't take it with you: Why ability assessments don't cross cultures. *American Psychologist, 52,* 1115–1124.

Greenfield, Patricia M.; Keller, Heidi; Fuligni, Andrew; & Maynard, Ashley. (2003). Cultural pathways through universal development. *Annual Review of Psychology, 54,* 461–490.

Greengard, Paul. (2001). The neurobiology of slow synaptic transmission. *Science, 294,* 1024–1030.

Greenwald, Anthony G. (1992). New Look 3: Unconscious cognition reclaimed. *American Psychologist, 47,* 766–779.

Greenwald, Anthony G.; Spangenberg, Eric R.; Pratkanis, Anthony R.; & Eskenazi, Jay. (1991). Double-blind tests of subliminal self-help audiotapes. *Psychological Science, 2,* 119–122.

Gregory, Richard L. (1968, November). Visual illusions. *Scientific American, 212,* 66–76.

Gregory, Richard L. (2003). Seeing after blindness. *Nature Neuroscience, 6,* 909–910.

Griffin, Donald R. (2001). *Animal minds: Beyond cognition to consciousness* (2nd ed.). Chicago: University of Chicago Press.

Grigorenko, Elena L. (2003). Epistasis and the genetics of complex traits. In Robert Plomin, John C. DeFries, Ian W. Craig, & Peter McGuffin (Eds.), *Behavioral genetics in the postgenomic era*. Washington, DC: American Psychological Association.

Gross, Charles G. (2000). Neurogenesis in the adult brain: Death of a dogma. *Nature Reviews Neuroscience, 1,* 67–73.

Gross, Samuel R.; Jacoby, Kristen; Matheson, Daniel; Montgomery, Nicholas; & Patil, Sujata. (2004, April 19). *Exonerations in the United States, 1989 through 2003*. Report issued by The University of Michigan Law School, Ann Arbor, MI. Retrieved June 8, 2004, from http://www.law.umich.edu/NewsAndInfo/exonerations-in-us.pdf

Grossman, Karin; Grossman, Klaus E.; Fremmer-Bombik, Eliszbeth; Kindler, Heinz; Scheuerer-Englisch, Hermann; & Zimmermann, Peter. (2002). The uniqueness of the child–father attachment relationship: Fathers' sensitive and challenging play as a pivotal variable in a 16-year longitudinal study. *Social Development, 11,* 307–331.

Grossman, Randi Priluck, & Till, Brian D. (1998). The persistence of classically conditioned brand attitudes. *Journal of Advertising, 27,* 23–31.

Grotevant, Harold D. (1987). Toward a process model of identity formation. *Journal of Adolescent Research, 2,* 203–222.

Grotevant, Harold D. (1992). Assigned and chosen identity components: A process perspective on their integration. In Gerald R. Adams, Thomas P. Gullotta, & Raymond Montemayor (Eds.), *Adolescent identity formation*. Newbury Park, CA: Sage.

Grutzendler, Jaime; Kasthuri, Narayanan; & Gan, Wen-Biao. (2002). Long-term dendritic spine stability in the adult cortex. *Nature, 420,* 812–816.

Guarnaccia, Peter J. (1993). Ataques de nervios in Puerto Rico: Culture-bound syndrome or popular illness? *Medical Anthropology, 15,* 157–170.

Gudykunst, William B., & Bond, Michael Harris. (1997). Intergroup relations across cultures. In John W. Berry, Cigdem Kagitcibasi, & Marshall H. Segall (Eds.), *Handbook of cross-cultural psychology* (2nd ed., Vol. 3). Boston: Allyn & Bacon.

Guinard, Jean-Xavier, & Brun, Patrice. (1998). Sensory-specific satiety: Comparison of taste and texture effects. *Appetite, 31,* 141–157.

Gunderson, John G. (1997). The borderline patient's intolerance of aloneness: Insecure attachments and therapist availability. *American Journal of Psychiatry, 153,* 752–758.

Gusnard, Debra A., & Raichle, Marcus E. (2001). Searching for a baseline: Functional imaging and the resting human brain. *Nature Reviews Neuroscience, 2,* 685–694.

Gustavson, Carl R.; Kelly, Daniel J.; Sweeney, Michael; & Garcia, John. (1976). Prey-lithium aversions: I. Coyotes and wolves. *Behavioral Biology, 17,* 61–72.

Gyatso, Tenzin. (2003, April 26). The monk in the lab. *New York Times,* p. A19. Retrieved April 26, 2003, from http://www.nytimes.com/2003/04/26/opinion/26LAMA.html

Haaga, David A. F., & Davison, Gerald C. (1991). Cognitive change methods. In Frederick H. Kanfer & Arnold P. Goldstein (Eds.), *Helping people change: A textbook of methods* (4th ed.). New York: Pergamon.

Habermas, Tilmann, & Bluck, Susan. (2000). Getting a life: The emergence of the life story in adolescence. *Psychological Bulletin, 126,* 748–769.

Habib, Michel; Gayraud, D.; Oliva, A.; Regis, J.; Salamon, G.; & Khalil, R. (1991). Effects of handedness and sex on the morphology of the corpus callosum: A study with brain magnetic resonance imaging. *Brain & Cognition, 16,* 41–61.

Haddock, Geoffrey; Zanna, Mark P.; & Esses, Victoria M. (1993). Assessing the structure of prejudicial attitudes: The case of attitudes toward homosexuals. *Journal of Personality and Social Psychology, 65,* 1105–1118.

Hagerty, Michael R. (1999). Testing Maslow's hierarchy of needs: National quality-of-life across time. *Social Indicators Research, 46,* 249–271.

Halaas, Jeffrey L.; Gajiwala, Ketan S.; Friedman, Jeffrey M.; & others. (1995, July 28). Weight-reducing effects of the plasma protein encoded by the obese gene. *Science, 269,* 543–546.

Halford, Graeme S. (2002). Information-processing models of cognitive development. In Usha Goswami (Ed.), *Blackwell handbook of childhood cognitive development*. Malden, MA: Blackwell.

Hall, Calvin S., & Van de Castle, R. L. (1966). *Content analysis of dreams*. New York: Appleton-Century-Crofts.

Hall, Christine C. Iijima. (1997). Cultural malpractice: The growing obsolescence of psychology with the changing U.S. population. *American Psychologist, 52,* 642–651.

Hall, Gordon C. Nagayama. (2001). Psychotherapy research with ethnic minorities: Empirical, ethical, and conceptual issues. *Journal of Consulting and Clinical Psychology, 69,* 502–510.

Hall, Judith A., & Matsumoto, David. (2004). Gender differences in judgments of multiple emotions from facial expressions. *Emotion, 4,* 201–206.

Halliday, Gordon. (1995). Treating nightmares in children. In Charles E. Schaefer

(Ed.), *Clinical handbook of sleep disorders in children*. Northvale, NJ: Aronson.

Halmi, Katherine A., Sunday, Suzanne R.; Strober, Michael; & others. (2000). Perfectionism in anorexia nervosa: Variation by clinical subtype, obsessionality, and pathological eating behavior. *American Journal of Psychiatry, 157*, 1799–1805.

Halpern, Diane F. (1998). Teaching critical thinking for transfer across domains: Dispositions, skills, structure training, and metacognitive monitoring. *American Psychologist, 53*, 449–455.

Halpern, John H.; Sherwood, Andrea R.; Hudson, James I.; Yurgelun-Todd, Deborah; & Pope, Harrison G. (2005). Psychological and cognitive effects of long-term peyote use among Native Americans. *Biological Psychiatry, 58*, 624–631.

Hamilton, Mykol C. (1988). Using masculine generics: Does generic he increase male bias in the user's imagery? *Sex Roles, 19*, 785–799.

Hamilton, Mykol C. (1991). Masculine bias in the attribution of personhood. *Psychology of Women Quarterly, 15*, 393–402.

Hammen, Constance. (2005). Stress and depression. *Annual Review of Clinical Psychology, 1*, 293–319.

Haney, Craig; Banks, Curtis; & Zimbardo, Philip. (1973). Interpersonal dynamics in a simulated prison. *International Journal of Criminology and Penology, 1*, 69–97.

Harlow, Harry F. (1953a). Learning by Rhesus monkeys on the basis of manipulation-exploration motives. *Science, 117*, 466–467.

Harlow, Harry F. (1953b). Mice, monkeys, men, and motives. *Psychological Review, 60*, 23–32.

Harlow, Harry F. (1953c). Motivation as a factor in new responses. In *Current theory and research in motivation: A symposium*. Lincoln: University of Nebraska Press.

Harris, Ben. (1979). What ever happened to Little Albert? *American Psychologist, 34*, 151–160.

Harter, Susan. (1990). Self and identity development. In S. Shirley Feldman & Glen R. Elliott (Eds.), *At the threshold: The developing adolescent*. Cambridge, MA: Harvard University Press.

Hauser, Marc D. (2000). *Wild minds: What animals really think*. New York: Holt.

Hawkins, John N. (1994). Issues of motivation in Asian education. In Harold F. O'Neil, Jr. & Michael Drillings (Eds.), *Motivation: Theory and research*. Hillsdale, NJ: Erlbaum.

Haydon, Philip G. (2001). Glia: Listening and talking to the synapse. *Nature Reviews Neuroscience, 2*, 185–193.

Heaps, Christopher M., & Nash, Michael. (2001). Comparing recollective experience in true and false autobiographical memories. *Journal of Experimental Psychology: Learning, Memory, & Cognition, 27*, 920–930.

Hearst, Eliot. (1999). After the puzzle boxes: Thorndike in the 20th century. *Journal of the Experimental Analysis of Behavior, 72*, 441–446.

Heart and Stroke Foundation of Canada. (1999). *The changing face of heart disease and stroke in Canada: 2000*. Ottawa, Ontario: Heart & Stroke Foundation of Canada.

Hebb, Donald O. (1955). Drives and the C. N. S. (central nervous system). *Psychological Review, 62*, 243–254.

Hebert, Liesi E.; Scherr, Paul A.; Bienias, Julia L.; Bennett, David A.; & Evans, Denis A. (2003). Alzheimer disease in the U.S. population: Prevalence estimates using the 2000 Census. *Archives of Neurology, 60*, 1119–1122.

Hedge, Alan, & Yousif, Yousif H. (1992). Effects of urban size, urgency, and cost of helpfulness: A cross-cultural comparison between the United Kingdom and the Sudan. *Journal of Cross-Cultural Psychology, 23*, 107–115.

Heiby, Elaine M.; DeLeon, Patrick H.; & Anderson, Timothy. (2004). A debate on prescription privileges for psychologists. *Professional Psychology: Research and Practice, 35*, 336–344.

Heider, Eleanor Rosch, & Olivier, Donald C. (1972). The structure of the color space in naming and memory for two languages. *Cognitive Psychology, 3*, 337–354.

Heine, Marilyn K.; Ober, Beth A.; & Shenaut, Gregory K. (1999). Naturally occurring and experimentally induced tip-of-the-tongue experiences in three adult age groups. *Psychology & Aging, 14*, 445–457.

Heinrichs, Markus; Baumgartner, Thomas; Kirschbaum, Clemens; & Ehlert, Ulrike. (2003). Social support and oxytocin interact to suppress cortisol and subjective responses to psychosocial stress. *Biological Psychiatry, 54*, 1389–1398.

Heinrichs, R. Walter. (1993). Schizophrenia and the brain: Conditions for a neuropsychology of madness. *American Psychologist, 48*, 221–233.

Heinrichs, R. Walter. (2005). The primacy of cognition in schizophrenia. *American Psychologist, 60*, 229–242.

Heller, Wendy; Nitschke, Jack B.; & Miller, Gregory A. (1998). Lateralization in emotion and emotional disorders. *Current Directions in Psychological Science, 7*, 26–32.

Hendrix, Mary Lynn. (1993). *Bipolar disorder* (NIMH Publication No. 93–3679). Rockville, MD: National Institute of Mental Health.

Henley, Nancy M. (1989). Molehill or mountain? What we know and don't know about sex bias in language. In M. Crawford & M. Gentry (Eds.), *Gender and thought: Psychological perspectives*. New York: Springer-Verlag.

Henry, William P.; Strupp, Hans H.; Shacht, Thomas E.; & Gaston, Louise. (1994). Psychodynamic approaches. In Allen E. Bergin & Sol L. Garfield (Eds.), *Handbook of psychotherapy and behavior change* (4th ed.). New York: Wiley.

Hepper, Peter G.; Shahidullah, Sara; & White, Raymond. (1990, October 4). Origins of fetal handedness. *Nature, 347*, 431.

Herbert, James D.; Lilienfeld, Scott O.; Lohr, Jeffrey M.; Montgomery, Robert W.; O'Donohue, William T.; Rosen, Gerald M.; & Tolin, David F. (2000). Science and pseudoscience in the development of eye movement desensitization and reprocessing: Implications for clinical psychology. *Clinical Psychology Review, 20*, 945–971.

Herbert, Tracy Bennett, & Cohen, Sheldon. (1993). Depression and immunity: A meta-analytic review. *Psychological Bulletin, 113*, 472–486.

Herman, Louis M. (2002). Exploring the cognitive world of the bottlenosed dolphin. In Marc Bekoff, Colin Allen, & Gordon M. Burghardt (Eds.), *The cognitive animal: Empirical and theoretical perspectives on animal cognition*. Cambridge, MA: MIT Press.

Herman, Louis M.; Kuczaj, Stan A., II; & Holder, Mark D. (1993). Responses to anomalous gestural sequences by a language-trained dolphin: Evidence for processing of semantic relations and syntactic information. *Journal of Experimental Psychology: General, 122*, 184–194.

Herman-Giddens, Marcia E.; Wang, Lily; & Koch, Gary. (2001). Secondary sexual characteristics in boys: Estimates from the National Health and Nutrition Examination Survey III, 1988–1994. *Archives of Pediatrics and Adolescent Medicine, 155*, 1022–1028.

Hermans, Hubert J. M. (1996). Voicing the self: From information processing to dialogical interchange. *Psychological Bulletin, 119*, 31–50.

Hersh, Seymour. (2004a, April 30). Torture at Abu Ghraib. *The New Yorker* (Posted online 4/30/04, issue of 5/10/04). Accessed on November 29, 2005 from http://www.newyorker.com/printables/fact/040510fa_fact

Hersh, Seymour. (2004b, May 9). Chain of command. *The New Yorker* (Posted online 5/9/04, print issue of 5/17/04). Accessed on November 28, 2004 from http://www.newyorker.com/printablers/fact/040517/fa_fact2

Hersh, Seymour. (2005). *Chain of command: The road from 9/11 to Abu Ghraib*. New York: HarperPerennial.

Hertel, Paula T., & Rude, Stephanie S. (1991). Depressive deficits in memory: Focusing attention improves subsequent recall. *Journal of Experimental Psychology: General, 120*, 301–309.

Hertz, Marguerite R. (1992). Rorschach-bound: A 50-year memoir. *Professional Psychology: Research and Practice, 23*, 168–171.

Herzog, D. B.; Nussbaum, K. M.; & Marmar, A. K. (1996). Comorbidity and outcome in eating disorders. *Psychiatric Clinics of North America, 19*, 843–859.

Herzog, Harold A. (2005). Dealing with the controversy of animal research in the classroom and beyond. In Chana K. Akins, Sangeeta Panicker, & Christopher L. Cunninham (Eds.). *Laboratory annimals in research and teaching: Ethics, care, and methods*. Washington, DC: American Psychological Association.

Hespos, Susan J., & Baillargeon, Renée. (2001). Infants' knowledge about occlusion and containment events: A surprising discrepancy. *Psychological Science, 12,* 141–147.

Hess, Ursula; Senecal, Sacha; Kirouac, Gilles; Herrera, Pedro; Philippot, Pierre; & Kleck, Robert E. (2000). Emotional expressivity in men and women: Stereotypes and self-perceptions. *Cognition & Emotion, 14,* 609–642.

Heth, Josephine Todrank, & Somer, Eli. (2002). Characterizing stress tolerance: "Controllability awareness" and its relationship to perceived stress and reported health. *Personality and Individual Differences, 33,* 883–895.

Hetherington, Marion M., & Rolls, Barbara J. (1996). Sensory-specific satiety: Theoretical frameworks and central characteristics. In Elizabeth D. Capaldi (Ed.), *Why we eat what we eat: The psychology of eating*. Washington, DC: American Psychological Association.

Hettema, Jennifer; Steele, Julie; & Miller, William R. (2005). Motivational interviewing. *Annual Review of Clinical Psychology, 1,* 91–111.

Hettema, John M.; Neale, Michael C.; & Kendler, Kenneth S. (2001). A review and meta-analysis of the genetic epidemiology of anxiety disorders. *American Journal of Psychiatry, 158,* 1568–1578.

Hetzel, Lisa, & Smith, Annetta. (2001). *The 65 years and over population: Census 2000 brief* (Series C2KBR/01–10). Washington, DC: U.S. Census Bureau. Retrieved February 20, 2002, from http://www.census. gov/prod/2001pubs/c2kbr01–10.pdf

Hewstone, Miles; Rubin, Mark; & Willis, Hazel. (2002). Intergroup bias. *Annual Review of Psychology, 53,* 575–604.

Heyman, Karen. (2003). The enriched environment. *The Scientist, 17*(9), 24–25.

Hickok, Gregory; Bellugi, Ursula; & Klima, Edward S. (2001, June). Sign language in the brain. *Scientific American, 184,* 58–65.

Hilgard, Ernest R. (1982). Hypnotic susceptibility and implications for measurement. *International Journal of Clinical and Experimental Hypnosis, 30,* 394–403.

Hilgard, Ernest R. (1986a). *Divided consciousness: Multiple controls in human thought and action*. New York: Wiley.

Hilgard, Ernest R. (1986b, January). A study in hypnosis. *Psychology Today, 20,* 23–27.

Hilgard, Ernest R. (1991). A neodissociation interpretation of hypnosis. In Steven J. Lynn & J. Rhue (Eds.), *Theories of hypnosis: Current models and perspectives*. New York: Guilford Press.

Hilgard, Ernest R. (1992). Divided consciousness and dissociation. *Consciousness & Cognition, 1,* 16–32.

Hilgard, Ernest R.; Hilgard, Josephine R.; & Barber, Joseph. (1994). *Hypnosis in the relief of pain* (Rev. ed.). New York: Brunner/Mazel.

Hilgard, Ernest R., & Marquis, D. G. (1940). *Conditioning and learning*. New York: Appleton-Century-Crofts.

Hilton, James L., & Darley, John M. (1991). The effects of interaction goals on person perception. In Mark P. Zanna (Ed.), *Advances in experimental social psychology* (Vol. 24). San Diego, CA: Academic Press/Harcourt.

Hilton, James L., & von Hippel, William. (1996). Stereotypes. *Annual Review of Psychology, 47,* 237–271.

Hines, Terence M. (1998). Comprehensive review of biorhythm theory. *Psychological Reports, 83,* 19–64.

Hines, Terence M. (2003). *Pseudoscience and the paranormal: A critical examination of the evidence* (2nd ed.). Buffalo, NY: Prometheus Books.

Hingson, Ralph; Heeran, Timothy; Zakoc, Ronda C.; Kopstein, Andrea; & Wechsler, Henry. (2002). Magnitude of alcohol-related mortality and morbidity among U.S. college students ages 18–24. *Journal of Studies on Alcohol, 63,* 136–144.

Hinshaw, Stephen P., & Cicchetti, Dante. (2000). Stigma and mental disorder: Conceptions of illness, public attitudes, personal disclosure, and social policy. *Developmental Psychopathology, 12,* 555–598.

Hirshkowitz, Max; Moore, Constance A.; & Minhoto, Gisele. (1997). The basics of sleep. In Mark R. Pressman & William C. Orr (Eds.), *Understanding sleep: The evaluation and treatment of sleep disorders*. Washington, DC: American Psychological Association.

Hobfoll, Stevan E.; Lilly, Roy S.; & Jackson, Anita P. (1992). Conservation of social resources and the self. In Hans O. F. Veiel & Urs Baumann (Eds.), *The meaning and measurement of social support*. New York: Hemisphere.

Hobfoll, Stevan E., & Stephens, Mary Ann Parris. (1990). Social support during extreme stress: Consequences and intervention. In Barbara R. Sarason, Irwin G. Sarason, & Gregory R. Pierce (Eds.), *Social support: An interactional view*. New York: Wiley.

Hobfoll, Stevan E., & Vaux, Alex. (1993). Social support: Resources and context. In Leo Goldberger & Shlomo Breznitz (Eds.), *Handbook of stress: Theoretical and clinical aspects* (2nd ed.). New York: Free Press.

Hobson, Charles, J., & Delunas, Linda. (2001). National norms and life-event frequencies for the revised Social Readjustment Rating Scale. *International Journal of Stress Management, 8,* 299-314.

Hobson, J. Allan. (1988). *The dreaming brain*. New York: Basic Books.

Hobson, J. Allan. (1995). *Sleep*. New York: Scientific American Library.

Hobson, J. Allan. (1999). *Consciousness*. New York: Scientific American Library.

Hobson, J. Allan. (2001). *The dream drugstore: Chemically altered states of consciousness*. Cambridge, MA: MIT Press.

Hobson, J. Allan. (2005, October 27). Sleep is of the brain, by the brain and for the brain. *Nature, 437,* 1254–1264.

Hobson, J. Allan, & McCarley, Robert W. (1977). The brain as a dream state generator: An activation-synthesis hypothesis of the dream process. *American Journal of Psychiatry, 134,* 1335–1348.

Hobson, J. Allan, & Stickgold, Robert. (1995). The conscious state paradigm: A neurological approach to waking, sleeping, and dreaming. In Michael S. Gazzaniga (Ed.), *The cognitive neurosciences*. Cambridge, MA: MIT Press.

Hobson, J. Allan; Stickgold, Robert; & Pace-Schott, Edward F. (1998). The neuropsychology of REM sleep dreaming. *NeuroReport, 9*(3), R1–R14.

Hockenbury, Don H., & Hockenbury, Sandra E. (1999, January 4). *Using pseudoscientific claims to teach scientific thinking*. Paper presented at the National Institute on the Teaching of Psychology, St. Petersburg Beach, FL.

Hoffman, Hunter G.; Granhag, Pär Anders; See, Sheree T. Kwong; & Loftus, Elizabeth F. (2001). Social influences on reality-monitoring decisions. *Memory & Cognition, 29*(3), 394–404.

Hoffman, Martin L. (1977). Moral internalization: Current theory and research. In Leonard Berkowitz (Ed.), *Advances in experimental social psychology* (Vol. 10). New York: Academic Press.

Hoffman, Martin L. (1988). Moral development. In Marc H. Bornstein & Michael E. Lamb (Eds.), *Developmental psychology: An advanced textbook*. Hillsdale, NJ: Erlbaum.

Hoffman, Martin L. (1994). Discipline and internalization. *Developmental Psychology, 30,* 26–28.

Hoier, Sabine. (2003). Father absence and age at menarche: A test of four evolutionary models. *Human Nature, 14,* 209–233.

Holahan, Carole K., & Sears, Robert R. (1995). *The gifted group in later maturity* (in association with Lee J. Cronbach). Stanford, CA: Stanford University Press.

Holden, Constance (2003). Future brightening for depression treatments. *Science, 10,* 810–813.

Hollander, Edwin P., & Julian, James W. (1970). Studies in leader legitimacy, influence, and innovation. In L. Berkowitz (Ed.), *Advances in experimental social psychology* (Vol. 5). New York: Academic Press.

Hollon, Steven D., & Beck, Aaron T. (2004). Behavior therapy with adults. In Michael J. Lambert (Ed.), *Bergin and Garfield's handbook of psychotherapy and behavior change* (5th ed.). New York: Wiley.

Holloway, Jennifer Daw. (2004a). Louisiana grants psychologists prescriptive authority. *APA Monitor, 35*(6), 20–24.

Holloway, Jennifer Daw. (2004b). New Mexico closing in on RxP implementation. *APA Monitor, 35*(7), 13.

Holmes, David. (1990). The evidence for repression: An examination of sixty years of research. In Jerome Singer (Ed.), *Repression and dissociation: Implications for personality theory, psychopathology, and health*. Chicago: University of Chicago Press.

Holmes, Stanley. (1994, April 25). The tortuous tale of a serial killer. *Newsweek*, p. 30.

Holmes, Thomas H., & Masuda, Minoru. (1974). Life change and illness susceptibility. In Barbara Snell Dohrenwend & Bruce P. Dohrenwend (Eds.), *Stressful life events: Their nature and effects*. New York: Wiley.

Holmes, Thomas H., & Rahe, Richard H. (1967). The Social Readjustment Rating Scale. *Journal of Psychosomatic Research, 11*, 213–218.

Holyoak, Keith J., & Spellman, Barbara A. (1993). Thinking. *Annual Review of Psychology, 44*, 265–315.

Hopkins, William D., & Cantalupo, Claudio. (2005). Individual and setting differences in the hand preferences of chimpanzees *(Pan troglodytes)*: A critical analysis and some alternative explanations. *Laterality, 10,* 65–80.

Hopkins, William D.; Russell, Jamie; Freeman, Hani; Buchler, Nicole; Reynolds, Elizabeth; & Schapiro, Steven J. (2005). The distribution and development of handedness for manual gestures in captive chimpanzees *(Pan troglodytes). Psychological Science, 16,* 487–493.

Hopkins, William D.; Stoinski, Tara S.; Lukas, Kristen E.; Ross, Stephen R.; & Wesley, Michael J. (2003). Comparative assessment of handedness for a coordinated bimanual task in chimpanzees (Pan troglodytes), gorillas (Gorilla gorilla) and orangutans (Pongo pygmaeus). *Journal of Comparative Psychology, 117,* 302–308.

Hopkins, William D.; Wesley, Michael J.; Izard, M. Kay; Hook, Michelle; & Schapiro, Steven J. (2004). Chimpanzees *(Pan troglodytes)* are predominantly right-handed: Replication in three populations of apes. *Behavioral Neuroscience, 118,* 659–663.

Hoptman, Matthew J., & Davidson, Richard J. (1994). How and why do the two cerebral hemispheres interact? *Psychological Bulletin, 116,* 195–219.

Horney, Karen. (1926/1967). The flight from womanhood. In Harold Kelman (Ed.), *Feminine psychology*. New York: Norton.

Horney, Karen. (1945/1972). *Our inner conflicts: A constructive theory of neurosis*. New York: Norton.

Hornig-Rohan, Mädy, & Amsterdam, Jay D. (1994). Clinical and biological correlates of treatment-resistant depression: An overview. *Psychiatric Annals, 24,* 220–227.

Horton, Robert S. (2003). Similarity and attractiveness in social perception: Differentiating between biases for the self and the beautiful. *Self and Identity, 2,* 137–152.

House, Robert J. (1977). A 1976 theory of charismatic leadership. In J. G. Hunt & L. L. Larsen (Eds.), *Leadership: The cutting edge* (pp. 189–207). Carbondale: Southern Illinois University Press.

House, Robert J.; Spangler, William D.; & Woycke, James. (1991). Personality and charisma in the U.S. presidency: A psychological theory of leader effectiveness. *Administrative Science Quarterly, 36,* 364–396.

Houshmand, Zara; Harringon, Anne; Saron, Clifford; & Davidson, Richard J. (2002). Training the mind: First steps in a cross-cultural collaboration in neuroscientific research. In Richard J. Davidson & Anne Harrington (Eds.), *Visions of compassion: Western scientists and Tibetan Buddhists examine human nature*. New York: Oxford University Press.

Howard, Ann. (1986). College experiences and managerial performance. *Journal of Applied Psychology, 71,* 530–552.

Howard, J. C. (2000). At-home work spurs risk management concerns. *National Underwriter, 18,* 6.

Howard, William, & Crano, William D. (1974). Effects of sex, conversation, location, and size of observer group on bystander intervention in a high risk situation. *Sociometry, 37,* 491–507.

Howe, Mark L. (2003). Memories from the cradle. *Current Directions in Psychological Science, 12,* 62–65.

Howes, Carollee. (1991). Caregiving environments and their consequences for children: The experience in the United States. In E. C. Melhuish & P. Moss (Eds.), *Day-care for young children*. London: Routledge.

HRFocus News Briefs. (2000, June). *HRFocus, 77,* 8–9.

Hubble, Mark A.; Duncan, Barry L.; & Miller, Scott D. (Eds.). (1999). *The heart and soul of change: What works in therapy*. Washington, DC: American Psychological Association.

Hubel, David H. (1995). *Eye, brain, and vision*. New York: Scientific American Library.

Huesmann, L. Rowell; Moise-Titus, Jessica; Podolski, Cheryl-Lynn; & Eron, Leonard D. (2003). Longitudinal relations between children's exposure to TV violence and their aggressive and violent behavior in young adulthood: 1977–1992. *Developmental Psychology, 39,* 201–221.

Hull, Clark L. (1943). *Principles of behavior: An introduction to behavior theory*. New York: Appleton-Century-Crofts.

Hull, Clark L. (1952). *A behavior system: An introduction to behavior theory concerning the individual organism*. New Haven, CT: Yale University Press.

Hume, K. Michelle, & Crossman, Jane. (1992). Musical reinforcement of practice behaviors among competitive swimmers. *Journal of Applied Behavior Analysis, 25,* 665–670.

Hunt, Earl, & Agnoli, Franca. (1991). The Whorfian hypothesis: A cognitive psychology perspective. *Psychological Review, 98,* 377–389.

Hunt, Stephen P., & Mantyh, Patrick W. (2001). The molecular dynamics of pain control. *Nature Reviews Neuroscience, 2,* 83–91.

Hunter, John E., & Hunter, Ronda F. (1984). Validity and utility of alternative predictors of job performance. *Psychological Bulletin, 96,* 72–98.

Huntjens, Rafaele J. C.; Postma, Albert; Peters, Madelon L.; Woertman, Liesbeth; & van der Hart, Onno. (2003). Interidentity amnesia for neutral, episodic information in dissociative identity disorder. *Journal of Abnormal Psychology, 112,* 290–297.

Huppert, Felicia A.; Johnson, Tony; & Nickson, Judith. (2000). High prevalence of prospective memory impairment in the elderly and in early-stage dementia: Findings from a population-based study. *Applied Cognitive Psychology, 14,* S63–S82.

Hurovitz, Craig S.; Dunn, Sarah; Domhoff, G. William; & Fiss, Harry. (1999). The dreams of blind men and women: A replication and extension of previous findings. *Dreaming, 9,* 183–193.

Hurvich, Leo M. (1981). *Color vision*. Sunderland, MA: Sinauer.

Huston, Ted L.; Ruggiero, Mary; Conner, Ross; & Geis, Gilbert. (1981). Bystander intervention into crime: A study based on naturally-occurring episodes. *Social Psychology Quarterly, 44,* 14–23.

Huttunen, Matti O.; Machon, Ricardo A.; & Mednick, Sarnoff A. (1994). Prenatal factors in the pathogenesis of schizophrenia. *British Journal of Psychiatry, 164*(Suppl. 23), 15–19.

Hyde, Janet Shibley. (1996). Where are the gender differences? Where are the gender similarities? In David M. Buss & Neil M. Malamuth (Eds.), *Sex, power, conflict: Evolutionary and feminist perspectives*. New York: Oxford University Press.

Hyman, Ira E., Jr., & Pentland, Joel. (1996). The role of mental imagery in the creation of false childhood memories. *Journal of Memory & Language, 35,* 101–117.

Hyman, Ray. (1994). Anomaly or artifact? Comments on Bem and Honorton. *Psychological Bulletin, 115,* 19–24.

International Human Genome Sequencing Consortium. (2004, October 21). Finishing the euchromatic sequence of the human genome. *Nature, 431,* 931–945.

Inui, Akio. (2001). Ghrelin: An orexigenic and somatotrophic signal from the stomach. *Nature Reviews Neuroscience, 2,* 1–9.

Isabella, Russell A.; Belsky, Jay; & von Eye, Alexander. (1989). Origins of infant-mother attachment: An examination of interactional synchrony during the infant's first year. *Developmental Psychology, 25,* 12–21.

Iversen, Iver H. (1992). Skinner's early research: From reflexology to operant conditioning. *American Psychologist, 47,* 1318–1328.

Iwamasa, Gayle Y. (1997). Asian Americans. In Steven Friedman (Ed.), *Cultural issues in the treatment of anxiety*. New York: Guilford Press.

Iwanaga, Makoto; Yokoyama, Hiroshi; & Seiwa, Hidetoshi. (2004). Coping availability and stress reduction for optimistic and pessimistic individuals. *Personality and Individual Differences, 36,* 11–22.

Izard, Carroll E. (1990a). Facial expressions and the regulation of emotions. *Journal of Personality and Social Psychology, 58,* 487–498.

Izard, Carroll E. (1990b). The substrates and functions of emotion feelings: William James and current emotion theories. *Personality and Social Psychology Bulletin, 16,* 626–635.

Jackson, Benita; Sellers, Robert M.; & Peterson, Christopher. (2002). Pessimistic explanatory style moderates the effect of stress on physical illness. *Personality and Individual Differences, 32,* 567–573.

Jacob, Suma; Kinnunen, Leann H.; Metz, John; Cooper, Malcolm; & McClintock, Martha K. (2001). Sustained human chemosignal unconsciously alters brain function. *NeuroReport, 12,* 2391–2394.

Jacob, Suma, & McClintock, Martha K. (2000). Psychological state and mood effects of steroidal chemosignals in women and men. *Hormones and Behavior, 37,* 57–78.

Jacobs, Barry L. (2004). Depression: The brain finally gets into the act. *Current Directions in Psychological Science, 13,* 103–106.

Jacobs, Bob; Schall, Matthew; & Scheibel, Arnold B. (1993). A quantitative dendritic analysis of Wernicke's area in humans: II. Gender, hemispheric, and environmental factors. *Journal of Comparative Neurology, 327,* 97–106.

Jacox, Ada; Carr, D. B.; & Payne, Richard. (1994, March 3). New clinical-practice guidelines for the management of pain in patients with cancer. *New England Journal of Medicine, 330,* 651–655.

James, Lori E., & Burke, Deborah M. (2000). Phonological priming effects on word retrieval and tip-of-the-tongue experiences in young and older adults. *Journal of Experimental Psychology: Learning, Memory, & Cognition, 26,* 1378–1391.

James, William. (1884). What is an emotion? *Mind, 9,* 188–205.

James, William. (1890). *Principles of psychology*. New York: Holt.

James, William. (1892). *Psychology, briefer course*. New York: Holt.

James, William. (1894). The physical basis of emotion. *Psychological Review, 1,* 516–529. (Reprinted in the 1994 Centennial Issue of *Psychological Review, 101,* 205–210)

James, William. (1899/1958). *Talks to teachers*. New York: Norton.

Jameson, Dorothea, & Hurvich, Leo M. (1989). Essay concerning color constancy. *Annual Review of Psychology, 40,* 1–22.

Jamison, Kay Redfield. (1993). *Touched with fire: Manic-depressive illness and the artistic temperament*. New York: Free Press.

Jamison, Kay Redfield. (2000). *Night falls fast: Understanding suicide*. New York: Vintage.

Janisse, Michel Pierre, & Dyck, Dennis G. (1988). The Type A behavior pattern and coronary heart disease: Physiological and psychological dimensions. In Michel Pierre Janisse (Ed.), *Individual differences, stress, and health psychology*. New York: Springer-Verlag.

Jarrett, Robin B.; Kraft, Dolores; Doyle, Jeanette; Foster, Barbara M.; Eaves, G. Greg; & Silver, Paul C. (2001). Preventing recurrent depression using cognitive therapy with and without a continuation phase. A randomized clinical trial. *Archives of General Psychiatry, 58,* 381–388.

Jarvis, Erich D.; Güntürkün, O.; Bruce, L.; Csillag, A.; Karten, H.; & The Avian Brain Nomenclature Consortium. (2005). Avian brains and a new understanding of vertebrate evolution. *Nature Reviews Neuroscience, 6,* 151–159.

Jefferson, James W. (1995). Lithium: The present and the future. *Journal of Clinical Psychiatry, 56,* 41–48.

Jewett, Megan E.; Wyatt, James K.; Ritz De Cecco, Angela; Khalsa, Sat Bir; Dijk, Derk-Jan; & Czeisler, Charles A. (1999). Time course of sleep inertia dissipation in human performance and alertness. *Journal of Sleep Research, 8,* 1–8.

Jilek, Wolfgang G. (1993). Traditional medicine relevant to psychiatry. In Norman Sartorius, Giovanni de Girolamo, Gavin Andrews, G. Allen German, & Leon Eisenberg (Eds.), *Treatment of mental disorders: A review of effectiveness*. Washington, DC: World Health Organization/American Psychiatric Press.

John, Elton. (2005, February 7). Quote from interview by Larry King on Cable News Network program "Larry King Live." Retrieved February 26, 2005, from http://transcripts.cnn.com/TRANSCRIPTS/0502/07/lkl.01.html

John, Oliver P. (1990). The "Big Five" factor taxonomy: Dimensions of personality in the natural language and in questionnaires. In Lawrence A. Pervin (Ed.), *Handbook of personality: Theory and research*. New York: Guilford Press.

Johns, Michael.; Schmader, Toni; & Martens, Andy. (2005). Knowing is half the battle: Teaching stereotype threat as a means of improving women's math performance. *Psychological Science, 16,* 175–179.

Johnson, Jeffrey G.; Cohen, Patricia; & others. (2001). Association of maladaptive parental behavior with psychiatric disorder among parents and their offspring. *Archives of General Psychiatry, 58,* 453–460.

Johnson, Katrina W.; Anderson, Norman B.; Bastida, Elena; Kramer, B. Josea; Williams,

David; & Wong, Morrison. (1995). Panel II: Macrosocial and environmental influences on minority health. *Health Psychology, 14,* 601–612.

Johnson, Marcia K.; Hashtroudi, Shahin; & Lindsay, D. Stephen. (1993). Source monitoring. *Psychological Bulletin, 114,* 3–28.

Johnson, Mark H. (2001). Functional brain development in humans. *Nature Reviews Neuroscience, 2,* 475–483.

Johnson, Mark H.; Dziurawiec, Suzanne; Ellis, Hadyn; & Morton, John. (1991). Newborns' preferential tracking of face-like stimuli and its subsequent decline. *Cognition, 40,* 1–19.

Johnson, Sheri L., & Roberts, John E. (1995). Life events and bipolar disorder: Implications from three biological theories. *Psychological Bulletin, 117,* 434–449.

Johnston, Daniel; Magee, Jeffrey C.; Colbert, Costa M.; & Christie, Brian R. (1996). Active properties of neuronal dendrites. *Annual Review of Neuroscience, 19,* 165–186.

Johnston, Timothy D., & Edwards, Laura. (2002). Genes, interactions, and the development of behavior. *Psychological Review, 109,* 26–34.

Joiner, Thomas E.; Brown, Jessica S.; & Wingate, LaRicka R. (2005). The psychology and neurobiology of suicidal beavior. *Annual Review of Psychology, 56,* 287–314.

Jones, Edward E. (1990). *Interpersonal perception*. New York: Freeman.

Jones, Edward E., & Nisbett, Richard E. (1971). *The actor and the observer: Divergent perceptions of the causes of behavior*. Morristown, NJ: General Learning Press.

Jones, Ernest. (1953). *The life and work of Sigmund Freud: Vol. 1. The formative years and the great discoveries: 1856–1900*. New York: Basic Books.

Jones, James M. (1991). Psychological models of race: What have they been and what should they be? In Jacqueline D. Goodchilds (Ed.), *Psychological perspectives on human diversity in America*. Washington, DC: American Psychological Association.

Jones, Mary Cover. (1924a). The elimination of children's fears. *Journal of Experimental Psychology, 7,* 382–390.

Jones, Mary Cover. (1924b). A laboratory study of fear: The case of Peter. *Pedagogical Seminary and Journal of Genetic Psychology, 31,* 308–315.

Jones, Mary Cover. (1975). A 1924 pioneer looks at behavior therapy. *Journal of Behavior Therapy and Experimental Psychiatry, 6,* 181–187.

Jones, Warren H., & Russell, Dan W. (1980). The selective processing of belief-discrepant information. *European Journal of Social Psychology, 10,* 309–312.

Jonnes, Jill. (1999). *Hep-cats, narcs, and pipe dreams: A history of America's romance with illegal drugs*. Baltimore: Johns Hopkins University Press.

Joyner, Kara, & Udry, J. Richard. (2000). You don't bring me anything but down: Adolescent romance and depression. *Journal of Health and Social Behavior, 41,* 369–391.

Judd, Charles M., & Park, Bernadette. (1993). Definition and assessment of accuracy in social stereotypes. *Psychological Review, 100,* 109–128.

Judge, Timothy A., & Watanabe, Shinichiro. (1993). Another look at the job satisfaction–life satisfaction relationship. *Journal of Applied Psychology, 78,* 939–948.

Juliano, Laura M., & Griffiths, Roland R. (2004). A critical review of caffeine withdrawal: Empirical validation of symptoms and signs, incidence, severity, and associated features. *Psychopharmacology, 176,* 1–29.

Julien, Robert M. (2005). *A primer of drug action: A concise nontechnical guide to the actions, uses, and side effects of psychoactive drugs* (10th ed.). New York: Worth.

Jung, Carl G. (1923/1976). Psychological types. In Joseph Campbell (Ed.), *The portable Jung.* New York: Penguin Books.

Jung, Carl G. (1931/1976). The structure of the psyche. In Joseph Campbell (Ed.), *The portable Jung.* New York: Penguin Books.

Jung, Carl G. (1936/1976). The concept of the collective unconscious. In Joseph Campbell (Ed.), *The portable Jung.* New York: Penguin Books.

Jung, Carl G. (1951/1976). Aion: Phenomenology of the self. In Joseph Campbell (Ed.), *The portable Jung.* New York: Penguin Books.

Jung, Carl G. (1963). *Memories, dreams, reflections* (Richard and Clara Winston, Trans.). New York: Random House.

Jung, Carl G. (1964). *Man and his symbols.* New York: Dell.

Jung, Carl G. (1974). *Dreams* (R. F. C. Hull, Trans.). New York: MJF Books.

Kaas, Jon H., & Collins, Christine E. (2001). Evolving ideas of brain evolution. *Nature, 411,* 141–142.

Kagan, Jerome. (2004, Winter). New insights into temperament. *Cerebrum, 6,* 51–66.

Kagan, Jerome, & Snidman, Nancy. (2004). *The long shadow of temperament.* Cambridge, MA: Harvard University Press.

Kagitçibasi, Cigdem. (1997). Individualism and collectivism. In John W. Berry, Cigdem Kagitçibasi, & Marshall H. Segall (Eds.), *Handbook of cross-cultural psychology* (2nd ed., Vol. 3). Boston: Allyn & Bacon.

Kahn, Edwin; Fisher, Charles; & Edwards, Adele. (1991). Night terrors and anxiety dreams. In Steven J. Ellman & John S. Antrobus (Eds.), *The mind in sleep: Psychology and psychophysiology* (2nd ed.). New York: Wiley.

Kahneman, Daniel, & Tversky, Amos. (1982). On the psychology of prediction. In Daniel

Kahneman, Paul Slovic, & Amos Tversky (Eds.), *Judgment under uncertainty: Heuristics and biases.* New York: Cambridge University Press.

Kaitz, Marsha; Lapidot, Pnina; Bronner, Ruth; & Eidelman, Arthur I. (1992). Parturient women can recognize their infants by touch. *Developmental Psychology, 28,* 35–39.

Kalat, James W. (1985). Taste-aversion learning in ecological perspective. In Timothy D. Johnston & Alexandra T. Pietrewicz (Eds.), *Issues in the ecological study of learning.* Hillsdale, NJ: Erlbaum.

Kalidindi, Sridevi, & McGuffin, Peter. (2003). The genetics of affective disorders: Past and future. In Robert Plomin, John C. DeFries, Ian W. Craig, & Peter McGuffin (Eds.), *Behavioral genetics in the postgenomic era.* Washington, DC: American Psychological Association.

Kamen, Dean. (2001, December 2). Quoted in John Heilemann: "Reinventing the wheel." *Time Online Edition.* Retrieved on February 25, 2005, from http://www.time.com/time/business/article/0,8599,186660-1,00.html

Kamin, Leon J. (1995). The pioneers of IQ testing. In Russell Jacoby & Naomi Glauberman (Eds.), *The Bell Curve debate: History, documents, opinions.* New York: Times Books.

Kampe, Knut K. W. (2001, October 10). Quoted in *MSNBC Science News*: "When eyes meet, the brain soars." Retrieved February 27, 2002, from: http://stacks.msnbc.com/news/641208.asp

Kampe, Knut K. W.; Frith, Chris D.; Dolan, Raymond J.; & Frith, Uta. (2001, October 11). Reward value of attractiveness and gaze. *Nature, 413,* 589.

Kamps, Debra M.; Leonard, Betsy R.; Vernon, Sue; Dugan, Erin P.; & Delquadri, Joseph C. (1992). Teaching social skills to students with autism to increase peer interactions in an integrated first-grade classroom. *Journal of Applied Behavior Analysis, 25,* 281–288.

Kandel, Eric A. (2001). The molecular biology of memory storage: A dialogue between genes and synapses. *Science, 294,* 1030–1038.

Kanner, Allen D.; Coyne, James C.; Schaefer, Catherine; & Lazarus, Richard S. (1981). Comparison of two modes of stress management: Daily hassles and uplifts versus major life events. *Journal of Behavioral Medicine, 4,* 1–39.

Kanwisher, Nancy. (2001). Faces and places: Of central (and peripheral) interest. *Nature Neuroscience, 4,* 455–456.

Kaplan, Craig A., & Simon, Herbert A. (1990). In search of insight. *Cognitive Psychology, 22,* 374–419.

Kaplan, Steve. (1990). Capturing your creativity. In Michael G. Walraven & Hiram E. Fitzgerald (Eds.), *Annual editions: Psychology: 1990/91.* Guilford, CT: Dushkin.

Karney, Benjamin R., & Bradbury, Thomas N. (1995). The longitudinal course of marital quality and stability: A review of theory,

method, and research. *Psychological Bulletin, 118*(1), 3–34.

Karni, Avi; Tanne, David; Rubenstein, Barton S.; Askenasy, Jean J. M.; & Sagi, Dov. (1994, July 29). Dependence on REM sleep of overnight improvement of a perceptual skill. *Science, 265,* 679–682.

Karson, Samuel, & O'Dell, Jerry W. (1989). The 16 PF. In Charles S. Newmark (Ed.), *Major psychological assessment instruments* (Vol. 2). Boston: Allyn & Bacon.

Kasl, Charlotte Davis. (1992). *Many roads, one journey: Moving beyond the twelve steps.* New York: HarperPerennial.

Kasser, Tim, & Sharma, Yadika S. (1999). Reproductive freedom, educational equality, and females' preference for resource-acquisition characteristics in mates. *Psychological Science, 10,* 374–377.

Kastenbaum, Robert. (1986). *Death, society, and the human experience.* Columbus, OH: Merrill.

Kastenbaum, Robert. (1992). *The psychology of death.* New York: Springer-Verlag.

Katkin, Edward S.; Wiens, Stefan; & Öhman, Arne. (2001). Nonconscious fear conditioning, visceral perception, and the development of gut feelings. *Psychological Science, 12,* 366–370.

Katkowski, David A., & Medsker, Gina J. (2001). SIOP income and employment: Income and employment of SIOP members in 2000. *The Industrial-Organizational Psychologist, 39,* 21–36.

Katz, David M. (1999). Caution urged on e-mail probes. *National Underwriter, 17,* 3.

Katz, Phyllis A., & Ksansnak, Keith R. (1994). Developmental aspects of gender role flexibility and traditionality in middle childhood and adolescence. *Developmental Psychology, 30,* 272–282.

Katzman, Robert. (1993). Education and the prevalence of dementia and Alzheimer's disease. *Neurology, 43,* 13–18.

Kaufman, Alan S. (1990). *Assessing adolescent and adult intelligence.* Boston: Allyn & Bacon.

Kaufman, Lloyd, & Kaufman, James H. (2000). Explaining the moon illusion. *Proceedings of the National Academy of Sciences, USA, 97,* 500–505.

Kaufmann, Dagmar; Gesten, Ellis; Santa Lucia, Raymond C.; & others. (2000). The relationship between parenting style and children's adjustment: The parents' perspective. *Journal of Child and Family Studies, 9,* 231–245.

Kawamura, Kathleen Y.; Frost, Randy O.; & Harmatz, Morton G. (2002). The relationship of perceived parenting styles to perfectionism. *Personality and Individual Differences, 32,* 317–327.

Kay, Paul, & Regier, Terry. (2003). Resolving the question of color naming universals. *Proceedings of the National Academy of Sciences, USA, 100,* 9085–9089.

Kaye, Walter H.; Klump, K. L.; Frank, G. K. W.; & Strober, Michael. (2000). Anorexia and bulimia nervosa. *Annual Review of Medicine, 51,* 299–313.

Kazdin, Alan E. (1982). The token economy: A decade later. *Journal of Applied Behavior Analysis, 15,* 431–445.

Kazdin, Alan E. (1994). Psychotherapy for children and adolescents. In Allen E. Bergin & Sol L. Garfield (Eds.), *Handbook of psychotherapy and behavior change* (4th ed.). New York: Wiley.

Kazdin, Alan E. (2001). *Behavior modification in applied settings* (6th ed.). Belmont, CA: Wadsworth.

Kazdin, Alan E. (2003). Psychotherapy for children and adolescents. *Annual Review of Psychology, 54,* 253–276.

Kazdin, Alan E., & Benjet, Corina. (2003). Spanking children: Evidence and issues. *Current Directions in Psychological Science, 12,* 99–103.

Keck, Paul E., Jr.; Marcus, Ronald; Tourkodimitris, Stavros; Ali, Mirza; Liebeskind, Amy; Saha, Anutosh; & Ingenito, Gary. (2003). A placebo-controlled, double-blind study of the efficacy and safety of aripiprazole in patients with acute bipolar mania. *American Journal of Psychiatry, 160,* 1651–1658.

Keck, Paul E., Jr., & McElroy, Susan L. (1993). Current perspectives on treatment of bipolar disorder with lithium. *Psychiatric Annals, 23,* 64–69.

Keesey, Richard E., & Hirvonen, Matt D. (1997). Body weight set-points: determination and adjustment. *Journal of Nutrition, 127,* 1875S–1883S.

Keesey, Richard E., & Powley, Terry L. (1986). The regulation of body weight. *Annual Review of Psychology, 37,* 109–133.

Keller, Martin B.; McCullough, J. P.; Klein, D. N.; Arnow, B.; Dunner, D. L.; Gelenberg, A. J.; & others. (2000). A comparison of nefazodone, the cognitive-behavioral analysis system of psychotherapy, and their combination for the treatment of chronic depression. *New England Journal of Medicine, 342,* 1462–1470.

Kelly, Ciara, & McCreadie, Robin. (1999). Smoking habits, current symptoms, and premorbid characteristics of schizophrenic patients in Nithsdale, Scotland. *American Journal of Psychiatry, 156,* 1751–1757.

Kelly, John F., & Moos, Rudolf. (2003). Dropout from 12-step self-help groups: Prevalence, predictors, and counteracting treatment influences. *Journal of Substance Abuse Treatment, 24,* 241–250.

Kelman, Herbert C. (2005). The policy context of torture: A social-psychological analysis. *International Review of the Red Cross, 87,* 123–134.

Keltner, Dacher, & Anderson, Cameron. (2000). Saving face for Darwin: The functions and uses of embarrassment. *Current Directions in Psychological Science, 9,* 187–192.

Keltner, Dacher, & Buswell, Brenda N. (1997). Embarrassment: Its distinct form and appeasement functions. *Psychological Bulletin, 122,* 250–270.

Kempermann, Gerd, & Gage, Fred H. (1999, May). New nerve cells for the adult brain. *Scientific American, 280,* 48–53.

Kempermann, Gerd; Kuhn, H. Georg; & Gage, Fred H. (1998, May 1). Experience-induced neurogenesis in the senescent dentate gyrus. *Journal of Neuroscience, 18,* 3206–3212.

Kempermann, Gerd; Wiskott, Laurenz; & Gage, Fred H. (2004). Functional significance of adult neurogenesis. *Current Opinion in Neurobiology, 14,* 186–191.

Kendall, Philip C.; Holmbeck, Grayson; & Verduin, Timothy. (2004). Methodology, design, and evaluation in psychotherapy research. In Michael J. Lambert (Ed.), *Bergin and Garfield's handbook of psychotherapy and behavior change* (5th ed.). New York: Wiley.

Kendler, Kenneth S.; Bulik, Cynthia M.; Silberg, Judy; Hettema, John M.; Myers, John; & Prescott, Carol A. (2000). Childhood sexual abuse and adult psychiatric and substance use disorders in women: An epidemiological and Cotwin control analysis. *Archives of General Psychiatry, 57,* 953–959.

Kendler, Kenneth S., & Diehl, Scott R. (1993). The genetics of schizophrenia: A current genetic-epidemiologic perspective. *Schizophrenia Bulletin, 19,* 261–285.

Kendler, Kenneth S.; Kessler, Ronald C.; Neale, Michael C.; Heath, Andrew C.; & Eaves, Lindon J. (1993). The prediction of major depression in women: Toward an integrated etiologic model. *American Journal of Psychiatry, 150,* 1139–1148.

Kendler, Kenneth S.; Neale, Michael C.; MacLean, Charles J.; & others. (1993). Smoking and major depression: A causal analysis. *Archives of General Psychiatry, 50,* 36–43.

Kendler, Kenneth S.; Thornton, Laura M.; Gilman, Stephen E.; & Kessler, Ronald C. (2000). Sexual orientation in a U.S. national sample of twin and non-twin sibling pairs. *American Journal of Psychiatry, 157,* 1843–1846.

Kessen, William. (1996). American psychology just before Piaget. *Psychological Science, 7,* 196–199.

Kessler, Ronald C. (1994, January 22). "Really serious conditions. . . ." Quoted in *Science News, 145,* 55.

Kessler, Ronald C. (2003a). Epidemiology of women and depression. *Journal of Affective Disorders, 74,* 5–13.

Kessler, Ronald C. (2003b, February). [*In-cites* interview with: Dr. Ronald C. Kessler]. *ISI essential science indicators.* Philadelphia: Thompson Scientific. Retrieved January 9, 2005, from http://www.in-cites.com/papers/DrRonaldKessler.html

Kessler, Ronald C.; Berglund, Patricia; Demler, Olga; Jin, Robert; Koretz, Doreen; Merikangas,

Kathleen R.; Rush, A. John; Walters, Ellen E.; & Wang, Philip S. (2003, June 18). The epidemiology of major depressive disorder: Results from the National Comorbidity Survey Replication (NCS-R). *Journal of the American Medical Association, 289,* 3095–3105.

Kessler, Ronald C.; McGonagle, Katherine A.; Zhao, Shanyang; Nelson, Christopher B.; Hughes, Michael; Eshleman, Suzann; & others. (1994). Lifetime and 12-month prevalence of DSM-III-R psychiatric disorders in the United States: Results from the National Comorbidity Survey (NCS). *Archives of General Psychiatry, 51,* 8–19.

Kessler, Ronald C., & Merikangas, Kathleen R. (2004). The National Comorbidity Survey Replication (NCS-R). *International Journal of Methods in Psychiatric Research, 13,* 60–68.

Kessler, Ronald C.; Price, Richard H.; & Wortman, Camille B. (1985). Social factors in psychopathology: Stress, social support, and coping processes. *Annual Review of Psychology, 36,* 531–572.

Kessler, Ronald C., & researchers from the World Health Organization. (2004, June 2). World Mental Health Survey Consortium: Prevalence, severity, and unmet need for treatment of mental disorders in the World Health Organization mental health surveys. *Journal of the American Medical Association, 291,* 2581–2590. Retrieved January 9, 2005, from http://jama.ama-assn.org/cgi/reprint/291/21/2581.pdf

Kibel, Howard D. (1993). Inpatient group psychotherapy. In Anne Alonso & Hillel I. Swiller (Eds.), *Group therapy in clinical practice.* Washington, DC: American Psychiatric Press.

Kiecolt-Glaser, Janice K. (1999). Stress, personal relationships, and immune function: Health implications. *Brain, Behavior and Immunity, 13*(1), 61–72.

Kiecolt-Glaser, Janice K., & Glaser, Ronald. (1991). Stress and immune function in humans. In Robert Ader, David L. Felten, & Nicholas Cohen (Eds.), *Psychoneuroimmunology.* San Diego, CA: Academic Press.

Kiecolt-Glaser, Janice K., & Glaser, Ronald. (1993). Mind and immunity. In Daniel Goleman & Joel Gurin (Eds.), *Mind/body medicine: How to use your mind for better health.* Yonkers, NY: Consumer Reports Books.

Kiecolt-Glaser, Janice K.; McGuire, Lynanne; Robles, Theodore, F.; & Glaser, Ronald. (2002). Emotions, morbidity, and mortality: New perspectives from psychoneuroimmunology. *Annual Review of Psychology, 53,* 83–107.

Kiecolt-Glaser, Janice K., & Newton, Tamara L. (2001). Marriage and health: His and hers. *Psychological Bulletin, 127,* 472–503.

Kiesler, Charles A., & Kiesler, Sara B. (1969). *Conformity.* Reading, MA: Addison-Wesley.

Kihlstrom, John F. (1992). Dissociation and dissociations: A comment on consciousness and cognition. *Consciousness & Cognition, 1,* 47–53.

Kihlstrom, John F. (1993). The continuum of consciousness. *Consciousness & Cognition, 2,* 334–354.

Kihlstrom, John F. (1995, September). On the validity of psychology experiments. *APS Observer, 8*(5), 10–11.

Kihlstrom, John F. (2001). Hypnosis and the psychological unconscious. In Howard S. Friedman (Ed.), *Assessment and therapy: Specialty articles from the Encyclopedia of Mental Health*. San Diego, CA: Academic Press.

Kihlstrom, John F. (2002). Demand characteristics in the laboratory and the clinic: Conversations and collaborations with subjects and patient. *Prevention & Treatment, 5,* np. Retrieved July 17, 2004, from http://journals.apa.org/prevention/volume5/pre0050036c.html

Kihlstrom, John F. (2004). An unbalanced balancing act: Blocked, recovered, and false memories in the laboratory and clinic. *Clinical Psychology: Science and Practice, 11,* 34–41.

Kihlstrom, John F. (2005). Dissociative disorders. *Annual Review of Clinical Psychology, 1,* 227–253.

Kihlstrom, John F., & Barnhardt, Terrence M. (1993). The self-regulation of memory: For better and for worse, with and without hypnosis. In Daniel M. Wegner & James W. Pennebaker (Eds.), *Handbook of mental control*. Englewood Cliffs, NJ: Prentice-Hall.

Kihlstrom, John F.; Glisky, Martha L.; & Angiulo, Michael J. (1994). Dissociative tendencies and dissociative disorders. *Journal of Abnormal Psychology, 103,* 117–124.

Kihlstrom, John F.; Mulvaney, Shelagh; Tobias, Betsy A.; & Tobias, Irene P. (2000). In Eric Eich, John F. Kihlstrom, Gordon H. Bower, Josheph P. Forgas, & Paula M. Niedenthal (Eds.), *Cognition and emotion*. New York. Oxford University Press.

Kimzey, Stephen L. (1975). The effects of extended spaceflight on hematologic and immunologic systems. *Journal of the American Medical Women's Association, 30,* 218–232.

King, D. Brett; Cox, Michaella; & Wertheimer, Michael. (1998). Karl Duncker: Productive problems with beautiful solutions. In George A. Kimble & Michael Wertheimer (Eds.), *Portraits of pioneers in psychology* (Vol. 3). Washington, DC: American Psychological Association.

Kinsella, Kevin, & Velkoff, Victoria A. (2001). *An aging world: 2001* (International Population Report, Series P95/01–1). Washington, DC: U.S. Government Printing Office, U.S. Census Bureau.

Kirchgessner, Annette L., & Liu, Min-tsai. (1999). Orexin synthesis and response in the gut. *Neuron, 24,* 941–51.

Kirsch, Irving. (1996). Hypnotic enhancement of cognitive-behavioral weight loss treatments: Another meta-reanalysis. *Journal of Consulting and Clinical Psychology, 64,* 517–519.

Kirsch, Irving, & Braffman, Wayne. (2001). Imaginative suggestibility and hypnotizability. *Current Directions in Psychological Science, 10,* 57–61.

Kirsch, Irving; Montgomery, Guy; & Sapirstein, Guy. (1995). Hypnosis as an adjunct to cognitive-behavioral psychotherapy: A meta-analysis. *Journal of Consulting and Clinical Psychology, 63,* 214–220.

Kirschenbaum, Howard. (2004). Carl Rogers's life and work: An assessment on the 100th anniversary of his birth. *Journal of Counseling and Development, 82,* 116–124.

Kitayama, Shinobu; Markus, Hazel Rose; & Kurokawa, Masaru. (2000). Culture, emotion, and well-being: Good feelings in Japan and the United States. *Cognition & Emotion, 14,* 93–124.

Kitayama, Shinobu; Markus, Hazel Rose; Matsumoto, Hisaya; & Norasakkunkit, Vinai. (1997). Individual and collective processes in the construction of the self: Self-enhancement in the United States and self-criticism in Japan. *Journal of Personality and Social Psychology, 72,* 1245–1267.

Klahr, David. (1992). Information-processing approaches. In Ross Vasta (Ed.), *Six theories of child development: Revised formulations and current issues*. London: Jessica Kingsley.

Klein, Donald F., & Wender, Paul H. (1993). *Understanding depression: A complete guide to its diagnosis and treatment*. New York: Oxford University Press.

Klein, Stephen B., & Mowrer, Robert R. (1989). *Contemporary learning theories: Instrumental conditioning theory and the impact of biological constraints on learning*. Hillsdale, NJ: Erlbaum.

Klerman, Elizabeth B.; Rimmer, David W.; Czeisler, Charles A.; & others. (1998). Nonphotic entrainment of the human circadian pacemaker. *American Journal of Physiology, 274,* R991–R996.

Klerman, Gerald L., & Weissman, Myrna M. (Eds.). (1993). *New applications of interpersonal psychotherapy*. Washington, DC: American Psychiatric Association.

Klerman, Gerald L.; Weissman, Myrna M.; Rounsaville, Bruce J.; & Chevron, Eve S. (1984). *Interpersonal psychotherapy of depression*. New York: Basic Books.

Kluft, Richard P. (1993). Multiple personality disorders. In David Spiegel (Ed.), *Dissociative disorders: A clinical review*. Lutherville, MD: Sidran.

Knafo, Ariel; Iervolino, Alessandra C.; & Plomin, Robert. (2005). Masculine girls and feminine boys: Genetic and environmental contributions to atypical gender development in early childhood. *Journal of Personality and Social Psychology, 88,* 400–412.

Knapp, Samuel, & VandeCreek, Leon. (2000). Received memories of childhood abuse: Is there an underlying professional consensus? *Professional Psychology: Research and Practice, 31,* 365–371.

Knecht, Stefan; Dräger, B.; Deppe, M.; Bobe, L.; Lohmann, H.; Flöel, A.; & others. (2000). Handedness and hemispheric language domi-nance in healthy humans. *Brain, 123,* 2512–2518.

Knight, Bob G.; Maines, Michele. L.; & Robinson, Gia S. (2002). The effects of sad mood on memory in older adults: A test of the mood congruence effect. *Psychology & Aging, 17,* 653–661.

Knowles, John B. (1963). Conditioning and the placebo effect: The effects of decaffeinated coffee on simple reaction time in habitual coffee drinkers. *Behavior Research and Therapy, 1,* 151–157.

Kochanek, Kenneth D., & Smith, Betty L. (2004, February 11). Deaths: Preliminary data for 2002. *National Vital Statistics Reports, 52,* No. 13. Atlanta, GA: Centers for Disease Control, U.S. Department of Health and Human Services. Retrieved January 7, 2005, from http://www.cdc.gov/nchs/data/nvsr/nvsr52/nvsr5213.pdf

Koffka, Kurt. (1935). *Principles of Gestalt psychology*. New York: Harcourt, Brace.

Kohen, Daniel P., & Olness, Karen. (1993). Hypnotherapy with children. In Judith W. Rhue, Steven J. Lynn, & Irving Kirsch (Eds.), *Handbook of clinical hypnosis*. Washington, DC: American Psychological Association.

Kojima, Masayasu; Hosoda, Hiroshi; Date, Yukari; Nakazato, Masamitsu; Matsuo, Hisayuki; & Kangawa, Kenji. (1999). Ghrelin is a growth-hormone-releasing acylated peptide from stomach. *Nature, 402,* 656–660.

Kolb, Bryan, & Whishaw, Ian Q. (1998). Brain plasticity and behavior. *Annual Review of Neuroscience, 49,* 43–64.

Koopowitz, Leslie Frank; Chur-Hansen, Anna; Reid, Sally; & Blashki, Miriam. (2003). The subjective experience of patients who received electroconvulsive therapy. *Australian & New Zealand Journal of Psychiatry, 37,* 49–54.

Koplan, Jeffrey P., & Dietz, William H. (1999, October 27). Caloric imbalance and public health policy. *Journal of the American Medical Association, 282,* 1579–1581.

Kopta, S. Mark; Lueger, Robert J.; Saunders, Stephen M.; & Howard, Kenneth I. (1999). Individual psychotherapy outcome and process research: Challenges leading to greater turmoil or a positive transition? *Annual Review of Psychology, 50,* 441–469.

Korabik, Karen; Baril, Galen L.; & Watson, Carol. (1993). Managers; conflict management style and leadership effectiveness: The moderating effects of gender. *Sex Roles, 29,* 405–420.

Koren-Karie, Nina; Oppenheim, David; Dolev, Smadar; Sher, Efrat; & Etzion-Carasso, Ayelet. (2002). Mothers' insightfulness regarding their infants' internal experience: Relations with maternal sensitivity and infant attachment. *Developmental Psychology, 38,* 534–542.

Koriat, Asher; Goldsmith, Morris; & Pansky, Ainat. (2000). Toward a psychology of memory accuracy. *Annual Review of Psychology, 51,* 481–537.

Kornfeld, Alfred D. (1989). Mary Cover Jones and the Peter case: Social learning versus conditioning. *Journal of Anxiety Disorders, 3,* 187–195.

Koss, Mary P., & Shiang, Julia. (1994). Research on brief psychotherapy. In Allen E. Bergin & Sol L. Garfield (Eds.), *Handbook of psychotherapy and behavior change* (4th ed.). New York: Wiley.

Kosslyn, Stephen M. (2001, May-June). Quoted in Andrew Cocke: "The science behind hypnosis." *BrainWork: The Neuroscience Newsletter, 11,* 7.

Kosslyn, Stephen M.; Ball, Thomas M.; & Reiser, Brian J. (1978). Visual images preserve metric spatial information: Evidence from studies of image scanning. *Journal of Experimental Psychology: Human Perception and Performance, 4,* 47–60.

Kosslyn, Stephen M.; Ganis, Giorgio; & Thompson, William L. (2001). Neural foundations of imagery. *Nature Reviews Neuroscience, 2,* 635–642.

Kosslyn, Stephen M., & Thompson, William L. (2000). Shared mechanisms in visual imagery and visual perception: Insights from cognitive neuroscience. In Michael S. Gazzaniga (Ed.), *The new cognitive neurosciences* (2nd ed.). Cambridge, MA: MIT Press.

Kosslyn, Stephen M.; Thompson, William L.; Costantini-Ferrando, Maria F.; Alpert, Nathaniel M.; & Spiegel, David. (2000). Hypnotic visual illusion alters color processing in the brain. *American Journal of Psychiatry, 157,* 1279–1284.

Kozorovitskiy, Yevgenia, & Gould, Elizabeth. (2004). Dominance hierarchy influences adult neurogenesis in the dentate gyrus. *Journal of Neuroscience, 24,* 6755–6759.

Kramer, Arthur F., & Willis, Sherry L. (2002). Enhancing the cognitive vitality of older adults. *Current Directions in Psychological Science, 11,* 173–177.

Kramer, Peter D. (1993). *Listening to Prozac: A psychiatrist explores antidepressant drugs and the remaking of the self.* New York: Viking.

Krantz, David S., & McCeney, Melissa K. (2002). Effects of psychological and social factors on organic disease: A critical assessment of research on coronary heart disease. *Annual Review of Psychology, 53,* 341–369.

Krausz, Michael, & Müller-Thomsen, Tomas. (1993). Schizophrenia with onset in adolescence: An 11-year followup. *Schizophrenia Bulletin, 19,* 831–841.

Kring, Ann M., & Gordon, Albert H. (1998). Sex differences in emotion: Expression, experience, and physiology. *Journal of Personality and Social Psychology, 74,* 686–703.

Krippner, Stanley. (1994). Cross-cultural treatment perspectives of dissociative disorders. In Steven Jay Lynn & Judith W. Rhue (Eds.), *Dissociation: Clinical and theoretical perspectives.* New York: Guilford Press.

Krosnick, Jon A.; Betz, Andrew L.; Jussim, Lee J.; & Lynn, Ann R. (1992). Subliminal conditioning of attitudes. *Personality and Social Psychology Bulletin, 18,* 152–162.

Kruger, Justin, & Gilovich, Thomas. (2004). Actions, intentions, and self-assessment: The road to self-enhancement is paved with good intentions. *Personality and Social Psychology Bulletin, 30*(3), 328–329.

Kübler-Ross, Elisabeth. (1969). *On death and dying.* New York: Macmillan.

Kuhl, Patricia K.; Andruski, Jean E.; Chistovich, Inna A.; Chistovich, Ludmilla A.; Kozhevnikova, Elena V.; Ryskina, Viktoria L.; & others. (1997, August 1). Cross-language analysis of phonetic units in language addressed to infants. *Science, 277,* 684–686.

Kuhl, Patricia K.; Williams, Karen A.; Lacerda, Francisco; Stevens, Kenneth N.; & Lindblom, Bjorn. (1992, January 31). Linguistic experience alters phonetic perception in infants by 6 months of age. *Science, 255,* 606–608.

Kuhn, Cynthia M., & Wilson, Wilkie A. (2001, Spring). Ecstasy on trial: Our dangerous love affair with Ecstasy. *Cerebrum, 3,* 22–33.

Kunda, Ziva, & Thagard, Paul. (1996). Forming impressions from stereotypes, traits, and behaviors: A parallel-constraint-satisfaction theory. *Psychological Review, 103,* 284–308.

Kunoh, Hiroshi, & Takaoki, Eiji. (1994). *3-D planet: The world as seen through stereograms.* San Francisco: Cadence Books.

Kupfer, David J., & Frank, Ellen. (2001). The interaction of drug- and psychotherapy in the long-term treatment of depression. *Journal of Affective Disorders, 62,* 131–137.

Kurdek, Lawrence A. (1995). Developmental changes in relationship quality in gay and lesbian cohabiting couples. *Developmental Psychology, 31,* 86–94.

Kurdek, Lawrence A. (2005). What do we know about gay and lesbian couples? *Current Directions in Psychological Science, 14,* 251–254.

Lachman, Margie E. (2004). Development in midlife. *Annual Review of Psychology, 55,* 305–331.

Ladd, George T., & Petry, Nancy M. (2003). Antisocial personality in treatment-seeking cocaine abusers: Psychosocial functioning and HIV risk. *Journal of Substance Abuse Treatment, 24,* 323–330.

LaFromboise, Teresa D.; Coleman, Hardin L. K.; & Gerton, Jennifer. (1993). Psychological impact of biculturalism: Evidence and theory. *Psychological Bulletin, 114,* 395–412.

LaFromboise, Teresa D.; Trimble, Joseph E.; & Mohatt, Gerald V. (1993). Counseling intervention and American Indian tradition: An integrative approach. In Donald R. Atkinson, George Morten, & Derald Wing Sue (Eds.), *Counseling American minorities: A cross-cultural perspective* (4th ed.). Madison, WI: Brown & Benchmark.

Lalonde, Justine K.; Hudson, James I.; Gigante, Robin A.; & Pope, Harrison G. (2001). Canadian and American psychiatrists' attitudes toward dissociative disorders diagnoses. *Canadian Journal of Psychiatry, 46,* 407–412.

Lamb, Michael E.; Sternberg, Kathleen J.; & Prodromidis, Margarita. (1992). Nonmaternal care and the security of infant-mother attachment: A reanalysis of the data. *Infant Behavior and Development, 15,* 71–83.

Lamb, Michael E.; Thompson, Ross A.; Gardner, William; & Charnov, Eric L. (1985). *Infant–mother attachment: The origins and developmental significance of individual differences in Strange Situation behavior.* Hillsdale, N.J: Erlbaum.

Lamb, R. J.; Kirby, K. C.; Morral, A. C.; Galbicka, G.; & Iguchi, Martin Y. (2004). Improving contingency management programs for addiction. *Addictive Behaviors, 29,* 507–523.

Lambert, Michael J.; Garfield, Sol L.; & Bergin, Allen E. (2004). Overview, trends, and future issues. In Michael J. Lambert (Ed.), *Bergin and Garfield's handbook of psychotherapy and behavior change* (5th ed.). New York: Wiley.

Lambert, Michael J., & Ogles, Benjamin M. (2004). The efficacy and effectiveness of psychotherapy. In Michael J. Lambert (Ed.), *Bergin and Garfield's handbook of psychotherapy and behavior change* (5th ed.). New York: Wiley.

Lampinen, James M.; Copeland, Susann M.; & Neuschatz, Jeffrey S. (2001). Recollections of things schematic: Room schemas revisited. *Journal of Experimental Psychology: Learning, Memory, & Cognition, 27,* 1211–1222.

Lampinen, James M.; Faries, Jeremiah M.; Neuschatz, Jeffrey S.; & Toglia, Michael P. (2000). Recollections of things schematic: The influence of scripts on recollective experience. *Applied Cognitive Psychology, 14,* 543–554.

Lamprecht, Raphael, & LeDoux, Joseph. (2004). Structural plasticity and memory. *Nature Reviews Neuroscience, 5,* 45–54.

Lancer, Charles E.; Lautenschlager, Gary J.; Sloan, Christopher E.; & Varcar, Philip E. (1989). A comparison between bottom-up, top-down, and bidirectional models of relationships between global and life facet satisfaction. *Journal of Personality, 57,* 601–624.

Lander, Hans Jürgen. (1997). Hermann Ebbinghaus. In Wolfgang G. Bringmann, Helmut E. Lück, Rudolf Miller, & Charles E. Early (Eds.), *A pictorial history of psychology.* Chicago: Quintessence.

Lange, Carl G., & James, William. (1922). *The emotions* (I. A. Haupt, Trans.). Baltimore: Williams & Wilkins.

Langer, Ellen, & Rodin, Judith. (1976). The effects of choice and enhanced personal responsibility for the aged: A field experiment in an institutional setting. *Journal of Personality and Social Psychology, 34,* 191–198.

Laruelle, Marc; Kegeles, Lawrence S.; & Abi-Dargham, Anissa. (2003). Glutamate, dopamine, and schizophrenia: From pathophysiology to treatment. *Annals of the New York Academy of Sciences, 1003,* 138–158.

Lashley, Karl S. (1929). *Brain mechanisms and intelligence.* Chicago: University of Chicago Press.

Lashley, Karl S. (1950). In search of the engram. *Symposia of the Society for Experimental Biology, 4,* 454–482.

Lask, Bryan. (1995). Night terrors. In Charles E. Schaefer (Ed.), *Clinical handbook of sleep disorders in children.* Northvale, NJ: Aronson.

Laskow, Gregory B., & Grill, Dennis J. (2003). The Department of Defense experiment: The Psychopharmacology Demonstration Project. In Morgan T. Sammons, Ruth Ullman Paige, & Ronald F. Levant (Eds.), *Prescriptive authority for psychologists: A history and guide.* Washington, DC: American Psychological Association.

Lasser, Karen; Boyd, J. Wesley; Woolhandler, Steffie; & others. (2000). Smoking and mental illness: A population-based prevalence study. *Journal of the American Medical Association, 284,* 2606–2610.

Latané, Bibb, & Darley, John M. (1970). *The unresponsive bystander: Why doesn't he help?* New York: Appleton-Century-Crofts.

Latané, Bibb, & Nida, Steve A. (1981). Ten years of research on group size and helping. *Psychological Bulletin, 89,* 308–324.

Laumann, Edward O.; Gagnon, John H.; Michael, Robert T.; & Michaels, Stuart. (1994). *The social organization of sexuality: Sexual practices in the United States.* Chicago: University of Chicago Press.

Laumann, Edward O., & Michael, Robert T. (Eds.). (2001). *Sex, love, and health in America: Private choices and public policies.* Chicago: University of Chicago Press.

Laumann, Edward O.; Paik, Anthony; & Rosen, Raymond C. (1999, February 10). Sexual dysfunction in the United States: Prevalence and predictors. *Journal of the American Medical Association, 281,* 537–544.

Laumann, Edward O.; Paik, Anthony; & Rosen, Raymond C. (2001). Sexual dysfunction in the United States: Prevalence and predictors. In Edward O. Laumann & Robert T. Michael (Eds.), *Sex, love, and health in America: Private choices and public policies.* Chicago: University of Chicago Press.

Laumann, Edward O., & Youm, Yoosik. (2001). Sexual expression in America. In Edward O. Laumann & Robert T. Michael (Eds.), *Sex, love, and health in America: Private choices and public policies.* Chicago: University of Chicago Press.

Laursen, Brett, & Collins, W. Andrew. (1994). Interpersonal conflict during adolescence. *Psychological Bulletin, 115*(2), 197–209.

Lavie Peretz. (1989). To nap, perchance to sleep—ultradian aspects of napping. In David F.

Dinges & Roger J. Broughton (Eds.), *Sleep and alertness: Chronobiological, behavioral, and medical aspects of napping.* New York: Raven Press.

Laviolette, Steven R., & van der Kooy, Derek. (2004). The neurobiology of nicotine addiction: Bridging the gap from molecules to behaviour. *Nature Reviews Neuroscience, 5,* 55–65.

Lawler, Edward E., III. (1973). *Motivation in work organizations.* Pacific Grove, CA: Brooks/Cole.

Lazarus, Arnold A. (2000). Will reason prevail? From classic psychoanalysis to New Age therapy. *American Journal of Psychotherapy, 54,* 152–155.

Lazarus, Richard S. (1991). Cognition and motivation in emotion. *American Psychologist, 46,* 352–367.

Lazarus, Richard S. (1993). From psychological stress to the emotions. A history of changing outlooks. *Annual Review of Psychology, 44,* 1–21.

Lazarus, Richard S. (1995). Vexing research problems inherent in cognitive-mediational theories of emotion—and some solutions. *Psychological Inquiry, 6,* 183–197.

Lazarus, Richard S. (1999). *Stress and emotion: A new synthesis.* New York: Springer.

Lazarus, Richard S. (2000). Toward better research on stress and coping. *American Psychologist, 55,* 556–773.

Lazarus, Richard S., & Folkman, Susan. (1984). *Stress, appraisal, and coping.* New York: Springer.

Leach, Carolyn S., & Rambaut, Paul C. (1974). Biochemical responses of the Skylab crewmen. *Proceedings of the Skylab Life Sciences Symposium, 2,* 427–454.

LeBlanc, Jacques. (2000). Nutritional implications of cephalic phase thermogenic responses. *Appetite, 34,* 214–216.

Lebow, Jay L., & Gurman, Alan S. (1995). Research assessing couple and family therapy. *Annual Review of Psychology, 46,* 27–57.

Lecomte, Tania, & Lecomte, Conrad. (2002). Toward uncovering robust priciples of change inherent to cognitive-behavioral therapy for psychosis. *American Journal of Orthopsychiatry, 72,* 50–57.

LeDoux, Joseph E. (1994a, June). Emotion, memory, and the brain. *Scientific American, 270,* 50–57.

LeDoux, Joseph E. (1994b). Memory versus emotional memory in the brain. In Paul Ekman & Richard J. Davisdon (Eds.), *The nature of emotion: Fundamental questions.* New York: Oxford University Press.

LeDoux, Joseph E. (1995). Emotion: Clues from the brain. *Annual Review of Psychology, 46,* 209–235.

LeDoux, Joseph E. (1996). *The emotional brain: The mysterious underpinnings of emotional life.* New York: Simon & Schuster.

LeDoux, Joseph E. (2000). Emotion circuits in the brain. *Annual Review of Neuroscience, 23,* 155–184.

Lee, Kimberly L.; Vaillant, George T.; Torrey, William C.; & Elder, Glen H. (1995). A 50-year prospective study of the psychological sequelae of World War II combat. *American Journal of Psychiatry, 152,* 516–522.

Lehman, Barbara J., & Crano, William D. (2002). The pervasive effects of vested interest on attitude-criterion consistency in political judgment. *Journal of Experimental Psychology, 38,* 101–112.

Leibenluft, Ellen. (1996). Women with bipolar illness: Clinical and research issues. *American Journal of Psychiatry, 153,* 163–173.

Leichtman, Michelle D., & Ceci, Stephen J. (1995). The effects of stereotypes and suggestions on preschoolers' reports. *Developmental Psychology, 31,* 568–578.

Leocani, Letizia; Locatelli, Marco; Bellodi, Laura; & others. (2001). Abnormal pattern of cortical activation associated with voluntary movement in obsessive-compulsive disorder: An EEG study. *American Journal of Psychiatry, 158,* 140–142.

Leon, Scott C.; Kopta, S. Mark; Howard, Kenneth I.; & Lutz, Wolfgang. (1999). Predicting patients' responses to psychotherapy: Are some more predictable than others? *Journal of Consulting and Clinical Psychology, 67,* 698–704.

Leonardo, E. D., & Hen, René. (2005). Genetics of affective and anxiety disorders. *Annual Review of Clinical Psychology, 57,* 117–137.

Lepore, Frederick E. (2001, Winter). Dissecting genius: Einstein's brain and the search for the neural basis of intellect. *Cerebrum, 3,* 11–26.

Lepore, Stephen J. (1993). Social conflict, social support, and psychological distress: Evidence of cross-domain buffering effects. *Journal of Personality and Social Psychology, 63,* 857–867.

Lerner, Melvin J. (1980). *The belief in a just world: A fundamental delusion.* New York: Plenum Press.

Lester, David. (1997). *Making sense of suicide: An in-depth look at why people kill themselves.* Philadelphia: Charles Press.

Lester, Gregory W. (2000, November/December). Why bad beliefs don't die. *Skeptical Inquirer, 24,* 40–43.

Leuchter, Andrew F.; Cook, Ian A.; Witte, Elise A.; & others. (2002). Changes in brain function of depressed subjects during treatment with placebo. *American Journal of Psychiatry, 159,* 122–129.

LeVay, Simon. (1991, August 30). A difference in hypothalamic structure between heterosexual and homosexual men. *Science, 253,* 1034–1037.

LeVay, Simon, & Hamer, Dean H. (1994, May). Evidence for a biological influence in male homosexuality. *Scientific American, 270,* 44–49.

Levenson, Hanna. (2003). Time-limited dynamic psychotherapy: An integrationist perspective. *Journal of Psychotherapy Integration, 13,* 300–333.

Levenson, Robert W. (1992). Autonomic nervous system differences among emotions. *Psychological Science, 3,* 23–27.

Levenson, Robert W.; Ekman, Paul; & Friesen, Wallace V. (1990). Voluntary facial action generates emotion-specific autonomic nervous system activity. *Psychophysiology, 27,* 363–384.

Levenson, Robert W.; Ekman, Paul; Heider, Karl; & Friesen, Wallace V. (1992). Emotion and autonomic nervous system activity in the Minangkabau of west Sumatra. *Journal of Personality and Social Psychology, 62,* 972–988.

Levine, Allen S., & Billington, Charles J. (1997). Why do we eat? A neural systems approach. *Annual Review of Nutrition, 17,* 597–619.

Levine, Robert V. (1997). *A geography of time: The temporal misadventures of a social psychologist, or how every culture keeps time just a little bit differently.* New York: Basic Books.

Levine, Robert V., & Norenzayan, Ara. (1999). The pace of life in 31 countries. *Journal of Cross-Cultural Psychology, 30,* 178–205.

Levy, Becca. (1996). Improving memory in old age through implicit self-stereotyping. *Journal of Personality and Social Psychology, 71,* 1092–1107.

Levy, Benjamin L., & Anderson, Michael C. (2002). Inhibitory processes and the control of memory retrieval. *Trends in Cognitive Science, 6,* 299–305.

Levy, Sheri R.; Freitas, Antonio L.; & Salovey, Peter. (2002). Construing action abstractly and blurring social distinctions: Implications for perceiving homogeneity among, but also empathizing with and helping, others. *Journal of Personality and Social Psychology, 83*(5), 1224–1238.

Lewontin, Richard. (1970, March). Race and intelligence. *Bulletin of the Atomic Scientists,* pp. 2–8.

Lewy, Alfred J., & Sack, Robert L. (1987). Phase typing and bright light therapy of chronobiological sleep and mood disorders. In Angelos Halaris (Ed.), *Chronobiology and psychiatric disorders.* New York: Elsevier.

Liddle, Rodger A. (1997). Cholecystokinin cells. *Annual Review of Physiology, 59,* 221–242.

Lieb, Roselind; Bronisch, Thomas; Höfler, Michael; Schreier, Andrea; & Wittchen, Hans-Ulrich. (2005). Maternal suicidality and risk of suicidality in offspring: Findings from a community study. *American Journal of Psychiatry, 162,* 1665–1671.

Lieberman, Matthew D. (2000). Intuition: A social cognitive neuroscience approach. *Psychological Bulletin, 126,* 109–137.

Lieberman, Robert Paul. (2000). The token economy. *American Journal of Psychiatry, 157,* 1398.

Liebowitz, Michael R.; Salmán, Ester; Jusino, Carlos M.; Garfinkel, Robin; Street, Linda; Cárdenas, Dora L.; & others. (1994). Ataque de nervios and panic disorder. *American Journal of Psychiatry, 151,* 871–875.

Liff, Zanvel A. (1992). Psychoanalysis and dynamic techniques. In Donald K. Freedheim (Ed.), *History of psychotherapy: A century of change.* Washington, DC: American Psychological Association.

Light, Kathleen C.; Smith, Tara E.; Johns, Josephine M.; Brownley, Kimberly A.; Hofheimer, Julie A.; & Amico, Janet. (2000). Oxytocin responsivity in mothers of infants: A preliminary study of relationships with blood pressure during laboratory stress and normal ambulatory activity. *Health Psychology, 19,* 560–567.

Lilie, Jamie K., & Rosenberg, Russell P. (1990). Behavioral treatment of insomnia. In Michel Hersen, Richard M. Eisler, & Peter M. Miller (Eds.), *Progress in behavior modification* (Vol. 25). Newbury Park, CA: Sage.

Lilienfeld, Scott O. (1998, Fall). Pseudoscience in contemporary clinical psychology: What it is and what we can do about it. *Clinical Psychologist, 51,* 3–9.

Lilienfeld, Scott O.; Lynn, Steven Jay; & Lohr, Jeffrey M. (Eds.). (2003). *Science and pseudoscience in clinical psychology.* New York: Guilford Press.

Lilienfeld, Scott O.; Wood, James M.; & Garb, Howard N. (2000). The scientific status of projective techniques. *Psychological Science in the Public Interest, 1,* 27–66.

Lilienfeld, Scott O.; Wood, James M.; & Garb, Howard N. (2001). What's wrong with this picture? *Scientific American, 284,* 80–87.

Lin, Ling; Faraco, Juliette; Kadotani, Hiroshi; Rogers, William; Lin, Xiaoyan; Qui, Xiaohong; & others. (1999, August 20). The sleep disorder canine narcolepsy is caused by a mutation in the hypocretin (orexin) receptor 2 gene. *Cell, 98,* 365–376.

Lindsay, D. Stephen, Hagen, Lisa; Read, J. Don; Wade, Kimberley A.; & Garry, Maryanne. (2004). True photographs and false memories. *Psychological Science, 15,* 149–154.

Lindsay, D. Stephen, & Read, J. Don. (1994). Psychotherapy and memories of childhood and sexual abuse: A cognitive perspective. *Applied Cognitive Psychology 8,* 281–338.

Lindsay, D. Stephen; Wade, Kimberley A.; Hunter, Michael A.; & Read, J. Don. (2004). Adults' memories of childhood: Affect, knowing, and remembering. *Memory, 12,* 27–43.

Lindsey, Delwin T., & Brown, Angela M. (2004). Commentary: Sunlight and "blue": The prevalence of poor lexical color discrimination within the "grue" range. *Psychological Science, 15,* 291–294.

Link, Bruce G.; Andrews, Howard; & Cullen, Francis T. (1992). The violent and illegal behavior of mental patients reconsidered. *American Sociological Review, 57,* 275–292.

Link, Bruce G., & Stueve, Ann. (1998). Commentary: New evidence on the violence risk posed by people with mental illness. *Archives of General Psychiatry, 55,* 403–404.

Links, Paul S. (1996). *Clinical assessment and management of severe personality disorders* (Clinical Practice No. 35). Washington, DC: American Psychiatric Press.

Little, Karley Y.; Krolewski, David M.; Zhang, Lian; & Cassin, Bader J. (2003). Loss of striatal vesicular monoamine transporter protein (VMAT2) in human cocaine users. *American Journal of Psychiatry, 160,* 47–55.

Liu, Dong; Diorio, Josie; Tannenbaum, Beth; Caldji, Christian; Francis, Darlene; Freedman, Alison; & others. (1997). Maternal care, hippocampal glucocorticoid receptors, and hypothalamic-pituitary-adrenal responses to stress. *Science, 277,* 1659–1662.

Livingstone, Margaret, & Hubel, David. (1988, May 6). Segregation of form, color, movement and depth: Anatomy, physiology, and perception. *Science, 240,* 740–749.

Lockard, Robert B. (1971). Reflections on the fall of comparative psychology: Is there a message for us all? *American Psychologist, 26,* 168–179.

Locke, Edwin A. (1976). The nature and causes of job satisfaction. In M. D. Dunnette (Ed.), *Handbook of industrial and organizational psychology.* Chicago: Rand McNally.

Locke, Edwin A., & Schweiger, David M. (1979). Participation in decision-making: One more look. In B. M. Staw (Ed.), *Research in organizational behavior* (Vol. 1). Greenwich, CT: JAI Press.

Lockhart, Robert S., & Craik, Fergus I. M. (1990). Levels of processing: A retrospective commentary on a framework for memory research. *Canadian Journal of Psychology, 44*(1), 87–112.

Loewenstein, George F.; Weber, Elke U.; Hsee, Christopher K., & Welch, Ned. (2001). Risk as feelings. *Psychological Bulletin, 127,* 267–286.

Loewenstein, Richard J. (1993). Psychogenic amnesia and psychogenic fugue: A comprehensive review. In David Spiegel (Ed.), *Dissociative disorders: A clinical review.* Lutherville, MD: Sidran.

Loftus, Elizabeth F. (1993). The reality of repressed memories. *American Psychologist, 48,* 518–537.

Loftus, Elizabeth F. (1996). *Eyewitness testimony* (Rev. ed.). Cambridge, MA: Harvard University Press.

Loftus, Elizabeth F. (2001). Imagining the past. *The Psychologist, 14,* 584–587.

Loftus, Elizabeth F. (2002). Memory faults and fixes. *Issues in Science and Technology, 18*(4), 41–50.

Loftus, Elizabeth F. (2003). Our changeable memories: Legal and practical implications. *Nature Reviews Neuroscience, 4,* 231–234.

Loftus, Elizabeth F.; Garry, Maryanne; Brown, Scott W.; & Rader, Marcella. (1994). Near-natal memories, past-life memories, and other memory myths. *American Journal of Clinical Hypnosis, 36,* 176–179.

Loftus, Elizabeth F., & Ketcham, Katherine. (1991). *Witness for the defense: The accused, the eyewitness, and the expert who puts memory on trial.* New York: St. Martin's Press.

Loftus, Elizabeth F., & Ketcham, Katherine. (1994). *The myth of repressed memory: False memories and allegations of sexual abuse.* New York: St. Martin's Press.

Loftus, Elizabeth F., & Palmer, J. C. (1974). Reconstruction of automobile destruction: An example of the interaction between language and memory. *Journal of Verbal Learning and Verbal Behavior, 13,* 585–589.

Loftus, Elizabeth F., & Pickrell, Jacqueline E. (1995). The formation of false memories. *Psychiatric Annals, 25,* 720–725.

Lohr, Jeffrey M.; Hooke, Wayne; Gist, Richard; & Tolin, David F. (2003). Novel and controversial treatments for trauma-related stress disorders. In Scott O. Lilienfeld, Steven Jay Lynn, & Jeffrey M. Lohr (Eds.), *Science and pseudoscience in clinical psychology.* New York: Guilford Press.

LoLordo, Vincent M. (2001). Learned helplessness and depression. In Marilyn E. Carroll & J. Bruce Overmier (Eds.), *Animal research and human health: Advancing human welfare through behavioral science.* Washington, DC: American Psychological Association.

Lonetto, Richard, & Templer, Donald I. (1986). *Death anxiety.* Washington, DC: Hemisphere.

Long, James E., Jr. (2005). Power to prescribe: The debate over prescription privileges for psychologists and the legal issues implicated. *Law & Psychology Review, 29,* 243–260.

Lonsdorf, Elizabeth V., & Hopkins, William D. (2005). Wild chimpanzees show population-level handedness for tool use. *Proceedings of the National Academy of Sciences, USA, 102,* 12634–12638.

Lord, Charles G.; Ross, Lee; & Lepper, Mark R. (1979). Biased assimilation and attitude polarization: The effects of prior theories on subsequently considered evidence. *Journal of Personality and Social Psychology, 37,* 2098–2109.

Lord, Robert G.; DeVader, Christy L.; & Alliger, George M. (1986). A meta-analysis of the relation between personality traits and leadership perceptions: An application of validity generalization procedures. *Journal of Applied Psychology, 71,* 402–410.

Louie, Kenway, & Wilson, Matthew. (2001). Temporally structured replay of awake hippocampal ensemble activity during rapid eye movement sleep. *Neuron, 29,* 145–156.

Lovallo, William R.; al'Absi, Mustafa; Pincomb, Gwen A.; Everson, Susan A.; Sung, Bong Hee; Passey, Richard B.; & Wilson, Michael F. (1996). Caffeine and behavioral

stress effects on blood pressure in borderline hypertensive Caucasian men. *Health Psychology, 15,* 11–17.

Lu, Lin; Hope, Bruce T.; Dempsey, Jack; Liu, Shirley Y.; Bossert, Jennifer M.; & Shaham, Yavin. (2005). Central amygdala ERK signaling pathway is critical to incubation of cocaine craving. *Nature Neuroscience 8,* 212–219.

Lu, Ying; Sweitzer, Sarah M.; Laurito, Charles E.; & Yeomans David C. (2004). Differential opioid inhibition of C- and A delta-fiber mediated thermonociception after stimulation of the nucleus raphe magnus. *Anesthesia & Analgesia, 98,* 414–419.

Luborsky, Lester, & Barrett, Marna S. (2006). The history and empirical status of key psychoanalytic concepts. *Annual Review of Clinical Psychology, 2,* 69–78.

Luders, Eileen; Rex, David E.; Narr, Katherine; Woods, Roger; Jancke, Lutz; Thompson, P.M.; & others. (2003). Relationships between sulcal asymmetries and corpus callosum size: Gender and handedness effects. *Cerebral Cortex, 13,* 1084–1093.

Luo, Jing, & Niki, Kazuhisa. (2003). Function of hippocampus in "insight" of problem solving. *Hippocampus, 13,* 316–323.

Luo, Yuyan; Baillargeon, Renée; Brueckner, Laura; & Munakata, Yuko. (2003). Reasoning about a hidden object after a delay: Evidence for robust representations in 5-month-old infants. *Cognition, 88,* B23–B32.

Lutz, Antoine; Greischar, Lawrence L.; Rawlings, Nancy B.; Richard, Matthieu; & Davidson, Richard J. (2004, November 16). Long-term meditators self-induce high-amplitude gamma synchrony during mental practice. *Proceedings of the National Academy of Sciences, USA, 101,* 16369–16373.

Lykken, David T. (1995). *The antisocial personalities.* Hillsdale, NJ: Erlbaum.

Lykken, David T.; McGue, Matthew; Tellegen, Auke; & Bouchard, Thomas J., Jr. (1992). Emergenesis: Genetic traits that may not run in families. *American Psychologist, 47,* 1565–1577.

Lynam, Donald R., & Gudonis, Lauren. (2005). The development of psychopathy. *Annual Review of Clinical Psychology, 1,* 381–407.

Lynch, Denis J.; McGrady, Angele; Alvarez, Elizabeth; & Forman, Justin. (2005). Recent life changes and medical utilization in an academic family practice. *Journal of Nervous and Mental Disease, 193,* 633–635.

Lyness, Scott A. (1993). Predictors of differences between Type A and B individuals in heart rate and blook pressure reactivity. *Psychological Bulletin, 114,* 266–295.

Lynn, Richard. (1987). The intelligence of the Mongoloids: A psychometric evolutionary and neurological theory. *Personality and Individual Differences, 8,* 813–844.

Lynn, Steven Jay; Lock, Timothy G.; Myers, Bryan; & Payne, David G. (1997). Recalling the unrecallable: Should hypnosis be used to

recover memories in psychotherapy? *Current Directions in Psychological Science, 6,* 79–83.

Lynn, Steven Jay, & Nash, Michael R. (1994). Truth in memory: Ramifications for psychotherapy and hypnotherapy. *American Journal of Clinical Hypnosis, 36,* 194–208.

Lytton, Hugh, & Romney, David M. (1991). Parents' differential socialization of boys and girls: A meta-analysis. *Psychological Bulletin, 109,* 267–296.

Maccoby, Eleanor E., & Martin, John A. (1983). Socialization in the context of the family: Parent-child interaction. In Paul H. Mussen (Ed.), *Handbook of child psychology: Vol. 4. Socialization, personality, and social development.* New York: Wiley.

MacDonald, Benie, & Davey, Graham C. L. (2005). Inflated responsibility and perseverative checking: The effect of negative mood. *Journal of Abnormal Psychology, 114,* 176–182.

MacKenzie, Brian. (1984). Explaining race differences in IQ: The logic, the methodology, and the evidence. *American Psychologist, 39,* 1214–1233.

Mackie, Diane M., & Hamilton, David L. (1993). Affect, cognition, and stereotyping: Concluding comments. In Diane M. Mackie & David L. Hamilton (Eds.), *Affect, cognition, and stereotyping: Interactive processes in group perception.* San Diego, CA: Academic Press.

Macrae, C. Neil, & Bodenhausen, Galen V. (2001). Social cognition: Categorical person perception. *British Journal of Psychology, 92,* 239–255.

Macrae, C. Neil; Milne, Alan B.; & Bodenhausen, Galen V. (1994). Stereotypes as energy-saving devices: A peek inside the cognitive toolbox. *Journal of Personality and Social Psychology, 66,* 37–47.

Magnavita, Jeffrey J. (1993). The evolution of short-term dynamic psychotherapy: Treatment of the future? *Professional Psychology: Research and Practice, 24,* 360–365.

Maguire, Eleanor A.; Gadian, David G.; Johnsrude, Ingrid S.; Good, Catriona D.; Ashburner, John; Frackowiak, Richard S. J.; & Frith, Christopher D. (2000). Navigation-related structural change in the hippocampi of taxi drivers. *Proceedings of the National Academy of Sciences, USA, 97,* 4398–4403.

Mahler, D. A.; Cunningham, L. N.; Skrinar, G. S.; Kraemer, W. J.; & Colice, G. L. (1989). Beta-endorphin activity and hypercapnic ventilatory responsiveness after marathon running. *Journal of Applied Physiology, 66,* 2431–2436.

Mahmood, Iftekhar, & Sahajwalla, Chandrahas. (1999). Clinical pharmacokinetics and pharmacodynamics of buspirone, an anxiolytic drug. *Clinical Pharmacokinetics, 36,* 277–287.

Mahowald, Mark W., & Schenck, Carlos H. (2005, October 27). Insights from studying human sleep disorders. *Nature, 437,* 1279–1285.

Maier, Steven F.; Seligman, Martin E.; & Solomon, Richard L. (1969). Pavlovian fear conditioning and learned helplessness: Effects of escape and avoidance behavior of (a) the CS=UCS contingency, and (b) the independence of the UCS and voluntary responding. In B. A. Campbell & R. M. Church (Eds.), *Punishment and aversive behavior*. New York: Appleton-Century-Crofts.

Maier, Steven F., & Watkins, Linda R. (2000). The neurobiology of stressor controllability. In Jane E. Gilham (Ed.), *The science of optimism and hope: Research essays in honor of Martin E. P. Seligman*. Philadelphia: Templeton Foundation Press.

Maj, Mario; Magliano, Lorena; Pirozzi, Raffaele; Marasco, Cecilia; & Guarneri, Manuela. (1994). Validity of rapid cycling as a course specifier for bipolar disorder. *American Journal of Psychiatry, 151*, 1015–1019.

Majid, Asifa; Bowerman, Melissa; Kita, Sotaro; Haun, Daniel B. M.; & Levinson, Stephen C. (2004). Can language restructure cognition? The case for space. *Trends in Cognitive Sciences, 8,* 108–114.

Malaspina, Dolores; Harlap, Susan; & others. (2001). Advancing paternal age and the risk of schizophrenia. *Archives of General Psychiatry, 58*, 361–367.

Malenka, Robert C. (2003). The long-term potential of LTP. *Nature Reviews Neuroscience, 4,* 923–926.

Malla, Ashok, & Payne, Jennifer. (2005). First-episode psychosis: Psychopathology, quality of life, and functional outcome. *Schizophrenia Bulletin, 31,* 650–671.

Mallinckrodt, Brent. (2001) Interpersonal processes, attachment, and development of social competencies in individual and group psychotherapy. In Barbara R. Sarason & Steve Duck (Eds.), *Personal relationships: Implications for clinical and community psychology*. Chichester, England: Wiley.

Maltz, Wendy. (1991). *The sexual healing journey: A guide for survivors of sexual abuse*. New York: HarperCollins.

Mandler, George. (1993). Thought, memory, and learning: Effects of emotional stress. In Leo Goldberger & Shlomo Breznitz (Eds.), *Handbook of stress: Theoretical and clinical aspects* (2nd ed.). New York: Free Press.

Mann, J. John; Waternaux, Christine; Haas, Gretchen L.; & Malone, Kevin M. (1999). Toward a clinical model of suicidal behavior in psychiatric patients. *American Journal of Psychiatry, 156*, 181–189.

Maquet, Pierre. (2001). The role of sleep in learning and memory. *Science, 294*, 1048–1052.

Maquet, Pierre; Laureys, Steven; Peigneux, Phillippe; Fuchs, Sonia; Petiau, Christophe; Phillips, Christophe; & others. (2000). Experience-dependent changes in cerebral activation during human REM sleep. *Nature Neuroscience, 3*, 831–836.

Marañon, Gregorio. (1924). Contribution à l'étude de l'action émotive de l'adrenaline. *Revue Francaise d'Endocrinologie, 2,* 301–325.

Marcelino, A.S.; Adam, A.S.; & others. (2001). Internal and external determinants of eating initiation in humans. *Appetite, 36,* 9–14.

Marcia, James E. (1991). Identity and self-development. In R. M. Lerner, A. C. Petersen, & Jeanne Brooks-Gunn (Eds.), *Encyclopedia of adolescence* (Vol. 1). New York: Garland.

Marco, Christine A., & Suls, Jerry. (1993). Daily stress and the trajectory of mood: Spillover, response assimilation, contrast, and chronic negative affectivity. *Journal of Personality and Social Psychology, 64,* 1053–1063.

Marcus, Gary. (2004). *The birth of the mind: How a tiny number of genes creates the complexities of human thought*. New York: Basic Books.

Marder, Stephen R.; Ames, Donna; Wirshing, William C.; & Van Putten, Theodore. (1993). Schizophrenia. *Psychiatric Clinics of North America, 16*, 567–587.

Marder, Stephen R., & Meibach, Richard C. (1994). Risperidone in the treatment of schizophrenia. *American Journal of Psychiatry, 151*, 825–835.

Margolin, Gayla, & Gordis, Elana B. (2000). The effects of family and community violence on children. *Annual Review of Psychology, 51,* 445–479.

Margraf, Jürgen, & Ehlers, Anke. (1989). Etiological models of panic: a) Medical and biological aspects; b) Psychophysiological and cognitive aspects. In Roger Baker (Ed.), *Panic disorder: Theory, research and therapy*. Chichester, England: Wiley.

Mark, Victor W., & Taub, Edward. (2003). Cortical reorganization and the rehabilitation of movement by constraint-induced therapy after neurological injury. In Luiz Pessoa & Peter De Weerd (Eds.), *Filling-in: From perceptual completion to cortical reorganization*. London: Oxford University Press.

Markman, Arthur B., & Gentner, Dedre. (2001). Thinking. *Annual Review of Psychology, 52,* 223–247.

Markus, Hazel Rose, & Cross, Susan. (1990). The interpersonal self. In Lawrence A. Pervin (Ed.), *Handbook of personality: Theory and research*. New York: Guilford Press.

Markus, Hazel Rose, & Kitayama, Shinobu. (1991). Culture and the self: Implications for cognition, emotion, and motivation. *Psychological Review, 98*, 224–253.

Markus, Hazel Rose, & Kitayama, Shinobu. (1994). The cultural construction of self and emotion: Implications for social behavior. In Shinobu Kitayama & Hazel Rose Markus (Eds.), *Emotion and culture: Empirical studies of mutual influence*. Washington, DC: American Psychological Association.

Markus, Hazel Rose, & Kitayama, Shinobu. (1998). The cultural psychology of personality. *Journal of Cross-Cultural Psychology, 29,* 63–87.

Markus, Hazel Rose, & Kunda, Ziva. (1986). Stability and malleability of the self-concept. *Journal of Personality and Social Psychology, 51,* 858–866.

Markus, Hazel Rose, & Nurius, Paula. (1986). Possible selves. *American Psychologist, 41,* 954–969.

Markus, Hazel Rose, & Wurf, Elissa. (1987). The dynamic self-concept: A social psychological perspective. *Annual Review of Psychology, 38,* 299–337.

Marlatt, G. Alan; Baer, John S.; Donovan, Dennis M.; & Kivlahan, Daniel R. (1988). Addictive behaviors: Etiology and treatment. *Annual Review of Psychology, 39,* 223–252.

Marler, Peter. (1967). Animal communication symbols. *Science, 35*, 63–78.

Marmie, William R., & Healy, Alice F. (2004). Memory for common objects: Brief intentional study is sufficient to overcome poor recall of US coin features. *Applied Cognitive Psychology, 18,* 445–453.

Marsella, Anthony J., & Dash-Scheuer, Alice. (1988). Coping, culture, and healthy human development: A research and conceptual overview. In Pierre R. Dasen, John W. Berry, & Norman Sartorius (Eds.), *Health and cross-cultural psychology: Toward applications* (Vol. 10, Cross-cultural Research and Methodology Series.). Newbury Park, CA: Sage.

Marshall, Grant N.; Wortman, Camille B.; Kusulas, Jeffrey W.; Hervig, Linda K.; & Vickers, Ross R., Jr. (1992). Distinguishing optimism from pessimism: Relations to fundamental dimensions of mood and personality. *Journal of Personality and Social Psychology, 62,* 1067–1074.

Marshall, Nancy L. (2004). The quality of early child care and children's development. *Current Directions in Psychological Science, 13,* 165–168.

Martens, Brian K.; Lochner, David G.; & Kelly, Susan Q. (1992). The effects of variable-interval reinforcement on academic engagement: A demonstration of matching theory. *Journal of Applied Behavior Analysis, 25,* 143–151.

Martin, Bruce. (1998, May). Coincidences: Remarkable or random? *Skeptical Inquirer, 22,* 23–28.

Martin, Carol Lynn, & Halverson, Charles F., Jr. (1981). A schematic processing model of sex typing and stereotyping in children. *Child Development, 52,* 1119–1134.

Martin, Carol Lynn, & Halverson, Charles F., Jr. (1983). The effects of sex-typing schemas on young children's memory. *Child Development, 54,* 563–574.

Martin, Carol Lynn, & Ruble, Diane. (2004). Children's search for gender cues: Cognitive perspectives on gender development. *Psychological Science, 13,* 67–70.

Martin, Carol Lynn; Ruble, Diane N.; & Szkrybalo, Joel. (2002). Cognitive theories of early gender development. *Psychological Bulletin, 128,* 903–933.

Martin, Carol Lynn; Ruble, Diane N.; & Szkry-balo, Joel. (2004). Recognizing the centrality of gender identity and stereotype knowledge in gender development and moving toward theoretical integration: Reply to Bandura and Bussey. (2004). *Psychological Bulletin, 130,* 702–710.

Martin, Laura. (1986). "Eskimo words for snow": A case study in the genesis and decay of an anthropological example. *American Anthropologist, 88,* 418–423.

Martin, Stephen D.; Martin, Elizabeth; Santoch, S. Rai; Richardson, Mark A.; & Royall, Robert. (2001). Brain blood flow changes in depressed patients treated with interpersonal psychotherapy or venlafaxine hydrochloride. *Archives of General Psychiatry, 58,* 641–648.

Martin, Stephen J.; Grimwood, Paul D.; & Morris, Richard G. M. (2000). Synaptic plasticity and memory: An evaluation of the hypothesis. *Annual Review of Neuroscience, 23,* 649–711.

Marucha, Phillip T.; Kiecolt-Glaser, Janice K.; & Favagehi, Mehrdad. (1998). Mucosal wound healing is impaired by examination stress. *Psychosomatic Medicine, 60,* 362–365.

Marx, Jean. (2004, July 16). Prolonging the agony: Researchers are deciphering the biological changes that can turn pain into a debilitating, chronic state. *Science, 305,* 326–329.

Masland, Richard H. (2001). The fundamental plan of the retina. *Nature Neuroscience, 4,* 877–886.

Maslow, Abraham H. (1943). A theory of human motivation. *Psychological Review, 50,* 370–396.

Maslow, Abraham H. (1954). *Motivation and personality.* New York: Harper.

Maslow, Abraham H. (1968). *Toward a psychology of being* (2nd ed.). Princeton, NJ: Van Nostrand.

Maslow, Abraham H. (1970). *Motivation and personality* (2nd ed.). New York: Harper & Row.

Mason, Paul T., & Kreger, Randi. (1998). *Stop walking on eggshells: Taking your life back when someone you care about has borderline personality disorder.* New York: New Harbinger.

Masson, Jeffrey M. (1984a). *The assault on truth: Freud's suppression of the seduction theory.* New York: Farrar, Strauss & Giroux.

Masson, Jeffrey M. (1984b, February). Freud and the seduction theory: A challenge to the foundations of psychoanalysis. *The Atlantic, 253,* 33–60.

Masters, William H., & Johnson, Virginia E. (1966). *Human sexual response.* Boston: Little, Brown.

Masters, William H.; Johnson, Virginia E.; & Kolodny, Robert C. (1995). *Human sexuality* (5th ed.). New York: HarperCollins.

Mataix-Cols, David; Rauch, Scott L.; Manzo, Peter A.; & others. (1999). Use of factor-analyzed symptom dimensions to predict outcome with serotonin reuptake inhibitors and placebo in the treatment of obsessive-compulsive disorder. *American Journal of Psychiatry, 156,* 1409–1416.

Matarazzo, Joseph D. (1981). Obituary: David Wechsler (1896–1981). *American Psychologist, 36,* 1542–1543.

Matson, Claire A.; Reid, Dana F.; Cannon, Todd A.; & Ritter, Robert C. (2000). Cholecys-tokinin and leptin act synergistically to reduce body weight. *American Journal of Physiology, 278,* R882–R890.

Matsumoto, David. (2000). *Culture and psychology: People around the world* (2nd ed.). Belmont, CA: Wadsworth/Thomson Learning.

Mattick, John S. (2004, October). The hidden genetic program of complex organisms. *Scientific American, 291*(4), 60–67.

Mavromatis, Andreas. (1987). *Hypnagogia: The unique state of consciousness between wakefulness and sleep.* New York: Routledge & Kegan Paul.

Maxmen, Jerrold S., & Ward, Nicholas G. (1995). *Essential psychopathology and its treatment* (2nd ed.). New York: Norton.

May, Mike. (2002, September 26). Quoted in British Broadcasting Corporation (BBC) transcript 9-26-02: *LiveChat: The man who learned to see.* Retrieved on August 2, 2004 at: http://www.bbc.co.uk/ouch/wyp/mikemayqa.shtml.

May, Mike. (2004). Quoted in Sendero Group: "Mike's journal." Retrieved August 2, 2004, from http://www.senderogroup.com/mikejournal.htm

Mayer, John D., & Salovey, Peter. (1993). The intelligence of emotional intelligence. *Intelligence, 17,* 433–442.

Mayer, John D., & Salovey, Peter. (1997). What is emotional intelligence? In Peter Salovey & David J. Sluyter (Eds.), *Emotional development and emotional intelligence: Educational implications.* New York: Basic Books.

Maynard, Ashley E., & Greenfield, Patricia M. (2003). Implicit cognitive development in cultural tools and children: Lessons from Maya Mexico. *Cognitive Development, 18,* 489–510.

McAdams, Dan P. (1992). The five-factor model in personality: A critical appraisal. *Journal of Personality, 60,* 329–362.

McAndrew, Francis T.; Akande, Adebowale; Turner, Saskia; & Sharma, Yadika. (1998). A cross-cultural ranking of stressful life events in Germany, India, South Africa, and the United States. *Journal of Cross-Cultural Psychology, 29,* 717–727.

McCaig, Linda F., & Burt, Catharine W. (2004, March 18). *National hospital ambulatory medical care survey: 2002 emergency department summary* (Advance Data From Vital and Health Statistics, No. 340). Hyattsville, MD: National Center for Health Statistics. Retrieved January 6, 2005, from http://www.cdc.gov/nchs/data/ad/ad340.pdf

McCartney, Kathleen; Harris, Monica J.; & Bernieri, Frank. (1990). Growing up and growing apart: A developmental meta-analysis of twin studies. *Psychological Bulletin, 107,* 226–237.

McClearn, Gerald E.; Johansson, Boo; Berg, Stig; Pederson, Nancy L.; Ahern, Frank; Petrill, Stephen A.; & Plomin, Robert. (1997, June 6). Substantial genetic influence on cognitive abilities in twins 80 or more years old. *Science, 276,* 1560–1563.

McClelland, David C. (1961). *The achieving society.* Princeton, NJ: Van Nostrand.

McClelland, David C. (1975). *Power: The inner experience.* New York: Irvington.

McClelland, David C. (1985a). How motives, skills, and values determine what people do. *American Psychologist, 40,* 812–825.

McClelland, David C. (1985b). *Human motivation.* Glenview, IL: Scott, Foresman.

McClelland, David C. (1987). Characteristics of successful entrepreneurs. *Journal of Creative Behavior, 21,* 219–233.

McClelland, David C. (1989). Motivational factors in health and disease. *American Psychologist, 44,* 675–683.

McClelland, David C.; Atkinson, John W.; Clark, Russell A.; & Lowell, Edgar L. (1953). *The achievement motive.* New York: Appleton-Century-Crofts.

McClelland, David C., & Winter, David G. (1971). *Motivating economic achievement.* New York: Free Press.

McClintock, Martha K. (1971). Menstrual synchrony and suppression. *Nature, 229,* 244–245.

McClintock, Martha K. (1992, October). Quoted in John Easton: "Sex, rats, and videotapes: From the outside in." *University of Chicago Magazine, 85*(1), 32–36.

McClintock, Martha K. (2001, July 25). Quoted in Marcella S. Kreiter: "Neurology: Brain smells out signals." *MedServ Medical News.* Retrieved November 8, 2001, from http://www.medserv.no/article/php?sid=666

McCoy, Robert. (1996). Phrenology. In Gordon Stein (Ed.), *The encyclopedia of the paranormal.* Amherst, NY: Prometheus Books.

McCrae, Robert R., & Costa, Paul T., Jr. (1990). *Personality in adulthood.* New York: Guilford Press.

McCrae, Robert R., & Costa, Paul T., Jr. (1996). Toward a new generation of personality theories: Theoretical contexts for the five-factor model. In Jerry S. Wiggins (Ed.), *The five-factor model of personality: Theoretical perspectives.* New York: Guilford Press.

McCrae, Robert R.; Costa, Paul T., Jr.; Martin, Thomas A.; Oryol, Valery E.; Rukavishnikov, Alexey A.; Senin, Ivan G.; Hrebíčková, Martina; & Urbánek, Tomás. (2004). Consensual validation of personality traits across cultures. *Journal of Research in Personality, 38,* 179–201.

McCrae, Robert R.; Costa, Paul T., Jr.; Ostendorf, Fritz; Angleitner, Alois; Hřebíčová, Martina; Avia, Maria D.; & others. (2000). Nature over nurture: Temperament, personality, and life span development. *Journal of Personality and Social Psychology, 78*, 173–186.

McCrae, Robert R.; Terracciano, Antonio; & Members of the Personality Profiles of Cultures Project. (2005). Universal features of personality traits from the observer's perspective: Data from 50 cultures. *Journal of Personality and Social Psychology, 88*, 547–561.

McDougall, William. (1908). *Introduction to social psychology*. London: Methuen.

McFadden, Lisa; Seidman, Edward; & Rappaport, Julian. (1992). A comparison of espoused theories of self- and mutual help: Implications for mental health professionals. *Professional Psychology: Research and Practice, 23*, 515–520.

McGaugh, James L. (2000). Memory—A century of consolidation. *Science, 287*, 248–251.

McGaugh, James L. (2004). The amygdala modulates the consolidation of memories of emotionally arousing experiences. *Annual Review of Neuroscience, 27*, 1–28.

McGeary, Johanna. (2004, May 17). The scandal's growing stain. *Time Magazine*. Accessed on December 7, 2005 from http://www.time.com/time/archive/printout/0,23657,994176,00.html

McGue, Matt; Bouchard, Thomas J., Jr.; Iacono, William G.; & Lykken, David T. (1993). Behavioral genetics of cognitive ability: A life-span perspective. In Robert Plomin & Gerald E. McClearn (Eds.), *Nature, nurture, and psychology*. Washington, DC: American Psychological Association.

McKean, Keith Joseph. (1994). Academic helplessness: Applying learned helplessness theory to undergraduates who give up when faced with academic setbacks. *College Student Journal, 28*, 456–462.

McKellar, Peter. (1972). Imagery from the standpoint of introspection. In Peter W. Sheehan (Ed.), *The function and nature of imagery*. New York: Academic Press.

McManus, Chris. (2004). *Right hand, left hand: The origins of asymmetry in brains, bodies, atoms and cultures*. Cambridge, MA: Harvard University Press.

McManus, Chris, & Bryden, M. Philip. (1992). The genetics of handedness, cerebral dominance, and lateralization. In Isabelle Rapin & Sidney J. Segalowitz (Eds.), *Handbook of neuropsychology: Vol. 6. Developmental neuropsychology* (Pt. 1). New York: Elsevier.

McNally, Richard J. (1987). Preparedness and phobias: A review. *Psychological Bulletin, 101*, 283–303.

McNally, Richard J. (1998, September 14). Quoted in Judy Foreman: "New therapy for trauma is doubted." *The Boston Globe Online*. Retrieved October 10, 2001, from http://www.globe.com/globe/search/stories/health/healthsense/091498.htm

McNally, Richard J. (2003). Progress and controversy in the study of posttraumatic stress disorder. *Annual Review of Psychology, 54*, 229–252.

McNally, Richard J. (2004) The science and folklore of traumatic amnesia. *Clinical Psychology: Science and Practice, 11*, 29–33.

McNally, Richard J., & Louro, Christine E. (1992). Fear of flying in agoraphobia and simple phobia: Distinguishing features. *Journal of Anxiety Disorders, 6*, 319–324.

McNeilly, Cheryl L., & Howard, Kenneth I. (1991). The effects of psychotherapy: A reevaluation based on dosage. *Psychotherapy Research, 1*, 74–78.

Mebert, Carolyn J. (1991). Variability in the transition to parenthood experience. In Karl Pillemer & Kathleen McCartney (Eds.), *Parent-child relations throughout life*. Hillsdale, NJ: Erlbaum.

Melanson, Kathleen J.; Smith, Françoise J.; Campfield, L. Arthur; & others. (1999). Blood glucose patterns and appetite in time-blinded humans: Carbohydrate versus fat. *American Journal of Physiology, 277*, R337–R345.

Mellers, Barbara A. (2000). Choice and the relative pleasure of consequences. *Psychological Bulletin, 126*, 910–924.

Melton, Lisa. (2005, December 17). Use it, don't lose it. *New Scientist, 188*, 32–35.

Meltzoff, Andrew N., & Moore, M. Keith. (1977). Imitation of facial and manual gestures by human neonates. *Science, 198*, 75–78.

Meltzoff, Andrew N., & Moore, M. Keith. (1983). Newborn infants imitate adult facial gestures. *Child Development, 54*, 702–709.

Melzack, Ronald, & Wall, Patrick D. (1965). Pain mechanisms: A new theory. *Science, 150*, 971–980.

Melzack, Ronald, & Wall, Patrick D. (1996). *The challenge of pain* (2nd ed.). Harmondsworth, UK: Penguin.

Mendlowicz, Mauro V., & Stein, Murray B. (2000). Quality of life in individuals with anxiety disorders. *American Journal of Psychiatry, 157*, 669–682.

Mennella, Julie A., & Beauchamp, Gary K. (1996). The early development of human flavor preferences. In Elizabeth D. Capaldi (Ed.), *Why we eat, what we eat: The psychology of eating*. Washington, DC: American Psychological Association.

Merckelbach, Harald; Arntz, Arnoud; Arrindell, Willem A.; & De Jong, Peter J. (1992). Pathways to spider phobia. *Behavior Research and Therapy, 30*, 543–546.

Merikle, Philip M., & Daneman, Meredyth. (1998). Psychological investigations of unconscious perception. *Journal of Consciousness Studies, 5*, 5–18.

Mervis, Carolyn B., & Rosch, Eleanor. (1981). Categorization of natural objects. *Annual Review of Psychology, 32*, 89–115.

Metcalfe, Janet, & Mischel, Walter. (1999). A hot/cool-system analysis of delay of gratification: Dynamics of willpower. *Psychological Review, 106*, 3–19.

Miceli, Maria, & Castelfranchi, Cristiano. (2000). Nature and mechanisms of loss of motivation. *Review of General Psychology, 4*, 238–263.

Michael, Robert T.; Gagnon, John H.; Laumann, Edward O.; & Kolata, Gina. (1994). *Sex in America: A definitive survey*. New York: Warner Books.

Michelson, David; Bancroft, John; Targum, Steven; Kim, Yongman; & Tepner, Rosalinda. (2000). Female sexual dysfunction associated with antidepressant administration: A randomized, placebo-controlled study of pharmacological intervention. *American Journal of Psychiatry, 157*, 239–243.

Mikalsen, Anita; Bertelsen, Bård; & Flaten, Magne Arve. (2001). Effects of caffeine, caffeine-associated stimuli, and caffeine-related information on physiological and psychological arousal. *Psychopharmacology, 157*, 373–380.

Mikkelsen, Edwin J. (2001). Enuresis and encopresis: Ten years of progress. *Journal of the American Academy of Child and Adolescent Psychiatry, 40*, 1146–1158.

Miklowitz, David J. (1994). Family risk indicators in schizophrenia. *Schizophrenia Bulletin, 20*, 137–149.

Milgram, Stanley. (1963). Behavioral study of obedience. *Journal of Abnormal Psychology, 67*, 371–378.

Milgram, Stanley. (1965/1992). Some conditions of obedience and disobedience to authority. In John Sabini & Maury Silver (Eds.), *The individual in a social world: Essays and experiments* (2nd ed.). New York: McGraw-Hill.

Milgram, Stanley. (1974). *Obedience to authority: An experimental view*. New York: Harper & Row.

Milgram, Stanley. (1980). Interview by Richard I. Evans. In Richard I. Evans (Ed.), *The making of social psychology: Discussions with creative contributors*. New York: Gardner Press.

Milgram, Stanley. (1992). On maintaining social norms: A field experiment in the subway. In John Sabini & Maury Silver (Eds.), *The individual in a social world: Essays and experiments* (2nd ed.). New York: McGraw-Hill.

Miller, Arthur G. (1986). *The obedience experiments: A case study of controversy in social science*. New York: Praeger.

Miller, George A. (1956/1994). The magical number seven, plus or minus two: Some limits on our capacity for processing information [Special centennial issue]. *Psychological Review, 101*, 343–352.

Miller, Gregory A., & Keller, Jennifer. (2000). Psychology and neuroscience: Making peace. *Current Directions in Psychological Science, 9*, 212–215.

Miller, Gregory E.; Cohen, Sheldon; & Ritchey, A. Kim. (2002). Chronic psychological stress and the regulation of pro-inflammatory cytokines: A glucocorticoid-resistance model. *Health Psychology, 21*, 531–541.

Miller, Patricia H. (1993). *Theories of developmental psychology* (3rd ed.). New York: Freeman.

Miller, Richard E., & Sarat, Austin. (1981). Grievances, claims, and disputes: Assessing the adversary culture. *Law & Society Review, 15,* 525.

Miller, Todd Q.; Smith, Timothy W.; Turner, Charles W.; Guijarro, Margarita L.; & Hallet, Amanda J. (1996). A meta-analytic review of research on hostility and physical health. *Psychological Bulletin, 119,* 322–348.

Miller-Jones, Dalton. (1989). Culture and testing. *American Psychologist 44,* 360–366.

Milne, Sarah; Sheeran, Paschal; & Orbell, Sheina. (2000). Prediction and intervention in health-related behavior: A meta-analytic review of protection motivation theory. *Journal of Applied Social Psychology, 30,* 106–143.

Milner, Brenda. (1970). Memory and the medial temporal regions of the brain. In Karl H. Pribram & Donald E. Broadbent (Eds.), *Biology of memory.* New York: Academic Press.

Milton, Julie, & Wiseman, Richard. (1999). Does psi exist? Lack of replication of an anomalous process of information transfer. *Psychological Bulletin, 125,* 387–391.

Milton, Julie, & Wiseman, Richard. (2001). Does psi exist? Reply to Storm and Ertel (2001). *Psychological Bulletin, 127,* 434–438.

Minda, John Paul, & Smith, J. David. (2001). Prototypes in category learning: The effects of category size, category structure, and stimulus complexity. *Journal of Experimental Psychology: Learning, Memory, and Cognition, 27,* 775–799.

Mindell, Jodi A. (1997). Children and sleep. In Mark R. Pressman & William C. Orr (Eds.), *Understanding sleep: The evaluation and treatment of sleep disorders.* Washington, DC: American Psychological Association.

Mineka, Susan, & Nugent, Kathleen. (1995). Mood-congruent memory biases in anxiety and depression. In Daniel L. Schacter (Ed.), *Memory distortion: How minds, brains, and societies reconstruct the past.* Cambridge, MA: Harvard University Press.

Mintzberg, H. (1973). *The nature of managerial work.* New York: Harper & Row.

Mirescu, Christian; Peters, Jennifer D.; & Gould, Elizabeth. (2004). Early life experience alters response of adult neurogenesis to stress. *Nature Neuroscience, 7,* 841–846.

Mischel, Walter. (1966). Theory and research on the antecedents of self-imposed delay of reward. *Progress in Experimental Personality Research, 3,* 85–132.

Mischel, Walter. (1996). From good intentions to willpower. In Peter M. Gollwitzer & John A. Bargh (Eds.), *The psychology of action: Linking cognition and motivation to behavior.* New York: Guilford Press.

Mischel, Walter. (2004). Toward an integrative science of the person. *Annual Review of Psychology, 55,* 1–22.

Mischel, Walter, & Shoda, Yuichi. (1995). A cognitive-affective system theory of personality: Reconceptualizing situations, dispositions, dynamics, and invariance in personality structure. *Psychological Review, 102,* 246–268.

Mischel, Walter; Shoda, Yuichi; & Mendoza-Denton, Rodolfo. (2002). Situation-behavior profiles as a locus of consistency in personality. *Current Directions in Psychological Science, 11,* 50–54.

Mischel, Walter; Shoda, Yuichi; & Rodriguez, Monica L. (1989, May 26). Delay of gratification in children. *Science, 244,* 933–938.

Mitchell, Laura. (2002). Take two aspirin and the Moonlight Sonata. *Psychologist, 15,* 362–363.

Mitler, Merrill M. (1994). Sleep and catastrophes. In Rosemary Cooper (Ed.), *Sleep.* New York: Chapman & Hall.

Moffat, Scott D.; Hampson, Elizabeth; & Lee, Donald H. (1998). Morphology of the planum temporale and corpus callosum in left handers with evidence of left and right hemisphere speech representation. *Brain, 121,* 2369–2379.

Moghaddam, Fathali M.; Taylor, Donald M.; & Wright, Stephen C. (1993). *Social psychology in cross-cultural perspective.* New York: Freeman.

Mogil, Jeffrey S.; Wilson, Sonya G.; Chesler, Elissa J.; Rankin, A. L.; Nemmani, K. V.; Lariviere, W. R.; & others. (2003, April 15). The melanocortin-1 receptor gene mediates female-specific mechanisms of analgesia in mice and humans. *Proceedings of the National Academy of Sciences, USA, 100,* 4867–4872.

Mohr, Charles. (1964, March 28). Apathy is puzzle in Queens killing: Behavioral specialists hard put to explain witnesses' failure to call police. *New York Times,* pp. 21, 40.

Mohr, David; Vedantham, Kumar; Neylan, Thomas; Metzler, Thomas J.; Best, Suzanne; & Marmar, Charles R. (2003). The mediating effects of sleep in the relationship between traumatic stress and health symptoms in urban police officers. *Psychosomatic Medicine, 65,* 485–489.

Mohr, David C. (1995). Negative outcome in psychotherapy: A critical review. *Clinical Psychology: Science and Practice, 2,* 1–27.

Mombaerts, Peter. (2004). Genes and ligands for odorant, vomeronasal, and taste receptors. *Nature Reviews Neuroscience, 5,* 263–278.

Monahan, John. (1992). Mental disorder and violent behavior: Attitudes and evidence. *American Psychologist, 47,* 511–521.

Mondimore, Francis Mark. (1993). *Depression: The mood disease* (Rev. ed.). Baltimore: Johns Hopkins University Press.

Montgomery, Guy H.; DuHamel, Katherine N.; & Redd, William H. (2000). A meta-analysis of hypnotically induced analgesia: How effective is hypnosis? *International Journal of Clinical and Experimental Hypnosis, 48,* 138–153.

Morelli, Gilda A.; Rogoff, Barbara; Oppenheim, David; & Goldsmith, Denise. (1992). Cultural variation in infants' sleeping arrangements: Questions of independence. *Developmental Psychology, 28,* 604–613.

Morgan, Christiana, & Murray, Henry A. (1935). A method of investigating fantasies: The Thematic Apperception Test. *Archives of Neurology and Psychiatry, 4,* 310–329.

Morgan, William P. (1993). Hypnosis and sport psychology. In Judith W. Rhue, Steven J. Lynn, & Irving Kirsch (Eds.), *Handbook of clinical hypnosis.* Washington, DC: American Psychological Association.

Morgenstern, Jon; Langenbucher, James; Labouvie, Erich; & Miller, Kevin J. (1997). The comorbidity of alcoholism and personality disorders in a clinical population: Prevalence rates and relation to alcohol typology variables. *Journal of Abnormal Psychology, 106,* 74–84.

Morrell, Julian, & Steele, Howard. (2003). The role of attachment security, temperament, maternal perception, and care-giving behavior in persistent infant sleeping problems. *Infant Mental Health Journal, 24,* 447–468.

Morris, John S.; Scott, Sophie K.; & Dolan, Raymond J. (1999). Saying it with feeling: Neural responses to emotional vocalizations. *Neuropsychologia, 37,* 1155–1163.

Morris, Michael W., & Peng, Kaiping. (1994). Culture and cause: American and Chinese attributions for social and physical events. *Journal of Personality and Social Psychology, 67,* 949–971.

Morris, Richard J. (1991). Fear reduction methods. In Frederick H. Kanfer & Arnold P. Goldstein (Eds.), *Helping people change: A textbook of methods* (4th ed.). New York: Pergamon.

Morrison, Adrian R. (2003). The brain on night shift. *Cerebrum, 5,* 23–36.

Moss, Cynthia. (2000). *Elephant memories: Thirteen years in the life of an elephant family.* Chicago: University of Chicago Press.

Motowidlo, Stephen J.; Hanson, Mary A.; & Crafts, Jennifer L. (1997). Low-fidelity simulations. In D. L. Whetzel & G. R. Wheaton (Eds.), *Applied measurement methods in industrial psychology* (pp. 241–260). Palo Alto, CA: Consulting Psychologists Press.

Mounts, Nina S., & Steinberg, Laurence. (1995). An ecological analysis of peer influence on adolescent grade point average and drug use. *Developmental Psychology, 31,* 915–922.

Moyer, Christopher A.; Rounds, James.; & Hannum, James W. (2004). A meta-analysis of massage therapy research. *Psychological Bulletin, 130,* 3–18.

Muchinsky, Paul M. (2000). *Psychology applied to work: An introduction to industrial and organizational psychology* (6th ed.). Belmont, CA: Wadsworth.

Mueller, Shane T.; Seymour, Travis L.; Kieras, David E.; & Meyer, David E. (2003). Theoretical implications of articulatory duration, phonological similarity, and phonological complexity in verbal working memory. *Journal of*

Experimental Psychology: Learning, Memory, and Cognition, 29, 1353–1380.

Mueser, Kim T.; Bellack, Alan S.; & Brady, E. U. (1990). Hallucinations in schizophrenia. *Acta Psychiatrica Scandinavica, 82,* 26–29.

Mueser, Kim T., & Glynn, Shirley M. (1993). Efficacy of psychotherapy for schizophrenia. In Thomas R. Giles (Ed.), *Handbook of effective psychotherapy.* New York: Plenum Press.

Mulhern, Sherrill. (1991). Embodied alternative identities: Bearing witness to a world that might have been. *Psychiatric Clinics of North America, 14,* 769–786.

Mullen, Mary K. (1994). Earliest recollections of childhood: A demographic analysis. *Cognition, 52,* 55–79.

Murphy, Sheila T.; Monahan, Jennifer L.; & Zajonc, Robert B. (1995). Additivity of nonconscious affect: Combined effects of priming and exposure. *Journal of Personality and Social Psychology, 69,* 589–602.

Murray, Henry A. (1938). *Explorations in personality.* New York: Oxford University Press.

Murray, Henry A. (1943). *Thematic Apperception Test Manual.* Cambridge, MA: Harvard University Press.

Murray, John B. (1995). Evidence for acupuncture's analgesic effectiveness and proposals for the physiological mechanisms involved. *Journal of Psychology, 129,* 443–461.

Murtagh, Douglas R. R., & Greenwood, Kenneth M. (1995). Identifying effective psychological treatments for insomnia: A meta-analysis. *Journal of Consulting and Clinical Psychology, 63,* 79–89.

Mustanski, Brian S.; Chivers, Meredith L.; & Bailey, J. Michael. (2002). A critical review of recent biological research on human sexual orientation. *Annual Review of Sex Research, 13,* 89–140.

Mustanski, Brian S.; Viken, Richard J.; Kaprio, Jaakko; Pulkkinen, Lea; & Rose, Richard J. (2004). Genetic and environmental influences on pubertal development: Longitudinal data from Finnish twins at ages 11 and 14. *Developmental Psychology, 40,* 1188–1198.

Musto, David F. (1991, July). Opium, cocaine and marijuana in American history. *Scientific American, 265,* 40–47.

Muth, Denise K.; Glynn, Shawn M.; Britton, Bruce K.; & Graves, Michael F. (1988). Thinking out loud while studying text: Rehearsing key ideas. *Journal of Educational Psychology, 80,* 315–318.

Myers, Mark G.; Steward, David G.; & Brown, Sandra A. (1998). Progression from conduct disorder to antisocial personality disorder following treatment for adolescent substance abuse. *American Journal of Psychiatry, 155,* 479–485.

Nadarajah, Bagirathy, & Parnavelas, John G. (2002). Modes of neuronal migration in the developing cerebral cortex. *Nature Reviews Neuroscience, 3,* 423–432.

Nairne, James S. (2002). Remembering over the short-term: The case against the standard model. *Annual Review of Psychology, 53,* 53–81.

Najib, Arif; Lorberbaum, Jeffrey P.; Kose, Samet; Bohning, Daryl E.; & George, Mark S. (2004). Regional brain activity in women grieving a romantic relationship breakup. *American Journal of Psychiatry, 161,* 2245–2256.

Nakazato, Masamitsu; Murakami, Noboru; Date, Yukari; Kojima, Masayasu; Matsuo, Hisayuki; Kangawa, Kenji; & Matsukura, Shigeru. (2001, January 11). A role for ghrelin in the central regulation of feeding. *Nature, 409,* 194–198.

Narrow, William E.; Rae, Donald S.; Robins, Lee N.; & Regier, Darrel A. (2002). Revised prevalence estimates of mental disorders in the United States: Using a clinical significance criterion to reconcile 2 surveys' estimates. *Archives of General Psychiatry, 59,* 115–123.

Nash, Michael R. (2001, July). The truth and the hype of hypnosis. *Scientific American, 285,* 46–49, 52–55. Retrieved January 14, 2002, from http://www.sciam.com/2001/0701issue/0701nash.html

Nathan, Peter E.; Stuart, Scott P.; & Dolan, Sara L. (2000). Research on psychotherapy efficacy and effectiveness: Between Scylla and Charybdis? *Psychological Bulletin, 126,* 964–981.

National Association for the Education of Young Children. (1998). *Choosing a good early childhood program.* Washington, DC: National Association for the Education of Young Children.

National Association for the Education of Young Children. (2005). NAEYC accreditation performance criteria: Teacher child ratios within group size. Retrieved on November 25, 2005 at: http://www.naeyc.org/accreditation/performance_criteria/teacher_child_ratios.html

National Center for Complementary and Alternative Medicine (NCCAM). (2002, March). *Research report: Acupuncture* (NCCAM Publication No. D003). Bethesda, MD: National Institutes of Health, Office of Alternative Medicine and Office of Medical Applications of Research. Retrieved August 1, 2004, from http://nccam.nih.gov/health/acupuncture/acupuncture.pdf

National Center for Health Statistics. (2000). *Prevalence of overweight and obesity among adults: United States, 1999.* Atlanta, GA: Centers for Disease Control and Prevention, National Center for Health Statistics, Health E-Stats. Retrieved May 25, 2001, from http://www.cdc.gov/nchs/products/pubs/pubd/hestats/3and4/sedentary.htm

National Center for Health Statistics. (2002a). *Health, United States, 2002, with chartbook on trends in the health of Americans* (DHHS Publication No. (PHS) 2002–1232). Hyattsville, MD: National Center for Health Statistics, U.S. Department of Health and Human Services, Centers for Disease Control and Prevention. Retrieved January 3, 2003, from http://www.cdc.gov/nchs/data/hus/ hus02.pdf

National Center for Health Statistics. (2002b). *Prevalence of overweight and obesity among adults: United States, 1999–2000.* Atlanta, GA: Centers for Disease Control and Prevention, National Center for Health Statistics, Health E-Stats. Retrieved January 3, 2003, from http://www. cdc.gov/nchs/products/pubs/pubd/hestats/obese/obse99.htm

National Center for Health Statistics. (2002c). *Prevalence of overweight and obesity among children and adolescents: United States, 1999–2000.* Atlanta, GA: Centers for Disease Control and Prevention, National Center for Health Statistics, Health E-Stats. Retrieved January 3, 2003, from http://www.cdc.gov/nchs/products/pubs/pubd/hestats/overwght99.htm

National Center for Health Statistics. (2004). *Health, United States, 2004: With chartbook on trends in the health of Americans.* Hyattsville, MD: National Center for Health Statistics. Retrieved January 6, 2005, from http://www.cdc.gov/nchs/data/hus/hus04.pdf

National Council on Aging. (1998, September 28). *News: Half of older Americans report they are sexually active and 4 in 10 want more sex, says new survey.* Washington, DC: National Council on Aging. Retrieved April 12, 1999, from http://www.ncoa.org/news/ archives/sexsurvey.htm

National Highway Traffic Safety Administration. (2003, March). *National survey of distracted and drowsy driving attitudes and behavior: 2002: Volume 1.* Washington, DC: National Highway Traffic Safety Administration. Retrieved on February 13, 2005, from http://www.nhtsa.dot.gov/people/injury/drowsy driving1/distracted03/DISTRFINFINRPt-8mar04.pdf

National Institute of Neurological Disorders and Stroke. (2001). *Restless legs syndrome fact sheet* (NIH Publication No.01-4847). Bethesda, MD: National Institutes of Health. Retrieved January 12, 2002, from http://www.ninds.nih.gov/healthandmedical/pubs/restlesslegs.htm

National Institute on Aging. (2002). *Alzheimer's disease: Unraveling the mystery* (NIH Publication No. 02-3782). Washington, DC: U.S. Department of Health and Human Services, National Institutes of Health. Retrieved July 10, 2004, from http://www.alzheimers.org/unraveling/unraveling.pdf

National Institutes of Health. (2000). *Statistics related to overweight and obesity* (NIH Publication No. 96-4158). Bethesda, MD: National Institutes of Health: National Institute of Diabetes & Digestive & Kidney Diseases. Retrieved May 25, 2001, from http://www.niddk.nih.gov/health/nutrit/pubs/statobes.htm

National Organization on Fetal Alcohol Syndrome. (2002). *What is fetal alcohol syndrome?* Retrieved November 2, 2002, from http://www.nofas.org/main/whatisFAS.htm

National Sleep Foundation. (2000). *Adolescent sleep needs and patterns: Research report and resource guide.* Washington, DC: National Sleep Foundation. Retrieved February 12, 2005, from http://www.sleepfoundation.org/publications/sleepandteensreport1.pdf

National Sleep Foundation (2002, April 2). *2002 "Sleep in America" Poll*. Washington, DC: National Sleep Foundation. Retrieved May 5, 2002, from http://www.sleep foundation.org/img/2002SleepInAmericaPoll.pdf

National Sleep Foundation. (2004, March). *2004 "Sleep in America" Poll: Final report.* Washington, DC: National Sleep Foundation. Retrieved August 20, 2004, from http://www.sleepfoundation.org/polls/2004SleepPoll FinalReport.pdf

National Television Violence Study (Vol. 1). (1996). Thousand Oaks, CA: Sage.

National Television Violence Study (Vol. 2). (1997). Thousand Oaks, CA: Sage.

National Television Violence Study (Vol. 3). (1998). Thousand Oaks, CA: Sage.

Naveilhan, Philippe; Hassani, Hessameh; & others. (1999). Normal feeding behavior, body weight and leptin response require the neuropeptide Y Y2 receptor. *Nature Medicine, 5,* 1188–1193.

NDCHealth. (2005). U.S. pharmaceutical industry data: Excerpts from *2005 Pharma Insight*. Accessed on December 18, 2005 at: www.ndchealth.com/press_center/uspharmaindustrydata/NDCHealth_2005PharmaInsight_excerptsfinal.ppt

Nederkoorn, Chantal; Smulders, Fren T.Y.; & Jansen, Anita. (2000). Cephalic phase responses, craving and food intake in normal subjects. *Appetite, 35,* 45–55.

Neher, Andrew. (1991). Maslow's theory of motivation: A critique. *Journal of Humanistic Psychology, 31,* 89–112.

Neisser, Ulric (Chair); Boodoo, Gwyneth; Bouchard, Thomas J., Jr.; Boykin, A. Wade; Brody, Nathan; Ceci, Stephen J.; & others. (1996). Intelligence: Knowns and unknowns. *American Psychologist, 51,* 77–101.

Nelson, Elliot C.; Heath, Andrew C.; Madden, Pamela A. F.; Cooper, M. Lynne; Dinwiddie, Stephen H.; Bucholz, Kathleen K.; Glowinski, Anne; McLaughlin, Tara; Dunne, Michael P.; Statham, Dixie J.; & Martin, Nicholas G. (2002). Association between self-reported childhood sexual abuse and adverse psychosocial outcomes: Results from a twin study. *Archives of General Psychiatry, 59,* 139–145.

Nelson, Katherine, & Fivush, Robyn. (2004). The emergence of autobiographical memory: A social cultural developmental theory. *Psychological Review, 111,* 486–511.

Nelson, Marcia Z. (2001). *Come and sit: A week inside meditation centers.* Woodstock, VT: Skylight Paths.

Nestler, Eric J. (2001). Molecular basis of long-term plasticity underlying addiction. *Nature Reviews Neuroscience, 2,* 119–128.

Nestler, Eric J., & Malenka, Robert C. (2004, March). The addicted brain. *Scientific American, 290,* 78–85.

Neter, Efrat, & Ben-Shakhar, Gershon. (1989). The predictive validity of graphological inferences: A meta-analytic approach. *Personality and Individual Differences, 10,* 737–745.

Newberg, Andrew B., & Iversen, Jeremy. (2003). The neural basis of the complex mental task of meditation: Neurotransmitter and neurochemical considerations. *Medical Hypotheses, 61,* 282–291.

Newport, Frank, & Stausberg, Maurta. (2001, June 8). *Americans' belief in psychic and paranormal phenomena is up over last decade.* The Gallop Organization, Poll Release, June 8, 2001. Retrieved June 9, 2001, from http://www.gallup.com/poll/releases/pr010608.asp

Ng, Debbie M., & Jeffery, Robert W. (2003). Relationships between perceived stress and health behaviors in a sample of working adults. *Health Psychology, 22,* 638–642.

Niaura, Raymond; Todaro, John F.; Stroud, Laura; Spiro, Avron; Ward, Kenneth D.; & Weiss, Scott. (2002). Hostility, the metabolic syndrome, and incident coronary heart disease. *Health Psychology, 21,* 588–593.

NICHD Early Child Care Research Network. (2001). Child-care and family predictors of preschool attachment and stability from infancy. *Developmental Psychology, 37,* 847–862.

NICHD Early Child Care Research Network. (2002). Child-care structure –> process –> outcome: Direct and indirect effects of child-care quality on young children's development. *Psychological Science, 13,* 199–206.

NICHD Early Child Care Research Network. (2003a). Does quality of child care affect child outcomes at age 4 1/2? *Developmental Psychology, 39,* 451–469.

NICHD Early Child Care Research Network. (2003b). Families matter—even for kids in child care. *Journal of Developmental & Behavioral Pediatrics, 24,* 58–62.

Nichols, M. James, & Newsome, William T. (1999, December 2). The neurobiology of cognition. Impacts of foreseeable science. *Nature, 402*(Suppl.), C35–C38.

Nickerson, Raymond S., & Adams, Marilyn J. (1982). Long-term memory for a common object. In Ulric Neisser (Ed.), *Memory observed: Remembering in natural contexts.* San Francisco: Freeman.

Nielsen, Tore A., & Stenstrom, Philippe. (2005, October 27). What are the memory sources of dreaming? *Nature, 437,* 1286–1289.

Nikles, Charles D.; Brecht, David L.; Klinger, Eric; & Bursell, Amy L. (1998). The effects of current-concern- and nonconcern-related waking suggestions on nocturnal dream content. *Journal of Personality and Social Psychology, 75,* 242–255.

Nisbet, Matthew. (1998, May/June). Psychic telephone networks profit on yearning, gullibility. *Skeptical Inquirer, 22,* 5–6.

Nishio, Kazumi, & Bilmes, Murray. (1993). Psychotherapy with Southeast Asian American clients. In Donald R. Atkinson, George Morten, & Derald Wing Sue (Eds.), *Counseling American minorities: A cross-cultural perspective* (4th ed.). Madison, WI: Brown & Benchmark.

Njenga, Frank G.; Nicholls, P. J.; Nyamai, Caroline; Kigamwa, Pius; & Davidson, Jonathan R. T. (2004). Post-traumatic stress after terrorist attack: Psychological reactions following the U.S. embassy bombing in Nairobi: Naturalistic study. *British Journal of Psychiatry, 185,* 328–333.

Nobler, Mitchell S.; Oquendo, Maria A.; Kegeles, Lawrence S.; Malone, Kevin M.; Sackeim, Harold A.; & Mann, J. John. (2001). Decreased regional brain metabolism after ECT. *American Journal of Psychiatry, 158,* 305–308.

Nolen-Hoeksema, Susan. (2001). Gender differences in depression. *Current Directions in Psychological Science, 10,* 173–176.

Nolen-Hoeksema, Susan. (2003). *Women who think too much: How to break free of overthinking and reclaim your life.* New York: Holt.

Norris, Joan E., & Tindale, Joseph A. (1994). *Among generations: The cycle of adult relationships.* New York: Freeman.

North, Carol S.; Nixon, Sara Jo.; Shariat, Sheryll; Mallonee, Sue; McMillen, J. Curtis; Spitznagel, Edward L.; & Smith, Elizabeth M. (1999). The psychiatric impact of the Oklahoma City bombing on survivors of the direct blast. *Journal of the American Medical Association, 282,* 755–762.

North, Carol S., & Pfefferbaum, Betty. (2002). Research on the mental health effects of terrorism. *Journal of the American Medical Association, 288,* 633–636.

Nosofsky, Robert M., & Zaki, Safa R. (2002). Exemplar and prototype models revisited: Response strategies, selective attention, and stimulus generalization. *Journal of Experimental Psychology: Learning, Memory, & Cognition, 28,* 924–940.

Oakley, Bruce. (1986). Basic taste physiology: Human perspectives. In H. L. Meiselman & R. S. Rivlin (Eds.), *Clinical measurement of taste and smell.* New York: Macmillan.

O'Brien, Charles P. (1997, October 3). A range of research-based pharmacotherapies for addiction. *Science, 278,* 66–70.

Ochse, R. (1990). *Before the gates of excellence: The determinants of creative genius.* New York: Cambridge University Press.

O'Connor, Daryl B., & Shimizu, Mikiko. (2002). Sense of personal control, stress and coping style: A cross-cultural study. *Stress and Health, 18,* 173–183.

O'Craven, Kathleen M., & Kanwisher, Nancy. (2000). Mental imagery of faces and places activates corresponding stimulus-specific brain regions. *Journal of Cognitive Neuroscience, 12,* 1013–1023.

O'Doherty, John; Rolls, E. T.; Francis, S.; Bowtell, R.; & McGlone, F. (2001). Representation of pleasant and aversive taste in the human brain. *Journal of Neurophysiology, 85,* 1315–1321.

Oettingen, Gabriele, & Gollwitzer, Peter M. (2001). Goal setting and goal striving. In A. Tesser & N. Schwarz (Vol. Eds.) & M. Hewstone & M. Brewer (Series Eds.), *The Blackwell handbook in social psychology: Vol l. Intraindividual processes*. Oxford, England: Blackwell.

Ogbu, John U. (1986). The consequences of the American caste system. In Ulric Neisser (Ed.), *The school achievement of minority children: New perspectives*. Hillsdale, NJ: Erlbaum.

Ogden, Jenni A., & Corkin, Suzanne. (1991). Memories of H. M. In Wickliffe C. Abraham, Michael Corballis, & K. Geoffrey White (Eds.), *Memory mechanisms: A tribute to G. V. Goddard*. Hillsdale, NJ: Erlbaum.

Öhman, Arne, & Mineka, Susan. (2001). Fear, phobias, and preparedness: Toward an evolved module of fear and fear learning. *Psychological Review, 108*, 483–522.

Öhman, Arne, & Mineka, Susan. (2003). The malicious serpent: Snakes as a prototypical stimulus for an evolved module of fear. *Current Directions in Psychological Science, 12*, 5–9.

O'Kane, Gail; Kensinger, Elizabeth A.; & Corkin, Suzanne. (2004). Evidence for semantic learning in profound amnesia: An investigation with patient H.M. *Hippocampus, 14*, 417–425.

O'Leary, K. Daniel, & Wilson, G. Terence. (1987). *Behavior therapy: Application and outcome* (2nd ed.). Englewood Cliffs, NJ: Prentice-Hall.

Olson, James M., & Zanna, Mark P. (1993). Attitudes and attitude change. *Annual Review of Psychology, 44*, 117–154.

Olson, Michael A., & Fazio, Russell H. (2001). Implicit attitude formation through classical conditioning. *Psychological Science, 12*, 413–417.

Olton, David S. (1992). Tolman's cognitive analysis: Predecessors of current approaches in psychology. *Journal of Experimental Psychology: General, 121*, 427–428.

Ones, Deniz S.; Viswesvaran, Chockalingam; & Schmidt, Frank I. (1993). Comprehensive meta-analysis of integrity test validities: Findings for personnel selection and theories of job performance. *Journal of Applied Psychology, 78*, 679–703.

Orlinsky, David E.; Ronnestad, Michael Hedge; & Willutzki, Ulrike. (2004). Fifty years of psychotherapy process-outcome research: Continuity and change. In Michael J. Lambert (Ed.), *Bergin and Garfield's handbook of psychotherapy and behavior change* (5th ed.). New York: Wiley.

Orne, Martin T., & Holland, Charles H. (1968). On the ecological validity of laboratory deceptions. *International Journal of Psychiatry, 6*, 282–293.

Ornstein, Peter A.; Ceci, Stephen J.; & Loftus, Elizabeth F. (1998). Adult recollections of childhood abuse: Cognitive and developmental perspectives. *Psychology, Public Policy, & Law, 4*, 1025–1051.

Otis, John D.; Cardella, Lucille A.; & Kearns, Robert D. (2004). The influence of family and culture on pain. In Robert H. Dworkin & William S. Breitbart (Eds.), *Psychosocial aspects of pain: A handbook for health care providers*. Seattle, WA: International Association for the Study of Pain, IASP Press.

Ottati, Victor, & Lee, Yueh-Ting. (1995). Accuracy: A neglected component of stereotype research. In Yueh-Ting Lee, Lee J. Jussim, & Clark R. McCauley (Eds.), *Stereotype accuracy: Toward appreciating group differences*. Washington, DC: American Psychological Association.

Overmier, J. Bruce, & Carroll, Marilyn E. (2001). Basic issues in the use of animals in health research. In Marilyn E. Carroll & J. Bruce Overmier (Eds.), *Animal research and human health: Advancing human welfare through behavioral science*. Washington, DC: American Psychological Association.

Owen-Howard, M. (2001). Pharmacological aversion treatment of alcohol dependence. I. Production and prediction of conditioned alcohol aversion. *American Journal of Drug and Alcohol Abuse, 27*, 561–585.

Oyserman, Daphna; Grant, Larry; & Ager, Joel. (1995). A socially contextualized model of African American identity: Possible selves and school persistence. *Journal of Personality and Social Psychology, 69*, 1216–1232.

Ozbayrak, Kaan R., & Berlin, Richard M. (1995). Sleepwalking in children and adolescents. In Charles E. Schaefer (Ed.), *Clinical handbook of sleep disorders in children*. Northvale, NJ: Aronson.

Ozer, Elizabeth M., & Bandura, Albert. (1990). Mechanisms governing empowerment effects: A self-efficacy analysis. *Journal of Personality and Social Psychology, 58*, 472–486.

Ozer, Emily J.; Best, Suzanne R.; Lipsey, Tami L.; & Weiss, Daniel S. (2003). Predictors of posttraumatic stress disorder and symptoms in adults: A meta-analysis. *Psychological Bulletin, 129*, 52–73.

Paik, Haejung, & Comstock, George. (1994). The effects of television on antisocial behavior: A meta-analysis. *Communication Research, 21*, 516–546.

Paillère-Martinot, M. L.; Caclin, A.; Artiges, E.; Poline, J. B.; Joliot, M.; & others. (2001). Cerebral gray and white matter reductions and clinical correlates in patients with early onset schizophrenia. *Schizophrenia Research, 50*, 19–26.

Paivio, Allan. (1986). *Mental representations: A dual coding approach*. New York: Oxford University Press.

Paivio, Allan. (1995). Imagery and memory. In Michael S. Gazzaniga (Ed.), *The cognitive neurosciences*. Cambridge, MA: MIT Press.

Palm, Kathleen M., & Gibson, Pamela. (1998). Recovered memories of childhood sexual abuse: Clinicians' practices and beliefs. *Professional Psychology: Research and Practice, 29*, 257–261.

Palmblad, J.; Petrini, B.; Wasserman, J.; & Akerstedt, T. (1979). Lymphocyte and granulocyte reactions during sleep deprivation. *Psychosomatic Medicine, 41*, 273–278.

Palmer, Emma J., & Hollin, Clive R. (2001). Sociomoral reasoning, perceptions of parenting and self-reported delinquency in adolescents. *Applied Cognitive Psychology, 15*, 85–100.

Palmer, John. (2003). ESP in the ganzfeld: Analysis of a debate. In James Alcock, Jean Burns, & Anthony Freeman (Eds.), *Psi wars: Getting to grips with the paranormal*. Charlottesville, VA: Imprint Academic.

Palmer, Stephen E. (2002). Perceptual grouping: It's later than you think. *Current Directions in Psychological Science, 11*, 101–106.

Palmeri, Thomas J., & Gauthier, Isabel. (2004). Visual object understanding. *Nature Reviews Neuroscience, 5*, 2303.

Panksepp, Jaak. (2000). The riddle of laughter: Neural and psychoevolutionary underpinnings of joy. *Psychological Science, 9*, 183–186.

Pannemans, D. L., & Westerterp, K. R. (1995). Energy expenditure, physical activity and basal metabolic rate of elderly subjects. *British Journal of Nutrition, 73*, 571–581.

Papa, Michael J.; Singhal, Arvind; Law, Sweety; Pant, Saumya; Sood, Suruchi; Rogers, Everett M.; & Shefner-Rogers, Corinne. (2000). Entertainment-education and social change: An analysis of parasocial interaction, social learning, collective efficacy, and paradoxical communication. *Journal of Communication, 50*, 31–55.

Papini, Mauricio R. (2002). Pattern and process in the evolution of learning. *Psychological Review, 109*, 186–201.

Papoušek, Mechthild; Papoušek, Hanus; & Bornstein, Marc H. (1985). The naturalistic vocal environment of young infants: On the significance of homogeneity and variability in parental speech. In Tiffany M. Field & N. Fox (Eds.), *Social perception in infants*. Norwood, NJ: Ablex.

Parens, Erik. (2004, January–February). Genetic differences and human identities: On why talking about behavioral genetics is important and difficult. *Hastings Center Report Special Supplement, 34*(1), S1–S36.

Parent, Anne-Simone; Teilmann, Grete; Juul, Anders; Skakkebaek, Niels E.; Toppari, Jorma; & Bourguignon, Jean-Pierre. (2003). The timing of normal puberty and the age limits of sexual precocity: Variations around the world, secular trends, and changes after migration. *Endocrine Reviews, 24*, 668–693.

Park, Bernadette; Ryan, Carey S.; & Judd, Charles M. (1992). Role of meaningful subgroups in explaining differences in perceived variability for in-groups and out-groups. *Journal of Personality and Social Psychology, 63*(4), 553–567.

Park, Crystal L.; Armeli, Stephen; & Tennen, Howard. (2004). Appraisal-coping goodness of fit: A daily Internet study. *Personality and Social Psychology Bulletin, 30,* 558–569.

Patapoutian, Ardem; Peier, Andrea M.; Story, Gina M.: & Viswanath, Veena. (2003). ThermoTRP channels and beyond: Mechanisms of temperature sensation. *Nature Reviews Neuroscience, 4,* 529–539.

Patterson, Charlotte J. (1995). Lesbian mothers, gay fathers, and their children. In Anthony R. D'Augelli & Charlotte J. Patterson (Eds.), *Lesbian, gay and bisexual identities across the lifespan: Psychological perspectives.* New York: Oxford University Press.

Paul, Diane B., & Blumenthal, Arthur L. (1989). On the trail of Little Albert. *The Psychological Record, 39,* 547–553.

Paul, Gordon L., & Menditto, Anthony A. (1992). Effectiveness of inpatient treatment programs for mentally ill adults in public psychiatric facilities. *Applied and Preventive Psychology, 1,* 41–63.

Pauli-Pott, Ursula; Mertesacker, Bettina; & Beckman, Dieter. (2004). Predicting the development of infant emotionality from maternal characteristics. *Development and Psychopathology, 16,* 19–42.

Pavlov, Ivan. (1904/1965). On conditioned reflexes. In Richard J. Herrnstein & Edwin G. Boring (Eds.), *A source book in the history of psychology.* Cambridge, MA: Harvard University Press.

Pavlov, Ivan. (1927/1960). *Conditioned reflexes: An investigation of the physiological activity of the cerebral cortex* (G. V. Anrep, Trans.). New York: Dover. Retrieved May 25, 2001, from http://psychclassics.yorku.ca/Pavlov/index.htm

Pavlov, Ivan. (1928). *Lectures on conditioned reflexes.* New York: International Publishers.

Pawlow, L. A.; O'Neil, P. M.; & Malcolm, R. J. (2003). Night eating syndrome: Effects of brief relaxation training on stress, mood, hunger, and eating patterns. *International Journal of Obesity & Related Metabolic Disorders, 27,* 970–978.

Payne, Christina, & Jaffe, Klaus. (2005). Self seeks like: Many humans choose dog pets following rules used for assortative mating. *Journal of Ethology, 23,* 15–18.

Payne, David G.; Neuschatz, Jeffrey S.; Lampinen, James M.; & Lynn, Steven Jay. (1997). Compelling memory illusions: The qualitative characteristics of false memories. *Current Directions in Psychological Science, 6,* 56–60.

Payne, John W.; Bettman, James R.; & Johnson, Eric J. (1993). *The adaptive decision maker.* Cambridge, England: Cambridge University Press.

Payton, Jack R. (1992, May 16). The sad legacy of Japan's outcasts. *Chicago Tribune,* Sect. 1, p. 21.

Pearce, John M., & Bouton, Mark E. (2001). Theories of associative learning in animals. *Annual Review of Psychology, 52,* 111–139.

Pedersen, Sara, & Seidman, Edward. (2004). Team sports achievement and self-esteem development among urban adolescent girls. *Psychology of Women Quarterly, 28,* 412–422.

Peeters, Frenk; Nicholson, Nancy A.; & Berkhof, Johannes. (2003). Cortisol responses to daily events in major depressive disorder. *Psychosomatic Medicine, 65,* 836–841.

Peirce, Robert S.; Frone, Michael R.; Russell, Marcia; & Cooper, M. Lynne. (1996). Financial stress, social support, and alcohol involvement: A longitudinal test of the buffering hypothesis in a general population study. *Health Psychology, 15,* 38–47.

Pendergrast, Mark. (1996). *Victims of memory: Sex abuse accusations and shattered lives* (2nd ed.). Hinesburg, VT: Upper Access.

Pennisi, Elizabeth. (2004, October 22). Searching for the genome's second code. *Science, 306,* 632–635.

Pepler, Debra J., & Craig, Wendy M. (1995). A peek behind the fence: Naturalistic observations of aggressive children with remote audiovisual recording. *Developmental Psychology, 31*(4), 548–553.

Pepperberg, Irene M. (1993). Cognition and communication in an African gray parrot (Psittacus erithacus): Studies on a nonhuman, nonprimate, nonmammalian subject. In Herbert L. Roitblat, Louis M. Herman, & Paul E. Nachtigall (Eds.), *Language and communication: Comparative perspectives.* Hillsdale, NJ: Erlbaum.

Pepperberg, Irene M. (2000). *The Alex studies: Cognitive and communicative abilities of gray parrots.* Cambridge, MA: Harvard University Press.

Pepperberg, Irene M., & Gordon, Jesse D. (2005). Number comprehension by a grey parrot *(Psittacus erithacus),* including a zero-like concept. *Journal of Comparative Psychology, 119,* 197–209.

Pérez-Stable, Eliseo J.; Herrera, Brenda; Peyton, Jacob, III; & Bonowitz, Neal L. (1998, July 8). Nicotine metabolism and intake in black and white smokers. *Journal of the American Medical Association, 280,* 152–156.

Perloff, Richard M. (1993). *The dynamics of persuasion.* Hillsdale, NJ: Erlbaum.

Pert, Candace B., & Snyder, Solomon H. (1973). Opiate receptor: Demonstration in the nervous tissue. *Science, 179,* 1011–1014.

Pervin, Lawrence A. (1994). A critical analysis of current trait theory. *Psychological Inquiry, 5,* 103–113.

Payne, John W.; Bettman, James R.; & Johnson, Eric J. (1993). *The adaptive decision maker.* Cambridge, England: Cambridge University Press.

Petersen, Ronald C. (2002). *Mayo Clinic on Alzheimer's disease.* Rochester, MN: Mayo Clinic Press.

Peterson, Christopher. (2000). Optimistic explanatory style and health. In Jane E. Gillham (Ed.), *The science of optimism and hope: Research essays in honor of Martin E. P. Seligman.* Philadelphia: Templeton Foundation Press.

Peterson, Christopher, & Bossio, Lisa M. (1993). Healthy attitudes: Optimism, hope, and control. In Daniel Goleman & Joel Gurin (Eds.), *Mind/body medicine: How to use your mind for better health.* Yonkers, NY: Consumer Reports Books.

Peterson, Christopher, & Bossio, Lisa M. (2001). Optimism and physical well-being. In Edward C. Chang (Ed.), *Optimism and pessimism: Implications for theory, research, and practice.* Washington, DC: American Psychological Association.

Peterson, Christopher; Maier, Steven F.; & Seligman, Martin E. P. (1993). *Learned helplessness: A theory for the age of personal control.* New York: Oxford University Press.

Peterson, Christopher; Seligman, Martin E. P.; & Vaillant, George E. (1988). Pessimistic explanatory style as a risk factor for physical illness: A thirty-five-year longitudinal study. *Journal of Personality and Social Psychology, 55,* 23–27.

Peterson, Lloyd R., & Peterson, Margaret J. (1959). Short-term retention of individual items. *Journal of Experimental Psychology, 58,* 193–198.

Petitto, Laura Ann; Holowka, Siobhan; Sergio, Lauren E.; Levy, Bronna; & Ostry, David J. (2004). Baby hands that move to the rhythm of language: Hearing babies acquiring sign languages babble silently on the hands. *Cognition, 93,* 43–73.

Petitto, Laura Ann; Holowka, Siobhan; Sergio, Lauren E.; & Ostry, David. (2001). Language rhythms in baby hand movements. *Nature, 413,* 35–36.

Petitto, Laura Ann, & Marentette, Paula F. (1991). Babbling in the manual mode: Evidence for the ontogeny of language. *Science, 251,* 1493–1496.

Petrovic, Predrag; Kalso, Eija; Petersson, Karl Magnus; & Ingvar, Martin. (2002, March 1). Placebo and opioid analgesia—Imaging a shared neuronal network. *Science, 295,* 1737–1740.

Petry, Nancy M.; Tedford, Jacqueline; Austin, Mark; Nich, Charla; Carroll, Kathleen M.; & Rounsaville, Bruce J. (2004). Prize reinforcement contingency management for treating cocaine users: How low can we go, and with whom? *Addiction, 99,* 349–360.

Pezdek, Kathy; Whetstone, Tony; Reynolds, Kirk; Askari, Nusha; & Dougherty, Thomas. (1989). Memory for real-world scenes: The role of consistency with schema expectation. *Journal of Experimental Psychology: Learning, Memory, & Cognition, 15,* 587–595.

Pham, Lien B., & Taylor, Shelley E. (1999). From thought to action: Effects of process- versus outcome-based mental simulations on performance. *Personality and Social Psychology Bulletin, 25,* 250–260.

Phan, K. Luan; Wager, Tor; Taylor, Stephan F.; & Liberzon, Israel. (2002) Functional neuroanatomy of emotion: A meta-analysis of emotion activation studies in PET and fMRI. *NeuroImage 16*, 331–348.

Phelps, Elizabeth A.; O'Connor, Kevin J.; Gatenby, J. Christopher; Gore, John C.; Grillon, Christian; & Davis, Michael. (2001). Activation of the left amygdala to a cognitive representation of fear. *Nature Neuroscience, 4*, 237–441.

Phillips, Antoinette S., & Bedeian, Arthur G. (1994). Leader-follower exchange quality: The role of personal and interpersonal attributes. *Academy of Management Journal, 37*, 990–1001.

Phillips, Jean M. (1998). Effects of realistic job previews on multiple organizational outcomes: A meta-analysis. *Academy of Management Journal, 41*, 673–690.

Phillips, Susan D., & Blustein, David L. (1994). Readiness for career choices: Planning, exploring, and deciding. *The Career Development Quarterly, 43*, 63–75.

Piaget, Jean. (1952). *The origins of intelligence in children* (Margaret Cook, Trans.). New York: International Universities Press.

Piaget, Jean. (1972). Intellectual evolution from adolescence to adulthood. *Human Development, 15*, 1–12.

Piaget, Jean. (1973). The stages of cognitive development: Interview with Richard I. Evans. In Richard I. Evans (Ed.), *Jean Piaget: The man and his ideas*. New York: Dutton.

Piaget, Jean, & Inhelder, Bärbel. (1958). *The growth of logical thinking from childhood to adolescence: An essay on the construction of formal operational structures* (Anne Parsons & Stanley Milgram, Trans.). New York: Basic Books.

Piaget, Jean, & Inhelder, Bärbel. (1974). *The child's construction of quantities: Conservation and atomism*. London: Routledge & Kegan Paul.

Pica, Pierre; Lemer, Cathy; Izard, Veronique; & Dehaene, Stanislas. (2004, October 15). Exact and approximate arithmetic in an Amazonian indigene group. *Science, 306*, 499–503.

Piliavin, Jane Allyn; Dovidio, John F.; Gaertner, Samuel L.; & Clark, Russell D., III. (1981). *Emergency intervention*. New York: Academic Press.

Pillemer, David B. (1998). *Momentous events, vivid memories*. Cambridge, MA: Harvard University Press.

Pillow, David R.; Zautra, Alex J.; & Sandler, Irwin. (1996). Major life events and minor stressors: Identifying mediational links in the stress process. *Journal of Personality and Social Psychology, 70*, 381–394.

Pinel, John P. J.; Assanand, Sunaina; & Lehman, Darrin R. (2000). Hunger, eating, and ill health. *American Psychologist, 55*, 1105–1116.

Pinker, Steven. (1994). *The language instinct: How the mind creates language*. New York: Morrow.

Pinker, Steven. (1995). Introduction: Language. In Michael S. Gazzaniga (Ed.), *The cognitive neurosciences*. Cambridge, MA: MIT Press.

Pinker, Steven. (1997). *How the mind works*. New York: Norton.

Piomelli, Daniele. (2003). The molecular logic of endocannabinoid signalling. *Nature Reviews Neuroscience, 4*, 873–884.

Pirke, Karl M. (1995). Physiology of bulimia nervosa. In Kelly D. Brownell & Christopher G. Fairburn (Eds.), *Eating disorders and obesity: A comprehensive handbook*. New York: Guilford Press.

Pitschel-Walz, Gabi; Leucht, Stefan; Bauml, Josef; Kissling, Werner; & Engel, Rolf. (2001). The effect of family interventions on relapse and rehospitalization in schizophrenia—A meta-analysis. *Schizophrenia Bulletin, 27*, 73–92.

Plake, Barbara S., & Impara, James C. (2001). *The mental measurements yearbook* (14th ed.). Lincoln: University of Nebraska Press, Buros Institute of Mental Measurements.

Plant, E. Ashby; Hyde, Janet Shibley; Keltner, Dacher; & Devine, Patricia G. (2000). The gender stereotyping of emotions. *Psychology of Women Quarterly, 24*, 81–92.

Platek, Steven M.; Critton, Samuel R.; Myers, Thomas E.; & Gallup, Gordon G., Jr. (2003). Contagious yawning: The role of self-awareness and mental state attribution. *Cognitive Brain Research, 17*, 223–227.

Plomin, Robert. (2003). General cognitive ability. In Robert Plomin, John C. Defries, & Peter McGuffin (Eds.), *Behavioral genetics in the postgenomic era*. Washington, DC: American Psychological Association.

Plomin, Robert, & Colledge, Essi. (2001). Genetics and psychology: Beyond heritability. *European Psychologist, 6*, 229–240.

Plomin, Robert; DeFries, John C.; Craig, Ian W.; & McGuffin, Peter. (2003). Behavioral genetics. In Robert Plomin, John C. DeFries, Ian W. Craig, & Peter McGuffin (Eds.), *Behavioral genetics in the postgenomic era*. Washington, DC: American Psychological Association.

Plomin, Robert; DeFries, John C.; McClearn, Gerald E.; & McGuffin, Peter. (2001). *Behavioral genetics* (4th ed.). New York: Worth.

Plomin, Robert, & McGuffin, Peter. (2003). Psychopathology in the postgenomic era. *Annual Review of Psychology, 54*, 205–228.

Plomin, Robert; Owen, Michael J.; & McGuffin, Peter. (1994, June 17). The genetic basis of complex human behaviors. *Science, 264*, 1733–1739.

Plomin, Robert, & Spinath, Frank M. (2004). Intelligence: Genetics, genes, and genomics. *Journal of Personality and Social Psychology, 86*, 112–129.

Poehlman, Eric T., & Horton, Edward S. (1995). Measurement of energy expenditure. In Kelly D. Brownell & Christopher G. Fairburn (Eds.), *Eating disorders and obesity: A comprehensive handbook*. New York: Guilford Press.

Poldrack, Russell A., & Wagner, Anthony D. (2004). What can neuroimaging tell us about the mind: Insights from prefrontal cortex. *Current Directions in Psychological Science, 13*, 177–181.

Polk, Thad A., & Newell, Allen. (1995). Deduction as verbal reasoning. *Psychological Review, 102*, 533–566.

Pope, Harrison G., Jr.; Gruber, Amanda J.; Hudson, James I.; Huestis, Marilyn A.; & Yurgelun-Todd, Deborah. (2001). Neuropsychological performance in long-term cannabis users. *Archives of General Psychiatry, 58*, 909–915.

Pope, Kenneth S. (1990). Therapist–patient sexual involvement: A review of the research. *Clinical Psychology Review, 10*, 477–490.

Pope, Kenneth S., & Brown, Laura S. (1996). *Recovered memories of abuse: Assessment, therapy, forensics*. Washington, DC: American Psychological Association.

Pope, Kenneth S., & Tabachnick, Barbara G. (1993). Therapists' anger, hate, fear, and sexual feelings: National survey of therapist responses, client characteristics, critical events, formal complaints, and training. *Professional Psychology: Research and Practice, 24*, 142–152.

Pope, Victoria. (1997, August 4). Day-care dangers. *U.S. News & World Report, 123*, 30–37.

Pope Davis, Donald B.; Liu, William M.; Toporek, Rebecca L.; & Brittan-Powell, Christopher S. (2001). What's missing from multicultural competency research: Review, introspection, and recommendations. *Cultural Diversity and Ethnic Minority Psychology, 7*, 121–138.

Population Communications International. (2004). *Telling stories, saving lives*. Retrieved September 5, 2004, from http://www.population.org/index.shtml

Porkka-Heiskanen, Tarja; Strecker, Robert E.; Thakkar, Mahesh; Bjørkum, Alvhild A.; Greene, Robert W.; & McCarley, Robert W. (1997, May 23). Adenosine: A mediator of the sleep-inducing effects of prolonged wakefulness. *Science, 276*, 1265–1268.

Porter, Kenneth. (1993). Combined individual and group psychotherapy. In Anne Alonso & Hillel I. Swiller (Eds.), *Group therapy in clinical practice*. Washington, DC: American Psychiatric Press.

Posada, German; Carbonell, Olga A.; Alzate, Gloria; & Plata, Sandra J. (2004). Through Colombian lenses: Ethnographic and conventional analyses of maternal care and their associations with secure base behavior. *Developmental Psychology, 40*, 508–518.

Posada, German; Jacobs, Amanda; Richmond, Melissa K.; Carbonell, Olga A.; Alzate, Gloria; Bustamonte, Maria R.; & Quiceno, Julio. (2002). Maternal caregiving and infant security in two cultures. *Developmental Psychology, 38*, 67–78.

Posner, Michael I., & DiGirolamo, Gregory J. (2000). Attention in cognitive neuroscience: An overview. In Michael S. Gazzaniga (Ed.), *The new cognitive neurosciences* (2nd ed., pp. 621–632). Cambridge,MA: MIT Press.

Powell, Douglas H. (2004). Behavioral treatment of debilitating test anxiety among medical students. *Journal of Clinical Psychology, 60,* 853–865.

Powlishta, Kimberly K. (1995a). Gender bias in children's perceptions of personality traits. *Sex Roles, 32,* 223–240.

Powlishta, Kimberly K. (1995b). Intergroup processes in childhood: Social categorization and sex role development. *Developmental Psychology, 31,* 781–788.

Pratkanis, Anthony R. (1992). The cargo-cult science of subliminal persuasion. *Skeptical Inquirer, 16,* 260–273.

Pratkanis, Anthony R., & Aronson, Elliot. (1992). *Age of propaganda: The everyday use and abuse of persuasion.* New York: Freeman.

Pratto, Felicia. (1996). Sexual politics: The gender gap in the bedroom, the cupboard, and the Cabinet. In David M. Buss & Neil M. Malumuth (Eds.), *Sex, power, conflict: Evolutionary and feminist perspectives.* New York: Oxford University Press.

Premack, Steven L., & Wanous, John P. (1985). A meta-analysis of realistic job preview experiments. *Journal of Applied Psychology, 70,* 706–719.

Prescott, Carol A., & Gottesman, Irving I. (1993). Genetically mediated vulnerability to schizophrenia. *Psychiatric Clinics of North America, 16,* 245–268.

Preti, George; Cutler, Winnifred B.; Garcia, C. R.; Huggins, G. R.; & Lawley, H. J. (1986). Human axillary secretions influence women's menstrual cycles: The role of donor extract of females. *Hormones and Behavior, 20,* 474–482.

Preuss, Ulrich W.; Meisenzahl, Eva M.; Frodl, T.; Zetzsche, T.; Holder, J.; Leinsinger, G.; & others. (2002). Handedness and corpus callosum morphology. *Psychiatry Research: Neuroimaging, 116,* 33–42.

Price, Donald D. (1999). *Psychological mechanisms of pain and analgesia.* Seattle, WA: International Association for the Study of Pain, IASP Press.

Price, Donald D. (2000, June 9). Psychological and neural mechanisms of the affective dimension of pain. *Science, 288,* 1769–1772.

Prinzmetal, William. (1995). Visual feature integration in a world of objects. *Current Directions in Psychological Science, 4,* 90–94.

Provine, Robert R. (1989). Faces as releasers of contagious yawning: An approach to face detection using normal human subjects. *Bulletin of the Psychonomic Society, 27,* 211–214.

Pujol, Jesus; Deus, Joan; Losilla, Josep M.; & Capdevila, Antoni. (1999). Cerebral lateralization in normal left-handed people: Studies by functional MRI. *Neurology, 52,* 1038–1043.

Pulakos, Elaine D., & Schmitt, Neal. (1995). Experience-based and structured interview questions: Studies of validity. *Personnel Psychology, 48,* 289–308.

Pullum, Geoffrey K. (1991). *The great Eskimo vocabulary hoax and other irreverent essays on the study of language.* Chicago: University of Chicago Press.

Purkey, William Watson, & Stanley, Paula Helen. (2002). The self in psychotherapy. In David J. Cain & Julius Seeman (Eds.), *Humanistic psychotherapies: Handbook of research and practice.* Washington, DC: American Psychological Association.

Quattrocki, Elizabeth; Baird, Adigail; & Yurgelun-Todd, Deborah. (2000). Biological aspects of the link between smoking and depression. *Harvard Review of Psychiatry, 8,* 99–110.

Quinn, Diane M., & Spencer, Steven J. (2001). The interference of stereotype threat with women's generation of mathematical problem-solving strategies. *Journal of Social Issues, 57,* 55–71.

Rabinowitz, Jonathan; Lichtenberg, Pesach; Kaplan, Zeev; Mark, Mordechai; Nahon, Danielle; & Davidson, Michael. (2001). Rehospitalization rates of chronically ill schizophrenic patients discharged on a regimen of risperidone, olanzipine, or conventional antipsychotics. *American Journal of Psychiatry, 158,* 266–269.

Rachlin, Howard. (1974). Self-control. *Behaviorism, 2,* 94–107.

Rachlin, Howard. (1995). The value of temporal patterns in behavior. *Current Directions in Psychological Science, 4,* 188–192.

Rachlin, Howard. (2000). *The science of self-control.* Cambridge, MA: Harvard University Press.

Racine, Eric; Bar-Ilan, Ofek; & Illes, Judy. (2005). fMRI in the public eye. *Nature Reviews Neuroscience, 6*(2), 159–164.

Rahe, Richard H. (1972). Subjects' recent life changes and their near-future illness reports. *Annals of Clinical Research, 4,* 250–265.

Raisman, Geoffrey. (2004). The idea that scandalized brain science. *Cerebrum, 6,* 21–34.

Rakic, Pasko. (2002). Neurogenesis in adult primate neocortex: An evaluation of the evidence. *Nature Reviews Neuroscience, 3,* 65–71.

Rakic, Pasko. (2004). Immigration denied. *Nature, 427,* 685–686.

Ramachandran, Vilayanur S. (1992a, May). Blind spots. *Scientific American, 266,* 86–91.

Ramachandran, Vilayanur S. (1992b). Filling in gaps in perception: Part 1. *Current Directions in Psychological Science, 1,* 199–205.

Randi, James. (1980). *Flim-flam!* New York: Lippincott & Crowell.

Randi, James. (1982). *The truth about Uri Geller.* Buffalo, NY: Prometheus Books.

Rapee, Ronald M.; Brown, Timothy A.; Antony, Martin M.; & Barlow, David H. (1992). Response to hyperventilation and inhalation of 5.5% carbon dioxide-enriched air across the DSM-III-R anxiety disorders. *Journal of Abnormal Psychology, 101,* 538–552.

Rapoport, Judith L. (1989). *The boy who couldn't stop washing: The experience and treatment of obsessive-compulsive disorder.* New York: Dutton.

Rapoport, Judith L. (1991). Basal ganglia dysfunction as a proposed cause of obsessive-compulsive disorder. In Bernard J. Carroll & James E. Barrett (Eds.), *Psychopathology and the brain.* New York: Raven Press.

Raskind, Murray A.; Peskind, Elaine R.; & others. (2004). The cognitive benefits of galantamine are sustained for at least 36 months: A long-term extension trial. *Archives of Neurology, 61,* 252–256.

Rasmussen, Steven A., & Eisen, Jane L. (1992). The epidemiology and clinical features of obsessive-compulsive disorder. *Psychiatric Clinics of North America, 15,* 743–758.

Rasmussen, Theodore, & Milner, Brenda. (1977). The role of early left brain injury in determining lateralization of cerebral speech functions. *Annals of the New York Academy of Sciences, 299,* 355–369.

Ratcliff, Roger, & McKoon, Gail. (1994). Retrieving information from memory: Spreading-activation theories versus compound-cue theories. *Psychological Review, 101,* 177–184.

Ratterman, R.; Secrest, J.; Norwood B.; & Ch'ien, A. P. (2002). Magnet therapy: What's the attraction? *Journal of the American Academy of Nurse Practitioners, 14,* 347–353.

Ravussin, Eric, & Danforth, Elliot, Jr. (1999, January 8). Beyond sloth—physical activity and weight gain. *Science, 283,* 184–185.

Rawlings, Steve W., & Saluter, Arlene F. (1995). *Household and family characteristics: March 1994* (U.S. Bureau of the Census, Current Population Reports, Series P20–483). Washington, DC: U.S. Government Printing Office.

Rawlins, William K. (1992). *Friendship matters: Communication, dialectics, and the life course.* Hawthorne, NY: de Gruyter.

Raynor, Hollie A., & Epstein, Leonard H. (2001). Dietary variety, energy regulation, and obesity. *Psychological Bulletin, 127,* 325–341.

Read, John, & Harré, Niki. (2001). The role of biological and genetic causal beliefs in the stigmatisation of "mental patients." *Journal of Mental Health, 10,* 223–235.

Regier, Darrel A.; Narrow, William E.; Rae, Donald S.; Manderscheid, Ronald W.; Locke, Ben Z.; & Goodwin, Fredrick K. (1993). The de facto U.S. mental and addictive disorders service system: Epidemiologic catchment area prospective one-year prevalence rates of disorders and services. *Archives of General Psychiatry, 50,* 85–94.

Register, Patricia A., & Kihlstrom, John F. (1986). Finding the hypnotic virtuoso. *International Journal of Clinical and Experimental Hypnosis, 34,* 84–97.

Register, Patricia A., & Kihlstrom, John F. (1987). Hypnotic effects on hypermnesia. *International Journal of Clinical and Experimental Hypnosis, 35,* 155–170.

Reis, Harry T.; Collins, W. Andrew; & Berscheid, Ellen. (2000). The relationship context of human behavior and development. *Psychological Bulletin, 126,* 844–872.

Reisberg, Daniel, & Chambers, Deborah. (1991). Neither pictures nor propositions: What can we learn from a mental image? *Canadian Journal of Psychology, 45,* 336–348.

Reisel, William D., & Kopelman, Richard E. (1995). The effects of failure on subsequent group performance in a professional sports setting. *Journal of Psychology, 129,* 103–113.

Reisenzein, Rainer. (1983). The Schachter theory of emotion: Two decades later. *Psychological Bulletin, 94,* 239–264.

Reiss, B. K. (1990). *A biography of Mary Cover Jones.* Berkeley, CA: Wright Institute.

Reiss, Diana, & Marino, Lori. (2001, May 7). Mirror self-recognition in the bottlenose dolphin: A case of cognitive convergence. *Proceedings of the National Academy of Sciences, USA, 98,* 5937.

Rejeski, W. Jack; Gregg, Edward; Thompson, Amy; & Berry, Michael. (1991). The effects of varying doses of acute aerobic exercise on psychophysiological stress responses in highly trained cyclists. *Journal of Sport and Exercise Psychology, 13,* 188–199.

Rejeski, W. Jack; Thompson, Amy; Brubaker, Peter H.; & Miller, Henry S. (1992). Acute exercise: Buffering psychosocial responses in women. *Health Psychology, 11,* 355–362.

Reneman, Liesbeth; Booij, Jan; de Bruin, Kora; & others. (2001). Effects of dose, sex, and long-term abstention from use on toxic effects of MDMA (Ecstasy) on brain serotonin neurons. *Lancet, 358,* 1864–1869.

Reneman, Liesbeth; Lavalaye, Jules; Schmand, Ben; deWolff, Frederik A.; & others. (2001). Cortical serotonin transporter density and verbal memory in individuals who stopped using 3,4-methylenedioxy-methamphetamine (MDMA or "Ecstasy"). *Archives of General Psychiatry, 58,* 901–906.

Renzulli, Joseph S. (1986). The three-ring conception of giftedness: A developmental model for creative productivity. In Robert J. Sternberg & Janet E. Davidson (Eds.), *Conceptions of giftedness.* New York: Cambridge University Press.

Repetti, Rena L. (1989). Effects of daily workload on subsequent behavior during marital interaction: The roles of withdrawal and spouse support. *Journal of Personality and Social Psychology, 57,* 651–659.

Repetti, Rena L. (1993). Short-term effects of occupational stressors on daily mood and health complaints. *Health Psychology, 12,* 125–131.

Repetti, Rena L., & Wood, Jenifer. (1997). The effects of daily stress at work on mothers' interactions with preschoolers. *Journal of Family Psychology, 11,* 90–108.

Rescorla, Robert A. (1968). Probability of shock in the presence and absence of CS in fear conditioning. *Journal of Comparative and Physiological Psychology, 66,* 1–5.

Rescorla, Robert A. (1980). *Pavlovian second-order conditioning: Studies in associative learning.* Hillsdale, NJ: Erlbaum.

Rescorla, Robert A. (1988). Pavlovian conditioning: It's not what you think it is. *American Psychologist, 43,* 151–160.

Rescorla, Robert A. (1997). Quoted in James E. Freeman. "Pavlov in the classroom: An interview with Robert A. Rescorla." *Teaching of Psychology, 24,* 283–286.

Rescorla, Robert A. (2001). Retraining of extinguished Pavlovian stimuli. *Journal of Experimental Psychology: Animal Behavior Processes, 27,* 115–124.

Reuter-Lorenz, Patricia A., & Miller, Andrea C. (1998). The cognitive neuroscience of human laterality: Lessons from the bisected brain. *Current Directions in Psychological Science, 7,* 15–20.

Revelle, William. (1995). Personality processes. *Annual Review of Psychology, 46,* 295–328.

Reynolds, David K. (1990). *A thousand waves: A sensible life-style for sensitive people.* New York: Morrow.

Rhodes, Richard. (2000, September 17). Hollow claims about fantasy violence. *New York Times,* Sect. 4, p. 19.

Ricaurte, George A., & McCann, Una D. (2001). Assessing long-term effects of MDMA (Ecstasy). *Lancet, 358,* 1831–1832.

Riccio, David C.; Millin, Paula M.; & Gisquet-Verrier, Pascale. (2003). Retrograde amnesia: Forgetting back. *Current Directions in Psychological Science, 12,* 41–44.

Rice, Laura N., & Greenberg, Leslie S. (1992). Humanistic approaches to psychotherapy. In Donald K. Freedheim (Ed.), *History of psychotherapy: A century of change.* Washington, DC: American Psychological Association.

Rice, Robert W.; McFarlin, Dean B.; & Bennett, Debbie E. (1989). Standards of comparison and job satisfaction. *Journal of Applied Psychology, 74,* 591–598.

Richelson, Elliott. (1993). Treatment of acute depression. *Psychiatric Clinics of North America, 16,* 461–478.

Richman, Laura Smart; Kubzansky, Laura; Masello, Joanna; Kawachi, Ichiro; Choo, Peter; & Bauer, Mark. (2005). Positive emotion and health: Going beyond the negative. *Health Psychology, 24,* 422–429.

Riegel, B.; Simon D.; Weaver, J.; Carlson, B.; Clapton, P.; & Gocka, I. (1996). *Ayurvedic medicine demonstration project* (1R21 RR09726–01). Bethesda, MD: Report submitted to the National Institutes of Health, Institute for Alternative Medicine.

Rieger, Gerulf; Chivers, Meredith L.; & Bailey, J. Michael. (2005). Sexual arousal patterns of bisexual men. *Psychological Science, 16,* 579–584.

Rilling, Mark. (2000). John Watson's paradoxical struggle to explain Freud. *American Psychologist, 55,* 301–312.

Rioult-Pedotti, Mengia-S.; Friedman, Daniel; & Donoghue, John P. (2000). Learning-induced LTP in neocortex. *Science, 290,* 533–536.

Rivas-Vasquez, Rafael A. (2003). Aripiprazole: A novel antipsychotic with dopamine stabilizing properties. *Professional Psychology: Research and Practice, 34,* 108–111.

Rivkin, Inna D., & Taylor, Shelley E. (1999). The effects of mental simulation on coping with controllable stressful events. *Personality and Social Psychology Bulletin, 25,* 1451–1462.

Roazen, Paul. (1999). *Freud: political and social thought.* Piscataway, NJ: Transaction.

Roazen, Paul. (2000). *The historiography of psychoanalysis.* Piscataway, NJ: Transaction.

Robbins, Ann S.; Spence, Janet T.; & Clark, Heather. (1991). Psychological determinants of health and performance: The tangled web of desirable and undesirable characteristics. *Journal of Personality and Social Psychology, 61,* 755–765.

Robbins, Steven B.; Lauver, Kristy; Le, Huy; Davis, Daniel; Langley, Ronelle; & Carlstrom, Aaron. (2004). Do psychosocial and study skill factors predict college outcomes? A meta-analysis. *Psychological Bulletin, 130,* 261–288.

Robiner, William N.; Bearman, Diane L.; Berman, Margit; Grove, William M.; Colón, Eduardo; Armstrong, Joann; Mareck, Susan; & Tanenbaum, Robert L. (2003). Prescriptive authority for psychologists: Despite deficits in education and knowledge? *Journal of Clinical Psychology in Medical Settings, 10,* 211–212.

Robins, Clive J., & Hayes, Adele M. (1993). An appraisal of cognitive therapy. *Journal of Consulting and Clinical Psychology, 61,* 205–214.

Robinson, Barbara S.; Davis, Kathleen L.; & Meara, Naomi M. (2003). Motivational attributes of occupational possible selves for low-income rural women. *Journal of Counseling Psychology, 50,* 156–164.

Robinson, Daniel N. (1993). Is there a Jamesian tradition in psychology? *American Psychologist, 48,* 638–643.

Robinson, Daniel N. (1997). Aristotle and psychology. In Wolfgang G. Bringmann, Helmut E. Lück, Rudolf Miller, & Charles E. Early (Eds.), *A pictorial history of psychology.* Chicago: Quintessence.

Robinson, John P., & Godbey, Geoffrey. (1998, February). No sex, please . . . we're college students. *American Demographics, 20*(2), 18–23.

Robinson, Michael D., & Clore, Gerald L. (2002). Belief and feeling: Evidence for an accessibility model of emotional self-report. *Psychological Bulletin, 128,* 934–960.

Robinson, Paul. (1993). *Freud and his critics.* Berkeley: University of California Press.

Robinson, Thomas N.; Wilde, Marta L.; Navracruz, Lisa C.; Haydel, K. Farish; & Varady, Ann. (2001). Effects of reducing children's television and video game use on aggressive behavior. *Archives of Pediatric and Adolescent Medicine, 155,* 17–23.

Robles, Theodore K.; Glaser, Ronald; & Kiecolt-Glaser, Janice K. (2005). Out of balance: A new look at chronic stress, depression, and immunity. *Psychological Science, 14,* 111–115.

Rochat, François; Maggioni, Olivier; & Modigliani, Andre. (2000). Captain Paul Grueninger: The Chief of Police who saved Jewish refugees by refusing to do his duty. In Thomas Blass (Ed.), *Obedience to authority: Current perspectives on the Milgram paradigm.* Mahwah, NJ: Erlbaum.

Rock, Irvin. (1995). *Perception.* New York: Scientific American Library.

Rodin, Judith. (1986, September 19). Aging and health: Effects of the sense of control. *Science, 233,* 1271–1275.

Rodin, Judith, & Langer, Ellen. (1977). Long-term effects of a control-relevant intervention with the institutionalized aged. *Journal of Personality and Social Psychology, 35,* 897–902.

Roediger, Henry L., III. (1990). Implicit memory: Retention without remembering. *American Psychologist, 45,* 1043–1056.

Roehrs, Timothy, & Roth, Thomas. (2001). Sleep, sleepiness, and alcohol use. *Alcohol Research and Health, 25,* 101–109.

Roenneberg, Till; Wirz-Justice, Anna; & Merrow, Martha. (2003). Life between clocks: Daily temporal patterns of human chronotypes. *Journal of Biological Rhythms, 18,* 80–90.

Rogers, Carl R. (1951). *Client-centered psychotherapy.* Boston: Houghton-Mifflin.

Rogers, Carl R. (1957a/1989). A note on "The Nature of Man." In Howard Kirschenbaum & Valerie Land Henderson (Eds.), *The Carl Rogers Reader.* Boston: Houghton Mifflin.

Rogers, Carl R. (1957b/1989). A therapist's view of the good life: The fully functioning person. In Howard Kirschenbaum & Valerie Land Henderson (Eds.), *The Carl Rogers reader.* Boston: Houghton Mifflin.

Rogers, Carl R. (1957c). The necessary and sufficient conditions of therapeutic personality change. *Journal of Consulting Psychology, 21,* 95–103.

Rogers, Carl R. (1959). A theory of therapy, personality, and interpersonal relationships, as developed in the client-centered framework. In S. Koch (Ed.), *Psychology: A study of a science: Vol. 3. Formulations of the person and the social context.* New York: McGraw-Hill.

Rogers, Carl R. (1961). *On becoming a person.* Boston: Houghton Mifflin.

Rogers, Carl R. (1964/1989). Toward a modern approach to values: The valuing process in the mature person. In Howard Kirschenbaum & Valerie Land Henderson (Eds.), *The Carl Rogers reader.* Boston: Houghton Mifflin.

Rogers, Carl R. (1977). *Carl Rogers on personal power: Inner strength and its revolutionary impact.* New York: Delacorte Press.

Rogers, Carl R. (1980). *A way of being.* Boston: Houghton Mifflin.

Rogers, Carl R. (1981/1989). Notes on Rollo May. In Howard Kirschenbaum & Valerie Land Henderson (Eds.), *Carl Rogers: Dialogues.* Boston: Houghton Mifflin.

Rogers, Carl R., & Skinner, B. F. (1956, November 30). Some issues concerning the control of human behavior: A symposium. *Science, 124,* 1057–1066.

Rolls, Edmund T. (2000). Memory systems in the brain. *Annual Review of Psychology, 51,* 599–630.

Romans, Sarah E.; Martin, M.; Gendall, K.; & Herbison, G. P. (2003). Age of menarche: The role of some psychosocial factors. *Psychological Medicine, 33,* 933–939.

Romer, Daniel; Jamieson, Patrick; Holtschlag, Nancy J.; Mebrathu, Hermon; & Jamieson, Kathleen Hall. (2003). *Suicide and the media.* Philadelphia, PA: Annenberg Public Policy Center of the University of Pennsylvania. Retrieved January 7, 2005, from http://www.annenbergpublicpolicycenter.org/07adolescentrisk/suicide/dec14%20suicide%20report.htm

Ronen, Tammie. (1991). Intervention package for treating sleep disorders in a four-year-old girl. *Journal of Behavior Therapy and Experimental Psychiatry, 22,* 141–148.

Rook, Karen S. (1992). Detrimental aspects of social relationships: Taking stock of an emerging literature. In Hans O. F. Veiel & Urs Baumann (Eds.), *The meaning and measurement of social support.* New York: Hemisphere.

Rorden, Chris, & Karnath, Hans-Otto. (2004). Using brain lesions to infer function: A relic from a past era in the fMRI age? *Nature Reviews Neuroscience, 5,* 812–819.

Rosch, Eleanor H. (1973). Natural categories. *Cognitive Psychology, 4,* 328–350.

Rosch, Eleanor H. (1978). Principles of categorization. In Eleanor H. Rosch & Barbara B. Lloyd (Eds.), *Cognition and categorization.* Hillsdale, NJ: Erlbaum.

Rosch, Eleanor H. (1987). Linguistic relativity. *Et Cetera, 44,* 254–279.

Rosch, Eleanor H., & Mervis, Carolyn B. (1975). Family resemblances: Studies in the internal structure of categories. *Cognitive Psychology, 7,* 573–605.

Rose, Jed E.; Behm, Frederique M.; Coleman, R. Edward; & others. (2003). PET studies of the influences of nicotine on neural systems in cigarette smokers. *American Journal of Psychiatry, 160,* 323–333.

Rosekind, Mark. (2003, April 8). Quoted in National Sleep Foundation press release: "Sleep is important when stress and anxiety increase, says the National Sleep Foundation." Washington, DC. Retrieved January 4, 2005, from http://www.sleepfoundation.org/PressArchives/stress.cfm

Rosen, Gerald M., & Lohr, Jeffrey. (1997, January/February.) Can eye movements cure mental ailments? *NCAHF Newsletter.* Retrieved October 15, 2001, from http://www.pseudoscience.org/rosen-and-lohr.htm

Rosen, Gerald M.; McNally, Richard J.; & Lilienfeld, Scott O. (1999). Eye movement magic: Eye movement desensitization and reprocessing a decade later. *Skeptic, 7*(4), 66–69.

Rosenbaum, David A.; Carlson, Richard A.; & Gilmore, Rick O. (2001). Acquisition of intellectual and perceptual-motor skills. *Annual Review of Psychology, 52,* 453–470.

Rosenberg, Harold. (1993). Prediction of controlled drinking by alcoholics and problem drinkers. *Psychological Bulletin, 113,* 129–139.

Rosenlicht, Nicholas, & Feinberg, Irving. (1997). REM sleep = dreaming: Only a dream. *Sleep Research Society Bulletin, 3*(1), 2–4.

Rosenman, Ray H., & Chesney, Margaret A. (1982). Stress, Type A behavior, and coronary disease. In Leo Goldberger & Shlomo Breznitz (Eds.), *Handbook of stress: Theoretical and clinical aspects.* New York: Free Press.

Rosenthal, Abraham M. (1964a, May 3). Study of the sickness called apathy. *The New York Times Magazine,* Sect. VI, pp. 24, 66, 69–72.

Rosenthal, Abraham M. (1964b). *Thirty-eight witnesses.* New York: McGraw-Hill.

Rosenthal, Norman E. (1998). *Winter blues: Seasonal affective disorder: What it is and how to overcome it* (Rev. ed.). New York: Guilford Press.

Rosenzweig, Mark R. (1996). Aspects of the search for neural mechanisms of memory. *Annual Review of Psychology, 47,* 1–32.

Rosenzweig, Saul. (1997). Freud's only visit to America. In Wolfgang G. Bringmann, Helmut E. Lück, Rudolf Miller, & Charles E. Early (Eds.), *A pictorial history of psychology.* Chicago: Quintessence.

Ross, Barbara. (1991). William James: Spoiled child of American psychology. In Gregory A. Kimble, Michael Wertheimer, & Charlotte White (Eds.), *Portraits of pioneers in psychology.* Washington, DC: American Psychological Association.

Ross, Lee. (1977). The intuitive psychologist and his shortcomings: Distortions in the attribution process. In Leonard Berkowitz (Ed.), *Advances in experimental social psychology* (Vol. 10). New York: Academic Press.

Ross, Lee, & Anderson, Craig A. (1982). Short-comings in the attribution process: On the origins and maintenance of erroneous social assessments. In Daniel Kahneman, Paul Slovic, & Amos Tversky (Eds.), *Judgment under uncertainty: Heuristics and biases*. New York: Cambridge University Press.

Rossier, Jerome; Dahourou, Donatien; & Mc-Crae, Robert R. (2005). Structural and mean level analyses of the five-factor model and locus of control: Further evidence from Africa. *Journal of Cross-Cultural Psychology, 36,* 227–246.

Rothbart, Mary K.; Ahadi, Stephan A.; & Evans, David E. (2000). Temperament and personality: Origins and outcomes. *Journal of Personality and Social Psychology, 78,* 122–135.

Rothbart, Mary K., & Putnam, Samuel P. (2002). Temperament and socialization. In Lea Pulkkinen & Avshalom Caspi (Eds.), *Paths to successful development: Personality in the life course.* New York: Cambridge University Press.

Rothbaum, Barbara O.; Hodges, Larry; Anderson, Page L.; Price, Larry; & Smith, Samantha. (2002). Twelve-month follow-up of virtual reality and standard exposure therapy for the fear of flying. *Journal of Consulting and Clinical Psychology, 70,* 428–432.

Rothenberg, Saul A. (1997). Introduction to sleep disorders. In Mark R. Pressman & William C. Orr (Eds.), *Understanding sleep: The evaluation and treatment of sleep disorders.* Washington, DC: American Psychological Association.

Rowe, David C. (2003). Assessing genotype-environment interactions and correlations in the postgenomic era. In Robert Plomin, John C. DeFries, Ian W. Craig, & Peter McGuffin (Eds.), *Behavioral genetics in the postgenomic era.* Washington, DC: American Psychological Association.

Rowe, Shawn M., & Wertsch, James V. (2002). Vygotsky's model of cognitive development. In Usha Gowsami (Ed.), *Blackwell handbook of childhood cognitive development.* Malden, MA: Blackwell.

Roy, Michael M., & Christenfeld, Nicholas J. S. (2004). Do dogs resemble their owners? *Psychological Science, 15,* 361–363.

Rozin, Paul. (1996). The socio-cultural context of eating and food choice. In H. L. Meiselman & H. J. H. MacFie (Eds.), *Food choice, acceptance and consumption.* London: Blackie Academic and Professional.

Rubin, Edgar. (1921/2001). Readings in perception. In Steven Yantis (Ed.), *Visual perception: Essential readings.* Philadelphia: Psychology Press.

Rubin, Nava. (2001). Figure and ground in the brain. *Nature Neuroscience, 4,* 857–858.

Ruiz-Miranda, Carlos R.; Kleiman, Devra G.; Dietz, James M.; Moraes, Ezequiel; Grativol, Adriana D.; Baker, Andrew J.; & Beck, Benjamin B. (1999). Food transfers in wild and reintroduced golden lion tamarins, Leontopithecus rosalia. *American Journal of Primatology, 48* (4), 305–320.

Ruscio, John. (1998, November/December). The perils of post-hockery. *Skeptical Inquirer, 22,* 44–48.

Russek, Linda G., & Schwartz, Gary E. (1997). Perceptions of parental caring predict health status in midlife: A 35-year follow-up to the Harvard Mastery of Stress Study. *Psychosomatic Medicine, 59,* 144–149.

Russell, James A. (1991). Culture and the categorization of emotions. *Psychological Bulletin, 110,* 426–450.

Rutherford, Alexandra. (2000). Radical behaviorism and psychology's public: B. F. Skinner in the popular press, 1934–1990. *History of Psychology, 3,* 371–395.

Rutherford, F. James, & Ahlgren, Andrew. (1991). *Science for all Americans.* New York: Oxford University Press.

Rutter, Michael L. (1997). Nature-nurture integration: The example of antisocial behavior. *American Psychologist, 52,* 390–398.

Ruvolo, Ann Patrice, & Markus, Hazel Rose. (1992). Possible selves and performance: The power of self-relevant imagery. *Social Cognition, 10,* 95–124.

Ryan, Richard M., & Deci, Edward L. (2000). Self-determination theory and the facilitation of intrinsic motivation, social development, and well-being. *American Psychologist, 55,* 68–78.

Ryan, Richard M., & Deci, Edward L. (2001). On happiness and human potentials: A review of research on hedonic and eudaimonic well-being. *Annual Review of Psychology, 52,* 141–166.

Ryan, Richard M., & La Guardia, Jennifer G. (2000). What is being optimized over development? A self-determination theory and basic psychological needs. In Sara Honn Qualls & Norman Abeles (Eds.), *Psychology and the aging revolution: How we adapt to longer life.* Washington, DC: American Psychological Association.

Sabbatini, Renato M.E. (1997, March–May). Phrenology: The history of brain localization. *Brain and Mind: Electronic Magazine on Neuroscience,* No. 1. Retrieved January 20, 2000, from http://www.epub.org.br/cm/n01/frenolog/frenologia.htm

Sachs, Gary S.; Lafer, Beny; Truman, Christine J.; Noeth, Mary; & Thibault, Amy B. (1994). Lithium monotherapy: Miracle, myth and misunderstanding. *Psychiatric Annuals, 24,* 299–306.

Sachse, Rainer, & Elliott, Robert. (2002). Process—Outcome research on humanistic therapy variables. In David J. Cain & Julius Seeman (Eds.), *Humanistic psychotherapies: Handbook of research and practice.* Washington, DC: American Psychological Association.

Sackeim, Harold A. (2001). Functional brain circuits in major depression and remission. *Archives of General Psychiatry, 58,* 649–650.

Sackeim, Harold A.; Haskett, Roger F.; Mulsant, Benoit H.; Thase, Michael E.; Mann, J. John; Pettinati, Helen M.; & others. (2001). Continuation psychotherapy in the prevention of relapse following electroconvulsive therapy: A randomized controlled trial. *Journal of the American Medical Association, 285,* 1299–1307.

Sacks, Michael H. (1993). Exercise for stress control. In Daniel Goleman & Joel Gurin (Eds.), *Mind/body medicine: How to use your mind for better health.* Yonkers, NY: Consumer Reports Books.

Sagi, Abraham; Koren-Karie, Nina; Gini, Motti; Ziv, Yair; & Joels, Tirtsa. (2002). Shedding further light on the effects of various types and quality of early child care on infant–mother attachment relationship: The Haifa Study of Early Child Care. *Child Development, 73,* 1166–1186.

Sakheim, David K., & Devine, Susan E. (Eds.). (1992). *Out of darkness: Exploring Satanism and ritual abuse.* New York: Lexington Books.

Salancik, G. R., & Pfeffer, J. (1977). An examination of needs satisfaction models of job satisfaction. *Administrative Science Quarterly, 22,* 427–450.

Salmán, Ester; Diamond, Kimberly; Jusino, Carlos; & others. (1997). Hispanic Americans. In Steven Friedman (Ed.), *Cultural issues in the treatment of anxiety.* New York: Guilford Press.

Salokangas, Raimo K.R.; Vilkman, Harry; Ilonen, Tuula; & others. (2000). High levels of dopamine activity in the basal ganglia of cigarette smokers. *American Journal of Psychiatry, 157,* 632–634.

Salovey, Peter; Mayer, John D.; & Rosenhan, David L. (1991). Mood and helping: Mood as a motivator of helping and helping as a regulator of mood. In Margaret S. Clark (Ed.), *Prosocial behavior: Vol. 12. Review of personality and social psychology.* Newbury Park, CA: Sage.

Saltzman, Ann L. (2000). The role of the obedience experiments in Holocaust studies: The case for renewed visibility. In Thomas Blass (Ed.), *Obedience to authority: Current perspectives on the Milgram paradigm.* Mahwah, NJ: Erlbaum.

Sandelowski, Margarete; Holditch-Davis, Diane; & Harris, Betty G. (1992). Using qualitative and quantitative methods: The transition to parenthood among infertile couples. In Jane F. Gilgun, Kerry Daly, & Gerald Handel (Eds.), *Qualitative methods in family research.* Newbury Park, CA: Sage.

Sanna, Lawrence J. (1999). Mental simulations, affect, and subjective confidence: Timing is everything. *Psychological Science, 10,* 339–345.

Sanna, Lawrence J. (2000). Mental simulation, affect, and personality: A conceptual framework. *Current Directions in Psychological Science, 9,* 168–173.

Saper, Clifford B.; Scammell, Thomas E.; & Lu, Jun. (2005, October 27). Hypothalamic regulation of sleep and circadian rhythms. *Nature, 437,* 1257–1263.

Sarason, Irwin G.; Sarason, Barbara R.; Pierce, Gregory R.; Shearin, Edward N.; & Sayers, Merlin H. (1991). A social learning approach to increasing blood donations. *Journal of Applied Social Psychology, 21,* 896–918.

Saskin, Paul. (1997). Obstructive sleep apnea: Treatment options, efficacy, and effects. In Mark R. Pressman & William C. Orr (Eds.), *Understanding sleep: The evaluation and treatment of sleep disorders.* Washington, DC: American Psychological Association.

Saufley, William H.; Otaka, Sandra R.; & Bavaresco, Joseph L. (1985). Context effects: Classroom tests and context independence. *Memory & Cognition, 13,* 522–528.

Savage-Rumbaugh, E. Sue. (1993). Language learnability in man, ape, and dolphin. In Herbert L. Roitblat, Louis M. Herman, & Paul E. Nachtigall (Eds.), *Language and communication: Comparative perspectives.* Hillsdale, NJ: Erlbaum.

Savage-Rumbaugh, E. Sue, & Lewin, Roger. (1994, September). Ape at the brink. *Discover, 15,* 91–98.

Savage-Rumbaugh, E. Sue; Shanker, Stuart G.; & Taylor, Talbot J. (1998). *Apes, language, and the human mind.* New York: Oxford University Press.

Saxe, Glenn N.; Chinman, Gary; Berkowitz, Robert; Hall, Kathryn; Lieberg, Gabriele; Schwartz, Jane; & van der Kolk, Bessel A. (1994). Somatization in patients with dissociative disorders. *American Journal of Psychiatry, 151,* 1329–1334.

Scanlon, Matthew, & Mauro, James. (1992, November/December). The lowdown on handwriting analysis: Is it for real? *Psychology Today, 25,* 46–53.

Scarr, Sandra, & Weinberg, Richard A. (1976). IQ test performance of black children adopted by white families. *American Psychologist, 31,* 726–739.

Schacter, Daniel L. (1995, April). Memory wars. *Scientific American, 272,* 135–139.

Schacter, Daniel L. (1998, April 3). Memory and awareness. *Science, 280,* 59–60.

Schacter, Daniel L. (2001). *The seven sins of memory: How the mind forgets and remembers.* Boston: Houghton-Mifflin.

Schacter, Daniel L.; Chiu, Peter C.Y.; & Ochsner, Kevin N. (1993). Implicit memory: A selective review. *Annual Review of Neuroscience, 16,* 159–182.

Schacter, Daniel L.; Norman, Kenneth A.; & Koutstaal, Wilma. (1998). The cognitive neuroscience of constructive memory. *Annual Review of Psychology, 49,* 289–318.

Schachter, Stanley, & Singer, Jerome E. (1962). Cognitive, social, and physiological determinants of emotional state. *Psychological Review, 69,* 379–399.

Schaie, K. Warner. (1994). The course of adult intellectual development. *American Psychologist, 49,* 304–313.

Schaie, K. Warner. (1995). *Intellectual development in adulthood: The Seattle Longitudinal Study.* New York: Cambridge University Press.

Schaie, K. Warner, & Willis, Sherry L. (1986). Can decline in adult intellectual functioning be reversed? *Developmental Psychology, 22,* 223–232.

Schaie, K. Warner, & Willis, Sherry L. (1996). *Adult development and aging* (4th ed.). New York: HarperCollins.

Schaller, Mark, & Cialdini, Robert B. (1990). Happiness, sadness, and helping: A motivational integration. In Richard M. Sorrentino & E. Tory Higgins (Eds.), *Handbook of motivation and cognition: Vol. 2. Foundations of social behavior.* New York: Guilford Press.

Scharff, Lisa; Marcus, Dawn A.; & Masek, Bruce J. (2002). A controlled study of minimal-contact thermal biofeedback treatment in children with migraine. *Journal of Pediatric Psychology, 27,* 109–119.

Schattschneider, Doris. (1990). *Visions of symmetry: Notebooks, periodic drawings, and related work of M. C. Escher* (p. 169, notes on p. 301). New York: Freeman.

Schatzman, Morton, & Fenwick, Peter. (1994). Dreams and dreaming. In Rosemary Cooper (Ed.), *Sleep.* New York: Chapman & Hall.

Scheibel, Arnold B. (1994, July). Quoted in Daniel Golden: "Building a better brain." *Life,* p. 66.

Schenk, Carlos H. (2003, February 2). Quoted in Chip Brown: "The man who mistook his wife for a deer." *New York Times Magazine.* Retrieved February 2, 2003, from http://www.nytimes.com/2003/02/02/magazine/02SLEEP.html

Schenck, Carlos H., & Mahowald, Mark W. (2002). REM sleep behavior disorder: Clinical, developmental, and neuroscience perspectives 16 years after its formal identification in SLEEP. *Sleep, 25,* 120–138.

Scherer, Klaus R., & Wallbott, Harald G. (1994). Evidence for universality and cultural variation of differential emotion response patterning. *Journal of Personality and Social Psychology, 66,* 310–328.

Schilling, Stephen L. (1999). The basics of a successful telework network. *HRFocus, 76,* 9–10.

Schlenker, Barry R., & Weigold, Michael F. (1992). Interpersonal processes involving impression regulation and management. *Annual Review of Psychology, 43,* 133–168.

Schmader, Toni, & Johns, Michael. (2005). Converging evidence that stereotype threat re-duces working memory capacity. *Journal of Personality and Social Psychology, 85,* 440–452.

Schmit, Julie. (2005, February 2). Impotence drugs selling slowly. *USA Today.* Retrieved March 2, 2005, from http://www.usatoday.com/news/health/2005-02-02-sexdrug-usatx.htm

Schneider, Barry H. (1998). Cross-cultural comparison as doorkeeper in research on the social and emotional adjustment of children and adolescents. *Developmental Psychology, 34,* 793–797.

Schneider, Kirk. (1998). Toward a science of the heart: Romanticism and the revival of psychology. *American Psychologist, 53,* 277–289.

Schneiderman, Neil; Ironson, Gail; & Siegel, Scott D. (2005). Stress and health: Psychological, behavioral, and biological determinants. *Annual Review of Clinical Psychology, 1,* 607–628.

Scholz, Joachim, & Woolf, Clifford J. (2002). Can we conquer pain? *Nature Neuroscience, 5*(Suppl.), 1062–1067.

Schooler, Jonathan W. (2001). Discovering memories of abuse in the light of meta-awareness. *Journal of Aggression, Maltreatment, & Trauma, 42,* 105–136.

Schooler, Jonathan W.; Ohlsson, Stellan; & Brooks, Kevin. (1993). Thoughts beyond words: When language overshadows insight. *Journal of Experimental Psychology: General, 122,* 166–183.

Schrater, Paul; Knill, David C.; & Simoncelli, Eero P. (2001). Perceiving visual expansion without optic flow. *Nature, 410,* 616–619.

Schredl, Michael; Frauscher, Saskia; & Shendi, Acram. (1995). Dream recall and visual memory. *Perceptual and Motor Skills, 81,* 256–258.

Schredl, Michael, & Montasser, Alyaa. (1997). Dream recall: State or trait variable? Part II. State factors, investigations, and final conclusions. *Imagination, Cognition and Personality, 16,* 239–261.

Schroth, Marvin L., & McCormack, William A. (2000) Current problems and resolutions—Sensation seeking and need for achievement among study-abroad students. *The Journal of Social Psychology, 140,* 533.

Schuckit, Marc A.; Smith, Tom L.; Daeppen, Jean-Bernard; Eng, Mimy; Li, T.-K.; Hesselbrock, Victor M.; & others. (1998). Clinical relevance of the distinction between alcohol dependence with and without a physiological component. *American Journal of Psychiatry, 155,* 733–740.

Schulman, Michael, & Mekler, Eva. (1985). *Bringing up a moral child: A new approach for teaching your child to be kind, just, and responsible.* Reading, MA: Addison-Wesley.

Schultz, Wolfram; Dayan, Peter; & Montague, P. Read. (1997, March 14). A neural substrate of prediction and reward. *Science, 275,* 1593–1599.

Schulz, Marc S.; Cowan, Philip A.; Cowan, Carolyn Pape; & Brennan, Robert T. (2004). Coming home upset: Gender, marital satisfaction, and the daily spillover of workday experience into couple interactions. *Journal of Family Psychology, 18,* 250–263.

Schwartz, Bennett L. (1999). Sparkling at the end of the tongue: The etiology of tip-of-the-tongue phenomenology. *Psychonomic Bulletin and Review, 6,* 379–393.

Schwartz, Bennett L. (2002). *Tip-of-the-tongue states: Phenomenology, mechanism, and lexical retrieval.* Mahwah, NJ: Erlbaum.

Schwartz, Jeffrey M.; Stoessel, Paula W.; & Phelps, Michael E. (1996). Systematic changes in cerebral glucose metabolic rate after successful behavior modification treatment of obsessive-compulsive disorder. *Archives of General Psychiatry, 53,* 109–117.

Schwartz, Michael W.; Woods, Stephen C.; Porte, Daniel, Jr.; Seeley, Randy J.; & Baskin, Denis G. (2000, April 6). Central nervous system control of food intake. *Nature, 404,* 661–671.

Scoville, William Beecher, & Milner, Brenda. (1957). Loss of recent memory after bilateral hippocampal lesions. *Journal of Neurology, Neurosurgery, and Psychiatry, 20,* 11–21.

Scully, Judith A.; Tosi, Henry; & Banning, Kevin. (2000). Life event checklists: Revisiting the Social Readjustment Rating Scale after 30 years. *Educational and Psychological Measurement, 60,* 864–876.

Sedikides, Constantine, & Anderson Craig A. (1994). Causal perceptions of intertrait relations: The glue that holds person types together. *Personality and Social Psychology Bulletin, 20,* 294–302.

Segal, Zindel V.; Williams, J. Mark G.; & Teasdale, John D. (2002). *Mindfulness-based cognitive therapy for depression: A new approach to preventing relapse.* New York: Guilford Press.

Segall, Marshall H. (1994). A cross-cultural research contribution to unraveling the nativist/empiricist controversy. In Walter J. Lonner & Roy Malpass (Eds.), *Psychology and culture.* Boston: Allyn & Bacon.

Segall, Marshall H.; Campbell, Donald T.; & Herskovits, Melville J. (1963). Cultural differences in the perception of geometric illusions. *Science, 193,* 769–771.

Segall, Marshall H.; Campbell, Donald T.; & Herskovits, Melville J. (1966). *The influence of culture on visual perception.* Indianapolis, IN: Bobbs-Merrill.

Segall, Marshall H.; Lonner, Walter J.; & Berry, John W. (1998). Cross-cultural psychology as a scholarly discipline: On the flowering of culture in behavioral research. *American Psychologist, 53,* 1101–1110.

Segerdahl, Pär; Fields, William; & Savage-Rumbaugh, Sue. (2006). *Kanzi's primal language: The cultural initiation of primates into language.* New York: Palgrave Macmillan.

Segerstrom, Suzanne C.; Castañeda, Jay O.; & Spencer, Theresa E. (2003). Optimism effects on cellular immunity: Testing the affective and persistence models. *Personality and Individual Differences, 35,* 1615–1624.

Segerstrom, Suzanne C., & Miller, Gregory E. (2004). Psychological stress and the human immune system: A meta-analytic study of 30 years of inquiry. *Psychological Bulletin, 130,* 601–630.

Segerstrom, Suzanne C.; Taylor, Shelley E.; Kemeny, Margaret E.; & Fahey, John L. (1998). Optimism is associated with mood, coping, and immune change in response to stress. *Journal of Personality and Social Psychology, 74,* 1646–1655.

Self, David W. (2005). Neural basis of substance abuse and dependence. In Benjamin J. Sadock & Virginia A. Sadock (Eds.), *Comprehensive textbook of psychiatry* (8th ed.). Baltimore: Lippincott/Williams & Wilkins.

Seligman, Martin E. P. (1970). On the generality of the laws of learning. *Psychological Review, 77,* 406–418.

Seligman, Martin E. P. (1971). Phobias and preparedness. *Behavior Therapy, 2,* 307–320.

Seligman, Martin E. P. (1990). *Learned optimism.* New York: Knopf.

Seligman, Martin E. P. (1992). *Helplessness: On development, depression, and death.* New York: Freeman.

Seligman, Martin E. P., & Maier, Steven F. (1967). Failure to escape traumatic shock. *Journal of Experimental Psychology, 37B,* 1–21.

Selye, Hans. (1956). *The stress of life.* New York: McGraw-Hill.

Selye, Hans. (1976). *The stress of life* (Rev. ed.). New York: McGraw-Hill.

Sendero Group. (2004). *Mike's journal.* Retrieved August 2, 2004, from http://www.senderogroup.com/mikejournal.htm

Senghas, Ann. (2004). Quoted in: "Children create new sign language," *BBC News,* 9/16/04. Retrieved December 9, 2004, from http://news.bbc.co.uk/go/pr/fr//1/hi/sci/tech/3662928.stm

Senghas, Ann; Kita, Sotaro; & Özyürek, Asli. (2004, September 17). Children creating core properties of language: Evidence from an emerging sign language in Nicaragua. *Science, 305,* 1779–1782.

Seta, John J., & Seta, Catherine E. (1993). Stereotypes and the generation of compensatory and noncompensatory expectancies of group members. *Personality and Social Psychology Bulletin, 19,* 722–731.

Sexton, Thomas L.; Alexander, James F.; & Mease, Alyson Leigh. (2004). Levels of evidence for the models and mechanisms of therapeutic change in family and couple therapy. In Michael J. Lambert (Ed.), *Bergin and Garfield's handbook of psychotherapy and behavior change* (5th ed.). New York: Wiley.

Shapiro, Francine. (1989a). Efficacy of the eye movement desensitization procedure in the treatment of traumatic memories. *Journal of Traumatic Stress, 2,* 199–223.

Shapiro, Francine. (1989b). Eye movement desensitization: A new treatment for post-traumatic stress disorder. *Journal of Behavior Therapy and Experimental Psychiatry, 20,* 211–217.

Shapiro, Francine. (1995). *Eye movement desensitization and reprocessing: Basic principles, protocols, and procedures.* New York: Guilford Press.

Shapiro, Francine, & Forrest, Margot Silk. (1997). *EMDR: The breakthrough therapy for overcoming anxiety, stress, and trauma.* New York: Basic Books.

Sharman, Stefanie J.; Garry, Maryanne; & Beuke, Carl J. (2004). Imagination or exposure causes imagination inflation. *American Journal of Psychology, 117,* 157–168.

Shavinina, Larisa V. (2001). Beyond IQ: A new perspective on the psychological assessment of intellectual abilities. *New Ideas in Psychology, 19,* 27–47.

Shedler, Jonathan; Mayman, Martin; & Manis, Melvin. (1993). The illusion of mental health. *American Psychologist, 48,* 1117–1131.

Sheldon, Kennon M.; Elliot, Andrew J.; Kim, Youngmee; & Kasser, Tim. (2001). What is satisfying about satisfying events? Testing 10 candidate psychological needs. *Journal of Personality and Social Psychology, 80,* 325–339.

Shepard, Roger N. (1990). *Mind sights: Original visual illusions, ambiguities, and other anomalies, with a commentary on the play of mind in perception and art.* New York: Freeman

Sherif, Muzafer. (1956, November). Experiments in group conflict. *Scientific American, 195,* 33–47.

Sherif, Muzafer. (1966). *In common predicament: Social psychology of intergroup conflict and cooperation.* Boston: Houghton-Mifflin.

Sherif, Muzafer; Harvey, O. J.; White, B. Jack; Hood, William R.; & Sherif, Carolyn W. (1961/1988). *The Robbers Cave experiment: Intergroup conflict and cooperation.* Middletown, CT: Wesleyan University Press.

Shermer, Michael. (1997). *Why people believe weird things: Pseudoscience, superstition, and other confusions of our time.* New York: Freeman.

Shields, Stephanie A. (2002). *Speaking from the heart: Gender and the social meaning of emotion.* Cambridge, England: Cambridge University Press.

Shiffrin, Richard M., & Nosofsky, Robert M. (1994). Seven plus or minus two: A commentary on capacity limitations. *Psychological Review, 101,* 357–361.

Shih, Margaret; Pittinsky, Todd L.; & Ambady, Nalini. (1999). Stereotype susceptibility: Identity salience and shifts in quantitative performance. *Psychological Science, 10,* 80–83.

Shinskey, Jeanne L., & Munakata, Yuko. (2005). Familiarity breeds searching: Infants reverse their novelty preferences when reaching for hidden objects. *Psychological Science, 16*, 596–600.

Shneidman, Edwin S. (1998). *The suicidal mind*. New York: Oxford University Press.

Shneidman, Edwin S. (2004). *Autopsy of a suicidal mind*. New York: Oxford University Press.

Shogi-Jadid, Kooresh; Small, Gary W.; Agdeppa, Eric D.; Kepe, Vladimar; Ercoli, Linda M.; Siddarth, Prabba; & others. (2002). Localization of Neurofibrillary tangles and beta-amyloid plaques in the brains of living patients with Alzheimer's disease. *American Journal of Geriatric Psychiatry, 10*, 24–35.

Shors, Tracey J.; Miesegaes, George; Beylin, Anna; Zhao, Mingrui; Rydel, Tracy; & Gould, Elizabeth. (2001). Neurogenesis in the adult is involved in the formation of trace memories. *Nature, 410*, 372–376.

Shotland, R. Lance, & Straw, Margret K. (1976). Bystander response to an assault: When a man attacks a woman. *Journal of Personality and Social Psychology, 34*, 990–999.

Shou, Mogens. (1993). *Lithium treatment of manic-depressive illness: A practical guide* (5th ed.). Basel: Karger.

Shulman, Ian D.; Cox, Brian J.; Swinson, Richard P.; Kuch, Klaus; & Reichman, Jaak T. (1994). Precipitating events, locations and reactions associated with initial unexpected panic attacks. *Behavior Research and Therapy, 32*, 17–20.

Shumaker, Sally A., & Hill, D. Robin. (1991). Gender differences in social support and physical health. *Health Psychology, 10*, 102–111.

Shuval, Judith T. (1993). Migration and stress. In Leo Goldberger & Shlomo Breznitz (Eds.), *Handbook of stress: Theoretical and clinical aspects* (2nd ed.). New York: Free Press.

Shweder, Richard A.; Mahapatra, Manamohan; & Miller, Joan G. (1990). Culture and moral development. In Jerome Kagan & Sharon Lamb (Eds.), *The emergence of morality in young children*. Chicago: University of Chicago Press.

Siegal, Michael. (2004, September 17). Signposts to the essence of language. *Science, 305*, 1720–1721.

Siegel, Jerome M. (2000, January). Narcolepsy. *Scientific American, 282*, 77–81.

Siegel, Jerome M. (2001). The REM sleep–memory consolidation hypothesis. *Science, 294*, 1058–1063.

Siegel, Jerome M. (2005, October 27). Clues to the functions of mammalian sleep. *Nature, 437*, 1264–1271.

Siegel, Judith M. (1990). Stressful life events and use of physician services among the elderly. *Journal of Personality and Social Psychology, 58*, 1081–1086.

Siegler, Robert S. (1992). The other Alfred Binet. *Developmental Psychology, 28*, 179–190.

Siegler, Robert S. (1996). *Emerging minds: The process of change in children's thinking*. New York: Oxford University Press.

Siegler, Robert S., & Ellis, Shari. (1996). Piaget on childhood. *Psychological Science, 7*, 211–215.

Silbersweig, David A.; Stern, Emily; & Frackowaik, R. S. J. (1995, November 9). A functional neuroanatomy of hallucinations in schizophrenia. *Nature, 387*, 176–184.

Silver, Eric; Mulvey, Edward P.; & Monahan, John. (1999). Assessing violence risk among discharged psychiatric patients: Toward an ecological approach. *Law and Human Behavior, 23*(2), 237–255.

Silverstein, Steven M.; Menditto, Anthony A.; & Stuve, Paul. (2001). Shaping attention span: An operant conditioning procedure to improve neurocognition and functioning in schizophrenia. *Schizophrenia Bulletin, 27*, 247–257.

Simon, Bernd; Pantaleo, Giuseppe; & Mummendey, Amelie. (1995). Unique individual or interchangeable group member? The accentuation of intragroup differences versus similarities as an indicator of the individual self versus the collective self. *Journal of Personality and Social Psychology, 69*, 106–119.

Simons, Christopher T., & Noble, Ann C. (2003). Challenges for the sensory sciences from the food and wine industries. *Nature Reviews Neuroscience, 4*, 599–605.

Singer, Tania; Verhaeghen, Paul; Ghisletta, Paolo; Lindenberger, Ulman; & Baltes, Paul. (2003). The fate of cognition in very old age: Six-year longitudinal findings in the Berlin Aging Study (BASE). *Psychology and Aging, 18*, 318–331.

Singhal, Arvind; Cody, Michael J.; Rogers, Everett M.; & Sabido, Miguel (Eds.). (2004). *Entertainment-education and social change: History, research, and practice*. Mahwah, NJ: Erlbaum.

Sirey, Jo Anne; Bruce, Martha L.; Alexopoulos, George S.; & others. (2001). Perceived stigma as a predictor of treatment discontinuation in young and older outpatients with depression. *American Journal of Psychiatry, 158*, 479–481.

Skinner, B. F. (1938). *The behavior of organisms: An experimental analysis*. New York: Appleton-Century-Crofts.

Skinner, B. F. (1948a/1976). *Walden two*. Englewood Cliffs, NJ: Prentice-Hall.

Skinner, B. F. (1948b/1992). Superstition in the pigeon. *Journal of Experimental Psychology: General, 121*, 273–274.

Skinner, B. F. (1953). *Science and human behavior*. New York: Macmillan.

Skinner, B. F. (1956). A case history in scientific method. *American Psychologist, 11*, 221–233.

Skinner, B. F. (1961, November). Teaching machines. *Scientific American, 205*, 90–102.

Skinner, B. F. (1966). Some responses to the stimulus "Pavlov." *Conditional Reflex, 1*, 74–78. (Reprinted in 1999 in the *Journal of the Experimental Analysis of Behavior, 72*, 463–465.)

Skinner, B. F. (1967). B. F. Skinner . . . an autobiography. In E. G. Boring & G. Lindzey (Eds.), *A history of psychology in autobiography* (Vol. 5). New York: Appleton-Century-Crofts.

Skinner, B. F. (1971). *Beyond freedom and dignity*. New York: Bantam Books.

Skinner, B. F. (1974). *About behaviorism*. New York: Knopf.

Skinner, B. F. (1979). *The shaping of a behaviorist*. New York: Knopf.

Slamecka, Norman J. (1992). Forgetting. In Larry R. Squire (Ed.), *Encyclopedia of learning and memory*. New York: Macmillan.

Smith, Andrew W.; Whitney, Helen; Thomas, Marie; Perry, Kate; & Brockman, Pip. (1997). Effects of caffeine and noise on mood, performance and cardiovascular functioning. *Human Psychopharmacology: Clinical and Experimental, 12*, 27–33.

Smith, Barry D.; Cranford, David; & Green, Lee. (2001). Hostility and caffeine: Cardiovascular effects during stress and recovery. *Personality & Individual Differences, 30*, 1125–1137.

Smith, David E., & Seymour, Richard B. (1994). LSD: History and toxicity. *Psychiatric Annals, 24*, 145–147.

Smith, Eliot R. (1993). Social identity and social emotions: Toward new conceptualizations of prejudice. In Diane M. Mackie & David L. Hamilton (Eds.), *Affect, cognition, and stereotyping: Interactive processes in group perception*. San Diego, CA: Academic Press.

Smith, Gerard P., & Gibbs, James. (1998). The satiating effects of cholecystokinin and bombesin-like peptides In Gerard P. Smith (Ed.), *Satiation: From gut to brain*. New York: Oxford University Press.

Smith, Marilyn C. (1983). Hypnotic memory enhancement of witnesses: Does it work? *Psychological Bulletin, 94*(3), 387–407.

Smith, Michael T.; Perlis, Michael L.; Park, Amy; & others. (2002). Comparative meta-analysis of pharmacotherapy and behavior therapy for persistent insomnia. *American Journal of Psychiatry, 159*, 5–11.

Smith, Timothy W. (1992). Hostility and health: Current status of a psychosomatic hypothesis. *Health Psychology, 11*, 139–150.

Smuts, Barbara. (1996). Male aggression against women: An evolutionary perspective. In David M. Buss & Neil M. Malumuth (Eds.), *Sex, power, conflict: Evolutionary and feminist perspectives*. New York: Oxford University Press.

Snyder, Solomon H. (1984). Drug and neurotransmitter receptors in the brain. *Science, 224*, 22–31.

Snyman, J.; Aamodt, M. G.; Johnson, D. L.; & Frantzve, J. (1991). Pre-employment paper-and-pencil testing: A quantitative review. *Journal of Police and Criminal Psychology, 7,* 11–25.

Solomon, Henry; Solomon, Linda Zener; Arnone, Maria M.; Maur, Bonnie J.; Reda, Rosina M.; & Roth, Esther O. (1981). Anonymity and helping. *Journal of Social Psychology, 113,* 37–43.

Solomon, Hester McFarland. (2003). Freud and Jung: An incomplete encounter. *Journal of Analytical Psychology, 48,* 553–569.

Solomon, Linda Zener; Solomon, Henry; & Stone, Ronald. (1978). Helping as a function of number of bystanders and ambiguity of emergency. *Personality and Social Psychology Bulletin, 4,* 318–321.

Solomon, Paul R.; Adams, Felicity; Silver, Amanda; Zimmer, Jill; & DeVeaux, Richard. (2002). Ginkgo for memory enhancement: A randomized controlled trial. *Journal of the American Medical Association, 288,* 835–840.

Solomon, Sondra E.; Rothblum, Esther D.; & Balsam, Kimberly F. (2004). Pioneers in partnership: Lesbian and gay male couples in civil unions compared with those not in civil unions and married heterosexual siblings. *Journal of Family Psychology, 18,* 275–286.

Son, Lisa K. (2004). Spacing one's study: Evidence for a metacognitive control strategy. *Journal of Experimental Psychology: Learning, Memory, & Cognition, 30,* 601–604.

Sood, Suruchi; SenGupta, Manisha; Mishra, Pius Raj; & Jacoby, Caroline. (2004). "Come gather around together": An examination of radio listening groups in Fulbari, Nepal. *Gazette: The International Journal for Communication Studies, 66,* 63–86.

Southwick, Steven M.; Vythilingam, Meena; & Charney, Dennis S. (2005). The psychobiology of depression and resilience to stress: Implications for prevention and treatment. *Annual Review of Clinical Psychology, 1,* 255–291.

Sowell, Elizabeth R.; Peterson, Bradley S.; Thompson, Paul M.; Welcome, Suzanne E.; Henkenius, Amy L.; Toga, Arthur W. (2003). Mapping cortical change across the human life span. *Nature Neuroscience, 6,* 309–315.

Sowell, Elizabeth R.; Thompson, Paul M.; Leonard, Christiana M.; Welcome, Suzanne E.; Kan, Eric; & Toga, Arthur W. (2004, September 22). Longitudinal mapping of cortical thickness and brain growth in normal children. *Journal of Neuroscience, 24,* 8223–8231.

Spangler, William D. (1992). Validity of questionnaire and TAT measures of need for achievement: Two meta-analyses. *Psychological Bulletin, 112,* 140–154.

Spanos, Nicholas P. (1987–1988, Winter). Past-life hypnotic regression: A critical view. *Skeptical Inquirer, 12,* 174–180.

Spanos, Nicholas P. (1991). A sociocognitive approach to hypnosis. In Steven Jay Lynn & Judith W. Rhue (Eds.), *Theories of hypnosis: Current models and perspectives.* New York: Guilford Press.

Spanos, Nicholas P. (1994). Multiple identity enactments and multiple personality disorder: A sociocognitive perspective. *Psychological Bulletin, 116,* 143–165.

Spanos, Nicholas P. (1996). *Multiple identities & false memories: A sociocognitive perspective.* Washington, DC: American Psychological Association.

Spanos, Nicholas P.; Burnley, Caroline E.; & Cross, Patricia A. (1993). Response expectancies and interpretations as determinants of hypnotic responding. *Journal of Personality and Social Psychology, 65,* 1237–1242.

Spanos, Nicholas P.; McNulty, Stacey A.; DuBreuil, Susan C.; & Pires, Martha. (1995). The frequency and correlates of sleep paralysis in a university sample. *Journal of Research in Personality, 29,* 285–305.

Spanos, Nicholas P.; Mondoux, Thomas J.; & Burgess, Cheryl A. (1995). Comparison of multi-component hypnotic and non-hypnotic treatments for smoking. *Contemporary Hypnosis, 12,* 12–19.

Spearman, Charles E. (1904). "General intelligence" objectively determined and measured. *American Journal of Psychology, 15,* 201–293.

Spencer, Natasha A.; McClintock, Martha K.; Sellergren, Sarah A.; Bullivant, Susan; Jacob, Suma; & Mennella, Julie A. (2004). Social chemosignals from breastfeeding women increase sexual motivation. *Hormones and Behavior, 46,* 362–370.

Spencer, Steven J.; Steele, Claude M.; & Quinn, Diane M. (1999). Stereotype threat and women's math performance. *Journal of Experimental Social Psychology, 35,* 1–28.

Sperling, George. (1960). The information available in brief visual presentations. *Psychological Monographs, 74*(Whole No. 48).

Sperry, Roger W. (1982). Some effects of disconnecting the cerebral hemispheres. *Science, 217,* 1223–1226.

Spiegel, David. (1993a). Dissociation and trauma. In David Spiegel (Ed.), *Dissociative disorders: A clinical review.* Lutherville, MD: Sidran.

Spiegel, David. (1993b). Social support: How friends, family, and groups can help. In Daniel Goleman & Joel Gurin (Eds.), *Mind/body medicine: How to use your mind for better health.* Yonkers, NY: Consumer Reports Books.

Spiegel, David; Bloom, J. R.; Kraemer, H. C.; & Gottheil, E. (1989). Effect of psychosocial treatment on survival of patients with metastatic breast cancer. *Lancet, 2,* 888–891.

Spiegel, David, & Cardeña, Etzel. (1991). Disintegrated experience: The dissociative disorders revisited. *Journal of Abnormal Psychology, 100,* 366–378.

Spiegel, Karine; Leproult, Rachel; & Van Cauter, Eve. (1999, October 23). Impact of sleep debt on metabolic and endocrine function. *Lancet, 354,* 1435–1439.

Spiegel, Karine; Tasali, Esra; Penev, Plamen; & Van Cauter, Eve. (2004). Sleep curtailment in healthy young men is associated with decreased leptin levels, elevated ghrelin levels, and increased hunger and appetite. *Annals of Internal Medicine, 141,* 846–850.

Spraggins, Reneé E. (2003, March). *Women and men in the United States: March 2002* (Current Population Reports, Population Characteristics, P20-544). Washington, DC: U.S. Bureau of the Census. Retrieved November 30, 2004, from http://www.census.gov/prod/2003pubs/p20-544.pdf

Springer, Sally P., & Deutsch, Georg. (1998). *Left brain, right brain: Perspectives from cognitive neuroscience* (5th ed.). New York: Freeman.

Squire, Larry R., & Kandel, Eric R. (1999). *Memory: From mind to molecules.* New York: Scientific American Library.

Squire, Larry R., & Knowlton, Barbara J. (1995). Memory, hippocampus, and brain systems. In Michael S. Gazzaniga (Ed.), *The cognitive neurosciences.* Cambridge, MA: MIT Press.

Squire, Larry R.; Ojemann, Jeffrey G.; Miezin, Frances M.; Petersen, Steven E.; Videen, Thomas O.; & Raichle, Marcus E. (1992). Activation of the hippocampus in normal humans: A functional anatomical study of memory. *Proceedings of the National Academy of Sciences, USA, 89,* 1837–1841.

Squire, Larry R.; Schmolck, Heike; & Buffalo, Elizabeth A. (2001). Memory distortions develop over time: A reply to Horn. *Psychological Science, 12,* 182.

Sroufe, L. Alan. (1995, September). Quoted in Beth Azar: "The bond between mother and child." *APA Monitor, 26*(9), 28.

Sroufe, L. Alan. (2002). From infant autonomy to promotion of adolescent autonomy: Prospective, longitudinal data on the role of parents in development. In John G. Borkowski & Sharon Landesman Ramey (Eds.), *Parenting and the child's world: Influences on academic, intellectual, and social-emotional development.* Mahwah, NJ: Erlbaum.

Stacy, Alan W.; Widaman, Keith F.; & Marlatt, G. Alan. (1990). Expectancy models of alcohol use. *Journal of Personality and Social Psychology, 58,* 918–928.

Stajkovic, Alexander D., & Luthans, Fred. (1997). A meta-analysis of the effects of organizational behavior modification on task performance, 1975–1995. *Academy of Management Journal, 40,* 1122–1149.

Stams, Geert-Jan J. M.; Juffer, Femmie; & Van Ijzendorn, Marinus H. (2002). Maternal sensitivity, infant attachment, and temperament in early childhood predict adjustment in middle childhood: The case of adopted children and their biologically unrelated parents. *Developmental Psychology, 38,* 806–821.

Stangor, Charles. (1995). Content and application inaccuracy in social stereotyping. In Yueh-Ting Lee, Lee J. Jussim, & Clark R. McCauley (Eds.), *Stereotype accuracy: Toward appreciating group differences.* Washington, DC: American Psychological Association.

Stangor, Charles, & Lange, James E. (1994). Mental representations of social groups: Advances in understanding stereotypes and stereotyping. In Mark P. Zanna (Ed.), *Advances in experimental social psychology* (Vol. 26). San Diego, CA: Academic Press.

Stangor, Charles, & Ruble, Diane N. (1987). Development of gender role knowledge and gender constancy. In Lynn S. Liben & Margaret L. Signorella (Eds.), *Children's gender schemata* (New Directions for Child Development Series, No. 38). San Francisco: Jossey-Bass.

Stanton, Annette L., & Snider, Pamela R. (1993). Coping with a breast cancer diagnosis: A prospective study. *Health Psychology, 12*, 16–23.

Statham, Anne. (1987). The gender model revisited: Differences in the management styles of men and women. *Sex Roles, 16*, 409–429.

Staub, Ervin. (1996). Cultural-societal roots of violence: The examples of genocidal violence and of contemporary youth violence in the United States. *American Psychologist, 51*, 117–132.

Staudinger, Ursula. (2001). Life-reflection: A social-cognitive analysis of life review. *Review of General Psychology, 5*, 148–160.

Staw, Barry M., & Ross, Jerry. (1985). Stability in the midst of change: A dispositional approach to job attitudes. *Journal of Applied Psychology, 70*, 469–480.

Steadman, Henry J.; Mulvey, Edward P.; Monahan, John; Robbins, Pamela Clark; Appelbaum, Paul S.; Grisso, Thomas; & others. (1998). Violence by people discharged from acute psychiatric inpatient facilities and by others in the same neighborhoods. *Archives of General Psychiatry, 55*, 393–401.

Steblay, Nancy Mehrkens. (1987). Helping behavior in urban and rural environments: A meta-analysis. *Psychological Bulletin, 102*, 346–356.

Steele, Claude M. (1997). A threat in the air: How stereotypes shape intellectual identity and performance. *American Psychologist, 52*, 613–629.

Steele, Claude M. (2003). Through the back door to theory. *Psychological Inquiry, 14*, 314–317.

Steele, Claude M., & Aronson, Joshua. (1995). Stereotype threat and the intellectual performance of African Americans. *Journal of Personality and Social Psychology, 69*, 797–811.

Steele, Claude M., & Josephs, Robert A. (1990). Alcohol myopia: Its prized and dangerous effects. *American Psychologist, 45*, 921–933.

Steig, Philip E. (2004, October 12). Quoted in Jamie Talan: "Christopher Reeve dies at 52." *Newsday.* Retrieved January 5, 2005, from http://www.newsday.com/other/education/ny-news101304.story

Stein, Elliot A.; Pankiewicz, John; Harsch, Harold H.; Cho, Jung-Ki; Fuller, Scott A.; Hoffmann, Raymond G.; & others. (1998). Nicotine-induced limbic cortical activation in the human brain: A functional MRI study. *American Journal of Psychiatry, 155*, 1009–1015.

Stein, Lincoln D. (2004, October 21). End of the beginning. *Nature, 431*, 915–916.

Steinberg, Laurence. (1990). Autonomy, conflict, and harmony in the family relationship. In S. Shirley Feldman & Glen R. Elliott (Eds.), *At the threshold: The developing adolescent.* Cambridge, MA: Harvard University Press.

Steinberg, Laurence. (2001). We know some things: Parent–adolescent relationships in retrospect and prospect. *Journal of Research on Adolescence, 11*, 1–19.

Steinberg, Laurence; Darling, Nancy E.; Fletcher, Anne C.; Brown, B. Bradford; & Dornbusch, Sanford M. (1995). Authoritative parenting and adolescent adjustment: An ecological journey. In Phyllis Moen, Glen H. Elder, Jr., & Kurt Luscher (Eds.), *Examining lives in context: Perspectives on the ecology of human development.* Washington, DC: American Psychological Association.

Stepfamily Association of America. (2005). *Frequently asked questions about stepfamilies.* Retrieved February 28, 2005, from http://www.saafamilies.org/faqs/faqs.htm

Stephens, Benjamin R.; & Banks, Martin S. (1987) Contrast discrimination in human infants. *Journal of Experimental Psychology: Human Perception and Performance, 13*, 558–565.

Stern, Kathleen, & McClintock, Martha K. (1998, March 12). Regulation of ovulation by human hormones. *Nature, 392*, 177.

Stern, Marilyn, & Karraker, Katherine Hildebrandt. (1989). Sex stereotyping of infants: A review of gender labelling studies. *Sex Roles, 20*, 501–522.

Stern, Peter. (2001). Sweet dreams are made of this. *Science, 294*, 1047.

Stern, Yaakov; Alexander, Gene E.; & Prohovnik, Isak. (1992). Inverse relationship between education and parietotemporal perfusion deficit in Alzheimer's disease. *Annals of Neurology, 32*, 371–377.

Stern, Yaakov; Gurland, B.; & Tatemichi, T. K. (1994, April 6). Influence of education and occupation on the incidence of Alzheimer's disease. *Journal of the American Medical Association, 271*(13), 1004–1007.

Sternberg, Robert J. (1986). *Intelligence applied: Understanding and increasing your intellectual skills.* San Diego, CA: Harcourt Brace Jovanovich.

Sternberg, Robert J. (1988). A three-facet model of creativity. In Robert J. Sternberg (Ed.), *The nature of creativity.* New York: Cambridge University Press.

Sternberg, Robert J. (1990). *Metaphors of mind: Conceptions of the nature of intelligence.* New York: Cambridge University Press.

Sternberg, Robert J. (1995). For whom the bell curve tolls: A review of The Bell Curve. *Psychological Science, 6*, 257–261.

Sternberg, Robert J. (1997). The concept of intelligence and its role in lifelong learning and success. *American Psychologist, 52*, 1030–1037.

Stevens, Gwendolyn, & Gardner, Sheldon. (1982). *The women of psychology: Vol. I. Pioneers and innovators.* Cambridge, MA: Schenkman.

Stevenson, Harold W., & Lee, Shin-Ying. (1990). Contexts of achievement: A study of American, Chinese, and Japanese children. *Monographs of the Society for Research in Child Development, 55* (Serial No. 221, Nos. 1–2).

Stevenson, Harold W.; Lee, Shin-Ying; & Stigler, James W. (1986). Mathematics achievements of Chinese, Japanese, and American children. *Science, 236*, 693–698.

Stevenson, Harold W., & Stigler, James W. (1992). *The learning gap: Why our schools are failing and what we can learn from Japanese and Chinese education.* New York: Summit Books.

Steward, Barbara. (2000). Changing times: The meaning, measurement and use of time in teleworking. *Time & Society, 9*, 57–74.

Stewart, V. Mary. (1973). Tests of the "carpentered world" hypothesis by race and environment in America and Zambia. *International Journal of Psychology, 8*, 83–94.

Stickgold, Robert. (2005, October 27). Sleep-dependent memory consolidation. *Nature, 437*, 1272–1278.

Stickgold, Robert; Hobson, J. Allan; Fosse, Roar; & Fosse, M. (2001). Sleep, learning, and dreams: Off-line memory reprocessing. *Science, 294*, 1052–1057.

Stipek, Deborah. (1998). Differences between Americans and Chinese in the circumstances evoking pride, shame, and guilt. *Journal of Cross-Cultural Psychology, 29*, 616–629.

Stogdill, Ralph M. (1948). Personal factors associated with leadership: A survey of the literature. *Journal of Psychology, 25*, 35–71.

Stone, Arthur A.; Cox, Donald S.; Valdimarsdottir, Heiddis; Jandorf, Lina; & Neale, John M. (1987). Evidence that secretory IgA antibody is associated with daily mood. *Journal of Personality and Social Psychology, 52*, 988–993.

Stone, Arthur A.; Neale, John M.; Cox, Donald S.; Napoli, Anthony; Valdimarsdottir, Heiddis; & Kennedy-Moore, Eileen. (1994). Daily events are associated with a secretory immune response to an oral antigen in men. *Health Psychology, 13*, 440–446.

Storm, Lance, & Ertel, Suitbert. (2001). Does psi exist? Comments on Milton and Wiseman's (1999) meta-analysis of Ganzfield research. *Psychological Bulletin, 127*, 424–435.

St-Pierre, Edouard S., & Melnyk, William T. (2004). The prescription privilege debate in

Canada: The voices of today's and tomorrow's psychologists. *Canadian Psychology, 45,* 284–292.

Strack, Fritz; Martin, Leonard L.; & Stepper, Sabine. (1988). Inhibiting and facilitating conditions of the human smile: A non-obtrusive test of the facial-feedback hypothesis. *Journal of Personality and Social Psychology, 54,* 768–777.

Straus, Joshua L., & von Ammon Cavanaugh, Stephanie. (1996). Placebo efects: Issues for clinical practice in psychiatry and medicine. *Psychosomatics, 37*(4), 315–326.

Straus, Murray A., & Stewart, Julie H. (1999). Corporal punishment by American parents: National data on prevalence, chronicity, severity, and duration, in relation to child and family characteristics. *Clinical Child & Family Psychology Review, 2,* 55–70.

Strickland, Bonnie R. (1995). Research on sexual orientation and human development: A commentary. *Developmental Psychology, 31,* 137–140.

Strober, Michael; Freeman, Roberta; Kaye, Walter; & others. (2001). Males with anorexia nervosa: A controlled study of eating disorders in first-degree relatives. *International Journal of Eating Disorders, 29,* 262–269.

Strupp, Hans H. (1996). The tripartite model and the Consumer Reports study. *American Psychologist, 51,* 1017–1024.

Stuart, Richard B., & Davis, Barbara. (1972). *Slim chance in a fat world.* Champaign, IL: Research Press.

Stutts, Jane C.; Wilkins, Jean W.; & Vaugh, Bradley V. (1999, November). *Why do people have drowsy driving crashes? Input from drivers who just did.* Washington, DC: AAA Foundation for Traffic Safety. Retrieved February 12, 2005, from http://www.sleepfoundation.org/ddsummit/CrashesAAAStudy.pdf

Styron, William. (1990). *Darkness visible: A memoir of madness.* New York: Vintage.

Substance Abuse and Mental Health Services Administration. (2002). *The National Household Survey on Drug Abuse Report.* Retrieved on November 2, 2002, from http://www.samhsa.gov/oas/nhsda/2klnhsda/vol1/highlights.htm

Suchman, Anthony L., & Ader, Robert. (1992). Classic conditioning and placebo effects in crossover studies. *Clinical Pharmacology and Therapeutics, 52,* 372–377.

Sue, Stanley; Zane, Nolan; & Young, Kathleen. (1994). Research on psychotherapy with culturally diverse populations. In Allen E. Bergin & Sol L. Garfield (Eds.), *Handbook of psychotherapy and behavior change* (4th ed.). New York: Wiley.

Suess, Gerhard J.; Grossmann, Klaus E.; & Sroufe, L. Alan. (1992). Effects of infant attachment to mother and father on quality of adaptation in preschool: From dyadic to individual organisation of self. *International Journal of Behavioral Development, 15*(1), 43–65.

Sullivan, Cath, & Lewis, Suzan. (2001). Home-based telework, gender, and the synchronization of work and family: Perspectives of teleworkers and their co-residents. *Gender, Work & Organization, 8,* 123–145.

Suls, Jerry, & Bunde, James. (2005). Anger, anxiety, and depression as risk factors for cardiovascular disease: The problems and implications of overlapping affective dispositions. *Psychological Bulletin, 131,* 260-300.

Sumerlin, John R., & Bundrick, Charles M. (1996). Brief Index of Self-Actualization: A measure of Maslow's model. *Journal of Social Behavior and Personality, 11,* 253–271.

Sun, Shumei S.; Schubert, Christine M.; Chumlea, William Cameron; Roche, Alex F.; Kulin, Howard E.; Lee, Peter A.; & others. (2002). National estimates of the timing of sexual maturation and racial differences among US children. *Pediatrics, 110,* 911–919.

Super, Donald E. (1990). Career and life development. In Duane Brown, Linda Brooks, & Associates (Eds.), *Career choice and development: Applying contemporary theories to practice.* San Francisco: Jossey-Bass.

Swan, Daniel C., & Big Bow, Harding. (1995, Fall). Symbols of faith and belief—Art of the Native American Church. *Gilcrease Journal, 3,* 22–43.

Swann, William B. (1984). Quest for accuracy in person perception: A matter of pragmatics. *Psychological Review, 91,* 457–477.

Swart, Lyle C., & Morgan, Cynthia L. (1992). Effects of subliminal backward-recorded messages on attitudes. *Perceptual and Motor Skills, 75*(3, Pt. 2), 1107–1113.

Swickert, Rhonda J.; Rosentreter, Christina J.; Hittner, James B.; & Mushrush, Jane E. (2002). Extraversion, social support processes, and stress. *Personality and Individual Differences, 32,* 877–891.

Swim, Janet K. (1994). Perceived versus meta-analytic effect sizes: An assessment of the accuracy of gender stereotypes. *Journal of Personality and Social Psychology, 66,* 21–36.

Swoboda, H.; Demal, U.; Krautgartner, M.; & Amering, M. (2003). Heightened embarrassability discriminates between panic disorder patients with and without agoraphobia. *Journal of Behavior Therapy and Experimental Psychiatry, 34,* 195–204.

Szechtman, Henry, & Woody, Erik. (2004). Obsessive-compulsive disorder as a disturbance of security motivation. *Psychological Review, 111,* 111–127.

Taft, Lois B., & Nehrke, Milton F. (1990). Reminiscence, life review, and ego integrity in nursing home residents. *International Journal of Aging and Human Development, 30,* 189–196.

Taguba, Antonio M. (2004). Article 15-6. Investigation of the 800th Military Police Brigade. Accessed on December 8, 20055 from: http://www.npr.org/iraq/2004/prison_abuse_report.pdf

Taheri, Shahrad; Lin, Ling; Austin, Diane; Young, Terry; & Mignot, Emmanuel. (2004, December). Short sleep duration is associated with reduced leptin, elevated ghrelin, and increased body mass index. (2004). *PloS Medicine, 1*(Issue 3, e62, 001-008). Retrieved December 17, 2004, from http://www.plosmedicine.org/archive/1549-1676/1/3/pdf/10.1371journal.pmed.0010062-p-L.pdf

Talarico, Jennifer M., & Rubin, David C. (2003). Confidence, not consistency, characterizes flashbulb memories. *Psychological Science, 14,* 455–461.

Tallman, Karen, & Bohart, Arthur C. (1999). The client as a common factor: Clients as self-healers. In Mark A. Hubble, Barry L. Duncan, & Scott D. Miller (Eds.), *The heart and soul of change: What works in therapy.* Washington, DC: American Psychological Association.

Talwar, Sanjiv, K.; Xu, Shaohua; Chapin, John K.; & others. (2002, May 2). Rat navigation guided by remote control. *Nature, 417,* 37–38.

Tanaka-Matsumi, Junko, & Draguns, Juris G. (1997). Culture and psychopathology. In John W. Berry, Marshall H. Segall, & Cigdem Kagitçibasi (Eds.), *Handbook of cross-cultural psychology: Vol. 3. Social behavior and applications.* Boston: Allyn & Bacon.

Tanford, Sarah, & Penrod, Steven. (1984). Social influence model: A formal integration of research on majority and minority influence processes. *Psychological Bulletin, 95,* 189–225.

Tart, Charles T. (Ed.). (1990). *Altered states of consciousness* (3rd ed.). San Francisco: HarperCollins.

Tart, Charles T. (1994). *Living the mindful life: A handbook for living in the present moment.* Boston: Shambhala.

Taylor, Donald M., & Porter, Lana E. (1994). A multicultural view of stereotyping. In Walter J. Lonner & Roy Malpass (Eds.), *Psychology and culture.* Boston: Allyn & Bacon.

Taylor, Shelley E., & Aspinwall, Lisa G. (1993). Coping with chronic illness. In Leo Goldberger & Shlomo Breznitz (Eds.), *Handbook of stress: Theoretical and clinical aspects* (2nd ed.). New York: Free Press.

Taylor, Shelley E.; Kemeny, Margaret E.; Bower, Julienne E.; Gruenewald, Tara L.; & Reed, Geoffrey M. (2000). Psychological resources, positive illusions,and health. *American Psychologist, 55,* 99–109.

Taylor, Shelley E.; Klein, Laura Cousino; Lewis, Brian P.; Gruenewald, Tara L.; Gurung, Regan A.; & Updegraff, John A. (2000). Biobehavioral responses to stress in females: Tend-and-befriend, not fight-or-flight. *Psychological Review, 107,* 411–429.

Taylor, Shelley E.; Lewis, Brian P.; Gruenewald, Tara L.; Gurung, Regan A. R.; Updegraff, John A.; & Klein, Laura Cousino. (2002). Sex differences in biobehavioral response to threat: Reply to Geary and Flinn (2002). *Psychological Review, 109*, 751–753.

Taylor, Steven; Thordarson, Dana S.; Maxfield, Louise; Fedoroff, Ingrid C.; Lovell, Karina; & Ogrodniczuk, John. (2003). Comparative efficacy, speed, and adverse effects of three PTSD treatments: Exposure therapy, EMDR, and relaxation training. *Journal of Consulting and Clinical Psychology, 71*, 330–338.

Taylor, Susan M., & Sackheim, Kathryn K. (1988). Graphology. *Personnel Administrator, 33*, 71–76.

Taylor, W. S., & Martin, M. F. (1944). Multiple personality. *Journal of Abnormal and Social Psychology, 39*, 281–300.

Terman, Lewis M. (1916). *Measurement of intelligence*. Boston: Houghton Mifflin.

Terman, Lewis M. (1926). *Genetic studies of genius* (2nd ed., Vol. I). Stanford, CA: Stanford University Press.

Terman, Lewis M., & Oden, Melita H. (1947). *Genetic studies of genius: Vol. IV. The gifted child grows up: Twenty-five years' follow-up of a superior group*. Stanford, CA: Stanford University Press.

Terman, Lewis M., & Oden, Melita H. (1959). *Genetic studies of genius: Vol. V. The gifted at mid-life: Thirty-five years' follow-up of the superior child*. Stanford, CA: Stanford University Press.

Terracciano, Antonio; McCrae, Robert R.; Brant, Larry J.; & Costa, Paul T., Jr. (2005). Hierarchical linear modeling analyses of the NEO-PI-R Scales in the Baltimore Longitudinal Study of Aging. (2005). *Psychology and Aging, 20*, 493–506.

Terrace, Herbert S. (1985). In the beginning was the "name." *American Psychologist, 40*, 1011–1028.

Tett, Robert P.; Jackson, Douglas N.; & Rothstein, Mitchell. (1991). Personality measures as predictors of job performance: A meta-analytic review. *Personnel Psychology, 44*, 703–742.

Thacker, Rebecca A., & Wayne, Sandy J. (1995). An examination of the relationship between upward influence tactics and assessments of promotability. *Journal of Management, 21*, 739–757.

Thase, Michael E. (2001). Neuroimaging profiles and the differential therapies of depression. *Archives of General Psychiatry, 58*, 651–653.

Thase, Michael E.; Entsuah, A. R.; & Rudolph, R. L. (2001). Remission rates during treatment with venlafaxine or selective serotonin reuptake inhibitors. *British Journal of Psychiatry, 178*, 234–241.

Thase, Michael E., & Jindal, Ripu D. (2004). Combining psychotherapy and psychopharmacology for treatment of mental disorders. In Michael J. Lambert (Ed.), *Bergin and Garfield's handbook of psychotherapy and behavior change* (5th ed.). New York: Wiley.

Thomas, Alexander, & Chess, Stella. (1977). *Temperament and development*. New York: Brunner/Mazel.

Thomas, Alexander, & Chess, Stella. (1986). The New York Longitudinal Study: From infancy to early adult life. In Robert Plomin & Judith Dunn (Eds.), *The study of temperament: Changes, continuities, and challenges*. Hillsdale, NJ: Erlbaum.

Thomas, Ayanna K.; Bulevich, John B.; & Loftus, Elizabeth F. (2003). Exploring the role of repetition and sensory elaboration in the imagination inflation effect. *Memory & Cognition, 31*, 630–640.

Thompson, Clara. (1950/1973). Some effects of the derogatory attitude toward female sexuality. In Jean Baker Miller (Ed.), *Psychoanalysis and women*. Baltimore: Penguin Books.

Thompson, Paul. (2001, September 25). Quoted in UCLA Researchers map: "How schizophrenia engulfs teen brains." University of California—Los Angeles press release. Retrieved March 6, 2005, from: http://www.loni.ucla.edu/~thompson/MEDIA/PNAS/Pressrelease.html

Thompson, Paul M.; Hayashi, Kiralee M.; Simon, Sara L.; London, Edythe D.; & others. (2004). Structural abnormalities in the brains of human subjects who use methamphetamine. *Journal of Neuroscience, 24*, 6028–6036.

Thompson, Paul M.; Hayashi, Kiralee M.; Toga, Arthur W.; & others. (2003). Gray matter loss in Alzheimer's disease. *Journal of Neuroscience, 23*, 994–1005. Retrieved July 10, 2004, from http://www.loni.ucla.edu/~thompson/PDF/ADwave.pdf

Thompson, Paul M.; Vidal, Christine; Gledd, Jay N.; Gochman, Peter; Blumenthal, Jonathan; Nicolson, Robert; & others. (2001). Mapping adolescent brain change reveals dynamic wave of accelerated gray matter loss in very early-onset schizophrenia. *Proceedings of the National Academy of Sciences, USA, 98*, 11650–11655.

Thompson, Richard F. (1994). Behaviorism and neuroscience. *Psychological Review, 101*, 259–265.

Thompson, Richard F. (2000). *The brain: A neuroscience primer* (3rd ed.). New York: Freeman.

Thompson, Richard F. (2005). In search of memory traces. *Annual Review of Psychology, 56*, 1–23.

Thompson, Suzanne C.; Nanni, Christopher; & Levine, Alexandra. (1994). Primary versus secondary and central versus consequence-related control in HIV-positive men. *Journal of Personality and Social Psychology, 67*, 540–547.

Thompson, Suzanne C., & Spacapan, Shirlynn. (1991). Perceptions of control in vulnerable populations. *Journal of Social Issues, 47*, 1–21.

Thompson, Vetta L. Sanders; Bazile, Anita; & Akbar, Maysa. (2004). African Americans' perceptions of psychotherapy and psychotherapists. *Professional Psychology: Research and Practice, 35*, 19–26.

Thompson-Pope, Susan K., & Turkat, Ira D. (1993). Schizotypal, schizoid, paranoid, and avoidant personality disorders. In Patricia B. Sutker & Henry E. Adams (Eds.), *Comprehensive handbook of psychopathology* (2nd ed.). New York: Plenum Press.

Thorndike, Edward L. (1898). Animal intelligence: An experimental study of the associative processes in animals. *Psychological Review Monograph Supplement, 2*(Serial No. 8).

Thorndike, Robert L. (1991). Edward L. Thorndike: A professional and personal appreciation. In Gregory A. Kimble, Michael Wertheimer, & Charlotte L. White (Eds.), *Portraits of pioneers in psychology*. Washington, DC: American Psychological Association.

Thorne, Barrie. (1993). *Gender play: girls and boys in school*. New Brunswick, NJ: Rutgers University Press.

Thornton, Bill. (1992). Repression and its mediating influence on the defensive attribution of responsibility. *Journal of Research in Personality, 26*, 44–57.

Thunberg, Monika, & Dimberg, Ulf. (2000). Gender differences in facial reactions to fear-relevant stimuli. *Journal of Nonverbal Behavior, 24*, 45–51.

Thurstone, Louis L. (1937). *Primary mental abilities*. Chicago: University of Chicago Press.

Tienari, Pekka; Sorri, Anneli; Lahti, Ilpo; Naarala, Mikko; Wahlberg, Karl-Erik; Moring, Juha; & others. (1987). Genetic and psychosocial factors in schizophrenia: The Finnish Adoptive Family Study. *Schizophrenia Bulletin, 13*, 477–484.

Tienari, Pekka; Wynne, Lyman C.; Moring, Juha; Lahti, Ilpo; Naarala, Mikko; Sorri, Anneli; & others. (1994). The Finnish Adoptive Family Study of Schizophrenia: Implications for family research. *British Journal of Psychiatry, 164*(Suppl.), 20–26.

Tindall-Ford, Sharon; Chandler, Paul; & Sweller, John. (1997). When two sensory modes are better than one. *Journal of Experimental Psychology: Applied, 3*, 257–287.

Todd, James T., & Morris, Edward K. (1992). Case histories in the great power of steady misrepresentation. *American Psychologist, 47*, 1441–1453.

Todd, Michael. (2004). Daily processes in stress and smoking: Effects of negative events, nicotine dependence, and gender. *Psychology of Addictive Behaviors, 18*, 31–39.

Toga, Arthur W., & Thompson, Paul M. (2003). Mapping brain asymmetry. *Nature Reviews Neuroscience, 4*, 37–48.

Tolman, Edward C. (1932). *Purposive behavior in animals and men*. New York: Appleton-Century-Crofts.

Tolman, Edward C. (1948). Cognitive maps in rats and men. *Psychological Review, 55*, 189–208.

Tolman, Edward C., & Honzik, Charles H. (1930a). "Insight" in rats. *University of*

California, Berkeley, Publications in Psychology, 4, 215–232.

Tolman, Edward C., & Honzik, Charles H. (1930b). Introduction and removal of reward, and maze performance in rats. *University of California, Berkeley, Publications in Psychology, 4,* 257–275.

Tolman, Edward C.; Ritchie, B. F.; & Kalish, D. (1946/1992). Studies in spatial learning. I. Orientation and the short-cut. *Journal of Experimental Psychology: General, 121,* 429–434.

Tomaka, Joe; Blascovich, Jim; Kelsey, Robert M.; & Leitten, Christopher L. (1993). Subjective, physiological, and behavioral effects of threat and challenge appraisal. *Journal of Personality and Social Psychology, 65,* 248–260.

Tomb, David A. (1994). The phenomenology of post-traumatic stress disorder. *Psychiatric Clinics of North America, 17,* 237–250.

Tooby, John, & Cosmides, Leda. (2000). Evolutionary psychology and the emotions. In Michael Lewis & Jeanette M. Haviland-Jones (Eds.), *Handbook of emotions* (2nd ed.). New York: Guilford Press.

Torrey, E. Fuller. (1992). Are we overestimating the genetic contribution to schizophrenia? *Schizophrenia Bulletin, 18,* 159–170.

Torrey, E. Fuller; Bowler, Ann E.; Rawlings, Robert; & Terrazas, Alejandro. (1993). Seasonality of schizophrenia and stillbirths. *Schizophrenia Bulletin, 19,* 557–562.

Torrey, E. Fuller; Bowler, Ann E.; Taylor, Edward H.; & Gottesman, Irving I. (1994). *Schizophrenia and manic-depressive disorder: The biological roots of mental illness as revealed by the landmark study of identical twins.* New York: Basic Books.

Torrey, E. Fuller; Miller, Judy; Rawlings, Robert; & Yolken, Robert H. (1997). Seasonality of births in schizophrenia and bipolar disorder: A review of the literature. *Schizophrenia Research, 28,* 1–38.

Trachtenberg, Joshua T.; Chen, Brian E.; Knott, Graham W.; Feng, Guoping; Sanes, Joshua R.; Welker, Egbert; & others. (2002). Long-term in vivo imaging of experience-dependent synaptic plasticity in adult cortex. *Nature, 420,* 788–794.

Trappey, Charles. (1996). A meta-analysis of consumer choice and subliminal advertising. *Psychology and Marketing, 13,* 517–530.

Trautman, Richard; Tucker, Phebe; Pfefferbaum, Betty; Lensgraf, S. Jay; Doughty, Debby E.; Buksh, Azra; & Miller, Peteryne D. (2002). Effects of prior trauma and age on posttraumatic stress symptoms in Asian and Middle Eastern immigrants after terrorism in the community. *Community Mental Health Journal, 38,* 459–474.

Triandis, Harry C. (1994). *Culture and social behavior.* New York: McGraw-Hill.

Triandis, Harry C. (1995). *Individualism and collectivism.* Boulder, CO: Westview Press.

Triandis, Harry C. (1996). The psychological measurement of cultural syndromes. *American Psychologist, 51,* 407–415.

Trope, Yaacov, & Fishbach, Ayelet. (2000). Counteractive self-control in overcoming temptation. *Journal of Personality and Social Psychology, 79,* 493–506.

Trull, Timothy J.; Widiger, Thomas A.; Lynam, Donald R.; & Costa, Paul T. (2003). Borderline personality disorder from the perspective of general personality functioning. *Journal of Abnormal Psychology, 112,* 193–202.

Tsang, Laura Lo Wa; Harvey, Carol D. H.; Duncan, Karen A.; & Sommer, Reena. (2003). The effects of children, dual earner status, sex role traditionalism, and marital structure on marital happiness over time. *Journal of Family and Economic Issues, 24,* 5–26.

Tschöp, Matthias; Smiley; David L.; & Heiman, Mark L. (2000, October 19). Ghrelin induces adiposity in rodents. *Nature, 407,* 908–913.

Tsien, Joe Z. (2000, April). Building a brainier mouse. *Scientific American, 282,* 62–68.

Tsuang, Ming T.; Stone, William S.; & Faraone, Stephen V. (2000). Toward reformulating the diagnosis of schizophrenia. *American Journal of Psychiatry, 157,* 1041–1050.

Tucker, Phebe, & Trautman, Richard. (2000). Understanding and treating PTSD: past, present, and future. *Bulletin of the Menninger Clinic, 64*(Suppl. A), A37–A51.

Tulving, Endel. (1983). *Elements of episodic memory.* Oxford, England: Clarendon Press/Oxford University Press.

Tulving, Endel. (1985). How many memory systems are there? *American Psychologist, 40,* 385–398.

Tulving, Endel. (1995). Organization of memory: Quo vadis? In Michael S. Gazzaniga (Ed.), *The cognitive neurosciences.* Cambridge, MA: MIT Press.

Tulving, Endel. (1997). Human memory. In Michael S. Gazzaniga (Ed.), *Conversations in the cognitive neurosciences.* Cambridge, MA: MIT Press.

Tulving, Endel. (2002). Episodic memory: From mind to brain. *Annual Review of Psychology, 53,* 1–25.

Tuomisto, Terhi; Tuomisto, Martti T.; Hetherington, Marion; & Lappalainen, Raimo. (1998). Reasons for initiation and cessation of eating in obese men and women and the affective consequences of eating in everyday situations. *Appetite, 30,* 211–222.

Turati, Chiara; Simion, Francesca; Milani, Idanna; & Umiltà, Carlo. (2002). Newborns' preference for faces; What is crucial? *Developmental Psychology, 38,* 875–882.

Turk, Dennis C., & Nash, Justin M. (1993). Chronic pain: New ways to cope. In Daniel Goleman & Joel Gurin (Eds.), *Mind/body medicine: How to use your mind for better health.* Yonkers, NY: Consumer Reports Books.

Turkheimer, Eric; Haley, Andreana; Waldron, Mary; D'Onofrio, Brian; & Gottesman, Irving I. (2003). Socioeconomic status modifies heritability of IQ in young children. *Psychological Science, 14,* 623–628.

Tversky, Amos. (1972). Elimination by aspects: A theory of choice. *Psychological Review, 80,* 281–299.

Tversky, Amos, & Kahneman, Daniel. (1982). Judgment under uncertainty: Heuristics and biases. In Daniel Kahneman, Paul Slovic, & Amos Tversky (Eds.), *Judgment under uncertainty: Heuristics and biases.* New York: Cambridge University Press.

Tversky, Amos, & Shafir, Eldar. (1992). Choice under conflict: The dynamics of deferred decision. *Psychological Science, 3,* 358–361.

Tweney, Ryan D. (1997). Edward Bradford Titchener (1867–1927). In Wolfgang G. Bringmann, Helmut E. Lück, Rudolf Miller, & Charles E. Early (Eds.), *A pictorial history of psychology.* Chicago: Quintessence.

Twenge, Jean M.; Campbell, W. Keith; & Foster, Craig A. (2003). Parenthood and marital satisfaction: A meta-analytic review. *Journal of Marriage and Family, 65,* 574–583.

Uchino, Bert N.; Cacioppo, John T.; & Kiecolt-Glaser, Janice K. (1996). The relationship between social support and physiological processes: A review with emphasis on underlying mechanisms and implications for health. *Psychological Bulletin, 119,* 488–531.

Ulett, George A., & Han, Songping. (2002). *The biology of acupuncture.* St. Louis, MO: Warren H. Green.

Ulett, George A.; Han, Songping; & Han, Jisheng. (1998). Electroacupuncture: Mechanisms and clinical application. *Biological Psychiatry, 44,* 129–138.

Underwood, Geoffrey (Ed.). (1996). *Implicit cognition.* New York: Oxford University Press.

U.S. Bureau of Labor Statistics. (2000). *Occupational outlook handbook.* Washington, DC: U. S. Department of Labor.

U.S. Census Bureau. (2002). *Statistical abstract of the United States: 2001* (121st ed.). Washington, DC: U.S. Government Printing Office.

U.S. Census Bureau. (2004a). *Annual Social and Economic Supplement: 2003 Current Population Survey, America's Families and Living Arrangements: 2003* (Current Population Reports: Series P20-553). Washington, DC: U.S. Census Bureau. Retrieved November 20, 2004, from http://www.census.gov/population/socdemo/hh-fam/tabMS-2.pdf

U.S. Census Bureau (2004b). Facts for features: Special Edition: Unmarried and single Americans week. Retrieved November 30, 2004, from http://www.census.gov/PressRelease/www/releases/archieves/factsforfeatures specialeditions/002265.html

U. S. Department of Health and Human Services. (1999). *Mental health: A report of the Surgeon General.* Rockville, MD: U. S. Department of Health and Human Services, Center for Mental Health Services, National Institute of Mental Health. http://www.nimh.nih.gov/-mhsgrpt/home.html (February 22, 2000)

U.S. Public Health Service. (1999). *The surgeon general's call to action to prevent suicide.* Washington, DC: U.S. Government Printing Office. Retrieved October 30, 2001, from http://www.surgeongeneral.gov/library/calltoaction/calltoaction.pdf

Uttal, William R. (2001). *The new phrenology: The limits of localizing cognitive processes in the brain.* Cambridge, MA: MIT Press.

Vallee, Bert L. (1998, June). Alcohol in the western world. *Scientific American, 278,* 80–85.

Van Agtmael, Tom; Forrest, Susan M.; & Williamson, Robert. (2001). Genes for left-handedness: How to search for the needle in the haystack? *Laterality: Asymmetries of Body, Brain & Cognition, 6,* 149–164.

Van Boven, Leaf; Kamada, Akiko; & Gilovich, Thomas. (1999). The perceiver as perceived: Everyday intuitions about the correspondence bias. *Journal of Personality and Social Psychology, 77,* 1188–1199.

Van Cauter, Eve. (1999, October 21). Quoted in "Lack of sleep ages body's systems." <http://www.psycport.com/news/1999/10/21/tbl-z/4265-0775-SLEEP-DEBT-MED.html> (1999, November 22).

Vandell, Deborah Lowe, & Corasaniti, Mary Ann. (1990). Child care and the family: Complex contributors to child development. In Kathleen McCartney (Ed.), *Child care and maternal employment: A social ecology approach* (New Directions for Child Development Series, No. 49). San Francisco: Jossey-Bass.

van den Boom, Dymphna C., & Hoeksma, Jan B. (1994). The effect of infant irritability on mother-infant interaction: A growth-curve analysis. *Developmental Psychology, 30,* 581–590.

van der Helm, Peter A. (2000). Simplicity versus likelihood in visual perception: From surprisals to precisals. *Psychological Bulletin, 126,* 770–800.

van Geert, Paul. (1998). A dynamic systems model of basic developmental mechanisms: Piaget, Vygotsky, and beyond. *Psychological Review, 105,* 634–677.

van Praag, Henriette (2005, September 20). Quoted in: "Exercise may reverse mental decline brought on by aging." Society for Neurosciences News Release. Accessed on 9/27/95 from http//apu.sfn.org/content/AboutSFN1/NewsReleases/pr_091405.html

van Praag, Henriette; Kempermann, Gerd; & Gage, Fred H. (2000). Neural consequences of environmental enrichment. *Nature Reviews Neuroscience, 1,* 191–198.

van Praag, Henriette; Schinder, Alejandro F.; Christie, Brian R.; Toni, Nicolas; Palmer, Theo D.; & Gage, Fred H. (2002, February 28). Functional neurogenesis in the adult hippocampus. *Nature, 415,* 1030–1034.

van Praag, Henriette; Shubert, Tiffany; Zhao, Chunmei; & Gage, Fred H. (2005). Exercise enhances learning and hippocampal neurogenesis in aged mice. *Journal of neuroscience, 25,* 8680–8685.

van Wyhe, John. (2000). The history of phrenology on the Web. Retrieved January 17, 2000, from http://www.jmvanwyhe.freeserve.co.uk/

Venables, Peter H. (1996). Schizotypy and maternal exposure to influenza and to cold temperature: The Mauritius study. *Journal of Abnormal Psychology, 105,* 53–60.

Verplanken, Bas, & Faes, Suzanne. (1999). Good intentions, bad habits, and effects of forming implementation intentions on healthy eating. *European Journal of Social Psychology, 29,* 591–604.

Vingerhoets, Ad J. J. M.; Cornelius, Randolph R.; Van Heck, Guus L.; & Becht, Marleen C. (2000). Adult crying: A model and review of the literature. *Review of General Psychology, 4,* 354–377.

Vink, T.; Hinney, A.; & others. (2001). Association between an agouti-related protein gene polymorphism and anorexia nervosa. *Molecular Psychiatry, 6,* 325–328.

Vlahov, David; Galea, Sandro; Resnick, Heidi; Shern, Jennifer; Boscarino, Joseph A.; Bucuvalas, Michael; & others. (2002). Increased use of cigarettes, alcohol, and marijuana among Manhattan, New York, residents after the September 11 terrorist attacks. *American Journal of Epidemiology, 155,* 988–996.

Volkow, Nora D.; Chang, Linda; Wang, Gene-Jack; Fowler, Joanna S.; Ding, Yu-Sin; & others. (2001). Low level of brain dopamine D2 receptors in methamphetamine abusers: Association with metabolism in the orbitofrontal cortex. *American Journal of Psychiatry, 158,* 2015–2021.

Volkow, Nora D.; Chang, Linda; Wang, Gene-Jack; Fowler, Joanna S.; Franceschi, Dinko; & others. (2001). Higher cortical and lower subcortical metabolism in detoxified methamphetamine abusers. *American Journal of Psychiatry, 158,* 383–389.

Volkow, Nora D.; Fowler, Joanna S.; & Wang, Gene-Jack. (2003). The addicted human brain: Insights from imaging studies. *Journal of Clinical Investigation, 111,* 1444–1451.

Volkow, Nora D.; Wang, Gene-Jack; Fowler, Joanna S.; & others. (1999a). Association of methylphenidate-induced craving with changes in right striato-orbitofrontal metabolism in cocaine abusers: Implications in addiction. *American Journal of Psychiatry, 156,* 19–26.

Volkow, Nora D.; Wang, Gene-Jack; Fowler, Joanna S.; & others. (1999b). Prediction of reinforcing responses to psychostimulants in humans by brain dopamine D_2 receptor levels.

American Journal of Psychiatry, 156, 1440–1443.

Vygotsky, Lev S. (1978). *Mind in society: The development of higher psychological processes* (Michael Cole, Vera John-Steiner, Sylvia Scribner, & Ellen Souberman, Eds. & Trans.). Cambridge, MA: Harvard University Press.

Vygotsky, Lev S. (1987). *Thinking and speech* (Norris Minick, Trans.). New York: Plenum Press.

Wadsworth, Barry J. (1996). *Piaget's theory of cognitive and affective development: Foundations of constructivism* (5th ed.). White Plains, NY: Longman.

Waelde, Lynn C.; Thompson, Larry; & Gallagher-Thompson, Dolores. (2004). A pilot study of a yoga and meditation intervention for dementia caregiver stress. *Journal of Clinical Psychology, 60,* 677–687.

Wagstaff, Graham F. (1999). Hypnosis. In Sergio Della Sala (Ed.), *Mind myths: Exploring popular assumptions about the mind and brain.* Chichester, England: Wiley.

Wahba, Mahmoud A., & Bridwell, Lawrence G. (1976). Maslow reconsidered: A review of research on the need hierarchy theory. *Organizational Behavior and Human Decision Processes, 15,* 212–240.

Waite, Linda J., & Joyner, Kara. (2001). Emotional and physical satisfaction with sex in married, cohabiting, and dating sexual unions: Do men and women differ? In Edward O. Laumann & Robert T. Michael (Eds.), *Sex, love, and health in America: Private choices and public policies.* Chicago: University of Chicago Press.

Wald, George. (1964). The receptors of human color vision. *Science, 145,* 1007–1017.

Waldman, Irwin D.; Weinberg, Richard A.; & Scarr, Sandra. (1994). Racial group differences in IQ in the Minnesota Transracial Adoption Study: A reply to Levin and Lynn. *Intelligence, 18,* 29–44.

Walker, Elaine; Kestler, Lisa; Bollini, Annie; & Hochman, Karen M. (2004). Schizophrenia: Etiology and course. *Annual Review of Psychology, 55,* 401–430.

Walker, J. Michael; Huang, Susan M.; Strangman, Nicole M.; Tsou, Kang; & Sanudo-Pena, M. Clara. (1999, October 12). Pain modulation by release of the endogenous cannabinoid anandamide. *Proceedings of the National Academy of Sciences, USA, 96,* 12198–12203.

Walters, Ellen E., & Kendler, Kenneth S. (1995). Anorexia nervosa and anorexic-like syndromes in a population-based female twin sample. *American Journal of Psychiatry, 152,* 64–71.

Walton, Kenneth G.; Schneider, Robert H.; Nidich, Sanford I.; Salerno, John W.; Nordstrom, Cheryl K.; & Merz, C. Noel Bairey. (2002). Psychosocial stress and cardiovascular disease, part 2: Effectiveness of the Transcendental Meditation program in treatment and prevention. *Behavioral Medicine, 28,* 106–123.

Walton, Richard E. (1973, Fall). Quality of work life: What is it? *Sloan Management Review*, pp. 11–21.

Wang, Gene-Jack; Volkow, Nora D.; Logan, Jean; & others. (2001). Brain dopamine and obesity. *Lancet, 357,* 354–357.

Wang, Qi. (2001). Culture effects on adults' earliest childhood recollection and self-description: Implications for the relation between memory and the self. *Journal of Personality and Social Psychology, 81,* 220–223.

Wang, Qi. (2004). The emergence of cultural self-constructs: Autobiographical memory and self-description in European American and Chinese children. *Developmental Psychology, 40,* 3–15.

Ward, Colleen, & Rana-Deuba, Arzu. (1999). Acculturation and adaptation revisited. *Journal of Cross-Cultural Psychology, 30*(4), 422–442.

Ware, Jacqueline; Jain, Kumud; Burgess, Ian; & Davey, Graham C. L. (1994). Disease-avoidance model: Factor analysis of common animal fears. *Behavior Research and Therapy, 32,* 57–63.

Washburn, D. (1997). Study shows rise in employee theft in 1996. *Home Improvement Market, 234,* 22.

Watson, Jeanne C. (2002). Re-visioning empathy. In David J. Cain & Julius Seeman (Eds.), *Humanistic psychotherapies: Handbook of research and practice.* Washington, DC: American Psychological Association.

Watson, John B. (1913). Psychology as the behaviorist views it. *Psychological Review, 20,* 158–177.

Watson, John B. (1916). The place of the conditioned-reflex in psychology. *Psychological Review, 23,* 89–116.

Watson, John B. (1919). A schematic outline of the emotions. *Psychological Review, 26,* 165–196.

Watson, John B. (1924/1970). *Behaviorism.* New York: Norton.

Watson, John B. (1930). *Behaviorism* (Rev. ed.). Chicago: University of Chicago Press.

Watson, John B., & Rayner, Rosalie. (1920/2000). Conditioned emotional reactions. *Journal of Experimental Psychology, 3,* 1–14. (Reprinted March 2000: *American Psychologist, 55*(3), 313–317)

Wayment, Heidi A. (2004). It could have been me: Vicarious victims and disaster-focused distress. *Personality and Social Psychology Bulletin, 30*(4), 515–528.

Weaver, Charles A., III. (1993). Do you need a "flash" to form a flashbulb memory? *Journal of Experimental Psychology: General, 122,* 39–46.

Weaver, Charles N. (1978). Job satisfaction as a component of happiness among males and females. *Personnel Psychology, 31,* 831–840.

Webb, Katie, & Davey, Graham C. L. (1993). Disgust sensitivity and fear of animals: Effect of exposure to violent or revulsive material. *Anxiety, Coping and Stress, 5,* 329–335.

Webb, Wilse B. (1975). *Sleep: The gentle tyrant.* Englewood Cliffs, NJ: Prentice-Hall.

Wechsler, David. (1944). *The measurement of adult intelligence* (3rd ed.). Baltimore: Williams & Wilkins.

Wechsler, David. (1977). *Manual for the Wechsler Intelligence Scale for Children* (Rev.). New York: Psychological Corporation.

Wechsler, Henry; Lee, Jae Eun; Kuo, Meichun; Seibring, Mark; Nelson, Toben F.; & Lee, Hang. (2002). Trends in college binge drinking during a period of increased prevention efforts: Findings for 4 Harvard Public School of Public Health College Alcohol Study Surveys: 1993–2001. *Journal of American College Health, 50,* 203–217.

Weinberg, Richard A. (1989). Intelligence and IQ: Landmark issues and great debates. *American Psychologist, 44,* 98–104.

Weinberg, Richard A.; Scarr, Sandra; & Waldman, Irwin D. (1992). The Minnesota Transracial Adoption Study: A follow-up of IQ test performance at adolescence. *Intelligence, 16,* 117–135.

Weinberger, Daniel R. (1995, June). Quoted in Joel L. Swerdlow: "Quiet miracles of the brain." *National Geographic, 187,* 2–41.

Weindruch, Richard. (1996). Caloric restriction and aging. *Scientific American, 274,* 46–52.

Weiner, Bernard. (1985). An attributional theory of achievement motivation and emotion. *Psychological Review, 92,* 548–573.

Weinstein, Lissa N.; Schwartz, David G.; & Arkin, Arthur M. (1991). Qualitative aspects of sleep mentation. In Steven J. Ellman & John S. Antrobus (Eds.), *The mind in sleep. Psychology and psychophysiology* (2nd ed.). New York: Wiley.

Weintraub, M. I.; Wolfe, G. I.; Barohn, R. A.; Cole, S. P.; Parry, G. J.; Hayat, G.; & others. (2003). Static magnetic field therapy for symptomatic diabetic neuropathy: A randomized, double-blind, placebo-controlled trial. *Archives of Physical Medicine and Rehabilitation, 84,* 736–746.

Weisberg, Robert W. (1988). Problem solving and creativity. In Robert J. Sternberg (Ed.), *The nature of creativity.* New York: Cambridge University Press.

Weisberg, Robert W. (1993). *Creativity: Beyond the myth of genius.* New York: Freeman.

Weiss, Howard M., & Shaw, James B. (1979). Social influences on judgments about tasks. *Organizational Behavior and Human Performance, 24,* 136–140.

Weisse, Carol Silvia. (1992). Depression and immunocompetence: A review of the literature. *Psychological Bulletin, 111,* 475–489.

Weissman, Myrna M.; Markowitz, John C.; & Klerman, Gerald L. (2000). *Comprehensive guide to interpersonal psychotherapy.* New York: Basic Books.

Weisz, Carolyn, & Jones, Edward E. (1993). Expectancy disconfirmation and dispositional inference: Latent strength of target-based and category-based expectancies. *Personality and Social Psychology Bulletin, 19,* 563–573.

Weisz, John R.; Rothbaum, Fred M.; & Blackburn, Thomas C. (1984). Standing out and standing in: The psychology of control in Japan and America. *American Psychologist, 39,* 955–969.

Wells, Gary L., & Loftus, Elizabeth F. (2003). Eyewitness memory for people and events. In Alan M. Goldstein (Ed.), *Handbook of Psychology: Vol. 11. Forensic psychology* (pp. 149–160). New York: Wiley.

Wells, Gary L.; Malpass, Roy S.; Lindsay, R. C. L.; Fisher, Ronald P.; Turtle, John W.; & Fulero, Solomon M. (2000). From the lab to the police station: A successful application of eyewitness research. *American Psychologist, 55,* 581–598.

Werker, Janet, & Desjardins, Renee. (1995). Listening to speech in the 1st year of life: Experiential influences on phoneme production. *Current Directions in Psychological Science, 4,* 76–81.

Wertheimer, Max. (1912/1965). Experimentelle Studien über das Sehen von Bewegung. *Zeitschrift für Psychologie, 61,* 162–163, 221–227. [Portions of original publication translated and reprinted in Richard J. Herrnstein & Edwin G. Boring (Eds.), *A source book in the history of psychology* (Don Cantor, Trans.). Cambridge, MA: Harvard University Press]

Wertsch, James V., & Tulviste, Peeter. (1992). L. S. Vygotsky and contemporary developmental psychology. *Developmental Psychology, 28,* 548–557.

West, Michael A. (1987). Traditional and psychological perspectives on meditation. In Michael A. West (Ed.), *The psychology of meditation.* New York: Oxford University Press.

Westen, Drew. (1990). Psychoanalytic approaches to personality. In Lawrence A. Pervin (Ed.), *Handbook of personality: Theory and research.* New York: Guilford Press.

Westen, Drew. (1998). The scientific legacy of Sigmund Freud: Toward a psychodynamically informed psychological science. *Psychological Bulletin, 124,* 333–371.

Wetherell, Julie Loebach; Gatz, Margaret; & Craske, Michelle G. (2003). Treatment of generalized anxiety disorder in older adults. *Journal of Consulting and Clinical Psychology, 71,* 31–40.

Wethington, Elaine; McLeod, Jane D.; & Kessler, Ronald C. (1987). The importance of life events for explaining sex differences in psychological distress. In Rosalind C. Barnett, Lois Biener, & Grace K. Baruch (Eds.), *Gender and stress.* New York: Free Press.

Wheeler, Mark E.; Petersen, Steven E.; & Buckner, Randy L. (2000). Memory's echo: Vivid remembering reactivates sensory-specific cortex. *Proceedings of the National Academy of Sciences, USA, 97,* 11125–11129.

Wheeler, S. Christian, & Petty, Richard E. (2001). The effects of stereotype activation and behavior: A review of possible mechanisms. *Psychological Bulletin, 127,* 797–826.

Whisman, Mark A. (2001). Marital adjustment and outcome following treatments for depression. *Journal of Consulting and Clinical Psychology, 69,* 125–129.

White, Geoffrey M. (1994). Affecting culture: Emotion and morality in everyday life. In Shinobu Kitayama & Hazel Rose Markus (Eds.), *Emotion and culture: Empirical studies of mutual influence.* Washington, DC: American Psychological Association.

White, Lon; Katzman, Robert; & Losonczy, Katalin. (1994). Association of education with incidence of cognitive impairment in three established populations for epidemiologic studies of the elderly. *Journal of Clinical Epidemiology, 47,* 363–371.

White, Robert W. (1959). Motivation reconsidered: The concepts of competence. *Psychological Review, 66,* 297–333.

Whorf, Benjamin L. (1956). Science and linguistics. In J. B. Carroll (Ed.), *Language, thought, and reality: Selected papers of Benjamin Lee Whorf.* Cambridge, MA: MIT Press.

Whyte, Jamie, & Schaefer, Charles E. (1995). Introduction to sleep and its disorders. In Charles E. Schaefer (Ed.), *Clinical handbook of sleep disorders in children.* Northvale, NJ: Aronson.

Widiger, Thomas A., & Clark, Lee Anna. (2000). Toward DSM-V and the classification of psychopathology. *Psychological Bulletin, 126,* 946–963.

Wilcoxon, Hardy C.; Dragoin, William B.; & Kral, Paul A. (1971). Illness-induced aversions in rat and quail: Relative salience of visual and gustatory cues. *Science, 171,* 826–828.

Wilfley, Denise E., & Rodin, Judith. (1995). Cultural influences on eating disorders. In Kelly D. Brownell & Christopher G. Fairburn (Eds.), *Eating disorders and obesity: A comprehensive handbook.* New York: Guilford Press.

Williams, A. C., Jr. (1938). Perception of subliminal visual stimuli. *Journal of Psychology, 6,* 187–199.

Williams, Martin H. (1992). Exploitation and inference: Mapping the damage from therapist-patient sexual involvement. *American Psychologist, 47,* 412–421.

Williams, Nigel M.; O'Donovan, Michael C.; & Owen, Michael J. (2005). Is the dysbindin *(DTNBP1)* a susceptibility gene for schizophrenia? *Schizophrenia Bulletin, 31,* 800–805.

Williams, Robert L.; Gökcebay, Nilgün; Hirshkowitz, Max; & Moore, Constance A. (1994). Ontogeny of sleep. In Rosemary Cooper (Ed.), *Sleep.* New York: Chapman & Hall.

Willinger, Marian; Ko, Chia-Wen; Hoffman, Howard J.; Kessler, Ronald C.; & Corwin, Michael J. (2003). Trends in infant bed sharing in the United States, 1993–2000: The National Infant Sleep Position Study. *Archives of Pediatrics and Adolescent Medicine, 157,* 43–49.

Wilson, Timothy D., & Dunn, Elizabeth W. (2004). Self-knowledge: Its limits, value, and potential for improvement. *Annual Review of Psychology, 55,* 493–518.

Wilson, Wayne. (1999). *The psycopath in film.* Lanham, MD: University Press of America.

Wimbush, James C., & Dalton, Dan R. (1997). Base rate for employee theft: Convergence of multiple methods. *Journal of Applied Psychology, 82,* 756–763.

Windholz, George. (1990). Pavlov and the Pavlovians in the laboratory. *Journal of the History of the Behavioral Sciences, 26,* 64–73.

Windle, Michael, & Windle, Rebecca C. (2001). Depressive symptoms and cigarette smoking among middle adolescents: Prospective associations and intrapersonal and interpersonal influences. *Journal of Consulting and Clinical Psychology, 69,* 215–226.

Winemiller, M. H.; Billow, R. G.; Laskowski, E. R.; & Harmsen, W. S. (2003). Effect of magnetic vs. sham-magnetic insoles on plantar heel pain: A randomized controlled trial. *Journal of the American Medical Association, 290,* 1474–1478.

Winkelman, John W.; Herzog, David B.; & Fava, Maurizo. (1999). The prevalence of sleep-related eating disorder in psychiatric and non-psychiatric populations. *Psychological Medicine, 29,* 1461–1466.

Winner, Ellen. (1997). Exceptionally high intelligence and schooling. *American Psychologist, 52,* 1070–1081.

Winner, Ellen. (1998, Winter). Uncommon talents: Gifted children, prodigies, and savants. *Scientific American Presents: Exploring Intelligence, 9,* 32–37.

Winokur, George; Coryell, William; Endicott, Jean; & Akiskal, Hapog. (1993). Further distinctions between manic-depressive illness (bipolar disorder) and primary depressive disorder (unipolar depression). *American Journal of Psychiatry, 150,* 1176–1181.

Witelson, Sandra F.; Kigar, Debra L.; & Harvey, Thomas. (1999). The exceptional brain of Albert Einstein. *Lancet, 353,* 2149–2153.

Wixted, John T. (2004). The psychology and neuroscience of forgetting. *Annual Review of Psychology, 55,* 235–269.

Wohlschläger, Andreas, & Wohlschläger, Astrid. (1998). Mental and manual rotation. *Journal of Experimental Psychology: Human Perception and Performance, 24,* 397–412.

Wolpe, Joseph. (1958). *Psychotherapy by reciprocal inhibition.* Stanford, CA: Stanford University Press.

Wolpe, Joseph. (1982). *The practice of behavior therapy.* New York: Pergamon.

Women's Sports Foundation. (2005). Title IX: Questions and answers. Retrieved March 1, 2005, from http://www.womenssports foundation.org

Wonderlic, E. F. (1998). *Wonderlic Personnel Test Manual.* Libertyville, IL: Wonderlic & Associates.

Wood, James M., & Bootzin, Richard R. (1990). The prevalence of nightmares and their independence from anxiety. *Journal of Abnormal Psychology, 99*(1), 64–68.

Wood, Jeffrey J., & Repetti, Rena L. (2004). What gets Dad involved? A longitudinal study of change in parental child caregiving involvement. *Journal of Family Psychology, 18,* 237–249.

Wood, Robert, & Bandura, Albert. (1991). Social cognitive theory of organizational management. In Richard M. Steers & Lyman W. Porter (Eds.), *Motivation and work behavior.* New York: McGraw-Hill.

Wood, Wendy; Rhodes, Nancy; & Bick, Michael. (1995). Working knowledge and attitude strength: An information processing analysis. In Richard E. Petty & Jon A. Krosnick (Eds.), *Attitude strength: Antecedents and consequences.* Hillsdale, NJ: Erlbaum.

Woods, Stephen C.; Schwartz, Michael W.; Baskin, Denis G.; & Seeley, Randy J. (2000). Food intake and the regulation of body weight. *Annual Review of Psychology, 51,* 255–277.

Woodward, Amanda L.; Markman, Ellen M.; & Fitzsimmons, Colleen M. (1994). Rapid word learning in 13- and 18-month-olds. *Developmental Psychology, 30,* 553–566.

Woodworth, Robert S. (1918). *Dynamic psychology.* New York: Columbia University Press.

Woodworth, Robert S. (1921). *Psychology: A study of mental life.* New York: Holt.

Woolf, Clifford J., & Salter, Michael W. (2000, June 9). Neuronal plasticity: Increasing the gain in pain. *Science, 288,* 1765–1768.

Wright, Kenneth P., Jr.; Hughes, Rod J.; Kronauer, Richard E.; Dijk, Derk-Jan; & Czeisler, Charles A. (2001). Intrinsic near-24-h pacemaker period determines limits of circadian entrainment to a weak synchronizer in humans. *Proceedings of the National Academy of Sciences, USA, 98,* 4027–4032.

Wu, Li-Tzy, & Anthony, James C. (1999). Tobacco smoking and depressed mood in late childhood and early adolescence. *American Journal of Public Health, 89,* 1837–1840.

Wundt, Wilhelm. (1874*). Grundzûge der physiologischen Psychologie* [Principles of physiological psychology], 5th ed.. Leipzig, Germany: Engelmann. (English version published by Macmillan, New York, 1904)

Yapko, Michael D. (1994a). Suggestibility and repressed memories of abuse: A survey of psychotherapists' beliefs. *American Journal of Clinical Hypnosis, 36,* 163–171.

Yapko, Michael D. (1994b). *Suggestions of abuse: True and false memories of childhood sexual trauma.* New York: Simon & Schuster.

Yarnell, Phillip R., & Lynch, Steve. (1970, April 25). Retrograde memory immediately after concussion. *Lancet, 1,* 863–865.

Yonkers, Kimberly A.; Dyck, Ingrid R.; & Keller, Martin B. (2001). An eight-year longitudinal comparison of clinical course and characteristics of social phobia among men and women. *Psychiatric Services, 52,* 637–643.

Yukl, Gary. (1989). Managerial leadership: A review of theory and research. *Journal of Management, 15,* 251–289.

Yukl, Gary; Guinan, P. J.; & Sottolano, D. (1995). Influence tactics used for different objectives with subordinates, peers, and superiors. *Group and Organization Management, 20,* 272–296.

Zajonc, Robert B. (1984). On the primacy of affect. *American Psychologist, 39,* 117–123.

Zajonc, Robert B. (1998). Emotions. In Daniel T. Gilbert, Susan T. Fiske, & Gardner Lindzey (Eds.), *Handbook of social psychology* (4th ed.). New York: McGraw-Hill.

Zajonc, Robert B. (2001). Mere exposure: A gateway to the subliminal. *Current Directions in Psychological Science, 10,* 224–228.

Zanarini, Mary C.; Williams, Amy A.; Lewis, Ruth E.; Reich, R. Bradford; Vera, Soledad C.; Marino, Margaret F.; & others. (1997). Reported pathological childhood experiences associated with the development of borderline personality disorder. *American Journal of Psychiatry, 154,* 1101–1106.

Zandi, Peter P.; Anthony, James C.; & others. (2004). Reduced risk of Alzheimer disease in users of antioxidant vitamin supplements: The Cache County study. *Archives of Neurology, 61,* 82–88.

Zandstra, Elizabeth H.; de Graaf, Cees, & van Trijp, Hans C.M. (2000). Effects of variety and repeated in-home consumption on product acceptance. *Appetite, 35,* 113–119.

Zeki, Semir. (2001). Localization and globalization in conscious vision. *Annual Review of Neuroscience, 24,* 57–86.

Zeman, Adam; Britton, Tom; Douglas, Neil; Hansen, Andrew; Hicks, Jane; Howard, Robin; & others. (2004). Narcolepsy and excessive daytime sleepiness. *British Medical Journal, 329,* 724–728.

Zernike, Kate. (2004, August 7). At abuse hearing, no testimony that G.I.'s acted on orders. *New York Times.* Accessed on 8/7/04 at http://www.nytimes.com/2004/08/07/international/middleeast/07abuse.html

Zhang, Xue-Jun; He, Ping-Ping; Liang, Yan-Hua; Yang, Sen; Yuan, Wen-Tao; Xu, Shie-Jie; & Huang, Wei. (2004). A gene for freckles maps to chromosome 4q32-q34. *Journal of Investigative Dermatology, 122,* 286–290.

Zhou, Jing, & George, Jennifer M. (2001). When job satisfaction leads to creativity: Encouraging the expression of voice. *Academy of Management Journal, 44,* 682–696.

Zickler, Patrick. (2001, May). National Institute of Drug Abuse (NIDA) *Research reports: Annual survey finds increasing teen use of ecstasy, steroids* (NIDA Notes, 16, No. 2). Retrieved January 14, 2002, from http://www.nida.nih.gov/NIDANotes/NNVol16N2/Annual.html

Zimbardo, Philip G. (1992). Foreword. In Stanley Milgram (Ed.), *The individual in a social world: Essays and experiments* (2nd ed.). New York: McGraw-Hill.

Zimbardo, Philip G. (2000a). Prologue: Reflections on the Stanford Prison Experiment: Genesis, transformations, consequences. In Thomas Blass (Ed.), *Obedience to authority: Current perspectives on the Milgram paradigm.* Mahwah, NJ: Erlbaum.

Zimbardo, Philip G. (2000b, Sept./Oct.). Quoted in Christina Maslach, Emperor of the edge. *Psychology Today.* Retrieved on 2-23-06 from http://www.psychologytoday.com/articles/pto-20000901-000032.html

Zimbardo, Philip G. (2004a). A situationist perspective on the psychology of evil: Understanding how good people are transformed into perpetrators. In Arthur G. Miller (Ed.), *The social psychology of good and evil.* New York: Guilford Press.

Zimbardo, Philip G. (2004b, May 9). 'Power turns good soldiers into "bad apples."' *Boston Globe.* Accessed on December 5, 2005 from: http:www.boston.com/news/globe/editorial_opinion/oped/articles/2004/05/09/power_turns_good_soldiers_into_bad_apples.html

Zimbardo, Philip G. (2005, January 19). You can't be a sweet cucumber in a vinegar barrel: A talk with Philip Zimbardo. *Edge: The Third Culture.* Accessed on 10/08/05 at http://www.edge.org/3rd_culture/zimbardo05_index.html

Zimbardo, Philip G.; Banks, W. Curtis; Haney, Craig; & Jaffe, David. (1973, April 8). The mind is a formidable jailer: A Pirandellian prison. *The New York Times Magazine,* pp. 38ff.

Zimbardo, Philip G., & Leippe, Michael R. (1991). *The psychology of attitude change and social influence.* New York: McGraw-Hill.

Zimbardo, Philip G.; Maslach, Christina; & Haney, Craig. (2000). Reflections on the Stanford Prison Experiment: Genesis, transformations, consequences. In Thomas Blass (Ed.), *Obedience to authority: Current perspectives on the Milgram paradigm.* Mahwah, NJ: Erlbaum.

Zimbardo, Philip G.; Weisenberg, Matisyohu; Firestone, Ira; & Levy, Burton. (1965). Communicator effectiveness in producing public conformity and private attitude change. *Journal of Personality, 33,* 233–256.

Zimmerman, Mark; McDermut, Wilson; & Mattia, Jill I. (2001). Frequency of anxiety disorders in psychiatric outpatients with major depressive disorder. *American Journal of Psychiatry, 157,* 1337–1340.

Zimring, Fred M., & Raskin, Nathaniel J. (1992). Carl Rogers and client/person-centered therapy. In Donald K. Freedheim (Ed.), *History of psychotherapy: A century of change.* Washington, DC: American Psychological Association.

Zinbarg, Richard E.; Barlow, David H.; Brown, Timothy; & Hertz, Robert M. (1992). Cognitive-behavioral approaches to the nature and treatment of anxiety disorders. *Annual Review of Psychology, 43,* 235–267.

Zola-Morgan, Stuart. (1995). Localization of brain function: The legacy of Franz Joseph Gall (1758–1828). *Annual Review of Neuroscience, 18,* 359–383.

Zubieta, Jon-Kar; Bueller, Joshua A.; Jackson, Lisa R.; Scott, David J.; Xu, Yanjun; Koeppe, Robert A.; Nichols, Thomas E.; & Stohler, Christian S. (2005). Placebo effects mediated by endogenous opioid activity on μ-opioid receptors. *Journal of Neuroscience, 25,* 7754–7762.

Zuckerman, Marvin. (1979). *Sensation seeking: Beyond the optimal level of arousal.* Hillsdale, NJ: Erlbaum.

Zuckerman, Marvin. (1994). *Behavioral expression and biosocial bases of sensation seeking.* New York: Cambridge University Press.

Zusne, Leonard, & Jones, Warren H. (1989). *Anomalistic psychology: A study of magical thinking* (2nd ed.). Hillsdale, NJ: Erlbaum.

Zweig, Richard A., & Hinrichsen, Gregory A. (1993). Factors associated with suicide attempts by depressed older adults: A prospective study. *American Journal of Psychiatry, 150,* 1687–1692.

Illustration Credits

Permission has been granted by Phoebe Beasley to use her artwork on the cover, in the chapter openers, and in the table of contents. Please find her work on the following pages: b, 38, 82, 126, 172, 216, 258, 296, 348, 394, 436, 474, 504, 546.

CHAPTER 1

2 © Louise Gubb/CORBIS SABA   **3** Peter Poulides/ Getty   **4** (*top*) Corbis; (*bottom*) Archives of the History of American Psychology, The University of Akron   **5** Corbis   **6** (*left*) Corbis; (*center*) Wellesley College Archives; (*right*) Archives of the History of American Psychology, The University of Akron   **7** Clark University   **8** (*top left*) Culver Pictures; (*top middle*) Underwood & Underwood/ Corbis; (*top right*) Archives of the History of American Psychology, The University of Akron; (*bottom left*) Courtesy of Carl Rogers Memorial Library; (*bottom right*) Courtesy of Brandeis University   **9** Courtesy of Suzanne Corkin   **10** © AP Photo/ David J. Phillip   **11** (*top*) Corbis/ Keren Su; (*bottom*) Corbis/Paul Souder   **12** Figaro Magahn/Photo Researchers   **14** (*top*) Spencer Grant/Photo Edit; (*bottom*) John Neubauer/PhotoEdit/PictureQuest   **15** Alissa Rosenhaft   **16** © Dan Piraro 1994. Reprinted with special permission of King Features Syndicate   **17** © Anderson Ross/Getty Images   **18** (*top*) © APS Observer/Sari Goodfriend; (*bottom*) Courtesy of the authors   **20** © 1999 by Sidney Harris   **21** © ImageState/Alamy   **24** (*top*) Telegraph Colour Library /FPG/Getty; (*bottom left*) Paul Almasy/Corbis; (*bottom right*) Jeremy Horner/Corbis   **26** Rockstar Games   **27** ©The New Yorker Collection 2002 David Sipress from cartoonbank.com. All Rights Reserved.   **29** (*top*) Courtesy of Dr. Craig Anderson; (*bottom*) Worth Publishers   **30** DOONESBURY © 2004 G. B. Trudeau. Reprinted with permission of UNIVERSAL PRESS SYNDICATE. All rights reserved.   **32** Bente Rettberg-Beck

CHAPTER 2

40 Ted Kawalerski/The Image Bank   **42** CNRI/Science Source/Photo Researchers   **45** Courtesy Tim Murphy and Gil Wier, The University of British Columbia   **48** John Chiasson/The Gamma-Liaison Network   **49** AP/Wide World Photos   **51** Biophoto Associates/Science Source/Photo Researchers   **54** Frank Siteman/Stock Boston   **56** Geoff Tompkinson/ SPL/Photo Researchers   **57** (*left*) AFP/ Getty Images; (*right*) © Dr. Frederick Lepore   **58** (*top right*) Hulton Getty/Liaison Agency; (*bottom*) M. James Nichols & William T. Newsome (1999, December 2). "The neurobiology of cognition." *Nature, vol. 402,* no. 6761   **59** (*top*) Richard Nowitz/Photo Researchers; (*bottom*) Nestle/Petit Format/Science Source/ Photo Researchers   **60** (*left*) Hank Morgan/Science Source/Photo Researchers; (*center*) Scott Camazine/Science Source/Photo Researchers; (*right*) Courtesy of R. A. Poldrack, Harvard Medical School   **61** M. E. Raichle, Mallinckrodt Institute of Radiology, Washington University School of Medicine   **62** Courtesy of Fred H. Gage, The Salk Institute, San Diego   **66** Martin M. Rotker   **69** Courtesy of Terence Williams, University of Iowa   **71** (*top*) National Library of Medicine Collection; (*bottom*) National Library of Medicine Collection   **72** Courtesy of Dr. William D. Hopkins   **73** Courtesy of the California Institute of Technology   **74** Dan McCoy/Rainbow   **75** (*top right and left*) Courtesy of Dr. Arne May, from Bogdan Draganski, Christian Gaser, Volker Busch, Gerhard Schuierer, Ulrich Boddahn & Arne May, (22 January 2004). Neuroplasticity: Changes in grey matter induced by training, *Nature 427,* 311–312; (*bottom*) © Mark Peterson/Corbis   **76** Bryn Alan   **77** Courtesy T. A. Jones and W. T. Greenough   **78** Lisa Poole/AP

CHAPTER 3

84 Florence Low   **85** Paul Conklin   **87** AFP/Corbis   **89** John Downer/ Planet Earth Pictures   **90** Lennart Nilsson/Bonnier Alba AB/Behold Man; Little, Brown & Company   **95** Patrick Collins   **98** Lennart Nilsson/ Bonnier Alba AB   **99** © 2002 Joeseph Scafuro   **100** Roy Botterell/FPG/ Getty   **104** Photonica   **105** Courtesy of the Authors Lennart Nilsson/ Bonnier Alba AB/Behold Man; Little, Brown & Company   **107** (*top*) Bettmann/Corbis; (*bottom*) Fabio Colombini/Animals Animals   **108** *Scott Adams. United Features Syndicate*   **109** Photodisc   **111** (*top*) Dan Piraro; (*bottom*) Julie Houck/Stock Boston   **112** (*left*) Mike Caldwell/Tony Stone/Getty; (*middle*) Superstock; (*right*) Steve McGurry/Magnum Photos   **113** (*top*) Hiroshi Kunoh. Originally published in 3-D Planet, Cadence Books, San Francisco. Reprinted by permission; (*bottom*) Florence Low   **114** Globus Brothers Studios/Corbis Stock Market   **115** Joel Meyerowitz   **116** Sol Mednick   **117** Shay Stevens Photography   **118** M.C. Eschers "Waterfall" © 2003 Cordon Art B.V. –Baarn- Holland. All rights reserved.   **119** (*top*) NASA/JPL/Malin Space Science Systems; (*bottom*) Dick Ruhl   **120** Michael A. Dwyer/Stock Boston   **121** Alyson Aliano   **122** W. Hill, Jr./The Image Works

CHAPTER 4

129 Colin Molyneux/The Image Bank   **130** Getty   **132** (*top*) Barbara Alper/ Stock Boston; (*bottom*) PhotoDisc/Getty Images   **131** Hank Morgan/ Rainbow   **134** GARFIELD © 1989 PAWS INC. Reprinted with permission of UNIVERSAL PRESS SYNDICATE. All Rights Reserved.   **135** Ted Spagna/Photo Researchers   **137** © David Lassman/Syracuse Newspapers/ The Image Works   **139** (*top*) Michio Hoshino/Minden Pictures; (*bottom*) Snodgrass/Photonica   **140** Carmen Taylor/AP   **141** The Granger Collection   **142** Joel Deutsch/Slim Films   **143** Robert Landau/Corbis   **144** © The New Yorker Collection 2006 Robert Mankoff from Cartoonbank.com All Rights Reserved.   **145** Courtesy of Dr. Allen R. Braun, Language Section, National Institute on Deafness and other Communication Disorders, NIH   **146** © The New Yorker Collection 1988 Charles Saxon from Cartoonbank.com All Rights Reserved.   **147** © The New Yorker Collection 1999 Gahan Wilson from Cartoonbank.com All Rights Reserved.   **148** (*top*) AKG/Photo Researchers, Inc.; (*bottom*) Courtesy of Dr. J. Allan Hobson   **150** Kyoko Hamada   **151** (*top*) Courtesy of the late Earnest Hilgard, Photo News and Publications Service, Stanford University; (*bottom*) Tony Freeman/PhotoEdit   **153** Courtesy of Stephen Kosslyn, Ph.D. and William L. Thompson, Dept. of Psychology, Harvard University   **155** Patrick Zachmann /Magnum Photos   **157** (*top*) Andrew Newberg, Hospital at the University of Pennsylvania; (*bottom*) R. Davidson/W. M. Keck Laboratory for Functional Brain Imaging and Behavior, University of Wisconsin   **172** (*top*) Paul A. Souders/Corbis; (*bottom*) Ronald Martinez/Allsport/Getty   **158** Reprinted with permission from the American Journal of Psychiatry, Copyright 2002. American Psychiatric Association. Goldstein, Rita Z. & Volkow, Nora D. (2002). Drug addiction and its underlying neurobiological basis: Neuroimaging evidence for the involvement of the frontal cortex. *American Journal of Psychiatry, 159,* 1642–1652.   **159** (*top*) Jake Schoellkopf/AP; (*bottom*) Bob Daemmrich/Stock Boston   **161** (*top*) Corbis; (*bottom*) © The New Yorker Collection 1993 Mort Gerberg from Cartoonbank.com All Rights Reserved.   **162** Greg Meadors/ Stock Boston   **163** (*top*) The Granger Collection; (*bottom*) Thompson, Paul M.; Hayashi, Kiralee M.; Simon, Sara L.; Lonkon, Edyth D.; et. al. (2004) Structural abnormalities in the brains of human subjects who use methamphetamine. Journal of Neuroscience, 24, 6028–6036.   **164** Kal Muller/ Woodfin Camp & Associates   **166** (top) Syracuse Newspaper/Zach Ornitz/ The Image Works; (bottom) Dr. Liesbeth Reneman, Academisch Medisch Centrum, Universiteit van Amsterdam, Amsterdam, Netherlands

CHAPTER 5

175 (*top*) Kerbs/Monkmeyer; (*bottom*) Stock Montage **176** Sovfoto **177** Bizzaro cartoon, ©12/30/02 Kings Features Stndicate **178** Michael Newman/PhotoEdit **179** Archives of the History of American Psychology, The University of Akron **181** Archives of the History of American Psychology, The University of Akron **182** (*left*) Duke University, Special Collections Library; (*right*) Gaslight Advertising Archives **183** (*top*) © 1998 CATHY GUISEWITE distributed by Universal Press Syndicate; (*bottom*) © David Bishop/FoodPix/Getty **185** Courtesy of Robert A. Rescorla/University of Pennsylvania **186** Darren Bennett/Animals Animals **187** Stuart Ellins, California State University **188** (*left*) Victoria McCormick/Animals Animals; (*right*) Joe McDonald/Animals Animals **189** (*top*) Courtesy of Columbia University; (*bottom*) Yale University Library **190** Bettmann/Corbis **192** (*top*) Stephen Mallon/Photonica; (*bottom*) Lucy Nicholson/Reuters/Corbis **194** Rob Schoenbaum/Time Life Pictures/Getty **195** (*top*) ©Ellen Senisi/The Image Works; (*bottom*) ©Baby Blues Partnership. Reprinted with special permission of King Features Syndicate **196** ©1996 Washington Post Writer Group **197** TimePix **198** Nina Leen, LIFE Magazine © Time Warner, Inc. **199** (*top*) Courtesy of the Authors; (*bottom*) Corbis **201** Jim Bourg/Reuters **202** Sanjiv K. Talwar, Dept. of Physiology and Pharmacology, SUNY Downstate Medical Center **203** Archives of the History of American Psychology, The University of Akron **204** ©The New Yorker Collection 1994 Sam Gross from Cartoonbank.com All Rights Reserved. **205** David J. Phillip/AP **206** Robert & Marion Bailey/Animal Behavior Enterprises **207** Courtesy Albert Bandura, Stanford University **208** Courtesy Albert Bandura, Stanford University **209** Courtesy of Population Communications International /Wencai Audio Video **210** © 1995 Watterson/Dist. By Universal Press Syndicate. Used by permission.

CHAPTER 6

218 PBJ Pictures/The Gamma-Liaison Network **219** Wernher Krutein/The Gamma-Liaison Network **220** Courtesy of Professor George Sperling **221** Travis Morisse/The Hutchinson News **224** © 1983 The New Yorker Collection from cartoonbank.com. Ed Fisher. **226** © Roy Ooms/Masterfile **227** A. Ramey/Stock Boston **231** Doug Pensinger/Allsport **256** Bob Schatz/The Gamma-Liaison Network **232** Courtesy of the authors **233** Corbis **238** Kelly Kerr/Tulsa World **239** Robbie McClaran **240** Reuters /Corbis **241** Brewer, W. F., and Treyens, J. C. (1981). "Role of schemata in memory for place." *Cognitive Psychology; 23,* Figure 1, pp. 207–230. **242** Courtesy of Sandy Hockenbury **243** Archives of the History of American Psychology, The University of Akron **245** Courtesy of Richard Thompson **246** Courtesy of Mark E. Wheeler, Randy L. Buckner, and Steven E. Petersen **247** © Karen Kuehn/Matrix International **248** Michael Colicos, UCSD **249** (*top*) Jonathan Daniel/Allsport; (*bottom*) Courtesy of Montreal Neurological Institute **250** Courtesy of Suzanne Corkin **251** (*left*) Bettman/Corbis; (*middle*) Franco Origlia/Getty Images; (*right*) Bettmann/Corbis **252** Dr. Paul Thompson, UCLA

CHAPTER 7

261 Mike Powell/Getty Images **262** Courtesy of Kathleen O'Craven, Rotman Research Institute **263** (*top*) Merlin Tuttle/Photo Researchers; (*bottom*) Flip Nicklin/Minden Pictures **266** © 2006 The New Yorker Collection. Cartoonbank.com, Christopher Weyant **269** Stephen Jaffe/Getty Images **271** Michael Newman/PhotoEdit **273** Courtesy Ann Senghas **274** (*top*) Courtesy Peter Gordon; (*bottom*) Frans Lanting/Minden Pictures **275** (*top*) *www.GreatApeTrust.org;* (*bottom*) © Arlene Levin-Rowe **276** Archives of the the History of American Psychology/The University of Akron **277** Archives of the History of American Psychology/The University of Akron **278** News Service, Stanford University **279** (*top*) Archives of the History of American Psychology, The University of Akron; (*bottom*) Laura Dwight/Photo Edit **281** Archives of the History of American Psychology, The University of Akron **282** (*top*) Archives of the History of American Psychology, The University of Akron; (*center*) Jay Gardner © 2004; (*bottom left*) John Blaustein/The Gamma-Liaison Network; (*middle*) Andre Forget/AP Wide World; (*right*) Chris Trotman/Corbis **283** ©The New Yorker Collection 2001 David Sipress from Cartoonbank.com. All Rights Reserved. **285** Mary Kate Denny/PhotoEdit **286** Robert A. Isaacs/Photo Researchers **289** (*top*) Tom Wagner/Saba Press Images/Corbis; (*bottom*) Garry Conner /PhotoEdit **290** Alexandra Avakian/Contact Press Images **293** Louis Lanzano/AP

CHAPTER 8

300 Peter Glass/Monkmeyer **301** (*bottom*) Tom Sanders/Adventure Photo & Film **302** Harlow Primate Laboratory, University of Wisconsin **302** Natalie Behring/Reuters/Archive **303** Natalie Behring/Reuters/Archive Photos **304** Corbis **305** Don Mason/Corbis Stock Market **306** Remi Banali/Liaison **307** © The New Yorker collection 2005 Alex Gregory from Cartoonbank.com. All Rights Reserved. **309** George D. Lepp/Corbis **310** Courtesy of Dr. Gene-Jack Wang, Brookhaven National Laboratory **311** (*top*) Jill Greenberg © 1996 The Walt Disney Co. Reprinted by permission of Discover Magazine; (*bottom*) Peter Kramer/Getty Images **313** Frans Lanting/Minden Pictures **315** TIME Magazine © 2006 Time Inc. Reprinted by permission. **316** (*left*) AP Photo/Haydn West; (*right*) Eric Gaillard/Corbis **317** AP Photo/Ron Edmonds **319** (*top*) Deborah Davis/PhotoEdit; (*bottom*) Frank Wartenburg/Corbis/The Picture Press **320** (*top left*) Tony Anderson/FPG; (*top right*) A. Bartels & S. Zeki, University College London **321** (*top*) Sotographs/The Gamma-Liasion Network; (*bottom*) *Dennis Degnan* / Corbis **322** (*top*) Pam Francis/The Gamma-Liasion Network/PhotoEdit; (*bottom*) George Tiedemann/ Corbis **324** Courtesy of Brandeis University **325** (*bottom*) Agence France-Presse/Corbis **326** Reuters New Media/Corbis **327** (*top*) Tony Freeman/PhotoEdit; (*bottom*) RNT Productions/Corbis **328** Charles Darwin, *The Expression of the Emotions in Man and Animals,* Definitive Edition. Paul Ekman (Ed.). New York: Oxford University Press, 1998. **329** © Zits Partnership. Reprinted with permission of King Features Syndicate. **330** Catherine Karnow/Corbis **331** Deborah Cannon/AP Photo **333** Courtesy of Antonio R. Damasio, Dept. of Neurology and PET Imaging Center, University of Iowa College of Medicine **334** (*top*) Louis Schakel/Michael Kausman/The New York Times Pictures; (*bottom*) From Matsumoto, D., & Ekman, P. (1989) Japanese and Caucasian Facial Expressions of Emotion. JACFEE. Photographs courtesy of Paul Ekman. **335** (*top*) From Eibl-Eibesfeldt, I. (1970). *Ethology: The Biology of Behavior.* New York: Holt. Photo courtesy of I. Eibl-Eibesfeldt; (*bottom*) Courtesy of Dacher Keltner, Dept. of Psychology, University of California, Berkeley **336** (*left*) Michael Dick/Animals Animals; (*right*) Alan & Sandy Carey **337** Art Wolfe/Photo Researchers **338** Corbis **340** Joel Gordon **342** Kathy Willens/AP Photo

CHAPTER 9

350 Courtesy Don and Sandy Hockenbury **352** (*top left*) Nancy Sheehan/PhotoEdit; (*top right*) © Jon Feingersh/Masterfile; (*bottom left*) © Ariel Skelly/Masterfile; (*bottom right*) M. Ferguson Cate/PhotoEdit **354** CNRI/Science Photo Library/ Photo Researchers **355** Biophoto Associates/Photo Researchers **356** (*left*) Petit Format/Nestle/Science Source/Photo Researchers; (*middle*) Petit Format/Nestle/Science Source/Photo Researchers; (right) Petit Format/Nestle/Science Source/Photo Researchers **357** (*top*) Photograph copyright of Anthony Young. From *First Glances* by Davida Y. Teller, *Journal of Investigative Opthalmology and Visual Science,* Vol. 38, 1997, pp. 2183–2203.; (*bottom left*) Elizabeth Crews/The Image Works; (*bottom right*) Petit Format/ Science Source/ Photo Researchers **359** Courtesy Don and Sandy Hockenbury **360** (*top*) Robert Marvin; (*bottom*) John Lei/Stock Boston **362** Stephen Agricola/ The Image Works **364** Romilly Lockyer/The Image Bank **366** (*top*) Myrleen Ferguson/PhotoEdit; (*center*) Tony Freeman/PhotoEdit; (*bottom*) Courtesy Don and Sandy Hockenbury **367** From *Good Night, Sleep Tight? Shh . . .* by Gyo Fujikawa. © 1990 Gyo Fujikawa **368** Bill Anderson/Photo Researchers **369** (*top*) Elizabeth Crews/The Image Works; **370** (*top*) Laura Dwight; (*bottom*) Bill Armstrong **371** Mug Shots/Corbis Stock Market **372** Courtesy of Renee Baillargeon, University of Illinois at Urbana-Champaign **373** Sovfoto/Eastfoto **374** © Ellen Senisi/The Image Works **376** Courtesy Don and Sandy Hockenbury **377** (*top*) Courtesy of Paul Thompson, Kiralee Hayashi, Arthur Toga, UCLA/Nitin Gogtay, Jay Giedd, Judy Rapoport/NIMH **378** (*top*) © Jeff Greenberg/The Image Works **379** Gary Conner /PhotoEdit **380** Sarah Putnam/The Picture Cube/Index Stock **382** David Young-Wolff /PhotoEdit **383** © 2006 The New Yorker Collection, Carolita Johnson from Cartoonbank.com. All rights reserved. **384** Michael Newman/PhotoEdit **385** © David Young-Wolff /PhotoEdit **386** © 2004, The Washington Post. Photo by Anthony Faiola. Reprinted with permission. **387** Joel Gordon

CHAPTER 10

396 Courtesy of Don Hockenbury   **397** Steve Chenn/Corbis   **398** Mary Evans/Sigmund Freud Copyrights/Photo Researchers   **399** (*top*) Culver Pictures; (*bottom*) Corbis   **401** (*top*) Tony Freeman/PhotoEdit   **402** Michael Newman/PhotoEdit   **403** Eric Futran/The Gamma-Liaison Network   **405** Paul Gish/Monkmeyer   **406** Karsh/Woodfin Camp & Associates   **407** (*top*) Paul Almasy/Corbis; (*bottom left*) Courtesy of Dept of Library Services, American Museum of Natural History. Photo by P. Hollembeak; (*bottom right*) Courtesy Dharma Publishing   **408** Photofest   **409** (*top*) Corbis; (*bottom*) Corbis   **410** TimePix   **411** Corbis   **412** Courtesy of Carl Rogers Memorial Library   **413** Jean Michel Turpin/The Gamma-Liaison Network   **414** Russell D. Curtis/Photo Researchers   **416** Courtesy of Albert Bandura, Stanford University   **417** Jean Hangarter/The Picture Cube/Index Stock   **419** Courtesy of Mary Cattell   **421** Courtesy of Dr. Turhan Canali, Stanford University   **422** Courtesy of Don Hockenbury   **423** Myrleen Ferguson Cate/PhotoEdit   **424** Photo by Jim Bailey/courtesy of Alan and Alvin Chow   **426** (*left*) Spencer Grant/PhotoEdit; (*right*) The Granger Collection, New York   **428** Lew Merrim/Photo Researchers

CHAPTER 11

438 Tony Freeman/PhotoEdit   **439** © The New Yorker Collection 2004 Robert Leighton from Cartoonbank.com   **440** Robert Brenner\PhotoEdit, Inc   **441** (*top*) Photofest; (*bottom*) Chicago Tribune Photo   **442** Knut Kampe, University College London   **443** Tom Smart/Deseret News/Getty Images   **444** AP Photo / Roberto Borea   **445** Philip & Karen Smith/Getty Images   **447** Samantha Sin/AFP/Getty Images   **448** © Bernard Napthine/Lonely Planet Images   **449** Courtesy of Zimbardo Collection / © Nila Winter   **450** Paul Warner/AP   **451** Dean Dunson/Corbis   **453** From Sherif, Muzafer; Harvey, O. J.; White, B. Jack; Hood, William R.; & Sherif, Carolyn W. (1961/1988). *The Robbers Cave Experiment: Intergroup Conflict and Cooperation.* Middletown, CT: Wesleyan University Press.   **454** From Sherif, Muzafer; Harvey, O. J.; White, B. Jack; Hood, William R.; & Sherif, Carolyn W. (1961/1988). *The Robbers Cave Experiment: Intergroup Conflict and Cooperation.* Middletown, CT: Wesleyan University Press.   **455** Courtesy Of The Solomon Asch Center for study of Ethnopolitical Conflict   **456** Allana Wesley White/ CORBIS   **457** (*top*) Courtesy of CUNY Graduate School and University Center; (*bottom*) Courtesy Alexandra Milgram. From the film *Obedience,* distributed by Penn State Media Sales   **458** Courtesy of Alexandra Milgram   **460** From the film *Obedience,* distributed by the New York University Film Library   **462** no credit   **463** AP Photo/ LM Otero   **464** Corbis   **465** The New York Times Pictures   **466** (*top*) Edward Hausner/The New York Times Pictures; (*bottom*) Skjold/The Image Works   **467** Dunn/Monkmeyer   **468** Michael Newman/PhotoEdit

CHAPTER 12

476 (*top left and right*) Carmen Tylor/AP; (*middle*) Paul Hawthorne/AP; (*bottom*) Ed Bailey/AP   **477** Myrleen Ferguson Cate/PhotoEdit   **479** (*top*) Tony Freeman/PhotoEdit; (*bottom*) Courtesy of Richard S. Lazarus/University of California, Berkeley   **480** Bebeto Matthews/AP   **481** Tina Fineberg/AP **482** Steve Liss/The Gamma-Liaison Network   **483** Edgar Fahs Smith Collection, University of Pennsylvania Library   **484** (*top*) © 1974 John Olson/People Weekly; (bottom) Omikron/Science Source/Photo Researchers   **485** (*top left and right*) From Petrovic, Predrag; Kalso, Eija; Petersson, Karl M.; and Ingvar, Martin. Placebo and opioid analgesia—Imaging shared neuronal network. Science, 295, 1737–1740   **486** (*top left*) Courtesy of Robert Ader, photo by James Montanus, University of Rochester; (*top right*) Courtesy of Nicholas Cohen, University of Rochester; (*bottom*) Courtesy of Janice Kiecolt-Glaser, Ohio State University College of Medicine   **488** Shaul Schwarz/Getty Images   **489** David Lassman/Syracuse Newspapers/The Image Works   **491** Robert Brenner/PhotoEdit   **493** Dan Habib/Corbis   **494** (*top*) Macduff Everton/The Image Works; (bottom) Joe Carini/The Image Works   **495** Piers Cavendish/Zuma Press   **496** Tony Freeman/PhotoEdit   **497** AP/Wide World Photos   **499** AP/Wide World Photos   **500** Joshua Griffler   **501** © 2005 The New Yorker Collection John Jonik from cartoonbank.com. All Rights Reserved.

CHAPTER 13

508 Photofest   **509** Reprinted with permission from *Diagnostic and Statistical Manual of Mental Disorders,* Fourth Edition, Text Revision. © 2000 by the American Psychiatric Association.   **510** Billy Barnes/PhotoEdit   **513** Treë   **514** ©The New Yorker Collection 2004 Roz Chast from Cartoonbank.com.   **515** Bernard Wolf   **516** (*top*) John Kaprician/Photo Researchers; (*bottom*) Seth Resnick   **517** Suzanne Plunkett/AP   **519** © 1996, American Medical Association from Archives of General Psychiatry, February 1996, Vol. 53. Courtesy of Jeffrey M. Schwartz.   **520** Eric Fenblatt/Corbis Sygma   **521** S.I.N./Corbis   **522** Courtesy of Dr. Lew Baxter and Dr. Michael Phelps, University of California, Los Angeles   **523** The Everett Collection   **524** Jeff Greenberg/PhotoEdit   **525** Courtesy of Dr. Elliot A. Stein, Dept. of Psychiatry, Medical College of Wisconsin   **526** Corbis (*for Twain and Plath*) and Robert Capa/Magnum Photos (*for Hemingway*)   **529** AP Photo/Bo Rader, Pool   **530** K. McGlynn/The Image Works   **532** John Caldwell   **533** Courtesy of Mental Health Clinical Research Center, University of Iowa   **534** Courtesy of David Silbersweig, M.D., Emily Stern, M.D., Cornell Medical Center   **535** A. Ramey/PhotoEdit   **539** Joe McNally/National Geographic Society Image Collection   **540** Courtesy of Dr. Paul Thompson, Dept. of Neurology, UCLA Lab of Neuro-Imaging & Brain Mapping Division   **542** Joel Gordon

CHAPTER 14

548 Bruce Ayres/Tony Stone Images   **549** Courtesy of LTC Debra Dunivin, Dept. of Psychology, Walter Reed Army Medical Center   **550** (*top*) Culver Pictures; (*bottom*) AP/Wide World Photos   **553** Michael Rougier, LIFE Magazine Inc.   **554** Richard Nowitz/Photo Researchers   **556** Innervisions   **557** Larson/Watson Papers, Archives of the History of American Psychology, The University of Akron   **558** Françoise Sauze/Science Photo Library/Photo Researchers   **559** (*top*) Bob Mahoney/The Image Works; (*bottom*) Bob Mahoney/The Image Works   **640** Courtesy of Wayne Simpson/Simtek, Inc.   **562** Courtesy of Albert Ellis   **563** Courtesy of Melvin Powers   **564** Courtesy of Aaron T. Beck, University of Pennsylvania Medical Center   **566** © The New Yorker Collection 2005 Tom Cheney from cartoonbank.com.   **567** (*top*) F. Pedrick/The Image Works; (*bottom*) Michael Newman/PhotoEdit   **568** Hank Morgan/Science Source/Photo Researchers   **571** Michael Newman/PhotoEdit   **572** Worth Publishers   **574** Steve Liss/The Gamma-Liaison Network   **575** (*left*) The Granger Collection; (*middle*) Corbis; (*right*) Culver Pictures; (*bottom*) Woodson, R. E., Jr., Youngken, H. W., Schlittler, E., and Schneider, J. A. (eds.). (1957).   **576** *Rauwolfia: Botany, Pharmacognosy, Chemistry and Pharmacology.* Boston: Little, Brown. Reprinted with permission.   **578** Courtesy of Bristol-Myers Squibb and Otsuka America Pharmaceutical   **579** Corbis   **580** Jonathan Nourok/Stone   **581** Courtesy of Arthur Brody, M.D., UCLA   **582** James Wilson/Woodfin Camp & Associates

APPENDIX B

B-2 Ralf Finn-Hestoft/Saba   **B-8** James Schnepf/The Gamma-Liaison Network   **B-10** Forrest Anderson/The Gamma-Liaison Network   **B-12** Pictor International/PictureQuest

Name Index

Subject Index